D1135036

THE WORLD OF

OPERA

The Story of Its Origins

A N D

the Lore of Its Performance

THE WORLD OF OPERA

OPERA

The Story of Its Origins

AND

the Lore of Its Performance

THE WORLD OF OPERA

The Story of Its Origins

A N D

the Lore of Its Performance

B Y

WALLACE BROCKWAY

& HERBERT WEINSTOCK

PANTHEON BOOKS

THE AUTHORS *wish to express*
their deep appreciation to
The Metropolitan Opera Guild
for allowing them
to cull its extensive collection of photographs
and for permission to reproduce
those used as illustrations here.

Contents

Illustrations

Plates

THE WORLD OF

OPERA

The Story of Its Origins

A N D

the Lore of Its Performance

THE WORLD OF

OPERA

The Story of Its Origins

AND

the Lore of Its Performance

CHAPTER I

The Birth of Opera

O PERA is the most protean of the musical arts, as its name proves. What could be more vague than the word itself? *Opera,* in Italian, means "work"; the longer form is *opera in musica,* "musical work." The term came slowly into use, the English, until recently not devoted to opera (occasional attacks of opera mania to the contrary notwithstanding), being the first to popularize it, whereas the Italians resisted it stubbornly long after it had been accepted in France and Germany. Apparently, they felt that it did not accurately describe what they had begun to create in the late sixteenth century. Among the terms they favored were *dramma per musica,* "music drama," which indeed they often failed to create, *favola,* "fable," appropriate to many an opera of even late vintage, and *melodramma.* The nomenclature of opera is a considerable subject in itself. A phenomenon arising from conventions and theories, opera, perhaps fortunately for its problem-ridden historians, is not a form in the sense that a sonata may be.

The most learned musicologists, knowing the precursors of opera like their ABC's, provide us with the complex phenomenology of these not-quites. Verbal entertainment with music is teasingly old, and many musicians and musical theorists have speculated, often fruitlessly, about its beginnings. Tinctoris, in the fifteenth century, and Zarlino, in the sixteenth, guessed amusingly on this fascinating subject, but they knew as little as their modern commentators, not one of whom can vitalize Greek music for us. Greek music haunted the fathers of opera—Greek music and, of course, its ideals. Meanwhile, composers, glorifying the Church or serving sovereigns, nobles, and the merely rich, pursued their various ways. For these the ideas of the classic past were not quite so alluring as they were to painters, sculptors, architects, and men of letters intent upon re-creating the antique. Such men as Palestrina and Orlando di Lasso, master masons of the piously erected cathedral of vocal polyphony, were in the Renaissance but not altogether of it. But the secular composers, fashioners of delightful madrigals, chansons, and what not, provided the music for pageants of various sorts, and were drawn into the great game of playing with the antique—the poets' texts demanded their participation. And some of these lavish treats might accidentally have turned into operas if the story line had been less errant and the dramatic emphasis stronger. Masques, *intermezzi, intermedii*—their strong point was apathy. They often delighted eye and ear, but rarely brought on a touch of catharsis.

Tomás de Victoria was adding the last jewel-like panes of stained glass to the great fabric of sacred polyphony when a few obscure men, unaware that the Renaissance was dying, made music's first formal obeisance to the antique. Cold-bloodedly, they created opera, which was the child of endless theorizing. Some of them began meeting in the palace of Giovanni Bardi, a Florentine noble, around the year 1580. Of this *camerata,* as Count Bardi's circle was called, perhaps Vincenzo Galilei is best known to posterity because of his son, the astronomer. He early (1581) published an attack on counterpoint, and this crucial document furnished the theories on which his associates based their practice. The *camerata,* early or late, could not claim a first-rate composer. Jacopo Peri and Giulio Caccini were well-known singers; Emilio de' Cavalieri was a dilettante nobleman whose crude experiments resulted in the thorough-bass; Ottavio Rinuccini was a dramatic poet; and Jacopo Corsi, another Florentine nobleman, to whose palace the *camerata* resorted after Bardi was called to Rome in 1592, dabbled at composing. Perhaps the latecomer Marco da Gagliano was the most musically gifted of the group.

Rinuccini provided the text—still extant—of *Dafne,* the first opera, most of which was composed by Peri; Corsi helped, and some uninteresting fragments of his workmanship survive. Otherwise the music is lost, and it is perhaps idle to waste reverence upon it. It was probably performed in 1597, though some authorities still insist that 1594 was the year. The score of the second opera, *Euridice,* survives; the details of its authorship are not wholly clear. Peri wrote most of it; Caccini added to it, apparently after Peri had made a complete first draft. Two years later, Caccini composed another *Euridice,* using excerpts from his own additions to the first *Euridice.*

The fact that the Peri-Caccini mosaic was staged as part of the festivities that followed a royal wedding need not disturb the accepted picture of the *camerata* as aloof idealists. All the theory could not have been talked through and written out (Caccini's enlargements on Galilei were notable and for a time notorious) for the mere sake of novelty.[1] The spectacle sufficed for the needed allure (the Italians were then, and for long remained, the most ingenious designers of stage machinery), and Peri and Caccini could afford to keep their heads in the clouds as magnificently as possible. And the high contracting parties would have brought the crowds without a single flourish of trumpets, the occasion being the marriage of Maria de' Medici to Henry IV of France, which was celebrated at Florence on October 6, 1600. As the reservations hedging his kingly state did not allow Henry to leave his own country to meet his bride, Maria's uncle, Ferdinando, Grand Duke of Tuscany, acted as his proxy.

Euridice, which has had several scholarly revivals in the twentieth century, could not have pleased the pleasure-loving princess, whose preference for rowdy harlequinades was well known and did not wane: history was to prove her quite uneducable. Rinuccini's solemn text evoked thin, feeble musical comment, much of it in what was then called *recitar cantando*—recitative—"a mean between speech and music." Yet, apart from a stubborn conviction that they were following the practice of Greek classical drama, Peri and Caccini proceeded along lines so sensible that they were, with variations dictated by the fads of the moment, re-enunciated throughout the history of opera. They insisted that the text be perfectly understood, that the words be sung according to the principles of natural declamation, and that the music project the drama of the words, not only in detail but also as a whole. But they felt, quite erroneously, that in the Greek drama not only the chorus but also the individual actors had sung their roles. It is most unlikely that the composers of the first *Euridice* intended to compete with the madrigal comedies, the first of which—Orazio Vecchi's *Amfiparnasso* (Modena, 1594)—slightly antedated the *première* of *Dafne.* These set entire plays to polyphonic music throughout, which tended to impair the dignity of situations that called only for a solo singer on the stage, though some composers had other singers accompany him behind a drapery. The madrigal comedy,

[1] Moreover, the revolt against polyphony was one of the phenomena—symptoms, possibly—of the oncoming baroque. The *camerata* was not unique in this, but its reasons for discarding polyphony for monody were peculiarly its own.

which for all its absurdity was amazingly successful, can scarcely be considered a true ancestor of opera.

Caccini and Peri, without commanding gifts to draw upon, without traditions to shore up their feeble inspiration, with nothing but the desire to bring to life the dramatic music of the ancient Greeks, produced operas of little value in themselves, serviceable only as rough models for future masters. In view of the sparseness of their operatic materials, it is just as well that the members of the *camerata* were less than geniuses. Stronger men might have forced the infant opera into a strait jacket of frozen forms from which it might have struggled vainly to escape. As it was, since their theory of the opera inevitably committed them to the subject matter of Greek and Roman mythology and history, they set a style in librettos that was amiably accepted by even the greatest composers of tragic opera for more than a century and a half. During this period, the characters of the serious musical stage were the gods and goddesses of the classical pantheons, with a riot of nymphs and dryads, heroes and demigods, fates and furies, along with a select group of historical statuary to bear them company.

Peri and Caccini, by their separate emphases and affinities, unconsciously marked the battle lines of opera's central dichotomy. Herein lay their importance. Peri wrote simply and starkly, always keeping the musical interest subordinated to the dramatic. Caccini, not only a singer himself but also father of the first prima donna, inverted the process: for him, the musical line was of the most passionate interest, and he decorated it with those vocal adornments—roulades, cadenzas, and other *fioriture*—which have ever since characterized the singer's opera. Even today, some composers consider a play as merely a peg on which to hang music, and they are fiercely opposed by others who hold that music should but underline the action of the drama. The greatest of operatic composers, no matter which side they publicly proclaim to be theirs, transform a text by their music, with the result that music remains the dominant actor. This is true of Mozart and even of Gluck at his most doctrinaire.

Opera in its infancy was lucky that Claudio Monteverdi, its first man of genius,[2] was not theory-bound. Until his fortieth year almost exclusively a writer of madrigals, Monteverdi was already a master composer

[2] Marco da Gagliano's *Dafne*, first performed at Mantua in 1608, indicates a composer of great talent, but Gagliano was too self-critical and timid to push on the operatic venture.

when the Florentine experiments attracted his interest. It is likely that he was in the small, invited audience that heard Peri and Caccini's *Euridice* on that epochal October 6 of the year 1600. Two years later, becoming master of the music to Vincenzo Gonzaga, the splendid tyrant who befriended Tasso, patronized Galileo, and murdered the "Admirable" Crichton, Monteverdi was encouraged to try his own hand at a *favola in musica*. Nothing seems to have come of this until February, 1607, when his *Orfeo* was staged in Mantua. Because of the sheerly musical interest of the score, as well as because it contains several still universally used operatic procedures, the date of its production is a milestone in the history of music. Already, the gap between Caccini and Peri and this bold innovator, who seems miraculously to have known exactly where he was going, is tremendous. A polyphonist of genius with an understanding of the techniques of many schools, in *Orfeo* he boldly experimented with the orchestra of the time where his own masters had been satisfied with a few not always happy combinations of instruments. Taking from polyphonic practice an acceptance of clashing melodies, he diversified the stream of *Orfeo* with the drama and excitement of often shrieking harmonies.

In *Orfeo* Monteverdi's orchestra [3] became an ensemble of diversified eloquence, specific instruments being used—singly, in choirs, or in combinations—to express every dramatic effect. Each character is differentiated from the others by his own instrumental accompaniment. For example, Orpheus is supported by the bass viola, Eurydice by violas, and Pluto by no less than four trombones. Charon bawls out his notes to the accompaniment of the *chitarrone,* a big—not to say gross—lute. All this has delighted the sophisticated modern ear. Monteverdi was especially partial to various sorts of keyboard instruments, lutes, and harps, whose chord-making possibilities allowed the richest harmonic texture. He used, but with discretion, the violin tremolo for pointing up moments of pathos, not foreseeing the bathetic ends to which less tasteful composers would take it.

A year later than *Orfeo,* Duke Vincenzo asked Monteverdi to write an opera for the wedding of his son Francesco to Margaret of Savoy. Before *Arianna* was completed, the composer's wife died, and the extraordinarily personal quality of the deserted Arianna's poignant lament may owe something to a direct transference of Monteverdi's grief. Six thousand invited guests are said to have heard the *première* of *Arianna*

---

[3] In his later operas, he returned to a miniature orchestra, mostly strings.

(May 28, 1608); apparently many of them went away with the tragic melody fixed in their minds—the lament was the first operatic hit song. It became familiar throughout Europe, and survives, though the rest of the score has been allowed to perish. It still has the power to move us, the key to its peculiarly modern quality being its audacious use of dissonance and the halting, dramatic melodic design, utterly new at the time. But Arianna's lament, which at the *première* is said to have moved thousands to tears, is only an early, if most striking, example of Monteverdi's uncanny psychological verity—a flair for realistic exposition of character that his countrymen, three hundred years later, were to try to recapture.

In 1612, his health undermined by the dank air of the Mantuan marshes, Monteverdi left the scene of his first successes and within a year was installed in Venice as master of the music to the Most Serene Republic, a post he held until his death some thirty years later. He blossomed in the luxurious capital of the doges. Successor at St. Mark's to a line of brilliant *maestri,* he did not in any way suffer by comparison. His so-called sacred works, like those of such preceding *maestri* as Willaert and the Gabrieli, often wavered on the edge of the profane: into them there entered more and more the spirit of the pleasure-loving city Veronese had wooed with ripe color and spacious line. In 1637, when the Tron family inaugurated at Venice the Teatro San Cassiano, the first public opera house, a new phenomenon was born overnight—opera as a popular spectacle, so passionately delighted in that its subsequent fortunes are at least as much part of folk as of musical history.

For that mildly earth-shaking event in the story of European culture, a now unknown opera—*Andromeda,* by Francesco Manelli—had been chosen. Venice had to wait two years before hearing something from Monteverdi's long-dormant theatrical muse. Even Francesco Cavalli, his pupil, who specialized in robust melodies of easy tunefulness, established his works on the boards of the San Cassiano more quickly. The elder master's *Adone,* performed at a new and more sumptuous house, ran continuously from late 1639 until the Carnival of 1640; meanwhile, his revived *Arianna* drew crowds to still another theater. It is hard to believe, despite the later example of Verdi, that the septuagenarian composer could have written the, at times, almost vernal sequences of *Il Ritorno d'Ulisse* and the fresh and vivid *L'Incoronazione di Poppea,* possibly the first historical opera. However, they were first performed shortly before his death in 1643, soon enough, happily, to let him savor the pleasure of being a popular favorite. The second of these two operas achieves a quite unusual balance between music and drama, soon to be destroyed by Monteverdi's own pupils.

Monteverdi, the mere enumeration of whose madrigals and church music fills several closely printed pages in a short-title catalogue, composed his few operas as a sort of fashionable side line. Although most of them have been lost, from those remaining we get more than a hint of the important revolution he undertook. His innovations were not the fumbling, graceless thinking aloud of a parched theorist, but the rapid, expressive strokes of a creative genius blocking out the architecture of a new medium, and hampered only by the flimsiest of precedents.

The mere presence of Monteverdi in Venice sufficed to start a local operatic tradition that was carried down the peninsula and to the courts of France and Austria. After Monteverdi's death, leadership among operatic composers was shared by his pupil, Francesco Cavalli, and Marcantonio Cesti, whose training had come from an early experimentalist in oratorio, Giacomo Carissimi. Both were important missionaries in carrying Italian opera beyond the Alps: Cavalli went to France at the invitation of Cardinal Mazarin, gained high position at court, and in 1660 had his opera *Serse* produced at the wedding fetes of Louis XIV and the Infanta María Teresa; Cesti, a Franciscan monk with a capable tenor voice, sought his fortune in Austria, where he was appointed vice-*Kapellmeister* to the Emperor Leopold I, the ugliest prince in Europe. Cavalli, whose sobriety and logic reduced to order certain chaotic elements of opera, replaced with *sinfonie,* brief instrumental pieces of atmospheric and descriptive character, the irrelevant little introductions previously used. He also tried, with less signal success, to reach a medium between bare recitative and the full-blown aria, evolving a kind of singing talk of monotonously Oriental effect. If these tendencies are extended in time, we can see their effects, remotely, in Gluck, Wagner, Debussy, and Alban Berg. Cesti, not at all solemn and far more facile (as against Cavalli's sheer carelessness), worked for his day: he truckled to the growing spirit of *festa* that was to take over Italy for more than a century, introducing comic relief into operas so starred with popular songs as to be little more than strings of arias.

Already, less than fifty years after the "invention" of opera, it had departed from the severe "Greek" ideals of Peri. The dominance of the singer, which Caccini, even as he pledged faith to classic austerity, helped to assure by the introduction of vocal ornamentation, had become absolute. Nothing of antiquity remained except the names of the characters, who were plunged into situations more fantastic than anything the fancy of Ovid could have invented. Operas began to become vehicles for popular singers, composers the slaves of the singers' whimsies. Thus, in its infancy, while it needed every ounce of strength to achieve reasonable form, opera frittered away its energies in pandering to the sensational and the ephemeral.

The sopranos came first—extravagantly feted creatures with voices of supernatural agility, some of whom ended up, if not ladies, duchesses. They were more than mere machines: composers, poets, bluestockings, they commanded the worshipful attentions of the discriminating. One of them, Leonora Baroni, won a double immortality because John Milton happened to hear her at a fashionable gathering at Cardinal Barberini's, and indited three Latin poems to her; she was, moreover, a lifelong friend of the witty Cardinal Rospigliosi, the most popular librettist of the day, who became Pope Clement IX. There was Francesca Caccini, the daughter of Giulio Caccini, for whom her father wrote the first operatic roulades, and there was, most spectacular of all, Adriana Basile, mother of great daughters—among them Milton's Leonora. This amazing woman, whose services were bid for by crowned sovereigns, and whose enormous salary at the Mantuan court was supplemented by unparalleled *pourboires* of brocaded gowns and precious gems, became homesick for her native Naples. Returning thither, the ennobled singer was hailed by the entire city, while the local academy of highborn dilettantes laid their eulogies at her feet.

After the sopranos came the *castrati*, artificially preserved male sopranos and altos, though their heyday was reserved for the age of Handel. Out of the obscurity of a church singer's life (for the choir seems to have been their cradle), these emasculated warblers came to challenge the pre-eminence of natural sopranos and altos. Intensively cultivated from early childhood, their voices were exotics we cannot well imagine— a woman's range produced with the power of a man's lungs. The effect was something pure and sexless, like a boy's voice in a mature throat. *Castrati* were introduced to circumvent the papal ban against women on the stage, and at first played only female roles—the Venus of Manelli's *Andromeda* was a *castrato*. Soon, however, their vocal gymnastics in these parts made audiences clamor for their use in male roles as well. Thus, the ridiculous spectacle of a eunuch as Hercules was soon taken for granted, shrill voice and all. As the opera mania spread over Europe, the demand for *castrati* soon became almost too great for the supply. France alone did not take to the eunuchs, but even there, as late as 1660, Padre Francesco Melani, a male soprano belonging to the Servite order, sang the role of Queen Amestris, Xerxes' paramour, in Cavalli's opera *Serse*.

Long before the seventeenth century had run its course, opera, which in 1600 had begun as the expensive toy of the jaded few, was established as the most popular form of musical entertainment in Italy. Moreover, it was an important commercial enterprise. The *commedia dell' arte* was hard pressed to keep its audiences, notably in its very capital, Venice, where by 1699 no less than ten opera houses were flourishing, increasing the prestige of, and in some cases enriching, the great families who ran them—Tron, Grimani, Giustiniani, Vendramin, Venier, and Labia.

Yet the theaters, except for a few luxuriously fitted-out loges, were anything but fine: they were dark and ill-smelling, and the seats were of rough wood. The managements concentrated their expenditures on popular singers and on fantastically elaborate staging. A seventeenth-century observer, quoted in Pompeo Molmenti's *Venice*, speaks rhapsodically of the glories of the productions at the San Cassiano and other theaters, expatiating on their "marvelous transformation scenes, their crowded stage, their ingenious mechanism, their flying figures, their scenery representing the heavens, Olympus, the ocean, royal palaces, forests, groves, and innumerable other enchanting spectacles." In one case, a sumptuous ballroom, brightly illuminated, was suspended over the permanent stage, and drawn up out of sight when not wanted. The overemphasis on stage architecture reminds us that the seventeenth century was an age of engineering triumphs. Before the baroque had entered its last phases, stage architecture and its incredible engines and machines matched in cost and complexity those permanent monuments of the age which still astonish and delight us.

By 1700, regional schools of opera had arisen and died in Florence, Venice, and Rome, and another was being born in the south, with the Neapolitan Alessandro Scarlatti, who was to formulate certain practices without which further evolution could not have taken place. The first Florentine operas had suffered from two chief defects: first, they were mere workings-out of a dubious theory; and second, like most self-conscious innovations, they were far less good than the best conventional work of the time, which happened to be the superb masterpieces of mature vocal polyphony. Peri and Caccini gave to their child little more than the gift of recitative, which in their uninspired view was only attaching a note to each syllable of metrical speech.

On the flickering flame of *le nuove musiche*—the monodic style of Peri and Caccini—Claudio Monteverdi had directed the bellows of his creative imagination. Himself an eminent polyphonist, he seems to have turned to opera because the old forms no longer gave scope to his expressiveness—the many strangenesses that make his madrigals far from orthodox show him desperate in the face of restrictions that are as much part and parcel of the conventional madrigal as the fourteen-line scheme is of the sonnet. Recitative, quite as starkly defined, could not satisfy him: as dramatic situations demanded, he spontaneously expanded the frame of the musical picture. He had no pedantic aversion to music itself, as the early Florentines, lost in their visions of Greece and Rome, seem to have had: he had, in short, no aversion to melody,[4] and he had a positive affection for harmony. Crises in the libretto drew from him the most lyrical of phrases or the most savage harmonies. He employed a nervous line capable of sudden departures, often amazingly florid, from the contours of the speech—irruptions of color which came to be called *coloratura*. These Monteverdi always conceived organically; some of his contemporaries and, even more, his immediate successors, coming speedily under the thumb of vain sopranos and altos of both sexes, subordinated their entire conception of opera to the manufacture of these display passages. With this trend allowed to run wild, opera was in danger of degenerating into a side show with which no serious composer could concern himself. Yet, for years to come, the best of composers worked complaisantly and at times brilliantly for that side show.

[4] Obviously, melody must be thought of as a relative term. It was left to the Neapolitans and their successors to give point to the familiar concept of Italy as the home of melody, where every street boy is born with a lilting tune on his lips. Melodically, the earliest composers of Italian opera were the opposite of lush.

CHAPTER II

Classical Austerity and Laughter

OPERA becomes more baffling as we proceed. At the very beginning, the presence of an original genius like Monteverdi gives us a feeling of security. Although one of his five operas has been totally lost, a great fragment survives from *Arianna,* and the other three are fairly often revived. Monteverdi thus seems to dominate the first half-century of opera, though it is doubtful whether his contemporaries felt that this was true about him. His *Orfeo* came precisely a decade after the now accepted date for *Dafne,* and *L'Incoronazione di Poppea* overlapped the early career of Cavalli and preceded that of Cesti by only seven years. So, while many have some idea of Monteverdi, few know anything of Cavalli, who wrote forty-one operas, and Cesti, who wrote fifteen.[1]

The strait jacket known as the repertoire interposes itself at this point, making a listener's history of the opera possible only to those with the longest purses and the energy to attend musical festivals in the most out-of-the-way places, not to speak of a preternatural watchfulness as to the birth and death dates that frequently spark the festivals. It may well be that the most sapient historian of opera has heard only a tithe of the high spots. First, some of the scores are lost. Thus we can never hear Francesco Manelli's *Andromeda,* used at Venice in 1637 to open the Teatro San Cassiano, the first public opera house in any town. Second, a score may be extant, but the resources to produce it are lacking. For

---

[1] Cavalli's *Didone* was revived at the Maggio Musicale Fiorentino of 1952, Cesti's *Orontea* (a masterpiece, to judge by the fragments alone), at the Settimana Musicale Senese of 1953.

example, *Chi soffre speri,* by Virgilio Mazzocchi and Marco Marazzoli, produced in the private theater of the Palazzo Barberini in Rome on February 27, 1639, was the first comic opera. Curiosity is not diminished by the fact that Milton and Cardinal Mazarin were among the guests. Third, revivals of historical curiosities, if given, are not likely to be repeated: the novelty, not the merits, attracts most of the audience. And so on . . .

How sadly the serious listener is served may be ascertained by scanning a list of twentieth-century revivals of operas composed before 1733, the date of Pergolesi's *La Serva padrona,* the first staple in the repertoire.[2] In this list thirteen composers are represented by twenty-three operas, but only Monteverdi (4), Lully (5), Purcell (3: two are not true operas), Keiser (2), and Telemann (2) are honored by more than one. A further list up to Gluck's *Orfeo* (1762), his first reform opera, prolongs the disappointment. Here twenty-five operas are divided among sixteen composers, but only Rameau (7), Pergolesi (2), Philidor, the famous chess player (3), and Thomas Augustine Arne (2) show more than a single opera revived. It would be possible to swell the list by including Handel and the earlier operas of Gluck, but the facts are clear. Aside from the efforts of certain recording companies, little is being done for the listener interested in pre-Gluckian opera.

Except, then, for Handel, the opera from Monteverdi to Gluck's *Orfeo,* roughly about one hundred and twenty years, must, with the single exception of *La Serva padrona,* be taken on faith. Despite opera's popularity during that period, it held to conventions that now argue against performance. At first, the austere declamation of the early music dramas served the natural proclivity of a limited group, and popularity came only after these rigors were relaxed. The public wanted songs, and then duets, and finally ensembles of three personages or more. When they came in, the old declamation, which in Monteverdi had touched the sublime, went out, and with it—temporarily—the sole dramatic contribution that early opera could claim. The excessive use of *recitativo secco* —dry recitative—represents the triumph of cynicism: the business of the plot had somehow to be unwound, and that as expeditiously as possible, with only bass viol and harpsichord affording a harmonic skeleton. As *recitativo secco* was often very rapid, the ear had to strain to hear

---

[2] In this context, to use the Metropolitan as a gauge would be parochial, even though it presented *La Serva padrona* during two widely separated seasons.

the hinges of action. Nevertheless, though the plots were chiefly taken from mythology or classical history known to most of the audience, opera tended to become a concert in costume.[3]

The concept of opera as a concert in costume need not bother us if we frankly admit that the spectacle side of opera so dear to the grown-up children of the baroque would have to be abandoned in a modern revival. Taxes are too high, and producers wince at the idea of chancing too much on a superspectacle like Rameau's *Les Indes galantes* as revived in Paris, at the Opéra. The real question is: can a cast be gathered to do justice to the musical side of a baroque opera? Because many roles were intended for *castrati*, this question can only be answered by many experiments that may end in discouragement (since desperate remedies are no longer possible). As to the assumption that the conventions of baroque opera are too remote for the twentieth-century listener, the first answer is that we are all used to shifting our time gears in reacting to visual works of art (see Malraux *passim*), to living with the conventions of Shakespeare's or Racine's theater, and to listening without too much perplexity to the sublime paradoxy of the B minor Mass.

Besides Cavalli and Cesti, many operatic composers, some of them famous and popular in their own day, intervene between Monteverdi and Scarlatti. The Florentine school, at once too lofty and too precious for long life, expired in thirty years, and Monteverdi's last operas, written and produced at Venice, began appearing only two years after the inauguration of the San Cassiano. Even in its sunset days Venice did things magnificently, and its operatic composers could not complain of meanness in production. Yet Cesti was wooed by the Hapsburgs, and for Vienna he composed, for an imperial wedding, his masterpiece, *Il Pomo d'oro,* based on the story of Paris and the artifices with which Juno, Minerva, and Venus tried to secure the award of the golden apple. Loewenberg doubts that *Il Pomo d'oro,* "with its huge apparatus," was ever revived after the Vienna performances in 1667–68. It called for twenty-four separate stage sets and various ballets, with a triple ballet at the end, when Leopold I presented his bride, the Infanta Margarita of Spain, with the golden apple as being superior to the three goddesses.

---

[3] Many an opera of the master eclectic and great original, Handel, has been called just that. The only conceivable answer is the quality of the music itself—Hasse's and Alessandro Scarlatti's and that of a few others—which we never hear, and never have a chance to hear.

But *Il Pomo* was merely a supreme superspectacle in an age of super-spectacles.

None of the operatic composers of the early era equaled the activity of Cavalli: forty-one operas in thirty years. Dying in 1676, seven years after composing his last operas, he lived to see the decline of the Venetian school that he had helped to found. The soil of the Most Serene Republic continued to breed composers, but before the end of the century some of the best found employment at Vienna or Naples, even occasionally at Florence or Rome. Antonio Draghi, Carlo Pallavicino, and Agostino Steffani were the most interesting of the *émigrés*. They are named in ascending order of importance. Draghi, who lived long enough to borrow from Scarlatti, seldom rose above the dull usefulness of un-critical fecundity: he left, besides other stage works, sixty-seven operas. Pallavicino, whose operatic average was one a year, showed imagination in using his limited orchestra. Steffani, who might have been one of the greatest composers of the late seventeenth and early eighteenth centuries had he not divided his time among music, statecraft, and diplomacy, had a native understanding of instruments (and of the human voice as but one of them, though ineluctably *prima inter pares*). Steffani's concept reconciled the monodic ideals of the *camerata* with the old contrapuntal tradition, and the result was, at its best, far nobler than the runaway favorites of the time, which joined comedy to easy, almost folksy melody. Among the Venetian stay-at-homes Giovanni Legrenzi alone showed a tolerant resistance to this sure-fire combination and was content to leaven his essentially serious stage works with comic touches.

But Venice was not destined to provide the perdurable recipe that remained more or less valid for Italian opera until the later operas of Verdi. Naples, in less than half a century, worked it out and provided at least one perfect model for its *buffa* aspect, in *La Serva padrona*. But before examining the paradoxical career of Alessandro Scarlatti, the true founder of the Neapolitan school, we must quote from J.-J. Lalande's *Voyage d'un français en Italie* (1769), written over forty years after Scarlatti's death. Here is the classic enunciation of the Neapolitan (later annexed by all Italians) as the race that is peculiarly musical: "Music is a special triumph of the Neapolitans. It seems as if in that country the membranes of the eardrums are more taut, more harmonious, more sonorous than elsewhere in Europe. The whole nation sings: gesture, tone of voice, rhythm of syllables, the very conversation—all breathe music and harmony. Thus Naples is the principal source of Italian music, of great composers and excellent operas." This—everything taken into account—outrageous statement, a glorious eulogy of Scarlatti and his pupils and followers, re-emphasizes the oddity of this great corpus of opera being all but unavailable in performance.

As if to compound the oddity, the fame of Alessandro Scarlatti, the most vital in operatic history between Monteverdi and Handel, has survived outside of most textbooks largely because his son Domenico was one of the most delectable composers of keyboard music who ever lived. Yet, judged by purely musical standards, the now obscure father was the greater of the two. But whereas many of Domenico's sparkling harpsichord sonatas are as fresh and acceptable as on the day they were composed, Alessandro's more than one hundred operas are such obvious period pieces that, as operas, they could be revived only in concert versions. Nor have his other compositions, wonderful as music, fared better, though many of his chamber cantatas would be enjoyable. What has happened to Scarlatti is what would have happened to Handel if he had composed nothing but operas. Most people will probably go to their graves without hearing a single note of some of the best music composed in the seventeenth century, but for this state of affairs Scarlatti himself, as a canny child of his time, is to blame: he gave that baroque age exactly what it wanted, and very few have wanted him since.

Scarlatti was a learned, meticulous craftsman who often had to earn his living by hastily contrived operas. In them, except those composed late in life, it is difficult to find complete proof of his erudition. The key to that resides in his chamber cantatas, of which he wrote hundreds. Many of these cantatas solve the most tortuous of technical problems, and it is fairer to describe them as beautiful puzzles than as operas for solo voice and continuo (there are almost six hundred of these). We can imagine Scarlatti, after a racking day trying to devise a usable operatic score for some royal theater, turning to problems in pure music, and pouring into them that perfect understanding of technique and form which he could use only restrictedly in his workaday life. His chamber cantatas bear much the same relation to his operas as *Die Kunst der Fuge* and *Das musikalisches Opfer* do to the *Cantor*'s labors of Bach. There, of course, the comparison ends, for the German did not have to worry overmuch about catering to the popular taste.

There is an apparently insoluble mystery about Scarlatti's origins and early life. Was he, as he occasionally described himself, a native of Palermo? Were his boyish studies guided by his father, or was his musical lore gained in two years with that same Carissimi who had taught Cesti, and whose only familiar work, until yesterday (when the glories of his great oratorios were first revealed to listeners outside Italy), was a strident love song, "Vittoria, vittoria," that is still all too familiar to recital audiences? Students have professed to find a strong trace of Alessandro Stradella in Scarlatti's early work, but where he could have heard an opera by that accomplished adventurer does not transpire.[4] If Stradella gave anything to young Scarlatti, it was a way with melody, but while the older man was given to maddening repetition of his tunes, his imitator knew when to stop. Also Scarlatti's individual treatment of accompaniments may have been stimulated by a study of Stradella's music.

The first of Scarlatti's operas that can be dated was produced in Rome in 1679, when he was about twenty years old. Rome had been the seat of a flourishing school of operatic composers, abetted by the deft dramatic poet Giulio Rospigliosi, who provided Roman composers with excellent librettos for over twenty years, giving up only when, in 1653 or thereabouts, it was obvious that he was destined for high ecclesiastical preferment (he became pope, as Clement IX, in 1667). Unhappily, the Roman operatic composers wrote little, but that little included such scores as Stefano Landi's *Sant'Alessio* (1632), far ahead of its time and of many a time to come, being about the inner life of a real human being; *La Galatea* (1639), by the famous male soprano Loreto Vittori, which is described as a pastorale of singular beauty; and Luigi Rossi's two operas, *Il Palazzo incantato* (1642) and *L'Orfeo* (1647), both masterly in detail, but as wholes without dramatic relevance. With the fall of the Barberini, their enormous private theater (holding three thousand) was closed, and Paris, whither the Barberini migrated with all their cultural paraphernalia, benefited. The Roman school was short-lived, but produced much that later operatic composers could adapt or imitate.[5]

Thus, by 1679, Rome had heard many fine operas. Fortunately, Scar-

---

[4] Stradella was as unfortunate after death as he was in life: possibly killed by a second set of assassins hired by an irate rival in love (after a first set had been charmed into harmlessness by his music), he became the subject of an opera by the composer of *Martha* and of a novel by F. Marion Crawford; moreover, his most famous composition, "Pietà, Signore," may have been one of Rossini's hoaxes.

[5] Without being a great composer, one of Scarlatti's Roman predecessors, Domenico Mazzocchi, was a clever innovator who advanced musical notation several steps. He was the first to use the signs $<$ and $>$ to indicate increasing and decreasing volume, as well as the abbreviations p (soft), f (loud), and tr (trill).

latti's *Gli Equivoci nel sembiante,* childish though it was in many ways, had hints of genius. It attracted the attention of Christina of Sweden, most notorious of Roman converts, and she immediately extended her dangerous patronage to the young Sicilian. Gustavus Adolphus' recreant daughter was a very strange woman; and those she befriended often lived to regret her generosity. Scarlatti, conductor in her private theater for over four years, came out unscathed. This was unusual, for Christina was as destructive in friendship as in wrath: she had her secretary killed, fought constantly with the almost sainted Innocent XI, and once, in an access of warmth, handshook Alexander VII so violently as to break bones in his fingers.

Although the first public opera house in Rome had been established as early as 1671, some of Scarlatti's Roman operas were performed in Christina's palace. The ex-queen's interest in secular musical entertainment was long-standing and obstinate: she had been a close friend of the charming, libretto-writing Clement IX, and even before his reign, during that of the irresponsible Alexander VII, cardinals thronged to her operas in such numbers that they were said to have been given "in consistory." In 1679, opera in Rome was mainly, because of varying papal sentiments, the toy of the high nobility, and Scarlatti's development was doubtless retarded because his first efforts were made under such unfavorable conditions—had he gone early to Venice or Florence, where opera was already a people's art, his career might have been even more brilliant than it turned out to be. It is possible that in 1684, when he left Christina's service, he was weary of working under straitened conditions. If so, he did little to improve them, for Naples, where he now went, had only the thinnest operatic tradition, and his post as court conductor to the Spanish viceroy, though nominally a step upward, limited his activities quite as much as before. Yet it would be a mistake to think of Scarlatti as vexed with his official duties: of his more than forty years of active composing, twenty-eight were spent in Naples and eleven in Rome. This is not the record of a man driven to rebellion and flight.

Scarlatti, indeed, was anything but a rebel: he was a standardizer of already existing, but not completely realized, musical forms. He invented little, established much. To the detriment of the dramatic unity of an entire work, he concentrated on perfecting a few elements. With all his great purely musical gifts, he stalled the evolution of opera as credible theater: not only did he wither whatever improvisatory freedom opera had when he came upon the scene, but he so congealed the patterns of various operatic elements that even so resourceful a composer as Handel had to turn to oratorio in order to free himself from the bondage of Scarlattian precedents. A casuist might say that by freezing its molds, Scarlatti made his most valuable contribution to opera, as he thereby forced the reforms of Gluck.[6] Only by using the orchestra rather than the harpsichord alone to accompany recitative, thus softening the contrasts between it and the aria, did he look forward to the tendencies that still seem to have the final word in the construction of opera.

Scarlatti's conception of the overture as a three-section, self-contained suite, consisting of an allegro, a *grave,* and another fast movement, is aesthetically above reproach; moreover, it is probably one of the several ancestors of the eighteenth-century sonata form. But its very self-sufficiency cut it away, except in general mood, from the body of the opera itself, and thus delayed the day when, at the hands of Gluck and Mozart, it was to be persuaded into the whole, either flowing effortlessly and without interruption into the action or anticipating it by suave quotation. But, to qualify: Scarlatti at times found his neat little overture a bit stultifying, and tried something related to the whole, as Handel, Jommelli, and a few others were also to try.

Likewise, Scarlatti's perfecting of the *da capo* aria (in which, after a contrasting part, the third section merely repeats the first), based on the sound aesthetic canon of statement, contrast, and recognition, stultified his own output and fathered an undramatic conception of opera which was to dominate the musical stage for more than half a century. Nothing less likely to carry forward the action of a libretto can be imagined than a series of these rigorously devised *da capo* arias: yet, beginning with *Teodora* in 1693, Scarlatti often used fifty or sixty of them to an opera. This, more than any other single element, was to deliver opera, a bound captive, into the singer's hands. Whatever the beauty of its separate pieces, a Scarlatti opera has no more dramatic unity than a Broadway musical comedy. It has, indeed, even less carefully planned organization than a good revue, whose very flouting of rhyme and reason can be a subtle thing. It is a concert of often impressively lovely songs connected precariously by recitative, and grafted, with slight relevance, onto a pseudoclassical libretto.

It is unreasonable to blame Scarlatti for concentrating on the purely

[6] He retained, even in his reform operas, the *da capo* aria, which seemed singularly appropriate to baroque opera, which was a series of moods (*affetti*). Gluck did not merely reform; he was too great a composer and man of the stage to do that. Vestigial remains of baroque-opera conventions have endured—and still endure.

musical aspect of opera and letting the dramatic go by the board. The Florentine fathers of opera had ostensibly started at the other extreme. That Monteverdi, whose few extant operas are superior to Scarlatti's as musical plays, had a conscious understanding of how to bring about a happy balance between the dramatic and musical elements is borne out by his letters. Yet his meditations to the contrary notwithstanding, he was in that happy position of being able to indulge his own bent unhampered; fortunately for the longevity of his works, he had a native flair for drama as well as musical gifts of the highest order. Moreover, living when the Renaissance was dying and the baroque had not fully asserted its character, and before the age of the unrestrained sway of tyrant singers, Monteverdi had no persistent demands to meet: the age had not yet formulated them. Scarlatti, apparently accepting the standards of the high baroque without a question,[7] discovered a popular formula which, until the end of his days, he was content to provide with ever-changing surface decoration.

Of Scarlatti's 115 operas, not half have been preserved, and of those extant many are incomplete. Most of them were designed for Rome or Naples, though a few were composed for Venice or Pratolino, the summer villa of Ferdinando de' Medici, outside Florence. To show to what lengths speculation on the flimsiest evidence can go, it is sometimes stated that the operas written for the Florentine prince were Scarlatti's finest, though scarcely a scrap of their music remains. To support this claim, Scarlatti's letters to Ferdinando, mentioning one of them—*Lucio Manlio*—as the best he had yet written, are brought forward. It is difficult to understand how these letters, which are typical high-flown fawnings on a patron, can be cited as proofs of anything except their author's eagerness to keep the prince happy. Artists have a way of talking a good picture, a good statue—or a good opera.

More convincing of the high quality of these lost Medicean operas is the score of *Il Mitridate Eupatore,* written for Venice during the period Scarlatti was working for Ferdinando. Fortunately, *Mitridate* survives in its entirety—a five-act tragedy with ballet. Written in a grand and elevated manner, the solemnity of which Scarlatti emphasized by the omission of the two comic characters whose presence had become a convention of serious opera, *Mitridate* registers a great advance over the hasty contrivances of his first Neapolitan period. Beautifully conceived, poetically felt, it exerts a pull on the feelings that the brilliant, hard, and showy *Tigrane,* a triumph of Scarlatti's second Neapolitan period, can-

[7] So did Bach and Handel, but each, in his separate way, had great dramatic gifts.

not. Possibly his most noted opera, but certainly not his best, *Tigrane* is nevertheless in some ways more interesting than the lovelier *Mitridate:* the comic scenes are frequent, diversified, and funny, affording a welcome contrast to the heroics of the ranting principals and foreshadowing the vivacities of *opera buffa;* also, this 105th of Scarlatti's operas, composed in 1715, shows that only six years before abandoning a long, practical career, he was tentatively approaching the use of orchestra itself as a full-fledged dramatic element.

By the time of his death in 1725, Scarlatti was a figure from the past. Younger men, among them Handel, had already usurped his popularity in Italy and had coolly appropriated the few devices his musical genius had wheedled into life—for instance, the *da capo* aria and reiterative instrumental interludes (*ritornelli*) in arias. These devices could be imitated, but his ultimate triumph—that inimitable sensuous melodic turn which is an irresistible element of great Italian opera—could only be emulated (or downright stolen). Scarlatti thereby followed in the path of Cavalli and Cesti, who obviously were haunted by the need to be melodic, and showed a way to the most effective of the Italian operatic composers —not merely his Neapolitan successors. Finally, his choice of the minor mode for expressing the elegiac or melancholy fits the sad, appealing, and noble-looking man who watches us gravely from the cracked and faded portrait painted by Francesco Solimena, himself a dominating figure of the Neapolitan baroque.

Scarlatti's last years were not without moments of quickening. His son Domenico, his most eminent pupil, had already set Italy afire with his playing of the harpsichord; in London and Portugal his operas were preferred to his father's. Now, in 1724, only a year before Alessandro Scarlatti's death, a young German came to him and implored to be taken on as a pupil. This was Johann Adolf Hasse, destined to write more than a hundred operas and to be, in some respects, Scarlatti's most faithful and successful disciple. It was Hasse who persuaded Scarlatti to receive, against his will, another young German, Johann Joachim Quantz, already suffering from that lucky love of the flute which was to bring him high fame as the teacher of the most renowned of flautists, Frederick the Great. "Scarlatti," wrote Quantz, "let me hear him on the harpsichord, which he played in a learned manner, though he did not possess as much agility as his son." There, unwittingly, Quantz pronounced Alessandro Scarlatti's epitaph: he was a learned man, and he was the father of Domenico.

Italian opera, Scarlattian in its general lineaments, was to conquer the world and to hold it in fee for many a year, though it might present superficially different faces in different countries. In the process, the leadership was to pass sometimes to England, sometimes to France, even sometimes to Germany and Austria, occasionally in the hands of Italians, more often in those of Italianate foreigners. Italy continued to be a thriving song factory, as it does to this day, but few of its workers produced anything lasting until the first warblings of that quenchless songbird, Gioacchino Rossini, early in the nineteenth century.

The Neapolitan school did not, in general, develop. For the most part, its operatic composers, whatever their gifts, surrendered to the singers—it is not strange that Niccolò (or Nicola) Porpora, whose operas were immensely popular, was the most famous singing teacher of the age. As such, in his old age, after he had taught Farinelli, Caffarelli, and other wonders, he was immortalized in George Sand's *Consuelo*.[8] Frederick Westlake, who knew Porpora's available scores, wrote that he "always wrote beautifully for voices," and indignantly refuted Burney's often-quoted sentence about his *Temistocle* (1718), an early opera: "I never saw music in which shakes were so lavished; Porpora seems to have composed the air 'Contrasto assai' in a shivering fit."

The long-lived Hasse still awaits not merely revival but sympathetic revival. Unlike the intolerably bland Antonio Caldara, Hasse must have pondered his designs, and many of them exist in two versions, some even in three, like his masterpiece *Artaserse,* which contained two of the several arias that Farinelli nightly sang to the melancholy Philip V of Spain. Quite apart from the disastrous Dresden fire, when his manuscripts, brought together and revised for the collected edition to be published at the King's expense (Augustus II was King of Poland as well as Elector of Saxony), were destroyed, Hasse suffered from the pleasure of being married to the lovely Faustina Bordoni, the greatest female singer of the age. Marriage, as well as his Neapolitan upbringing, compelled him to compose singers' operas, besides which most of his stage works were written to librettos by Metastasio, whose sole interest emphasized the necessity of his limpid texts' being sung to equally limpid music. And surely, no one could complain that Hasse's music was not lovely, for it shed beauty in and out of season. Yet he attempted to vary his style to fit the mood, treated the *da capo* aria as a form rather than as a pattern, and

[8] The famous *castrato* Antonio Uberti, who lived to teach the great Mme Mara, called himself **Porporino** after his master.

occasionally attained a poignant expressiveness, technically attributable to his nice understanding of orchestral and vocal combinations. As not a single one of Hasse's operas exists in a modern edition, we must rely on fragments published in musical histories.

Dying in 1783, Hasse outlived the much younger Niccolò Jommelli and Tommaso Traetta, born respectively in 1714 and 1727, and was not survived long by Antonio Sacchini, who died in 1786. These later Neapolitans expressed their dissatisfaction with their heritage fragmentarily; but at least, as much-courted travelers, they showed from time to time that old patterns had to be discarded or at least revised. Sacchini, the most disgruntled, but also unhappily an idler, ended up as an avowed disciple of Gluck. Jommelli, whose loyalty to Metastasio limited his development, nevertheless took note of both German and French procedures, whereas Traetta, a searching intellectual, fell under the influence of Rameau, though he seems never to have gone to France. Both owed to Germany a scholarly understanding of orchestration, but neither worked himself free of Neapolitan bonds. Yet a good modern writer's reference to their "lace-valentine texture" seems unnecessarily harsh.

These Neapolitan operatic composers, some of them earnestly questing and undeniably intelligent and self-critical (Jommelli's musicianship has been compared to Gluck's to the latter's discredit), if not utterly forgotten, are commemorated only by special pleaders, notably by that delicate eclectic of twilight yesterdays, Vernon Lee. Their music-making was not contemptible: some of their airs might pass as Scarlatti's. They had a correctness and elegance that are the ineluctible qualities of their age, and they were sweet, tender, and sometimes subtle melodists. A few isolated airs rise above this accomplished craftsmanship; but these musical poets of the eighteenth century in Italy, without the enduring boldness needed for big issues, lacked, similarly, staying power. They are interim men, hangers-on of traditions that took many years in dying.

More vigorous, because it did not rely on the stultified traditions of *opera seria* and, from the least promising beginnings, forced a respectable place for itself, was *opera buffa*. This variety of comic opera stemmed from the broadly farcical interludes with which, even before the days of opera itself, comic leavening had been inserted between the acts of an otherwise serious play. These *intermezzi,* as they were called at their first appearance in the sixteenth century,[9] had no connection whatever with

---

[9] A more ancient lineage is claimed for them, carrying their genealogy back to the interludes in medieval times and even to the Roman *saturae*.

the play in which they appeared and at first were merely comic songs or madrigals without dramatic content. Serious operatic composers, by retaining these *intermezzi,* weakened further the already feeble structural integrity of their tragedies—or comedies; but no doubt they wished to satisfy their audiences' persistent hankering after the rough-and-tumble of the *commedia dell' arte.* Even Alessandro Scarlatti did not disdain to compose *intermezzi;* by his time, however, they had developed certain conventions of their own, sometimes being musical Punch-and-Judy shows. As soon as plots began to be fitted to them, it was inevitable that the *intermezzi* would expand to self-sufficiency, often being lifted from the parent opera, and produced and published separately. At the moment when, having drawn to itself all the comic elements of the old opera, especially the two conventional farce characters, the *intermezzo* became the *opera buffa,* the distinction between it and *opera seria* was sharply defined.

Many composers of opera tried their hands at *buffa,* once it was established. The great Carlo Goldoni wrote librettos for the patrician Leonardo Leo and for the deft Baldassare Galuppi.[10] The *buffe* developed along broad, simple lines; so much so, in fact, that in 1733, when the model *buffa—La Serva padrona*—was produced, it depended for its effects on the general atmosphere of horseplay, the use of two strongly contrasted characters (there were three characters in all, one of them mute), and a time-honored plot that rang every conceivable change on the comic aspects of jealousy. First used between the acts of one of its composer's serious operas, *La Serva padrona* almost immediately received independent performance, and within a few years was a favorite throughout the peninsula. In 1752 it started a riot among the Parisian intellectuals, arousing Rousseau and the Encyclopedists, as well as the aged Rameau—in his role, of course, of master theoretician. Its fame continued to spread and is not yet extinct.

Giovanni Battista Pergolesi, the contriver of this long-lived trifle which runs little more than half an hour, had such an incredible and melodramatic life that he has ended up as the subject of two operas. Except for having died in his bed rather than by poison, and at the age of twenty-six instead of seventeen, Pergolesi might be termed the Chatterton of Italian music. He might better be compared to Mozart: legend has

[10] Whose *Il Filosofo di campagna,* the most popular *buffa* between Pergolesi's *La Serva padrona* and Piccinni's *La Buona Figliuola,* has been revived at least thrice in the twentieth century.

been busy blackening their names with exaggerated charges of profligacy and extravagance. Appealing figures both, they worked hard and earnestly against time, frequently on large and ambitious works, and died disregarded and penniless. Legend, furthermore, has said that Pergolesi completed his *Stabat Mater* on his deathbed: unfortunately for the parallel to Mozart's dying before he could finish the Requiem, Pergolesi wrote the *Stabat Mater* when he was only nineteen and in excellent health. This is the *Stabat Mater* Rossini regarded so highly that he hesitated—but in vain—to set the same text himself. His version, not inferior to Pergolesi's, is—to modern ears—even more theatrical. In our own times, Igor Stravinsky has done his bit to keep green the name of the composer of *La Serva padrona:* in 1920, for the Ballet Russe, he pieced together a charming collection of tunes attributed to Pergolesi and called the result *Pulcinella.* While it is possible to name Pergolesi, somewhat loosely, the father of comic opera, *La Serva padrona* may have been, in its creator's mind, one of the least of his artistic children, for the very reason that it had first appeared as an *intermezzo* in his opera *Il Prigionier superbo,* which signally failed.

La Serva padrona was the first important *buffa.* Most practitioners of *buffa,* notably those who worked at it exclusively, have been obscure, but some of its occasional devotees have been geniuses. Cimarosa, its next great exponent in Italy, seems—though mostly for chronological reasons—to belong to another age: born only thirteen years after Pergolesi's death, he died in the nineteenth century, having composed his single masterpiece, *Il Matrimonio segreto,* in Vienna the year after the death of Mozart, himself a genius of *buffa.* That same year, 1792, Italy's greatest manufacturer of gaiety, Rossini, was born. The line may not yet be extinct: Ermanno Wolf-Ferrari, whose *Il Segreto di Susanna* is in the most sparkling tradition, died as recently as 1948.

Earthier and more robust than *opera seria, opera buffa* steadfastly refused to employ the services of *castrati,* sturdily insisting that full-grown men were either tenors, baritones, or basses, and women sopranos or contraltos. Thus it escaped in some measure the dictatorship of the singers, who thought of opera only as a testing ground for their agility. Nevertheless, by the beginning of the eighteenth century the star system had so fastened itself on opera that librettists and composers were often the servants of the singers.

The librettists, if they had a shred of originality (which was not often the case), found themselves hedged in by restrictions at every point.

The libretto was more rule-bound than the French classic drama: big parts had to be written for the principals, whether the logic of the story admitted such procedure or not (this sad state of affairs continued well into the nineteenth century); the order of the scenes in which the principals and secondary performers were to shine was based on a jealously preserved scheme of precedence that might tax the hair-splitting talents of the editors of *Burke's Peerage*. Not only were the sequence and timing of solo and concerted numbers as inflexibly ordered as the laws of the Medes and the Persians, but also the prerogatives of the principals had to be so nicely balanced that the writing of a libretto, even without these extra complications a difficult task, became as involved as a Chinese puzzle. Is it, then, strange that the librettos were seldom dramatic?

As for the poor composer who had to respect what pitiable fragments of drama were handed to him, he was not even allowed the luxury of fitting to the poetry the most appropriate music he could conceive. If a jealous singer felt himself slighted in the allotment of scenes, the wretched musician was often obliged to interpolate a number utterly irrelevant to the already twisted scheme of action. Finally, there was no guarantee that the singers would be satisfied with the music as written: many an operatic performance degenerated into a carnival of ad-libbing, with each entrant playing to the gallery with every vocal trick at his command.

A few strong composers tried to oppose the singer's despotism, but as long as they worked within the frame of the old opera, with its undramatic sequence of set scenes, orchestral *ritornelli,* and *da capo* arias, they were beaten before they started. Their audiences were not with them, but with the singers, as Handel was to discover more than once. Rebel composers and rebel librettists were needed who would house-clean opera from top to bottom. And a small rebellious minority in the audience was needed, too—a minority that would be interested in the dramatic unity of music and action.

CHAPTER III

Handel

WHEN the Saxon Heinrich Schütz arrived in Venice in 1609 to study with one of the brilliant *maestri* of St. Mark's Chapel, opera was still an unfledged novelty. Although Schütz was pre-eminently interested in religious music, he possessed the genius and the common sense to master both the contrapuntal style of the Venetian school and that of *le nuove musiche,* which had come to light in Florence but a few years earlier and was advancing the cause of monody, without which opera either would have become something different or would not have flourished at all. After his return to Germany, Schütz served as one bridge from the era of the great Italian contrapuntalists to that of Bach and Handel. His profound musical education and obvious abilities made him much sought after, and when he at last settled in Dresden, it was as *Kapellmeister* to the Elector Johann Georg I. A dozen years later, in 1627, he was called upon to provide special music for the wedding of the Elector's daughter Sophie to the Landgrave of Hesse-Darmstadt.

Schütz sent to Italy for the score of Peri's *Dafne.* It arrived safely, but in Italian. In one of the earliest examples of mistaken earnestness of the sort, it was decided to have the honeyed Italian syllables translated into German by the philosopher-poet Martin Opitz. This precipitated one of those musicolinguistic crises which so often and so unnecessarily confront opera impresarios: it was found that Opitz's lines did not satisfactorily fit Peri's music. So Schütz had to adapt some of the music to Opitz's lines and probably to add some music of his own to piece out the ceremonial prologue and five acts.

Thus, more than three centuries ago, the problem of performing opera in a language other than that of the libretto to which its score was originally composed, of attempting to make the text of an opera understandable to a new group of listeners—the problem, in short, that Americans and Englishmen know as "opera in English"—was conceived, faced, and unsatisfactorily solved. No satisfactory solution of it has ever been found; in truth, by its nature the problem is insoluble.

Obviously, an understanding of the text is essential to real understanding of an opera; efforts to secure this understanding by translation spring from an entirely commendable intention. The objections to performance in translation are, however, manifold and insuperable. Some important ones are phonetic: certain vowel sounds can be heard fully only when sung at certain pitches; some languages are relatively stressless, whereas others—English and German, for example—are heavily stressed. The most sensitive composers have respected these considerations, consciously and unconsciously, wherever possible. Other translation difficulties have to do with syntax: the order in which words occur often dictates the line of a melody and the ebb and flow of speed and of relative loudness and softness. Still other difficulties have to do with the differing temper of various languages: terseness, diffuseness, concentration, various imponderables. To translate a libretto—or even the text of a song—from one language to another, keeping all these factors in mind, and produce a text that can be sung without altering the music is impossible.

Christoph Willibald von Gluck, a great master of opera, faced the difficulties and solved them in the only possible way. When he produced *Orphée et Eurydice,* the French version of his Italian *Orfeo ed Euridice,* he largely recomposed the music. Unhappily, composers are usually dead or indifferent when translation of one of their operas seems desirable, and are not involved in translating the music into the new language. Nor is another musician, however talented and well trained, ever justified in tampering with a composer's notes in order to make them fit words for which they were not intended.[1]

[1] To bring the problem to the United States and England again, it would be far better for everyone concerned if we should drop the meaningless cry of "opera in English," insist upon having good bilingual printed librettos, study the two texts side by side before a performance, and come to understand the texts and music together as librettist and composer intended them to be understood. Needless to say, English can be sung as well as any other language: as has been proved many times, operas composed to English texts can be sung so that they can be understood though, mournfully, they usually are not.

Returning to Schütz, it was probably on April 13, 1627, at Schloss Hartenfels near Torgau in Saxony, that *Daphne,* not only the first opera performed in Germany but also the first German opera, was first heard. The fuss attendant upon its production may have discouraged not only Schütz, who seems never to have had a hand in another opera though he lived another forty-five years, but also many of his successors who might otherwise have been tempted to set German texts. Serious opera in German did not establish itself for nearly two centuries, though opera in Italian by both Germans and foreigners attained a great vogue in Germany before the end of the seventeenth century.

To measure the full effects of the Thirty Years' War on the creative energy of Continental Europe is impossible, but it unquestionably proved ruinous to any vigorous expression of German genius. The *Daphne* of Schütz and Opitz, produced in the full tide of the war, remained unique; also, because its score was destroyed by fire in 1760, only the text surviving, its quality is a matter for guesswork. Opera remained the occasional diversion of courtly life throughout the German states until shortly after the opening of an opera house in Hamburg in 1678, whereafter an active school of musicodramatic writers sprang up in that old Hanse town. Of these early German opera composers, the most interesting, because he was perhaps the most gifted, was Johann Wolfgang Franck, who provided the Hamburg theater with fourteen operas in half as many years. But since in all probability audiences will never hear even a measure from Franck's operas, his fame is more likely to rest on the facts that he was one of the first composers to set one of his own texts (*Aeneas,* 1680) and that he was one of the few murderers ever to achieve distinction as a composer: in a jealous fury, he stabbed his wife and killed a fellow musician.

Franck's young contemporary Reinhard Keiser also led a violent and unkempt life, but he bulks larger in the history of music because he influenced Handel's career. The extraordinary Keiser bestrode musical Hamburg, with few intermissions, for forty years, reigning as musical dictator at the opera house and even insinuating himself into the cathedral revenues as a canon. Bounder, spendthrift, and prolific composer of stage pieces and religious works quite as lively, he lifted Hamburg to musical supremacy in Northern Europe. He wrote more than one hundred operas, sometimes at the rate of eight a year. These works, estimated to contain no less than 4,500 separate airs, often are melodically attractive and at times show a sense of dramatic verity. But most of

them were composed to German texts of such wretched workmanship
and parched imagination that it is small wonder that by 1740, a year after
Keiser's death, not a single one of his operas held the boards, which were
thenceforward given over to settings of more polished Italian texts.[2]

Far more notable than Keiser's varied services to Hamburg was his
hiring, in 1703, as second violinist in the opera orchestra, an eighteen-
year-old youth from Halle who, writing to Italian librettos and producing mostly in England, was destined to become the first great German
musician to compose operas. This was George Frideric Handel, for such
was the way that Georg Friedrich Händel signed his name for the forty
most productive years of his life. He composed his first stage work when
Keiser grew tired of setting a partial translation into German (some
sections being left in Italian) by Friedrich Christian Feustking of an
Italian libretto remotely derived from a Spanish play by Lope de Vega.
Handel took it up and quickly composed *Almira,* the leading tenor role
to be sung by his friend Johann Mattheson, who wrote operas but was
even more immersed in musical theory. Coming shortly after a duel between the two young friends, the bilingual *Almira,* which had forty-two
arias in German and fifteen in Italian, proved to be not merely a compliment to Mattheson's vocal and histrionic abilities, but also, and more
importantly, an omen of Handel's flair for the stage.

After *Almira*'s *première* on January 8, 1705, it ran for about twenty
performances. Keiser, who endured no successful rivals near his throne,
was enraged, though he could have taken Handel's maiden effort as a
tribute to himself: stylistically, it was his own child.[3] Happily for the
general peace, Handel's second effort, *Nero,* first sung on February 25,
1705, was a failure and provided Keiser with what he took to be an opportunity to read a lesson to his froward subordinate: he himself set the
librettos of both *Almira* and *Nero* to show how it should be done. But the
Hamburgers would have none of his Queen of Castille or his first fiddling
Caesar, and *Octavia,* his second Nero opera, failed as miserably. What
had been meant to finish Handel ended by finishing Keiser for the time
being. Johann Saurbrey, the new director at the opera, was friendly to

[2] One of the few recent opportunities to hear music by Keiser was afforded,
curiously, by *Der tolle Kapellmeister* (1929), an operetta by Benno Bardi produced in Berlin. Based on Keiser's life, it quoted lavishly from his operatic music.

[3] In the last act of *Almira* occurs a sarabande that haunted Handel's mind. He
used its melody several times later—most effectively, perhaps, in the well-known
"Lascia ch'io pianga" in *Rinaldo* (1711).

Handel, but Mattheson, who had sung in Handel's *Nero,* turned jealously against him, and the young Saxon decided to try his fortunes elsewhere.

A half-invitation from one of the minor Medici may have been decisive in attracting Handel to Italy. For something like four years, until early in 1710, he posted up and down the peninsula, studying styles, playing the harpsichord and organ, and tossing off his earliest near-oratorios. At first he was feted rather as a performer than as a composer, outshining even the scintillant Domenico Scarlatti, with whom he seems occasionally to have vied in friendly contest. His first Italian opera, *Rodrigo,* in which the leading soprano role was written for La Bombace (the famous soprano Vittoria Tarquini), may not have been performed, though some reports have it sung in Florence, adding that Handel's reward was a little money and a set of dishes from Alessandro Scarlatti's penurious patron, Ferdinando de' Medici.

But *Agrippina,* mounted in Venice at the Grimani family's fine Teatro San Giovanni Crisostomo (the libretto was by Cardinal Vincenzo Grimani, viceroy of Naples), on December 26, 1709, made official the news that Handel was to be reckoned with in the world of Italian opera. This second of his approximately forty Italian operas was sung twenty-seven times during the Carnival season and remained in the repertoire for almost a quarter of a century when operas were mostly as frail as the virtue of their heroines. *Agrippina* brought him fame and his future. Not only were several members of its original cast to sing for him later in London, but, also, an absorbed spectator from the dogal loge at each night of that unprecedented run in 1709–10 was Prince Ernst Augustus, whose brother, the Elector Georg Ludwig of Hanover, was heir presumptive to the British throne. Once before, the Prince (the first of that very special group, the Handelians,[4] as partisan in their way as the Wagnerians) had invited Handel to become *Kapellmeister* at Hanover. Now he renewed the offer, and Handel, strangely, with Venice at his feet, accepted.

By 1711, tired in less than one year of the stodgy splendors of Herrenhausen, the Elector Georg's imitation Versailles, Handel was in Lon-

---

[4] Perhaps the most vociferous of those who have exalted Handel above all other composers was Samuel Butler, author of *The Way of All Flesh,* to whom Bach was less than dirt beneath Handel's feet. Butler composed two oratorios, Handelian in everything but spirit, to librettos by his future biographer, H. Festing Jones, a descendant of Michael Christian Festing (1680?–1752), who had known Handel personally.

don on leave. *Rinaldo,* his first opera there, was produced to tremendous acclaim on February 24, 1711. What he saw in England evidently pleased him more than the easier charms of Italy, for though expiration of his leave from Hanover forced him to return to the Continent, he was back in London as soon as he could decently plead for another vacation. The decisive factor in wedding Handel to England was not the single fact that *Rinaldo* had won a great success there: in similar circumstances, when *Agrippina* was being sung night after night in Venice, he had turned his back on Italy. Handel was innately as English as the English, and he recognized his soil the moment he touched it. Thenceforth, for almost half a century, he was to remain in London, making only a few hurried, brief excursions abroad. Every year putting on another pound or two of flesh, every year becoming more John Bullish, he eventually became one of the town's honored monuments. Among the great dead in Westminster Abbey, none is less foreign than the man who was christened Georg Friedrich Händel.

The paradox of Handel's career is that, despite his intense Englishness, he dealt a crippling blow to opera in English. Except for a rare sport, usually in some comic genre, no English operas have established themselves fully to this day. And, indeed, English opera was most often a halfhearted thing. Beginning during the latter days of the Commonwealth as a way of circumventing the Puritan ban against stage plays, it took feeble wing from the hand of Sir William D'Avenant, poet laureate and playwright of parts, who amused himself by letting it be noised about that he was Shakespeare's bastard. Pleasant coxcomb that he was, D'Avenant had all the blatant confidence, though not the genius, that might have been expected in a love child of England's greatest poet; and when, in 1656, he advertised an experiment as *The Firste Dayes Entertainment at Rutland House by Declamations and Musick; after the manner of the Ancients,* he was not, as the last phrase might have seemed to indicate, aping Peri and Caccini. He was merely playing a trick on the Protector: he wanted his dramatic poems set to music so that they could be staged legally.

Several months later, D'Avenant followed *The Firste Dayes Entertainment* with what is often called the first English opera, *The Siege of Rhodes,* likewise staged at his private dwelling, Rutland House, about September 10, 1656. Given without dancing and without the scenic display characteristic of Continental presentations of opera, this miscellaneous effort enlisted the varying talents of five composers: Henry

Lawes, Captain Henry Cooke, Matthew Locke, Dr. Charles Coleman, and George Hudson, the last two composing only instrumental music. Locke also sang in the first performances.

Public response to *The Siege of Rhodes* encouraged D'Avenant to lease a theater for the performance of opera, with some difficulty wangling a license from the prevailingly bluenosed regime. *The Cruelty of the Spaniards in Peru* and *The History of Sir Francis Drake* were thus produced at the Cockpit, and, finally, *The Siege of Rhodes* was lengthened for revival there. It was doubtless about one of these, staged amid the troubles attending the distintegration of the timid rule of Richard Cromwell, that John Evelyn, under the date of May 6, 1659, entered in his diary: "I went to visit my brother in London and next day to see a new opera, after the Italian way in recitative music and sceanes much inferior to the Italian composure and magnificence: but it was prodigious that in a time of such public consternation such a vanity should be kept up or permitted. I being engaged with company could not decently resist the going to see it though my heart smote me for it."

During the reigns of James I and Charles I, the masque and, increasingly, its cousin the pastoral drama with music had flourished. One of the most famous of these, with a text by Milton, had been heard at Ludlow Castle in 1634 when John Egerton, Earl of Bridgewater, had been installed as Lord Lieutenant of Wales and the Marches: it was *Comus*, with music by the composer-singer Henry Lawes.[5] Nearer the condition of opera and farther from that of word-accompanied dance-pantomime-spectacle was a masque heard for the first time near the end of Charles II's reign, John Blow's *Venus and Adonis*, a near-opera in a prologue and three acts to a text whose author has not been determined. When it was performed in London, probably about 1684, the role of Venus was assigned to one of the King's mistresses, Mary Davies—and Mary Tudor, her daughter by the King, took the part of Cupid.

The restoration of the Stuarts in 1660 had reopened the theaters for spoken plays. English opera, thus having lost its *raison d'être* as a substitute (and masques and pastoral dramas continuing to be largely semi-

[5] *Comus*, with the Milton text revised and added to by Dr. John Dalton, was presented successfully, with an entirely new score by Thomas Augustine Arne, at the Drury Lane Theatre, London, in 1738. Milton's poem was also used, in Italian adaptation by Paolo Rolli, as the basis of a *pasticcio* opera, *Sabrina*, heard at His Majesty's Theatre in the Haymarket on April 26, 1737, Rolli having also selected and arranged the music.

amateur entertainments for court and nobility), ceased to breathe but did not quite expire. Foreign musicians became the rage under the Francophile Charles II, but few operas—and those mostly French—were heard in London. Not until some months after the resurrection of the national consciousness which accompanied the arrival of William of Orange on English shores did English opera also revive and, in one of its few hours of splendor, throw off a masterpiece. At Josias Priest's school for young ladies in Chelsea, probably at Christmastide, 1689, was sung *Dido and Aeneas,* the work of Blow's pupil Henry Purcell, a thirty-year-old musician in the royal service, "the greatest natural genius that the country has produced, and one of the greatest of any country or any period."

Nephew of a man who had sung a leading role in *The Siege of Rhodes* and son of another seasoned court musician, this active, vigorous, worldly pluralist is a baffling figure. The simplest explanation of Purcell's failure to produce, during a lifetime about as long as Mozart's, the sovereign masterpieces that might reasonably have been expected from so commanding a genius is that he was born either too early or too late. In some of his compositions he seems a belated Elizabethan: his mastery extended to every phase and form of the art of music as it had been de-. veloped up to his own time in England, and had he lived in the time of the great Queen, he might have so participated in its exuberance and joyful life as to have crowned the achievements of the school of Gibbons, Byrd, and Bull. In other compositions he seems a premature composer of another sort, looking ahead into the eighteenth century, but lacking the glass with which to see it. Living in a relatively barren age of English music, he had to vex himself with finding the right garments to clothe his ideas and to fritter away his tragically brief time in doing so. In this process, he poured out a flood of works, more than a few of them great music. But had he been able to draw upon a living tradition, particularly a living formal tradition, as the eighteenth-century composers were to do, he would now be known not only as England's greatest composer but also as the peer of Bach and Handel.

Unhappily, this man, who in his profusion of occasional odes, welcome hymns, and catches showed lively awareness of the life around him, went back, in his only true opera, to a classical subject instead of following the lines of possible interest opened up in *The Siege of Rhodes* and D'Avenant's other librettos. If Purcell had taken D'Avenant's hint, the reaction against the increasingly stultified classical libretto might have occurred half a century before it did, and might have come from a serious rather than a comic direction. But Purcell took what was handed to him. To a humdrum, fatuous text by Nahum Tate, noted along with Colley Cibber as the most egregious of the Shakespearean adapters, he composed *Dido and Aeneas*.

The prologue and three brief acts of Purcell's opera are crammed with all the complex machinery we are now accustomed to find in opera: dancing, recitative and arias, ensembles, instrumental interludes, and choral numbers. Each act is held together within the framework of a very few persistently used key signatures: Act I, for instance, hovers around C major and C minor. In a long act this might become unbearably monotonous, but Purcell's speed and concentration are always such that the effect is right and inevitable. In fact, the pace is almost too swift: Purcell does not give his audience enough time to relax and savor the succession of delights. Fortunately, the finest thing in the opera—Dido's heartbreaking lament, "When I am laid in earth"—comes last. The hearer, having experienced this emotional purge, might resent the immediate irruption of another number, however fine.

Purcell went on to compose a wealth of incidental music for plays, twice supplying so much music, indeed, that the resulting work comes very close to opera. Such, for example, is *King Arthur or The British Worthy,* a "dramatick opera" in a prologue, five acts, and an epilogue, which John Dryden had intended as the sequel of his *Albion and Albanius*. First heard in London at Dorset Gardens in May or June, 1691, it stands wavering on the border between masque, music-accompanied play, and opera. Equally difficult for categorizers is *The Fairy Queen,* an adaptation of Shakespeare's *A Midsummer Night's Dream* by unknown hands. Again Purcell was generous with music for the production of this play at Dorset Gardens in April, 1692. But never after *Dido and Aeneas* did an occasion or a libretto spur him to compose another continuous score that can certainly and without equivocation be called that of an opera. *Dido and Aeneas* all but vanished from the stage for nearly two centuries, and thus did not influence the course of dramatic music in England. It was the cornerstone of a structure that was never to be reared, for though Purcell influenced Handel, contributing markedly to that quality in the Saxon's music which we recognize immediately as "English," that influence did not exert itself so much on Handel's operas as on his oratorios. Purcell's unique way of wringing pure music from emotions— his peculiar intensity—disappeared from England with its author.

Purcell's death in 1695 removed from the scene the one English genius who might have established English opera on solid foundations. An influx of foreigners followed. As early as Charles II, French and Italian singers had begun invading the island, where their spectacular vocal prowess was much prized. As early as 1661, D'Avenant was employing a *castrato* in *The Siege of Rhodes,* but because he was a poor specimen of the artificial breed, the populace did not take to him. The great male soprano Siface appears to have sparked the vogue for *castrati,* which swelled to such proportions that the English, simultaneously attracted and repelled, tried vainly to stem the current by forcing very high natural tenors to add falsetto notes at the top of their registers. The counter-tenors [6] were, operatically speaking, but a stopgap. Siface flourished under the Catholic Stuarts, but found England inhospitable after the Battle of the Boyne. When he departed, Purcell commemorated the event by a little harpsichord piece, *Sefauchi's Farewell.*

Other *castrati* were to follow Siface shortly. Meanwhile, there appeared in London in 1692 the first important female singer to make a career in England, Margherita de l'Épine—whom H. Sutherland Edwards, in his study of the phenomenon, was to call the first prima donna. As early as 1703, handbills announcing "positively the last time of her singing on the stage during her stay in England" were being passed out: this serves to date a familiar prima-donnaish frailty, for the *signora* continued for fifteen years longer to warble in London, and never left England at all. Further, in 1703 the best part of her career was ahead of her. Two years later she sang songs before and after the performance of Thomas Clayton's *Arsinoë,* the libretto of which was probably pieced together from an Italian source by Peter Motteux, famous for his pioneering translation, with Sir Thomas Urquhart, of Rabelais. As *Arsinoë* was sung in English, De l'Épine underwent the humiliation of hearing her English-born rival, Mrs. Tofts, carry off honors in the opera itself. *Arsinoë* was a success. But Clayton's next opera, *Rosamond,* which boasted a libretto by Addison, failed miserably, dealing a formidable blow to the faction struggling to maintain opera in English.

The Italians, composers and singers alike, were not slow to fill the gap. While the disappointed Clayton retired to Ireland, and there spread the blessings of opera with English texts, Italian artists slowly but surely

---

[6] A countertenor is a physically intact male singer whose voice has been trained to rise above normal adult pitch. The resulting tones aspire to relatively full-throated falsetto.

began to take over the musical stage. Bilingual operas, sung partly in English and partly in Italian, marked an intermediate period. Finally, in January, 1710, London heard its first uncompromisingly Italian opera—*Almahide*—which brought together a galaxy of brilliant Italian singers, including, besides De l'Épine, the *castrato* Valentini, who had been a contralto until his voice changed, whereupon he had become a glorious soprano. Unhappily, the names of the librettist and composer of *Almahide* are not known: [7] what was more important, perhaps, was that this historic opera required the services of two prima donnas and at least two *castrati*. The stage was set for Handel.

And Handel was ready. What might have been the effect upon his future activities if the first opera with which he was to challenge the already securely entrenched Italian composers had been some trifle of the Clayton caliber? Fortunately for him, the opera that he composed in two weeks under the loving eye of Aaron Hill, a prince of eighteenth-century impresarios, was a masterpiece, *Rinaldo*. Its libretto, by Giacomo Rossi, deals with the tale of Rinaldo and Armida from Tasso's *Gerusalemme liberata*. The cast that Hill and Handel had assembled for the *première* at the Queen's Theatre on February 24, 1711, was superb. It included Giuseppe Maria Boschi, leading basso of the era, and the *castrato* Nicolini, whose nightingale tones seemed to have been awaiting exactly the airs that Handel had assigned to him. London, on which *Rinaldo* fell like a bombshell full of delights, carried the opera on its lips for months. Years later, when Dr. Johann Christoph Pepusch concocted that marvelous *pasticcio* [8] known as *The Beggar's Opera,* he could not get his hated rival's airs out of his mind, and found them good enough to borrow. During its first season, *Rinaldo* played to fifteen crowded houses; it was being revived as late as 1731. On the profits from printing songs from its tuneful score, John Walsh laid the foundation of his sizable fortune as a music publisher.

Handel led a crowded life as a purveyor of stage music for so many years that to chronicle the composition, production, and reception of all of his operas and near-operas would be as monotonous as chronicling all the separate transactions of any businessman. For Handel became a

---

[7] Some reason exists for supposing that the score may have been by Giovanni Battista Buononcini, of whom more later.

[8] *Rinaldo* itself was almost a *pasticcio,* though all of Handel's own baking: some of its sections he simply recast from earlier operas. Its high spots are Rinaldo's soprano "Cara sposa" and Almirena's "Lascia ch'io pianga."

businessman—a speculator who made and lost fortunes, intermittently displaying a superb nose for what the public could be wheedled into buying. Nothing tells more eloquently his feeling of responsibility to himself as a shrewd dealer and man of substance than his half-amused, half-bitter remark after the blazing success of John Walsh's edition of songs from *Rinaldo*—from which the publisher seems to have earned about fourteen hundred guineas, Handel not even twenty—that Walsh should compose the next opera and he would publish it.

Until 1719, Handel, though engaged in a number of musical activities of the highest importance to his development, especially as a composer of oratorios, was jockeying for a position as an impresario and supplier of popular operas which he could not be sure of until he had regularized his relations with the new dynasty. For when Queen Anne died childless after a tragic round of childbearing, her successor was that Elector Georg of Hanover whom Handel had, in a sense, deserted for the attractions and potentially fat profits of London. Since George I, for all his objectionable qualities, loved music, he could not long remain vexed by the insubordination of so good a composer. So, after some perfunctory pouting, he showed up at performances of a revival of *Rinaldo* on July 2 and 9, 1715. All was forgiven.

By 1719, therefore, when the parvenu but powerful Duke of Newcastle and some of his friends were seeking a general director for an opera company to be called, by the King's permission, the Royal Academy of Music, George naturally suggested his friend Handel. Only one year before the bursting of the South Sea Bubble, selling ten thousand pounds' worth of shares in the Royal Academy was an easy matter, especially when His Majesty led off the list of subscribers with one thousand pounds. Lavishness keynoted the venture. Handel went to the Continent to secure singers, not only hiring the *castrato* known as Senesino and the soprano Margherita Durastanti, but also rehiring Boschi, who had shone so splendidly in *Rinaldo*. Both Durastanti and Boschi had sung in *Agrippina* in Venice ten years earlier.

In their desire to be magnificent, the directors of the Royal Academy sowed the seeds of discord by engaging what they termed "associate composers," among them Giovanni Battista Buononcini. This gifted but haughty and addlepated Italian, thirteen years Handel's senior, and with notable successes in his past, willingly and foolishly acceded to the wish of a group of dissidents within the Academy that he allow himself to be set up as Handel's rival. When the inevitable storm finally burst, the King was found supporting his compatriot; the great Duke of Marlborough, who was almost tone-deaf, was one of those in the Buononcini camp.

Radamisto, the first Handel opera presented under the auspices of the Royal Academy, opened at the King's Theatre in the Haymarket without benefit of an overt schism in the ranks of the shareholders, but also— except for Margherita Durastanti—without benefit of the stellar cast Handel had hired abroad: the other singers, still under contract on the Continent, could not appear. *Radamisto* was a sensation, nonetheless, surely in part because of Polissena's magnificent soprano aria "Ombra cara." [9] It achieved ten or eleven performances between April 27, 1720, and the closing of the Royal Academy season on June 25. So persistent was its success—it was to be revived often—that Continental musicians soon heard of it; in 1722 Handel's old friend and enemy Johann Mattheson staged it in Hamburg, having renamed it *Zenobia* after its heroine and having left the airs in Italian, though he himself composed recitatives in German to replace the Italian dialogue. In England, Handel's star shone brightly. The opposition momentarily felt dashed. But in the autumn of 1720 Buononcini's *Astarto,* his first London opera, was staged for Senesino's London debut and all but equaled the popularity of *Radamisto.*

The battle lines were drawn: the shareholders divided into two camps. Even the most sanguine Handelians could not hope for easy victory. The dramatically inclined suggested a contest between the composer rivals, decision to be awarded to him who wrote the finer act of a three-act opera, the opening act of which—doubtless to square things all around —was assigned to a vague nonentity whose name was either Mattei or Amadei. Handel's third act of *Muzio Scevola* (1721) won him a bootless victory: the adherents of Buononcini, who were in reality using Handel as a substitute target in their rage against their English-hating German monarch, would not acknowledge defeat in a fair fight.

The struggle between the alien lords of opera seesawed back and forth for seven years, during which polite—and sometimes not so polite— factionalism raged. For a time it seemed that Buononcini might win out: his light, sensuously tuneful operas proved irresistible to a large section of high society. In an attempt to strengthen his hand, Handel kept im-

[9] Sir John Hawkins reported that Handel thought "Ombra cara" and "Cara sposa" from *Rinaldo* the best arias he had ever composed. Psychologists might study the fact that Handel, a permanent bachelor, should have rated so high two tributes to faithful spouses.

porting more and more vocal stars, until London became a vast cage of singing birds. There was Senesino, with whom the future Empress Maria Theresa had deigned to sing duets. His incredible roulades, however, did not save the melodious, Buononcini-like *Floridante,* which Handel had designed as a winner in 1721. When Buononcini replied to *Floridante* with two hits (one of them his masterpiece, *Griselda*), Handel fell into temporary despair. He had the further humiliation of seeing his Italian rival, then at the top of his fame, asked to compose the music for Marlborough's funeral. Bitterness made Handel rash. He had heard of Francesca Cuzzoni, a young Italian contralto who was then the wonder of Venice; sound unheard, he sent her an offer of the then unbelievable sum of two thousand pounds per year. Cuzzoni arrived, ugly, intractable, every pound a prima donna. Handel tamed her so well that she re-established her master overnight by a magnificent performance at the *première* of his *Ottone* on January 12, 1723. Others in the cast were Boschi and Gaetan Berenstadt, both eminent bassos, Senesino, and the English favorite, Anastasia Robinson, a soprano-become-contralto who had also sung in *Floridante.* So mortified was Mrs. Robinson by the audience's marked preference for Cuzzoni that she shortly retired from the stage and became a countess.[10]

For a time, as in Handel's *Flavio* (1723), Cuzzoni and Senesino were enough. Buononcini's strength was ebbing, and Handel fortified his position by composing two of his best scores, the first, *Giulio Cesare* (1724), to an absurd rigmarole by Nicola Francesco Haym. The second, *Tamerlano* (1724), provided with an equally harebrained pseudohistorical text by that same favorite collaborator, built up to a massive musical climax.[11] It was unusually intense emotionally: Handel was starting to think aloud about his oratorio style. He was showing wisdom, for his audiences were beginning to tire of Italian opera, whether in Buononcini's light, lascivious manner or as invigorated by Handel's buoyant masculinity and tolerance of dignified pathos. Also, the shareholders of the Royal Academy of Music, with their distinguished genius for spend-

[10] An unacknowledged one for a long time: her husband, Charles Mordaunt, Earl of Peterborough, was a snob. He loved her, however, in his fashion, and once publicly flogged Senesino for hurling coarse words at Anastasia. The romance of Peterborough and Anastasia gave George Meredith the subject of his novel *Lord Ormont and His Aminta.*

[11] Its score calls for two clarinets, one of that instrument's two known appearances in Handel composition.

ing its profits, were terrified by empty seats. Instead of prudently cutting their budget, these scatterbrained lords did precisely the opposite: they sent for Faustina Bordoni, called *la nuova sirena* by her enchanted countrymen. One of the most appealing figures in the history of the musical stage, this lovely woman put a high price on her great abilities as a mezzo-soprano. Like Cuzzoni, she asked two thousand pounds per year, and got it.

Cuzzoni and Senesino were almost enough stars for *Rodelinda* (1725) —one of Handel's finest operas—and *Scipione* (1726). But then, as if daring the fire of the gods, Handel associated Faustina with them in his next opera, *Alessandro,* which opened on May 5, 1726, and at once achieved the rare success of eleven performances within one month. Handel had carefully composed roles of equal importance and display for the two Italian divas. They were already rivals, having made their debuts together in Venice seven years earlier. Fireworks were expected (probably hoped for) at once, but for a time the ladies contented themselves with singing gloriously to packed houses at the Haymarket Theatre and acting toward one another with the cold decorum of Latins struggling to repress natural emotions.

Suddenly, after the season ended, hell broke loose. The ladies' followers began it by wearing party emblems—a Cuzzoni scarf, a Faustina riband. Soon a Cuzzoni and a Faustina were entered in the Newmarket races. By the middle of 1727, the battle had waxed so hot that the protagonists themselves finally joined in, spitting out rather than singing duets with each other. On the night of the closing of the Royal Academy's eighth season, June 6, 1727, the offering (not that anyone cared) was *Astianatte,* Buononcini's last London opera. A fight broke out in the pit and rapidly spread to the stage. To everyone's joyful relief, it was climaxed when Cuzzoni and Faustina flew at each other and, despite the presence in the audience of Caroline, Princess of Wales, began pulling each other's hair.

The Royal Academy of Music lasted but one year more. Handel, who had become a British subject, swearing allegiance to George I as His Britannic Majesty on February 14, 1727, tried, with *Riccardo primo,* to woo the public with a patriotic theme. But even Faustina, Cuzzoni, and Senesino could not make Englishmen stomach an Italian-singing Richard the Lion-Hearted. The ever-resourceful Handel then wrote to the young Roman poet Metastasio, already the acknowledged prince of librettists, and besought a life-saving text from him. He received a workmanlike compilation of semihistorical data concerning Cyrus the Great, which he incontinently turned over to Haym, who butchered it. The resulting collaboration, *Siroë,* was in rehearsal when, on January 29, 1728, London went to the first performance of *The Beggar's Opera.* The fate of the Royal Academy was sealed: it closed its now useless doors in June.

The men who contrived *The Beggar's Opera* were cleverer than they knew. John Gay, its librettist, was a spoiled and witty party poet with a talent for broad, if not leering, salaciousness. Dr. Johann Christoph Pepusch, a transplanted Prussian theorist and authority on old music, had an equally lively talent for appropriating melodies that happened to be lying about, whether folk tunes or scraps of Purcell and Handel. *The Beggar's Opera* both satirized the government of Sir Robert Walpole and parodied Italian opera—for the excellent reasons that Gay had a grudge against the Whigs and that Pepusch, whom Handel had supplanted as private musician to the extravagant Duke of Chandos, wanted to get even with his fellow German.

Gay and Pepusch offered their exhilarating novelty at the psychological moment. London was sick to death of assorted myths and historical snippets from Greece and Rome, not to mention more outlandish places. It was bored with the stiff attitudes and run-of-the-mill fustian of pseudo-classical characters spouting in a foreign jargon. So Gay, taking a flimsy but not incredible tale and peopling it with an unsavory crew of derelicts, footpads, and ladies and gentlemen of the highway who might have stepped from Hogarth prints, contrived knowingly spiced dialogue interspersed with lyrics of a saucy and scurrilous nature. Pepusch adapted to these naughty trifles various tunes of widely varied provenance. His sole original contribution to the score was an overture and one song.

Only an analyst with a blind *parti pris* could find in *The Beggar's Opera* a unity much more solid than that of a typical Handel stage piece, but its sprightly tempo and easy comprehensibility, plus the obvious lilt of its tunes, made it an instant and conquering success, running for a record-establishing sixty-two nights the first season. After its thirty-sixth performance, Gay boasted that he had already pocketed about eight hundred pounds (his manager made five times that amount in the same period). Polly, the heroine of the piece, made the fortune of Lavinia Fenton, who created the role. While still active on the stage, she became the mistress of Charles Paulet, Duke of Bolton; she retired to become his wife and eventually to inherit much of his vast estate.

Soon *The Beggar's Opera* overran the British Isles. Even the people of

Minorca heard it—though it seems unlikely that they understood it better than the Londoners understood Italian opera. Within twenty-five years of its first night, it was sung in Paris and New York; in the latter place, it preceded Italian opera by almost half a century.

But Handel, who after the failure of the Academy had gone into partnership with John James Heidegger, an uncomely dwarf known as "the Swiss Count," evidently interpreted the success of *The Beggar's Opera* as a passing fad. True, women of fashion were carrying its ballads on their fans or obstructing their living quarters with "Polly" or "Macheath" screens. But had they not acted the same way when his two rival canaries had been dividing London? Was there not, for example, the "Cuzzoni" dress of brown and silver which had added to the success of his opera *Rodelinda* (1725) and given fashionable London dressmakers a new color scheme?

Yes, definitely, *The Beggar's Opera* was a craze. So, perhaps, Handel thought as he doggedly set about concocting his twenty-fifth Italian opera, *Lotario* (1729). That he saw no *Mene, mene* on the wall is proved by the fact that he took no pains with its libretto or music, and stolidly used it to introduce a soprano of surpassing ugliness, Anna Maria Strada del Pò, known as "The Pig." Only in 1730, by reimporting Senesino and counting on the affection of London for some of his old scores, did Handel manage once more to crowd the theater night after night. *Poro*, a new opera with a ripe Oriental book based on Metastasio, was wildly acclaimed in 1731. Critics called it Handel's greatest work, and the presses of John Walsh groaned to supply the demand for the airs that Senesino had made fashionable.

Feeling again that he was on top, Handel rather sentimentally revived his first London opera, *Rinaldo*. Then another blow fell. A heat wave wilted London and opera. When it had subsided, Handel's audiences were nowhere, and though he continued to compose Italian operas for ten years more—eighteen of them, in fact—he seems to have realized at last that he could never regain his pre-eminence through them. After 1731, magnificently revising *Esther,* an oratorio he had composed in 1720, he inaugurated his great series of English oratorios. By these works he was to prove again that the English language can be set singably to great music, and he again became the musical god of the English people.

Beginning in 1733, the opposition to Handel crystallized in a group known unofficially as the "Opera of the Nobility." Semipolitical in character, it ranged itself under the banner of the rebellious Frederick, Prince of Wales, and the young Duke of Marlborough. As its official composer it secured the Neapolitan Niccolò Porpora, almost exactly Handel's contemporary, a man of talent and determination. Weaning Cuzzoni and Senesino away from Handel's company, which had been regrouped in 1728 as the New Royal Academy, was easy, but this merely divided the meager audiences between the two companies. Porpora did not begin to fill his theater, in Lincoln's Inn Fields, until he succeeded in hiring the greatest *castrato* of them all—Carlo Broschi, called Farinelli.

This golden-voiced creature burst upon London on October 29, 1734, in a setting of Metastasio's *Artaserse* largely by Johann Adolf Hasse, who originally had composed it for Faustina Bordoni in 1730, the year of their marriage. That performance by a singer who was never to appear in a Handel opera was notable because it signed one more death warrant for Handel's operatic career. It was even more notable for one of those rare gestures of approval from one star singer to another. After Farinelli had completed his first aria, the veteran Senesino, also singing that night, strode over to his junior rival and impulsively embraced him.

The excellence of performers who lived before the days of gramophone records must be judged by the written opinions that seem most trustworthy; the fact that tradition is almost unanimous in calling Farinelli the first of singers is strong evidence of his surpassing merit. Reputedly of noble birth, he was, it was said, a *castrato* by accident and not by design: grievously injured while out riding, he had had to submit to the effeminizing operation or die. It happened that the voice thus induced became the most beautiful ever heard—after laborious training by Porpora and other masters of *bel canto*. When Farinelli went to London in 1734, this handsome, intelligent man had already chalked up extraordinary triumphs in Italy and Austria, and for three years he held London in his pocket. When even his powers could no longer shore up Italian opera there, he left for France, where Louis XV presented him with a royal portrait framed in diamonds.

Traveling in regal style, Farinelli then proceeded into Spain, no doubt intending merely to get homage for his voice at the court before returning to the scenes of his earlier successes. He remained in Madrid a quarter of a century. Philip V, the melancholy Bourbon who dragged out a painful existence under the thumb of a domineering wife, was enchanted by his exotic guest and would not let him leave. For ten years, at an annual stipend of fifty thousand francs, this strange David solaced his harmless Saul with a program of soporific monotony—a nightly program that was never varied. Among the three (or perhaps four) songs that Farinelli sang some thirty-five hundred times to the demented monarch were two from *Artaserse,* the very opera by Hasse with which he had first dazzled London.

When Philip died and Ferdinand VI reigned in his place, Farinelli became more powerful through the magic of his singing, and even took a hand in ruling Spain. But when Ferdinand went insane and died and his half-brother Charles III ascended the throne, Farinelli was hustled out of Spain.[12] The year was 1759, and the singer was fifty-four. He was too old to return to opera, but he carried into retirement a vast fortune amassed during his many years as a popular and court favorite. Charles III was not vindictive: he not only allowed the erstwhile favorite to carry his gold away with him, but also continued his salary, insisting, however, upon residence outside Spain's dominions. Although Farinelli might well have preferred to settle in his native Naples, he could not (it was then in Spanish territory); eventually he chose Bologna, and spent the remaining twenty-one years of his life there in luxurious ease. Dr. Charles Burney, the inquisitive and indefatigable father of the author of *Evelina,* visited Farinelli there in 1771, and brought away a glowing account of the remarkable man who, almost forty years before, had temporarily ruined Handel.

But only temporarily. The career of Handel shows amazing vigor and buoyancy—qualities that can be recognized again and again in his music. Refusing to admit that disaster really mattered, and perhaps thinking that Farinelli's overwhelming success depended upon his being a soprano, whereas the Academy's *castrati* had mostly been altos, Handel in 1736 revived *Ariodante* with the high-voiced Conti replacing the contralto Carestini as the heroine. Conti was a most peculiar fellow: it was said that the first time he heard Farinelli sing he was so overcome that he not only wept but also fainted dead away in despair of being able to match the wonders of his rival's singing. Nonetheless, Handel cast him again in the *première* of his *Atalanta* on May 12, 1736. By then, however, really serious trouble was impending. When Handel opened a season

---

[12] Daniel-François-Esprit Auber wrote, in *Le Part du diable, ou Carlo Broschi* (1843), a rather charming semicomic opera about the happier part of Farinelli's Spanish adventure. No male soprano being available in 1843, Auber gave the role of the great *castrato* to a woman. Wagner's friend Hermann Zumpe and the popular Spanish composer of *zarzuelas* Tomás Bretón composed operas on the same theme.

at the Theatre Royal, Covent Garden, with a revival of *Alcina* on November 6, the rival company, then newly under the direction of Hasse, replied seventeen days later by putting on its director's *Siroë*. Into the fray Handel tossed two new operas: *Arminio* (January 12, 1737) and *Giustino* (February 16). When the arrival of Lent forbade the production of operas, he continued the season with oratorios. All to no avail: his financial troubles simply increased. On April 13 he suffered a paralytic stroke that immobilized his right arm. Some weeks later still another new opera, *Berenice,* achieved only four performances between its *première* on May 18 and the end of the season on June 15. Handel temporarily admitted defeat and went off to Aix-la-Chapelle to take the cure.

After the catastrophic season of 1737, Handel composed only three more operas, though he lived twenty-two active years longer. One of the three was his only essay at comic opera—*Serse,* a work of great ingenuity, distinction, and charm, which, with a little trouble, could be revived today. And *Serse* contains the most famous (though surely not the finest) of Handel's operatic arias, the all-too-immortal "Ombra mai fù," erroneously known as the "Largo." The last of the three—*Deidamia*—was produced in 1741. But 1741 was more memorable in the history of music for another reason: in that year, doubtless, Handel was beginning to shape *Messiah,* the vast fabric that was to set his name alongside that of Johann Sebastian Bach.

And it is as the composer of *Messiah, Israel in Egypt,* and other oratorios that Handel remains familiar as a composer of vocal music. The best of the oratorios are more impressively dramatic than any of Handel's operas; some of them, *Semele* in particular, have been performed as operas with striking effect. Part of the superior dramatic impact of the oratorios lies not so much in any measure-by-measure excellence of their music itself as in the mighty surge of the great choruses, little used in the operas—which almost entirely neglect choral numbers. When writing for the opera stage, Handel was hampered by traditions of usage and construction, which had been so rigorously codified by the beginning of the eighteenth century that only violent revolution could have freed the frozen dramatic element.

Handel was no revolutionary. He took opera as he found it and left it in exactly the same state. Even the best Handel opera is likely to seem to most modern lovers of opera a concert of lovely airs and heroic or pathetic recitatives interspersed with a much larger number of machine-made airs and recitatives couched in an always pleasant but often very

conventional idiom. A kind of theatrical thoughtlessness, even insouciance, must seem to the modern opera enthusiast to cling to this prodigal
manufacturer of music on those occasions when he strings his good, his
mechanical, and his fair-to-middling numbers on the threads of a stilted,
rambling, often altogether inconsequential libretto.

The poor librettist was not wholly to blame. He might hit upon a
powerful theme like that of *Rinaldo*. He might, like Metastasio, have a
genuine poetic gift. But the obligation to provide set arias for each of the
principal singers at fixed points in each act, to end his story happily with
all the living principals joining in a so-called "chorus" at the close of
the last act, and to conform to any number of other laws was as stifling to
him as to any desire the composer might harbor to create musical continuity. Add to these rules of operatic dramaturgy the general literary
conventions of the time—foppishness, extravagance, exalted diction,
plumed heroics, strained pseudoclassicism—and it is little wonder that
even the best librettos that Handel and other operatic composers of his
day had to put up with strike many people today as mere verbiage.

Yet this view is surely, at least in part, merely a refusal on our part
to meet halfway the first half of the eighteenth century. No art whatever
exists without acceptance of well-defined conventions by both its creators
and its public. One of the conventions of the Handelian opera was virtu-
osic singing of a particular sort—properly called *bel canto*—which endured well into the nineteenth century, but was all but killed by the
different sort of singing demanded by Wagner, by the later Verdi, by
Puccini, and by many more recent composers. But since World War II a
revival of *bel canto* seems to have been initiated. And with it, performances of Handel's operas without the interference of too heavy an edi-
torial hand have begun to look possible. At the same time, music-lovers
have demonstrated increasing interest in and affection for music earlier
than Mozart. This conjunction of events forcefully suggests that restag-
ings of Handel's operas have not only become increasingly possible but
also would find a sympathetic public waiting. And indeed his *Alcina*
(1735) has served admirably as a vehicle for the phenomenal Joan
Sutherland.

Placed, like Bach, in a historic position that required him to be a conservative, a great summer-up rather than a pioneer, Handel seems to have
regarded an opera much as a modern tunesmith regards a musical
comedy: as a vessel into which a number may be inserted without much
consideration of its environment, but with a great deal of consideration

for the star who needs it or must have it at that exact point—and who will put it over. Handel was sure of his Senesinos and Cuzzonis and Faustinas even after they could no longer put over his operas merely by singing his arias superbly. He asked himself no questions about his concept of opera even when the whole audience melted away, deserting to Gay and Pepusch. He had no way of knowing that *The Beggar's Opera* was the precursor of his adopted land's only sound vernacular opera— that light, comic, broadly mocking strain which was to culminate in the delicious flummery of Gilbert and Sullivan. Nor, of course, could he foresee the operatic forms of Gluck and Mozart.

Handel's operas are occasionally revived. The so-called German "Handel Renaissance" (initiated in 1920 by Dr. Oskar Hagen, the historian of art, with a revival of *Rodelinda* at Göttingen) had produced nine of them in highly controversial versions there (and ten more in other German towns) when World War II broke out and cut short the ambitious project of restaging them all. In the United States, the scholarly Werner Josten staged several of them at Smith College with critical *réclame;* concert performances, usually in sharply abbreviated versions, occasionally turn up. During the Handel bicentenary celebrations of 1959, several of his operas were staged in Europe and by semiprofessional troupes in the United States. Still, it seems unlikely that any Handel opera will soon banish Gluck's *Orfeo ed Euridice* (composed only three years after Handel's death in 1759) from its honored place as the oldest serious opera still often professionally staged.

CHAPTER IV

The French Way: Part One

A CHILL modern way of examining phenomena which flout the sentimentality of tradition finds characteristic expression in André Piganiol's well-known dictum: "The [Roman] Empire did not die a natural death. It was assassinated." Whether an oversimplification or not, this cuts through vast structures of hypothesis. The method can be applied to the history of opera, for it dissipates the mystery of opera's not beginning in France or in England, despite the presence in those countries of circumstances quite as favorable for forcing it into being. A godlike spectator with one eye on Paris and another on Florence might allow himself a smile warranted by his prescience. The historian, with only a sampling of all the facts to go by, must content himself with the reflection that Florence possessed the unique catalyst for the occasion. Yet, as we sift names and documents, just as we cannot fix upon the precise assassin of the Roman Empire, neither can we finally decide whether Giovanni Bardi, Jacopo Corsi, or still another deserves the title of operatic midwife.

That opera originated in Italy, and not in France, is a historical fact that wobbles slightly under the microscope, and depends somewhat upon the question: When is an opera not an opera? In view of opera's not being a succinct form (though with endless recognizable varieties), the answer is not easy. It is generally agreed, however, that the *ballet de cour,* a combination of poetry, music, and dance which entertained the French court for roughly a century, from the middle of the sixteenth to the middle of the seventeenth, does not belong to the operatic genre. Under the later Valois, ballets of sumptuous magnificence crowded out all other court entertainments. It is obvious that when poetry and music were added to dancing, opera might come into being, almost accidentally. Polyphony was going out, monody was coming in, and the moment had arrived for the great adventure of the solo voice. The *Ballet comique de la royne* (1581), produced under the supreme direction of Balthasar de Beaujoyeulx—whom Brantôme called the "best violin-player of Christendom"—at a cost of more than half a million dollars at the present rate, must have been a close thing. For it is pointed out that the plot is trifling (the French King foils the sorceries of Circe); much the same indictment might be made of certain operas contrived today.

What might have happened if M. de Beaujoyeulx's entertainment had not been so expensive cannot be predicted, but those who have heard and seen Rameau's *Les Indes galantes* will at least know whither *Le Ballet comique de la royne* was tending. However, in the rapid budgeting that followed, the chance for opera was swamped in the litter of shoestring festivities that served the outgoing Valois and incoming Bourbons. It was not until the minority of Louis XIV, when Cardinal Mazarin, an Italian, was ruling France, that the court heard its first opera, doubtless because the chief minister, desirous of importing amenities and luxuries from his native land, also wished, for political reasons, to surround himself with Italians. Keenly aware that entertainment helped to keep the masters of a people subdued, the wily cardinal imported an opera company whole.

Orfeo, by the now utterly obscure Luigi Rossi (an unwearied fashioner of more than one hundred cantatas),[1] was produced in France in 1647. Possibly because it was commissioned expressly for Paris, it has been called, quite inexactly, the first opera given there. It had at least two predecessors, both apparently given in 1645. Despite Mazarin's anxiety to popularize the new form of entertainment (he had a French analysis of the libretto of *Orfeo* handed out before the performance), the lords and ladies reacted coldly. We must attribute their apathy to pre-Fronde sullenness, not to critical acumen. Under happier conditions, the fact that the *dramma* had moved well away from the *musica* would not have spoiled their fun. But the historian must report that the frequently beautiful music has almost nothing to do with the serious or comic elements strung out to fill the required time. *Orfeo* has a most eloquent lamentation on the death of Eurydice: it is set for four sopranos and uses dissonance with the sureness of effect of a master writing three hundred years later.[2]

[1] He was the most important composer between the first operatic generation and that of Cavalli and Cesti.

[2] Just as the sixteenth century reached the heights in the religious lamentations

Mazarin was still master of France when Cavalli's *Serse* was produced at the Louvre in 1660 during the wedding fetes of Louis XIV and María Teresa of Spain. It fared somewhat better, though the reception given to the Servite father who sang the role of Queen Amestris was far from flattering—he was a *castrato,* and the French did not like him. However, Cavalli was asked back, two years later, when he staged his masterpiece, *Ercole amante.* Even this admirable work did not establish opera in Italian, and at that date it would not have been unreasonable to predict that unless a French twist was given to *dramma per musica,* it would survive in France only as an occasional plaything of the court.

Less reasonable to predict would have been that the man to give opera a French twist was the pushing young Florentine who had been commissioned to introduce some of his popular dance tunes into both *Serse* and *Ercole amante.* These commissions to a man who had been Louis' friend when he was still a crowned puppet under Mazarin's thumb were signs that the Sun King was rising and would shed his rays over a very French France. *Ercole amante* was a compatriot's epitaph on Mazarin, who had just died: Lully's dances in *Ercole* were the future. For a dozen years this brilliant, rough, and unscrupulous *compositeur du roi,* risen from an underscullion's greasy tasks to the domination of music in France, forged and tempered the instruments of his art. In 1664, the year of his perfectly attested marriage (the contract was witnessed by Louis XIV, María Teresa, and the Queen Mother, Anne of Austria), he began a happy collaboration with Molière which just missed producing the first French opera, but which did father such masterpieces as *Le Mariage forcé, Le Bourgeois gentilhomme,* and *Pourceaugnac,* with apt and sprightly incidental music. Racine also collaborated with Lully.

In 1671, the Molière-Lully team sired *Psyché,* a work so close to full-fledged opera that only a miracle of omission kept it in the category of *comédies-ballets.* So the honor of composing the first[3] French opera

---

(Palestrina's for the three days preceding Easter), the seventeenth is notable for the great secular lamentations that begin with Monteverdi's "Lamento d'Arianna" and end with Purcell's lament of Dido.

[3] In truth, not exactly the first. Of two preceding French operas there is not a scrap left: Michel de La Guerre's *Le Triomphe de l'Amour sur des bergers et bergères* (1655) and the first Cambert-Perrin collaboration, *Pastorale* (1659). What remains of *Pomone* does not suffice for making a prediction that Cambert and Perrin, if left alone by Lully, would themselves have made a recognizable national opera for France.

went, through sheer accident, to a team of well-known hacks, the poet Pierre Perrin and the tunesmith Robert Cambert. Their pleasantly melodious five-act pastorale—*Pomone*—was successfully produced in March, 1671. Cambert followed with another opera, but it was not staged: the envious Lully had intrigued to such effect that within a year Cambert had to flee to England, where he was eventually murdered by his valet.

Lully, like Louis, now reigned alone, and he celebrated his *coup d'état* by joining forces with Philippe Quinault, a dramatic poet of considerable talent if not actual genius. The pair's first effort was a plotless pastoral, *Les Festes de l'Amour et de Bacchus,* whose success augured well for further collaboration. They therefore tried something more ambitious and unified, and thus created the first of the so-called *tragédies en musique*—*Cadmus et Hermione,* staged on April 27, 1673. This tragic opera (*tragédie-lyrique*) [4] was the first of a series of fifteen such (twelve of them with books by Quinault), all admirable in proportion, careful in workmanship, and nice in declamation. While we are unlikely to hear the statement proved by performance, the collaboration of Lully and Quinault may be compared in effectiveness with those of Gluck and Calzabigi, Mozart and Da Ponte, Verdi and Boito, Wagner and Wagner. Quinault received 4,000 livres a year for his share of the work. Lully apparently paid himself more lavishly: dying in 1687, he left, in addition to four substantial pieces of city property, a fortune estimated at 342,000 livres.

Lully was a voluminous workman: besides the fifteen operas that he wrote in fourteen years, ballets, pastorals, dances, songs, instrumental pieces of many kinds, and church music were furnished to his avid patrons, at whose head stood the most insatiable of them all—the generally unmusical Louis XIV, who, nevertheless, composed pretty trifles, and who desperately wanted to be amused and praised. The King, self-conscious, vainglorious architect of a new France, applauded *Cadmus et Hermione* with such obvious pleasure that Lully, an observant courtier, realized that he had hit upon a workable formula. He found no reason to change it, for it was already a French thing. Tailor-made, highly conventionalized, almost intemperately artificial, yet supremely correct, it naturally appealed to a monarch and a court who considered the grandly

[4] *Tragédie-lyrique* and *opera seria:* historically, the former must be considered a literary genre with music, the latter a musical genre with some literary pretexts, but the difference was not slavishly observed.

dull façades of Versailles the height of architectural perfection. When Lully's *Alceste* was staged in 1674, Louis asserted that he would hear it every day if he was in Paris.

Like every important institution that flourished in the France of the *grand siècle,* opera was a spectacle. Sumptuous costumes, elaborate décors, and incredibly ingenious and complex stage machines—of Italian ancestry—that were like vastly magnified clockwork toys made even the most severe *tragédie* essentially a visual delight. *Tableaux* and *divertissements,* for all the world like costly side shows, ministered to momentarily flagging appetites. But these attractions paled beside the incidental ballets, for which Lully often saved his finest effects. Ballet had acquired such popularity among the nobility during its first century of existence in France that it was a shrewd stroke of business on Lully's part to introduce it into his operas. Once there, be it noted, it stayed—not only in the native products, but also in imported operas, whether or not their composers had provided for one in the original design (Wagner's dilemma over the Paris production of *Tannhäuser* is a most flagrant example of this French determinism). Lully, armed with a bottomless budget and a tradition of costliness, was prepared to spend any amount of money and inject any innovation necessary to make his ballets the wonder of the times. He was the first to make use of trained male ballet dancers, though occasionally, as in days past, the King himself and some of the great lords eagerly deigned to impersonate Jupiter and Apollo and their separate trains.

Because Lully's operas were given at court, they were lavishly mounted, but this circumstance of production must not be confused with their essential structure and musical character. If submitted to analysis, these entities prove, with certain qualifications, to be surprisingly close relatives of the early Florentine operas. On the one hand, we must admit their costly swathe of superficialities: these the agents of the *camerata*'s lofty theories would have abhorred. On the other hand, neither Peri nor Caccini, nor even Gagliano, could command Lully's fine orchestration and his beautifully carved melodies. And Lully's operas have other, more obvious novelties. They begin with a so-called "French overture" invented by Lully himself; it was in two, sometimes three, sections—slow, quick and fugal, slow. Equally unfamiliar to Peri and Caccini would have been the accompanied recitatives which are among the strongest dramatic elements of a Lully score. Strangest of all, no doubt, would have been the vigorous and lofty choruses, sometimes as mighty as those

Peri's *Euridice,* in the Boboli Gardens, Maggio Musicale Fiorentino, 1960; production by Franco Zeffirelli

Rameau's *Les Indes galantes,* Entrée III, at the Opéra, Paris, 1952

Handel's *Giulio Cesare*, Act III, at La Scala, Milan, 1956–57 season; scenery and costumes by Piero Zuffi; Nicola Rossi-Lemeni as Giulio Cesare

Gluck's *Orfeo ed Euridice*, Act III, at the Holland Festival, 1952; Kathleen Ferrier as Orfeo

Mozart's *Die Entführung aus dem Serail,* Act II, at the Teatro della Pergola, Maggio Musicale Fiorentino, 1958; Fritz Ollendorf (Osmin), Murray Dickie (Pedrillo)

Mozart's *Die Zauberflöte,* Act II, at the Budapest Opera, January 27, 1956; scenery and costumes by Gusztáv Oláh

Beethoven's *Fidelio,* Act I, at the Netherlands Opera, Amsterdam; Nel Duval (Marzelline), Guus Hoekman (Rocco), Gré Brouwenstijn (Leonore)

Weber's *Oberon,* Scene 2, at the Opéra, Paris, 1954; scenery and costumes by Jean-Denis Malclès

Rossini's *Il Barbiere di Siviglia,* at the Hamburg State Opera, 1941; production by Günther Rennert

Rossini's *L'Italiana in Algeri,* Act I, at the Teatro della Pergola, Maggio Musicale Fiorentino, 1960; production by Franco Enriquez; Marcello Cortis (Taddeo), Fedora Barbieri (Isabella), Paolo Washington (Mustafà)

Bellini's *Beatrice di Tenda,* Act II, Scene 2, at La Scala, Milan, 1961; Joan Sutherland as Beatrice

Donizetti's *Poliuto* (*Les Martyrs*), Act II, Scene 2, at La Scala, Milan, 1960; scenery and costumes by Nicola Benois; Maria Callas (Paolina), Ettore Bastianini (Severo), Nicola Zaccaria (High Priest)

Spontini's *La Vestale*, Act II, at La Scala, Milan, 1954; production by Luchino Visconti; scenery and costumes by Piero Zuffi

Gounod's *Faust,* Act II, at the National Opera, Sofia, Bulgaria, 1957

Gounod's *Faust,* Act II, at the Israel National Opera, Tel-Aviv; Georges Vaillant (Méphistophélès), Ulli Schocken (Siébel)

Bizet's *Carmen*, Act II, at the Hamburg State Opera, 1958–59 season; production, scenery, and costumes by Wieland Wagner; Toni Blankenheim (Zuniga), Kerstin Meyer (Carmen), Rudolf Schock (José)

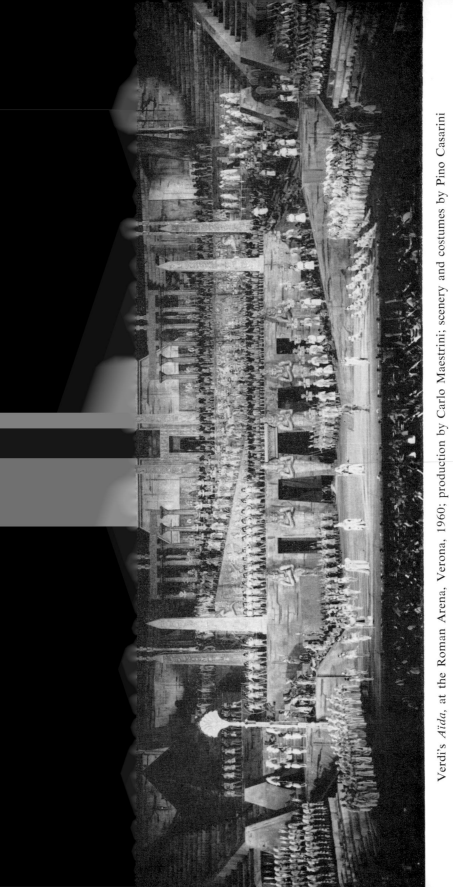

Verdi's *Aïda*, at the Roman Arena, Verona, 1960; production by Carlo Maestrini; scenery and costumes by Pino Casarini

Verdi's *Un Ballo in maschera,* Act III, Scene 3, at La Scala, Milan; production by Margherita Wallmann; scenery and costumes by Nicola Benois

Verdi's *Falstaff,* Act II, at the Holland Festival, 1956; production, scenery, and costumes by Franco Zeffirelli; Fernando Corena as Falstaff

Wagner's *Lohengrin,* Act II, at the Festspielhaus, Bayreuth, 1954; production by Wolfgang Wagner; Birgit Nilsson (Elsa), Astrid Varnay (Ortrud)

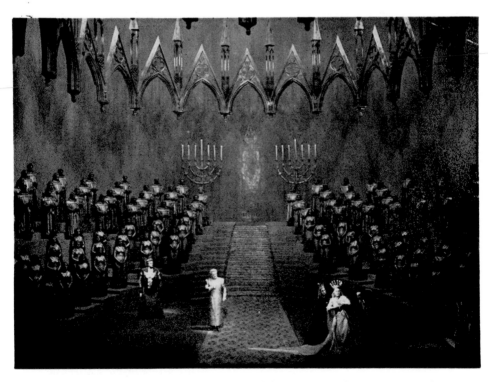

Wagner's *Lohengrin,* Act II, at the Festspielhaus, Bayreuth, 1958; production by Wieland Wagner; Keith Engen (Heinrich), Sandor Konay (Lohengrin), Astrid Varnay (Ortrud), Leonie Rysanek (Elsa), Ernest Blanc (Telramund)

Wagner's *Der fliegende Holländer,* Act I, at the Opernhaus, Frankfurt-am-Main, 1957; production by Hans Hartleb; scenery by Hein Heckroth

Wagner's *Das Rheingold,* closing scene, at the Festspielhaus, Bayreuth, 1955; production by Wieland Wagner

Berlioz' *Les Troyens*, Act III, at Covent Garden, London, 1957; production by Sir John Gielgud; scenery and costumes by Mariano Andreu; Blanche Thebom as Dido

Offenbach's *Les Contes d'Hoffmann,* Prologue, at the Komische Oper, Berlin, 1958; production by Walter Felsenstein; scenery and costumes by Rudolf Heinrich; Irmgard Arnold (Niklausse), Hanns Nocker (Hoffmann)

Massenet's *Don Quichotte,* the Belgrade Opera, at Fort Revelin, Dubrovnik, Yugoslavia; production by Mladen Sabljic; Miroslav Cangalovic as Don Quichotte

of Handel. But the Florentines would quite have understood their descendant's approach to the central problem of reconciling the dramatic and the musical: Lully evidently viewed his task as the heightening and underscoring of a poetic text. He fitted the music to the words, and did not torture the words to fit the music. Nor was he a vocalist's pander. Italian-born though he was, Lully understood the subtlest problems of French prosody, treating its rich, tricky assonances with positive reverence, and evolving an admirable style of French declamation that is at once musical and dramatically eloquent. Yet he was no doctrinaire, and was bound by no philosophy of opera: his frequent interpolations of purely instrumental snatches, irrelevant except as sheer irruptions of beauty, prove that he let himself go whenever he felt like it.

Writing in *The Spectator* in 1711, Addison, after praising Lully for fitting his music to the French language, continues:

> The Chorus in which that Opera abounds, gives the Parterre frequent Opportunities of joining in Consort with the Stage. This Inclination of the Audience to Sing along with the Actors, so prevails with them, that I have sometimes known the Performer on the Stage to do no more in a Celebrated Song, than the Clerk of a Parish Church, who serves only to raise the Psalm, and is afterwards drown'd in the Musick of the Congregation. Every Actor that comes on the Stage is a Beau. The Queens and Heroines are so Painted, that they appear as Ruddy and Cherry-cheek'd as Milk-maids. The Shepherds are all Embroider'd, and acquit themselves in a Ball better than our *English* Dancing-Masters. I have seen a couple of Rivers appear in red stockings; and *Alpheus,* instead of having his head covered with Sedge and Bull-Rushes, making Love in a fair full-bottomed Perriwig, and a Plume of Feathers; but with a Voice so full of Shakes and Quavers that I should have thought the Murmurs of a Country Brook the much more agreeable Musick.

Lully's talent was protean, expressive of humor, heroism, and pathos. His instrumentation was not always, for the best of reasons, the most nearly correct—indeed, in this department of his art he was something of an experimentalist. Certain products of his laboratory were deliciously absurd: once, to suggest the rocking of Charon's boat, he used the identical rhythm and counterpoint he had previously used in describing the hero's wrath in *Roland* (1685), which he considered his best opera. But Louis XIV, who listened suspiciously to sprightly melodies and brilliant passages (unless they happened to be the rollicking military marches in which Lully was surpassing), liked what his Italian favorite wrought for him, which explains much concerning both Lully's good qualities and his defects. Particularly does it explain the empty grandeur of some of his airs. Magniloquence is the blight on acres of Lully, but what is good is very, very good. It has style, elevation, character, sometimes real dramatic expressiveness. We do not demean the age of Boileau and Molière by calling it also the age of Lully.

Rameau, the next great composer of the French school of opera, was but four years old when Louis XIV's *maître de musique* died prematurely from the effects of striking his foot sharply with his long, wandlike baton while conducting a *Te Deum* to celebrate the King's recovery from an illness. Since Rameau did not write his first important opera until he was over fifty, there was a considerable interval during which the influence of Lully persisted, coloring the work of the lesser men of that transition. Although the names of these minor composers—Campra, Montéclair, Destouches—are almost unknown today, some of them were in themselves interesting, and produced music of mild charm. As the rage for ballet went on unabated, they saved some of their best melodies and dance tunes for that genre. An amusing incident, showing clearly that the art of deifying kings did not pass with the Grand Monarque, is connected with the public performance of Destouches's ingenious ballet *Les Éléments*. When it was first given at Versailles, the young Louis XV danced in it, and was routinely complimented by various characters of the ensemble. When the ballet was staged in Paris, however, a bust of the King had to do service for his role: quite as fulsome compliments were addressed to this immobile dancer.

Mythology and the old romances still furnished these interim composers with most of their stories, but occasionally a Biblical theme was selected. Montéclair, whose music is not without wit, had great success with the lugubrious story of Jephtha, that rather foolhardy judge of Israel who, having promised to sacrifice to Jehovah, in return for victory over the Ammonites, "whatsoever cometh forth of the doors of my house to meet me," was greeted by his only child. Rameau, at the time of *Jephté*'s success a middle-aged man still struggling for recognition, had once tried his own hand at a sacred subject. His choice was Samson, around whom Handel was to build one of the most impressive of his oratorios, but who was never the subject of a popular opera until Saint-

Saëns thought of putting the emphasis on the enchantress Delilah.[5] Rameau's reading of the long-tressed Hebrew hero never reached the stage: its performance was interdicted at the last moment, apparently because it was feared that the libretto, by a rising publicist named Voltaire, might give offense to the religious.

It is perhaps typical of a professional organist like Rameau to try to storm the portals of the Académie Royale de Musique (the official name of the Opéra), admission to which was essential for a profitable career as an operatic composer, with a Bible story. He soon saw that he was mistaken, and hired the Abbé Pellegrin, known as the *curé de l'opéra,* to sift the good old reliable subject matter of Racine's *théâtre* for a libretto likely to be acceptable to the authorities. Pellegrin chose the fairly threadbare story of Phaedra and Hippolytus, and extracted a promise from Rameau to pay him five hundred livres if *Hippolyte et Aricie* failed.[6] At rehearsal, however, he was so delighted with the music that he impulsively tore up the bond at the end of the first act.

The first performance of *Hippolyte et Aricie,* at the Académie, on October 1, 1733, was a success, despite the fact that a critical, almost savage opposition broke into full cry at once. During the four years that elapsed between *Hippolyte* and the *première* of Rameau's overwhelmingly popular masterpiece, *Castor et Pollux,* in 1737, his colleagues and a very large section of the public directed against him the most poisonous shafts, usually in the name of tradition and Lully. This was an ironical situation for the man who was to become the champion of French music, but it is understandable. Before coming to the operatic stage, Rameau had been an outsider—a mere theoretician whose best jobs had been in the organ lofts of provincial cathedrals. In short, he did not rate: his own transformation into the very symbol of *la musique française* was far in the future, though Campra had perhaps shown in which direction the wind would blow when, long before the days of Rameau's canonization as the patron saint of French music, he remarked that *Hippolyte et Aricie* had enough stuff in it for ten operas and that its composer would someday outshine all his contemporaries.

That peripatetic historian of music Charles Burney, writing an exact

[5] Even *Samson et Dalila* was originally written as an oratorio.

[6] We do not know what the Abbé was to receive if the opera succeeded, but unless this was stipulated, the arrangement was one of the most quixotic in history, and struck at the very root of the law of contract.

quarter-century after the death of Rameau, gave a detailed description of *Castor et Pollux,* "long regarded in France as the masterpiece of this composer":

> The overture is the best of this author, upon Lulli's plan. The opening symphony is beautiful; but why the same melody was not applied, in the same measure, to the poetry, I know not, unless the versification required a change of time; but, in that case, why write the symphony on a subject that would not suit the words? But those eternal changes in the measure, which teaze and disappoint the ear of all that are used to other Music, is general in serious French operas, and seem as much the fault of the poet as musician. It is, however, wonderful, that this defect was not sooner discovered. The overcharged tenderness of Rameau's Music appears in all his slow movements, which are in one style, and generally in triple time. This master perpetually discovers himself to be a great harmonist; but inured to a bad taste and style of composition, as well as to bad singing, he has only augmented the defects of his predecessors, and rendered what was rude and clumsy in Lulli, still more offensive, by endeavours at sweetness or high seasoning. The appoggiaturas, or leaning notes, being so frequently incorporated in the harmony, renders it crude, and the hanging on every note, as if unwilling to relinquish it, checks and impedes the motion of the air, and gives it a slow and languid effect, however likely the theme on which it is composed. Every passage in such a melody resembles a French heroic verse:
>
> > "Each is an *Alexandrine,* through the song,
> > That like a wounded snake, drags its slow length along." [7]
>
> The opening of the second act: *Que tout gémisse,* is very fine, and the pathos well applied; but the subsequent air, which is cast in an admirable mould, is spoiled by frequent and unnecessary changes of measure; and yet in spite of these defects, and the vocal outrages of Mademoiselle Arnould, I was more pleased and affected by this scene, than any other I ever heard at the French serious opera. The march, which has few appoggiaturas in it, is like other Christian Music.
>
> The *prélude tendre,* at the opening of the third act, abounds with too many of these drags, which being equally harsh to the ear and injurious to the pulsation, seem to prevent the performer from ever

---

[7] Adapting Pope, *An Essay on Criticism,* l. 357f.

falling on his feet; and bar eleventh, the chord of the superfluous fifth, which makes all nature shudder, except our Gallic neighbours, is here continued so long that it distorts the countenance of every other hearer, like *hiera picra*. The major minuet, page 121, after so long and tiresome a minority, is rich in harmony and graceful in melody. The voice is worse used by the composer than the most insignificant instrument. For after several symphonies that are extremely promising, and the ear has been made to expect a continuation of the prefatory strain, nothing is given to the vocal part but broken accents and dislocated measures. In the *chaconne,* which is admirable, the measure is well marked and well accented. . . . More genius and invention appear in the dances of Rameau than elsewhere, because in them, there is a necessity for motion, measure, and symmetry of phrase. And it may with truth be said, that nothing in Lulli's operas was imitated or adopted by the rest of Europe, but the style of his overtures, or in Rameau's, but the dances.

Not only is this an interesting bit of contemporary spectator criticism, but it is also an object lesson for music critics who are conscientious about their task. Those strictures which are Burney's prejudices against novelties or departures from his own rigorous ideas sound today merely irrelevant and old-fogyish. But when the fussy Doctor tested things by universal principles, his native sharpness led him to opinions that are as valid today as when he wrote them. The harmonic and rhythmic strangenesses that offended Burney are Rameau's chief claim to fame. From a purely musical point of view, he was a sorely needed innovator, both theoretically and in practice. As Burney declares, the instrumental sections are the best parts of Rameau's operas: he wrote well enough for the voice, but often inspiredly for instruments, introducing new ones and searching out new secrets of orchestral color. In his overtures he not only foreshadowed the romantic program overture of almost symphonic scope that Berlioz was to bring to maturity, but also more clearly defined the sonata tendency that has characterized the symphony from that day to this.

The staying power of Rameau's operas is such that every one of the major ones has been revived in the twentieth century. *Les Indes galantes* (1735) has become one of the staples of the Opéra—it was used on June 16, 1952, to open the Paris season. It is an overwhelming series of spectacles—a prologue followed by three entrées—but it is barely an opera, and indeed, it was called a *ballet héroïque,* that is, a ballet with words and music, both vocal and instrumental. Much of it is grand and lofty (the music given to the Turks, Peruvians, and Persians of the three *entrées* can scarcely be called indigenous). It is, perhaps, a series of diverse essays in the grand style, and leaves us with the conviction that Rameau, so languidly interested in operatic form, was not a great composer of operas, but a great composer who wrote operas. Yet, as many examples show, he could rise to a dramatic occasion, and perhaps he might have left truer operas had not his audiences had so unmitigated a taste for mere *divertissement.*

This man, who completed his first successful opera when he was fifty-one, was still writing for the stage when he was nearly eighty. He had finally achieved a brilliant position, almost as favored by Louis *le bien-aimé* as Lully had been by Louis *le grand,* but without stilling vicious tongues. He had merely exchanged one set of enemies for another. Starting out as a reputed enemy of the national school as represented by the worshipers of Lully, he ended by being a French national school of his own, quite as venerated as Lully had ever been.

In 1752, a troupe of Italian comic singers arrived in Paris to help lighten a musical season that had got off to a bad start with a deadly fiasco by Destouches. These lively artists, known in France as *Les bouffons,* staged Pergolesi's *La Serva padrona* with such thumping success that the old stand-bys of the Académie Royale, who wrote almost nothing but *opera seria* in French, found their position threatened. The situation became doubly serious when parties began to range themselves under the *buffa* and *seria* banners: the supporters of French opera found a protector in the King; the Italian party in the Queen, who took their side mainly because Mme de Pompadour had steered the King to the nationalists. Jean-Jacques Rousseau, always spoiling for a good fight, led a motley band of Encyclopedists to the defense of the *bouffons,* remarking that all true connoisseurs were with them, and that, anyhow, "There is neither measure nor melody in French music, because the language itself is not susceptible of either." It did not matter that he himself had taken some pains to disprove the precise truth of this statement by putting together, in *Le Devin du village,* a pastoral opera both in the French style and in the French language that remained in the repertoire of the Opéra until 1829, and has since been revived.

Thus was precipitated, because of the coolness between Louis XV's mistress and his Polish wife, the renowned *guerre des bouffons*—an extraordinary war with but a single battle, and that lost by the victors. The Queen's Corner (so called because the Italianists took to sitting beneath her loge) had recruited, besides Rousseau, Baron Grimm, Diderot, and D'Alembert, and was threatening the King's Corner (musical, but chic), when the single battle occurred. The director of the Opéra-Comique, where the *bouffons* held forth, produced a comic opera in French, announcing it as the work of a Viennese Italian. When the Queen's Corner had applauded itself silly, the director announced that his "Viennese Italian" was a fable and that the composer of *Les Troqueurs* was a native-born Frenchman, Antoine d'Auvergne, who had used a libretto by a Parisian poet. Thus, by a Trojan-horse trick, were Frenchmen made to swallow—and like—*opera buffa* in their own tongue. While the wails of the victors mingled with those of the defeated, few remembered that, almost ten years before, Rameau, chief of the nationalists, had himself unsuccessfully presented an *opera buffa* of the selfsame type as *Les Troqueurs*.

The point of the *guerre des bouffons* (if, indeed, it had one) was that comic opera with spoken dialogue was made respectable in France. The stranglehold of the stiff, undramatic *opera seria* had been broken, and Paris was ripe for the "reforms" of Gluck.

CHAPTER V

The Age of Gluck

CHRISTOPH WILLIBALD GLUCK (who became "von" Gluck only when knighted by Benedict XIV in 1756) was not a child prodigy. His biography is as arresting as a case history in slow development. The dates are significant not only in his biography, but also in the history of opera. Gluck was born in 1714; he wrote his first opera, *Artaserse*—to a libretto by Metastasio, be it noted—in 1741, his first important opera in 1762. To be sure, the latter was *Orfeo ed Euridice,* still (except for the frivolous *La Serva padrona*) the oldest opera in the standard repertoire. But in 1762 Gluck was still five years away from the attempts at intellectual-operatic reform that were to make him one of the half-dozen surpassing figures in opera's story. The history of his slow, but at last gloriously fruitful, evolution belongs almost as much to literature as to music.

The key to Gluck's major difference from his immediate predecessors and most of his contemporaries is the fact that, probably early in his composing career, he began to look at librettos, first with a critical eye, and finally with a jaundiced one. The difference was intellectual before it was musical. Monteverdi was a master of intense emotional effects that now seem archaic and curiously romantic. Lully, often ragged-edged, can sometimes exhilarate and invite to dancing, at others impress with solemn grandeur. Alessandro Scarlatti, as melodious as an antique Schubert, displays a logic that operatic music seldom achieves. Handel is as fertile and resistless as the Nile flood, and Rameau, scholarly, a little crabbed, yet resourceful beyond his age, sums up a nation's musical past with true magnificence. In single aspects of his art, Gluck could not match them. His achievement is less spectacular in detail, but wider in scope: it is, in short, the product of a man with some intense ideas. Stated simply, it is the conception of opera not as just music plus libretto, but, rather, as a thoroughly new entity including them both—an amalgam, fused and compact. Gluck's predecessors, great and small, no matter what their intelligence (and certainly four out of the five men named above were vigorously intelligent), either used music as a background accompaniment to a text or submerged a text in music. Neither of those ways was Gluck's when he rose to his greatest mastery.

In either of those approaches, the poor lyric poet failed to get his just due—even when he seemed to be getting more, as in the first Florentine operas. What must those pioneering works have been like when first performed? Extraordinarily thin musically. Perhaps effective dramatically —but with the drama irrelevantly impeded by a trickle of musical sound. It is no wonder that the vaunted classical severity of the *camerata* (which was, of course, only pseudoclassical) gave way quickly to "abuses" and "corruptions." Opera had to develop (if not grow up), and if it hobbled forward and jumped sporadically, that was mainly because its librettists and composers entertained such wild and widely varied conceptions of their distinct roles, one of the wildest being that their roles were indeed distinct. When the pendulum had swung completely away from Florence, the florid school came into its own, extraordinarily thin as to drama, its often superb music impeded by a supernumerary line of words. Is it any wonder that then the librettists, thwarted at every turn, pleaded with the world to judge their wares by the circumstances of their production?

"When I write for music, the last person I consider is myself. I think of the singers, I think very much of the composer, I think of the pleasure of the audience; and if my dramas were only represented and not read, I should dare to hope for more justice of judgment." These are the words, not of a hack librettist grinding out adapted *opera seria* texts for Handel or Buononcini, but of the great Venetian playwright of comedy, Carlo Goldoni. They were written in 1756, only six years before Gluck's *Orfeo ed Euridice,* and at a time when Metastasio's pre-eminence had secured for his fellow craftsmen a sensible improvement in status. It was not by librettos damped down in any such spirit of submissiveness that Goldoni at last altered the course of Italian spoken drama.

Ottavio Rinuccini, the earliest librettist of them all, was a poet of talent who avoided the pitfalls of originality by sticking close to his Greek models. Had it been possible to maintain Rinuccini's lofty conception of the libretto, his successors would not so quickly have lost their dignity. Unhappily for them, and for generations of operagoers ever since, the singer—whose labor should be to reveal the text and create character in the light of the music the composer has provided—disdained to accept this rewarding and lofty role, choosing instead to indulge in exhibitionism. Degeneration at opera's roots (which speedily followed) resulted from overfloriation at the top: the librettist, in order to earn a little money, had to work for the composer, and the composer, also in order to live, had to work for the singer, whom audiences adored. The principal reason a serious attempt to reform the opera was delayed so long was that the opera pleased just as it was. In England, when the florid opera ceased to please, opera in effect died out, to be revived (an exotic, as it had begun there) decades later. In countries where it was a popular vernacular entertainment, opera was changed, almost by *force majeure,* before dissatisfaction with it had been widely voiced.

Italy, more because of the stubborn conventionality of its audiences than because of any lack of imagination in its composers and librettists, was not to be a storm center of attempts at change, though rebellion stirred even there. The leaders of the later Neapolitan school—men like Niccolò Jommelli and Tommaso Traetta—were uncomfortably aware that something was amiss with *opera seria.* Separately or together, they anticipated practically every item on the Gluckian program of reform, which, incidentally, was not given to the world in a single fulmination, but was disclosed progressively in both polemic and practice. Indeed, the forward-looking Jommelli and Traetta were criticized harshly for impairing Italian purity by taking too extensive hints from the French and the Germans (as Rossini was to be charged with advanced Teutonism, and Verdi with Wagnerism). What defeated them, perhaps even more certainly than the invincible, understandable complacency of their audiences, was their equally invincible and understandable respect for the excellent fashionable dramatists of their day, particularly the two Caesarean poets—that is, official poets to "Caesar," the Holy Roman Emperor—of the Vienna court, Apostolo Zeno and Metastasio.

Zeno, born in Venice in 1668 and dying there in 1750, was an intelligent professional man of letters. In 1710 he joined Scipione Maffei, the historian and excellent dramatist, and the eminent physician and student of the *castrato* voice, Antonio Vallisnieri, in founding the influential *Giornale dei letterati d'Italia.* Occupying the post of Caesarean poet at Vienna for about eleven years (1718–29), Zeno then took up a similar position in Venice, where he wrote numerous librettos, many of them in collaboration with Pietro Pariati (1665–1733). Such of his beautifully constructed texts as *Faramondo* (used by Handel), *Temistocle* (set by Porpora), *La Griselda* (which Alessandro Scarlatti made into the last of his more than one hundred operas), and *Lucio Papirio dittatore* (set by Hasse) [1] were used over and over throughout the eighteenth century —and even later—both as Zeno wrote them (alone or with Pariati) and as revised, rewritten, and renamed by others.

The most famous and most often employed of Zeno's librettos was *Lucio Vero,* under several titles the text of a dozen operas stretching at least from Antonio Pollarolo's *Lucio Vero* (1700) to various operas called *Vologeso, re dei Parti* (Sacchini, Jommelli, and others), and in 1811, a *Berenice, regina d'Armenia* by the Neapolitan Nicola Antonio Zingarelli. Zeno also wrote the libretto of the first Hamlet opera—the *Ambleto* of Francesco Gasparini (1705)—and one of the earliest operas based on *Don Quixote*—Francesco Conti's *Don Chisciotte in Sierra Morena* (1719). When the Stuttgart Hoftheater was inaugurated on September 14, 1912, part of the performance was a partial singing of Jommelli's *Il Vologeso* (its text a revision of *Vologeso, re dei Parti,* in turn a revision of the *Lucio Vero* that Zeno had written in Venice more than two centuries earlier); the first performance of the Jommelli opera had occurred on February 11, 1766, at Ludwigsburg, a few miles north of Stuttgart.

But successful as Apostolo Zeno and his librettos were, he was dimmed by his successor as Caesarean poet. Metastasio, born Pietro Trapassi, would have been an amazing figure in any age. The romantic reader can find enough interest in this obscure Roman's swift rise to fame and power, in his love affairs, in his Platonic attachment to the beautiful, virtuous Countess Althann, in his final achievement of domestic sobriety. [2] Metastasio lived eighty-four years and wrote scores of librettos for opera and oratorio—wrote them, after an extraordinarily brief apprenticeship, with a felicity of versification and singability, with an understanding of arresting detail, which soon raised him to unquestioned primacy in his profession.

Such sureness of touch did not go unrewarded: the foremost composers

[1] Renamed *Quinto Fabio,* Zeno's *Lucio Papirio dittatore* was heard in Modena in 1778 in a setting by Dmitri Stepanovich Bortnyansky, the Russian composer whose collected works (mostly religious music) in ten volumes were to be edited by Tchaikovsky, nearly driving him insane from boredom.

[2] The story is told remarkably in Vernon Lee's remarkable book *Studies of the Eighteenth Century in Italy.*

turned to Metastasio for their texts as unerringly as we go to a telephone directory for a telephone number. Hundreds of operas were composed to his librettos (Loewenberg says that they number "far more than a thousand"). His first important *dramma per musica* was *Didone abbandonata,* the first setting of which—by Domenico Sarro—was sung on February 5, 1724, at the Teatro San Bartolommeo, Naples. Of the forty known settings of his *Artaserse,* three are by Hasse, who loyally set almost all of Metastasio's texts. Besides Faustina's prolific husband, Handel, Jommelli, Traetta, Galuppi, Gluck, Paisiello, Piccinni, and Porpora repaired constantly to Metastasio's verse. Mozart and Haydn occasionally used Metastasio librettos. As late as 1819, so shrewd a purveyor of public delights as Giacomo Meyerbeer was setting Metastasio's *Semiramide riconosciuta,* which had been used earlier by Leonardo Vinci, Hasse, and Gluck. The *terminus ad quem* of the uncanny attractiveness of this stage poetry may have been 1838, when Giovanni Pacini turned to the sadly shopworn *Temistocle* as a peg for his pseudo-Rossinian cadences.[3]

As soon as we leave the romance and statistics concerned with Metastasio, we get into trouble: aesthetically he is a hard nut to crack. Of late decades the target of almost unrelieved denigration by writers on opera, Metastasio deserves their arrows as little as he deserved the almost unique deification accorded to him by Hasse and many other composers. He immeasurably improved the general design of *opera seria,* shearing away many excrescences—and often reducing the number of acts from five to three. An inspired master of prosody (his best librettos can be read, in Italian, for the sheer pleasure of their literary excellence), he wrote verses made for singing, the products of an infallible ear and the habit, which he shared with Philippe Quinault, Lully's librettist, of writing his librettos at the harpsichord. Perhaps because he himself was an amateur composer of close to professional status, he helped to restore the chorus to a useful place in opera. He counseled the many composers who sat at his feet to use accompanied recitative more abundantly.

So far, all to the good. But Metastasio the poet customarily used an idiom so involved, twisted, and convolute as to drown in a torrent of rhetoric the very dramatic effects at which he seemed to be aiming most carefully. Further, though his stage works were logical and sequential,

[3] If, indeed, it was not 1840, the year of Baltasar Saldoni's *Cleonice, regina di Siria,* which may have been composed to Metastasio's *Demetrio,* originally supplied to Antonio Caldara more than a century earlier.

they had not sufficient dramatic intensity to animate their elaborate structures. Conflict and catharsis are mostly lacking. The characters are, with few exceptions, mere outlines of men and women, semianimated moral qualities; the stories themselves are not of life: they are courtly charades or, worse, sermons. He was not a Racine.

Gluck, who was eventually to join hands with one of Metastasio's most cogent critics and thus begin to break the stranglehold of the libretto cartel, started out seeming to be an unquestioning admirer of the Caesarean poet. He set almost twenty of Metastasio's librettos in all, three of them after his "revolt" had been begun. Gluck's musical debut was almost as tame as Richard Wagner's was to be, and he developed far less rapidly than Wagner. A percipient critic, surveying the first decade of Gluck's operatic career (during which he composed some sixteen run-of-the-mill, and sometimes worse than run-of-the-mill, Italian operas), might well have dismissed him as just another polite fabricator of court entertainments. His first opera, a setting of Metastasio's eternal *Artaserse,* was staged at Milan's Teatro Regio Ducale in 1741. Obvious and stereotyped, it was liked. Gluck was a popular mediocre composer long before he became a reluctantly accepted great one. He failed only in London, where, too, Handel told him off and gave him good advice.

Gluck's operas of the early and middle 1750's show flutters of his particular sort of originality. In 1755, to a simple, moving story by an anti-Metastasian who occupied the strategic post of director of the imperial court opera, Gluck composed a significant score, *L'Innocenza giustificata.* Something of his future can be read, not in the whole work, but in some of its single numbers. Its librettist, Count Giacomo Durazzo, would gladly have gone further, and might have been competent to handle the literary phase of a rebellion. But in 1755, though forty-one, Gluck was so little ready to take over the musical phase that he larded *L'Innocenza giustificata* with arias to Metastasio verses—and thereafter lapsed into his timeserving ways and turned out four additional examples of his neo-Milanese patchwork. Durazzo himself did not set Gluck aflame, but at least he served as catalyst in one of the most fruitful associations in the history of opera: in 1761 he introduced his favorite composer to an exchequer official recently arrived from Paris (he had been born in Leghorn)—Raniero de' Calzabigi.

The new librettist, the very form and spelling of whose name are as controversial as are the extent and originality of his part in the imminent reforms, was probably born, like Gluck, in 1714. Casanova, who was his friend, described him as "a great conniver, familiar with financial dealings, acquainted with the business of all countries, well versed in history, a *bel esprit,* poet, and great lover of women." At first not merely an admirer but openly an imitator of Metastasio, Calzabigi was obliged to give the Roman's texts finical scrutiny when preparing a critical edition of them; his adoration did not survive. This edition, brought out in Paris in 1755, included a prefatory dissertation on Metastasio by its editor. In it, after analyzing the *tragédie-lyrique* of Quinault and Lully, Calzabigi let fall the following pregnant observations:

> If in the end the same ground plan could be reconciled with the exigencies of truth; if once purely human actions were to unfold themselves to the exclusion of pagan divinities and all that smacks of the devil and of magic; in short, all that is beyond things within the control of human beings, there is no doubt that a delightful whole would result from the interplay of a large chorus, the dance, and a scenic action whose poetry and music would be united in a masterly way.

Although the knowledgeable reader saw the names of Lully and Quinault referred to in these remarks, he must have realized that they were in part directed against Metastasio. But that aging poet, far from taking offense at the dissertation, retained it in his own edition of his works. The question of whether Metastasio felt Calzabigi's barbs at all or secretly agreed with his detractor [4] must depend on an estimate of Metastasio's intellectual powers. Diagnosing a disease is not equivalent to possessing the power to cure it.

Calzabigi the reformer was anything but a bluenose. Like several notable librettists earlier than the spotless Boito, he was something of a scoundrel—and no less than Casanova, his very good friend and well-wisher, is authority for the statement. Calzabigi left Paris in 1761 too hurriedly for decency and achieved an important government post in Vienna with suspect rapidity. Long after his association with Gluck, Calzabigi, who seems eventually to have blossomed forth as a species of international financier, is discovered managing—and mismanaging—

---

[4] To dismiss Metastasio as indifferent to some problems of musicodramatic reform would be a mistake. He was, for example, vehement against the style of music that was, he wrote, "making the theater resound no longer with any applause other than that given to displays of execution, with the vain inundation of which she has hastened her own disgrace after having first occasioned that of the mangled, disfigured, and ruined drama."

government lotteries and providing money at exorbitant rates of interest to impecunious princes. All this is incidental to the essential qualities that he placed at the disposition of art. Intelligent, widely read, truly cultivated, the devotee of a thousand intellectual passions, Calzabigi also had the boldness needed to put into action ideas about which other gifted men had been content to theorize. The libretto that, at Count Durazzo's bidding, he presented to Gluck in 1761 sounded a warning to Metastasians that a new era was coming.

Metastasio himself needed no warning. In 1751 he had written that Gluck "has surprising fire, but he is mad." Five years later, writing from Vienna to Farinelli, he lamented: "The opera that will be represented tonight in the public theater will certainly meet with applause. What is there which would not please on such a day [the celebration of the birthday of Maria Theresa's husband, the Emperor Francis I]? The drama is my *Re pastore,* set by Gluck, a Bohemian composer whose spirit, noise, and extravagance have supplied the place of merit in many theaters of Europe, among those whom I pity, and who do not form the minority of the folks of this world. Thank God, we have no want of such auditors here." Compare this with the words of Alfred Einstein (1936), who had the advantage of looking back on *Il Re pastore* as one integer of Gluck's entire career: "There is much beautiful and carefully fashioned music in the work, but not a single feature that exceeds the most conventional of conventions. . . . Yet on the whole the work is no more than the response to a command from the throne of which Gluck acquitted himself with decency."

In 1761, Gluck was finally prepared to do justice to a credible vehicle. The same year, composing a long and elaborate dramatic ballet based remotely on Molière's Don Juan play, *Le Festin de pierre,* he had responded with constructive intelligence to another demand for reform—the great dancer Noverre's insistence that the stereotyped, listless *ballet de cour* be transformed into a more dramatic and lifelike form of entertainment. Naturalness, expressiveness, truth in depicting human manners and emotions: those were Noverre's demands. They were also Calzabigi's, and Gluck was as ready for Calzabigi's ambitious program as he had been for Noverre's. Readier, perhaps, for in *Orfeo ed Euridice,* first produced at the Vienna Burgtheater on October 5, 1762, with the famed male contralto Gaetano Guadagni as Orpheus, he composed one of the sovereign masterworks of the musical stage.

Orfeo is far from perfect either dramatically or musically. A few years later, Calzabigi would have had more theatrical tact than to ruin a simple, moving story with a preposterous happy ending. True, there was a tradition of happy endings, a tradition that appealed strongly to the soft hearts of operagoers. But Calzabigi would never have been worthy of the best in Gluck if he had decided to cater always to such aesthetically infantile predilections. Nor would he err again in making an opera substantially a monologue for its hero. The fact that Eurydice, entering belatedly, must behave like a ravishing deaf-mute until the sudden outburst of galvanic excitement which brings on her second demise is not calculated to intensify the drama, the histrionic abilities of most sopranos being what they are. The role of Amor, whose thankless privilege it is to turn the tragedy into a farce, is the kind of supernumerary, actually hostile to the drama itself, which Calzabigi never again employed so blatantly. Gluck made fewer mistakes (apart from the mistake of not forcing Calzabigi to improve the text). The flaws in *Orfeo* derive mostly from elements of the old *opera seria* which Gluck and Calzabigi together had not been able to exorcise. The worst, perhaps, was Gluck's composing a comparatively dull overture of doubtful relevance. Almost as bad was a third act that even the presence of his most famous single aria does not save after the double miracle of two nearly perfect acts.

Yet *Orfeo*'s tremendous virtues so outweigh its faults that the most intelligent audiences of two centuries have rejoiced in it. Evidence survives that it was concocted in cold blood as the opening document of a revolt; not the least of its triumphs is that in proper performance it shows no trace of self-consciousness. Calzabigi's contributions were simplicity, ease of language, large understanding of situation and character, and all but complete disregard of the complex formulas for libretto construction set by Zeno and Metastasio (which does not mean that he was their equal in other respects). Calzabigi was stating no more than the truth when he wrote, in a letter published in the *Mercure de France* on August 21, 1784: "I hope that you will agree . . . that if Gluck created dramatic music, he did not create it out of nothing. I furnished him with the material, the chaos, if you wish; the honor of this creation, then, is common to us both."

Gluck contributed, besides the simple, unaccountable fact of his genius, a response to the subtlest implications of Calzabigi's book. No more appropriate music has ever been composed—and surely appropriateness is the essential quality of operatic music—though Gluck would achieve later a more delicate balance between drama and music as he sloughed off more and more elements of *opera seria* that were no longer in any way relevant to his purposes. In no other score, moreover, did Gluck manage so many temptations to stop the show. The magnificent scene at the gates of Erebus, beginning with the hellish dance of the Furies (borrowed from his own *Don Juan*) and ending with Orpheus' pathetic plea to be allowed to seek his beloved among the shades, punctuated with explosive shouts of *"No!"* from the Furies, is the sheer stuff of drama. The scene in the Elysian Fields, with the ecstatic, solemn "Che puro ciel" and serenely lovely Dance of the Happy Shades is perhaps Gluck's purest musical claim to stand with the very greatest of composers. In the Dance, the flute usurps the place of the human voice and produces utterly unique magic. Finally—as hummability is at least a minor touchstone of the art for all good operagoers—there is "Che farò senza Euridice," a melody so beautiful and self-sufficient that only the most accomplished singer can keep it securely within the framework of the opera's structure. Yet "Che farò" presents so many difficulties of interpretation that Gluck himself said of it: "Make the least change in it, either in the tempo or in the turn of expression, and it will become an air for a puppet show."

The revolutionary *Orfeo* was not received with enthusiasm by Vienna, which was so annoyed or bewildered by the bread and cold water of this strange, Doric score that it supported only eight performances in nearly nine months. For five years Gluck turned back to the mellifluous verbiage of Metastasio and his imitators: there were scant signs that more operas like *Orfeo* would increase his fortune—at least in Vienna and Italy, otherwise his reliable markets. Upsurges of high drama in *Telemacco* (Burgtheater, Vienna, January 30, 1765) show that Gluck was not entirely satisfied with potboiling. And in 1764 (Burgtheater, January 7) he had produced the last of his comic operas, *La Rencontre imprévue,* not only the only full-length comedy he produced, but also the only one of his comedies to reflect the reforms he and Calzabigi were trying to effect in more solemn operas. The text, adapted by L.-H. Dancourt from an earlier French vaudeville by Alain-René Lesage, the author of *Gil Blas,* and D'Orneval, was a thoroughly amusing and viable opera text. In modern revivals, which have served to establish the excellence of both libretto and music, the opera has often been called *Les Pèlerins de la Mecque.*

No, potboiling was not to Gluck's taste. And yet, in *Alceste,* his next collaboration with Calzabigi, he himself made—and may have persuaded his librettist to make—concessions to the baroque style, though this is a work of even greater sobriety and sternness than *Orfeo ed Euridice.* The libretto brings forward once more the useless female friends of the heroine who had cluttered up the scenery in many a Zeno and Metastasio libretto. Quite as odd is Gluck's return to *recitativo secco* after having banished it summarily from *Orfeo.*

These evasions of uncompromising reform would attract less notice if *Alceste* had not been published, two years after its production at the Vienna Burgtheater on December 26, 1767, with a preface by Calzabigi signed, and unquestionably concurred in, by Gluck. Except for the per-oration—several lengths of soft soap for the ego of the dedicatee, the future Leopold II—this fiery, unblushingly sensible manifesto deserves quotation in full:

YOUR ROYAL HIGHNESS,

When I undertook to write the music for *Alceste,* I resolved to divest it entirely of all those abuses, introduced into it either by the mistaken vanity of singers or by the too great complaisance of com-posers, which have so long disfigured Italian opera and made of the most splendid and most beautiful of spectacles the most ridiculous and wearisome. I have striven to restrict music to its true office of serving poetry by means of expression and by following the situations of the story, without interrupting the action or stifling it with a useless superfluity of ornaments; and I have believed that it should do this in the same way as telling colors affect a correct and well-ordered drawing, by a well-assorted contrast of light and shade, which serves to animate the figures without altering their contours. Thus I did not wish to arrest an actor in the greatest heat of dialogue in order to wait for a tiresome *ritornello,* nor to hold him up in the middle of a word on a vowel favorable to his voice, nor to make display of the agility of his fine voice in some long-drawn-out passage, nor to wait while the orchestra gives him time to recover his breath for a cadenza. I did not think it my duty to pass quickly over the second section of an aria of which the words are perhaps the most impassioned and important, in order to repeat regularly, four times over, those of the first part, and to finish the aria where its sense may perhaps not end, for the con-venience of the singer who wishes to show that he can vary a passage capriciously in a number of guises; in short, I have sought to abolish all the abuses against which good sense and reason long have cried out in vain.

I have felt that the overture ought to apprise the spectators of the nature of the action to be represented and to form, so to speak, its argument; that the concerted instruments should be introduced in proportion to the interest and intensity of the words, and not leave that sharp contrast between the aria and the recitative in the dialogue, so as not to break a period unreasonably or wantonly disturb the force and heat of the action.

Furthermore, I believed that my greatest labor should be devoted to seeking a beautiful simplicity, and I have avoided making displays of difficulty at the expense of clarity; nor did I judge it desirable to discover novelties not naturally suggested by the situation and its expression; and there is no rule that I have not thought it right to set aside willingly for the sake of an intended effect.

Such are my principles. By good fortune, my designs were wonderfully furthered by the libretto, in which the celebrated author, devising a new dramatic scheme, had substituted heartfelt language, strong passions, interesting situations, and an endlessly varied spectacle for florid descriptions, unnatural paragons, and sententious, cold morality. . . .

Few will deny that the collaborators worked in the spirit of this epochal and cold-bloodedly intelligent document even when they violated its letter. A libretto even more simply worded and more dramatically focused than *Orfeo*'s gave Gluck his inspiration. A bodingly tragic overture moving straight into the action [5] (of which, indeed, it forms part) magnificently gives flesh to one of the promises of the manifesto. The first act sets the forces of fate in motion; the second sees them operating toward an inevitably violent end; the third provides a happy ending not unpalatable in so far as it is inherent in the whole drama. Furthermore, the joy of this *dénouement* is not degraded (or should not be—opera directors can force the issue) by a pagan neighborhood fiesta such as concludes the unsatisfactory last act of *Orfeo*.

Alceste failed. "For nine days," complained one of the smart set at the *première,* "the theater has been closed, and on the tenth it opens with a

---

[5] So straight that this favorite concert number could not be heard apart from the opera if it were not for the special ending composed for it by Wagner.

Requiem." But this time Gluck waited only three years and one potboiler before returning to the charge with *Paride ed Elena,* in some respects the most ambitious of his stage works. Calzabigi, collaborating with Gluck for the last time, handed him what can only be called a study in ethnic contrasts (Sparta versus Phrygia), made all the more interesting by the astonishing discovery that Helen of Troy was a prude. A silly business without motion or climax, it is simply the story of Paris' wooing of Helen (who is merely affianced to Menelaus). *Paride ed Elena* mostly lacks drama, but it happens to contain much splendid music, as well as Gluck's most passionate love song, "O del mio dolce ardor." [6]

The Viennese did not like the five acts of *Paride ed Elena,* which was sung for the first time at the Burgtheater on November 3, 1770. But then their dislikes and likes meant little to Gluck: he was beginning to find the atmosphere of Austrian rigidity hostile to the new direction he wanted to go in. He was now stubbornly determined on exodus—otherwise he might have reconsidered, if only to be near and to support the youthful Antonio Salieri, his first pupil, whose brilliant career was just starting. He began to haunt the French embassy, hinting at preferment in Paris, where his imperial pupil, the Archduchess Marie Antoinette, was established as the much-indulged wife of the Dauphin Louis. Gluck wangled so well that when he set out with his family for France some four years later, he carried with him parts of the score of an opera in French whose production in Paris was all but assured. And this time, Calzabigi having disappeared after a scandal, Gluck's librettist was his master wangler at the embassy—Marie-François-Louis Gand-Leblanc, Bailli du Rollet.

Paris, for so many years a proud beehive of reaction, had just laughed itself out of lethargy during the *guerre des bouffons,* and was probably the only city in the world in which Gluck could have carried his intentions to their logical conclusions. As far as the nationalists—the *rameauistes* and the King's Corner—were concerned, much of the logic in Gluck's logical conclusions consisted of the fact that he had most of a French opera in his traveling bags. More important, finally, the Encyclopedists, though lingeringly Italianate, were sympathetic to Gluck's ideas,

---

[6] Alfred Einstein described "O del mio dolce ardor" as "nothing else than a cavatina in a minor key in the later Neapolitan operatic style." It can only be hoped that he intended this as praise of Jommelli, Sacchini, and Traetta rather than derogation of Gluck. More illuminating seems Einstein's remark that the response of Helen to Paris in Act II is an "expression of irony—surely something new in the history of opera."

and he was assured of vigorous intellectual support. Marie Antoinette, too, was importantly in the picture. An impressive cast was assembled for the *première* of *Iphigénie en Aulide:* the great Sophie Arnould, at the full of her powers, created the name role, Joseph Legros was the Achilles, and the presence of Vestris, *"le dieu de la danse,"* lent the necessary aura of divinity. Du Rollet's libretto was based on Racine; everything looked propitious when the curtains of the Opéra parted on the night of April 19, 1774, with Marie Antoinette in the royal loge.[7]

Before the *première* of *Iphigénie en Aulide,* Gluck had been one of a dozen celebrated composers for the stage; after it, he was without a peer in France. For the moment, Paris was delightfully stunned. The witty Abbé Arnaud, director of the influential *Gazette de France,* echoed the general enthusiasm when he said of a certain melody in *Iphigénie,* "With that air one might found a religion." Mme du Deffand, who confessed to Horace Walpole that "M. Glou's" opera bored her to death, was almost a minority of one. There was reason for the opera's magnificent reception: *Iphigénie en Aulide,* more than any other of Gluck's operas, puts its best foot forward at once—the magnificent and magnificently relevant overture leads without pause into a strong situation, which it immeasurably heightens. The score, except in the last scene, sustains this tension; time and again, despite the librettist's sober presentation of a chain of psychological conflicts, the music threatens to boil over. Gluck followed his text with painstaking fidelity, but provided accents that were far beyond the talents of Du Rollet. In the provision of such accents—in knowing surely what music could do better than words—Gluck showed his genius.

So powerful was the effect of some scenes in *Iphigénie* that members of the audience forgot that they were witnessing make-believe, and were with difficulty restrained from rushing onto the stage to deliver the hapless princess of Mycenae. The fact that none of Gluck's operas is likely to have this effect on a modern audience does not mean that they have lost vitality. Our aural palate has become accustomed to the rich fare and spices of Verdi and verism and the heady wines of pure and neo-Wagnerism. By one of the familiar ironies of history, we who are used to the

---

[7] She would become Queen of France exactly three weeks later, for Louis XV died on May 10, 1774. The resulting period of mourning interrupted the successful run of *Iphigénie en Aulide* after its fifth performance. Alfred Loewenberg records that it was sung again on January 10, 1775, and by 1824 had achieved 428 performances at the Opéra alone.

scarifying vocalism of Strauss's *Elektra* have come to consider as stylized and unexciting the opera of Gluck, which in its own day was condemned as the death of singing. To get all of the drama from *Iphigénie,* we must borrow the ears of the eighteenth century, which had never heard Wagner [8] or Strauss, Verdi or Puccini, Berg or Stravinsky.

During the two years following *Iphigénie en Aulide,* Gluck reworked *Orfeo* and *Alceste* to French translations of their original librettos. These adaptations are not wholly satisfactory. *Orphée et Eurydice* was nevertheless a success. Had Parisian conditions allowed the use of *castrati, Orfeo* might not have been so stringently revised. As it was, the role of Orpheus had to be transposed and in part recomposed for a tenor— Legros, who had contributed so much to the initial success of *Iphigénie.* This upset the key relationships, and to remedy that unwelcome difficulty, it has become the custom for a woman to sing the role in the original key.[9] To compensate, however, Gluck added a lot of superb new music to the revised score.

Besides Legros, the principals at the first performance of *Orphée et Eurydice,* on August 2, 1774, included Arnould as Eurydice and Rosalie Levasseur as Amor. For the revival of November 18, 1859, at the Théâtre-Lyrique, Hector Berlioz, a worshiper of Gluck, crossed the versions of 1762 and 1774 in a way that allowed the incomparable Pauline Viardot-García to espouse the role of Orpheus. It turned out to be the greatest triumph of a great career. Berlioz, who was, anyhow, in love with Viardot-García, poured out a rhapsodic tribute to her impersonation. Of her singing of "J'ai perdu mon Eurydice" ("Che farò senza Euridice"), he wrote:

> Mme Viardot treated it as it ought to be treated, that is to say, as what it is, one of those prodigies of expression which are well-nigh incomprehensible for vulgar singers, and which are, alas! so often desecrated. She delivered its theme in three different manners: at first in a slow movement, with suppressed grief; then, after the episodic adagio:

[8] Or, for that matter, Wagner's version of *Iphigénie en Aulide,* parts of which resemble *Lohengrin.* Not only did he substantially rewrite both words and music, but he also interpolated stretches of music of his own contriving. As the crowning touch of this ambiguous devotion, he introduced the goddess Artemis into the cast of characters.

[9] Orpheus is sometimes sung by a tenor; such a version has been available in recordings.

Mortel silence!
Vaine espérance!

sotto voce, pianissimo, with a trembling voice choked by a flood of tears; and, finally, after the second adagio, she took up the theme in a more animated movement, withdrawing from the body of Eurydice, beside which she had been kneeling, and rushing away, mad with despair, toward the other side of the stage, the very picture of frenzy in her outcries and sobs. I shall not attempt to describe the excitement of the audience at this overwhelming scene. Certain maladroit auditors even so far forgot themselves as to cry *"Bis!"* before the sublime passage:

Entends ma voix qui t'appelle,

and great difficulty was experienced in imposing silence upon them. Some persons would cry "Bis!" for the scene of Priam in the tent of Achilles or for Hamlet's "To be or not to be."

The operation performed on *Alceste* for the Paris production (April 23, 1776) became even more flagrant than that on *Orfeo,* especially because Gluck was not the only surgeon in attendance.[10] While Gluck was out of town, official busybodies at the Opéra allowed François-Joseph Gossec to insert into the last act of the score his rewriting of an old and forgettable aria from one of Gluck's earlier works and assign it to a character foreign to the original Vienna version. Alfred Einstein cogently suggested that an ideal presentation of *Alceste,* like one of *Orfeo,* would consist of a combination of the best elements of the Vienna and Paris scores. All that we could ask is a musician of Gluck's ability to make the selection of elements.

Shortly after the Paris *première* of *Alceste* there entered upon the scene a mild-mannered, big-hearted Italian composer of most respectable gifts whose unwanted distinction it was to be carried aloft as the banner of the gathering opposition to Gluck. Left to himself, Nicola Piccinni might have continued his spectacularly successful career in Italy, to which he had been purveying well-liked operas for many years; he would then have occupied a less ambiguous position in histories of music, for he was a composer of great talent and attractiveness. In the first place,

[10] No one, however, who is familiar with Alcestis' great supplication as "Divinités du Styx" is likely to be satisfied with the original Italian version, "Ombre, larve, compagne di morte," with its peculiarly lame rhythm and meter.

the reasons for his importation into France display a mystifying confusion in the minds of his patrons. Their reasoning is all highly reminiscent of the time when some people in London decided to pit a little fribble of a man like Buononcini (by no measure a composer of Piccinni's stature) against a force of nature like Handel, apparently forgetting that a good fight requires opponents of almost equal weight. Piccinni, fourteen years Gluck's junior, had written many hits, most of them *opere buffe.* At thirty-two he had composed *La Buona Figliuola,* which had set Rome, then Italy, then all Europe, to laughing. Only an Englishman could have appreciated its richest humor: it was based on Samuel Richardson's solemn *Pamela.* The librettist, however, was Carlo Goldoni. Piccinni had also trafficked with *opera seria,* usually with indifferent success. Two years before his French visit of 1776, however, he had fished out an old Metastasio warhorse entitled sometimes *Alessandro nell' Indie* (as which it has been set by, among others, Baldassare Galuppi and Johann Christian Bach), sometimes *Cleofide* (Hasse), and sometimes *Poro* (Handel and Gluck himself [1743])—and had set it to quite unexpected *réclame.* That sealed his fate. He was imported not as a composer of *opera buffa,* in which he could have outdistanced Gluck handily, but as a master of *opera seria* or something like it, in which he was manifestly Gluck's inferior. Even before the innocent Piccinni had stirred out of Italy, he had received his credentials. Unfortunately for him, they were sealed orders.

The ultimate credit for staging the contest between the German and the Italian must go to that useless favorite of romantic history, Marie Antoinette. Assurance of her protection had taken Gluck to Paris; the same assurance was extended to Piccinni. Like the serpent at Eve's ear, the crafty and malicious historiographer of royal France, Jean-François Marmontel, had whispered that it would be fun to have the protagonists set the same libretto. The Queen agreed that this would indeed be fun, and Marmontel accordingly sent to each composer his own revamping of *Roland,* a text by Philippe Quinault which Lully had set in 1685. Gluck got wind of the plot, and not only refused indignantly to add another pen-stroke to the uncompleted score but also wrote to his friend Du Rollet denouncing the trickery and stating that he had thrown his share into the fire. Du Rollet published the letter. Instantly, Paris divided into Gluckists and Piccinnists. Hundreds went to pay court to Piccinni, who had just arrived, accompanied by his large family and a complete ignorance of the French language.

Some of Gluck's followers admitted uneasily that he possibly had lost the first trick by thus refusing to compete. Their fears were quieted somewhat by the news that their idol was at work on another of Quinault's tried-and-true librettos, the *Armide* that Lully had used for his masterpiece in 1686. What Gluck produced, with the quickly regained favor of the public, was not, to be sure, another step forward in his revolutionary march, but a lumbering old-fashioned five-acter. *Armide* (September 23, 1777) is notable chiefly for the care that he lavished on the dramatic creation of Armida herself, an unwholesome sorceress (out of Tasso) of profoundly erotic tastes—an eighteenth-century foreshadowing of Wagner's Kundry. Ironically, when Piccinni's *Roland* was produced five months later, it was found that he had composed it to a neat three-act text by Marmontel at which Calzabigi need not have blushed. Neither man had won—or perhaps they had won each other's battles.

Much of *Armide* is romanticism before its time. In the midst of much eighteenth-century music that had not entirely freed itself of baroque features of *opera seria,* the most renowned aria in *Armide*—"Plus j'observe ces lieux"—seems almost out of place, so much does it resemble the sensuousness of much nineteenth-century French opera. The same quality recurs more than once, notably three acts later in the duet of parting between Armida and Rinaldo, with what Einstein aptly called "an infinity of simple melody." And, harking back to the music for the Furies in *Orfeo* which he had taken from his ballet *Don Juan,* Gluck in this fifth act provided the court ballet with music of great beauty which often summons up the ample grandeur of Rameau. Were the rest of *Armide* a worthy setting for these wonders, it would be a great opera. But, alas, much in Quinault's libretto was not at all germane to Gluck's purposes; what *Armide* demonstrates most clearly is that librettos, like everything else, are intimately related to their era: what was all grist for Lully's mill was only intermittently of use to Gluck. And so *Armide* is a patchwork of the best, the merely good, and the frankly perfunctory.

While the absurd, protracted conflict of the Gluckists and Piccinnists, in which the points at issue never were clearly defined, ended by embroiling almost every articulate Parisian, the two men around whose names the battles raged stood above the noise and turmoil. Gluck and Piccinni rather liked each other. Gluck treated the Italian with scrupulous courtesy and a fairness pleasant to record of a man whose conduct toward his colleagues had not always been free of chicanery and double-dealing. Piccinni admired his unwanted rival, whose importance to the evolution of opera he fully appreciated. When Gluck died, Piccinni attempted vainly to get subscribers for annual concerts in memory of the man to whom, in his own words, "the lyrical theater owes as much as the French drama owes to Corneille." [11]

The last set piece of fireworks in the Gluck-Piccinni "war," which turned out to be the deadest squib of all, was a silly bit of treachery that resulted in the chief actors' finally composing music to librettos based on the same classical story, *Iphigénie en Tauride*. Gluck's was produced first (May 18, 1779), proved to be his greatest work, and settled the question, not of his principles, but of his pre-eminence. The director of the Opéra had handed him a faithful, straightforward adaptation of Euripides. Gluck's purposeful mind recognized its possibilities and provided it with his finest dramatic score. Piccinni tampered with the text handed him and, having boasted about his speed in composition, turned in his opera two years later than Gluck (it was produced on January 23, 1781). That was exactly two years too late: when Piccinni's *Iphigénie* finally reached the boards of the Opéra, it suffered at least as much from comparison with Gluck's austerely classical masterpiece as from the unhappy circumstance that the leading lady at the *première* was visibly drunk. "This is not *Iphigénie en Tauride*," Sophie Arnould decided. "It is 'Iphigénie en Champagne.' " The most loyal Piccinnists could not withstand so fateful a combination of blows. Furthermore, by 1781 Paris was beginning to forget the feud, which died of peaceful old age.

Iphigénie en Tauride not only is unique among Gluck's operas; it is also the undeniable ancestor of much in the operas of Cherubini, Spon-

---

[11] Piccinni's career remained consistently checkered. After Gluck went home for his last few stately, honored years in Vienna, Piccinni was again cast for a seesaw role when Antonio Sacchini arrived in Paris. When, in 1786, several years after his arrival, this newcomer died in despair over Parisian fickleness, Piccinni stepped forward to pronounce his unhappy compatriot's funeral oration. His own finest operas all postdated Gluck's departure in 1779: *Iphigénie en Tauride* (1781, to a different libretto from the one Gluck had used), *Didon* (1783), and *Le faux Lord* (1783), the last to a libretto by his son Giuseppe Maria. The Revolution drove Piccinni back to Naples, where for nine years he sank into wretched poverty. Then he decided to see France again. Napoleon befriended him, even creating for him a tiny post at the Conservatoire. But when Piccinni died in 1800, he was buried in the potter's field. No colleague pronounced an oration over his tomb.

tini, Berlioz, Wagner, and Strauss. It combines, that is, a true feeling of the classical Greek (felt, of course, through an eighteenth-century sensibility) with an intense interest in the characterization of individual protagonists. The choruses, brilliantly used, no longer are technically "Greek," in that they do not comment on the action or the crises, but supply backgrounds of vocal color. The brief prelude leads without interruption into the action. From that point on, it is clear that Gluck's musicodramatic genius has won out over his noble theories: this is a great musicodramatic unit because here wonderfully melodious and expressive music has taken over the action, sending it forth again, mixed with the directing words of the text, as an overpoweringly effective series of grand airs, choruses, dances, and ensembles. The separate airs and other numbers are frequently very beautiful and moving in themselves, but the final proof of their greatness can be measured by the amounts of both beauty and effectiveness which they lose when divorced from the entirety of *Iphigénie en Tauride*.

After the second of his Iphigenia operas, Gluck lingered in Paris only long enough to compose his last opera, *Echo et Narcisse,* which was a failure when presented at the Opéra on September 24, 1779. He suffered several apoplectic seizures, returned to Vienna, and went into comfortable retirement, dying on November 15, 1787. Even if his reform of opera had been completely and wholeheartedly carried out—which it certainly was not—it could not have reformed opera completely: opera is an incorrigible. Any "reform" turns out to be merely a set of specific circumstances, unlikely to endure, and certainly not effectively imitable. Gluck possessed no magic formula that even he could copy. He had the creative intelligence to see how the dramatic and musical elements of opera could be balanced effectively in a particular way. He had, however, to face new problems with every libretto he undertook to fuse into a single entity with music. His musical idiom was not greatly different from that of his most gifted contemporaries. He made better use of it, employed it more dramatically and justly, but only when elements in the libretto carried him to heights normally above him.

Gluck taught what few have been able to learn: that a genuine musicodramatic unity can be achieved, its continuity maintained. In 1782, just after the slothful old reformer had commanded a special performance of Mozart's *Die Entführung aus dem Serail,* he delightedly asked the youthful composer to his fine house in the suburbs of Vienna. He wined and dined him—and no doubt there was plenty of talk about music and about opera. What Gluck did not, could not, know was that much of the future of opera lay not with himself—the already half-forgotten reformer —but in part with such of his (and Piccinni's) descendants as Cherubini and Spontini, in larger part with this young heir of Hasse and the Neapolitans as well as of *opera buffa.*

CHAPTER VI

Mozart

IN the slightly more than one hundred and fifty years of operatic history before the appearance of Gluck's series of masterpieces, no one had succeeded in producing that fusion of music and drama which obliterates every trace of opera's hybrid ancestry. It would be cheating to mention Monteverdi or Purcell: anyhow, praise would be neutralized by a damning "considering the time and the resources at hand." It would not be cheating to mention Pergolesi's *La Serva padrona* (1733), for it is—for all its brevity—a perfect thing. But our dignity does not permit us to allow that the first artistically satisfactory opera is a *buffa.* No, let us begin with sublimity: let us begin with *Orfeo ed Euridice,* after which the continuity of occasional perfection was established almost without a break.

Gluck's creative life stopped in 1782, just when Mozart was beginning to write his more astonishing series of masterpieces (the reformer of opera died in 1787, the year of *Don Giovanni*). Only three months intervened between Mozart's death and the birth of Rossini, whose *Il Barbiere di Siviglia* was the next miracle. Since Rossini survived until 1868, he lived to witness not only the births of all the composers [1] of the greatest operatic masterpieces since his own, but also the creation of several of these masterpieces. Wagner had composed *Tristan, Die Meistersinger,* and most of the *Ring* before Rossini died. Verdi was still a quarter-century away from *Otello* and *Falstaff,* but he had already composed works that portended genius. Mussorgsky was working on the first version of *Boris Godunov.* Bizet had done little that was not mediocre. Finally, Debussy and Strauss, respectively six and four in 1868, existed only as problems to their parents.

[1] Alban Berg (1885–1935) excepted.

Mozart is the most baffling member of this royal line. Gluck was a theorist whose best operas perfectly ground his axes. Rossini, whose *Barbiere* is Mozart with a difference, deliberately founded French grand opera.[2] Wagner, another theorist, made opera the vehicle of philosophy, vastly extended the orchestra's role, and discovered the musical equivalent of the loins.[3] Verdi, assuming in old age, and with equal grace, the masks of high comedy and high tragedy, achieved in pithy, gnomic saying and tragic soliloquy the perfect foil to Bayreuth's dark suggestiveness and eloquent, sensual narrative. Bizet and Mussorgsky, attacking problems of color, style, and dramatic accent, solved them in varying yet oddly related ways, and immeasurably enriched the whole musical palette. Debussy, a Wagner in reverse, returning to the ideals of Peri and Caccini, made a single dream opera of whispers and asides and further broke down the musical spectrum into shades, tints, and tonalities. Then came Strauss, the Saint Paul of Wagnerism and the Mohammed of the libido, who nevertheless poured out the most effervescent champagne in an opera of waltzes. The line has come temporarily to an end with Berg's *Wozzeck,* the only opera finished by this febrile, perfervid child of post-war years.

To capture Mozart's quality in a phrase, or even a series of phrases, is impossible. No composer, not excepting Schubert, deals so exclusively with the pure stuff of music, working always in seeming abandon and utter unself-consciousness with self-sufficient patterns of sound. While the metaphysics of Mozart's music can be discussed to the point of verbosity, attempts to give it a program do well if they produce one germane phrase in twenty pages of exegesis. Music that has literary, philosophical, or pictorial overtones and intentions can, of course, be described: faced with Mozart, literature admits itself defeated, and recourse must be had to the grammar of formal analysis. The problem becomes more complicated when it is realized with what versatility he uses the several styles at his command. Would we not be inclined to divide his widely varying masterpieces among several geniuses, if we did not feel that only Mozart could have written any of them?

Furthermore, Mozart did not hew to a line. The routine musicologist finds his career untidy: he quite obviously had no sense of a mission in

[2] Meyerbeer's claim to this fantastic realm is not forgotten. See pp. 213 ff.

[3] In *Jessonda* (1823), Ludwig Spohr veered close to the explicit raptures of *Tristan und Isolde* (1865).

life. His exquisite sense of the fitness of things, coupled with his ability to do always what was needed, helps to resolve the apparent contradictions of his career. For instance, he brought Italian *opera buffa* to perfection and also launched its cousin the Singspiel on the road to artistic respectability. The former achievement was, if anything, the more remarkable of the two. Taking that *buffa* tradition much as he found it, and doing almost nothing to change its essentials, by the most delicate *ad hoc* adjustments and qualifications he composed operas that are living today, while his models have survived only as museum pieces. (Some of them, it is fair to say, deserve resuscitation.) Apparently working without definite dramatic theories,[4] and taking any libretto pushed his way, he created a gallery of characters comparable to the creations of a great novelist—characters whose being is built solidly out of situation, music, and words. In this respect, in the creation of operatic characters in the round, Mozart has never been excelled: compared to his personages, Gluck's are but embodied emotions, the later Wagner's embodied philosophical and nationalistic concepts.[5] The final miracle—paradox, if you will—of *Le Nozze di Figaro, Don Giovanni,* and *Die Zauberflöte* is that the creations of the wonder child of the most crystalline reaches of the eighteenth century should have become recognized touchstones of universal art.

Until 1781, when he wrote *Idomeneo,* Mozart's career as an operatic composer is of interest only to close students of precocity and of influences and tendencies. His early efforts, while marvels of mimicry and technical ease, are otherwise immature and tentative. One of the earliest, *Bastien und Bastienne* (1768),[6] dating from his twelfth year, has been revived: it is a curiosity—and nothing more. Metastasio furnished two of his librettos; a third has been attributed to Calzabigi. From *Il Re pastore,* written when Mozart was nineteen, comes an exquisite aria that is still often heard in the recital hall, "L'amerò, sarò costante." In all these early operas there are pages that for modern ears diffuse the antique

---

[4] Mozart's famous dictum (in a letter to his father, October 13, 1781) that "in an opera the poetry must be altogether the obedient daughter of the music" must be remembered and forgotten. In practice, he turned it around when he felt like it, and usually saw to it that music and poetry were *his* obedient daughters.

[5] It does not need charity to except Hans Sachs and his Eva.

[6] Its libretto, by Friedrich Wilhelm Weiskern, is a German version of Charles-Simon Favart's parody of Rousseau's *Le Devin du village.*

charm characteristic of most eighteenth-century music that is not actually bad.[7] When Mozart showed the first sure signs that he had grown up as an operatic composer, he celebrated his coming of age with an opera that nodded courteously but without conviction to Gluck's ideals. Mozart happened to be closer personally to Gluck the year of *Idomeneo* than at any other time.

Idomeneo, re di Creta is an old-fashioned *opera seria,* with all the conventions connoted by the term. In the plenitude of his powers, Mozart carried the load lightly and was able, by fulfilling the uttermost demands of these conventions, to fill the decadent form with incredible vitality. By brilliantly summarizing the very best that the *opera seria* could ever do, Mozart so effectively killed it off that the species soon became utterly moribund.

There is a special grandeur to *Idomeneo,* some of it traceable to the restrained *hommage à Gluck* and to its theme (though not to its plot, which is as silly as any parody libretto ever evolved). But with all its grandeur, *Idomeneo* cannot throw off its formal shackles—if it could, it would not be an *opera seria.* To be magnificent and synthetic is the central paradox of *Idomeneo*'s existence: from a wretched *esse* Mozart drew a sublime *posse.* At this point the warning enters. Mozart's genius, which might have delighted in setting one of the livelier Platonic dialogues, became bored with the stark manifestations of Greek fate. No one can question the elevation of Mozart's style when he chooses to be elevated, but it stops short of the marmoreal: his forms are too plastic to assume the static magnificence of Gluck's collection of classical statuary. There is just enough willfulness, just enough spirit of play, in *Idomeneo* to mar its Greek-tragedy pretensions; and those who can read the signs, even in the first five measures of the fine and basically serious overture, must see that this is the work of a potential master of comedy, not quite happy in the company of Agamemnon's daughter, which role was created, as far as modern audiences are concerned, by Elisabeth Schumann—in Richard Strauss's revision of the score.[8]

[7] Not to labor the point too much, all but the most puerile of eighteenth-century composers could command an international style that made for pleasant enough background noise. Mozart could command it, and so could Bach, and so could practically every other great name of the century. And as they could, so they did, frequently.

[8] A radical revision, based largely on Mozart's own reworking of the score for a single performance at Prince Auersperg's (Vienna, March, 1786). But because

After *Idomeneo,* which had been composed for the Munich carnival of 1781, Mozart turned to a relatively unexplored phase of the musical stage. This was the Singspiel, of rather obscure, and far from respectable, history. The Singspiel, very simply, is an opera in German containing spoken dialogue: it is the German counterpart of *opéra-comique* and the English ballad opera. Depending on one's ability to trace ancestry to un-promising origins, the Singspiel, in 1781, could have been regarded as an antique or a parvenu. It was very remotely descended from medieval religious plays. More realistically, it seems to date back to a German translation of *The Devil to Pay,* one of the most successful imitations of *The Beggar's Opera.* After being the rage in England for some seasons, this was taken up in Germany, where in 1766, in a version composed by J. A. Hiller, it rivaled its popularity in England. Hiller, who eventually became the first conductor of the Gewandhaus concerts at Leipzig, has been called the father of the Singspiel. Deservedly so. The phenomenal box office for *Der Teufel ist los* made him study the art of writing for large audiences. He learned to forget his Italian training: he bought his puff paste in Paris but served it up as a German dish. With their many folksy numbers, Hiller's Singspiels, like the ballad operas whence they derived, were as broad as the popular taste—by strict definition, merely farces with music.

Despite Mozart's flair for the light comic, his connection with the Singspiel came about accidentally. Josef II, that not quite great son of Maria Theresa, had a passion for culture that was none the less sincere for being a thing of whim and crotchets. Having helped to put German spoken drama on a firm footing in Vienna, in 1778 he decided to lend his imperial favor to opera in German. This meant, in effect, that the Burgtheater would have to rely chiefly upon the Singspiel. But the very first offering, being of the Hiller, or North German, type, did not appeal to the Viennese, and Mozart's commission owed as much to his Italianate predilections as to the local appetite for *buffa* sung in German.[9]

---

a competent Electra could not be found for this performance, the part was cur-tailed. This points up the old scholars' maxim that a last draft is not necessarily the best.

[9] The ensuing facts about the composition of *Die Entführung* are clear enough (some tortuous details about the libretto have been purposely skipped), but it is worth saying that its historical importance has been overestimated. Moreover, the Singspiel did not die in the nineteenth century because of the dearth of good scores: its lightweight quality could not survive the onset of romanticism, which

Gottlieb Stephanie the Younger, an official at the Burgtheater, borrowed a libretto, rewrote it, and gave it to Mozart. That it was not his to give made no difference to this knavish actor-manager-quasi-playwright, who was famous for his complicated schemings and for a version of *Macbeth* even more melodramatic than Shakespeare's. In August, 1781, Mozart began to set *Die Entführung aus dem Serail* in a great hurry, having been told that it would be used to entertain the Grand Duke Paul of Russia, who was arriving in six weeks. But that personage delayed his coming, and when he finally arrived, Gluck's *Alceste* was sung instead. The reasons for this substitution are not clear, but one possibility may have been that *Die Entführung* was considered too frivolous for the gloomy heir apparent of all the Russias. Not until July 16, 1782, was this delicate peepshow into seraglio life presented at the Burgtheater.

Die Entführung suffers from a variety of faults, any one of which might have been fatal to the work of a less gifted composer. In the first place, the Pasha Selim, one of the six characters, is musically mute, which means that, in an opera, he is dramatically forceless. It does not seem that Mozart's failure to make Selim sing arose from a well-considered intention to produce a specific effect: it is more likely that either he could not invent peculiarly Selimlike music or he could not find a singer for the music he thought suitable for a Turkish pasha. If, however, he (or his librettist) purposely limited the noble Turk to spoken conversation, the result was no more dramatically effective than when, fifty years later, Auber, in *Masaniello,* went to the extreme of having the *première danseuse* mime the role of the dumb girl. In Auber, the effect is at least fey; in Mozart, it is merely inept.

The nonvocalizing Selim is surrounded, but scarcely supported, by a group of characters who (with one exception) are, for Mozart, wooden without parallel. The heroine is simply not characterized at all: she is as much a vocalist as Selim is not—a singing-school star. Finally, *Die Entführung* cannot be viewed as a musical unity. It is, instead, a medley of styles, some used with nice appreciation of their character, others haphazardly. In short, it has no central unmistakable manner from which diversions are excusable as legitimate sources of contrast or underlinings of character. In this exaggerated eclecticism, true contrast is lost.

---

at first took itself too seriously to allow humor. Besides, Ditters von Dittersdorf, Florian Leopold Gassmann, Johann Schenk, and even Haydn wrote Singspiels that were structurally convincing and musically satisfying.

Die Entführung boasts one superb character—the major-domo Osmin, first of the great line of Mozart's *buffa* varlets, ancestor of Leporello and Monostatos. Time and again, it breaks into gay and delicious song. Occasionally, there is something even finer: Constanze's *scena* in Act II— "Martern aller Arten"—is rather too magnificent for its surroundings. *Die Entführung* is a comic opera verging on farce; "Martern aller Arten" is noble and sublime, belonging in spirit to *Die Zauberflöte* and technically to the very highest phase of Mozart's art. In it we can detect the beginning of a new symphonic conception of opera, German in practice but not obviously national. Yet it is only a beginning, for there is a certain naïveté, by no means artless, in treating the voice as but one of several concertizing instruments. But this aria, Osmin's comic interludes, the vivacious drinking song, Pedrillo's serenade, and the absurdly anachronistic, utterly amusing Chorus of Janissaries are not what has kept *Die Entführung* alive.[10] It is, rather, the belief that, being the first full-length opera in German by an undisputed master, it must necessarily be the first great German opera, and therefore worth performing. We see beginnings in *Die Entführung,* not decisions—there is no undisputed mastery of a genre. What performability it has depends upon how high a value is to be set upon reproducing in costume an eighteenth-century concert of vocal music, some of it extremely beautiful.

While working on *Die Entführung,* Mozart kept his demanding father informed by letter of the vicissitudes of its creation, and nowhere did he suggest that the libretto was the mediocre thing it most certainly is. True, details displeased him, and he imperiously changed them. But here, as in his earlier correspondence, there are few signs that Mozart ever seriously analyzed the qualities a good libretto should have. He was willing to bend the verse to his will without scruple, the more particularly as he had a talent for adroit jingles. Unlike Gluck, he seems to have been

[10] Certainly, the "Turkish" music that captivated both Mozart and his audience has little of the titillation of novelty to us. Between its *première* in 1781 and the collapse of the Burgtheater as a state-subsidized project in 1788, Vienna heard *Die Entführung* thirty-four times—the city never again so favored Mozart. It was performed in thirty-three cities before Mozart's death in 1791. In the score Mozart uses his favorite "Turkish" instrument—the triangle—like a toy that never becomes a bore. The Oriental atmosphere of Pedrillo's serenade, or romanza, is delectable— if it really exists. Anyhow, we must risk the guess that in Mozart's own day going to *Die Entführung* was a bit like going to the circus. Today much of the tonal topicality is missing.

quite indifferent to any speculations about the wholeness of opera. In this negligent attitude, he was true to himself: all his life he worked miracles with material that happened to come his way and which he accepted with, at the worst, a petulant resignation. A flagrant example of his noncritical attitude where all except the pure stuff of music was concerned is in his song-writing. Like Schubert, he set any stray verse that came his way—and as a catchpenny hauler he was less lucky than Schubert, who often found Goethe or Heine in his net.[11] There is reason to believe that if a good libretto or two had not all but been thrown at him, Mozart would have gone on pouring glorious music into unworthy vessels.

This dark picture of Mozart's incuriousness about one of the central problems of opera needs some slight qualification. If it was indeed he, and not the librettist, who suggested that Beaumarchais's *Le Mariage de Figaro* would make a good opera, he must be credited with having hit upon one of the most inspired ideas in the history of art. That the nature of the inspiration was on a par with that of the first chance dramatization of the season's runaway novel is no more valid criticism than the fact that Paisiello's *Il Barbiere di Siviglia* (1782), a setting of the first half of the same story, had all Europe talking. *Figaro,* Beaumarchais's sequel to *Le Barbier de Séville,* had created a scandal in Paris, which made it tremendously popular. When Mozart accepted a libretto made from it by Lorenzo da Ponte, Josef II's Latin secretary and theater poet, he had met his Calzabigi.

Da Ponte was just the man to undertake a delicate and dangerous task of this sort. *Le Mariage de Figaro* was not only ribald: it was also political dynamite, and a less intrepid and practiced wrangler would not have touched it. But Da Ponte was an altogether odd sort; an unfrocked priest, a converted Jew, a former university professor, and a boon companion of Casanova, he was an eel in wiggling into and out of domestic and political scandals. Mozart was but an incident in his life: after presenting him with three excellent librettos, Da Ponte resumed a wandering life that took him by way of London, where he taught Italian, wrote more librettos, and failed as a bookdealer, to New York, where he established a series of spasmodic and rapidly crumbling business enterprises. There, after failing to support himself and his wife by the sale of tobacco,

[11] Of course, the *Lied* practically did not exist in the classic era. But Mozart wrote songs, some of them to trumpery lyrics. Alfred Einstein classified "Das Veilchen" as "a lyric *scena.*"

groceries, or strong waters, he turned again to opera, and made musical history by helping Manuel del Popolo Vicente García to present the first Italian opera company in New York. The year was 1825, and as García was the mighty sire of three great children—Maria Malibran, Pauline Viardot-García, and Manuel Patricio García—the last of whom died as late as 1906, the influence of that amiable reprobate Da Ponte seems to span the centuries. Born in 1749, and thus Mozart's senior by seven years, he learned his craft from Metastasio, whom he knew intimately. In the United States, where he died in 1838, he sat for his portrait to Samuel F. B. Morse, and was patronized by Clement C. Moore, who wrote "The Night Before Christmas." Da Ponte ended his days as a teacher of Italian at what is now Columbia University, where there exists the Da Ponte professorship of Italian.

Even in 1786, Da Ponte was not a man to quail before the prospect of Josef II's wrath. In six weeks, he was presenting the libretto to the Emperor in person. Whereupon, according to his more or less truthful *Memoirs,* the following remarkable dialogue ensued:

"What?" he [the Emperor] said. "Don't you know that Mozart, though a wonder at instrumental music, has written only one opera, and nothing remarkable at that?"

"Yes, Sire," I replied quietly, "but without Your Majesty's clemency I would have written but one drama in Vienna!"

"That may be true," he answered, "but this *Mariage de Figaro*—I have just forbidden the German troupe to use it!"

"Yes, Sire," I rejoined, "but I was writing an opera, and not a comedy. I had to omit many scenes and to cut others quite considerably. I have omitted or cut anything that might offend good taste or public decency at a performance over which the Sovereign Majesty might preside. The music, I may add, as far as I may judge of it, seems to me marvelously beautiful."

"Good! If that be the case, I will rely on your good taste as to the music and on your wisdom as to the morality. Send the score to the copyist."

Had all of Josef II's decisions been as wise as this, history would have passed a more favorable verdict on him than that he meant well. *Le Nozze di Figaro* evoked, on its first performance (May 1, 1786),[12] an

---

[12] The English-born Nancy Storace, then eighteen years old, was the original Susanna.

ovation of such proportions that Mozart must have felt that he had found a formula of success. Every number was encored, and the Austrian counterparts of that very *ancien régime* at which Beaumarchais had directed his shafts howled their delight, apparently not realizing that in the insolent Almaviva, with his brutal indifference to the feelings of social underlings, they were seeing themselves. In a very short time, Prague, which thenceforth became a center of hysterical Mozartolatry, discovered *Le Nozze*. Mozart went there to conduct it, and was deified. Not only did golden kronen flow into his pockets, but also a fat contract for a new opera was signed. The Viennese shelved *Le Nozze* that same season in favor of *Una Cosa rara,* a delightful enough trifle by a young Spaniard, Vicente Martín y Soler, which happened to contain a number that began the Viennese waltz craze. But the Praguers, who never tired of *Le Nozze,* were also on the side of history: it is still one of the unfailing joys of Western civilization wherever that civilization is intact, and occasionally where it is not. Oddly, Italy has not responded to this most characteristic creation of the greatest of *buffa* composers. Its own plethora of operas, good, bad, and indifferent, spewed forth by living favorites, has been partly accountable for this situation. A rather different concept of *buffa* may also have militated against *Le Nozze*'s complete acceptance there.[13]

It has often been said that *Le Nozze di Figaro* is the easiest of Mozart's great operas to stage under modern conditions. Almost the opposite of this statement is true. Certainly, it needs no such elaborate staging as that for *Don Giovanni* (which is of such a challenging nature that when the Residenztheater, Munich, which possessed the first revolving stage in Europe, wanted to show it off for the first time [1896], they chose *Don Giovanni*). Nor does it ask for miracles of vocal agility such as are required to sing Ottavio in the *Don* or the Queen of the Night in *Die Zauberflöte*. True, furthermore, the audience is not required to suspend disbelief in barefaced nonsense as it is in *Die Zauberflöte*. But these are feathers if weighed against the difficulty a modern audience has in trying to sense unity in what has become, through constant hearing via radio, concert, transcription, and home music-making, a succession of gems.

This unhappy situation is not, of course, Mozart's fault: he perfectly turned the book into music, perfectly sustained characterization, per-

[13] Mozart, whose comic operas are unquestionably in the Italian *buffa* tradition (it all but submerged *Die Entführung*), has been called the "greatest of Italian *buffa* composers." Types of *buffa* are discussed throughout this book, notably under Rossini, Verdi, and Wolf-Ferrari. Puccini also could use *buffa* most adroitly.

fectly established the wholeness of the opera. Equally, it is not the audience's fault: Mozart worked with such inspiration coupled with such flawless craftmanship that each section stands, if possible, too obviously on its own merits. One would like, finally, to say that the singers are not to blame, but unfortunately they are usually only too willing to regard their parts as done if they only do a good singing job in a recital that happens to be divided into acts. Only in a performance in which the listener is resolved to hear an opera and not a collection of songs sung by a galaxy of stars,[14] and in which impresario, stage director, and each member of the cast are equally resolved to give due emphasis to the development of the drama, can *Le Nozze* be the complete experience it should be. These optimum conditions place upon the lover of Mozart and of opera at its best a strenuous if not onerous obligation: he must go hopefully to every performance of *Le Nozze,* for only about once in a generation does a perfect creation emerge.

Le Nozze is not the overture, "Se vuol ballare," "Non più andrai," "Voi che sapete," "Deh vieni, non tardar," and a dozen or more other airs or ensemble numbers, including the splendidly contrived group finales, revolutionary in conception and far-reaching in influence. It is not the unrivaled series of living, rounded characters—Figaro, Susanna, Cherubino, Count Almaviva, the Countess, Dr. Bartolo, and the rest. It is the peerless *jeu d'esprit* which knows where it is going from the first note of the lightsome and exactly right, perfectly proportioned overture to the joyous finale, when the reconciled principals announce that they are about to turn night into day. Complex as the plot is, the opera proceeds unerringly to its destination. *Le Nozze* carries the profound internal reality of its own made world and has the razor-sharp edge of seriousness that the mature satire of Beaumarchais deserves. Opera could justify its existence on the basis of *Le Nozze di Figaro* alone. One or two operas as great were composed by Mozart himself and by perhaps half a dozen others: they are different in kind, not better.

Da Ponte's eminent role in the collaboration that created *Le Nozze* must not be underestimated, particularly in view of the next book he gave to Mozart. Undoubtedly he saw exactly where his composer's strength lay: it was in the ability to create drama by means of vigorously painted portraits, and Da Ponte realized, therefore, that his own duty was to provide the types into which Mozart could breathe life. A significant passage from his *Memoirs* shows how he served Mozart in com-

[14] Although galaxies of stars are rarer than they used to be.

parison with another composer: "For Mozart I chose *Don Giovanni,* a subject that pleased him mightily; and for Martini [Da Ponte's name for Martín y Soler] *L'Arbore di Diana.* For him I wanted an attractive theme adaptable to those sweet melodies of his. . . ." Paraphrased, Da Ponte says that Diana's tree is good enough for a composer of pretty tunes,[15] but for Mozart nothing less than one of the great primal figures of European literature will do. At the same time, he was also helping Salieri to turn a French opera into an Italian one. When Josef II remarked that he would never succeed in doing all three jobs at once, Da Ponte replied: "Perhaps not, but I am going to try. I shall write evenings for Mozart, imagining that I am reading the *Inferno;* mornings I shall work for Martini, and pretend I am studying Petrarch; my afternoons will be for Salieri—he is my Tasso." The Emperor was pleased to say that Da Ponte's parallels were well chosen.

Don Giovanni is not the flawless thing *Le Nozze di Figaro* is. Although, like all of Mozart's operas, it was designed as a musical unit (for instance, it begins and ends in the same key, and the big moments of the action are in either that key or closely related keys), it does not produce an effect of coherent structure. The reasons for this are twofold: first, it is never given in the original version—Mozart himself began the orgy of revision that managers and singers have been indulging in ever since; second, the libretto is a patchwork of Da Ponte and conventional scenes and stock characters borrowed from other writers. The circumstances under which the poet worked suggest that he did not give full attention to his task:

> I returned home and went to work. I sat down at my table and did not leave it for twelve hours continuous—a bottle of Tokay to my right, a box of Seville to my left, in the middle an inkwell. A beautiful girl of sixteen—I should have preferred to love her only as a daughter, but alas . . . !—was living in the house with her mother, who took care of the family, and came to my room at the sound of the bell. To tell the

---

[15] The historian, who should be able to see everything in its proper perspective, is nevertheless piqued that Martín y Soler was, in his day, more successful than Mozart. But *Una Cosa rara* is delicious; it was revived at Barcelona in 1936. Martín y Soler left Vienna for St. Petersburg, where he became court composer to Catherine II, who wrote the librettos for two of his operas. For no apparent reason, her mad son Paul appointed him a privy councilor.

truth the bell rang rather frequently, especially at moments when I felt my inspiration waning.

In some ways, this sounds like the ideal recipe for writing about Don Juan, but even Byron did not combine reality and fiction in such a reckless manner when he was working on his interpretation of the great philanderer.

Don Giovanni suffers mainly from Da Ponte's failure to surround the magnificently built-up character of the Don with strong independent personalities. Just as Leonore dwarfs the rest of the *Fidelio* cast, so, with one or two exceptions, the Don dwarfs all the other personages of the action. The juvenile lead, Ottavio, is a ninny, and Donna Anna, leader of the betrayed ladies, is a female ninny, maybe by design.[16] The chief exception, significantly, is the Don's familiar and servant—the comic, cowardly toad at his ear, Leporello. The Commendatore, the instrument of justice, is never more than an animated statue. Masetto and Zerlina, on whom much of the delicately silly byplay of the opera depends, have been given such delicious music that we are almost induced to believe that they are more than conventionalized rustics. Neither the functions nor the portrayals of these characters are so definite as those in *Le Nozze*. The Don (or Leporello—which comes to the same thing) is so strongly realized that even when he is off the stage, his personality towers over the action. This is, of course, a triumph of characterization, but it tends to weaken conflict and, by overheightening contrast, reduce it to ineffectiveness. Thus, *Don Giovanni* is a superb projection of character, but a feeble drama.

There is a story that Mozart, who arrived in Prague with the score of *Don Giovanni* only partially complete, did not get around to composing the overture until the night before the final rehearsal, and that his wife had to keep him awake with a jug of punch and the reading of fairy tales. The result of this reported last-minute rush was a perfect dramatic *Vorspiel* that contents itself with portending the clash of opposing forces. It merges with the action, and soon we hear Leporello's "Madamina, il catalogo" (that brazen list of the Don's conquests with which Feodor

[16] It is obvious that Mozart's sympathies were all with Donna Elvira, as the orchestra shows when the Don and Leporello are playing the most outrageous tricks on her. This is one of his great strokes: the use of orchestral comment to project eternal truth in contrast to the transiency of the moment.

Chaliapin invariably disrupted the performance). Shortly after that comes "Là ci darem la mano," loveliest of all duets. Straight to the end follows a wealth of wonderful airs and ensembles, rising in the second act to its florid peak in "Il mio tesoro," a tenor showpiece of excessive difficulty and great melodic beauty. But of course the most popular excerpt from *Don Giovanni* is the minuet toward the end of the first act. It is used as music for a party in the Don's palace, and at its first appearance is played by a small orchestra on the stage.

All these elements add up to an opera that is neither comic nor tragic, but an artful mingling of the two that comes—if correctly performed—close to life.[17] The Don, alternately comic, pathetic, and villainous, and a blend of all these when music and action are most intense, becomes—in the last great scene—a fully realized hero of nineteenth-century romanticism. His engulfment by the flames of Hell is far indeed from Orpheus at the gates of Erebus, but only next door to Weber and Marschner. There is a symphonic power, not of a classical kind, and certainly found in no one else before Beethoven, in this tremendous finale. Mozart himself was to explore this vein further, chiefly in the Requiem and *Die Zauberflöte,* and the Don's damnation scene was to influence the zealots of romanticism.

Don Giovanni, which evoked lusty bravos from Prague at its first performance, on October 29, 1787, had favorable repercussions in Vienna. About one month later, Gluck having died, Mozart was appointed to succeed him as *Kammerkomponist* to Josef II. Although the Emperor seemed, in cutting the annual stipend of the post from 2,000 to 800 gulden, to be passing judgment on the respective merits of Gluck and Mozart, it was fortunate for the latter that he received the preferment when he did. For Vienna, when it heard *Don Giovanni* in May, 1788, cold-shouldered it. Entrenched at court, however insignificantly, Mozart was certain of a few crumbs, even though Salieri, for personal reasons, as well as because of his position as Gluck's spiritual heir, opposed everything he did. And as Salieri had just become court conductor and was

---

[17] This, despite the incredible difficulties that Mozart had to cope with, particularly the caprices of the singers, who either asked for numbers that would show them off or refused numbers that were beyond their powers. Composing *Don Giovanni* was a tough job that only a great man of the theater could possibly finish. Even today, after decades of sympathetic study, the opera we hear may be devoid of the finale that the whole drama demands.

himself a darling of the Viennese opera-lovers, his opposition was almost blighting. As it was, Mozart's ever being employed again for the Vienna stage may have rested on the happy accident of *Figaro*'s being revived there in August, 1789, with record-breaking success. On its heels followed an order from the Emperor for a comic opera, which was to be rushed through to completion.

Mozart and Da Ponte, once more his collaborator, obeyed: the manuscript score of *Così fan tutte,* with its countless abbreviations, testifies to the composer's anxiety to finish in time. Josef II survived the successful *première,* on January 26, 1790, by less than a month. With his death, Mozart lost his most understanding collaborator, for Da Ponte had relied solely on the Emperor for his position at court: now he had to flee for his life—whether from debtors, politicians, or vengeful husbands is not clear.

With misfortune stalking him and almost ready to pounce, Da Ponte gave to Mozart one of the most sparkling products of his wit, and that despite the fact that neither he nor the composer had anything to say about the plot itself. It was based on certain recent happenings in Vienna that had so delighted the Emperor (discouraged about everything else in the world) that he ordered them to be immortalized. Few librettos have been so denigrated, largely for moral purposes, and indeed it seems odd that the virtuous Josef sponsored it. Briefly, two gentlemen, goaded by a cynical oldster, test their sweethearts' fidelity by returning to them in disguise. The ladies succumb to the rich-seeming "Albanians," and just as a double wedding is about to be celebrated, the young men make their identities known. All ends happily to the moralizing refrain: "Così fan tutte"—"That's Women for You!" The plot will probably impress most modern readers as vapid rather than immoral. It would be interesting to know what Beethoven, whose puritanical morals were outraged by *Figaro* and *Don Giovanni,* thought of this. It is significant that when Barbier and Carré, the shrewd librettists of Gounod's *Faust,* tried to find a more palatable story for a French version of *Così fan tutte,* the best they could think up was a translation of Shakespeare's insipid *Love's Labour's Lost.*

While *Così fan tutte* has not won as many admirers as Mozart's three other great operas, it nevertheless has merits of its own to which they cannot pretend. Possibly because of the circumstances of its creation, it has a period quality that approaches realism. We find Mozart the analyst of types rather than the creator of individuals.[18] The characters have no motor force of their own but must respond to the touch of that merciless, teasing, galvanic wire. Don Alfonso, the one initiator of all the opera's imbroglios, is, in one respect, nothing but our old friend the *deus ex machina*. But this is a superficial evaluation, and though his role in the opera is confined, with a single short exception, to recitative, Don Alfonso is, in another respect, one more in that immortal gallery of dramatic middlemen that begins with Osmin and ends with Papageno. Of this gallery, Don Alfonso is in one way the most interesting: he is more cerebral than his compeers—he represents a point of view, a philosophy of a sort, not perhaps of the highest order, but nevertheless consistent and unmistakable. Through him speak those worldly-wise teammates Mozart and Da Ponte. Don Alfonso's complement is the ladies' maid, Despina, who never quite achieves his solidity, but who is an unforgettable figure of fun. A creature of disguises, she seems, in her notary's gown, like a parody Portia; and the enormous, somehow shocking spectacles she wears as the doctor have the powerful conventionality of a Greek mask.

All of Mozart's operas have their special problems for the listener. That of *Così fan tutte* comes from the importance of the recitative, which, instead of being used secondarily to connect the dramatic rises, is the very *élan vital* of the action. Reading the text through is a requisite to listening, nor will the task be a bore: it is Da Ponte at his wittiest and most sarcastic best, as deft and sure as Beaumarchais himself. Only by reading it can we fully recognize how Mozart has made music the distillation of this satire: until then, we must be prepared to find *Così fan tutte* amorphous and, at best, a harebrained projection of nitwittery. But when the argument is known in full, then everything in the musical scheme falls into its ordained place, and what emerges is one of Mozart's most aerial and imaginative structures—the most operatic of lyric plays. That we miss a succession of magical airs such as we find in *Figaro* may disappoint some. This is not a flaw; it results from a different, perhaps a more difficult, technique. Seduction does not come at once, as it does in *Figaro;* but when it does come, it is likely to be quite as complete if less intense.

Between *Die Entführung* and *Figaro,* Mozart had written a trifling but pretty one-act Singspiel called *Der Schauspieldirektor* (1786) that is still

[18] In other operas, Mozart occasionally did not take the trouble, or have the energy, to create individuals, and so was satisfied with mere types—quite another matter.

occasionally heard, sometimes with a different libretto. Now, between *Così fan tutte* and the completion of *Die Zauberflöte,* he wrote another trifle, but one of huge proportions. This was *La Clemenza di Tito* (1791), whose Metastasio libretto had already been set by such old-time masters as Gluck, Hasse, Leonardo Leo, a minor stripling of the Scarlatti family, and a dozen others. As archaic in style as if it had been composed by any of these men, Mozart's version, provided with a libretto liberally but not successfully recast for the occasion, is the poorest dramatic work of his maturity. Possibly the circumstances of its composition have much to do with this—it was written to order in eighteen days, the consignees being the loyal burghers of Prague, the occasion the crowning of Leopold II as King of Bohemia. It shows some evidence of haste, for which Mozart's mounting illness was a sufficient excuse. (That he allowed a favorite pupil, Franz Xaver Süssmayr, to compose parts of the *recitativo secco* has been unduly stressed: subletting this task was not unusual.) Further, he was not happy in trying to cope once more—after the triumphant decisions of *Idomeneo*—with the by then creaking machinery of *opera seria.* For once, Mozart composed a lifeless score whose grand austerities might have come properly from a Gluck, to whom they would have been native. The chief criticism of *La Clemenza di Tito* is that it is not often like Mozart. Oddly enough, it gained a very considerable popularity that did not languish until the nineteenth century was well advanced; it has often been revived during Mozart festival years. Even more strangely, it was the first Mozart opera to reach London, an early enthusiast being the Prince Regent, who lent the full score from his own library to the King's Theatre, Haymarket, for that first production (March 27, 1806).

La Clemenza di Tito, to its further extenuation, had the ill fortune to be composed while both *Die Zauberflöte* and the Requiem, works on which Mozart was lavishing his most sublime inspirations, were in progress. On them he had staked his hopes, respectively, of final triumph as a composer for the stage and for immortality. He died before finishing the Requiem, but lived to conduct the opening performance of *Die Zauberflöte,* on September 30, 1791. That *première* was far from a triumph, and unfortunately the composer was too ill to witness the quick turning of the tide. News of it did, however, trickle into the death chamber, cheering him when he could get his mind off the unfinished Requiem. But even the cheer had a quality of the macabre in it, for it consisted of his taking his watch in hand and timing the performance as, every evening at curtain time, it began to unroll in his imagination. Sixty-six days after that first frigid reception at the Theater auf der Wieden, Mozart was dead.

Fully to appreciate *Die Zauberflöte* as one of the great flawed works of art, one must wrestle with the task of trying to understand its libretto in terms of the period that produced it and of its meaning to Mozart. Read with these considerations in mind, what seems on the surface the veriest jumble of complicated nonsense takes on a certain mad logic.[19] Emanuel Schikaneder, its fabricator [20] and one of Mozart's childhood friends, tried to cram into this strange mélange of parable, fairy tale, and blatant, gallery-wooing extravaganza all the esoteric symbolism and grandiose revelations of the Grand Oriental Lodge of Freemasons, of which both he and Mozart were members. As if this were not enough, Schikaneder is alleged to have woven into this crazyquilt a rather belated attack on the *Realpolitik* of Maria Theresa. Those who believe this last pretend to read in the vicious, quite incredibly malignant Queen of the Night the housewifely features of that Queen Victoria of the eighteenth century, who had once dandled Mozart on her knee. Similarly, they identify the wily Monostatos with the Jesuits, and Prince Tamino with the virtuous Josef II.

Mozart set the text with intense seriousness. After all, he was as good a Mason as Schikaneder, and besides, the libretto offered opportunities for every kind of musical treatment, ranging from a more solemnly religious style than he ever used in his Masses to the most unqualified slapstick. If one were to hear a recital that contained the high priest Sarastro's exalted utterances—"O Isis und Osiris" and "In diesen heil'gen Hallen," the Queen of the Night's icy pyrotechnics, and the ripely tender duet—"Bei Männern, welch Liebe fühlen"—between Pamina and the birdman Papageno, he would be justified in not believing them to be parts of the same work. (That they are all Mozart he could never doubt.) A good performance of *Die Zauberflöte* does, if with difficulty and not without a

[19] Witness Goethe's remark that "it takes more culture to perceive the virtues of *Die Zauberflöte* text than to point out its defects." But "culture" scarcely seems the operative word.

[20] Although Schikaneder has had to shoulder all the blame for the text, it has long been claimed that he was importantly assisted in its fabrication by Johann Georg Metzler, who played the part of the first slave at the *première*. He went under the name of Karl Ludwig Giesecke and died professor of mineralogy at Dublin in 1833. The claim has been denied. In any event, *Die Zauberflöte* derives ultimately from the philosophical novel *Sethos* (1731), by the Abbé Terrasson.

sense of strain triumphantly overcome, establish the unity Mozart saw in the book.[21] Even the usual performance is not a thankless experience, for never is the music less than Mozart at his most apt. Each number, if exposed to careful scrutiny, is found to be flawless of its kind and un- cannily right in its place. And its greatest moments, whether of sub- limity, buffoonery, amorousness, playfulness, or villainy, are not sur- passed, if they are equaled, in any of Mozart's other masterpieces. The characterization in *Die Zauberflöte* is less eloquent than that in *Figaro* because the characters are frankly symbols and, as such, faithfully ex- emplified, notably by the use of identifying tonalities.

It is difficult to classify *Die Zauberflöte*. Technically a Singspiel, it seems like a farce oratorio in costume. Its comic interludes, however, are incidental: they perform, and perfectly, the same function as Shake- speare's often dubious comic relief. *Die Zauberflöte,* as one is fairly admonished by the solemn strains of the magnificent overture, is pri- marily a religious work. The scene of purification in the second act is fit music for an Eleusinian initiation. Sarastro's was called by Bernard Shaw the only music that would not sound out of place in the mouth of God. Nor, similarly, are the arias of the Queen of the Night out of place in the mouth of that female devil. Certainly, the two are ideal protag- onists in this quasi-mystical struggle between the forces of good and evil. Musically and spiritually, *Die Zauberflöte* is a more convincing paean to life transcendental than the agonizing sublimities of the Requiem.

While Mozart's other great stage pieces, though operating in frame- works from the past and cheerfully accepting equally hoary conventions, pullulate with ideas for the future, *Die Zauberflöte,* not less great, was too much the product of a special need and of a unique personality's obliga- tions to his most intimate being, to be easily imitable. Thus, in general, it has had no easily recognizable descendants. The mold died with the maker.

[21] Although it is evident that Schikaneder and Metzler-Giesecke changed their minds about their characters in the middle of the first act, and performed the psychological equivalent of making the sun rise in the west, it was Mozart's triumph that he *did* manage to establish the unity.

CHAPTER VII

Opera in Germany

STRIVINGS after a national opera in Germany were competently frustrated by the stranglehold of Italian opera, some of whose best—and most conservative—practitioners were themselves German. Besides Hasse, whose melodious scores testified to his uncritical devotion equally to the Neapolitan style and to Metastasio (whose favorite composer he was), there were Karl Heinrich Graun and Johann Gottlieb Naumann. As official composer to Frederick the Great, who worshiped Hasse to distraction, Graun aped the style of his somewhat older contemporary at a remove that sufficed to preserve his dignity. His *Montezuma* (1755), written to a libretto by Frederick, is one of the few eighteenth-century operas dealing with a comparatively modern subject. Naumann, during his sojourn at the court of the enlightened Gustavus III at Stockholm, wrote *Cora och Alonzo* to a Swedish libretto, and this was heard for the hundredth time in 1882, the occasion being the centenary of the Stockholm opera house.[1]

Had opera been left to composers of this stripe (no matter how gifted),

[1] *Piramo e Tisbe*, a Hasse intermezzo, was revived at Cologne (in German) as late as 1939. Graun's *Montezuma* was revived at Saarbrücken (in German) in 1936. (Needless to say, Frederick II had written the original libretto in French prose, which had then been translated into Italian verse by the court poet.) Whether the Swedes still occasionally revive *Cora och Alonzo* is not known, but the amiable Naumann's memory should be cherished by them, for he wrote *Gustaf Wasa* to a text by J. H. Kellgren, based on a "sketch" (Loewenberg says "scenario") by Gustavus III. This opera, first produced at Stockholm in 1786, had been heard there 134 times by 1823; it was often revived during the nineteenth century, and parts of it were heard as recently as 1923.

a German national opera would not likely have been born. It is true that the comic strain was to find an outlet in the Singspiel, but meanwhile the serious opera quickly came to a dead end after heroic but not very far-sighted efforts. When Anton Schweitzer, an earnest enough composer, joined forces with the poet Wieland, they cold-bloodedly planned to rout Metastasio with an opera called *Alceste* (1773). Note the date: eleven years after the first opera of the Gluckian reform. Although *Alceste* is a very serious opera in five acts, its style shows plainly that avoiding *opera seria* is the chief desideratum, but makes no challenging assertions of its own. Yet the opera is sung, there is no spoken dialogue, and the voices of German romanticism are somewhat stronger than the baroque clichés that remain.[2] A second attempt in the same general direction boldly seized upon a subject from German history. But *Günther von Schwarzburg*—music by Ignaz Holzbauer, libretto by Anton Klein—did not keep the idea of national German opera afloat, though a bright observer like Mozart wrote ardently of Holzbauer's music and even echoes it in *Die Zauberflöte*. Nevertheless, the collaborators had a rather grandiose sense of destiny, and *Günther* was the first German opera published in full score (1776, a year before its production).

As the Singspiel soared upward to operatic status in Mozart's *Entführung* and to positive apotheosis in *Die Zauberflöte,* only to decline slowly in the hands of Wenzel Müller and Johann Schenk, who composed in terms of a spectacular box office, the great national opera remained just around the corner. It was obvious that it would be the musical revelation of German romanticism, the first if not altogether fine raptures of whose literary pioneers had already been spent by the time of the revised *Fidelio* (1814) and *Der Freischütz* (1821). Musically, what intervened between Schweitzer's *Alceste* and these two very dissimilar achievements was the invention of the melodrama by Georg Benda (1722–95), *Kapellmeister* at Gotha for twenty-eight years. Mozart, who liked the melodrama well enough to use its principles in parts of *Zaïde,* defined it thus: "Not a note is sung, only spoken; in fact it is a recitative with instruments, only the actor speaks instead of singing." In a small way, *Ariadne auf Naxos* (1775), Benda's first melodrama, was epochal, and both Beethoven and, more importantly, Weber took hints from this new musicodramatic form.[3]

[2] This elaborately orchestrated, somewhat cumbersome work was revived at Weimar in 1933.

[3] Benda's *Ariadne* and *Medea* (1775) have been frequently revived in Germany;

Strict adherence to a chronological scheme would at this point be both embarrassing and illogical. Just as *Fidelio* is an isolated phenomenon, Beethoven is an autonomy. No matter how *Fidelio* is finally assessed, and no matter what its influence (real or false because of a devotion to Beethoven's music *tout court*), it can never be brought into court as a document of German romanticism, and thus we can safely postpone a more detailed examination of the literary climate, with its relevant musical analogues, that fostered the genius of Carl Maria von Weber.

When one considers Ludwig van Beethoven as an operatic composer, facts and figures impose an inevitable significance. It may be said that this composer of nine symphonies, eleven overtures, sixteen string quartets, thirty-two full-fledged piano sonatas, and innumerable other opus numbers distributed among various categories also wrote an opera. Beethoven appeared just when Mozart, one of the most skillful and understanding of musical dramatists, and Haydn, who thought in sonatas and had only the most parochial conception of the nature of opera,[4] had managed by their separate activities to challenge the supremacy of the human voice in music. Haydn was the first composer to achieve greatness almost exclusively by instrumental means, unless the term "greatness" be construed to include such a master, working commonly in small, as Domenico Scarlatti. Yet, in 1795, when Haydn had dried the ink on his last great symphony and Mozart was already four years dead, it was still a question whether the orchestra would assume first place in the world of music. Beethoven, by a mighty resolution, answered it for the orchestra, and since his time the voice has never regained its sovereignty outside of Italy. That country became the voice's last stronghold, and has remained so. And, to show how the emphasis was changing in opera itself, the center of operatic gravity shifted from country to country as did the rallying place of the most assertive figures.

Fidelio is but one of many problems in the artistic life of a man who

---

there have been several twentieth-century productions of both. In France, Horace Coignet and Jean-Jacques Rousseau had written the first melodrama, *Pygmalion* (1770), but Benda could not have heard this before his own experiments, though he later successfully set a *Pygmalion* (1779) to a German translation of Rousseau's text.

[4] Despite the splendor of his surroundings, Haydn had to cope with parochialism at the country court of the Esterházys. In opera, he accepted the Italian modes, whereas otherwise he was, in his own words, "forced to be original." Because Haydn's operas were model pieces, they have not unnaturally been revived.

would not be a whit less famous if he had never composed a line of operatic music. The problem ought to be seen in perspective, without excessive
claims or excessive faultfinding. Its importance stretches into infinity, not
because of its intrinsic qualities, but because its influence on later composers has been stated in exaggerated terms. It is well to remember that
Fidelio is merely Opus 72 in the mammoth corpus of Beethoven's work.
Critics and biographers, noticing that Beethoven was often on the verge
of composing another opera, have asserted that the reason he failed to
follow through was his inability to find another congenial libretto. Many
librettos, certainly, came to his attention; for one reason or another, he
either rejected or forgot them. He carried on long, laborious correspondence with several leading writers of the day, only at last to give up in
despair. He was a very difficult man to please: his ethical bent was strong
—he therefore preferred simple situations in which evil was punished
and good rewarded. Plot as such scarcely interested him at all. As for
characters, he saw them more clearly as symbols of right or wrong than
as human beings. With such desiderata for his book, it is not surprising
that his one opera is not, as an opera, very effective. What is surprising
is that Beethoven composed an opera at all. That he never wrote another
is susceptible to the common-sense explanation that he was a conscious
enough artist to realize that he could achieve his aims better in the forms
of instrumental music.

One of Beethoven's favored excuses for rejecting a proffered libretto
was that it had already been set by someone else or resembled another
libretto. As by the early nineteenth century every pre-Marxian or pre-
Freudian situation under the sun had already been used by stage poets,
Beethoven could be easy in his mind that he would never have to write
another opera. That he had not at first demanded originality is proved
by the ancestry of *Fidelio, oder Die eheliche Liebe,* the libretto of which
was an adapted translation by his friend Josef Ferdinand von Sonnleithner
of a French original, Jean-Nicolas Bouilly's *Léonore, ou L'Amour conjugal,* which Pierre Gaveaux had set for the Opéra-Comique (1798) and
Ferdinando Paër had set in Italian translation for Dresden in 1804.
Bouilly, its first begetter, had taken the incidents from an episode of
which he had had direct knowledge while serving as a government ad-
ministrator in the provinces, near Tours, during the Terror. But neither
Gaveaux nor (if he knew of the opera) Paër could chill Beethoven's almost adolescent infatuation with this altogether usual tale once he had
set his heart on it. More accurately, his heart was set on the heroine and

on the heroic role she plays in saving her husband's life at the risk of her own.

Beethoven's connection with the stage had begun in 1791, when he was twenty-one years old, with some dance tunes he composed for a ballet. This music, foisted upon the public of Bonn as the work of his patron, Count Ferdinand von Waldstein, did nothing to advance its real composer's reputation. Ten years later he tried again, this time in Vienna, with an overture and dance numbers for an allegorical ballet, *Die Geschöpfe des Prometheus*. It is bright, attractive music, but definitely does not display Beethoven in a very dramatic mood. Yet Emanuel Schikaneder, Mozart's librettist for *Die Zauberflöte,* heard it and (he was still grimly holding on as impresario of the Theater an der Wien) invited Beethoven to compose an opera for him. The solicitation came at the height of a war between Schikaneder and Baron Braun, chief at the Hoftheater, each of whom had been fighting for years to keep the other from getting the Vienna *première* of every new opera by Luigi Cherubini—whom, incidentally, Beethoven much admired. Braun had just outwitted his rival by going to Paris with a black-and-white proposition for Cherubini. In desperation, Schikaneder approached both Beethoven and the facile, entirely suave half-charlatan Georg Joseph Vogler, immortalized in Browning's *Abt Vogler* and notable in the history of opera as a teacher of both Carl Maria von Weber and Giacomo Meyerbeer. Schikaneder produced the *abbé's* opera, *Samori,* on May 17, 1804, but before Beethoven could get his offering ready, the veteran impresario was forced to the wall. His theater was bought out by Baron Braun. Schikaneder, whose managerial troubles were as grievous, though not as various, as Handel's, tried several schemes for recouping his losses. They failed, and he went insane on a trip to Budapest. After much suffering, he died poverty-stricken in Vienna in 1812.

Baron Braun at once renewed the contract with Beethoven, who had become so noteworthy a figure in Vienna by this time that he could dare to dictate to the management of the Hoftheater just the kind of libretto he would deign to set.[5] Sonnleithner's text called for an opera in three acts, which is what Beethoven composed, disregarding the fact that the type of plot doomed the first two acts to triviality or inaction, or both. Working passionately through the summer of 1805, trying, testing, ex-

[5] It appears that Beethoven had done nothing for Schikaneder, and had been negotiating with Braun even before disaster overtook the Theater an der Wien.

panding, contracting, trying again, and for many reasons repeating the process over and over, Beethoven completed the opera by the fall.

Leonore (as it was then called) was produced at Schikaneder's former house on November 20, 1805, played three consecutive nights, and was a dismal failure, partly because of its intrinsic faults, but also partly because Napoleon had just occupied Vienna and the audience consisted mostly of his soldiers. Despite this mitigating circumstance, Beethoven reacted violently, almost despairingly, and began to rewrite the opera, though only after threatening to put the score on the ash heap. With no great difficulty, friends had made him desist from that destruction; one of them, Stephan von Breuning, had agreed to overhaul the libretto. Thus was the first revision of *Leonore* engineered. Breuning condensed the first two acts into one and shortened the former third act. These changes were good, but they were not enough. *Leonore* was tried out again at the Theater an der Wien on March 29, 1806; this time it began to show some small signs of popularity. Beethoven, however, now quarreled with his impresario, demanded—and got—the score back, chucked it into a trunk, and left it there for eight years.

The second revision, shorter than most standard-repertoire operas, undertaken by the competent dramatist and play doctor Georg Friedrich Treitschke, is largely responsible for the version presented today. Treitschke expanded the finales of both acts, making them dignified and impressive; that of the second act, indeed, has been so built up as to require a change of scene. Furthermore, he painstakingly went through the text and made good German of it. His was a creditable job, though the basic material was so refractory that even his most conscientious work could not balance the two acts. Beethoven's revisions of the music followed, outdoing Treitschke's revisions of the text. This final overhauling, while clearly the most stageworthy, is a patchwork of Beethoven's early and middle periods, and therefore lacks the spontaneity and stylistic unity of the first and second versions. Reputedly undertaken at the request of some singers from the Kärntnerthortheater, this final version was produced there on May 23, 1814, as *Fidelio*. Beethoven had fought to the last against changing the name, but it was probably pointed out to him that the name Leonore uses when disguised as a boy only temporarily conceals Leonore the woman. And the great, immediate success of *Fidelio* no doubt helped to console the sulking hero.

One of the numerous problems of *Fidelio* is to uncover the reasoning behind Beethoven's complicated shuffling and reshuffling of the over-tures. First, let us ponder their chronology. The "Leonore" Overture No. 1 may conceivably have been composed first and discarded by its composer in the mistaken belief that it was too slight for the opera. But as there was talk of using it for a Prague performance in 1807, it may just as con-ceivably have been composed then. The Prague performance fell through, and there is no clear record of "Leonore" No. 1's having been performed publicly during Beethoven's life. With No. 2 we are on firmer ground: it was used at the *première* of the first version of *Leonore* (though, to complicate the complicated, an alternative version of it survives). A revised and much enlarged form, now called "Leonore" No. 3, preluded the Breuning revision of 1806. This, too, was scrapped in the 1814 ver-sion, for which Beethoven composed what is still called the "Fidelio" Overture.

The "Leonore" Overture No. 1 is comparatively light; it would serve well enough if it had to introduce no more than the trivial events in the first act of this ill-balanced opera. If it was written first, it signifies that Beethoven in the beginning felt called upon not to sum up the entire drama, but merely to provide an adequate curtain raiser. With "Leonore" No. 2, his mind was obviously beginning to focus upon the heroic pro-clivities of his heroine: this music, germane enough to Act II, already begins to tower over Act I. Its expansion—the magnificent symphonic poem known as "Leonore" No. 3—is intolerable in the opera, and the widespread custom [6] of playing it between the first and second scenes of Act II or elsewhere can be excused only as an understandable desire to get in, willy-nilly, the best music inspired in Beethoven by the Leonore theme. Between 1806 and 1814, Beethoven would seem to have returned to his original feeling about the sort of overture required by his opera. The "Fidelio" barely suggests the depths of Leonore's soul and busies itself chiefly with the more human drama of the first act. That Beethoven

---

[6] Could Gustav Mahler, who introduced this custom at the Metropolitan Opera House, have thought that this orchestral interlude produced a Wagnerian effect? Just as ingenious, but more excusable, was Artur Bodanzky's metamorphosis of *Fidelio* from the Singspiel Beethoven had composed into a grand opera. He ac-complished this by changing the spoken dialogue into recitative and adding ac-companiments of his own. As the Singspielness of *Fidelio* is irrelevant, nothing was thereby lost; but the fact remains that the opera was no longer all Beethoven's. At all events, the *Fidelio* that audiences hear in most opera houses usually, in one detail or another, adds one more revision to the two Beethoven himself undertook.

had set his face against the heroic Nos. 2 and 3 is proved by the fact that, the "Fidelio" not being ready for the 1814 *première,* he used the shallow "Ruins of Athens" Overture for that event. The "Fidelio" was used at the second performance, on May 26.

As operatic history continues to be made and unmade, and as taste changes for better or for worse, it seems likely that the only parts of *Fidelio* to be heard frequently will be the two most magnificent of the overtures—"Leonore" No. 2 and "Leonore" No. 3—which Beethoven, in a belated understanding of dramatic effectiveness, discarded. In the past, *Fidelio* has secured stage revivals for two reasons. First, an opera by Beethoven—because it was by Beethoven—would be bound to secure a hearing every now and then. Second, the role of Leonore has proportions and possibilities that must inevitably attract an ambitious dramatic soprano who can manage the German language and has the lungs for the prison scene.

Fidelio has neither catchy tunes nor pervasive dramatic strength, at least one of which is essential for operatic popularity and longevity. While Beethoven was thoroughly captivated by his noble-acting heroine, the score presents evidence that the libretto itself rather bored him. And no wonder: *Fidelio* has the most conventional of patterns. Beginning as a comedy—opening indeed into a scene of broad farce involving minor characters—it works up to a situation of crisis from which the protagonists are rescued in the nick of time. Despite the revisions, only two characters emerge with sufficient sharpness to have engaged Beethoven's deepest interest. And one of these, the scoundrel Pizarro, it must be admitted, is something of a stock villain. So Leonore, the beloved heroine after whom Beethoven had insisted upon naming the opera until the final revision, remains the only full-bodied human being in the book. And even Leonore, as Beethoven built her up far beyond the stature of those around her, becomes a superwoman, very essence of very *Frau* (for it is impossible to think of her as the Spanish woman she is supposed to be), and finally discards human lineaments. As if to provide this epical creature with a comfortable arena in what is, after all, a comic opera, Beethoven prolongs and magnifies the resolution of the crisis in a ceremonial paean of unearthly joy which is startlingly different in key from the genial good humor and slapstick of the earlier portions. Mozart could, and did, combine farce, comedy, and tragedy; Beethoven did, and could not. It is significant that of all Mozart's operas, Beethoven preferred *Die Zauberflöte,* a very dangerous model from which to borrow even scraps.

In pondering Beethoven's working out of *Fidelio,* we need to forget playwrights and play doctors and come directly to the central truth. Very simply, Beethoven lacked a sense of the theater. He did not know what constituted a stageworthy play or opera,[7] and was not interested in working out those minutiae of characterization and incident which give motion and life to a stage spectacle. Not a scene of *Die Zauberflöte* but bears the unmistakable stamp of its composer; in *Fidelio* long stretches might have come from the pen of any workmanlike German of the time who knew Mozart, Cherubini, and Beethoven. Long stretches, too, could be moved about without loss or gain, so little are they related to the action. Yet, after all the vexations that preceded the final version, Beethoven to the end of his life believed passionately in *Fidelio,* and on his deathbed stated: "Before all others [of my works] I hold it worthy of being possessed and used for the science of art." Behind these arcane words there may have been a theory that Beethoven did not take the trouble to enunciate at his leisure.

Once these manifest operatic defects in *Fidelio* have been admitted, much remains which we should not willingly sacrifice. The overtures aside, these are moments, rare indeed, but exceedingly powerful when they arrive, when the action demands a special expenditure of creative energy in the expression of a single dominating emotion—hatred, love, joy. Beethoven excelled in such concentrations. For that reason, Pizarro's "Ha, welch'ein Augenblick" is a distillation of rage; Leonore's "Abscheulicher, wo eilst du hin?" a hymn of faith in the power of love; and the Leonore-Florestan duet, "O namenlose Freude!" an ode to joy. It is precisely in "Abscheulicher" that Leonore surrenders her more human traits to become, like a German Beatrice, an abstract ethical force. This aria, too, like a "Martern aller Arten" of more magnificent proportions, looks forward to the great *scene* of Beethoven's disciples, Weber and Wagner, and to a new conception of the dramatic role of the human voice. Yet, wonderful though it is, flawlessly as it lights up a noble conception of womankind, it just as relentlessly shows up Beethoven's basic inattention to the real problems of opera. "Abscheulicher" freezes the action in a heroic attitude and substitutes a generality for an individual. Taking this mightiest moment of *Fidelio* as a test, we can see why an

[7] But when he was examining the finale of the second act of *Der Freischütz,* he burst out: "I see what he means. . . . I feel it is the real thing." This was his reaction to one of the touchstones of German romantic opera—a great musico-dramatic achievement.

unsurpassed creator of dramatic music was unable to evolve a successful music drama.

In terms of the Germany of the early nineteenth century, *Fidelio* scarcely added a frieze to the great temple that had been planned by Schlegel and his collaborators. For, with music included among the contributing arts, a great musicodramatic work was most urgently wanted. And, apart from the fact that *Fidelio* was primarily a symphonic composer's incursion into obviously hostile territory, in genre it belonged to the rescue-opera type that had emerged, as a natural product of the French Revolution, with *Les Rigueurs du cloître* (1790) of Henri Montan Berton (1767–1844) and was to infest the Continental repertoire until the early 1820's. The romantic penumbra that frames Beethoven's *opera omnia* has confused the issue for more than a century, for his romanticism belonged as much to his personality as to his music. And personally he was as much an idealist as a romantic: quite another thing.

As an idealist, Beethoven had reacted enthusiastically to Napoleon, whose better aspect gleamed forth before the farcical drama of his self-coronation on December 2, 1804. Beethoven then canceled the dedication to Bonaparte of the "Eroica" Symphony, and lived to rejoice in the downfall of the "gran uomo" who had disappointed him and to deplore the system that replaced the Napoleonic hegemony.

The Congress of Vienna, which finished the hopes of Napoleon, also shriveled the hopes of that pseudoclassicism which the Emperor had made part of the panoply of his glory. Throughout Europe, the folk was awakening—by the proxy of artistic middlemen—to a lively sense of itself, of its background, traditions, and strength. Romanticism (the name aestheticians have elected to call this phenomenon) first appeared in different countries at different times, and in each country it wore a special face. There is, for instance, little relation between English romanticism, which, though responding to Continental radiations, went to the facts of nature for its primary source and material, and German romanticism, in which a wondering, childlike, and sometimes childish interest in folklore, particularly of the supernatural and grisly order, was from the first most evident. Also evident from the first was the intense nationalism of the German variety. Germany, with its scores of large and small states, had been crushed by the French: naturally, its arts now became German through and through. England, which had not been touched physically by Napoleon, had no spiritual need to assert its national individuality in its arts.

Just as Stein, architect of the modern Prussian state, discovered in the soul of his people, at a crucial moment, the iron that was ultimately, with England's help, to defeat Napoleon, so it was the critics and aestheticians and philosophers who discovered in the folk the base metals from which German romanticism was forged. The movement was engineered and stage-managed from the top: the concepts came before the creations. Such a man as Ludwig Tieck pointed out the path of German romantic literature before many feet had trodden it. The truth is that he and his fellow zealots were working passionately for a German expression, and secondarily for art. Many of the creations of their disciples are strangely dual—made to order and yet wild and undisciplined. For romanticism, despite its authoritarian, semipolitical activations, was partly a rebellion against the rules. The result was that the average romantic artist—writer, musician, painter, sculptor—was wild and undisciplined, without being anything else. The pride of the stock, the golden fruit of the tree, was, of course, Goethe. It is possible to call him the greatest of the German romantics; he was equally the greatest of the classicists: in short, he was an eclectic who took what he wanted wherever he happened to find it.

There are portents of romanticism in Mozart, most particularly in *Don Giovanni,* and there is just a hint of it even in the young classicist Beethoven. But the immediate inspiration of full-cry German musical romanticism was literary. While every shudder and excess cannot be laid at their door, two men of letters, Johann Paul Friedrich Richter and Ernst Theodor Amadeus Hoffmann, famous in their own days but unread now, concentrated in their work tendencies that proved most attractive to composers. The first of these, familiarly known as Jean-Paul, was a voluminous novelist, critic, and general essayist, abounding in playful humor, unbridled imagination, and patches of the exotic and grotesque. The second was a kind of German Poe, less careful as an artist, but as fanciful, horrific, and macabre. He delighted in projecting himself, as a character, into his writings—in fact, Offenbach's *Les Contes d'Hoffmann* is based on three fantastic adventures that he pretended had befallen him. A composer of tendentious operas, Hoffmann yearned, as did Weber, Schumann, Berlioz, and Wagner (like him, writers as well as musicians), after the synthesis of music and literature. Because he summed up all the more obvious aspects of the German romantic movement, Hoffmann exercised an influence far beyond his merits.

Hoffmann's most interesting opera, *Undine* (1816), musically traces its ancestry to the *haute noblesse*—that is, Gluck and Mozart—but its libretto, by Friedrich de La Motte-Fouqué, concerns the machinations of a wretched water sprite, and the classical cadences are given a romantic twist, notably in supernatural situations. It foreshadows the darkling mood of *Der Freischütz,* which was to come only five years later. Other German operatic composers besides Hoffmann had long since turned to fairy lore, magic, and the supernatural in general, along with *gemütlich* folk elements. There was an *Oberon* as early as 1790, a *Titania* dating from 1801. The first *Faust* opera, based on Goethe's poem, came from the pen of the musical theorist Ignaz Walter in 1797. Some of these adumbratory romantics, whose operas we are not likely to hear unless we remove to Germany for surprise revivals, made their mark and attracted their audiences, but their musical style did not match their hair-raising librettos. An exception must be made for Josef Weigl (1766–1846), whose *Schweizerfamilie* (1809), a Singspiel, struck an authentically romantic note that gladdened the hearts of sentimental Germans for almost a century.

The year 1817 was epochal in the career of German romanticism, for it was then that Friedrich Kind presented Carl Maria von Weber with the libretto of *Der Freischütz.* In certain fields, the movement was already in lush maturity, but it was awaiting a salient musical expression of sufficient proportions and popularity to challenge the efforts of classical and pseudoclassical musicians, native or foreign, plying their trade in the German states. Weber was marked from birth to sweep German music into the romantic camp: he was qualified by heredity, experience, and special talents. There were, of course, huge chunks of romanticism in Schubert and even in the later Beethoven, not to mention lesser men, but the work of the former was, except in his own small circle, unknown, while Beethoven's, except in *Fidelio,* was in classical forms.[8] Schubert's songs were too delicately wrought and intimate to be effective rallying points. *Fidelio* might have served had it been more popular, more theatrical, more stageworthy. In effect, it was merely a huge straw in the wind.

Weber's training for his mission included a childhood in traveling theatrical companies and a young manhood in operatic work, ranging from prompting to directing (at the age of twenty-six) the Prague opera house. Further, his personal life, disordered by the unpredictable behavior of a rogue father who dabbled in music, playwriting, acting, pol-

[8] The archclassicist composer could not resist the man, whose idealism found much that was attractive in some of the romantic catchwords. As opera has no forms (often not any form), *Fidelio* did not clash with Beethoven's ideals.

itics, and lithography, was itself a romantic extravaganza. Weber felt the strong call of the new, still heterogeneous Germany, and in 1814 had composed a group of patriotic songs and choruses that had touched the hearts of millions of his countrymen. The next year came his fervidly nationalistic cantata, *Kampf und Sieg,* about which an old Prussian fire-eater of high rank had been pleased to remark: "With you I hear nations speaking." It was only natural, then, that Friedrich Augustus, King of Saxony, seized upon this redoubtable patriot when, in 1816, he was look-ing around for a *Kapellmeister* for German opera at Dresden. But this was a political appointment, pure and simple, and the King, who doted on Italian opera, may have thought that his new employee would not take his job too seriously. If so, Friedrich Augustus had mistaken his man.

From the first, Weber fought tenaciously for the prerogative of the German opera. But the native fare was scanty, and the *Kapellmeister* had to content himself with staging Meyerbeer, then at his most Rossin-ian, and Méhul's *Joseph* (in German, of course), a cantatalike opera in a dignifiedly lyrical vein. Oddly enough, he waited six years to give a Dresden performance of *Fidelio,* which he had staged in Prague as early as 1814. In moments that he could snatch from onerous official duties, petty squabbles, literary efforts, composition of ceremonial folderol, tour-ing as a piano virtuoso, getting married, and begetting his first child, Weber was himself preparing to swell the German repertoire. He was not utterly without experience as an operatic composer: four [9] of his efforts, including the delightful little Singspiel *Abu Hassan* (Munich, 1811), had reached the boards. Most characteristic of these (in a Weber-ian sense) was *Silvana,* a rewriting of a Singspiel he had composed and produced at the age of thirteen. *Silvana* was tried out at Frankfurt-am-Main in September, 1810, but since a female balloonist was making an ascent outside the town, not only was the house practically empty but also some of the singers, in their frenzy to get a glance at the spectacle, skipped whole arias. The *première* was therefore far from propitious, but Weber always had a tenderness for *Silvana* and in his palmier days revived it. The libretto is outrageously, absurdly romantic—and the heroine is a mute. The score abounds in effects instantly recognizable as Weber's.

[9] This number includes *Das Waldmädchen,* written and produced when he was fourteen, and *Peter Schmoll und seine Nachbarn,* written in 1801–2. Details of the latter's production in 1803 are unknown, and its libretto is lost. Nevertheless, with a new "dialogue" by K. Eggert, *Peter Schmoll* was revived at Lübeck in 1927.

After *Abu Hassan,* no new opera by Weber was mounted for ten years, and then it was one based on a story that he had been considering when the idea for *Abu Hassan* struck him. *Der Freischütz,* the cornerstone of German romantic opera, was achieved in the most haphazard and vacillating manner. Far from seeming to be pursued by a Teutonic demon that would not let him rest from his task of destiny, Weber acted quite unlike a man about to make history. He discovered the story in 1810, but it was not until seven years later that he began talking it over with Kind. He then wrote excitedly to his wife: "Friedrich Kind is going to begin an opera book for me this very day. The subject is admirable, interesting, and horribly exciting. . . . This *is* super-extra, for there's the very Devil in it. He appears as the Black Huntsman; the bullets are made in a ravine at midnight, with spectral apparitions around. Haven't I made your flesh creep upon your bones?" This was February, 1817. Kind, doubtless fired by Weber's enthusiasm, produced a libretto in ten days. Immediately, the composer's interest seemed to flag. During the remainder of that year, he squeezed out only one aria and a few rough sketches. Three days were all of 1818 that he devoted to the score. In March, 1819, he sketched the first-act finale in one day, and then abandoned work for six months. Suddenly, he apparently regained his old enthusiasm and completed *Der Freischütz* between September, 1819, and May, 1820, writing the overture last.

Piqued by Dresden's seeming indifference to the prospects of German opera, and infuriated by its officials' contemptuous treatment of himself as an operatic composer, Weber promised *Der Freischütz* to Berlin, then the seat of a vast if undiscriminating expansion in all the arts. There he was evidently appreciated, for Count Brühl, intendant of the court theaters, pledged his word that the new opera would be the first to be sung at the Schauspielhaus. Weber stuck to his part of the bargain: when the opening of the Schauspielhaus was delayed for a year, he simply laid *Der Freischütz* aside, and went about his other business. Copenhagen heard a sample of the opera when Weber went there on tour: the ever popular overture received its first acclamation. In 1821, when the Schauspielhaus was finally ready, *Der Freischütz* was billed for June 18.

Meanwhile, however, something had happened to depress Weber's friends: Gaspare Luigi Pacifico Spontini, a composer of vast operatic canvases, and extraordinarily honored in France, had secured the lucrative post of royal music director in Berlin in 1819. He had already tested, with flattering success, Prussian response to his music, and the Berlin *première* of his lavish *Olimpie,* with a libretto translated by Hoffmann, was scheduled for May 14, little more than a month before *Der Frei-schütz. Olympie* was so magnificent as a spectacle that the Berliners were hypnotized into believing that the music was better than it really was. Weber alone kept his head, certain that his own opera was a masterpiece. So calm, indeed, was he that between rehearsals he composed the still-famous *Concertstück.* When the Prussian capital heard *Der Freischütz* on that sixth anniversary of Waterloo, it was found that Spontini had met his Wellington.

Various operas have established the reputations of their composers overnight, but the wild acclamation that greeted *Der Freischütz* was something special. The excited temper of the audience was evident from the moment the overture was encored, the ardor being heightened by the fiery applause of the many members of the *Landswehr,* all of whom had, during the fateful years of the Napoleonic crisis, thrilled to Weber's pa-triotic songs and choruses. Representatives of the arts were there in force, including Hoffmann, young Felix Mendelssohn, and Heine, nor was soci-ety less brilliantly shown off at this historic performance. From his peers Weber received the accolade he seems to have anticipated—after the opera was over, Hoffmann crowned him with a laurel wreath. But his final triumph came from a wider quarter. Before six months had elapsed, *Der Freischütz* had been presented to clamorous audiences throughout Germany and had become a loved favorite of the people, which it re-mains. In Vienna, even a truncated version caused by an imperial ban on the Devil himself, as well as on the guns and bullets that are essential to the opera's salient scene, could not stem this wildfire. Finally, on January 26, 1822, Dresden was converted. And, on March 2, 1825, less than four years after its world *première,* New York heard *Der Freischütz,* in English.[10]

Although it is not always presented as one, *Der Freischütz* was origi-nally a Singspiel, with a great deal of the plot carried forward by spoken dialogue. While Tieck, the great spokesman of romanticism, sneeringly remarked that it was just another Singspiel, he could not deny that it was brimming over with true-blue romantic feeling. It was (and this was an aspect of *Der Freischütz'* success that Weber came to resent) the sort of thing that ordinary people, especially those without artistic sophistica-tion, took to their hearts and kept there. It is tremulous with emotion (not excluding sentimentality), full of shudders, full of plot, and extremely

[10] It is not clear which of the several English versions was used.

proper—Agatha, the heroine, is more nicey-nice than Parsifal; not un-naturally, this role was chosen for the operatic debut of Jenny Lind, on March 7, 1838, at Stockholm. It is drenched with that quality for which only German has a word—*Gemütlichkeit*—and the very fact that the peculiarly heart-warming and folksy Hunting Chorus, from Act III, was, and in its native land still is, the most popular number from the opera shows that it was this quality that first captivated Germany.

The overture sums up all these qualities, being an enormously clever patchwork not only of musical segments but also of theatrical effects and moods. It is played constantly by both symphony orchestras and bands. Outside Germany, very little more of the opera survives in popular musical memory. Occasionally, a soprano with a big enough voice will revive the dramatically tender "Leise, leise," and even more rarely a tenor may be heard in the still fresh "Durch die Wälder," an ingenuous evocation of woodland spirit. In the entire history of the Metropolitan Opera, only seventeen performances are recorded.

Of the historical importance of *Der Freischütz* there can be no doubt. Meyerbeer and Wagner owed much to it, and so did lesser men, includ-ing Marschner and, in his own despite, Spohr. It is difficult not to hear echoes of it in Rossini's *Guillaume Tell*. What Weber passed on to those men was not only such specific things as new orchestral effects, both in general color and in the handling of separate instruments, but also a broad understanding of music for the stage. He gave them a new atmos-phere to play with, to draw out into subtleties, and, finally, to spiritualize. This new atmosphere was, of course, musical romanticism—the some-thing that throbs through *Der fliegende Holländer, Tannhäuser,* and *Lohengrin,* and through Schumann's overture to *Manfred* and Berlioz' *Harold en Italie.* Unfortunately, it also pulses blatantly through the over-tures of Suppé and whole cohorts of imitators of that king of imitators. It is a currency that has become so debased that we thoughtlessly extend to the model the stigma of the counterfeit. Too much din of this variety has assailed our ears—too many challenging horns, too many slow, moon-bathed introductions and galloping finales—for us to be able to "hear" *Der Freischütz* as Weber conceived it (with its unquestionable originality) and as those first audiences heard it (with its unquestionable impact of novelty).

Der Freischütz had made Weber the operatic man of the hour in Ger-many. Yet, after the first savor of the laurels, he began to feel vaguely annoyed over his new-found fame. Tieck's sneer rankled, and so did

Spohr's sincere but rancorous criticism. In a sense, it was the very popularity of *Der Freischütz* that Weber came to regard as an aspersion on his professional honor. He yearned to be, not a popular composer, but the creator of works that would meet Tieck's exacting standards. This state of mind led him to the most serious mistake of his career—the decision to compose, at all costs, an opera on a loftier level—one that would revel in the supernatural but would forsake the folk for the nobility.

At this juncture, Domenico Barbaia, who had already squeezed several excellent operas out of Rossini, sent Weber a commission to compose, for the Kärntnerthortheater in Vienna, an opera *à la Freischütz.* Weber accepted the commission, but not the specification. In his headlong flight toward ill luck, he wheedled from Helmine von Chézy, a loony if aristocratic *littérateuse,* one of the wildest and most unsettable librettos in the history of opera. Eleven times did the book suffer revision without becoming half as stageworthy as would have been a translation of *Cymbeline,* basically the same story. Compared to his snail's pace on *Der Freischütz,* Weber worked on the new opera at fever speed. Begun on December 15, 1821, *Euryanthe* was completed in less than a year, despite the fact that, as an opera, it had to have much more music than *Der Freischütz,* not being allowed to use the spoken dialogue that is a feature of the Singspiel.

Barbaia did not get around to scheduling *Euryanthe* until 1823, and when Weber set out for Vienna, in September of that year, he was a tired, ailing man. In his job, in the face of enmity from his co-workers, royal negligence, and ceaseless petty annoyances, he had been burning up his energies, already sadly wasted by tuberculosis. Yet he threw himself into the rehearsing of *Euryanthe* with his accustomed abandon and was not daunted by singers' complaints—requests for the insertion of special arias, star billing, and so on—and the adverse criticism of his friends, professional and nonprofessional. Except for certain reservations about the libretto, Weber seems to have been as complacent about the high quality of *Euryanthe* as he had been about that of *Der Freischütz* —he was certain that it was a good opera. True, young Franz Schubert, who had succumbed completely to the folk magic of the earlier opera, was cool about the new, which he heard in rehearsal and pronounced lacking in melody. This must have annoyed Weber, for when Schubert showed him the score of one of his own ill-fated operas, he said that first operas, like first puppies, should be drowned. This remark, in turn, must have incensed Schubert, for later he spoke even more acidly of *Eu-*

Tchaikovsky's *Pique-Dame,* Act II, Scene 2, at the Opera, Rome, 1956;
Antonio Annaloro (Herman), Gianna Pederzini (Countess)

Rimsky-Korsakov's *Christmas Eve,* at the Stadttheater, Zurich, 1959; production by Karl Heinz Krahl; scenery by Max Roethlisberger; Mary Daven-
port as the Tsarina

Dvořák's *Rusalka,* Act II, at the Janáček Opera, Brno, Czechoslovakia

Janáček's *The Cunning Little Vixen,* Act I, at the Janáček Opera, Brno, Czechoslovakia, 1958; production by Oscar Linhart; scenery by Josef A. Sálek; Cecilie Strádalová (Vixen), František Roesler (Ranger)

Cilèa's *Adriana Lecouvreur,* dress rehearsal at the Teatro San Carlo, Naples, 1960; Mariano Caruso (L'Abate di Chazeuil), Ettore Bastianini (Michonnet), Renata Tebaldi (Adriana)

Leoncavallo's *Pagliacci,* Act I, at La Scala, Milan, 1955–56 season; Clara Pe-rella (Nedda), Giuseppe di Stefano (Canio)

Puccini's *La Bohème,* Act II, at the Roman Arena, Verona, 1957; production by Carlo Maestrini; settings by Nicola Benois

Puccini's *Madama Butterfly,* Act II, at the Lyric Opera, Chicago, 1960; production by Christopher West; Mildred Miller (Suzuki), Leontyne Price (Cio-Cio-San)

Puccini's *Turandot*, Act III, Scene 2, at La Scala, Milan, 1958; production by Margherita Wallmann; scenery by Nicola Benois; Giuseppe di Stefano (Calaf), Birgit Nilsson (Turandot)

Strauss's *Salome,* at Covent Garden, London, 1949; setting by Salvador Dali; Ljuba Welitsch as Salome

Strauss's *Die Frau ohne Schatten,* Act II, Scene 1, at the War Memorial Opera House, San Francisco, 1959; scenery by Jean-Pierre Ponnelle; Irene Dallis (Nurse), Mino Yahia (Barak), Edith Lang (Empress)

Berg's *Wozzeck,* Act III, Scene 4, at Covent Garden, London, 1952; production by Sumner Austin; Parry Jones (Captain), Frederick Dalberg (Doctor)

Poulenc's *Les Dialogues des Carmélites,* Act III, Scene 4, at La Scala, Milan, 1957; production by Margherita Wallmann; settings by Georges Wahkévitch

Křenek's *Jonny spielt auf,* Scene 11, at the Metropolitan Opera House, New York, 1929; scenery by Joseph Urban; Lawrence Tibbett as Jonny

Prokofiev's *War and Peace*, Act I, Scene 2, at the Teatro Comunale, Maggio
Musicale Fiorentino, 1953; production by Tatiana Pavlova; Fedora Barbieri
(Helene), Rosanna Carteri (Natasha)

Stravinsky's *The Rake's Progress*, Act I, Scene 1, at the Teatro La Fenice,
Venice, 1951; Elisabeth Schwarzkopf (Ann Trulove), Robert Rounseville
(Tom Rakewell), Otakar Kraus (Nick Shadow), Raphaël Arié (Trulove)

Pizzetti's *Assassinio nella cattedrale*, Interlude, at La Scala, Milan, 1958; production by Margherita Wallmann; settings and costumes by Piero Zuffi; Nicola Rossi-Lemeni as Tommaso Becket

Walton's *Troilus and Cressida*, Act I, at La Scala, Milan, 1956; settings by Piero Zuffi; David Poleri (Troilus), Dorothy Dow (Cressida)

Britten's *Albert Herring,* the Komische Oper, Berlin, at the Théâtre Sarah Bernhardt, Paris, 1959; production by Walter Felsenstein; Erwin Wohlfahrt as Albert

Britten's *A Midsummer Night's Dream,* at Covent Garden, London, 1961; production by Sir John Gielgud; scenery and costumes by John Piper; Joan Carlyle (Tytania), Geraint Evans (Bottom)

Menotti's *The Medium,* at the Ethel Barrymore Theater, New York, 1947; Leo Coleman (Toby), Marie Powers (Madame Flora), Evelyn Keller (Monica)

Barber's *Vanessa,* Act II, at the Metropolitan Opera House, New York, 1958; production by Gian-Carlo Menotti; settings and costumes by Cecil Beaton; Eleanor Steber (Vanessa), Nicolai Gedda (Anatol), Giorgio Tozzi (Old Doctor), Regina Resnik (Old Baroness), George Cehanovsky (Majordomo), Rosalind Elias (Erika)

The Metropolitan Opera
House, New York, from
the auditorium

The Metropolitan Opera House, New York, from the stage; opening night of
the 1960–61 season; Thomas Schippers, conductor

The Royal Opera House, Covent Garden, London

The Grand Escalier d'Honneur of the Opéra, Paris

The Teatro alla Scala, Milan, from the stage; Victor de Sabata, conductor

The Teatro della Pergola, Florence, from the stage

The rebuilt Vienna State Opera, October, 1957

The new Staatsoper, Hamburg, 1955

ryanthe: "This is no music. This is no finale, no concerted piece according to the rules of art. It is all striving after effect. And he finds fault with Rossini! It is utterly dry and dismal."

So, too, thought Vienna, which had just risen from a feast of its beloved Rossini. By comparison, *Euryanthe* was funeral meats. Although the three hours consumed by the *première* of the opera, on October 25, 1823, would not seem long by modern standards, they bored the local wits, who cruelly said that Weber was evidently writing for eternity. The critics were more forthright, but quite as harsh. Strangely enough, *Euryanthe* persisted for twenty performances that season before being retired for many years. It has never been a lasting success anywhere. The Metropolitan has given it only nine times in all, the last performance being in 1915.[11] Weber pieced together, in one of his précis overtures, the best of the opera's purely musical inspirations, and that is still often heard. As for the rest, even the several pleasantly lyrical airs are never resurrected. Weber had failed in his chief purpose of writing an opera that would prove his status as a serious composer, and was left with the chill comfort of a studied encomium from Ludwig Tieck. Yet, again, *Euryanthe,* like *Der Freischütz,* exerted considerable influence on the course of opera, for from its elaborate first scene—a full-dress ceremonial at the court of Louis VI of France—stem in part those similar scenes of pomp and circumstance that Meyerbeer used in *Les Huguenots,* Wagner in *Tannhäuser* and *Lohengrin,* and Verdi in several operas, notably *Aida.*

As early as the rehearsals of *Euryanthe,* Weber was in agonizing ill

[11] Commenting on the 1915 revival at the Metropolitan, for which Toscanini was responsible, Henry Edward Krehbiel wrote, in the *New York Tribune,* apparently with a straight face: "It is the lovely manner and perfection with which Weber had wedded the drama and the music which make *Euryanthe* an almost incredible work." At no place in his review did Krehbiel refer adversely to the libretto. The absurdity of the *Euryanthe* libretto has so imposed itself on those who have some knowledge of operatic history that it is all but impossible to listen even to a concert performance of the opera with innocent ears—especially if the program contains a précis of the plot. Speaking of Rolf Lauckner's 1922 "thorough revision of the libretto," Sir Donald Francis Tovey (*Essays in Musical Analysis,* IV, 56) reported "a straightforward and impressive drama which perfectly supports Weber's music. . . . The patchiness (of Weber's score) was mainly due to the nonsensical dramatic situations, and it vanishes with their removal. . . . I was astonished at the effect the new text has upon the many tragic and complex passages which suffered from their absurd original background." Unfortunately, we find no record that *Euryanthe* was ever presented with the Lauckner libretto.

health. Now he began to die. Nothing could save him except complete
inactivity, but the harrying duties of his position, as well as his neurotic
financial fears, would not permit him to rest. For a time, public coldness
to *Euryanthe* suspended his operatic activities, though *Der Freischütz*
was going on from success to success, abroad as well as in Germany. For
fifteen months, Weber composed nothing. Then, when his anxiety for
the future welfare of his increasing family had reached an acute stage, a
commission for a new opera came from the actor-manager Charles Kemble, lessee of Covent Garden. The offer specified an English libretto and
a world *première* conducted by the composer. Weber, fully realizing that
the exertions of learning a new language, composing a full-length opera,
and daring the rigors of an English journey in winter would be fatal to
him, very properly acted like a shrewd barterer and jacked up his price—
to one thousand pounds, said his pupil and friend Sir Julius Benedict.
Agreement was reached, and Weber set to work on his last opera,
Oberon, or *The Elf King's Oath.* He was given the option of setting *Faust,*
but refused this much more fruitful subject because it had already been
made into an opera by his critical friend Ludwig Spohr.

Oberon was composed under even more difficult circumstances than
Weber may have anticipated. He had been punctilious in learning English, but his librettist in London was not equally so in sending him the
libretto. It arrived act by act at intervals of a month, and the composer
was thus forced to begin work before seeing the complete book or knowing in detail the exact development of the plot. When its development did
become manifest, it was found to be quite the most fantastic concoction
of the English antiquarian, herald, playwright, and novelist, James Robinson Planché—almost as convoluted and absurd as *Euryanthe,* which
it resembled in being the story of true love tested. While Weber kept in
the back of his mind a plan to turn *Oberon,* translated for performance
in Germany, into a true opera, for the London version he contented himself with a Singspiel in English, alternating music and lengthy expository
bits of spoken dialogue. In his frantic eagerness to finish the work before
death finished him, Weber adapted sections from his own earlier operas
—the finale of *Oberon,* for example, is lifted chiefly from *Peter Schmoll
und seine Nachbarn,* composed twenty-five years earlier.

Weber broke his trip to London by stopping in Paris, where he visited
his idol, Cherubini, and his chief detestation, Rossini. The meeting with
the former was the consummation of a tiny mutual-admiration society,
but it was Rossini who gave the dying man the excellent advice to turn

back. Weber, however, was determined to stand by his contract and see his family better provided for. He manfully went through his agony, heartened by the circumstances of the production. An ideal cast had been assembled: Mary Anne Paton, the Rezia, and John Braham, the Sir Huon, were the idols of the English public; almost as popular was the Fatima, Lucia Elizabeth Vestris. Moreover, he pronounced the orchestra the best he had ever heard. He conducted the *première* of *Oberon* on April 12, 1826, and several succeeding performances, but at the dreadful price he and his friends had foreseen—three months to a day after his arrival in London, he died there in his sleep.

The trip to England had at least been lucrative for Weber's heirs: his average daily earnings during his ninety days there were the equivalent of sixty dollars. His artistic success was less unqualified. What *Oberon* would have been like had Weber lived to revise it, it is difficult to guess, but certainly in its present form it leaves much to be desired. Nor have its inadequacies been effectively masked by the fumbling remedies of the patchwork artists of varying degrees of grandeur, from Benedict to Bodanzky, who have sweated over the score. Unhappily, *Oberon* has a central organic disease—chronic rather than acute—that defies the blue-pencilings and additions of learned musical doctors.

As Weber left it, *Oberon* is, at first blush, a clumsy play, preceded by his best overture and interrupted by fine outbursts of song. There is a sort of mutual courtesy between the action and the music that does not allow them to get in each other's way—they alternate but, on a first examination (for one can no longer speak of hearing it except in Continental opera houses), do not seem to co-operate. A closer familiarity with the score shows that, whatever Weber's plans were for turning *Oberon* into a grand opera, the whole Singspiel has a quite remarkable concision that is not nullified by the trying libretto, which he presses to the service of a radical musicodramatic dialectic. Its compactness, its very brevity, is the law of its being. It is by no accident that *Oberon* is among the shortest of all operas, for Weber stringently stripped it of all but essentials.

The musical reflection of the drama's play and contrast gleams accumulatively through the overture—it uses no less than seven motives drawn from the opera. Besides being one of the most adroitly calculated pieces of stage music ever written, by its sheer loveliness it casts a radiance over the whole of the opera. The *scena* "Ocean, thou mighty monster," which the overture quotes copiously, has few peers in the repertoire: it is surely Weber's most brilliant writing for the voice—symphonic in scope, epic in style, and too taxing for any but the most gifted of dramatic sopranos and for those, too, with the strength needed for singing "Abscheulicher, wo eilst du hin?" and the *Liebestod*. The rest of the opera is lavish in melodic loveliness and orchestral color. In some respects, *Oberon,* with the "horns of Elfland faintly blowing," is Weber's most wonderful and certainly most poignant contribution to opera.

Thus, the most famous operatic composer of the early nineteenth century left three immortal operas of which only the first is regularly performed (in Germany), even after—in two cases—the most auspicious beginnings. Let us start with *Oberon,* the last of the three. Despite Weber's popularity in England both personally and as a composer—*Der Freischütz* had been a notable attraction there for some years—*Oberon* scarcely outlived the furore attending the performances the composer himself conducted.

Euryanthe has always been unfortunate, though Weber secured the seventeen-year-old Henriette Sontag for the title role, thus helping to launch one of the most brilliant operatic careers of the century—a career that brought this poor girl a countess's coronet and unstinted professional and domestic happiness.[12]

Der Freischütz has been the most widely retained of all Weber's operas. New York has heard it in German, French, Italian, and English. After a single performance at the Metropolitan in the season of 1884–85, a quarter of a century intervened; then sixteen repetitions were bunched into twenty years, the last in 1929, when Elisabeth Rethberg appeared triumphantly as Agatha. In France, the opera, though in an abominable distorted version that aroused the bitter maledictions of Berlioz, attained a success that at first rivaled its vogue in Germany. The perpetrator of this scandal was François-Henri-Joseph Blaze, better known as Castil-Blaze, a respectable enough musicologist but a fiendish Procrustes to what he considered intractable operas, who in the course of his nefarious activities operated similarly on stage works by Mozart, Rossini, and Donizetti.

In 1824, Castil-Blaze prepared a translation and adaptation of both the book and music of *Der Freischütz,* called it *Robin des bois,* and had it presented at the Odéon. The performance was so sloppy that it was

[12] After triumphs in the United States, she had just begun a season in Mexico City when she was attacked by cholera, and died within a few days, on June 17, 1854. She was forty-eight years old.

hissed off the stage, and Blaze wisely withdrew it for revision, particularly of the casting. But when it was staged again, many of those who had hissed the first performance of *Robin* returned to vent their spite on the refurbishment. When Blaze saw how the wind was blowing, he papered the house night after night for more than a week. At that point, popular curiosity was strained to such a point that demand broke through his all-sold-out artifice, and legitimate ticket sales forced 327 consecutive performances.[13] Not realizing that what they were seeing and hearing was a caricature, the French romantics—Victor Hugo among them— went into ecstasies over *Robin des bois.* Before the craze evaporated, articles of dress and other objects were named after *Robin.* Only Berlioz, the purist, continued to object, though it is worth noting that years later, when he himself was in a position of authority at the Opéra, he felt called upon to adapt Weber's score to certain realistic exigencies of production.

In Germany, at Weber's death, only five years after the *première* of *Der Freischütz,* there was already the beginning of a flourishing school of romantic opera, the strongest member of which was, without question, the young man who for two years had served as joint-*Kapellmeister* (with Weber and his hated Italian colleague, Francesco Morlacchi) at Dresden. This was Heinrich Marschner, who had industriously studied Weber's operas to give added atmosphere and stage effects to his own already romantic style. Marschner, besides being musically clever and a humorist of the broadest sort, was a pleasing melodist. His first great success, *Der Vampyr,* almost sensually indulged a leaning toward the macabre, the supernatural, and the grotesque. He followed this with *Der Templer und die Jüdin,* a version of *Ivanhoe.* His most famous opera, however, was *Hans Heiling* (1833), which was until recently popular in Germany. The libretto, by Mendelssohn's friend Eduard Devrient, deals with gnomes and human beings, the sort of mixture that we are already familiar with through the librettos of Weber. Wagner was strongly influenced by Devrient's book and Marschner's music, particularly in *Der fliegende Holländer.* Marschner, indeed, through his longer span of years, was the bridge between Weber and Wagner.

Besides Marschner, other German romantic opera composers—excepting that strange composite, Meyerbeer—fade into insignificance.

---

[13] Castil-Blaze's treatment of *Euryanthe* was even more highhanded. Taking large slices of it, mixing them with slices of Beethoven, Meyerbeer, Rossini, and others, and using a comic book, he achieved the pastiche known as *Le Forêt de Sénart.* This, however, did not have the success of *Robin des bois.*

Mention must be made of the peculiarly stiff-necked violin virtuoso Ludwig Spohr, whose *Faust* (not after Goethe) and *Jessonda* (whose heroine is the ancestress of such disparate figures as Lakmé and Lohengrin's Elsa) had a fleeting success. Chorley accurately dismissed him as ". . . Spohr, who had a strange desire for being—that which he could not be—fantastic and supernatural (and showed a choice in his opera books as curiously courageous as his music was timidly orderly). . . ." For instance, *Jessonda* included a daring scene of suttee, an institution of which the Europe of that day had not heard.

Also, there was Otto Nicolai, whose prankish, good-humored overture to *Die lustigen Weiber von Windsor* [14] is practically the only survivor of a mass of half-romantic, half-Rossinian operas. Rather more individualized was Gustav Lortzing, a broad painter of genre pictures built on vigorous *Volkslieder* themes. He wrote an opera about Hans Sachs that antedated Wagner's portrayal of him in *Die Meistersinger* by more than twenty years, as well as a sentimental comedy of contrasts, *Zar und Zimmermann,* which has retained its hold on the German public.

Finally, there was the oversweet Friedrich, Freiherr von Flotow, whose *Martha, oder Der Markt zu Richmond* (usually sung in Italian, as *Marta*) is absolutely indestructible. It is, perhaps, as well contrived an operetta as *Blossom Time,* though inferior in tunes simply because Flotow adhered chiefly to his own inspirations to work on, whereas Sigmund Romberg had Schubert's. Even so, the best-known number in *Martha* is "The Last Rose of Summer," an Irish folk melody interpolated by Flotow himself. Only slightly less famous (it once was a swing best seller) is the lachrymose tenor air "M'appari," which sounds as if it had escaped from the pen of Donizetti, but, instead, had been interpolated from one of Flotow's earlier operas.

A man like Flotow would not have been recognizable to Weber as one of his legitimate progeny, so pervasive had become the softening, relaxing influence of the melodymongers of the South. The more effete descendants of Weber ended by surrendering to this influence with almost indecent abandon; Wagner, more solidly protected by the buckler of Teuton *Kultur,* did not.

[14] The opera was produced at the Academy of Music, New York, on February 5, 1886, in an English translation by H. E. Krehbiel. In 1905, at the Berlin Hofoper, it was the vehicle of Frieda Hempel's operatic debut.

CHAPTER VIII

The Divine Opera-Grinder

GIOACCHINO ROSSINI, who turned out operatic masterpieces as early in life as his artistic ancestor Mozart, lived more than twice as long. But at thirty-seven he abandoned opera to devote his lively talents to the full-time job of being an international wit and, at last, one of the most sought-after of Parisian hosts. Although we have become used to thinking of Rossini as an aging gentleman, at once comic-looking and portentous, with an all too obvious wig perched on his head (he wore more than one when the weather turned chill), his life as a creator of operas was as brief as Mozart's. But whereas the great Austrian was untimely cut off by death, Rossini suddenly and without previous warning turned off the faucet of his inspiration when there was no sign that it would ever run dry. Aside from the happy fact that in later years he returned to music occasionally—to compose his *Stabat Mater* and *Petite Messe solennelle,* a few official hymns, and a flurry of delicious piano trifles which he called *Péchés de vieillesse*—the Rossini who had dazzled the operatic world from 1810 on ceased to exist in 1829. By thus killing off one of the most attractive of opera composers, Rossini served only the professional musicologist, who, as it is, often finds some difficulty in differentiating sharply among the thirty-eight operas of his nineteen years of diabolic fecundity.

Only a dozen or so of the most brilliant fish in this shoal need concern us—and of those, only a few as wholes. Rossini himself was a most dismal prophet of his prospects for survival, foreseeing a continuing future for only the third act of *Otello,* the second of *Guillaume Tell,* and all of *Il Barbiere di Siviglia.* Time, fortunately, has proved him too much the pessimist and, in general, far too modest. *Il Barbiere* remains fixed in opera-house use (and too often in opera-house routine) everywhere. And since World War II, others of Rossini's merry delights have begun to reassert their convincing claims. A number of overtures and arias have always been heard. Rossini's sad self-evaluation was made when he was old and, despite his effervescing sense of humor, embittered by a sense of unjust neglect. The fame of Giacomo Meyerbeer was at flood, and Rossini was seeing the works of his very slightly older contemporary—operas in an eclectic, cosmopolitan style in which he himself could not feel comfortable—crowd him from the stage, apparently leading his own operas to retreat toward oblivion.

With a sheerly musical endowment that has seldom been surpassed, Rossini nevertheless does not seem to have realized that the liveliest of his works, by their very nature, had, in the long run, to be preserved. The long run was, in his case, long indeed. For at the end of the nineteenth century, a perilous moment arrived when musical criticism was dominated by German nationalists of an extraordinarily ponderous and assertive type (and by their plenipotentiaries in non-Germanic countries). Then Rossini's cause seemed lost indeed, along with that of almost everyone except Wagner and Beethoven. Our own century has increasingly rediscovered Rossini as a musical genius, and were he alive today, he would no doubt pronounce a *bon mot* over the comparative fates of Meyerbeer's operas and his own. While *Il Barbiere di Siviglia* still makes the rounds; while audiences in opera houses and listening to records at home are afforded increasingly frequent opportunities to delight in *L'Italiana in Algeri, Il Turco in Italia, La Cenerentola, Le Comte Ory,* and much (but never all) of *Guillaume Tell;* while symphony orchestras continue to schedule overtures from a half-dozen or more Rossini operas, Meyerbeer goes all but totally unheard.

Rossini started out—in 1810, with the one-act *La Cambiale di matrimonio*—as a composer of eighteenth-century *opere buffe,* and it will save time to admit that his greatest triumphs were scored in his own version of that genre. In 1816, *Il Barbiere di Siviglia,* heard first at Rome on February 20 as *Almaviva o sia l'inutile precauzione,*[1] established his fame without qualification, and it is *Il Barbiere* that today most keeps that fame brightly burnished in the opera houses of the world. Yet when Francis Toye wrote that "it may be doubted whether any previous opera, Mozart's *Entführung* and Cimarosa's *Matrimonio segreto* not excepted,

[1] Not until August 10, 1816, at the Teatro Contavalli in Bologna, was the opera billed as *Il Barbiere di Siviglia.*

had ever before been characterized by such sparkle, such a wholly irresponsible sense of fun," he was referring, not to *Il Barbiere,* but to its
fifteenth predecessor, *La Cambiale di matrimonio,* Rossini's first try,
which that cherubic country bumpkin had dashed off at the age of
eighteen.

La Cambiale di matrimonio is a curiosity and more than a curiosity.
First heard at Venice's Teatro San Moisè on November 3, 1810, it had a
libretto by Gaetano Rossi based on a peculiar *farsa* by Camillo Federici.
Ringing some reasonably fresh changes on the hoary plot of a girl in
love with an attractive young man, but forced to fight her father's determination to marry her to a more prosperous older man, the libretto deals
with "English" people of high tone (Sir Tobias Mill and his daughter,
Fanny) and with a preposterous "Canadian" known as Slook. It opens
with the unfledged prototype of all Rossini overtures, and contains, in
Fanny's aria "Come tacer," music that was rescued for fame when Rossini transformed it into the duet "Dunque io son" in *Il Barbiere di
Siviglia.* Once sung in Vienna as *Der Bräutigam von Canada, La Cambiale di matrimonio* is also occasionally still heard in Italy.

Francis Toye, whose *Rossini: A Study in Tragi-Comedy* is an enchanting book, was perhaps a little uncritical of his hero. But his rippling delight in *La Cambiale* echoed that of its first audiences, whose demands
for more and ever more Rossini led him to compose five operas in 1812
and four in 1813. Of the first group, *La Scala di seta,* another one-acter,
has a libretto which Gaetano Rossi derived from the libretto of Pierre
Gaveaux's opera *L'Échelle de soie* (1808), in which François-Antoine-
Eugène de Planard had rung still other changes on the story of the girl
who cannot see eye to eye with her guardian as to whom she shall marry.
La Scala di seta leads off with the earliest of Rossini's popular overtures.
Someone called this bubbling piece "a brightly colored puppy chasing its
tale," and it introduced the *crescendo à la Rossini* (of which more later).
La Scala di seta was produced first at the Teatro San Moisè, Venice, on
May 9, 1812, and it has seldom been staged since.

Of the 1813 group of Rossini operas, one, *Il Signor Bruschino* (in the
light-footed overture to which the violinists tap on their music stands
with the wood of their bows), was used as a pleasant if inappropriate
curtain raiser to Strauss's *Elektra* at the Metropolitan Opera House in
1932–33. When first given—again at Venice's Teatro San Moisè, late in
January, 1813—it was not a success; it has, however, been revived with
some frequency since the 1840's. Another of Rossini's 1813 crop was

Tancredi, a two-act *melodramma eroico* with a dire, tragic libretto by Gaetano Rossi out of Tasso's *Gerusalemme Liberata* and Voltaire's *Tancrède.* From it the charming and eternal "Di tanti palpiti" emerged to become internationally familiar, helping to make the opera Rossini's first ambassador to the non-Italian world.

A third of the 1813 group, *L'Italiana in Algeri,* is the earliest Rossini opera to have been performed widely during this century, its genuinely funny two-act libretto by Angelo Anelli [2] having given Rossini exactly what he was equipped to accept: his first really big chance to be entirely himself. Blessed with one of his ever attractive overtures, *L'Italiana* is especially abounding in ensemble numbers, of which the quintet at the end of Act I—beginning "Confusi e stupidi"—may be without rival for incisiveness and pace. Funnier, though less swift in flight, is the second-act initiation of Mustafà, Bey of Algiers, into the order of *Mangiatacci* (those who eat and keep quiet). The arias for the mezzo-soprano Isabella, the tenor Lindoro, who loves her, and Mustafà (bass) are only a shade less brilliant. Unhappily, *L'Italiana* trails off in a weak, sentimental ending. But when a Giulietta Simionato sings the archrole of Isabella, *L'Italiana* splendidly justifies the reputation it began to create at Venice's Teatro San Benedetto (later renamed Teatro Rossini) on May 22, 1813.

The Teatro alla Scala, Milan, was the scene, on August 14, 1814, of the *première* of Rossini's second collaboration with the prolific Felice Romani,[3] who had concocted the book of *Aureliano in Palmira.* This pendant to, or mirror image of, *L'Italiana in Algeri* was *Il Turco in Italia.* Not quite so sparklingly demented as *L'Italiana,* and perhaps too much like it for the demands of the Milanese, *Il Turco* was neither a failure nor a success. It did travel to foreign lands, however, and the recent revival of florid singing has found it intermittently restored to the stage. The Teatro alla Scala was the setting for its first notable twentieth-century revival; after not having been heard in Milan for 130 years, it was successfully presented there on April 15, 1955, with Maria Callas as Fiorilla.

By 1816, the miraculous year of *Il Barbiere di Siviglia,* though the *serio* aspect of Rossini's operatic art was still in the groping state (it was

---

[2] Anelli had written this libretto for Luigi Mosca, whose opera based on it was presented at the Teatro alla Scala, Milan, on August 16, 1808, nearly five years before Rossini's.

[3] Romani (1788–1865) was responsible for many librettos used by Simon Mayr, as well as for those of Bellini's *La Sonnambula* and *Norma* and Donizetti's *L'Elisir d'amore* and *Lucrezia Borgia.*

always to remain in part synthetic), he had perfected its *buffo* aspects. Every detail of farce and featherweight comedy came to him easily. He had a healthy, guileless love of fun and nonsense—triviality even—and a genius for clothing them spontaneously in music, a genius that bubbled up irrepressibly even when he was writing his admirable, influential exercises in *opera seria*. His earliest *opere buffe* were mainly in the tradition of Pergolesi, Cimarosa, and Paisiello, and were couched in the gleaming eclectic style of the late eighteenth century. From those men and their manners, he borrowed their best effects without sacrificing the unquestionable originality of touch that had appeared as early as *La Cambiale di matrimonio*. That originality was present in effervescence, in a stanchless uncorking of melodic and rhythmic champagne, an intoxicating *brio*. He may have borrowed many details, but he borrowed so cleverly that they became his own. He was familiar with Mozart's operas and with Haydn—he had conducted *Die Schöpfung* in Bologna in his nineteenth year. From them, very possibly, he learned the lessons of painstaking craftsmanship of a sort rare among his Italian contemporaries. Almost from the beginning, he refused to accommodate his vocal lines to any old accompaniment, and produced beautifully contrived scores. Even before the gorgeously fashioned *Semiramide* (1823), in which the orchestra would blaze forth with exuberance and volume previously suggested in Italy only in the now almost forgotten operas of the Italianized German, Johann Simon Mayr, his hankering after big orchestral effects had earned him the nickname of the "Little German." It would later lead to his being called, sometimes in deprecation, "M. Crescendo."

All of Rossini's carefulness was not lavished on the orchestra. In *Elisabetta, regina d'Inghilterra,*[4] one of the two operas he composed in 1815, he applied himself assiduously to the problem of the singer. The opera in question was tailor-made to fit the vocal gifts, histrionic abilities, personality, and appearance of Isabella Colbran, then the mistress of the impresario Domenico Barbaia, Rossini's chief at the Teatro San Carlo, Naples, but later his own mistress and finally his wife.[5] Because of her

[4] With a fine disregard for geography and history, Rossini borrowed, for this opera about the Virgin Queen, both the overture and the finale of his *Aureliano in Palmira* (1813).

[5] The situation that evolved at Naples was laughably like aspects of Stendhal's description of a typical opera company in an Italian town many times smaller than Naples: "The mechanism of an Italian theater is as follows. The manager is frequently one of the wealthiest and most considerable persons in the little town

amiability toward him, the young composer—Colbran was seven years his senior—was emboldened to take the liberty of writing out in full the vocal ornaments. In the Italian operas of Rossini's immediate predecessors and contemporaries, composers appeared to have forgotten (if they had ever heard of) one of the lessons of Gluck's reform: they had left vocal ornamentation to the abilities, ingenuity, and whims of individual singers. Today, as in Lully's time or in Gluck's operas from 1760 on, it is taken for granted that the singers will perform what the composer wrote, adding nothing, subtracting nothing, altering nothing.[6] But it required courage on Rossini's part to begin emancipating the composer

---

he inhabits. He forms a company consisting of a *prima donna, tenore, basso cantante, basso buffo,* a second female singer, and a third *basso.* He engages a *maestro,* or composer, to write a new opera, who has to adapt his own airs to the voices and capacities of the company. The libretto, or poem, is purchased at the rate of from sixty to eighty francs from some unlucky son of the Muses, who is generally a half-starved *abbé,* the hanger-on of some rich family in the neighborhood. The character of the parasite, so admirably painted in Terence, is still to be found in all its glory in Lombardy, where the smallest town can boast of five or six families with incomes of three or four hundred a year. The manager, who, as has already been said, is generally the head of one of these families, entrusts the care of the financial department to a *registrario,* generally a pettifogging attorney who holds the situation of his steward. The next thing that usually happens is that the manager falls in love with the *prima donna;* and the progress of this important *amour* gives ample employment to the curiosity of the gossips. The company, thus organized, at length gives its first performance after a month of cabals and intrigues, which furnish conversation for the whole period. This is an event in the simple annals of the little town, of the importance of which the people of large places can form no idea. During months together, a population of eight or ten thousand persons does nothing but discuss the merits of the forthcoming music and singers with the eager impetuosity that belongs to the Italian climate. The first performance, if successful, is generally followed by twenty or thirty more presentations of the same piece; after which the company breaks up. This is what is called a *stagione* or season; the last and best of which is that of the carnival. The singers not engaged in any of these companies are usually to be found at Milan or Bologna, where they have agents whose business it is to find them engagements or maneuver them into situations when opportunity offers."

[6] This is, of course, theory only. Standards of fidelity are still not so high in opera as in instrumental music. The singer, if important or popular enough, still adds and subtracts and alters, particularly when a passage is very difficult, for opera singers of our time are seldom the gymnasts their predecessors seem to have been.

from tyrant singers. It was also in *Elisabetta*—Giovanni Schmidt's libretto for which startlingly parallels the plot of Scott's *Kenilworth,* published five years later—that Rossini dropped *recitativo secco* and first wrote an *opera seria* in which all the recitative was supported by the orchestral strings. And in *Tancredi* he already had upset the moldy tradition that the bass voice was essentially comic and therefore useless in serious opera.

It was no novice, then, who, in the space of a fortnight in the winter of 1816, cast a double *défi* to the world by setting the first play of Beaumarchais's Figaro trilogy. Mozart already had spun a golden web from *Le Mariage de Figaro,* the second play; the aged, revered Paisiello, whom the Neapolitans worshiped only less than San Gennaro, had set *Le Barbier de Séville* under the title of *Il Barbiere di Siviglia.* Rossini was far from being an upstart: he had several tremendous hits to his credit and had earned the right to dare the lightning. But under the circumstances, he was rashly brave, for his own *Barbiere* was the second of two operas he had composed for Rome, and the first of them—*Torvaldo e Dorliska* (Teatro Valle, December 26, 1815)—had seemed a dismal failure.

Attempting to preclude indignation on the part of Paisiello and his cohorts, Rossini called the new opera *Almaviva, o sia l'inutile precauzione.* Useless precaution indeed! At the *première* at the Teatro Argentina on February 20, 1816, the Paisiellians had posted a leather-lunged anti-claque, which found its pretext for abuse when the great Spanish tenor Manuel del Popolo Vicente García tuned his guitar on the stage before accompanying himself to its plunkings, a piece of stage business that modern audiences, educated by the antics of realistic singing actors and actresses, would certainly love. Rossini, inclined like many wits to black pessimism, decided that his new opera was a fiasco and rushed home to sleep it off. There he remained the second night; he was shamming sickness in bed when friends burst in on him to announce that the Romans rather liked his second offering. It ran out the week, which ended the season. Elsewhere it gathered popularity, slowly at first, then swiftly. When Rome heard it again five years later, it was the rage of Europe and had been sung in an abbreviated English version in New York. It ended by becoming probably the most popular opera of the nineteenth century, praised by such a motley collection of Rossini's colleagues as Beethoven, Schubert, Berlioz, Wagner, and Brahms. Not precisely fashionable today, *Il Barbiere di Siviglia* has survived all changes of fashion and seems likely to survive many more.

Il Barbiere is arranged audaciously. Rossini sets the pace with one of his most charming overtures, and then, fairly early in Act I, hinting at the vocal delights to come, brings forth "Largo al factotum," Figaro's whirlwind lament of an overworked Jack-of-all-trades. There is no letdown: in fact, *Il Barbiere* is one of those rare stage works we leave with a sense of having been cheated—we actually wish there had been more.[7] The rapid-fire action does not lag; the witty, copious inventiveness never slackens. Because that inventiveness is not of the same sort as Mozart's, we do not, as we ransack the score, find as many separate memorable numbers as make *Le Nozze di Figaro,* though a unity, one of the most richly varied of vocal concerts. Rossini is always apt, but he is not of Mozart's order as a supreme melodist.

In composing *Il Barbiere,* Rossini was constantly the vessel of the *buffo* spirit, and his first services were given to it; Mozart's first services were always to music. Take the highest spots of *Il Barbiere* and analyze them: "Una voce poco fà," cleverly located in the action, is primarily a florid display piece; the Calumny Song almost entirely loses its significance when separated from its context—it is negligible as music, flawless as *opera buffa.* Rossini set the broad, mocking, thoroughly irreverent Beaumarchais play to a tee; Mozart, though respecting his libretto, took off from it for a display of his own unique magic.[8]

As now usually presented, *Il Barbiere* displays several odd features. The overture is not the one that Rossini composed for the Rome *première:* that was unfortunately misplaced early in the opera's life. It may have been a peculiarly interesting piece: it was based on authentic Spanish melodies given to Rossini by García. The overture now used, however much it may sound as though designed specifically for *Il Barbiere,* had served as the overture to two of Rossini's *opere serie*—*Aureliano in Palmira* (1813) and *Elisabetta, regina d'Inghilterra*—before being used here, a further proof of the essentially *buffo* character of his genius. Too, Rosina, the heroine who for ages has been a giddy soprano of the most incorrigible variety, began life as a mezzo-soprano (the origi-

---

[7] This refers to the arbitrarily cut version we almost always hear. How many of us can know Almaviva's aria "Ah, il più lieto, il più felice," the chief melodic phrase of which reappears in Angelina's "Non più mesta" in *Cenerentola?*

[8] The mistake of confounding the farcial genius of Rossini with the comedic genius of Mozart is of some antiquity: on November 16, 1837, at the National Theater, New York, a mixture of *Le Nozze di Figaro* and *Il Barbiere di Siviglia* was presented as *The Two Figaros.*

nal Rosina was Signora Giorgi-Righetti). Sopranos, who have nearly always been more popular than contraltos or mezzos, could not bear to leave so juicy a role outside their own hunting grounds; they simply ordered it to be transposed and transported there. We do not know either the date or the name of the first perpetrator of this role-snatching, though it may have been the Paris debut of Henriette Sontag, in June, 1826. In recent decades, the coloratura contralto or mezzo-soprano having undergone something of a rebirth, Rosina has often been happily restored to her original range.

A third curiosity of many stagings of *Il Barbiere* is "Manca un foglio," Dr. Bartolo's famous aria in Act II, which was composed by a comparative nonentity named Romani, though "A un dottor'," the fine aria that Rossini composed for this scene, exists. Item: Romani's "Manca un foglio" is much easier to sing than Rossini's "A un dottor'," which latter, however, now is frequently restored to its rightful position in the opera. Finally, there is Rosina's Lesson Scene, about the absurdities of which oceans of ink have been spilled. Rossini composed some delightful music for her singing lesson, "Contro un cor che accende amore," but when Rosina's voice changed, it was discarded; interpolations of almost any sort were substituted at sopranos' whims. In flagrant cases of egocentricity, Rosina has been known to exercise her birdlike voice for more than half an hour, choices of vehicle ranging from such simple heart songs as "Home, Sweet Home" (the astute preference of Adelina Patti, who thereby rested her voice) and "Annie Laurie" to the Mad Scene from *Lucia di Lammermoor* and inane vocal variations that are merely losing contests with the flute.

The period from December, 1816, to May, 1817, was the most efflorescent in Rossini's career, for in those six months were bunched the *premières* of three of his best operas. *Otello,* heard at Naples on December 4, was the first—and in some respects the most beautiful—of them. Rossini's only Shakespearean opera is deeply interesting both historically and psychologically. First, it was laid at the feet of Isabella Colbran, whose acting talent Rossini admired sincerely, and with whom he was in love. Further, the story itself (despite the distortions of Shakespeare perpetrated by its librettist, the Marchese Francesco Berio di Salsa) really affected Rossini, stimulating him to a serious, almost passionate style quite in keeping with it. *Otello* is surprisingly free from that undertone of banter which had given a note of unintentional levity to his gravest earlier efforts. Nineteenth-century critics exhausted their superlatives while swooning over the tragic beauties of its third act. And indeed Desdemona's Willow Song—"Assisa a piè d'un salce" (which somehow suggests, in its form and antique harmonies, Verdi's later Willow Song) —and her prayer, "Deh! calma, o ciel," deserved their praise.

In *Otello,* too, Rossini finally abandoned the lingering traces of the old *recitativo secco.* In *Tancredi,* three years earlier, he had accompanied the recitative with strings; now, using the full orchestra, he was able to treat scenes as unified musical wholes. Audiences accepted this innovation without murmur, but the librettist's bold retention of Shakespeare's tragic ending alienated many spectators, some of whom spoiled the calculated dramatic effect by shouting out to warn Desdemona that the Moor was approaching to kill her. Nothing, however, stopped the spontaneous enthusiasm for Rossini's reading of the pathetic story. Within a few years, *Otello,* like a tragic companion to *Il Barbiere di Siviglia,* became one of the standard operas of the world. The fame of Verdi's masterly *Otello* has helped to drive this old-time favorite from the boards, but an occasional revival in concert form continues to assert its vitality.

Rossini's other two operas of this period were as frivolous as *Otello* was grave. Of these, the first was a setting of the Cinderella story with all the magic elements removed from it by the composer's order, possibly because he had a native dislike for such stuff, possibly because stage machinery was so clumsily managed in the Italian opera houses of the era as to render illusionist tricks too risky. This excision left it with a libretto, by Jacopo Ferretti,[9] which is far from unamusing and is almost realist in its acerbity. *La Cenerentola* was, like *Il Barbiere,* a comparative failure on its opening night—January 25, 1817, at the Teatro Valle in Rome—but as its subtitle (*La Bontà in trionfo*) predicted, it went on to become a smash hit of long duration. The score is, in spots, as fresh and witty as that of *Il Barbiere,* but it is a patchwork, the self-borrowing (in which, like Handel and many other composers, Rossini indulged constantly) here being at times quite inept. But that would not have caused *La Cenerentola* to disappear from the boards for so many years. The real cause of its vanishing was the eclipse of florid singing, for it contains in some ways the most difficult vocal music that Rossini ever composed, particularly that for the name part, which requires that phenomenon long thought extinct—a mezzo with coloratura agility. The recent resto-

[9] In the fashion of the times, Ferretti had in actuality merely adapted a French libretto, by Charles-Guillaume Étienne, which had been made into an opera by Niccolò Isouard (Opéra-Comique, Paris, February 22, 1810).

ration of *La Cenerentola* to intermittent performance has signalized the rebirth of florid singing in the throats of such ladies as Conchita Supervia, Giulietta Simionato, and Marina de Gabarain. A mezzo who can sing Cinderella's final "Nacqui all'affanno" and "Non più mesta accanto al fuoco" can sing anything, technically speaking.

On May 31, 1817, little more than four months after the Rome *première* of *La Cenerentola,* the Teatro alla Scala at Milan witnessed what Stendhal, in his delightful, unreliable *Vie de Rossini,* called the most successful first night he ever attended, that of *La Gazza ladra.*[10] Rossini took special pains with this preposterous mixture of frivol and melodrama, for he was not in the good books of the Milanese, who were demonstrating a perverse taste for the German operas of Peter von Winter [11] and others. To scotch this wandering, Rossini determined to outsmart the Germans on their own terms: he gave the orchestra a much more important role than had been his custom; he went to unusual lengths to spin out music suitable to each character; and he stole from the monstrously prolific Winter the idea of concealing dramatic lag by inserting a dramatically irrelevant prayer. So effective was this device that Rossini thereafter used it *ad nauseam.*

The overture to *La Gazza ladra* is really dramatic, and so, too, is much of the vocal score. This engrossing and highly flavored tale of aborted tragedy brought about by the thieving pranks of a magpie is likely to be one of the now comparatively little-known Rossini operas to be restored to intermittent revival. Until it is, however, most of us must be content with the appetite-whetting overture, one of the most adroit adventures in musical suspense ever devised, and with very occasional hearings of such delightful arias as the Podestà's first-act "Il mio piano è preparato" and Ninetta's first-act "Di piacer mi balza il cor."

La Gazza ladra was the opera with which Lorenzo da Ponte and his partner, the Chevalier Riva-Finoli, inaugurated the first New York theater built solely for the production of opera. The Italian Opera House,

[10] Giovanni Gherardini, apparently otherwise unknown to fame, had adapted this libretto from a French play, *La Pie voleuse,* a collaboration by Jean-Marie-Théodore Baudouin d'Aubigny and Louis-Charles Caigniez.

[11] Peter von Winter (1754–1825) composed dozens of operas, no less than twenty-six Masses, and whole libraries of oratorios, cantatas, and other church music. His greatest hit was *Das unterbrochene Opferfest,* first produced at Vienna on June 14, 1796, which Alfred Loewenberg described as "about the most successful German opera between *Zauberflöte* (1791) and *Freischütz* (1821)."

located at Church and Leonard streets, in a then fashionable, now completely commercial, district, was opened on November 18, 1833. Philip Hone, a former mayor of New York, was present, and left this lively account of the evening in his diary:

> The opera, they say, went off well for a first performance; but to me it was tiresome, and the audience was not excited to any degree of applause. The performance occupied four hours—much too long, according to my notion, to listen to a language which one does not understand; but the house is superb, and the decorations of the proprietors' boxes (which occupy the whole of the second tier) are in a style of magnificence which even the extravagance of Europe has not yet equaled. I have one-third of box No. 8; Peter Schermerhorn one-third; James J. Jones one-sixth; William Moore one-sixth. Our box is fitted up with great taste with light blue hangings, gilded panels and cornice, armchairs, and a sofa. Some of the others have rich silk ornaments, some are painted in fresco, and each proprietor seems to have tried to outdo the rest in comfort and magnificence. The scenery is beautiful. The dome and the fronts of the boxes are painted in the most superb classical designs, and the sofa seats are exceedingly commodious. Will this splendid and refined amusement be supported in New York? I am doubtful.[12]

For five years after *La Gazza ladra,* Rossini manufactured a series of stereotyped operas, few of them successes. First (Teatro San Carlo, Naples, November 11, 1817) came *Armida,* with a text that Giovanni Schmidt had derived from Tasso. Never very popular in Italy, it won a passing success in Vienna and Germany in German translation; it was revived in 1952 at the Florence Maggio Musicale as a starring vehicle for Maria Meneghini Callas. Next came *Adelaïde di Borgogna,* which appears to have been forgotten completely. But the next opera, billed as an *azione tragico-sacra,* was *Mosè in Egitto* (Teatro San Carlo, Naples, March 5, 1818). With its solemn text by Andrea Leone Tottola, its bold use of the bass voice—both Moses and Pharaoh rumble in the lowest register—and its once universally popular choral prayer in Act III, "Dal

---

[12] What Hone apparently wished to have supported was not the performance of *La Gazza ladra* and other Italian operas, but the lavish interior decorations of the opera house and the social whirl that went with them. In any event, his doubts were justified: the Italian Opera House as such lasted for two years, after which a decade passed before Italian opera made another stand in New York.

tuo stellato soglio," [13] *Mosè in Egitto* not only became an international favorite but was also subjected to an unparalleled series of alterations, changes of text, deletions, and insertions, as well as to performance as an oratorio.

Mosè in Egitto was followed by four operas that for more than a century have been only items in a catalogue: *Adina, Ricciardo e Zoraïde, Ermione,* and *Edoardo e Cristina.* The small success of several of these is perhaps summed up in the fact that *Edoardo e Cristina* (Teatro San Benedetto, Venice, April 24, 1819) contained nine numbers from *Adelaïde di Borgogna,* seven from *Ermione,* and three from *Ricciardo e Zoraïde.* Rossini, whose melodic fountain may have appeared to be going dry, was merely resting up. The jets gushed forth again in *La Donna del lago* (Teatro San Carlo, Naples, September 24, 1819), a fantastic adaptation by Andrea Leone Tottola of Scott's *The Lady of the Lake,* its relation to which is about that of *Lucia di Lammermoor* to *The Bride of Lammermoor.* For twenty-five years, *La Donna del lago* turned up in opera houses everywhere, especially to the delight of sopranos, who always triumphed with "Oh mattutini albori."

Returning once more to Milan and the Teatro alla Scala, Rossini produced, on December 26, 1819, the first opera to be based on a text by the then thirty-four-year-old Alessandro Manzoni: *Bianca e Faliero* had a libretto by Felice Romani derived from Manzoni's tragedy *Il Conte di Carmagnola.* Despite the presence of the once-popular cavatina-cabaletta "Della rosa il bel vermiglio"–"O serto beato," *Bianca e Faliero* achieved only moderate success. Little better fate befell *Maometto II* (Teatro San Carlo, Naples, December 3, 1820), with a libretto by Cesare della Valle, Duke of Ventignano; but *Maometto II* was destined to be reborn six years later as a successful French opera entitled *Le Siège de Corinthe.* Bad luck and, it may be, careless workmanship continued to dog Rossini's footsteps. *Maometto II* was succeeded by *Matilde di Shabran,*[14] the *première* of which (Teatro Apollo, Rome, February 24, 1821) was conducted by Paganini, and which became somewhat popular without adding to Rossini's reputation or enduring fame. And *Matilde di Shabran* was in turn followed by *Zelmira* (Teatro San Carlo, Naples,

[13] The famous prayer was not a part of the opera as originally sung at Naples, but was added for a revival there on March 7, 1819.

[14] For this libretto, Jacopo Ferretti had reached back thirty years for François Benoît Hoffman's text for Méhul's *Euphrosine* (Paris, September 4, 1790), which he then recast.

February 16, 1822), which used another of those transmogrified French texts (by Tottola, borrowed by him from a 1762 tragedy of Pierre-Laurent Buirette de Belloy), which Rossini himself conducted in both Vienna and London, and which boasted another of those cavatina-cabaletta display pieces once beloved by pyrotechnical sopranos: "Ciel pietosa, ciel clemente"–"Ma, che sento." These operas showed him still marking time, seemingly in a rut.

Although neglected, these operas of the 1817–22 period show how indomitable Rossini could be when convinced of the worth of certain innovations. In them, against constant and often violent protests—a music-lover once confessed that he had entertained seriously the notion of murdering the composer because of the two drum-rolls in the overture to *La Gazza ladra*—he continued to build up the role of the orchestra, to assign important roles to bassos, and to write out all the vocal ornaments. Since most of these operas were composed for Isabella Colbran, whom Rossini finally married in 1822, he was unopposed in this last innovation. And because the novelties of treatment were his, they were eventually adopted by other Italian composers. The final result was that, except for its peculiar Latinness and sensuousness of melodic turn, Italian opera tended to become more like German. Actually, there was give and take between the two schools, and Richard Wagner himself was not uninfluenced by Rossini.

In 1822–23, Rossini composed the heaviest and last of his serious Italian operas, *Semiramide* (Teatro La Fenice, Venice, February 3, 1823). Ironically, this long, ponderous, almost Meyerbeerian opera was composed right after he had made a triumphal visit to Vienna, where Beethoven had given him that famous advice which he was to ignore almost entirely: "Give us more *Barbers!*" Incest is the theme, Babylon the locale of the text that Gaetano Rossi had carved from Voltaire's tragedy. The more earnest operagoers of the mid-nineteenth century persisted in considering Rossini's *Semiramide* the masterpiece of this essentially *buffo* spirit (for to them nothing so apparently scatterbrained as *Il Barbiere di Siviglia* could seem to be his finest work). In reality, it is a circus of ingenious tricks—a collection of shudders and shams brought together with a ruthless eye to effect.

Aside from several affecting numbers, *Semiramide* displays Rossini at far from his best. The overture survives, popular still with "pops" orchestras and brass bands: it is shameless claptrap in which a few innocuous ideas are blown up and stretched out in chains of those patented crescendos which were always among the most obvious signatures of Rossini's style. The overture fairly represents the poorer sections of the opera, but it gives no idea of the vocal extravagances of this astonishing score, including the mezzo-soprano's "Ah' quel giorno ogni rammento" and the soprano's luscious "Bel raggio lusinghier." Rossini called it a "tragic melodrama," and so, in more senses than one, it is. And yet, Bernard Shaw no doubt told only the exact truth when he wrote: "The general opinion, especially among literary men who affected music, used to be that there was an Egyptian grandeur about *Semiramide*, a massiveness as of the Great Pyramids, a Ninevesque power and terror far beyond anything that Beethoven had ever achieved." In the twenty years after its *première*, *Semiramide* spread across Europe, as well as to Malta, Mexico, Havana, Algiers, and Valparaiso.

Semiramide closed Rossini's Italian career, during which he had composed thirty-three operas in thirteen years. A circuitous tour finally took him to Paris. There, within five years, he ended his operatic life with a tally of one official opera-cantata in Italian and four operas in French. The ceremonial piece—*Il Viaggio a Reims ossia L'Albergo del giglio d'oro*—first heard in Paris, at the Théâtre-Italien, June 19, 1825—was intended to celebrate the crowning of Charles X, who provided Rossini with a well-paid government post. It was nonetheless a complete failure, playing for only three nights.

Of Rossini's four French operas, two were rewritings of earlier Italian works; two were original, or partly original. All of them, significantly, were produced after Rossini had had a hand in launching Giacomo Meyerbeer in France by an almost piously careful production of *Il Crociato in Egitto*, thereby unwittingly paving the way for his own exile from the Parisian stage. But Meyerbeer's first flaming success—*Robert le diable*, 1831—did not occur until after Rossini had borrowed enough from Meyerbeer to enable him to become a founding father of French grand opera, and thereafter had stopped composing operas altogether. Rossini lived on for almost forty years after composing his last opera, growing to resent Meyerbeer's usurpation of his own former place. Meyerbeer, however, never spoke of Rossini except with warmest admiration and gratitude.

Before attempting anything of importance for the French stage (*Il Viaggio a Reims* is a patchwork of old Rossiniana and national airs, and does not enter the argument), Rossini, from his strategic outlook as director of the Théâtre-Italien, studied the technique of French singing, the tastes of his potential public, and, finally, the French language. As his personal coach, he secured the eminent tenor Adolphe Nourrit, who created many roles in famous operas. Never had this precocious, bouncing Italian boy of thirty-odd years worked harder or more conscientiously. He was stimulated by new and better conditions: a larger, more highly trained orchestra, superior and more reliable stage machinery, and more time in which to think things out.

Le Siège de Corinthe was Rossini's first French opera. It did much to hush the criticism, bolstered by *Il Viaggio a Reims,* that he was an unrepentant confectioner of pastiches. Produced at the Opéra on October 9, 1826,[15] *Le Siège* was helped by its music and, more decisively, by its libretto, the work of Louis-Alexandre Soumet and Giuseppe Luigi Balocchi. Dealing with a high-minded Greek girl who refuses to marry her childhood sweetheart because, having become Sultan of Turkey, he has ill-treated her people, the text inflamed the audience, all fashionably pro-Greek, to riotous acclamation. Rossini had so slaved over the score, a rewriting of *Maometto II,* as practically to have composed a new opera. Already he had seen that he must adapt his Italian style somewhat for French performers. *Le Siège de Corinthe,* therefore, takes some steps toward a simpler, more direct emotional line; though as big as *Semiramide,* it is far less elaborate.[16]

In *Le Siège de Corinthe,* Rossini had capitalized, doubtless deliberately, on a political vogue. In *Moïse et Pharaon, ou Le Passage de la Mer Rouge,* a rewriting of *Mosè in Egitto,* he dealt with subject matter that was dramatic enough but forbidding in character. The original *Mosè* had been received well in Paris: *Moïse* became Rossini's most signal French success.[17] Adolphe Nourrit and Laure Cinti-Damoreau, the tenor and

[15] Twenty-four days earlier, a typical Rossini pastiche not of his own baking had been served at the Odéon. Called *Ivanhoé,* and thus reflecting again the widespread popularity of Scott, it contained music from *La Gazza ladra, Mosè in Egitto, Tancredi,* and *Semiramide.* An Italian composer, Antonio Pacini, had adapted this hodgepodge to a libretto by two Frenchmen. *Ivanhoé*—such were the oblivious customs of the period—was translated into English as *The Maid of Judah* and played in London, Dublin, New York, and Philadelphia. It was even sung at Coburg in German.

[16] Interestingly, Italian versions of *Le Siège de Corinthe* were fairly popular in Italy from about 1828 to 1867.

[17] In Italy from about 1830 on, *Mosè in Egitto* alternated in a confusing seesaw with an Italian version of *Moïse* usually identified simply as *Mosè nuovo.*

soprano who had been cheered at the *première* of *Le Siège de Corinthe,*
and Nicolas Levasseur, a much-admired bass, were in the cast of *Moïse*
when it was first presented at the Opéra on March 26, 1827. The scenery
used in the Israelites' passage of the Red Sea (which was made of real
water) behaved unworthily, but the sneers and titters that momentarily
ran through the crowd were soon drowned in applause. Its four acts, with
their depressing text by Giuseppe Luigi Balocchi and Victor-Joseph
Étienne de Jouy, were not found to be too long.

Moïse established Rossini as a respected French composer. As if to
prove its Frenchness, it even had a ballet, the music of which he had
drawn in part from his *Armida,* which alone of his Italian operas has a
ballet. But in the French version, as in the Italian, the mighty choruses,
particularly the prayer, became the opera's chief attractions for the
public. Their almost Handelian largeness and strength, along with the
Biblical theme, were responsible for the opera's strange fortune in England and the United States, where it reigned for many years as a favorite
oratorio.[18] Balzac judged *Moïse* to be "a tremendous poem in music,"
and from the Conservatoire the usually frosty Cherubini sent down word
that he was pleasantly surprised.

Moïse was nothing if not solemn, but Rossini was not fatally altered.
At heart still the *farceur,* he followed his Biblical giant with a delicate,
somewhat naughty shaft of wit. *Le Comte Ory* (Opéra, August 20,
1828), written around a featherbrained legend only half whipped into
shape by a pair of librettists (Charles-Gaspard Delestre-Poirson and
Eugène Scribe, the latter the most quenchless French librettist of
the nineteenth century and one of the founders of French grand opera),
was a palpable hit. Considering that the score of *Le Comte Ory* consists
of most of the score of *Il Viaggio a Reims,* plus twelve new numbers, it is,
not surprisingly, not another *Barbiere* (and it would certainly have scandalized Beethoven). Where the earlier opera is brilliant and brisk, *Le
Comte Ory* is elegant and graceful. In *Il Barbiere* there is much shaking
with laughter; the French comedy more often contents itself with knowing smiles, arch slyness, and sheer musical cleverness. It has attractions

---

[18] To meet the English censors' requirement that no Biblical personages be
represented in the theater, *Moïse*'s Italian ancestor already had suffered comic
misadventures, emerging first as an opera about Peter the Hermit and later, with
infusions of Handel, as an oratorio called *The Israelites in Egypt*—which may
help to explain why, after visiting England, Rossini decided to become a Frenchman.

that cry out for revival—a cry that has only since World War II begun to be answered, notably at Glyndebourne.

Le Comte Ory was an enthusiasm of that leading non-Rossinian, Hector Berlioz, and rightly so. No opera of Rossini's contains more delightful music, a fact long hidden because the Italians, who until recently were allowed almost exclusive purveyorship of Rossini, never took to it. Also, its libretto, swift and funny for an act and a half, then collapses into banal sentimentality. Berlioz said an apposite thing when he wrote that *Le Comte Ory* "forms a collection of diverse beauties which, if divided up ingeniously, would suffice to make the fortune of not one, but two or three operas." Its high spot is unquestionably the second-act trio, "A la faveure de cette nuit obscure," of which Francis Toye said: "For loveliness of melody, originality of harmony, charm of part-writing, it is beyond praise, worthy of Mozart at his best."

French comic-opera composers, notably Offenbach, Lecocq, and Auber, did homage to *Le Comte Ory* by borrowing its very atmosphere, just as Rossini had taken hints for it from their predecessors Grétry, Hérold, and particularly Boieldieu, whose influential *La Dame blanche* (an opera that Georges Bizet came to hate with almost monomaniacal violence) had been produced only three years earlier than *Le Comte Ory*. Should an impresario ever succeed again in gathering together the kind of French company that made Oscar Hammerstein's Manhattan Opera House one of the brightest memories of opera in America, he should remember that a whole repertoire lies at his disposal, among the first items of which might well be Rossini's *Le Comte Ory*.

For his next opera, which turned out to be his last, Rossini mustered all his strength to create an overwhelming masterpiece—a grand opera on a heroic scale. He had proved himself a master of music; now he aspired to be a doctor of music as well. Toward his degree, he wrote a dissertation entitled *Guillaume Tell*. His reward was that critics applauded rapturously while the people listened with respect. He produced a four-act compendium of grand-operatic resourcefulness which became as famous—and about one-fiftieth as popular—as *Il Barbiere di Siviglia*. *Tell* has exerted a big influence, but is in itself regarded as a magnificent embarrassment. It excites admiration: it is obviously serious, even sincere. Its proportions mark out a certain grandeur and its characters are evoked with painstakingly achieved psychological verisimilitude. It marks another big step toward the symphonization (which many would call the degradation) of opera. It closely foreshadows Wagner's special way of using the leitmotiv. And, with Auber's *La Muette de Portici,*[19] it marked the true birth, after some false labor, of French grand opera—which Richard Wagner was to interpret as opera's last development before the advent of his own "music drama." Yes, *Guillaume Tell* excites admiration; in part, however, it also excites profound boredom.

One of *Guillaume Tell*'s handicaps was the disparity between its great length and its contents: in 1856, when the directors of the Opéra staged an uncut performance of it, the unsuccessful experiment cost each member of the audience six hours. Yet, critical acclaim had kept it intact through fifty-six performances during the season of its *première* (Opéra, August 3, 1829). A fine cast, with whose principals—Cinti-Damoreau (Mathilde), Nourrit (Arnold), Levasseur (Walter), and Henry Bernard Dabadie (Tell)—Rossini had already worked, had helped to get the opera off to a running start. Records show that *Guillaume Tell* had been performed at the Opéra 868 times up to 1912; but that tells only part of the history. After the first season, drastic cuts were made in it. The acts were telescoped or dropped one by one, until the result was truncated beyond recognition. Nothing but the overture and Act II remained at last, and they were used to raise the curtain on other, less lengthy works. Outside France, the fortunes of *Tell* have been mediocre, though dozens of cities have at one time or another staged one or another version of it in every language from Italian and German to Swedish and Slovenian. Nothing seems to win it a lasting public.

The four acts of *Guillaume Tell* contain enough fine music for an absorbing three-acter. Unfortunately, the music is wedded to an adaptation

[19] Historically, *La Muette de Portici* (1828), which is as well known under the title of its Italian incarnation, *Masaniello,* can claim a more important role than *Guillaume Tell,* which it antedated by more than one year and a half. By a curious coincidence, Daniel-François-Esprit Auber was, like Rossini, chiefly a composer of comic opera. Like *Tell,* too, *La Muette* is very long (five acts) and is based on the political struggles of an oppressed people—Neapolitans this time. Musically, it is greatly inferior to *Tell;* scenically, it looks forward to Meyerbeer's gorgeous ceremonial pageants. Besides having a leading lady who is a mute, it is a tissue of improbabilities. It ends, as Edward J. Dent observed, with the heroine's leap "from the balcony of the royal palace at Naples into the crater of Vesuvius, a distance of some eight or nine miles." A performance of *La Muette* at Brussels in 1830 served as the tocsin to set off the Belgians' rebellion against the suzerainty of Holland. In one of the few modern performances of the opera in America—at the Lexington Theater, New York, on October 25, 1915—Anna Pavlova was the dumb girl, a role that she later portrayed in a spectacular motion picture.

(by Victor-Joseph Étienne de Jouy and Hippolyte-Louis-Florent Bis) of Schiller's *Wilhelm Tell* which is cast iron in its intractability and listless in its undramatic verbosity. If Rossini had hoped to arouse enthusiasm by depicting the heroism of a suffering people, and thus repeat the success of *Le Siège de Corinthe,* his librettists failed him. Wherever they squeezed an ounce of drama from a situation, the shrewd Italian blew it up musically into a pound. His handling of the gathering of the cantons in Act II is somehow epic; something about these choruses calls to mind the bigger, differently styled, but scarcely more impressive ceremonials in Meyerbeer and Wagner. "Sombre forêt" has palpable atmosphere, almost as delicately sensed as if Weber had composed it. The trio sung by Arnold, Tell, and Walter ("Quand l'Helvétie") is strenuous, male, and convincing. Tell's third-act prayer ("Je te bénis . . . Sois immobile") and Arnold's lyric "Asile héréditaire" in Act IV are other genuine excellences.

Most famous of all, of course, is the ever-popular overture, which has no thematic relation to the much-cut version of *Tell* now occasionally heard. In it, Rossini propounded the best-known of the many examples of "crescendo à la Rossini," his special—and effective—way of cumulating excitement by simultaneously quickening tempo and increasing loudness. Performed by a great orchestra under a sensitive conductor, the overture remains a thrilling and dramatic experience, program music standing midway between the "Pastoral" Symphony of Beethoven and the "Scotch" Symphony of Mendelssohn, the overtures of Berlioz, and countless pages of Wagner.

Guillaume Tell ended Rossini's career as an opera composer. The reasons for his succeeding forty years of aloofness from the stage remain guesswork. What is certain is that he is unique in the annals of music in giving up voluntarily while still the all but unchallenged ruler of a rich empire. Rossini's knowledge of that empire was total: he had devoted nineteen years of genius and exceedingly active effort to making it so. The instruments of his success were unmistakable: an unsurpassed sense of the theater, based on native flair and on experiences in the leading opera houses of Europe; a comprehensive musicianship as much at ease with the orchestra as with the voice; a detective's nose for ferreting out new talent; and managerial tact and astuteness. To these essentials he had added tempered audacity in innovation; unceasing melodic inventiveness; taste and elegance not so infallible as his most ardent admirers might have wished him to have, but of combined strength and delicacy when in full play; and—to leave the best to the last—a wit broader and more robust than Mozart's, but quite as resilient and accessible.

Considering the road that Rossini traveled from *La Cambiale di matrimonio* toward *Guillaume Tell* and the milestones that he set up along it, his nineteen active operatic years appear not brief, but extraordinarily long. This progress was not to be predicted on the basis of *La Cambiale* and the other works of his minority, but it will not seem miraculous if we remember that Rossini was a considerable genius who traveled widely in Europe and reacted, despite his pretended laziness, to all the aesthetic forces operative in his time. In *opera buffa* he found an idiom of his own almost at once, and in this idiom, which he indeed made unique, he changed least—though *Le Comte Ory* has a new tang, perhaps because *opéra-bouffe* is never precisely *opera buffa*.

Change was more marked in Rossini's *opere serie*. His earlier examples are static historical charades, eighteenth-century carry-overs that would have left him (like the pre-*Orfeo* Gluck) less than half alive as an enduring composer—and even that only in a detailed musical encyclopedia. But just as his childish ears had been exposed to Jommelli, Pergolesi, and Paisiello, so he later heard Mozart, Haydn, Beethoven, and Weber. The result was that his last operas taught much to Bellini and Donizetti and reached hailing distance of Verdi; his French operas became a school for Meyerbeer, Auber, and Offenbach. In atmosphere and texture they are romantic through and through; only at times does the melodic contour betray their classic origins. In the end, as this Italian reacted more and more to French influences, he came to regard himself almost as a French composer. As a matter of fact, Rossini, unlike the German Meyerbeer—who cherished an illusion of successfully achieved Gallicization, but remained a cosmopolitan—was always deliciously and completely Italian no matter what foreign languages he learned to speak and to speak well.

CHAPTER IX

Bellini and Donizetti

UNTIL modern times, the art of singing was practiced at its best by special virtuosos, the *castrati,* both sopranos and contraltos, many of whom later became great singing teachers," Teodoro Celli has written. "They were masters of the *stile fiorito,* the flowery style . . . in which melodic lines were ornamented with embellishments—roulades, arpeggios, fragments of scales, mordents, single and double appoggiaturas, chromatic runs, trills—all of which light sopranos perform even today, though only in one (the 'coloratura') incarnation. Precisely because of those embellishments, the style based on them was called *bel canto.* It remains one of the glories of Italian art because of the masterworks that it elicited from so many composers." Without serious rivals among those composers were Rossini, Bellini, and Donizetti.

Earlier Italian composers had borrowed little from the operatic manners of neighboring nations. Many of them traveled, tending not only to preserve their own national traits jealously, but also to Italianize music in the countries in which they worked. With the exception of Lully, who went to France at an early and impressionable age, and of such Neapolitans as Jommelli, Sacchini, and Traetta, they remained Italians abroad or on their native soil. Foreign musicians visited Italy at the risk of becoming as Italian as their hosts. Handel, Hasse, Gluck, Mozart—all succumbed for a time or forever to the lure of that disorderly and poverty-stricken land, rich only in history, sunlight, song, and color. Beethoven and Weber did not take the Italian tour, and so hit upon new, genuinely German styles of operatic writing.

Rossini was the most important Italian musician to be influenced by foreign styles since the contrapuntalists had borrowed polyphonic gambits from the Flemings. His last development was toward further orchestral weight in opera—toward Beethoven, that is; and this Parisian Italian lived long enough to regret not having had an academic start in Germany. "For," as he said disarmingly to Wagner, "I had some talent and a certain intuition." Although he had effected wide changes in the operatic pattern, it may not have seemed so to this bewigged, gently acidulous old man, so quickly had Meyerbeer stepped in to take the reins in France, so completely had Rossini's own countrymen gone on being unregenerately Italian. They accepted him as *papà,* but not as *père.* To a less realistic man than Gioacchino Rossini it might have been humiliating that his Italian disciples, from Bellini through Donizetti and the younger Verdi, owed little or nothing to the thoughtful works of his maturity and far too much to those somewhat stereotyped *opere serie* and heedless *buffo* pieces of his nonage. At times it seemed that all they wanted from him was his melodic stintlessness, understanding of the voice, and elegance of ornamentation—and he knew that more than these should go into the making of an opera.

When Rossini was a great man in the French capital, wielding an influence comparable to Cherubini's at the Conservatoire, he did everything he could to help along the chances there of his most talented compatriots. He paved the way effectually for Giuseppe Mercadante, and that prolific composer of some sixty operas (more than Rossini himself composed) died a member of the Académie des beaux-arts. More important to the story of opera was his sponsoring of Bellini and Donizetti. The way he chivvied Bellini about the weakness of his orchestration (in 1834, however, when it was all but too late, with the culprit about to die) proves that he was not content merely with luring his protégés to Paris. He wanted them to see things his way. Fortunately, his method of persuading—with Bellini, in any case—was of the gentlest. Rossini's usual public manner, compounded of wit, *brusquerie,* and sarcasm, might have paralyzed the delicate, oversensitive young Sicilian.

The problem of giving advice to Bellini was a difficult one for several reasons. Having heard that Rossini was cynical and grasping, he was inclined to suspect his motives. Rossini, on his part, thought that Bellini had regressed since his third opera, *Il Pirata* (1827), in the direction of untoward simplicity. That Bellini came not only to trust but eventually to worship Rossini, even doctoring his last opera, *I Puritani,* according to Rossini's prescriptions, is a tribute to the older man's diplomacy and a gauge of what the young musical talents lost when, in 1836, their generous mentor fled from the artistic capital of the world to seek temporary retirement in an Italian provincial town.

In viewing the history of opera, as in viewing the history of music in general, we are too used to allowing certain imposing figures, some great, others not great, to usurp the stage. In the opera of the first half of the nineteenth century, Weber, Rossini, and Meyerbeer bulk so large that other composers seem to have huddled in the background, so many shadowy supernumeraries. No view could be more false. During those five decades, those eminent shapers of operatic destiny had as their associates such men—each of real significance in the unfolding chronicle of the art—as Marschner, Cherubini, Spontini, Boieldieu, Bellini, Donizetti, and Auber. But it is our own place in history which makes them seem obscure. In their own days they were great men, worthy and feared rivals of the giants who have made the most noise in the history books. Furthermore, two of them, Cherubini and Spontini, were veritably worshiped, and Rossini, even at the height of his prestige, never equaled the dictatorial license that Spontini was encouraged to indulge. If active survival of several operas by Weber, Rossini, and Meyerbeer could be contrasted with complete disappearance of other men from the active repertoire, then the myopia of history might at least be explained rationally. But the fact is that only one opera by Rossini and one by Donizetti belong among the perennial popular favorites. The historian has the unhappy habit of giving space to men in proportion to their influence on the future of their art.

Bellini, who had little influence on the history of opera in the most limited sense, and so is dismissed with a few lines in most modern textbooks, bulked very large indeed from the 1830's on. His influence was exerted on singing and on the history of music in general. More than any other composer, more even than Rossini or Donizetti, he summed up and extravagantly displayed a style of singing which became first impossible and then unfashionable—or vice versa—and which has begun to be revived only in recent decades. *Bel canto,* literally "beautiful song," is a phrase susceptible to many interpretations. The style relies primarily on agility, accuracy, and variety of timbre in music rich in embellishments; at its finest, it achieves dramatic projection through them. It is partial to long passages of simple, affecting melody alternating with outbursts of vocal scrollwork,[1] the latter often inserted for no better reason

[1] This partiality explains the very common occurrence in *bel canto* operas of the double aria—the slow, melodious cavatina followed by the rapid, difficult cabaletta.

than that they illustrate the essence of *bel canto* itself. *Bel canto* really makes the voice a wind instrument. Its perfect practitioners have always made sounds of quite unearthly beauty, moving the listener quite as a miracle would move him, so well do they do something that it seems superhuman or inhuman to do at all. Whether *bel canto* disappeared because people grew tired of it or because its foremost practitioners fell off in everything but weight is a question. What is certain is that it did temporarily disappear, and with it a formidable part of Bellini's reputation. And the dramas on which the later Verdi and his Italian and French contemporaries based their operas of high romanticism called for—and called forth—an entirely different style of composition and singing.

Bellini has had his revenge. A melodist of genius, he introduced into music an atmosphere that was quickly imitated by his contemporaries, became an easy adjunct with the next generation, and still echoes, sometimes in the least likely places, throughout the world. What was that atmosphere? A hushed, neurotic ecstasy, a sort of gently languorous orgasm in moonlit, bloom-pervaded gardens. Long before Verlaine, it was always in Bellini's heart. Chopin heard it, and it is the very stuff of his sulphurous, elegant nocturnes.[2] Thereafter, almost immediately, began its degradation and cheapening. Liszt sobbed out his player's heart to the tune of unsuccessful simulacra of these long, singing melodies, these throaty cantilenas with their heartbreaks stabbed out in exacerbating repetitions of the same torturing tone. After Liszt, the Bellinian melody proliferated like a cancer, and found its way into the creative language of even the most austere composers. It was not only the Rubinsteins and Alabievs and Massenets who succumbed to it: you can hear it in Brahms, Wagner, Tchaikovsky, and Debussy, glinting out like fool's gold from its less showy matrix. One whiff of this Sicilian perfume, and—

> *My heart aches, and a drowsy numbness pains*
> *My sense, as though of hemlock I had drunk,*
> *Or emptied some dull opiate to the drains*
> *One minute past, and Lethe-wards had sunk . . .*

Thus Keats, Bellini's senior by only six years, after listening to a nightingale. To quote what Alabiev did after listening to Bellini would not be kind. Anyhow, with the debasing of his most characteristic and original note into the linked sweetness of dinner music long drawn out, an-

[2] Needless to say, perhaps, its presence in performances of most of Chopin's other pieces was no part of his intention.

other part of Bellini's reputation was erased, further proof that reputation has little relation to influence.

The frail Bellini was always able to find backers. Born of relatively poor parents in a Sicilian town, he found patrons there to send him through music school in Naples. There the noted Nicola Zingarelli, whose pert, lightsome songs still are occasionally heard, guided his talent for easy melody and sentimental phrase. At Carnival time of 1825, when Bellini was twenty-two years old, the same Barbaia who had furthered Rossini's career and had given *Euryanthe* to an ungrateful Vienna heard the young man's first opera, a school exercise, which was presented in the theater of the Conservatorio San Sebastiano at Naples. It was made possible for his first professional opera, *Bianca e Gernando,*[3] to be given at the Teatro San Carlo in 1826 (in revised form, and with the hero Fernando once more, it was to open Genoa's new Teatro Carlo Felice on April 7, 1828). It was successful enough to stimulate Barbaia into ordering another opera and to cure at once any feeling of unprofessionalism which Bellini might have had. His luck held: the librettist whom he found was Felice Romani, the best in Italy, who was to supply the texts of all but the last of the eight operas that he would compose over the next decade. And the cast for the *première* of *Il Pirata* at La Scala, Milan, on October 27, 1827, included the golden-voiced Giovanni Battista Rubini and Henriette-Clémentine Méric-Lalande, a popular French soprano. *Il Pirata* was a genuine hit. Bellini's fame spread beyond Italy when it was heard within five years in Vienna, Dresden, London, Madrid, Paris, and New York. Also, Rossini tendered his compliments.

Because three of Bellini's four last operas are the only ones we have been at all likely to hear, the others have been reduced to little more than their titles. But remarkably gifted casts gained for most of them a measure of success. For instance, when *La Straniera* was first sung at La Scala on February 14, 1829, with a cast including Caroline Unger, Méric-Lalande, and Tamburini, Bellini was called to the stage thirty times. On the other hand, when *Zaïra* was sung at the opening of Parma's new Teatro Ducale on May 16 of that same year, with Méric-Lalande and Lablache, but with the two other leading roles in inept hands, it was unsuccessful, dragging through eight performances and then never being heard again. This taught Bellini that a man's career cannot be entrusted

[3] *Gernando* is not a misprint: originally called Fernando, the character had to be renamed because the heir apparent to Francis I, King of the Two Sicilies, was called Fernando.

to incompetent throats: thereafter, he stipulated in his contracts the singers to be assigned to the leading roles—and never failed completely again.

This partial usurpation of what had been regarded as the manager's role marks an important development in the production of opera. The composer has now become so important that the opera house wanting the prestige of a *première* must accede to his demands that full justice be done to his work. And the singer's tyranny has become a legitimate one: he no longer dictates to the composer, but has been moved to his (and her) proper place on the auction block, a precious something on whose best efforts the success of an opera largely depends.

Bellini's next hit, first heard at Venice's Teatro La Fenice on March 11, 1830, was a Shakespearean opera, *I Capuletti ed I Montecchi,* to a Romani libretto that Niccolò Vaccai had set for the Milanese as *Giulietta e Romeo* five years before.[4] This opera had a curious history. First, Bellini had worked into its score parts of the ruins of his unhappy *Zaïra.* And then, beginning in 1832, *I Capuletti ed I Montecchi* began to be mutilated, its last act being replaced by that of Vaccai's *Giulietta e Romeo.* But the opera has never fallen entirely out of the repertoire in Italy, and toward the end of the nineteenth century Bellini's own last act was restored to it in performance.

Late in 1830 it happened that the Teatro Carcano at Milan had a fine group of singers at its disposition. Unwilling to waste such good fortune, the directors commissioned an opera apiece from Bellini and Donizetti. Fatefully for the future of a seventeen-year-old peasant boy named Giuseppe Verdi, the censor stepped in and forbade Bellini to finish his setting of a Romani libretto based on Victor Hugo's *Hernani:* the subject was too hot for a Europe suffering one of its periodic spasms of revolution. So Romani, who was supplying Donizetti with a safe biography of Anne Boleyn, gave Bellini an even safer one about the tragicomic vicissitudes of a female sleepwalker. Henry VIII's addlepated queen reached the stage, as *Anna Bolena,* on December 26, 1830, three months before *La Sonnambula.* Although Donizetti's opera was the first to win him a

[4] When Bellini had not yet been born, his future teacher Zingarelli had, in 1796, composed a *Giulietta e Romeo* for La Scala. But even that had not been the beginning of the operatic career of the Veronese lovers: in 1793 Daniel Steibelt had composed in French, for the Théâtre Feydeau, Paris, a *Roméo et Juliette* that warrants mention in books on orchestration, being said to have been the first opera calling for a Chinese gong.

reputation outside Italy, Bellini scored heavily over his much more practiced rival. When Pasta and Rubini finished their performance of *La
Sonnambula* on March 6, 1831, they had launched one of the most
nearly indestructible masterpieces of the florid style and had been first
to sign a register that was to contain the names of the greatest sopranos
and tenors of many ensuing decades.

The really tremendous vogue once enjoyed by *La Sonnambula*—it was,
for example, the first serious opera to be heard in Chicago (July 29,
1850)—is easy to understand. A brief musical story, notable for its un-
willingness to spin itself out to irrelevant lengths, this little opera is primarily a delightful entertainment. The well-constructed, uninvolved, if
(to the skeptic and sometimes ribald modern mind) rather silly, libretto
was exactly right for the effusions of Bellini's muse: it offered simple
situations, obvious emotions, strong contrasts. Of them Bellini made the
most, unless realism be considered a *sine qua non* of "the most," which
it certainly was not in 1831. *La Sonnambula* is as romantic as *Der Freischütz,* but its romanticism is Italian, delicately tinted by what was doubtless a superficial acquaintance with the current fashions in European literature. An idyllic, positively sentimental note here can be traced to
that faded chronicler of a hopeless love, Bernardin de Saint-Pierre.

This idyllic note, miscalled "elegiac," was then Bellini's peculiar forte,
and he illustrated it in *La Sonnambula* with melodies such as never had
been heard before—melodies that seem at their most characteristic here
because here they are in their purest form. The line of Amina's song in
"Ah! non credea" is impeccable in draftsmanship and is traced in silver-
point. It is utterly irresistible even when sketched out in a piano's faulty
legato, and something inexpressibly better when sung by a great soprano.
The ending of this aria illustrates one of Bellini's (and *bel canto*'s)
strengths: when Amina begins to warble whole cascades of embellishments, these *fioriture* seem to rise inevitably as the only possible resolution of the built-up emotion. Compare this cavatina with the more showy,
almost Rossinian cabaletta that follows soon after—the famous rondo
"Ah! non giunge"—and judge what was Bellini's special métier.

The *réclame* Bellini reaped because of *La Sonnambula* brought him
a new commission from La Scala. This time the fecund Romani turned
to the Gallic Druids to spin a libretto that Schopenhauer, usually a man
of stern common sense, called the best in existence. *Norma* was constructed with loving care and provided with exactly the richly pathetic
scenes to set Bellini's pen to sighing. Late in 1831, the score was ready.

On December 26, at La Scala, it was staged with the kind of cast which Bellini demanded. Pasta (who only a little more than nine months earlier had created the part of Amina in *La Sonnambula*) sang the tragic priestess Norma, Giulia Grisi the Adalgisa, and Domenico Donzelli the Roman proconsul and deceiver Pollione. At the *première, Norma* failed utterly and without qualification. But not Bellini's luck: his expensive cast and the Scala management rallied to him, confident that the opera had the stuff of which successes are made. They played it until it succeeded— and at last it succeeded so well that in fame and staying power it has outstripped Bellini's other operas.

Norma is as dramatic as *La Sonnambula* is undramatic. Further, Romani's libretto is more theatrically dramatic than Bellini's music. Despite the multiple beauties of the score, the story would better have suited Verdi's vigorous genius—the musical line does not always sound germane to the romantic violence of the book. It has been said that Bellini was weakest when not composing arias. The overture to *Norma* is an example of his moments of noninspiration: melodramatic and banal claptrap, it is quite unsuited to the tragedy it preludes. Nor can the construction of the opera be called altogether craftsmanlike: the country along the road between arias and ensemble numbers remains remarkable for its intemperate listlessness. Although not boiled down to a formula, these dull musical turnpikes are as boring as the most formula-ridden passagework. If *Norma* did not contain its few great arias and affecting duets, it would surely yield its stubborn fragments of popularity to *La Sonnambula,* which is, on the whole, far more rewarding to listen to today.

But *Norma* has "Casta diva," that miraculous exercise in the *bel canto* balance between suavity and florid vocal tracery. And after "Casta diva"—it comes early in the opera—a few other luscious numbers hold us in our seats until the end. One is the second-act duet for Norma and Adalgisa, "Mira, o Norma." Another is the fine bass aria with chorus, "Ah! del Tebro." It would be a mistake to pretend that these ripe, expressive melodies are cleverly spaced: even in his shrewdest score, Bellini seldom gives the feeling of conscious dramatic competence. More, he often appears to have lacked intention and foresight as those qualities are translated by a master of drama. Bellini was, in his way, a force of nature, however minor. "Casta diva" is a wonderfully flowing lyric. But lyrics alone do not make an opera—if they could, Franz Schubert's operas would not have been stillborn. Only the magical singing of a Rosa Ponselle at the height of her powers or the intense personal drama of a Maria

Callas can do for *Norma* what Romani must have had in mind when he penned its libretto—make it into a deeply stirring human drama.

For all practical purposes, *Norma* was the last but one of Bellini's operas. True, he composed two more stage works. But *Beatrice di Tenda* (La Fenice, Venice, 1833) suffered from a libretto that Bellini had found uninspiring. The second, however, though it reached the stage and went on to equal *Norma* in renown, was even more a curiosity than the other two. This was *I Puritani di Scozia,* whose librettist, Count Carlo Pepoli, justified its title by boldly locating Plymouth in Scotland. *I Puritani* was a departure for Bellini in another sense: it was not for Italy, but for Paris. Rossini had persuaded the Théâtre-Italien to commission it, and his presence in France had helped Bellini to decide upon settling there.

While Bellini was composing *I Puritani,* Rossini was clucking around his protégé like a stout hen around a scrawny chick. Not only did he make suggestions in general, but he also criticized the music page by page, line by line. Bellini was suspicious of this mothering at first, having heard that the Swan of Pesaro was devoid of the softer parental emotions. But he was already under the spell of the composer of *Guillaume Tell*— which, after twelve hearings, he was comparing to *La Divina Commedia.* Then Rossini the social genius got him. In short, Bellini capitulated, and for the remaining months of his brief life loved his new friend without qualification. Finally, he fell so much under the spell that when *I Puritani* was produced at the Théâtre-Italien on January 25, 1835, it was almost as much Rossini's last opera as Bellini's. The master's touch is evident mainly in the strong, earnestly worked-out orchestration and in the brevity of the *longueurs* between arias and ensemble numbers. Finally, *I Puritani* contains two bass roles, one of them the weightiest that Bellini ever composed.

Literally nothing else was so important about *I Puritani* as its original cast, particularly the four principal singers for whom Bellini had designed it. First of these was Giulia Grisi, the Elvira. Next was Rubini, the Arturo, who was responsible both for the pristine fame of the opera and for the almost complete desuetude into which it fell for a long time after he retired from the stage. For Rubini boasted, besides his famous shake, a voice of phenomenal range, from bass E to treble B—three octaves and a half with ease, and more on occasion. Arturo's *tessitura* therefore lies very high, and the role—and the opera—practically died with Rubini: to sing Arturo, the average tenor must indulge in a lot of falsetto squeaking—or beg for transposition. Third in the cast was Tamburini, the Riccardo. Luigi Lablache, the greatest bass of the age, who had been chosen for the honor of singing in the Mozart Requiem at both Haydn's funeral and Beethoven's,[5] was the Giorgio, rounding out what came to be called the "Puritani Quartet." For years they toured Europe, and every operatic composer dreamed of writing for them. Even after Rubini was replaced by Mario, the Quartet survived, just as famous as ever; for it, in 1834, Donizetti composed *Don Pasquale*.

The almost complete disappearance of *I Puritani* from most opera houses is regrettable. It has a flimsy book, and parts of it often have to be transposed into odd keys in order to be sung at all. But it is, if not Bellini's most characteristic music, his most mature and dramatic. It has not only passages of real musical characterization, but also a vigor lacking in long stretches of *La Sonnambula* and *Norma*. Elvira's Mad Scene in Act II (she has another in Act III [6])—with its affecting opening lines, sung offstage, "O rendetemi la speme, o lasciatemi morire"—requires only a willingly achieved suspension of disbelief to be marvelously touching. It culminates in "Qui la voce," which has been called the most sheerly beautiful aria ever composed (it is also the most Scottish thing in the score, bearing a fleeting resemblance to the tune of "Annie Laurie"). Surely "Qui la voce" is musically on a much higher level than the languorous waltz to which Lucia loses her mind. Elvira, too, in the Rossinian "Son vergin vezzosa," shows herself a girl of spirit. The ensemble finale, with principals and chorus (for *I Puritani* is *melodramma serio,* not *tragedia lirica,* for which reason the hero and heroine are alive at the end), is a strong, vivacious essay at part-writing, an indication that the dying Bellini had untouched reserves of creative strength.

Bellini had not yet said his complete say when he died, aged thirty-three, eight months after the *première* of *I Puritani*. Had he lived, he might have deflected somewhat the stream of operatic development in France.

Bellini became more spectacular dead than he had been alive. His funeral was stage-managed by four composers, with Cherubini and Rossini at their head. A special musical department, presided over by that audacious orchestral conductor of generous impulse and uncertain tempo,

---

[5] He was not singing bass on both occasions. On the earlier one (1809), he was a boy contralto.

[6] It was the year for mad scenes: *Lucia di Lammermoor* came only nine months later.

François-Antoine Habeneck, arranged a unique funeral service: part of the Requiem was sung to a melody from *I Puritani,* the executants being the Russian tenor Nicholas Ivanoff and three-quarters of the Puritani Quartet—Lablache, Rubini, and Tamburini.

Bellini's death and Rossini's continuing abstention from the stage left the commanding position in the field of Italian opera to the copious Donizetti. The least obviously original of the three, Donizetti provided a stylistic link between them and the young, rapidly maturing Verdi of *Ernani* and *Luisa Miller.* With many touches of Rossini's verve and grace, Bellini's *bel canto* and languid suavity, and even Verdi's urgent realism, Donizetti lacked a quickly recognizable strong musical personality of his own. He was a virtuoso composer and did not avoid altogether displaying the virtuoso's common defects. In the space of about twenty-six years, he composed nearly seventy operas (some of them, to be sure, one-act frivolities). A surprisingly high percentage of them contains beautifully expressive writing, but many of them have little dramatic coherence. He once composed a one-acter (*Il Campanello di notte,* 1836) in nine days; the last act of *La Favorite,* one of his most successful scores, was spun off in a few hours.

That the results of this slapdash haste are not seventy masterworks, that many of Donizetti's operas are marred by feeble passagework, drearily monotonous accompaniments, grateful acceptance of whatever occurred to him, is not surprising. He held in good-natured contempt anyone who worked more deliberately than he did. When he was told that Rossini had composed *Il Barbiere di Siviglia* in thirteen days, he commented: "Why not? He's so lazy." In this he was the opposite of Bellini, who once wrote to Giovanni Ricordi, his publisher, to demand firmly but politely four times the usual fee for an opera, his reason being that he composed only one opera while other men wrote four (he probably meant Donizetti, of whom he was inclined to be icily contemptuous).

Donizetti exaggerated the tendency, encouraged by Rossini, to look in almost any direction for a libretto. In Rossini this freedom of choice liberated an element of creativeness. Donizetti, inheriting it and laboring desperately to make money and assuage the unhappinesses of his tragic life, construed it as license to accept any book. Glancing over the astonishing list of his operas, one visualizes him poring over a terrestrial globe, suddenly darting down to fix a pin in some, to him, exotic spot, and thinking in triumph: "Here I shall erect another opera." In *La Regina di Golconda*—which, on May 12, 1828, became the first new opera to be heard at Genoa's five-week-old Teatro Carlo Felice—he reached India's coral strand; his closest approach to Greenland's icy mountains was Liverpool, which he celebrated in *Emilia di Liverpool* (1824), about an evidently not very fussy girl who dwelt in a hermitage there. From his titles alone comes evidence of interest in such other ill-assorted locales as Burgundy, Livonia, Granada, Saardam, Kenilworth, Calais, Rome, Foix, Paris, Castile, England, and Chamounix. The oddly titled *Otto Mesi in due ore* (*Eight Months in Two Hours*) was laid in Siberia. Did *Il Diluvio universale* (*The Universal Deluge,* 1830) end on Ararat? In any case, these operas are a very far cry from Greek and Roman myth, the subject matter of the earliest operas, and nearly as far from the heroic exploits, historic and pseudohistoric, of *opera seria.* Rossini had opened a Pandora's box when he had turned to Shakespeare, Scott, and actual modern history for the books to display his musical inventiveness. The last ill doubtless still lies in that box. Since Paul Hindemith dramatized a daily news report in *Neues vom Tage,* all bets have been canceled.

The first thirty-four of Donizetti's operas, fruits of his labors from 1816 to 1830, have left little trace behind. Then, with his thirty-fifth opera, he rang the bell with *Anna Bolena,* with a libretto by Romani, first heard at Milan's Teatro Carcano on December 26, 1830. It was a bell destined to clang and clamor, tinkle and knell, through thirty-six more operas, and to echo and re-echo through every opera house in the world, but then to be dimmed and muffled until it began to be heard again more clearly in the 1940's and 1950's. It sometimes seemed a bell of impure alloy, but it often emitted a silver tone. Of the operas after *Anna Bolena, Lucia di Lammermoor* has remained a fixture steadily wherever opera has been given, and others have been returning gradually to life after hibernation.

The glory of *Anna Bolena* was dimmed, seemingly forever, with the disappearance of the great trio that sang it in its abounding youth: Pasta as Anne Boleyn, Rubini as Percy, Lablache as Henry VIII. But it unexpectedly took a new lease on life at La Scala, Milan, during the 1956–57 season when its splendid revival with Maria Callas as Anne Boleyn and Giulietta Simionato as Jane Seymour proved that it was, both musically and dramatically, a very good opera indeed. To English-speaking audiences it will always present one surprise: in Act III occurs a close facsimile of the melody they always have known as "Home, Sweet Home." Will not every loyal Englishman and American swear that Sir Henry

Bishop, perpetrator of "Lo, Here the Gentle Lark," was the only fabricator of this most epidemic of heart songs? Where, then, did Donizetti get the tune he worked into *Anna Bolena?* Did he borrow it from Bishop, who years before appliquéing it to John Howard Payne's libretto in his opera *Clari, or The Maid of Milan* (1823) had both published it as a Sicilian folk melody and used it in another opera? Possibly it was exactly what Bishop at first had said that it was—a Sicilian folk melody—and not his own brain child, as he succeeded in establishing in a court of law —after it became famous.

Not so edifying in sentiment as "Home, Sweet Home," but musically more compelling, was the aria "Una furtiva lagrima," which made the fortune of the sparkling *buffo* score that Donizetti composed two years after *Anna Bolena.* This was *L'Elisir d'amore,* to another Romani text, first heard at the Teatro della Canobbiana, Milan, on May 12, 1832. Although it is inferior to *Don Pasquale* among Donizetti's comic operas (and scarcely the equal of *La Fille du régiment*), it is witty enough to demonstrate the sheen of Donizetti's wit. During parts of the early twentieth century it seemed more popular than any Donizetti opera but *Lucia,* in part because the role of Elvino (a tenor, who sings "Una furtiva lagrima") was a favorite with Enrico Caruso. He was singing it at the Brooklyn Academy of Music on December 11, 1920, when he was stricken with the pleurisy of which he died eight months later.

Within sixteen months of *L'Elisir,* Donizetti composed four operas of which not a measure has been heard across footlights for many decades. Then Romani supplied him with a viable, violent, grotesque, and— at that time—conventional twisting of the story of that now whitewashed Renaissance heroine Lucrezia Borgia. Even as operatic melodramas go, this absurd version of an absurd play by Victor Hugo was too full of corpses. Yet to it Donizetti wrote a series of delightful melodies, some of them quickening into genuine dramatic utterance. Only occasionally in *Lucrezia Borgia,* first heard at La Scala, Milan, on December 26, 1833, did Donizetti achieve the violent, convincing, melodramatic vitality that had marked *Anna Bolena* as something new, something we now recognize as a foretaste of Verdi. Yet most of these melodies are forgotten. There is one still-famed exception—a drinking song, or *brindisi,* sung by a contralto roughneck: it is even more charming, shallow, and lightheaded than the rest. It sounds just like something from a Savoy opera.

Five operas after *Lucrezia Borgia,* Donizetti created his most enduringly popular opera, *Lucia di Lammermoor* (Teatro San Carlo, September 26, 1835). As if anticipating its destined success, he shaped it specifically for two of the most notable star singers of the time, Fanny Persiani and Gilbert Duprez. For its libretto, a skeletonizing of Scott's *The Bride of Lammermoor,* he forsook Romani, the hero of a hundred texts, for Salvatore Cammarano, who eighteen years later was to provide Verdi with the libretto of *Il Trovatore. Lucia* triumphed immediately: the exhilaration of the stormy *première* sent the physically unstable Donizetti to bed with a fever. It raced through Europe like wildfire, reaching London on April 5, 1838, when Persiani and Rubini were the doomed lovers.

That *Lucia di Lammermoor* remains a popular fixture, in the class that also holds *Don Giovanni, Aïda, Carmen, Faust, Pagliacci, Cavalleria rusticana,* and the Wagner, Puccini, and Strauss favorites, at first seems astonishing. The libretto is unrelievedly gloomy and without distinction, as inferior to the novel from which it was taken as that novel is to the best of Scott. Good as much of the music is, it is not markedly better than that of many other Donizetti scores that have had no such enduring popularity. Present-day singers capable of executing faithfully its prodigious vocal difficulties while projecting the dramatic crises out of which they grow have not been numerous.

Lucia was for decades saved for perennial performance by two of its numbers, the Sextet and the Mad Scene. The first was in every operatic whistler's home and street repertoire; the second, however, is a mystery within a mystery: for all its fame, it would probably stump nine out of ten called upon to hum or sing it in a music-memory contest. But the score contains much more than those two warhorses. Many other musically and dramatically effective numbers are listened for by every hardened operagoer (who usually is eager to compare one singer's performance of them with another's). Lucia's cavatina, "Regnava nel silenzio," is a pensive, melancholy melody of Bellinian cast which truly characterizes Lucia, not least when it quickens into the inevitable cabaletta, the ecstatic "Quando rapita in estasi." Edgardo's final aria, "Fra poco a me ricovero," the climax of the anticlimactic final scene, gives almost Verdian expression to despair.

The Sextet, "Chi mi frena in tal momento," has been called the greatest ensemble number in Italian opera by people who have listened inattentively to the Quartet from *Rigoletto* and the closing Octet of *Falstaff,* to mention only two of its superiors. But it has much more than its catchiness and its way of going wild at the repeated climax in a burst of unrestrained florid grandeur. Such is its sweep that it seems as though the six personages involved had to get it out of their systems or burst. It cannot serve, as the *Rigoletto* Quartet can when properly sung, to add touches to the characters involved in singing it; but it does express passionate involvement and it is brimming with vitality. Hackneyed though it became, it has the indefinable something that convinces and endures.

Quite different is the Mad Scene, that long sketch for a bravura demonstration by a great singing actress. It is not a basket of fruity tunes; in its decorous, calculated pace, it completely lacks spontaneity. In the Mad Scene as usually performed, the florid soprano, who (like the florid alto, tenor, baritone, and bass) had threatened to unbalance opera from its very birth—and none the less when she had been a *castrato*—achieved her single-minded purpose. In that traditional performance, the already enfeebled action of *Lucia* halted for some fifteen minutes (usually punctuated with applause) for an exhibition of machinelike virtuosity which had small dramatic relevance and little more that was musical. As Paul England once described it in a witty *précis:* "The heroine now wanders on to the scene to show us that, whatever the state of her mind may be, she has her voice under perfect control." It is only when that soprano's voice, under perfect control, has been made the vehicle for a display of virtuoso characterization as well, tearing at the listener with understanding of a human mind going in and out of eclipse, that Donizetti's artistic wisdom has been justified.

Whatever one may think of overprolonging the Lesson Scene in *Il Barbiere di Siviglia,* at least the libretto provides against the chief absurdity by motivating the interruption of the action. Various composers of the nineteenth century, faced with the task of pleasing a star soprano, artificially used a "mad scene" as an excuse for allowing her to sing acres of *fioriture* that only an insane woman would think of singing, but that no insane woman would have the control to sing. Anna Bolena in Donizetti's opera and Imogene in Bellini's *Il Pirata* are notable examples. Commenting on this convention (which, like all similar conventions, could be turned to justified account by a good musical dramatist), H. Sutherland Edwards, an entertaining nineteenth-century writer on musical matters, wrote:

> The exceptional personage in serious opera is the light soprano who does *not* go mad—as, for instance, Gilda in *Rigoletto.* Martha, in the opera of that name, only abstains from becoming insane because

Lionel, the tenor, saves her the trouble by becoming insane in her place. Catherine, in *L'Étoile du nord,* is crazy from the beginning almost to the end of the third act; Dinorah is, throughout the opera to which she gives her name, as mad as the proverbial March hare, and she becomes madder still after the climax at the end of the second act —that critical juncture at which the reason of nine heroines, of the "light" order, out of ten gives way. The ordinary operatic heroine trusts in the first act, is deceived in the second, and goes mad in the third. She is without character, and is remembered not as an individual, but as a member of a large and uninteresting class of melodious lunatics.

In the four years following *Lucia,* Donizetti composed nine operas. Only a few of them retain glimmers of active life. In 1836, as already mentioned, he composed the one-act *Il Campanello di notte* in little more than one week, his philanthropic purpose being to provide a friendly impresario with the means of evading bankruptcy.[7] *Poliuto* (1840, but composed in 1838) induced a king of Naples (not of a witty race) to make a *mot.* Adolphe Nourrit, who was to sing it, had the reputation of being a radical, and Ferdinand II forbade the performance. Nourrit expostulated, explaining that Poliuto, despite his depraved-sounding name, was a saint. "Keep," thundered indignant majesty, "the saints in the calendar, and do not bring them on the stage." So Salvatore Cammarano's Italian libretto, based on Corneille's *Polyeucte,* had to be translated into French by Scribe; when the opera finally achieved performance at the Opéra in Paris, on April 10, 1840, it was no longer *Poliuto,* but *Les Martyrs.*[8]

Exactly the opposite fate befell Donizetti's next opera, *Le Duc d'Albe,* composed in part in 1839, but never completed. The original French libretto was by Scribe and Charles Duveyrier. After Donizetti's death, the opera was completed by a fellow Bergamasque, Matteo Salvi, to an Italian translation of the libretto by Angelo Zanardini. It was heard for

[7] During the 1830's, in which decade Donizetti brought forth no less than twenty-seven operas, he scarcely knew failure. Many of his operas that are now completely unknown won major successes throughout Europe and even in North and South America.

[8] As these lines were being written, La Scala, Milan, opened a season with a revival of *Poliuto* starring Maria Callas. It is never safe to pronounce a Donizetti opera completely dead.

the first time at the Teatro Apollo, Rome, on March 22, 1882. When it was revived as part of the Spoleto Festival of Two Worlds of 1959, the conductor, Thomas Schippers, tried to purify the score of everything not Donizetti's own—and the producer, Luchino Visconti, found some of the 1882 sets in a Rome warehouse and used them, refurbished, as the excelling backgrounds for this curiously Verdi-like opera.

Donizetti's tenth opera after *Lucia* had better luck. *La Fille du régiment,* produced at the Opéra-Comique, Paris, on February 11, 1840, was Donizetti's first produced opera to a French libretto, and it achieved such enduring popularity in Paris that by 1916 it had been sung there something like a thousand times. As *La Figlia del reggimento* it fared almost as well in Italy. And when Jenny Lind took it up, it became a favorite with the nice-thinking subjects of Queen Victoria, who were pleased to overlook the heroine's uncouthness in view of her moral rectitude. For *La Fille* is a miracle play: the *vivandière* Marie, though she swears like the troopers she has lived among, is, in her heart of hearts, pure Windsor Castle.

In whatever language sung, *La Fille* is so thin musically as to be more operetta than opera. It is not to be mentioned with *Don Pasquale,* Donizetti's comic masterpiece. What Mendelssohn might have produced if he had turned his undramatic mind seriously to opera may be surmised from his once having snubbed a group of musicians who were making fun of *La Fille,* saying pontifically: "I should like to have written that myself." Yet Marie the *vivandière* is never quite dead. A war fever is always likely to resurrect her. Singing this role during the early days of the American Civil War, Clara Louise Kellogg (who had learned to play the drum for the occasion) aroused a patriotic tempest. In her reminiscences she exults over the possibility that several young men may have joined up as a result of it.

Fifty-seven years later, three days after the signing of the Armistice that ended World War I, Frieda Hempel, singing the role of Marie at the Metropolitan, stepped out of her role twice, once to sing (why?) Proch's "Variations," once to sing, rather *en retard,* Ivor Novello's great patriotic lied, "Keep the Home Fires Burning." And as soon as Lily Pons was announced to sing Marie in December, 1940, during World War II, pictures of the vivacious diva in military costume graced the Sunday supplements. She learned to play the drum. She was inducted into a regiment of the United States Army as an honorary member. Without a war fever, however, the successful revival of *La Fille* depends upon the presence of a florid light soprano who is also a deft comedienne.

Ten months after *La Fille du régiment* was successfully presented to society at the Comique, Donizetti was represented at the Opéra (December 2, 1840) by a full-fledged grand opera complete with ceremonial scenes, ballet, and all the other trappings of the *Guillaume Tell*–Meyerbeer school of stage-crowding. *La Favorite* was as heavy as *La Fille* was light. It was pseudohistorical, being based on a long, nasty skit by two Frenchmen (one of them Scribe, of course) about the mother of Pedro the Cruel of Castile, a woman who had done much to corrupt the morals of fourteenth-century Spain. The presence in the cast of Rosine Stolz, the Opéra's reigning star, and in her own quiet way as remarkable as Pedro's mother,[9] did not bring immediate success to this most solid and impressive of Donizetti's tragic operas. Again translation and rechristening followed: as *La Favorita* the opera has had a long, sanguinary career.

For an opera containing so many expressively beautiful pages, *La Favorite* opens suspiciously with an ambiguous overture, its first section Bach *à l'italienne*, moving unreasonably into the jumpiest kind of motion-picture music. The first two acts contain good numbers, but also ballet music so infernally tum-tummy (did Donizetti influence Verdi in this, too?) as almost to send one home discouraged at this point. In Act III, however, things begin to happen consecutively in the music as well as in the libretto. First comes a baritone aria, "A tanto amor," nervous and sensitive in line, its eloquence heightened by the interjections and asides of the infatuated tenor and mezzo; its pointedness is entirely Verdian. A few moments later, Leonora pours forth her love in "O mio Fernando," one of the sultriest outbursts of passion in pre-Verdian opera and proof that the Donizetti of *Anna Bolena* was not yet dead. The finale of this act has found admirers in the most alien camps. It is a large, amply conceived, altogether impressive ensemble of the principals and the full chorus. Something of its proportions may be deduced from the fact that it runs to thirty-nine pages even in piano score.

Act IV of *La Favorite*, though no longer than the finale of Act III, constitutes Donizetti's most honorable claim as a great musicodramatic

[9] After first marrying a commoner (but a powerful one—he was manager of the Théâtre de la Monnaie at Brussels), Stolz successively espoused a baron, a count, and a duke, accomplishing these social steps up after her forty-fifth year. She died Duchesse de Bassano at Paris in 1903 at the age of eighty-eight.

composer. It lends weight to the most lurid false picture of "inspiration," having been scribbled off in a few hours. The music is here wonderfully responsive to the demands of the libretto: as an artistic statement of a harrowing situation brought to a violent climax, it is flawless. It is so good, in fact, that it must raise the question of why the man who composed it did not do likewise more often. The tenor aria "Spirto gentil" [10] is only less famous than "Una furtiva lagrima": at times no less than twenty separate recorded versions of it have been available.[11]

Between *La Favorite* and *Don Pasquale,* three years and more operas intervened. One of them was a light, featherbrained tear-jerker about the mortgage on the old homestead, the farmer's pure daughter, the rich villain, and the faithful lover, *Linda di Chamounix.* Its original success, at the Kärntnerthortheater, Vienna, on May 19, 1842, is easily explained by the cast of five bright stars: Persiani, Marietta Brambilla, Mario, Tamburini, and Lablache. Still, but for a mad scene and the tripping first-act coloratura aria "O luce di quest'anima," it might not have survived. Because of them, largely, every notable coloratura of the second half of the nineteenth century and even noncoloraturas of the twentieth have tried the role of Linda.

Brilliant as that first cast of *Linda di Chamounix* had been, Donizetti composed (and in part adapted the libretto of) *Don Pasquale* for one of unsurpassed glamour, nothing less than the Puritani Quartet, with Mario replacing Rubini, but with Grisi, Tamburini, and Lablache as of old. The opportunity evidently quickened his flagging senses and warmed his sometimes confused imagination, for this *opera buffa,* first heard in Paris, at the Théâtre-Italien, on January 3, 1843, suggested that Rossini's comic muse might have to vacate the throne on which for so many years she had been sleeping. Slighter, less mordant, less incredibly abounding than *Il Barbiere di Siviglia, Don Pasquale* is furiously alive with its own unfailing brand of delight. Fortunately, this swiftly written score, composed in between eight days and three weeks (certainty about

---

[10] As this number was drawn from the incomplete score of *Le Duc d'Albe,* Donizetti's spectacular speed in writing Act IV is partly—but only partly—explained. Interestingly, the libretto that Scribe had written for *Le Duc d'Albe* he rewrote in 1854 for Verdi: it became *Les Vêpres siciliennes.*

[11] Another of Donizetti's 1840 operas waited until May 7, 1860, for its *première*—at the Opéra-Comique. This was *Rita, ou Le Mari battu,* in one act. A pointlessly prolonged joke, it has been revived in recent years, most often by amateur and semiamateur troupes.

this point is impossible), had no time or space for the lachrymosity that often had marred Donizetti's other comedies. It is primarily, inflexibly, a great comedy of central situation.[12] Stemming from Pergolesi and Cimarosa as well as from Rossini, it stands in the line that seems to have ended with the acidulous humor of Puccini's *Gianni Schicchi* and the more polite and suave, but just as crisp, social comment of Wolf-Ferrari's *Il Segreto di Susanna.*

One of the most remarkable things about *Don Pasquale* is its unspoiled freshness, astonishing in the sixty-ninth opera of a man who had been purveying all sorts of vehicles for all sorts of singers and all sorts of audiences for twenty years, and who was, at the time of its composition, on the verge of a collapse that was to end in imbecility and, within five years, death. It shares with the best comic works of the Italian schools, Puccini's excepted, a singular youthful quality on which years have no effect. There is springtime in *Don Pasquale,* and though the music is not of great weight, it is of precious metal. In short, the charm persists. The chattery, saucy overture, a potpourri of good things from the opera, is Donizetti's best. The barefaced nonsense of the plot is matched by the high-spirited, often farcical numbers, which reach their most delicious absurd in the prolonged quartet at the end of Act II. Of the solos, it is difficult to choose between Norina's entrance aria, "So anch'io la virtù," a pert, madcap melody, wonderfully hummable, a shrewd underlining of the situation, and Ernesto's serenade, "Com'è gentil," a delicious love song of unmistakably Latin allure, with mandolinlike effects from the chorus.

During the rehearsals before the *première* of *Don Pasquale,* both Donizetti and the principals felt that the extra something essential to putting an opera across was lacking. Rummaging about in a pile of his manuscripts, Donizetti found an aria, which he then sent to Mario with the words "Sing this to Norina in the garden scene." This was "Com'è gentil," with which, as Lablache strummed a lute accompaniment behind the scenes, the great tenor brought the fashionable Parisian audience to its feet on the opening night. Lablache himself as Don Pasquale was so remarkable as to draw the following tribute from the usually faultfinding Henry Fothergill Chorley:

[12] Donizetti and Michele Accursi (pseudonym of Giovanni Ruffini) had borrowed both the central situation and much of its detailed working-out from a libretto by Angelo Anelli which Stefano Pavesi had composed with great success for La Scala in 1810, *Ser Marc'Antonio.*

It used to be said in Paris that the bouquet which the dear, silly hero of the farce-opera wore in the coat which stuck to him with as terrible a closeness as the outside garment of a sausage does to the contents within, was offered, night after night, by anonymous admirers. But throughout the entire farce of Lablache's performances nothing was more admirable than his entire avoidance of grossness or coarse imitation. There was, with him, that security which only belongs to persons of rare and admirable tact; and, with that security, the highest power of expressing comedy, tragedy, or grotesque,—because it belongs to one who will risk nothing hazardous, but who is not afraid of daring anything extraordinary. When I hear of this person's style, and that person's high note, and when I think of Lablache, I am tempted to feel as if I had parted company with real comic genius on the musical stage for ever!

Donizetti's finest comic opera proved to be his last success. For *Don Pasquale* was followed by a comparative failure each in Vienna, Paris, and Naples. *Maria di Rohan*, first heard in Vienna on June 5, 1844, provided the mighty Giorgio Ronconi, during a later performance in St. Petersburg, with the opportunity to indulge in a flight of facial acrobatics which is worth a footnote as illustrating the operatic acting of the period.[13]

Public coolness to *Dom Sébastien, roi de Portugal* (Opéra, Paris, November 13, 1843), appears to have hastened Donizetti's mental disintegration: it was a five-act historical pageant opera that he regarded as his chef d'oeuvre.[14] *Caterina Cornaro* (Naples, January 12, 1844) was his last opera. He died four years later in his native Bergamo. A photograph of him and his nephew Andrea, taken at Paris after his paralysis and insanity became nearly total, belongs with Repin's well-known portrait

[13] Ronconi had boasted to Nicholas I that he could, while singing, express tragedy with one side of his face, comedy with the other. As Clara Louise Kellogg told it in her *Memoirs of an American Prima Donna*, the night of *Maria di Rohan*, Ronconi "managed to turn one side of his face, grim as the Tragic Mask, to the audience, while the other, which could be seen only from the Imperial Box, was excessively humorous and cheerful. The Czar was greatly amused and delighted with the exhibition." Doubtless it was a lonesome gay spot in a gory evening.

[14] Donizetti was neither a fool nor a popinjay—and ought we not somehow to have the opportunity to judge for ourselves whether he was right or wrong about *Don Sébastien?*

of Mussorgsky among the most terrifying depictions of human disintegration.

Donizetti's career and works will continue to take up what may seem like a disproportionate number of pages in histories of opera—disproportionate to the number of performances given across the world to many of the operas discussed. He provided grateful roles for the leading singers of one of singing's golden eras, and as long as a few singers are capable of matching the use of their voices with memories of that age, *Lucia di Lammermoor* and *Don Pasquale* certainly, several of his other operas probably, will continue to be heard. He belongs to a category of creators which always is difficult to assess: those prolific men of not quite the first rank who more than once—and at times in sustained works—have snatched at genius, striking with complete success high above their own average.

CHAPTER X

The French Comic Spirit

THE impudent incursion of the *bouffons* into Paris in 1752 had had other sequels besides the well-intentioned reforming efforts of Gluck. One, perhaps the most natural, result was the rise of a considerable school of French composers who, though they also wrote in other styles, directed their major efforts toward invoking and illustrating the comic spirit. Their origins are obscure, as remote as one wishes to make them. It is not impossible that, late in the thirteenth century, the *trouvère* Adam de la Halle composed, in his pastorals with music and dialogue—the best-known of which is *Le Jeu de Robin et de Marion*—the original ancestors of *opéra-comique*. The solemn tone of some of these calls to mind the curiousness of certain French musical terms. Thus, *opéra-comique* may be, but is not necessarily, comic—the defining factor being that it must contain spoken dialogue. Further, *opéra-bouffe* (almost, but not quite, equivalent to *opera buffa,* for whose *recitativo secco* it often substitutes spoken dialogue) is *opéra-comique,* but not all *opéra-comique* is *opéra-bouffe,* as a moment's attention to *Carmen,* most famous of all *opéras-comiques,* shows.

Whether Adam de la Halle's pieces were ancestral to *opéra-comique* or not, French comic opera slept until roused by the noise of the *bouffons.*[1] Roused completely, that is, for even the classic-minded Rameau

---

[1] The comedy ballets of Molière and Lully—notably *L'Amour médecin* (1665), *Monsieur de Pourceaugnac* (1669), and *Le Bourgeois gentilhomme* (1670)—were still other ancestors of *opéra-comique,* if not of *opéra-bouffe.* So, too, were the *vaudevilles* played at the Théâtre de la Foire, for they were often parodies of *opera seria.* It was these "fair theaters" which gave place directly, about 1715, to the Théâtre de l'Opéra-Comique.

had composed an *opéra-bouffe* of moderately hilarious temper. But the year of the *bouffons*—1752—Jean-Jacques Rousseau compiled and composed, in *Le Devin du village,* a comic piece that won a popular currency far beyond that of Rameau's. The busy philosopher of Geneva thus offhandedly set the stage for a persistent school of French operatic composers, sometimes flourishing, sometimes languishing, but finally the most special product of the French musical stage.

As is frequently the case in the illogical, checkered story of French music, the first recognizable figure of this industrious race of frippery-sellers was an Italian immigrant, one Egidio Romualdo Duni. Further to complicate the matter, he wrote (or compiled—for some students think many of his numbers borrowed) his first French comic opera in Parma at the suggestion of Duke Philip, enough of a Bourbon to give the whole transaction a French twist from the start. This opera, *Le Caprice amoureux ou Ninette à la cour* (1755), often known simply as *Ninette à la cour,* was so well received in Paris that Duni removed thither and worked there for the remaining twenty years of his life. He soon found imitators of, if not his style, then his way of tickling the public palate.

The precarious state of infant French *opéra-comique* may be deduced from the character of Duni's early colleagues. The first, François-André Danican, better known under his father's assumed name of Philidor, was primarily a chess player of international celebrity.[2] Another, Pierre-Alexandre Monsigny, was maître d'hôtel to the Duc d'Orléans when seized by the ambition to become a light-opera composer. When Philidor and Monsigny composed their first operas, they no doubt thought of composition as a side line. Although Philidor remained true to chess, Monsigny gave up household economics for the more satisfactory pursuit of fashionable adulation and, finally, the glory of membership in the Institut. While Marie Antoinette was playing at rusticity and turning over in her mind plans for the Petit Trianon, Monsigny was delighting Parisian exquisites of both sexes with his naïve scores, simple melodies, transparent accompaniments, and unquestioned charm. But neither Duni nor his two confreres proved sufficiently vital to give real sap to a comic-opera tradition.

André-Ernest-Modeste Grétry, born in 1741 a few leagues outside France itself, but ultimately more Parisian than Jean de Paris, was a timid Belgian who was pushed up to eminence by the right people—

[2] The most prodigious of child prodigies have commonly excelled in three somehow internally related disciplines: mathematics, chess, and music.

pushed onto the scene when the resourcefulness he so abundantly had was most needed to shore up the uncertain fortunes of French comic opera. A rich Belgian prelate had sent him to Rome, and after eight years of study in the riotous capital of Clement XIII, he set out vaguely for Paris. En route, he stopped off at Geneva, where Voltaire refused to write a libretto for him, but assured him that Paris was indeed the place for a young artist. Success came to Grétry with absurd ease. He had been in Paris for less than a year as a petted protégé of the Swedish ambassador when his *Le Huron* (1768) was produced with great éclat. With a text that Marmontel had based on Voltaire's silly conception of an American Indian's innocence and of a girl who dies of shame after sacrificing her honor to save her lover's life, *Le Huron* made a powerful appeal to audiences inoculated with the fashionable Rousseauism of the day.

With *Lucile,* another piece in sentimental vein, this time to a libretto that the eminent and slickly suave Marmontel had based on a story of his own writing, Grétry found himself established. *Lucile* (1769) contains a didactic, smugly virtuous quartet—"Où peut-on être mieux qu'au sein de la famille?"—that swept France for fifty years and was employed for the least likely occasions. Its homey sentiment rose like incense to the bourgeois Louis XVI during the short-lived reaction in his favor just before the period of inflexible hatred set in. And—final irony—to the poor dupes of Napoleon's *grande armée,* the decent, humdrum burgher celebrated in the quartet became identified with the figure of the Little Corporal surrounded by his guards.

Grétry was twenty-eight years old when he produced his first true *opéra-bouffe, Le Tableau parlant* (1769), in one act. Apotheosis followed. He was compared to Pergolesi, and his admirers began to call him "the Molière of French music." Adulation could go no further. Mme Vigée-Lebrun was to paint him, Dr. Charles Burney to pronounce him the idol of the Parisians, and Napoleon to pay him court. Nothing could exceed the exceeding greenness of this earliest laurel. Diderot and the other Encyclopedists, still fighting the already decided *guerre des bouffons,* took up this new Pergolesi, and the cautious, opportunistic young man was soon the lion of the *salons.* Social success was his, and after he composed two short operas for Marie Antoinette's wedding festivities, he became a court favorite. One of these was *Les Deux Avares,* a really amusing two-act score full of delicious program effects—just the sort of thing to captivate the not-too-spoiled young girl the Dauphine still was.

In 1770, the year of *Les Deux Avares,* Grétry's career was only five years old, but it was already apparent that he was not to be a reformer. His was a static talent more or less dependent on momentary inspiration, though he had a respectable enough academic background. Grétry was not a thinker, and though he associated with the wits and savants of the capital, from D'Alembert to Mme de Staël, from Baron Grimm to Mlle de Lespinasse, he was not really one of them. As a musician, he had the strength and weaknesses of a dilettante, and he never mastered more than the rudiments of musical architecture. He appears to have escaped the influence of the theory-loving Rameau, who had died only the year before Grétry reached Paris. Also, though he worshiped Rousseau, he was never infected with a passion for big general ideas or a feeling that he had been born to remake the world. He wrote melodies because they occurred to him, but his harmony was unadventurous and his orchestration wan, again in contrast to Rameau, who had evolved a lavish orchestra and used varied and telling harmonies. Only twenty-six instruments are called for in a typical Grétry score, and it was sneeringly said of his harmony that one might drive a coach and four between the bass and the first violin.

What charmed Grétry's public was the spontaneity of his melodies. Speaking in 1817, Carl Maria von Weber said: "It would be impossible to equal the really exquisite purity of his melodies, which are always inspired to suit the exigencies of the moment and not according to stereotyped forms." Equally winning were the aptness of his pictorial effects and the happy way he joined words and music. Few French composers have surpassed Grétry in the perfection of a declamatory style. Characteristically, he admired Haydn's charming, insignificant operas, but was put off by Mozart, whose stage works he dismissed impatiently: "Mozart puts the pedestal on the stage and the statue in the orchestra." He himself, unfortunately, was never tempted to commit the same error. To compensate for his lack of adventurousness, he was ingenuously self-analytical. "I received from Nature the gift of appropriate melody," he said, "but she denied me that of strict and complicated harmony."

Grétry, child of nature, discreet courtier, had a handsome career as long as the *ancien régime* survived, and then a tolerable one under the Terror. Still a courtier and basically without political opinions, he knew how to bend with the storm. Mme du Barry shed precious tears over his *Zémire et Azor* (1771) and granted him a pension. Marie Antoinette stood godmother to one of his three pretty daughters. When the whimsical Austrian found opera that pleased her more than his, he retired from the scene so gracefully as to seem to be conferring a compliment on her taste. Pensions and sinecures were showered upon him. A street in Paris bore his name. Amiable and well balanced, he received these honors without losing his head. His only meeting with Rousseau passed off badly, but he bore his hero no grudge; in 1796, long after the philosopher's death, Grétry purchased the Hermitage, the house that Rousseau had occupied at Montmorency.

The Revolution interrupted but did not halt Grétry's career. It confiscated his property, but after some hesitation did not prohibit performances of his works. By the time Napoleon took the center of the stage, *le citoyen* Grétry had become one of the venerated musicians of the First French Republic. The Emperor restored and then augmented his honors. Grétry died at the Hermitage in 1813. Had he lived on into the reign of Louis XVIII, he might have acquired even greater rewards, for had he not flattered that prince, then Comte de Provence, thirty years before by setting *La Caravane du Caire,* a libretto in the preparation of which both the Comte and Louis XVI are said to have had a part? *La Caravane* (1783) became a great hit at the Opéra in 1784, and before Louis XVIII's death in 1824 was approaching its five-hundredth performance there.

Despite Grétry's almost invariable good luck, he did not go through life uncriticized. His *Céphale et Procris,* sung at Versailles in 1773 for the marriage of the future Charles X to Maria Theresa of Sardinia, boasted Sophie Arnould; when it was produced in Paris at the Opéra in 1775 Arnould's place was taken by her successor, Rosalie Levasseur. This did not keep La Harpe from calling *Céphale* feeble, or Mlle de Lespinasse from finding it "rather anemic." This dissatisfaction, even among his friends, with Grétry's far from searching music was heightened the very next year by the production of Gluck's first Paris opera. But when the local demand for Grétry dwindled to performances on Sunday —the unfashionable day—he could console himself with the knowledge that his operas were being performed simultaneously in half a dozen European countries.

By refusing to greet Piccinni on his arrival in Paris, Grétry unintentionally seemed to take sides in the Gluck-Piccinni strife. The Piccinnists took their revenge by creating disturbances during performances of Grétry's operas. Fortunately, on October 21, 1784, when his masterpiece, *Richard Coeur-de-Lion,* was produced at the Comédie-Italienne, most of this animus against him was a thing of the past, and, after a mildly successful *première,* in which exception was taken to the ending,[3] this opera, slightly altered to disarm future criticism, soon became epidemic. Its fame spread almost immediately to England, where two versions, one of them adapted by Mozart's friend Thomas Linley to an English translation by "Gentleman John" Burgoyne, the absent-minded blunderer of Saratoga, strove with each other to hold the town.

Today, when the rest of *Richard,* like most of Grétry, is forgotten, Blondel's air—"Ô Richard, ô mon roi!"—gets an occasional hearing. The opera's popularity during the last fifteen years of the eighteenth century and well into the nineteenth can now scarcely be imagined. During the Terror, citizens were guillotined for no more heinous crime than singing its royalist strophes, and the fact that Grétry had composed it placed him in momentary peril. The air became, in fact, the Bourbon anthem, though all manner of men sang or hummed its deliberately archaic measures. That dour republican John Quincy Adams went around repeating to himself the doleful lines "Ô Richard! L'univers t'abandonne": he had failed of re-election, and no doubt liked to picture himself as a ruler abandoned by the universe. Although most of Grétry's earlier success had been made with lighter works, his most enduring reputation came from *Richard,* a serious opera.

Richard Coeur-de-Lion was in every sense the summit of Grétry's achievement. Although he lived almost thirty years after its *première,* and through 1792 wrote at least one opera each year—and did not stop composing operas until 1804—he gradually declined as a composer. The honors Grétry received under Napoleon were paid to the shade of greatness. In 1785 he had presented what may have been literally the first Rabelaisian opera: *Panurge dans l'isle des lanternes;* in 1790, his mediocre *Pierre le grand* (with a libretto by the same Bouilly who had written the *Léonore* on which the text of Beethoven's *Fidelio* was to be based) was almost the last French opera to depict royalty in a favorable light during the Revolution; the following year, his *Guillaume Tell* was a successful effort at coat-turning. Much like the officials of modern totalitarian states, the revolutionary committees were soon ordering French artists of every conviction to produce works of propaganda. It was not enough, the bureaucrats ruled, for a work to be neutral: it must be violently pro-Revolution.

[3] *Richard Coeur-de-Lion* began as a three-act opera. In 1785, however, it was expanded into a four-act version—which played only two or three times, after which it returned to three acts.

Among those who responded without scruple to the government's demands was the former archcourtier Grétry. In December, 1793, posters appeared announcing his one-act opera *La Fête de la raison,* evidently intended as a placatory offering to the ideally cool-headed deity who was to usurp the place of *le bon Dieu* on the lips, if not in the hearts, of all prudent revolutionaries, and whose installation in Nôtre Dame was soon to take place. But the authorities read the libretto and were themselves revolted; Grétry was forced to apply his tunes to new subject matter. As *La Rosière républicaine,* celebrating the planting of the tree of liberty, this was presented at the Opéra in September, 1794. Some idea of the tone of these made-to-order revolutionary operas may be gathered from the fact that one scene of *La Rosière,* depicting nuns seduced into dancing lasciviously, was described by *Le Journal de Paris* as "very gay." A ballet suite taken from this opera, more sweetly staid than gay, is one of the few compositions by Grétry still occasionally heard.

One of the most extraordinary performances of the era was a ribald antiroyalist business called *Le Congrès des rois,* composed communally by a dozen more or less distinguished musicians, bringing together such disparate spirits as Grétry, the sober Cherubini, the fashionable Kreutzer (to whom Beethoven dedicated the sonata made famous by Tolstoy), Nicolas Dalayrac, and the young, still-struggling Étienne-Nicolas Méhul. It was topical without being accurate: kings, betrayed by their mistresses (a shaft directed ineffectually at the faithful Du Barry, who had just been guillotined), are forced to disguise themselves as sans-culottes to escape vengeful justice. The skit might have had point through one brief act, but in three long acts it became merely tiresome. It lasted one performance and was lucky for only one of its collaborators. Méhul received an appointment at the Comédie-Italienne and an annual stipend of one thousand livres.

Méhul's reward was rightfully earned, for of the entire group no one was more enthusiastically for *liberté, égalité, fraternité* than he. In fact, Méhul became unofficial composer extraordinary to the French Revolution. Before its energies had dribbled away into muddle, he had composed countless hymns, chants, and cantatas celebrating its transient deities and shibboleths. His "Chant du départ," first sung in July, 1794, for a time vied in popularity with the "Marseillaise." It was the marching song of the conscript armies of the Republic, and to the ragged legions who went impudently to match themselves with the tried, well-accoutered armies of Austria copies of it were distributed by the tens of thousands.

Its words flowed from the pen of Marie-Joseph de Chénier, whose brother André was, at the moment of its writing, awaiting execution for those imprudent deeds which Umberto Giordano and his librettist, Luigi Illica, were to construe as heroism a century later in *Andrea Chénier*. When this same Marie-Joseph de Chénier proposed a *conservatoire de musique* (which still exists), the authorities give Méhul the most important sign of their satisfaction by making him its first inspector of instruction.

During the lifetimes of Grétry and Méhul, the two men were referred to as respectively the Molière and the Corneille of French music, an illuminating comparison if not interpreted too nicely, for it points up the essential antithesis between the lighthearted *liégeois* and the more earnest peasant lad from the foothills of the Meuse. Like Grétry, Méhul had gone to Paris as a green boy, but he had not conquered the city so easily. He did not know the ropes—in fact, never got to know them as well as Grétry. Nor did a letter of introduction to Gluck, who was busy staging *Iphigénie en Tauride,* bring him anything more tangible than advice to give up the idea of composing for the Church and take to the stage.

Méhul reacted slowly to this advice. Not until September 4, 1790, was his first opera—*Euphrosine, ou Le Tyran corrigé*—staged in Paris at the Comédie-Italienne. The following year, he selected a poem that had won a government prize. *Cora,* with a libretto based on Marmontel's *Les Incas,* was a failure. With a few exceptions using execrable texts, Méhul's operas usually enjoyed an opening spurt of popularity followed by a languishing take at the box office and final dissolution. Despite the charming music that he lavished on them, they did not succeed. The amiable Méhul, almost stupidly humble, blamed the ultimate failures of his operas not on his flawlessly inept taste in librettos, but on his delightful music. Time and time again he begged the pardon of his hack librettists for spoiling their precious handiwork.

And yet Méhul got along and had his successes. His public understood even when he did not. Within thirteen years of his arrival in Paris, two of his operas had been received warmly enough to bring him an enviable position among the musicians of the capital. In his small way, he got caught in a social whirl. Even in the days before Mme Récamier began to wear Directoire gowns, he was welcome at her *salon,* and among his other friends he numbered Talma, the tragedian, Rouget de Lisle, and many of his fellow composers, including Gossec, Grétry, and Boieldieu. In 1794, Méhul definitely was on the way up, and perhaps for that reason was momentarily in peril: in those days, success (no matter whose) was enough to make the nervous authorities listen to any tale brought them by a jealous ill-wisher.

Méhul's opera *Mélidore et Phrosine,* a tale of incest, was forbidden because the libretto "was not sufficiently republican in spirit. . . . The word 'liberty' does not appear once." The sacred word was obediently inserted at frequent intervals, the censors—callous to incest—were appeased, the opera was produced, and Méhul's head was safe for the time being. The opera was denounced again, this time for "unseemly extravagance in the costumes": as this detail was outside Méhul's province, he very sensibly ignored the new charge. Considering his hairbreadth escapes as he peacefully pursued his musical career in revolutionary France, it is little wonder that Méhul changed easily from sincere republicanism to no less sincere Bonapartism and served enthusiastically as an official of the Empire.

The Terror was almost spent when Méhul, already on intimate terms with the man who was to become Emperor of a vaster France than had existed before, heralded the changing times by composing an opera with a king as hero. Perhaps this is crediting Méhul with too much consciousness in the matter: he may merely have taken the first story that came his way, and the bold one may have been the busy Bouilly, who managed for many years to provide the leading composers of France with librettos. *Le Jeune Henry,* based on an incident from the youth of Henry IV, was thin in plot—too silly to be presented for more than a night or two. It was heard at the Opéra-Comique on May 1, 1797; at its third performance the composer was called out for an ovation. The offending white plume of Navarre had been forgotten in the loveliness of the music.

The *ouverture de chasse* in *Le Jeune Henry* got a hold on Parisian hearts. It had to be repeated twice on the opening night, and for thirty years was used as a kind of entr'acte. Called "La Chasse du jeune Henry," it is a sparkling bit of program music, frankly, even naïvely, delighting in realistic tricks and touches—a swift, courtly hunt carried on amid vicissitudes of weather, the whole mildly presaging the most famous of operatic program overtures, that to Rossini's *Guillaume Tell.* It is no accident that, though *Le Jeune Henry* was unsuccessful and now has been silent for a century or more, "La Chasse" still is played and has been recorded. Méhul, who later turned to composing symphonies patterned on Haydn's, was almost invariably most expressive as an instrumental composer. In an otherwise sloppy transitional period, during which melodies were allowed to speak all too barrenly for themselves, Méhul was notable for the exquisite joinery of his musical craftsmanship.

Méhul is often catalogued as a founder of the French light-opera school that culminated in Auber and Offenbach. Actually, his particular forte was not only serious opera, but a form of serious opera of such intense sobriety and devout elevation that it can only be called opera-oratorio. In 1799 he presented, in *Ariodant,* a score of grave beauty and fastidious workmanship which occupies a place of some importance in the history of the leading-motive technique. Beethoven studied this score, and it influenced him in his own cautious use of leading motives in *Fidelio.*

In 1806, Méhul presented *Les Deux Aveugles de Tolède,* the frisking overture to which can still delight us. And in 1807, when his usually dim star was burning with unwonted splendor, he came forth with his master-piece, *Joseph,* at the Opéra-Comique on February 17. It is a work of lyrical fecundity with few traces of the deft gaiety so often associated with Méhul's name. This movingly noble work shows that his real master was not his elder colleague Grétry, but in truth the great Austrian whom he, a faltering novice, had sought out thirty years before. The loftiness and austerity with which Gluck had mantled his pagan legends Méhul claimed for the Biblical story of Joseph and his evil brothers. Unfortunately, *Joseph* has the usual undistinguished Méhul libretto. Cohesive enough, it is devoid of love interest, a lack that has not endeared it to French operagoers. In Germany, however, *Joseph* came to be regarded almost as an indigenous work, probably because the rising masters of the New German School [4] saw in it some faint prevision, and that not wholly accidental, of their ideals.

Classic in declamation, classic in harmonic mood, *Joseph* turned its face toward the rising romantic sun in its free-singing melodic line. A study of the score is amply rewarding, and not only in pure aural delight: it reveals throughout a musical scholar of ranging taste, curiosity, and liberal refinement. The overture and the prelude to Act II carry us persistently to the best traditions of Haydn and Mozart; Joseph's attractive recitative and air in Act I—"Vainement, Pharaon" and "Champs paternels!"—are new territory, at least for considerable stretches. No

[4] The early popularity of *Joseph* in Germany coincided with the rise of the New German School of painters, the so-called "Nazarenes"—Johann Friedrich Overbeck was their leader—whose aim was to make art once more the handmaid of religion.

wonder that Weber, who staged *Joseph* lovingly at Dresden in 1817, after judicious qualification as to its "drab tone," went on in all but rapturous strains about this work "imbued with a sentiment, a pathos, a purity of line and composition beyond compare." No wonder that Richard Wagner called it "a magnificent work, which transported me to a higher world."

Méhul lived until 1817, but the last decade of his life was an anticlimax spent pleasantly enough in a rose garden where, with the same scholarly, loving solicitude that he had lavished on his music, he produced some rare blossoms. At his funeral, the oration was fittingly pronounced by another and greater musical scholar, Cherubini; among the mourners were Méhul's friend Boieldieu and his pupil Hérold, both of whom mimicked the cleverest effects of his comic style.

Grétry and Méhul, like Garrick in Reynolds' famous picture, were torn between the Tragic and the Comic Muse. François-Adrien Boieldieu suffered no conflict of that sort. He chose early in life to be a composer of comic operas, and he did comparatively little else. He had composed eleven mediocre operas before his twenty-fifth birthday (the tenth of them a collaboration with Cherubini); his twelfth, squeezed in just before that date, showed shrewdness in supplying what his Parisian audience wanted. *Le Calife de Bagdad* (1800) would be rated a smash hit today: it ran intermittently at the Opéra-Comique for thirty-six years. Despite its Oriental theme, the opera makes no attempt to sound Oriental —Boieldieu was nothing if not unadventurous. Oriental stories were the rage in those dawn days of French romanticism, but Boieldieu, knowing the easy melodies his Frenchmen knew they liked, was not risking even a Turkish march. Cherubini was scandalized by the adulation being paid to *Le Calife*. "Wretch!" he is reported to have exclaimed to Boieldieu with heavy playfulness as he accosted the younger man in the lobby of the theater: "Aren't you ashamed of such undeserved success?" Instead of answering (like everyone else, Boieldieu was a little frightened by Cherubini), he enrolled with the formidable Italian for a stiff course in counterpoint.

His head swimming with glory, Boieldieu quickly married—and married a shrew. Repenting as quickly, he fled to Russia, where he remained for eight years, exposed to the dazzling barbaric edges of its folk music and proving immune to them. He came, he saw, he stopped his ears, and, like the gentle lamb he was, served as *maître de chapelle* to the sponsor of the Holy Alliance. During this comparative suspension of life, he

penned several harmless Parisian operas. They gave him practice, stead-
ied his hand, and in the eyes of the Autocrat of All the Russias took
nothing from his stature. But the St. Petersburg winters were inclement,
and when Russia and France went to war in 1810, Boieldieu seized the
pretext and returned home loaded—as was the custom in those polite,
hypocritical days—with imperial largess. Two years later, he was fully
re-established as one of Paris' musical darlings. In that fateful year
1812, when Napoleon was losing his all in the east, Boieldieu treated
his admirers to a romantic flummery called *Jean de Paris*. Based on one
of the several fundamental plots, it deals with a prince who wants to be
loved for himself alone, and therefore woos his lady as a rich bourgeois.

By 1817, Boieldieu's position was such that he succeeded to the seat
in the Institut left vacant by the death of Méhul, thereby literally humiliating to death his rival Niccolò Isouard, a sulky Maltese who seems to
have believed that he could bully his way to fame by smothering the
musical stage in hastily executed operas. Meanwhile, for another eight
years Boieldieu also went on grinding out fragrant trivialities that proved
Cherubini's lectures to have been given in vain. Then, fifty years old,
Boieldieu found gold again. The Scott cult was at its height, and Scribe,
at the opening of a career that was to leave in its wake more than five
hundred librettos, had patched together *La Dame blanche* from parts of
The Monastery and *Guy Mannering*. The resulting story has found admirers, though its spectral trappings, fake horrifications, and tortuous
mazes seem unadulterated fustian. Scribe's book contains every sort of
situation except a tragic one.

For the profundity and high imagination that Boieldieu lacked, he
substituted, in *La Dame blanche,* attractive surfaces, a fancy buoyant
and carefree, and a finely tempered and tireless wit. Moreover, the opera
is, without being windy or diffuse, borne forward through its three long
acts by a musical ebullience that never flags. In this opera, in fact, Boieldieu carved out a small, not unprincely territory all his own. When *La
Dame blanche* became the most popular comedy of its day, its creator
modestly disclaimed his right to the more fantastic tributes by saying
that perhaps the Parisians were merely tired of Rossini—who, incidentally, was a devotee of Boieldieu's melodious opera.

La Dame blanche has been called the French counterpart of *Der
Freischütz;* it has been pointed out that it is an expansion of the chanson,
as Weber's masterpiece is of the old *Volkslied*. All this is in part true, but
La Dame also contains musical quotations from Scotland and not a few

touches of pure 1825 Paris vaudeville. Something of the brimming-over quality of Weber's melodies is in *La Dame blanche,* and the Germans discovered it, for the opera was long a favorite east of the Rhine. Its popularity in France became so long-lived (it reached its thousandth singing at the Opéra-Comique on December 16, 1862) that Georges Bizet developed a monomaniacal hatred of it, especially when his own operas showed no sign of exercising even a small fraction of its hold on the public.

Although he was only in his middle fifties, Boieldieu was occupied chiefly with spending the liberal, much-needed pension that Thiers had bestowed upon him when, in the vintage year 1831,[5] Louis-Joseph-Ferdinand Hérold, most brilliant of Méhul's pupils, produced his still-remembered *Zampa.* For about twenty years, this prodigiously active composer, one of the first Prix de Rome winners, had been pouring out, sometimes far from shoddily, shoals of symphonies, ballets, sonatas, operas, and musical miscellanies. Wonderful things had been predicted of the boy Hérold, who in the course of the years turned into a feverishly productive near-genius running a doomed race with tuberculosis. In the whole history of music no other man has wasted away so energetically. He died in 1833, just short of forty-two, lamenting with almost his last breaths that he had just begun to understand the musical stage. He had learned a great deal, nevertheless, and two operas produced in consecutive years bear witness to his great gifts.

Zampa, an *opéra-comique,* though not a *bouffe,* was the first of Hérold's masterworks. Like *La Dame blanche,* it has the sort of grisly plot that Weber loved. Furthermore, it is not much inferior in color and dramatic intensity to the German's operas. Although nothing is done today to prove it, Hérold is even Weber's superior in stageworthiness. His connection with the leading Parisian opera houses was as long and intimate as Weber's with those in Germany. Nor does the analogy end there: *Zampa*'s overture, once so dazzling and even startling, and now so hackneyed as to seem sleazy, is reminiscent of a Weber potpourri.

Without sacrificing romance or verve, Hérold proceeds through the difficult exposition of an implausible book. His invention seldom falters; his tempo is always right. The romantic note is effectively sounded throughout, but without Weber's overinsistence. Hérold, too, is less senti-

---

[5] From March to December, 1831, these operas received their first performances: Bellini's *La Sonnambula* and *Norma,* Hérold's *Zampa,* and Meyerbeer's *Robert le diable.*

mental, having a saving feeling for measure. In some respects he is perhaps closer to Marschner than to Weber, not least of all when his brilliance occasionally razors off into shrillness. To condescend to *Zampa* because brass bands play its overture, or because it is a French *opéra-comique,* is, in these days of German and Italian domination of opera houses, to confess oneself afraid of adventure. *Zampa* is difficult to produce: the name role, probably written for the eminent tenor-baritone Jean-Baptiste-Marie Chollet, requires his type of wonderfully useful freak range. Chorley amusingly described an 1844 London staging of *Zampa.* Persiani, usually so resourceful, was reduced to confusion when placed vis-à-vis a tenor who was not very good and was quite incapable of singing Zampa's low notes.

The Germans took *Zampa* to their hearts, though often with the vocal extremities of Zampa himself excised. The French have preferred Hérold's more lighthearted masterwork, *Le Pré aux clercs* (1832). The scene is Paris, the story is from a Mérimée historical novel—in short, the whole thing is unqualifiedly French. More dashing than *Zampa,* it had chalked up nine hundred and ninety-nine performances at the Comique by October 10, 1871, when Marie-Caroline Miolan-Carvalho sang in the thousandth. Maurice Cauchie, a specialist in the field, called *Le Pré aux clercs* "the culminating point of *opéra-comique,* French and foreign." It is the work of a man who had mastered his medium and therefore had leisure to devote his talents to those details which lend finish and point. The bold innovator Berlioz complained of Hérold's chromatic heterodoxies; even today Hérold's late scores retain a faint but recognizable exoticism. The overture to *Le Pré aux clercs,* which is not played so often as it deserves, gives us that experience of refreshing novelty of which we are deprived by the overture to *Zampa.* Nor is the complete score of *Le Pré* inferior to that of *Zampa*—it is more scintillant and has unity of style and many witty moments.

One month after the *première* of *Le Pré aux clercs,* Hérold—with the imperishable Cherubini waiting to pronounce the *éloge*—gave in to phthisis. Less than two years later, Boieldieu died and an epoch in French comic opera came to an end.

Boieldieu's place was taken by Auber, who already had shown himself in a dual role: the composer of the generally serious *La Muette de Portici* and of a large number of *opéras-comiques* so frivolous in both text and music as to be little more than operettas. Auber was a musical lightweight, but what he did was fastidiously clean in detail and had real dash. Rossini said that Auber "may have produced light music, but he produced it like a great musician." There was a large, unceasing demand for his entertainments, which he supplied lavishly, in good times and bad, until nearly the end of the Second Empire. A notable wit and man of the world, he put much of his own neat, dandified personality into his sophisticated scores. Some of them, such as *Le Cheval de bronze* (1835, later made into a grand opera), *Le Domino noir* (1837), and *Les Diamants de la couronne* (1841), became staple revivals for light-opera companies; excerpts from them still are occasionally heard. But the only one of Auber's comic operas that has held the stage, albeit precariously outside France, is *Fra Diavolo* (1830), a romantic tale by Scribe of brigandage in the Papal States.

Auber's leaning toward operetta exerted an influence even on the sober Halévy, who, a few months after completing his grim tragedy *La Juive,* wrote the sparkling *L'Éclair* (1835), the scenes of which are laid in colonial Boston. The next year, Adolphe Adam, a deeply religious man who poured out of the same shallow phial operas, ballets (including the immortal *Giselle*), and Masses, brought out *Le Postillon de Longjumeau,* a naïve business that was soon heard around the world.

The retreat from *opéra-comique* to operetta became a rout with the advent of the German-born Jacques Offenbach, who crystallized the nineteenth-century version of the latter type. During the Second Empire, this son of a cantor in a Cologne synagogue fought his way to the top in theatrical Paris, supplying the incorrigibly superficial subjects of Napoleon and Eugénie with more than ninety operettas in twenty-five years. Most of them are mere names today, though the overtures to several of them—*Orphée aux enfers* (1858), *La Belle Hélène* (1864), *La Grande Duchesse de Gérolstein* (1867)—keep some of their best tunes alive (as does the Offenbach potpourri that Manuel Rosenthal arranged for the ballet *Gaîté parisienne*). Their tunes, however, made only some part of their total effect, which depended upon the wit, irony, and satire with which they viewed both momentary and enduring aspects of human life. And so, in recent years, the Metropolitan Opera's attempt to prove that *La Périchole* (1868) in English translation and without style will do as well as Johann Strauss's *Die Fledermaus* in English translation and without style has succeeded in proving just that—but nothing at all about what would happen if an Offenbach operetta were to be staged as it was composed and staged before Sedan.

Unhappily, Offenbach survives chiefly through a work that started out as a play and ended as almost a grand opera. This is *Les Contes d'Hoff-mann,* which Jules Barbier and Michel Carré [6] (the librettists of, among many other operas, Gounod's *Faust*) based on three fantastic episodes from E. T. A. Hoffmann's fanciful autobiography. Produced as a play as early as 1851, it was then shelved until Offenbach, nearing the end of his career, took it up for refashioning. He died before completing the score, and the New Orleans–born Ernest Guiraud arranged and orchestrated most of it with an expert's hand. It opened at the Opéra-Comique on February 10, 1881, and was repeated there one hundred times before that year ran out. In December it was staged at the Ringtheater in Vienna. On the second night of what promised to be a long run, a great fire broke out in the building, causing much loss of life and temporarily putting the opera on the black list of superstitious singers.

Reminiscent in some ways of the episodic construction of many Russian operas—*Les Contes* consists of three separate episodes in the hero's life united only by the tenuous thread of disillusionment—it is far less interesting as music. It presents a facsimile of musical unity in the clever sentimentality of its idiom and its unflawed superficiality. The banal Barcarole, a duet for mezzo and soprano whch Offenbach had borrowed from his German opera *Die Rheinnixen* (1864), is now hackneyed besides. It not unfairly represents the entire score, in which the Legend of Kleinzach and the merely stunt Doll's Song come as moments of relief. As the culmination of a long career, *Les Contes d'Hoffmann* forcibly suggests that Offenbach was right in sticking close to operetta much of his life. For, in truth, the best of his operettas exceed *Les Contes d'Hoffmann* in quality in almost every department of musicodramatic construction.

Offenbach has had many followers to imitate or ring changes on his formulas for comic opera. Some of them have been almost worthy of their master in the matter of providing an evening's entertainment. Some of them have earned large fortunes doing just that. But none of them has contributed anything lasting to the story of opera, however large the number of pages they may occupy deservedly in a history of the Parisian theater.

[6] After the vocal score was first published, Carré's name was dropped—wherefore Barbier alone is often wrongly credited with having written the original play.

CHAPTER XI

Damaged Demigods

FRENCH opera has been under a cloud for so long a time everywhere except in France that only the unlikely combination of a new Oscar Hammerstein I and a new Mary Garden could bring it back into the full light of day elsewhere. Operatic cycles do move, however, and both the public and the managers of opera houses will some day have to look around them for new staples. Even lovers of *Aïda* at times reach satiety; worshipers of *Der Ring des Nibelungen* are now fewer than they once were. At a foreseeable moment, the most loyal Puccinian will hear with languid ear that Floria Tosca, for the ten-thousandth time, is assigned to kill Baron Scarpia and cast herself from the battlements of the Castel Sant'Angelo while the orchestra, as Joseph Kerman wrote, "screams the first thing that comes into its head, 'E lucevan le stelle.' " The standard repertoire of opera houses will not always be top-heavy with Verdi, Wagner, Strauss, and Puccini to the point of keeping other masters silent. Looking over a roster of the Metropolitan Opera House's entire repertoire since it opened on October 22, 1883, we shall not find *La Dame blanche* represented by only a single performance, and *Richard Coeur-de-Lion, Joseph, Zampa,* and *Le Pré aux clercs* by none at all.

At present it is impossible to hear these operas, which a century and more ago delighted audiences quite as sophisticated as any our own age can muster. Now they are considered too old-fashioned for remounting. By the same token, should we then not wonder at the thousands in all countries who still find delight in the pictures of David and Ingres, the *Confessions* of Rousseau, the early outpourings of Victor Hugo? Obviously, anyone can decide to look at pictures or read books—he has only to have access to a gallery or a library. But in order to hear music, and peculiarly in order to hear opera, he requires a whole series of middlemen not always to be found. Prominent in such a series is the manager with the will to take a chance with costly adventure.

Critical disinterest in French opera, excepting the antique Lully and archaic Rameau, the Trojan epic of Berlioz, and the isolated phenomena of *Carmen* and *Pelléas et Mélisande,* may be taken for granted. This disinterest may have helped to poison the managerial mind. But by some curious quirk of criticism, three great Italians who worked importantly in Paris during the period of Grétry, Méhul, Boieldieu, and Hérold have been exempted from the blight that criticism has managed to cast over the French opera composers. The case of Rossini is worth mentioning again: he did not always escape denigration; he is, in fact, only now in process of becoming seen again as more than the composer of *Il Barbiere di Siviglia.* Of the other two Italians, Cherubini and Spontini, the first has ever been a sacred cow hung with wreaths from the hands of the musical mighty, from Beethoven to Brahms. Not a musical theorist or historian but writes of him with verbal genuflections. Yet, had Cherubini's descendants to live on royalties from performances of his twenty-five operas, for whole decades they would not possess a crust of bread among them. In the entire course of its history, Covent Garden has listed only a thin scattering of performances of three Cherubini operas; the Metropolitan, which has got around to producing *Diana von Solange,* the masterpiece of Prince Albert's brother, Ernst II of Saxe-Coburg-Gotha, has never staged a work by Cherubini. All the critical pother has, in his case, been to no avail. Critics pull little weight in the manager's sanctum on the other side of the opera-house box office.

The neglect of Cherubini resembles poetic justice, of course. He spent his extremely long life terrifying people: he was personally a formidable man, and he knew everything. A kind of perpetual mailed fist of Parisian musical life, he kept the lore and laws of all ages at his fingertips. Even Beethoven, whom he visited in Vienna something in the manner of the Angel of the Lord descending upon Jacob, stood in awe of him. With admirable simplicity, Haydn merely called him the greatest of living composers. Of all his contemporaries—he lived from 1760 to 1842—Berlioz alone had the temerity and originality to send in a minority report. Liszt, it is true, disliked him—for a very Lisztian reason: the Tuscan-born Cherubini had refused him admission to the Paris Conservatoire on the ground that he was not French. In short, the man who gazes out with such somber oppressiveness, such chill melancholy, from the depths of Ingres's great portrait was an ogre. Opera managers are understandably frightened by his ghost.

Cherubini was a great theorist: the famous *traité* that bears his name (and was largely written by Halévy) is standard. He was a great religious composer: his Mass in F, one hundred measures longer than Beethoven's *Missa solemnis,* need not cover its face before that other masterwork. Upon Cherubini's shoulders, no doubt, the mantle of Palestrina eventually fell. He composed, besides, a single symphony and considerable amounts of chamber music, each piece of which is a formal model of what chamber music is erroneously supposed to be by those who dislike it. Examining this music without further data, one would be unlikely to suppose that its composer also wrote operas. Actually, he wrote more than two dozen. The first twelve, written to Italian librettos, scarcely count: they appear to have been clever imitations of the musical patter of Paisiello and other charming Neapolitans. In these frivolities [1] we no more foresee the mature Cherubini of *Médée* and *Les Deux Journées* than we could foresee the mature Gluck in his early Italian and Viennese periods. Cherubini's youthful efforts, Metastasian illustrations and all, brought him his portions of success and failure, and left the path of opera cluttered but undeflected. At one moment it seemed that Cherubini might emulate the career of Handel: an invitation to England ended with his appointment as court composer and the composition of more Italian operas. Fortunately for his future greatness, perhaps, this lasted but one year, whereupon he moved on to France. With this change of locale, the best of his creative life may be said to have begun.

The outlines of Cherubini's mature style became evident even to the critics when his first French opera, *Démophon,* to a libretto that Marmontel had taken from Metastasio's *Demofoonte,* had its *première* at the Paris Opéra on December 5, 1788. This cold music was received coldly. As Cherubini did not produce another opera of his own for three years, contenting himself with inserting new attractions into the popular scores of Cimarosa and Paisiello, a few may have suspected that he was abandoning his neo-Gluckism. No supposition could have been wider of the mark. All this time he was maturing plans for a more rigorous interpretation of dramatic verity in musical terms. He hurled his new *défi* at the Parisian populace on July 18, 1791 (Théâtre Feydeau), just two months before the Prague *première* of Mozart's last opera, *La Clemenza di Tito.*

[1] The first comedy among them, heard at Venice in 1783, has a charming title: *Lo Sposo di tre, marito di nessuna (Husband of Three, Married to None).*

This was *Lodoïska,* its libretto a three-act text by Claude-François Fillette Loraux.

Cherubini's intellectual integrity and artistic daring were unlikely to make friends for him with audiences who, because of the rising temper of the times, were fast losing the ability or desire to criticize fairly. Yet *Lodoïska* won through: two hundred performances marked its first-year triumphs, and as many more were demanded later by Cherubini's infatuated public. The opera is an odd object for adulation: the spectacular story of a wild, impossible Poland is flagrant romantic gush, whereas the music is severe, restrained, classical in timbre, a music for grave, animated statues. The enthusiasm aroused by those marmoreal strophes meant that the dawn of French imperial classicism already was breaking. *Lodoïska,* magnificent in its inertness, was elaborately worked out, richly and—by comparison with the French operas of the era—heavily orchestrated. Melodies it has, some of them both beautiful and movingly expressive, all of them somewhat solemn in character. When *Lodoïska* became a favorite in New York for about two decades after a performance in English at the Lafayette Theater on December 4, 1826, the chief reason for its popularity seems to have been the scene in which the heroine was rescued by numerous imitation Tatars riding real horses onto the stage.

Cherubini, to whom political circumstances were kind only in his crabbed old age, was not to be allowed to proceed logically with his operatic work. The Revolution in its full frightfulness intervened, and Cherubini, a suspected royalist, fled to Normandy, where he puttered about a secularized, well-stocked monastery. Only when Robespierre was six months dead and the Terror practically over did he venture to try another work on a purged Paris. *Elisa, ou Le Voyage aux glaciers du mont Saint-Bernard,* first heard at the Théâtre Feydeau on December 13, 1794, had a two-act libretto by Jacques-Antoine de Révéroni Saint-Cyr. The unwonted tenderness of many of its pages has forced Cherubini's solemn biographers into an orgy of face-saving explanation: his father had died, and he wrote the new opera before he had had a chance to clamp his usual iron grip on his natural human emotions. What really had happened was that some of his natural Italian fluency for melody had been allowed to seep into an otherwise well-mannered score. This has not prevented the critics from declaring *Elisa* "too learned, too German." The libretto is "pinnacled dim in the intense inane," and the libretto cut *Elisa's* career short.

There is something touching about Cherubini's persistence as an operatic composer. Things were always delaying his progress or deflecting his course. After *Elisa,* it was the founding of the Paris Conservatoire, to whose board of study inspectors he, as the leading musical pundit in France, was promptly appointed along with Gossec, Grétry, Méhul, and Jean-François Lesueur. Routine absorbed him. As an official of the Directoire government, he was called upon to compose sundry republican hymns and ceremonial pieces, a chore to which he was, it must be admitted, eminently well suited. As he poured out those windy evocations, his creative mind became a crystal-clear, superhumanly unruffled repository of pure theory, all of which, unfortunately, he used whether occasion demanded it or not, down to the last hemidemisemiquaver. What, one cannot help wondering, was blowing down the corridors of that mighty mind as it manufactured *Le Salpêtre républicain,* a chorus to be chanted at the opening of a new saltpeter works? What, as it poured out musical odes on the 18th Fructidor, the 1st Vendémiaire, and all the other holidays of the revolutionary months? [2] The precise answers are lacking, but certainly it was nothing revolutionary, unless revolution be construed narrowly as moving against the currents of musical fashion.

What kind of revolutionary Cherubini really was became certain when his next opera, *Médée,* was heard at the Théâtre Feydeau on March 13, 1797, the text in three acts having been based on Euripides by François-Benoît Hoffman. In *Médée,* his mold for serious opera was finally set. It established his true role in the history of opera: he was to be its Justinian, recodifying the laws of Gluck, making them more stringent, applying them without pity for singers or audiences, and proceeding everywhere with unresilient justice. Measure was his god, and he finally came to regard genuine innovation as the devil. His whole program is implicit in *Médée,* which is a great opera—and the title role of which is one of the most taxing ever assigned to a soprano. The scarcity of sopranos who can sing the role of Medea—not to mention both sing and act it—is often advanced as a reason for not staging the opera. Quite apart from this, there have been other reasons, among them the sort of beauty the opera

---

[2] What does any composer think while grinding out the official pieces demanded by a government? In the case of an Elgar, the answer is too obvious, but the problem becomes more difficult when it involves a Richard Strauss writing a hymn for the opening of the Olympic Games at Garmisch-Partenkirchen or a Prokofiev turning out a Cantata for the Twentieth Anniversary of the October Revolution to texts snippeted from Karl Marx, Lenin, and Stalin.

undoubtedly has. Cherubini, rightly going over Hoffman's head and directly back to Euripides, took Greek mythology and drama at their word. Neither the protagonists of *Médée* nor the searing music that Cherubini composed for them are cherishably human. In that sense, we are soon reminded that Jason was a hero, Medea herself scarcely less.[3]

The overture to *Médée* is of the sort that Beethoven tried out for *Egmont* and hoped to use for *Fidelio,* a microcosm of the whole opera, not in the sense of a potpourri but in a more imaginative, more evocative way. It is all done irreproachably on a scale vaster than opera previously had used. Only Cherubini's inability to write easily memorable melodies can explain the fact that this stark, overpoweringly dramatic opera, instinct with lofty beauty, has not held operatic stages always, everywhere. But *Médée* was never a popular favorite. When the acid Auber was asked his opinion of it and replied dryly, "C'est la musique bien faite," he probably echoed the consensus.

On January 16, 1800, however, Cherubini brought out at the Théâtre Feydeau a considerably more human opera, a *comédie-lyrique* still definitely on the grand side, which won immediate and enduring vogue. This was *Les Deux Journées,* known equally well as *Der Wasserträger* and *The Water Carrier.* At last the dramatically unsophisticated Italian had found a libretto of such excellence that Goethe, who knew good melodrama when he read it, spoke of it as a model. This superior book came from the unevenly inspired fancy of Jean-Nicolas Bouilly, often no better than a scribbler. Beethoven's admiration for the libretto of *Les Deux Journées* indirectly resulted in Bouilly's unhappy collaboration with Josef Ferdinand von Sonnleithner and in Beethoven's acceptance of their faulty *Leonore.*

Besides begrudging Cherubini the libretto of *Les Deux Journées* Beethoven positively venerated its music. The score of Cherubini's opera

---

[3] The Cherubini *Medea* that has begun to be heard widely since its revival at the Maggio Musicale Fiorentino in 1953 for Maria Meneghini Callas is not the *Médée* heard in Paris in 1797. The original, in French, included spoken dialogue. This was replaced, for a performance in German at Frankfurt am Main on March 1, 1855, with recitatives composed by Franz Lachner. The usual modern version keeps Lachner's recitatives, uses Carlo Zangarini's translation of the text into Italian, and continues that revision of the score which Cherubini himself began, by cutting some five hundred measures when the opera was heard, in a German translation by Beethoven's friend Georg Friedrich Treitschke, at Vienna on November 6, 1802.

constantly lay on his worktable. The two composers had many traits in common, but not enough to explain why so much of *Les Deux Journées* now sounds like Beethoven. Cherubini did not copy the younger man; Beethoven studied Cherubini with such love that some of the Italian's turns of musical phrase unceremoniously passed over into his admirer's musical idiom. The overture to *Les Deux Journées* sounds only a little less Beethovian than the more frequently performed overture to Cherubini's 1803 opera, *Anacréon*. It abounds, for example, in those reflective pauses that Beethoven was to use with such dramatic force, and it includes two or three melodies that might have occurred to him but which he would have developed more boldly. These resemblances, had Cherubini noted them, would have irritated him greatly: he had little appreciation for Beethoven's music, of which he once said plaintively: "It makes me sneeze." A theoretician rather than a truly searching master of theory, he sneered at the "Leonore" No. 3: "I can't tell what key it's in," thus at once disavowing his own influence and outlining his own limitations.

Les Deux Journées is, in truth, the excelling achievement of a second-flight Beethoven. It loomed much larger than that before such composers as Weber, Mendelssohn, and Ludwig Spohr. The last threw away caution (for him a difficult gesture), professing himself "intoxicated with delight by its music." These transports were reasonable: *Les Deux Journées* is the most immediately appealing of Cherubini's operas, the most melodious and human, the least mythological or statuesque. He gets through its three acts without freezing or terrifying his hearers and without making it too clear that he is letting them overhear something surpassingly noble and learned. In short, the unpleasant edges of the man's personality show here less than elsewhere. For Cherubini, *Les Deux Journées* comes close to simple, unaffected entertainment, and several of its melodies are extraordinarily beguiling. The opera is much more than historically interesting; its complete neglect outside Germany is inexcusable. Its restaging would certainly pay artistically; it might even pay at the box office.

Cherubini dedicated *Les Deux Journées* to Gossec—a fine example of his tactlessness, for he had pompously refused to allow himself the pleasure of dedicating it to Haydn, saying, "No, as yet I have written nothing worthy of such a master." Nor did he, if we judge him by his own high standards. The history of Cherubini's later career as a composer for the stage is, with the exception of a single opera, unedifying. *Anacréon, ou L'Amour fugitif,* sung at the Opéra on October 4, 1803, has not much more than its delightfully fresh overture to hold the modern listener. *Faniska,* with a libretto by Sonnleithner, is the exception.

Produced at the Kärntnerthortheater, Vienna, on February 25, 1806, in the presence of a crowd of notables which included Haydn and Beethoven, *Faniska*—it was a Singspiel in German—was lively enough to take an important role in establishing Cherubini's fame throughout Central Europe. As he tarried in Vienna, no doubt basking in the approbation of his admired colleagues, Napoleon, flushed from victory at Austerlitz, took up residence there. Although the Emperor and Cherubini had never hit it off, the latter, to his surprise, was appointed director of music at Schönbrunn. But this led to nothing back in Paris, and after three operas designed in part to force Napoleon to give him some court position commensurate with his unquestioned eminence, Cherubini retired bitterly from the field. Operatically speaking, he was heard from only in 1813—on April 6, at the Opéra—when Napoleon attended the *première* of his relatively unsuccessful three-act opera (to a text Victor-Joseph Étienne de Jouy had built on Jean-Pierre Claris de Florian's novel *Gonzalve de Cordoue*) *Les Abencérages ou L'Étendard de Grenade.* After *Les Abencérages* had been heard less than two dozen times, Cherubini held aloof from the stage for twenty years.

In retirement, Cherubini at first scarcely drew a stave. He ostentatiously gardened; he affixed small landscape pictures to the walls of his retreat. During the Hundred Days, the Legion of Honor, which had been denied him when it had been given to Gossec, Grétry, and Méhul, at last became his. Louis XVIII appointed him to the Institut and finally made him superintendent of the king's chapel. But by then these sinecures were being showered on him because of another career, one on which he had embarked almost accidentally in 1809, when, during one of his periodic sulks, he had been wheedled into composing the Mass in F, the large proportions and splendor of conception of which show that his early Palestrinian studies and imitations were to have magnificent late results. When, in 1822, Cherubini was made director of the reconstituted Conservatoire, it was to the foremost living religious composer that the honor was given.

Eleven years later—in 1833, the year of Auber's *Gustave III,* Bellini's *Beatrice di Tenda,* Marschner's *Hans Heiling,* and a quartet of Donizetti operas including *Lucrezia Borgia*—the seventy-three-year-old Cherubini once again tried the stage. *Ali Baba ou Les Quarante Voleurs,* heard at the Opéra on July 22, 1833, turned out to be the last fruit of a withering bough. It was, in fact, largely a rewriting of *Koukourgi,* an unperformed opera that Cherubini had composed forty years earlier. *Ali Baba* was a failure despite a star-studded cast got together to do homage to the master, and including Nourrit, Levasseur, Cinti-Damoreau, and Cornélie Falcon, the last in the second of the brief six years of a singing career so remarkable that sopranos of her type are still called *falcons.* The sole interest of what Berlioz called an "operatic fossil" is as an example of tenacity: *Ali Baba* was heard fifty-three years after Cherubini's first opera, *Quinto Fabio,* which had been sung at Alessandria, in Lombardy, in 1780. Only Verdi was to beat this record, and then only by one year: *Falstaff* was to be heard fifty-four years later than *Oberto.*

After *Ali Baba,* Cherubini as a composer began to run down like a clock, though he mitigated not at all his rigorous rule at the Conservatoire. In 1838, Paris heard the first performance of his last important work, the Requiem in D minor. In 1841, mindful of his own greatness, Cherubini sat for Ingres. The portrait, in which the Muse, holding a lyre in one hand, spreads her other hand above the composer's head as though in blessing, turned out well. Cherubini graciously sent Ingres a token of appreciation, a little canon to a text of his own. It was his last composition. Two months later, he died. It was March 15, 1842, and Cherubini was eighty-one.

Thus ended the long life, the reign, of a most accomplished musician. This Italian, son of a minor musician at the Teatro della Pergola at Florence, had spent much of his life in a capital synonymous with tolerance, but remained a puritan who regarded music as a high calling and practiced it conscientiously always. For devotion to his task, for painstaking workmanship, he is not surpassed in the whole history of music. Yet it may be questioned whether he should have devoted so much of his time to the composing of operas. As a religious composer, using formulas that it was possible to burnish and perfect, and in a field where his whole character responded, Cherubini stayed in the first rank. His finest Masses, and especially those written for the coronations of Louis XVIII and Charles X, have emotional richness that is amazing to those who know him by his operas alone. Except for *Médée* and *Les Deux Journées* and *Faniska,* the operas are a little parched. Of this thwarted genius of the stage, Sir Donald Francis Tovey wrote, with his customary acumen: "If his melodic invention had been as warm as Gluck's his immensely superior technique in every branch of the art would have made him one of the greatest composers that ever lived. But his personal character shows in quaint exaggeration the same asceticism that in less sour and more negative form deprives even his finest music of the glow of that lofty inspiration that fears nothing." [4]

In 1807, after Cherubini's return to Paris from Vienna, and just when his star seemed to be favorably in conjunction with Napoleon's, he—and most of the leading French operatic composers—failed to win a newly inaugurated decennial opera prize contest sponsored by the Emperor. This desirable plum of ten thousand francs went most unexpectedly to a man who had given few signs of becoming a strong contender. The winning opera, *La Vestale,* was written to a libretto that Cherubini had rejected. Its composer, Gaspare Spontini, was a pushing young Italian from an obscure hill town. The lucky winner found a powerful faction leagued against him: the promised prize money never was awarded. But this was a secondary consideration with Spontini: in the Empress Josephine he found a champion who could dissipate all opposition merely by commanding a performance of *La Vestale* at the Opéra, where it was sung on December 16, 1807. Its success was so great that Cherubini was discouraged: *La Vestale* as much as anything was responsible for his self-imposed exile, shortly after, from the boards. Like Rossini faced with the popularity of Meyerbeer, he had no taste for the struggle. His withdrawal saved the balance of power in musical Paris: it is doubtful that the capital could have supported two composers whose classicizing was so stringent.

Spontini, arriving in Paris in 1803, had tried to win its public with much the same line of Neapolitan trivialities that Cherubini had begun with—and with as small results. He struck, if not a more serious, at least a more somber, note in 1804, when, on November 27 at the Opéra-Comique, his *fait historique, Milton,* was produced. The libretto by Étienne de Jouy and Michel Dieulafoy was based on episodes from John Milton's life, surely an unusual subject for dramatic comment. *La Vestale* was composed the next year. Such a grand, gloomy subject Gluck would have loved, and he would not have been in a position to criticize severely the happy ending brought about by the kind offices of a *dea ex machina,* Vesta. For this somewhat highfalutin libretto, Spontini provided a carefully composed score, which—during the two years that elapsed before its *première*—he turned over and over on the lathe of his imagination, revising, adding, subtracting, pruning, polishing, and then starting the

---

[4] Tovey's epitaph is just. Clearly, however, it does not underwrite neglect of Cherubini's best operas by impresarios who can find reasons for continuing to stage, say, Giordano's *Andrea Chénier.*

process over. He had a passion for perfection which, beginning with *La Vestale,* rode him mercilessly for the rest of his life. The final result of his wrestlings was a score of impressive magnificence, elaborate, heavily orchestrated, and conscientiously varied with the rise and fall of its action and the comings and goings of its characters, whose personalities and crises always are mirrored in the music.[5]

La Vestale is classical in texture, and has been called Gluckian. Certainly, Julia's magnificent aria "Tu che invoco" is exactly that, though Spontini probably learned much of what is in it from his teacher, Piccinni, Gluck's rival. Allowing for small idiosyncrasies of manner, *La Vestale* might have come from the workshop of Cherubini. Close investigation yields larger differences: Spontini seems less crabbed, less static, than his fellow Italian, has more ear for theatrical effect, and—though his personal history gives the lie to such an allegation—more warmth. Otherwise, Spontini might, except in the actual profile of a musical phrase, be a continuation of Cherubini, composer of *Médée.* As for technical innovation, the pompous and self-glorifying composer told Richard Wagner, forty years later, that in *La Vestale* he had ushered the suspension of the sixth into orthodox harmony and had first used the big drum in the orchestra.

La Vestale established Spontini in Paris. In Germany, whither it soon found its way, it long remained verdant. In the mid-forties, when Wagner was on the way up in the course of one of his many rises and descents, he staged it at Dresden, inviting the elderly composer to rehearse and conduct it. This invitation grew out of Wagner's sincere admiration for Spontini's music, and it is to his credit that the admiration survived a visitation from the ancient martinet. Even at seventy, Spontini ruled orchestra and singers with an iron hand—and an ebony baton, with an ivory ball at each end, which he wielded like a field marshal. By the time of the performance, Spontini's were the only intact nerves in operatic Dresden, and Wilhelmine Schröder-Devrient, who had been the erring Vestal, feigned illness to speed Spontini's departure.

[5] Like Cherubini's *Médée,* *La Vestale* has come to be known almost exclusively as translated into Italian. The libretto (left unused both by Boieldieu, for whom Étienne de Jouy had written it, and by Méhul, to whom it was offered) was Italianized more than once—by Niccolò Perotti for a Dresden performance in 1810 and by Giovanni Schmidt for the first singing in Italy (Teatro San Carlo, Naples, September 8, 1811).

New York had to wait until 1925 to hear *La Vestale*. But as early as January 6, 1888, the Metropolitan Opera House was the scene of a most spectacular production of Spontini's next opera, *Fernand Cortez*. This setting by an Italian of a French libretto about the Spanish conquest of Mexico was sung in an English-speaking city by Germans, in German. "The people employed in the representation," Henry Edward Krehbiel wrote, "rivaled in numbers those who constituted the veritable Cortez's army, while the horses came within three of the number that the Spaniard took into Mexico." That would have pleased Spontini, who by the time of *Fernand Cortez* (1809) had gone far on his career of vast spectacle-operas, in which he preceded both Rossini and Meyerbeer.

After its *première* at the Paris Opéra on November 28, 1809, *Fernand Cortez* became immensely popular, among its most enthusiastic sup-porters being Napoleon, who hoped that the villainous portrayal of the conquistadors would intensify the French people's dislike of the Span-iards (it was the eve of the Peninsular War)—by no means the first time politics had looked to opera for help. In 1817, after interest in the opera had abated somewhat, Spontini revised it throughout, shuffling the three acts with a thoroughness that only he could have devised. What was heard at the Metropolitan was a translation of the revised version. More theat-rical than *La Vestale,* this misreading of Mexican history is also more noisy—from it, Wagner drew inspiration for the thunders of *Rienzi*.

Having said the last musical word on a Roman theme and a Spanish-Mexican one, Spontini, after a decade devoted to the raising of musical taste in Paris, to becoming a great conductor able to assert the importance of rehearsals, and to tortuous intrigues and conduct of a peculiarly dom-ineering sort, turned his attention to Greco-Macedonian culture. Olym-pias, the mother of Alexander the Great, was the heroine of his third great opera. Voltaire's tragedy was the basis of the book that was pre-sented to Spontini for musical commentary. The last act alone engaged him for four years. Finally, on December 22, 1819, *Olimpie* was staged at the Paris Opéra, and for the first time since his transmogrification into a despot, Spontini failed. He was not daunted, but set heroically to work revising the music to a revised libretto. Version No. 2 had a happy end-ing, and was altogether more "operatic" in its book than the first. In German translation by E. T. A. Hoffmann, it was sung in Berlin on May 14, 1821. It was acclaimed, but Spontini set his face against so easy a success: he prepared still another version, which was received warmly in Paris on February 28, 1826; and with that he was content. But *Olimpie,* which some writers have called the best of his operas, and on which he bestowed the most labors, brought him the sharpest disappointment.

In 1819, Friedrich Wilhelm III of Prussia, long an admirer of Spontini, made him chief *Kapellmeister* and general music director at Berlin. Rather like a maharaja who receives a salute of nineteen guns at home and seventeen abroad, Spontini was also provided by the considerate monarch with the title of superintendent general of the royal music, to be used while traveling outside Prussia. The title was fine; even better was the salary—the fattest in musical Germany. After a year or so of insignificant official efforts, Spontini chose the second version of *Olimpie* to introduce his real self to the Berlin public. Nothing approaching the elaborateness and vastness of the resulting production had been seen there before, and when the curtain went up on the *première,* there had already been a royal reprimand because of the cost of the forty-two rehearsals, the fabulously expensive settings and costumes, and the lavishness of the entire project. But the King forgave all when he saw how Spontini had spent all that money. Berlin gasped. Spontini triumphed, and for forty-four days was the most talked-about composer in Europe.

Then June 18, 1821, brought forth *Der Freischütz,* and Weber tumbled Spontini from the skies. It was a popular catastrophe, for, almost from the beginning, Spontini, by his arrogance and grasping self-assertiveness, had alienated his colleagues and subordinates. Faced with a new spirit in music, he grew more and more unbending, choleric, overweening: the new spirit was completely outside his comprehension. He was only forty-seven when the triumph of German romanticism stripped him of the substance of power; he retained the shadow of it for twenty years—in short, as long as his royal protector lived. One of his last official acts was an attempt to thwart the advancement of young Felix Mendelssohn.

But even if the old warhorse was not equipped by innate temperament, background, or accomplishment to understand the nature of the artistic forces surging about him, and most expressively characterized in Weber and Marschner, he was not a fool. He attempted to regain his rule by meeting the enemy on what he supposed to be its own ground. In the mind of this sublime egocentric, the idea that Weber offered the Germans nothing more than a national libretto led immediately to the decision to vanquish the Saxon whippersnapper with a German opera of his own. The theme he selected was lofty, the heroine no less than an unfortunate lady of the House of Hohenstaufen.[6] As far as the book by Ernst Raupach was concerned, the three-act opera was German through and through. But the music was in Spontini's own style—a strange and sometimes greatly effective composite most aptly called Roman Imperial. The scale was grander than ever, the first act alone being long enough to provide an evening's entertainment.

By an arrangement possibly unique in the annals of opera, the vast first act of *Agnes von Hohenstaufen* was sung separately, sent up as a sort of trial balloon, on May 28, 1827. Two years later, on June 12, 1829, the entire three acts of this finically embroidered medieval tapestry were gradually unrolled at Berlin's Königliches Opernhaus. The circumstances attending this solemn *première* made the opera very German indeed, though its music was not: it was staged as part of the celebrations connected with the wedding of Prince Wilhelm of Prussia, later the first ruler of united Germany, to Augusta of Weimar. *Agnes von Hohenstaufen* was revived eight years later in a much-revised version, but Germany remained indifferent. It proved to be Spontini's last completed opera, though he lived until 1851.

Spontini's last years were troubled. Before losing his position in Berlin, he committed various indiscretions, culminating in an insult to the new King of Prussia, Friedrich Wilhelm IV, a friend to everything in the arts (grandeur excepted) which Spontini detested. Indictment for *lèse-majesté* followed, along with a threat of imprisonment. On April 2, 1841, Spontini appeared to conduct *Don Giovanni,* which was, with Gluck's *Armide,* the only opera not of his own composition that he deigned to produce in Berlin. He was hissed from the podium; his long tenure of office was at an end. The King forgave him his misdeeds, provided him with a pension not one groschen less than his salary, and sent him out of the country. He became a wanderer, honored—though not always welcomed —everywhere. He was decorated by the King of Denmark; Gregory XVI made him a count. Already he was a member of the Institut de France. Even to him, however, it gradually became apparent that he was a relic from the past. Although he never doubted the superiority of that past, neglect by the present hurt. Attacks of melancholia became frequent. He be-

---

[6] This was not actually Spontini's first German opera, but only his first important one. The first had been *Nurmahal, oder das Rosenfest von Caschmir,* with a libretto Carl Alexander Herklots based on Thomas Moore's *Lalla Rookh* (Berlin, May 27, 1822).

came deaf. In 1851, he died, leaving his very large fortune to the poor of Majolati, his native village. So, after all the quarrels and storms, the ill-humors and pontifications, the end was edifying.

Spontini's life may be read as tragedy or high comedy, depending upon the emphases. The temptation is to see him too unrelievedly as a figure of fun. Often there is something a little comic even in his music, which can sound emptily pompous, merely noisy, unreasonably orotund. But a composer whom the ungracious Wagner praised and whom Berlioz worshiped just next to Gluck was not a mediocrity. Not all of Spontini's effects are pompous: some have the authentic classical ring, speak with a rare, individual nobility. In that orchestral din, those piled-on brasses, not all is just sound and fury. At times these volumes speak with real eloquence. Technically, Spontini was scarcely less accomplished than Cherubini. The acts of his operas not only are unities within themselves, but also flow into each other, thus giving each of his four major operas satisfying formal design. Wagner realized this and studied Spontini's scores to great effect, nor was Spontini's brilliant handling of choruses lost on him. There is much in the theory that the composer of *Die Meistersinger* was at least as much in debt to Spontini as to Meyerbeer.

CHAPTER XII

Berlioz

HECTOR BERLIOZ is one of those people—and there are several in each of the major arts, not to speak of the multitudes in the minor ones —whose idiom is so personal that the part of prudence is to leave them out of a general survey. Thus, Bernard Berenson could not fit Carlo Crivelli into the Venetian Painters (1894), apologizing for the omission in a graceful, allusive paragraph with a line that could be the epitaph for many of these idiosyncratics: "(He) does not belong to a movement of constant progress. . . ." Certainly, it applies to Berlioz. Into that part of criticism which consists of finding ancestors and descendants, he fits badly, or scarcely at all. In a survey of opera, therefore, he is included not as a step in the evolution of the art, but because he composed several operas interesting in themselves. He was not a traditionalist: he did not sum up any of the previously accepted styles of operatic composition; he was not a radical: he did not overturn the fabric of opera as he found it and put something totally new in its place. Nor did he write his operas according to a theory of his own devising. His style of operatic writing has something of the accidental about it: it happened once and may never happen again. The final challenge of this tortured, difficult man, who was so conscious of his originality, might have been the *défi:* Imitate me if you can.

In discussing any segment of Berlioz' career, the natural temptation is to go off on a tangent about his melodramatic life, to weigh the fact and fiction in his own fascinating writings about himself, and to take sides prematurely for or against his merits as a composer—to talk about everything except the point at issue, the music itself. Ten or fifteen years ago such evasions had point: no one, not even the French, had heard enough of the larger Berlioz to be party to an intelligent discussion. While the situation is gradually being rectified, we still—an occasional notable exception aside—await performances of many of his works, notably the operas. Berlioz almost evaporates in piano scores, for the sum total of his radicalism is, apart from certain harmonic and melodic personalisms, a way of thinking in terms of orchestral sound. It is no wonder, then, that the baffled critic, unable to hear Berlioz' major compositions often enough or to appreciate their effectiveness on his own piano or by silent score-reading, used to fall back on the consoling cushion of biographical detail.

Berlioz was a little over thirty years old when he began to work, not on his first opera, but on the first one that reached the stage. Barely more than a decade before, in 1823, when he was the most callow of music students, he had dared to write, out of his voluminous ignorance of the essentials of composition, a something which at the time he very much wished to see produced, though in later years he was grateful that it had remained on paper. As so much of even the later Berlioz is variable in quality, we need not regret the loss of *Estelle et Némorin*. Three years later in 1826, a student of Lesueur, for whom he felt an affectionate but patronizing respect, he tried again. This time he dropped the project before completing it. The pleasant overture—superior prentice music— to *Les Francs-Juges* survives, and whole chunks of the rest of the opera, which has vanished as such, later cropped out in various works, particularly the *Symphonie fantastique*.

Although all the music Berlioz composed for the next few years was highly dramatic, even theatrical, in quality, it was not until 1834 that he got around to beginning another opera. To show, however, that his thoughts were never far away from the stage, he kept experimenting with overtures and cantatas—*Le Roi Lear* (1831) is the most attractive of the former and is an occasional concert number. Tovey has pointed out that though this is a tragic work, it is written in a bright major key— an arresting example of Berlioz' very personal way of interpreting a situation. It is possible that some of his interpretations were entered upon in a spirit of adventurousness that wandered fatally near to *blague*.

After 1833, when he married the heroine of his *idée fixe*—the impossible Henrietta Smithson, an Irish actress of disputed merit—Berlioz gave up the most salient extravagances in his music, though he did not renounce melodrama in his life. Artistically, he settled down, and as in him everything went by contraries, began to do his best work. He chose what, in view of his recent marriage, could scarcely be called a tactful libretto—the story of Benvenuto Cellini, his libretto for which was promptly rejected by the Opéra-Comique. This did not discourage Berlioz, who had started to set it as soon as it was delivered to him, and pecked at it sporadically for the next four years. By the time it was completed, it had been accepted by the Opéra, and Berlioz had taken time off to compose, besides small pieces, one of the most impressive of his achievements—the *Grande Messe des morts,* a requiem for those who had been killed when Fieschi's bomb failed to assassinate Louis-Philippe.

Berlioz' first staged opera was not a success: in four months *Benvenuto Cellini* reached only four performances, and was then dropped. Various causes were alleged for its failure: a coterie of musicians was ranged against it; Duprez, generally a favorite, and certainly a competent artist, muffed the title role; Habeneck, the conductor at the Opéra, and one of Berlioz' bêtes noires, is said to have conspired against it. At any rate, at the *première,* on September 10, 1838, the overture alone was encored, and most of the rest was hissed. Much of this animosity may have been directed at the composer, who had a talent for putting people's backs up, but quite as much was undoubtedly directed at the music itself. It was not cacophonous; it was not extravagant as was so much of Berlioz' early music—but definitely it was strange. Some of it would still seem strange —most of it, however, is like Auber or fledgling Wagner—for reasons that were as valid a hundred years ago as today: Berlioz' whole concept of musical idea is outside the main lines of development, and from the hearer's point of view, the great length of his single melodic phrases make them seem, to all but the most tutored ears, not melodies at all. Today, the commonest adverse criticism of Berlioz is that he has no tunes and, doubtless, that was the commonest criticism of 1838. Testimony to the contrary by all those who have qualified themselves to listen intelligently cannot change public insistence that melody resemble either the repetitive patterns of Italian song or those packed germinal phrases which are almost atavistically recognized as "Wagner" even if their source is not precisely that.

Benvenuto Cellini lay untouched for fourteen years, except that in 1844 Berlioz took certain sections, mainly vocal, from the finale of the second act, and recast them in purely instrumental form. The result was the most brilliant and popular of his overtures, the *Carnaval romain.* In 1851, at the request of Liszt, who admired Berlioz, had an unselfish interest in furthering the spread of his music, and yet proclaimed him a charlatan, he began rewriting the entire opera, for Liszt had promised to produce it at Weimar. The next year, after further revisions suggested during rehearsals, it was produced there most successfully on March 20. Unfortunately, Berlioz was in England conducting the concerts of the New Philharmonic Society, and was not present either to taste success or to witness the beautifully disciplined performance Liszt had somehow managed to draw from his small forces. However, in November of that year, Liszt twice repeated *Cellini* to honor Berlioz on a visit to Weimar. As the Germans were by way of taking him up because he had been repudiated by the barbarous French, the warmth that greeted these repetitions did Berlioz' ego a lot of good, but also gave him the unhappy idea of having the opera staged in London. Of that miserable performance at Covent Garden, on June 25, 1853, Chorley wrote: *"Benvenuto Cellini* failed more decidedly than any foreign opera I recollect to have seen performed in London," and that despite the fact that the composer himself, one of the best conductors of the age, directed.

Berlioz' next opera had a fantastic history: it began, five years before *Benvenuto Cellini,* as a suite of songs, then developed into a cantata, and was finally made into an opera—twenty-four years after the composer's death. *La Damnation de Faust* grew out of his youthful enthusiasm for Goethe's poem, which, however, he knew only in a prose translation by the exotic Gérard de Nerval. He became so infatuated with it that he could not tear himself away. The first fruit of this mad obsession was a song cycle—*Huit Scènes de Faust*—of cantatalike aspect; this he published at his own expense in 1829. As Berlioz never had much money, this meant consuming passion, and the Faust idea continued to smolder in him until 1846. That year, in the midst of a tour through Central Europe, he became inflamed with the idea of Hungarian independence, and for a concert in Budapest made a shattering orchestration of the piously revered patriotic *Rákóczy March.* This created such a sensation that, though it had no relation to either Goethe's poem or Nerval's translation (or his own emendations of both), he incorporated it into the first part of the "dramatic legend"—really a cantata—he was concocting out of fragments of the *Huit Scènes* and some new material.

Krehbiel, who, with some justification, called *La Damnation de Faust* "a thing of shreds and patches," amusingly described how the work was strung together:

Traveling from town to town, conducting rehearsals and concerts, he wrote whenever and wherever he could—one number in an inn at

Passau, the Elber scene and the Dance of the Sylphs at Vienna, the peasants' song by gaslight in a shop one night when he had lost his way in Pesth, the angels' chorus in Marguerite's apotheosis at Prague (getting up in the middle of the night to write it down), the song of the students, "Jam nox stellata velamina pandit," (of which the words are also Berlioz'), at Breslau. He finished the work in Rouen and Paris, at home, at his café, in the gardens of the Tuileries, even on a stone in the Boulevard du Temple.

Finally it reached completion and was presented to the public on December 6, 1846. As if anticipating its operatic destiny, *La Damnation de Faust* was given, not in a concert hall, but at the Opéra-Comique. Again the French would have nothing of Berlioz (who had paid the production expenses)—they did not like cantatas, however lively, and the work fell flatter than *Benvenuto Cellini*. The next year, Berlin heard it, and the Germans, being consistent too, liked it better. But it was in England that *La Damnation* was most appreciated: the English took it as a very pious work, and after 1880, when Sir Charles Halle gave it at Manchester, it soon became a festival feature. What these performances had become by 1893 is best suggested by Shaw, in a critique in his best and rowdiest manner, ending with the sad reflection that "the damnation has been lifted from the work. It has been 'saved,' so to speak."

The next operation on the helpless carcass of *La Damnation de Faust* was performed, appropriately, at Monte Carlo, the very year that Shaw was scoffing at the tameness of the Albert Hall rendition. The surgeon was the Rumanian composer Raoul Gunsbourg, who at that time was impresario of the local opera house. Whatever the flaws of Gunsbourg's adaptation (which continues to flurry the purists), he had the right idea: *La Damnation de Faust* is more opera than oratorio, and in this way, if in no other, resembles a composition that set out to seek its fortunes in much the same condition—Saint-Saëns' *Samson et Dalila*. Jean de Reszke ensured the success of the Gunsbourg *première,* and when Monte Carlo heard it again, nine years later, he joined Melba and Maurice Renaud to make a truly stellar cast.

After *La Damnation de Faust* (which, we must remember, was not an opera), Berlioz was extremely busy for almost ten years giving concerts, conducting operas, writing criticisms, and waging war with his musical contemporaries. He was a driven man, at times finding it hard to earn enough to live on, though an impressive amount of evidence has been gathered to show that, with all his ups and downs, Berlioz was a hardheaded businessman. To Théophile Gautier, he was one of the three supreme romantics of French art, the other two being Victor Hugo and Delacroix. For all three, romanticism paid off: Hugo, the shrewdest of them, died very rich; in their last years Delacroix and Berlioz were certainly well-to-do.

But neither the great man of letters nor the great painter had to struggle for so long a time as Berlioz did. After *La Damnation,* though an endless number of projects entered into his whirling brain, the idea of composing another opera was apparently not foremost in his thoughts, even in a period that was by no means barren of big works. In 1854, he completed the oratorio *L'Enfance du Christ,* an almost faultless score, fastidiously set for small orchestra, solo voices, and chorus, notable for sobriety of style, yet tenderly expressive: Giotto in music. Its wide success did something to offset the disappointment of not being appointed to the post of director of the Hofoper at Dresden, despite the efforts of Liszt and Hans von Bülow, both immensely influential personages.

The next year brought further compensations: Liszt had never relaxed his good soldiering to gain for Berlioz a sympathetic and, if possible, large following, and in 1854 had put on a miniature Berlioz festival in Weimar. While there, the revived composer was seized upon by Liszt's mistress, the earnest but gaga Princess Carolyne Sayn-Wittgenstein. They had long, serious talks, during which Berlioz doubtless mentioned his old passion for Virgil. Naturally, the Polish-born Princess had had the same passion, and she immediately suggested that Berlioz compose an opera about the Trojans at Troy and their vicissitudes after the fall of the city. Their mutual fascination persisted, and in a letter to the Princess, written just after the *première* of a shortened version of *Les Troyens* in 1863, he spoke of the opera as "our work"—a phrase that led at least one scholar to guess that she had written a scenario for Berlioz' guidance. But the book of the opera, such as it is, comes from the *Aeneid* and Berlioz.

In 1856, by the time he was ready to work on *Les Troyens,* the availability of a government sinecure, as well as a small inheritance from his father, had given Berlioz comparative leisure and some financial ease. Semipublic readings of the libretto of *Les Troyens*—his own fabrication of whole sections of the *Aeneid* (owing something, no doubt, to his conversations with the Princess) mingled with straight Virgil—aroused anticipatory enthusiasm about the opera, and Berlioz went plowing ahead hopefully. Although much of this very long composition was written at top speed, it was not finished until March, 1858. Then began the lengthy, pride-draining business of trying to sell the idea of producing this seven-act epic to an opera house, and Berlioz was as unwearying as his weakened physical condition would allow (he had what was then called "neuralgia of the intestines") in hawking it from one manager to another.

It seemed that his round of humiliation would never end. It was especially scarifying when a gleam of hope brightened for a moment, then waned the next. For instance, as early as 1858 Napoleon III was showing interest in *Les Troyens,*[1] and in 1861, when he summoned Berlioz to dine with him, the composer must have gone hopefully into the presence. But Napoleon was not a real lover of music: he did nothing for the wretched man who thought that he was going to die, and could not bear to die without once having heard what he believed to be his masterpiece. The worst case of hope frustrated came the same year, when it looked as if the Opéra might accept *Les Troyens.* However, in 1863, Léon Carvalho, impresario of the Théâtre-Lyrique, and one of the original enthusiasts for the work, promised to produce it late that year. But even this did not mean victory: Carvalho could not run the risk of mounting the excessively long opera complete. Therefore, Berlioz reluctantly divided it into two unequal parts, and the second, longer part—*Les Troyens à Carthage*—was sung twenty-two times that season, beginning on November 4.

Berlioz' press was mainly laudatory, and if there were some dissenting comments, he could explain them by the fact that he had never given quarter in his own critiques. His accusations, in his *Mémoires,* against Carvalho, whom he declares responsible for the opera's disappearance after the first season, can be dismissed as the ravings of a sick man. Generally, the people who meant something artistically were impressed, Meyerbeer being in the van of those who did not hesitate to call the opera a masterpiece. The simple truth is that the public did not like *Les Troyens à Carthage* enough to warrant either its restaging or, more, the production of the opera as a unit. Indeed, Berlioz died without ever having heard the first part—*La Prise de Troie.*

At last, twenty-one years after Berlioz' death, Felix Mottl, famous for his Wagnerism, consummated, on the nights of December 6 and 7, 1890, a long devotion to an unpopular cause by giving the world *première* of

[1] No doubt the classical subject had its share in attracting Napoleon III, who later wrote a life of Julius Caesar, who had claimed descent from Aeneas.

Les Troyens—in German. Not Paris, but Karlsruhe, a provincial but progressive little town in the Rhineland, was vouchsafed to be the scene of this epic event. Both parts have since been sung at the Opéra, but when Paris hears the "complete" opera, it is in a grotesquely telescoped perversion that is forced into a single evening. Except for a solitary production at Brussels, in French, in 1906, apparently the only reverent treatment it has received since 1890 has been accorded it in Great Britain. Dr. Erik Chisholm staged *Les Troyens* intact in Glasgow in 1935, and in 1957 and 1958 it was mounted lovingly and almost at full length at Covent Garden, though in English. Neither part of the work seems to have been mounted in the United States by a regular opera house, though semiprofessional productions have been tried.

The spirit of *Les Troyens* is surely not that of the *Symphonie fantastique,* though it is recognizably the same composer's. Here, at last, is Berlioz' *éloge* to Gluck, the more glorious because so long meditated during the constantly interrupted tranquillity that he was able to steal for himself. The young Berlioz would not have thought the score of *Les Troyens* romantic music: it is a classical work with romantic touches derived as faithfully from Virgil as an unreconstructed original like Berlioz would allow. Its existence is a challenge to those who would plant a sign marked "classical" or "romantic" on an area, for it fuses the romantic and the classical with the experience of one who knows the deeper hells beneath each of these rallying cries.

This tremendous tale of the capture of Troy, the love of Dido and Aeneas, and Aeneas' leave-taking to keep his date with destiny (as the opera closes, the chorus chants "Italie! Italie!" and the Capitol looms in the background like a Mediterranean Valhalla) runs for four hours and a half, not counting intermissions. Opera managers, willing to subject their patrons to *Parsifal* at least once a year (for piety's sake?), can find reasons for depriving these same patrons of Berlioz' most ambitious work. Most of us, therefore, must judge the merits of *Les Troyens* from the printed score and from excerpts, whether recorded or heard in the concert hall, assisted by reports of those fortunate musical observers who heard the Glasgow essay of the entire work in 1935, which disclosed, as Sir Donald Tovey testified, "one of the most gigantic and convincing masterpieces of music-drama," or the Covent Garden performances begun in 1957. Even a knowledge of *Les Troyens* confined to Hylas' "Vallon sonore," Aeneas' "Inutiles regrets," and the "Chasse royale et orage" could persuade us to echo Tovey's pronouncement. With a knowledge, by ear, only of patches, one salient fact is at once apparent: wherever the voice is used, it reigns supreme, whether in the noble declamatory style of the recitatives or in the passionately conceived arias, "the whole," as Léon Vallas has said, "bathed in a rich orchestration."

Les Troyens was Berlioz' last opera but one. His swan song was, in size, a mere two-acter, in spirit a bit of fooling, in genesis a commission from the Baden-Baden theater. It was written around *Much Ado About Nothing,* a subject Berlioz had toyed with thirty years before. With a curious inattention to Shakespearean spelling, he called his little comic opera *Béatrice et Bénédict.* Conducting its *première* at the opening of the Baden-Baden theater on August 9, 1862, Berlioz was in such agonizing pain that he could not savor the warmth with which he and his diverting music were received. He was inordinately pleased with the libretto (his own) and particularly with touches of comedy that he had added to Shakespeare's text. Had his own sense of humor been in the best working condition at the time, he might have thanked the gods that *Béatrice et Bénédict* first saw the light in so musically sophisticated a town as Baden-Baden, for its best comedy number is the rehearsal of a fugal wedding song by choristers and instrumentalists—not likely to appeal to the untutored. But the opera as a whole is pretty and most cleverly devised: it should be known by more than its overture; it deserves occasional production.

It would be pleasant to recount how Berlioz ended his tortured, misunderstood career on a note of comedy because, like Verdi penning *Falstaff* in his eightieth year, he had finally won through to some kind of inner serenity. Unfortunately, the truth is that this feckless piece had no relation at all to Berlioz' state of mind: Baden-Baden had ordered a comic opera, and he had filled the order. *Béatrice et Bénédict* was not only his last opera; it was also his last considerable composition of any sort. Berlioz was a ruin—a man wilting away of a spiritual malaise; the physical decay was secondary. A few more years, a few footling trifles, and then the end, on March 8, 1869.

No one in the whole range of musical history—no one, that is, with comparable gifts—tried so hard for merited recognition and failed so disastrously. Posthumous reward has been delayed, and even now the battle to proclaim Berlioz one of the unquestioned masters has not been won. Before the nineteenth century was over, he had the fame conferred by imitation: Saint-Saëns said that a whole generation modeled itself on Berlioz, and his influence extended to Debussy. Richard Strauss listened equally to Wagner and Berlioz, as did many lesser men, including Ernest Reyer. Still needed to bring the picture of Berlioz into focus are more performances. When that picture does emerge completely, we will know to what a large extent Berlioz is inimitable.

To compare Berlioz with a man who struggled as hard and almost as long as he, but with quite different results: Wagner gained his comparatively quick victory first by the tangible seductiveness of the mere externals of his music; Berlioz has no such physical allure, no such easy sensuality. It was possible, once one was accustomed to the novelties of the Wagnerian vocabulary, to lie back and bathe in the drugging clouds of sound. Berlioz invites to no such physical languors: to appreciate his long-breathed melodies requires a constantly attentive ear; to hear him at all, in fact, means listening every minute. (Unfortunately, his *longueurs* are notorious, and his sole large work entirely without them is *L'Enfance du Christ.*) It means forgoing most of the sensuous appeal that his contemporaries exuded with romantic fervor, and collaborating, as a listener, imaginatively and intellectually with the music. Berlioz' music offers appeals to the emotions, but rarely to the loins.

On the face of it, Berlioz chose a hard path for a would-be popular composer of opera: he has been called, with exact justice, a creator of great melodies, but he wrote few tunes—the "Danse des sylphes" and "Menuet des feux-follets" from *La Damnation de Faust* are early and exceptional. He wrote vocal passages that are nightmares to singers, not only because they are difficult to sing, but also because conquering them brings no startled applause from the audience. And, finally, this most theatrical of men was without that sense of the theater which knows instinctively how to prepare for, and underline, dramatic effects. He made the tactical error of absorbing the drama into the music instead of keeping music and drama wedded to each other in a fair marriage. Wagner often made the same error, but he was saved from popular neglect by his rich sensory attractiveness; Berlioz had no such palliative to offer, and thus, in his case, the error was almost fatal. It has reduced his first surviving opera (such occasional performances as those by the Carl Rosa company in England in the 1950's aside) to two overtures, one a successful afterthought. It has maimed his greatest opera and for a long time all but kept it from the stage.

Berlioz is usually brought forth as the typical rebel romantic, particularly by those whose knowledge of his work is limited to two or three concert warhorses. The most considerable of these, the *Symphonie fan-*

tastique and *Harold en Italie,* were youthful extravagances. It is disappointing to those who judge Berlioz by those flagrant and beguiling works not to find the Byronic touch in his later compositions. It is particularly disappointing to those who read the libretto of *Benvenuto Cellini* before hearing its music. The truth is that after 1834, those early porings over the scores of Gluck in the library of the Conservatoire began to have their sequel: the pull of classicism became so intense that Berlioz gave way. By the time of *Les Troyens,* he was very possibly the least romantic composer in Europe, and the only vestige of his rebelliousness was his umbrellalike thatch of untamed hair. By that time, too, he was really elect to set Virgil's great story.

Grand-Opera Fanfare

GIACOMO MEYERBEER died at Paris on May 2, 1864. On April 28, 1865, *L'Africaine,* the opera that he considered his masterpiece, was given a spectacular *première* at the Paris Opéra; so universal was his fame that before the year was over, the opera had been heard also in London, Madrid, Bologna, Berlin, Antwerp, New York, and The Hague. From 1831 on, Meyerbeer had been the most famous of active operatic composers—a man so powerful in the opera house that Rossini had retired from the lists partly because he would not struggle against so dangerous a rival. For thirty-three years the living Meyerbeer had reigned; for a decade after his death he exercised a ghostly sovereignty. Then came Bayreuth, and the operatic world began to recognize a new master.

During the bloody Wagnerian revolution, many a musical princeling was guillotined and yet managed to survive. In Meyerbeer's case, the procedure was not so peremptory (because more difficult), but, when it was completed, it proved thorough. Although Meyerbeer's hold on the stage lasted into the first decade of the twentieth century, the public had long ceased to worship him, and the great all-star revivals of *Les Huguenots* and *Le Prophète* were for the purpose of animating what the more advanced critics proclaimed to be corpses. In time, these proclamations took effect: fewer and fewer operatic nights were devoted to this supreme master of theatrical legerdemain. *Robert le diable,* the opera that first enthroned Meyerbeer, has not been heard at Covent Garden since the 1890's or at the Metropolitan Opera since that theater's first season, 1883–84. *Les Huguenots,* the most popular of his scores, has not been sung at Covent Garden since a disastrous revival in 1927, or at the Metropolitan since 1914. Meyerbeer has not been represented at the Metropolitan since February 24, 1933, its final performance of *L'Africaine*.

The reasons for the demise of Meyerbeer after a promise of almost endless longevity are to be sought for as much in the facts of his life as in the intrinsic qualities of his operas. He was tireless in offering a helping hand to deserving fellow artists, and this attractive quality worked for his posthumous ruin. He made the central mistake of being kind to Wagner and, at the same time, of being a success while Wagner was a failure. Furthermore, he was born ten or fifteen years too early to share in the blessings of the Wagnerian dispensation. Finally, though a German, Meyerbeer—and this caused his friend Weber untold agony of spirit— was anything but a German composer. His first successful operas were written in Italian to a Rossinian pattern, his last ones in French in a cosmopolitan polyglot lingo all his own. Wagner never forgave him. Besides, while any musical ignoramus could point to Wagner's pilferings from the rich Meyerbeerian hoard, when did Meyerbeer borrow anything from Wagner?

From decent gratitude—a period of short duration—Wagner's attitude toward Meyerbeer changed to hatred manifested chiefly as reiterated denunciation. Meyerbeer was made to figure as the Antichrist of Wagnerism, and as pious Wagnerians came to dominate both music and music criticism, joyously perpetuating the *Meister*'s feuds, his enemy's reputation became blacker and blacker. Some have suggested that Wagner hated Meyerbeer primarily because he was a Jew, but a chronological analysis of Wagner's anti-Semitic sayings and writings suggests that it was the other way around: Wagner hated Jews primarily because Meyerbeer was one. The task of destroying Meyerbeer was easy. Meyerbeer labored during one of those periods in which opera is dominated not by purely musical or predominantly dramatic considerations, but by absorption with theatrical effect. Nothing shifts fashions so easily and rapidly. One of the few extended modern defenses of Meyerbeer occurs, properly, in Bernard Van Dieren's remarkable book entitled *Down Among the Dead Men*.

Meyerbeer, one of music's spoiled children, was born rich and remained rich. He was prodigiously gifted, so gifted that he could choose from among several possible careers. He could, it is said, have become the foremost piano virtuoso of the period. Instead, he turned to opera, and by the day he became twenty-one had produced a score (*Jephthas Gelübde,* Munich, December 23, 1812) so learned and solemn that it sounded like an oratorio. It was to a German text, as was his second opera, *Wirth und Gast, oder Aus Scherz Ernst* (Stuttgart, January 6, 1813).[1] Both were received so indifferently by his countrymen that when Salieri, no doubt previsaging a parallel between Meyerbeer's career and Gluck's, advised him to visit Italy to learn how to write for the voice, he leaped at the idea.

Meyerbeer arrived in Venice in 1815, during the protracted *Tancredi* madness, and was converted at once to Rossini. Two years later came the first of his six unadulteratedly Rossinian operas, *Romilda e Costanza* (Padua, July 19, 1817). Several of these were successful and reached staging in various parts of Europe. But by the time the last of them was composed (1822), Meyerbeer was becoming dissatisfied with himself. His plumes were borrowed, and the fascination of Italy had become easier to exorcise. Weber, who had been Meyerbeer's fellow student at the curious academy of the arts conducted by that learned charlatan the Abbé Vogler, staged one of Meyerbeer's Italian operas at Dresden and also, hoping to recall the expatriate to his German senses, restaged *Wirth und Gast.* Because Meyerbeer had a high regard for Weber, he tried to compose another German opera (*Das Brandenburger Thor,* 1823), but failed so miserably that it never reached the stage. This disaster catapulted him back to Venice. There, in 1824, his last and most successful Italian opera was performed (La Fenice, March 7).

Il Crociato in Egitto is a fascinating score. In this big spectacle opera based on stories of the Crusades, and with a libretto by the same Gaetano Rossi who had fabricated the book of Rossini's *Semiramide,* Meyerbeer stands at the crossroads. Gone is his earlier obsession with pure lyric tunes, gone the easy, undramatic flow of his earlier Italian operas. This is the work of a restive Rossinian. In it, a seer might have detected signs of Meyerbeer's future: those few but affectionately contrived *coups de théâtre,* those rumblings of a still-muffled orchestra, those moments of eloquent declamation, that pomp and glitter—were not these the very elemental devices of that eclectic style which Meyerbeer was at last to devise as his own?

At the Fenice *première* of *Il Crociato in Egitto,* Giovanni Battista Velluti, the last of the great *castrati,* took the soprano part of Armando, the Christian knight. When the opera was heard in London in 1825—the

[1] *Jephthas Gelübde,* sung twice, appears to have disappeared, but *Wirth und Gast* was to turn up at Vienna in 1814 as *Die beiden Kalifen* and at Dresden in 1820 as *Alimelek.*

first by Meyerbeer [2] to be played there—with Maria Malibran and Maria Caradori-Allan, he again sang Armando. The Earl of Mount Edgcumbe, a dilettante critic and composer, said of this belated representative of a once-great class of singers:

> At the moment when he was expected to appear, the most profound silence reigned in one of the most crowded audiences I ever saw, broken on his entering by loud applauses [*sic*] of encouragement. The first note he uttered gave a shock of surprise, almost of disgust, to inexperienced ears; but his performance was listened to with attention and great applause throughout, with but few audible expressions of disapprobation speedily suppressed. . . . To the old he brought back some pleasing recollections; others, to whom his voice was new, became reconciled to it, and sensible of its merits, while many declared that to the last his tones gave them more pain than pleasure. However, either from curiosity or real admiration, he drew crowded audiences, and no opera but the *Crociato* was performed to the end of the season.

In *Il Crociato,* Meyerbeer knows with fair certainty whither he will go, and when it was produced successfully in Paris, he did not hesitate to take the next obvious step. Being a man with leisure to command, he spent the next five years forging the instruments of his craft. By 1831 he was ready to show the world of Paris—which had become his home— what he really could do. He labored on his setting of a five-act text by Eugène Scribe and Germain Delavigne for four years, constantly shifting details in its welter of inordinate complexities. So costly were the stage properties demanded by the score that they probably explain why Louis Véron, the new director at the Opéra, demanded a financial guarantee from Meyerbeer, though he was already a composer of high standing.

The guarantee could have been dispensed with: when *Robert le diable* came to the stage on November 21, 1831, its success was so gigantic as to ensure the stability of Véron's regime. True, the little bourgeois of genius—impresario, doctor, journalist, and politician—had collected a resplendent foursome of chief singers, and had given the mimed role of the Abbess to the leading female dancer of the period, Maria Taglioni. Julie Dorus-Gras was the Alice, Laure Cinti-Damoreau the Isabelle, Nourrit the Robert, and Levasseur the Bertram. But for once it scarcely

[2] A performance of the overture to *Il Crociato,* at the Bowery Theater, New York, on May 9, 1833, was advertised as the first music by Meyerbeer to reach America.

mattered what these excelling artists did: they were all unwittingly engaged in an inevitable revolution. For if Auber's *La Muette de Portici* (1828) and Rossini's *Guillaume Tell* (1829) had not fixed the pattern for French grand opera, that pattern was set, and for the rest of the century, that night in 1831. Cinti-Damoreau had played a truly leading role in this revolution: she had sung in the *premières* of all three operas.

Meyerbeer cast the deciding vote for the new order, for Rossini had abandoned the operatic stage after the ambiguous triumph of *Tell,* and Auber, having laid one of the foundation stones of French grand opera, soon renounced this serious role for one closer to his twinkling nature. It was Meyerbeer, the serious student not only of musical styles but also of all cultural history, the conscious eclectic, who established the nineteenth-century spectacle opera, the opera of constant effects and ever-changing picture and pageantry. He found, as a coadjutor, a scenic designer of such talent that it has been said that *Robert le diable* could not have come off without his realistic, sumptuous settings and ingenious mechanical devices. This was Pierre Cicéri, whom an ungrateful Paris would be calling old-fashioned by 1836. The score was suited to both the frenziedly romantic Scribe-Delavigne libretto and Cicéri's investiture. It was, that is, grandiose, searchingly characteristic, highfalutin, and grotesque, on the verge of the Gothic. And yet, for all its flushed orchestral coloring, often produced by then recondite combinations of instruments (one of its melodies is scored for four kettledrums), for all its reiterated rhythmic patterns, *Robert* was not yet pure Meyerbeer. He had not yet found the right proportions for the preternaturally clever patchwork he was to make his own.

The spirit of Rossini had not proved easy to dispel: *Robert* teems with those tunes that Meyerbeer had learned how to write in Venice—graceful, fluent, singable, and somehow slipping from the memory while Rossini's remain. *Robert* is still too noticeably a pastiche: the ingredients are present, but not mixed by the integrating hand of a master *confiseur.* The absurdly macabre, curiously effective scene of Bertram's invocation, when the Fiend summons the ghosts of a company of immoral nuns to take part in a bacchanale, becomes a tableau of high self-sufficiency that could only be Meyerbeer's. But the most famous aria in the opera—Alice's "Robert, toi que j'aime"—could be from any of Meyerbeer's scores—or from those of several other composers.

Getting his next opera ready occupied Meyerbeer for five years after the *première* of *Robert le diable.* It was about a fictitious episode during the Massacre of St. Bartholomew, and, to prepare himself for composing suitable music for it, he saturated himself in the history, memoirs, diaries, and other documents of that dramatic period. Nor did he neglect the painting and sculpture of the time. Scribe again had supplied the libretto, this time with some assistance from Émile Deschamps. They gave Meyerbeer for *Les Huguenots* [3] a very long five-act text in which the fifth act is preposterously anticlimactic. As originally planned, the libretto called specifically for five sopranos, five tenors, and six deep male voices, from bass-baritone to *basso profondo.* The mob scenes called for choruses of unexampled size. The settings required included a banquet hall in a château, a garden with bathing pools, the Pré-aux-Clercs (a field on the banks of the Seine), a salon in a sumptuous Paris mansion, and a barricaded street during the massacre. The giant tocsin bell cast especially for this last scene still occupies a large space in the storerooms of the Paris Opéra. At the end of the third act, a gaily decorated nuptial barge must move down the river.

The Meyerbeerian orchestra, already almost as large as Wagner's, has, in *Les Huguenots,* to be augmented by several archaic instruments. Dancing is called for in three separate acts, though in the truncated version used in later years the very elaborate ballet in Act V vanished when that act was sheared off. What all this added up to, of course, was a vast historical extravaganza—a series of detailed canvases reminiscent of boldly figured tapestries. It was treated musically with the gusto and psychological aptness to which a historical theme that truly appealed to him always roused Meyerbeer.

The opening night of *Les Huguenots,* at the Opéra, fell, inappropriately, on one of Rossini's rare birthdays—February 29, 1836. The leading female role of Valentine was assigned to the great Cornélie Falcon, who had made her debut four years earlier in a repetition of *Robert le diable.* Three of the other stellar parts went to veterans of *Robert's première:* Dorus-Gras was Marguerite de Valois, Nourrit was Raoul, and Levasseur was Marcel. The opera was well received, but was not at all the sort of instantaneous hit *Robert* had been. On the basis of its

[3] Alfred Loewenberg pointed out the vicissitudes of this title in predominantly Catholic cities. In Munich it became *Die Anglicaner und Puritaner,* in Vienna *Die Welfen und die Gibellinen,* in Florence *Gli Anglicani,* and in Rome *Renato di Croenwald.*

first few performances, Meyerbeer could not foresee that *Les Huguenots* would finally become the favorite among all his operas and would ring up one thousand singings at the Opéra in seventy-five years.

The immediate popular reaction to *Les Huguenots* was reticent for several reasons. It was far from being a duplication of *Robert:* it contained nothing but Meyerbeer. Also, while it presented a succession of tableaux, each treated with a gloating sense of its contents, Meyerbeer had yet managed to lend a false feeling of unity to each of the five acts by appearing to rob the set numbers of their autonomy. Although *Les Huguenots,* despite being a tissue of foreign styles, was unquestionably French, it was not Paris that finally hit upon the most renowned way of exploiting it. Had the French impresarios but realized what they had, they could have made even larger fortunes from it. The wilier impresarios of London and New York grasped the fact that if a star singer could be secured for each of the opera's seven definitely stellar roles, unheard-of prices could be charged. In their hands, *Les Huguenots* again and again became the superb show that Meyerbeer must have wanted it to be, a glittering seven-ring circus.[4]

Les Huguenots is rich in characteristic arias and ensembles: Meyerbeer neglected none of his stars in his conscientious effort to let his characters portray themselves. Marcel, the bigoted Huguenot, has the first stop-the-show air, "Piff, paff," a bragging soldier's song of vindictiveness. Urbain (a travesty role) has a florid, mock-formal cavatina, "Nobles seigneurs, salut!" whose very lack of dramatic impact comments on the character's functions. Act II begins with Marguerite's extraordinary florid paean of love for her native land, "O beau pays de la Touraine," which modulates into a second air, the combination forming one of the most wearing *scene* in operatic literature. Valentine, never awarded any *fioriture,* never singing anything important alone, figures dramatically in several ensemble numbers, especially the great duet with Raoul, "O ciel! où courez-vous?" in Act IV, the most passionate love music that Meyerbeer ever created. But the theatrical climax of the opera has occurred earlier in Act IV, in the tremendous double scene of

---

[4] What these seven-starred nights became in London and New York is visible in the cast of a performance at the Metropolitan on December 26, 1894: Lillian Nordica (Valentine), Nellie Melba (Marguerite de Valois), Sofia Scalchi (Urbain), Jean de Reszke (Raoul), Édouard de Reszke (Marcel), Victor Maurel (Nevers), and Pol Plançon (St.-Bris). The best seats that night were seven dollars, for the period an exorbitant amount.

the oath-taking and the benediction of the swords. The fact that Meyerbeer could follow this gigantic, full-blooded scene of furor, fanaticism, and conspiracy with a love duet that kept listeners breathless proved his indisputable mastery. Act IV, in its entirety, forms one of those entities of action, text, and music toward which all opera ideally aspires. Here Meyerbeer was a first-rate composer of opera.

Edgar Istel has justly called Act IV of *Les Huguenots* "a play within a play." Wagner, archenemy of Meyerbeerism, could never deny its power. In 1840, before he turned on his benefactor, Wagner wrote of it in strophes of wild rhapsody; eleven years later, after excoriating Meyerbeer in *Oper und Drama,* he tempered his words with an admission that beside the love scene "none but the most finished works of musical art are worthy to be set." Even after his own beatification at Bayreuth, Wagner was honest enough to admit the strange power of this act. One evening during a sojourn in Italy, he mentioned having been moved by an opera that he had heard the day before. When asked what it was, he answered, after some hesitation: "I shall let you know if you promise me not to speak about it. Now then—yesterday evening I was at *Gli Ugonotti,* and was positively wrought up by that fourth act. I implore you not to let a soul know about it—otherwise the Wagnerians will flay me alive!" Fortunately, the future Princess von Bülow, who was present during this confession, told the story to a recording angel.

Meyerbeer's enemies said that he, a Jew, was making capital out of the wickednesses and dissensions of Christians: in *Robert le diable* he had introduced a chorus of lascivious nuns; in *Les Huguenots* he had aired the bloody feuds between French Catholics and Protestants. In his next important opera, *Le Prophète,* he illustrated pages from the heretical disputes of the Anabaptists. In 1842, Friedrich Wilhelm IV of Prussia appointed Meyerbeer his general music director at Berlin; at about the same time, Scribe handed him a libretto based on unpleasant events in the life of John of Leiden, the Dutch heresiarch. They were much to Meyerbeer's liking. In fact, years earlier he had considered such a book for his favorite tenor, the unhappy Nourrit—who had abandoned the Opéra in 1837 and committed suicide two years later. Once more Meyerbeer immersed himself in the lore of a remote period. Within one year he had completed the score of *Le Prophète.* But his duties in Berlin, including as they did the composition of a German opera and the staging of *Euryanthe* and *Rienzi,* retarded its production, which he would not permit without his supervision.

Meyerbeer's last German opera, *Ein Feldlager in Schlesien,* was a setting of a three-act libretto by Ludwig Rellstab, who described it as *Singspiel in Lebensbildern aus der Zeit Friedrichs der Grossen.* Meyerbeer composed it especially for the rededication, on December 7, 1844, of the Königliches Opernhaus, which had been badly damaged by fire on August 18, 1843. It was mildly successful, and Jenny Lind scored one of her early successes in it when it was restaged in Vienna in 1847 as *Vielka.* Meyerbeer was to adapt six numbers from it for a French text of the opera brought out at Paris in 1854 as *L'Étoile du nord.*

By the time Meyerbeer was able to oversee the production of *Le Prophète* in Paris, Gilbert Duprez, Nourrit's successor as first tenor of the Opéra, had retired to teach singing, and the best of the available tenors in the company was not competent to sing the role of Jean as originally composed. Meyerbeer therefore tried a daring experiment. Pauline Viardot-García, the greatest mezzo-soprano of the era, was available. By reducing the roles of Jean and his betrothed, Berthe, and by building up the role of Fidès, Jean's mother, Meyerbeer created the first great mother role in nineteenth-century opera. Doing so involved wholesale reconstruction of the score. Paris therefore did not get its first opportunity to see and hear another of its idol's grand historical spectacles until April 16, 1849. On that night the role of Jean was assigned to Hippolyte Roger, a useful but not spectacular tenor. Viardot-García wrought one of her remarkable triumphs. But Meyerbeer himself received no ovation. Had he set *Le Prophète* in the style of *Les Huguenots,* he might have imposed the new opera upon the public at once, but he was too responsive to text to be able to copy himself. The sequence of *Robert le diable* and *Les Huguenots* was soon paralleled, however, and Paris began applauding *Le Prophète* wildly.

That *Le Prophète* caught on at all was a victory, for the experiment of making an older woman the real heroine of an opera was risky, and Meyerbeer had done anything but soften that blow by making the hero an execrable creature. Both on the Continent and in England, the earliest success of *Le Prophète* was largely a personal one for Viardot-García, who was said to have suggested many detailed changes to Meyerbeer. As Fidès is by far the biggest thing in the opera, its continuing life came to depend on finding other singing actresses with the right range of voice.

It is unfortunate that Meyerbeer, who had by then achieved indisputable supremacy on the musical stage, did not compose *Le Prophète* on the bold, simple lines of a mother-son drama. Instead, he crowded it with a multitude of tableaux, some of them theatrically effective if dramatically irrelevant, others mere period scenes smelling of research and uninspired historic conscientiousness. As a result, *Le Prophète* displays a hysterical and disheveled quality less pertinent to the riot of the times Meyerbeer was trying to portray than to the chaos Scribe handed him, and to which the score is party. The best that can be said of Scribe's book is that it supplied Meyerbeer with opportunities for providing a spoiled public with samples of practically all the devices in his huge bag of musical tricks. For taking full advantage of these opportunities instead of seizing upon the essentials of Scribe's book and making the magnificent drama that was there for the taking, Meyerbeer has been accused of being consciously untrue to himself. But, as Cecil Gray wisely said: "Meyerbeer has often been wrongly reproached with insincerity; he simply lacked entirely any very strong or definite convictions. He was an artistic opportunist from want of a clear sense of direction rather than from a lack of moral integrity or conscience."

Le Prophète contains many individual numbers of distinction, several others of considerable fame. Most popular of all is the pompous and very circumstantial Coronation March in Act IV, in which Meyerbeer perfectly struck the generic note. He never invented a more universally familiar tune. Not quite in the same category is the Skaters' Quadrille in Act III, an engagingly rhythmic number that Liszt contorted into a satanically clever and difficult encore piece for piano. The same master arranger sank his claws into the dour, turbulent chant of the Anabaptists, "Ad nos, ad salutarem undam," which recurs as a sort of musical basting throughout the score, and from it concocted a muzzy and magniloquent fantasia and fugue for organ. There are better things in the opera than these. Two of Fidès' solos stand out: "Ah! mon fils" is consoling motherhood powerfully expressed; "Donnez, donnez," a tremulously affecting expression of sorrow. Few airs in mezzo-soprano–contralto literature are finer than these. Differently effective is Fidès' scornful, passionate "O prêtres de Baal." Jean's music is, on the whole, less interesting, and Berthe's is perfunctory.

Between *Le Prophète* and *L'Africaine,* Meyerbeer's last and, in some ways, most magnificent opera, intervened two scores, both designed for the Opéra-Comique, both intended (even if Meyerbeer did not see it that way) for a featherbrained type of coloratura display. The first of these was *L'Étoile du nord,* with a three-act libretto by Scribe, into which numbers from *Ein Feldlager in Schlesien* were rabbeted. The impossible hero of this impossibility was Peter the Great, the heroine the peasant girl he was to seat on the throne beside him. *L'Étoile* all but died out with Meyerbeer's death, a brief career for an opera that had its *première* on February 16, 1854. It was kept alive in its youth by the miraculous agility with which Jenny Lind coped with two flutes in the mad scene from the last act, and by the intelligence that Luigi Lablache brought to the role of Peter's boon companion. Today *L'Étoile* seldom shines even momentarily on the concert stage, for few contemporary sopranos can safely try the cruel *tessitura* of Catherine's mimetic bouts with the flutes in "Là, là, là, air chéri."

The second of these *opéras-comiques* was *Le Pardon de Ploërmel,* later more familiar as *Dinorah.* For the book of this fatuous Breton tale, Meyerbeer deserted Scribe for Jules Barbier and Michel Carré, the librettists of Gounod's *Faust,* the *première* of which preceded that of *Le Pardon*—April 4, 1859—by only one month. The music is of the slightest and lightest, entirely apt for the idiotic girl who idiotically wanders through the three acts. Except for the gracious baritone aria "Ah! mon remords te venge," the opera is an empty coloratura vehicle. It contains the most famous single aria that Meyerbeer ever composed, the giddy, tripping, trifling, mindless waltz song "Ombre légère," which gave the opera precarious, temporary hold on the boards.

Dinorah was the last of his operas that Meyerbeer was destined to hear, but not the last that he composed. Back in 1838, Scribe had handed him a fantastic libretto about an African slave girl. By 1849, the score was finished, but by then Meyerbeer was not satisfied with either Scribe's work or his own. He therefore asked for a new libretto; after endless bickering, Scribe—who at one time had withdrawn the libretto angrily— gave him a revised version in 1852. This included for the first time the figure of the opera's present hero, Vasco da Gama, after whom it was temporarily named, and who had been suggested to Scribe by the fact that Jessonda, in Spohr's opera of that name, falls in love with another Portuguese navigator, Tristan da Cunha. Nothing in the life of Vasco da Gama remotely resembled the foolish sequence of events in Scribe's text, and his "African slave girl," Selika, is obviously an East Indian. But these details did not deter Meyerbeer from doing his usual job of research or from worrying the score to completion in eight years. It was ready in 1860, but production was delayed four years while the finically fastidious composer changed details even after the opera had been put into rehearsal. But Meyerbeer was seventy-two years old, and this time procrastination was fatal. He completed the copying of the final corrections at his house in the rue Montaigne on May 1, 1864, and the next day he died. Less than a year later, after three of Meyerbeer's friends [5] had shifted many scenes around to produce harmony between score and libretto (as they conceived its requirements), the opera was sung for the first time.

Much of the delay between the finishing of the score in 1860 and the *première* at the Opéra on April 28, 1865 (six weeks before the Munich *première* of *Tristan und Isolde*), had been caused by casting difficulties. The first Selika—Marie Sax, a former *variétés* artist—was not of Meyerbeer's choosing. Far outshining his fellows in the cast was the almost mythically famous Jean-Baptiste Faure, who sang the baritone role of Nelusko. Emilio Naudin followed the dictates of Meyerbeer's will by creating the role of Vasco da Gama. Not until July 22, and then at Covent Garden, London (where, translated into Italian, the opera had become *L'Africana*), was the role of Selika sung by Pauline Lucca, the great singing actress whom Meyerbeer himself had coached in the role. Hermann Klein called Lucca's impersonation of the passionate slave "a supreme achievement to be mentioned in the same breath with the Rosina of Adelina Patti and the Marguerite [*Faust*] of Christine Nilsson."

L'Africaine is peculiar. Although its separate numbers are the most disciplined of those in any Meyerbeer opera, the whole is a throwback to the hysterical days of *Robert le diable,* when he had been just beginning to understand the necessity of creating a personal speech out of the several idioms he could speak. Plainly pieced together over a long span of time, as plainly written from several unreconciled points of view, it is not a successful opera. But it has a generally gorgeous and somber score marred only by *longueurs* of spotless academic writing. It is scenically as spectacular as *Les Huguenots,* but its music is less showily theatrical. The false touches that blemish the music of *Le Prophète,* but which there can be excused as results of a misreading of history, are much more egregious in *L'Africaine,* whose fake Orientalism resulted from a faulty reading of an alien culture. (Meyerbeer, furthermore, seems to have been uncertain about which alien culture he was trying to evoke.)

But when Meyerbeer succeeded in *L'Africaine,* it was perhaps on the

[5] One of them, the formidable music critic François-Joseph Fétis, in some places cruelly maltreated Meyerbeer's ingenious orchestration, ineptly substituting a saxophone for the bass clarinet out of friendship for Adolphe Sax, a fellow Belgian who had invented the instrument.

highest musical level he attained. "Ô Paradis," the fine tenor aria in Act IV, with its continuation, "Conduisez-moi vers ce navire," remains so surpassingly lovely as to seem an act of serendipity. Quite as dramatic is Nelusko's primitive evocation of Adamastor, deity of sea and storm, in Act III—"Adamastor, roi des vagues." Most effective of the pseudo-Oriental numbers is Selika's second-act lullaby, "Sur mes genoux, fils du soleil," an air of entrancing tenderness. And in the final Vasco-Selika duet, "Ô transports, ô douce extase," Meyerbeer almost reopened the vein of passion he had found in the last duet of Valentine and Raoul in *Les Huguenots.* As in two or three others of his scores, there are enough fine things in *L'Africaine* to make it tragic that Meyerbeer never managed to produce a single opera in which he was consistently at his best throughout. Such an opera would unquestionably have been among the most remarkable musicodramatic works ever composed.

"*Aïda* is musically little more than a grandiose pendant or sequel to *L'Africaine.*" Thus Cecil Gray, carelessly exaggerating: *Aïda* grew from Verdi's whole experience, from his own abilities as they had developed, not exclusively—or even largely—out of hints taken from Meyerbeer. Even though Meyerbeer's best tricks can be found in scores by the most unlikely composers, he really founded no school. He was like a teacher whose influence persists in detail long after the broader aspects of his instruction have been repudiated. There are Meyerbeerian elements in *Aïda* and other Verdi scores, in *Rienzi,* in many French operas of the nineteenth century. But the only opera by another that might have come from Meyerbeer's own atelier is the passionately written *La Juive,* by Jacques-François-Fromental-Élie Halévy, seven years his junior. And even *La Juive,* composed when only *Il Crociato in Egitto* and *Robert le diable* existed to show the direction of Meyerbeer's maturing, was less a slavish imitation than one natural expression of a man whose character was much like Meyerbeer's—scholarly, devoted to craftsmanship, eclectic. Halévy, in his best opera, is almost as much Cherubini's pupil as Meyerbeer's friend.

In one respect, *La Juive* rises superior to any score by Meyerbeer: it is more genuinely felt, establishes an integrity, preserves a unity, with a persistence that might have carried the more gifted Meyerbeer to musical greatness. Halévy, unlike Meyerbeer, never allowed his flair for experimentation to run away with him: it is almost always religiously controlled. The tragedy of the perfectly schooled Halévy was that he was facile and prolix, setting without enthusiasm almost thirty texts, most often catchpenny books. In Scribe's *La Juive,* for all its rant and fustian, he found for once a dramatic story to set his devoutly Jewish imagination on fire.

The intellectual Nourrit, who had an advisory voice in the shaping of several Meyerbeer scores, played an even more important role vis-à-vis *La Juive.* He was weary of portraying amorous young men, and therefore persuaded Halévy to make Eléazar, the heroine's father, a tenor rather than the expected baritone or bass. He is said even to have written the words to Eléazar's thrilling aria in Act IV—"Rachel! quand du Seigneur." He was naturally the Eléazar of the opening performance at the Opéra on February 23, 1835. The Rachel was Cornélie Falcon, the Eudoxie was Julie Dorus-Gras, and the Cardinal was Levasseur. A little later, Viardot-García became an unexcelled Rachel.

The fact that Meyerbeer and Halévy are now both all but unsung reflects a change in fashion, a sad change from the point of view of variety for the repertoire. Who knows? Perhaps one or another of the world's great opera houses will be able someday soon to mount *Les Huguenots, Le Prophète, L'Africaine,* or *La Juive* with a cast of great singers, with stage designers and managers of real insight into period aptness. The amazing machines, lying inactive for so long, may then soar into action again, giving off the heat and light that delighted many thousands of listeners not so very long ago.

CHAPTER XIV

Valhalla

SOME time after the Easter of 1842, Wilhelm Fischer, stage manager of the Dresden Hofoper, had to worry about scenery for a new five-act opera of unprecedented amplitude by a man whose only past stage performance had been a fiasco so thorough that it had completed the ruin of the company that had produced it. Fischer was required, substantially, to put medieval Rome on the stage, not forgetting its principal ruins, and to provide, as a denouement, for the destruction of the Capitol, without setting the theater afire or breaking the heads of his singers. The costume designer, Ferdinand Heine, was faced with an equally harrowing task: he had to get 537 period costumes ready for the dress rehearsal. Although Fischer and Heine could not realize it when they received their orders, their most onerous duty was to work with the dynamic little man who had composed the opera to his own libretto, and who was, at twenty-nine, already the leading fuss-budget in central Germany.

No detail of costuming, scene painting, choral work, or dancing was too minute for the personal intervention of Richard Wagner. With *Cola Rienzi, der Letzte der Tribunen,* he had set out to surpass Meyerbeer at his own game; he was not to be balked by mere material limitations. Novice though he was, he had secured the services of several noted singers, among them Wilhelmine Schröder-Devrient and Joseph Aloys Tichatschek, a Bohemian tenor. Miraculously, though after numerous delays, *Rienzi* reached its opening night on October 20, 1842, and Wagner had his first taste of popular favor. Although self-confident to the point of arrogance, he was afraid that *Rienzi* had failed that first night, despite the fact that the audience remained in the theater from six to eleven-fifteen, and was applauding loudly at the end of the fifth act. He rushed to the theater at eight the next morning, bent on slashing his opera to a more tolerable length.[1] Tichatschek, who was enraptured with the music of the name role, forbade the major cuts and gradually convinced the agitated composer that *Rienzi* just as it was had been a success.

There was no reason why *Rienzi* should not have succeeded: very little about it was new. The libretto, which Wagner himself had written, basing it on Bulwer-Lytton's novel, was a historical pageant of a familiar type—Meyerbeer called it the best he had seen. The music was vigorous, noisy, harmonically conventional, and, in one or two numbers, notably the Prayer, catchy. Nothing about the style was experimental or likely to rile the most sensitive devotee of Meyerbeer's complicated eclecticism. In fact, anyone examining Wagner at this point in his history and knowing nothing of the very different score tucked away in his belongings, could be forgiven for dismissing him as an imitation Meyerbeer not without talent. Nor would he have been likely to change his mind if he had examined the scores of the unperformed *Die Feen* (1833) [2] or the self-consciously licentious *Das Liebesverbot,* an unfortunate comic opera (Wagner had based his text on Shakespeare's *Measure for Measure*), chiefly Auberian in approach, to which the good people of Magdeburg had objected so strenuously that it had been abandoned after its first night, March 29, 1836. Nothing in Wagner's first three operas showed that the disciple was at hand for whom Weber, passionate about a real German composer who could go on from where he himself had left off, had prayed. In 1842, Wagner seemed to be going the international way.

Only by reason of being Wagner's first operatic success and by a certain rude gusto does *Rienzi* stand out from the general run of second-rate operas of its period.[3] Even were it to vanish from the boards completely (it is seldom given), *Rienzi* would be remembered for its still popular, slapdash, patchwork overture, whose unctuousness triumphant

[1] From 1843 on, the Dresden authorities at times solved the problem of *Rienzi's* inordinate duration by giving it in two parts—*Rienzis Grösse* and *Rienzis Fall*—on successive evenings. Can this first have given Wagner the idea of a cycle of operas occupying several performances?

[2] Wagner had been dead five years when *Die Feen* was finally staged in Munich in 1888 under the direction of the *Meister's* favorite conductor, Hermann Levi. It is not the only opera with a text derived from Carlo Gozzi's *La Donna serpente:* Alfredo Casella produced his opera by that name in 1932.

[3] Interestingly, Wagner's first success followed Verdi's—with *Nabucodonosor* (*Nabucco*)—by only a little more than seven months.

is the first faint (though noisy) premonition of that aspect of Wagner's artistic nature which would fulfill itself ultimately in the least attractive pages of *Parsifal*. In the body of the opera itself, Wagner's willingness to get on by borrowing styles wherever he chose is nowhere better evidenced than in the tumultuous finale to Act I, which Eduard Hanslick, the eminent Viennese critic, later described well, to Wagner's fury, as a mixture of Donizetti and Meyerbeer and an anticipation of Verdi.

Those who think of Wagner primarily in terms of *Der Ring des Nibelungen,* and therefore come unprepared to *Rienzi,* without knowledge of its antecedents, are in for rude shocks. At first blush, it is an old-fashioned opera, in some of its elements rather like certain operas produced in Paris from the Revolution on. It is, in fact, just the sort of thing a clever borrower with a complete knowledge of fashionable styles in opera picked up during eight years of conducting and stage-managing in the provinces would be likely to contrive.

Closer examination of the score of *Rienzi* shows more to it than at first meets the ear. The music is integrated with the action in a very ingenious way not altogether novel: certain of the characters and salient situations have musical themes that appear and reappear with them. In short, here was the most extensive use up to that time of the leading-motive idea, which was as old as the invention of opera itself, and which had been used by Monteverdi in *L'Incoronazione di Poppea,* by Mozart —notably in *Don Giovanni* and *Die Zauberflöte*—and by many other composers. In *Rienzi,* however, Wagner was not employing the leitmotiv as an occasional device, as earlier men had employed it and as he himself had in *Das Liebesverbot:* here it was a cohesive element, not merely a way to sharpen dramatic stab. *Rienzi* contains more than thirty leitmotivs, all clearly audible to those who bother to listen for them. They are not the sort of leitmotivs used in the *Ring;* they are not conceived for the same purpose or used in the same way. They are not the brief, gnomic, vibrating phrases that—developed, altered, combined, and reshuffled— make up the close, shimmering web that the later Wagner magically wove. They are long-lined, static labels, by their very nature not susceptible to symphonic treatment in the Beethovian style that Wagner adopted as his own last manner.

Rienzi grew out of nothing more personal to Wagner than his passion for the romantic novel and his determination to succeed as an operatic composer. *Der fliegende Holländer,* however, was the first chapter in a musical autobiography that was to be completed only forty years later, when he blotted the last notes of *Parsifal*. It is a tremendous picture of sea and storm: Wagner, fleeing from Riga in 1839, had endured a four-week crossing from Pillau to Gravesend that was, according to his own description, rather more terrible than the first voyage of Columbus. The *Holländer* spins an epic tale of a sinful man redeemed by the self-sacrificing love of a woman. Wagner embarked on it partly as a love gift to his first wife, Minna Planer, whom, at least during the composition of Acts I and II, he considered the angel of his own redemption; before completing the final act, he had begun to discover that so mentally limited an angel could not redeem Richard Wagner. Added to these ingredients, even if not specifically identifiable in the libretto and score, were grinding destitution and months of failure in Paris, where he completed the opera in 1841.

Wagner sent the score of *Der fliegende Holländer* to Berlin with a personal plea to Meyerbeer, then general music director there. Accepted provisionally, the opera was still unproduced, despite Meyerbeer's efforts in its behalf, when *Rienzi,* also helped to the stage by Meyerbeer's influence, scored its success in Dresden in 1842. Wagner then impatiently withdrew it from Berlin, and it was accepted for production in Dresden. Its *première* occurred on January 2, 1843, with Schröder-Devrient as the faithful Senta (originally called Minna) and Johann Michael Wächter, the original Orsini in *Rienzi,* in the baritone role of Vanderdecken, the Flying Dutchman. The opera contained no tenor role important enough for Tichatschek, who was consoled by the knowledge that Wagner was composing another opera in which he again would have the name part.

Der fliegende Holländer started out by being as much a debacle as *Rienzi* had been a hit. It was given four times at Dresden, which then dropped it for more than twenty-two years. There were various reasons for its failure, not least of them being *Rienzi,* whose qualities were such as to make the Dresdeners yearn for the same thing with the label changed. Instead of dazzling historical pageantry, gaudy scenery, polychromatic costumes, they were offered three acts of unmitigated somberness, dark scenery, and dreary costumes. Instead of bright, blaring, brassy music, much of it to jolly rhythms, they received gloomy, thunderously whispered surges of man and the elements—music that might give one a sharp headache, but was hard to remember. It had been a mistake to produce this untuneful stuff in the pleasant social capital of Saxony, where Weber's untiring efforts to stir up interest in German opera—

words and music both—had apparently been in vain. For the *Holländer* was as obviously a Weberian opera as *Rienzi* had been a Meyerbeerian one: in it, Weber would have recognized for the first and perhaps the last time his true disciple. In some respects, it was a direct descendant of *Der Freischütz;* in others, it was as wholly new as *Der Freischütz* itself had been when it dethroned Spontini in Berlin.

Der fliegende Holländer is the first symphonically constructed opera, the first opera in which the music grows out of a few germinal themes, grows continuously without being divided into autonomous entities. It was not the first opera to possess unity, but it was the first to possess the sort of musical unity that had been achieved first in the mature development of the symphony. True, in the *Holländer,* the music drama—that superb side show to the main operatic edifice, that side show which Wagner was to make his own—had not yet arrived. For example, he had not yet thrown aside the separate-number pattern and other conventions of the older opera (in some respects, of course, he never dispensed with them entirely). Vanderdecken's carefully prepared-for scene in Act I— "Die Frist ist um"—clearly evidences this, while Senta's ballad—"Traft ihr das Schiff im Meere an"—is, for all its Valkyrielike ho-hos, an old-fashioned set number of the French *romance* type, equipped with exciting music of unmistakably Wagnerian cast. After allowing for the magnificent things in *Der fliegende Holländer,* it is possible to commiserate with the Dresden audiences: the opera is ingenious, and undeniably represents a gigantic step in the evolution of one of the significant operatic composers of the nineteenth century, but those who heard it for the first time could not guess from that evidence its composer's destiny as the musical *Übermensch.* Much of *Der fliegende Holländer* is dull, and the Dresdeners had a reasonable preference for entertainment.

Tannhäuser, the opera in which Tichatschek had been promised the name role, was produced at Dresden on October 19, 1845. Schröder-Devrient was the Venus, Wagner's niece Johanna the Elisabeth. The shrewd Venus had warned Wagner against this casting, protesting with humorous candor that she herself was too stout to make a credible goddess of love (a protest that her biography belies), that the nineteen-year-old Fräulein Wagner was too immature to grasp the role of Elisabeth, and that the bluff Bohemian tenor would misread Tannhäuser. At the first performance the principals were little more than figures of fun, and the opera suffered accordingly. The shoddy second-hand scenery added to the audience's annoyance, and Wagner, who had become assistant conductor at the Hofoper, was in despair, particularly because the bellowing tenor had strained his voice so badly as to make further singing of the opera impossible for more than a week. But new sets for the big singing-contest scene arrived, and the interim, moreover, had given Wagner time to drill his singers in the interpretative niceties of their roles. The second performance was poorly attended, but was received so much more enthusiastically than the first that *Tannhäuser* was started on the road to a popularity that has never waned.

As most often played today, with the expanded Venusberg music composed for the Paris production of 1861, *Tannhäuser* has the further lure of a tone poem of singular blandishments, couched in the mature musical style of the composer of *Tristan und Isolde*. The overture starts at once with Wagner's best-known tune, the Pilgrims' Chorus, and works itself up into a triumphal frenzy. The opera is a succession of high spots, beginning with the Bacchanale and Tannhäuser's Hymn to Venus in Act I; going on from Elisabeth's nobly joyful salute to the Hall of Song, "Dich, teure Halle," through the pompous ceremonial march, to the songs of the contending singers, including Wolfram's serene "Blick' ich Umher," in Act II; and from the Pilgrims' Chorus through Elisabeth's Prayer to Wolfram's third-act apostrophe to the evening star, "O du mein holder Abendstern," which has become almost as hackneyed as the Pilgrims' Chorus.

Even as a product of 1845, *Tannhäuser* is an ambiguous work. Its libretto does not represent Wagner's most advanced convictions about the functions of a libretto; moreover, it mingles myth and history in a way that he would not have admitted even a very few years later. On the other hand, the music—not to speak of the Paris additions—is, besides being more attractive on the surface than that of *Der fliegende Holländer*, of greater technical interest. The texture of the score is more specifically Wagnerian than anything preceding it: the rich complexity of *Tristan* and the other bona fide music dramas is here plainly previsaged in harmony, orchestration, and ways of using leitmotivs. Here, too, are moments of that overripe sensuousness deepening into sexuality—that indulgence in torrid musical color for its own sake—which was to mark the *Meister*'s, in this sense, strangely un-Germanic hand right up to, and in, *Parsifal*.

Therein lies the ambiguity: a largely old-fashioned libretto is fitted with music speeding ahead to a new condition of—despite its composer's pet theories—symphonic self-sufficiency. The music of *Tannhäuser* was new, advanced, but a final element was lacking: it had not yet cohered ideally, had not shaped its own inevitable pattern. It is the stuff of the future music drama just before the last moment of illumination. For that reason, no doubt, it seems almost to retrogress from the *Holländer,* whose all but uninterrupted unity of musicodramatic mood gives it a superficially closer resemblance to the *Ring.* In the *Holländer,* Wagner was working with simpler, more easily malleable elements, and so success was easier. In *Tannhäuser,* he boldly enlarged his scope and began trying to achieve something far more difficult than a mere unity of mood. He did not wholly succeed, but he took a step forward.

Tannhäuser is historically bound up with Wagner's personal vicissitudes. When he was scurrying over the frontier into Switzerland as a political refugee in 1849, Liszt, his future father-in-law, was preparing to stage it at Weimar. It was the first opera that Wagner managed, a dozen years after that, to peddle in Paris, and it was with *Tannhäuser,* despite the inspiredly clever music that he composed especially to seduce the ballet-mad habitués of the Opéra, that he suffered the most wounding setback of his middle career. The second performance in French, on March 18, 1861, with Marie Sax as Elisabeth and Albert Niemann as Tannhäuser (the first Wagnerian role of one of the most eminent of Wagnerian tenors), was the occasion of a notorious riot when members of the Jockey Club, having come too late to witness the choreographic splendors of Lucien Petipa, brutally expressed their disapproval of the ballet's being in the first act. After a third performance, during which the opposition again raged, Wagner insisted upon withdrawing the opera despite definite signs of a popular reaction in its favor.

Wagner had supervised and conducted the Dresden *première* of *Tannhäuser.* When *Lohengrin,* his next opera, was first staged, he was a fugitive from Saxon justice living in exile in Switzerland; he did not himself hear the opera until 1861, by which date it had had dozens of performances in thirteen cities. It was Liszt, not wholly convinced of the practicability of producing this "superideal" opera, and with skimpy forces in the pit and on the stage, who took upon his resigned shoulders the task of introducing yet another revolutionary opera by his unreasonable friend. The scene was the tiny Hoftheater at Weimar, already one of the magnets of artistic life on the Continent; the date was August 28, 1850. Wagner had completed *Tannhäuser* in April, 1845, in the summer of which year, after toying with ideas that he eventually shaped into the librettos of *Die Meistersinger von Nürnberg* and *Parsifal,* he wrote the poem of *Lohengrin*. The music was composed in odd sequence: Act III first, then Acts I and II, followed by the Prelude—a mode of procedure familiar to students of the *Ring*. The scoring was completed in 1848. Now, two years later, Wagner was fretting for news from Weimar.

The first news was bad: the lengthy work had not worn well with the first-night audience, and Liszt, clever though he was in making ends meet where others could not, was unable to do it justice with second-rate singers and an orchestra of only thirty-eight men. Some of the singers were all but paralyzed with fear by the difficulty of their roles. Liszt, having done what could be done, told the bad news to Wagner, who, besides being in exile, was recuperating from a badly managed love affair with another man's wife. The failure of *Lohengrin* completed his prostration—temporarily.

Yet, after a slow, listless beginning, *Lohengrin,* appearing to gather strength from within itself, leaped over Germany in nine years: by 1859, it had been heard in fourteen German towns, Riga, and Prague. Charles Lamoureux used *Lohengrin* in 1887 to test the readiness of Parisian operagoers to listen to Wagner with ears that had forgotten the Jockey Club's riots against *Tannhäuser*. A dozen years before that, the Wagner craze had seized upon London so intensely that two competing houses had presented *Lohengrin* only a few days apart. As so often with these rivalries, the one that managed to be first on the scene did the inferior job; both performances suffered in appropriateness from being sung in Italian.

Lohengrin is the summit of nineteenth-century German romantic opera; in many respects it is Wagner's finest stage work, as it is certainly his most nearly perfect in musicodramatic balance. In it, he arrived at a rare equilibrium of his intensely demanding, often nonco-operative talents as poet-dramatist and absolute composer. The book of *Lohengrin* is passable poetry and better drama. The music is expressive of the book; it chooses, moreover, a lofty but ingratiating lyricism, as distinct from mere easy melody as it is from mere background music. The story does not provide just breathless, episodical plot; neither is it distended by those soggy chunks of undigested philosophizing which slow up the action of Wagner's later stage pieces. In *Lohengrin,* the crudities of *Rienzi* and the *Holländer* have largely been exorcised. So, too, the Latin echoes of *Tannhäuser* are no more. *Lohengrin* is a thoroughly German work, which goes far toward explaining its exemplary unity. In it, Wagner finally quiets the restless shade of Carl Maria von Weber; here German opera, as the composer of *Der Freischütz* conceived it, comes of age, and though Wagner does not, after *Lohengrin,* cease to consider himself the prophet of German music, his experiments become the highly individual out-pourings of his egocentric psyche. In *Lohengrin,* finally, most of the drama is still taken up by the voices, though the powerful, brilliantly used orchestra, not yet encouraged to smother the singers' prerogatives, takes part in it to an extent unprecedented in the operas of earlier com-posers.

After surveying Wagner's heroic achievement, it is impossible not to understand, and to sympathize with, Ernest Newman's wistful sum-ming-up of his reactions to *Lohengrin:* "The Wagner of this period reaches the supreme height of his powers in *Lohengrin;* and as one watches that diaphanous web unfold itself, one is almost tempted for the moment to regret that the daemon within him drove him on so relent-lessly to another style."

Those not fully acquainted with the cranky theorist in Wagner, an-other name for the "daemon" that drove him on to the *reductio ad ab-surdum* of the *Ring,* find it hard to understand why he could not consider the style of *Lohengrin* the sufficient earnest of his ideas. *Oper und Drama,* written just after the first performance of *Lohengrin,* helps to explain this apparently perverse flight from his own near-perfection. In that remarkable book he ventilated the oddly arbitrary ideas that the musician should be the servant of the poet and that the poet should use only myth. *Lohengrin* still contains a tiny core of history, and in it the balance between music and drama is so subtly maintained, so ideally even, that the relentless application of theories could only destroy it. Musically, Wagner has by this time created a new instrument—a con-tinuously unfolding web of sounds evolved from a collection of brief leitmotivs susceptible to symphonic treatment. In *Lohengrin,* too, the orchestra has become a wonderful medium of its own enchantments—a thing of varied hues and lights, predominantly shimmering in effect, brought about by using the separate timbres and colorations of the instru-mental families in a way new to music. In *Lohengrin,* this sensuous agent is held justly in check, but the potentialities of its unleashing were so obvious that Wagner became intoxicated with them, though he surely never recognized that central fact in his later aesthetic.

A final proof of the maturity of the style of *Lohengrin* is that the opera as a totality is more attractive, has more impact, than any one of its parts. The only flaws in its continuity occur exactly when Wagner lapses into a careless, loose idiom out of his past—these halts, as old-fashioned as anything in *Rienzi,* and far more wounding in this otherwise seasoned score, can be typified by the humdrum, mock-joyous Bridal Chorus. The Prelude to Act III is less a lapse back to an earlier idiom than a lapse in taste. Its appalling bumptiousness and rudeness of statement glare all the more because the opera opens with another Prelude that is beautifully proportioned and exquisitely expressed.

Lohengrin proved to be, except for the inspired recession in *Die Meistersinger,* the last of Wagner's operas. *Tristan und Isolde* was the first of his music dramas, but its *première* occurred fifteen years after that of *Lohengrin,* and many important things happened to Wagner in the intervening time. First among these was the evolution of the concept of *Der Ring des Nibelungen*—a moment in the history of the arts that can be compared to Gibbon's decision to write *The Decline and Fall of the Roman Empire.* But whereas Gibbon, as he listened to the monks singing the Roman service at the Ara Coeli, saw his idea whole, Wagner was at work on his for a long time before he realized what it was. In 1848, two years before the Weimar production of *Lohengrin,* he had written the poem of *Siegfrieds Tod.* Three years later, he realized tardily that an epic about Siegfried's death would not exert the desired impact unless it followed an earlier poem of the hero's first exploits. *Der junge Siegfried* was the result.

The next year—1852—was big in eventfulness for Wagner. He met Otto Wesendonk and his wife, Mathilde, who for five years were to be among the chief pawns in his dramatic quest of love. He also, partly because of Mathilde's warm sympathy, completed the poems of the *Ring.* He had begun to sense the cyclic nature of his Siegfried story, and so to put himself somewhat in the position of his future audiences. Thus, he began to ask himself questions about the parentage of the young Siegfried,[4] and realized that he had to tell the story of that incestuous generation. And when he had told it, in *Die Walküre,* he persuaded himself that a basic motivation was needed to propel his three poems along their proper path. The theft of the Rhinegold, which started all the mischief, was therefore made the subject of a further prefatory poem, *Das Rheingold.* Finally, after *Die Walküre* and *Das Rheingold* had been written, in

[4] In regard to Lohengrin, Wagner not only answers this question of parentage in *Lohengrin* itself, but answers it, rather more fully than is necessary, in *Parsifal,* his definitive biography of Lohengrin's father. Who Lohengrin's mother was, however, Wagner neglected to make clear.

that order, Wagner returned to rewrite *Der junge Siegfried* (eventually called just *Siegfried*) and *Siegfrieds Tod* (eventually called *Götterdämmerung*). The entire cycle, entitled *Der Ring des Nibelungen,* was printed in 1853 in most luxurious format.

The poems of the *Ring* had been written in reverse chronological sequence over a period of five years. The music, composed in proper sequence, took twenty-one years to complete, and was, moreover, interrupted by, among other things, the composition of two other large stage works. Wagner began to compose *Das Rheingold* in 1853, and finished scoring it in 1854. At once he set to work on *Die Walküre,* which he completed in 1856. That same year, he began *Siegfried,* which was well under way when, in July, 1857, he dropped it for eight years: his love for Mathilde Wesendonk had burst the dike, and he had become obsessed by a desire to symbolize their yearnings in a music drama about a—to him—similar pair of lovers, the legendary Tristram and Yseult.

Under the love-filled glances of Mathilde (Wagner and his wife had moved to the Asyl, a small house on the grounds of the Wesendonk estate in suburban Zurich), he was hectically active, though Mathilde was far from occupying all his waking thought. He labored on the poem of *Tristan und Isolde,* thought sporadically of Parsifal and the legend of the Holy Grail, and wondered how he might rid himself of Minna, his wife. Some of the music for *Tristan* was composed before the inevitable explosion occurred. During the coolness that followed it, he completed the score, partly at Venice, partly at Lucerne. The final measures were scored on August 8, 1859. During the succeeding five years, Wagner was constantly on the move, struggling for place, harassed by debt, failing miserably in Paris again, and at last beginning unprecedentedly to question his unquestionable vocation. Yet, in the midst of this almost unalleviated anguish, he conceived the idea of *Die Meistersinger von Nürnberg* as a comic pendant to *Tannhäuser,* and even wrote the poem and composed the prelude and part of the first act before wearily laying the idea aside.

Overnight, Wagner's situation changed. Called to Munich by the impulsive young Ludwig II of Bavaria, the fifty-year-old composer found himself the indulged and powerful male sultana of this strange monarch. Neither personally nor as an artist did he waste time. Having parted from his wife in 1862, he was soon having a love affair with a young woman who was the illegitimate daughter of one of his best friends and the legitimate wife of another—Cosima Liszt, who was married to a promising Saxon musician, Hans von Bülow. In 1865, Frau von Bülow bore Wagner a daughter, who was christened Isolde. Exactly two months later, on June 10, with Bülow conducting, Munich was the scene of the first official triumph of Wagnerism: *Tristan und Isolde,* almost six years old, was performed. Had the reaction of that audience been decisive in determining Wagner's position or the future of *Tristan,* one might have been untenable, the other black. Faced with music that really was new, the audience listened with polite, cold attention. It was Ludwig, again, who saved Wagner by his candidly effusive enthusiasm, accompanied by a command for three repetitions. With them, *Tristan* ended its career for several years: Ludwig Schnorr von Carolsfeld, the "heroic tenor" who had sung Tristan, died, and Wagner could find no one to replace him even if Malwine Schnorr von Carolsfeld, the first Isolde, had consented to resume her role immediately with someone else in her late husband's place.

In *Tristan und Isolde,* we are permitted to examine the most nearly perfect carrying-out of Wagner's theories about music drama. The score has uninterrupted continuity. The old set numbers now appear to have vanished completely; even the division into acts is, for the first time, rather a method of giving musicians and audience time to relax than a manner of showing that one musicodramatic unit is complete and another about to begin (though, of course, Wagner's "curtains" are most often brilliantly timed). The ceaseless musical flow appears natural and spontaneous: in the Prelude, Wagner plants the seeds out of which the whole opera seems to grow. In a drama whose central situation inevitably involved tremendous intensity of expressiveness, this technique of continual exfoliation is uncannily apt. So, too, is the chromatic harmony that produces constant, painfully gradual motion, a psychological inching-along that is the musical artist's only *perpetuum mobile* because it does not demand periodical resolutions giving the effect of full stops.

In *Tristan,* that tale of intractable forbidden passion, the pressure increases, the tension mounts, until human nature no longer can bear it. But Tristan and Isolde, though flesh, are also creatures of myth; more importantly, they are also the tempest-battered phantasms of Wagner's ceaseless imaginings. Happily, the line of passion ebbs as well as surges, thus supplying the needed contrast that every work of art must have. Those parts of the score which have been excerpted widely—the *Liebesnacht,* for example, and the *Liebestod*—are simply those long moments when intensity multiplies itself to the consummate thrust. When so excerpted, they suffer from being torn out of their contexts: they are climaxes alone, without reason or result.

Tristan und Isolde overflows with beauty, beauty of a very special, rarely created sort. It is a beauty set richly amid connotations of sexual craving and fulfillment; reactions to it are bound to be more belligerently personal, more conditioned by individual experience, than are those to most works of art. The most intelligent child in the world would find *Tristan* a mystery, but not at all the sort that Wagner intended it to be. Among those capable of understanding it fully, some will always find it a salutary, healing purge; others will find it vaguely, yet agreeably, disturbing; still others will be disgusted. To these last, *Tristan und Isolde* resembles pornography. The average operagoer, equable in state of mind and point of view, is unlikely to be reduced to delirium or driven to moral outburst: to him, *Tristan* is tremulously beautiful, often exciting, but not devoid of boring calms.

It is on the purely musical level alone that *Tristan* is a nearly perfect carrying-out of Wagner's theorizing. When the musician subordinates himself to the poet (doubtless in the belief that one half of himself is cooperating with the other), the music drama falls into most peril. In short, the obligation of getting along with the plot, of producing the central crises, involved Wagner in narrative doldrums that can be compared to the passagework in a mechanical pseudoclassical sonata. When the lovers are together on the stage, and the story therefore tells itself, Wagner's theories collapse like a sand castle. The musician reigns, and Tristan and Isolde might as well be exchanging mumbo-jumbo as the words they do exchange. The text is there; only the music matters. Far from being poetry's handmaiden, the music of *Tristan* glories in untheatrical self-sufficiency, and ends by making us forget everything but itself. (This is often fortunate, for the speeches that Wagner assigned to the protagonists even in the climaxes are, on occasion, verbose drivel.)

Die Meistersinger von Nürnberg, the next of Wagner's operas to reach production, bears as curious a relation as *Tristan* to his biography. *Tristan* clearly is an opera of self-projection, Wagner confessing his passion across the footlights. *Die Meistersinger,* apparently the most detached and objective of all his later works, can be construed as quite as autobiographical. During the composition of most of it, Wagner was carrying on—and unquestionably consummating—the most fervid love relationship of his life. *Tristan* was the expression of desires fulfilled either clandestinely or not at all; *Die Meistersinger* was completed after he had settled down, at Triebschen in Switzerland, with the woman who was to become his second wife. The legal barriers to a happy affair with Cosima, still Bülow's wife, were as numerous as those to one with Mathilde Wesendonk. But Mathilde had been adoring and timid, whereas Cosima was adoring and eager. The first had been hedged in by bourgeois convention; the other, natural daughter of Franz Liszt and the Comtesse d'Agoult, was a willing accomplice. She and Wagner understood each other perfectly at once, entered freely and without arresting scruple upon the life they wanted—a life that turned out, from their points of view, to be entirely satisfactory. With Mathilde, Wagner had had to cry out his passion unspent; no such need colored his life with Cosima. In *Die Meistersinger* there is reflected, from his new relationship, love bounteous and harvested.

Back in 1845, Wagner had dallied with the idea of a stage work about Hans Sachs, the poet-cobbler of Nuremberg, but the project remained in seminal condition for sixteen years. By 1861, when he embarked on the poem of *Die Meistersinger,* the original conception of a comic treatment of the same sort of *Sängerfest* which had yielded dramatic effects in *Tannhäuser* had been augmented by other ideas connected intimately with his artistic theories and personal vicissitudes. First, it was to glorify German art. Second, it was to lampoon, in the twisted figure of the maladroit Sixtus Beckmesser, those critics—and particularly Eduard Hanslick, a power of the Vienna press—who were luckless enough to be less than convinced Wagnerians.

With stanchless gusto and great good spirits, Wagner wrote his best dramatic poem: it is humanly credible, often truly funny, and poetic throughout. The energy that served him for this task carried him through the overture [5] and some of Act I, at which point the combined drive of his troubles and his ambitions carried him off on a tangent. When, after many wanderings and the episode with King Ludwig, he took up *Die Meistersinger* again, at Triebschen in 1866, he completed it in little more than one year. Under a royal patronage manifestly less effulgent than that which had dictated the first performance of *Tristan, Die Meister-*

[5] Ernest Newman pointed out, in Volume III of his masterly life of Wagner, that because the melody common to the overture and the *Preislied* was composed before the present words of the *Preislied* were written, Wagner was here going counter to his aesthetic doctrine that the music must in all cases result from the poem.

singer was given its *première* at Munich on June 21, 1868, with Bülow (still Cosima's husband) conducting, and with Hans Richter in charge of the chorus. The cast, though all but unknown to compilers of musical encyclopedias, was excellent. Edward Dannreuther, writing in 1889, called this the best Wagnerian performance he had ever seen.

Die Meistersinger immediately took the town, then Germany. And why should it not have? This hearty, lustily created big comedy of manners evoked sixteenth-century Germany. Everything about it was right, beginning with the locale: Nuremberg, most flavorsome of towns, in which in Wagner's time a seen past lingered on every stone, and where the imaginative could summon up the late-medieval atmosphere of guilds, journeymen, and apprentices. The libretto was right, though to be so it had had to break with some of Wagner's aesthetic: there is no element of myth in *Die Meistersinger,* which is all human and credibly everyday historical. To a poem that carries conviction and radiates charm, Wagner had added music of varied and often surpassing beauty and life. It was music that he could not have employed to body forth the doings of gods and goddesses, or even of superlovers like Tristan and Isolde. To create such music at all, he had to recede some distance from the hypotheses that had produced *Tristan* and that, constricted into dogma, were to challenge dissent in the *Ring* and *Parsifal.*

Die Meistersinger opens with an overture constructed, rather like that to *Tannhäuser,* on a few telling themes from the body of the opera, themes treated with wonderful semicontrapuntal ingenuity. It is an old-fashioned potpourri overture so cannily contrived as to seem novel. It is entirely appropriate to the largely good-natured entertainment that follows. Curiously, in glorifying German art Wagner had returned to the old idea of opera as entertainment, but on a plane so lofty that invidious comparison could never be made. For his purposes here, a potent germ like the Prelude to *Tristan* would have been quite inappropriate. Too, he had chosen for much of the melodic idiom the type of song-theme which the actual Mastersingers had sung, and had even introduced melodies surviving from their era. Thus, while he continued to use leitmotivs, he could not entwine these longer-phrased melodies into the sort of shifting, turning, unceasing musical mesh which had been so logical for expressing the fatally indestructible passion of Tristan and Isolde. Also, the condition of the *Meistersinger* melodies called for predominantly diatonic harmony: periodical resolutions were inevitable, and a partial return to the set-number scheme was concomitant. Finally, the primary plot-requisite of a singing contest is recognizable separate numbers: thus, the young, lyrical *Preislied* correctly stands out from the rest of the score.

Each of Wagner's operas has, in addition to its essential Wagnerian something, one special quality that distinguishes it from the others. Thus, *Rienzi* is brash and gaudy, *Der fliegende Holländer* menacingly somber, *Tannhäuser* exultant, festive, and contrite, *Lohengrin* lyric, light-shot, and noble, *Tristan* passionate and hallucinated. *Die Meistersinger* is warm and earthily human: its joys, its high-singing raptures, its light-hearted wit, its lovingly mingled wisdom and humor, and even its satire —sometimes woundingly barbed—are human. Hans Sachs is one of the towering figures of opera; in him, Wagner most nearly approaches the German conception of the poet, the *Dichter* who speaks wisely for the nation. His greatest moments, as in "Wahn! Wahn!"—that magnificent monologue on the world's madness—have the eloquence of speech and the persuasion of music. Yet Sachs, though his amplitude of understanding can encompass the world, never alone reaches the plane that Wagner reserved, with wonderful dramatic sense and sympathy, for the quintet in the last act, one of the supreme ensemble numbers of all opera. There, in Wagner's finest (almost his only) true ensemble number, with the *Volk* standing symbolically on the side lines, Sachs and the two pairs of lovers whom he has befriended hymn their mutual joys in rhapsodic cantillation. It provides the most impressive outpouring of that communal spirit which is diffused throughout the opera, and which Wagner expresses in such different numbers as the purposely clumsy, waltzlike Dance of the Apprentices, with its comical stumbling rhythms, and the ceremonially pompous March of the Meistersinger, perfect music for self-sufficient men of good will engaged in civic festival.

Except for a brief spell immediately after the first hearing of *Tristan und Isolde,* Wagner did not work at the *Ring* seriously again until after the *première* of *Die Meistersinger* in 1868. Despite a growing coolness on King Ludwig's part, the fact that at that performance the monarch had shared his box with the composer joined the patent enthusiasm of the people for his music to give Wagner some hope that his vast four-part music drama, if composed, would have a chance of production. By September, 1869, he had completed the preliminary score of *Siegfried;* the next month he began *Götterdämmerung,* which, after some interruptions, was complete in full score by November, 1874. As Wagner in the meantime had finished the full score of *Siegfried,* that date meant the achievement of a project on which he had been engaged, in one way or another, for twenty-six years.

Wagner's desire—nay, his determination—was to give the *Ring* only in cyclic form in a theater built especially for its production, but the Bavarian King was equally determined to hear the separate parts, on which he justifiably felt that he had a lien. Thus, it was by royal command that the *Vorabend* to the trilogy,[6] *Das Rheingold,* was sung at Munich on September 22, 1869, and that *Die Walküre* was sung there on the following June 26. That was as far as Ludwig got. By the time the final two scores were ready, the specially designed Festspielhaus at the little Bavarian town of Bayreuth was well in process of erection. After heroic struggles by Wagner, his friends, and his well-wishers all over the world, the money for the completion of the theater and Wagner's adjacent home —Wahnfried—was finally got together.[7] When the first Bayreuth Festival was announced for 1876, the theater was far from ready, and for a time there was some doubt that the essential funds would be forthcoming. But the fanatically determined Wagner cut down obstacles as they arose. His natural choler stopped short of apoplexy even when he learned that the dragon ordered for *Siegfried* had been sent to Beirut in Syria rather than Bayreuth in Bavaria. Finally the invitations were released with a feeling of certainty that the invited notables stood an excellent chance of hearing the four scheduled performances. The composer's luck held: the Festspielhaus opened on August 13, 1876.

Because a less conspicuously stellar cast assembled for *Das Rheingold* than would appear in each of the succeeding music dramas, which are peopled by the more important characters of the epic cycle, the first audience had its best chance not only to listen to the strange sounds issuing from orchestra and singers and to watch the bizarre antics of the players, but also to survey the house itself and to realize that half the brilliance and high society of Europe was present. Hans Richter conducted (as he did throughout the Festival), and in addition to Heinrich Vogl, a well-known Tristan, as Loge, Franz Betz, who had created the role of Hans

[6] In Wagnerian terminology, *Der Ring des Nibelungen* consists of a "fore-evening," or prelude—*Das Rheingold*—and three music dramas: *Die Walküre, Siegfried,* and *Götterdämmerung.*

[7] A small part—$5,000—of the more than $250,000 needed for the theater alone came from the "American Centennial March" that Wagner composed in 1876 for a world's fair in Philadelphia.

Sachs, as Wotan, and Eugen Gura as Donner, Lilli Lehmann sang the relatively minor role of Woglinde, swimming next to her sister Marie as another Rhinemaiden. To Lehmann fell the dangerous honor of pronouncing the doggerel lines with which the massive machinery of the *Ring* is set in motion: "Weia! Wage! Woge, du Welle, walle zur Wiege! wagala weia! wallala, weiala weia!"

In *Die Walküre,* given on August 14, the Brünnhilde was Amalie Materna, the Siegmund was Albert Niemann, the Wotan Franz Betz, Lilli Lehmann Helmwige, her sister Marie Ortlinde; Wagner's niece, Johanna Jachmann-Wagner, by then turned fifty, and with her great days well behind her, had the bit part of Schwertleite. After *Die Walküre,* the guests were allowed a one-day breathing spell. The Festival was resumed on August 16 with *Siegfried.* This, unlike the first two performances, was a world *première.* Georg Unger, hand-picked by Wagner, sang the title role; Materna and Betz continued as Brünnhilde and Wotan (here called The Wanderer). Finally, on August 17, the last of the cycle, *Götterdämmerung*—another world *première*—brought forward, besides Materna and Unger, Gura in the new role of Gunther, Johanna Jachmann-Wagner as a Norn, and the Lehmann sisters again as Rhinemaidens.

After *Götterdämmerung,* that almost unparalleled audience dispersed to talk about the most controversial event in the history of opera. Wagner himself was left, after two repetitions of the entire *Ring,* the most discussed artist alive. At the age of sixty-three, he was faced with a deficit of thirty thousand dollars.

How many of the fifteen hundred guests left the first *Ring* in dazzled but puzzled rumination is not recorded, but as that is the effect the *Ring* still has on its novices, probably a large percentage of those first audiences left Bayreuth in that state. Tchaikovsky was there, and his final reaction can be found in a letter that he wrote to his brother Modest:

As a theatrical spectacle the work aroused my interest and charmed me by its wonderful staging. As music it is incredible nonsense in the midst of which there are occasional flashes of extraordinary and amazing beauty. . . . With the last chords . . . I felt as though I had been set free from captivity. Perhaps the *Nibelungen* is a great masterpiece, but it is certain that there never was anything more boring and long drawn out than this spun-out composition. . . . Yet if the *Ring* bores one at times, if much of it is at first incomprehensible and vague, if Wagner's harmonies are at times open to objection as being too complicated and manufactured, if his theories are false—even if the results of his vast labor should at last disappear into oblivion and the Festspielhaus fall eternally to sleep, yet *Der Ring des Nibelungen* is an occurrence of the greatest importance to the world and an epoch-making work of art.

If played continuously, the *Ring* would last something over twelve hours—and understanding it depends upon a fund of complex special knowledge which is imparted as the dramas themselves unfold. Listening intelligently to the *Ring* cannot be an idle pastime: the mind must be kept ever alert, the ear sharply tuned. Nor can the dreamily closed eye—that favorite device of passionate music-lovers—be indulged in: details of costume, scene-shifting, and gesture are freighted with significances whose comprehension is essential to understanding the action. As the *Ring* is Wagner's most audacious experiment in the use of the leitmotivs, every one of them must be understood, not only when it first appears alone, but also when it reoccurs changed, twisted, and contrapuntally joined with one or more other leitmotivs. This would be difficult enough if there were only ten or a dozen to keep in one's head, but thirty appear in *Das Rheingold* alone, and sixty more must be struggled with before the curtains close on *Götterdämmerung:* analyzing the *Ring,* Ernest Newman found it necessary to quote 198 leitmotivs, fragments, and transformations. In addition to the musical and dramatic meanings conveyed by the sights and sounds, Wagner intended them to convey philosophical and symbolical ones as well.

Listening to the *Ring* is a task at first. Assuming, however, that we have familiarized ourselves with the entire machinery of the cycle, by constant attentive listening and watching supplemented by many hours of collateral reading in the huge *Ring* literature and by playing the leitmotivs over and over again, what do we have when it is all known? Not, all too clearly, that one supersynthesis of all the arts which Wagner intended. Our not finding that supersynthesis was for a long time blamed upon the always faulty, frequently ridiculous ways of staging the *Ring.* But even Wagnerians have now largely discarded that excuse.

No performance of the *Ring* could so hypnotize the informed listener as to hide completely the gross crudities of the four-part poem that serves as its libretto. It is repetitious, often gaseous, very often silly. The fact that he wrote it backwards compelled Wagner to synopsize parts of the dramas still to be written. He composed the music in chronological sequence, but without excising the synopses as he joined poems and music. The audience therefore has often to listen to long monologues in which one of the characters retells what has already taken place on the stage or has already been told. Other monologues, as well as an occasional dialogue, expound none too original chunks of philosophy, putting the action completely to sleep. A hardheaded thinker remarked that Wagner mistook the epic for the dramatic. A logical outcome of this odd error is Wagner's emphasis of certain elemental figures—Wotan, Erda, the dragon Fafner, and the dwarf Alberich, for example—who have little or no means for communicating humanly with the audience. Wagner's insistence on working exclusively with myth thus backfired. The epic figures whose tragedy is their humanness bear the focus of audience interest throughout the entire *Ring,* even when Wagner planned his specific situations otherwise.

The *Ring* poem contains enough truly dramatic material for two good librettos; that material has been distributed through hours and hours of undramatic verbiage. As Wagner was an inspired musical translator, and as he earnestly set every word, phrase, and nuance of his poem, the music of the *Ring,* as an entity, suffers from the selfsame faults that vitiate the libretto. Where the text is dull, the music is dull; where it flashes into life or leads naturally into a lyric interlude, Wagner does not miss the chance. He becomes, as necessity dictates, a supreme musical dramatist, a protean tone poet—in short, a program symphonist without equal. The *Ring* is inevitably a spotty performance, rather like an overland journey from New York to California, with all the variability of landscape, so much of it unfortunately poor. But there are canyons and torrents, grand mountains, mighty rivers—and it is these that keep Wagnerians going to hear the *Ring* long after the first occasion on which some of us have begun to think that the whole cycle should be condensed into concert performance. Even four evenings of the *Ring* are not too much if measured in terms of the high spots it would otherwise require years of concertgoing to hear.

Between the Prelude to *Das Rheingold* and the stupendous last half-hour of *Götterdämmerung* occur some of the most magnificent passages not only in opera, but in all music. They are orchestral pages pure and simple, whether voices take part in them or not: by the time Wagner was scoring the *Ring,* he had come to treat the human voice as but one of the most important instruments of a tremendously expanded orchestra. In

practice, he had unconsciously completed a right-about-face: far from
making music and the other arts handmaidens of poetry, he had stifled
all but music under a passion for symphonic sound. However one judges
his later music dramas as music, they could be construed as anti-operas,
an unannounced declaration of war against the lyric stage. As thinker,
stage revolutionary, and poet, Wagner is a tarnished figure. As musician,
he is secure among the great. Fashion may tend to continue diminishing
his vogue, but never to the degree that it has diminished the vogue of
Meyerbeer. In *Lohengrin, Tristan, Die Meistersinger,* and parts of the
Ring, he added enduringly to the artistic heritage of all imaginable time.

After the mighty *Ring,* after the comparative flawlessness of *Lohengrin, Tristan,* and *Die Meistersinger,* Wagner, though ill and weary, was
not content to rest until he had added a religious music drama to the already imposing roster of his works. The theme of salvation had haunted
him all his adult life, appearing in one form or another in every one of
his operas from *Rienzi* on: sometimes, as in *Tannhäuser,* supplying the
mainspring of the drama; sometimes, as in *Die Meistersinger,* developed
as only one of many motives. Now, when his life was petering out, and he
had achieved personal beatification (Wahnfried, Wagner's house, stood
in relation to the Festspielhaus much as a bishop's house does to a cathedral), he was in the mood to turn again to this idea and give it a more
pious twist. His mind was crowded with the religious lore of the ages,
from Buddhism to Christianity. It was crowded, too, with fragments of
philosophies, including many dubious ideas of his own.

In 1845, Wagner had considered a poem about the Holy Grail and
the perfect, spotless knight who found it—Parsifal, the father of Lohengrin. Twenty years later, as a favor to Ludwig of Bavaria, who was en-
tranced by the idea, he sketched the story, though not in poetic form. The
apotheosis of 1876 at Bayreuth was the impetus needed to produce the
actual libretto. This was completed in April, 1877, and published that
year. Composition progressed slowly: Wagner was constantly ailing and
was engaged in a struggle to pay off the Bayreuth deficit and raise money
for a second Festival. He intended to restrict all performances of *Parsifal*
to Bayreuth, hoping that compulsory attendance at the sacred music
drama, at stiff prices, would help to pay off the deficit.

The second Festival was assured by January, 1882, and *Parsifal,* which
was to be its only attraction, was finished. By late spring, rehearsals were
under way. On July 26, 1882, at a private performance that ranked high
among the social events of that year, *Parsifal* had its world *première.*
Hermann Winkelmann created the title role, Materna that of the sorceress

Kundry [8]—direct descendant of the Armida out of Tasso who had been dear to eighteenth-century librettists. The Gurnemanz, Klingsor, and Amfortas were respectively Emil Scaria, Karl Hill, and Theodor Reichmann. Conducting was Hermann Levi, a Jew whom the intermittently anti-Semitic Wagner had inconsistently chosen to usher in this holy Christian mystery.

In *Parsifal,* most of Wagner's great qualities have ripened beyond palatability. He had set himself a task of integration too difficult for the solving genius of mortal man. The poem is a rope of shoddy; in it, the luminosity of *Tristan* and much of the *Ring* has turned to the phosphorescence of decay. "You see," according to James Gibbons Huneker, "a lot of women-hating men, deceiving themselves with spears, drugs, old goblets, all manner of juggling formulas, and yet being waited upon by a woman—a poor, miserable witch. . . . In Act II, you are transported to the familiar land of Christmas pantomime. There a bad magician seeks to destroy the castle of the noble knights, and evokes a beautiful phantom to serve his purpose. There are spells, incantations, blue lights, screaming that makes the blood run cold. . . ."

In short, *Parsifal* is silly. Through episodes fit only for one of those interminable Italian marionette shows which depict Boiardo or Ariosto down to the last comma, the guileless Parsifal wanders in sickly innocence, while the voice of that ancient man Gurnemanz endlessly explains. How could anyone, how could even Wagner, make credible music drama out of this sanctimonious, neurotic, completely undigested twaddle?

Thus, *Parsifal,* even more than the *Ring,* must be judged on the merits of its music alone. And as music it suffers from defects as grave as, and not very different from, those of the libretto. All the portentous machinery that oftentimes worked miracles with the unpromising episodes of the *Ring* is here set in motion with singularly stale and flat results. It is set in motion, but almost nothing moves. The wheels go around—the leitmotivs appear, develop, and intermingle; the huge orchestra is made drunk with color and winy harmony; the scenery has an unholy life of its own. For five hours the gyroscopic action continues while the musical miracle fails to take place. Either these legends, rituals, philosophies, did not really stir Wagner to the depths or, as some critics have supposed, his creative power had so failed with his health that little was left him except the dry bones of his aesthetic theories and his astonishing tech-

[8] Adelina Patti once made the incredible statement that Wagner had composed the role of Kundry for her. According to the diva, she declined the honor because the sorceress has "too much screeching" to do.

nique. His sensuous evocations have become shrill and strident, as if the creator himself had sickened of passion. And the contrasting purity—the themes given to Parsifal himself—is of a pale, negative hue with as little relation to childlike innocence as to masculine self-denial. The lapses into straight narrative exposition—always a weakness with Wagner—in *Parsifal* completely stultify the action. Hours of the music drama are plainly dreary. Nor can much of the whole be salvaged, for even the recognized high spots tend to flounder in this slough of musical despond. The Good Friday Spell, for instance, has, for all its beauty of statement, so low a vitality that after several dozen measures its result is so much maunder. Compare the Prelude, perhaps the best music in *Parsifal,* with that to *Lohengrin:* the latter is a flood of light, the former a memory of that light. One is the sun, the other a glimmer of candles well out of the open air. That, finally, is *Parsifal:* the creation of a weary sorcerer poring wearily over musty books full of incantations and abracadabras.

Parsifal supplied Wagner with his last opportunity to force upon the public a conception of opera so radical that Bayreuth had had to be built to demonstrate it. Not only was the subject matter calculated to inspire a reverential attitude, but also all the circumstances of its production were focused in the same direction. To Wagner, the audience was as much a participant in a perfect presentation of music drama as the rest of his forces: it was to provide the appropriate ambiance, the atmosphere without which the music drama could not, in fact, successfully be performed. Moving away from the conception of opera as entertainment, he substituted one of lofty, ritualistic seriousness. Because he thought of the works of his maturity as syntheses of all the arts, and therefore wholly enriching, he did not think it too much to ask special conduct and complete concentration from his audiences.

At Bayreuth, every small detail was prearranged with an eye toward unity of effect, even the musical themes to be played for reassembling the audience after intermissions being stipulated by Wagner. He supervised everything about productions, with the exception of drilling orchestra and chorus—that function was, however, safely in the hands of men who had dedicated their very existence to the service of Wagner and his ideals. Not content with being the first composer of operas to set only librettos of his own writing and with having designed, down to the smallest acoustical detail, a great hall especially adapted to his music, Wagner ordered the scenery, designed the costumes, chose the singers, and made mandatory minutiae of voice and gesture. His wishes were respected, or at least paid lip service to, until after World War II. Then his grandsons

—Wieland and Wolfgang, the sons of Siegfried—simplified and modernized the staging. Their "experiments" succeed or do not succeed—and in either case demonstrate that even in the holy of holies it is no longer possible to present chemically pure Wagner.

Applause and encores would have marred the continuity of Wagnerian music dramas; they were banished. For the same reason, latecomers were not admitted until an intermission. This was a long distance from the days when people cooked spaghetti in their loges, played chess, or indulged in chatter that drowned out whatever was rising from the orchestra pit and stage. The irrelevancies of virtuoso singers were forbidden in Wagner's operas—even the spoiled Max Alvary was not allowed to sing an encore, add a special passage of vocal flourish, or interpolate some music that he and the audience happened to like. The most practical commandments of Wagner in respect to conduct of both performers and audience still hold in the best-run opera houses and concert halls, and thus guarantee to the modern music-lover a chance to listen undisturbed.

Ironically, Wagner founded so short-lived a school of opera that it can scarcely be said to have had an existence at all. *Hänsel und Gretel,* the best opera of Engelbert Humperdinck, most notable of Wagner's unquestioning disciples, is not recognizably Wagnerian to the average listener, so cleverly is the idiom watered down for the child consumer. It is, of course, a masterpiece of its kind. Curiously, the only other even partially successful operas modeled earnestly on the Wagnerian *Aesthetik* were composed by Frenchmen. Such were Ernest Reyer's *Sigurd* (1884) and *Salammbô* (1890) and Vincent d'Indy's *Fervaal* (1897), none of them musically of the first order. Richard Strauss was undilutedly Wagner in his first attempt at opera, *Guntram* (1894); after that, his derivations became more indiscriminate as he became more certainly himself.

What Wagner most effectively gave to opera *per se* was liberty and scope, not, primarily, modes of expression or—fortunately—subject matter.[9] Music in general was his real heir: no composer since Wagner has remained uninfluenced in either harmony or orchestration by his revolutionary practice.

[9] One full-fledged Wagnerian disciple, August Bungert (1845–1915), tried an epic cycle of four music dramas, his own books for which were adaptations of episodes from Homer: *Homerische Welt.* The third section, *Odysseus Heimkehr,* produced at Dresden in 1896, was moderately successful, and was followed by the first part, *Kirke* (Dresden, 1898), the second part, *Nausikaa* (Dresden, 1901), and the last part, *Odysseus Tod* (Dresden, 1903). Bungert mildly suggested that he, too, should have his Festspielhaus, but in vain.

CHAPTER XV

A Perfect Opera

BORN in 1838, a quarter of a century after Wagner, and living about half as long, the unpretentious and bourgeois Georges Bizet left, besides works of all kinds and all qualities, one perfect opera. He invites comparison with Wagner, who entertained the most absurdly exaggerated conception of the artist and his sacred calling. R. G. Collingwood might have been thinking of him when, in his amusingly perspicacious *The Principles of Art,* he wrote: "In the later nineteenth century the artist walked among us as a superior being, marked off even by his dress from common mortals; too high and ethereal to be questioned by others, too sure of his superiority to question himself, and resenting the suggestion that the mysteries of his craft should be analyzed and theorized about by philosophers and other profane persons." Bizet was as old-fashioned, and as prosaic, as the Greeks and Romans about his art, which to him, as to them, meant "a craft or specialized form of skill, like carpentry or smithying or surgery." He wrote no tracts, expounded no theories, but expressed his opinions in a bluff, unfastidious way. He did not air philosophical or religious profundities in his music. In his cool and clearheaded understanding of what constitutes a musician's role, he did his jobs as they came along as well as he knew how. He regarded secular music as something that should be essentially entertaining. In that hardheaded, unsentimental point of view, Bizet looked ahead to the unashamedly sybaritic but scrupulously fastidious point of view that Debussy was fond of expressing and illustrating.

Had Bizet been innately a romantic, the circumstances of his early career might have turned his head. A child prodigy, he was admitted to the Conservatoire at the age of nine, reaping a considerable harvest of medals. When not yet twenty, he won in rapid succession Offenbach's prize for a one-act operetta for the Bouffes-Parisiens [1] and the Prix de Rome, among the judges in the former contest being Scribe and Bizet's future father-in-law, the composer Halévy. The piece for the Bouffes sparkled like a patent homage to Rossini (it may have been just that, for the old master presented his portrait to Bizet shortly after). In short, *Le Docteur Miracle,* after eleven performances, suffered the deserved fate of brazen eclecticism and was heard no more. At least it gave pleasure, which *Clovis et Clotilde,* Bizet's Prix de Rome cantata, decidedly did not. Three years in Rome resulted in much student work, of which *Don Procopio,* a nice bright child of Donizetti's *Don Pasquale,* was an enticement of the Monte Carlo season of 1906. Had it been given in Bizet's lifetime, his reputation as a musical wit would have been firmly established with his coming of age.

With *Les Pêcheurs de perles,* his next extant score, produced at the Théâtre-Lyrique in 1863, Bizet reached the eclectic's paradise of superb joinery. Besides borrowing from himself (fitting the "Pleni sunt coeli" of *Clovis et Clotilde* to the words "O Brahma divin" shows a nice irreligiosity), he ransacked—besides his old favorite Weber—Gounod, Félicien David, Verdi, and Meyerbeer. That he also despoiled Wagner is a canard—he had scarcely heard any of the *Meister's* works at this time. But the positive plethora of Gounod-like melodies in *Les Pêcheurs* should have assured its immediate success (after Bizet's death it eventually became one of the fixtures at the Opéra-Comique). Berlioz, writing his last critical article, proved his great powers as a critic by adroitly separating the best qualities of *Les Pêcheurs* from the mediocre ones. Besides Bizet's brilliant scoring, he noted his use of exoticisms, time-tried in our day but original in 1863. In these Bizet may have taken a hint from Félicien David, but whereas David had used them statically, as an end in themselves, Bizet used them as dramatic emphases.

Had Eugène Cormon and Michel Carré's libretto been less lifeless, Bizet might have bettered his efforts. He did his best for a libretto that is feeble and for characters who are sticks. Nevertheless, in the midst of much that is perfunctory and derivative, there are evidences of a composer of vigor, imagination, and dramatic power. Further, there are moments of lyric beauty, points of color and song, and a way with themes that points to the future composer of *L'Arlésienne* and *Carmen.*

[1] Bizet divided the prize money with Alexandre Lecocq (1832–1918), who later scored huge success with *La Fille de Mme Angot* and *Giroflé-Girofla.* The winning compositions ran alternately at the Bouffes for a brief time.

In almost every way, *Les Pêcheurs* is superior to Bizet's next opera,[2] *La Jolie Fille de Perth,* which has been described nastily as "a long way after Scott." It was written to order for the Théâtre-Lyrique, which had made a fair profit out of *Les Pêcheurs.* The new score, produced in 1867, was not precisely a failure—worse, it was a success dissipated by bad luck. The performance was good, and the press liked it so much that a new favorite seemed in the making. One by one the singers sickened, the replacements were inadequate, and finally the Lyrique collapsed financially. *La Jolie Fille* was not healthy enough to survive: she was essentially a thing of shreds and patches. Reyer, a keen critic, had practically said so in his generous review in the *Journal des débats.* Again the master of his orchestra, Bizet again relied on Gounod, Verdi, Weber, and Meyerbeer, but this time with a nicer understanding of the proprieties of borrowing—in fact, assimilation has now become the better word, and the pervasive quality of the score can properly be called Bizetian. The failure of *La Jolie Fille de Perth,* blasting Bizet's stage hopes, came just when he was ready to use a pen that was truly his own.

As of the close of the year 1869, Bizet's prospects were not much above those of a talented hack. He had just married the daughter of his old friend and teacher Halévy, who had died seven years before, and in an access of filial piety he had undertaken to complete the score of his father-in-law's last opera, *Noë.* This Biblical extravaganza wanted orchestration and a last act, both of which Bizet supplied with flaccid adequacy. His creative energies were being frittered away on arranging other men's work for a living and on salon pieces of the utmost triviality. The big career open to him seemed to be that of a pianist, though even at this dark period the ailing Berlioz was sufficiently perspicacious to note that Bizet had to be taken into account primarily as a composer: others dismissed him as a brilliant runner-up to Saint-Saëns, another acclaimed piano virtuoso whose operatic triumphs were in the future.

Yet, two years were to change Bizet, the chief influences being his very happy marriage and the horrors of the Franco-Prussian War and the

---

[2] Next, that is, of his performed operas: something called *Ivan le terrible* was composed for the Lyrique in 1865. Why Bizet withdrew it on the eve of its performance and then offered it to the Opéra is not known; anyhow, mention of it riled him after the Opéra turned it down. Those who heard an apparently incomplete version at Mühringen in 1946 report a very grand grand opera indeed, almost submerged by Meyerbeer and Gounod but kept afloat by Bizet's increasing mastery of orchestration.

Commune. The first brought him not only a wife, but also her considerable inheritance, which freed him from the sordid and petty tasks of Paris' frightfully underpaid Grub Street. The second made him think not only of life and art in general, but also of his own life and art. He had served some time as a fusilier, and had witnessed many bloody scenes. When the Commune had slaughtered its last victims, and he was able to move to a pleasant country house, a new Bizet, more serious, and with an increased understanding of the realities of life, entered upon a thoughtful phase of a career [3] that had previously been lived in scatterbrained half-consciousness. Fortunately, his experiences did not turn him into a solemn, nondoing theorist, for he retained intact his native balance and *esprit* and never allowed his seriousness, particularly about himself, to weigh him—or his creations—down.

The change was quickly evident. Early in 1871, a commission from the Comique resulted in a neatly executed little masterpiece of pointed humor. *Djamileh,* Louis Gallet's adaptation of a poem by Alfred de Musset, did not enjoy a dramatic libretto, but at least it was easy to follow and had some sparkle in its language. Bizet worked tirelessly at it for several months, and on May 22, 1872, the first real sample of his rapidly maturing style was offered to the Parisians. They stood *Djamileh* for only eleven performances. The indifference of the public enraged Saint-Saëns, who wrote: "The ruminating bourgeois, potbellied and ugly, sits in his narrow stall, regretting separation from his kind; he half opens a glassy eye, munches a bonbon, then sleeps again, thinking that the orchestra is a-tuning." The discreet boldness of the score, some of which was stigmatized as Wagnerism by the critics (who used the term to cover every deviation from textbook rule), was doubtless responsible for some of the public apathy and annoyance. Also, the libretto, frankly immoral (but insufferably listless) may have shocked some of the good bourgeois whom Saint-Saëns derided. A decade later, when Parisian manners and morals had once again assumed their wonted liberality, the little one-acter would have had a better fate.

[3] *La Jolie Fille* marked the end of Bizet's willingness to pass slipshod work and an immature conception of a project as a whole. Ever ready to welcome intelligent criticism, he meditated upon the severe but relevant words of Johannès Weber, the musical critic of *Le Temps,* after the *première* of *La Jolie Fille,* and finally sent him the well-known letter wherein he renounced the "school of *flonflons,* trills, and falsehoods." He did not, for the sake of the golden proportion that he finally achieved, renounce wit and lightheartedness.

A faintly perfumed exotic, *Djamileh* shows with what success Bizet had sloughed off his derivations in little more than two years. Without the almost fatal facility that came perilously close to turning the composer of *Les Pêcheurs de perles* into a clever but inert imitator, *Djamileh* has the moments of unsureness that betray an experimenting hand. But, as Ernest Reyer, Wagner's chief disciple in France, pointedly said: "The musician who falters as he makes a step forward is more interesting than the musician who shows us the ease with which he steps backward." *Djamileh,* with its apt, insinuating music, its happy strokes of characterization, and its witty contrasts of broad *bouffe* and sensuous, melancholy lyricism, cries out for resurrection. It vies easily with other such excellent curtain raisers as *Il Segreto di Susanna, Gianni Schicchi,* and *Il Signor Bruschino,* and would be a decided relief from *Cavalleria rusticana* or *Pagliacci.* Gustav Mahler's gallant effort to revive *Djamileh* in Vienna, though successful, has not been imitated in either the United States or Great Britain.

Bizet's next work for the theater was not an opera, but twenty-seven pieces of incidental music to Alphonse Daudet's *L'Arlésienne.* These are important because they show what Bizet was capable of when given subject matter that aroused his talents for dramatic portraiture. Previously, he had accepted without question the librettos that came his way. *L'Arlésienne,* a brilliantly nervous play about the fierce, passionate types of the Midi, gave him a whole gallery of vividly differentiated individuals, presented in the contrasted situations of melodrama. Bizet not only draws the characters with harsh, telling strokes, but also surrounds them with the native colors of sun-intoxicated Provence. Yet he works with singular delicacy—with sureness of definition. Bizet underlines Daudet's situations but does not usurp the dramatist's function.

The step forward from *L'Arlésienne* to *Carmen* is no such long stretch as that from *La Jolie Fille de Perth* to *L'Arlésienne.* In this incidental music Bizet has already arrived at a mastery of the orchestra that he never surpassed. He is no innovator—no one will speak of "Bizet's orchestra" as one speaks of Wagner's or Strauss's—and, if anything, he created his best effects with even slighter means than those used by his more conventional colleagues. His one act of daring in *L'Arlésienne* was to include a saxophone (for which he wrote beautifully), an instrument at that time still connotationally innocuous. The whole orchestra called for only twenty-six players.

L'Arlésienne was produced at the Théâtre du Vaudeville, Paris, on

October 1, 1872, with scattered acclaim for both the play and the music. And now, though the former is dead [4] the music is more popular than ever, as presented in two suites arranged for symphony orchestra, the first by Bizet himself, the second by his friend Guiraud. Even before Bizet had begun the incidental music to *L'Arlésienne,* he had been approached by the Comique to do a full-length opera to a libretto by his wife's cousin, Ludovic Halévy, and Henri Meilhac. With a boldness amazing for those stuffy times, the subject chosen was Prosper Mérimée's *succès de scandale* of the year 1845, *Carmen.*

The choice was daring; the libretto was not. For in order to make *Carmen* at all acceptable to the management of the Comique, then presided over by the strait-laced Camille du Locle (one of the literary middlemen of *Aïda*), the sordid, consistently vicious tale of an unreclaimed gypsy tart had to be denatured and translated into the realm of relatively polite license. For bourgeois consumption, the librettists robbed Carmen of her spouse, made the *espada* Escamillo (in the story a mere *picador* named Lucas) her sole infidelity to Don José, instead of merely an unimportant one of many, and, finally, created, in the simple-hearted Micaëla, a symbol of pure womanhood as a foil to the hard-boiled cigarette girl. In this delousing process, the librettists did a truly wondrous job on Carmen herself, washing her, clothing her in decent, finally splendid raiment, and cleaning up her language. In short, the heroine whom Halévy and Meilhac gave to Bizet was, comparatively speaking, a lady, though with enough brass, vigor, and viciousness left to make her a happy contrast to the spineless, lachrymose, and inanely sentimental heroines of most operas of that time.

Literary purists as well as psychologists have railed at Meilhac and Halévy for distorting the careful verity of Mérimée's always credible tale, but they must be exonerated of blame. As realistic practitioners of their craft, they had to bow to audience scruples as well as to produce that rare kind of drama which music fits naturally. They did their job surpassingly well, so well in fact that it has been said of the libretto that, slightly adapted, it would be quite tolerable as an unaccompanied stage play. It cannot be pretended that dramatic autonomy is the only criterion of a good libretto, but as that of *Carmen* supplies throughout the necessary points for musical exposition, the answer is sufficiently made. In *Djami-*

[4] More dead, in fact, than *L'Arlesiana,* the opera that Francesco Cilèa, an Italian verist, made from Daudet's drama in 1897. Enrico Caruso, who first became famous in *L'Arlesiana,* did much to keep it alive.

leh, and even more in *L'Arlésienne,* Bizet had shown what he could do if the inflammatory material happened to come his way. And when he saw the libretto of *Carmen,* he knew at once that with it he could create a masterpiece. His self-confidence in this instance is a completely clear example of his realistic understanding of what he was doing. When twelve hundred pages of sketch lay on his worktable, he could see the earnests of his conscientiousness. From that point the project took wings: he arranged, polished, and orchestrated this material in two months.

Bizet was utterly confident of success as the curtain rose on the first performance of *Carmen,* at the Opéra-Comique, on March 3, 1875. He had spared no pains, and the management, though dubious about the morals of the plot, had co-operated nobly. The cast was excellent, at its head being Célestine Galli-Marié, who had created the role of Mignon in Ambroise Thomas's opera eight years before. The audience was large and widely representative. The opera was well but not enthusiastically received, and the press was well-mannered without being cordial. Accounts of Bizet's reactions vary: at best he left the Comique the first night in a mood of mild disappointment. Shortly afterwards, his always fragile health failed more visibly, and, on June 3, he unexpectedly died.

Immediately the legend sprang up that a broken heart, brought on by the failure of *Carmen,* had killed Bizet. But *Carmen* had scarcely been a failure. The night Bizet died, it was being performed for the twenty-third time at the Comique, and it was repeated twenty-seven more times during the season of 1875–76. This run was far in excess of the average enjoyed by new operas, and the box-office receipts were considerable. And it wasn't merely the friendship of Camille du Locle, the director of the Comique, which prompted that timid organization to order another opera from Bizet. Bizet, who was usually resilient, could not throw off depression; he became morbid, and after hearing a gifted young singer do something for Schumann's *Manfred,* he cried out: "What a masterpiece, but what despair! It's enough to make you long for death." As Bizet was suffering from angina, morbidity and despair certainly did not improve his condition. To this extent the legend of his dying from a broken heart is true.

What prevented *Carmen* from catching on in a big way from the very start? First, in a "family" theater, the shocking libretto. Second, the tragic nature of the story and its tragic end: audiences at the Comique were used to operas that would answer roughly to the English phrase "comic opera," rather than to tragic works that were *opéras-comiques* merely because they contained spoken dialogue. Finally, there was some prejudice against Carmen, chiefly from the conservative wing of the critical press, because it contained harmonic vagaries that could easily be mislabeled Wagnerian; the French Wagnerians, led by Adolphe Jullien, did not find the score Wagnerian enough: it was, Jullien wrote in *Le Français,* "nothing but a long string of compromises." These were all reasons that may have caused the timid Du Locle to leave *Carmen* on the shelf after the first season. Before Paris heard it again, it had established itself elsewhere, notably at Vienna, where the spoken dialogue was discarded in favor of accompanied recitatives by Guiraud that are now accepted as integral parts of the opera except in France. As this occurred in 1875, the tradition for the use of the recitatives is almost as old as the opera itself. Brussels followed with an extraordinarily successful production, and by the end of 1878 *Carmen* had been given in the United States, England, Russia, Italy, and Germany, besides several towns in the French provinces. In 1880 Tchaikovsky was prophesying that within a decade it would become the most popular of all operas.

Finally, eight years after the *première,* Carvalho, Du Locle's breezy successor at the Comique, was bulldozed by Ludovic Halévy into restaging it. The revival took place on April 23, 1883, and though the performance was bad—so bad that the audience yowled its complaints of the whole sad affair—press and public joined in hailing *Carmen* as a masterpiece. When, in October of the same year, Galli-Marié was brought back to re-create her role, the result was a triumph. By 1887, *Carmen* had reached its three-hundredth performance at the Comique,[5] and on December 23, 1904, its one-thousandth was duly solemnized. In 1911, a Paris newspaper took a poll of opera popularity among its readers: *Carmen* was first with 26,116 votes; *Manon,* its nearest competitor, was more than 5,000 votes behind. When (1959) *Carmen* was moved to the Opéra, it was approaching its three-thousandth performance at the Comique, thus continuing to hold the runaway record. France echoes José's cry: "Carmen, je t'aime." Elsewhere, though not the prime favorite at the biggest houses, in the provinces it is a staple with every tiny company that boasts operatic ambitions.

In the years that have elapsed since the original production of *Carmen,* the reasons that militated against immediate acclaim have utterly lost

[5] In 1890, Galli-Marié, then fifty years of age, headed a special Comique cast got together to raise funds for a Bizet monument. Her principal associates were Melba, Jean de Reszke, and Lassalle.

their force. The libretto is effective, but far from shocking a generation that now considers *Salome* tame. The tragic ending is so seasoned a convention that we accept it without thought, the corollary to that being that most operas are produced so shoddily that it is rare to hear an effectively comic comic opera or an effectively tragic tragic one. Finally, Bizet's harmonic vagaries have become as friendly to the ear as the most limpid passages of Mendelssohn, and even to mislabel them Wagnerian would not scare us. Half of the best numbers in the score are today popular—in the exact sense of the word: the Habanera, the Seguidilla, and the Toreador Song are as familiar as anything in music. Crowding on them are such numbers as the Gypsy Song, Don José's *air de fleur,* Micaëla's song, and several instrumental entr'actes.

Much of *Carmen* is assumed to have the quality of Spanish folk melody, though Spaniards have never thought so. The myth has thrived on the fact that most pseudo-Spanish music imitates one or another part of *Carmen.* The most truly authentic Spanish music in the opera, in both sound and source, is probably the entr'acte before Act IV, which Bizet may have borrowed from a totally forgotten stage work by the elder Manuel García. What really happened was that Bizet, who knew a lot of Spanish music, and had assimilated its essential characteristics— rhythms, harmonies, colors, melodic piquancies—used this fund of technical resource toward the creation of a theatrical and convincing Spain of his own. That he never tried to fortify his conception of Spain by visiting the actuality shows how little interest he had in trying to re-create anything except as imaginary reality.

Within that reality (and it is an easy one to accept), Bizet has worked miracles. The most striking of these is his evocation of an all-pervasive atmosphere. The music of *Carmen* is itself a landscape, an ambiance, a Mediterranean atmosphere in which, until the last curtain falls, we exist with the protagonists.[6] The characters are aptly, inevitably placed in this landscape, but placed without losing their individualities—if anything, they gather strength from it. Carmen, even when she is not on the stage, dominates the action: the opera is tilted toward her, and yet preserves an exquisite balance. She is unforgettable—a symbol, yet a complete personality. She is one of the living characters of opera, and those who are pawns in her dangerous game are less vital only because to have given

[6] *Carmen* became, to Nietzsche, after his disillusionment with Wagnerism, the symbol of the "Mediterraneanized" art that he so admired, not quite as a, or in its, reality, in his later years.

them equal stature with her would have ruined the effect for which Bizet was striving.

Don José, a tragic weakling, is presented as the precise sort of awkward but charming bumpkin who might easily attract the wayward gypsy, but would be unable to cope with her. Escamillo is a popinjay, a braggart, a great man of the world on a small scale, who, in his unmoved self-assurance, gives just the right contrast to José's helplessness. Bizet presents the logic of Carmen's preference for the dashing *espada* with devastating clarity. Finally, there is Micaëla, good, wholesome, simple of heart—but not of mind, as she is usually played. Have ever the lines of battle been more clearly drawn? That much, perhaps, is obvious from the libretto. But Bizet did not lazily permit the libretto to do his work for him. The protagonists and their conflict are all in the music—in its bite and acerbity, its dry wit and acid elegance, its spleen and banter, its sun and somberness, set off by interludes of unabashed sentimental lyricism. Here is as nice a balance of musical and dramatic elements as can be found in opera: they add up to a perfect work of art. In neatness of statement, variety of exposition, and poignancy of conclusion, *Carmen* is unsurpassed.

CHAPTER XVI

The French Way: Part Two

IT took Georges Bizet twelve years after the production of his first professionally performed opera (*Les Pêcheurs de perles,* 1863) to achieve the masterwork with which he ended his career at thirty-six: *Carmen* (1875). Charles Gounod, his senior by exactly twenty years, waited until he was thirty-three to write his first opera. An ex-student of theology who had become interested primarily in religious music, he turned to opera because it offered, at the moment, the only road to riches for a serious French musician. Even so, only eight years elapsed between *Sapho* (1851), his first essay, and *Faust,* the most successful of his operas. And though Gounod lived another thirty-four years after *Faust,* he never bettered that fourth of his twelve operas: none of the others is of its quality, and none of them nearly equaled it in popularity. Bizet never doubted that the stage was his real métier. Gounod approached it with doubt, almost with a sense of guilt, and that he succeeded more quickly than his younger colleague was owing to his voluptuous, insinuating melodies, not to any special flair for drama—with which, indeed, he was not normally endowed. Into opera after opera, Gounod projected a new sort of melody, less technical than spiritual in its novelty. This was a yearning, sometimes cloying upsurge partaking of both ecstasy and prurience, a note that has done its part in vitiating much of French music since his day, being evident in the works of composers as different as César Franck and Jules Massenet, as well as in the early effusions of Claude Debussy.

That commanding woman of affairs and great artist, Pauline Viardot-García, did much to shape Gounod's first resolve to write an opera. *Sapho,* about the unhappy poetess of ancient Lesbos, not about the magnanimous heroine of Alphonse Daudet's romance (which inspired Massenet's *Sapho*), was therefore written for a mezzo-soprano. Viardot-García had it produced at the Opéra in Paris on April 16, 1851. Although commercially a failure, it was reviewed with enough kindness to give Gounod hope that his efforts would ultimately succeed. Berlioz praised the last act, which contains the only number that still is occasionally heard: "O ma lyre immortelle." Three years after *Sapho*, Gounod tried again at the Opéra, with a very long five-acter based on Matthew Gregory Lewis' fantastic novel, *The Monk*. The libretto by Scribe and Germain Delavigne was so poor a thing that it had been refused by Meyerbeer, Halévy, Verdi, and Berlioz [1] before Gounod accepted it. The career of *La Nonne sanglante* paralleled that of *Sapho*. Produced on October 18, 1854, it received pleasant notices and no public support.

Gounod was somewhat dashed but did not despair. His many famous friends—was he not, after all, a Prix de Rome?—urged him to persevere. *Le Médecin malgré lui*, his third attempt, to a libretto consisting of Molière's play as tampered with by Gounod himself and the later highly renowned libretto-writing team of Jules Barbier and Michel Carré, was staged at the Théâtre-Lyrique on January 15, 1858, by Léon Carvalho. With *Le Médecin* Gounod had found in Barbier and Carré collaborators with whom he could work harmoniously. To them, accordingly, he turned when he needed another libretto to set for Carvalho.

Gounod had traveled through Germany after his sojourn in Rome, and had fallen somewhat under the spell of the German romanticists, particularly Goethe. For years he had been mulling over *Faust* as a possible source of operatic material, and it is possible that he had already composed music for it before he asked Barbier and Carré to adapt some of the poem for him. It is conceivable that a great dramatist or even a very shrewd librettist—someone of the stature of Strauss's private man of letters, Hugo von Hofmannsthal—could condense the most stageworthy elements of Goethe's *Faust* into an evening-long libretto that would possess elements of credibility and yet retain the poetic force that made the original the central work of German romantic literature. (The Italian librettist-composer Arrigo Boito managed to preserve some of both in his own adaptation of Goethe for his opera *Mefistofele* [1868].) Barbier and Carré were not men of that size. Their operation, apart from their selection of scenes—which phase of their work was not in itself bad— was fundamentally a castration. They turned *Faust* into a sexless boudoir comedy acted outside the gate of Heaven.

[1] Not to mention Félicien David, Albert Grisar, and Antoine-Louis Clapisson.

The hero of Barbier and Carré's morality play is a spineless ninny whose character lacks utterly those possibilities of growth which Goethe developed in Part II of his drama. In short, the French Faust is not Faustian. Marguerite is as weakly conceived, even though more comparable to the original Gretchen of Part I.[2] But with Mephistopheles the librettists missed the point completely. Goethe made him an experimenter with human passions, a lineal descendant of the skeptical Satan of the Book of Job. Gounod's literary team vulgarized him, turning him into a flashily dressed pimp; there is no good dramatic reason, as far as their libretto can show, why he should ever have been anything more. Characters of low intensity and small interest, Faust, Marguerite, and Mephistopheles are aptly placed in a commonplace plot that can be summarized as a demonstration of the evil results of paying too high a price for the pleasures of seduction.

The measure of Gounod's genius may be gauged by the fact that his musical treatment of the libretto acquiesces in its commonplace. Nowhere in his score does the music penetrate beneath the surfaces that satisfied Barbier and Carré. Gounod was a bright academic musician; in one respect he went far beyond textbook facility. His command of orchestration was in advance of his time (in a nonsymphonic period of French music, he composed two expert, lightly charming symphonies), characterized by a freedom and spaciousness that allowed him to progress from tuneful banality to tuneful banality with spurious audacity. His harmonies, never in advance of his time, were seasoned with archaic modal usages reflecting his painstaking study of early Church composers. His writing for the voice is often brutally insensitive, lying generally too high or too low for the type of voice specified.[3] As a dramatist in tone, as an interpreter of situations, he was without imagination; his developments of crises are invariably pedestrian.

Gounod might have gone on composing one unsuccessful opera after another but for his unique gift of pathetic melody shallowing off into bathos. With that gift momentarily at flood, he succeeded, in *Faust,* in riding roughshod over his otherwise fatal deficiencies, creating one of the most popular of operas. With few exceptions, the many very familiar

[2] Goethe, dramatizing man's fate, is always most interested in the problems of his hero. Women, whether Gretchen in Part I or the many legendary creatures of Part II, is as much an abstraction in *Faust* as in the poetry of John Donne.

[3] One long-lasting technical innovation is to Gounod's credit: he invented, for Marguerite, the type of soprano now called "lyric."

numbers from *Faust* convey the crushing sweetness of salon music. That they have perfumed charm is unquestionable, but their almost total lack of dramatic sinew leaves their use in an opera incredible. With *Faust* as a precedent, fortune must await the *pasticheur* with the temerity to string together the *Caprice viennois,* the *Simple aveu,* the third *Liebestraum,* and other favorites of dining-room ensembles, provide them with a homiletic libretto, and call the result an opera.

Much of the popularity of *Faust* has always depended upon the ease with which many of its tunes lightly touch universal emotions. These are sentimentality, religiosity, vague aspiration—those directionless gropings of adolescence not always wholly sloughed off by even the most sophisticated and mature. They pervade the score, but at certain places one or another of them can be isolated in pure state. Siébel's song in Act II is tremulous with jellylike passion, and is not improved by being sung by a soprano in boy's clothes. The final trio—"Anges purs, anges radieux!"—has a jolly, unctuous tune quite devoid of deep religious feeling —and so, despite the assurance of the libretto that Marguerite is about to soar toward Heaven, her feet remain comfortably anchored to the stage. Where Gounod has failed to turn on his limited battery of sentimental effects, we get, in *Faust,* straight salon music, sometimes excellent of its kind, sometimes mediocre, always irrelevant. Its very use of a restricted emotional palette, coupled with its sugary charm, sufficed to make *Faust* a favorite with Victorians throughout the world. As Victorianism is a state of being rather than a temporal aberration, *Faust* continues to enjoy marked, if declining, popularity. Helpless juniors who inherited from parents and grandparents the necessity of hearing *Faust* are now elders who hand on the same obligation to their children. Its tunes have taken on the aspect of a group of friends so old and familiar as not to be questioned, much less listened to with critical attention.

The history of *Faust* in France can be summarized by saying that on December 31, 1934, it received its two-thousandth Paris performance. It began humbly enough when, on March 19, 1859,[4] it was staged at the Théâtre-Lyrique, with Marie Miolan-Carvalho, the manager's wife, as Marguerite, and with a cast that was otherwise secondary except for the Siébel, Constance Nantier-Didiée. Its greatest popularity in France dates from March 3, 1869, when the Opéra, which had cold-shouldered Gounod after his second failure, but then had recanted in 1862 to stage *La*

---

[4] *Faust* was, like *Carmen,* originally an *opéra-comique:* it had spoken dialogue. It became a grand opera in April, 1860.

Reine de Saba, another failure of the by then world-famous composer, put on a grandiose production of *Faust,* with its most brilliant luminary, Christine Nilsson, as Marguerite, supported by Faure as Mephistopheles. Twenty-five years later, on December 14, 1894, Paris had heard *Faust* one thousand times—an average of once every nine days. Its popularity then began to slacken: the second thousand performances took forty years to complete—only one performance each fortnight.

After *Faust,* Gounod composed eight operas (nine, if his complete revision of *Sapho* in 1894 be counted), only two of which—*Mireille* and *Roméo et Juliette*—were received with enthusiasm. The first of these, with a libretto that Michel Carré drew from Frédéric Mistral's poem-story in Provençal, *Mireïo,* was saved at its *première* (March 19, 1864, at the Théâtre-Lyrique) only by Mme Miolan-Carvalho's talents. It contains some charming lyrical passages and many proofs that Gounod was an indifferent musical dramatist. Mireille's graceful, pyrotechnical waltz song, "Hirondelle légère," is only less well known than Juliette's. Something about *Mireille* suits it to special outdoor performance: one of its well-remembered modern revivals occurred in the open air at Saint-Rémy-de-Provence, where Gounod had composed much of it, in 1934; another was spectacularly staged in 1954 at Les Baux, in the Val d'Enfer where much of Mistral's story takes place. But the opera cannot otherwise be said to remain in the active repertoire.

Roméo et Juliette has often been, like *Faust,* in the standard repertoire of major non-Italian opera houses. At its world *première,* at the Lyrique on April 27, 1867, with Miolan-Carvalho as Juliette, it was acclaimed; it ran one hundred consecutive performances, easily asserting itself as the most popular opera ever written on this Shakespearean theme.[5] It then moved triumphantly to the Comique, and finally ended at the Opéra, where it has remained a beloved fixture (between November 28, 1888, and January 7, 1898, it was sung there five hundred times).

The libretto by Barbier and Carré concentrates on the central love interest more exclusively than Shakespeare did, and the opera is therefore a lyrical effusion rather than a drama. It lacks a Mephistopheles—

[5] The most admirable of its precedessors had been Bellini's *I Capuletti ed i Montecchi,* thirty-seven years before. Composers have been attracted to the subject at least since Georg Benda's *Romeo und Julie* was sung at Gotha (in German) in 1776. Riccardo Zandonai's *Giulietta e Romeo,* first heard at Rome in 1922, was based less on Shakespeare than on the sources from which he had taken the basic materials for his poetic drama, principally Bandello.

who, absurd as he is, provides *Faust* with a sort of crude contrast. The librettist-invented Stephano, a mezzo-soprano page boy, is an obvious parallel to Siébel in *Faust*, as the music in general is a faint reminder of that of the earlier opera. One of Gounod's admirers called *Roméo* "a series of love duets," not meaning the phrase as a compliment. The sensuous lyricism of *Faust* reappears in *Roméo,* but washed out and carried to extremes. As a fusion of music and drama, the opera fails. As sentimental entertainment, it succeeds rather better—if the lovers happen to be an attractive pair animated by sufficient intelligence to keep their performance of both action and music from melting into amorphous stickiness. Unlike *Faust,* which first brought into unseemly prominence a type of melody which was to haunt French music for fifty years, *Roméo et Juliette,* which was more of the same thing, exerted absolutely no influence on the progress or degradation of opera.

Faust, *Mireille,* and *Roméo* were the most effective results of Gounod's operatic career. He composed a round dozen of operas, not all of the other nine being worthless. *Philémon et Baucis* (1860), for example, a little one-acter written for the theater of the gaming rooms at Baden-Baden, but later stretched to three acts for the Lyrique (and then reduced to two for the Opéra), has some piquancy and charm, altogether polished surfaces, and a static libretto. Not even Gounod's position as the Grand Old Man of French opera could save his final stage works from humiliating fiasco. The recluse of the splendid house on the Boulevard Malesherbes, half priest, half voluptuary, remained [6] until his death the composer of *Faust.* When that end came in 1893, Gounod was regarded throughout much of the Western world as solidly seated among the titans of music, a place to which his beautifully kept patriarch's beard seemed to assure his title. Even ten years before his death, when those wise men responsible for beautifying the auditorium of the Metropolitan Opera House decided to grave upon the proscenium arch the six foremost names in operatic history, they set on the left side Gluck, Mozart, and Verdi; on the right, Wagner, Beethoven, and Gounod.

In the Master's heyday, his most dangerous French competitor was the formidable academician and nightmare of budding original talents, Ambroise Thomas, seven years his senior. Like Berlioz and Gounod a

[6] Except in England, and fleetingly in the oratorio societies of the United States, where his large religious works made him seem, temporarily, a second Mendelssohn. They are musically much like *Faust,* perhaps a shade more sensual, certainly as saccharine.

pupil of Jean-François Lesueur and a Grand Prix de Rome, Thomas came from behind to win. After thirty years of middling success as a composer of *opéras-comiques,* ballets, and grand operas, at the age of fifty-five he brought forth *Mignon,* an equally conventional stage piece that overnight forced Gounod to realize that a rival had appeared on the native heath. Two years later, Thomas almost repeated this success with *Hamlet.* After that, though he lived nearly thirty years and did not entirely abandon composition, he figured chiefly as Auber's much-feared successor at the Conservatoire. Official honors smothered his unoriginal talents while his *Mignon* vied with *Faust* in keeping Goethe's fame green. During the fete attendant on the one-thousandth *Mignon* (May 13, 1894), Thomas received the grand cross of the Legion of Honor. Less than two years later, in 1896, he died in his eighty-fifth year.

Those ghoulish tamperers with masterpieces, Barbier and Carré, supplied the books for both of Thomas's principal operas. Having watered down *Faust* into small beer, they did much the same with *Wilhelm Meister:* in selecting episodes for *Mignon* from Goethe's philosophical novel, they conscientiously removed most of the philosophy and all of the literary distinction. The result is something exuberantly skittish and totally incredible, ending with a happy tying-together of loose ends in a hysterical jollification unusual even on the operatic stage. Miraculously, Barbier and Carré took a segment from a predominantly tragic story, carried it within shouting distance of its natural denouement, and then sidestepped it with a slick device of mistaken identities. Thomas conscientiously followed the result, not Goethe's thoughtful, poetic narrative.

At sporadic intervals, as in the translation of that charming lyric "Kennst du das Land," when the librettists allow Goethe the poet to have his say, Thomas rises to the occasion. In that lovely air, "Connais-tu le pays," Gounod-like in contour, but somehow more convincing than most of Gounod as a fragment of dramatic expression, Thomas is at his best. Two or three other spots in the opera equal it. When the libretto is stale, flat, and unprofitable, Thomas is stale, flat, and unprofitable, and is not averse to adding a bit of silliness of his own. A ponderable part of *Mignon*'s remaining popularity depends upon the polonaise, "Je suis Titania," which is put into the mouth of the middle-aging coquette, and which is one of the most addlepated display pieces ever composed. It is the Marguerite's Jewel Song and Juliette's Waltz Song of *Mignon,* but in this kind of fluff Thomas showed himself much inferior to Gounod. Altogether, *Mignon* is compact of shreds and patches.

Thomas's other success, *Hamlet,* followed the pattern of *Mignon,* with Barbier and Carré once more mutilating a great work of art and Thomas once more carefully setting the letter of their libretto. The reckless trio had impudently selected a subject that already had balked, besides Domenico Scarlatti, a score or more of lesser men. The tortured melancholia of the Prince of Denmark was not material for the action operas of the age of Thomas, and could not well have been used until operatic music had profited by the psychological suggestivity of a Debussy or a Strauss. *Hamlet* was not half so successful as its predecessor, despite the instant popularity of Ophelia's mad scene. Its *première* at the Opéra, on March 9, 1868, however, was brilliant, Nilsson warbling exuberantly as Ophelia under the convincingly dour eye of Faure as Hamlet.

France took to *Hamlet* at once, but the opera has been far from lucky elsewhere. Hamlet, in the first place, is a baritone—an audacity of casting that audiences, spoiled by mellifluous tenors, did not easily tolerate. Then, too, the libretto, which did not worry Frenchmen generally unfamiliar with Shakespeare, puzzled or infuriated Englishmen and Americans, who could not condone making Polonius an accomplice at the old king's murder and thus giving Hamlet a legitimate excuse for not marrying Ophelia. Finally, it was difficult for English-speaking hearers to accept the interpolated Drinking Song on its own merits. Yet, when *Hamlet* did occasionally succeed, it was often because a stirring baritone stopped the valid proceedings with that very interpolation. Also, Ophelia goes mad and distributes her withered flowers to a flossy waltz tune that is an exciting obstacle race for a coloratura. Naturally this florid creation, if sung by an accomplished technician, produces an astonishing effect.

Gounod and Thomas were typical serious-opera composers of the gilt-and-white splendors of Napoleon and Eugénie's Paris, just as Auber and Offenbach were its entertainers in a lighter vein. Their suave, burnished surfaces, their decorative details, their melodic voluptuousness, their long, complicated, and expensive ballets—all this reflects the heavy, sense-drugging luxury of the Second Empire as clearly as it is reflected in the deft brushwork of Winterhalter. Gounod and Thomas were heirs to the grandiosity of Meyerbeer—to his tricks, but not to his streak of dramatic genius. They faded, literally, after Sedan, and when the curtain rose again on the operatic scene, a new group of men was making the stage works of an embittered and chastened people. Wagnerism, so long fought against, entered French music almost at the moment when Germany humiliated France. Yet the French Wagnerians, as an official school, never enjoyed popularity: they cast themselves as opponents of native taste, and to the end their productions reeked of the ivory tower. Even so gifted a man as Ernest Reyer half stultified his talents by pious imitation of Wagner (and Berlioz).

The first men to gain the applause of post-1871 Paris were totally uninfluenced by Wagner, whose circle was definitely among the literary, artistic, musical intellectuals. Léo Delibes was not of that esoteric group. To his fingertips a practical man of the theater, before attempting an opera he had had a long and glittering career as a fabricator of sparkling operettas and ballets. Several of the former obtained large box-office success in the two years just before the Franco-Prussian War, while excerpts from two of his ballets—*Coppélia* (1870) and *Sylvia* (1876)—became dining-hour staples. *Coppélia* equaled the popularity of *Giselle,* a ballet by Delibes's master, Adam, himself a disciple of Boieldieu. From Adam, and even more clearly from Auber and Offenbach, Delibes picked up some elements of his brisk, sophisticated style. In 1873, with *Le Roi l'a dit,* he began to compose operas for the Comique. After a second, *Jean de Nivelle* (1880), the third lifted him overnight to fame equaling that of his elder operatic contemporaries—those entrenched academicians whose chief business, according to Camille Saint-Saëns, was plotting against the stage careers of Delibes, Bizet, and himself. The lucky inspiration was *Lakmé,* produced at the Comique on April 14, 1883.

The libretto of *Lakmé,* the work of Philippe Gille and Edmond Gondinet, is quite as silly as anything that Gounod or Thomas ever set, but it takes place in a storybook India that allowed the composer to invent a number of seductive pseudo-Oriental melodies and introduce a nautch ballet. Delibes treated the melodramatic and tragic plot with a discretion calculated to spare the sensitivities of his hearers: at its most intense, *Lakmé* is pleasantly sad, charmingly wistful, lyric but not dramatic. The Oriental coloring, depending upon reiterated harmonic and rhythmic tricks, palls sharply after Act II, which, moreover, contains most of the best music—the famous Bell Song occurs in Act II. Its history shows that it is little more than a vehicle for an attractive coloratura. Otherwise it has no power over listeners; even as superficial entertainment, it is far less satisfying than *Coppélia.* Yet, flimsy though the score is, it remained the best-known of Delibes's four operas, the last of which, *Kassya*—though boasting a libretto based on a tale by the shocking Sacher-Masoch and completed by Massenet after Delibes's death—was an utter failure.

A more interesting composer than Delibes, but less successful, was

Édouard Lalo, now remembered chiefly for the almost violin concerto that he called *Symphonie espagnole*. A man of superior intellect, widely informed in the means of his art, Lalo might have composed great music if his creative imagination had equaled his knowledge. He was primarily symphonic in outlook, and his operas were not the most personal of his works. Of the three, only *Le Roi d'Ys,* based on a Breton folk legend, had any career. It had its *première* at the Comique on May 7, 1888, and was slow in getting to London and New York, though it had a New Orleans hearing in 1890. Elsewhere, the overture, a subtly orchestrated symphonic movement, was popular long before the opera itself was performed; indeed, this had been true even in Paris ten years before the Comique *première,* for Lalo had let it be performed separately. During the 1921–22 season, the Metropolitan Opera finally staged *Le Roi d'Ys,* thus fulfilling a promise first held out in the prospectus of the German season of 1889–90. Beniamino Gigli as Mylio had the star number, the lovely *aubade* "Vainement, ma bien-aimée," based on a haunting Breton song. But even a cast that also included Frances Alda, Rosa Ponselle, Giuseppe Danise, and Léon Rothier failed to carry the opera beyond the five performances of that season. Its signal lack of success outside France contrasts glaringly with the almost baneful popularity of the piano piece that Debussy based on the same legend of a Breton town inundated by the waves of an avenging sea, *La Cathédrale engloutie.*

One characteristic of the French operatic composers of the second half of the nineteenth century seems to have been an inability to make more than a single permanent addition to the repertoire. Gounod is only apparently an exception, for *Roméo et Juliette* now hovers precariously on the edge of oblivion. Thomas's *Hamlet* is in even worse straits. Delibes never had an effective second-string opera, and it is doubtful that Lalo can now be said to be in the repertoire at all. Bizet remains chiefly the composer of *Carmen.* Saint-Saëns suffered from the same inability, in his case all the more striking because in several genres of instrumental music he left compositions that still are regularly performed. He tried long and earnestly to gain an equal repute in the opera house, but of his thirteen attempts, composed between 1864 and 1911, only one—*Samson et Dalila*—endured in any practical sense of the word. Some of the others were sumptuously produced, but almost all of them failed. *Henry VIII* won a certain vogue in France, but it is unknown elsewhere except for its graceful ballet music.

Saint-Saëns was one of the foremost piano virtuosos of the nineteenth century. His playing was concise, perfectly finished, and exquisitely ordered, but most often lacked warmth and fervor. The same formal perfection and polish characterized most of his compositions. But he largely overcame this deficiency of feeling in the carefully worked-out *Samson,* begun in 1868 and completed in 1872. He was so proficient technically that his creative ease often degenerated into automatic writing; in *Samson,* this fatal facility never won full sway—throughout, the composer modeled his work. In it, too, his melodic gift was not only abnormally consistent, but also rose to unusually high levels. Always a frighteningly competent second-flight composer of utmost respectability, he came close, in *Samson et Dalila,* to the stature demanded by a story of inherent vitality.

The heroic mold of the temptress Delilah would suggest that Saint-Saëns himself was enthralled by her: the rich sensualism of the music by which her character is built up is far from typical of him. Delilah engages him so strongly that the other figures, Samson included, are secondary, and it is significant that the erring Hebrew hero has few solo moments of arresting interest, whereas two of Delilah's solos—"Printemps qui commence" and "Amour, viens aider ma faiblesse"—always stop the show. Even the tremendously famous duet, "Mon coeur s'ouvre à ta voix," is arranged to give the impression of being a mezzo-soprano solo with tenor chimings-in. Only the ballet music can compete with Delilah. Altogether, the score, when properly performed—which means both sung and acted—is vastly entertaining, even, at moments, thrilling. Throughout, *Samson* shows the work of an admirable musician—colorful, but not to excess, cleverly orchestrated, dramatic. The choral writing is solid and telling, and even the seeming lack of balance caused by Saint-Saëns' passion for his enchantress is evened up by the tenseness of the struggling Samson, who does not, appropriately, display heroic stature until, at the final curtain, he pulls down the Temple of Dagon on the heads of the Philistines.

Samson et Dalila has had a curious history. When Saint-Saëns had completed it, no French opera house would stage it despite the fact that he was already very distinguished. Its alleged seriousness and gloom were cited against it. Fragments of it were performed publicly, and Pauline Viardot-García gave the second act at her summer place, herself singing Delilah. Liszt, from whom Saint-Saëns had already borrowed copiously while perfecting his instrumental style, then came forward with his usual generosity, offering to stage the opera at Weimar. There, accordingly, a

German version, with Ferdinand Lemaire's French libretto translated by Richard Pohl, was brought out on December 2, 1877. The next year, Brussels heard a concert performance of *Samson* in French, and that original version was first staged in France at Rouen on March 3, 1890. Seven months later, on October 31, it reached Paris, but still not the Opéra (it was sung at the Théâtre Eden), which did not capitulate until November 23, 1892. Since then, in France, *Samson* has joined the small company of such overplayed favorites as *Faust, Mignon, Carmen,* and *Manon.*

An Anglo-Saxon prejudice against presenting Biblical characters on the stage led to oratorio performances of *Samson et Dalila,* in English, in both England and the United States. In the former country it was not heard as an opera until 1909, at Covent Garden. New Orleans, a predominantly Catholic city of liberal cosmopolitan cast, secured the first American *Samson,* January 4, 1893, at the French Opera House.

Gounod, Thomas, Delibes, Lalo, and Saint-Saëns form an interesting group for the student of musical development in opera. It would be unfair to say that, had they never lived, music would be what it is, for some of them exerted a powerful influence on salon music, both sacred and profane, and at least Lalo and Saint-Saëns wrote instrumental music of wide popular appeal. They had imitators, chiefly diluters of whatever originalities they could detect in their models. The eclectic Massenet is closely linked to this group, but stands apart by reason of his sensitivity to other influences, from Wagner to *verismo,* and the fact that his operatic activity extended well into the twentieth century. The importance of Gounod, Thomas, and the others depends only upon the additions they made to the repertoire, and on that basis Lalo, in some purely musical respects the best of them all, can scarcely be included. They added largely to operatic lore, gave a gallery of new roles to aspiring singers, and found, at least with one opera each, the secret, temporary or lasting, of box-office success. And the secret? In their cases, it seems to have been an ability to write charming, easily remembered melodies. Whether those melodies were relevant or irrelevant to libretto and situations seems scarcely to have mattered.

CHAPTER XVII

The Russians

THE belief that the history of Russian opera began on December 9, 1836, with the first performance, in St. Petersburg, of Mikhail Ivanovich Glinka's *A Life for the Tsar,* has stubbornly refused to yield to the pressure of the facts. Russian opera was almost a century old when the first of Glinka's two masterpieces was first given. Nor can it be claimed that *A Life for the Tsar* was a revolutionary work: its difference from the many Russian operas that had preceded it lay chiefly in its superior quality. But Glinka came to be recognized as the father of the self-conscious, noisily assertive Russian nationalist school, and it was his followers, propagandists all, who decided to begin the history of native opera with this patriotic piece cast, except for details exaggerated by the nationalists, in a conventional Italian style.

The truth is that a kind of Russian opera was flourishing as early as the reign of the Empress Anne (d. 1740), who imported an Italian troupe in 1734. Francesco Araja, its head, who had composed *La Forza dell' amore e dell'odio* for the Carnival season of 1734 in Milan, produced it at St. Petersburg on February 9, 1736, apparently the first opera given on Russian soil. For the text of the first opera written expressly for Russia Araja chose to set Metastasio's *Semiramide riconosciuta,*[1] presented on February 9, 1737. Not until 1755 did Araja set a Russian text: *Cephal i Prokris (Cephalus and Procris)*, by Alexander Petrovich Sumarokov, "the first gentleman in Russia," according to Prince D. S. Mirsky, "to choose the profession of letters." By the middle of the reign of Catherine II (1762–96), the importation of Italian musicians was in full swing:

[1] This may have been the first setting of this famous libretto, which served, under one name or another, almost thirty composers.

among the facile melodists whom she brought in were Galuppi, Traetta, Paisiello, Sarti, and Cimarosa. The Spaniard Martín y Soler, another missionary of the school of Naples, died in St. Petersburg—despite his neurotic hatred of his mother's cultural program, the Emperor Paul had created him a privy councilor.

The great Catherine had favored her Italians with an occasional libretto, after it had been edited by her secretary. It merits note that this sophisticated princess, the correspondent of Diderot and Voltaire, always chose Russian subjects: one of them was a satire on the brilliant Gustavus III; another, in which Sarti had a hand, was written in the style of Shakespeare, "without observing the traditional rules of the stage." The Italians, left to their own devices, ignored Russian texts.[2] Some of the Russians, though musically but feeble imitators of the Italians, set Russian texts about Russian subjects. The short-lived Evstignei Ipatovich Fomin (1761–1800) wrote *Melnik* (1779), a comedy that survived well into the nineteenth century, and *Amerikantsi* (*The Americans*), which should have some value as a curiosity. Alexei Titov (1769–1827) wrote many operas in dilute Mozart, while Alexei Verstovsky (1799–1862), like Glinka a pupil of that Chopinist before Chopin, John Field, succeeded so well with his Italian imitations that he ended as manager of the Imperial Opera at Moscow. His great moment as an operatic composer came the year before *A Life for the Tsar,* and it was a moment that did not quite wane until the last revival at Moscow in 1897. His *Askoldova mogila* (*Askold's Tomb*), first given at Moscow in September, 1835,[3] seemed to meet the not very precise contemporary demands for a regenerated national opera. It uses gypsy tunes and street songs with an alluring boldness, but the texture of the music is thin. More interesting are the humorous touches and the clever reliance on Weber in dealing with the supernatural. A fourth composer of this period is Alexander Alabiev (1787–1851), who, though he turned out a profusion of completely forgotten operas, is occasionally heard in the opera house for the curious reason that coloratura sopranos, following precedents set by

[2] An honorable exception was the Venetian Catterino Cavos (1775–1840), most of whose operas used Russian texts. One of them, the successful *Ivan Susannin*, anticipated the subject matter of *A Life for the Tsar*. When Glinka's opera came out, Cavos, who was managing director of all the imperial theaters, proclaimed its superiority to his own treatment of the theme.

[3] *Askold's Tomb* was sung, in Russian, at the Théâtre Français, New York, in 1869.

Viardot-García and Patti, sometimes sing his show song, "The Nightingale" in the Lesson Scene of *Il Barbiere di Siviglia*. Liszt transcribed this song for piano solo, and Glinka's last completed composition was an arrangement of it for small orchestra to accompany a singer.

Titov and Alabiev were army officers, and Verstovsky was a civil engineer: it almost seems as if they set a pattern of amateurism or dilettantism for Russian composers. Almost without exception, the Russian masters of the nineteenth century did their composing as a side line or came to it somewhat late, after another career. Even Glinka, the child of rich landholding gentry, worked in a government office for some years before laziness rather than a passion for music made him resign. He remained a dilettante all his life.[4] The Great Five all led extramusical lives, at least for a while. Balakirev was a railway employee; Cui was a lieutenant-general of engineers; Borodin was a chemistry professor; Mussorgsky was a small-time civil servant; and Rimsky-Korsakov was a naval officer. Tchaikovsky was a government attorney. Only Rubinstein, the child prodigy, was a musician from the very beginning. It was this lack of technical grounding and continuous practice that flawed many inherently interesting Russian compositions, and in some cases delayed their acceptance, particularly by critics. But these very lacks were, in the case of the nationalist composers, frequently twisted into strengths, and to them the Five owed a good portion of their spontaneity, audacity of experiment, and strangeness—in the best sense of the word.

Glinka is more interesting than most fathers of schools, and for the unreasonable reason that he was personally quite insignificant. The mere mention of his name aroused Tolstoy to a tempest of moral indignation —Mikhail Ivanovich was such a worthless, sensual fellow! Tchaikovsky expressed astonishment that so commonplace a man could be so good an artist. That Glinka was worthless and a libertine cannot be deduced from his music: that he was commonplace is, on occasion, all too obvious. Most of his work is banal, and even the best of it is spotted with banalities. In most respects, *A Life for the Tsar* is a continuation of the stuff turned out by the Titovs and Verstovskys.[5] But it is, in one sense, a revo-

---

[4] Repin's famous portrait of Glinka the composer—he is lying on a sofa, his head against a pillow, a sheet of music on his lap, and a meditative pencil at his lip—could epitomize the Oblomov of a generation later. Goncharov could have used the last nine years of Glinka's life as a model for the spiritually paralyzed hero of his immortal casebook of the Russian gentleman's soul.

[5] The libretto, by Baron G. F. Rosen, is more than a reworking of Prince A. A.

lutionary work, the product of an impatient mind. In its acres of imitation Bellini we meet with strange formal devices Bellini would have considered quite unnatural: the same year as *Das Liebesverbot,* not one note of which Glinka could possibly have heard, he used a system of theme repetition more extensive and more effective than Wagner was to achieve for many a year. These themes are not the pulsating nodes that Wagner favored eventually, but longer, more lyric phrases, quoted unchanged. Otherwise, except for lavish use of Slavic color in places, *A Life for the Tsar* is a deftly orchestrated, harmonically unadventurous, and dramatically feeble piece.

A Life for the Tsar was popular: it was patriotic,[6] easy to understand, elegantly old-fashioned. Other Russian gentlemen had produced operas of this kind, though not such good ones. The Tsar gave the happy little composer a ring valued at four thousand rubles and appointed him master of the Imperial Chapel. For a few years he was referred to as a genius. Then he made a mistake: he wrote a second opera in a quite different style, and had it produced on December 9, 1842, the sixth anniversary of *A Life for the Tsar.* His friends could not make head or tail of it; its complexities shocked society; and the critics, many of whom considered themselves artistic radicals, were not quite prepared for *Ruslan and Lyudmila.* The Grand Duke Mikhail Pavlovich told Liszt that instead of arresting refractory officers he punished them by ordering them to a performance of *Ruslan,* and thought Liszt was making a bad joke when he referred to Glinka as a genius.

In some respects, Glinka's erstwhile admirers had reason to be annoyed at him: *Ruslan*'s verse libretto, a silly wandering fairy tale, though based on Pushkin, had been filtered through the foggy minds of at least five collaborators, and finally tampered with by the good-natured composer himself. It is utterly lacking in dramatic interest—a fact of which Glinka seems to have been strangely unaware. Dostoevsky alone not only tolerated but adored the libretto, and constantly dragged his family to performances of the opera. In it he saw an elaborate political allegory —a kind of Slavic *Zauberflöte.*

Shakhovskoy's text for *Ivan Susannin.* It had to be: Glinka caught fire at once, and sketched out most of the opera before Rosen wrote a single verse.

[6] Nationalism was not considered good taste by some of the conservatives. They called *A Life for the Tsar* "music for coachmen." Glinka, an aristocrat who spoke French quite as well as his critics, replied: "What does it matter, since the men are superior to their masters?"

But in a world where bad librettos were the rule, another bad one was not enough to alienate critics and public. The music itself was the offender. Its harmonic, rhythmic, and melodic audacities spoke a new musical language that Glinka had, to a large extent, invented. Partly from hints taken from Russian and Oriental folk music, partly from his own knack for exotic combination, Glinka had evolved that unmistakable, highly colored idiom which obviously differentiates Russian from other types of music. *Ruslan and Lyudmila* is an opera of examples, and from it almost every Russian composer since Glinka's day has borrowed freely whenever he has wished to be Russian. What Tchaikovsky said of Glinka's orchestral fantasia *Kamarinskaya* (1848) could have been said with modifications about *Ruslan:* "The present Russian symphonic school is all in *Kamarinskaya,* just as the whole oak is in the acorn." When *Ruslan* was first given, it sounded just as foreign to Russian critical ears as the first Russian music sounded to the ears of foreigners. It sounded, that is, discordant, barbaric, and just a trifle improper.

Glinka's neglect at home was compensated for by the adulation of later Russian composers, both nationalist and cosmopolitan. To the former he was an idol, and the latter regarded him as a god who was not absolutely to be trusted. When he died in 1857, he was, except to a few enthusiasts of advanced views like Liszt and Berlioz (both of whom had visited Russia), unknown beyond the borders of his native land.[7] However, for all his dilettantism and casualness, Glinka had a sense of his mission and a feeling that the future was with him. Only the year before his death, in deciding upon who was to supervise the musical education of a favorite niece, he hit upon Mili Alexeievich Balakirev, the future leader of the Five, then but nineteen years old. "No one else has ideas so like my own," he told his sister. "One of these days he will be a second Glinka." This prediction was not precisely carried out, but Balakirev did indeed live to become the most powerful preacher of Glinka's ideas. It was Balakirev who conducted a Prague performance of *Ruslan and*

---

[7] Meyerbeer, whose advanced views were known only to himself and his valet, must be excepted. He went out of his way to court Glinka. When the latter was in Berlin in 1857, Meyerbeer, as music director to the King of Prussia, included the trio from *A Life for the Tsar* in the annual court concert. Glinka, delighted, attended. He suffered a chill after leaving the overheated palace and died two days later.

Lyudmila in 1867, but that was as far west as he carried his master's music.

When Russian music spread to Western Europe, and then to the United States, and particularly when books had been written about it, Glinka's fame became international. But as far as his two operas are concerned, he is like one of those great unread classics of literature which everyone reveres and no one knows. Neither opera has been given as a whole in the United States, and performances any place outside Russia have been few.[8] Of the operatic music of Glinka, only the high-spirited little overture to *Ruslan* is widely familiar, and that, except for the use of the whole-tone scale, fifty years before Debussy, is notoriously uncharacteristic of the original material in *Ruslan.*

Alexander Sergeievich Dargomizhsky, the eldest of the younger men, began as a passionate disciple of Glinka, and ended, after borrowing from him what he pleased, by going off in another direction. Glinka's strength was lyrical, Dargomizhsky's dramatic. The former produced his best and most attractive effects with the long, singing line; Dargomizhsky, by comparison, is gnomic and short-winded. His sole training in musical theory consisted in copying out the five notebooks Glinka had taken down during studies in Berlin—in contrast to the earnest, ambitious Dargomizhsky, Glinka was musically erudite. Furthermore, whereas Glinka always had native flair to rely on in cases of theoretical uncertainty, Dargomizhsky needed much more technique than he ever commanded. His deficiencies were always bringing him up sharp against problems he could not solve.

Dargomizhsky's *Russalka,* based on a Pushkin fairy tale, and produced at St. Petersburg on May 4, 1856, immediately showed that Russian opera had enlisted a master of characterization, especially in the extremes of tragedy and comedy. In general color deriving strongly from Glinka, it struck out boldly with a powerful type of declamation, halfway between aria and recitative, and particularly telling when a realistic effect was intended. *Russalka,* because of a skimpy production, was only a moderate success, though before Dargomizhsky died in 1869 he had the satisfaction of seeing it well established in the Russian repertoire.[9] In its early career, the opera gave fine opportunities for the singing and

[8] A French version of *A Life for the Tsar* was sung at Covent Garden in 1887, with Julián Gayarré, the Basque tenor, as Susannin.

[9] New York heard *Russalka,* in Russian, in 1922.

acting of the phenomenal Ossip Afanassievich Petrov, who created the role of the Miller with the same sensitive intelligence he brought to that of Susannin in *A Life for the Tsar,* and of Ruslan in *Ruslan and Lyudmila.* In later years, Fyodor Ivanovich Chaliapin, Petrov's renowned successor, made the Miller, especially in the scenes of his insanity, one of his supreme interpretations.

Russalka brought Dargomizhsky the flattering attention of Balakirev and his two acolytes, César Antonovich Cui and Modest Petrovich Mussorgsky. But his demanding and vainglorious nature left him only Cui, the most trivial of the Five. Not until the spring of 1866, when work was well under way on another opera, *The Stone Guest,* which was to express without compromise or dilution all of Dargomizhsky's musical ideals, did the younger talents again cluster around him. Then the jealous and fame-loving man, who in 1862 had petulantly asked a friend, "In what respect am I inferior to Glinka?" [10] found himself the center of an idolatrous group, among it at least two geniuses. It was for some years like a not ignoble page from the Renaissance. Then the master died, his work unfinished, the orchestration not even begun.

In any other country, this might have meant the end of *The Stone Guest,* but as the Russian composers had already formed the habit of writing each other's works, and as Nikolai Andreievich Rimsky-Korsakov was already on hand, its career had only just begun. Cui finished the first scene (or tableau, as it was called), and Rimsky orchestrated the whole. It was his first major midwife's job, and though the opera failed when it was finally produced at the Maryinsky, on February 16, 1872, Rimsky wrote complacently: "I was content with my orchestration and quite delighted with the opera." Thirty years later, his professorial conscience began to bother him, and he did the job over, characteristically "softening here and there the extreme harshness and harmonic follies of the original."

The Stone Guest, an exact setting of Pushkin's version of the Don Juan legend, has three well-differentiated characters—Don Juan, Donna Anna, and Leporello. As early as 1857, Dargomizhsky had written his artistic credo in a letter to a friend. It ended with this significant sentence: "I wish the notes to express exactly what the words express: I want truth." His method of arriving at this truth was that of using an unmiti-

[10] The answer of his friend—it was Yuri Arnold, the critic—is worth recording: "My dear Alexander, you are endowed with sufficient sagacity to be able to find the answer for yourself."

gated "melodic recitative" (his own words), its rise and fall dictated by the accent, meaning, and inflection of the words. The voice was more important than the orchestra. In the hands of a first-class composer, equally impatient of Italian models and inspired by certain developments in Western music, notably Gluck's and Wagner's, these intentions would have served admirably in helping to emphasize the heightened stature of the three principal characters. At certain moments, they served Dargomizhsky as well as he could have wished. But he was too sketchily endowed to carry his own theories to ends other than those provided by dry-as-dust logic—for page after page of *The Stone Guest,* we wonder what has happened to the creative artist. And so, today, the chief interest in that much-labored-over score is that it contains harmonies more advanced than anything else done that side of the twentieth century. It even dispenses with key signatures. It is, in very truth, a theorist's playground. It had a visible influence on greater men than Dargomizhsky, and Mussorgsky, particularly, was much in its debt in his finest work. Unlike Glinka's *Ruslan* and Dargomizhsky's own *Russalka, The Stone Guest* would probably be thankless in revival. Outside Russia it is all but unknown.

Standing well away from the disciples of either Glinka or Dargomizhsky, Alexander Nikolaievich Serov, quite apart from the fascination of his mercurial personality, demands attention because he happened to compose the Russian operas that became most popular in nineteenth-century Russia. Primarily a practicing critic, Serov found himself at loggerheads not only with the nationalists but also, at one time or another, with almost every musician in Russia. During a trip to Germany in 1858, this irrepressible hero-worshiper (who was always changing heroes) became enslaved to Wagnerism. The next year, meeting Wagner himself in Switzerland, he clinched the one musical loyalty that lasted until his death. But when he came to compose an opera himself, Serov was not unimpeachably a Wagnerian. He had heard both *Tannhäuser* and *Lohengrin,* and his first opera, *Judith,* based on a familiar Biblical story, is full of echoes of them. But as there are many strong dashes of Meyerbeer in *Judith,* the total effect resembles early Wagner—*Rienzi,* for example. Produced at the Maryinsky Theater on May 28, 1863, *Judith* was a big success, somewhat to Serov's surprise (his career, up to that time, had been anything but a series of triumphs) and altogether to the chagrin of his many enemies in every conceivable camp.

Serov, the critical analyst, dissected the reasons for the popularity of

Judith, and designed his next operatic venture on the basis of his findings. He realized that his strength lay in playing the Meyerbeerian gambit all the way. He had a story in mind, but no definite libretto. Almost in parody of Meyerbeer's method of working in tableaus, Serov conceived his story as a series of sensational situations, each to be a sensational stage picture. He adapted words to the music for these situations as he went along. *Rogneda,* the outcome of this peculiar method of work, was crowned with the tumultuous success at which Serov, an unrelenting critic of false ideals in other men's work, had aimed. Within five years of its *première* at the Maryinsky, on November 8, 1865, *Rogneda* had been given seventy times at that theater alone, besides many performances elsewhere in Russia. It is a work of small musical value, but so much is happening on the stage all the time that it has much the appeal of a circus. There was point in Dargomizhsky's remark: "Why shouldn't Serov's operas succeed? He has camels in one and real dogs in the other."

The effect of this double success was to rid Serov of his feeling of insecurity as a composer and also to soften his temper. He became almost friendly to the nationalists, lectured admiringly on Glinka and Dargomizhsky, and even got on easy terms with the Rubinstein group of conservative cosmopolitans. Having assured himself of their respect, he then tried to give musical expression to his Wagnerism, choosing a sordid drama by the gloomy Ostrovsky. He made the experiment of fusing Glinka and Wagner, but did not get far. An Italian operatic company, starring Patti, Lucca, and Mario, came to St. Petersburg, and Serov forgot Wagner for Patti and the kind of music she liked to sing. Laying aside the almost completed *Hostile Power,* he started a thoroughly Italianate vehicle for her, based on George Sand's *Consuelo.* This rash inconsistency was too much for the gods: he died on February 1, 1871, without having completed either opera. *Consuelo,* indeed, was never finished, but *Hostile Power,* completed by the pedantic Nikolai Feopemtovich Soloviev,[11] added measurably to his fame.

Of the Five, the core of that nationalist group with which Serov was at war most of his life, four—all except Balakirev—wrote operas. Cui, a busybody who aspired to the leadership of the Five whenever Balakirev was absent, had more theoretical grounding than most of his colleagues, having once studied with the great Polish nationalist composer Stanislaw Moniuszko, and so found his claims respected. Vocally a vigorous and

---

[11] He told Rimsky-Korsakov to "go back to school" after he had found a misprint in *Pskovityanka.*

caustic asserter of Balakirev's most cherished ideals, Cui had the same difficulty as Serov in carrying over his critical opinions into musical creation. A Russian nationalist without a drop of Russian blood (he was half French, half Lithuanian), Cui wrote purportedly nationalist operas that, on analysis, show themselves to be based solidly on Auberian models with strong transfusions of Schumann. Passionately desirous of feeling every throb of the nationalist pulse (natural conduct for a future lieutenant-general of engineers), Cui had been in the van of those who had seen Dargomizhsky's importance, and it is obvious that he considered his own lackluster scores as inspired by Dargomizhsky rather than by Glinka. The best of his ten operas, all mediocre, is *William Ratcliff*, based on a Scots blood-bath coagulated by Heinrich Heine.[12] Cui's chief contribution to the cause of Russian opera was his unresting championing of it—he lived until 1918—in French and Belgian periodicals. He never realized that his own operas, only two of which, ironically, have Russian stories, were not contributions to nationalist music.

The eldest of the Five, and next to Mussorgsky its commanding genius, was Alexander Porfirievich Borodin, a bastard descendant of the ancient kings of Imeretia, a part of the Caucasus. One of the most attractive figures in the history of Russian art, Borodin was devoid of that morbid introspection which makes the biographies of many of his confreres, when read in succession, seem repetitive: he was sunny in disposition, optimistic, easygoing, unassuming, and brilliantly gifted in several fields. Unfortunately for music, he had some of the defects that often accompany those virtues. A creative chemist of all except the highest genius, a pioneer in the field of education for women, and a composer of rare originality, he lacked that personal ambition which might have driven him to the very top in any one of his interests, instead of next to the top. What Bernard Shaw said of Haydn—that he "would have been among the greatest had he been driven to that terrible eminence"—might more fittingly have been said of Borodin. As it is, his two greatest works—the Third Symphony and *Prince Igor*—remained unfinished: in the first case death overtook him as he dawdled, and in the second the fructifying self-confidence was not there to make him complete it. One of the most tragic situations in the history of music as an evolving art is that in his last years, Borodin expressed delight instead of annoyance when Rimsky-Korsakov offered to complete *Igor*.

[12] This little matter of three murders, a suicide, and a case of insanity also inspired operas by Xavier Leroux and two Italian verists, Pietro Mascagni and Emilio Pizzi. Like the characters, none of these survived.

When Borodin died in 1887, it was eighteen years since he had begun to work on *Prince Igor,* but only a small fraction of that time had gone into the opera. Vladimir Vassilievich Stassov, the great nationalist critic who, though not a composer himself, directed, quite as much as Balakirev, the thinking of the Five, had suggested the subject to Borodin, who was attracted to it because of its Caucasian setting. Basing it on two ancient chronicles, Stassov wrote out a ten-page scenario that Borodin followed, gradually and constantly altering it and writing the actual libretto as he composed separate numbers. Everyone who heard these fragments was enthusiastic, as Borodin himself testified: "It is curious to see how all the members of our set agree in praise of my work. While controversy rages among us on every other subject, all, so far, are pleased with *Igor*—Mussorgsky, the ultrarealist, the innovating lyricodramatist; Cui, our master; Balakirev, so severe as regards form and tradition, and Vladimir Stassov himself, our valiant champion of everything that bears the stamp of novelty or greatness." But Borodin progressed slowly: among his multifarious activities music came after chemistry, and had to be pieced in when time allowed. "In winter," Borodin explained, "I can only compose when I am too unwell to give my lectures. So my friends, reversing the usual custom, never say to me, 'I hope you are well,' but 'I do hope you are ill.' "

When Rimsky-Korsakov and young Alexander Glazunov, Borodin's musical executors, began searching through his effects, they found, of *Prince Igor,* only a few scenes, individual arias, and sketches and memoranda for the rest. None of the opera was orchestrated, and no complete libretto was at hand. Rimsky at once saw his duty and communicated it so persuasively to his collaborator that Glazunov wrote a full-dress overture based on a few themes from the fragments of the score. All of Act III except the opening march is from Glazunov's pen. Rimsky arranged and orchestrated the rest. The result is therefore something of a hodgepodge: to Borodin's male vitality and Oriental primes were added the flaccid touches of Glazunov's classicizing mind and the tempered, oversweet exoticism of Professor Rimsky-Korsakov. These conscientious musical executors strove to denature a product that might have proved too barbaric, too heady, if taken raw. They fussed at *Igor* until it was respectable enough for the stage, and accordingly, on November 4, 1890, it was produced at the Maryinsky Theater, Rimsky afterwards observing, "Both Glazunov and I were pleased with our orchestration and additions."

Prince Igor was a success, but the management of the Maryinsky soon

took the precaution of cutting Act III and finally of dropping it altogether. This left of Glazunov's handiwork only the overture, and even
that was omitted when the opera at last reached New York, in Italian,
on December 30, 1915. The Metropolitan's decision to produce *Prince
Igor* came as a result of the interest in Russian opera aroused by the first
American performance of *Boris Godunov* two years earlier. Toscanini
had enthusiastically taken it under his wing, intending to conduct it, but
left the company in the spring of 1915, when a natural desire to offer his
services to Italy, which had just entered World War I, gave the tempera-
mental conductor an excellent excuse for putting into effect his oft-
expressed intention of withdrawing from the annoyances to which, he
alleged, he was subjected at the Metropolitan. So it was Giorgio Polacco
who conducted this important *première*. The principal roles were taken
by Alda, Amato, and Didur. New York was not as responsive as the
management had hoped, and after eight repetitions spread over three
successive seasons, *Prince Igor* was dropped permanently from the Metropolitan repertoire.

In France, where it had the benefit of a Diaghilev production, with
Chaliapin as Prince Galitzky, *Igor* fared better. In London, Sir Thomas
Beecham added it to the Covent Garden repertoire in 1912, with Chaliapin again as Galitzky, and there it drew large and warmly appreciative
audiences. Its survival, in the United States at least, is usually limited to
the ballet music—the Polovtsian Dances from Act II, almost always
without the chorus—that Fokine used for one of his most vivid and
popular choreographic creations. This is not opera's loss, but music's:
full of attractive pages, some of them transcending its surface color and
dynamism, *Prince Igor* is structurally invertebrate, of no significance in
the morphology of operatic forms. Its influence has not been as a totality,
but its tradition-unencumbered harmonies, the Orientalisms that sprang
from the Georgian composer's native convictions, and its brutal, free
rhythmic patterns sank deeply into the imaginations of such disparate
men as Debussy and Stravinsky.[13]

But more important than Borodin in influencing later composers was

[13] Before leaving Borodin we must note his first stage work, *Bogatyri* (*The
Valiant Knights*), an opera farce parodying Serov's *Rogneda*. Produced anony-
mously in Moscow in 1867, *Bogatyri* was half Borodin, half adaptations of Meyerbeer, Rossini, Offenbach, Serov, and others. Although it was said to have been
hilarious (at least musically), it failed. When it was revived at the Kemerny
Theater, Moscow (with a new libretto), in 1936, it was banned by the Soviet
authorities after a few performances.

Modest Petrovich Mussorgsky, the youngest but one of the Five. The legend of this singularly gifted man as a naïve, untutored, and bungling worker of accidental miracles, all of them marred by a child's technique, is one of the most serious blunders of the muse of history. Mussorgsky was even more cultivated than Borodin: he was a man of good education and sound musical training, and his whole life, with the exception of the last few tragic years, was a continuous process of further self-education. Curiosity was his passion, and he pursued it relentlessly after hours spent first as a subaltern in the Preobrazhensky Guards and later in a routine government job. It has been fashionable, as an extension of the legend, to call Mussorgsky a dilettante, but he had a sharp critic's knowledge of the art movements of his day, and the creative imagination to draw from them materials to be used in his own work. Without being political-minded, he knew the significance of what was going on about him and had a sane appreciation of what the liberation of the serfs meant to Russia. The realistic trend in literature and painting, with their fresh and vigorous interest in the folk, interested him keenly. Such a work as *Pictures at an Exhibition* suggests that his sharp eye for visual detail and personal idiosyncrasy would have enabled him to become a painter or novelist of power if his métier had not been music. It was natural for such a man to find his model in Dargomizhsky, that indomitable searcher for truth.

Mussorgsky's first protracted attempt to write an opera occurred before he was twenty years old. The subject—Flaubert's *Salammbô,* a novel with a wealth of realistic surface detail, but with no reality at the core—defeated him. He was much happier with Gogol's *Marriage,* a genre comedy of *petit bourgeois* life. Like Dargomizhsky with *The Stone Guest,* what Mussorgsky started to set, in June, 1868, was the play itself, not a libretto based on it. One act was finished in piano score—twenty-seven days' work—and then it was laid aside while he began to think ahead. When the one act was performed privately early in October, everyone except Stassov, while admitting the eloquence of Mussorgsky's declamation and the vividness of his character drawing, thought that he had, at one point or another, gone too far in the rawness of his harmonies. Even Dargomizhsky, who sang one of the roles (Mussorgsky himself and Rimsky-Korsakov's future wife also took parts), had reservations. Stassov, fifteen years the composer's senior, alone was enraptured by what he heard and at once assumed toward Mussorgsky the double role of father and prophet of his greatness. By his very enthusiasm, Stassov prevented Mussorgsky from completing *Marriage* [14]: he told him excitedly about Pushkin's Russo-Elizabethan drama, *Boris Godunov,* and from then on Gogol was forgotten.

Working rapidly, Mussorgsky finished *Boris* between the fall of 1868 and December 27, 1869. It was rejected overwhelmingly by the accept-ance committee of the Maryinsky, six votes being cast against it and only one—probably that of the Czech composer-conductor, Eduard Franzevich Napravnik—for it. Aside from scandalous harmonies and the lack of a big female role, *Boris* sinned in treating an episode in Rus-sian history far from popular with the authorities—and the committee-men were nothing if not politicians. Mussorgsky began to rework *Boris* at once, paying no attention to any strictures except those about the necessity of enlarging Marina's part. Before the revision was completed in 1872, he resubmitted the opera, which was again rejected.

This time, however, a strong bloc not only of Mussorgsky's friends but also of the curious of all parties was infuriated by the arrogant stand of the Maryinsky committee. In February, 1873, the stage manager of the theater had several excerpts from *Boris* performed at his benefit, and later in the same year Y. F. Platonova, an admired staff soprano, is said to have refused to renew her contract unless the opera was staged. What-ever the cause of their change of heart, the committeemen finally agreed to produce *Boris Godunov.* The *première* took place on February 8, 1874, with Platonova as Marina and Petrov as Varlaam. Before the sea-son was over, nine repetitions had been called for, and, according to Rimsky, Mussorgsky's character sharply changed for the worse. Despite the organized opposition of those whom Stassov called "the old men, the indifferentists, the routinists, and the worshipers of banal operatic mu-sic," *Boris'* popularity persisted through 1876, at which point the bar-barous cuts and unrepaired decay of the production began to tell against it.

Mussorgsky's unmitigated *Boris* (even at the *première* it had been slightly cut) was first heard only after publication of the two original versions in 1928, under the auspices of the State Music Publishers, Mos-

[14] A concert version was given at Rimsky-Korsakov's in 1906 and a stage version (with piano accompaniment) at St. Petersburg in 1910. Fully orchestrated, *Marriage* was the curtain raiser at the first production of *The Fair at Sorochintzy* (Petrograd, 1917). In 1931, Mikhail Ippolitov-Ivanov, an elder heir of the Five, and one of the official composers of the Soviet Union, presented a version of *Marriage:* the first act was Mussorgsky's; the other three acts were his own.

cow. At Sadler's Wells, in 1935, English audiences clamorously expressed their complete satisfaction with it. Ordinarily, we are not permitted to hear either of Mussorgsky's versions, but a wholesale reworking by Rimsky, and only sections of that. The great orchestrator was impelled by friendly piety and a sincere belief that, though a great genius, Mussorgsky did not quite know what he was doing. In reality, this meant only that Rimsky did not agree with what Mussorgsky had done.

In the middle nineties, Rimsky began his revision, but, fatally facile though he usually was, he found *Boris* a soul-racking experience. As late as 1906, he was working, in an agony of conscientiousness, on parts he had been criticized for omitting in his first edition. When he died in 1908, sections still lacked the suave touch of the master polisher. The ideas of the *Boris* usually heard are Mussorgsky's; the surfaces, the trappings, are Rimsky's. It is all very splendid, very glittering, very Muscovite even, if you will—but it is not Mussorgsky. His jolting abruptness, his harsh, cruel harmonies, have been restored away. Naturally, a modernist critic would be expected to prefer the original—did not the junior Edwin Evans once suggest that if editing had indeed to be done, someone like Stravinsky undertake the job?—but it was the temperately conservative Olin Downes who, after hearing one of the composer's own drafts in Russia, wrote: "The music of *Boris* as a whole is far superior, far more dramatically truthful and modern in texture in Mussorgsky's original version than in the Rimsky-Korsakov editing."

In order to appreciate *Boris,* it is essential not to approach it with a *parti pris,* particularly a Wagnerian one. Mussorgsky was not trying to compose a constantly unfolding Wagnerian music drama. Wagner in his maturity conceived of opera symphonically, while Mussorgsky built *Boris* block by block, conceiving it as a series of tone episodes. Wagner's musical means were complex, elaborate; Mussorgsky's were simple, bare. The unity of *Boris* is obtained by the establishment of mood and by the fierceness of the psychological concentration. Mussorgsky's separate characterizations are unforgettably credible and in the round, inviting comparison with Mozart's. His characterization of crowds is even more remarkable, for he painstakingly thought of them not as mobs, but as groups of individuals occasionally forced into mob action. He was allowed the luxury of writing this way because in Russia the most insignificant member of the chorus thought of himself as an individual artist and created his part with the same care as a principal. *Boris* re-creates life: its foremost virtue is vitality, not conventional beauty. The score is packed with the results of close observation of people in every walk of life and doing every conceivable thing: the miracle of Mussorgsky's achievement is in no way diminished by the circumstance that many of the elements of sixteenth-century Russian life survived almost unchanged in his own day.

Boris requires for its interpretation artists of a very special sort. It is no accident that though other singers of justly acquired repute have sung the name part, it has been all but inextricably connected with Chaliapin. Critics have accused him of using *Boris* as a vehicle for one of his stunt performances, but it is a fact that in it he created a never-to-be-forgotten personality—one which, incidentally, Mussorgsky would probably have applauded. Not playing—at the Metropolitan and other American houses—with actors of ability equal to his own, Chaliapin tended to throw *Boris* off balance. The result was that unity seemed better preserved when a less robustly intellectual singer was the Tsar. But to twist this illusion into a criticism of Chaliapin is to make a tacit plea for mediocrity.

The first American *Boris* had the advantage of a production brought as near perfection as the circumstances allowed: Toscanini rehearsed it for two months, and so the Metropolitan orchestra and chorus never more gloriously fulfilled themselves than on March 19, 1913, when the opera had its American *première*. But this impeccable conductor could not find sixteen principals, not to speak of an enormous chorus, who sang Russian or could even be imbued with an understanding of Russian ideas of declamation. So this performance, so flawless in many purely musical respects, began with the handicap of slighting many equally important dramatic values. The Polish Adamo Didur was as admirable as any non-Russian-singing Boris can be, but as he and all his colleagues sang in Italian, the force and dramatic stress of Pushkin's Russian words, which Mussorgsky had converted into musical sound syllable by syllable, were necessarily lost. The décor, brought wholesale from Paris, was as atmospherically correct as the presence, in major roles, of such otherwise excellent but incurably non-Slavic artists as Homer, Anna Case, Andrés de Segurola, Rothier, and Althouse (making his debut) was jarring. Yet despite these disadvantages, *Boris* had a terrific impact, and box-office receipts heartened Gatti-Casazza (ordinarily no friend to innovation), who had said, in a rather *ex cathedra* strain immediately after the *première:* "I consider *Boris* the most important performance artistically that I have given at the Metropolitan." His enthusiasm did not abate, though he never got around to staging *Boris* to Mussorgsky's original score—an action that he seriously contemplated after 1926, when the Russian State Publishing House republished it. This radical step was not taken at the Metropolitan until the directorship of Rudolf Bing, and then as edited by Karol Rathaus. In 1960, however, the Metropolitan dodged the issue differently, using for the first time the "version" of *Boris* prepared by Shostakovich.

Mussorgsky began two other operas, but never finished either. During the last years of his life, when excessive alcoholism had undermined his physical and moral being, one group of his well-wishers was giving him one hundred rubles a month to finish the tragic *Khovanshchina,* while another was giving him eighty to finish the comic *Fair at Sorochintzy.* The result was that when he died, on March 28, 1881, nothing of either was in final form. Fortunately for friends eager to construct wholes out of the unconnected parts, large sections of both were amply sketched out. The facts in the later history of both are quickly told. Rimsky-Korsakov orchestrated and completed *Khovanshchina,* publishing it in 1883. *The Fair at Sorochintzy* found four separate architects, each of whom carried it to completion in his own way: the first (1913) was by I. Saknovsky, and was a hopeless hybrid; the octogenarian Cui produced his version in 1917; Nikolai Tcherepnin, evidently adding as little as possible from his own pen, tried out a third version, in French, at Monte Carlo in 1923; finally, Vissarion Shebalin gave Moscow his reading of Mussorgsky's ideas in 1930.

The Fair at Sorochintzy, begun as a relaxation from what Mussorgsky called his "two heavyweights," *Boris* and *Khovanshchina,* was always a stepchild—and shows it. Parts of it are said to be extremely funny, but unhappily only to Russians, for the humor is too regionally topical for foreigners. For those who understand the point of the situations, the music is forceful, and there are not lacking, even for non-Russians, bursts of Mussorgsky's bold and vivid characterization. Yet the music as a whole is disappointing, and uncharitable critics who heard the Metropolitan performance, on November 29, 1930, frankly said that the best thing in the score was the already familiar, interpolated *Night on Bald Mountain,* which is more Rimsky than Mussorgsky.

Khovanshchina, which has properly had a more lively history in the United States than *The Fair,* is a worthy pendant to *Boris.* Musically, and in particular orchestrally, it has long sections quite as impressive, as beautiful, as anything in *Boris.* The libretto of *Khovanshchina,* which is based on a fugitive idea of Stassov's, and which Mussorgsky developed by cribbing the needed historical information from a multitude of books, evidently stirred him far more than the excellent Gogol story around which he wrote *The Fair.* Its theme—the conflict between the old and the new in seventeenth-century Russia—was exactly the sort of thing to inflame a typical man of the liberating sixties.

Khovanshchina, even more than *Boris,* showed Mussorgsky as inimitable: he could be idolized, but he could found no school. It epitomizes his willingness to sacrifice beauty for truth in the interest of realistic expression. Although *Khovanshchina* is much less dramatic than *Boris,* its variety of precise characterization, often achieved by a deliberate, spelling-out *Sprechstimme,* keeps it alive. Yet the opera has a central flaw: its diffuseness, its lack of dominating characters around whom conflict should inevitably rage. It seems as if Mussorgsky tried to show as many different types as he possibly could, and the result is that the stage is too often filled with an unindividualized confusion—a confusion which may be very much like life itself, but which lacks sufficient dramatic concentration to focus our attention. Our sympathies have to shift so often that eventually we have none at all. Rosa Newmarch hit off a fine comparison when she said: *"Khovantchina* reminds us of those early ikons belonging to the period when the transport of pictures through the forests, bogs, and wilderness of Russia so restricted their distribution that the religious painter resorted to the expedient of representing on one canvas as many saints as could be packed into it."

Nikolai Andreievich Rimsky-Korsakov, the youngest of the Five, and, next to Tchaikovsky, the most popular of all Russian composers, would never have made the mistake of crowding too many saints into one ikon. The story of his fifty years as an active composer, from his fumbling musical ABC's to that last period when he was the most revered master of techniques outside Germany, is one of constant self-discipline, husbanding of forces, polishing, filing, tempering, and revising. Had Rimsky confined this self-discipline to himself and not extended it to the works of others—some of them original geniuses—he would have left a fairer name.

Unfortunately, rather like the pest who has some inner drive always to touch fresh paint, this unrelenting *magister musicae* felt it his duty to Rimsky-Korsakovize the "flawed" scores of Dargomizhsky, Borodin, and Mussorgsky, to correct their excessive audacities, to give them an alien suavity, and, in short, to provide them with a shimmering outer garment not precisely their own. A sample of Rimsky's noble self-dedication follows: "Only when I have revised the whole of Mussorgsky's works shall I begin to be at peace and feel that my conscience is clear; for then I shall have done all that can and ought to be done for his compositions and his memory." Thus, as Mrs. Newmarch acidly observed, "When it came to a question of what he believed to be an offense against art, he saved his friend's musical soul at the expense of his originality." We must agree that Rimsky's high-minded smugness is infuriating. But it is irrelevant to a fair judgment of his own compositions, which are among the most delicious fruits of the Russian musical efflorescence.

Yet, any evaluation of Rimsky's fifteen operas (and the same stricture can be applied to his songs and instrumental pieces) must begin with the admission that these fruits come all too obviously from a single tree. Gerald Abraham, a most reliable guide through the labyrinth of Russian music, has pointed out that Rimsky "practically sums up the aesthetic contribution to music of the entire group." At one point or another in his operas, the influence of each of his great Russian contemporaries, as well as of Glinka, is patent. Nevertheless, so pervasive is Rimsky's own musical personality that though it is possible to mistake one of his operas for another, it is quite impossible to mistake any one of them for the work of anyone else.

Rimsky's first opera, *Pskovityanka,* dates from the years of his closest intimacy with Mussorgsky: begun in 1868, it was finished in 1872. This was a crude affair—an imitation of his friend's mingling of Dargomizhsky and folk music—but was produced with ponderable success in 1873, partly because of the political connotations of some of the music (Rimsky, at twenty-nine, was already a liberal, and had had censor trouble). In the following three years, during which he was working hard at harmony and counterpoint, he must have fretted about the crudities of *Pskovityanka,* for even before beginning a second opera, he spent two years completely polishing this first one and adding a prologue. The second version, notable chiefly for casting out whatever attractive roughness he had achieved in the first, introduced much extraneous matter by way of displaying his newly found technical knowledge. No one liked it, and it was never produced, its sole virtue even to its perpetrator being its solid respectability. Eleven years later, Rimsky started on a second revision, during which the prologue was detached and made into a one-act opera, *Boyarynya Vera Sheloga.*

The third *Pskovityanka* was finished in 1893, and five years later provided, in the role of Ivan the Terrible, one of the earliest of Chaliapin's triumphs. For years, Rimsky had been revising his works, and he was able, after [15] the completion of the third *Pskovityanka,* to make this curious pronouncement of virtuous self-examination: "I closed my account with my past. Not one of my major works of the period before *May Night* [his second opera, composed in 1878] remained in its original form." This final version of *Pskovityanka* has become known, particularly in France, as *Ivan le terrible.*

Never again did Rimsky-Korsakov labor so hard and drearily on an opera as he did on *Pskovityanka. May Night,* his next opera, was a facile essay in the Glinka style, and overflows with bright folk color of an agreeable if not very memorable sort. Still in the Glinka mode, he composed *Snegurochka* on a text by the popular dramatist Ostrovsky. It was composed under very happy circumstances, and Rimsky threw himself into the work with gusto. The subject—a fantastic fairy tale of pagan Russia —appealed to him, and he wrote much of the vocal score at a country paradise outside Moscow, where every sight and sound awoke in him the pantheistic feelings that seem to have inspired heathen tales of the type of *Snegurochka.* Although it was first produced under trying circumstances (its great length necessitated cuts that he resented, and, moreover, his wife was recovering slowly from her first childbirth), Rimsky, years later, when a feeling that his powers were permanently on the wane had induced in him a mood of sad reminiscence, spoke with loving pride of *Snegurochka,* which the critics had treated harshly. He felt then, in 1893, that *"Snegurochka* is not only my best opera, but, on the whole, perhaps the best of all contemporary operas." [16] One naturally wonders exactly what he meant by "contemporary," but there is no doubt that it is a charming score.

In 1881, when *Snegurochka* was finished, Rimsky was not the supreme orchestral wizard that he was to become within a few years, but even so, the relatively simple score is already charged with that magic, that sense of fantasy, peculiar to him. The delicately gamboling song of Lehl, in Act III, is one of his loveliest inspirations, while the Dance of

---

[15] Or possibly in 1891, when the second revision was half done. Rimsky's own statement is somewhat obscure on this point, but either interpretation is admissible.

[16] The man who could offer himself such consolation was obviously on the way to recovery. Ten more operas were to come from him before death alone stopped his composing, fifteen years later.

the Buffoons, from the same act, is as broadly bumbling as its name implies. It would seem that these and several other numbers would endear *Snegurochka* to any audience with a shred of childlike wonder left, but when the opera was produced, in French, at the Metropolitan, on January 23, 1922, almost forty years to a day after its Moscow *première,* it was received without apparent interest. The much-loved Bori was the Snow Maiden, and the almost idolized Bodanzky led the orchestra—but a few performances each in two seasons sufficed to sate New York's appetite. London has shown as little interest in *Snegurochka.*

During the fifteen years that elapsed between the completion of *Snegurochka* and that of *Sadko* in 1896, Rimsky-Korsakov composed two other operas, the first of which, *Mlada,* had a curious history. About 1870, S. A. Gedenov, director of the imperial theaters, invited Cui, Borodin, Mussorgsky, and Rimsky to compose a collaborative pageant opera with ballet. The first of them faithfully completed his mediocre share, but the others abandoned the project after halfhearted attempts. In 1888, years after the Five had broken up (both Borodin and Mussorgsky were dead), Anatol Liadov suggested that Rimsky revive the idea for himself alone. But there was a curse on *Mlada* from the very beginning, and Rimsky's own score was manufactured rather than created. He himself came to dislike it so much that he actually forgot its name, and the public, to which it was presented in 1892, wearied of it quickly.

Even worse was the fate of Rimsky's attempt to reset that legend of Vakula the Smith which had fascinated Tchaikovsky so much that he had tried twice to make a successful opera out of it. No sooner had Tchaikovsky been buried than Rimsky set his own version of the legend, calling it *Christmas Eve.* Like *Mlada,* this suffered from being a synthetic thing, and so, when it was put into production in 1895, Napravnik not unjustly insisted on stringent cutting. Rimsky, the Procrustes of other men's creations, could not bear to have the length of his own altered, and his nerves were cruelly exacerbated. Even worse were last-minute cuts and changes in the libretto demanded, after the dress rehearsal, by outraged members of the imperial family, who could not endure seeing their ancestors—or even their ancestors' tombs—on the stage. So both the Romanovs and the Rimskys were conspicuously absent from the *premiére,* and altogether circumstances helped the opera into early desuetude.

Christmas Eve was the first extended work Rimsky attempted after a serious nervous breakdown. Shortly after beginning it, he started another opera, likewise of mixed antecedents, legendary and historical. This seven-acter, produced in 1898, was *Sadko,* except for *Le Coq d'or* the most popular of his stage works. The libretto was his own, its story of an itinerant guzla player who falls in love with the Ocean King's daughter supplying him with the fantastic background he could illustrate so aptly with his gorgeous pictures. In it, he carefully steered clear of tragedy, though there is enough suspense in the action to make the story worth following. In the libretto he set himself no task that his musical powers could not execute. He provided it with dazzling ballet music and sinuous chromatic melodies, particularly, in Act IV, in the Song of the Viking Guest, for bass, and the tenor Song of the Hindu Guest, known the world over as the "Song of India," overwhelmingly his most popular fragment.

No other composer could have competed with Rimsky in creating the submarine never-never land of *Sadko.* The effects are all his own, but he accepted tools from others in creating them: from Balakirev and Borodin he extracted a way of achieving national color, from Liszt a pungent chromaticism, from Wagner a fuller use of leitmotivs than he had ever before attempted in an opera, and from Liszt's tone poems, via Wagner, a dramatic organization of whole scenes on a symphonic basis. That Rimsky was perfectly conscious of these borrowings is obvious, and he once rebuked a too idolatrous friend with the caustic admonition: "Study Liszt and Balakirev more closely, and you'll see that a great deal in me is—*not* me."

Between *Sadko* and Rimsky's last operatic masterpiece, *Le Coq d'or,* the completion of which was practically coincidental with his death in 1908, he composed, besides four Russian operas, three with foreign subject matter. The third of the non-Russian group, *Mozart and Salieri* (1897), is altogether the most curious of Rimsky's operas. Based on Pushkin's reading of the now discredited idea that Mozart was poisoned by the jealous Salieri, it superimposes Dargomizhsky's idea of musical "truth" on a deliberate imitation of Mozart's musical style. In the original production, Chaliapin was a convincingly fiendish Salieri, and for some years this was one of his favorite impersonations.

The four Russian operas of the same period are of varying interest. The least attractive of them, *The Tsar's Bride* (1898)—Russian folk tunes with a dash of Bizet—is among the few Rimsky operas heard in New York (New Amsterdam Theater, May 9, 1922, in Russian). Rimsky followed it with *The Legend of Tsar Saltan* (1899–1900), one of the most glowing of his scores, again with Wagnerian machinery and symphonically built-up scenes. Act III contains the brilliantly contrived "Flight of the Bumblebee," an amusing evocation of that insect's erratic flight and droning noise. The *première* of this opera, at Moscow on November 3, 1900, was conducted by Ippolitov-Ivanov, himself one of Rimsky's pupils and a composer of numerous operas flatteringly imitative of his master.[17]

The Legend of Kashchey the Deathless (1901–2) is an advanced score, pitting diatonic harmonies against chromatic in an attempt to point up the differentiation beween human and supernatural elements. The last of the four Russian operas was *The Tale of the Invisible City of Kitezh* (1903–4). Except for the fact that Rimsky went on to write one more opera, this might be called his *Parsifal*. Strongly influenced, like *Kashchey*, by Wagner's lengthy essay on the sacred and the profane, this opera is almost its Slav counterpart in sumptuous religious ceremonial, pervasive mysticism, moments of heated fleshliness. Yet this glittering score lacks drama, has something of the stasis of a Byzantine mosaic.

In 1905, at a time when Russian blunders in the war with Japan were reflected in local disorders of a revolutionary nature, Rimsky, by his defense of the rights of student dissenters, broke with the authorities and unexpectedly found himself the hero of the liberal groups. When a temporary ban on his music had been lifted, it became tremendously popular. Meanwhile, these events contributed strongly to Rimsky's feeling of disillusionment and spiritual malaise. On September 4, 1906, while summering at the Lake of Garda, he wrote finis to his autobiography, thinking that his career as a composer was at an end. He had seriously underestimated his powers: before 1906 was over, he had entered the cockcrow theme of *Le Coq d'or* in his notebook and thus was on the eve of his finest achievement in the operatic field. His rage over governmental stupidity in the war with Japan was bearing fruit, and for once in his life he felt a violent personal drive to make music.

As Rimsky found precisely the arsenal of his own scorn in Pushkin's fairy-tale satire on the officialdom of an earlier day, it is all the more unfortunate that he did not live to witness the first triumphant performance of the opera at Moscow, on October 7, 1909, almost two years after his death. The libretto of *Le Coq d'or* is as preposterous, as hard to follow, as that of *Die Zauberflöte,* and for the same reason: we do not possess

[17] It does not seem likely that Ippolitov-Ivanov's *The Last Barricade,* a Soviet opera written in the composer's seventy-fifth year, conforms to the old fantastic model.

the entire key to either. We are told that the bumbling King Dodon represents Nicholas II, that the council of war in Act I mirrors the bureaucracy that bungled things for Russia, but we do not know the functions of most of the other characters and situations. Yet Rimsky, like Mozart, holds us with his music, whether the libretto adds up to something or not. In *Le Coq d'or,* he is altogether at his best, even though the score has not the drugging richness of some of the others—*Kitezh,* for instance. To compensate, Rimsky's flair for the typical, the onomatopoeic, and the illustrative was never more sure. His piquant harmonies, flowing melodies, prismatic colors, and shifting rhythms create with their own magical touch the fairy-story world. Throughout, his deft, transparent orchestration answers each vibration of the lissome fantasy.

Rimsky just escaped being a genius—a situation that he himself recognized—but the escape was sufficient to make his music, cleverly contrived and beautifully put together though it is, finally unsatisfactory to dwell with. With him, it is the first impression that counts, and it is fair to say that the first impression is often magnificent, as is indeed natural in the works of an artist who founded so many of his effects on pageantry and ceremonial. It is not only that these effects have a certain easily recognizable family resemblance, but also that repeated hearings of any one Rimsky composition, even such dazzling masterworks as *Le Coq d'or* and *Scheherazade,* bring no new experiences. Aridity derives logically from Rimsky's lack of conviction in what he was doing. This is no theorizing after the fact—he condemned himself out of his own mouth: "I doubt if you would find anyone in the whole world more incredulous of everything supernatural, fantastic, phantasmal, or lying beyond the grave, and yet as an artist it is just *these* things that I love above all. And *ceremonial*—what could be more intolerable than ceremonial? . . . Yet with what delight I have depicted 'ceremonial' in music! No—I'm definitely of the opinion that art is essentially the most enchanting and intoxicating of lies!" Further, this archtheorist had no views on opera that could carry him far beyond the superficial: "Opera is essentially a false artistic genre, but alluring in its spaciousness and endless variety of forms." These are not the words of a pioneer.

Standing considerably apart from his Russian nationalist contemporaries, but not quite so far as certain of his critics have asserted, is Piotr Ilyich Tchaikovsky. The composer of almost a dozen operas, the first written when he was still a prentice at his craft, and the last after all of his major works except the Sixth Symphony, he was generally unsuccessful in this genre. This intensely subjective man could convincingly set only librettos that contained characters with whom he could sympathetically identify himself, and it is precisely in *Eugene Onegin* (1878) and *Pique-Dame* (1890), his most popular operas, that he found protagonists who reflected his own spiritual struggles. The chief appeal of these scores is the deeply felt lyricism that ebbs and rises with his own collaboration with the stage characters, and it is through this lyricism that the audience is reached.

For *Eugene Onegin* and *Pique-Dame* are fundamentally little more than projections of Tchaikovskyan mood. Formally, their composer did nothing to enrich opera: content to fall back on the easily learned structure of Meyerbeer, he filled it out with melodies that, at their convincing and beautiful best, are quite beyond the German's short-winded muse. Tchaikovsky totally lacked Meyerbeer's genius for the theatrically apt, and the moments of dramatic power in his operas are accidentally wrought by the lyric passages themselves. The glib use of Italian and French musical phraseology is the irrelevant mimicry of a master assimilator, as is his occasional, and almost invariably undramatic, use of leitmotivs. Tchaikovsky was an eclectic less by conviction than by the circumstances of self-education, and he as willingly took for his purposes a Russian folk tune as a phrase or two from the Occidental past. Thus, to deny Slavic influence in Tchaikovsky's work is to deny his whole *modus operandi*.

Tchaikovsky was thirty-nine years old when the Pushkin-inspired *Eugene Onegin* was produced for the first time in 1879. It failed, but what hurt him more than the public indifference was the hostile silence of Anton Rubinstein, who had traveled from St. Petersburg to Moscow to hear it. As the creator of numerous colossal stage works,[18] the great pianist was regarded by the then far less renowned Tchaikovsky as an oracle. After five years of neglect, *Onegin* was restaged at St. Petersburg by imperial command, and the acclaim was so vociferous that after that night Tchaikovsky's fame snowballed.

The belated success of *Onegin* was proportionate to the emotion that Tchaikovsky had bestowed on the work. He had traveled into the very heart of the poem, and at one time had written: "I was in love with Tatiana and furious with Onegin for his coldness and heartlessness." Yet, despite his personal reactions, Tchaikovsky managed to lower the in-

[18] Not one of which has succeeded in deflecting the course of opera one millimeter.

tensity of *Onegin*. What came forth was by and large pretty romantic opera of old-fashioned cast. Although Onegin himself does a lot of attitudinizing, he barely reveals himself as the type of tragic Byronism until the last act. Unhappily, the finest aria is reserved for his friend Lenski. For the heroine Tchaikovsky displays the respect of a well-mannered Russian gentleman for a sympathetic young lady who manages her life badly. The truth is that this rather tame, disciplined, and of course quite lovely opera could have stood suffusions of the very emotionalism that so embarrassed Tchaikovsky's latter-day critics. As if to emphasize the gap between the incandescent poem and Tchaikovsky's setting, the ballet music, as is to be expected, is charming.

And so is the ballet music to *Pique-Dame* (1890), which is also based, via Tchaikovsky's brother, on Pushkin. One of the great moments in the opera is the old Countess's singing of a Grétry air: here situation and song are dramatically matched, which is not usual in Tchaikovsky the composer of operas. But from the start *Pique-Dame,* which at its best has scenes of great intensity, was a triumph, and it has kept its place securely next to the relatively static *Eugene Onegin.*

Russian opera as such produced little effect on the formal development of opera, chiefly because it never emancipated itself from the episodic. On the purely musical side, the story is different. First in driblets, then in a widening stream, Russian music—its harmonies, rhythms, color, sheer vitality, and fresh feeling for instrumental timbres and combinations—flowed into the receptive artistic imagination of Western European musicians. When Debussy first cupped his ear to its pungent sounds, it was an exotic outlander from the East. When Stravinsky, Rimsky-Korsakov's most famed pupil, had become the admitted leader of modern music (outside of the German-speaking world, which, even in its most arid period of devitalized theorizing, refused to surrender leadership), it seemed for a time that the tributary stream would altogether absorb the indulgent parent. Quickly, that crisis passed, and today Russian music has lost its pre-eminence and become but one of the many sources of whatever richness modern music may possess.

CHAPTER XVIII

Verdi

FOR the Germans, 1813 was a great year. At the battle of Leipzig, Napoleon suffered the defeat that broke the spine of his power, and in the town of Leipzig itself was born Wilhelm Richard Wagner, who was to assert the greatness of German music and become its symbol. The same year, at Stuttgart, young Giacomo Meyerbeer managed to have his second German opera, *Wirth und Gast,* produced, and so raised delusory hopes among his admirers, particularly Carl Maria von Weber, that he was to be a prophet of musical Teutonism. In 1813 German opera was not much, and an impartial observer could have been forgiven for believing that it had begun with Mozart's *Die Entführung aus dem Serail* and *Die Zauberflöte* and ended with Beethoven's *Fidelio.* Everywhere the Italians, pure and adulterated, had their few feeble rivals on the run. In Paris, Cherubini reigned, and Spontini, though under a passing cloud, had great things still ahead of him. Even in Russia Italian composers and their imitators amused the court of Alexander I and his great nobles.

In Italy, too, 1813 was an *annus mirabilis.* Rossini, twenty-one—and only three years a practicing maker of operas—found his fecundity almost unequal to the task of satisfying his enraptured admirers: he gave them *Il Signor Bruschino, Tancredi,* and two other operas that year, and still they clamored for more. Finally, the same year, far from the great world of Paris, the decaying splendors of Venice, and the solid bourgeois comforts of Leipzig, there was born, in an insignificant village of a paltry Italian state, Giuseppe Verdi.

During the twenty-six years that elapsed between Verdi's birth and the staging of his first opera, *Oberto, Conte di San Bonifacio,* the face of opera in Italy was changing. Rossini turned himself into a composer of French operas and then retired from active composition. Bellini went his brief and limpid way. Donizetti, with four good years ahead of him, reached the peak of his career. Not having been much exposed to Rossini's late French operas, with their heavier orchestration and richer harmonies, Italy in 1839 was still supporting composers content with diatonic harmonies, flowing tunes, the barest of guitarlike accompaniments, and a nicely assorted bouquet of vocal effects. The composers of *bel canto* operas were the rage. Verdi, to judge by the mildly successful *Oberto,* was to be one of them: the score was at once labeled Bellinian—and both looks and sounds that way. *Oberto* was the conventional nineteenth-century adaptation of *opera seria;* its comic successor, *Un Giorno di regno* (1840), was an old-fashioned *opera buffa.*

Without accepting as dogma the belief that only suffering can produce great works of art, it can be said that Verdi's third opera, *Nabucodonosor,* which shows an astonishing advance over his first two efforts, was composed after the death of his only son, his only daughter, and his wife. *Nabucco*—as it soon came to be known—is the product of an individual, and already shows traits that can be pointed back to as Verdian. It has drive and rude vigor that well compensate for an appalling libretto,[1] frequent *gaucheries,* and stretches of pure banality. In the words of Francis Toye, the characters "live separate and genuine musical lives of their own." *Nabucco* is, indeed, so full of more than promise (that word is an insult to the chorus "Va pensiero sull'ali dorate") that it seems surprising that nine years and twelve operas were to pass before Verdi created a thoroughly satisfying opera.

Why did Verdi develop so slowly? The chief reason is that, not being a man of contemplative intellect, he worked things out by experiencing them—by the trial-and-error system. By comparison, Wagner, once his serious career as an operatic composer had begun, advanced swiftly because he thought things out and then tried them. He considered the whole libretto problem long and earnestly, for example, and wrote his own librettos because he knew that no one else could give him exactly the ones he must have. Verdi, on the other hand, shows few signs of ever having thought about the libretto as an abstract aesthetic problem. He was generally willing to accept any book that came to his hand (at least, until late in his career) as long as it contained dramatic crises, the more violent the better. His letters show him haggling with his librettists over

---

[1] By Temistocle Solera, it had been turned down by Otto von Nicolai, later the composer of *Die lustigen Weiber von Windsor.*

details, but rarely piercing to the essential weaknesses of their texts. Once he had accepted a libretto, he attacked its detail with shrewdness and acumen, but he might have composed fewer operas and developed faster if he had learned earlier to question the worthwhileness of subject matter.

Far from trying to foist upon an unwilling public a new conception of opera, as Wagner did, Verdi considered himself a devoted servant of the public. He was eventually to lead opera away from *bel canto* to a form of naturalistic romanticism (which would easily change in other hands into *verismo*). But the changes he ultimately effected in the fabric of the musical drama were results of an honest craftsman's determination to give that public the best he had in him, not of any conscious revolutionary determination to reform either opera or operagoers. In his early days, before his public became international, when it was confined to an Italy in the throes of the long-drawn-out struggle for liberty and unity, Verdi was so much its servant that he gave it good rousing patriotic tunes more often than the music most properly demanded by the situations of the libretto.

I Lombardi alla prima crociata, which followed *Nabucco,* was produced at La Scala, Milan, on February 11, 1843. It shows at their worst the faults of a Verdi groping his way toward maturity. On the credit side, it has his flair for dramatic emphasis, apt underlining of character, and dynamic melody. Also partly on the credit side, but partly not, is its full, vigorous, sometimes noisy scoring, certainly a relief after the most feeble of Donizetti's accompaniments, but at its worst too reminiscent of the town band. This sort of scoring was demanded by the rabble-rousing tunes that his admirers could turn into marching songs and battle cries. Deep on the debit side are the libretto, again by Solera—a thoroughly incredible hodgepodge of high-flown romantic pseudo-history—and those several places where Verdi's nervous masculinity shrills off into strident vulgarity or his easy tunefulness thins out into banality.

It cannot be said that Verdi's fifth opera, *Ernani,* which was the first to carry his name beyond the Alps, was much of an improvement: in it, the bad simply does not outweigh the good, as it definitely does in *I Lombardi.* The libretto, an adaptation of Victor Hugo's *Hernani* (one of Verdi's unquestioned beliefs was that any good play would necessarily supply a good libretto), was the first furnished him by Francesco Maria Piave, a hard-working mediocrity whom the composer uncritically favored for eighteen years—until, that is, Piave was incapacitated by paralysis.

The four operas that succeeded *Ernani* [2] advanced Verdi's development not one inch except as, because of the way he worked, the mere experience of composing them helped him. Then came *Macbeth,* which was to cause him more heartburnings, over many years, than any of his other works. He was passionately attached to it. [3] He wanted, through it, to offer fitting homage to Shakespeare, his lifelong idol. Unfortunately, *Macbeth*—composed to a Piave text and first produced at the Teatro della Pergola, Florence, on March 14, 1847, turned out to be not a total failure (a failure might at least have closed that chapter permanently) but one of those odd changelings which contain, amid many excellences, some weakening flaw. Because he loved the excellences, Verdi accepted the recognized flaw as a challenge: he toyed and sometimes toiled at reconstructing it off and on for eighteen years. It was his ill fortune that Piave's original libretto was poor, that his own contributions to it were no better, that his friend Andrea Maffei's later retouchings were still worse—and, finally, that the French translation for the 1865 Paris production was the worst of all. [4]

Verdi had only himself to blame for not realizing, after his first disappointment with *Macbeth* in 1847, that it required not revision but complete rewriting. Yet, as the revising he did do for Paris belonged to his maturity, he very much improved his first musical ideas and added some splendid new ones. An edited version of that later score has been enthusiastically applauded in many opera houses in recent years. It is chiefly in Verdi's advanced idiom, but even those sections left as he first let them be

[2] *I due Foscari* (Rome, November 3, 1844), *Giovanna d'Arco* (Milan, February 15, 1845), *Alzira* (Naples, August 12, 1845), and *Attila* (Venice, March 17, 1846).

[3] Verdi was only one of a number of composers who have been fascinated by *Macbeth.* They began with John Milton's friend Matthew Locke, whose incidental music for the play dates from 1672 and has been called "a pure emanation of genius." Beethoven's notebooks contain preliminary sketches for the overture and opening chorus of a projected opera on the subject. Completed *Macbeth*s exist by the French violinist Hippolyte Chélard, whose libretto was furnished by the composer of the "Marseillaise," and by Ernest Bloch, whose version was first produced in Paris in 1910. Shostakovich's *Lady Macbeth of Mzensk* (really *A Lady Macbeth from Mzensk*) has nothing whatever to do with Shakespeare.

[4] That production at the Théâtre-Lyrique was a failure. Saint-Saëns, who had been attracted to *Macbeth* as a subject, commented bitterly in his memoirs: "I suggested to Carvalho that I write a *Macbeth* for Madame Viardot. Naturally enough, he preferred to stage Verdi's *Macbeth.* It was an utter failure and cost him thirty thousand francs."

staged show how definitely he had been laboring toward a new conception of opera even then. In 1848, writing to Salvatore Cammarano, one of his librettists, about a projected performance of the original *Macbeth* at Naples, he aired some then radical ideas about unified musico-dramatic effect:

> I understand that you are rehearsing *Macbeth,* and as this opera interests me more than any other, I ask you to allow me to say a few words about it. Mme Tadolini is, I believe, to sing Lady Macbeth, and I am astounded that she should have undertaken the role. You know how highly I think of Mme Tadolini, and she knows it too; but in all our interests I think it necessary to remark that she has too great qualities for this part! This may seem an absurdity! Mme Tadolini has a beautiful face and looks good, and I would have Lady Macbeth ugly and wicked. Mme Tadolini sings to perfection, and I would not have Lady Macbeth sing at all. Mme Tadolini has a wonderful voice, clear, liquid, and powerful, and Lady Macbeth's voice should be hard, stifled, and dark. Mme Tadolini's voice is the voice of an angel, and Lady Macbeth's should be the voice of a devil. Please bring these remarks to the notice of the directors of Maestro Mercadante, who will understand my ideas better than anyone, and of Mme Tadolini herself, and do what you think for the best.

It was along the lines suggested by those remarks, rather than by means of leitmotivs and other Wagnerian techniques, that Verdi would approach a sort of musical drama that certainly is not Wagnerian, but is quite as valid. He never labeled his most highly developed scores "music dramas" or advertised his innovations, and Wagner was therefore looked upon as the only reformer. Verdi's reticence in that direction was natural, for though there is evidence that he at last discovered whither he was, however deliberately, going, he never wrote theory music as such. Until the publication of his correspondence many years after his death, the public had no way of knowing that Verdi had had conscious aims of any formulated sort. Only if audiences listened analytically to his best operas seriatim, from *Macbeth* on, could they deduce the fact that Verdi was as much a creative revolutionist as Wagner.

Macbeth as it is performed today contains some marvelous pages. To mention only a few of them, there is Lady Macbeth's soaring second-act aria, "La luce langue," in which she looks forward to becoming Queen of Scotland; there is the magnificent *scena* and duet finale of Act III,

"Ora di morte"; there is, above all, the superbly conceived and master-fully executed Sleepwalking Scene, "Una macchia è qui tuttora." English and American operagoers often must adjust themselves to some scenes full of (to them, but not to Italians) unintentional humor.

Of the six operas between *Macbeth* and *Rigoletto,* only two retain much interest, one for historical reasons, the other for musical. *I Masna-dieri* (Florence, March 14, 1847), based by Piave on Schiller's *Die Räuber,* was the first opera that Verdi composed expressly for foreign production. Its reception at its London *première* (Her Majesty's Theatre, July 22, 1847) was none too happy despite Jenny Lind's presence as its heroine. Henry Fothergill Chorley, whose antipathy to Verdi's music was to be almost lifelong, pontificated: "Her Amalia . . . could not have pleased had it been given by Saint Cecilia and Melpomene in one, so utterly worthless was the music."

Chorley was quite as stringent about *Luisa Miller* (Teatro San Carlo, Naples, December 8, 1849) when it was first given in London in 1858: "There are staccato screams in it enough to content any lover of shock-ing excitement; but the entire texture of the music implies (I can but fancy) either a feeble mistake or else a want of power on the part of an artificer who, obviously (as Signor Verdi does), demanding situation and passion and agony to kindle the fire under his cauldron, has also only one alphabet, one grammar, one dictionary, whatsoever the scene, what-soever the country—one cantabile, one spasmodic bravura, one feverish crescendo, as the average tools by pressure of which the stress on the public is to be strained out."

But *Luisa Miller* is much better than that. It starts with the advantage of a superior book, which Salvatore Cammarano had based on Schiller's *Kabale und Liebe,* and which must not be judged by the fact that its three acts are entitled respectively "Love," "Intrigue," and "Poison." It is put together with great care and cunning (it is an unusually erudite score for this period in Verdi's development), and shows Verdi treating new types of situation and character. The manner in which simple, effective touches are produced by learned musical means adumbrates *Falstaff;* the intimacy of the situations and the homeliness of the characters look forward to *La Traviata.* Far from being the monstrosity that Chorley makes it out to be, *Luisa Miller* is comparatively restrained in tone, al-together a work of considerable charm. Its overture is one of the best that Verdi ever composed.

What Chorley was denouncing—he was, of course, entirely correct in finding *Luisa Miller* something comparatively new—was the end of the great period of Italian *bel canto* opera, with its magic worked by *fioriture, messa di voce,* and subtle vocal control, the era of Grisi, Pasta, and Malibran among female singers, of their extraordinarily agile counterparts among tenors, baritones, and basses. The days of Cherubini, Bellini, and Donizetti were passing. Verdi, after all, had read *Hernani:* he belonged to the high noon of romanticism, when the shadows of naturalism were already to be predicted. He required more violent means toward more violent results. It is possible to laugh at Chorley, but it is impossible not to share a little the emotion that resulted in his blind striking out at the end of an era that could produce *Medée, La Sonnambula,* and *Lucia di Lammermoor.* He could not, in 1858, foresee *Aïda, Otello,* and *Falstaff,* the crowning masterworks of the Italian operatic era of which *Luisa Miller* was perhaps the first certain harbinger.

Everything about *Rigoletto,* Verdi's seventeenth opera, proclaims it a masterpiece. As usually staged, it is anything but a masterpiece— through no fault or omission of Verdi's. In it, he began breaking down the barriers between individual numbers and the encompassing action, tending toward a more continuous musical and dramatic flow; he arrived at a mastery, just this side of supreme, of character creation, and he reached a new ability to evoke and project atmosphere. He was merely stating the truth when, being urged to transfer to a much-altered libretto music he had already completed, he retorted: "My music—good or bad as it may be—is written in no casual manner." In much of *Rigoletto,* music has been fused indissolubly with action. Only when Verdi fails to examine carefully the dramatic requirements of a situation, and falls back upon traditional rule of thumb and operatic conventions useful to earlier men but unsuited to his new purposes, does he show that he has not yet entirely arrived.

Let us cite the three vocal touchstones of *Rigoletto,* which—so vicious has the opera-house tradition become—are now almost the only reasons why the opera remains popular. "Caro nome," with its exquisite melody meant as a hushed, rapt, and wondering meditation, comes off most often as a bravura exposition by whatever lady may be displaying her vocal athleticism at the time. "La donna è mobile," that perfect signature of a perfect libertine, establishes the Duke's character at once—if it is sung as a means of conveying its meaning; it is used in the last scene to point the tragic irony of the entire opera. The tenor who plants himself downstage, and then sings for applause, destroys Verdi's intentions. Finally, the great quartet, "Bella figlia dell'amore," is a triumph of emotional counterpoint, with each character assigned an apt, individual melodic line. Verdi's aim was to give Rigoletto and Gilda, the Duke and Maddalena, each a personal separateness. As "Bella figlia" is usually rendered, it sounds as if the four of them had decided to get together for an evening of part-singing. Is it any wonder that *Rigoletto* is often dismissed by otherwise sensitive people as mere organ-grinder's music, a succession of tunes that you like or do not like?

The tenseness of political conditions in 1850 was responsible for many changes in the book of *Rigoletto*. Drawn from Hugo's *Le Roi s'amuse,* a ferocious melodrama built around the libertine Francis I, it came near to sharing the fortunes of the play. Hugo had dared to defy the government of Louis-Philippe, and the play had been banned after its first night. The Austrian censors objected violently, as much on moral as on political grounds, to *La Maledizione*—the original name of Piave's libretto. Verdi stood firm on essentials, but grudgingly agreed to change the French king into an unidentified duke of Mantua. He battled to the end against changing the hunchback Rigoletto into a normal human specimen and for retaining the sack in which Rigoletto finds the dying Gilda, disposing with withering logic of the objection that these elements were too repulsive.

As Verdi wrote: "In my opinion, the presentation of this character, so deformed and ridiculous outside, so full of love and passion within, is a fine idea. Indeed, it was precisely on this account that I chose the subject." Things came to such a pass that the disputants—Verdi, Piave, and the secretary of the Fenice at Venice, who naturally had to see eye to eye with the censor—signed an agreement that determined the final shape of the libretto. Incredibly, the resulting text is one of the scant five or six thoroughly good texts that Verdi ever managed to get at. Victor Hugo, who began by detesting *Rigoletto* as much as he had detested *Ernani,* ended up as its unstinting admirer.

From its first performance at the Fenice on March 11, 1851, *Rigoletto* was a hit. Verdi had been a well-known composer; *Rigoletto* bore him immediately to pre-eminence. After running like wildfire the length of the peninsula, where censorship difficulties forced it to assume fabulously absurd *noms de guerre* such as *Viscardello, Clara di Perth,* and *Lionello,* within four years it was heard in Austria-Hungary, Germany, England, France, and the United States. By 1922 it had been sung in New York in Italian, German, English, and Russian. It everywhere remains a true staple of the operatic repertoire.

After finishing *Rigoletto,* Verdi returned to an old love of horrifying aspect, a gory and wonderfully labyrinthine Spanish tragedy, called *El Trovador,* by Antonio García Gutiérrez. Salvatore Cammarano and, after his death in 1852, Leone Emmanuele Bardare achieved a libretto with all essential crises intact, but all explanatory connectives omitted. The result is a series of ellipses quite undecipherable without reference to the original play. With mounting doubts, Verdi nevertheless set the book in either four or six weeks—in either case, a wonder of swiftness. When, on January 19, 1853, the day of the *première* of *Il Trovatore* came around, the Tiber had turned much of nearby Rome into a shallow lake. Yet the queue at the Teatro Apollo began gathering early that morning despite weather and advanced prices. The performance, by no means perfect, was a triumph commensurate with that of *Rigoletto,* like which *Il Trovatore* circumnavigated the globe in a few years. Many critics refused, however, to ride with the audiences: calling upon the names of Rossini, Bellini, and Donizetti, they pronounced *Il Trovatore* the death of *bel canto.*

The critics were both right and wrong. Whole sections of *Il Trovatore* have departed from the *bel canto* manner. But the magnificent aria for Leonora, "D'amor sull'ali rosee," is in the full *bel canto* manner—or should be: it is now far too often left almost trill-less as sung by sopranos without training in the true difficulties of *bel canto* singing. But *bel canto* singing has not vanished completely from this earth even today. The critics were correct in implying that Verdi was composing music that required vigorous dramatic singing, most often at the expense of flawless ornaments and agile *messa di voce.* And *Il Trovatore* must have sounded to the more elderly lovers of the old time as though Verdi had composed it to annoy them.

At forty, hale in his prime, after the artistic restraint of *Rigoletto,* Verdi had let himself go with hearty abandon. *Il Trovatore* is, for longish stretches, strident, muscular—and spontaneous. Artistically not the satisfying fusion of libretto and music which *Rigoletto* is, it bursts with tunes of frank and healthy vulgarity. Sensitive critical lovers of music can be forgiven for shuddering at what is most barefacedly noisy in *Il Trovatore,* but not for dismissing the entire opera with a sneer. In addition to the charm of "D'amor sull'ali rosee" and of "Il balen," a love lyric that Verdi seldom surpassed, it has an inspired last act of mingled wistfulness and human tragedy. Also, in *Il Trovatore* Verdi created, a full thirty-five years before *Otello,* one of his most profoundly understood and affecting characters. In the best sense, Azucena, the gypsy mother, is the moving force of the opera, its *raison d'être* even. She is no lopsided abstraction of undiluted mother love, but a many-sided woman of recognizable humanness. She is the descendant of Eléazar in *La Juive* and of Fidès in *Le Prophète*—but the descent is purely chronological. "Stride la vampa!" and "Ai nostri monti," her duet with Manrico, are revelations of character antithesis, not the irrelevant barrel-organ tunes they have wastefully been allowed to become.

After two ringing successes, Verdi came up with a failure. Going against all operatic conventions, he selected a libretto with scenes laid in his own time. The characters wore costumes that could have been seen daily on the streets of Paris. As opera was still largely a show, this was indeed radical. His heroine was a courtesan and tubercular. There were plenty of objections to her on both counts: it was not nice to show such laxity in a heroine, and for a singer to die of tuberculosis was obviously ridiculous. Dumas's *La Dame aux camélias,* from which Piave expertly had drawn the libretto, might have been convincing in itself, but as an opera, with a stout, obviously healthy heroine, *La Traviata*[5] was too much for the first-night audience at the Fenice, on March 6, 1853, forty-six days after the Rome *première* of *Il Trovatore.*

Worse than hissing, that first audience for *La Traviata* burst into uproarious laughter at the most pathetic moments and left no doubt in Verdi's mind that his painstaking labors had gone for nothing. *"La Traviata* was a fiasco yesterday. Is it my fault or the singers'?" he asked. "Time will decide." On May 6, 1854, again in Venice (Teatro San Benedetto), *La Traviata* was restaged with a credibly slender soprano and with costuming of the Louis XIII period. Venice revised its verdict, and *La Traviata* at once joined its two predecessors in public favor. The absurd costumes were adhered to until 1904, when Gemma Bellincioni, whom Verdi considered the best Violetta, reverted to the crinolines of Dumas—which by then had taken on a charming period character of their own.

Historically speaking, *La Traviata* marks the first successful attempt to tap a vein that Verdi himself had prospected, some years before, in *Luisa Miller,* and even more in the poorly received *Stiffelio* (1850), later unsuccessfully re-historicized as *Aroldo* (1857): realistic treat-

[5] The literal translation of this title would be "The Strayed Girl."

ment in opera of scenes and situations from contemporary life, involving characters whose sole importance resides in their own personal dramas. In turning to them, Verdi tacitly abandons the classical theory that tragedy is the downfall of the mighty and the royal, and temporarily abandons the world of grand opera proper, the world of *la haute politique,* of monarchs and courtiers, of great wars, involved plots, ceremony, and ritual. This bold departure recognizes, of course, the triumph of the *bourgeoisie:* previously, the *bourgeoisie* had been admitted into comic opera. Verdi was the first to make its tragedies the stuff of serious opera.[6]

Luisa Miller had been a step in this direction: the characters were ordinary enough, but the scene was located two centuries back. *Stiffelio* tactlessly went the whole way in dealing with a domestic tragedy of nineteenth-century Germany, in itself not wholly unpalatable, but confusing to Verdi's Catholic audiences because its chief character was a married clergyman. *Stiffelio* did not please; Verdi's attempted remedy seems to prove that he was not yet ready for his own audacity. In *Aroldo,* the 1857 revision, he moved the locale to Scotland and England in the period of the Crusades and turned the characters into ladies and knights, but left the central psychological conflict unchanged, not realizing that its implications were essentially of the nineteenth century. It is significant that he bungled the job of revision in that particular way after seeing *La Traviata* changed from failure into success by a mere back-dating. When *Aroldo* found few more admirers than *Stiffelio,* he realized that he had no infallible way of salvaging these domestic pieces, and so never returned to them. They were to be taken up again, as the world well knows, by his Italian successors.

La Traviata is almost a chamber opera. Sensitive to the kind of music demanded by the libretto, Verdi composed the entire score on a smaller scale than was his wont. It is one of his few essays in sheer charm, the very antithesis of the thrust of *Il Trovatore.* By comparison, *La Traviata* is quiet, almost monochromatic in spots, and would doubtless gain in effect if presented in theaters smaller than the world's leading opera houses. It calls for intimacy, and in an enormous hall much of its pathos is dissipated between stage and audience. It is not only its heroine's opera, but also the vehicle of a frail, exquisite personality—a fact that Verdi did not forget, though most producers and stage managers do. The lovely

[6] The "ordinary" folk who people such an opera as Bellini's *La Sonnambula* are presented as picturesque rather than grimly real, however real some of their situations become.

preludes to Acts I and III,[7] so different from his noisier overtures, are the signatures of certain aspects of Violetta's character and condition. The *scena* that closes Act I abundantly proves Verdi's ability to take old, seemingly outworn forms and use them unerringly as instruments of psychological verisimilitude. "Ah! fors è lui," followed by "Sempre libera," is an old-fashioned cavatina developing into a rapid, pyrotechnical cabaletta. Earlier composers and Verdi himself had used this formula for any type of character, but here it is related, shaped with loving care, to the clearly conceived personality of Violetta and to her state of mind as it shifts at this stage of the story. It is creative dramatic music, carrying the story forward in a way only music can. And so, often by other threadbare devices handled with freshness and relevance, Verdi eloquently brings the moving story to its inevitable tragic finale.

During the eighteen years between *La Traviata* and *Aïda,* Verdi composed five completely new operas,[8] four of which have retained a precarious hold on the stage. Successful and rich at forty, Verdi could afford the luxury of meditating before putting pen to paper, and of working with care and deliberation after he started. Besides, he was the squire of an estate, with a gentleman farmer's interest in his land, and was for a time involved in politics at the insistence of his friend Cavour. The gaps between Verdi *premières* began to widen: *La Traviata* is 1853, *Les Vêpres siciliennes* 1855, *Simon Boccanegra* 1857, *Un Ballo in maschera* 1859, *La Forza del destino* 1862, *Don Carlos* 1867, and *Aïda* 1871. More time, however, did not always mean better results. Of the operas of this period, only *Aïda* is, as a totality, equal to *La Traviata,* though most of the others show progress in Verdi's command of musicodramatic techniques. Only one of the group, the earliest, is relatively poor stuff.

Les Vêpres siciliennes was Verdi's first commission from the Paris Opéra. He executed it with a timidity usually foreign to his nature, though he did flare up at the makeshift historical canvas that Scribe, in a tactless and unconciliatory mood, painted with his most careless brush. Faced with the need to set a libretto in French, the already vexed composer did the natural thing: he left his own evolving style in Italy and

---

[7] At the Metropolitan Opera House, as in many other theaters, *La Traviata* is given in four acts, the first and second scenes of the original Act II being called respectively Act II and Act III, and the original Act III thus becoming Act IV.

[8] The unsuccessful *Aroldo,* produced at Rimini on August 16, 1857, was a rewriting of the equally unsuccessful *Stiffelio,* first heard at Trieste on November 16, 1850.

wrote imitation Meyerbeer (*vide* the bolero "Mercè, diletti amiche").
The results could have been foretold. In the interminable five-act opera,
heard first on June 13, 1855, only the overture—which freakishly happens to be the best that Verdi ever composed—is first-rate. The bastard
French ballet music is frightful trash. The poorness of the vocal music
might be ascribed to Verdi's unfamiliarity with French declamation, but
when he recast the opera for Italy (where it was called *Giovanna di
Braganza, Giovanna di Guzman, Giovanna di Sicilia,* and *Batilde di
Turenna* before finally settling down as *I Vespri siciliani*), he did not
improve it noticeably.

Simon Boccanegra is another matter. Like *Macbeth,* it was revised
many years after its *première,* and therefore includes elements from two
distinct periods of Verdi's development. First produced at the Fenice in
Venice on March 12, 1857, in its final version it belongs to the long interregnum between *Aïda* and *Otello.* Piave had no forthright *Dame aux
camélias* to work on, but another of the lengthy, intricately involved
dramas by Antonio García Gutiérrez, the Spaniard who had written *El
Trovador.* Just as Cammarano had muffed the job of abridging *El Trovador,* producing a puzzle to which only readers of García Gutiérrez hold
the key, so Piave got out of his difficulty only by reducing *Simon Boccanegra* to nonsense. Arrigo Boito, called in to doctor the text for the
1881 revision, was almost completely defeated by the task, and left the
libretto but little improved. Ironically, in providing a new scene for
which Verdi composed the most moving music of the later version, Boito
slowed the action down to immobility. *Simon Boccanegra* remains an
opera of almost unrelieved gloom. The chief character is tediously, in-
humanly noble, and there simply is insufficient drama to go around during a prologue and three acts with a large cast of characters. Yet Verdi
never worked more strenuously, and he ended by composing for *Simon
Boccanegra* some of his richest pages. The music should keep the opera
in the repertoire; the libretto has threatened, since the days of both its
premières, to relegate it to oblivion, leaving us only its great dramatic
apostrophe, "Il lacerato spirito."

After leaving *Un Ballo in maschera* in silence for a quarter of a century, the Metropolitan Opera revived it on December 2, 1940, not only
as a season opener but also as the first opera put forward by the resident
company after the purchase of its aging opera house. Sumptuously
mounted, it was well received by the first-nighters. It was nevertheless,
in many details, an absurd performance. The scenes were said to be laid

in Stockholm, but the audience was asked to believe in two Swedish conspirators named Sam and Tom. In a laudable attempt to return the opera to the Sweden of Gustav III, which the librettist naturally had had in mind for a story dealing with that monarch's assassination, the Metropolitan had contented itself, unfortunately, with a half measure.

Antonio Somma, Verdi's librettist for what was originally called *La Vendetta in domino,* had been forced by the Neapolitan censors, over-jittery because of a recent attempt on Napoleon III's life, to move the scene of the story to Boston (possibly because of the relaxed political conditions, no one had objected to Auber's setting of Scribe's *Gustave III, ou Le Bal masqué* at Paris in 1833); this forced him to change King Gustavus into a titled colonial governor. The 1940 Metropolitan version restored the original locale, but not the identities of Gustavus—who, incredibly, remained "Riccardo, conte di Warwick"—or the other personages of the drama. Such shilly-shallying does no good for the cause of opera, and there were many to criticize uncharitably this well-meant evasion of the problem.

It is unlikely that *Un Ballo in maschera,* which was first heard at the Teatro Apollo, Rome, on February 17, 1859, would become a popular opera even if restored completely to the conditions that Somma and Verdi originally had in mind. The plot is unwieldy, obvious, and unintegrated; the music is only intermittently relevant. It is another milestone on Verdi's route between one period of mastery and another. As such, it is interesting. For example, Gustavus-Riccardo, a later edition of the Duke in *Rigoletto,* has the variety of a human being. More important is the introduction into a tragic opera of an elegant, witty, foppish, feather-brained creature who might have stepped out of the pages of *Le Nozze di Figaro,* so clearly does the Oscar of *Un Ballo* show his descent from Cherubino and—going back to the beginnings of opera—the Page in Monteverdi's *L'Incoronazione di Poppea.* This shows that Verdi, taking every advantage of the opportunities his librettist had afforded him, was ready to project a whole world, which, however predominantly tragic, had interludes of something else. Even the conspirators, Sam and Tom, are not without moments of lightness, while the wronged and vengeful Renato is much redeemed by the beauty of his great aria, "Eri tu." The sorceress Ulrica is perhaps a stock witch, but the somewhat matte character of Amelia is relieved by the plastic beauty of more than one of her arias.

La Forza del destino was composed to order for the Imperial Opera in St. Petersburg.[9] Its reception there on November 10, 1862, won Verdi a decoration from Alexander II and frigid attention from an audience half hostile because of a Russian composers' cabal against the Latin invader. Verdi took his new opera to Madrid, where it was more warmly received, partly because the Spaniards were already familiar with the minutiae of the very detailed drama, by Angel Pérez de Saavedra, Duque de Rivas, a well-known liberal, on which Piave had based the libretto. Still, *La Forza del destino* was not a hit of the sort Verdi had known, and in 1869 he tried for a larger, more enthusiastic public by shortening the opera somewhat. This helped measurably but does not justify the cut-up, positively deformed versions of the opera often presented.

La Forza del destino carried Verdi a step further toward his second artistic maturity. The ever-increasing attention he was paying to the shaping of character is apparent throughout, though in the cases of Leonora and, to a smaller extent, some of the other people in the story, much of the music—in itself intensely moving—is attached to beings whose lack of free will invests them with the nature of managed puppets. The roster of characters shows another interesting recruit. Just as Verdi had introduced the comic-opera figure of Oscar into *Un Ballo in maschera,* so here he imported from *opera buffa* the bluff, roistering friar, Melitone—a character whose presence speaks volumes for Verdi's broadened understanding of life's diversity. Melody pours forth unstintedly, but it is modeled with a growing attention to total effect, is along more spacious, longer-breathed lines. The orchestral writing has abandoned the sometimes tedious naïveté of the earlier operas, is at once subtler, more integral, and more solid. Without ever dominating the singers, the orchestra claims attention as an essential dramatic ingredient.

Although Verdi was moving relentlessly, and wholly in his own way, toward a conception of opera which can be called music drama as legitimately as anything of Wagner's, *La Forza* still has easily detachable set numbers, not a few of which are known from concert performance. Apart from "Solenne in quest'ora," that splendidly dramatic tenor-

[9] Under a Moscow dateline, *The New York Times* of June 22, 1962, announced that Italian researchers working in Leningrad had found a complete original score of *La Forza del destino* with notes by Verdi that "reveal new aspects of the composer's technique," including "radical changes in the fourth act." Other finds (mostly in the Kirov Theater library) included unknown or little-known operas by Catterino Cavos, Cimarosa, and Paisiello and early operas on the subjects used for Mozart's *Don Giovanni* and Beethoven's *Fidelio.*

baritone duet, the type of which Verdi had adumbrated eloquently in *Les Vêpres siciliennes* (the "Quando al mio sen" of the Italian version), they range from the elaborately worked-out overture through Leonora's pitiful prayer, "Madre, pietosa vergine," and her tragic last-act outburst, "Pace, pace, mio dio," through Don Alvaro's lamenting "O tu che in seno agli angeli" to "Non imprecare," the fine trio for the Abbot and two of the chief victims of destiny, Leonora and her brother.

The difference between *La Forza del destino* and *Don Carlos,* which succeeded it five years later, is, except for subject matter, purely formal. In the first, the tendency to repudiate set numbers was becoming obvious; in the second, it was all but accomplished. *Don Carlos* is, however imperfectly, a music drama. Unhappily for Verdi, it was made for the Paris Opéra, which meant a libretto in French—a language for which he composed insensitively. In 1867, it also meant a libretto in the manner preferred by Meyerbeer, whose long dictatorship had been cut short by death only three years earlier. It meant, also, ballet music, the composition of which, then and always, invited Verdi to banality. It meant, finally, working with collaborators imperfectly acquainted with the processes of Verdi's thoroughly Italian mind. Many misunderstandings arose in the course of the collaboration, and it is small wonder that the product of this *mésalliance* was a hybrid of unstable character, sometimes musically equal to Verdi's best earlier works—even hinting at what was to come during his last years—and sometimes of boring flatness.

The librettists, Joseph Méry and Camille du Locle, took Schiller's *Don Carlos* and painstakingly stripped it of everything except the circumstances of its encompassing gloom. Verdi, unable to cast off the heavy traditions of the Opéra, set all five acts in a style formally all his own, but texturally part Meyerbeer. And, in general effect, *Don Carlos* was comparable to those vast pageants to which the composer of *Les Huguenots* and *Le Prophète* was partial. Neither Verdi nor his public was ever satisfied with it in either French or Italian, and though it was revised twice (he first removed Act I and then restored most of it), scattered modern performances have demonstrated that not even a four-act version selecting the cream of the three versions, but disregarding Verdi's final decision in favor of his first act, can make *Don Carlos* convincing or popular.

Don Carlos is dotted with grand pages that lose only part of their effectiveness when heard as extracts from the opera. Most renowned of them are Philip II's bitter "Ella giammai m'amò," the Princess Eboli's "O don fatale," Rodrigo's "O Carlo, ascolta," and Elizabeth of Valois's "Tu che la vanità." They indicate that Verdi had been defeated only by his willingness to accept an inadequate libretto. His mature style was shaped: for its effective display, it waited only on a congruous and dramatic book. It may be asked what that mature style was. It was, simply, Verdi's first and only style, subjected to refining, polishing, observation from a hundred different points of vantage, meditation, so changing its original manifestations that it came to be something quite new. The trial-and-error method instinctively followed by this practical worker for the operatic stage had resulted in the sloughing off of everything uncongenial to the perfect projection of musicodramatic values. In 1869, when Verdi was fifty-six years old, already the composer of twenty-three operas, and had only just achieved the final tuning of this instrument, he was at last not inclined to labor on a book unworthy of his genius.

Therefore, when Ismail Pasha, Khedive of Egypt, invited him to compose an opera on an Egyptian theme to celebrate the opening of the Suez Canal, Verdi had to be wooed. After two flat refusals, he consented to examine a scenario—the barest skeleton of an outline—by the French archaeologist Auguste-Édouard Mariette, known as Mariette Bey. Verdi liked it and authorized Camille du Locle, one of the librettists of *Don Carlos,* to write a French libretto based on it. This was translated into Italian by Antonio Ghislanzoni, for whom Verdi had developed the highest regard after Ghislanzoni had made a revision of the text of *La Forza del destino.* Closely consulting on every phase of the script not only with Verdi but also with his wife, the erstwhile singer Giuseppina Strepponi, a woman of acute intelligence who had sung in her future husband's earliest operas, Ghislanzoni produced a conventional, entirely dramatic libretto full from start to finish of those strong situations which delight the heart of a born theatrical composer.

The Franco-Prussian War having hindered the plans of many of the polyglot personages involved, *Aïda* missed the opening of the Suez Canal. Cairo, however, got the *première* two years later, on December 24, 1871, but without Verdi, who had been irritated by all the fanfare. He was present, however, at *Aïda*'s Italian *première,* at La Scala, Milan, on February 8, 1872. The acclamations that rang through La Scala that night foretold the unique career in store for *Aïda,* which soon became—and to this day has remained—if not the most popular of all operas, then certainly one of the two or three most popular.

What has made *Aïda* so beloved? The answer is to be found in the combination of many masterfully controlled elements. In exactly right proportions, *Aïda* has the lure of pageantry and ceremonial, of exotic coloring and locale, of exciting dramatic climaxes and moving lyric interludes—all against a background of beautiful melody treated with harmonic richness and orchestrated with a pertinence toward which Verdi had been striving, not always with success, for years. *Aïda,* also, is peopled with individuals who are interesting in themselves, whose characters shift, change, and develop in our eyes and ears. Their emotions are made easy to understand, and the actions richly varied without being complicated.

Aïda has everything—even that bit of cheapness which makes the whole world kin. In this score, which in performance gushes forth so abundantly in untrammeled spontaneity, everything is calculated so nicely that it is almost impossible not to wonder if Verdi measured out the right portion of cheapness, too. The proportion in the score is small, but in performance it is often so overemphasized as to dominate. Verdi could not foresee, for instance, such productions as that which Colonel Mapleson sponsored in Chicago in 1886, when six hundred state militiamen and an extra chorus of three hundred and fifty swelled the triumphal march in Act II to Barnumidian size.

The very effective opening scene begins with "Celeste Aïda," which gives many insensitive tenors the chance to turn a particularly Verdian effect into banality by shouting out the final B flat instead of singing it *pianissimo* as Verdi requests in the score. The chief glories of the opera —the Nile Scene in Act III and the whole final act—fortunately come late enough so that even the most fashionable members of society (who nearly always miss the inconveniently early "Celeste Aïda") can hear them. They are exquisitely beautiful, poignant, and affective tableaux, each dynamic and integrated into the musicodramatic entity. Although Verdi would still move on to more subtle musical speech, *Aïda* is a great masterpiece. After many years of patient experimentation, often disappointing in its results, Verdi had arrived, for the second time in his still-eventful career, at complete mastery.

Sixteen years passed between *Aïda* and *Otello,* the first of the two astonishing masterpieces of Verdi's old age. During that long interval, he composed only his deftly constructed String Quartet (1873) and, in the following year, the magnificent "Manzoni" Requiem. But he was not otherwise in retirement. He traveled extensively, particularly when the overwhelming success of the Requiem brought incessant demands for his presence to conduct it—demands he was loath to refuse, feeling the obligation as a patriotic one. Precisely halfway to *Otello,* Arrigo Boito, whom Verdi had regarded coldly for many years because of Boito's youthful criticism of his music, was reconciled to him. In 1879, Boito, besides having written the librettos of Franco Faccio's *Amleto* (1865) and Amilcare Ponchielli's *La Gioconda,* was himself the librettist-composer of *Mefistofele,* an opera that had begun to gain popular suffrage slowly after its production at La Scala on March 5, 1868. He had so changed his estimate of Verdi that, despite his own considerable fame, he was more than willing to put aside his own musical ambitions to become Verdi's Lorenzo da Ponte.

Someone—it was probably Tito Ricordi, Verdi's publisher—suggested that Boito construct a book after Shakespeare's *Othello:* Boito was a Shakespeare devotee and had already extracted a libretto from *Hamlet.* Verdi, consulted in the matter, held back for a number of reasons. In addition to a lingering suspicion of the converted Boito, he did not care to shelve either his old idea of an opera to be based on *King Lear* or that of one on a comic subject. Finally, Rossini's *Otello* still held the stage, and Verdi was not eager to challenge the old master. However, he was soon won over. Boito entrenched himself in Verdi's esteem by undertaking the thankless task of revising the text of *Simon Boccanegra* for a La Scala revival in 1881. By 1885, Verdi had begun to set Boito's *Otello.* The opera was completed in 1886, but the meticulous production plans delayed the *première,* at La Scala, until February 5, 1887.

Supplied at last with a libretto that was not only highly adequate as a theatrical vehicle but also a work of literary distinction, Verdi—at seventy-three more than ever hypersensitive to the demands of his text —rose to the perfect opportunity and wrote the most magnificent of his tragic operas. The new fruit that a long period of silent growth had brought to Verdi's orchard was indubitably his own. He had always been a supreme melodist: in *Otello* he remained one. But his uses of melody had changed. In *Aïda* he had invoked a sweeping lyrical sentence to proclaim, there and forever, a certain character; in *Otello,* melodies much less broad, and in most cases less lyrical, reveal seriatim the facets of character. The method does not, at first hearing, exert so much attraction as the one that Verdi had discarded. But the man who composed *Otello* was more interested in the subtleties of psychological verisimilitude than even the man who had composed *Aïda.* The chief characters in *Otello* reveal themselves constantly until the moment of their usually violent ends: it is literally true, for example, that Otello discloses the last creative fact about himself only with his last breath.

The music of *Otello* is of almost infinite variety. The pure, untroubled love scene in Act I is a shimmering, ecstasy-filled, lyrically tender flood of song. The "Oath" duet in Act II contrasts malign craft with agonized doubt shading into blind jealousy, doing so not only by the type of musical lines allotted respectively to Iago and Otello, but also by the shrewd exploitation of the psychological qualities of the baritone voice and the tenor. In Act III, when Otello and Desdemona sing their duet, for Otello purity is sullied and tenderness soured; his scornful, raging spasms of sound spew out against her confused innocence. While the beauty of the score is sometimes forgotten in the intensity of the crowding drama, not a few pages of it have an intense loveliness. The final scene is as nearly flawless as anything Mozart ever wrote. It is all the more moving because the gross violence is preceded by Desdemona's exquisite Willow Song ("Salce, salce") and poignant "Ave Maria," and followed by Otello's quiet suicide soliloquy, which, quoting the kiss motive from Act I, at once intensifies the tragedy, fills out the character of the Moor, and clarifies the aesthetic problem of rounded unity.

Because Verdi was seventy-three years old when *Otello* was produced, it was reasonable to think, as he himself thought, that it was to be his last major composition, that after it he would enter well-earned retirement. But 1887 was not yet over when rumors were heard of another Verdi opera—this time a comedy, probably based on *Don Quixote*. The rumors were half right. In 1890, at a dinner party, Boito proposed a toast to "Potbelly," which mystified the company until Giulio Ricordi blurted out "Falstaff!" After deeply sincere hesitation, chiefly occasioned by his advanced age, Verdi had given in to the persuasive arguments of Boito, buttressed by those of Giuseppina, and had consented to set a book drawn from *The Merry Wives of Windsor* and *Henry IV*. Until the score was almost complete, Verdi pretended that he was composing it only for his own amusement and might either never complete it or give it only privately at Sant'Agata, his country villa near Busseto. Boito provided a libretto so superior in design and detail that Verdi, usually overzealous in finding ineptitudes in detail, asked for not a single change. Despite the fact that he gave only two hours a day to its composition, having read that working longer than that was dangerous for old men, he finished *Falstaff* in less than two years.

Before *Falstaff* reached its *première* at La Scala on February 9, 1893, two dangers threatened its production. The first was Verdi's probably justifiable apprehension that a house as large as La Scala would impair the effect of what was essentially a chamber opera. The other was his near-break with Victor Maurel, when the great baritone, who had created the role of Iago in *Otello,* fruitlessly insisted that he be given the exclusive right to the role of Sir John. Both dangers were overcome. Fifty-three years after Verdi's only other comic opera, his second was heard by an audience that equaled the Bayreuth pilgrims in social and intellectual brilliance. For two of the three acts, enthusiasm was at a peak. The acclaim was less warm for Act III, but *Falstaff* looked like a success. With few exceptions, the critics responded rapturously. But these presages were not to be trusted. In Italy, the octogenarian composer's personal popularity was reflected in homage paid to this last of his masterpieces. But *Falstaff* waned after his death in 1901. Except in England, and there only in spurts, it has never become a truly popular opera.

Yet there can be no doubt that this *Falstaff* is one of the very greatest of comic operas, the worthy laughing pendant to the tragic *Otello*. It belongs to the select company of *Le Nozze di Figaro, Il Barbiere di Siviglia,* and *Die Meistersinger.* It employs the same musical idiom that Verdi had used for the most tragic purposes in *Otello*, but with well-defined adjustments. The pace is breathless to the verge of temerity—the opera's lack of recognizable points of repose is in part responsible for the public's difficulty in responding to it. It is literally too fast for many listeners, who would find many of their difficulties evaporating after a second or a third hearing. The melodies often have lives rounded in a singer's breath, and the set-number scheme has almost vanished—structurally, *Falstaff* is little more like old-fashioned Italian *opera buffa* than *Die Meistersinger* is. The melody is so abundant and ever-changing that it loses its identity as melody, becoming an extraordinarily beautiful and persuasive dramatic speech. Characterization is swift and magical: traits are ticked off at trigger speed, often in a few gnomic measures. In his late seventies, Verdi had emerged as a master orchestrator of so refined and sensitive a touch that each syllable seems to get its own apposite treatment. Yet there is, in *Falstaff,* no feeling of excess.

The score of *Falstaff* can be studied as a textbook of what instrumentation can be made to carry of wit and brilliance, but it is not closet writing. From an orchestral crescendo trill that is a favorite of admiring theorists to the eight-voice fugue that spins this genial burlesque to its close, there is no cessation of tactfully applied musical erudition. All this, spooling from the creative fancy of a mellowed genius, serves the comic spirit generously, poetically, luminously. Ranging from the robust good humor, the lovable humanity, the rollicking obscenity of Sir John to the dewy, tremulous love of Nanetta and Fenton and the earthy cacklings of the Merry Wives, *Falstaff* has the variety demanded by its characters, by this particular little world of Shakespeare. For, by some extreme artistic miracle, it is even English.

CHAPTER XIX

Italian Opera after Verdi

THE achievement of Arrigo Boito in providing Verdi with two librettos of surpassing excellence would suffice to keep his name fresh in any history of the opera. His selflessness in turning aside from the composition of his *Nerone* has often been pointed out, but it would be more accurate to say that a divided allegiance delayed his musical career. Moreover, an examination of his operas, for which he also wrote the librettos, shows that Boito's choice was a proof of his critical acumen: his literary gifts surpassed his musical. An intellectual of volatile temper, sensitive, refined, squeamish, and a touch feminine, Boito, who had devoured libraries of theory by his early twenties, could ponder and polish a musical phrase until it lost not only its bloom but also its connection with neighboring phrases on either side. Yet he managed to write one opera—*Mefistofele*—not too sicklied over with the pale cast of thought. After that, he labored over *Nerone,* his second and last opera, for fifty-four years. He did not live to see this unwieldly epic of decadent Rome performed: six years after his death, Toscanini, who had helped to put the finishing touches to the score, conducted its *première* at La Scala on May 1, 1924. Received with riotous enthusiasm by a distinguished audience, *Nerone,* which is harmonically of great interest, nevertheless has not emigrated to the United States or England. The character of the music, with its scholarly infusions of Bach and Wagner, may be deduced from a suggestive incident: in 1902, after permitting *Nerone* to be announced for La Scala, this most encyclopedic of closet musicians withdrew it, saying that he did not "know" harmony, and was going to study it in lovely, remote Sermione, on the shores of Garda, where Catullus had meditated almost two thousand years before. Simplifying the libretto might have helped *Nerone*'s chances, for its complexities can scarcely be grasped at a single hearing.

Mefistofele was merely a youthful example of the hesitant processes of this exacerbated mentality. It was first produced at La Scala on March 5, 1868, its unqualified failure creating a riot and retiring it for seven years, during which Boito subjected it to a major overhauling. Faust lost his baritone voice and became a tenor, and the opera, much shortened, was presented again on October 4, 1875, this time at Bologna. The revised version succeeded: since then it has been performed over five thousand times in Italy and has had fitful spells of popularity elsewhere. Examination of the fastidiously doctored score shows that Boito had studied the techniques of many masters—Beethoven, Berlioz, and Brahms among them. It shows him, more ambitious than Messrs Barbier, Carré, and Gounod, striving to compass the whole of Goethe's presentation of the struggle between good and evil. But it shows him less musically vital than Gounod, to whom he might well have given some of his sheer power of intellect in exchange for a saving sensuality. The music is clever, but alternates between being parched and thin and being boisterously noisy. It has little life of its own, but certain performers, notably Chaliapin, its most famed Devil, have been able to galvanize it with their own vitality. Nevertheless, certain numbers stand out, notably the wistful "Lontano, lontano" (added in the revised version), the exciting "L'altra notte," the fresh "Dai campi, dai prati," and the impressive "Sabba classico." Although *Mefistofele,* like so many revolutionary documents (Boito's devotion to Beethoven was expressed in a pondered modern idiom), has aged a bit, the score was ransacked for ideas by many of Boito's younger contemporaries, even possibly by Verdi himself. Huneker's summing up of the situation is essentially true: "Boito seems to have been the pivotal point of the neo-Italian school—himself remaining in the background—while the youngsters profited by his many experimentings."

Less interesting than Boito as a person and as a musical thinker, but quite as influential in the course of Italian opera because he taught Mascagni, Puccini, and Franco Leoni, was Amilcare Ponchielli, the composer of *La Gioconda* and of several other works whose popularity was confined to Italy. Although he began composing operas in his early twenties, he did not achieve a success until he was almost forty. This was a revision of an early effort—*I Promessi Sposi,* which was based on Manzoni's famous novel, and which doubtless drew a large measure of its popularity from that fact. Coming in 1872, when Verdi, with the completion of *Aïda,* might have been expected to retire permanently, *I Promessi Sposi* indicated Ponchielli as Verdi's successor, and indeed, during the rest of his comparatively brief career—he died in 1886, one year before the production of *Otello*—he enjoyed the position of heir apparent. *La Gioconda* was the first of his four tremendous successes at La Scala. Of the remaining three, *Il Figliuol prodigo* (1880), a Biblical opera of spectacular character, has been called his finest work—an opinion to be taken on trust by Americans, as the opera has never been performed here.

For all practical purposes, *La Gioconda* is Ponchielli. Its impressive career astoundingly exceeds its merits, though the reasons for its popularity are apparent. Starting out with a second-rate blood-and-thunder melodrama by Victor Hugo, Ponchielli called in Boito to make a credible libretto from this *Angelo, tyran de Padoue.* He failed.[1] The libretto, unusual in that each act has its own title, is not credible. But it is violent and melodramatic, and the music is just like it. Krehbiel spoke happily of the "hot vigor" of the work—a phrase that can refer to both the music and the libretto. It abounds in glaring contrasts, robust declamation, bravura finales, and—what has probably contributed most to its popularity—unmistakable if sometimes banal lyric sweep. Musically, Ponchielli is more compelling than Boito, though less an innovator and less careful in producing his effects. The point is, he does produce them—by wrapping up his own free-flowing melody in packages collected from such international entrepreneurs as Meyerbeer, Halévy, Verdi, even Wagner.

La Gioconda has been called one of the ancestors of *verismo*—that realistic way of treating the violent, the sordid, and the everyday which became endemic in Italy during the 1890's and which gradually spread to other countries. Yet, the well-known excerpts from *La Gioconda* are mostly not typical of a veristic opera: the Dance of the Hours is timeless salon music of not the highest order; "Cielo e mar," "Voce di donna," "Stella del marinar," and "Pescator, affonda l'esca" are lyrical numbers whose honesty of conviction barely saves them from banality; "Suicidio!" alone carries into the concert hall the predominant violence of the score, but even that is less veristic than Verdian.

---

[1] The libretto was given out to be the work of Tobia Gorrio (an anagram of Arrigo Boito), but there is no evidence that Boito used this subterfuge to hide any shame he may have felt about his handiwork.

Verismo may be said to have burst into full bloom as the result of a prize contest for one-act operas sponsored by the Milan music-publishing house of Edoardo Sonzogno. Second price went to *Labilia,* by Nicola Spinelli, a twenty-five-year-old Turinese whose later *A basso porto* (1894) has been heard in New York. First money plucked from obscurity a wan-faced starveling of twenty-seven, Pietro Mascagni, whose entry was entitled *Cavalleria rusticana.* When it was first produced at the Teatro Costanzi, Rome, on May 17, 1890, with Bellincioni and Stagno as Santuzza and Turiddu, the acclamations were such that there could be no reasonable doubt that a new popular favorite had arrived. It was soon resounding throughout Italy, and within two years had been heard in Berlin, New York, London, and Paris. Its success was everywhere immediate, and has endured.

Mascagni composed more than a dozen operas after *Cavalleria,* and not one of them has had, at best, more than a passing *succès d'estime.* His career, by and large, was that of an impertinent coxcomb. Encouraged still further by the popularity of *L'Amico Fritz* (1891), an adaptation of one of Erckmann-Chatrian's tamer tales, and *Iris* (1898) (a mock-Japanese tear-jerker) but not moved to self-criticism by several flat failures, Mascagni arranged to have the *première* of his *Le Maschere* take place simultaneously (1901) in seven of Italy's most important cities.[2] This arrogant action was greeted with the sharp rebuff merited by the poor quality and imitative character of the music, Rome alone, with the composer on the podium, giving it a slight suffrage. In Milan, a knowing audience signified by catcalls of "Ah! Puccini, viva Puccini!" that one source of Mascagni's borrowings was only too obvious. At Genoa, *Le Maschere* was not allowed to proceed to the end. After this fiasco, Mascagni's operations were on a more modest scale, though there was no evidence of deflated ego. In 1917, *Lodoletta,* based on a Ouida story that Puccini had experimented with, achieved a mild world fame, and in 1918 even secured performance from a by then skeptical Metropolitan management, the cast being headed by Farrar and Caruso. *Lodoletta* failed to establish itself in New York, as did *L'Amico Fritz,* despite Calvé, and *Iris,* despite a *première* with Eames, Caruso, and Scotti (1907), a revival with Bori, under Toscanini (1915), and a final try with Rethberg, Gigli, De Luca, and Pinza (1931). Next to the 260 Metropolitan *Cavallerias,* the total of twenty-six performances achieved by *L'Amico Fritz, Iris,* and *Lodoletta* makes a telling commentary on the

[2] Naples was two days late.

consistent falling off, after a single youthful spurt, of Mascagni's inspiration.

Mascagni put everything he had into *Cavalleria*—like the familiar author of one successful autobiographical novel, he could not repeat. Before setting down a note on paper, he had been possessed by the raw strength of Giovanni Verga's crude Sicilian tale, and when the strident chords of the finale flashed across his mind, he started, beginning with the end, to whelm down the music. All his impetuosity and young passion went into it, and it all but flames with conviction. He was desperately poor, and *Cavalleria* was written literally out of his need. Melodies flooded his imagination, and he let them gush forth without criticism. Had Mascagni been able to continue tapping this source, he might eventually have secured for himself a place comparable to that Verdi had secured before composing *Rigoletto*. Unfortunately, Mascagni could neither do that nor go on to an *Aïda* or a *Falstaff;* for his immortality he had to depend on *Cavalleria rusticana*. Its fiery lyricism, its black-and-white contrasts, its sultry Southern passions, its pervading catchiness— these are small change for the ferryman of the Styx, but the Intermezzo alone would assure passage. *Cavalleria* is the apotheosis of hurdy-gurdy, and is occasionally somewhat better.

The career of *Pagliacci,* the other foundation stone of *verismo,* has been at least as spectacular as that of *Cavalleria.* This two-acter, composed, like the earlier work, for the publishing house of Sonzogno, was first given at the Teatro dal Verme, Milan, on May 21, 1892, with Toscanini conducting. Besides Ancona (Silvio), the cast was given éclat by its Tonio, Maurel, who had been instrumental in getting the opera produced. Its success showed that *Cavalleria* had a rival, but how serious a one was not immediately revealed.

Ruggero Leoncavallo, a man of very considerable intelligence, wrote his own librettos, sometimes from episodes known to him personally. Such was *Pagliacci,* which was based on a murder committed by a member of a company of strolling players at a Calabrian village. As Leoncavallo's father had been the presiding judge at the actor's trial, the incident was indelibly graved on the composer's mind. This did not save him from being sued unsuccessfully for plagiarism by Catulle Mendès, who claimed that the central situation was stolen from his *La Femme de tabarin*. The libretto of *Pagliacci* is an excellent frame for the broad melodies, flavorsome declamation, and crashing volumes that Leoncavallo devoted to it. It is rank melodrama, but most theatrically believable and simple to follow. Like *Cavalleria, Pagliacci* was exciting stuff in the nineties, and it still is. For now, when we are so inured to the raw speech of *verismo* that its novelty is gone, the power of these brief operas—a typical performance of the two-act *Pagliacci* is four minutes shorter than one of the single act of *Cavalleria,* which requires seventy-three minutes —is their pace, their terse, unpadded drama, and their melodic largess. *Pagliacci* contains some of the most familiar music ever composed: the Prologue, a curious bit of theatrical formalism whose roots go back to the infant beginnings of opera, to Peri's *Dafne,* is one of these; the other is "Vesti la giubba," the big sob song that has become the *locus classicus* of the clown with the broken heart. There are other high spots in a score that is melodically attractive throughout.

Mascagni had composed *Cavalleria rusticana* out of an urgent need to keep himself and his family alive; Leoncavallo had composed *Pagliacci* out of an equally urgent need to make good. He was thirty-four, and his life had been full of failure. *Chatterton,* his first opera, had been on the verge of production when the impresario absconded; his second, *I Medici*—originally intended to be the first opera of a trilogy, *Crepusculum,* the other units of which (*Girolamo Savonarola* and *Cesare Borgia*) never were completed—languished in the Ricordi files until Leoncavallo, impatient to hear himself performed, began dickering with the rival house of Sonzogno. Then came his one great success, and thereafter the parallel with Mascagni again became only too bitterly apparent. The yellowing scores of *Chatterton* and *I Medici* were dusted off and offered to the public without success.

Then Leoncavallo composed *Zazà,* hoping with it to equal the success of the play, which was familiar to multitudes of Englishmen and Americans because of Mrs. Leslie Carter's portrayal of the heroine. The score has undoubted merits, and for a time *Zazà* filled opera houses throughout the world. But its vogue died after a decade, and even in Italy it is only occasionally heard. During Geraldine Farrar's last years at the Metropolitan *Zazà* persisted because of her vivid interpretation. Indeed, so much was she admired in the part that it was chosen for her operatic farewell on April 22, 1922. Since that afternoon, *Zazà,* which had been heard at the Tivoli Opera House, San Francisco, as early as 1903, has not been sung in the United States. Leoncavallo, without encouragement except from the unabating popularity of *Pagliacci,* went on grinding out operas up to his death in 1919. One of them, *Der Roland von Berlin,* was composed to order for Wilhelm II, whose favorite composer Leoncavallo was, and devotes itself earnestly to the business of glorifying early Hohen-zollerns. Even the Prussian capital, where it had its *première* on December 13, 1904, accorded *Der Roland* only polite applause.

Giacomo Puccini, most fortunately endowed of the verists, early or late, was the last of the group to arrive.[3] There is a marked resemblance between the beginnings of his career and those of Mascagni and Leoncavallo, though each worked out differently in detail.[4] All, however, suffered from penury and despair. Puccini, whose musical ancestors were almost as numerous as Bach's, failed to win even honorable mention in a competition for a one-act opera sponsored by Edoardo Sonzogno. But he had friends—Boito and Ponchielli among them—who believed in *Le Villi*, the loser, and through their efforts it came to production at the Teatro dal Verme, Milan, on May 31, 1884. The forlorn hope was a huge success, and thus, under the rosiest auspices, was launched one of the most successful musical careers of modern times. Made over into a two-acter, *Le Villi* became the rage in Turin, and finally attained La Scala. It was the sole success Puccini was to experience for almost ten years. This young man, whose flair for the stage was to become a byword, next accepted an impossible libretto based on one of Musset's wildest verse melodramas, set it earnestly and capably, and had it produced at La Scala on April 21, 1889. The book had defeated him: *Edgar* was a fiasco, and it took courage for the house of Ricordi, which by this time had a vested interest in Puccini's career, not to falter in their support. They had not too long to wait: the promising score of *Manon Lescaut* was completed in 1892, and its promise redeemed early the next year.

The agony of work that went into the book of *Manon Lescaut* was symptomatic of the trouble Puccini never ceased having with his librettos. Had he had Leoncavallo's ability to write his own, he might have been saved years of painful search for suitable material, and we might have double the output of nine full-length and three one-act operas that he

[3] Except the talented Franco Leoni, another Ponchielli pupil, who, though a fecund composer of operas, is known in America only by *L'Oracolo* (1905), based on a Chinese horror story, which offered Antonio Scotti the chance for one of his best and most popular portrayals. The great baritone played the role of Chim-fen no less than forty-four times at the Metropolitan, and bade farewell to that house, as well as to opera, as the evil Chinese on January 20, 1933, after a New York career of thirty-four years.

[4] Puccini and Leoncavallo were almost exact contemporaries; Mascagni was five years their junior.

left, after an active career of forty years, at his death in 1924. In the case of *Manon Lescaut,* the very fact that he selected a version of the same Abbé Prévost story that had already been set with conspicuous success by Massenet showed that he was desperate for opera-worthy material to which he could respond with warmth. Before the libretto satisfied him, five men, including Giulio Ricordi and the two playwrights who were eventually to provide his most viable books—Giuseppe Giacosa and Luigi Illica—had wrestled with it, and Puccini himself had added the finishing touches. It was well worth the effort, for when *Manon Lescaut* finally reached its *première* at the Teatro Regio, Turin, on February 1, 1893, it was immediately realized, in native musical circles, that Mascagni and Leoncavallo were in danger of being eclipsed, though this opinion was not immediately echoed abroad. At the London *première,* for instance, Bernard Shaw was the lone critic who realized that Puccini, not Mascagni or Leoncavallo, was the step after Verdi in Italian opera.

Like Verdi, Puccini reached his first maturity in his middle thirties: *Manon Lescaut* was his *Rigoletto.* In it are, though not frequently in final form, the elements of his musical individuality. Sweet, pungent, and diverse harmonies, lush romantic melodies, calculated contrasts, schooled effects carried out with pared means—such are the qualities of *Manon Lescaut,* and such, often in more exaggerated guises, are those of *La Bohème, Tosca,* and *Madama Butterfly,* and, to a somewhat lesser extent, of the later operas. From Des Grieux's aria, "Donna non vida mai," in Act I, descended the many throbbing love songs that can be depended upon to stop the show. Even the Intermezzo, "La Prigionia," which is a small tone poem, has the harmonic tang, feminine charm, and intimate flavor that were to remain the characteristics of Puccini's instrumental interludes. Thus he early established the hallmarks of his manner and told his admirers what to look for. He did not often disappoint them thereafter by departing flagrantly from these stylistic norms. This is not to say that he had a static talent: he improved upon what he had, without adding much that was new. The point is that, except for one period of fumbling, he did improve, and consistently. *Manon Lescaut* set the pattern, too, by having a thoroughly credible libretto, but it was far more disjointed than any an experienced and self-confident Puccini would ever again allow collaborators to devise for him.

On February 1, 1896, at the Teatro Regio, Turin, Toscanini conducted the *première* of Puccini's fourth opera, *La Bohème,* three years to a day after that of *Manon Lescaut.* The facts of its composition uncover one of the several discreditable episodes in the life of this shrewd and feline man. Before *Manon Lescaut* was completed, Puccini was already toying vaguely with a new idea—an opera about Buddha. His friend Leoncavallo sent him a libretto of his own devising, based on episodes from Henri Murger's *Scènes de la vie de Bohème*. Puccini rejected it without much thought. Some time after the launching of *Manon Lescaut,* he infuriated Leoncavallo by announcing calmly that Giacosa and Illica had given him an excellent libretto based on the Murger novel. Leoncavallo, who meanwhile had decided to set his own libretto, protested that the idea belonged to him, only to be told that there would be two *Bohèmes*. Puccini's opera came out first and, though at the beginning only modestly acclaimed, was such a success at Palermo that, even after most of the orchestra had left the theater, the audience demanded, and got, a repetition of the finale, with the principals in their street clothes. Had Puccini's opera failed, instead of becoming one of the most popular operas in the world, Leoncavallo might have forgotten the episode. As it was, his own opera (eventually renamed *Mimi Pinson*) was tepidly received and Leoncavallo never forgave Puccini.

Not until he developed a passionate interest in his material could Puccini begin to translate a libretto into music. He set this new opera *con amore,* for not only did the incidents in the libretto remind him of his own student days in Milan, but also he had fallen in love with the pathetic little heroine, Mimi. The score is Puccini at his best and worst. At his worst, he is mawkish, cloying, and sticky with adolescent sentimentality. At his best, he is eloquently dramatic, psychologically sound, and adroit in carrying passionate rapture along on the crest of swelling melody. In *La Bohème,* he is not only all these things but most of them *in excelsis.*

A testimonial to the power of *La Bohème* is the fact that it provokes definite reactions: one either surrenders wholeheartedly to it or one rejects it completely. But no one, not even those most put off by its sentimental excesses, will deny that *La Bohème* is a credible story turned into an effective stage piece by music that provides a throbbing flesh for the story's skeleton. It is possible to dislike Mimi and Rodolfo, but it is the healthy dislike one feels for some real people, not for vague abstractions or mere types such as crowd most of the operas of Donizetti or Gounod. The music makes them real, gives them personality. And some of that music is so familiar that the gramophonic history of *La Bohème* would make a small volume in itself. Complete and slightly abridged recordings

have been numerous and multilingual, while such excerpts as "Che ge-
lida manina," "Si mi chiamano Mimi," Musetta's Waltz Song, and Mimi's
Farewell have been recorded countless times each.

The history of the libretto of Puccini's next opera is quite as unsavory
a morsel as that of the libretto of *La Bohème*. Sometime in the late
eighties, Puccini had seen Sarah Bernhardt in Sardou's *La Tosca* and
seemingly had not been attracted to the drama. A good decade later,
Verdi was quoted as having said that only his age kept him from setting
Sardou's play. Then Puccini remembered that when he had heard Bernhardt, he had been able perfectly to follow the argument of the play without understanding the language in which it was written. This was ample
evidence to the theatrical-minded composer that *La Tosca* contained
the elements of a good libretto. But he found that Illica had already
sketched a libretto of *La Tosca* for Alberto Franchetti, a wealthy composer of the Meyerbeerian school. That the idea was ethically Franchetti's
was but a slight barrier to Illica and Ricordi, who, as soon as they learned
that Puccini was interested, bamboozled poor Franchetti into releasing
the sketch. They argued that the material was too vile for operatic treatment and immediately presented the skeleton libretto to Puccini. Then
Illica and Giacosa, with suggestions from Ricordi and Puccini himself,
not to mention a plethora of useless comment from the doddering Sardou,
finally put together a satisfactory book.

The Puccini score had its first hearing at the Costanzi, in Rome, on
January 14, 1900, and barely escaped being a fiasco: rumors were rife
that enemies of Puccini's success were out to "get" him, and when some
latecomers caused muttering in the audience, the management, fearing
the worst, rang down the curtain. As nothing dangerous developed, they
raised it again, and the first *Tosca* proceeded eventlessly to its conclusion.
The next morning, vicious newspaper criticisms echoed the arguments
Illica and Ricordi had used dishonestly to Franchetti. But despite the
fact that they called the story noisome, and charged that the torture scene
by its very nature debased the art of music, *Tosca* soon established itself
as Puccini's third big success.

Tosca is the most thrilling of Puccini's operas—heart-in-the-mouth
entertainment from the three rasping chords that open it with the villainous Scarpia's signature to the end of Act II. Tosca's suicide scream does
not suffice to make acceptable a third act that is curiously undramatic.
The libretto is an unrelieved horror story, made up of such elements as
attempted rape, torture, murder, execution, and suicide. The villain is

black and sardonic, the hero white and angelic; only Tosca herself is human—in the libretto. By his music, however, Puccini managed to make the whole gory affair acceptable as a story. Much of the stage business could not be set to music, and for long stretches, therefore, the composer contented himself with writing clever musical illustrations and evocations of atmosphere. But where passions, whether black or white, fused, Puccini provided lyricodramatic floods of song and heightened declamation, often a telling coalescence of the two. In song, he frequently retained some of the quality of speech, as can be seen in such climaxes as "Recondita armonia," "Vissi d'arte," and "E lucevan le stelle."

All his life an aesthetic blotter, Puccini, during the *Tosca* period, was absorbing late Verdi, him of *Otello,* in every receptive fiber. And he was also beginning to point like a vane to each new wind in the musical sky —to profit by what his contemporaries outside Italy were doing. He was becoming an internationalist (without ever relinquishing his claims to his share in the heritage of Italian melody), and even in 1900 his harmonies were diverging sharply from tradition. He reacted like an intellectual. For instance, in *Tosca* he experimented with the whole-tone scale, with ecclesiastical modes, and with outright harmonic heresies.

How international Puccini was becoming could more easily be told after examining the score of his next opera, *Madama Butterfly.* It is not merely that this is an American's story of a fictional Japan, limned with a realistic intent that never quite succeeds. It makes use of authentic Japanese tunes—during the period of *Butterfly*'s composition, Puccini conscientiously imported records from Japan—and quotes "The Star-Spangled Banner." Moreover, it meets the issue of harmonic modernity even more bravely than *Tosca* did. Puccini did not quite achieve homogeneity of style with these disparate and perhaps immiscible elements, though Dyneley Hussey perhaps overstated the case when he spoke of *Butterfly*'s "impure style . . . in which the Japanese and American tunes were never completely absorbed into the texture of the music but stick out of it like so many almonds on top of a trifle." In short, Puccini's music is finally as artistically incredible as the milieu he had to illustrate —a half-real, half-Gilbert-and-Sullivan Japan. When it is not being picture-postcard Japanesy, when it is at its best, that is, it is the good old Italian sweeping lyricism with which Puccini had seduced the world in *Bohème* and *Tosca.* And in "Un bel di, vedremo," Cio-Cio-San's rapturous paean of hope, he composed what has become the best known of all his arias.

The history of the composition of *Madama Butterfly* parallels in some details that of *Tosca*. When Puccini was in London in 1900, he saw the play that David Belasco and John Luther Long had made from the latter's magazine story, "Madam Butterfly." Although he understood little English, he was as gripped as he had been by Sardou's drama. In short, he fell in love with Cio-Cio-San, and soon secured rights to the use of the play as the basis of a libretto. Giacosa and Illica, turned loose on the tale, did their best—and last—job. Puccini set to work with feverish eagerness and, despite a serious motor accident, completed it in, for him, record time. It received its *première* at La Scala on February 17, 1904, and failed miserably. The fact that it was in two very long acts did not help it, but more serious was the flouting of tradition, both musical and theatrical. The harmonies, though still only transitional, were strange, and the costuming did not square with romantic notions. Probably none of these considerations would have been decisive against the immediate success of the opera had not the temper of the Milanese audience been raised to choler by echoes, real or fancied, of *Bohème*. Characteristically, they felt that they were being cheated—having paid to hear a new opera, they demanded that all of it be new. Another, less exacting audience might at once have declared for *Madama Butterfly*. As it was, after a few revisions, the most important of which was making a new division into three acts, it was staged triumphantly at Brescia on May 28, 1904, and soon spread its wings abroad.

It was just before the Metropolitan *première* of *Madama Butterfly* that Puccini announced to the press that he was going to collaborate on an opera with David Belasco, with whom he had struck up a friendship during the negotiations over the Long-Belasco play. He was exaggerating: Belasco was not a librettist and wrote only in English. What Puccini had in mind was something based on Belasco's hit melodrama, *The Girl of the Golden West*. But Giacosa had died, and Illica by himself was unsatisfactory to Puccini. Returned to Italy, the composer entered upon an unhappy period, both professionally and personally. For many months he looked vainly for a likely librettist and finally found one who could block out the general lineaments of the story and another who could help to give them life.

The book was finished, and Puccini had just begun to compose *La Fanciulla del West* (for such is its hybrid title), when his violently jealous wife disrupted his existence by driving to suicide a housemaid whom she had accused publicly of being the composer's mistress. Signora Puccini was tried, and convicted, for criminal slander after a post-mortem examination had proved baseless her charges of sexual intimacy. Puccini paid heavily to keep his wife out of prison, and for a time left her, though he eventually again lived with her and more or less happily. After almost a year's interruption, he returned to *La Fanciulla del West,* and finished it in October, 1910. Unfortunately, Puccini never had a greater need for reassurance, and this time it was denied him. Although the Metropolitan, which had ordered *La Fanciulla,* listened to it cordially enough, its fate elsewhere was close to harsh. Even in Italy, where Puccini occupies a throne next to Verdi's, the work has never come into real favor.

Even if the music of *La Fanciulla* were better than it is, the libretto would prove an all but insuperable bar to sincere appreciation. Singers dressed up as frontiersmen and shouting Italian in a Wild West saloon (the Polkadot) cannot be regarded, particularly by Americans, as the vessels of opera that any self-respecting person can take seriously. If this obstacle deprived us of the ability to listen properly to some of Puccini's best music, rewriting the book might be worth the trouble. But much of *La Fanciulla* is almost as hopeless musically as it is theatrically. The shadows of Puccini's life do not show in it, but the lack of inspiration that visited him because of them is often evident. Technical care is in the score, the attempt to capture the American flavor by use of native tunes, the gestures of a master craftsman—all are there, and yet fail utterly to animate this musical mule. In fact, *La Fanciulla* must have made some of Puccini's warmest admirers fear that the cometlike ascent had ended. *La Rondine,* which issued stillborn from his pen in 1917, after seven long years of waiting, was a poor Viennese-waltz operetta— which, nevertheless, Lucrezia Bori used, on March 21, 1936, as her farewell to opera. It must have made them shudder for his future. At fifty-nine, it is not easy to make a comeback.

Before *La Rondine* was begun, however, Puccini had composed part of a most spectacular comeback—a "triptych" of three contrasting one-act operas. As early as 1914, he had almost finished the first, *Il Tabarro,* a brutal lens focused on a Parisian slum tragedy. While completing it, after delays caused by the war and the composition of *La Rondine,* he was still searching for two more short librettos to fill out his scheme. Then Giovacchino Forzano, who had already provided Mascagni with the book of *Lodoletta,* came forward with two ideas, the first the story of a nun with an unhappy past, the second the droll story of a hoax perpetrated in Dante's Florence.

Early in 1918, all three sections of *Il Trittico* were ready—*Il Tabarro,*
Suor Angelica, and *Gianni Schicchi.* Tito Ricordi closed with the Metropolitan for the world *première,* and there, accordingly, on December 14,
1918, it was given. Puccini was not present (it was only a month after
the Armistice), and the operas were received with an indifference his
presence might have prevented. Claudia Muzio and Geraldine Farrar
created the chief female roles in *Il Tabarro* and *Suor Angelica* respectively, but despite the popularity of these dramatic singing actresses, neither opera succeeded at the Metropolitan, from which both disappeared
after two seasons. Although the Italian *première* of *Il Trittico,* at the
Costanzi, Rome, on January 11, 1919, with Toscanini conducting and
the King and Queen present, was an unparalleled personal triumph for
Puccini, this brilliant send-off was not effective in establishing Parts I
and II of the trilogy in the affections of the people. Throughout the rest
of Europe, their fate was almost as dismal. *Gianni Schicchi's* destiny was
quite different. Florence Easton, Giuseppe De Luca, and Adamo Didur
covered themselves with glory at the world *première,* and slowly, definitely, the opera made its way.

Il Trittico shows Puccini gaining stature as a serious musician. In
conception, design, and execution, it seems beyond the potentialities of
the callow young melodist of *Le Villi,* and not to have been expected of
the adroit romanticist who contrived *La Bohème. Il Tabarro* does not
deserve its present obscurity. Plotted along simple, direct lines, it is a
small masterpiece of uncompromising realism which musically works out
the psychological problem with inexorable logic. It is a thriller, but not
of the garish Mascagni-Leoncavallo school, for the music starkly, hon-
estly hews to the action. *Suor Angelica* is impressionistic, almost Debussyan in its subtle evocation of atmosphere. As is so often the case
with neglected works, this was, of *Il Trittico,* the composer's favorite,
but, by providing too many audience hurdles, he had made himself responsible for its failure. There are too many incidents too loosely integrated for the one-act frame, and the fact that all the voices in a largely
feminine score are female tends to produce a soporific tedium.

Gianni Schicchi is a quite un-Puccinian masterpiece. While his in technique, spiritually it is the child of *Falstaff.* The libretto, though actually
based by Forzano on a casual hint in *La Divina Commedia,* bears a
curious resemblance to Ben Jonson's *Volpone.* It is good malicious fun
all through, and has just enough going on to make the one act perfect
entertainment. The music is fast, witty, brilliantly apt, and overflowing

—particularly when Gianni holds the center of the stage—with a kind of benevolent malice. It is a flawless score, with one exception, and that its best-known fragment—the lushly Italian "O mio babbino caro," psychologically apt but, in its context, musically irrelevant.

Before his death on November 29, 1924, Puccini had completed all but the last scene of one of the most interesting operatic scores of the century. This was *Turandot,* with a libretto by Giuseppe Adami, who had written the book of *Il Tabarro,* and Renato Simoni, a poet who was something of a Sinologue. As Puccini's admiring biographer, Vincent Seligman, says in *Puccini among Friends,* "A Persian legend from the *Thousand and One Nights;* a Chinese fairy tale of a cruel Princess, whose hatred at last turned to love; a Venetian Masque; a play of Gozzi, a poem of Schiller, an overture of Weber—from such discordant elements was Puccini's masterpiece born." He worked on the score of *Turandot* for four years, and when he went to the Brussels hospital in which he died, he took thirty-six manuscript pages of sketch material and notes for the finale with him.

After Puccini's death, these pages were handed over to Franco Alfano, an intelligent second-rater whose name once was slightly green in the United States because of Mary Garden's revival, in French, of his elderly *La Risurrezione.* Alfano, consulting Toscanini, who had discussed *Turandot* in detail with Puccini, completed it sympathetically—that is, without distortion—and it was presented at La Scala on April 25, 1926, with Rosa Raïsa (Turandot), Maria Zamboni (Liù), Miguel Fleta (Calaf), and Giacomo Rimini (Ping). Toscanini conducted.

Turandot is interesting chiefly because in it post-Verdian Italian operatic music, veristic and romantic, meets and momentarily merges with the surge of influences from Northern and Eastern Europe—the post-Wagnerism of Strauss, the atonality of Schoenberg, and the polyrhythms and savage colors of Stravinsky. Whereas in *Madama Butterfly* Puccini had imported Japanese gramophone records for his exotic *appliqué* work, in *Turandot* he made a serious study of Chinese music and emerged with results reminiscent of Debussy's dilettante reactions to Javanese and Annamese music. If this somewhat self-conscious experimentation smacks of the *fin de siècle,* as does also the unabated nervous tension in the big *scene,* in this complex score Puccini never forgets that he is creating a musicodramatic work, and is almost invariably master of his materials—even in the pages left for Alfano's editing. *Turandot* is Puccini—the ever-changing master of musical theater—all the way through, with a heightened genius for pathetic utterance that supremely convinces in the music that he gave to the pitiable Liù. Where the ultramodern elements fail to mix with the indigenous musical speech, *Turandot* may sound like *Butterfly* with "wrong notes." Flawed though it is, and lacking the final polish that Puccini might have given it, *Turandot* worthily crowns his career of increasing knowledge. With something less than the highest genius, he might have gone on because of his insatiable intellect, his unimpaired melodic gift, and his technical mastery, to create in his old age works as far ahead of *Manon Lescaut* as *Falstaff* was of *Ernani*. At sixty-six, he died too young.

In Puccini, Verdi had found a not unworthy successor, while in their early *Cavalleria rusticana* and *Pagliacci,* Mascagni and Leoncavallo had at least given a somewhat specious novelty to the musical scene. But their contemporaries and followers in Italy, especially Mascagni's, were largely a sorry lot, ever finding cruder, more blatant ways of repeating the same old shockers. They were, with few exceptions, pattern workers, and the exceptions, despite technical ease, all too often added up to the jejune.

Among the lesser verists, Francesco Cilèa, Umberto Giordano, and Riccardo Zandonai have varying claims to mention. Of Cilèa's five operas, two—*L'Arlesiana* (1897) and *Adriana Lecouvreur* (1902)—are notably connected with the career of Enrico Caruso, who made his first great success in the first, and created the rôle of Maurizio in the second at the Scala *première*. When Giulio Gatti-Casazza chose *Adriana* to open the Metropolitan season of 1907–8, the imposing cast of Caruso, Scotti, and Marcel Journet might have carried it into the permanent repertoire had not Lina Cavalieri, "the most beautiful woman in the world," been a bad singer and an indifferent actress. While *L'Arlesiana* is forgotten, *Adriana Lecouvreur,* about the unhappy love of the great French actress for the fickle Maréchal de Saxe, still packs the opera houses of Italy. It is a charming rather than a powerfully dramatic score, and at present is a favorite with Renata Tebaldi.

Verismo seems run of the mill in Giordano, who had, nevertheless, a most successful career. No less than four of his dozen operas—*Andrea Chénier, Fedora* (1898), *Madame Sans-Gêne* (1915), and *La Cena delle beffe* (1924)—were considered sufficiently stageworthy to be produced at the Metropolitan, while a fifth—*Siberia* (1903)—was a little-liked novelty of Hammerstein's second season at the Manhattan Opera House. *Andrea Chénier,* with a libretto by Illica, is easily the most popular of Giordano's operas, and is in some ways his most engaging. Full of obvious melodies, bold declamation, and effective stage tricks, it is, despite its title, a good vehicle for a dramatic soprano of large voice and a weakness for heroics. It is exactly contemporary with *La Bohème,* having been first given at La Scala in 1896.

Zandonai, who as a student received from Mascagni's lips the gospel of verism, followed his master, at some distance. Several of his operas have had continuing success in Italy, where he was eulogized by both Boito and Puccini, but he had little success in establishing himself elsewhere. In the United States, for example, only two of his operas are known, and those not well. The first, *Conchita,* with a sadistic Spanish libretto after Pierre Louÿs, was heard in San Francisco in 1912 and came east the next year with Tarquinia Tarquini, the original Conchita and Zandonai's future wife. The second, *Francesca da Rimini,* with a libretto by Tito Ricordi from the D'Annunzio play, had an all-star cast when it was first produced at the Metropolitan on December 22, 1916, among the players being Frances Alda, Edith Mason, Mabel Garrison, Sophie Braslau, Giovanni Martinelli, Pasquale Amato, and Angelo Bada. Orchestral sophistication, a limited flair for the theater, and almost nothing original to say characterize Zandonai's scores. Like Giordano, he sometimes provides a memorable moment when he allows the orchestra to have its say while the action is suspended temporarily.

No mere imitators, yet measurably removed from the experimental modernist school, were such men as Ferruccio Busoni, Ottorino Respighi, Italo Montemezzi, and Ermanno Wolf-Ferrari. An American will find difficulty in assessing Busoni as an operatic composer, for none of the operas of the great pianist,[5] teacher, theorist, and musical philosopher has been performed here. Busoni was, in musical preferences, rather more German than Italian, and his ardent, almost mystical preaching of Liszt and Wagner was scarcely preparation for a truly modern idiom. Those who have heard his four stage works recognize in them the utterance of a lofty and original, but not lyrically gifted, man. Busoni took his operatic compositions most seriously and wrote them to his own librettos. His most considerable opera, *Doktor Faust,* was completed after his death by his pupil, the erudite Philipp Jarnach, and was presented at

---

[5] Another famous pianist with almost as tireless a pen was Eugen d'Albert, whose *Tiefland* has been described as a "German *Carmen.*" Despite its immense popularity in Germany, his adopted land, *Tiefland* survived only four performances at the Metropolitan, though Destinn was entrusted with the chief role. The *première* there occurred on November 23, 1908.

Dresden in 1925. Of it, Edward J. Dent said, "Busoni's real masterpiece is *Doktor Faust,* a work in which he sums up the experiences of a lifetime; it is a drama on a spiritual plane far removed from the normal operatic level, and it will remain one of those operas, like *Les Troyens* of Berlioz, which are revived and presented only at rare and solemn intervals." [6]

The popular composer of *Le Fontane di Roma, I Pini di Roma,* and other sumptuously accoutered orchestral works of derivative nature was persistent in his attentions to the theater. But though he experimented with numerous types, from comic opera to lyric tragedy, not to mention several of his own devising, Respighi succeeded signally, to the detriment of his stage pieces, in remaining a symphonic composer. He became, after Puccini's death, Italy's outstanding composer, and everything he wrote was eagerly performed, all too often with a success that ignored his failure to use pertinently the form he had selected. His operas (some of which he evasively labeled "a story," or "a mystery," or anything he chose) revealed his lack of understanding of the interrelation of orchestra and singers in a musicodramatic whole. They are episodic tone poems with words added. *La Fiamma,* about a witch, was the most acclaimed of his operas. One of them, after Hauptmann's play *Die versunkene Glocke,* was first heard as *La Campana sommersa* in the United States, a year after its *première* in Hamburg in German. The Metropolitan, on November 24, 1928, produced it with Elisabeth Rethberg, Martinelli, De Luca, and Ezio Pinza in the chief roles, Tullio Serafin conducting. Respighi, on hand for this *première,* said fulsomely, "In heaven itself I could not wish for such a production!"

Busoni died in 1924, full of honors and of exasperation at a world that did not understand him, at the age of fifty-eight. Respighi was not quite fifty-seven when death cut short his prolific activity in 1936. Montemezzi

[6] Professor Dent, whose wit flashes out even in his rather solemn biography of Busoni, succeeded only in establishing him as a musical sage almost too great to be listened to. *Doktor Faust,* one of the important documents of neoclassicism, is still on the shelf. As to its music, Donald Jay Grout's analytical footnote (*A Short History of the Opera*) reads like a cry of despair: "The music is not atonal, but tonality is nearly always blurred by one or more of the following devices: pandiatonic chords, parallelism, dissonances against pedal points or ostinato motives, linear dissonant counterpoint, modality and organum-like chords, cross relations, atonal melodies (often including octave transposition of single notes in the line), and polytonal chord combinations."

and Wolf-Ferrari were born five months apart, in 1875 and 1876 respectively. The elder (died 1952) was also the less gifted. Like Mascagni and Leoncavallo, he was primarily a one-opera man, though three of his five operas were produced at the Metropolitan. *Giovanni Gallurese* and *La Notte di Zoraïma* were undoubtedly staged in the hope of cashing in on the prestige of the composer of *L'Amore dei tre re*. They failed utterly.

The very successful *L'Amore dei tre re* is happy in an original libretto by Sem Benelli, somber, powerful, and direct. Fortunately, Montemezzi did not overreach his talents in setting the Benelli book, but was content to provide a musical atmosphere for the action. The result is very satisfactory: without being great music, *L'Amore dei tre re* is an artistic unit executed with taste and restraint. The music responds admirably to the situations and shouts only when they do. This is primarily an absorbing stage play with excellent background music. Philip Hale succinctly described its achievement: "Montemezzi has done in an Italian way for an Italian drama what Debussy in an ultra-modern French way did for the Belgian Maeterlinck."

All four of Wolf-Ferrari's best-known operas were composed to Italian texts, but produced first in Germany to German versions of the librettos. As his name suggests, the composer himself was half German, half Italian. He was similarly divided in artistic loyalties: roughly, his heart was with the Italians, his head with the Germans—Italian melody and sparkle, German soundness and technique. At his best, in three *opere buffe,* he suggests a diminutive modern Mozart. These have been successful in Europe, but in America they have been all but cold-shouldered and still await their due.

The second of these *opere buffe,* the delicious one-act *Il Segreto di Susanna,* was the first to be introduced in New York, where the Philadelphia-Chicago Opera Company, at the Metropolitan, presented Caroline White and Mario Sammarco in the singing roles of the Countess and the Count, with Francesco Daddi in the only other role, that of the mute servant, Sante. The resident company gave its first performance of *Il Segreto* on December 13, 1912, with Farrar, Scotti, and Bada. Bori, however, rather than Farrar, became associated with the role of the Countess, and the revival of 1920–21 was staged in her honor. White and Bori, the latter at Ravinia Park, really popularized *Il Segreto* in Chicago, but it has not been heard at the Metropolitan since 1922.

Even less enduring was Manhattan's response to *Le Donne curiose,* which was a Toscanini triumph at its Metropolitan *première* on January 3, 1912, while *L'Amore medico,* also with Toscanini, having been brought forward unstrategically near the end of the season, on March 25, 1914, suffered almost immediately an undeserved eclipse. Who was to blame? Surely not Gatti-Casazza, who had given to his best conductor Farrar, Jadlowker, and Scotti in *Le Donne curiose,* Bori, Pini-Corsi, and Rothier in *L'Amore medico.* Not the critics, most surely, who were enthusiastic to a man. Nor can the audience be fairly blamed. The truth is that Wolf-Ferrari's brittle evocations of the past—seventeenth-century France, eighteenth-century Venice, and mid-Victorian Piedmont—are too delicate for a vast house like the Metropolitan, where fragile shafts of wit, subtle raillery, and pervasive intimacy are crushed by vast, gilt-surrounded open spaces.

What was once Wolf-Ferrari's best-known, and in America—especially in Chicago—most popular opera, *I Gioielli della Madonna,* a gory Neapolitan melodrama, is the most flagrant latter-day example of Mascagnitis. It can and should be dismissed with the descriptive word that headed Huneker's review of it—"Paste!" Pitts Sanborn called it a Neapolitan *Louise,* which may be precisely true. It is hard to believe that *I Gioielli* is not the calculated—and very successful—potboiler of a most accomplished craftsman, so far is it, in style and quality, from his best work. It is so brash, so catchily tuneful, so thoroughly vulgar, that it reads like a malicious parody of *Cavalleria rusticana.*

At first blush, it had seemed as if the post-Verdian descendants of Ponchielli—the verists, that is—had enlarged the scope of opera, but as the newness of their works dulled, it became evident that they had contributed next to nothing [7] to its development, though they had enlarged its effective repertoire very considerably. They are important in the history of the opera house as a going concern, not of the art form allegedly fostered therein. Nor can all their gifts to the effective repertoire be put down to the credit of *verismo,* for the pure verist strain began to peter out in multiple trickles almost as soon as it appeared. Puccini was never completely a convinced verist, and in *La Bohème,* for instance, he often got swept away into purely romantic utterance. Wolf-Ferrari, except in

---

[7] Is this too summary a way to dismiss the elimination of recitative from Italian opera? We think not, for Verdi had made that elimination inevitable. The substitution of continuous arioso, that flowing style of vocal speech which compromises between pure aria and pure recitative, was seized upon as a veristic *sine qua non,* and has held its ground.

the egregious *Gioielli,* exploited a tradition antedating romanticism, stemming from Mozart, Cimarosa, and Pergolesi.

Verismo, which was inclined to set itself up as realism, just as Zola had come to think of his *naturalisme* as a faithful mirror held up to reality, defeated its professed purpose by its emphasis on certain aspects of life to the almost total exclusion of others. As it approached the condition of Grand Guignol puppetry, the broader and more sensitive talents began to drift away from *verismo,* realizing that it was but one of several methods of treating dramatic material, however contemporary and "true to life." The result, until experimental modernism set in, was a growing eclecticism, chiefly along veristic lines. *Turandot,* produced in 1926, was at once the last, most sumptuous, and, in its very outlandishness, most typical result of this eclecticism, and a presage, significant as coming from one nurtured on the early promises of *verismo,* of Italy's final plunge into the vortex of the modern schools.

CHAPTER XX

Richard Strauss

W<small>AGNER</small> died in 1883. The most important music composed in Germany during the next two decades was a series of big orchestral works by Richard Strauss. They began with *Aus Italien* in 1887 and ended with the *Sinfonia domestica* in 1903. Although all nine of them achieved *succès de scandale,* they did not all win the public that they shocked. But such of them as *Don Juan, Tod und Verklärung, Till Eulenspiegels lustige Streiche, Also sprach Zarathustra,* and *Don Quixote* established the right of a young man who had begun as a conventional composer to assume the leadership of the *Zukunftsmusiker,* those Musicians of the Future orphaned by the deaths of Wagner and Liszt. Even as early as *Aus Italien,* Strauss had hinted, in overt theatricality and programmatic drama, that it would not be long before its composer would be writing operas. Were not these tone poems substantially operas without words and stage action—Wagnerian music drama grafted onto the symphonic poem of Liszt? Strauss's choice was wise: it was less risky to carry the symphonic poem a step farther than to try, in the high noon of Wagner's apotheosis, to do the same with opera. But in 1893, when Wagner had been dead ten years, Strauss himself was a *Meister.* And so he composed *Guntram,* his first opera. A really popular opera was not to come from him for a dozen years: when *Salome* was produced in 1905, Strauss had completed all of his largest orchestral pieces except *Eine Alpensinfonie* (1915).

In the tone poems, Strauss had perfected his own manner, an unmistakable way of arranging musical ideas of any provenance whatever. But when it came to composing *Guntram,* this most assured of eclectics rejected his own manner in favor of borrowing everything—type of subject matter and musical style—from Wagner. Like Wagner, too, he wrote his own libretto, basing it upon those ideas of redemption through love which had haunted Wagner's mind from *Die Feen* to *Parsifal*. The very names of the principal characters—Guntram, Freihild, and Friedhold— might have come from the *Ring*. The music, even to the profiles of its melodies and its closely imitative way of using leitmotivs, led straight back to Bayreuth. *Guntram* may be interpreted either as a public procla- mation that Strauss believed himself equipped to vie with Wagner, using the *Meister's* own weapons, or as a confession that he had not yet devised his own language for the opera house. When *Guntram* was staged on May 10, 1894, at Weimar, most critics voted it tiresome. Strauss himself got two things from the 1894 production: a realization that the public would not stomach his imitation of Wagner—and a wife, Pauline de Ahna, who had sung the role of Freihild. Fourteen years later, Ernest Newman, submitting a minority report, wrote: "Altogether *Guntram* is a great work, the many merits of which will perhaps some day restore it to the stage from which it is now most unjustly banished." And indeed, Strauss was to revise the opera in 1940 for a restaging at Weimar—but the revision did not prove to be a restoration.

In his second operatic venture, Strauss leaped ahead by securing a li- bretto that was as much of a shock to some as his tone poems had been. Shock then was a *sine qua non* of Strauss's technique: he had to have it to work successfully in either concert hall or opera house. The libretto of *Feuersnot,* drawn by Baron Ernst von Wolzogen from his own play *Singgedicht,* is not only shocking but also obscene, combining Rabelais and the German idea of the comic—not a bland mixture. It also con- tained attacks—perhaps suggested by Wagner's assault on the critic Eduard Hanslick as Beckmesser in *Die Meistersinger*—on men who had showed contempt for Strauss's earlier efforts. For this farce, Strauss amended his Wagnerism in two ways. He allowed simple tunes, naïve, folksy, and banal, to contaminate the Wagnerian stream, and from his tone poems he brought over a connoisseur's understanding of harmonic *Schrecklichkeit.* This tempered use of unresolved dissonances, unpre- pared modulations, and warring contrapuntal lines meant that Strauss was all but ready to project into opera his carefully elaborated dual per- sonality. When *Feuersnot* was first sung at Dresden on November 21, 1901, it found him arrived, but with some of his luggage unpacked. It won the meager success that its trial-flight character deserved; it is now seldom revived.

Then Strauss let himself go with *Salome,* in one bound reaching an operatic position as advanced as that which he had attained, years earlier, with purely instrumental music. Rather as a coup, he had managed to secure Oscar Wilde's notorious poetic play, which Germans of that day considered only less lofty than Goethe or Shakespeare. Except for a few brief excisions, Strauss accepted Hedwig Lachmann's faithful German translation of the play just as it was—a self-contained work of minor art so jeweled, static, and immalleable that it did not require music, with which it would not have mixed well.

Strauss did not attempt to mix play and music. Instead, he composed a tone poem with voices as added orchestral instruments, the result designed to accompany a stage spectacle of an aggressively sense-stimulating nature. For the suggestive, heavily scented, rigidly mannered text, he wrote music that exaggerated each of its qualities. The score tells more than it says, is downright aphrodisiac, and ends in a tetanic catalepsy. Throughout *Salome,* the music so overshadows the stage action as to reduce it to mime. Even the greatest of dramatic singers cannot (and probably should not) overcome completely the posed, almost hieratic stasis of the drama. Strauss's *Salome* is more decadent than Wilde's play; it takes itself more seriously. Or, perhaps, it only seems to—with the Strauss of the early 1900's one is never certain. Now that its magnificent tissue has begun to wear a little thin, revealing the cotton shoddy to which the gold threads were stitched, it is tempting to write *Salome* off as a supercraftsman's cold-blooded fabrication. But what remains of the opera is enough, when a powerful singing actress takes the title role, to provide a thumping good evening in the opera house.

Salome, first staged at Dresden on December 9, 1905, dazzled the world with its piled-up brilliance, its quivering energy, its batteries of shattering effects. Because that magnificent envelope contained little, it was certain at last to be seen for what it was: a symptom of the bustling imperial Germany of the early twentieth century, with its boasts, its strutting muscularity, its sumptuary excesses, its wide-open exploration of sexual peculiarities, its glee in the superficials of progress. *Salome* supplied another course of the continuous German champagne banquet of Wilhelm II's expanding empire. It was, though not in any Weberian sense, a national opera. Those able to see through the dazzle detected the synthetic core and said that Strauss lacked conviction. They said that *Salome* had no inwardness; it was whispered about that Strauss's creative peak had been passed. Ending a monograph on Strauss in 1908, Ernest

Newman struck this ominous note: "His new opera, which is to be produced early next year, will probably show whether he is going to realize our best hopes or our worst fears."

Strauss's next opera was *Elektra*. It confirmed the worst fears of many: it was louder, more cacophonous, more unrelievedly psychopathic. *Salome* had emitted an odor of mingled attar and decay; *Elektra* omitted the perfume, and the decay clearly had advanced into decomposition. Here, they said, was stench in terms of music. Hugo von Hofmannsthal, writing the libretto, they said, had distorted Sophocles and made him hideous; Strauss had further uglified the result. It was the end, they said, and Strauss, besides being degenerate, was certainly insane. There could be no doubt that so foul a betrayal of art would soon shrivel up and disappear.

Elektra has done nothing of the sort. Performance after performance has confirmed the opinion, expressed cautiously at first, but then with ever-growing conviction, that *Elektra* is a tragic masterpiece of the very first order. It has not faded: it is as shattering, as profound in terror, as on the night of its *première*. What we can now hear that many of its first baffled listeners could not—their interest being consumed by its most obvious, less significant aspects—is the abiding conviction that holds *Elektra* together. The noise,[1] the supposed cacophony, the reek of neuroses and unleashed passions—all have solidly integral functions. In short, *Elektra* deals with the naked psyche, which knows no reticences. Within the limits imposed by the climactic character of the story, the characters achieve a wholeness that remains the best proof of Strauss's searching care in projecting personalities. So intense was that care in *Elektra* that the tender lyricism of certain interludes escapes the banality that was all too often Strauss's only counterpoise to the horrible and the grotesque.

Elektra is formally and technically more satisfactory than *Salome,* and like it is in one act. Little in the excellent libretto or the music is extraneous to the display of Elektra's disastrous struggle with Fate. To this great issue, Strauss's sure-fire theatrical devices—his pictorialism, his automatic program-making, his underlining of each situation, how-

---

[1] Having created the role of Klytemnestra at the world *première* of *Elektra* at Dresden in 1909, Ernestine Schumann-Heink relinquished that plum forever. She told Henry T. Finck that during the rehearsals Strauss had shouted at Ernst von Schuch, the conductor: "But, my dear Schuch, louder, louder the orchestra; I can still hear the voice of Frau Heink!"

ever small—are tributary. For in *Elektra* he kept his unstanchable cleverness in its place. The extreme chromaticism and dissonance—which sometimes seem willful in *Salome*—are always relevant in *Elektra,* in which they are more abundantly employed. *Elektra,* too, is more singable than *Salome.* The voice parts, instead of doubling instruments in the orchestra, provide throughout the notes of color which sustain the balance of the palette. In *Salome,* the tone-poem base and the stage action all but dispossess the voice; in *Elektra,* Strauss, a master of declamation, establishes the parity of the vocal line without sacrificing the equilibrium of the opera. He does not damp down the orchestra: the singers must work hard. But they work to effect.

At the world *première* of *Elektra* in Dresden on January 25, 1909, the Klytemnestra was Ernestine Schumann-Heink, who never sang the role again after that performance. "It was frightful," she said. "We were a set of mad women. There is nothing beyond *Elektra.* We have lived to reach the farthest boundary in dramatic writing for the voice with Wagner. But Strauss goes beyond him. His singing voices are lost. We have come to a full stop. I believe that Strauss himself sees it." Schumann-Heink was mistaken about many things, but correct in sensing that Strauss would, in some measure, recant in his next stage work.

"This time I shall write a Mozart opera," Strauss said. *Der Rosenkavalier* was the result. Again Hofmannsthal supplied the libretto, this time a farce satire with pathetic overtones set in the Vienna of the mid-eighteenth century. It was written in a broad Viennese dialect that shocked its first Vienna audiences, though many of them used the same idiom. Hofmannsthal's book is a masterly mélange of the ridiculous, the coarse, and the sad, to all of which Strauss gave due consideration. This time he disappointed the expectations of those who had come to regard him as exclusively a purveyor of pathological thrillers or clinical studies. *Der Rosenkavalier* is shocking but not psychotic. The affair between the Marschallin and the seventeen-year-old Octavian is only mildly perverse; Baron Ochs is merely a lecherous country squire.[2] But the libretto is surely no more suggestive than that of *Le Nozze di Figaro* or *Così fan tutte;* compared with *Feuersnot, Salome,* or *Elektra, Der Rosenkavalier* is healthy, bawdy fun, with just a tinge of Hofmannsthal's overripeness.

[2] The complete original text is far more outspoken than the version frequently staged. In the latter, the Marschallin is discovered sitting on a sofa rather than in bed, and some very frank lines have been excised.

Der Rosenkavalier was first sung at Dresden on January 26, 1911. It has become a popular fixture in large opera houses everywhere, being the most popular opera composed since *Madama Butterfly*. The chief reason is its uncommon allure. Not only is *Der Rosenkavalier* the most digestible of Strauss's large operas, but it is also one of the most digestible modern stage works using post-Wagnerian harmonic technique. It is his most lush work, a single lyric outpouring. Oddly, in his "Mozart opera," Strauss cast his spells largely as Viennese waltzes, but the answer to those who would have preferred that he use gavottes and minuets is that his anachronism comes off: Strauss orchestrates a waltz as brilliantly as Ravel. Besides, a gavotte or minuet scored for the full *Rosenkavalier* orchestra would be incorrigibly overdressed.

It would have been better if Strauss had not brought up Mozart, for then *Der Rosenkavalier* could have been judged entirely on its merits, which are great. By coupling his own name with Mozart's, Strauss invited attack from his ill-wishers, among whom was the brilliant and opinionated Cecil Gray, who for years pursued him with unmitigated scorn. "The divinely innocent and virginal Mozartean muse cannot be wooed and won like an Elektra or a Salome," Gray wrote; "all we find in *Der Rosenkavalier* is a worn-out, dissipated *demi-mondaine,* with powdered face, rouged lips, false hair, and a hideous leer. Strauss' muse has lost her chastity. Does he himself actually believe that *Der Rosenkavalier* is like *Figaro?* Are we to regard this declaration as a pathetic self-deception, or as the last crowning perversity? It would be difficult to say, and it is perhaps more charitable to infer the former."

The man who could create the sheer delight of the senses that is the Presentation of the Silver Rose need not have called falsely on the name of Mozart. But Strauss lacked proportion about himself as damagingly as he lacked proportion about the complexity and loudness of his orchestration. *Der Rosenkavalier,* for all its charm, is overfreighted, too noisy, too elaborate for its libretto. A smaller orchestra would have helped. As scored, the emotions of the characters swim up larger than life, and the orchestral riot that breaks forth when, for the first time, the Marschallin's lover leaves her without a kiss is only one sample of a grave disproportion. Also, the opera will always seem, to many otherwise delighted listeners, simply too long, even in the somewhat shortened version almost always performed. These represent major lapses in taste, but not flaws serious enough to prevent *Der Rosenkavalier* from brimming over with lush beauty. Nor is that all. It is peopled with convincing characters, two of whom—the Marschallin and Baron Ochs—are unforgettable full-lengths.

Writing in 1927 of the two most famous of Strauss's post-*Rosenkavalier* operas, Cecil Gray said: "The impurity of style and juxtaposition of dissimilar idioms which was always one of his outstanding faults is carried to a disconcerting extreme in *Ariadne auf Naxos* [1912] and *Die Frau ohne Schatten* [1919]. In the first, Mozart dances a minuet with Mascagni, and Handel with Offenbach; in the second, Wagner is reconciled to Brahms, and Mendelssohn to Meyerbeer. Needless to say, this admixture of styles is not effected with any deliberate satirical intention, but from sheer lack of taste and cynical indifference." Gray's attitude was not unique; many critics said that in his later works, Strauss's indulgence in other people's styles—not to mention the special style of *Der Rosenkavalier*—had got out of bounds.

The later operas, it was noted, had enjoyed titanically publicized *premières*. All of them had solved separate technical problems; all of them contained pages that did not shame the creator of *Elektra* and *Der Rosenkavalier*. But, alas!—so the argument went on—only pages. Strauss was seen as having fallen victim to something closely akin to premature senility. None of his later stage works was granted the cohesiveness, the vigor, or the pervading imagination that had unified *Salome* and its two successors. The technical victories were saluted and described as of dazzling brilliance, but were said to have been over materials awkwardly, or not at all, related to their surroundings, or with materials either appallingly banal or shoddily imitative of Strauss's own past inspirations.

Toward at least some of the Strauss operas later than *Der Rosenkavalier,* however, both critical and audience attitudes began to change, notably in the years after World War II. Of these later operas, the one that aroused the most excited hopes was *Ariadne auf Naxos,* chiefly because it followed immediately on the heels of *Der Rosenkavalier.* The main feature of a Strauss festival at Stuttgart, with the composer himself conducting its *première* on October 25, 1912, it turned out to be a *divertissement* tacked on to a performance of Molière's *Le Bourgeois gentilhomme* (itself with Strauss's vivacious incidental music, in part a modern treatment of Lully's original score). The trick in Hofmannsthal's libretto is a good one: a farce mixed with serious drama, the story of the abandoned Ariadne and the arrival of her savior, Bacchus, being interrupted by five traditional masks from the *commedia dell'arte*.[3] Strauss used an orchestra of thirty-seven players, which intensified the opera's intimate quality, but left it unattractive for very large opera houses even after he had detached it from *Le Bourgeois gentilhomme* and given it a Prologue. When staged appropriately, however, it is an opera of very considerable effectiveness and attraction.

Strauss composed *Ariadne auf Naxos* in two distinct musical idioms that are very adeptly rabbeted together. For Ariadne herself and for Bacchus, the music is of almost Gluckian elevation and severity. For Zerbinetta and the four other masks, it is of *opera buffa* levity, even skittishness. Ariadne's magnificent aria "Es gibt ein Reich" is wonderfully different from Zerbinetta's complex burlesque aria, "Grossmächtige Prinzessin," which latter, being one of the most taxing and difficult solos ever composed, was perhaps incidentally intended to give the *coup de grâce* to the traditional coloratura display piece. Inconsequential *Ariadne auf Naxos* may be, but within its self-respected limitations it everywhere displays the mind and hand of an operatic master worker.

Seven years elapsed between the first version of *Ariadne* and the appearance of Strauss's next opera, *Die Frau ohne Schatten*. When heard at the Vienna Opera on October 10, 1919, this setting of still another Hofmannsthal text proved to be as big as *Ariadne auf Naxos* had been small. Something like an attempt to provide a sequel to *Die Zauberflöte* in terms of *Parsifal*, this extremely homiletic allegory was not a success. Only in recent years has it been developing a loyal, and very vocal, small body of intense admirers, most of whom consider it Strauss's greatest work. It requires exceedingly elaborate staging, a larger supply of really first-rate singing actors than is often available, and a willingness on the part of listeners to stay in the theater the very long time required by its extremely complex (some would say muddled) libretto. Few would now describe *Die Frau ohne Schatten* as an indication of creeping senility; it almost inevitably suggests, however, a light attack of megalomania.

Writing his own libretto for the first time since *Guntram,* Strauss in 1924 brought forth at Dresden (November 4) a "Bürgerliche Komödie mit sinfonischen Zwischenspielen" in two acts: *Intermezzo.* Embarrassingly based on an uncomfortable incident in his own domestic life (Frau Strauss, misreading a letter addressed by a lady to someone else, had taken

---

[3] Two separate entertainments have been prepared for the delectation of M. Jourdain's guests. But Jourdain suddenly orders that they be presented simultaneously rather than seriatim—and *Ariadne auf Naxos* is the result.

it to be a proof of infidelity on her husband's part and had flown into a jealous rage), it is little more than an evanescent *jeu d'esprit.* Comparatively speaking, *Intermezzo* has won few performances. Being autobiography, it should perhaps not be criticized too harshly for sounding like scraps found on the workroom floor after Strauss had completed *Der Rosenkavalier.*

Rebounding from the small dimensions of *Intermezzo* much as he had rebounded from those of *Ariadne auf Naxos* to the giantism of *Die Frau ohne Schatten,* Strauss next seized upon his fifth Hofmannsthal text and turned out the two-act, somewhat Meyerbeerian, pseudo-Greco-Trojan-Egyptian *Die ägyptische Helena,* the flatness of which was a libel on Helen of Troy. Never successful anywhere, even at its Dresden *première* of June 6, 1928, it has won few admirers despite the genuine humor of some of its situations, the unimpaired expertness of Strauss's musical carpentry, and the opportunities it provides for splendid stage pictures. Part of the difficulty with *Die ägyptische Helena* lies in its being an advanced case of Strauss's fixed love for the soprano voice: Helen herself, Hermione, Aithra, Aithra's First and Second Slaves, and the First and Second Elves are all sopranos.[4] This fixation on voices of very high range, whether or not exactly appropriate to the sex or character indicated by the librettist, also shows clearly in the ambiguousness of that female Cherubino, Octavian of *Der Rosenkavalier,* and in the wholly unconvincing attempts to sound like a boy required of the curiously brought-up Zdenka of *Arabella.*

Hugo von Hofmannsthal died in 1929, leaving Strauss the libretto of a Viennese musical comedy which he had drawn from his novelette entitled *Lucidor.* Strauss, remembering (not always vividly) *Der Rosenkavalier,* set it as *Arabella,* as which it was first heard at Dresden on July 1, 1933. The most consistently performed of Strauss's later stage pieces, it has nevertheless never satisfied completely even its ardent admirers. In its remarkably close resemblance to earlier Strauss, in its all but complete lack of fresh or original musical ideas, it finally cannot help suggesting senility—or, at least, the aridity of a once-green field. Charming, sentimentally pretty, some of its melodies are; in its ensembles it is at moments a convincing period piece. As the work of an unknown composer, it would be a hopeful augury; as the considered thoughts of a man of nearly seventy, *Arabella* is very uncomfortably superficial.

[4] "The All-Knowing Muschel," described as "a crystal ball with a voice," is, however, a contralto.

Of the five operas that Strauss composed after *Arabella,* little need—or can—be said. *Die schweigsame Frau,* heard at Dresden on June 24, 1935, is an extraordinarily raucous affair based on Ben Jonson's *Epicœne* or *The Silent Woman.* The libretto was written by Stefan Sweig; this collaboration with a Jew temporarily made Strauss *persona non grata* with Adolf Hitler, who, moreover, resented his past collaboration with another "non-Aryan," Hofmannsthal. After its performance at Munich on July 24, 1938, the one-act *Friedenstag,* its text a political morality play by Joseph Gregor along lines acceptable to the Nazi regime—though it celebrates peace [5]—restored to favor the old gentleman who had composed it. When *Friedenstag* was sung at Munich on October 15 of that year, it shared the bill with a Strauss *première:* that of *Daphne,* the one-act text of which was a "bükolische Tragödie" by Joseph Gregor. This quiet opera ends on an empty stage, with the tree that was Daphne vocalizing wordlessly.

Strauss was seventy-four when that double bill of *Friedenstag* and *Daphne* was heard at Munich. It was too late to hope that he could still, especially in a Reich on the verge of a terrible war, collect his scattered forces sufficiently to compose another opera worthy of his masterpieces. But the end was not yet. On October 28, 1941, the Munich Staatsoper heard the first performance of *Capriccio,* text by the conductor Clemens Krauss and Strauss himself. This turned out to be a closet opera with a totally untheatrical text made up of a long discussion about the qualities desirable in an opera libretto. *Capriccio* has its fascinations, but they are rather for other composers and librettists, students of operatic history, and intellectual critics than for opera audiences.

Strauss died at Garmisch on September 8, 1949. Almost three years later, the last of his fourteen operas was staged at the Festspielhaus, Salzburg (August 14, 1952). With a text by Joseph Gregor based on an idea by Hugo von Hofmannsthal, whom it was once again safe to mention, *Die Liebe der Danae* afforded many of its listeners a pleasant surprise: though grandiose, it was not so bad as they had feared. Unlike Verdi, whose longevity he came near to equaling, Richard Strauss had lived too long for the vitality of his reputation. Although such retroactive criticism

[5] Dyneley Hussey wrote: "Joseph Gregor has packed into one scene lasting little more than an hour the horrors of the Thirty Years' War and the relief that came to a devastated Germany at its ending," adding that the final scene is "a great hymn to Peace" and that the opera is "a finely dramatic work, though not musically very interesting."

is poorly grounded and often wildly unfair, there can be little doubt that the thinness and comparative unoriginality of the operas of Strauss's last three decades cast a pall of doubt over his earlier operas—except the small handful of unquestioned masterpieces with which he holds a leading position in the repertoire of opera houses everywhere, and by which alone it is fair to assay the fineness of his talents as a composer of operas.

CHAPTER XXI

From Massenet to Debussy

No realist could feel that French opera had sustained an irreparable loss with the death of Gounod in 1893. The man who, thirty-four years earlier, had created a sentimental masterpiece in *Faust* had long since ceased to be an active worker in the field.[1] From his foremost colleague, the octogenarian Thomas, nothing new could be expected after the silence of a decade. But Saint-Saëns was at the height of his stanchless, if not overvigorous, fecundity, and moreover, Gounod's true successor had already declared himself. *Manon,* in some respects Massenet's most satisfactory opera, was already nine years old, and showed that the disciple was in no way inferior to the master—he was just more of the same thing. While there is a distinct sense of anticlimax in Italian opera after Verdi, there is none in French opera after Gounod. Verdi was an irreplaceable genius, Gounod a typical *chef d'école.* Thus, the composer of *Otello* and *Falstaff* set standards beyond the capability of even so gifted a man as Puccini, whereas the composer of *Faust* and *Roméo et Juliette* established nothing more than a fashion. After accepting that fashion uncritically, to be his successor—and Thomas's—required a flair for the theater and a store of sentimental emotionalism. These Massenet had in abun-

[1] To repeat, Gounod simply retreated into quite sincere if showy religiosity, but not because he had failed. This explains his not following up the immense success of *Roméo et Juliette.* His return to opera ten years later is a true mystery, and it is scarcely surprising that his last three operas, all hastily executed, failed. But *Faust* continued to reign at the Opéra, *Roméo* at the Lyrique. And it should not be forgotten that Massenet and many others were familiar with the verdant beauties of *Mireille* and the wit and good manners of *Le Médicin malgré lui* and *Philémon et Baucis.*

dance; besides, he was a wily craftsman. His success was inevitable: he found French opera set in patterns acceptable to the widest public, and tirelessly, in a long series of stage pieces with music, he did nothing to change it.

Jules Massenet, for all his desire to please, is less pompously banal than Gounod. He had surer taste, which usually kept him from taking on subjects too large for his limited palette, and which held the intensity of his discipleship within decent limits. Certain elements of Gounod's recipe for success he never borrowed, probably for reasons of temperament: he has no bumptiousness, no knack of contriving thumping tunes, no Soldiers' Chorus. Gounod and Massenet were both unctuous, but nothing in the latter, not even Thaïs' death in an incredible odor of sanctity, approaches the holy bilge of the *Faust* finale. What restrains Massenet is a pervasive sense of proportion, a latent wit that does not allow stage sanctity to be anything more than stage sanctity. But he and his audiences pay for his taste: he lacks energy, his scores are almost overtly feminine (he was soon nicknamed "la fille de Gounod"), and, in avoiding overseriousness, he often sacrifices conviction. His best, most believing pages are devoted to love, deliciously on—but hardly ever over —the precipice of sexual delight. There is an excess of sugar in his musical stream, and yet, except in two or three instances (notably the "Méditation" from Act II of *Thaïs*) he never cloys as Gounod sometimes seems purposely to do.

As musicodramatic works of art, the operas of Massenet are not to be taken seriously. In his long career as a working composer, he was first and last a purveyor of entertainment. As such, he was enormously successful, and as such he should be judged. His operas, with few exceptions, are, in effect, plays with music—alternatives for theatergoers, not musts for operagoers. They require, for effective projection, not singers but actors and actresses who can sing. Many of them were composed with specific actors and actresses in mind, and his conception of opera as entertainment is a cornerstone of Massenet's art. While his way of working achieved its purpose at the time, it has proved a long-range loss. Some of Massenet's scores, successful when first produced, waned with the passing of the singers for whom they were written, and soon expired. In the United States, the retirement of Mary Garden and Geraldine Farrar shelved several of Massenet's most entertaining works, and in France itself only a small proportion of his twenty-seven publicly performed operas [2] holds the stage. Even more than with most operas, to hear a well-sung, but poorly acted and staged, performance of a Massenet score is not to have heard it at all. The same has been peculiarly true of the large majority of French operas ever since, and contributes saliently to their early disappearance from the repertoire in a world of operas mostly staged badly and acted execrably.

Not until his fifth performed opera—*Manon*—did Massenet find a subject that brought out in happiest proportion his most reliable assets. A precocious Prix de Rome, he had begun his operatic career in a comic mood successfully in *Don César de Bazan,* his second try. Two further essays in comedy followed. After two oratorios came *Le Roi de Lahore,* on a subject from Hindu mythology which brought him ponderable success, including praise from Tchaikovsky. In it, his characteristic idiom is further uncovered: the famous arioso from Act IV, "Promesse de mon avenir," is a full-blown example of Massenet's sensual-ecstatic love music.

Hérodiade was even more successful. Its *première,* at the Théâtre de la Monnaie, Brussels, on December 19, 1881, won the composer a personal ovation. Its Paris first (oddly, in Italian), three years later, with Maurel and the De Reszkes, confirmed his growing reputation. It is curious that this typical French grand opera, with, in this case, a touch of Meyerbeer to correct the Gounodian blandness, did not reach the Opéra until forty years after its composition. By November 8, 1909, when *Hérodiade* was first sung in New York—seventeen years later than in New Orleans—Massenet had become so popular in the United States that *Manon* was being used, the same evening, to open the Metropolitan's Brooklyn season. *Hérodiade,* opening Hammerstein's fourth, and final, season at the Manhattan, had Gerville-Réache as Herodias, Cavalieri as Salomé, Dalmorès as Jean, and Renaud as Herod. It has much perfumed, voluptuous music, including "Vision fugitive" (only yesterday sung to death), but it has not reached the Metropolitan, and for obvious reasons. It is not the competent evening's pastime Massenet guarantees at

---

[2] One of them, *Marie-Magdeleine,* came into being as an oratorio (1873), with Viardot-García as the Magdalen. Reformed prostitutes, brought into favor with romanticism, had been the rage since Hugo's *Marion Delorme* (1831), and all Paris crowded into the Odéon to hear Massenet's suggestive pages. For the naughtiness of the music cannot be doubted: the austere D'Indy might have had it in mind when he spoke of Massenet's "érotisme discret et quasi-religieux."

his best, and, moreover, Strauss's version of much the same events, in *Salome,* has made Massenet's opera seem, by comparison, suitable for student performances at a female academy.

For his next opera, Massenet went to a touching love story that had already attracted such diverse talents as Halévy, Balfe, and Auber, the last of whom turned out a score that was a favorite of Charles Dickens. This was the eighteenth-century *L'Histoire de Manon Lescaut et du chevalier des Grieux,* by the Abbé Prévost, which Henri Meilhac and Philippe Gille adapted for Massenet. First produced at the Opéra-Comique, on January 19, 1884, *Manon* was an instantaneous and enduring success. By October 16, 1893, it had chalked up two hundred performances at the Comique, and had brought more than a million francs into the box office. With it, Massenet assumed the leadership of French opera and, as he was professor of composition at the Conservatoire from 1878 to 1896, of French music as a whole, so venerated was the eminence from which he imposed his idiom. After *Manon* everything from his pen was breathlessly awaited. He soon saw this charming score coursing through the civilized world, Liverpool leading the way with an English version in 1885.

When Puccini set the same subject matter almost ten years after the *première* of Massenet's *Manon,* many wondered at the boldness of the junior who had dared invite comparison with a work to which a large section of the European public was almost idolatrously attached. But it is now plain that Puccini had only its popularity to fear. His *Manon Lescaut* is, in some respects, a more interesting score than *Manon,* its superior in dramatic unity and impact. When he composed *Manon Lescaut,* Puccini was not yet the master of dramatic craft he grew into only a few years later, and he was not equipped to set his libretto with the rich theatrical sophistication that Massenet had acquired. A few years later, Puccini might have insisted on changes in the libretto which would have made it as good a thing as Meilhac and Gille's—the anticlimactic fourth act, with Manon's by that time unaffecting death outside New Orleans, would have been junked, and Act III capped as neatly as the last act of *Madama Butterfly.* Even as it is, the atmosphere of *Manon Lescaut* is boldly close to that of Prévost's tale, and so has a more astringent quality than that of *Manon,* where the amoral baggage has been ladyfied into an erring frail, and the rather shady Chevalier des Grieux robbed of his vices. Not all of this was accomplished by the librettists; a large part must be credited to Massenet's talent for the charming and the idyllic, and much of *Manon*'s popularity—it had been given 1,975 times at the Opéra-Comique by December 31, 1960, 1,649 of them in the preceding half-century—depends on the concentration of those qualities.[3]

Manon is the best representative of the type of opera Massenet made peculiarly his own, a type so beloved by the public that, even during his lifetime, there was much more or less expert poaching on his preserve. Short, voluptuously sweet melody, entrancing but rarely ambitious harmonies, and pervading feminine charm come effortlessly from Massenet. These operas throb throughout with a somniferous lack of energy, and lull the listener by their genteel tameness. Cupping his ear to Gounod and Thomas for the *tournure* of his melodic ideas, Massenet cribbed devotedly certain structural devices, notably the use of leitmotivs (which he interpreted with academic smoothness and lack of imagination), from Wagner. In *Esclarmonde* (1889), he simply rewrote Wagner for the French market, and fastidiously emasculated him in the process. The official French Wagnerian, Reyer, said enigmatically that *Esclarmonde* had many "délicieuses surprises." Generally, Massenet was content to keep his Wagnerism as a spicing and leave the rest to his native ancestors.

Every year or so, a new opera—and sometimes two—made its way from Massenet's atelier to the stage. Usually they were successes, but with such a strong family likeness that what is true of one is true of most of them.

More than a dozen of Massenet's operas have reached New York and —during Mary Garden's active career there—Chicago, and there is no doubt that they have been as well represented in some European capitals. But outside France, few have managed to maintain themselves on the boards, and in the United States, only *Manon* and *Thaïs,* the latter precariously, can be said to be in the repertoire. Besides these, several— *Werther, La Navarraise, Sapho, Le Jongleur de Notre Dame,* and *Don Quichotte*—invite comment because of variation from the mold or because of unusual historic interest.

[3] In a one-act "epilogue" to *Manon,* presented at the Comique in 1894, Massenet showed a moralizing Des Grieux playing the strict uncle to his youthful nephew, and forbidding him to marry the girl of his choice because she is poor and a commoner. He relents when the girl, dressing up to look like a portrait of Manon that Des Grieux always has by him, turns out to be Manon's niece. Hence the title, *Le Portrait de Manon.*

Thaïs is a pattern opera of high quality. It has the "Méditation," [4] and it has a title role that, having been written for Sibyl Sanderson, a dazzling young American singer whom Massenet intensely admired, not unnaturally continued to captivate ambitious young sopranos, from Mary Garden to Marjorie Lawrence. It has, also, a smoldering book based on Anatole France's suave and superficial re-creation of early Christian Alexandria, and therefore calls for the most sumptuous efforts of a Joseph Urban. It is high entertainment of a kind that demands no collaboration on the part of the audience. The shifting between murky, sensual religiosity and elegant Eastern pornography affords a contrast that is extraordinarily piquant.

Werther is an opera of the *Manon* type, with strong infusions of weak verism. The undramatic libretto is derived from Goethe's *Die Leiden das jungen Werther,* and Massenet, who was not at his best in portraying virtuous women, set it without conviction. It has, therefore, some of the pensive charm of that generally dull book which was influential in starting a Continental suicide wave. Even though its hero (like Goethe's) shoots himself on Christmas Eve, Massenet's *Werther* can be depended upon to produce no such violent reaction. It is, in fact, something of a bore, though the music is so skillfully contrived that musically it represents an advance on his other stage works. As early as *Manon,* Massenet was flirting with Wagner—and perhaps the worst thing that can be said about this clever composer is that he tried to reconcile Wagner with Gounod and thus get the best of two conflicting worlds. The orchestra and the vocal line may often seek quite separate ends. Unfortunately, both Werther and Charlotte are a bit tiresome (who now reads *The Sorrows of Werther?*). Nevertheless, Jean de Reszke had an affection for the title role and gave the opera its first spurt of popularity in America (Metropolitan, April 19, 1894). Primarily a tenor's opera [5]—"Pourquoi moi reveiller?" is almost as popular as "Le Rêve" from *Manon*—nevertheless, it owed its few later American resuscitations to Farrar and Garden, both of whom thought Charlotte a good acting role.

Hammerstein, at the height of his Massenetis, gave New York a more

---

[4] It had turned up originally in the incidental music to *Les Érinnyes,* Leconte de Lisle's drama casually borrowed from Aeschylus. Although the Parnassian poet faltered in adapting from the Greek, Massenet erred more discordantly when he set Electra's libation to her father, the dead Agamemnon, to the "Méditation."

[5] Yet Massenet rewrote Werther's part for the silver-voiced Italian baritone, Mattia Battistini.

piquant sample of his idol's unconvincing flirtation with verism. This was *Sapho* (1897), a setting of Daudet's novel (then considered shocking) of the Paris demimonde. Massenet had composed it for Calvé, but Garden sang it for Hammerstein. Long after New York had forgotten *Werther* and *Sapho,* Garden was interpreting with unaltered verve both Charlotte and Fanny Legrand for enthusiastic Chicagoans. But *Sapho* was the waning of a flirtation which had had its moment of real passion in 1894, when Massenet, taking the measure of *Cavalleria rusticana,* turned out, in *La Navarraise,* an imitation of *verismo,* changing it subtly into *vérisme.*

Massenet had composed *La Navarraise* with Calvé in mind, and for Covent Garden, where it was heard on June 20, 1894, with Alvarez, Gilbert, Plançon, and Dufriche supporting her. Neither Calvé nor Sir Augustus Harris, manager of the theater, failed Massenet. The performance was worthy of Belasco in its violent verisimilitude, and Calvé was demonic. Bernard Shaw, giving that *première* his rare stamp of approval, reported that "she was a living volcano, wild with anxiety, to be presently mad with joy, ecstatic with love, desperate with disappointment, and so on in ever culminating transitions through mortification, despair, fury, terror, and finally—the mainspring breaking at the worst of the strain—silly maniacal laughter." In short, this violent, swift, and noisy opera runs the gamut of *Cavalleria.* Calvé was the Anita of the first Paris and Metropolitan (December 11, 1895) productions. *La Navarraise* fitted her so well that no one since has been able to do Anita justice. Gerville-Réache came closest to it, but two such gifted singing actresses as Farrar and Garden all but failed in their interpretations of the Navarraise.

Just as Massenet rewrote the title role of *Werther* for Battistini, he remodeled, at Garden's request, the tenor role in *Le Jongleur de Notre Dame* for soprano. Never was a remodeling more fortunate. Jean, the hero of Anatole France's little story, *L'Etui de nacre,* on which the opera is based, is a rather feminine adolescent more suitable for female than male impersonation, and Garden played Jean with the tenderness of real inspiration. She first sang the role at the Manhattan, on November 27, 1908, with Renaud as Boniface, a part he had created at the Monte Carlo *première,* and with Dufranne. So identified did the opera become with her characterization that when Hammerstein attempted to please a small group of traditionalists (*Le Jongleur* was less than eight years old at the time) by reverting to a male Jean, he had to add *Cavalleria* to the bill in order to fill a house that would have been all but empty for a Gardenless

Jongleur. With Garden's retirement, *Le Jongleur* vanished from American opera houses, and it is unlikely that it will reappear unless another singing actress of her stamp comes to the fore—a tenor could scarcely undertake a role still so inextricably connected with her name. Musically, the loss is negligible. *Le Jongleur* is Massenet at his least original and most eclectic, with such diverse sources as plainchant, Gounod, and Debussy at his blandest contributing to a background of vague charm and suave religiosity. Garden transcended it: her moving and pathetic performance lent the opera factitious importance.

Le Jongleur dates from 1902. During the next ten years, Massenet unwisely composed, among other things, three ponderous operas on classical themes, in which he tried to be profound, marmoreal, and Gluckian. But the capabilities were not there, and all three, despite strenuous efforts by the devoted contralto Lucy Arbell, failed to attract audiences. In 1910, however, at Monte Carlo, Raoul Gunsbourg produced *Don Quichotte,* and Massenet had his last success—which he owed, once again, to a great artist. Chaliapin interpreted the Don with such sympathy and pathos that the opera was in demand for twenty-five years when he could be secured for the role. The libretto is a marvelously silly concoction, the music workmanlike but devoid of melodic inspiration. With these tawdry materials, Chaliapin, by *force majeure* and sheer personal magnetism, worked wonders.

Massenet was the last French operatic composer to combine fecundity with success. He continued the Gounod-Thomas tradition into the twentieth century, making it palatable by spicing it heavily (the French have ever been masterful with sauces) with Wagnerian harmonies, Debussyan atmosphere, any number of veristic tricks, and his own lack of adventurousness. He added nothing, but his obvious interest in stepping up the histrionic side of the singers' function and the entertainment side of the opera as a whole (though in the latter his activities often misfired) influenced a whole generation of composers, most of them thoroughly second-rate.

A tireless pedagogue, Massenet taught many of his later competitors, though the best of them—Alfred Bruneau and Gustave Charpentier—revolted, owing, in their most vital aspects, little to him. Bruneau, for instance, most of whose operas were settings of Zola stories, used Wagnerian means to produce veristic results. Charpentier, as eclectic as his master, but apparently more sincere, and with more individuality of approach, was as meager in output as Bruneau was fertile. Yet, in some respects, *Louise,* the first of his two operas, was epoch-making.

The story of Charpentier as a composer is that of a man obsessed with his own struggles and dreams and with the city in which he struggled and dreamed. In a very real sense, most of his music is autobiographical, that for *Louise* and its much later sequel, *Julien,* being more obviously so only because they are attached to Charpentier's own librettos about an unhappy Parisian artist. *Louise* is a paean to the multifaceted Paris of the artist's imagining—a prolongation, in rhapsodic strophes, of Murger's *vie de Bohème.* His lifelong interest in stimulating the mental and artistic life of the poor working girls of Paris, especially sempstresses like his Louise, and his perpetual Bohemianism of garb and manner had their roots in a preoccupation with his own Montmartre past. To the first of his essentially vulgar operas, these obsessions gave conviction, vigor, and a kind of mesmeric force. Charpentier's weakness—failure to grow up, flight into an idealized past—is *Louise*'s strength, contributing to its best pages a brimming youthfulness and to its worst a tasteless mooncalfishness. When it was first produced, *Louise* was attacked as a glorification of vice: in fact, it has the total amorality of a man drugged by the vision of a certain kind of existence. Musically, the vision is scored to Wagner, Puccini, and Massenet. For many of his leitmotivs, Charpentier took the street cries of Paris. He accepted Puccini's romantic reading of verism, and enlisted Massenet's voluptuous melodic line for his sentimental and erotic crises, notably in the lush "Depuis le jour." The result was sure-fire, and *Louise* was hailed—and reviled—in a way that made it seem rather more important than it was.

Louise opened at the Opéra-Comique on February 2, 1900, and conquered at once. From being just another Prix de Rome, Charpentier was catapulted to international fame, and he was fortunate in finding, though not immediately, a singing actress who for more than thirty years put Louise among the first, if it was not indeed the very first, of an impressive series of musical portraits. This was Mary Garden, who was in Paris awaiting her opportunity when the Charpentier opera burst upon the scene. She did not create the name role, but understudied Marthe Rioton, the first Louise, who was in ill-health. Her chance came two months after the *première,* when Rioton was unable to go on for the third and fourth acts, and Garden found herself, after this world debut, catapulted much as Charpentier had been.[6] *Louise* had been sung 956 times at the Comique

[6] Telling Carl Van Vechten of her debut, Garden said: "The audience, you may be sure, was none too pleased at the prospect of having to listen to a Mlle Garden of whom they had never heard. Will you believe me when I tell you that I was never less nervous? . . . I must have succeeded, for I sang *Louise*

through 1950, when it was remounted with décors by another celebrant of Paris, Maurice Utrillo.

In the sequel to *Louise,* the curious, pathological, thoroughly anti-climactic *Julien* (1913), Charpentier confessed his inability to do more than walk around the old battlefield, pointing out the landmarks. It is *Louise* over again—without the drama, the novelty, the passionate youthful charm. At the Metropolitan, in 1914, despite Farrar and Caruso in the leading roles, *Julien* could not get beyond a fifth performance. To keep the record of Charpentier's Louiseolatry straight, it should be added that he provided a special bit of music for Grace Moore's motion picture based on the opera, which was made in Paris in the late 1930's.

One person who was not impressed by *Louise* was Claude Debussy, the outstanding genius of modern French music. A onetime Wagnerite, Debussy was, by the time *Louise* began to carry everything before it, in full flight from the spells and sensual enchantments of Bayreuth. Even as Charpentier was celebrating his first triumphs, Debussy was compounding a counterirritant. In 1892, he had seen a performance of Maeterlinck's mystical, complexly symbolic *Pelléas et Mélisande,* and had been attracted to this offshoot of *imagisme,* the French variety of which, in the poetry of Mallarmé and Verlaine, had already inspired some of his loveliest songs, as well as the *Prélude à L'Après-midi d'un faune.* He started to write incidental music for the Maeterlinck play, changed his mind at mid-career, and then decided to use most of the play itself, only very slightly altered, as the libretto of a full-length opera that would be a Gallic *défi* to Wagnerism.

Just as Debussy's earlier operatic efforts had proved abortive, it seemed that he might never finish this one: one version that he carried to its end did not pass his exquisite critical eye. It may have been, despite him, too Wagnerian. He began a new version in 1895, and finished it seven years later. The production was the culmination of a newspaper scandal: Maeterlinck had insisted vainly that the role of Mélisande be given to his common-law wife, Georgette Leblanc, who had played it in the speaking version. But Albert Carré, the manager of the Comique, had already promised the role to Mary Garden, and despite threats of a duel, legal action, and all types of other nuisances, he stuck to his promise. The *première,* on April 30, 1902, suffered from factional fighting

over two hundred times at the Opéra-Comique after that. The year was 1900, and I had made my debut on Friday, April 13."

within the theater. Debussy was too independent a spirit to be discomfited by the scorn and abuse of the French music critics, among whom Romain Rolland was a notable exception. Rolland called *Pelléas et Mélisande* "one of the three or four outstanding achievements in French musical history."

But the music critics and artistic diehards from all camps were quickly overruled by the persistent enthusiasm of a discriminating and influential wing of the Paris public. To this, at first, slightly cultish popularity the excellence of the Comique cast contributed largely. Garden turned in a well-nigh perfect performance, which she continued to polish until it became one of the superlative experiences provided by the singing stage. Her piquant French, always with a delicious alien note, served her particularly well as Mélisande, "a princess from a far land." Jean Périer, her vis-à-vis, was a singer of exquisite refinement, and besides—what is of urgent importance in this opera—as poetically personable as Garden herself. Their colleagues were also first-rate artists: Gerville-Réache was Geneviève, Dufranne was Golaud, and Felix Vieuille was Arkel. André Messager, a second-rate composer but a conductor of genius, led the orchestra.

Debussy's artistic conscience, working against a Wagnerism he had come to loathe, failed him, for *Pelléas* is, in one sense, more Wagnerian than Wagner. In it, the ideal of Peri and Caccini, of Gluck, of Wagner—that the music of an opera should obsequiously serve the text—found so comprehensive an embodiment that its score is all but without significance if separated from text and action. In fact, had the critics been somewhat more perceptive, they might have attacked Debussy, not as a Wagnerian heretic, but as one who had carried Wagner's professed ideals to the point of *reductio ad absurdum.*

But all that the critics could see were the superficials, which were remote from anything in Wagner's practice: the orchestra, reduced rather than expanded, until it is scarcely more than a chamber ensemble; the vocal line a susurrus of muffled half-voices conversing to music, moving up and down in languid intervals (*Pelléas* is, quite as much as Wilde's *Salomé,* Whistler's "nocturnes," and Conder's fans, self-consciously *fin-de-siècle*); the absence of the slightest hint of lyric separateness; and the nervous insistence on muffled volume. Moreover, while Debussy created a music drama that, as such, Wagner could not have criticized, in every other way he diverged from the *Meister,* most glaringly when ringing the changes on Wagnerian devices. For example, instead of using the Wagnerian leitmotiv, he evolved what Vincent d'Indy called "pivot themes," which "send out harmonic rays in all directions, rays that serve to present the musical speech in the ambiance suited to it." Also, Debussy's use of separate timbres—and combinations of timbres—to hallmark certain situations and symbolic ideas had been hinted at only in the most rudimentary manner by Wagner.

On the basis of superficials, the challenge was taken up, and awkwardly, by traditionalists, in 1902. Now, when *Pelléas* is no longer a shocking work—gone are the days when it was possible to refer, as one New York critic did in 1908, to its "combinations of tones that sting and blister and pain and outrage the ear"—these same superficials may baffle those who approach the opera for the first time. *Pelléas et Mélisande* did not establish an easily imitated pattern, and operas that have followed it do not prepare us for listening to it.[7] There are those to whom *Pelléas,* symbol-freighted, twilit, exhaling alternately *tedium vitae* and passionate frustration, will always be a trying experience. The real point is that any open ears, however prejudiced, however conditioned, will find experience in *Pelléas.* For those most susceptible to it, it has the compelling intensity of a dream, beautiful, piteous, evanescent, and, above all, true to its own poetic reality.

---

[7] Frederick Delius' *A Village Romeo and Juliet* might, if we had opportunities to hear it. Originally produced at Berlin in 1907 as *Romeo und Julia auf dem Dorfe,* it later received performance in England through the enthusiasm of Sir Thomas Beecham. The frequently played intermezzo, "The Walk to the Paradise Garden," is typical of the music in the opera. An English-born German, who spent some of his life in Florida and most of it in France, Delius was at his best a second-rate Debussy. His only other opera of interest, *Koanga,* is a setting of George W. Cable's *The Grandissimes,* a once-famous American novel of the vanished South.

CHAPTER XXII

A Digression on Folk Opera

IN Italy, France, and Germany, the distinct national musical idioms, quoting, derived from, or based on the usages of local folk song, were largely dissolved in the shifting stream of the classic and romantic schools. This absorption had not taken place in Russia when Glinka and his nationalizing followers first used folk tunes and colors in their operas. They therefore suggested to composers in such other countries as possessed more or less clearly differentiated national idioms a technique for incorporating elements of those idioms into opera. Glinka was not the first to put folk and folklike music into an opera, but he was the first to depend for many of his special effects upon the untamed strangeness of such a national idiom or group of idioms. In Russia, the folk opera, which was in part a rebellion against imported—in particular, Italian—elegancies, happened to beget a succession of talented men whose national color was caught up in the evolution of larger issues, and so transcended the circumscribed condition of folk art. The folk opera came into being precisely in countries that felt a spiritual need to assert their national selfhood. Even *Der Freischütz* was, besides being a romantic protest against the influence of foreigners, a voice of resurgent, post-Napoleonic Germany.

The national opera struck roots early in Poland, where a movement to keep the national culture alive and to win back political independence from the three countries that had gobbled her up won the support of many artists and intellectuals. Among them was Stanislaw Moniuszko, ten years Chopin's junior, a prolific composer of songs. Moniuszko, unlike his Russian counterparts, was a highly trained musician; he became successively a church organist, a conductor at the Warsaw Opera, and a conservatory professor. Among his fifteen operas, *Halka* has become a touchstone of Polish culture. Given first in an amateur production at Vilna on December 20, 1847, it received professional mounting in that city on February 16, 1854. A two-act tragedy of peasant life, it was later enlarged to four acts, in which form it began its highly successful career at Warsaw on January 1, 1858, reaching its thousandth performance there on October 8, 1935.

Halka seems to lack the force and individuality to remain on non-Polish stages. Moniuszko clearly patterned its structure after Glinka's most famous opera, but the Polish folk element is asserted vigorously throughout, particularly in scenes in which the stage action is dancing. The chief weakness of *Halka,* as with *A Life for the Tsar,* is the conventionality of its transitions. Although several of Moniuszko's later operas—most notably *Straszny dwór* (*The Haunted Castle,* Warsaw, September 28, 1865)—demonstrated greater certainty in solving structural problems, none of them has approached *Halka* in continued popularity. Wherever large numbers of Poles gather, a performance of *Halka* becomes a foreordained ceremony.

The Czechs, another national group held in subjection, produced a more vigorous school of nationalistic music. Its leader was Bedřich Smetana, a composer of charm and definite, if limited, genius. Smetana wrote many operas, all of which contain numbers separately salvageable for concert performance. Several of his operas have remained popular in Czechoslovakia, and one of them—*Prodaná nevěsta* (*The Bartered Bride*)—became the best known and most widely performed of all folk operas. His first opera, *Braniboři v Čechách* (*The Brandenburgers in Bohemia*), had been heard in Prague on January 5, 1866. *The Bartered Bride* was produced there only a little less than five months later (May 30, 1866).

The Bartered Bride was originally a two-act Singspiel, but was heard in two different revised versions in 1869 and in its final three-act form in 1870. It is now usually presented with the spoken dialogue replaced by accompanied recitative. It is a lighthearted, swiftly paced, vividly colored, and rhythmically vigorous panel of Bohemian peasant life, in effect a very superior operetta. Its original libretto, by Karel Sabina, is said to be riotously funny, and much of its broad humor has survived translation into both German (in which it is often sung—as *Die verkaufte Braut*—outside Czechoslovakia) and English. The energetic, boldly scored overture, the first-act polka, the "Stuttering Song" and furiant in Act II, and the lyrical "Alone at last" in Act III have become universal favorites. There is a hint of Mozart in this graceful, apposite music, and the booby Wenzel is not too remote a cousin to Papageno.

Less successful than *The Bartered Bride* was Smetana's *Dalibor,* given its *première* at Prague on May 16, 1868, as part of the ceremonial laying of the cornerstone of the new National Theater (the opera itself was sung in a huge temporary building). Although a pseudohistorical tragedy of Bohemian life, *Dalibor* was less pictorially bright and folklike, more "international" in idiom, than *The Bartered Bride*—and it was therefore attacked as Wagnerian by the Prague critics. It was dropped after only five performances; two attempts to revive it failed; only two years after Smetana's death in 1884 did *Dalibor* finally catch on in Prague.

Much happier for Smetana—who had undergone the horror of becoming completely deaf in 1874—was the fate of his sixth opera, *Hubička (The Kiss),* a smaller, more intense successor to the comedy of *The Bartered Bride.* Composed simultaneously with the well-known string quartet subtitled *From My Life,* which is in part compacted of personal tragedy, *The Kiss* is almost gay. Its libretto, by the pseudonymous Czech poetess Eliška Krásnohorská, deals charmingly with the difficulties of young peasants in love. The opera was staged at Prague on November 7, 1876, and was an immediate and lasting success, perhaps because in it, again, Smetana had evoked the folk colors of Bohemia with lyrical expressiveness.

Two operas later, Smetana came up with what many students of Czech music regard as his masterpiece: *Libuše* (Libussa was a mythical eponymous ancestress of the Czech nation). It was chosen for the opening of the new National Theater on June 11, 1881; when that building burned to the ground shortly after, another theater was quickly erected to take its place—and that building, too, was inaugurated (1883) with *Libuše.* This symbolic evocation of the past and future of the Czechs occupies among Smetana's serious operas the position of *The Bartered Bride* among his comedies. His harmonic idiom had begun to evolve swiftly away from the relative simplicities of folk usage, but the unmistakable Czech coloration still marks *Libuše* as the music of a highly talented composer responsive to folk colors.

Antonín Dvořák, Smetana's successor as the dean of Czech music, achieved his most striking results as an instrumental and religious composer. As a composer of operas, Dvořák was prolific but not, by and large, fruitful. Of his ten operas, one was a failure so complete that it was never published or revived; others won considerable suffrage among Prague audiences, but failed to survive transplantation outside their native land. Only the ninth—heard thirty-one years after Dvořák had composed the first—won any real success abroad. This was *Rusalka* (Prague, March 31, 1901), Jaroslav Kvapil's libretto [1] for which handled the theme of love between a mortal man and a girl who is or has become a sprite or undine, which is also the theme of Dargomizhsky's *Russalka,* Adam's *Giselle,* Tchaikovsky's *Swan Lake,* and Puccini's *Le Villi.* The opera is drenched in Czech coloring, which is most persuasively emotional and lyric in the undine's apostrophe to the moon in Act I, an aria that has long led a concert life of its own.[2]

Among the many operas of Leoš Janáček, only *Její pastorkyňa* (1904), better known outside Czechoslovakia as *Jenufa* or *Her Foster Daughter,* was at all known abroad up to the time of World War II. Janáček was not so much a Czech composer as a locally Moravian one; his music therefore shows Polish and Russian influences generally absent from the music of his colleagues. He evolved a very individual style, terse, ejaculatory, and, because he was a lifelong propagandist of Moravian culture and artistic nationalism, dyed with the raw primes of local folk music. *Jenufa,* which does not quote a single authentic folk tune, has the quality of folk opera projected by veristic means. After its *première* at Brünn (Brno) on January 21, 1904, it waited twelve years for a Prague production. Two years later, with a performance in Vienna, it began a tour of the world that took it to, among many other opera houses, the Metropolitan in New York.

[1] Kvapil borrowed for his libretto some ideas from Gerhart Hauptmann's highly successful play *Die versunkene Glocke,* on which Ottorino Respighi based his opera *La Campana sommersa* (1927).

[2] A third Czech opera composer of nationalizing tendency has remained all but unperformed outside Czechoslovakia, though sometimes popular there. He was Zdenko Fibich (1850–1900). His ten operas, produced between 1874 and 1900, include *Hippodameia,* a "melodramatic triptych"—*The Wooing of Pelops* (1890), *Tantalus' Atonement* (1891), and *Hippodameia's Death* (1891). *Sarka* (Prague, December 28, 1897) has been considered his masterpiece; it is an intensely national folk opera. Fibich died on October 15, 1900; on November 9, *The Fall of Arcona,* his last opera, was produced in Prague. Overshadowed by both Smetana and Dvořák, Fibich was nonetheless a highly individual composer, introspective and romantic in his musical moods.

Benefiting from the renaissance of opera which followed World War II, others of Janáček's increasingly individualistic and harmonically stringent operas have begun to win fame and audiences outside Czechoslovakia. Most successful of them has been *Kata Kabanová,* with a libretto based on A. N. Ostrovsky's play *Groza (The Storm).* First heard at Brünn on October 23, 1921, *Kata Kabanová* has been described by Paul Stefan as "the story of a Slavonic Madame Bovary" and "a mighty tone-painting of provincial life." Also heard outside Czechoslovakia have been *Lišky příhody bystroušky (The Sly Little Vixen,* Brünn, 1924); *Več Makropulos* (Brünn, 1926), with a libretto by Janáček based on Karel Čapek's play of the same name, known to English-speaking play-and-movie-goers as *The Makropoulos Secret;* and the posthumously produced *Z Mrtvého domu* (Brünn, April 12, 1930), for the text of which the composer had adapted Dostoievsky's *The House of the Dead.*

For a time in the late 1920's and early 1930's it seemed that *Svanda dudák (Schwanda the Bagpipe-player),* Jaromir Weinberger's bizarre folklore opera, might be winning a permanent position in the international repertoire. Based on a popular Czech folk tale that has been set at least three other times by Czech composers, *Schwanda* began, in Prague on April 27, 1927, a blazingly successful career that soon took it to most European countries and both South and North America, usually in German translation. It was enormously popular in Czechoslovakia until the Nazi invasion, after which it was temporarily silenced there (Weinberger had neglected to have himself born an Aryan). Elsewhere it is now all but unperformed. Its vivacious, ingratiating polka and fugue are concert perennials, however, and its revival is altogether likely. The title of another of Weinberger's several operas may well strike an American as peculiar: it is *Lidé z Pokerflatu,* a five-act setting of a libretto based on Bret Harte's *The Outcasts of Poker Flat,* and it was first produced at Brno in 1932.

Neighboring Hungary long cherished a national opera almost exactly as Poland cherished *Halka.* It was Ferenc Erkel's *Hunyady László,* a four-act nationalist, patriotic, pseudohistorical opera by a distinguished conductor and professor of music. It was given its *première* at Budapest on January 27, 1844, when patriotic ferment was intense. Although the opera, in which folk notes repeatedly are sounded, is all but unknown outside Hungary, at least its title is familiar to collectors of vocal records. For in 1850 Erkel added to the score especially for Anne de la Grange, a

French soprano who had gone to Hungary to study the role, a wildly difficult aria. And of that aria, referred to on the label as "Ah, Rebe . . . ," Lillian Nordica once made a magnificent recording. If it is really characteristic of the rest of *Hunyady László,* then Erkel made use of various sorts of folk music, not only that of the true Magyars but also the distinctive forms of the gypsies and other minority groups.[3]

Hunyady László was the second of Erkel's several operas. The third, *Bánk-Bán,* ranks just below it as a Hungarian national favorite. Completed in 1849, it was not heard until March 9, 1861. At once it rivaled the popularity of *Hunyady László,* being sung so often—frequently on or about the ides of March, a Hungarian national holiday—that by 1934 it had rolled up a total of about three hundred performances in Budapest. Erkel lived from 1810 to 1893, and when the Magyar Királyi Operaház was opened in Budapest on September 27, 1884, he provided it with an opera dealing with the life of King Stephen, *István király.* The new opera, in four acts, was coupled on the inaugural program with Act I of *Bánk-Bán*—and Act I of *Lohengrin.*

The influential Karl Goldmark trailed after Wagner in his scores, showing almost no interest in the indigenous music of his native land: his first and most famous opera, composed to a German text, was *Die Königin von Saba* (Vienna, March 10, 1875). It is full of pseudo-Oriental themes and instrumental effects. A better era for true Magyar music dawned when two of the most distinguished of Hungarian composers, Béla Bartók and Zoltán Kodály, began to study the native peasant tunes and dances in a collaborative effort to isolate the ethnic strains—and, incidentally, to convince the outside world that the so-called "Hungarian" music of Franz Liszt was not Hungarian at all (as Liszt well knew), but the café music of gypsy orchestras.

Much of Bartók's music was influenced by these studies, but he also evolved one of the most distinctive idioms of twentieth-century music, as is evident in even so early a work as his only opera, *A Kékszakállú Herceg Vára* (*Duke Bluebeard's Castle*). This one-act treatment of the Bluebeard legend was heard for the first time at Budapest on May 24, 1918. It has only three characters—two human protagonists and a splendidly exploited orchestra. Bartók's fame as a composer has guaranteed the little opera many stagings elsewhere, but its uninterrupted somber-

---

[3] Erkel was also the instrument by which one of the most famous of Hungarian melodies gained world distribution, for it was he who introduced Hector Berlioz to the "Rákóczy" March in 1846.

ness may have kept it from becoming fixed in the international repertoire.

In the lusty Singspiel *Háry János* (Budapest, October 16, 1926), Zoltán Kodály created a genuine ballad opera of great distinction. With its episodic construction (it is in five parts and an epilogue), strong rhythms, gaudily resplendent orchestration (which calls for a cimbalom), and coarse, earthy humor, it is a series of vivid splashes of color. A suite of highlights from *Háry János,* with vocal lines assigned to various instruments, has become a familiar orchestral staple. Kodály almost equaled the success of *Háry János* when, in 1932, his *Székely Fonó* (*The Szekely Spinning-Room*) was heard in Budapest. Seven years earlier, he had provided a brief cabaret musical comedy with its score; *Székely Fonó* revised and renamed that score in the form of another one-act ballad opera, as which it soon became popular in Hungary and was heard in Italian, German, and English translations.

Spain glories in a persistent, flourishing folk-music tradition of extraordinary potency. Just as Russian music drew some of its distinctive tang from Oriental sources, so Spanish music is set off from other European national idioms by the racial and national contacts of the Spanish people—gypsy, Moorish, Arabian, Jewish. As long ago as 1774, a Spanish Jesuit, Antonio Eximeno, promulgated in Italian the doctrine that the music of each nation should reflect the character of its folk melodies and folk dances. Never was a doctrine adopted more eagerly. Spanish folk music not only has been taken up eagerly by native composers, but also has become a kind of international style, sometimes brilliantly adapted, but more often debased and watered down. It has been favored especially by salon composers of little or no originality.

The first modern Spanish composer of any real importance was Felipe Pedrell, a Catalan. Scholarly, meticulous in his craft, and a conscientious disciple of Eximeno, Pedrell left behind him many operas, none of which ever had more than passing success. He lacked some element essential for succeeding in the land of that epidemic operetta-musical comedy, the *zarzuela,* and his importance resides chiefly in his influence as a teacher of many noteworthy Spanish musicians, including Isaac Albéniz, Enrique Granados, and Manuel de Falla. *I Pirenei* (Barcelona, January 4, 1902), with an originally Catalan text translated into Italian, was the most successful of Pedrell's unsuccessful operas. Its successor, *La Celestina,* was hailed as a Spanish *Tristan und Isolde* by the French critic Camille Bellaigue. *La Celestina* is described as compounded almost equally of

Wagner and mysticism, with hints of Slavic influence and inserted bits of old liturgical chants and Moorish, Catalan, and Spanish folk tunes. When the embittered Pedrell died in 1922, at the age of eighty-one, three of his pupils had become world-famous: he had outlived two of them— Albéniz by thirteen years, Granados by six.

Albéniz, whose *Iberia* and other piano pieces are in the permanent repertoire, was a prolific compounder of *zarzuelas,* those several varieties of operettalike musical shows with spoken dialogue and dancing, closely akin to the French *vaudeville* and richly topical in material. Literally tens of thousands of *zarzuelas* have been written and performed since the early seventeenth century.[4] As an operatic composer, Albéniz may have suffered as the result of a curious contract he made with Francis Money-Coutts (later Baron Latimer), a wealthy English banker with literary aspirations, who for seventeen years paid the Spaniard a pension on condition that Albéniz set his librettos to music. Of the resulting operas, some were grandiose three-act affairs of the most solemn sort. Only one of that variety was produced: *Enrico Clifford* (Barcelona, May 8, 1895); its English libretto had been translated into Italian for performance in a partly Catalan-speaking Spanish city. The only partly successful result was *Pepita Jiménez* (Barcelona, January 5, 1896), for which Money-Coutts had based his static libretto on Juan Valera's well-known tale. It too was sung in Italian. It has penetrated beyond the Pyrenees. Although execrably constructed and mostly undramatic, it makes extensive use of delightful folk tunes. A German-Italian-English-Spanish super-*zarzuela, Pepita Jiménez* clearly reveals, as Gilbert Chase pointed out, that Albéniz was primarily a keyboard composer.

Unique among operas is Enrique Granados' *Goyescas,* which was actually built up (or, perhaps more accurately, thinned down) from two piano suites of the same title. The first Spanish opera ever to reach New York's Metropolitan Opera House—and in Spanish, too—this tragedy, based on Granados' meditations on Goya's portrayal of early nineteenth-century Spanish life, is so loosely put together and ineptly orchestrated as to lose much of the piquancy and insinuating appeal of the original piano pieces. But at least its coloring is authentically Spanish, as the composer was at pains to point out in contrasting *Goyescas* and *Carmen.* In defense of the orchestration, it must be noted that its noise and blatancy

[4] Foreign operas were produced in Spain from the very earliest days, but *zarzuelas* monopolized the stage in so far as native composers were concerned. True opera by Spaniards is a comparatively recent institution in Spain.

are often characteristic of the *zarzuela,* to which genre *Goyescas* would belong if it had spoken dialogue. The most effective music in the opera is an intermezzo that Granados composed especially for the Metropolitan world *première* of January 28, 1916, when he was in the audience. Returning to Europe on the S. S. *Sussex,* Granados died when the ship was torpedoed by a German submarine. He was not yet forty-nine years old.

A man who might have composed viable Spanish operas if he had lived longer than twenty-eight years, and who came close to composing such an opera when he was only twenty-six, was José María Usandizaga, a Basque who studied composition under Vincent d'Indy. In three months of 1913, he set a text by Gregorio Martínez Sierra, *Las Golondrinas.* When first heard, at the Teatro Price, Madrid, on February 4, 1914, it was a three-act *zarzuela;* after Usandizaga's death on October 5, 1915, his brother Ramón carefully worked out the small amount of additional material required to turn *Las Golondrinas* into an opera, as which it was then heard at the Liceo, Barcelona. It is an astonishingly strong, tragic work, notable for the way in which Usandizaga managed the difficult matter of writing truly original melodies and harmonic investitures without sacrificing the essentials of Spanish coloring. It may well be the best Spanish opera composed by anyone, and it makes vivid a desire to hear Usandizaga's earlier *Mendi-Mendyian* (1910) and the setting of Gregorio Martínez Sierra's *La Llama* which he completed just before his death.

Manuel de Falla, whose music, like that of Albéniz, has done most to popularize the true Spanish idiom, composed three operas, only two of which have been performed (the third, *Fuego fatuo,* a comic piece making use of Chopin melodies, has never been printed or produced). The first—*La Vida breve*—was composed when Falla was not yet thirty, to a text by Carlos Fernández Shaw, a prolific supplier of *zarzuela* texts. It received its *première* in a French translation at Nice on April 1, 1913, eight years after it had won its composer the first prize in a competition at the Real Academia de Bellas Artes de San Fernando. It shows a personality steeped in folklore and murky old wives' tales—a personality, moreover, profoundly pessimistic in cast. The musical idiom that Falla chose, and which he preferred for years, came from Andalusia, where Moorish and gypsy influences are strongest and where *cante flamenco* and *cante hondo,* melismatic types of semi-Oriental chanting, still flourish. Although much of *La Vida breve* sounds like folk music, it is not: it is Falla's spontaneous use of a musical language he had learned in childhood. However spontaneous, it is none the less subtle, and Falla has not hesitated to add to it sophistications brought from beyond Spain's northern border. His work evidences not only the influence of foreign composers who had written "Spanish" music, but also the technical results of elegant borrowing, especially from Debussy and Stravinsky.

La Vida breve, which in 1926 became the second opera in Spanish to be heard at the Metropolitan Opera, New York, is based on a tragic story of love between social unequals. It is a ballet-opera, with the dancing used more vitally and integrally than is the custom in opera. It contains effective vocal passages, but its most memorable—and most familiar—music is the dances, which were conceived and composed with exquisite care and lovingness. *El Retablo de Maese Pedro,* the first public performance of which was heard at Madrid on March 23, 1923, is the setting of an episode from *Don Quixote* as a lyric scene for puppets or marionettes and live singers. The music is shaped after Falla's free adaptation of Spanish popular music at the time of Cervantes, but unhappily for the effect of the score, the adaptation was not sufficiently free. Running to monotony, especially in the long outbursts for the boy, it clearly shows Falla's late, narrowly classicizing, antiquarian tendency.

Taken all in all, Spanish nationalist opera—Spanish nationalist music in general—has not lived up to the hope that Pedrell held for it. Its great composers, one and all,[5] have a habit of receding into the middle distance just when they might be expected to rise above the surface allure that they all, in company with second- and third-rate Spanish composers, carry at their fingertips. Cecil Gray cruelly summed up the case against their music: "It is always pleasant to listen to, but reveals no distinctive personality. Spanish national music has so far produced no Borodin or Mussorgsky, but only three Rimsky-Korsakovs—which is three too many. To English ears, their work all sounds like endless variations on one Spanish folk-song, provided with an elaborate accompaniment of castanets and similar exotic percussion instruments."

Nor has Spanish America, despite its richness in the crossed breeds of Spanish and indigenous Indian music, provided sturdy examples of folk opera. The only opera of the Mexican Carlos Chávez, *Panfilo and Lauretta,* first heard in New York on May 9, 1957, was composed to an English libretto by Chester Kallman. Heard later in Spanish translation

[5] Joaquín Turina, who lived until 1949, won no name as a composer of operas. His *Margot,* heard at the Teatro de la Zarzuela, Madrid, on October 10, 1914, was a *comedia lírica* composed to a three-act libretto by Gregorio Martínez Sierra.

in Mexico City, it became *El Amor propiciado*. It takes place in Renaissance Italy, and its musical language has little or no trace of Mexican local color—apart, perhaps, from some passages of rhythmic insistence which passingly suggest Indian drummings.

Even Brazil, where the imported musical idiom loses its edges, as the Spanish language does where Spain shades into Portugal, and where a large portion of African is added to the Portuguese and Indian, has failed to inject folk operas into the international repertoire. Folk opera has shown persistence in Brazil without—as far as can be determined—distinction. Beginning with Antonio Carlos Gomes, who mingled Amazon Indian themes with a hurdy-gurdy conception of Verdi in his once-famous *Il Guarany,* first heard in Italian at La Scala, Milan, on March 19, 1870, and his equally Italian *Lo Schiavo,* mounted at Rio de Janeiro on September 27, 1889, the roster of Brazilian operatic composers has lengthened. Its most noted name is Heitor Villa-Lobos, whose operas may be expected to show the same mixture of undisciplined talent and tasteless mediocrity which characterizes the rest of his enormous output. His *Izaht,* in four acts, received a concert performance at Rio de Janeiro on April 6, 1940; his opera for children, *A Menina das nuvens* (*The Little Girl from the Clouds*) was staged there on November 29, 1960.

It would be pointless to list the folk operas of the Balkans, Scandinavia, or Switzerland. Nothing about folk opera elsewhere gives any reason for believing that second-flight composers in countries without major operatic tradition would produce operas one whit more interesting than those of third-flight Italian, French, or German opera composers. They must be picturesque, tuneful, brightly colored; they would be obvious members of one far-flung family. The Russian nationalists, and to a smaller extent their Czech brethren, constitute exceptions only in their genius and their few enduring operas.

CHAPTER XXIII

American Opera

IN contrast to the story of operatic performance in America, the history of American opera is mostly sad. But even sad stories must be told.

In its early phases, American opera is peopled by solitary lost souls valiantly, sedulously, and for the most part vainly attempting to ape foreign graces, and those not always of the most unimpeachable sort. Going irrelevantly hand in hand with this subservience to foreign styles was, from the very beginning, a militant profession of faith in American music. As was natural, when musical stage works first came to be composed in the Colonies, they followed the pattern of *The Beggar's Opera* and its family—ballad operas and *pasticci.* The librettos of those interesting American antiques have survived in many cases, but almost invariably their music has vanished.

One of the most ambitious of early American stage works, however, was an oratorio opera by Francis Hopkinson, a signer of the Declaration of Independence who also took part in the designing of the Stars and Stripes. *The Temple of Minerva,* set to Hopkinson's own semihistorical allegory in honor of the alliance with France, was performed in Philadelphia in 1781 in the presence of George and Martha Washington and the French Minister. The music is lost, but the libretto, published in the *Freeman's Journal* of Philadelphia on December 19, 1781, shows that it was made up of solos, choruses, and ensemble numbers, and was preceded by an overture. Hopkinson was born in Philadelphia in 1737 (he was the first student to enter the institution of learning which has become the University of Pennsylvania), and claimed, in a letter to Washington which accompanied a gift of some of his songs,[1] to be the first native of

---

[1] The publication, entitled *Seven Songs,* contains eight.

the United States to have "produced a musical composition." Washington, replying in the most charming of his manners, said: "I can neither sing one of the songs, nor raise a single note on any instrument to convince the unbelieving. But I have, however, one argument which will prevail with persons of true estate (at least in America)—I can tell them that *it is the production of Mr. Hopkinson.*" It is sad that the work that might, by some stretching of the term, be called the first American opera survives, like Peri's *Dafne,* only in its text.

Anne Julia Hatton, a sister of Mrs. Siddons, wrote the book for a ballad opera by the already unsavory name of *Tammany,* which dealt with a Cherokee chief of that name and his unfortunate encounters with Spanish explorers. Its composer, James Hewitt, an exact contemporary of Beethoven, conducted its *première* at the John Street Theater, New York, on March 5, 1794. Most of the airs were given to the heroine, Manana, which suggests that the piece was probably commissioned by John Hodgkinson, an English singing actor of the time, for his wife Arabella, also a singer. Benjamin Carr, also English-born, pioneered with Hewitt in music publishing, and composed the popular opera *The Archers, or Mountaineers of Switzerland,* to an adaptation of Schiller's *Wilhelm Tell* in an anonymous libretto called *Helvetic Liberty, or The Lass of the Lakes,* adapted by William Dunlap, a founder of the National Academy of Design. Some of the music of *The Archers* has survived. A third composer of ballad operas was Victor Pelissier, a French French-horn player who, using a libretto extracted by Elihu Hubbard Smith from *The Vicar of Wakefield,* composed *Edwin and Angelina,* which achieved its single performance at the John Street Theater, New York, on December 19, 1796, with the Hodgkinsons in the cast. Again, only a fragment of the music has survived, though the text was printed.

Shortly after the War of 1812, foreign opera companies began to cross the Atlantic. The Garcías came in 1825, the Montressor troupe in 1832. Finally, in 1838, arrived Arthur and Ann Seguin, an energetic English couple who toured the United States and Canada extensively. Lorenzo da Ponte, Mozart's librettist, was an indefatigable propagandist for Italian opera in Philadelphia and New York. In New Orleans, opera has been established from 1810 on, having been inaugurated with a performance of Paisiello's *Il Barbiere di Siviglia* in French (dialogue directly from Beaumarchais's play appears to have been spoken) on July 12, 1810.

American composers responded slowly and timidly to these stimuli. The first American grand opera reached the stage in 1845. It was William

Henry Fry's *Leonora;* the composer's brother Joseph Reese Fry had based its libretto on Bulwer-Lytton's popular play *The Lady of Lyons.* Given its *première* at the Chestnut Street Theater, Philadelphia, on June 4, 1845, by the Seguin company, *Leonora* ran for twelve nights. Although another of the composer's brothers, Edward R. Fry, was manager of the Astor Place Opera House in New York in 1848 and 1849, *Leonora* was not heard in New York until 1858, and then at the Academy of Music. More than seventy years later, in May, 1929, excerpts from it were presented in New York in a concert version arranged by Otto Kinkeldey. The audience found it excruciatingly funny, much to the annoyance of certain critics with a sense of history. W. J. Henderson asked acerbly whether, "properly mounted and sung, Fry's ambitious opus would not, in its archaic way, furnish better diversion than [Strauss's] *Egyptian Helen.*"

As evidence of the qualms and uncertainty with which American composers were working at opera, it is significant that Fry, always a belligerent proponent of opera in English, not only allowed *Leonora* to be translated into Italian for performance in New York, but chose non-American subject matter both for it and for his only other opera, *Notre Dame de Paris,* after Victor Hugo, which was produced in Philadelphia on May 4, 1864, only slightly more than four months before Fry's death; it was later heard in New York with Theodore Thomas conducting.

A refreshing exception to the qualms and uncertainty was George Frederick Bristow, a very influential musician who not only preached but also composed wholly American opera. His *Rip Van Winkle,* to a text drawn from Washington Irving's tale by Jonathan Howard Wainwright, was brought out at Niblo's Garden, New York, on September 27, 1855, and ran for a month. Temporarily it seemed destined to become a sort of American *Bohemian Girl.* When Bristow died in 1898 at the age of seventy-two, this Brooklyn-born composer was engaged on his second opera, *Columbus.*

During the fifty-two years that elapsed between the Academy of Music performance of Fry's *Leonora* in 1858 and the 1906 Boston *première* of Frederick Shepherd Converse's *The Pipe of Desire*—later the first opera by an American composer to be staged at the Metropolitan Opera in New York [2]—countless operas by citizens of the United States were

---

[2] John Knowles Paine, teacher of half the composers and critics of the day before yesterday, died in 1906 without having heard a performance of his only opera, *Azara,* on the Aucassin and Nicolette theme. Concert excerpts from it

composed, though many of them did not reach performance. Amid welters of dust-laden and almost certainly mediocre scores and names of scores (for many operas known to have been composed have vanished utterly), we come upon the flashy, eccentric Louis Moreau Gottschalk compounding two unwieldly pseudohistoric operatic tragedies, young Walter Damrosch and Victor Herbert writing their first operas, and several earnest females contriving dramatic inanities entitled *Narcissus, Priscilla,* and *Last Summer.* Neither New York's Academy of Music— New York's chief opera house from 1854 to the early 1880's—nor its more dominating successor, the Metropolitan, paid serious attention to these desperate efforts to compose an American opera.

The portals of the sacred temple of music located on Broadway between Thirty-ninth and Fortieth Streets did not swing ajar to an American opera until the unhappy joint management of Giulio Gatti-Casazza and Andreas Dippel opened them a chink reluctantly to admit Frederick Shepherd Converse's *The Pipe of Desire*—a one-acter to a text by George Edward Barton which had been heard in Boston four years earlier. The date was March 18, 1910. Alfred Hertz conducted; the cast included the Kentucky-born Riccardo Martin as Iolan; Louise Homer of Pittsburgh as Naoia; Clarence Whitehill of Iowa as The Old One; and Herbert Witherspoon of Buffalo, New York, as the First Gnome. The other opera on the boards that night was *Pagliacci.* In its only other performance at the Metropolitan, *The Pipe of Desire* (March 24, 1910) shared the bill with *Cavalleria rusticana* and a Glazunov ballet entitled *Hungary.*[3]

The Pipe of Desire had received a medal awarded by David Bispham, the renowned Quaker baritone who was an untiring partisan of opera in English. As matters turned out, that was insufficient reason for performing it at the Metropolitan. The libretto proved rambling, insipid, and poorly adapted to singing. As a result, the all-American stars thought-

---

prove interesting enough to suggest that Heinrich Conried may have been wrong when he decided not to produce it at the Metropolitan.

[3] *The Pipe of Desire,* however, was sung on March 31, 1910, at the newly opened New Theater during the Metropolitan Opera Company's attempt (nineteen performances in all) to move at least some performances uptown: the New Theater occupied the block on Central Park West between Sixty-third and Sixty-fourth Streets, but little removed from Lincoln Square. Soon renamed the Century, it was torn down about 1930.

fully provided by the management were—except for Clarence Whitehill
—unintelligible. The imitative music demonstrated an inept Wagnerism.
The audience might have accepted a text in English which it could not
understand (large sections of it were used to not understanding German,
Italian, and French texts) if only the music had said anything. Converse [4]
did not remain a passive Wagnerian. In 1927, his *Flivver Ten Million,* a
symphonic fantasy about the ten-millionth Ford automobile, showed him
critically and humorously *au courant* with twentieth-century life and
twentieth-century harmony.

Victor Herbert, the melodious Irishman and eminent cellist, had composed most of his famous operettas before his first opera reached the
Metropolitan. This was *Natoma,* its libretto by Joseph Deighn Redding
based on a story of early California. It reached New York on February
28, 1911, three days after its *première* in Philadelphia and London, in
which latter city a special performance, the purpose of which was to preserve British copyright, was given at Ladbroke Hall. The Metropolitan
performance was not by a resident company, but by a cast drawn from
the roster of Oscar Hammerstein's Philadelphia-Chicago Opera Company and conducted by Cleofonte Campanini. The cast was notable, including both Mary Garden (Natoma) and John McCormack (Merrill).
H. T. Parker succinctly described *Natoma* as "a dull text set to mediocre
music," but praised the staging and Garden's vivid performance as the
Indian heroine. But H. E. Krehbiel reported the action reduced to nonsense by the stage business. The opera itself, scantily provided with the
unforgettable tunes that had made Herbert's fortune, has vanished,
but the Dagger Dance and Natoma's Spring Song are still occasionally
heard.

Victor Herbert's second opera, *Madeleine,* its one-act text by Grant
Stewart patterned after a French play, was given its world *première* by
the resident Metropolitan company at a matinée on January 24, 1914,
when it was billed with *Pagliacci.* Giorgio Polacco conducted; the leading
roles went to Frances Alda, Paul Althouse, Antonio Pini-Corsi, and
Andrés de Segurola. In it, Herbert had abandoned the American scene
for an eighteenth-century French setting: a star of the Opéra is the
heroine. The undramatic libretto was judged to be accompanied by gen-

[4] Converse wrote several other operas—one of which, *The Sacrifice,* to his
own text, but with lyrics provided by John Albert Macy, was heard in Boston on
March 3, 1911.

erally wooden music. *Madeleine* achieved four performances that season, none in any other.

In the early days of their joint management, Gatti-Casazza and Dippel, momentarily quieting their native conservatism, offered a prize of ten thousand dollars for the best opera composed by an American, the text to be in English. Horatio W. Parker, a very respected professor of music at Yale University, and already the composer of *Hora Novissima*, the best-turned-out oratorio an American had composed, won the prize with a gloomy work about the ancient Britons. The librettist of *Mona*, Brian Hooker—who achieved some fame for his translation of Rostand's *Cyrano de Bergerac*—conceived his listless lyrics as a protest against female suffrage: Mona, a princess of Britain, brings about the death of Gwynn, her lover (who is really—like Pollione in *Norma*—a Roman), by insisting on playing a man's part in the world. Parker was unfortunate in the libretto, dramatic only in spots, and even more unfortunate in the cast assigned to *Mona*. At the Metropolitan *première,* on March 14, 1912, Alfred Hertz conducted; Louise Homer was Mona; her associates included Rita Fornia, Herbert Witherspoon, Albert Reiss, and—as Gloom, son of Enya and Arth—William Wade Hinshaw. Alone among the principals, Reiss seemed to have a grasp of his role. Yet, despite obstacles to success, *Mona* succeeded. Both critics and the public expressed generous admiration and lively interest. No American opera had received comparable praise from competent critics, and the action of Gatti-Casazza in withdrawing it from the Metropolitan repertoire after four performances casts suspicion on his many politic professions of interest in American music. The failure of later managers to revive it extends that suspicion to them.

For *Mona* is, despite occasional tediousness and a churchiness not always confined to devotional scenes (and which is, moreover, rather Anglican than druid), a good opera. It shows a firm grasp of the operatic resources of the period. The text is expertly set for singability. The declamation carries eloquence; the instrumentation has aptness and distinction, and through the entire three acts there are moments of great individuality. *Mona* is frequently both beautiful and persuasive, and it is remarkably free from the unctuousness that mars the work of many oratorio and cantata composers. In fact, one of Parker's most individual characteristics is a biting, astringent tone. Nor is he, in *Mona*, structurally uninteresting: twenty years before Alban Berg's *Wozzeck,* he assigned characteristic keys to various personages of the drama. But there is little of the closet about *Mona,* which is realistically created for life on the stage.[5]

Walter Damrosch, long a familiar figure on the American musical scene, began composing operas in the nineteenth century. His first, *The Scarlet Letter,* with a libretto that George Parsons Lathrop had based on his father-in-law's famous novel, showed that Damrosch had inherited from his noted father, the conductor Leopold Damrosch, a devotion to Wagner which expressed itself, in his case, in extended imitation. Whatever authenticity the libretto had was obliterated at the opera's first performance by a largely German cast headed by Johanna Gadski, who murdered the language and banished any semblance of American illusion. The *première* took place on February 10, 1896, in Boston; the opera was heard at the Metropolitan, New York, though not by the resident company, on March 6 of the same year. Soon *The Scarlet Letter* was laughingly and aptly referred to as "the *Nibelungen* of New England." [6]

Damrosch's *Cyrano de Bergerac,* produced at the Metropolitan by the resident company on February 27, 1913, placed the New York critics at a disadvantage. The four-act libretto had been derived from Rostand's famous five-act play by one of their most distinguished confreres, W. J. Henderson of *The Sun;* the composer was the conductor of the Symphony Society of New York. They treated Henderson somewhat more gently than they treated Damrosch, whose musical borrowings were noted laughingly. H. E. Krehbiel wrote: "It offers nothing which points even remotely to a solution of the problem of English or American opera." When the opera was sung again, its inordinate length [7] had been reduced,

---

[5] Parker won another ten-thousand-dollar prize—this time offered by the National Federation of Women's Clubs—with his only other opera, *Fairyland,* to another three-act text by Brian Hooker, which was first heard in Los Angeles on July 1, 1915.

[6] The Italo-American composer Vittorio Giannini wrote his own English libretto for his version of *The Scarlet Letter,* which was declined by the Metropolitan as being musically too Italian for Hawthorne, but was produced in Germany, at Hamburg, on June 2, 1938, as *Das Brandmal.*

[7] Irving Kolodin wrote that Henderson had asked Damrosch how long *Cyrano* would run, and that the composer had replied: "Oh, four or four and a half hours." The astonished librettist could say only "What!" Damrosch remarked: "Well, take *Meistersinger.*" He had misjudged his questioner. "But, Walter," Henderson replied, "you're not Richard Wagner."

but after the shortened version had been sung four times, *Cyrano de Bergerac* disappeared from the repertoire.

The reception of *Cyrano* appears to have discouraged Damrosch for almost a quarter of a century: he did not dare the critical thunders again until May 12, 1937, when Edward Everett Hale's *The Man Without a Country* was graduated from McGuffey's Readers, via a two-act libretto by Arthur Guiterman, to the stage of the Metropolitan, an opera with both singing and speaking roles. This *première* was one attraction of a special spring season of nineteen performances; it served to introduce, as Mary Rutledge, the remarkable soprano Helen Traubel. But the opera itself was reviewed enthusiastically by Lawrence Gilman,[8] and won a single repetition the following season. Then it, too, abruptly vanished from the repertoire. In 1942, when Damrosch was eighty, his final stage piece, *The Opera Cloak,* aroused only apathy when it was produced in New York—but not at the Metropolitan.

Only two of the several operas and operettas of Charles Wakefield Cadman, composer of "At Dawning," "I Hear a Thrush at Eve," and other gems of the semipopular repertoire, reached fully professional stage production. The first was *Shanewis,* Nelle Richmond Eberhardt's two-act libretto for which recounted the tragic tale of a white man infatuated with an Indian girl. Cadman had long been interested in American Indian

[8] A characteristic example of American opera criticism near its nadir, Gilman's review reads, in part: "His newest opera is, it may be affirmed at once, not only the best that Mr. Damrosch has given us, but it has an astonishing freshness of feeling, an infectious gusto. It is impossible to doubt that Mr. Damrosch enjoyed enormously the fun of writing it—almost as much as he quite obviously enjoyed the fun of conducting it last night, with an engaging mixture of expert watchfulness over the performers' treatment of his score and of measureless benevolence when things went to his liking.

"Mr. Damrosch has dealt simply and unpretentiously with a simple and unpretentious tale. He has not attempted to give us a music-drama à la Richard (Strauss or Wagner). He has paid no heed to the siren temptings of ultra-modern composers. His music moves fluently, with apt and appropriate relation to what is happening on the stage and in the hearts of his characters. It stops to let them speak, or it accompanies discreetly their spoken words. Once in a while, it goes alone on its own, as in the orchestral prelude to the second act. Sometimes the music is richly flavored with tinctures of the past, sometimes it is straight Damrosch. It would be fantastic to expect a sensitive musician to conduct as much great music by other men as Mr. Damrosch has done without some of it becoming part of his mental tissue."

music, which he presented in treacle-and-whey versions, and the salient lyrical moments of *Shanewis* displayed the qualities of some of his concert ballads—such as "From the Land of the Sky-blue Water." W. J. Henderson astonishingly wrote that Cadman "has shown a greater command of the technic of opera than any of his predecessors among American composers introduced at the Metropolitan, and while his music is not always distinguished, it is, by reason of the judgment in its treatment, never, or rarely at any rate, without direct and simple effectiveness." At its *première* on March 23, 1918, with Roberto Moranzoni conducting and Sophie Braslau in the title role, it shared the bill with the *première* of Henry F. Gilbert's ballet *The Dance in Place Congo,* the latter conducted by Pierre Monteux. It achieved a total of eight performances in two seasons, and was not heard again.

Cadman's other opera to reach a major house was *A Witch of Salem,* in which, Edward Moore wrote, Mrs. Eberhardt had "turned away from the romance and dance rhythms of the Indians to a drab tale of puritan Massachusetts in 1692." When the opera was heard at the Auditorium, Chicago, on December 8, 1926, it was judged not bad. Mr. Moore reported that "tongues were set wagging again about the value of the English language in opera." *A Witch of Salem* could not long cling to the Chicago Opera's stage, but it was sung many times later in amateur and semiamateur performances.

Quite as insignificant as Cadman as a writer for the serious musical stage, and as mysteriously favored by important opera companies, was Henry Hadley, whose first opera to be sung in the United States,[9] *Azora, Daughter of Montezuma,* with a three-act text by David Stevens, received its *première* at the Auditorium, Chicago, on December 26, 1917. It was a stirring occasion that looked like success. It was repeated the following week. "Then," wrote Edward Moore, "Hadley called upon Campanini [Cleofonte Campanini, then director of the Chicago company] to discuss the question of putting on *Azora* in the forthcoming New York season. Campanini was unenthusiastic, not to say cold. . . . Greatly surprised, Hadley argued that in two performances there had been two full houses. Campanini admitted the full houses, but stated that there were times when the Chicago Opera Association unfortunately found it advisable to issue passes in order to fill up large gaps in the theater seats. 'How many people do you think bought main floor seats for your second performance?' he wanted to know. Hadley opined that

[9] Hadley's *Safie,* a one-act opera composed to an English text but sung in German, was heard at Mainz on April 4, 1909.

there might have been five hundred. 'Too many, much too many,' said Campanini. . . . Hadley kept revising his estimate downward and Campanini's smile kept growing more sardonic. Finally he sent for the box-office statement, which had the official figures. Outside of the regular subscribers for this night, exactly five persons had bought seats on the main floor."

Three years later, the Metropolitan, undiscouraged by clear indications that Hadley was not an opera composer, staged his *Cleopatra's Night* on a double bill with a Caruso–Florence Easton–Scotti *Pagliacci,* thus guaranteeing it a full house. Alice Leal Pollock's two-act adaptation of Théophile Gautier's *Une Nuit de Cléopâtre* had supplied Hadley with cause for many pages of pseudo-Oriental sinuosities, especially prevalent during a protracted bacchanale. But not even ambitious orchestration could rescue the score from creeping dullness. The date of the *première* was January 31, 1920. In two seasons, it was sung seven times, missing by one performance the record set by *Shanewis.*

Remembered now, if at all, because Mary Garden suggested its composition and sang in it, is Hamilton Forrest's *Camille.* What can Forrest have been thinking as he composed an opera in a prologue and three acts based on his own version of Dumas's *La Dame aux camélias*? It is true that Rossini composed *Il Barbiere di Siviglia* when Paisiello's already existed, and Puccini his *Manon Lescaut* in the face of Massenet's *Manon.* On December 10, 1930, this excessively non-Verdian opera became the first new work heard at the Civic Opera House, Chicago (which had opened on November 4, 1930, with *Aïda*). As *Mary Garden's Story* puts it succinctly: "There were other people who thought there were a few good moments in *Camille,* but I'm afraid none of those people were in Chicago. It was a pretty dismal failure there." No one else was tempted to stage the complex, idiomatically modern opera. The name of its composer does not even appear in the standard encyclopedias of music. *La Traviata* remained unchallenged.

For a time more fortunate than any other American-born composer of opera was the versatile Deems Taylor. His first full-length opera, *The King's Henchman,* established a record for longevity among American works staged at the Metropolitan,[10] only to have that record broken by his second opera, *Peter Ibbetson.* The first reached fourteen perform-

---

[10] It was the first full-length American work to be presented there since 1917, when Reginald De Koven's tuneful but completely unimportant *The Canterbury Pilgrims*—an operetta rather than an opera—was given its world *première* there on March 8, Artur Bodanzky conducting.

ances in three seasons; the second was heard during four seasons for a total of sixteen times. Taylor was happy in his choice of librettists. Edna St. Vincent Millay provided the book for *The King's Henchman,* and Constance Collier helped the composer with her many years of theatrical experience when he decided to adapt as a libretto her dramatic version of George du Maurier's *Peter Ibbetson.*

When the Metropolitan commissioned *The King's Henchman,* Taylor was known chiefly as a witty journalist and as a composer of light orchestral works. The success of the *Henchman,* after its *première* on February 17, 1927—with Tullio Serafin conducting and a huge cast headed by Florence Easton, Edward Johnson, and Lawrence Tibbett—made him one of the most envied of American composers. Commentators blinded neither by the magnificence of the production nor by spleen hailed Taylor as the clever eclectic he was. Pitts Sanborn, tracing the musical genealogy of the opera, had to mention the names and works of Puccini, Debussy, Massenet, Mussorgsky, Charpentier, Rimsky-Korsakov, and Grieg, but concluded grimly: "For the most part, *The King's Henchman* is based firmly upon Wagner." The opera was front-page news, quite a feat for an American music drama of tenth-century England.

New York heard Taylor's second opera four years later, on February 7, 1931. *Peter Ibbetson* had been completed by means of a five-thousand-dollar grant from the Juilliard Foundation, and it was awaited with taut interest. The demonstration at the *première* verged on the hysterical: thirty-six curtain calls, the tears of many listeners, and a public embrace from Walter Damrosch were among the composer's immediate rewards for a score as unoriginal as *The King's Henchman,* but quite as adroit a job of joinery. Johnson and Tibbett again starred as interpreters of Taylor-made music, and Lucrezia Bori—in superb voice and beautiful in the period costumes—was Easton's peer in intelligibility. This time, in addition to numerous reminiscences of other composers, Taylor introduced French folk songs for sentimental effects. *Peter Ibbetson* established another precedent: on December 26, 1933, it became the first American opera ever to open a Metropolitan season.[11]

Despite the popularity of *The King's Henchman* and *Peter Ibbetson,* neither of them has been revived since being dropped from the Metropolitan repertoire. Taylor's third opera, *Ramuntcho,* composed to his own text derived from Pierre Loti, received its *première* at the Academy

[11] A matinee performance of *Hänsel und Gretel* the preceding day was counted as preseasonal.

of Music, Philadelphia, in February, 1942. It seems no more likely than the earlier operas to occupy a spot in the living repertoire.

The immediate success of Taylor's first two operas would seem to have made the Metropolitan management temporarily more attentive to American works. The middle thirties would have become a notable era in the history of the American musical stage if only the operas chosen by the Metropolitan had proved to be as worthy of that honor as their press agents claimed. The Russian-born Louis Gruenberg's *The Emperor Jones* was the first, and in many ways the best, of the three new American works that North America's foremost opera company adopted. The setting of Eugene O'Neill's melodrama was in itself a bold and admirable departure, but the composer's failure to capitalize upon certain effectively theatrical portions of the play was widely and justifiably criticized. Yet many pages of the score, particularly choral passages, show a dramatic talent at work. The use of a half-sung, half-spoken vocal declamation was frequently happy. Tibbett, as Jones, made the most of this device in his intelligently elaborated characterization. Altogether, the effect produced by *The Emperor Jones* at its *première,* a matinée, on January 7, 1933, with Serafin conducting, was of frustrated excellence.

The Emperor Jones was not Gruenberg's only opera. On November 19, 1931, his *Jack and the Beanstalk,* its three-act text "A Fairy Opera for the Childlike" by John Erskine, had been produced at the Juilliard School in New York. On September 7, 1937, the Columbia Broadcasting System, over a nation-wide network, presented his setting of a text derived from W. H. Hudson's *Green Mansions.* Commissioned by CBS, and designed specifically to be broadcast, it proved amorphous, falsely exotic, and lacking in dramatic impact. Gruenberg, it had become clear, was not the answer to the insistently repeated question: can American opera exist?

Certainly, however, *The Emperor Jones* was in all ways superior to Howard Hanson's *Merry Mount,* like Cadman's *A Witch of Salem* a tale of witchcraft, the libretto being a Nathaniel Hawthorne tale adapted by Richard L. Stokes. Heard first in concert form at Ann Arbor, Michigan, on May 20, 1933, *Merry Mount* reached the Metropolitan on February 10, 1934. This effort by a scholarly but uninspired musician had a pinched Nordic air that deceived few. Again Tibbett covered himself with glory, this time as Wrestling Bradford, but unprecedented heights of unintelligibility were reached by the Swedish Göta Ljungberg as Lady Marigold Sandys. It would be wholly irrelevant to compare with *The*

Emperor Jones the last American novelty of Gatti-Casazza's regime. The retirement of that veteran *régisseur* after flinging John Laurence Seymour's *In the Pasha's Garden* to the howling critics was not unfitting. As given its world *première,* on a double bill with *La Bohème,* at a matinée on January 24, 1935, it had literally nothing but Tibbett, by that date the strong man of American opera, and the novelty of scenery by Frederick J. Kiesler. Three performances that season constituted its Metropolitan career.

When the Edward Johnson regime had begun, it was not surprising that Tibbett was requisitioned to sing the villainous cuckold Guido in the Dutch-born Richard Hageman's *Caponsacchi.* This completely un-original opera in a prologue, three acts, and an epilogue was a setting of a libretto that Arthur Goodrich had based on a play by himself and Rose Palmer; the play in turn had been drawn from Robert Browning's *The Ring and the Book,* and therefore had its scenes in Rome and Arezzo in the seventeenth century. Heard at the Metropolitan on February 4, 1937, five years after its world *première* at Freiburg, Germany, *Caponsacchi* recalled Hageman's impressive academic background and the fact that he had composed several ingratiating songs. Its reception—it piled up a total of two performances—was not calculated to encourage the Metropolitan's interest in American opera.

A career different in variety and durability was inaugurated at the Academy of Music, Philadelphia, on April 1, 1937, when Fritz Reiner conducted there an *opera buffa* by a twenty-five-year-old Italian-American named Gian-Carlo Menotti. Six days later, *Amelia Goes to the Ball,* for which Menotti himself had written the libretto, was repeated at the New Amsterdam Theater, New York. As a cautious feeler, the Metropolitan took it on, staging it on March 3, 1938, as a curtain raiser for a hair-raising performance of Strauss's *Elektra* starring Rose Pauly. It was not, of course, really *Amelia Goes to the Ball:* it was *Amelia al ballo,* and Pitts Sanborn, after calling it merry and delightful, added: "To make an end of it all, *Amelia* is an agreeable example of modern Italian opera, vivacious and tuneful, sung in English. American it is not, except through geographical accident." Heard six times in two seasons, *Amelia* was then unaccountably dropped by the Metropolitan.

Menotti was to be heard at the Metropolitan again. On February 20, 1942, his brief, banal, and oversymbolic *The Island God,* again to his own libretto, was heard as the second half of a double bill with *Pagliacci.* Enduring for only three performances, it chalked up the first notable failure of Menotti's career. That career, played out largely in dramatic theaters through the agency of such pseudo-Puccinian semioperatic thrillers as *The Medium* (1946), *The Consul* (1950), and *The Saint of Bleecker Street* (1954), such puffs of smoke as *The Telephone* (1947), and such radio-television semioperas as *The Old Maid and the Thief* and the Christmas oleophone *Amahl and the Night Visitors,* has become an intensely publicized success story. Menotti's talent has appeared to be theatrical rather than musicodramatic, though his music is often charming, as in the ballet *Sebastian* and the semiballet, accompanied by madrigals, *The Unicorn, the Gorgon, and the Manticore.* Too often, however, his so-called operas melodramatically rape good or even serious ideas, producing something amorphous lying between honest musical comedy and *Kitsch de frisson.* He seemed (1958) to be returning toward opera with *Maria Golovin,* but nothing in his production has suggested that he will become a composer of the caliber of Cilèa, Wolf-Ferrari, Giordano, or Pizzetti, or that he is likely to compose either a genuine American opera or a major opera of any nationality.

The primarily instrumental composer Samuel Barber set a four-act libretto by Menotti as *Vanessa,* which was first heard at the Metropolitan Opera on January 15, 1958. The text, wandering somewhat diffusely in an unnamed Scandinavian or Slavic atmosphere, read and sounded a little like Chekov and Isak Dinesen. The music, thoroughly eclectic, rose to memorable stature only toward the end of the long opera, when a quintet with a melody reminiscent of Kurt Weill was expertly handled for ensemble characterization. Because the musical investiture improved as the opera progressed, people said that Barber was learning how to write opera as he went along, and that his second opera would be the real test. What is to be hoped is that the second opera will have a stronger, more dramatic, more logical text; such a text might draw from Barber stronger, more dramatic, more logical music. The splendor with which the Metropolitan staged *Vanessa* remained palpably in excess of the opera's qualities.[12] It fared much better in a somewhat shortened and otherwise revised version (in Italian translation) heard at the Spoleto Festival of Two Worlds in the summer of 1961.

[12] Solely to keep the record clear, mention must be made of another American opera staged at the Metropolitan. This was Bernard Rogers' *The Warrior,* with a libretto by Norman Corwin. When it received its world *première* as a curtain raiser for a matinée *Hänsel und Gretel* on January 11, 1947, it was as the winner of a competition sponsored by the Alice M. Ditson Memorial Fund. In the New

In his varied and busy career, George Gershwin, using a text based on DuBose Heyward's *Porgy,* turned out an opera that has been heard by more people the world around than have ever heard any other American opera. *Porgy and Bess,* which opened at the Colonial Theater, Boston, on September 30, 1935, was flawed by some of that pretentiousness which marred Gershwin's music whenever he deserted musical comedy. The opera, in fact, was at its best precisely in those spots at which it most closely approached musical comedy: "It ain't necessarily so" and "I got plenty o' nuttin'." The lovely "Summertime" has an elegiac quality at which Gershwin had only hinted earlier. Some of it has entered the stream of "standard numbers" so completely as to have begun to seem almost folk music, and it appears likely that parts of *Porgy and Bess* will outlast anything thus far composed for opera by more solemn, more academic American composers.

Positively reticent as a musical modernist is Virgil Thomson, the acidulous critic. His operatic fame rests on two works to apparently nonsensical, but always singable and amusing, texts adapted from Gertrude Stein. The first was *Four Saints in Three Acts,* "an opera to be sung." Produced with imagination and exquisite taste, and played with verve, knowingness, and delight by an all-Negro cast, this modest opera was one of the most attractive entertainments of its decade in New York. After a *première* on February 8, 1934, in Hartford, Connecticut, under the auspices of the Society of Friends and Enemies of Modern Music, it upset predictions by becoming a hit on Broadway. It is anything but a complicated score: it perfectly and understandably sets the satirically surrealist text, often seeming to suggest more than it says. The chief assets of this delicious music are aptness, simplicity, transparency—and unabashed triviality. *Four Saints* is the opposite of epochal. It has been revived several times, whole or in part.

Thomson's second opera, *The Mother of Us All,* with Maurice Gros-

---

York *Sun,* Irving Kolodin wrote: "As conventional opera, *The Warrior,* which had its première in the Metropolitan Opera House on Saturday afternoon, is not much more successful than the generality of American scores which have preceded it in the institution's history. As a species of musical theater, there is a good deal more to be said for it. All that can be said for it, however, does not add to the requirements of a repertory opera house." This version of the Samson-Delilah story, almost devoid of singing—it made use of chanting, declamation, speech, and shouting, some of it in the *Sprechstimme* manner—was heard again on January 31, after which it was heard no more.

ser again preparing the scenario from a Stein text, was first heard on May 7, 1947, at Brander Matthews Hall, Columbia University. A fantastic mélange of American history and legend, it boasts such characters as John Adams, Thaddeus Stevens, Ulysses S. Grant, Lillian Russell, Daniel Webster, Gertrude Stein, "Virgil T.," Anthony Comstock, and Jo the Loiterer. The "Mother" of the title is Susan B. Anthony. The opera, doing without the "Spanish" effects of *Four Saints,* reiterates the virtues of the earlier work, and often comes infuriatingly close to making logical sense. It too has been revived. Thomson's operas are almost alone among American examples of the genre in succeeding perfectly within their chosen limits, which admittedly are confined.

Finally, there is Aaron Copland, a musician of vast cleverness, erudition, and vitality, one of the two or three most gifted of American composers. He has composed two operas, both of somewhat specialized nature. *The Second Hurricane* was written to be sung by young people from eight to eighteen. It was first produced, under Orson Welles's direction, at the Grand Street Theater, New York, on April 21, 1937. A credible, simple story of modern American life by Edwin Denby joined to music utterly uncomplicated, direct, and briskly melodious, it nevertheless left few desiring to hear it again.

Copland's second opera, commissioned through the League of Composers by Richard Rodgers and Oscar Hammerstein II, is *The Tender Land,* with a libretto by Horace Everett (pseudonym). A story of Midwestern family life in the early 1930's, it shows signs of conception for semiamateur performance. Somewhat hobbled by a libretto of uncertain style, it makes no large gestures. It was first heard in professional performance at the New York City Center, during a season of the New York City Opera, on April 1, 1954. Too careful, perhaps, too little lyrical and expansive and dramatic, it left many admirers of Copland wondering if he is temperamentally or stylistically gifted for the composition of true opera.

The story of American opera easily deliquesces into a catalogue of almosts, nears, and certainly-nots. The epidemic spread of opera workshops in universities and elsewhere; the multiplication of amateur and semiprofessional local opera companies—all this has produced a spate of small-scale American operas. Mostly they aim at little, and all but achieve it. Too often they show no understanding of what an opera libretto is or ought to be, little insight into the art of writing for singing actors, and appalling poverty of musical invention. Even their successes stand outside the main stream of operatic history, to which, indeed, they seldom aspire to belong. They have almost no appeal for true lovers of the many-lived art that began so long ago in Florence and continues to-day to attract hundreds of thousands of listeners each year to the world's great opera houses.[13]

[13] The Ford Foundation has contributed large sums of money to the cause of furthering the performance and creation of American opera. It made large operatic grants, one early in 1959 to the New York City Opera Company to aid in the performance of existing works, one late in the same year to the Metropolitan, New York City, Chicago Lyric, and San Francisco companies for the mounting of operas to be created for the purpose. The first grant resulted in a spring, 1959, season during which the following operas, musical comedies, and plays with incidental music were sung at New York's City Center: Gian-Carlo Menotti's *Maria Golovin* and *The Medium;* Kurt Weill's *Street Scene;* Douglas Moore's *The Ballad of Baby Doe* and *The Devil and Daniel Webster;* Lee Hoiby's *The Scarf;* Carlisle Floyd's *Wuthering Heights* and *Susannah;* Robert Ward's *He Who Gets Slapped;* Norman Dello Joio's *The Triumph of St. Joan;* Marc Blitzstein's *Regina;* and Hugo Weisgall's *Six Characters in Search of an Author.* Perhaps stung by justified criticism of this appalling mélange, the New York City Opera opened its next season with a double bill made up of Stravinsky's *Oedipus Rex* and Orff's *Carmina Burana,* "operas" that resembled at least *Street Scene* and *Regina* in not being operas in any common usage of that word.

The later, and larger, grant of $950,000 envisaged the mounting of twelve new American operas by the Metropolitan, Chicago Lyric, and San Francisco companies at the rate of one each every other season—and of six new American operas by the New York City Opera at the rate of one or more each year after 1960. Nothing in the history of American opera warrants the belief that eighteen (or twelve, or six) American operas of anything close to the quality of the operas in the standard repertoires of the world's theaters will be evoked by this well-meant, but almost certainly impotent, philanthropy. The first four results were heard in 1961. On September 18, the San Francisco Opera presented Norman Dello Joio's *Blood Moon;* the New York City Opera followed with Douglas Moore's *The Wings of the Dove* (libretto after the Henry James novel) on October 12 and Robert Ward's *The Crucible* (libretto after the play of the same name by Arthur Miller) on October 26; finally, the Chicago Lyric Opera staged Vittorio Giannini's *The Harvest* on November 25. Aside from the customary flourishes of brittle enthusiasm—notably for *The Wings of the Dove* and *The Crucible*—and the equally customary blank denunciations—notably of *Blood Moon*—they failed to prove that philanthropy can produce viable opera likely to win devotees or remain long in the repertoire.

CHAPTER XXIV

A Modern Galaxy

THE twentieth century has not been a predominantly operatic period. With the notable exceptions of a few men who had already established themselves in the late years of the nineteenth century—Puccini and Strauss, most particularly—many of the best composers of this century's first fifty years turned to ballet when they composed for the stage. Part of this straying from the more traditional interest was the old business of following the leader. Much of it can be ascribed to the enthusiasm of the famous balletomane, connoisseur of the arts, and impresario, Serge Diaghilev, who began collecting his extraordinary group of staff composers before the close of the first decade of this century. For his sumptuous and fashionable Ballet Russe some of the finest early twentieth-century music was composed: Stravinsky provided *Petrouchka* and *Le Sacre du printemps,* Ravel *Daphnis et Chloë,* and Falla *El Sombrero de tres picos.* Many of the scores commissioned by Diaghilev have become permanent additions to ballet; suites from some of them remain concert fixtures. The exciting theatricality, in the most complimentary sense of the word, of much modern ballet music suggests what opera might have gained if the times had provided it with a Diaghilev of its own to draw these great talents to the sung musical drama more often and to guide them in making it as vigorous a reflection of the era as the Ballet Russe.

Interesting operas have been composed, of course. Absence from the repertoire—that collection of masterpieces and fortuitous choices—does not argue lack of merit. A few modern operas may be given renewed chances of immortality sooner or later, though that change will entail a mild revolution in the opera house. It will be a revolution that turns around to the past (the conventional kind, in short): it will hark back to those not so distant days when, with reason and natural appetite, impresarios and audiences were alike eager for novelties. The standard repertoire as now conceived is a forced modern invention that the old fogies of Mozart's, Weber's, and Meyerbeer's times would have found baffling. In an age of creative quiescence, operatically speaking, the record may be read this way: times for the performance of opera are relatively healthful; times for audiences are relatively varied; times for composers are pinched. The healthiest times for all concerned will have returned when the enduring good operas of whatever period, provenance, and category must share the season with likely newcomers.

Modern opera as one department of modern music could be divided into a dozen or more categories on the basis of style alone. It is simpler, and certainly more illuminating, to consider it a three-ring circus with a few delightful side shows. By and large the first ring is filled with descendants of the Russian nationalists; the second is given over to composers acknowledging Wagner, Strauss, and certain of the earlier German romantics as their ancestors; in the last we find a small group, some of whom ape the tricks of those in the first ring, but all of whom remain Parisians, compatriots of Debussy despite their foreign dominoes. Those in the first two rings make the most noise.

Igor Stravinsky, a onetime pupil of Rimsky-Korsakov, began by producing brilliant imitations of his master. His first opera, *Le Rossignol,* started when he was twenty-five and completed six years later, displays the conflicting interests of an extraordinarily vital artist developing at tremendous speed. The first act, begun in 1908, is reminiscent of *Le Coq d'or* not only in musical style but also in atmosphere; the second and third acts, completed in 1914, are asserted in the polyrhythmic, then advanced idiom, not yet carried to extremes, which was to make Stravinsky one of the central musical figures of the first half of the century. The opera was presented in Paris by Diaghilev on May 26, 1914. When it was first heard at the Metropolitan, on March 6, 1926, with Marion Talley as the Nightingale, Adamo Didur as the Emperor of China, and Ralph Errolle as the Fisherman, *Le Rossignol* began a run of six performances in two seasons. Irving Kolodin commented amusingly on the New York *première:* "The use of a French text for *Le Rossignol* lent an almost League of Nations internationalism to this production— the settings were by Serge Soudeikine, a Russian; the conductor [Tullio Serafin] was Italian; the leading singer an American; and the Oriental background originated in a story by Hans Christian Andersen!" Stravinsky later drew on the score of the opera for his symphonic poem entitled *Le Chant du rossignol.*

Stravinsky's second opera, *Mavra,* was composed when he had already begun to turn his back on the "terrible" style that had brought him world renown, and in *Mavra* his growing neoclassicism was apparent. This brittle one-act *opéra-bouffe* had its *première* in Paris on June 3, 1922.[1] It was heard in the United States when Maria Kurenko excelled as Parasha in a performance at the Academy of Music, Philadelphia, on December 28, 1934.

The third, and by far the most important, of Stravinsky's operas was composed to a text entitled *The Rake's Progress,* a collaborative libretto in English verse by W. H. Auden and Chester Kallman. A deliberate return to the eighteenth century and earlier in formal structure, this often beautiful and moving opera suffers from the fact that the subtleties and exceedingly refined beauties of its text are immune to operatic treatment and that the Rake himself, Tom Rakewell, has sacrificed all true rakishness to an admirable philosophic point. Quickly regarded as one of the greatest of twentieth-century operas, *The Rake's Progress* was first heard at the Teatro La Fenice, Venice, on September 11, 1951. Stravinsky conducted, and leading roles were sung by Elisabeth Schwarzkopf (Anne Trulove), Jennie Tourel (Baba the Turk, a bearded lady), Robert Rounseville (Tom Rakewell), and Otakar Kraus (Nick Shadow). Without becoming a widely popular opera, *The Rake*—which one Italian critic described as having "drawn an enormous question mark on the blackboard of contemporary music"—has gone on to performances in most principal cities of the Western world. It did not respond well to being plunged into the huge auditorium of the Metropolitan Opera House in New York, but was apparently at its right size at Glyndebourne.

The musically less influential Serge Prokofiev was much more productive as an operatic composer than Stravinsky. His persistent interest in the stage began very early: his first opera, *The Giant,* was composed to his own libretto when he was nine years old. Eight operas later, in

---

[1] *Mavra* was on a double bill with the *première* of a curious little entertainment —a "burlesque chamber opera"—called *Renard.* Stravinsky's fondness for hybrid musicodramatic forms was evinced further in several other works, notably *Les Noces villageoises* (1923), "choreographic Russian scenes with song and music," as he himself described it, and *Oedipus Rex* (1927, concert form; 1928, stage version), an oratorio-opera completely without dramatic impact, but impressive because of its superb choruses.

1948, his last opera, *A Tale About a Real Man,* was produced in Leningrad. That it was a private performance could not prevent party-line critics from blasting away at it so successfully that no public production followed. Between *The Giant* and that last bitter rejection, he had composed *Magdalena* (1913); *The Gambler,* after Dostoevsky (1916);[2] his most famous stage work, *The Love for Three Oranges,* after Carlo Gozzi (1921); *The Flaming Angel,* after a story by Valery Bryusov (1919); *Simeon Kotko* (1939); *Betrothal in a Convent* (1940); and *War and Peace,* after Tolstoy (1941–52).

The Love for Three Oranges is a fantastic fairy-tale opera in which Rimsky-Korsakov's highly developed idiom for expressing decorative aspects of the supernatural has been Prokofievized. The text, derived from Gozzi's *fiaba* entitled *L'Amore delle tre melarancie,* was Prokofiev's own; it was translated into French by Vera Janacopulos for the world *première,* which took place at the Chicago Auditorium on December 30, 1921, during Mary Garden's directaship[3] there. Sumptuously staged amid décors by Boris Anisfeld, it failed to arouse enthusiasm, being far too "modern" for the audiences then. It has persisted, however, and not only because of the hackneyed March and Scherzo from it, so often played by symphony orchestras; and it is occasionally heard, from Ljubljana to New York, in which latter city the New York City Opera Company staged it first in 1949.

The Love for Three Oranges remains delightful. It is concise, witty, vivid, and thoroughly entertaining in the way its music perfectly catches the insouciant spirit of the Venetian tale. Some of the score's rhythmic exuberance derives from Stravinsky as clearly as Prokofiev's *Scythian Suite* (from the ballet *Ala and Lolly*) derives from *Le Sacre du printemps.* But it is no musical shocker. Prokofiev's marked, unique talent for sarcasm and satire gets full play in this epigrammatic, vigorously tuneful score.

Altogether different is *The Flaming Angel,* a tempestuous tale of a sixteenth-century *Lanzknecht* in love with a beautiful girl who is con-

---

[2] *The Gambler* was ready for production—Albert Coates was to be the conductor—at the Maryinsky Theater in what was then Petrograd, when the Revolution intervened. The performance never took place. The *première* of this grim, sardonic version of Dostoievsky's *Igorok* actually occurred in Brussels, at the Théâtre de la Monnaie, on April 29, 1929.

[3] This is not a misprint: Miss Garden insisted for a time that she was the directa, not director, of the Chicago Opera Association.

vinced that she has been loved by an angel of fire and who is at last condemned to be burned alive by the Inquisition. The opera is curiously Teutonic in atmosphere even before Mephistopheles and Faust enter as characters in the last act. In part a very intense study of hallucinatory psychical hysteria, it rises to real dramatic power whenever Renata, the heroine (and certainly the character who interested Prokofiev), has a seizure or deliberately turns to the invocation of occult powers. *The Flaming Angel* won sensational attention when it was performed, for the first time, at a Venice festival in 1955, since when it has been heard elsewhere in Europe and has gone on gaining enthusiastic adherents. Prokofiev himself considered it his best opera.

Of Prokofiev's other operas, both *Simeon Kotko* (Moscow, June 23, 1940) and *War and Peace* (Leningrad, June 12, 1946), a gigantic panorama, suffer from ideological pressures, appearing to belong to the unhappy class of Prokofiev's official, state-inspired creations. The eminence of Tolstoy's great novel has induced production of *War and Peace* in condensed versions,[4] both staged and on television, outside the Soviet Union. But *Simeon Kotko,* with a patriotic libretto by Valentin Kataiev dealing with civil war in the Ukraine, has proved all but completely unexportable.

A far happier opera in every sense is *Betrothal in a Convent* (or *Cloister* or *Nunnery*). Even in semiamateur, small-scaled production as *The Duenna* (the name of the Sheridan play on which its libretto was based), this sparkling tomfoolery justified Martin Cooper's description of it as "a light, often elegantly written comedy in which Spanish pastiche is a considerable element." Devoid of both *diablerie* and political tendency or implication, it remains unmistakably Russian, unmistakably Prokofiev. It was sung for the first time at Leningrad on November 3, 1946. In the Western world, at least, the years' selectivity seems likely to single it out—perhaps alongside *The Love for Three Oranges* and *The Flaming Angel*—for living preservation among Prokofiev's operas.

Neither Stravinsky nor Prokofiev ever composed an opera that blew up as much controversy as was caused by Dmitri Shostakovich's *Lady Macbeth of Mzensk*. Completed in 1932, produced at the Little Theater in Leningrad on January 22, 1934, this harshly realistic setting of a

[4] Its complete cast of characters in the uncut version asks for seventy-two solo singers, though some of the roles permit doubling and tripling. For its first performance in Western Europe (Florence, 1953), it was produced in a version condensed by Artur Rodzinski.

libretto by the composer and Y. Preis tells the story of a bourgeois woman
—a kind of Russian Emma Bovary—who, out of boredom, takes a lover,
murders her husband, is exiled to Siberia, and commits suicide. Shostakovich commented with drastic, outspoken musical naturalism on this
sordid material, interspersing his musical photography and phonography
with pertinent lyrical banalities of cloying saccharinity. The opera presents, in short, much the same mixture of brash vitality and long-drawn-
out sentimentalizing which is familiar in Shostakovich's symphonies.
The particular mixture in *Lady Macbeth of Mzensk,* however, has
authentic reasonableness as illustrating the text. Also, some of the
entr'acte music remains among the most satisfactory that Shostakovich
has written.

Lady Macbeth of Mzensk became a success almost immediately.
Heard in Moscow two days after the Leningrad *première,* it was at first
accepted as a crushing satire on bourgeois manners. Then it reached
America, first, on January 31, 1935, at Severance Hall, Cleveland, and
five days later at the Metropolitan Opera House, New York, both times
performed by the Art of Musical Russia and the Cleveland Orchestra,
conducted by Artur Rodzinski. It was received with applause to match
the deafening noise of the score, though with some inclination to boggle
at orchestration that in one scene unquestionably mimics the sounds
of sexual intercourse. Early in 1936, however, as if to censure naughty
Russians for flocking to hear it, the awful voice of *Pravda* thundered
(in an article notable for muddy thinking), declaring the opera a
decadent, bourgeois-catering work wicked in its antimelodic snobbish-
ness. The acclaim of fashionable foreign audiences seems to have provoked *Pravda*'s attack. For an hour it appeared that Shostakovich, until
then a prize exhibit of Soviet culture, might be forced into apparent
silence. But common sense gradually asserted itself: *Lady Macbeth of
Mzensk* was, at least for the time being, suffered to go on portraying
sex-mad bourgeois society. Shostakovich restored himself to the good
graces of the authorities by writing the Fifth Symphony, which, having no
scandalous libretto, could be construed as containing an acceptable
ideology.

Without the opportunity to hear the probably minor operas of certainly minor Soviet composers, a discussion of them could only degenerate into cataloguing. Nothing heard of the music of the Kabalevskys,
Khatchaturians, Shebalins, and Dunayevskys suggests that their operas
would loom large by the side of, say, Stravinsky's *The Nightingale* and

The Rake's Progress, Prokofiev's *The Love for Three Oranges* and *The Flaming Angel.* Still, the possibility persists—at least until some of them have been made available by complete recording or in worthy professional production—that the Iron Curtain has been impoverishing the West. Whether or not we should ever be able to swallow librettos of socialist realism and pseudo-Marxian dialectic in carefully censored tones must remain another question.

The Russians, by and large, have subsisted on their own musical past, with the addition of some borrowings from Western Europe, notably from Wagner and Debussy. The Italians, on the contrary, except for those who have followed, more or less blind and deaf, *verismo,* the *opera buffa* tradition, Verdi, or Puccini, have been frantic experimentalists—tasters of bewildering and finally inert eclecticism, connoisseurs of ultimate shudders even down the cul-de-sac of atonality and dodecaphonism. With all their unquestioned ingenuity, eagerness, and industry, they have failed to produce a twentieth-century composer of opera of anything like the first significance.

Take Ildebrando Pizzetti, for instance, a seasoned composer of staggering technical competence whose *Fedra* (libretto by Gabriele D'Annunzio) was first produced as long ago as March 20, 1915. He has composed in almost every musical form, in many forms voluminously. But no definite musical personality has evolved. As a composer for the stage he seems destined not to survive, a sort of *Cavalleria*-less Mascagni, though he has composed a dozen operas and incidental music for many plays. Only one of his operas, but that possibly his best, the carefully constructed *Fra Gherardo* (Milan, May 16, 1928), has been staged in an American opera house, first at Buenos Aires, and then, on March 20, 1929, at the Metropolitan. It was given respectful attention, but neither the composer's own libretto about a medieval religious fanatic nor his finical delving into modal harmonies mingled with nonstructural, exterior modernistic touches could endear this one-third of a noninterrelated trilogy to the public. Four Metropolitan performances sufficed.

On March 1, 1958, when Pizzetti was past seventy-seven, another of his operas won world-wide notice. To a literal translation by Monsignor Alberto Castelli of T. S. Eliot's *Murder in the Cathedral,* he had composed, in two acts and an intermezzo, an oratoriolike, necessarily static, and—for most of its length—uninteresting score that not even a truly magnificent Scala production could altogether animate. *Assassinio nella cattedrale* has been heard elsewhere since, but it does nothing to remove

Pizzetti from the unhappy class of perfectly respectable men of music who always garner honors despite the fact that their destiny is to have each successive work greeted with the exclamation "Interesting!" and then promptly or shortly shelved and forgotten. Who now remembers (to pull three names at random from the list of Pizzetti's operas) *Debora e Jaele* (1922), *L'Oro* (1947), or *Cagliostro* (1953)?

Nor does that more gifted man, Gian Francesco Malipiero, the hermit of beautiful Asolo in the Venetian hinterland, add up to much more than Pizzetti as a composer, despite his more violent gyrations. Malipiero has been another self-librettist, and his operatic books most often ring with jangled, disjunctive poetry. So, too, do his scores. Malipiero has believed, and justly, that Italian music has fallen on evil days. His remedies—for he has tried several—are drastic, ranging from a complete rejection of the development of Italian music since Monteverdi (for example, he has relentlessly attacked Verdi) to the importation of new systems by Hindemith and Schoenberg. Further to complicate his texture, *Petrouchka* and *Le Sacre du printemps* echo through some of his scores, as do Gregorian chant and the polyphonic patterns of Palestrina. Malipiero never has displayed the consistency of the small mind. He is not even averse to using a scandalously overripe Neapolitan tune.

Malipiero began his operatic career in 1914 at Rome with an opera called *Canossa;* since then he has been operatically industrious. Among his many stage works, perhaps the best known is a titanic trilogy called *L'Orfeide,* which, on a vast scale, makes mock of civilization. No part of it [5] is what we are accustomed to think of, even in a loose sense, as opera. Not only do its dramatic sequences lack continuity for all except scholars capable of supplying bridges across their lacunae, but also Malipiero's musical style is too consistently discordant ever to enlist large numbers of affectionate singers or listeners.

If the number of operas written and produced were the sole criterion, Italy would, with Germany, still be the home par excellence of opera.

---

[5] The construction of *L'Orfeide* is arrestingly complex. It is in three large parts: *La Morte delle maschere, Sette canzoni,* and *L'Orfeo ossia L'Ottava canzone. Setti canzoni,* which was heard at the Paris Opéra as *Sept chansons* on July 10, 1920 (more than five years before the whole vast trilogy was presented in German translation at Düsseldorf on October 30, 1925), is made up of what the composer called *sette espressioni drammatiche* (roughly "seven dramatic expressions"), each of which has a title: *I Vagabondi, A Vespro, Il Ritorno, L'Ubbriaco, La Serenata, Il Campanaro,* and *L'Alba delle ceneri.*

Among the numerous twentieth-century Italians who have actively enlarged operatic dictionaries was Alfredo Casella, who came late to opera —he was nearly fifty when *La Donna serpente,* his first essay in the form, was played at the Teatro Reale, Rome, on March 17, 1932. The formally aloof, neoclassical work, with its then-contemporary harmonic and rhythmic idioms, was received with loud applause, in part because Casella had been viewed as unofficial composer extraordinary to the Mussolini regime (one of his later effusions was a lay oratorio on the Italian conquest of Ethiopia). On September 6 of that same year, at Venice's Teatro Goldoni, a brace of short Casella works was first heard. One half of it, *La Favola d'Orfeo,* was a semioperatic setting of Politian's *favola* that had been put to music first as early as 1472; the other half was a wordless "symphonic drama" called *Panthea.* Casella went back to glorifying the assault on Ethiopia in the one-act mystery *Il Deserto tentato,* written to a crude text by Corrado Pavolini. This Fascist balderdash was a much-praised feature of the Maggio Musicale Fiorentino, where it was sung for the first (and almost the last) time on May 6, 1937.

The slightly older Francesco Balilla Pratella, a voluminous fashioner of opera, attached himself briefly to the hopefully violent group of "futurists" headed by the poet and general jackanapes Filippo Tommaso Marinetti. But Pratella's operas were almost laughably innocuous despite their usually hysterical programs. Basically Mascagnian,[6] his most fearsome gesture turned out to be a timid approach to Debussy. His *L'Aviatore Dro,* first sung at Lugo on September 4, 1920, retains some interest as an early attempt to treat aviation operatically. Far more vital was another such try, *Volo di notte* (Florence, May 18, 1940), a one-act setting of Antoine de Saint-Exupéry's *Vol de nuit* by the most talented of the Italian generation born at the turn of the century, Luigi Dallapiccola, at that time a rigorous atonalist-dodecaphonist. Dallapiccola has also composed *Il Prigioniero,* a one-act opera with prologue heard by radio in 1949 and staged at Florence on May 20, 1950. When the Italian critic Massimo Mila said that in *Il Prigioniero* the presence of human actors on the stage seemed almost an encumbrance, the entire dramatic life having passed into the music, he made a critical charge to which too many recent operas, Italian and non-Italian, must plead guilty. Dallapiccola's *Job* (a *sacra rappresentazione*), first heard at Rome on October

---

[6] Mascagni himself, it must be remembered, was winning *premières* through the 1930's.

31, 1950, has music so autonomous that critics and audience wondered why it should have been staged at all.[7]

Deriving in about equal measures—seriatim, not simultaneously— from Casella and Schoenberg, Dallapiccola's almost exact coeval, Goffredo Petrassi, has also wrestled with problems of opera without solving them. His *Il Cordovano*, the one-act libretto of which he himself had adapted from Cervantes, turned out to be a strange emulsion of comic text and solemn music when it was performed at La Scala, Milan, on May 12, 1949. Petrassi's *La Morte dell' aria*, dealing seriously with the modern artist's serious psychic-aesthetic-practical dilemmas, was sung at the Teatro Eliseo, Rome, on October 23, 1950, and proved to be a lyric work—often with suggestions of madrigal style—borne down by Tito Scialoja's overcomplex libretto. It shared a triple bill with two other one-acters: Alberto Savinio's *Orfeo vedova* and the last work of the veteran Vincenzo Tommasini, memorable chiefly for his balletic arrangement of pieces by Domenico Scarlatti, *Le Donne di buon umore*. Tommasini died two months later at the age of seventy-two.

As a final reflection on a bustling, but not very important, industry, it should be said that scores of young, dedicated Italians try valiantly to prove their citizenship in the serial universe, turning out experiments that show courage and considerable ingenuity, all based on a terrifying logic. Most of them, however, are technically impeccable. Apparently, they fail to communicate, for the one quality they all seem to have in common is transience.

In France the operatic scene is less happily cluttered. Neither the French pseudo-Wagnerians nor the Debussyites established lasting schools. The men who have made marks on opera since *Pelléas et Mélisande* have had only Gallicism in common as they have individualistically taken roads of their own choice. Paul Dukas composed only one opera, *Ariane et Barbe-Bleue*, like Debussy setting a play much as Maurice Maeterlinck had written it. *Ariane* dates from May 10, 1907 (Opéra-Comique, Paris, where by 1950 it had been sung seventy-nine times), when the beautiful Lucienne Bréval was a superb heroine. The opera mingles Debussyan and Wagnerian influences without detriment

---

[7] Mention must be made of Riccardo Pick-Mangiagalli, a Bohemian-Italian composer, if only because his *L'Ospite inatteso* seems to have been the first opera to have been given its *première* by radio (Milan-Turin-Genoa network, October 25, 1931), and because his first opera, *Basi e bote* (Teatro Argentina, Rome, March 3, 1927), was written to a libretto by Arrigo Boito.

to sparkling wit and highly expressive orchestration as foreign to *Tristan* as to *Pelléas,* both of which are satirically quoted in the score, in which Mélisande herself is also a character. This delightful opera, bringing refreshing precision to the muzzily symbolic *théâtre* of Maeterlinck, has been heard too seldom outside Paris.

Albert Roussel, a forceful and intensely original composer of Dukas's generation, flirted with the stage in several ways—as ballet, as *opéra-bouffe,* as incidental music, and twice as opera-ballet: *La Naissance de la lyre,* produced at the Opéra, Paris, July 1, 1925, with a libretto by Théodore Reinach, and—Roussel's masterpiece in many French critics' view—*Pâdmâvatî* (Opéra, June 1, 1923). Louis Laloy's exotic libretto dealing with a beautiful Hindu princess and a khan from Mongolia would have invited many earlier and contemporary French composers to the Delibes–Florent Schmitt variety of pseudo-Orientalism. Roussel's powerful score avoids them completely, treating the tale to an investiture of acrid harmonies and subtle rhythms.

A one-opera man was Maurice Ravel,[8] after Debussy the leading musical talent of modern France. Unfortunately, *L'Heure espagnole,* though marked by the best of Ravel's musical qualities—wit, bite, alluring rhythm, irruptions of icy passion, and utter mastery of the orchestra —does not bring them together in their best ensemble. Ravel is often tagged as an impressionist, which he rarely was. In *L'Heure espagnole,* reacting against both romanticism and the tag ends of impressionism, he moved off in the direction of classical *bouffe.* His world-wide reputation and enormous popularity served to win this opera about a clock-maker's flirtatious wife many more productions than it might have been able to garner on its merits and appeal to audiences alone. In Paris it has been heard both at the Opéra-Comique (world *première,* May 19, 1911) and at the Opéra.

Still another one-opera man was the picturesque, sardonic, more-discussed-than-listened-to Erik Satie, a *petit-maître* whose naïve originality bore him nearly to greatness. Partly Scottish, Satie brought to a lifelong consuming interest in music the devastating logic of a perfect fool and an ebullient flair for nonsense. But his only opera, *Socrate,* a

[8] Ravel's *L'Enfant et les sortilèges* qualifies as a wholly delightful near-opera, near-pantomime, and almost-ballet. First heard—and seen—at Monte Carlo on March 21, 1925, this superb setting of a Colette morality about abused toys, animals, objects, and their revenge makes use of an adapted jazz idiom and of an orchestra including whistles, woodblocks, and cheese-graters.

three-part setting of selections from Victor Cousin's French translations
of Plato's Dialogues (Paris, February 14, 1920; first public stage performance, Prague, May, 1925), was gravely conceived and more gravely
executed. It represents the ultimate application of Satie's long-meditated
theories of art: *Socrate* goes more than one step beyond Debussy in
never interfering with the flawless integrity of the text, never underlining or commenting upon specific actions or words, but merely reacting to the atmosphere of the Dialogues. Satie's score is never picturesque,
never descriptive: *Socrate* is mood music, ideal music, of a rarefied sort
that approaches the concepts of Peri and Caccini. Of everything that the
theater and the opera house have taught us to consider dramatic, *Socrate*
is scrupulously free.

Satie, besides his effect on extramusical art, strongly influenced one
so-called school of composers—*Les Six*—and was for a time saluted as
father of another. The latter—the *École d'Arcueil*—fizzled out in a
blaze of mediocrity, but several of the soon-separated *Six,* originally
sponsored in brilliant manifestoes by Jean Cocteau, became composers
of true distinction. Three of them, the Provençal Darius Milhaud, the
Swiss Arthur Honegger, and the Parisian Francis Poulenc, were attracted
significantly to opera.

Milhaud responded like a healthy reed to influences ranging from
Stravinsky to Brazilian, Provençal, and traditional Hebraic tunes. His
many operas are widely diversified in subject matter, size, and treatment.
He is as capable of doing a trilogy on the *Oresteia* of Aeschylus as of
tossing off a piece of musical nut brittle like *Les Malheurs d'Orphée,*
in which that time-honored *chanteur* is treated with supreme, super-
Offenbachian indignity. In 1927, Milhaud wrote three "minute" operas
(*L'Enlèvement d'Europe, L'Abandon d'Ariane,* and *La Délivrance de
Thésée*) of astonishing brevity (about ten minutes each). Set to subjects from tragic Greek myth, these pungently discordant, rigidly compressed musical crises remain among the most vivid manifestations of
operatic neoclassicism. *L'Enlèvement d'Europe,* in eight scenes despite
its extreme brevity, was first heard at Baden-Baden on July 17, 1927; [9]
the other two were sung at Wiesbaden on April 20, 1928—and all were
sung in German.

Milhaud's most sensational opera has been *Christophe Colomb,* to a

[9] As part of a four-part bill of *premières,* the other three parts being Ernst Toch's
Die Prinzessin auf der Erbse, Paul Hindemith's *Hin und Zurück,* and Kurt Weill's
Aufstieg und Fall der Stadt Mahagonny.

libretto by Paul Claudel, under whom Milhaud had served in the French legation in Rio de Janeiro. This two-part opera in twenty-seven scenes has been described succinctly by Nicolas Slonimsky as "containing elements of Greek drama (the use of suasive chorus), mystery play (allegory), music drama (use of musical mottoes), expressionist technique (Columbus conversing with his second self), symbolism and modern newsreel methods (the use of motion pictures). . . ." *Christophe Colomb,* which has obvious affinity to German expressionist drama, was produced, not in Paris, but at the Berlin Staatsoper, in German, on May 5, 1930, under the direction of Erich Kleiber.[10]

Milhaud has composed more than a dozen operas ranging in length and manner all the way from the three "minute" operas to the grandiose *Maximilien* (Opéra, Paris, January 4, 1932),[11] its three-act French libretto by Armand Lunel being a translation of a German text drawn from Franz Werfel's play *Juarez und Maximilian,* and *David,* a five-act spectacle in twelve scenes, again with text by Lunel, which was first sung in Jerusalem in concert form on June 1, 1954 and then staged at La Scala, Milan, on January 2, 1955. But productions of these operas have remained rare; none of them has ever been mounted at either Covent Garden or the Metropolitan, for example. The trouble with much of Milhaud's music is that he does not seem to have been sufficiently self-critical.

The late Arthur Honegger was much less prolific than Milhaud; also, his compositional style became more compact, dense, and solemn than that of any of the other *Six.* Like many of his contemporaries, he tended to create dramatic stage works that could not readily be classified— dramatic psalms, mimed symphonies, lyric tragedies without action, and so on. The earliest of them, the *psaume dramatique, Le Roi David,* to a text by René Morax, director of the Mézières folk theater, was first performed at Mézières, Switzerland, on June 11, 1921, and has even been staged. But it is actually a concert oratorio, as which it has retained some power to move and shock.

The folk theater at Mézières also commissioned Honegger to provide incidental music for Morax's Biblical drama, *Judith;* this was later transformed into a three-act opera that was first sung at Monte Carlo on

[10] In 1952—his opus 318—Milhaud composed an entirely new *Christophe Colomb,* this time as incidental music for a production of the Claudel play.

[11] With *Christophe Colomb* and *Bolivar* (Paris Opéra, May 12, 1950), *Maximilien* forms a sort of "American" trilogy.

February 13, 1926. As produced at the Auditorium, Chicago, on January 27, 1927, with Mary Garden in the name role, *Judith* was acclaimed as a work of genius—and lasted two performances. Its most striking features are the grandeur of its choral masses and its bloodcurdling finale, a strident, chaotic pyramid of noises built up as the heroine rushes from the Assyrian general's tent with his severed head. Other Honegger stage works that attracted more than passing attention were an operetta, *Les Aventures du roi Pausole,* based on Pierre Louÿs's novel, and humorously obscene in tone (Bouffes-Parisiens, Paris, December 12, 1930); an *oratorio dramatique* with text by Paul Claudel, *Jeanne d'Arc au bûcher,* in eleven scenes, first heard at Basel, Switzerland, on May 12, 1938; and two scores written collaboratively with Jacques Ibert: a five-act opera, *L'Aiglon,* with text derived from Edmund Rostand's play about the King of Rome (Monte Carlo, March 11, 1937), and an operetta entitled *Les Petites Cardinal* (Paris, February 20, 1938).

By general consent, however, Honegger's most impressive opera is *Antigone,* first sung at the Théâtre de la Monnaie, Brussels, on December 28, 1927. The strong, spare three-act libretto by Jean Cocteau (after Sophocles) was set with stark power, a Lullyan type of continuous recitative being heard above a strong, sharply dissonant orchestral web. Honegger added to the kinetic urgency by disregarding a French operatic custom of placing the important first syllables of text words on unaccented or weakly accented beats—instead he repeatedly gave them strong accents. The opera is devoid of arias, and contains none of the decorative features, balletic or otherwise, of many large French operas; it hews unmitigatedly to the business of clothing the text (without word repetitions) in expressive music.

Much less prolific of stage pieces, but more certainly a possible contributor to the living repertoire of opera, has been Francis Poulenc. Although he was tempted by the singing stage as early as 1920 (when his *comédie-bouffe, Le Gendarme incompris,* was heard), he first attracted notice in the operatic world when his delicious and somewhat Ravelesque two-act *opéra-bouffe, Les Mamelles de Tirésias,* to a suggestive satirical text by Guillaume Apollinaire, was successfully staged in Paris at the Opéra-Comique on June 10, 1947. The tongue-in-cheek seminonsense about a feminist girl whose breasts (represented by balloons) float away when she determines to leave her husband and become a man, but return when she changes back into a girl and rejoins her husband (who, by means of an incubator, has had thousands of children in a single day), was set by Poulenc to his inimitable mixture of sentiment and deliberately vulgar "popular" music. The harmless obscenities of the text are mirrored faithfully in the brash, highly singable score.

Another side of Poulenc's talent, already evident, took on further stature with his religious opera *Les Dialogues des Carmélites,* sung at La Scala, Milan, in Italian, on January 26, 1957, and later that year at the Paris Opéra in French. The text, dealing with a community of Carmelite nuns driven from their convent by the French Revolution, and at last suffering martyrdom, has been based by Georges Bernanos on a novel by Gertrude von Le Fort and a scenario by Philippe Agostini and R. V. Bruckberger. Poulenc set the twelve tableaux of its three acts to lyric, conservative (some say "old-fashioned") music of continuous charm, singability, and intermittent dramatic relevance. *Les Dialogues,* unquestionably one of the most approachable of serious modern operas, has won numerous performances in several countries and seems likely to occupy a small permanent position in the enduring international repertoire.

On February 6, 1959, the Opéra-Comique, Paris, did something to restore itself to a long-lost position of importance in the operatic world: it presented the world *première* of Poulenc's one-act, one-character opera, *La Voix humaine.* Critics were divided as to whether Jean Cocteau's monologue-play was good operatic material, but were nearly unanimous in their praise of the great skill with which the composer had fitted the role of "She" ("He" never appears, being just a voice on the telephone) to the special talents of Denise Duval, who later displayed them in the role at the Piccola Scala, Milan, in New York (concert performance), and elsewhere. *La Voix humaine,* coming after the *Carmélites,* strengthened Poulenc's position as one of the most versatile of contemporary composers of opera.

Among the Teutonic composers, Arnold Schoenberg, that Viennese academe of vast erudition, stands first because of his audacious experiments and far-flung influence in many fields of composition. Although even now, so long after the epochal *Erwartung* (1909), the atonal music of Schoenberg and its later elaborate tone-row regimentation can be known well to but a small handful of concertgoers and closet musicians, his position as a force shaping twentieth-century music has been parallel to that of Stravinsky. Schoenberg began as a sentimentally lush romanticist, colored without notable violence by both Wagner and Brahms (not to mention Debussy), but by the time he began to compose for the stage he had quite left behind that early foolishness, and had begun to develop those complex mathematical formulas which made him the Einstein of music.

Erwartung, a one-act monodrama (or "mimodrama") to an expressionist text by Marie Pappenheim, employs a gigantic orchestra and a single soprano, who is required to demonstrate that she seeks her lover, stumbles upon his corpse, and thereupon—in a manner suggesting Isolde over the body of Tristan—rises into an exaltation of mystical love. It is deafeningly dissonant, but unquestionably powerful. Not clearly an opera at all, *Erwartung* might better be called a solo cantata. Composed in 1909 and published in 1916, it was heard for the first time at Prague on June 6, 1924, as the closing attraction of a festival of the International Society for Contemporary Music. Of this attempt to make a single character bear not only the action but also its environing implications, Schoenberg's fiercest admirers have asserted that in it he brought a new musical dispensation into being—a grandiose way of reporting that he had tried certain harmonic neoterisms and introduced novelties of declamation that were later developed further, notably in the tremulously beautiful and eloquent *Pierrot Lunaire,* a dramatic song cycle dating from 1912, and in his other operas.

Four months after the Prague *première* of *Erwartung,* Schoenberg's second stage work, *Die glückliche Hand* (composed in 1913), was sung at the Vienna Volksoper (October 14, 1924). In it, a baritone voice carries the chief commentary (Schoenberg's own text), while two other soloists occasionally join in, dancers mime the action, and a chorus of twelve voices speaking on musical tones provides a mystical overtone. Here is Schoenberg's much-favored *Expresionismus,* and *in excelsis.* And here, as in *Erwartung,* a swollen orchestra is busily employed in laying on a thick impasto of apparently willful dissonance and the vocal line is jagged and wide-spreading.

In 1929, Schoenberg finished *Von Heute auf Morgen,* a one-act opera employing the twelve-tone technique of composition throughout. Unlike *Erwartung* and *Die glückliche Hand,* it is not of continuous texture, but is plotted out in recognizably discrete arias and recitatives. Although this is a comic opera (the text is credited to a pseudonymous "Max Blonda"), *Von Heute auf Morgen* remains impenetrable to non-Schoenbergians, a forbidding congeries of musical means organized by what was unmistakably a profound musicomathematical mind, but failing to express anything recognizably human. The orchestra's odd sound does not derive entirely from the unwonted presence of such instruments as saxophone and flex-a-tone, which latter Curt Sachs described as a "metal plate whining under the pressure of the player's thumb." *Von Heute auf Morgen,* first heard at Frankfurt-am-Main on February 1, 1930, has been little performed since.

When Schoenberg died on July 13, 1951, he left unfinished a large operatic setting of his own text, *Moses und Aron.* Two acts of this Biblical drama had been completed in 1932, but he had taken up the third act, too late, only in 1951. The two completed acts were broadcast from Hamburg on March 12, 1954, and were heard in stage investiture at Zurich on June 6, 1957, during a festival of the International Society for Contemporary Music. *Moses und Aron* would, if completed, have been formally something between a Handel oratorio and true grand opera,[12] complete with huge but discreetly used orchestra (including piano, celesta, mandolins, and guitars) a ballet, and a staggering number of choristers. Moses (bass) employs *Sprechgesang,*[13] that peculiarly Schoenbergian version of text spoken on tones; Aaron, however, is a *Heldentenor.*

How far Schoenberg's considerations had removed him from the experienced universe of opera is well suggested by these sentences, intended as praise of *Moses und Aron,* from one of his celebrants, Peter Yates: "Schoenberg's art, like Bach's, is rigorous because it could not be otherwise. In them conscience was joined with duty and delight. Both were rejected by the spokesmen of the crowd.[14] Their art is inclusive, not exclusive; their admirers learn to enter one by one. Schoenberg's often simple, naïve expression of his inward necessity has given laughter to sophisticated critics. Twice he has answered in such manner that, overhearing, they may be ashamed: in the music for mixed chorus, Peace on Earth [*Friede auf Erden*], and in this tragic opera, an *ur*-form by which the inward spirit may measure the manifold activities and decisions of outward, political man."

[12] René Leibowitz, a convinced Schoenbergian, pointed out the influence here of Schoenberg's professed admiration for Puccini, and of *Turandot* in particular.

[13] In the score Schoenberg wrote: "The tempo of Moses' speech is governed by the music; the tone intervals should serve only for declamatory outline and characterization. This is *Sprechstimme,* the voice rising and falling relative to the indicated intervals, and everything being bound together with the time and rhythm of the music except where a pause is indicated."

[14] But was this true of Bach?

To many serious-minded, informed lovers of opera and of the art of music, nonetheless, Schoenberg's operas, like the body of his music in general, do not seem to bring us any *"ur*-form," but to proclaim instead the final disintegration of late Viennese psychological romanticism, to be the last highly complicated wavering of the line descending from Beethoven and Schubert through Brahms, Bruckner, and Mahler to that temporary ultimate in antimusical nonexpressiveness, the gnomic, overdelicate puzzle music of Anton von Webern, and to the psychoses-projecting scores of Alban Berg. That any of Schoenberg's operas will ever become prized possessions of the "crowd"—that they will ever, that is, achieve the genuine life represented by frequent performance—continues to seem very unlikely.

Down a curious operatic byway glimmer the works of Hans Pfitzner, largely unrecognized outside the German-speaking lands, but often looked upon with awe there. His stage career began on April 2, 1895, when *Der arme Heinrich,* to a text by James Grun, was staged at Mainz. Attracted in part by that very intense Germanness which has operated against Pfitzner's music outside his parents' native land (he himself, inappropriately, was born in Moscow), Humperdinck and others treated this harmlessly Wagnerian opera as a sign of flaming genius. Pfitzner followed it with *Die Rose vom Liebesgarten* (Elberfeld, November 9, 1901: revised version, Frankfurt-am-Main, May 5, 1939), to another Grun libretto, to the still further plaudits of enraptured German musicians of conservative tendencies. His most famous opera, *Palestrina* (Munich, June 12, 1917, with Bruno Walter conducting), well justifies Donald Jay Grout's description of his musical language as "deriving fundamentally from Wagner," but "modified by a more diatonic melody, a certain asceticism of feeling, long dwellings on mystical, subjective moods, and frequently dissonant contrapuntal texture with long-breathed melodies." *Palestrina,* crushingly static in nature, deals with Pfitzner's own version of the legend that Palestrina "saved" the art of music by composing his *Missa Papae Marcelli* in sufficiently simple, singable, and clearly understandable texture to satisfy the criticisms of overelaboration issued by the Council of Trent. Few doubted that Pfitzner was pointing out his own musical position.

Fourteen years after the ecstatically received *première* of *Palestrina,* Pfitzner's *Das Herz* was staged simultaneously at the Berlin and Munich opera houses. With a text by Hans Mahner-Mons (pseudonym of Hans Possendorf), it proved to be influenced by the trend toward separate-number operas in more advanced harmonic idioms, but was by no means radical. Like his earlier operas and his three-act "Christmas fairy story" *Das Christelflein* (Munich, December 11, 1906), *Das Herz* has had a career only within areas dominated by Germans and those who speak German. Pfitzner's reputation as a Nazi during World War II (he was exonerated by a de-Nazification court at Munich in 1948), accompanied as it was by a diminution of interest in his music, embittered him. He died in poverty at Salzburg in 1949.

Alban Berg, Schoenberg's most gifted pupil, subscribed in a very individual manner to the tenets of the master, but added many elements, most of them drawn from his profound study of the rich musical past. Berg, a belated romantic of the poetic persuasion, could not apply Schoenberg's most relentless theories without qualification. Compared with Schoenberg's operatic styles, Berg's is emotionally and humanly expansive and communicative: he is compact not from inner compulsion, but only when the urgent needs of a given dramatic situation demand compactness. Mingled with the modern harmonist is a broad lyricist of somewhat Schumannesque cast serving to make more palatable the scholarly patterns of his musical thought.

In *Wozzeck* (1914–21), a three-act opera in fifteen scenes, Berg had already created a thoroughly new, very complex, and enormously effective method of character-definition by assigning special harmonic sequences, capable of infinite variation and development, to each protagonist. Although this method is clearly an adaptation of the theories behind Wagner's leitmotiv and its application, Berg cast aside (as have so many more recent composers of opera) Wagner's endless musical web. Instead, he worked in a series of musical patterns—fugue, sarabande, gigue, gavotte, and others—each related with poetic illumination to the situation and the characters involved. In *Lulu* (1928–34), these ideas were developed and refined, always with such lambent intelligence and true musicianship that Berg's death before he had orchestrated the last act of *Lulu* was an artistic catastrophe.[15]

Wozzeck was recognized immediately as a great opera. This immensely powerful setting of Berg's own condensed adaptation of a disjunct twenty-five-scene play by Georg Büchner (1813–37) was performed 166 times

---

[15] Nicolas Slonimsky comments on the peculiar manner in which *Lulu* combines "purity of the classical design" with "a curious literalism of musical action." The erotomane heroine, he points out, "kills her last husband with five consecutive bullets on the ascending chromatics of the violins, C-sharp, D, E-flat, E, F. . . ."

in twenty-nine cities during the first eleven years after its *première* at the Berlin Staatsoper on December 14, 1925. This furore would not have been extraordinary as a greeting to a ripe veristic work like *I Gioielli della Madonna,* but *Wozzeck,* written largely in a difficult, dissonant idiom, would not have seemed in advance to be an easy work to assimilate. It is extremely difficult to produce adequately—the Berlin *première* required 136 rehearsals, and the score calls for four separate instrumental ensembles of widely varying make-up, one of them including instruments from a military band. Finally, the composer had, if anything, overemphasized rather than played down the psychosexual sordidness of Büchner's drama.

The early performances of *Wozzeck* created such violent partisanship pro and con that some of the topical literature about it was collected in a sizable volume. Time has neither stilled the controversy nor diminished the attraction that the opera itself exerts on musicians, musicologists, and operagoers. Indeed, it has become established as one of the major works of the twentieth-century musical stage along with *Pelléas et Mélisande,* the best of Puccini and Richard Strauss, and *The Rake's Progress.*

In Berg's few compositions later than *Wozzeck,* he increasingly employed dodecaphony, the elaborate, flexible system of basing a whole musical work on a single "tone-row" of twelve tones, none of them repeated until all have been heard. In 1928, he began to compose his second opera to a telescoped version of two related "tragedies of sex" by Frank Wedekind; when he died in 1935, *Lulu* was complete in sketch, but he had not fully orchestrated the third act (Schoenberg later completed the orchestration). What Berg had completed was staged at Zurich on June 2, 1937. Fortunately, he had arranged a suite for orchestra from numbers in the score, and this very interesting music is occasionally to be heard. Had he lived to complete *Lulu,* Berg might possibly have made it a worthy companion to *Wozzeck,* despite the unrelenting harshness of its discords and its total absence of the pathetic, gripping drama of his first opera.

Utterly antithetical to the romantic recluse Berg, Paul Hindemith, the prosaic, workaday craftsman, early made a profession of being a practical musician able to turn out under contract any kind of music. Hindemith's once tenaciously held point of departure, from which he later receded somewhat, is the precise opposite of art for art's sake. In his mind there was every reason why a work of art should have a specific usefulness; he was the leading exponent, that is, of *Gebrauchsmusik.* Because Hindemith had mastered several styles, not all of his operas conform to this fetish. An amusing *Gebrauchsoper* is his *Neues vom Tage* (1929), one of the episodes of which makes use of the widespread habit of singing in the bathtub,[16] while another includes a business letter set chorally.

Hindemith began as a romanticist making use of classical forms in a way suggested by the once highly regarded Max Reger. Innate inclinations quickly drew him toward a more incisive, impersonalized anti-Wagnerian style. *Cardillac* (Dresden, November 9, 1926), his first full-length opera, with a libretto by Ferdinand Lion based on E. T. A. Hoffmann's macabre *Das Fräulein von Scuderi,* is a clever modern adaptation of some of the manners of Handel's chamber music. In it Hindemith made use of classical patterns much as Berg used them in *Wozzeck* and *Lulu.* Although *Cardillac* was eagerly awaited, and had a considerable measure of success after its *première,* its neoclassical dryness has not helped its chances of survival even in a revised version (Zurich, June 20, 1952).

At Baden-Baden on July 17, 1927, Hindemith's *Hin und Zurück* proved to be unique in the annals of opera. This one-act *film sketch mit musik* made amusing play with the idea of a motion picture being run through a projector backwards. A man shoots his adulterous wife, a physician enters, and the woman dies; then the opera runs backwards as the woman returns from death to life, the doctor walks backwards through the door, the husband moves his gun from shooting position back into his pocket—and the little opera ends with everything exactly where it was in the beginning.

Much better known because of the popularity of the symphony that Hindemith arranged from its score, *Mathis der Maler* has more vital stuff in it. It was inspired by authenticated incidents in the life of Matthias Grunewald, painter of the Isenheim Altar, from which the stage settings and costumes were derived when the opera received its Zurich *première*

---

[16] In his useful booklet *Opera,* the late Edward J. Dent said of *Neues vom Tage:* "The libretto was amusingly modern, and the sensation of the opera was a scene in which the heroine, lying in a bath at a hotel, sang the praises of electric heating —'constant hot water, no horrid smell or danger of explosion,' etc. When the work was announced for performance at Breslau, the local gas company applied for and obtained an injunction, as this song was considered damaging to their trade. Opera is taken seriously in Germany."

on May 28, 1938. The opera would undoubtedly have been produced immediately in Germany had not Hindemith's style or styles of music been interdicted by the Nazi regime as *Kulturbolshewismus,* and he himself, though an "Aryan," eventually driven into exile. In later years, having returned to Germany, Hindemith saw his static but impressive five-scene opera, *Die Harmonie der Welt,* mounted at the Prinzregenten-theater, Munich, on August 11, 1957. Like his other operas, this one would seem to lack both of the requisites of which any opera must have at least one if it is to survive: memorable melody and vivid drama.

Gebrauchsmusik enlisted, at least temporarily, two other influential composers: Kurt Weill and Ernst Křenek. Weill, an artist of limited, uneven, but unquestionable inspiration, who sometimes let down his audiences with apparent *sang-froid,* wrote two particularly interesting near-operas, both collaborations with Bertolt Brecht, the poet, dramatist, stagecraftsman, and later Communist apologist who was regarded as the originator of the *Gebrauchsmusik* movement. The earlier, *Aufstieg und Fall der Stadt Mahagonny* (Leipzig, March 9, 1930), satirizes something resembling a decadent New York in music that alternates the hectic, the obscene, and the nerve-fraying. A series of discrete numbers, it rises to something like rhapsodic greatness in the sizzlingly ecstatic Alabama Song. Jazz is imitated with greater plasticity and irony in *Die Dreigroschenoper.* Weill, who spent his later years in America, frittered away his talents in a series of musical comedies of small distinction and incidental music of even less: long personal contact with the realities of American theatrical music appeared to rob him of his ability to satirize it effectively.

Most famous of jazz operas, *Jonny spielt auf,* by the learned and innately serious Křenek, who consistently missed greatness by little, may be considered the successful aberration of a solemn experimentalist. His most appreciable serious opera, *Karl V* (Prague, June 15, 1938; revised version, Düsseldorf, May 11, 1955), was composed in his own fearsome interpretation of Schoenberg's most arcane harmonic technique. *Jonny* was the typical opera of a period during which Europe—and Central Europe in its own intense, particular way—was discovering American jazz and then almost completely distorting it, sometimes as mockery, sometimes out of ineptitude and lack of understanding. *Jonny* was an explosive product: noisy, hilarious, riotous with half-directed energy, it captured the imagination of Europe soon after its *première* at Leipzig on

February 10, 1927. Shortly it had been translated into eighteen languages and given in more than one hundred cities. Somewhat bowdlerized, it was a novelty—in reality a curiosity—of the 1928–29 season at the Metropolitan. It entirely failed to convince Americans that European music, in the person of Křenek, had the slightest understanding of what the real jazz spirit was. After seven performances that season, *Jonny spielt auf* dropped permanently out of sight in America.

A disappointing career, beginning in deserved glory during adolescence and petering out in mediocrity during maturity, was that of the Austrian Erich Wolfgang Korngold. Beginning as a child, with music patently showing the imprint of Richard Strauss, Korngold composed two one-act operas—*Violanta* and *Der Ring des Polykrates* (Munich, March 28, 1916)—which were staged before his nineteenth birthday. With *Die tote Stadt* (Hamburg and Cologne, December 4, 1920) he won a brilliant success. This lush, lyrical setting of a text that Paul Schott had based on Georges Rodenbach's novel *Bruges-la-Morte,* reached Vienna and New York within one year and was soon played widely in Europe; the role of Marietta became one of Maria Jeritza's notable impersonations; a solo arrangement (known as "Mariettas Lied") for soprano of the soprano-tenor duet "Glück, das mir verblieb" for a time became a staple of *prima donna* recitals.

One more of Korngold's operas retained enough of the sensuous freshness and vitality of his early music to create a stir. This was *Das Wunder der Heliane* (Hamburg, October 7, 1927). The rest of Korngold's career (he died in Hollywood in 1957) was a decline in quality and originality, slow at first but then swift, until at last he seemed to have nothing left but mechanical competence.

A singular musical figure, capable of attracting both devotees and intense detractors, is Carl Orff, who, though born in 1895, evoked no large attention until 1937; his real international fame spread only after the end of World War II. His reworking of medieval student songs as a not-quite-opera, *Carmina Burana* (a "scenic oratorio"), first produced at Frankfurt-am-Main on June 8, 1937, exploits strong, repetitive rhythms, bare harmonies, *ostinati,* and crying vocal colors to produce an arresting effect that diminishes on rehearings. It was the first part of a semi-operatic trilogy, *Trionfi,* of which the two similar, related parts are *Catulli Carmina* (Städtische Theater, Leipzig, November 6, 1943) and *Il Trionfo d'Afrodite* (La Scala, Milan, February 13, 1953), both dealing with sexual excitement and even frenzy. They sound fascinatingly like nothing else ever composed, but do not finally communicate much more than surface excitement.

Another side of Orff's talent is represented by the "Bavarian play with music," *Die Bernauerin* (Stuttgart, June 15, 1947) and the comic one-act fable *Die Kluge* (Frankfurt-am-Main, February 20, 1943), the latter based on the Grimm tale "The Story of the King and the Wise Woman." Although these show little of Orff's attempt, as a neoclassicist, to go back to old monodic forms, they continue his coy flirtation with opera, each of his stage works being designated finically as a genre of its own. (*Carmina Burana* is subtitled "Cantiones profanae"; *Catulli carmina,* "Ludi scaenici"; *Il Trionfo d'Afrodite,* "Concerto scenico"; the early *Der Mond,* first heard at Munich on February 5, 1939, "Ein kleines Welttheater.") His *Antigonae,* on a text that Friedrich Hölderlin derived from Sophocles, is a full-fledged opera, but when the Württembergische Staatsoper, Stuttgart, staged his *Comoedia de Christi Ressurectione,* with Wieland Wagner as producer, on April 21, 1957, it turned out to be "An Easter Play." During the middle and late 1940's and the 1950's Orff was widely performed.

Less spectacular and unmistakable are the operas of Werner Egk, Gottfried von Einem, Boris Blacher, and the Swiss Rolf Liebermann.

Egk began his operatic career with *Columbus,* composed for radio performance, but staged at Frankfurt-am-Main on January 13, 1942. An able conductor and erudite musician, Egk appears to lack convincing power as a musical dramatist. Such of his operas as *Circe* (Städtische Oper, Berlin, December 18, 1948) and *Irisch Legende* (Festspielhaus, Salzburg, August 17, 1955) have not held the stage. But with *Der Revisor* (*The Inspector General*), after Gogol (Rokoko-Theater, Schwetzingen, May 9, 1957), he found a comic libretto particularly responsive to his somewhat academic-modern style, composing an opera that won interested attention and considerable praise.

Gottfried von Einem, an Austrian born in Switzerland, began his operatic career with *Dantons Tod,* a powerful work to a libretto by Boris Blacher based on a dramatic poem by Georg Büchner, author of *Wozzeck.* Its production at the Salzburg Festspielhaus on August 6, 1947, gave Einem a reputation with which he has had some difficulty keeping up, despite the adeptness with which he has shaped harmonic *derniers cris* to singability and the aural tolerance of audiences. His *Der Prozess,* with a libretto adapted by Boris Blacher and Heinz von Cramer from

Franz Kafka's novel, first heard at the Salzburg Festspielhaus on August 17, 1953, was hailed with enthusiasm in German-speaking countries, but has not traveled well. Blacher himself, born in China of Estonian-German parents, is a formidable musicologist and experimenter, as well as a distinguished teacher. His *Fürstin Tarakanowa,* heard at Wuppertal in 1941, caused little stir, but his "dramatic nocturne" *Die Nacht-schwalbe* (Städtische Theater, Leipzig, February 29, 1948) made a very loud noise indeed, largely because of its subject, which was stigmatized as "noisome." He seemed a chastened man when his less highly flavored *Romeo und Julia,* in one act, was heard at the Salzburg Festspielhaus on August 9, 1950, but succeeded in stirring up another tornado of discussion with his *Abstract Opera No. 1* (Frankfurt-am-Main, June 28, 1953), a sort of anti-opera requiring three soloists, two speaking actors, chorus, and orchestra.

Rolf Liebermann is a half-convinced Schoenbergian who also dallies on occasion with older manners and with jazz. His *Leonore 40/45,* described as an "opera semiseria," was sung at the Stadttheater in Basel on March 25, 1952; a related work, *Penelope,* was heard at the Salzburg Festspielhaus on August 17, 1954. But greater interest was evoked when *The School for Wives,* with a libretto by Heinrich Strobel (who has written all of Liebermann's texts), was sung at Louisville, Kentucky, on December 3, 1955, perhaps because it was free of the overlay of allegorical significance from which the earlier operas had suffered. But Liebermann's best-known composition is not a stage work: it is a widely played Concerto for Jazz Band and Orchestra (1954).

Liebermann was born in Zurich. The French area of Switzerland is most notably represented in modern opera by the Genevan Frank Martin. His *Le Vin herbé,* the text of which he had drawn from Joseph Bédier's retelling of the Tristram story, is halfway between an opera and an oratorio; it was sung for the first time at Zurich on March 26, 1942. More strictly an opera is *Der Sturm* (Vienna Opera, June 17, 1956), based on Schlegel's translation of Shakespeare's *The Tempest.* Martin's musical style is characterized by an increasingly individualized fusion of procedures inherited from French music of the turn of the century and from César Franck with the more advanced harmonic ways of the atonalists and dodecaphonists.

In England, a slowly cresting wave of renewed interest in opera has been accompanied by an occasionally nationalistic and insular feeling about native composers and native performers. The best results of this rebirth have brought international fame to Benjamin Britten, whose brilliant eclecticism makes impossible a single statement about his musical style. As a young man of only twenty-seven, he heard his first opera, *Paul Bunyan,* with a text by W. H. Auden, sung in New York (Columbia University, May 5, 1941). Four years later (June 7, 1945), the result of a commission from the Koussevitzky Foundation, his *Peter Grimes* reopened the Sadler's Wells Theatre in London, which had been closed by World War II. This powerfully grim tale of a fishing village, with a libretto that Montague Slater had based on a section of George Crabbe's *The Borough,* went on, after its *première,* to frequent repetitions in England and elsewhere. The suite of "Sea Interludes" which Britten arranged from its score became familiar as played by symphony orchestras. Many lovers of opera thought (and, unhappily for Britten's reputation, continue to this day to think) *Peter Grimes* theatrically the most viable English opera since *Dido and Aeneas* two and one half centuries earlier.

Britten's next opera (Glyndebourne, July 12, 1946), *The Rape of Lucretia,* suffers from a mannered, static (though very frank) retelling of the Tarquin-Lucrece episode by Ronald Duncan. This is a chamber opera requiring only eight singers (two of whom are a male and a female "chorus") and seventeen instrumentalists. The composer's spreading fame secured numerous stagings for *The Rape of Lucretia.* But much closer to the vitality of *Peter Grimes* is its successor, the comic *Albert Herring.* The text for this amusing spoof was based by Eric Crozier on a Maupassant tale transferred to an English locale.[17] *Albert Herring* was a star attraction of the Glyndebourne Festival on June 20, 1947, with Britten conducting.

Britten's next opera (Covent Garden, December 1, 1951) proved to be almost as much a literary event as a musical one: its libretto is by E. M. Forster, a recasting of Herman Melville's *Billy Budd.*[18] It cre-

---

[17] When the hero is crowned King of the May because no local girl can pass the chastity test required of a May Queen, he drinks what he believes to be lemonade, but which is really champagne—at which point the small orchestra emits a thin version of the motive of the love potion from *Tristan und Isolde.*

[18] Britten was not the first composer to produce an operatic treatment of Melville's Handsome Sailor. Giorgio Federico Ghedini, a prolific Italian composer twenty-one years Britten's senior—and composer, too, of *L'Ipocrita felice,* an operatic treatment of Max Beerbohm's *The Happy Hypocrite* (Piccola Scala,

ated advance international interest that was not sustained by its lack of action and monotonous absence of female vocal color, being in this exactly opposite Puccini's *Suor Angelica,* which suffers from lack of tenor, baritone, and bass tones.

Elizabeth II was crowned in Westminster Abbey on June 2, 1953. Six days later, at Covent Garden, Britten's *Gloriana,* with a text by William Plomer allegorically praising the new Queen in the person of Elizabeth I, revived an old-time custom of operatic compliments to reigning monarchs. More sustenance for Britten's slightly ebbing reputation as a stage composer was supplied by *The Turn of the Screw,* with a text by Myfanwy Piper based on Henry James's ambiguous story (Teatro La Fenice, Venice, September 14, 1954). And when the first performance of Britten's setting of *A Midsummer Night's Dream,* with a text derived from Shakespeare by himself and Peter Pears, was sung at the Aldeburgh Festival (June 11, 1960), negative criticism was limited to remarks about the composer's having assigned the role of Oberon to a countertenor and having written not very funny parodies of several sorts of opera in the Pyramus and Thisbe scene. *A Midsummer Night's Dream,* which was scheduled for performances elsewhere even before its *première,* seemed not to have pulled Britten's reputation back to the high level of *Peter Grimes.*[19]

Three other contemporary English composers have shone forth, each most notably with a single opera, as men of the stage. On December 3, 1954, Covent Garden was the scene of the *première* of Sir William Walton's *Troilus and Cressida,* a three-act opera with non-Shakespearean text by Christopher Hassall. A machine that works (despite the libretto's flat lack of distinction) and lyrically singable, *Troilus and Cressida* added nothing new to opera (it was compared to Zandonai's *Francesca da Rimini* of 1914) except a plausible addition to the repertoire. Much

---

Milan, March 10, 1956)—had composed a *Billy Budd* that was given its *première* at the Teatro La Fenice, Venice, on September 7, 1949.

[19] A special place in the corpus of Britten's stage work is occupied by "an entertainment for young people in two parts and three acts," *Let's Make an Opera.* The text by Eric Crozier and the Britten score are alike designed to allow youthful amateurs to take roles. Since its first performance at Aldeburgh on June 14, 1949, *Let's Make an Opera,* a real example of *Gebrauchsmusik,* and almost certainly descended from Paul Hindemith's *Wir bauen eine Stadt* (Oxford, July 25, 1931), has been performed widely in schools and by organizations of children.

more interesting, though also much more unsure of itself, was Michael Tippett's *A Midsummer Marriage* (Covent Garden, January 27, 1955), a gallimaufry set to his own overloaded and oversymbolized text. Tippett is a composer of eccentric originality, however, and the purely musical values of the score enlisted numerous admirers who could not swallow the libretto's significance and message.[20] And on July 23, 1957, at the Sadler's Wells Theatre, the Australian-English Arthur Benjamin's *A Tale of Two Cities,* libretto after Dickens by Cedric Cliffe, proved to be a workable spectacle devoid of any remarkable distinction.

[20] The late Cecil Smith's summing-up of his first impressions of *A Midsummer Marriage* demands quotation: "Tippett wrote his own libretto, and crowded it full of naïve, obscure symbolisms derived from Jungian psychology, Hindu philosophy, classic mythology, and any other arcane sources he could lay hands on. The plot, if that is the proper term for such chaos, centered upon the attempt to attain a satisfying relationship between the sexes. Two couples were involved. A Pamina-Tamino pair, Jenifer and Mark, were upper-class questers; they had to climb a staircase leading nowhere, disappear into a grotto barred by gates nobody else could open, and steam themselves in a mystic fire of regeneration before they were fit to enter a pseudo-Greek temple and live in the dreary but uplifting company of a He-Ancient and a She-Ancient. A Papagena-Papageno pair, Bella (a stenographer) and Jack (a mechanic), took matters more lightly, talking about having a baby and working matters out quite easily. Mixed up in the labyrinthine allegory were Jenifer's hard-bitten father, representing Big Business; Sosostris, a clairvoyante; and a pretentious ballet in which the male dancer (successively a hare, a fish, and a bird) was repeatedly ill-used by a predatory female dancer (successively a hound, an otter, and a hawk). Unintentional comic relief was furnished at the première by the male dancer, Pirmin Trecu, who could not count Tippett's irregular beats and kept clashing cymbals together long after the zero moment had passed in the orchestra."

Annals of Performance

Annals of Performance

1. Admeto, re di Tessaglia (Handel)

Three acts; text an adaptation (probably by Niccolò Francesco Haym, possibly by Paolo Antonio Rolli) of Aurelio Aureli's L'Antigona delusa da Alceste (first set by Pietro Andrea Ziani in 1660); London, Haymarket Theatre, January 31, 1727 (not February 11, as stated by Alfred Loewenberg).

The original cast included Faustina Bordoni (Alceste), Francesca Cuzzoni (Antigona), Anna Dotti (Orindo), Senesino (Admeto), Antonio Baldi (Trasimede), Giuseppe Maria Boschi (Ercole), and Signor Palmerini (Meraspe). During its run of nineteen nights, *Admeto* was heard by Johann Joachim Quantz, Frederick the Great's famous flautist, and probably by Voltaire. During this successful season, Handel formally applied for naturalization as a British subject.

Admeto was the last Handel opera revived during his lifetime, on March 12, 1754. As part of the so-called Handel Renaissance, it was played at Brunswick on October 14, 1925, in a German arrangement by Hans Dütschke. It was also one of the four Handel operas (the others being *Giulio Cesare, Poro,* and *Ariodante*) staged at the Theater des Friedens, Halle, in 1959,

as part of the celebration by the composer's birthplace of the bicentenary of his death.

2. Adriana Lecouvreur (Cilèa)

Four acts; libretto by Arturo Colautti, after a play by Augustin-Eugène Scribe and Ernest Legouvé; Milan, Teatro Lirico, November 6, 1902.

The cast of the Milan *première* included Francesco Pandolfini, Ghibaudo, Enrico Caruso, and Giuseppe de Luca; Cleofonte Campanini conducted. Before reaching London, the opera had been staged in Lisbon, Barcelona, Buenos Aires, Warsaw, Cairo, and Odessa in Italian; in German at Hamburg; and in French at Geneva and Antwerp. The first London performance, Covent Garden, November 8, 1904, in Italian, found the composer present. Campanini again conducted, and the cast was headed by Rina Giachetti (Adriana), Eleanora de Cisneros (Princesse de Bouillon), Giuseppe Anselmi (Maurizio), and Mario Sammarco (Michonnet). Four performances that season and two in 1906 (with Giovanni Zenatello replacing Anselmi and Leopoldo Mugnone conducting) ended the Covent Garden career of Cilèa's opera.

Campanini was conducting at the

rival Manhattan Opera House when the Metropolitan Opera House gave the first New York performance of *Adriana Lecouvreur* on November 18, 1907, opening the season. Rodolfo Ferrari spiritlessly conducted a performance in which Caruso repeated the role he had created at Milan; others in the cast were Lina Cavalieri (Adriana), Josephine Jacoby (Princesse de Bouillon), Antonio Scotti (Michonnet), and Marcel Journet (the Prince). Repeated eleven days later with the same cast, the opera then disappeared from the Metropolitan annals. It was announced for revival during the 1961–62 season as a starring vehicle for Renata Tebaldi, who had sung the title role in many places, including (1957) Chicago, but this production later was canceled and then re-announced for 1962–63.

Adriana Lecouvreur always has held a small place in the active repertoire in Italy, where in recent decades the title role has been favored by—among many others—Mafalda Favero, Maria Caniglia, Magda Olivero, and Tebaldi.

3. L'Africaine (Meyerbeer)

Five acts; libretto by Augustin-Eugène Scribe; Paris, Opéra, April 28, 1865.

Meyerbeer died on May 2, 1864; *L'Africaine*, the last of his operas, was produced with enormous success almost one year later. He had wanted Pauline Lucca for the role of Selika, but because she could not sing in French, the role went to Marie-Constance Sasse (or Sax), an ex-*variétés* artist. The cast also included Marie Battu (Inez), Jean-Baptiste Faure (Nelusko), Emilio Naudin—as specified in the composer's will (Vasco da Gama), and Louis-Henri Obin (High Priest of Brahma). Within little more than ten months, *L'Africaine* was sung at the Opéra 100 times; in twenty-eight years the tally of performances reached 485.

In Italian, as *L'Africana,* and much curtailed, the opera was heard at Covent Garden, London, less than three months after its Paris *première:* Lucca was the Selika, Mme Fioretti the Inez, Theodor Wachtel the Vasco da Gama, Francesco Graziani the Nelusko, and Sir Michael Costa the conductor, on July 22, 1865. Three months later, on October 21, the opera opened a season in English at Covent Garden with Louisa Fanny Pyne as Selika, Helen Lemmens-Sherrington as Inez, and Henry Haigh as Vasco da Gama. The Italian version had been sung four times that season; the English one reached a total of thirty-five performances.[1] The regular Covent Garden season of 1873 opened on April 1 with *L'Africana,* with Anna d'Angeri as Seiika and Ernest Nicolini as Vasco da Gama. Nicolini's future wife, Adelina Patti, sang her first Selika at Covent Garden on June 14, 1879, when Alwina Valleria was the Inez, Nicolini the Vasco da Gama, and Jean Lassalle the Nelusko in his London debut. During the 1880 season, Édouard de Reszke sang his first Don Pedro. On June 4, 1888, the Covent Garden cast of *L'Africana* included Lillian Nordica, Margaret Macintyre, Jean and Édouard de Reszke, and Lassalle; the future Edward VII and Queen Alexandra were in the house, and the opera was greeted rapturously. Nonetheless, its two performances that season proved to be its final ones at Covent Garden.

New Orleans, often the first city in the United States to hear new Meyerbeer operas, did not stage *L'Africaine* until December 18, 1869, in French. Earlier, New York had heard it in

---

[1] At the Imperial Opera House, Vienna, in 1869, as *Die Afrikanerin,* Meyerbeer's opera served to introduce a popular operetta singer to grand opera. Her name was Amalie Materna, and she eventually won her greatest fame as Brünnhilde at Bayreuth in 1876.

Italian (December 1, 1865), at the Academy of Music, with Zucchi as Selika, Mazzoleni as Vasco da Gama. Lucca was heard as Selika at the Academy on September 30, 1872. The Metropolitan's sixth (fifth all-German) season having opened on November 28, 1888, with *Les Huguenots,* its first production of *L'Africaine* was heard nine days later (December 7). Anton Seidl conducted, and the cast included Fanny Moran-Olden (Selika), Sophie Traubmann (Inez), Julius Perotti (Vasco da Gama), Adolf Robinson (Nelusko), and Emil Fischer (Don Pedro and High Priest of Brahma); the opera was repeated four times that season. The all-German seasons having passed, *L'Africana* was heard at the Metropolitan on January 15, 1892, with Nordica (Selika), Mathilde Bauermeister (Anna), Maria Pettigiani (Inez), Jean de Reszke (Vasco da Gama), Lassalle (Nelusko), and Édouard de Reszke (Don Pedro).

On February 13, 1895, the Metropolitan presented *L'Africana* with Nordica, Bauermeister, Lucille Hill (Inez), Francesco Tamagno (Vasco da Gama), Mario Ancona (Nelusko), and Édouard de Reszke (Don Pedro). Miss Hill fainted during Act II, and the versatile Bauermeister, stepping out of her menial role as Inez's attendant, Anna, assumed that of Inez for the rest of the performance. On February 27, 1899, with Nordica, both De Reszkes, and Pol Plançon doubling as the High Priest of Brahma and the Grand Inquisitor, Victor Maurel was first heard at the Metropolitan in his admired singing of Nelusko. Another remarkable Metropolitan cast was that of March 15, 1901: Lucienne Bréval (Selika), Suzanne Adams (Inez), Jean de Reszke (Vasco da Gama), Giuseppe Campanari (Nelusko), Marcel Journet (Don Pedro), and Plançon again doubling the two minor roles.

Enrico Caruso sang his first Vasco da Gama at the Metropolitan on January 11, 1907, opposite Olive Fremstad (Selika), Marie Rappold (Inez), Riccardo Stracciari (Nelusko), Plançon (Don Pedro), and Journet (High Priest of Brahma and Grand Inquisitor). After that season, *L'Africana* lapsed at the Metropolitan until Artur Bodanzky conducted it there on March 21, 1923, with Rosa Ponselle (Selika), Queena Mario (Inez), Marion Telva (Anna), Beniamino Gigli (Vasco da Gama), Giuseppe Danise (Nelusko), Adamo Didur (Don Pedro), and Léon Rothier (High Priest of Brahma and Grand Inquisitor). During the thirty-five performances that this revival ran up in eleven seasons, Elisabeth Rethberg was also heard as Selika. At the last Metropolitan performance to date (February 24, 1934), she was the Selika, Queena Mario the Inez, Giovanni Martinelli the Vasco da Gama, Armando Borgioli the Nelusko, Virgilio Lazzari the Don Pedro, and Ezio Pinza both the High Priest of Brahma and the Grand Inquisitor. After fifty-eight performances in twenty-three seasons, Meyerbeer's last opera left the Metropolitan without ever having been sung there in the original French. No Meyerbeer opera has been staged professionally in New York since 1934.

More recent revivals of *L'Africaine,* though not numerous, have probably outnumbered those of any other Meyerbeer opera. Tullio Serafin conducted a notable one in Verona's Roman Arena in 1932, with a cast that included Bruna Rasa, Gigli, Armando Borgioli, and Righetti. When the opera was revived in Rome five years later, Serafin and Gigli were again active; Maria Caniglia, Licia Albanese, Mario Basiola, and Giacomo Vaghi were also in the cast. A Vienna staging in that same year (1937) was conducted by Karl Alwin with a cast including Anny Konetzni, Gerhart, Alfred Piccaver, Alfred Jerger, and Zec. And at Berlin in 1951, the cast of a revival included Elfriede Wasserthal, Irma Beilke, Hans

Beirer, Josef Metternich, and Josef Greindl.

4. Die ägyptische Helena (Strauss)

Two scenes; libretto by Hugo von Hofmannsthal; Dresden, Opernhaus, June 6, 1928.

Fritz Busch conducted the world *première* of *Die ägyptische Helena;* the cast included Elisabeth Rethberg (Helena), Curt Taucher (Menelas), Maria Rajdl (Aithra), Friedrich Plaschke (Altair), Guglielmo Fazzini (Da-ud), Annaliese Petrich (Hermione), and Helene Jung (Die Muschel). Since that date it has had relatively few performances. It was heard in Vienna five days after the Dresden *première,* and in Berlin on October 7 of that same year, when Leo Blech conducted, and the cast included Maria Müller, Gita Alpar, Rudolf Laubenthal, and Friedrich Schorr. From 1933 until World War II, Viorica Ursuleac was the Helena of the few scattered performances in Germany and Austria, usually under the baton of her husband, Clemens Krauss. At a Munich revival in 1956, however, the Helena was Leonie Rysanek.

Die ägyptische Helena seems never to have been staged in London or Paris. But the Metropolitan Opera, New York, presented it, largely as a starring vehicle for Maria Jeritza (Helena), on November 6, 1928. Artur Bodanzky conducted, and others in the cast were Laubenthal (Menelas), Helen Eisler (Hermione, a role deleted in the four repeat performances), Editha Fleischer (Aithra), Clarence Whitehill (Altair), Jane Carroll (Da-ud), and Marion Telva (Die Muschel). After a final performance on December 19, the opera disappeared permanently from New York.

5. Aïda (Verdi)

Four acts; libretto by Antonio Ghislanzoni, after a French prose text by Camille du Locle based on a plot outline by Auguste-Édouard Mariette (Bey); Cairo, Khedival Theater, December 24, 1871.

The Cairo *première,* not attended by Verdi, was conducted by Giovanni Bottesini. The cast included Antonietta Pozzoni (Aïda), E. Grossi (Amneris), Pietro Mongini (Radames), F. Steller (Amonasro), P. Medini (Ramfis), Costa (King of Egypt), and Bottardi (Messenger). The *première* in Italy, at La Scala, Milan, on February 8, 1872, was conducted by Franco Faccio. The cast included Teresa Stolz[1] (Aïda), Maria Waldmann (Amneris), Giuseppe Fancelli (Radames), Francesco Pandolfini (Amonasro), and O. Maïni (Ramfis). Naples, Trieste, and Buenos Aires heard *Aïda* before it reached New York, the Academy of Music, on November 25, 1873, in Italian, with Ottavia Torriani (Aïda), Annie Louise Cary (Amneris), Italo Campanini (Radames), and Victor Maurel, in his American debut (Amonasro). The first performance in France, in Italian, occurred at the Théâtre-Italien, Paris, on April 22, 1876, with Stolz, Waldmann, Angelo Masini (Radames), and Édouard de Reszke, making his operatic debut (Ramfis). The opera was sung sixty-seven times at the Italien during the succeeding four years. When it was first heard in French, again at the Italien, on August 1, 1878, President Jules Grévy made a speech and created Verdi a grand officer of the Legion of Honor. London first heard *Aïda* at Covent Garden on June 22, 1876, in

---

[1] For whom Verdi added "O cieli azzurri" to the score. Of German stock though born in Bohemia, Stolz was a favorite of Verdi's; she excelled as Aïda and as Leonora in *La Forza del destino,* and made her farewell appearance at La Scala on June 30, 1879, in the "Manzoni" Requiem.

Italian. Enrico Bevignani conducted. The cast included, incredibly enough, Adelina Patti (Aïda), as well as Sofia Scalchi (Amneris), Ernest Nicolini (Radames), Antonio Cotogni (Amonasro), and Anacleto Bagaggiolo (Ramfis).

The Metropolitan did not get around to *Aïda* until its fourth (third German) season, on November 12, 1886. Anton Seidl conducted. The cast included, as Aïda, Therese Herbert-Förster, wife of the orchestra's first cellist, Victor Herbert, as well as Marianne Brandt (Amneris), Carl Zobel (Radames), Adolf Robinson (Amonasro), and Emil Fischer (Ramfis). W. J. Henderson reported in *The New York Times:* "It was evident . . . from last evening's performance that different conductorship and, in some instances, different singers must be had if Italian opera, pure and simple, is to be sung with German words at the Metropolitan. Many of the most beautiful and striking passages lost all their effect through the unconscionable dragging of the tempos by Herr Seidl, many symmetrical and melodic strains were drawn out of shape by a tendency to excessive emphasis on the part of the performers, and in the labors of almost all the artists there was discerned a want of refinement in feeling and expression." After the downfall of the German regime at the Metropolitan, *Aïda* became and remained Italian. It has

been sung more times than any other opera in Metropolitan history, 460 times through the 1961–62 season. It is also one of the few operas to have been sung at the Metropolitan twice within a single week.[2]

Aïda was the first opera sung in Paris by the Metropolitan troupe when it visited there in 1910. Arturo Toscanini conducted.[3] Emmy Destinn was the Aïda, Enrico Caruso the Radames. On November 16, 1908, Giulio Gatti-Casazza began his twenty-six years at the Metropolitan helm[4] with a performance of *Aïda* that presented both Toscanini and Destinn to American audiences for the first time; Caruso again was the Radames; the Amonasro was Antonio Scotti, the Ramfis Adamo Didur, and the Amneris Louise Homer.

Aïda, too, has been the opera to supply the Metropolitan with more than one of its most unintentionally dramatic moments. The announced Amneris for a performance on November 27, 1902, was Homer. But she was unable to appear, and Carrie Bridewell was substituted for her. Midway in the second act, however, Bridewell got into severe vocal difficulties. A rush call was sent out for Eugenia Mantelli, who was appearing in vaudeville at the time, and it was she who completed the opera. Others in what must by then have been a nervous cast were Emma Eames (Aïda), Emilio de

---

[2] On November 3, 1924, Tullio Serafin made his Metropolitan debut as the conductor of the opening night *Aïda*, with a cast that included Elisabeth Rethberg (Aïda), Margarete Matzenauer (Amneris), Giovanni Martinelli (Radames), Giuseppe Danise (Amonasro), and José Mardones (Ramfis). Serafin was to conduct every opening night at the Metropolitan until that of December 26, 1933—the sequence of operas being *Aïda*, 1924; *La Gioconda*, 1925; *La Vestale*, 1926; *Turandot*, 1927; *L'Amore dei tre re*, 1928; *Manon Lescaut*, 1929; *Aïda*, 1930; *La Traviata*, 1931; *Simon Boccanegra*, 1932; and *Peter Ibbetson*, 1933. Serafin conducted at the Metropolitan for the last time on March 29, 1934, when the opera was *Linda di Chamounix*. Why this man, admittedly

one of the ablest conductors of Italian opera, and still actively conducting when these words were written twenty-eight years later, never returned to the Metropolitan—which has housed many of his inferiors—remains a mystery of operatic lore.

[3] Twenty-four years earlier, *Aïda* had served to speed this most famous of conductors on his career. At Rio de Janeiro, on June 25, 1886, a staff conductor had been hissed from the podium; his place was taken by Toscanini, then a nineteen-year-old cellist in the theater orchestra; he brought the opera to a triumphant conclusion.

[4] Gatti's regime had tried its wings in Brooklyn two days earlier with a splendidly cast *Faust* (see No. 80).

Marchi (Radames), Scotti (Amonasro), Édouard de Reszke (Ramfis), and Marcel Journet (King of Egypt). And during a Saturday matinee broadcast of *Aïda* on February 26, 1938, Giovanni Martinelli, the Radames, was seized by illness during the first act and tottered from the stage. The curtain was lowered while the Metropolitan audience waited and the radio-station orchestra filled the air waves with dreary salon music. Then the hastily summoned Frederick Jagel replaced Martinelli and *Aïda* proceeded to its conclusion.

A telling indication of the perennial appeal of *Aïda* to New York audiences is afforded by a listing of some of the singers who have taken its leading roles at the Metropolitan. The Aïdas have included Lilli Lehmann, Lillian Nordica, Félia Litvinne, Eames, Nellie Melba, Celestina Boninsegna, Destinn (*d*),[5] Mariette Mazarin (*d*), Claudia Muzio, Rosa Ponselle, Elisabeth Rethberg (*d*), Maria Müller, Dusolina Giannini (*d*), Gina Cigna (*d*), Rose Bampton,[6] Daniza Ilitsch, Ljuba Welitch, Stella Roman (*d*), Zinka Milanov, Antonietta Stella (*d*), Renata Tebaldi, Leonie Rysanek, Leontyne Price, and Galina Vishnevskaya (*d*).

Metropolitan Amnerises have included Brandt, Mantelli, Marie Bréma, Homer (*d*), Edyth Walker (*d*), Margarete Matzenauer, Sigrid Onégin (*d*), Karen Branzell, Carmela Ponselle (*d*), Maria Olszewska, Cyrena Van Gordon (*d*), Bruna Castagna (*d*), Kerstin Thorborg, Rose Bampton, Blanche Thebom, Elena Nikolaidi, Margaret Harshaw, Fedora Barbieri, Nell Rankin (*d*), and Jean Madeira. The role of Radames has been sung by Jean de Reszke, Francesco Tamagno, Albert Saléza, Caruso, Riccardo Martin, Martinelli, Edward Johnson, Giacomo Lauri-Volpi, Jagel

(*d*), Set Svanholm (the first tenor since Jean de Reszke to sing Radames and Tristan in one Metropolitan season), Torsten Ralf (who respected Verdi's demand for a pianissimo high B flat at the end of "Celeste Aïda"), Kurt Baum, Ramón Vinay, Mario del Monaco, and Carlo Bergonzi (*d*).

The role of Amonasro has been sung at the Metropolitan by Maurel, Mario Ancona, Giuseppe Campanari, Scotti, Pasquale Amato, Giuseppe Danise (*d*), Michael Bohnen, Friedrich Schorr, John Charles Thomas, Lawrence Tibbett, Leonard Warren, Robert Merrill, George London (*d*), Robert McFerrin (*d*),[7] and Ettore Bastianini. As Ramfis have been heard Édouard de Reszke, Pol Plançon, Journet (*d*), Léon Rothier, José Mardones (*d*), Ezio Pinza, Nicola Moscona (*d*), Jerome Hines, Cesare Siepi, and Giorgio Tozzi.

On November 3, 1910, the first resident company to try for success at the then twenty-year-old Auditorium in Chicago shrewdly chose *Aïda* for its opening gambit. Cleofonte Campanini conducted. The cast included Jeanne Korolewicz (Aïda), Eleanor Broadfoot—who by a fortunate marriage had been enabled to abandon that name for the more euphonious Eleanora de Cisneros (Amneris), Amadeo Bassi (Radames), Mario Sammarco (Amonasro), and Nazzareno de Angelis (Ramfis). Oscar Hammerstein's New York debacle had been Chicago's gain: the resident Chicago aggregation was substantially the one that had been making operatic history at the Manhattan Opera House.

Interestingly, *Aïda* opened the Cairo opera season in 1959, almost eighty-eight years after its world *première* there. Franco Mannino conducted, and

---

[5] A (*d*) here indicates Metropolitan debut.
[6] In 1940 Bampton sang Aïda on January 19 and March 2, Amneris on January 26.
[7] With his debut as the Ethiopian king on January 27, 1955, McFerrin became the second Negro to sing a leading role at the Metropolitan, Marian Anderson having been heard as Ulrica in *Un Ballo in maschera* twenty days earlier.

the cast of Italian singers included Simona dell'Argine (Aïda), Franca Sacchi (Amneris), Mario Filippeschi (Radames), and Gino Bechi (Amonasro).[8]

6. Alceste (Gluck)

Three acts; libretto by Raniero de' Calzabigi; Vienna, Burgtheater, December 26 (not December 16, as often stated), 1767; the reworked French version, with text translated by Marie-François-Louis Gand-Leblanc, Bailli du Rollet, was first sung at the Opéra, Paris, April 23, 1776 (with parts of Act III rearranged by François-Joseph Gossec).

The Alceste of the original Vienna production was Antonia Bernasconi. The first cast of the French version included Marie-Rosalie Levasseur (Alceste), Joseph Legros (Admète), M. Gelin (Grand-Prêtre), and M. Larrivée (in the added role of Hercule). Up to 1866 it seems to have been sung 313 times at the Opéra. It was sung at the Opéra-Comique, Paris, for the first time on May 30, 1904, when Alexandre Luigini conducted and the cast included Félia Litvinne (Alceste), Léon Beyle (Admète), Hector Dufranne (Grand-Prêtre), and Gustave Huberdeau (Oracle). Following Pauline Viardot-García's Parisian triumph as Orphée, Berlioz revised *Alceste* for her, transposing the title role down. This version was staged at the Opéra on October 21, 1861. On February 8, 1926, the Opéra again presented *Alceste;* François Ruhlmann conducted, and the cast included Germaine Lubin (Alceste) and Georges Thill (Admète).

By the end of the eighteenth century, *Alceste,* in many languages and versions, had been sung in Germany, Italy, Copenhagen, Stockholm, Russia, and Budapest. It did not reach New York until January 24, 1941, when—Germaine Lubin, announced to sing the title role, not being on hand—the Alceste was Marjorie Lawrence. Ettore Panizza conducted, and the rest of the cast included René Maison (Admète) and Leonard Warren (Grand-Prêtre); in some of the four later performances the Alceste was Rose Bampton, the Admète Frederick Jagel, and the Grand-Prêtre Francesco Valentino. After March 19, 1941, the opera was not heard at the Metropolitan until, in English translation, it was presented (as *Alcestis*) on March 4, 1952, with Kirsten Flagstad (making her controversial return to the house after an absence of nearly eleven years) as Alcestis, Brian Sullivan as Admetus, and Paul Schöffler as the High Priest; Alberto Erede conducted. In some later singings, Set Svanholm was the Admetus, Valentino the High Priest. The season's final *Alcestis,* April 1, was Flagstad's farewell appearance at the Metropolitan. In the same English translation, slightly revised, but with a new and tasteless setting, *Alcestis* was revived at the Metropolitan on December 9, 1960, as the vehicle for the Metropolitan debut, in the title role, of the American soprano Eileen Farrell.

London heard *Alceste* for the first time when a visiting company from the Paris Opéra presented it at Covent Garden on May 6, 1937. Philippe Gaubert was the conductor, and the cast included Germaine Lubin (Alceste),

[8] *Aïda* and the several slightly less popular Verdian operas have made Verdi the most frequently performed operatic composer not only in Italy but also in the United States and in the German-speaking world. A survey of operatic performances during the 1960–61 season in Austria, West and East Germany, and Switzerland, as quoted in *The New York Times* of January 5, 1962, showed Verdi far in the lead, with 2,146 performances. Below that enormous figure followed Mozart, with 1,900; Puccini, with 1,531; Wagner, with 920; Lortzing, with 875. Far below the composer of *Zaar und Zimmermann* were to be found Prokofiev, with 351; Britten, with 245; Stravinsky, with 233; Orff, with 170, Schoenberg, with 71; and Hindemith, with 69.

Georges Jouatte (Admète), Martial Singher (Grand-Prêtre), Charles Cambon (Apollon), and Charles Paul (Un Hérault); the performance was not repeated. The opera was heard at Glyndebourne in 1953 and 1955 with Magda Laszlò as Alceste, Richard Lewis as Admète; in a 1958 revival, the Alceste was Consuelo Rubio; Vittorio Gui conducted.

7. Alcina (Handel)

Three acts; libretto, after Ariosto's Orlando Furioso, *probably by Antonio Marchi; London, Covent Garden, April 16, 1735.*

The cast of the first performance of *Alcina* consisted of Anna Maria Strada del Pò (Alcina), Giovanni Carestini (Ruggiero), Cecilia Young—*i. e.,* Mrs. Arne (Morgana), Maria Caterina Negri (Bradamante), John Beard (Oronte), Gustavus Waltz (Melisso), and William Savage (Oberto [1]); Marie Sallé danced. Within two years, *Alcina* achieved twenty-four performances. During Handel's lifetime, it was likewise sung at Brunswick, at first partly in German, but then wholly in Italian.

As part of the German Handel revival, *Alcina* was staged at Leipzig on June 14, 1928, in a German translation by Herman Roth. But the most notable modern revival of the opera began in England on March 19, 1957, when the Handel Opera Society staged it at the St. Pancras Town Hall. Joan Sutherland sang the title role, the Ruggiero was a male soprano, John Carvalho, and the Bradamante was Monica Sinclair. Charles Farncombe conducted the Boyd Neel Orchestra, and other roles were sung by Emerentia Scheepers (Morgana) and John Kentish (Oronte). As part of the bicentenary commemoration of Handel's death, the Royal Swedish Opera of Stockholm staged *Alcina* lavishly in

1959 with a cast headed by Margareta Hallin, Elisabeth Soederstroem, Kerstin Meyer, and Ingvar Wixell.

The most spectacular modern performance of *Alcina* was first seen at the Teatro La Fenice, Venice, on February 19, 1960. Franco Zeffirelli had produced it in magnificent baroque style. Sutherland was the triumphant heroine, making her Italian debut; Sinclair had shifted to the role of Ruggiero; others in the cast were Oralia Domínguez (Bradamante), Nicola Monti (Oronte), Plinio Clabassi (Melisso), and Cecilia Fusco (Morgana). This production later was seen in Dallas, Texas (November 16, 1960), with Nicola Rescigno conducting; Sutherland and Sinclair made their United States debuts in the roles they had sung in London; others in the Dallas cast were Blanche Thebom (Ruggiero), Luigi Alva (Oronte), Nicola Zaccaria (Melisso and Atlantes), and Joan Marie Moynagh (Morgana).

8. Amelia Goes to the Ball (Menotti)

One act; libretto by the composer (Amelia al ballo), *but translated from Italian into English by George Meade for the* première; *Philadelphia, Academy of Music, April 1, 1937.*

Amelia Goes to the Ball was first heard in New York at the New Amsterdam Theatre, in English, on April 11, 1937. The Metropolitan Opera staged it, with Ettore Panizza conducting, on March 3, 1938, on a double bill with Strauss's *Elektra.* In the Metropolitan cast were Muriel Dickson (Amelia), John Brownlee (Husband), Mario Chamlee (Lover), Helen Olheim (Friend), and Norman Cordon (Chief of Police). The response to the little opera brought it only six performances in two successive seasons. *Amelia al ballo* was first heard as the composer

---

[1] According to accounts of the time, Savage sang portions of the role of Oronte as well.

wrote it, in Italian, at San Remo, Italy, on April 4, 1938.

9. L'Amico Fritz (Mascagni)

Three acts; libretto by Nicola Daspuro (under the pseudonym of P. Suardon), after the novel L'Ami Fritz by Erckmann-Chatrian; Rome, Teatro Costanzi, October 31, 1891.

At the world *première*, a world-famous Carmen and the original Don José—respectively Emma Calvé and Paul Lhérie—created the roles of Suzel and Fritz Kobus; others in the cast were Fernando de Lucia and Synnemberg. The opera was Mascagni's most successful after *Cavalleria rusticana*, and is still performed with some frequency in Italy. Calvé again was the Suzel when Covent Garden, London, heard *L'Amico Fritz* for the first time on May 23, 1892, again with De Lucia; others in leading roles were Giulia Ravogli and Eugène Dufriche. Eleven performances spaced out through two seasons sufficed.

When the Metropolitan Opera, New York, got around to staging *L'Amico Fritz,* on January 10, 1894, Enrico Bevignani conducted, Calvé was the Suzel and De Lucia the Fritz; others in the cast were Mario Ancona (Rabbi David), Antonio de Vaschetti (Hanezo), N. Mastrobuono (Federico), Sofia Scalchi (Beppe), and Mathilde Bauermeister (Caterina). The opera lapsed after two performances, but lapsed back into life—three performances—during the 1923–24 season; on November 15, conducted by Roberto Moranzoni, it shared a double bill with Franco Leoni's *L'Oracolo*. Lucrezia Bori (Suzel), Miguel Fleta (Fritz), Giuseppe Danise (Rabbi David), and Merle Alcock (Beppe) headed the cast. A notable American performance of *L'Amico Fritz* was that given by the San Francisco Opera Company on October 2, 1924. Gaetano Merola conducted; the Suzel was Thalia Sabanieeva, Tito Schipa was Fritz and

the roles of Rabbi David and Hanezo were sung, respectively, by Giuseppe de Luca and Paolo Ananian. Mascagni himself, who was conducting Italian performances of *L'Amico Fritz* as late as the 1941 Florentine Maggio Musicale, seems never to have conducted the work in the United States.

10. L'Amore dei tre re (Montemezzi)

Three acts; libretto by Sem Benelli, after his own play of the same name; Milan, Teatro alla Scala, April 10, 1913.

The world *première* of *L'Amore dei tre re* was conducted by Tullio Serafin; the cast included the San Francisco-born Luisa Villani (Fiora), Edoardo Ferrari-Fontana (Avito), Carlo Galeffi (Manfredo), and Nazzareno de Angelis (Archibaldo). Less than a year later, on January 2, 1914, the opera was first heard outside Italy when the Metropolitan Opera, New York, presented it under the baton of Arturo Toscanini, to whom its American success has been attributed. But even though he knew how to work his effects, he had to have the right cast. The singers at the Metropolitan *première* appear to have transcended what could have been expected of them: Lucrezia Bori (Fiora), Ferrari-Fontana, in his American debut (Avito), Pasquale Amato (Manfredo), Adamo Didur (Archibaldo), and, in the small role of A Young Woman, Sophie Braslau. Also, as W. J. Henderson noted, the opera was approved by the Monday-night subscribers, and therefore survived. When it was revived on March 14, 1918, after a two-season interval, Didur and Amato survived from the first Metropolitan performance, but Enrico Caruso was the Avito and Claudia Muzio the Fiora. Caruso did not find the role congenial, but Giovanni Martinelli did when he sang Avito on April 6; Muzio's physical equipment was considered too ample for Fiora, but her performance was thrilling vocally. In later performances during that season, José Mardones was greatly admired as Archibaldo, but Florence Easton definitely was too "womanly" for the very young Fiora.

The return of Bori's Fiora (February 3, 1921) was welcomed; this time her Avito was Beniamino Gigli (later Edward Johnson), and the other leading roles were sung by Giuseppe Danise (Manfredo) and Didur (Archibaldo). Alterations in casting sometimes found Lawrence Tibbett as Manfredo, Pavel Ludikar as Archibaldo. With Metropolitan performances of *L'Amore* having passed the forty mark, the opera was revived again on December 27, 1939, under the Johnson management. The level of conducting had declined to that of a Gennaro Papi; of the leading singers—Helen Jepson (Fiora), Armand Tokatyan (Avito), Richard Bonelli (Manfredo), and Ezio Pinza (Archibaldo), only Pinza preserved the regal tone—which was wasted on a Fiora like Jepson. In later performances, Virgilio Lazzari was a fine Archibaldo, but the once careful casting of the opera was no longer. On February 7, 1941, Montemezzi himself conducted *L'Amore* at the Metropolitan, with Grace Moore (Fiora), Charles Kullmann (Avito), Bonelli, and Pinza. For an institution that already had done so well by *L'Amore,* Montemezzi provided some special entr'acte music. Generally, his reading of the score was praised as much as Moore's acting was derided. In the opera's last Metropolitan avatar to date, Dorothy Kirsten was the Fiora (December 1, 1949) under the listless conducting of Giuseppe Antonicelli; the cast also showed Kullman, Robert Weede (Manfredo), and Lazzari; in the small role of A Youth, Paul Franke made his Metropolitan debut, initiating a long career of distinction as a supporting singer. *L'Amore* was heard at the Metropolitan for the last time at a matinee on January 15, 1949.

On January 26, 1920, the Chicago Opera Company took its famed production of *L'Amore dei tre re* to the Lexington Theater, New York, with Mary Garden's spectacular Fiora (the only role she ever sang in Italian). Her Avito was Edward Johnson, thus making his New York debut. Garden's Fiora was an achievement that, once seen and heard, never could be forgotten. Almost as much as her Mélisande and her Louise, it became a paragon against which the interpretations of all other sopranos were measured—and found wanting.

The London history of *L'Amore* began somewhat later than its New York history. Covent Garden first produced the opera on May 27, 1914, with Louise Edvina a vocally perfect Fiora, her associates being Giulio Crimi (Avito), Francesco Cigada (Manfredo), and Didur (Archibaldo), all of them close to superb. *L'Amore* lasted only three performances, and a revival in 1930 added two more, the second of these being magnificent, with Vincenzo Bellezza conducting and the cast headed by Rosa Ponselle (Fiora), Francesco Merli (Avito), Giovanni Inghilleri (Manfredo), and Pinza (Archibaldo). Since that performance, on July 4, 1930, *L'Amore dei tre re* has not been heard at Covent Garden. It has, however, been heard elsewhere throughout the world, and is still revived occasionally in Italy.

11. Andrea Chénier (Giordano)

Four acts; libretto by Luigi Illica; Milan, Teatro alla Scala, March 28, 1896.

The chief roles at the *première* were sung by Avelina Carrera, Giuseppe Borgatti, and Mario Sammarco. Although *Andrea Chénier* reached New York as early as November 13, 1896, and a visiting production by the Boston National Opera Company was heard there in 1917 (with Luisa Villani, Giovanni Zenatello, Georges Baklanoff, and Francesca Peralta), the work was not produced at the Metropolitan Opera House until March 7, 1921, with Claudia Muzio (Madeleine), Beniamino Gigli (Chénier), Giuseppe Danise (Gérard), and Adamo Didur (Mathieu). Madeleine was one of Muzio's most moving impersonations. Elisabeth Rethberg, Florence Easton, and Rosa Ponselle sang Madeleine as its thirteen uninterrupted seasons went by. The opera was dropped in 1933, and returned to the repertoire —and then very briefly—only in 1954. Zinka Milanov, Mario del Monaco, Leonard Warren, and Salvatore Baccaloni were in the revival.

Manchester was the first English town to hear *Andrea Chénier* (in English, however), on April 2, 1903. Covent Garden, London, produced it first on November 11, 1905, with Phoebe Strakosch, Zenatello, and Sammarco. Enrico Caruso, Emmy Destinn, and Sammarco could not, of course, be bettered, and while they were available together, *Chénier* enjoyed great popularity. Margaret Sheridan was an admirable Madeleine; she was as unlucky in her first Chénier (Giacomo Lauri-Volpi) as she was lucky in his successor (Gigli).

Angel of Fire (Prokofiev)

See *The Flaming Angel* (No. 86).

12. Anna Bolena (Donizetti)

Two acts; libretto by Felice Romani; Milan, Teatro Carcano, December 26, 1830.

Donizetti had composed more than thirty operas [1] when the international success of *Anna Bolena* made him a personage mentioned with Rossini and Bellini. The original cast of *Anna Bolena* included Giuditta Pasta (Anna), Elisa Orlandi (Giovanna Seymour), Giovanni Battista Rubini (Percy), and Filippo Galli [2] (Enrico VIII). The first performance outside Italy occurred at the Haymarket, London, on July 8, 1831, in Italian.[3] It was sung at the Théâtre-Italien, Paris, the first Donizetti opera heard in the French capital, on September 1, 1831. It was staged in Mexico City in February 1836, very probably with Galli in his original role, as he was with the Mexico City Opera at the time.

The first *Anna Bolena* in the United States was sung at New Orleans, in French, in November 1839. New York (August 2, 1843) and Philadelphia (October 7, 1843) both heard it first in French. It was sung in New York in English on May 7, 1844, and in Italian on January 7, 1850. It has never been staged at the Metropolitan.

During Marietta Alboni's first season at Covent Garden, she sang in *Anna Bolena* the secondary (travesty) role of the page Smeton. On July 11, 1850, Pasta, then fifty-two years old, sang scenes from *Anna Bolena* in London; according to Benjamin Lumley, "She moved like a mighty shadow of the past before the eyes of the spectators; but it was the shadow of a shade." At Drury Lane in 1871, Mapleson revived *Anna Bolena* for Therese Tietjens (Anna), with Clarice Sinico (Giovanna Seymour), and Luigi Agnesi (Enrico VIII).

Alfred Loewenberg states that the "latest revivals in Italy were at Milan 20 January 1877; Brescia August 1879; and Leghorn 11 August 1881." But in more recent years it has been heard at Doni-

---

[1] His first professionally staged opera was *Enrico di Borgogna* (Venice, November 14, 1818). Of the many between it and *Anna Bolena*, almost nothing is now heard. Those which might best repay revival probably are *L'Ajo nell'imbarazzo* (Rome, 1824) and *L'Esule di Roma* (Naples, 1828).

[2] Galli (1783–1853) had been a highly suc-

cessful tenor, but a grave illness had affected his voice, and he became a distinguished bass. It was for him that Rossini had composed the role of Fernando in *La Gazza ladra* and the title role of *Maometto II* (1820).

[3] The standard cast at the Haymarket became Giulia Grisi (Anna), Rubini (Percy), and Luigi Lablache (Enrico VIII).

zetti's birthplace, Bergamo. And on April 14, 1957, it was triumphantly revived at La Scala, Milan, in a Luchino Visconti production with magnificent scenery by Nicola Benois. The conductor was Gianandrea Gavazzeni, a native of Bergamo who has published a book on Donizetti; the cast included Maria Meneghini Callas (Anna), Giulietta Simionato (Giovanna Seymour), Gabriella Carturan (Smeaton), Gianni Raimondi (Percy), Nicola Rossi-Lemeni (Enrico VIII), and Plinio Clabassi (Hervey). Many critics thought it Callas' greatest role; Simionato was greatly praised also, though it was noted that she is a mezzo-soprano whereas the original Giovanna Seymour, Orlandi, had been a soprano, for which reason Simionato's more deeply colored voice altered the balance intended by the composer. When the opera was repeated in 1958, Cesare Siepi took over the role of Enrico VIII. Simionato made her New York debut in a concert performance with the American Opera Society during the 1957–58 season, as Giovanna Seymour, with Arnold Gamson conducting, Gloria Davy as Anna Bolena, and Kenneth Smith as the King.

13. Arabella (Strauss)

Three acts; libretto by Hugo von Hofmannsthal, after his story "Lucidor"; Dresden, Opernhaus, July 1, 1933.

Clemens Krauss conducted the Dresden world *première* of *Arabella*. Frau Krauss (Viorica Ursuleac) had the title role, and other principals were Friedrich Plaschke (Graf Waldner), Camilla Kallab (Adelaide), Margit Bokor (Zdenka), Alfred Jerger (Mandryka), Martin Kremer (Matteo), Karl Albrecht Streib (Elemer), Kurt Böhme (Dominik), Arno Schellenberg (Lamoral), and Ellice Illiard (Fiakermilli). Vienna and Berlin had heard it in German, Olmütz in Czech, and Stockholm in Swedish before the end of 1933. Stagings in Basel and—in French translation by Raoul Gunsbourg—Monte Carlo followed early in 1934. On May 17 of that year, *Arabella* was staged at Covent Garden, London, during a season under the management of Geoffrey Toye and Sir Thomas Beecham. Krauss conducted, and the five principal roles were sung by those who had sung them at the Dresden *première* (Ursuleac, Bokor, Illiard, Kremer, Jerger). The four performances of that season were not received with much show of enthusiasm by either critics or audiences. *Arabella* was not heard at Covent Garden again until the Bayerische Staatsoper of Munich visited there in September, 1953. *Arabella* opened that eleven-day season on September 15, when Rudolf Kempe conducted, and leading roles were sung by Lisa della Casa (Arabella, a role she has sung often and in many places), Benno Kusche (Waldner), Ira Malaniuk (Adelaide), Gerda Sommerschuh (Zdenka), Hermann Uhde (Mandryka), and Erika Köth (Fiakermilli). This time the London critics liked it better (Ernest Newman said flatly that he had misjudged it in 1934), and it was well attended for five performances. It has not been heard since then at Covent Garden.

The Metropolitan Opera, New York, staged *Arabella* for the first time on February 10, 1955. Rudolf Kempe conducted, and principal roles were sung by Ralph Herbert—his Metropolitan debut (Waldner), Blanche Thebom (Adelaide), Eleanor Steber (Arabella), Hilde Gueden (Zdenka), George London (Mandryka), Brian Sullivan (Matteo), and Roberta Peters (Fiakermilli). The opera was sung in the English translation of John Gutman. On January 7, 1957, Lisa della Casa's internationally famous characterization of Arabella was heard at the Metropolitan. When, on November 18, 1960, the opera returned to the Metropolitan repertoire after a four-season absence, Martha Lipton was the Adelaide, Anneliese Rothenberger—

in her Metropolitan debut—the Zdenka, and Laurel Hurley the Fiakermilli.

14. Ariadne auf Naxos (Strauss)

One act; libretto by Hugo von Hofmannsthal; first version (as postlude to Molière's Le Bourgeois gentilhomme, itself with incidental music by Strauss), Stuttgart, Königliches Hoftheater, October 25, 1912; revised version, Vienna, Opera, October 4, 1916.

When Max Reinhardt produced Hugo von Hofmannsthal's German version of Molière's *Le Bourgeois gentilhomme* (as *Der Bürger als Edelmann*) [1] at the Kleines Haus of the Stuttgart Königliches Hoftheater on October 25, 1912, the performance included both Strauss's incidental music to the play and, tucked in at the end to replace the "Turkish ceremony" of Molière, the tiny opera called *Ariadne auf Naxos*. Strauss conducted, and the cast of *Ariadne* was made up of Mizzi (soon known as Maria) Jeritza (Ariadne), Hermann Jadlowker (Bacchus), M. Junker-Burchardt (Najade), Lilly Hoffman-Onégin [2] (Dryade), Erna Ellmenreich (Echo), Margarethe Siems (Zerbinetta), Albin Swoboda (Harlekin), George Meader (Scaramuccio), Reinhold Fritz (Truffaldin), and Franz Schwerdt (Brighella).

Although the cumbersome play-with-music-plus-opera was not regarded as successful, the first *Ariadne* was heard in Zurich, Prague, Berlin, Amsterdam, and London. The London performance (His Majesty's Theatre, May 27, 1913) presented Sir Herbert Beerbohm Tree (Monsieur Jourdain) and Phyllis Neilson-Terry (Dorimène) in Somerset

Maugham's English translation of *Le Bourgeois gentilhomme;* Sir Thomas Beecham conducted, Eva von der Osten was the Ariadne, Otto Marak was the Bacchus, and Hermine Bosetti was the Zerbinetta. Beecham was again the conductor when a similar version was revived by the Glyndebourne company at the Edinburgh Festival of 1950; Miles Malleson, who this time had made the English translation, was the Jourdain, and the leading members of the operatic cast were Hilde Zadek (Ariadne), Peter Anders (Bacchus), and Ilse Hollweg (Zerbinetta).

When experiments with *Ariadne auf Naxos* as a small opera separated from the Molière play did not prove successful, Hofmannsthal wrote a new prelude to the opera; Strauss not only composed the music for the prelude, but also revised that of the opera itself. This new version was first heard at the Vienna Opera on October 4, 1916, with Franz Schalk conducting and the following cast: (in the prologue) August Stoll (Haushofmeister), Hans Duhan (Musiklehrer), Lotte Lehmann, substituting for the indisposed Marie Gutheil-Schoder (Komponist), Béla von Környey (Tenor), Selma Kurz (Zerbinetta), Neuber (Harlekin), Hermann Gallos (Scaramuccio), Julius Betetto (Truffaldin), and Maria Nemeth (Brighella); (in the opera) Jeritza (Ariadne), Környey (Bacchus), Charlotte Dahmen (Najade), Hermine Kittel (Dryade), Carola Jovanovic (Echo), Kurz (Zerbinetta), Duhan (Harlekin), Gallos (Scaramuccio), Betetto (Truffaldin), and Georg Maikl (Brighella).

The revised *Ariadne auf Naxos* soon was being staged in Germany, Hungary, and the Netherlands. It reached Covent Garden, London, on May 27, 1924,

---

[1] The translation originally had been made in 1751 by one Bierling, who called it *Der adelige Bürger*. Hofmannsthal had adapted Bierling's version for Reinhardt.

[2] So listed on the program, this was Sigrid Onégin, whose full name was Elizabeth Elfriede Emilie Sigrid Hoffman. Her husband,

a composer-pianist who billed himself as Eugene Onégin, was really Eugene Lvov, a grandnephew of Alexis Lvov, who had composed the Russian (tsarist) national anthem. She had made her operatic debut, as Carmen, only thirteen days earlier, also at Stuttgart (October 10, 1912).

when Karl Alwin conducted a cast including Lehmann (Ariadne), Elisabeth Schumann (Komponist), Maria Ivogün (Zerbinetta), and Karl Fischer-Niemann (Bacchus). The opera was sung only twice. When the Dresden State Opera Company visited Covent Garden in 1936, Strauss conducted a single performance of *Ariadne* there on November 6, with Marta Fuchs (Ariadne), Elsa Wieber (Komponist), Erna Sack (Zerbinetta), and Torsten Ralf (Bacchus). *Ariadne* has not been heard at Covent Garden since then.

Ariadne auf Naxos has never been staged at the Metropolitan Opera House in New York, but is announced there for the 1962–63 season. The first American performance was sung at Philadelphia on November 1, 1928, when, as Echo, Helen Jepson made her operatic debut. When the opera was heard in New York for the first time, at the Juilliard School on December 5, 1934, it was sung in an English translation by Alfred Kalisch. The first New York performance by professionals was staged by the New York City Opera Company at the City Center on October 10, 1946. The prologue was sung in an English translation by Lewis Sydenham; the opera itself was sung in German. Laszlo Halasz conducted, and the cast included Polyna Stoska (Komponist), Vasso Argyris (Tenor-Bacchus), Virginia Mac-Watters (Zerbinetta), and Ella Flesch (Prima Donna-Ariadne).

The opera has been heard in the United States many times in both concert and staged performances. When the San Francisco Opera Company staged it in 1957, the prologue was sung in Leopold Sachse's English translation, the opera itself in German. Leonie Rysanek was the Ariadne, Helen George the Komponist, Rita Streich the Zerbinetta, and Richard Lewis the Bacchus. When San Francisco heard *Ariadne* again in 1959, Streich and Lewis returned, but Eileen Farrell was Ariadne,[3] Sena Jurinac the Komponist.

At Munich's Residenztheater in the summer of 1938, *Ariadne* was conducted by Clemens Krauss and sung by a remarkable cast including Adele Kern (Zerbinetta), Viorica Ursuleac—Krauss's wife (Ariadne), and Torsten Ralf (Bacchus). At the Florentine Maggio Musicale of 1959, *Ariadne* was heard with Teresa Stich-Randall as Ariadne, Helga Pilarczyk (Komponist), and Erika Köth (Zerbinetta). But the most frequent homes of this opera during the 1950's were Vienna and Salzburg. Familiar casts offered Lisa della Casa and Hilde Zadek as Ariadne; Jurinac, Christa Ludwig, and Irmgard Seefried as the Komponist; Streich, Köth, and Hilde Gueden as Zerbinetta; Rudolf Schock as a much-admired Bacchus; and Paul Schöffler and Alfred Poell in notable characterizations of the Musiklehrer.

In Paris, where *Ariadne* had been heard in German at the Théâtre des Champs-Elysées on September 10, 1937, it was staged at the Opéra-Comique in a French version by Paul Spaak on April 30, 1943. The principal roles were sung by Germaine Lubin (Ariadne), Janine Micheau (Zerbinetta), Marisa Ferrer (Kompositor), Hélène Bouvier (Dryade), and Georges Jouatte (Bacchus). Roger Desormière conducted. At a performance on June 7, 1950, the Ariadne was Georgette Camart, Micheau was again the Zerbinetta, and the other leading roles were sung by Margaret Mas (Kompositor) and Jean Giraudeau (Bacchus). Up to the end of that season, the opera had been sung fifteen times at the Comique.

Strauss was by no means the first composer to treat the story of Ariadne. After Monteverdi's now largely lost *Arianna* of 1608 came the lost *Ariane ou Le Mariage de Bacchus,* first heard in London in 1674, and usually attrib-

---

[3] Farrell had sung this role in a concert performance by The Little Orchestra Society at Town Hall, New York, on January 7, 1957, when the prologue was omitted. The Zerbinetta was Mattiwilda Dobbs, the Bacchus Albert Da Costa.

uted to Robert Cambert; Johann Sigmund Kusser's *Ariadne* (Brunswick, 1692); Nicola Porpora's *Arianna e Teseo* (Vienna, 1714); Benedetto Marcello's *Arianna* (composed in 1727, but first performed at Venice in 1913); Handel's *Arianna in Creta* (London, 1734); Johann Friedrich Edelmann's *Ariane dans l'isle de Naxos* (Paris, 1782); Massenet's *Ariane* (Paris, 1906); and Darius Milhaud's parodistic *L'Abandon d'Ariane,* one of his three "opéras-minutes" (first staged at Wiesbaden in 1928 as *Die verlassene Ariadne*). Paul Dukas's *Ariane et Barbe-bleue* has nothing to do with the classical character of Ariadne.

15. Ariane et Barbe-bleue (Dukas)

Three acts; libretto a little-altered version of Maurice Maeterlinck's play of the same name; Paris, Opéra-Comique, May 10, 1907.

François Ruhlmann conducted the Albert Carré production when *Ariane et Barbe-bleue* was given its *première* at the Opéra-Comique. The cast was: Georgette Leblanc-Maeterlinck (Ariane), Cécile Thévenet (La Nourrice), Suzanne Brohly (Sélysette), Marthe Bakkers (Ygraine), Hélène Demellier (Mélisande), Berg (Bellangère), Régina Badet (Alladine), Félix Vieuille (Barbe-bleue), Louis Azéma (Un Vieux Paysan), Lucazeau (Premier Paysan), Tarquini (Deuxième Paysan). It had been heard seventy-nine times at the Comique (often with Suzanne Balguérie as Ariane, Germaine Cernay as Sélysette, and, as late as 1927, Vieuille in his original role) when it was first presented at the Opéra, under Philippe Gaubert's direction, on January 25, 1935. On the latter occasion, the cast was: Germaine Lubin (Ariane), Ketty Lapeyrette (La Nourrice), Almona (Sélysette), Yvonne Gervais (Ygraine), Doniau-Blanc (Mélisande), Renaudin (Bellangère), Henri

Etcheverry (Barbe-bleue), Henri Médus (Un Vieux Paysan), Chastenet (Premier Paysan), and Madlen (Deuxième Paysan).

On April 2, 1908, *Ariane et Barbe-bleue* was performed at the Vienna Volksoper in a German translation by Harry La Violette. It had also been sung in French in Brussels (January 2, 1909) when it was first staged in America, at the Metropolitan Opera, New York, on March 29, 1911. Arturo Toscanini conducted; the cast was as follows: Geraldine Farrar (Ariane), Florence Wickham (La Nourrice), Jeanne Maubourg (Sélysette), Leonora Sparkes (Ygraine), Rosina Van Dyck (Mélisande), Henrietta Wakefield (Bellangère), Léon Rothier (Barbe-bleue), Georges Bourgeois (Un Vieux Paysan), Bernard Bégué (Premier Paysan), and Basil Ruysdael (Deuxième Paysan). The opera was followed by a ballet *divertissement* conducted by Josef Pasternack and danced by Anna Pavlova, Mikhail Mordkin, and the *corps de ballet.* When the opera was repeated on January 31, 1912, the cast of the preceding year was intact except for the replacement of Wickham as the Nurse by Margarete Matzenauer, to the sensible improvement of the pervading French style. Having been given four times during the 1910–11 season and three during that of 1911–12, *Ariane et Barbe-bleue* then lapsed into a Metropolitan silence from which it never has returned.

Dukas's only opera was staged, however, at La Scala, Milan, on April 17, 1911, in an Italian translation by Giovanni Pozza (Pavel Ludikar was the Barbe-bleue), as well as at Buenos Aires, Madrid, Basel, Prague, and Amsterdam. It finally reached Covent Garden, London, in the original French, on April 20, 1937, with the conductor and leading singers who had been heard in it at the Paris Opéra two years before. This participation in the Covent Garden season by the Parisian forces was part of the Coronation Year festivities. *Ariane* was heard twice. Later performances of it outside France have been very few.

16. Arianna (Monteverdi)

Prologue and eight scenes; libretto by Ottavio Rinuccini; performed at the court theater, Mantua, May 28, 1608.

Staged late in 1639 to open the third Venetian opera house, the Teatro San Moisè. The libretto survives intact, the score only in a few fragments (including the famous "Lamento d'Arianna"); the surviving scene was staged at Karlsruhe in January, 1926.

17. Armida (Rossini)

Three acts; libretto by Giovanni Schmidt, after Tasso's Gerusalemme liberata; Naples, Teatro San Carlo, November 11, 1817.

Although *Armida* was also staged at La Scala, Milan, on November 5, 1836, it did not really catch on in Italy. In *Annals of Opera,* the late Alfred Loewenberg reported his inability to find records of any performances in Paris, London, or New York, but recorded a Buenos Aires performance, in Italian, on February 5, 1828. A version in German by Joseph von Seyfried, however, heard first at Vienna on December 11, 1821, achieved some popularity, being staged also in Budapest, Prague, Graz, Hamburg, Berlin, and Bucharest.

The 1952 Florence Maggio Musicale, as part of an extensive program of Rossini productions, staged *Armida.* Tullio Serafin conducted, and the cast included Maria Meneghini Callas, Francesco Albanese, Mario Filippeschi, and Alessandro Ziliani. Cynthia Jolly, reporting on "Opera in Post-War Italy" for *Opera Annual, 1954–1955,* said that it "received a mixed press without substantially altering musical opinion of Ros-

sini: the libretto and an over-elaborate vocal line disturbed contemporary critics, even though Callas probably equalled La Colbran." [1]

18. Armide (Gluck)

Five acts; libretto by Philippe Quinault, after Tasso's Gerusalemme Liberata (libretto originally written for Lully, whose Armide et Renaud was first heard at the Opéra, Paris, on February 15, 1686); Paris, Opéra, September 23, 1777.

The first Armide was Marie-Rosalie Levasseur. The opera was sung at the Opéra until 1837, and was revived there on April 12, 1905; by 1913, it had been sung there 392 times. During the eighteenth century, it was also heard at Versailles, Kassel, Hanover, Copenhagen, and Stockholm. In Berlin, where it was first sung on May 20, 1805, in a German translation by Julius von Voss, it was heard intermittently until 1889. Richard Wagner conducted a notable revival at Dresden on March 5, 1843, and when the opera was sung at Karlsruhe in May, 1853, in a German translation revised by Eduard Devrient, it had recitatives by Joseph Strauss. The first performance in Italy appears to have been that at the Teatro San Carlo, Naples, in a translation by Angelo Zanardini, March 11, 1890.

Armide reached London, Covent Garden, on July 6, 1906, in French; André Messager conducted, and the cast included Lucienne Bréval (Armide) and Léon Laffitte (Renaud). On June 6, 1908, Covent Garden heard the opera in German; Hans Richter conducted, and the much-praised Armide was Emmy Destinn. A German version was sung there also on May 1, 1928; Frida Leider was the Armide, Walter Widdop the Renaud. In its first American per-

[1] Isabella Colbran, Rossini's first wife, was the Armida of the Naples *première* in 1817.

formance, *Armide* opened the Metropolitan season on November 14, 1910. Toscanini conducted, and the cast was: Olive Fremstad (Armide), Leonora Sparkes (Sidonie), Jeanne Maubourg (Phénice), Alma Gluck (Lucinde), Louise Homer (Haïne), Marie Rappold (Naïade), Enrico Caruso (Renaud), Dinh Gilly (Ubalde), Andrés de Segurola (Aronte), Pasquale Amato (Hidraot), Angelo Bada (Chevalier Danois), and Albert Reiss (Artémidore). The scenic designs, by Puvis de Chavannes, were greatly admired. Since its seventh Metropolitan performance, on March 18, 1912, *Armide* has not been seen in New York in professional staging.

Aroldo (Verdi)

See *Stiffelio* (No. 224).

19. Assassinio nella cattedrale (Pizzetti)

Two acts and an intermezzo; libretto from Monsignore Alberto Castelli's Italian translation of T. S. Eliot's Murder in the Cathedral; *Milan, Teatro alla Scala, March 1, 1958.*

The audience at the world *première* of Pizzetti's *Assassinio nella cattedrale,* was impressed most by the magnificent sets and costumes designed by Piero Zuffi, the direction of Margherita Wallmann, the conducting of Gianandrea Gavazzeni, and the performance of "L'Arcivescovo Tommaso Becket" by Nicola Rossi-Lemeni. Others in the cast were Leyla Gencer (Prima Corifea), Gabriella Carturan (Seconda Corifea), Aldo Bertocci (Un Araldo), Mario Ortica (Primo Sacerdote), Dino Dondi (Secondo Sacerdote), and Nicola Zaccaria (Terzo Tentatore). For the gala repetition on April 12, President Giovanni Gronchi and most members of the

diplomatic corps from Rome were in the house.

A staging of *Assassinio nella cattedrale* was announced for the Empire State Music Festival at Ellenville, New York, for August 21, 1958. But a storm necessitated postponement—and then cancellation of the whole festival, the tent in which performances were to have been given having been seriously damaged. The postponed performance was heard at Carnegie Hall, New York, on September 17, 1958. It was not a concert performance as such, but a sort of compromise—with scenery, costumes, and stage action adapted to the limitations of the Carnegie Hall stage. Rossi-Lemeni repeated the role he had created. Laszlo Halasz conducted the Symphony of the Air, Kurt Adler had prepared the extremely important chorus, and other singers in the cast were Martina Arroyo, Margery Mayer, Giulio Gari, Calvin Marsh, Hugh Thompson, John Druary, and Morley Meredith. The performance was repeated on September 22.

Rossi-Lemeni's superb, subtle characterization of Thomas à Becket was seen and heard at Rome on December 26, 1958, with the composer conducting, when *Assassinio nella cattedrale* opened the opera season there at the Teatro dell'Opera; it was repeated in Mexico City, Barcelona, and Lisbon. It was heard, too, at the Teatro San Carlo, Naples. But when the Empire State Music Festival, relocated at the Sterling Forest Research Center, finally succeeded in presenting the opera—during the summer of 1959—the Thomas was Plinio Clabassi, who had sung the role at Trieste in a production staged by Ernest de Weerth, designed by Orlando di Collalto, and conducted by Bruno Bartoletti. Halasz again conducted, and others in the cast included Theresa Stratas, Phillip Maero, Gari, Rudolf Petrak, Thompson, and Joseph Rouleau.

A special concert-oratorio performance of *Assassinio nella cattedrale* was sung in the Vatican on January 5, 1959, so that Pope John XXIII might hear it (it was said to be the first opera ever performed within the walls of the Vatican). The seventy-eight-year-old Pizzetti was present to receive the greetings of the seventy-seven-year-old pontiff.

20. Un Ballo in maschera (Verdi)

Three acts; libretto by Antonio Somma, an almost literal translation of Augustin-Eugène Scribe's five-act libretto for Auber's Gustave III ou Le Bal masqué *(Paris, Opéra, February 27, 1833); Rome, Teatro Apollo, February 17, 1859.*

Felice Orsini's attempt on the life of Napoleon III on January 14, 1858, encouraged the censors at Naples to forbid staging there of an opera dealing with the assassination at a masked ball of Gustavus III, King of Sweden, an opera intended by Verdi to be called *Gustavo III* first, then *Una Vendetta in domino.* (That original version of the opera was staged at Copenhagen on September 25, 1935—eight years after a less inflammatory version had been staged at Stockholm on February 12, 1927, the opera's first singing in Sweden.) With the help of Somma, Verdi then rejected the censors' suggestion that the opera be named *Adelia degli Adimari* and altered the locale and the identities of the characters, placing the story in Massachusetts and changing the King of Sweden into "Riccardo, conte di Warwick." Modern stagings of the opera have taken steps of varying lengths back in the direction of the original libretto, sometimes (as at the Metropolitan Opera in 1940) restoring the Swedish locale but leaving the names of the characters foolishly unchanged, at others not only going the whole way back to Verdi's original conception, but also insisting somewhat

sensationally upon the homosexual characteristics of Gustavus III.

The cast of the Roman *première,* on February 17, 1859, included Julienne Dejean (Amelia), Pamela Scotti (Oscar), Zelinda Sbriscia (Ulrica), Gaetano Fraschini (Riccardo), Leone Giraldoni (Renato), S. Santucci (Silvano), C. Bossi (Samuel), and G. Bernardoni (Tom);[1] the conductor was Emilio Angelini. Despite thirty curtain calls, flowers tossed onto the stage, and a traditional spraying from the top of the theater of glistening confetti, the opera was not a real success. Illness among the singers also lessened its chances of numerous performances, and the season ended after it had been sung only six times (it picked up a little, at the same theater, during the next two years). Its extra-Italy career began at Lisbon on April 15, 1860, when it was sung there in Italian.

Although the Théâtre-Italien, Paris, had the first important performance outside Italy (January 13, 1861)—for that occasion, the locale was changed to Florence—real drama surrounded the London *première* five months later, June 15, 1861. Colonel Mapleson already had Luigi Arditi rehearsing it at the Lyceum Theatre when Frederick Gye, his rival at Covent Garden, decided to race for the first-performance honors. The casts were well matched: Mapleson had, among other notables, Therese Tietjens, Antonio Giuglini, and Enrico delle Sedie; Gye had Marie Miolan-Carvalho, who had created the role of Marguerite in Gounod's *Faust,* Mario, and Constance Nantier-Didiée, a popular but short-lived soprano from the African island of Réunion.[2] Mapleson won the race by one week.

On April 21, 1873, the noted French baritone Victor Maurel made his Lon-

---

[1] These hapless conspirators had been called, for a time only, Mazeppa and Ivan.

[2] The Covent Garden program listed the usual Samuel and Tom as Armando and Angri.

don debut at Covent Garden as Renato in *Un Ballo in maschera;* the most noted of his colleagues on that occasion was the Ulrica, Sofia Scalchi. On July 3, 1888, Jean de Reszke made one of his few appearances in the role of Riccardo. On June 29, 1904, Enrico Caruso sang the role at Covent Garden for the first time, when the opera was revived there after a lapse of sixteen years; his colleagues were Giannina Russ (Amelia), Antonio Scotti (Renato), Selma Kurz (Oscar), and Nina Frascani (Ulrica). During an autumn season of that same year, under the aegis of a company visiting from the Teatro San Carlo, Naples, *Un Ballo* was heard with casts including Celestina Boninsegna, the American Eleanora de Cisneros, Emma Trentini, Francesco Vignas, and Mario Sammarco. During the spring-summer season just before the declaration of war in 1914, Covent Garden casts for *Un Ballo* showed such names as Destinn, Caruso, Martinelli, and Gilly.

Restored to the repertoire in the first postwar season, *Un Ballo in maschera* was conducted by Sir Thomas Beecham on June 17, 1919, the cast including Destinnová (Emmy Destinn), Giovanni Martinelli, and Dinh Gilly. After 1919, the opera was not heard until the Imperial League of Opera season in 1935; on September 30 of that year, Eva Turner was the Amelia, and others in the cast were Stella Andreva, Constance Willis, and Dino Borgioli.

Opening an autumn season at Covent Garden on October 23, 1952, *A Masked Ball,* in the late Edward J. Dent's translation, was the center of an extraordinary operatic tempest. Helen Werth, a German soprano, was demonstratively disapproved of by the gallery as Amelia. The next day it was decided that she could not undertake the role again the day after that. Attempts to enlist Hilde Zadek, Gré Brouwenstijn, Elfriede Wasserthal, and Dorothy Dow as a replacement ended unsuccessfully. Finally,

brought from Italy, the Brazilian soprano Constantina Araujo arrived at London airport so late on the day of the performance that the curtain had to be held for twenty minutes. She sang in Italian while her colleagues voiced Professor Dent's English; she announced that Renato (whom the others called Anckarstroem, the scene having been returned to Sweden) was going to be banished to "Inghilterra," though Dent had him going to Finland —and she triumphed, being brought forth for eight curtain calls. At more recent Covent Garden performances, Tito Gobbi has been greatly admired as Anckarstroem-Renato and Brouwenstijn has been excellent as Amelia.

New York heard *Un Ballo* before it had reached London; it was presented at the Academy of Music on February 11, 1861. Lilli Lehmann (who, some years earlier, had sung Oscar in Italian at Berlin in a company headed by Desirée Artôt, a onetime flame of Tchaikovsky's) was the first Metropolitan Amelia, when, on December 11, 1889, this Italian opera about the murder of a Swedish king metamorphosed into a Cavalier governor of a Puritan settlement in the wilds of New England was sung in German. Others in that cast were Betty Frank (Oscar), Emmy Sonntag-Uhl (Ulrica), Julius Perotti (Riccardo), and Theodor Reichmann (Renato); Anton Seidl conducted.

After four performances that season, *Ein Maskenball* disappeared from the Metropolitan. *Un Ballo in maschera* was first sung there on February 23, 1903, by a stupendous cast including Johanna Gadski, Louise Homer, Fritzi Scheff, Emilio de Marchi, Giuseppe Campanari, Édouard de Reszke, and Marcel Journet, despite which the opera was withdrawn after a single performance, only to reappear on February 6, 1905, with an even more imposing collection of artists to sing it: Eames, Homer, Bella Alten, Caruso, Scotti, Plançon, and Journet. These held for two performances only. Another eight years passed before, on November 22, 1913, Giulio Gatti-Casazza tried *Un Ballo* again with an all-star cast— Destinn, Margarete Matzenauer, Frieda Hempel, Caruso, Pasquale Amato, Andrés de Segurola, and Léon Rothier. It endured for only ten performances scattered over three seasons, after which came a long break until 1940.

On December 2, 1940, the opening night of the first season after the purchase of the Metropolitan Opera House by the resident company, *Un Ballo* was revived. Sumptuously mounted, and with an aggregation of singers headed by Zinka Milanov (Amelia), Kerstin Thorborg (Ulrica), Andreva (Oscar), Bjoerling (Riccardo), and—in his Metropolitan debut—Alexander Sved (Renato), it was well received by the first-nighters. It opened another season on November 10, 1947,[3] this time with Daniza Ilitsch as Amelia, Margaret Harshaw (Ulrica), Pierrette Alarie (Oscar), Jan Peerce (Riccardo), and Leonard Warren (Renato). After that season, it lapsed until January 7, 1955, when Marian Anderson (then nearly fifty-three years old, having been a famous singer for almost thirty years) made her operatic debut as Ulrica, an event that proved more sentimental and political than musicodramatic.[4] Under the baton of Dimitri Mitropoulos, her colleagues that night were Milanov (Amelia), Roberta Peters (Oscar), Richard Tucker (Riccardo), and Warren (Renato). Ulrica proved to be Anderson's only operatic role. The cast of *Un Ballo* had changed completely when, on March 19, 1959, it was heard at the Metropolitan for the fifty-sixth time. Mary Curtis-Verna (Amelia), Regina Resnik (Ulrica), Mildred Allen

(Oscar), Barry Morell (Riccardo), and Mario Sereni (Renato). The opera was restaged on January 25, 1962 (sixty-four performances by the end of the 1961–62 season), with the action restored to Sweden. The text sung was not without traces of *Un Ballo's* muddled history. For instance, the chief plotter was identified as Captain Johan Anckarstroem, though when a document containing the name Renato was read aloud, he said, "Il mio nome." Nello Santi made his debut as a Metropolitan conductor, and the principals were Leonie Rysanek (Amelia), Jean Madeira (Ulrica), Anneliese Rothenberger (Oscar), Carlo Bergonzi (Gustaf III), and Robert Merrill (Anckarstroem).

21. Il Barbiere di Siviglia (Rossini)

Two acts; libretto by Cesare Sterbini, after Beaumarchais's Le Barbier de Séville; *Rome, Teatro Argentina, February 20, 1816, as* Almaviva o sia l'inutile precauzione (*present title first used at Bologna on August 10, 1816*).

At the Rome *première*, Rossini conducted; the cast included Geltrude Giorgi-Righetti and Manuel del Popolo Vicente García (Almaviva). The opera was sung in London, in Italian at the Haymarket Theatre, March 10, 1818, with García as the Almaviva, and in English at Covent Garden on October 3, 1818, as arranged by Sir Henry Rowley Bishop, with Maria Dickons as Rosina (she had sung the same role in Mozart's *Le Nozze di Figaro* in 1812). An English version, probably Bishop's, reached New York on May 3, 1819, when the cast included Miss

---

[3] Although this was called the official opening night of the 1947–48 season, it had been preceded, three nights before, by a "Special Pre-Season Gala Performance" of *Don Giovanni*.

[4] Anderson was the first Negro to sing a leading role at the Metropolitan. She has been followed by such other Negro singers as Robert McFerrin, Mattiwilda Dobbs, Gloria Davy, and Leontyne Price.

Leesugg and Thomas Phillips. It became the first opera to be sung in Italian in New York when the García company opened a season at the Park Theater on November 29, 1825. The cast included the future Maria Malibran (Rosina); her father, Manuel del Popolo Vicente García (Almaviva); her brother Manuel Patricio García—who lived until 1906 (Figaro); and her mother, Señora García (Joaquina Briones), in the minor role of Berta.

Il Barbiere was first heard in Paris, in Italian, at the Théâtre-Italien, on October 26, 1819. The first performance in Castil-Blaze's French translation occurred at the Grand Théâtre, Lyon, on September 19, 1821. During its first performance at the Opéra-Comique, Paris, on November 8, 1884, the Rosina, Marie Van Zandt, was unable to continue after Act I, and was replaced by Cécile Mézeray. When *Le Barbier* was first performed at the Paris Opéra, on May 18, 1933, the Rosina was Fany Heldy, the Almaviva Miquel Villabella. By 1950, the opera had been sung 662 times at the Opéra-Comique alone, 387 of them in this century. First heard in Berlin in German, at the Königliches Opernhaus on June 18, 1822, it has been sung multilingually around the world, performances having been given even in Java, Australia, China, Palestine, and Morocco.

The Metropolitan Opera House offered *Il Barbiere* during its first season, on November 23, 1883. Augusto Vianesi conducted; the cast included Marcella Sembrich (Rosina—she sang Proch's Theme and Variations, Ries's "Wiegenlied," and Förster's "Ich liebe dich" during the Lesson Scene), Emily Lablache (Berta), Roberto Stagno (Almaviva), Giuseppe del Puente (Figaro), Baldassare Corsini (Bartolo), Giovanni Mirabella (Basilio), Ludovico Contini (Fiorello), and Amadeo Grazzi (An Official). Through the 1957–58 season, *Il Barbiere* had been heard at the Metropolitan 183 times, since when it has remained unsung.

The popularity of *Il Barbiere* has not suffered from changes in operatic fashion. A much-praised staging at La Scala, Milan, in 1952, conducted by Victor de Sabata, had a cast including Giulietta Simionato, Ferruccio Tagliavini, Gino Bechi, Nicola Rossi-Lemeni, and Melchiorre Luise. A Chicago Lyric Opera staging in 1958 showed this remarkable cast: Simionato (Rosina), Anna Maria Canali (Berta), Alvinio Misciano (Almaviva), Tito Gobbi (Figaro), Fernando Corena (Bartolo), Paolo Montarsolo (Basilio), and Henri Noel (Fiorello).

Rosina has been a favored role of countless sopranos and mezzo-sopranos. Many chose it for debuts and first appearances at important opera houses. Among them have been Giulia Grisi, Maria Malibran, Fanny Persiani, Marietta Alboni, Maria Caradori-Allan,[1] Henriette Sontag, Pauline Viardot-García, Adelina Patti, Angiolina Bosio, Luisa Tetrazzini, Nellie Melba, Marcella Sembrich, and Conchita Supervia. Then there have been Frieda Hempel, María Barrientos, Mabel Garrison, Amelita Galli-Curci, Lily Pons (the only role she ever sang at Covent Garden), Toti dal Monte (of whom, in this role, Ernest Newman wrote that "she sang well when she had not to act, and acted well when she had not to sing"), Jennie Tourel (Metropolitan debut, March 14, 1945), Margherita Carosio, Bidu Sayão, Victoria de los Angeles, Erna Berger, Patrice Munsel, Roberta Peters, Giulietta Simionato, and Maria Meneghini Callas.

To list the historic Figaros would be to call the roll of the most eminent baritones of the past and present. They

---

[1] More familiar in oratorio than in opera, Caradori-Allan became the first big foreign star to sing opera in the United States when she appeared in *Il Barbiere* at Niblo's Garden, New York, in 1837.

would include Michael William Balfe,[2] Antonio Tamburini, Giorgio Ronconi, Giuseppe Campanari, Mario Ancona, Jean de Reszke (before he moved up into the tenor range), Mario Sammarco, Riccardo Stracciari, Pasquale Amato, Titta Ruffo (Metropolitan debut, January 19, 1922), Giuseppe de Luca (Metropolitan debut, November 25, 1915), John Charles Thomas, John Brownlee, Robert Merrill, and Ettore Bastianini. Noted Almavivas have included Giovanni Battista Rubini, Mario, Alessandro Bonci, John McCormack, Charles Hackett, Tito Schipa, Ferruccio Tagliavini, Giuseppe di Stefano, and Cesare Valletti. Outstanding Basilios have been Édouard de Reszke, Feodor Chaliapin, Vanni Marcoux, Ezio Pinza, Italo Tajo (Metropolitan debut, December 28, 1948), and Cesare Siepi. Luigi Lablache was a famous Bartolo, in which role Salvatore Baccaloni and Fernando Corena have excelled in recent years.

renka. It had been put together too hurriedly, and the effect was Germanic, not Czech. By the time of the 1955 revival, it was felt that the opera was too small for the great spaces of Covent Garden, but nevertheless it was produced. The results were satisfactory, Elsie Morison being a particularly charming Marenka.

Smetana's opera had its New York first at the Metropolitan on February 19, 1909, with Emmy Destinn, Carl Jörn, Albert Reiss, and Adamo Didur. The 1926 revival, notable chiefly for Michael Bohnen's Kezal, also starred Maria Müller, Rudolf Laubenthal, and George Meader. The revival, in English, on February 28, 1941, was by no means perfect, but Jarmila Novotna was a sympathetic if rather too elegant Marenka. Charles Kullmann (Jenik— formerly Hans) turned in one of his best interpretations, and special praise was lavished on the care bestowed on the smallest roles.

22. The Bartered Bride (Smetana)

Three acts; libretto by Karel Sabina; Prague, Czech Theater, May 30, 1866.

In Czechoslovakia *Prodaná Nevěsta* is incredibly popular: in 1938 it was having its fourteen-hundredth performance in Prague. It was produced at the Drury Lane Theatre, London, in German, on June 26, 1895. Hermine Bosetti, Minnie Nast, and Fran Naval participated in the Covent Garden *première* on January 24, 1907. The 1930 revival, though well conducted by Barbirolli, did not hold the public, nor was Beecham's revival in 1939 effective, despite Hilde Konetzni's Ma-

23. La Battaglia di Legnano (Verdi)

Three acts; libretto by Salvatore Cammarano; Rome, Teatro Argentina, January 27, 1849.

Although *La Battaglia di Legnano* was applauded riotously at its *première*, it has never become a really successful opera. It has at times been given under the title *L'Assedio d'Arlem*, with plot and characters stringently altered. It was revived at La Scala, Milan, on January 19, 1916, and has been sung in Germany as both *Die Schlacht von Legnano* and *Das heilige Feuer*. A highly praised recent revival occurred on May 10, 1959, at the opening of the Florentine Maggio Musicale. In the presence of President Giovanni Gronchi of Italy, the opera was conducted by Vittorio Gui, and the cast included Leyla Gencer (Lida), Gas-

[2] The future composer of *The Bohemian Girl*, a singer before he succeeded as a composer, made his operatic debut as Figaro at Rossini's behest, at the Théâtre-Italien, Paris, in 1827.

tone Limarilli (Arrigo), Giuseppe Taddei (Rolando), and Paolo Washington (Barbarossa).

24. Beatrice di Tenda (Bellini)

Two acts; libretto by Felice Romani; Venice, Teatro La Fenice, March 16, 1833.

The cast of the Venice *première* included Giuditta Pasta (Beatrice), Anna Delserre (Agnese del Maino), Alberico Curioni (Orombello), and Orazio Cartagenova (Filippo Maria Visconti). Far from successful on its first night, the opera won adherents at the five additional performances, the last of which closed the Fenice season on Sunday, March 24. Never as much performed as *La Sonnambula, Norma,* or *I Puritani,* it nevertheless was heard in London as early as March 22, 1836; at the Théâtre-Italien, Paris, on February 8, 1841; at New Orleans on March 21, 1842; and at New York on March 18, 1844. In German translation, as *Das Castell von Ursino* (literal rendering of an Italian title used for it at Trieste in 1837), it made the rounds of German opera houses. It was heard with some frequency throughout Italy during the rest of the nineteenth century, and was revived at Bellini's birthplace, Catania, on January 1, 1935. A notable recent revival was staged at the Teatro Massimo, Palermo, to open a season, on January 12, 1959. Vittorio Gui, who conducted, also edited the score somewhat—removing, for example, a final cabaletta, taken from Bellini's *Bianca e Fernando* at Pasta's insistence. Leading roles were sung by Consuelo Rubio (Beatrice), Ilva Ligabue (Agnese del Maino), Juan Oncina (Orombello), and Giuseppe Taddei (Filippo Maria Visconti). Joan Sutherland made her New York debut in a concert performance of this opera at Town Hall

under the auspices of the American Opera Society on February 21, 1961. Nicola Rescigno conducted; others in the cast were Marilyn Horne, also in her New York debut (Agnese), Richard Cassilly (Orombello), and Enzo Sordello (Filippo). *Beatrice di Tenda* returned to La Scala, Milan, in May, 1961, with Sutherland in the title role, Giuseppe Campora (Orombello), Dino Dondi (Filippo), and the much-admired Raina Kabaivanska (Agnese). Antonino Votto conducted.

25. Béatrice et Bénédict (Berlioz)

Two acts; libretto by the composer, after Shakespeare's Much Ado About Nothing; *Baden-Baden, August 9, 1862.*

Berlioz conducted the world *première*. This delightful little opera has had almost no stage history, although in his *Memoirs* (Ernest Newman's version) Berlioz wrote: "This work is difficult of performance, especially in the men's parts, but I think it one of the most spirited and original I ever wrote. Unlike *Les Troyens,* its production entails no expense."

Béatrice et Bénédict was heard in German translation at Weimar in 1863, in Karlsruhe in 1888, in Vienna in 1890, in Leipzig in 1913, and in Plauen in 1929. It was given at Glasgow, in English, on March 24, 1936. The first Paris performance, not a notable success, was at the Opéra-Comique on June 4, 1890. What appears to have been the first performance in the United States was a concert version presented at Carnegie Hall, New York, on March 21, 1960, by The Little Orchestra Society. Thomas Scherman conducted, and the cast included Irene Jordan (Béatrice), Adele Addison (Héro), Madelyn Vose (Ursule), Michel Sénéchal (Bénédict), Robert Goss (Somarone), and Hugh Thompson (Claudio).

26. The Beggar's Opera

Three acts; libretto by John Gay; London, Lincoln's Inn Fields, February 9, 1728.

The Beggar's Opera was performed sixty-two times during its first season, a record not broken by another English stage production until 1822. The overture and one of the 69 airs seem to have been composed by John Christopher Pepusch; of the other 68 airs, 51 are taken to be English, Irish, Scottish, and French folk songs, the other 17 being generally attributed to John Barret (2), Giovanni Bononcini (1), Henry Carey (2), Jeremiah Clarke (2), John Eccles (1), Girolamo Frescobaldi (1), Francesco Geminiani (1?), Handel (2), Purcell (3), Lewis Ramondon (1), and John Wilford (1).

During the first year after its production in London, *The Beggar's Opera* was also heard at Dublin, Dover, Norwich, Bath, Newcastle, Canterbury, Bristol, Sandwich, Deal, Glasgow, Haddington, Bury, Colchester, Ipswich, and Edinburgh. Its success soon became world-wide. It was played in Jamaica in 1733 and in New York on December 3, 1750. It has been heard in French and German, and nineteenth- and twentieth-century revivals in England and the United States have been extremely numerous. The most successful of all productions was that arranged and orchestrated by Frederick Austin; this opened at the Lyric Theatre, Hammersmith, London, on June 5, 1920, and ran consecutively for 1,463 performances; it has been revived there several times since.

For Kurt Weill's setting of a modern version of Gay's text, see *Die Dreigroschenoper* (No. 61).

27. Benvenuto Cellini (Berlioz)

Two acts; libretto by Léon du Wailly and Jules Barbier; Paris, Opéra, September 10, 1838.

Despite its fine music and splendid cast, *Benvenuto Cellini* failed at the première; the principals were Gilbert-Louis Duprez (who unhappily muffed the name role), Julie Dorus-Gras, and Rosine Stoltz; there were four performances (after which the opera was not sung in France until 1913, when it opened the Théâtre des Champs-Élysées and was sung six times). Liszt revived it at Weimar fourteen years later. Both this remarkable revival and the production at Covent Garden, on June 25, 1853, were carefully reported by Henry Fothergill Chorley, who said of the English experiment: "*Benvenuto Cellini* failed more decidedly than any foreign opera I recollect to have seen performed in London." Chorley's careful analysis was fair for the time, and moreover, seems to anticipate much not altogether hostile writing about Berlioz today—in short, the old perplexities have endured. Enrico Tamberlik had the name role, and Berlioz himself conducted. Jacques Barzun noted that *Benvenuto Cellini* "enjoyed a veritable run in Germany between 1880 and the First World War," reaching a total of some six hundred singings in a dozen German cities. But Gustav Mahler's affection for the opera did not help the Vienna production in 1911.

The Carl Rosa Opera Company staged *Benvenuto Cellini* at the Sadler's Wells Theatre, London, on April 9, 1957, using the spoken dialogue that Berlioz replaced with recitative in 1852. Arthur Hammond conducted; the cast included Estelle Valery (Teresa), Pauline Allen (Ascanio), Charles Craig (Cellini), John Faasen (Fieramosca), Frederick Wood (Pompeo), Stanislav Pieczora (Cardinal Salviati), and Donald Campbell (Balducci). Although the production was called by Harold Rosenthal "a noble try, but one really beyond the company's capabilities," it became something of a repertoire regular. A far more adequate revival was seen and heard for the first time at the

Stadsschouwburg, Amsterdam, on June 25, 1961, as part of the fourteenth Holland Festival. Georges Prêtre conducted, the sets were by François Ganeau, and the producer was Marcel Lamy. Leading roles were sung by Gerry de Groot (Teresa), Nicolai Gedda (Cellini), Wim Koopman (a tenor, in the mezzo-soprano travesty role of Ascanio), Scipio Colombo (Fieramosca), Guus Hoekman (Salviati), Jos Borelli (Pompeo), and Chris Reumer (Innkeeper).

28. Betrothal in a Convent (Prokofiev)

Four acts; libretto by Mira Mendelson, after Richard Brinsley Sheridan's The Duenna; *Leningrad, Kirov Theater, 1946.*

Confusingly, this opera is widely known in the United States as *The Duenna*—and in England as *Betrothal in a Monastery* and even *Betrothal in the Monastery*. In the summer of 1948 it was given fifty-three performances by the Lemonade Opera Company at the Greenwich Mews Playhouse, New York, as *The Duenna,* in an English translation by Jean Karsavina. The music had been arranged for two pianos by the conductor, Sam Morgenstern, and leading roles were sung by Ruth Kobart (Duenna), Dean Mundy (Louisa), June Gallaher (Rosina), Robert Sprecher (Jerome), James Cosmos (Mendoza), Harry Wayne (Ferdinand), Donald Devor (Antonio), and Lewis Brooks (Carlos).

Betrothal in a Convent was produced in Germany for the first time in November, 1957, at Leipzig. Heinz Fricke conducted, the production was by Friedrich Ammermann, and the cast included Maria Croonen, Ingeborg Kollmann, Ferdinand Birgmann, Katrin Wölzl, Lothar Anders, Wilhelm Klemm, Georg Wegener, Helmut Eyle, and Paul Reinecke. In 1958, the East Berlin

Staatsoper staged it in a production by Erich-Alexander Winds, with scenery by Heinz Pfeiffenberger; Lovro von Matacic conducted. The first Italian production of the opera—as *Matrimonio al Convento*—occurred at the Teatro San Carlo, Naples, in the spring of 1959. Directed by Alessandro Brissoni, with sets by Giancarlo Bartolini Salimbeni, the opera was conducted by Fabien Sevitzky. The cast included Belen Amparan (Duenna), Roseta Noli, Giuseppe Valdengo (Ferdinand), Francesco Albanese (Jerome), Fernando Corena (Mendoza), Agostino Lazzari, and Guido Mazzini. The opera does not seem to have been heard in England.

29. Billy Budd (Britten)

Four acts; libretto by E. M. Forster and Eric Crozier, after the story by Herman Melville; London, Covent Garden, December 1, 1951.

Britten conducted the world *première* of this all-male opera (the score calls for five tenors, nine baritones, three basses, boys' voices, and a boy's spoken role). Among the singers were Peter Pears (Captain Vere), Theodor Uppmann, in his Covent Garden debut (Billy Budd), and Frederick Dalberg (Clagart). Heard twelve times that season, *Billy Budd* thereafter left the Covent Garden repertoire. Substantially the London cast was heard in Paris the following year. A few other mountings followed, including one in German, at Wiesbaden, in 1952.

30. La Bohème (Puccini)

Four acts; libretto by Giuseppe Giacosa and Luigi Illica; Turin, Teatro Regio, February 1, 1896.

Arturo Toscanini (he was then twenty-nine) conducted the world *première* of *La Bohème*. The cast was: Cesira Ferrani (Mimi), Camilla Pasini (Musetta), Evan Gorga (Rodolfo), Antonio Pini-Corsi (Schaunard), Alessandro Polonini (Benoit and Alcindoro), Dante Zucchi (Parpignol), Tieste Wilmant (Marcello), Michele Mazzara (Colline), and Felice Foglia (Sergente dei Doganieri). The public took to the opera only gradually, and its real success dates from a Palermo production on April 13, 1896, with Leopoldo Mugnone conducting; Ada Giachetti, Enrico Caruso's common-law wife, was the Mimi.

La Bohème reached England on April 22, 1897, in English, at the Comedy Theatre, Manchester, where it was billed as *The Bohemians;* Alice Esty and Robert Cunningham respectively were the Mimi and the Rodolfo. Still in English, it had its first Covent Garden hearing that same year, and was not very well received. Nellie Melba first sang Mimi at Covent Garden on July 1, 1899, and she liked the role so well —and London liked her so well in it —that until she retired, it became practically her property; she was finally to sing it from a wheel chair. Melba's love for Mimi, or for herself as Mimi, persuaded the London public to take *La Bohème* to its bosom, though certainly it would have established itself solidly in any event. Her chief associates for the first Italian *Bohème* at Covent Garden were Zélie de Lussan (Musetta), Fernando de Lucia (Rodolfo), and Mario Ancona (Marcello).

Bliss became rapture when, on May 22, 1905, Melba and Caruso sang their first Covent Garden *Bohème* together (they already had sung it in New York). One of Melba's interim Rodolfos was Emilio de Marchi, and in 1913 she again was partnered by Caruso, "By Desire of Their Majesties." Giovanni Martinelli was a very fine Rodolfo. In 1919, Melba, at fifty-eight, still was singing a full-scale Mimi, with Thomas Burke (Rodolfo) and Alfred Maguenat (Marcello); it was, however, her last season. It is almost shocking not to find her name on the 1920 Covent Garden roster. Miriam Licette and Tudor Davies marked quite a descent from Melba and Caruso. But Melba appeared in the role of Mimi as a guest artist as late as 1923 (even later elsewhere). In 1928, Margherita Carosio, a debutante Musetta, was not much more than "properly shrill" among her poorish associates, the best of whom was the Rodolfo, Aureliano Pertile. The advent of Beniamino Gigli strengthened the possibility of an acceptable *Bohème,* but perfection was not achieved despite isolated fine performances: Joan Cross as Mimi, Angelo Minghetti as Rodolfo. At its best the Mimi of Eidé Noréna was delightful, but she was erratic. Elisabeth Rethberg's Mimi was delightful vocally but not otherwise. Grace Moore's was not considered equal to the Mimis of her "illustrious predecessors"—a comment that could be applied to most of her interpretations. Ezio Pinza had long declared himself a superlative Colline. Heddle Nash's Rodolfo became all but impeccable. Comedy was inserted into an English-language *Bohème* when Elisabeth Schwarzkopf, Ljuba Welitch, Rudolf Schock, and Paolo Silveri produced various types of accents. One of the stupid accidents of opera in English—in the most gruesome sense of the phrase— was the nonre-engagement of the Belgian soprano Suzanne Danco, a truly great singer, because her accent did not please. Of the more recent Covent Garden productions of *La Bohème,* not much that is either good or interesting can be said.

The history of *La Bohème* at the Metropolitan, where it may overtake *Aïda* as the opera performed there most often, parallels its Covent Garden history—excelling casts at first, then gradual deterioration into mediocrity or worse, all based on the cynical, sound assumption that a performance of this sure-fire favorite will fill the house under any conditions. Although *Bohème* had been sung in New York as early as 1898, the Metropolitan did not stage it until December 26, 1900, with Melba as Mimi. Signora Occhiolini (Musetta), hastily produced because Fritzi Scheff was ill, was poor, but the others in the cast were excellent (and later in the year Scheff proved her special aptitude for Musetta): Albert Saléza, Giuseppe Campanari, Charles Gilibert, Marcel Journet, and Eugène Dufriche. *La Bohème* was dropped for one season, but then returned, to miss but a single season (1959–60) to date—a phenomenon unique in Metropolitan history. By the end of the 1960–61 season, it had been heard 400 times at the Metropolitan; eight performances were added to this tally during 1961–62.

In Melba's absence, Marcella Sembrich sang Mimi, but was judged too refined; her Rodolfo was Caruso, whose Central Park Zoo adventure added piquancy to the situation. Geraldine Farrar, Bella Alten, Herman Jadlowker, and Antonio Scotti formed an agreeable group of Bohemians in 1910. Frances Alda's Mimi, beginning without much promise, so had improved by 1917 that she deserved her Rodolfo, John McCormack, whose flawless style may possibly have been drawn too fine for Puccini. The death of Caruso made way for Gigli. It is perhaps not clear why Grace Moore was admired as Mimi, but there can be no doubt that Edward Johnson (Rodolfo) and Editha Fleischer (Musetta) gave her perfect support. Seasoned operagoers cherish warm memories of Lucrezia Bori as Mimi.

One of the best *Bohèmes* of its year was that of November 24, 1938, when Jussi Bjoerling was the Rodolfo, Mafalda Favero the Mimi; the whole ensemble took fire from the faultless achievements of these two. Jarmila Novotna would have been a perfect Musetta if her voice had been larger

—this deficiency troubled her entire Metropolitan career. In 1940, Salvatore Baccaloni began to show off his great *buffo* in some of the opera's secondary roles. Dorothy Kirsten suggested her true line of development in her first Mimi, far better suited to her voice than florid exploration; Jan Peerce (Rodolfo) and Martial Singher (a splendid Marcello) were among her associates. Stella Roman was even better than Kirsten, notably in her conception of the character. Licia Albanese and Ferruccio Tagliavini were agreeably paired as Mimi and Rodolfo. Richard Tucker became an outstanding interpreter of Rodolfo during the 1950's, but an outstanding Mimi is not so easy to indicate. Apparently Victoria de los Angeles tired of the role—certainly she was vocally flawless as Mimi.

31. Boris Godunov (Mussorgsky)

Prologue and four acts; libretto by the composer, "after Pushkin and Karamzin": that is, after Pushkin's historical drama of the same name (1831) and Nikolai Mikhailovich Karamzin's History of the Russian Empire *(1819–26) (Pushkin himself had followed Karamzin to such an extent that he even carried over Karamzin's sentimentality); St. Petersburg, Maryinsky Theater (in a slightly cut version), January 27 (O.S.), 1874.*

The St. Petersburg *première* was notable for the magnificent performances of Ossip Afanasyevich Petrov (Varlaam) and Yulie F. Platonova (Marina). After approximately twenty-five performances, the government censor banned *Boris*, which was not heard again until 1896, fifteen years after Mussorgsky's death, this time in Rimsky-Korsakov's edition, which he was to change further in a final revision (1906–8). For many years Rimsky's second version was the one generally used.

For the first performance outside Russia—in a Diaghilev production at the Opéra, Paris, on May 19, 1908—the first Rimsky version was used, with cuts. Feodor Chaliapin's Boris, combined with the splendors of the production, brought triumph. *Boris* had been heard in Italian, Czech, Swedish, Polish, Russian, and French in Europe and South America before it finally reached New York on March 19, 1913. Arturo Toscanini conducted this Metropolitan production, with Adamo Didur (Boris), Louise Homer (Marina), Paul Althouse (Dmitri), Anna Case (Feodor), Andrés de Segurola (Varlaam), and Léon Rothier (Pimenn). Chaliapin's Boris was first heard in the United States at the Metropolitan on December 9, 1921, with a predominantly inferior cast singing Italian while he sang Russian. Later performances that season convinced critics and public that he was the supreme singing actor of the era. It was to Giulio Gatti-Casazza's credit that, despite his tendency not to innovate, he kept *Boris* uninterruptedly in the repertoire for seventeen seasons (1912–29). It was revived for Ezio Pinza in 1938, but Boris never was one of his best roles, and the real impression was made by Kerstin Thorborg's Marina. Alexander Kipnis sang and acted a more impressive Boris in the 1942–43 season. Notable Borises of later Metropolitan performances have been Cesare Siepi, Jerome Hines, Nicola Rossi-Lemeni, and George London (who also has sung the role successfully in Russian in Russia).

The Metropolitan used versions of the Rimsky-Korsakov versions until March 6, 1953, when Mussorgsky was presented "pure"–that is, as "edited" by Karol Rathaus and translated into English by John Gutman. This partial step in the right direction was retraced when, on October 27, 1960, the Metropolitan presented *Boris,* still in English, in a version "revised and edited by Dmitri Shostakovich" in which the orchestra often sounded more Dmitri than Modest. When NBC-TV, on March 26, 1961, televised *Boris,* Rimsky-Korsakov was brought back and John Gutman retained; the impressive Boris of this unsatisfactory performance was Giorgio Tozzi, who later (September 21, 1961) sang the role with the San Francisco Opera Company under the baton of Leopold Ludwig.

Boris Godunov has had a far more restricted career in England, but at least it had a more auspicious start there—on June 24, 1913, when Chaliapin and a company sponsored jointly by Serge Diaghilev, Sir Joseph Beecham, and Sir Thomas Beecham, gave an all-Russian *Boris* during a memorable Drury Lane season. For London, Chaliapin was the one and only Boris for some years; often he was surrounded by Italian-singing confreres, among whom Salvatore Baccaloni (Varlaam) was notable. After 1929, Covent Garden heard no memorable *Boris* until the title role was taken over in 1949 by the finest of latter-day Godunovs, the Bulgarian Boris Christoff. He alone sang in Russian, and the score used was eclectic. Covent Garden had heard the opera in English in 1948, and though the version had been Mussorgsky 1874, the singers had been disappointing (Paolo Silveri as Boris most damagingly). On October 31, 1958, Covent Garden produced *Boris* in a version including almost all of the score from the original and revised versions as Mussorgsky had composed them—and sung entirely in Russian. Rafael Kubelik conducted, Christoff was the Boris, and others in the cast included Regina Resnik (Marina), Josephine Veasey (Feodor), Edith Coates (Hostess), Noreen Berry (Nurse), Joan Carlyle (Xenia), John Lanigan (Shuisky), Joseph Rouleau (Pimenn), David Kelly

(Varlaam), David Tree (Missail), Geraint Evans (Shchelkalov), Otakar Kraus (Rangoni), Duncan Robertson (Simpleton), and Josip Gostic (Dmitri). London had been afforded an opportunity to hear Mussorgsky's opera as he himself wanted it to be.

32. La Cambiale di matrimonio (Rossini)

One act; libretto by Gaetano Rossi, founded on a comedy by Camillo Federici; Venice, Teatro San Moisè, November 3, 1810.

During Rossini's lifetime, this, his first opera to be staged, was also performed in Barcelona, Trieste, and Vienna. Of several twentieth-century revivals, one was staged at Pesaro, Italy —his birthplace—on the 144th anniversary of his birth, February 29, 1936. It was also sung at the Stadttheater, Vienna, on September 22, 1937, and at the Forty-fourth Street Theater, New York, on November 8, 1937. One of the most recent stagings occurred at the Palais des Beaux-Arts, Brussels, in 1957; Angelo Questa conducted, and the cast included Dora Gatta, Petre Munteanu, Leo Pudis, and Melchiorre Luise.

One aria from *La Cambiale di matrimonio*, "Come tacer," was reused by Rossini in *Il Barbiere di Siviglia*, where it figures as the duet beginning "Dunque io son. . . ."

33. Il Campanello di notte (Donizetti)

One act; libretto by Donizetti, after La Sonnette de nuit, *a vaudeville by Léon-Lévy Brunswick, Mathieu-Barthélemy Troin, and Victor Lhérie; Naples, Teatro Nuovo, June 6, 1836.*

Donizetti is said to have composed this one-act opera in one week in order to save an impresario from the necessity of declaring bankruptcy. It was an immediate success in Italy, where it was at times billed as *Il Campanello dello speziale*. It was heard at the Lyceum, London, in Italian on November 30, 1837, and at St. James's Theatre twenty years later, November 14, 1857. In Paris, it opened the Fantaisies-Parisiennes on December 2, 1865, as *La Sonnette*, translated into French by Jules Ruelle. New York heard it in an English translation by Sydney Rosenfeld, at the Lyceum Theater on May 7, 1917. On April 15, 1957, the Piccola Scala, Milan, revived *Il Campanello di notte* as half of a double bill with Donizetti's *Rita*. Nino Sanzogno conducted, Fernando Corena was excellent as the aging apothecary whose dispensary bell rings infuriatingly throughout his wedding night, and Rolando Panerai excelled as the jokester who, in many disguises, does the bell-ringing.

34. Capriccio (Strauss)

One act; libretto by the composer and Clemens Krauss, after the Abbate Giovanni Battista Casti's Prima la musica e poi le parole, *first set by Antonio Salieri; Munich, Staatsoper, October 28, 1942.*

The first performance of *Capriccio* was conducted by Clemens Krauss. His wife, Viorica Ursuleac, sang the role of the Countess, and was supported by Hildegard Ranczak, Taubmann, Hans Hotter (Olivier), Walter Höfermayer, and Georg Hann. When Karl Böhm conducted it at Zurich two years later, the Countess was sung by Maria Cebotari, who was supported by Marta Rohs, Anton Dermota, Erich Kunz, and Paul Schöffler. At Salzburg in 1950, Böhm again conducted, but the cast was headed by Lisa della Casa, with Elisabeth Höngen, Dermota, Hans Braun, Wolff, and Schöffler; Wilma Lipp made much of the Italian Soprano's little. Rudolf Kempe was the conductor of a Vienna production in 1951 in which Christel Goltz was the Countess. London heard two notable singings of the little opera during a visit by the Bayerische Staatsoper to Covent Garden in September, 1953, the first on September 22. Robert Heger conducted; leading singers included Maud Cunitz (Countess), Erika Köth (Italian Soprano), Herta Töpper (Clairon), Richard Holm (Flamand), Karl Schmitt-Walter (Count), Lorenz Fehenberger (Olivier), Benno Kusche (La Roche), and Franz Klarwein (Italian Tenor). A notable staging of *Capriccio* was that of the Vienna Staatsoper in 1960. Karl Böhm conducted and the leading roles were sung by Elisabeth Schwarzkopf (Countess), Christel Goltz (Clairon), Dermota (Flamand), Schöffler (La Roche), and Walter Berry (Olivier).

The first professionally staged performance of *Capriccio* in the United States was given by the Santa Fe (New Mexico) Opera on August 1, 1958. John Crosby conducted, and leading members of the cast were: Maria Ferriero (Countess), Judith Raskin (Italian Soprano), Regina Sarfaty (Clairon), Loren Driscoll (Flamand), Robert Trehy (Count), Robert Rue (Olivier), John Macurdy (La Roche), and Nico Castel (Italian Tenor).

35. I Capuletti e i Montecchi (Bellini)

Four parts; libretto (written originally for Niccolò Vaccai, whose Giulietta e Romeo was successfully staged at the Teatro della Canobbiana, Milan, on October 31, 1825) based on Shakespeare's Romeo and Juliet by Felice Romani; Venice, Teatro La Fenice, March 11, 1830. The opera contains music transferred to it by Bellini from his notably unsuccessful Zaïra, which had inaugurated the new Teatro Regio, Parma, on May 16, 1829. In turn, many later performances of I Capuletti e i Montecchi were mutilated by the substitution of Vaccai's final act for Bellini's.

The cast of the original Fenice production of *I Capuletti* included Giuditta Grisi, Maria Caradori-Allan, and Lorenzo Bonfigli; the opera was sung eight times in ten days, closing the season on March 21. It was soon being sung throughout Europe and in both Americas. In Italian, it was heard at the Théâtre-Italien, Paris, on January 10, 1833, at London on the following July 20, and at the Königsstädtischestheater, Berlin, on June 5, 1834. After being sung in Havana, Mexico City, Rio de Janeiro, Valparaiso, and Trinidad, *I Capuletti* finally reached the United States at Boston in May, 1847. It was sung at Philadelphia on August 6, 1847, at New York on January 28, 1848. Translations into German, Hungarian, Russian, Czech, Danish, French, and Polish were shortly made.

On June 13, 1848, *I Capuletti ed*[1] *i Montecchi* was revived at Covent Garden with Jeanne Castellan (Giulietta) and Pauline Viardot-García (Romeo). The opera has never been staged at the Metropolitan. It is still occasionally sung in Italy, a notable staging having occurred at Turin on December 26, 1934. In concert form, it was presented at Carnegie Hall, New York, in October, 1958, by the American Opera Society; Arnold U. Gamson conducted, and the cast included Giulietta Simionato, Laurel Hurley, Ezio Flagello, David Smith, and Richard Cassilly. One of the reasons for the comparative infrequency of performances of this opera may be the difficulty that modern audiences find in seeing a female singer in travesty as Romeo.

In addition to Vaccai's and Bellini's operas, other settings of the Romeo and

---

[1] Although the "and" of the original title seems to have been *e*, the more pedantically correct *ed* was substituted somewhere along the way.

Juliet tragedy include: Georg Benda's pioneering *Romeo und Julie* (1776); Daniel Steibelt's *Roméo et Juliette* (1793), said to have been the first opera in which the score calls for a Chinese gong; the *Giulietta e Romeo* (1796) of Nicola Antonio Zingarelli, Bellini's teacher at Naples; Filippo Marchetti's *Romeo e Giulietta* (1865); Gounod's *Roméo et Juliette* (1867); Richard d'Ivry's *Les Amants de Vérone* (1878); and Riccardo Zandonai's *Giulietta e Romeo* (1922), which shows the results of research by its librettist, Arturo Rossato, into Shakespeare's sources, Bandello in particular. Frederick Delius's *Romeo und Julia auf dem Dorfe* (1907) has no more to do with Shakespeare than has Shostakovich's *Lady Macbeth of Mzensk*.

36. Cardillac (Hindemith)

Three acts; libretto by Ferdinand Lion, after E. T. A. Hoffmann's Das Fräulein von Scuderi; Dresden, November 9, 1926.

Cardillac was staged for the first time at Dresden on November 9, 1926. Fritz Busch conducted. Shortly later, it was heard at Vienna (March 3, 1927), Prague (March, 1927), Berlin (June 30, 1928), and other Central European cities. On December 18, 1936, it was given a concert performance at Queen's Hall, London, in an English translation by Felix H. White. At the Teatro La Fenice, Venice, in 1948, the opera was conducted by Nino Sanzogno; leading roles were taken by Boris Christoff and Raimondo Torres. Hindemith later made a revised version of *Cardillac*, and this was heard for the first time at Zurich on June 20, 1952.

37. Carmen (Bizet)

Four acts; libretto by Henri Meilhac and Ludovic Halévy, after Prosper Mérimée's tale; Paris, Opéra-Comique, March 3, 1875.

Célestine Galli-Marié, who had created the title role in Ambroise Thomas' *Mignon* at the Opéra-Comique in 1866, was the Carmen of the *première* there on March 3, 1875. Louis-Michel Deloffre conducted, and the rest of the cast consisted of Marguerite Chapuy (Micaëla), Mlle Ducasse (Frasquita), Esther Chevalier (Mercédes), Paul Lhérie (Don José), Joseph Bouhy (Escamillo), M. Potel (Le Dancaïre), M. Barnoldt (Le Remendado), M. Duvernoy (Moralès), Eugène Dufriche (Zuniga), M. Nathan (Lillas Pastia), M. Teste (Un Guide). In Act II, "La Flamenca" was danced by Mlles Blandini and Anckté. By the evening of the night during which Bizet died (June 3), the opera had reached its thirty-third performance; the original production was played for the forty-eighth and last time on February 15, 1876, after which *Carmen* was not heard in Paris for seven years.

The cast for the Paris revival on April 23, 1883—when Charles Lamoureux conducted—was headed by Adèle Isaac, who is said to have made Carmen into a perfect lady. Only Chevalier, Barnoldt, and Teste remained of the original cast. The opera, poorly rehearsed and mounted, was booed by the audience, but nevertheless was clearly launched on its almost unparalleled popularity. It was heard seventeen times during that spring season. Then, on October 22, 1883, Galli-Marié returned to the title role in a fine restaging of the original production. In her *Bizet and His World*, Mina Curtiss says that the twenty-six performances between November 3 and December 31 of that year brought approximately $40,300 into the Comique box office.[1]

By November 25, 1892, when Emma

[1] In 1890, Galli-Marié, then fifty years of age, headed a special Comique cast assembled to raise funds for a Bizet monument. Her principal associates on that occasion were Nellie Melba (Micaëla), Jean de Reske (Don José), and Jean Lassalle (Escamillo).

Calvé's Carmen was heard for the first time at the Comique (Galli-Marié went backstage to congratulate this most famous of her successors), *Carmen* had been heard there more than five hundred times. When the Comique moved from its temporary home in the Théâtre-Sarah Bernhardt to the present Salle Favart, the opening performance in the new hall was the 756th *Carmen* (December 8, 1898), with Georgette Leblanc in the title role, Léon Beyle as Don José, and Max Bouvet as Escamillo; Alexandre Luigini conducted. The Comique's 1,000th *Carmen* was heard on December 23, 1904 (Calvé as Carmen, Edmond Clément as Don José, Hector Dufranne as Escamillo); its 1,700th on April 30, 1923 [2] (Suzanne Brohly as Carmen, Lucien Muratore as Don José, Hubert Audoin as Escamillo); its 2,000th on June 29, 1930.

On October 25, 1938, the centenary of Bizet's birth, the Comique presented its 2,271st *Carmen* (Renée Gilly as Carmen, Solange Delmas as Micaëla, Mario Altéry as Don José, Martial Singher as Escamillo). The 2,500th presentation was reached at a matinee on June 1, 1947 (Solange Michel as Carmen, Jacqueline Brumaire as Micaëla, Édouard Kriff as Don José, Julien Giovanetti as Escamillo). By November 10, 1959, when, as one step in a tragically needed housecleaning of the national theaters, *Carmen* was transferred to the Opéra, it had been sung about 3,000 times at the Comique (2,897 on January 1, 1958). The lavish new production at the Opéra (100 supers, 100 choristers, 40 dancers, 13 horses, 1 monkey, 2 donkeys) was conducted by Roberto Benzi, an ex-child prodigy then twenty-two; the Carmen was a twenty-eight-year-old newcomer, Jane Rhodes. During the 1960–61 season, the Metropolitan Opera, having first introduced the Swedish Kerstin Meyer as Carmen (debut, October 29, 1960), gave the opera some new life in New York by presenting Mlle Rhodes in a single performance of it (the 375th in the house) on November 7, 1960, her United States debut. Mlle Rhodes' intelligent characterization made more noticeable than ever the fact that the Metropolitan *Carmen* stood in acute need of a re-creation as nearly complete as the one in which she had starred in Paris.

The lore about non-Parisian productions of *Carmen* is so vast that only a sliver of it can be given here. The first singing outside Paris occurred at Vienna on October 23, 1875, on which occasion the recitatives composed by Ernest Guiraud were first used. Brussels followed on February 3, 1876 (five hundred performances by October 11, 1913). Then came Antwerp, Budapest (in Hungarian), St. Petersburg (in Italian), and Stockholm (in Swedish). London first heard *Carmen* in Italian, on June 22, 1878, at Her Majesty's Theatre; the cast included the great American singing actress Minnie Hauk (Carmen), Alwina Valleria (Micaëla), Italo Campanini (Don José), and Giuseppe del Puente (Escamillo); Sir Michael Costa conducted. The opera was produced in Dublin on September 9, 1878, and reached New York, still in Italian, on October 23 of that year. At that Academy of Music performance, Hauk, Campanini, and Del Puente repeated their London roles. *Carmen* was heard at the Opernhaus, Berlin, on March 12, 1880, in German (five hundred performances by 1935). It was staged in Christiania, Norway, that same year—and on May 7, 1900, was restaged to inaugurate the new Norwegian State Opera House there. *Carmencita and the Soldier,* the Moscow Art Theater's famed adaptation of the Bizet opera, was first heard at Moscow on June 4, 1924. And, among dozens of other mountings in a variety of languages, *Carmen* was sung at Tokyo in Japanese on March 24, 1935.

---

[2] On this occasion, contrary to Parisian custom, the spoken dialogue was replaced by the recitatives written by Ernest Guiraud, familiar to non-French audiences.

Minnie Hauk, the first London and New York Carmen, was a difficult young woman. She refused to undertake the role for Mapleson's company at Her Majesty's unless she was allowed to choose the rest of the cast, all of whom began by objecting to their roles as too slender for their talents and position. Campanini pointed out that his only love duet was with the *seconda donna,* as his conventional Italian tenor's mind labeled Micaëla. Del Puente suavely suggested that Mapleson had sent him a chorus man's part accidentally, and Valleria's objections were much the same. Before the season was over, the chief delinquents were learning from the applause how good their assignments were. They learned to love the roles so much that Campanini became a famed Don José, and Del Puente has seldom been surpassed as the bull-fighter.

During the Metropolitan Opera's first season, it gave the Italian version of *Carmen,* again enlisting Valleria, Campanini, and Del Puente, but substituting Zelia Trebelli for Hauk; Cleofonte Campanini conducted. On November 25, 1885, during the Metropolitan's second all-German season, the company discarded the Guiraud recitatives for spoken dialogue in a performance that witnessed the debuts of both Lilli Lehmann (Carmen) and Max Alvary (Don José); Anton Seidl conducted; his wife, Auguste Seidl-Kraus, was the Micaëla, and the Escamillo was Adolf Robinson. Hauk made her Metropolitan debut as Carmen on February 20, 1891, the conductor being Walter Damrosch, the other principals Marie Jahn (Micaëla), Andreas Dippel (Don José), and Theodor Reichmann (Escamillo). As the

names suggest, this too was a performance in German.

Meanwhile, other prima donnas were flaunting their Carmens on European and American stages. In a proprietary sense, the role passed from Galli-Marié to Hauk to Calvé, who first sang it in America for the Metropolitan's bold experiment with the original French on December 20, 1893, when her colleagues were Emma Eames (Micaëla), Jean de Reszke (Don José), and Jean Lassalle (Escamillo). This production established Calvé, in American minds at least, as the peerless Carmen, Eames as a Micaëla difficult to better. As H. E. Krehbiel remarked, Calvé's Carmen became a fad, and for years the public would hear no other. Many professional critics agreed that her impersonation was the most satisfactory. Herman Klein, for instance, called her the greatest, adding: "Albeit I find it hard to differentiate between her and [Pauline] Lucca,[3] whose conception had in it more originality but less of the pure Spanish type.[4] To what extent, if any, Calvé had had an opportunity of studying the Carmens who preceded her, I cannot say. Nor do I believe for a moment that she consciously imitated any of them. The fact remains, nevertheless, that her delineation seemed to combine the most fascinating characteristics of each in turn. It had the calm, easy assurance, the calculated, dominating power of Galli-Marié's; it had the strong sensual suggestion and defiant resolution of Minnie Hauk's; it had the pantherlike quality, the grace, the fatalism, the dangerous, impudent coquetry of Pauline Lucca's; it had the sparkle, the vim, the Spanish insouciance and piquancy of Zélie de Lussan's."[5]

---

[3] Lucca was the first Covent Garden Carmen, May 27, 1882, when the other principals were Valleria (Micaëla), one M. Lestellier (Don José), and Bouhy.

[4] But is this a desideratum for a gypsy?

[5] De Lussan was the first to sing Carmen in French at Covent Garden—at a peculiar performance on July 28, 1890. Regina Pinkert

was the Micaëla, Jean de Reszke the Don José, and Jean Lassalle the Escamillo. The peculiarity lay in the management's having Luigi Mancinelli conduct the first and final acts, Enrico Bevignani the second act, and Alberto Randegger the third. Harold Rosenthal reports that one critic asked why Luigi Arditi had not been invited too, and that

Again other singers tried vainly to wrest the title from the reigning gypsy, the most successful among them being the Italo-Swiss mezzo Clotilde Bressler-Gianoli, whose coarse, strident interpretation was based more directly on Mérimée than on Meilhac, Halévy, and Bizet. This ill-fated singer—she died at the age of thirty-six—made her bid when Calvé's voice was declining, but the Calvé tradition was so persistent that its ghost was not laid in New York until Geraldine Farrar, a former Micaëla, tried the role. Farrar was New York's favorite Carmen from her debut as the *gitane,* on November 19, 1914, with Toscanini conducting, and with a spectacular supporting cast including Frances Alda (Micaëla), Caruso (Don José), Pasquale Amato (Escamillo)— not to mention Sophie Braslau (Mercédes), Léon Rothier (Zuniga), and Désiré Defrère [6] (Morales)—down to her last singing of the role, on April 17, 1922 (matinee), when Orville Harrold was her Don José, José Mardones her Escamillo.

Farrar's tenure of the role of Carmen was marked by various amusing incidents, among them a scuffle with Caruso that Carl Van Vechten reported in his entertaining *Music and Bad Manners:* "Mme Geraldine Farrar, just returned from a fling at three five-reel cinema dramas, elected to instil a bit of moving picture realism into *Carmen.* Fresh with the memory of her prolonged and brutal scuffle in the factory scene as it was depicted on the screen, Mme Farrar attempted something like it in the opera, the first act of which was enlivened with sundry blows and kicks. More serious still were her alleged assaults on the tenor (Mr. Caruso) in the third act which, it is said, resulted in his clutch-

ing her like a struggling eel, to prevent her interference with his next note. There was even a suggestion of disagreement in the curtain calls which ensued."

Since Farrar's retirement, no singer has come forward with a conception of Carmen so original as to make it unmistakably her own. In Europe, the striking gypsy of Conchita Supervia was both adored and disliked, and in more recent years the impersonations of Giulietta Simionato and Jean Madeira have divided critics and audiences. In the United States, post-Farrar Carmens have included Florence Easton, Maria Jeritza, Rosa Ponselle, Bruna Castagna, Rose Pauly, Marjorie Lawrence, Gladys Swarthout, and Risë Stevens. On January 16, 1936, Gertrud Wettergren, a Scandinavian contralto, called upon to replace Ponselle in a hurry, sang the title role in Swedish while her Metropolitan confreres stuck to French. Even the sketchiest résumé of Carmen lore cannot omit to note that Ernestine Schumann-Heink included the gypsy in her enormous repertoire of more than one hundred and fifty roles, or that in Chicago Mary Garden, though not truly a superb interpreter of Carmen, made the role her own for many years.[7]

38. Castor et Pollux (Rameau)

Five acts; libretto by Pierre-Joseph Bernard; Paris, Opéra, October 24, 1737.

Given 254 times at the Opéra until 1785, *Castor et Pollux* was chosen by Pierre de Jélyotte, the celebrated countertenor, in his farewell to the scene of his many triumphs. It has often been revived in the twentieth century, but ap-

---

George Bernard Shaw remarked "that all Harris's three conductors rolled into one would not make a [Hans] Richter or a [Franco] Faccio!"

[6] This was the Metropolitan debut of the man who was later, for many years, stage manager of the house.

[7] Garden was perhaps not primarily a great interpreter: her unique art consisted in creating whole a gallery of characters whose definitions had been left shadowy by librettist or composer, or both.

parently never in the United States. Translated into English by G. F. Mac-Crone and Dennis Arundell, it was performed at Oxford on November 22, 1934. *Castor et Pollux* was an outstanding feature of the Maggio Musicale at Florence on April 27, 1935, when a Paris Opéra cast was heard.

39. Cavalleria rusticana
(Mascagni)

One act; libretto by Guido Menasci and Giovanni Targioni-Tozzetti, after the play by Giovanni Verga; Rome, Teatro Costanzi, May 17, 1890.

Gemma Bellincioni and her husband, Roberto Stagno, were the Santuzza and Turiddu at the world *première,* a smash hit at the end of which the composer took some forty curtain calls. This success swiftly became international; as early as December 26, 1890, the opera was heard in Hungarian at Budapest as conducted by Gustav Mahler.

Philadelphia (September 9, 1891), Chicago, and Boston were the first cities in the United States to hear *Cavalleria;* the only notable member of the Philadelphia cast was the Alfio, Giuseppe del Puente. Translated into English, *Cavalleria* reached the Casino Theatre, New York, on the afternoon of October 1, 1891, and, in another production, the Lennox Lyceum that same evening. Three months later, on December 30, 1891, the Metropolitan first produced it, with Augusto Vianesi conducting a double bill that also included the first Metropolitan production of Gluck's *Orfeo ed Euridice.* The cast was: Emma Eames (Santuzza), Giulia Ravogli (Lola), Mathilde Bauermeister (Lucia), Eduardo Camera (Alfio), and Fernando Valero (Turiddu). Since that day, *Cavalleria* has been out of the Metropolitan repertoire possibly a dozen seasons: it was in solidly from 1908 to 1939.

On December 22, 1893, the Metro-politan first married *Cavalleria* and *Pagliacci,* a marvelous bargain, with Nellie Melba as Nedda, Emma Calvé as Santuzza. As was to be expected, Calvé was a much-admired Santuzza, and was soon joined by Antonio Scotti in one of his best roles, Alfio. Arturo Toscanini's first Metropolitan *Cavalleria* (paired with Puccini's *Le Villi*) occurred on December 17, 1908, and enlisted the services of Emmy Destinn, Maria Gay, Marie Mattfeld, Enrico Caruso, and Pasquale Amato. Florence Easton began her Metropolitan career as Santuzza on December 7, 1917. Destinn's return as Santuzza, on Christmas Night, 1919, found her as admirable as ever; in later performances, her Turiddu was Beniamino Gigli. Maria Jeritza was a dramatic Santuzza, as was Rosa Ponselle; Elisabeth Rethberg was somewhat lacking in the essential fire. A much later *Cavalleria* paired Zinka Milanov and Richard Tucker, agreeable as to voice, incredible as to acting, as the lovers; in the 1952–53 season, the roles were sung by Fedora Barbieri and Jussi Björling. A sizzling new Santuzza was presented on October 31, 1959, when Giulietta Simionato, in her first Metropolitan season, sang opposite Jan Peerce's first Metropolitan Turiddu. Interesting information about the Metropolitan's very numerous *Cavalleria* performances (275 through the 1959–60 season) is relatively slight because the managements often have been willing to produce so certain an attraction with only one or two good singers out of a cast of five.

Signor Lago, impresario, introduced *Cavalleria rusticana* to London at the Shaftesbury Theatre on October 19, 1891, with Adelaide Musiana (Santuzza), Marie Bréma (Lola), Grace Damian (Lucia), Francesco Vignas (Turiddu), and Brambara (Alfio); Luigi Arditi conducted. As almost everywhere, the opera took on immediately. Lago presented it thrice weekly until late November—and then nightly until

December 12. Covent Garden had to wait until May 16, 1892, when *Cavalleria* opened one of Sir Augustus Harris' seasons; Luigi Mancinelli conducted, and the principal roles were sung by Calvé, Giulia Ravogli, Fernando de Lucia, and Eugène Dufriche. During that season and the next, it ran up thirty-six performances; it achieved its one-hundredth singing on December 28, 1907. More recently, however, its popularity at Covent Garden has diminished to zero; it has not been in the repertoire since 1946. Covent Garden, too, had resorted to mediocre casts, certain that the opera's popularity would surmount all *gaffes*. In 1928, the Santuzza of Eva Turner brought comment that she was "equal to the best Italians."

During 1940, Mascagni, then seventy-six, conducted fiftieth-anniversary performances of *Cavalleria* at Venice, Rome, and Milan.

40. La Cenerentola, ossia La Bontà in Trionfo (Rossini)

Two acts; libretto by Jacopo Ferretti, based on a French libretto by Charles-Guillaume Étienne set by Niccolò Isouard and sung at the Opéra-Comique, Paris, on February 22, 1810; Rome, Teatro Valle, January 25, 1817.

Geltrude Giorgi-Righetti was the Angelina-Cenerentola of the Rome *première*. Enormously successful throughout Italy, the opera was soon heard in many European countries, North and South America—and became, on February 12, 1844, at Sydney, in an English translation by Richard Thompson, the first opera ever staged in Australia.

London first heard *Cenerentola*, in Italian, at the Haymarket Theatre on January 8, 1820; Covent Garden first heard it on April 13, 1830, as *Cinderella, or The Fairy and the Little Glass Slipper,* in an English adaptation by Michael Rophino Lacy. On that occasion the cast included Mary Anne Paton (Cinderella) Miss Cawse (Clorinda), Miss Hughes (Thisbe), Joseph Wood (Felix, Prince of Salerno–Don Ramiro), and G. Penson (Baron Pumpolino–Don Magnifico); Lacy had interpolated into it selections from three other Rossini operas: *Armida, Maometto II,* and *Guillaume Tell,* the last produced in Paris the preceding year. In 1848, at Covent Garden, the role of Angelina was sung by Marietta Alboni.

The traveling troupe headed by Manuel del Popolo Vicente García took *Cenerentola* to New York, playing it there on June 27, 1826. The Lacy–Covent Garden version was sung in New York, in English, on January 24, 1831. Paris heard the opera in Italian, at the Théâtre-Italien, on June 8, 1822. At the Opéra-Comique, October 25, 1932, Conchita Supervia, greatest modern interpreter of the role of Angelina, was supported by Dino Borgioli (Don Ramiro), Ernesto Badini (Dandini), Vincenzo Bettoni (Don Magnifico), and Carlo Scattola (Alidoro); Tullio Serafin conducted. When Supervia appeared in this part at Covent Garden, London, on June 14, 1934, her supporting cast included Borgioli, Ezio Pinza (Don Magnifico), and Emilio Ghirardini (Dandini); Gino Marinuzzi conducted, and the choreography by Ninette de Valois was performed by Alicia Markova and Robert Helpmann.

Since the death of Supervia in 1936, the role of Angelina has been sung by Gianna Pederzini, Fedora Barbieri, and Giulietta Simionato. In the Glyndebourne staging of 1952, Mina de Gabarain was the Angelina; she was supported by Juan Oncina, Sesto Bruscantini, and Ian Wallace; Vittorio Gui conducted. At the Teatro di Corte del Palazzo Reale, Naples, in the fall of 1958, *Cenerentola* was conducted by Mario Rossi; the Angelina was Teresa Berganza, and others in the cast were Ornella Rovero, Miti 'Truccato Pace, Nicola Monti, Bruscantini, Mario Petri, and Leonardo

Monreale. At the City Center, New York, the New York City Opera's production, heard on some occasions in Italian, on others in a poor English translation, has been notable chiefly for its stylishness, achieved with spare means, and for the singing of Frances Bible as Angelina. Berganza made an electrifying New York debut at Carnegie Hall on April 10, 1962, in an American Opera Society concert performance of *Cenerentola* with Nicola Rescigno conducting and superb comic support from Fernando Corena and Ezio Flagello.

41. Christophe Colomb (Milhaud)

Two parts (twenty-seven scenes); libretto by Paul Claudel; Berlin, Staatsoper, May 5, 1930.

Erich Kleiber conducted the world *première* of *Christophe Colomb*, in a German translation by Rudolf Stephen Hoffmann. Sometime later, it was sung in French, at Nantes, under the baton of Pierre Monteux. Manuel Rosenthal conducted the first Paris performance, in concert form, which was broadcast from the Salle Pleyel on December 6, 1936. On January 16, 1937, Milhaud himself conducted a London broadcast in an English translation by Arnold Perry. It was sung in Czech in Prague, and on January 17, 1940, was broadcast from Antwerp in a Flemish translation by Anton Van de Velde. In 1952, Milhaud completed a score for ten instruments—he himself called it "background music with only an occasional lyric passage"—for Jean-Louis Barrault's stage production of the Claudel play on which the opera originally had been based. And in 1952, Dimitri Mitropoulos conducted the New York Philharmonic at Carnegie Hall in a concert performance of the opera; the singers included Dorothy Dow, David Lloyd, Mack Harrell, John Brownlee, and Norman Scott. It was staged at the Teatro dell'Opera, Rome, in 1954, with Gabriele Santini conducting a cast that included Gian Giacomo Guelfi and Miriam Pirazzini.

42. Le Comte Ory (Rossini)

Two acts; libretto by Augustin-Eugène Scribe and Charles-Gaspard Delestre-Poirson; Paris, Opéra, August 20, 1828.

Rossini's first new [1] opera to a French text was a clear success. By January 18, 1884, it had been heard at the Opéra 434 times. It has never been enthusiastically supported in Italy, though it was translated into Italian quickly, and was sung in Venice in 1829 and in Milan and Rome in 1830, and was revived at Turin, Teatro Regio, in 1930.

Le Comte Ory reached London, in Italian, at the Haymarket Theatre, on February 28, 1829, and New York, in French, on August 22, 1831. As the final new production of the 1854 Covent Garden season, on August 8, it presented Angiolina Bosio (Comtesse Adèle), Mlle Marai (Isolier), Gioacchino Lucchesi (Comte Ory), and Joseph-Dieudonné Tagliafico (Raimbaud). It opened the following season on April 13, 1855, with Bosio and, as Comte Ory, Italo Gardoni, son-in-law of Antonio Tamburini.

In 1954, at the Edinburgh Festival, the Glyndebourne Festival Opera revived *Le Comte Ory* in a production by Carl Ebert. After seven performances there, the production was repeated at Glyndebourne six times in 1955, eight in 1957 (Act II being televised on one occasion), and ten in 1958, during which year the company also presented four performances of *Le Comte Ory* at

---

[1] "New" here needs some hedging: the score of *Le Comte Ory* contains twelve newly composed numbers, the rest of it having been borrowed by Rossini from his very unsuccessful tribute to the coronation of Charles X, *Il Viaggio a Reims ossia L'Albergo del giglio d'oro*, produced in Paris at the Théâtre-Italien on June 19, 1825.

the Théâtre-Sarah Bernhardt in Paris, with Vittorio Gui conducting the Royal Philharmonic Orchestra and a cast including Sari Barabas (Comtesse Adèle), Monica Sinclair (Ragonde), Fernanda Cadoni (Isolier), Juan Oncina (Comte Ory), Xavier Depraz (the tutor), and Heinz Blankenburg (Raimbaud).

Perhaps encouraged by the success of Glyndebourne's effort with *Le Comte Ory*, the Städtische Oper, Berlin, mounted a Carl Ebert production of the opera in 1957. Richard Kraus conducted, and the cast included Sari Barabas (Comtesse Adèle), Lisa Otto (Isolier), Nada Puttar (Ragonde), Ernst Häfliger (Comte Ory), Karl Kohn (the tutor), and Ernst Krukowski (Raimbaud). Similarly, but with less well admired results, the Piccola Scala, Milan, staged the opera in January, 1958, to open its season. The scaling-down necessitated by the smallness of theater and stage worked against the success of the venture, though Nino Sanzogno's conducting was praised, and the cast included Graziella Sciutti as the Countess Adèle, Teresa Berganza as Isolier, and Juan Oncina as Count Ory.

43. The Consul (Menotti)

Three acts; libretto by the composer; Philadelphia, March 1, 1950.

Lehman Engel conducted the Philadelphia and New York (March 15, 1950) *premières* of *The Consul*, with the following singers in the leading roles: Patricia Neway (Magda Sorel), Marie Powers (The Mother), Gloria Lane (The Secretary), Maria Marlo (The Foreign Woman), Cornell Mac-Neil (John Sorel), and Leon Lishner (Chief Police Agent). With Thomas Schippers conducting, much the same cast was heard at the Cambridge Theatre, London, in 1951. *The Consul* was staged in German at Hamburg and Zurich that same year. Also in 1951,

Nino Sanzogno conducted its Italian *première*, at La Scala, Milan, when the cast included Clara Petrella, Marie Powers, and Gian Giacomo Guelfi. The Vienna *première*, still in 1951, had a cast headed by Hilde Zadek, while Inge Borkh sang Magda Sorel in Berlin (1951) and Munich (1952). In a 1954 revival by the Sadler's Wells company in London, the role was sung by Amy Shuard. *The Consul* still is often revived throughout Europe.

44. Les Contes d'Hoffmann (Offenbach)

Four acts (nowadays, most usually a prologue, three acts, and an epilogue); libretto by Jules Barbier and Michel Carré—doubtless Barbier did the larger part of the work, for Carré was not mentioned in any edition after the first; Paris, Opéra-Comique, February 10, 1881.

Les Contes was repeated at the Opéra-Comique one hundred times in 1881. After a revival at the Théâtre-Lyrique in 1893, it again moved to the Comique in 1911, where it has been given over six hundred times. The heroine of the *première* was Adèle Isaac, who sang Stella, Olympia, Giulietta, and Antonia —a feat now rarely performed—with Alessandro Talazac as Hoffmann. The opera's second stopping place was the Vienna Ringtheater, which burned down the night of the second performance. Austria and Germany therefore looked askance at the work for a quarter of a century, though Berlin gave performances in German at the Friedrich-Wilhelmstädtisches Theater in 1884. On November 17, 1905, Hans Gregor produced a new version, notable for the act revision that is now so widely used, for the Kurfürsten-Oper; it had been given there five hundred times by September 24, 1909.

Les Contes reached New York, at the

Fifth Avenue Theater, on October 16, 1882, but it was not until Oscar Hammerstein sponsored it at his Manhattan Opera House that its American popularity began. This *première,* on November 14, 1907, brought together Alice Zepilli, Eleanora de Cisneros, Charles Dalmorès, Maurice Renaud, and Charles Gilibert. The cast of the Metropolitan *première,* on January 11, 1913, included Frieda Hempel, Olive Fremstad, Lucrezia Bori, Jeanne Maubourg, Umberto Macnez, Adamo Didur, Dinh Gilly, Léon Rothier, and Andrés de Segurola. A particularly deft interpreter of the doll Olympia was Mabel Garrison.

Later productions included Lawrence Tibbett's impersonations, in the old Renaud manner, of Hoffmann's four evil geniuses: Lindorf, Coppelius, Dappertutto, Miracle—on the whole disappointing because of his staginess. Possibly the finest Metropolitan *Contes* was that conducted by Sir Thomas Beecham (December 10, 1943), "a high point of his Metropolitan effort" (Irving Kolodin), with Raoul Jobin (Hoffmann), Ezio Pinza (Coppelius and Miracle), Patrice Munsel (Olympia), Lily Djanel (Giulietta), and Jarmila Novotna (Antonia); Martial Singher, as Dappertutto, was making a most distinguished Metropolitan debut. After ten years' absence from the Metropolitan, *Les Contes d'Hoffmann* was used, not very judiciously, to open the 1955–56 season, with Pierre Monteux conducting and with Singher playing four roles in the best Opéra-Comique tradition; Richard Tucker was a rather Italianate Hoffmann haunted by Roberta Peters, Risë Stevens, and Lucine Amara.

Les Contes was a relative latecomer to London, with its *première* at the Adelphi on April 17, 1907. Beecham gave a stylish production during his "opéra-comique" season at His Majesty's in 1910, with John Coates as Hoffmann and Maggie Teyte, Emma Nevada, and Zélie de Lussan as the three women of ill fate. Another Beecham

Contes, this time at Covent Garden, was a masterpiece of fine styling, but Dino Borgioli was not in good voice for Hoffmann, and Bernadette Delprat, doubling Giulietta and Antonia, sang the latter role exquisitely but was not luscious enough for the former; Stella Andreva was a flawless Olympia; Ezio Pinza doubled Coppelius and Miracle. Later productions at Covent Garden were, one and all, capriciously cast, even though *Les Contes* was selected to open the 1954–55 season, when Hermann Uhde sang Lindorf, Coppelius, Miracle, and Dappertutto with equal authority and tonal splendor; unhappily the name role had been given to Julius Patzak, barely a phantom of greatness, but remembered as a famous Hoffmann of the German stages.

In a notable motion picture version of *Les Contes d'Hoffmann,* in English, Sir Thomas Beecham conducted; the principal roles were sung by Robert Rounseville (Hoffmann), Dorothy Bond (Olympia), Margherita Grandi (Giulietta), Ann Ayars (Antonia), and Bruce Dargavel (Coppelius, Dappertutto, Dr. Miracle). The sound track was later made available on phonograph records.

45. Le Coq d'or (Rimsky-Korsakov)

Three acts; libretto by Vladimir I. Byelsky, after a satirical fairy tale by Pushkin; Moscow, October 7, 1909.

Le Coq d'or, popular in Russia, is Rimsky's only opera to achieve a true success outside Russia. Serge Diaghilev first gave it, in Russian, at the Opéra, Paris, on May 24, 1914, and later that year, on June 15, a Russian company sang it at the Drury Lane Theatre, London. It was revived, in English, at Covent Garden by Sir Thomas Beecham on November 5, 1919, with Sylvia Nelis (Queen of Shemakha) and Foster Richardson (Dodon). Mattiwilda Dobbs

(Queen of Shemakha) scored a great triumph in the revival of January 7, 1954, with Howell Glynne superb as Dodon. María Barrientos and Adamo Didur had these roles at the first New York production (Metropolitan, March 6, 1918)—"one of the great productions of the whole Gatti period, with its imaginative decor by Willy Pogany, its marshaling of vocal and mime talent to fill the ingenious Fokine plan of double casting, and, of course, the insinuating leadership of Pierre Monteux" (Irving Kolodin, *The Story of the Metropolitan Opera*). Before Lily Pons made her charming impression as the Queen of Shemakha in 1937, the role had been sung by such differently endowed singers as Amelita Galli-Curci, Thalia Sabanieeva, and Marion Talley. Dodon was one of Ezio Pinza's more exaggerated interpretations. Alessio de Paolis was always a memorable Astrologer. *Le Coq d'or* has been out of the Metropolitan repertoire since March, 1945. On October 11, 1955, the San Francisco Opera Company revived *Le Coq d'or*. Erich Leinsdorf conducted, Mattiwilda Dobbs displayed her admired Queen of Shemakha, and the Dodon was Lorenzo Alvary.

46. Così fan tutte (Mozart)

Two acts; libretto by Lorenzo da Ponte; Vienna, Burgtheater, January 26, 1790.

The Fiordiligi of the Vienna *première* was the sensational Adriana Ferraresi del Bene; Francesco Benucci—who had created the role of Figaro—was Guglielmo. The frank libertinism of the text seemed to shock straight through the nineteenth century and well into the twentieth. Alfred Loewenberg states: "No other opera, perhaps, has been subjected to so many different versions and attempts to 'improve' the libretto." Although *Così fan tutte* was heard in Lon-

don as early as May 9, 1811,[1] it was never popular there until recently—Sir Thomas Beecham's 1911 revival was not wholly successful.

In the United States, the opera was not heard until March 24, 1922, when the Metropolitan offered Florence Easton as Fiordiligi, Lucrezia Bori as Despina, Frances Peralta as Dorabella, George Meader as Ferrando, Giuseppe de Luca as Guglielmo, and Adamo Didur as Don Alfonso. Twelve performances in four seasons were enough for New York. It may be said that the Glyndebourne revival under Fritz Busch in 1934, with Ina Souez, Luise Helletsgruber, Irene Eisinger, Heddle Nash, Willi Domgraf-Fassbänder, and Vincenzo Bettoni in leading roles, started *Così* on the road to popularity. Glyndebourne took it to the Edinburgh Festival of 1948 with Suzanne Danco, Eugenia Zareska, Hilde Gueden, Petre Munteanu, and Erich Kunz. Finally, on December 28, 1951, as an innovation of the new Bing regime at the Metropolitan, a stylish revival—in English, however—brought acclaim to the efforts of Eleanor Steber, Blanche Thebom, Patrice Munsel, Richard Tucker, Frank Guarrera, and John Brownlee. In the fall of 1959, at the New York City Center, the New York City Opera Company also staged an English *Così fan tutte,* with Phyllis Curtin (Fiordiligi), Frances Bible (Dorabella), Judith Raskin (Despina), John Reardon (Guglielmo), John Alexander (Ferrando), and James Pease (Don Alfonso). Miss Curtin made her Metropolitan Opera debut on November 4, 1961 (matinee) in the house's thirty-seventh *Così;* Teresa Stich-Randall had made her Metropolitan debut, also as Fiordiligi, on the second night of the season (October 24, 1961).

From the Salzburg Festival of 1960 came credible reports of a delicious *Così*

---

[1] On October 1 of that year, too, Napoleon sat through a private performance at Compiègne.

fan tutte at the Landestheater; Karl Böhm was the conductor, and the cast was: Elisabeth Schwarzkopf (Fiordiligi), Christa Ludwig (Dorabella), Graziella Sciutti (Despina), Waldemar Kmentt (Ferrando), Hermann Prey (Guglielmo), and Karl Dönch (Don Alfonso).

47. Dalibor (Smetana)

Three acts; libretto by Josef Wenzig, but translated into Czech by Ervín Špindler for the première; *Prague, Czech Theater, May 16, 1868.*

At the world *première*, the two leading roles were sung by Benevic-Mikova (Milada) and Lukes (Dalibor). By March 10, 1924, the opera had been sung in Prague three hundred times. At a Vienna revival in 1938, in German, Bruno Walter conducted, and the cast included Hilde Konetzni, Esther Rethy, Mazaroff, Destal, and Alexander Kipnis. At a Berlin revival, in a new German translation (1940), the cast included Tiana Lemnitz, Hilde Scheppan, Franz Völker, Rudolf Bockelmann, and Josef von Manowarda. Although *Dalibor* won popularity in Central Europe (it has been heard in Croatian, Slovenian, Polish, Hungarian, and Bulgarian, in addition to German, Flemish, and Russian), it appears never to have been staged in France, England, or America.

48. La Damnation de Faust (Berlioz)

Five acts; text for the original legende dramatique *by the composer and Almire Gandonnière, after Gérard de Nerval's French version of Goethe's* Faust; *adapted for the operatic stage by Raoul Gunsbourg; Monte Carlo, February 18, 1893.*

Jean de Reszke was the Faust of the world *première*. Nine years later, also at Monte Carlo, his Faust was supported by Nellie Melba (Marguerite) and Maurice Renaud (Méphistophélès). The opera first reached England on February 3, 1894, at Liverpool. It was used, in Paris, to commemorate the centenary of Berlioz' birth, on December 11, 1903, with Emma Calvé, Albert Alvarez, and Renaud. Strangely, London did not hear *La Damnation* until May 26, 1933, when an Italian version at Covent Garden brought forward Gina Cigna, Giovanny Voyer, and Cesare Formichi, with Sir Thomas Beecham conducting. The *Times* lauded Beecham as "the true hero of the evening." The operatic version has been popular in Italy since its *première* (Milan, Teatro dal Verme, April 21, 1893, only two months after the world *première*); a 1947 production at La Scala, with Gabriella Gatti, Mario Binci, and Tito Gobbi, was notable. If the sparse and apparently garbled newspaper dispatch can be trusted, the Paris Opéra opened its 1940 season with *La Damnation*. The audience was composed largely of German officers and Spanish Falangists: there was no gaiety.

In 1906, New York, which in 1880 had become acquainted with the cantata form of *La Damnation* as interpreted by Leopold Damrosch, was afforded a view of the opera on the evening of December 7. On that memorable occasion, Geraldine Farrar, only two weeks old as a Metropolitan debutante, was Marguerite; she was supported by Charles Rousseliere, who had begun life as a blacksmith in Algeria, as Faust, while Pol Plançon was the greatly admired Méphistophélès. Five performances that season constitute its Metropolitan career to date, but scarcely had the last note of the fifth performance died away when Oscar Hammerstein gave New York another opportunity to compare Berlioz' with Gounod's *Faust*, which was then (as always) popular. The Manhattan cast included Charles Dalmorès and Renaud.

49. Daphne (Strauss)

One act; libretto by Josef Gregor; Dresden, Opernhaus, October 15, 1938.

At its world *première*, conducted by Karl Böhm (to whom the opera is dedicated), *Daphne* shared a double bill with Strauss's *Friedenstag*, another one-act opera, which had been heard for the first time, at Munich, on the preceding July 24. The title role was sung by Margarete Teschemacher; Torsten Ralf was the Apollo. Productions were later offered at Berlin (with Maria Cebotari as Daphne), Graz, and other German and Austrian cities. There was a Flemish-language production at Antwerp in 1939; when the opera was staged at La Scala, Milan, in 1942, Gina Cigna was the Daphne; Rose Bampton sang the role in Buenos Aires in 1948, and the Daphne of later German stagings was most often Annelies Kupper; more recently, Leonie Rysanek has sung the role.

The American *première* of *Daphne*, in concert form, was presented by The Little Orchestra Society at Town Hall, New York, on October 10, 1960, with Thomas Scherman conducting. Principal roles were sung by Gloria Davy (Daphne), Florence Kopleff (Gaea), Jon Crain (Apollo), Robert Nagy (Leukippos), and Lawrence Davidson (Peneios). The German diction of the singers was harshly criticized.

50. Les Deux Avares (Grétry)

Two acts; libretto by Charles-Georges Fenouillot de Falbaire de Quincey; Fontainebleau, October 27, 1770.

The first two performances at Fontainebleau were private. The opera was first produced publicly at the Comédie-Italienne, Paris, on December 6, 1770. London heard it in English, as *The Two Misers,* at Covent Garden on January 21, 1775. The Dublin production of 1781 was similarly titled; it was subtitled *The Mufti's Ghost.* It came to the United States in 1786: New York, July 17. The opera was revived in Paris, at the Opéra-Comique, as late as 1893, and at Versailles, by students of the Paris Conservatoire, in 1939.

51. Les Deux Journées (Cherubini)

Three acts; libretto by Jean-Nicholas Bouilly; Paris, Théâtre Feydeau, January 16, 1800.

Julie Scio was the first Constance, and the *première* developed into a tumultuous ovation. Number after number was encored, and when it was all over, Cherubini might have been excused for believing that he had won the people. Almost two hundred performances followed in the same year, and then Paris began to cool. The enthusiasm passed to Germany, and that country has remained loyal to the opera, as *Der Wasserträger.* About *Les Deux Journées* do not cling those stories of famous casts which cluster about other, less successful, operas. The roles are evenly distributed, and so do not appeal to jealous stars. Perhaps the most brilliant cast was assembled for a Drury Lane production in 1872. Sir Michael Costa conducted, the Constance was Therese Tietjens, the Mikeli, Luigi Agnesi; Mathilde Bauermeister and Marie Roze (Mrs. Henry Mapleson) sang smaller roles. Sir Charles Santley later distinguished himself as the Water Carrier.

52. Les Dialogues des Carmélites (Poulenc)

Three acts (twelve tableaux); libretto by George Bernanos after a novel by

Gertrude von Le Fort and a scenario by Philippe Agostini and Father Raymond V. Bruckberger; Milan, Teatro alla Scala, January 26, 1957.

"Seldom has such an international audience collected for a world première. Naturally the French were there *en masse*. Musical authorities, impresarii of most of the opera houses of the world came flying to Milan; motion-picture producers, artists, composers. Almost a hundred Italian and foreign critics alone were there. Even royalty was present, including the Sultan of Morocco, maharajahs, and visiting aristocracy." Thus Ernest de Weerth, reporting for *Opera News* the first performance anywhere of *Les Dialogues des Carmélites*. Nino Sanzogno was in the pit of La Scala on that evening of January 26, 1957, the production had been staged by Margherita Wallman, and the highly effective sets were by Georges Wakhévitch. The large cast singing the Italian translation included Virginia Zeani (Blanche de la Force), Gianna Pederzini, Nicola Filacuridi, Leyla Gencer, Gigliola Frazzoni, Eugenia Ratti, Vittoria Palombini, Fiorenza Cossotto, Alvinio Misciano, Antonio Pirino, Scipio Colombo, Arturo La Porta, Michele Cazzato, Armando Manelli, and Carlo Gasperini.

On June 21, 1957, the *Dialogues* was presented for the first time at the Paris Opéra, Pierre Dervaux conducting. Because of the difference between Maurice Jacquemont's staging and Suzanne Lalique's sets and costumes and their Milanese predecessors, Poulenc supplied some new orchestral passages linking the tableaux. Denise Duval was Blanche de la Force; others in the cast included Denise Scharley (Première Prieure), Régine Crespin (La Nouvelle Prieure), Rita Gorr (Mère Marie), Liliane Berton (Soeur Constance), Janine Fourrier (Mère Jeanne), Gisèle Desmoutiers (Soeur Mathilde), Xavier Depraz (Le Marquis de la Force), Jean Giraudeau (Le Chevalier de la Force), and Louis Rialland (L'Aumonier).

As part of the festival of performances signalizing the opening of the new Opera House in Cologne, *Les Dialogues des Carmélites* was sung there in German in the summer of 1957 in a production by Erich Bormann. Wolfgang von der Nahmer conducted, and the cast included Lillian Benningsen, Natalie Hinsch-Gröndahl, Reinhold Bartel, and Bormann. Still in 1957, the San Francisco Opera Company staged the *Dialogues* in an English translation by Joseph Machlis, at the War Memorial Opera House. The direction, costumes, and settings were by Harry Horner. Erich Leinsdorf conducted, and the cast included Dorothy Kirsten (Blanche de la Force), Leontyne Price (Nouvelle Prieure), Claramae Turner (Première Prieure), Blanche Thebom (Mère Marie), Sylvia Stahlman (Soeur Constance), Ralph Herbert, Jon Crain, and Harve Presnell. On December 8, 1957, the NBC-TV Opera Company telecast a version of the opera in the Machlis translation. Peter Herman Adler conducted, and leading roles were sung by Elaine Malbin (Blanche), Patricia Neway (Première Prieure), Price (Nouvelle Prieure), Rosemary Kuhlman (Mère Marie), Judith Raskin (Soeur Constance), Robert Rounseville (Chevalier), and Arthur Newman (Marquis). And before 1957 was out, the opera had been heard also in Trieste (November 23) as conducted by Oliviero de Fabritiis and sung by a cast including Nora de Rosa, Pederzini, Elda Ribetti, Luciana Serafini, Alfredo Kraus, and Renato Cesari.

Les Dialogues des Carmélites reached Covent Garden, London, on January 18, 1958. Rafael Kubelik conducted; the producer and stage designer were those of the Milan *prèmiere*, Wallman and Wakhévitch. The cast included Elsie Morison (Blanche), Jean Watson (Première Prieure), Joan Sutherland

(Nouvelle Prieure), Sylvia Fisher (Mère Marie), Jeannette Sinclair (Soeur Constance), John Lanigan (Chevalier), and Jess Walters (Marquis). At a repeat performance on June 23, 1959, Regina Resnik achieved a personal success for her personification of the Première Prieure. When the opera was heard during the spring season at the Teatro dell'Opera, Rome, the Wallman direction and Wakhévitch sets still were on display, but Franco Capuana conducted. Gabriella Tucci was the Blanche de la Force; others in the cast were Pederzini (Première Prieure), Magda Olivero (Mère Marie), Elisabetta Barbato (Nouvelle Prieure), Alda Noni (Soeur Constance), Enzo Mascherini (Marquis), and Giacinto Prandelli (Chevalier). During 1958, the *Dialogues* was also heard at Lisbon and at the Royal Opera, Ghent, the latter as produced by Karel Locufier, conducted by Robert Ledent, and with a cast that included Lucienne Delvaux (Première Prieure), Huberte Vecray (Mère Marie), Geri Bruninx (Nouvelle Prieure), Marian Balhant (Blanche), and Lia Rottier.

The Vienna Staatsoper presented, in German, a Wallman-Wakhévitch production of *Les Dialogues des Carmélites* (called *Die Gespräche der Karmeliterinnen*) early in 1959. Hans Hollreiser conducted, and the cast included Irmgard Seefried (Blanche), Elisabeth Höngen, Christel Goltz (Mère Marie), Anneliese Rothenberger (Soeur Constance), Hilde Zadek, Rosette Anday, Alfred Poell, Anton Dermota, and Ivo Zidek.

53. Dido and Aeneas (Purcell)

Prologue and three acts; libretto by Nahum Tate; London, Josias Priest's Boarding School at Chelsea, December (?), 1689.

The first performance, by amateurs, was in all probability part of a Christmas celebration. Although some public performances, in altered form, may have been given in London in 1700 and 1704, the first stage revival did not occur until, during the bicentenary celebrations of Purcell's death, it was staged in London by the Royal College of Music on November 20, 1895, with additional accompaniments supplied by Charles Wood. It was heard in New York, in a concert presentation of Artur Bodanzky's edition, on January 13, 1924, and at the Juilliard School of Music in Edward J. Dent's edition on February 18, 1932. As part of the Maggio Musicale at Florence in May, 1940, it was staged in an Italian translation by Mario Labroca, with reorchestration by the conductor, Vittorio Gui. The most notable modern revival occurred at the Mermaid Theatre, London, during the 1951 Festival of Britain, when the leading roles were sung by Kirsten Flagstad, Maggie Teyte, and Thomas Hemsley; Geraint Jones conducted. A remarkable pre-celebration of the tercentenary of Purcell's birth occurred at the Villa Olmo, Lake Como, late in 1958, when all the singers were Anglo-Americans then in Italy: Gloria Davy (Dido), Cynthia Jolly (Belinda), Ann Reynolds (Sorceress), Romana Pearson-Righetti and Morag Durie (Witches), Edward de Falce (Aeneas), and Douglas Faber-Smith (Sailor); Ennio Gerelli conducted, and the text was sung in English.

Dinorah (Meyerbeer)

See *Le Pardon de Ploërmel* (No. 172).

54. Djamileh (Bizet)

One act; libretto by Louis Gallet, after Alfred de Musset's Namouna; Paris, Opéra-Comique, May 22, 1872.

When *Djamileh* had its *première* at the Opéra-Comique, the title role was in the inadequate hands of a curious semiamateur, the Baronne de Presles, known as Aline Prelly, who had been a renowned Second Empire beauty as Mlle de Pomeyrac. Henri Gauthier-Villars once called her "the voiceless Venus." At that first performance, the other important roles were sung by M. Duchesne (Haroun), M. Potel (Splendiano), and M. Julien (Un Marchand d'esclaves); Louis-Michel Deloffre conducted. After the ten (or eleven—the records are unclear) performances of that season, Bizet's opera was not heard at the Comique again until, to celebrate the centenary of his birth (but actually two days late for that event, which had been pre-empted by the Comique's 2,271st Carmen), it was restaged on October 27, 1938. Gustave Cloëz conducted; the cast included Jennie Tourel (Djamileh), Louis Arnoult (Haroun), Roger Bourdin (Splendiano), and Alban Derroja (Un Marchand d'esclaves). Since the eleven performances of that season, Djamileh has not been heard at the Comique.

No record has been found of a professional stage performance of Djamileh in the United States. By the beginning of the twentieth century, however, it had been sung in Swedish, Italian, English, Czech, German, Russian, and Hungarian—and has since been heard additionally in Croatian, Spanish, Danish, and Serb. Dublin heard the opera, in English, on September 10, 1892, in a translation by Joseph Bennett, and it was staged for three performances at Covent Garden, London, in 1893. Alberto Randegger conducted, and the cast included Mlle Gherlsen (Djamileh), Charles Bonnard (Haroun), and Coutellier (Splendiano). On January 22, 1898, Gustav Mahler conducted a much-praised production, in German, at the Vienna Opera. There have been only scattered revivals in more recent decades. Under the direction of Thomas Scherman, The Little Orchestra Society gave Djamileh in concert form at Town Hall, New York, on December 7, 1959; Frances Bible was the Djamileh, Leopold Simoneau the Haroun, and Gregory Simms the Splendiano.

55. Don Carlos (Verdi)

Five acts (now usually presented in four); libretto by François-Joseph Méry and Camille du Locle, after Schiller's drama; Paris, Opéra, March 11, 1867.

The unhappy history of Don Carlos began with its premiére at the Opéra on March 11, 1867, at the height of that year's Exposition Universelle, when Emil Perrin conducted. The two leading stars of the cast—Marie-Constance Sasse (or Sax), the Elisabeth de Valois, who had also created the role of Selika in Meyerbeer's L'Africaine, and Jean-Baptiste Faure, the Rodrigo—did not perform as brilliantly as usual, and when the Empress Eugénie, offended by heretical opinions expressed by one of the characters, ostentatiously turned her back to the stage, the evening definitely was chilled. Nonetheless, Don Carlos was sung forty-three times that season, since when it has not been heard in Paris in French.

London was the next city to hear Don Carlos, which was sung at Covent Garden (in an Italian translation by Achille de Lauzières) on June 4, 1867. The leading singers of that cast were Pauline Lucca (Elisabetta), Antonietta Fricci (Eboli), Emilio Naudin (Don Carlos), Francesco Graziani (Rodrigo), Petit (Filippo), and Anacleto Bagaggiolo (Grande Inquisitore). The opera was sung seven times that season and two the next, and then lapsed until Sir Thomas Beecham conducted it on June 1, 1933, with a cast including Gina Cigna, Nini Giani, Ulysses Lappas, Giacomo Rimini, Fernando Autori, and Giulio Tomei. The opera was again regarded as a failure, winning only three singings. *Don Carlos* at Covent Garden produced the overwhelming effects of which it is capable only on the night of the centenary celebration of the present house, May 9, 1958. Presented almost complete in a five-act performance set and costumed by Luchino Visconti and admirably conducted by Carlo Maria Giulini, it boasted a remarkable cast: Gré Brouwenstijn (Elisabetta), Fedora Barbieri (Eboli), Jon Vickers (Don Carlos), Tito Gobbi (Rodrigo), Boris Christoff (Filippo), and Marco Stefanoni (Grande Inquisitore). Harold Rosenthal wrote of it that it "is not only one of the finest operatic productions ever seen or heard at Covent Garden, but it serves to vindicate completely the art of Grand Opera," but he lamented the few cuts made in the score, notably the scene in which the mob breaks into the prison to demand Don Carlos' release.

Don Carlos had been heard in many European cities, as well as in Malta and Buenos Aires, when it first reached New York, in Italian, on April 12, 1877, at the Academy of Music. More than forty-three years later, the Metropolitan staged *Don Carlos* for the first time, in an eclectic version edited by its conductor, Gennaro Papi. On December 23, 1920, Rosa Ponselle had the nominal heroine's role of Elisabetta (W. J. Henderson called her performance "neither queenly nor tear-compelling"), but the real heroine of the occasion was Margarete Matzenauer (Eboli), especially for her singing of "O don fatale." Also much admired were Giovanni Martinelli (Don Carlos), Giuseppe de Luca (Rodrigo), Adamo Didur (Filippo), and Louis d'Angelo (Grande Inquisitore). On December 2, 1922, Feodor Chaliapin, singing the role of Philip II, was applauded so vociferously for his singing of "Ella giammai m'amò" that he felt able, singlehanded, to break the Metropolitan's rule against encores. To the matinee audience's astonishment, he walked to the front of the stage, indicated to Papi where

to start over, and repeated the end of the aria. That performance was also notable for the restoration of the super-Meyerbeerian Inquisition scene, in which Léon Rothier, as the Grand Inquisitor, demonstrated his greatness as a singing actor. Irving Kolodin remarked that the cast was "led, but not directed, by Papi." After Chaliapin repeated his encore-giving at a performance on December 13, *Don Carlos* left the Metropolitan for twenty-eight seasons.

On November 6, 1950, the first season of the Metropolitan under the managership of Rudolf Bing opened with an opera called, for reasons never made entirely clear, *Don Carlo*. On that night, Margaret Webster became the first woman ever to have staged an opera at the Metropolitan, and house debuts were made by Lucine Amara (A Heavenly Voice), Barbieri (Eboli), Delia Rigal (Elisabetta), and Cesare Siepi (Filippo); the Don Carlos was Jussi Björling, Robert Merrill was the Rodrigo, and Jerome Hines the Grand Inquisitor. In the festive atmosphere, the scenery and costumes of Rolf Gerard were enthusiastically given a share of the acclaim. By April 10, 1959, this mounting of the opera had run the Metropolitan tally for *Don Carlos* up to 42. By November 6, 1960, the cast had undergone so many substitutions that it was no longer recognizable; Mr. Bing now had Mary Curtis-Verna as Elisabetta, Nell Rankin as Eboli, Martina Arroyo as A Heavenly Voice, Giulio Gari as Don Carlos, Mario Sereni as Rodrigo, Giorgio Tozzi as Philip II, and Hermann Uhde as the Grand Inquisitor. In some intervening performances, Hines had become the Philip II, Blanche Thebom had been heard as Eboli, Hans Hotter as the Grand Inquisitor, Eleanor Steber and Leonie Rysanek as Elisabetta, Paolo Silveri and Merrill as Rodrigo.

Don Carlos continues to be staged throughout Europe. In 1926, Toscanini conducted it at La Scala, Milan, with a cast including Bianca Scacciati, Cobelli, and Trantoul. Clemens Krauss was the conductor at the Vienna Opera on May 10, 1932, when the opera was presented in a version revised by Franz Werfel and Lothar Wallerstein; the cast included Viorica Ursuleac, Gertrud Rünger, Franz Völker, Emil Schipper, and Josef von Manowarda. At the Teatro La Fenice, Venice, in 1938, Margherita Grandi was intensely admired as Elisabetta in a performance conducted by Vittorio Gui. A staging at the 1950 Florentine Maggio Musicale had the remarkable cast of Maria Caniglia, Ebe Stignani, Mirto Picchi, Paolo Silveri, Boris Christoff, and Giulio Neri; Tullio Serafin conducted. And at the Salzburg Festival, on August 13, 1958, Herbert von Karajan led a cast of international texture, including Sena Jurinac, Christa Ludwig, Eugenio Fernandi, Ettore Bastianini, Siepi, Nicola Zaccaria, and Stefanoni. Critics objected that the Felsenreitschule provided an unsuitable ambiance for *Don Carlos* and that Gustaf Gründgens' production was dull and monotonous.

56. Don Giovanni (Mozart)

Two acts; libretto by Lorenzo da Ponte, after Giovanni Bertati's Don Giovanni o sia Il Convitato di pietra; *first performed at Prague, October 29, 1787, possibly with slight interpolations or substitutions in the text by Giacomo Casanova, who was in the audience.*

So great was *Don Giovanni*'s success that Domenico Guardasoni, the stage manager, told Mozart and Da Ponte that "as long as they lived there would never be any more bad seasons" (Edward J. Dent, *Mozart's Operas*). And it indeed remained Prague's favorite opera, being given there 532 times within a century; Berlin and Vienna were not far behind. *Don Giovanni* may well have been the favorite opera of the nineteenth century: its adventures

would fill a very large book. The adaptations it underwent all too often meant the most scandalous mutilation. After its miserable *première*, in French, at the Paris Opéra on September 17, 1805, before the Empress Josephine, the French were not to hear a more or less truthful *Don Giovanni* until Gaspare Spontini brought it forward at the Théâtre-Italien, in Italian, on September 2, 1811, with the following cast: Niccolò Tacchinardi (Don Giovanni), Luigi Barilli (Leporello), Gaetano Crivelli (Don Ottavio), Francesca Festa (Donna Anna), Signora Benelli (Donna Elvira), and Maria Anna Barilli (Zerlina).[1]

Not quite thirty years after its *première* in Prague, *Don Giovanni* was introduced to England. On April 12, 1817, William Ayrton staged it at the Haymarket, with Giuseppe Ambrogetti and Sebastiano Naldi as the Don and Leporello respectively. It was repeated more than twenty times the first season, but in less than two months there was a rival version in English, with the music most cynically "adapted" by Henry Rowley Bishop, whose score became standard for English performances both in England and in the United States for a number of years. But the Italian text, with Mozart's score followed with reasonable fidelity, gradually asserted itself, and the long lists of singers who have interpreted the chief roles contain many great names: as Donna Anna, Giulia Grisi, Pauline Viardot-García, Therese Tietjens, Emmy Fursch-Madi, Eugenia Pappenheim, Lillian Nordica, Félia Litvinne, Emmy Destinn, Frida Leider, Elisabeth Rethberg, and Ljuba Welitch; as Donna Elvira, Lillian Nordica,[2] Suzanne Ad-

---

[1] Hector Berlioz' *Soirées de l'orchestre* (1854—over forty years after the Spontini production) is the authority; *Lo Spettacolo* (1954, *sub* Barilli-Bondoni, M. A.) assigns Donna Anna to this singer.

[2] Hardened operagoers will remember that singers often shift roles in an opera. Nordica had made her world debut, at Milan, as

ams, Lotte Lehmann, Elisabeth Schwarzkopf, and Sena Jurinac; as Zerlina, Angiolina Bosio, Fanny Persiani, Maria Malibran, Adelina Patti (her only Mozart role), Minnie Hauk, Pauline Lucca, Sigrid Arnoldson, Zélie de Lussan, Fritzi Scheff, Maggie Teyte, Elisabeth Schumann, Mafalda Favero, and Hilde Gueden; as Don Giovanni, Antonio Tamburini, Mario, Jean-Baptiste Faure, Sir Charles Santley, Jean de Reszke, Francesco d'Andrade, Victor Maurel, Maurice Renaud, Antonio Scotti, Mariano Stabile, Ezio Pinza, and George London; as Leporello, Luigi Lablache, Giorgio Ronconi, Karl Formes, Édouard de Reszke, Marcel Journet, Antonio Pini-Corsi, and Virgilio Lazzari; and as Don Ottavio, Mario, Enrico Tamberlik, Formes, Emilio Naudin, Thomas Salignac, Enrico Caruso, John McCormack, Heddle Nash, Richard Tauber, and Leopold Simoneau. Herman Klein, in *The Golden Age of Opera,* called the 1869 cast the "historic 'cast of the century' " and, in *The Reign of Patti,* "perhaps the most remarkable operatic combination of the nineteenth century." The principals (unhappily Klein does not name the Leporello) were Tietjens, Christine Nilsson, Patti, Faure, and Mario. Another memorable group, under Hans Richter, consisted of Destinn (London debut), Adams, Alice Nielson (a recruit from the light-opera stage who acquitted herself admirably as Zerlina), Renaud, Journet, Salignac, and Charles Gilibert (Masetto). The first Glyndebourne performance, in 1936, enlisted Ina Souez, Luise Helletsgruber, Audrey Mildmay, John Brownlee, Salvatore Baccaloni, and Koloman von Pataky.

The Garcías brought *Don Giovanni* to New York on May 23, 1826, at the Park Theater, with the elder Manuel—

a tenor—as the Don, and the younger Manuel as Leporello; the elder Manuel's wife was Donna Elvira, and his daughter Maria (later the famous Malibran) was Zerlina. Early in its first season the Metropolitan Opera House welcomed *Don Giovanni* on November 29, 1883, with Fursch-Madi, Nilsson, Marcella Sembrich, Giuseppe Kaschmann, Giovanni Mirabella, and Italo Campanini. On December 27, 1899, Antonio Scotti, as the Don, made his Metropolitan debut, supported by Nordica, Adams, Sembrich, Édouard de Reszke, and Salignac. Maurel and Renaud divided honors as the finest of New York Dons, the latter at the Manhattan Opera House. On January 23, 1908, the Metropolitan revived *Don Giovanni* with a superb cast led by Emma Eames, Johanna Gadski, Sembrich, Scotti, Feodor Chaliapin, and Alessandro Bonci. The four performances that season were the last there until November 29, 1929, when Leonora Corona, Rethberg, Editha Fleischer, Pinza, Pavel Ludikar, and Beniamino Gigli had the leading roles. Later in the season the cast was much strengthened when Corona and Rethberg were replaced respectively by Rosa Ponselle (as Donna Anna she was magnificent) and Maria Müller. A favorite cast of the thirties included Zinka Milanov, Jarmila Novotna, Bidu Sayão, Pinza, Tito Schipa, and Baccaloni, with Bruno Walter on the podium. Recent Metropolitan principals have been: as Donna Anna, Welitch, Rose Bampton, and Margaret Harshaw; as Donna Elvira, Eleanor Steber and Lucine Amara; as Zerlina, Nadine Conner, Patrice Munsel (her first performance in the role rescued her career), and Roberta Peters; as Don Giovanni, Paul Schöffler, Cesare Siepi, and London; as Leporello, Baccaloni, Alexander Kipnis, and Erich Kunz; and as Don Ottavio, Schipa, Charles Kullmann, the inadequate James Melton (pushed by the Texas Company, sponsors of the Metropolitan radio

---

Donna Elvira. Patti, a sensible type, knew that she was just right as Zerlina, and never cast her eyes on the role of Donna Anna. Not all singers have been equally wise.

broadcasts), Jan Peerce, Richard Crooks, and Cesare Valletti.

Speaking of *Don Giovanni*'s long vacation (1908–29) from the Metropolitan, as well as of McCormack's altogether untouched talents as a singer of Mozart at that house, Irving Kolodin writes, in *The Story of the Metropolitan Opera 1883–1950* (revised edition, p. 320): "Protestations that *Don Giovanni* had to be avoided for lack of a cast seem pointless when one imagines the results that could have been achieved by Scotti, De Luca (Leporello), McCormack, Easton (Donna Anna), Hempel (Donna Elvira), and Farrar (Zerlina)." A notable performance of *Don Giovanni* by the San Francisco Opera Company on October 20, 1959, under the conductorship of Leopold Ludwig, had this cast: Sena Jurinac (Dona Anna), Leontyne Price (Donna Elvira), Pierrette Alarie (Zerlina), George London (Don Giovanni), Lorenzo Alvary (Leporello), Richard Lewis (Don Ottavio), Mino Yahia (Commendatore), Theodor Uppman (Masetto).

On September 24, 1961, the new Deutsche Oper in West Berlin was opened with a *Don Giovanni* staged by the company's departing general manager, Carl Ebert. President Heinrich Lübke of West Germany and Mayor Willy Brandt of West Berlin were in the invited audience to hear Dietrich Fischer-Dieskau (Don Giovanni), Elisabeth Grümmer (Donna Anna), Pilar Lorengar (Donna Elvira), Erika Köth (Zerlina), Donald Grobe (Don Ottavio), Ivan Sardi (Masetto), Walter Berry (Leporello), and Josef Greindl (Commendatore) under the baton of Ferenc Fricsay.

57. Don Pasquale (Donizetti)

Three acts; libretto by Donizetti and Michele Accursi (pseudonym of Giovanni Ruffini), a rewriting of Angelo Anelli's Ser Marc'Antonio (first set by Stefano Pavesi, Teatro alla Scala, Milan, September 26, 1810); Paris, Théâtre-Italien, January 3, 1843.

The cast of the original Paris production included four of the foremost singing stars of the era: Giulia Grisi (Norina), Mario (Ernesto), Antonio Tamburini (Malatesta), and Luigi Lablache (Pasquale). It was first sung in French at the Théâtre de la Monnaie, Brussels, on August 4, 1843; the same translation was sung at the Théâtre-Lyrique, Paris, on September 9, 1864. It was restaged at the Théâtre du Château-d'Eau on January 20, 1886. When the Opéra-Comique staged it on June 20, 1896, Lucien Fugère was the Pasquale, Edmond Clément the Ernesto. The opera was heard at the Comique for the eleventh, and last, time on February 4, 1904. At the Palais de Chaillot on December 20, 1943, Vina Bovy was the Norina.

Milan was the first Italian city to hear *Don Pasquale* (La Scala, April 17, 1843), followed later that year by Turin and Naples. It was sung in London at Her Majesty's Theatre, in Italian, on June 29, 1843, and at the Princess's Theatre on October 23 of that year in an English translation by Thomas H. Reynoldson. When Covent Garden staged the opera, under Sir Michael Costa's direction, it had three of the members of the original Paris cast—Grisi, Mario, and Lablache—and Giorgio Ronconi as Malatesta. With the appearance of Tamburini in 1855, the Covent Garden performances of June 28 and July 7 had all four of the leading members of the Parisian cast of twelve years before. Adelina Patti sang Norina at Covent Garden during 1862, her second season there; when she sang the role during the 1865 season, with Mario (Ernesto), Ronconi switched from the role of Malatesta to that of Don Pasquale.

At Covent Garden in the spring of 1905, a revival of *Don Pasquale* brought forth Hermine Bosetti as Norina, with Charles Gilibert (Don Pasquale), Victor Maurel (Malatesta), and Francesco Bravi (Ernesto). The next notable production of the opera in England occurred at Glyndebourne in 1938, when Fritz Busch conducted and the cast included Audrey Mildmay (Norina), Dino Borgioli (Ernesto), Mariano Stabile (Malatesta), and Salvatore Baccaloni (Don Pasquale).

Don Pasquale was first heard in New York in English on March 9, 1846, and in Italian on November 29, 1849. Its Metropolitan *première* took place on January 8, 1900, as half of a double bill with *Cavalleria rusticana;* the cast was Marcella Sembrich (Norina), Thomas Salignac (Ernesto), Antonio Scotti (Malatesta), Antonio Pini-Corsi (Don Pasquale), and M. Queyla (Notary), with Emilio Bevignani conducting. When the Metropolitan gave performances at the New Theater in the 1909–10 season, *Don Pasquale* was heard there on December 23, 1909, with Bernice de Pasquali (Norina), Alessandro Bonci (Ernesto), Scotti (Malatesta), and Pini-Corsi (Don Pasquale). Lucrezia Bori, in her first season at the Metropolitan, sang Norina on April 5, 1913, with Arturo Toscanini conducting, Umberto Macnez (Ernesto), Scotti, and Pini-Corsi. After four performances during that season and the next, *Don Pasquale* was unheard at the Metropolitan until February 23, 1935 (matinee), when it shared a double bill with the first metropolitan performance of Pergolesi's *La Serva padrona*. On that afternoon of Gatti-Casazza's last season, Ettore Panizza conducted, Bori repeated her greatly admired Norina, Tito Schipa was the Ernesto, Giuseppe de Luca the Malatesta, and Ezio Pinza the Pasquale. On December 21, 1940 (matinee) *Don Pasquale* was heard again, this time with Bidu Sayão (Norina), Nino Martini (Ernesto), Francesco Valentino (Malatesta), and Salvatore Baccaloni (Don Pasquale). On a double bill with Puccini's *Il Tabarro* at a matinee on January 5, 1946, Fritz Busch conducted a *Don Pasquale* with Sayão, Martini, Baccaloni, and an excellent Malatesta, John Brownlee. The twenty-five-year-old American conductor Thomas Schippers made his Metropolitan debut on December 22, 1955, with *Don Pasquale*. Roberta Peters was the Norina, Cesare Valletti the Ernesto, Frank Guarrera the Malatesta, and Fernando Corena the Don Pasquale; the bill was filled out with a dancing of the Rossini-Britten ballet *Soirée*. Later that season, Hilde Gueden and Laurel Hurley were also heard as Norina, and Enzo Sordello replaced Guarrera.

Early in 1957, at the Teatro San Carlo, Naples, *Don Pasquale* presented Rosanna Carteri as Norina, Gianni Raimondi as Ernesto, Renato Capecchi as Malatesta, and Corena in what was on the way to becoming a classic portrayal of Don Pasquale. On July 15 of that year, at the annual Holland Festival, Eugenia Ratti sang Norina, Mario Spina was a fledgling Ernesto, Scipio Colombo played Malatesta, and the Don was Guus Hoekman. Still attracting audiences everywhere, the opera was heard widely in 1958, some of its landing places having included Monterrey (Mexico), Barcelona, Genoa, Tel-Aviv, Buenos Aires, and Bilbao.

58. Don Quichotte (Massenet)

Five acts; libretto by Henri Cain, after Cervantes' novel and Jacques Le Lorrain's comedy, Le Chevalier de la longue figure *(1906); Monte Carlo, February 19, 1910.*

This opera, Massenet's last great success, numbered Lucy Arbell (Dulcinée) and Feodor Chaliapin (Don Quichotte) among its leading artists at the Monte

Carlo *première*. Although it reached the London Opera House on May 18, 1912, *Don Quichotte* never got to Covent Garden, and Oscar Hammerstein's efforts to make it popular in London were a sorry experience for him. It had come to the United States, at New Orleans, on January 27, 1912, and soon was taken into the repertoire of the Philadelphia-Chicago Opera Company, with Mary Garden, Vanni Marcoux, and Hector Dufranne. They introduced it to New York on February 3, 1914, during the Philadelphia-Chicago company's final visit to the Metropolitan Opera House. The Metropolitan revived it for Chaliapin at a matinee on April 3, 1926, and it lasted through five performances in two seasons. Chaliapin was notably successful, but neither Florence Easton nor Giuseppe de Luca was outstanding.

59. La Donna del lago
(Rossini)

Two acts; libretto by Andrea Leone Tottola, after Sir Walter Scott's The Lady of the Lake; Naples, Teatro San Carlo, September 24, 1819.

Very successful, *La Donna del lago* within five years of its *première* had been sung in many Italian cities, as well as in Germany, Portugal, Austria, Malta, Hungary, England, Spain, Russia, and France—and had been translated into both German and English.

The first London production, in Italian, was heard on February 18, 1823, at His Majesty's Theatre. It was first heard in English at Drury Lane on January 4, 1827. When another English version was staged at Covent Garden (translation by Mark Lemon, music

arranged by James Howard Tully) on January 31, 1843, the role of Malcolm Graeme was sung by Mary (Mrs. Alfred) Shaw, an English contralto who had made her operatic debut at La Scala, Milan, on November 17, 1839, and who had thus been present at a history-making occasion: the opera on that night was the *première* of *Oberto, conte di San Bonifacio,* the first staged work of Giuseppe Verdi.[1] Others to assume the role of Malcolm Graeme at Covent Garden in later years included Marietta Alboni, Elena Angri (1849, with Mario as James I, Sims Reeves as Roderick Dhu), and Mlle de Méric (not to be confused with Méric-Lalande), the last on April 25, 1850, in a cast that included Giulia Grisi as Elena, Mario as James I, Enrico Tamberlik as Roderick Dhu,[2] and Zelger as Douglas of Angus; not satisfied with the music allotted to Roderick Dhu, Tamberlik introduced into it a cabaletta from Rossini's 1822 opera, *Zelmira.*

After a Rome performance of *La Donna del lago* in 1823, Giacomo Leopardi wrote: "At the Teatro Argentina we have *La Donna del lago;* it is stupendous music, and would move me to tears if the gift of tears had not been taken away from me." Critics were not ready to go quite that far, but were nevertheless much more than respectful, when the opera was revived at the 1958 Maggio Musicale in Florence (Teatro della Pergola). Tullio Serafin conducted, and the cast included Rosanna Carteri (Elena), Cesare Valletti (Uberto—that is, James I), Eddy Ruhl (Roderick Dhu, alias Rodrigo), Irene Companeez (Malcolm Graeme), and Paolo Washington (Douglas of Angus).

La Donna del lago was sung in New York on August 25, 1829, in French,

[1] Mrs. Shaw was only thirty, and at the peak of her abilities, when her husband, Alfred Shaw the painter, went insane and died. This tragedy so affected her vocal cords that she had to leave the stage. The year was 1844, and she lived until 1876.

[2] Roderick Dhu had originally been a tenor, but Rossini himself had altered the role so that Antonio Tamburini, a baritone, could sing it in Paris in 1824.

and on December 16, 1833, in Italian. Philadelphia heard it in Italian on April 21, 1834. But there seems to have been no modern revival in the United States.

60. Le Donne curiose
(Wolf-Ferrari)

Three acts; libretto by Luigi Sugano, after Carlo Goldoni's play of the same name, but translated from Italian into German (as Die neugierigen Frauen) *by Hermann Teibler for the* première; *Munich, November 27, 1903.*

Wolf-Ferrari's opera had been heard in German, Flemish, Polish, Hungarian, and Swedish before, on January 3, 1912, it was sung for the first time in Italian—at the Metropolitan Opera, New York, with Arturo Toscanini conducting. It might have seemed destined for more than the eight performances in two successive seasons which made up its Metropolitan history; the leading singers were: Geraldine Farrar (Rosaura), Jeanne Maubourg (Beatrice), Hermann Jadlowker (Florindo), Antonio Scotti (Lelio), Antonio Pini-Corsi (Pantalone), and Adamo Didur (Ottavio). The opera was heard in Italy for the first time, at La Scala, Milan, on January 16, 1913. It is still occasionally to be heard in both Italy and Germany, but has never been staged at Covent Garden, London. It is still very revivable, as are others of Wolf-Ferrari's operas.

61. Die Dreigroschenoper
(Weill)

Prologue and eight scenes; text a German translation of John Gay's The Beggar's Opera *by Elisabeth Hauptmann, with lyrics by Bertolt Brecht, some of them based on poems by François Villon and Rudyard Kipling; Berlin, Theater am Schiffbauerdamm, August 31, 1928.*

A smash hit in Germany (an estimated four thousand performances in 120 theaters), *Die Dreigroschenoper* was quickly produced in translation in Poland, Holland, Denmark, Russia, Hungary, France, the United States (as *The Threepenny Opera,* translated by Clifford Cochran and Jerrold Krimsky, New York, Empire Theater, April 13, 1933), and—in concert form—England.

Marc Blitzstein's "Americanized" adaptation, known as *The Threepenny Opera,* accompanied by an eight-man instrumental ensemble (piano, two saxophones, two trumpets, trombone, banjo, and percussion), and with the original Jenny of the 1928 Berlin performance—Lotte Lenya, Kurt Weill's widow—opened at the Theater de Lys, New York, on March 10, 1954, ran for three months, and then had to close after ninety-six performances because the small theater had to honor a booking arrangement made earlier. The small, highly stylized production reopened at the same theater with a preview on September 19, 1955, and ran until December 17, 1961, having been played for 2,611 continuous performances with a total box office exceeding $2,500,000. Of the 709 performers who had taken the roles during this six-year run, not one of those who had been in it when it opened was still in the cast on the night when it closed. This was the longest continual run of any sort of musical show in the history of the American theater. During this run, at least one of the songs became a popular hit on radio and jukebox.

62. Il Duca d'Alba (Donizetti)

Four acts; libretto by Augustin-Eugène Scribe; first heard, in an Italian version translated by Angelo Zanardini and completed by Matteo Salvi, Rome, Teatro Apollo, March 22, 1882.

Donizetti failed to complete *Le Duc d'Albe* during 1839, though it was worked on in view of a deadline of January 1, 1840, but left it incomplete when he began work, instead, on *La Favorite* (into which, as "Spirto gentil," he transferred Marcello's aria "Ange si pur"). The opera became entangled in legal actions involving the Opéra, the first of which Donizetti won, the second of which—brought after the composer's death—was decided in favor of Donizetti's heirs when the score proved to be incomplete. In 1881, Signora Giovannina Lucca, having acquired the manuscript of *Le Duc d'Albe,* asked the director of the Conservatory at Milan, Antonio Bazzini, and two of his professors of composition— Cesare Dominiceti and Amilcare Ponchielli—to examine it with a view to possible staging. They found that it had no overture; that in Act I a chorus lacked orchestration; that in Act II recitatives were lacking and choruses had not been orchestrated; that in Acts III and IV Donizetti had sketched in only a bass, with sparse indications of instrumentation. Several vocal numbers had not been composed at all. In many respects, then, the opera heard at Rome in 1882 was in large part from the uninspired pen of Matteo Salvi, the Donizetti pupil to whom the task of completing the score had been entrusted. It could not, in any case, have been pure Donizetti.

The original cast, at the Teatro Apollo in 1882, included Julian Gayarré (Marcello), Bruschi-Chiatti (Amelia), Eugenio Giraldoni (Duca d'Alba), and Silvestri (Daniele); Marino Mancinelli conducted. The opera was well received by an extraordinarily brilliant audience that included Queen Margherita, and soon was produced at Naples, Turin, Bergamo, Barcelona, and Malta. Scribe meanwhile had rewritten the libretto, altering its locale and the names of its protagonists, and had handed it to Verdi: in that guise, it became the libretto of *Les Vêpres siciliennes* (Paris, Opéra, June 13, 1855).

When it was decided to revive *Il Duca d'Alba* at the 1959 Spoleto Festival of Two Worlds, the staging was entrusted to Luchino Visconti, the editing of the score to the conductor Thomas Schippers. Visconti, scouting for suitable scenery in Rome, found the original 1882 sets, after designs by Carlo Ferrario, in a warehouse, and had the costumes designed so that (to quote the Spoleto program) "with the sets, they would form a coherent whole, evoking the atmosphere and the taste of an opera production of the 1880's." Schippers painstakingly compared the two existing printed versions of the score with the original manuscript, removing as much of Salvi's handiwork as possible and generally trying to restore a truly Donizettian style, at the same time reducing the four acts to three.

Il Duca d'Alba, in this restored version, but still keeping Angelo Zanardini's Italian text, opened the Spoleto festival, at the Teatro Nuovo, on June 11, 1959. Schippers conducted, and the cast consisted of Ivana Tosini (Amelia), Renato Cioni (Marcello), Enzo Tei (Carlo), Luigi Quilico (Duca d'Alba), Wladimiro Ganzarolli (Sandoval), and Franco Ventriglia (Daniele). It was sung seven times and stagings elsewhere were soon projected.

The Duenna (Prokofiev)

See *Betrothal in a Convent* (No. 28).

63. Duke Bluebeard's Castle (Bartók)

One act; libretto by Béla Balázs; Budapest, May 24, 1918.

Bartók's only opera later was heard in German translation in Frankfurt-am-Main (1922) and Berlin (1929). After a revival in Hungarian at Budapest in 1937, the production was taken to the Florentine Maggio Musicale, being presented there on May 5, 1938. The New York City Opera Company staged it at the New York City Center in 1952, the cast consisting of Ann Ayars and James Pease. In a broadcast over the BBC, London, in 1953, the two roles were sung by Joan Cross and Arnold Matters. When the opera was staged at Sadler's Wells in 1954, Victoria Elliott was the Judith, David Ward the Bluebeard. In numerous performances in Switzerland, Italy, and elsewhere in Europe, Ira Malaniuk has been a notable Judith. The return to life of the Opéra-Comique, Paris, under the administration of that house and the Opéra by A.-M. Julien, was especially marked in October 1959, when Francis Poulenc's *La Voix humaine* shared a double bill with an admirable *Duke Bluebeard's Castle*, very well and stylishly sung by Xaver Depraz and Berthe Monmart.

64. Edgar (Puccini)

Four acts (later revised as three); libretto by Ferdinando Fontana, after Alfred de Musset's poetic drama La Coupe et les lèvres; *Milan, Teatro alla Scala, April 21, 1889.*

At the Milan *première* on Easter, 1889, Franco Faccio conducted, and leading roles were sung by Romilda Pantaleoni (Tigrana), Aurelia Cattaneo (Fidelia), and Giovanni Battista de Negri (Edgar). It was sung only three times. Puccini's three-act revision, made during the following summer, was intended for production at La Scala in the spring of 1890. Negri's illness prevented the carrying out of this plan, however, and the revised version was first heard at Ferrara on February 28, 1892. It was also sung in

a splendid production at Madrid on March 19, 1892, with Luigi Mancinelli conducting and a cast headed by Giuseppina Pasqua (Tigrana), the twenty-one-year-old Luisa Tetrazzini (Fidelia), and Francesco Tamagno (Edgar). Puccini revised *Edgar* again for a production at Buenos Aires on July 8, 1905, which he attended. It has never been staged professionally in either the United States or England.

65. Elektra (Strauss)

One act; libretto, after Sophocles, by Hugo von Hofmannsthal; Dresden, Königliches Opernhaus, January 25, 1909.

Ernst von Schuch conducted the world *première* of *Elektra* at Dresden on January 25, 1909, with the following cast: Ernestine Schumann-Heink (Klytemnestra), Annie Krull (Elektra), Margarethe Siems (Chrysothemis), Johannes Sembach (Aegisthus), and Karl Perron (Orestes). When the opera was presented in Berlin exactly three weeks later, Leo Blech was the conductor, the Elektra was Thila Plaichinger, and the Chrysothemis was an American soprano, Frances Rose. Vienna followed on March 24, 1909, when Marie Gutheil-Schoder sang the title role; the Klytemnestra was Anna von Mildenburg, the Orestes Hermann Weidemann. At La Scala, Milan, on April 6, 1909—ten weeks after the Dresden *première*—*Elektra* was sung in an Italian translation by Ottone Schanzer.

New York and London were to hear *Elektra* early in 1910, but it would not reach Paris until 1932, the year, too, when it would finally get to the Metropolitan. One year and one week after Dresden, Oscar Hammerstein staged *Elektra* at the Manhattan Opera House, New York (February 1, 1910), in a French translation by Henri Gauthier-

Villars. The Klytemnestra, Jeanne Gerville-Réache, renounced the role after that performance, as Schumann-Heink had renounced it after the world *première,* but the Elektra, Mariette Mazarin, was made of sterner stuff. Although she fainted after the performance, she recovered to sing it again six days later—and five days after that sang Elektra in the afternoon and Salomé in Massenet's *Hérodiade* in the evening. Hammerstein's Orestes was Gustave Huberdeau. The holy band of Manhattan critics was almost unanimous in denigrating *Elektra,* but the public hurried to see Mazarin's surpassing characterization, which was along truly Sophoclean lines. On March 24, 1910, Hammerstein's Manhattan company gave its final two performances: a *Salome* with Mary Garden at the matinee, a Mazarin *Elektra* in the evening.

Eighteen days after the New York *première,* Sir Thomas Beecham conducted the London *première* (Covent Garden, February 19, 1910). Edward VII and Queen Alexandra were in the audience, and the occasion was a tremendous triumph for Beecham, Strauss, and everyone else involved in it. This was the cast: Mildenburg (Klytemnestra), Edyth Walker, an American (Elektra), Rose (Chrysothemis), Maurice d'Oisly (Aegisthus), and Weidemann (Orestes). Strauss conducted the season's sixth and seventh performances —"at a fee," Harold Rosenthal has noted, "of two hundred pounds on each occasion." During the second of these special performances (March 15), Queen Alexandra received Strauss, Beecham, and Frank Rendle, the lessee-manager of Covent Garden, in her box. Before the ninth and final performance of that season, London also had heard the original Dresden Elektra, Annie Krull (March 17 and 19).

London's apparent liking for *Elektra* did not last. At one of the several revivals there, Bruno Walter conducted (May 26, 1925), beginning the evening with a reading of *Tod und Verklärung.* His cast was: Maria Olczewska (Klytemnestra), Gertrud Kappel (Elektra). Rosel Landwehr (Chrysothemis), Fritz Soot (Aegisthus), and Friedrich Schorr (Orestes). After two performances that season, the opera was not heard at Covent Garden again until 1938. Beecham conducted on May 5, 1938, and the Elektra was the truly demoniac Rose Pauly; with her on the stage were Kerstin Thorborg (Klytemnestra), Hilde Konetzni (Chrysothemis), Fritz Wolff (Aegisthus), and Herbert Janssen (Orestes). Despite the intense enthusiasm of the critics, *Elektra* again achieved only two performances that season. Until a production of Janáček's *Jenufa* in 1956, the poorest box office showing at Covent Garden after World War II had belonged to *Elektra.*

All this was changed in 1957. On November 16 of that year, replacing the indisposed Christel Goltz, Gerda Lammers won a resounding triumph as Elektra in a Covent Garden revival conducted by Rudolf Kempe, convincing several London critics that she was one of the truly great singing actresses. With her were Georgine von Milinkovic (Klytemnestra), Hedwig Müller-Bütow (Chrysothemis), and Otakar Kraus (Orestes).

In New York, the first Metropolitan *Elektra,* a matinee on December 3, 1932, was magnificently conducted by Artur Bodanzky, but the terrible drama of the opera seems to have eluded the singers, Karin Branzell (Klytemnestra), Kappel (Elektra), Göta Ljungberg (Chrysothemis), Rudolf Laubenthal (Aegisthus), and Schorr (Orestes). Ljungberg was later promoted to the title role; Branzell vacated that of Klytemnestra for Olczewska. The opera was sung six times that season, and then was not heard again until January 7, 1938, when Pauly (who had sung the role in a New York Philharmonic-Symphony performance, Artur Rodzinski conducting, on March 18, 1937) established herself as the greatest Elektra in New York operatic history. Preceded by a *Gianni Schicchi* with Lawrence Tibbett, the *Elektra* had, besides Pauly, Thorborg (Klytemnestra), Irene Jessner (Chrysothemis), Paul Althouse (Aegisthus), and Schorr (Orestes). Seven performances were rung up during two consecutive seasons.

The *Elektra* unveiled at the Metropolitan on February 18, 1952, was notable chiefly for the conducting of Fritz Reiner. The cast, which entirely failed to erase memories of that of 1938, was headed by Elisabeth Höngen as Klytemnestra, Astrid Varnay as Elektra, Walburga Wegner as Chrysothemis, Set Svanholm as Aegisthus, and Hans Hotter as Orestes. The opera returned to the Metropolitan stage again on February 13, 1961, when Joseph Rosenstock's accurate, unimpassioned conducting was overriden by the fine singing of Inge Borkh (Elektra), Frances Yeend, in her Metropolitan debut (Chrysothemis), and Jean Madeira (Klytemnestra). The great Elektra of Lammers was heard at the Metropolitan on March 16, 1962, spectacularly supported by Madeira and a more fiery Rosenstock. Some critics did not understand, but the audiences did. Regina Resnik's impassioned Klytemnestra returned on April 19, the twenty-seventh Metropolitan *Elektra* in thirty years.

A typical Salzburg *Elektra* was heard in the Festspielhaus there on August 16, 1957, with Borkh, Lisa della Casa (Chrysothemis), Jean Madeira (Klytemnestra), Max Lorenz (Aegisthus), and Kurt Böhme (Orestes); Dimitri Mitropoulos was the conductor. Borkh had made her American debut, on September 25, 1953, with the San Francisco Opera, as Elektra in a performance conducted by Georg Solti (also in his American debut); the rest of the cast on that occasion included Klose (a third United States debut), Ellen Faull (Chrysothemis), Ludwig Suthaus

(his American debut, as Aegisthus), and Paul Schöffler (Orestes).

66. L'Elisir d'Amore (Donizetti)

Two acts; libretto by Felice Romani after Augustin-Eugène Scribe's Le Philtre, the setting of which by Daniel-François Auber had been produced at the Paris Opéra on June 20, 1831; Milan, Teatro della Canobbiana, May 12, 1832.

The original cast of *L'Elisir d'amore* included Sabina Heinefetter (Adina), Giuseppe Frezzolini [1] (Dulcamara), Henry-Bernard Dabadie (Nemorino), and Genero (Belcore). The opera was an immediate and enduring success. Interestingly, the first non-Italian cities to hear it (all in 1833 and 1834) were Barcelona, Madrid, Lisbon, and Berlin. It reached London, the Lyceum Theatre, in Italian, on December 10, 1836; in an English translation by Thomas H. Reynoldson it was sung at the Surrey Theatre on May 29, 1839, and at Drury Lane on June 24, 1839. At Covent Garden during 1847, the Adina was Fanny Persiani, supported by Luigi Salvi (Nemorino), and Agostino Rovere (Dulcamara). During 1848, the soprano Emma Romer sang Adina at Covent Garden in an English version entitled *The Love Spell*. The 1850 season brought forth two notable Adinas, Pauline Viardot-García and Jeanne Castellan, both supported magnificently by Mario (Nemorino), Antonio Tamburini (Belcore), and Giorgio Ronconi (Dulcamara). On June 15, 1852, Angiolina Bosio made her London debut, at Covent Garden, as Adina, with Antonio Galvani (Nemorino), Ottavio Bartolini (Belcore), and Ronconi (Dulcamara). During 1855, Italo Gardoni, Tamburini's son-in-law, sang Ne-

---

[1] A noted *buffo cantante,* Frezzolini was the father of the soprano Erminia Frezzolini.

morino in his first Covent Garden season. Adelina Patti was presented as Adina in 1862, her second Covent Garden season. After a protracted absence from Covent Garden, *L'Elisir d'amore* was sung there again on September 13, 1950, during a visit by a company from La Scala, Milan. Franco Capuana conducted, and the cast included Margherita Carosio (Adina), Ferruccio Tagliavini (Nemorino), Tito Gobbi (Belcore), and Italo Tajo (Dulcamara).

L'Elisir d'amore, in English, was heard in New York on June 18, 1838; the original Italian version was heard there on May 22, 1844. Numerous other performances were sung in New York during the nineteenth century, but the Metropolitan Opera House did not stage the opera until January 23, 1904, when Arturo Vigna conducted and the cast included Marcella Sembrich (Adina), Isabelle Bouton (Giannetta), Enrico Caruso (Nemorino), Antonio Scotti (Belcore), and Archangelo Rossi (Dulcamara). During the 1906–7 season at Hammerstein's Manhattan Opera House, Alessandro Bonci was greatly admired as Nemorino. He was heard in the role at the Metropolitan on Christmas Night, 1908, with Sembrich, Giuseppe Campanari (Belcore), and Concetto Paterna (Dulcamara); the other half of the double holiday bill was a *Cavalleria rusticana* conducted by Arturo Toscanini, with Emmy Destinn as Santuzza and Riccardo Martin as Turiddu. Caruso did not sing the role of Nemorino at the Metropolitan from 1904 to 1916, returning to it on December 30 of the latter year opposite Frieda Hempel (Adina), Antonio Scotti (Belcore), and Adamo Didur (Dulcamara); later that season, María Barrientos was the Adina. Barrientos was also the Adina when Act III of *L'Elisir d'amore* was presented at a gala performance on March 22, 1919, to celebrate Caruso's twenty-fifth anniversary in opera. Besides singing the Nemorino in that act, Caruso sang Canio in Act I of *Pagliacci* and

John of Leyden in the Coronation Scene of *Le Prophète.*

At the Brooklyn Academy of Music on December 11, 1920, the Metropolitan company was presenting a Caruso *L'Elisir d'amore* when the great tenor broke down, coughing up blood. He tried vainly to complete the performance. Not realizing how sick he really was, Caruso sang Alvaro in *La Forza del destino* at the Metropolitan on December 13, Samson in *Samson et Dalila* on December 16, repeated his Eléazar in *La Juive* (which had opened the season on November 15, 1920) on December 24—and never sang again. He had sung 607 performances at the Metropolitan; he died at his birthplace, Naples, on the following August 2.

L'Elisir d'amore, thought of as "Caruso's opera," was not heard again at the Metropolitan until March 21, 1930, when Tullio Serafin conducted, Beniamino Gigli was the Nemorino, and the rest of the cast included Nina Morgana (Adina), Giuseppe de Luca (Belcore), and Ezio Pinza (Dulcamara). When the opera became the second heard during the 1932–33 season, the greatly praised Nemorino was Tito Schipa, with Editha Fleischer replacing Morgana. After that season, *L'Elisir* again lapsed, returning on November 28, 1941, to give New York its first opportunity to hear and see Salvatore Baccaloni's monumental Dulcamara; others in the cast, under Ettore Panizza's baton, were Bidu Sayão (Adina), Bruno Landi (Nemorino), Francesco Valentino (Belcore), and Mona Paulee (Giannetta). After still another interim, the opera was heard again on the second night of the 1948–49 season, again with Baccaloni and Sayão; Tagliavini was the Nemorino, Giuseppe Valdengo the Belcore. On January 23, 1949, Giuseppe di Stefano replaced Tagliavini, the Adina was Marilyn Cotlow, and Italo Tajo was heard as Dulcamara. At the last performance of that revival of *L'Elisir* at the Metropolitan (February 19, 1949),

Patrice Munsel was the Adina, Di Stefano the Nemorino, John Brownlee the Belcore, and Tajo the Dulcamara. The Metropolitan again restaged the opera on November 25, 1960 (its fifty-eighth performance in the house), with generally admired sets and costumes designed by Robert O'Hearn. The Adina was Elisabeth Soederstroem; the other principal roles were sung by Dino Formichini, in his Metropolitan debut (Nemorino), Frank Guarrera (Belcore), and the excellent Fernando Corena (Dulcamara).

In the spring of 1957, the Rome Opera staged *L'Elisir d'amore* in a three-act version, with Rosanna Carteri miscast as Adina, Tagliavini as Nemorino, Sesto Bruscantini as Belcore, and Giuseppe Taddei as Dulcamara. When the opera was heard at the Stoll Theatre, London, on May 30, 1957, Renata Scotto delighted the audience as Adina; others in the cast were Luigi Pontiggia (Nemorino), Enzo Sordello (Belcore), and Leo Pudis (Dulcamara). At the Edinburgh Festival, on August 31, 1957, Carteri showed herself a much-improved Adina; Di Stefano rather overdid the comic side of Nemorino, Giulio Fioravanti was the Belcore, and Corena excelled as Dulcamara; Nino Sanzogno conducted. *L'Elisir* is still frequently performed throughout Europe, particularly in Italy and Germany.

67. The Emperor Jones
(Gruenberg)

Seven scenes; libretto by Kathleen de Jaffa, after Eugene O'Neill's play of the same name; New York, Metropolitan Opera House, January 7, 1933.

Lawrence Tibbett had the role of Brutus Jones at the world *première,* being well supported by Pearl Besuner (Old Native Woman) and Marek Windheim (Henry Smithers). There were ten performances in two consecutive seasons. Tibbett's spectacular impersonation was heard in San Francisco on November 17, 1933 (when the opera shared a double bill with *Il Segreto di Susanna*). Wilfred Pelletier conducted; the supporting cast included Raymond Marlowe as Smithers and Myrtle Leonard as the Old Native Woman. Tullio Serafin, who had conducted *The Emperor Jones* at the Metropolitan in 1933, remembered it fondly enough to revive it in Italy in 1952, with Brutus Jones changed into an Italian emperor; the role was sung by Nicola Rossi-Lemeni. Also, *The Emperor Jones* had previously been revived, in Dutch, at Amsterdam.

68. L'Enfant et les sortilèges
(Ravel)

Two parts; libretto by Colette; Monte Carlo, Opera, March 21, 1925.

The world *première* of Ravel's two-part *fantaisie lyrique* at Monte Carlo was conducted by Victor de Sabata. Principal roles were taken by Marie-Thérèse Gauley (L'Enfant), Dubois-Lauger (Le Feu, La Princesse, Le Rossignol [1]), Julien Lafont (Le Fauteuil), and Henri Fabert (Le Vieillard arithmétique, La Rainette). The work was mounted at the Opéra-Comique, Paris, on February 1, 1926, when Albert Wolff conducted and the cast included Gauley (L'Enfant), Germaine Féraldy (La Feu, La Princesse, Le Rossignol), Mathilde Calvet (La Maman, La Tasse chinoise), Madeleine Sibille (La Libellule), Antoinette Reveille (Un Pastoure, La Chauve-souris), Roger Bourdin (L'Horloge, Le Chat), Louis Guenot (Le Fauteuil, L'Arbre), René Hérent (Le Vieillard arithmétique, La Rainette), and Georges Génin (La Théière).

---

[1] Ravel specified that the roles of Le Feu, La Princesse, and Le Rossignol are to be sung by a single *soprano léger*, those of Le Vieillard arithmétique and La Rainette by a single tenor.

On May 17, 1939, *L'Enfant et les sortilèges* was performed at the Opéra, Paris, for the first time. Philippe Gaubert was the conductor. But on May 17, 1950, it returned to the Comique under the baton of André Cluytens, with Martha Angelici (L'Enfant), Solange Delmas (Le Feu), Renée Tarn (La Princesse), Solange Michel (La Maman, La Tasse chinoise), Willy Tubiana (Le Fauteuil, L'Arbre), Julien Thirache (L'Horloge, Le Chat), Pierre Giannotti (La Rainette), Le Prin (Le Vieillard arithmétique), and Serge Rallier (La Théière). Through that season, it had received thirty performances at the Comique.

Outside France, *L'Enfant* was staged at Brussels on February 11, 1926, at San Francisco on September 19, 1930—with Gaetano Merola conducting and a cast that included Queena Mario—and at the Florentine Maggio Musicale (by a group from the Paris Opéra) on May 2, 1939, with Fernando Previtali conducting. It was also heard in Czech at Prague in 1927 and in German at Leipzig that year, at Vienna in 1929. When it was staged at La Scala, Milan, in 1948, Victor de Sabata conducted, and the cast included Suzanne Danco and Pierre Giannotti.

A notable performance of *L'Enfant et les sortilèges* (billed as *The Spellbound Child* and sung in a free translation by Jane Barzin and Lincoln Kirstein) was staged at New York's Central High School of Needle Trades on November 20, 1946, by the Ballet Society. Leon Barzin conducted the orchestra of the National Orchestral Association, nineteen solo singers, and a twenty-four-member chorus of the National Music League, all of whom—the auditorium having no orchestra pit—were on floor level between the spectators and the stage. In superbly imaginative costumes and décor by Aline Bernstein, George

Balanchine had staged the work as a ballet,[2] the chief dancers being Gisella Caccialanza, Ruth Gilbert, Georgia Hiden, Tanaquil LeClercq, Elise Reiman, Beatrice Tompkins, Paul (later Jacques) d'Amboise, and William Dollar.

69. Die Entführung aus dem Serail (Mozart)

Three acts; libretto by Gottlob Stephanie, being no more than a revision of a libretto by Christian Friedrich Bretzner; Vienna, Burgtheater, July 16, 1782.

Caterina Cavalieri (Constanze), Therese Teyber (Blonde), Johann Valentin Adamberger (Belmonte), Ernst Dauer (Pedrillo), and Ludwig Fischer (Osmin) were the principals of the *première*, with Mozart conducting. It was an immediate hit and received thirty-four performances before the Burgtheater closed its doors in 1788. Its popularity had spread to Moscow by 1810. It was first given at Covent Garden, in English, on November 24, 1827, labeled simply *The Seraglio*. Lucia Elizabeth Vestris, the Blonde, was the star of these proceedings; J. B. Cramer added airs. Throughout the nineteenth century, English audiences heard no *Entführung* that would have satisfied purists, and some productions had recitatives by Luigi Arditi or Julius Benedict. Maria Ivogün and Elisabeth Schumann were respectively Constanze and Blonde in the Covent Garden revival in 1927 under Bruno Walter. The 1938 revival there under Sir Thomas Beecham (". . . he danced his way through the score with incomparable elegance") brought forward Erna Berger, Irma Beilke, Richard Tauber, Heddle Nash, and Ludwig Weber.

Performances of *Die Entführung* in the United States have been sporadic since the Brooklyn *première*, under the auspices of the Brooklyn Operatic Cir-

---

[2] Only the role of the Child was sung and acted by the same person, a twelve-year-old boy named Joseph Connoly.

cle, on February 16, 1860. The Metropolitan Opera staged it for the first time on November 29, 1946, in English, with Emil Cooper conducting sluggishly and an unsparkling cast including Eleanor Steber (Constanze), Pierrette Alarie (Blonde), Charles Kullmann (Belmonte), John Carter (Pedrillo), and Dezso Ernster (Osmin). Four performances that season sufficed. At Stratford, Connecticut, Erich Leinsdorf conducted another English version, very stylishly staged, on May 30, 1956, as part of the Mozart bicentennial celebrations; the singing cast included Sarah Fleming, Sylvia Stahlman, William Lewis, Norman Kelley, and Richard Humphrey; the spoken role of the Pasha Selim was taken by Basil Rathbone. In still another English translation, the New York City Opera Company staged *Die Entführung* on October 30, 1957, at the City Center (using the Stratford sets and costumes). The cast included Phyllis Curtin, Virginia Haskins, Robert Rounseville, David Lloyd, and Richard Humphrey; Carlton Gauld was the Pasha Selim, and the conductor, Peter Hermann Adler, was making his bow with the company. But perhaps the most enjoyable performance of *Die Entführung* of recent memory in New York was the concert version (again, alas, in English) presented at Town Hall on March 31, 1950, by The Little Orchestra Society, with Thomas Scherman conducting. Erna Berger as Constanze was superb; not far behind her were Genevieve Warner as Blonde, Rounseville as Belmonte, Norman Kelley as Pedrillo, and Jerome Hines as Osmin. When a comparable cast sings the text as Mozart composed it, perhaps *Die Entführung* yet may take

its deserved position among the most popular of the Mozart operas.

70. Ernani (Verdi)

Four acts; libretto by Francesco Maria Piave, after Victor Hugo's play Hernani; *Venice, Teatro La Fenice, March 9, 1844.*

At the Fenice *première* of *Ernani,* the Elvira was Sofia Löwe; other roles were assigned to Carlo Guasco (Ernani), Antonio Superchi, and Antonio Selva. The opera triumphed, and was soon to make Verdi's name international. It traveled quickly throughout Italy,[1] and was the first Verdi opera to reach London, at Her Majesty's Theatre, in Italian, on March 8, 1845. When the opera was announced for production in Paris, Victor Hugo successfully objected to the use of *Ernani* as its title, claiming (justly) that the libretto traduced his drama. It was therefore produced at the Théâtre-Italien, on January 6, 1846, as *Il Proscritto ossia Il Corsaro di Venezia.* It was heard in New York for the first time at the Park Theater, on April 15, 1847, and was also sung as the opening production of the Astor Place Opera House [2] (of which the principal lessee was Salvatore Patti, father of the famous Adelina), on November 22, 1847. Boston heard it on April 23, 1847. It was staged at San Francisco in February, 1851, the first grand opera to be sung there.

When *Ernani* reached Covent Garden, London, in 1847, during that house's first season as a permanent opera theater, Enrico Tamburini found the bari-

---

[1] Because of censors suspicious of Victor Hugo's play, *Ernani* was sometimes given under other such titles as *Elvira d'Aragona* (Palermo, 1845) and *Il Corsaro di Venezia* (Naples, 1847).

[2] *Ernani* was the last opera to be heard (March 1, 1881), at the Teatro Capranica, Rome, the second of that city's public opera houses, which had opened on January 6,

1679, with the *première* of Bernardo Pasquini's opera *Dov'è amore è pietà.* The Capranica was later used for some years as a movie theater. The first Roman public opera house, the Teatro Tordinona (Torre di Nona), was opened on January 8, 1671, with a performance of Francesco Cavalli's *Scipione Africano.*

tone role of Don Carlos uncomfortably high—and it was therefore sung by Marietta Alboni, a contralto, her principal colleagues being Mlle Steffanoni (Elvira), Luigi Salvi (Ernani), and Ignazio Marini (Silva). During the 1852 season, Angiolina Bosio sang Elvira—and the following year a Covent Garden cast included Enrico Tamberlik (Ernani) and Giorgio Ronconi (Don Carlos). *Ernani* was revived at Covent Garden several times—in 1873 for Patti (Elvira), with Pietro Mongini (Ernani), Francesco Graziani (Don Carlos), and Anacleto Bagaggiolo (Silva).

The Metropolitan Opera staged *Ernani* for the first time (New York had not heard the opera since an Academy of Music production in 1882) on January 28, 1903. The cast included Marcella Sembrich, who was singing Elvira for the first time, Mathilde Bauermeister (Giovanna), Emilio de Marchi (Ernani), Antonio Scotti (Don Carlos), and Édouard de Reszke, in his final Metropolitan season (Silva). After three singings that season, *Ernani* lapsed at the Metropolitan until December 8, 1921, when Rosa Ponselle was the Elvira, and her colleagues were Minnie Egener (Giovanna), Giovanni Martinelli (Ernani), Giuseppe Danise (Don Carlos), and José Mardones (Silva), Danise being a replacement for an indisposed Titta Ruffo, who was to have made his Metropolitan debut that night, but did not sing Don Carlos until a matinee on January 28, 1922. On December 17, 1928, the Metropolitan's excelling Silva was Ezio Pinza, still with Ponselle, Martinelli, and Ruffo. The most recent Metropolitan revival, November 23, 1956, with Dimitri Mitropoulos conducting, was an unfortunate one for the Don Carlos, Leonard Warren, whose preposterous costume was greeted with a wave of laughter by the audience as he moved onto the stage; others in the cast were Zinka Milanov (Elvira), Mario del Monaco (Ernani), and Cesare Siepi (Silva).

Notable revivals of *Ernani* in Europe have included one at La Scala, Milan, in 1935, when the Elvira was Gina Cigna, with Francesco Merli (Ernani), Armando Borgioli (Don Carlos), and Tancredi Pasero (Silva); at Berlin in the same year with Tiana Lemnitz (Elvira), Marcel Wittrisch (Ernani), Herbert Janssen (Don Carlos), and Michael Bohnen (Silva); at Rome in 1951 with Caterina Mancini (Elvira), Gino Penno (Ernani), Paolo Silveri (Don Carlos), and Boris Christoff (Silva); and at the Teatro San Carlo, Naples, on November 27, 1960 (opening night), with Margherita Roberti (Elvira), Del Monaco (Ernani), Ettore Bastianini (Don Carlos), and Nicola Rossi-Lemeni (Silva). Of the last, Ernest de Weerth wrote: "Since Chaliapin there has not been a comparable singing actor on the operatic stage."

71. Erwartung (Schoenberg)

One act (four scenes); libretto by Marie Pappenheim; Prague, June 6, 1924.

Schoenberg's *Mimodrama* for a single character was produced in Prague on June 6, 1924, at the end of the second festival of the International Society for Contemporary Music. It was then fifteen years old, for Schoenberg had completed it on September 12, 1909. After the Prague *première,* it was heard at Wiesbaden on January 22, 1928, at Berlin on June 7, 1930, and—in a French translation by J. Wetterings—in Brussels on May 6, 1936. The little opera was broadcast from London on January 9, 1931, and has had occasional performances more recently. The 1958 Holland Festival presented it on a double bill with Schoenberg's *Von Heute auf Morgen.* Hans Rosbaud conducted the Hague Residentie Orchestra, the opera was produced by Hans Hartleb, and the décors were by Ita Maximovna. Helga

Pilarczyk sang the single role, the Wife. And on June 23, 1959, a season at the Teatro Colón, Buenos Aires, was opened with a double bill of *Erwartung* and Luigi Dallapiccola's *Volo di notte*. The Schoenberg was produced by Otto Erhardt, conducted by Robert Kinsky, and sung by Sofia Bandin. *Erwartung* received its United States *première* at Lisner Auditorium, Washington, D. C., under the auspices of the Opera Society of Washington, on December 28, 1960. Pilarczyk made her American debut; Robert Craft conducted; the Schoenberg *Mimodrama* shared a double bill with Stravinsky's *Le Rossignol,* conducted by the composer.

72. L'Étoile du nord
(Meyerbeer)

Three acts; libretto by Augustin-Eugène Scribe; Paris, Opéra-Comique, February 16, 1854.

Into the score of this opera about Peter the Great and his consort, Meyerbeer had introduced six rewritten numbers from the last of his German operas, *Ein Feldlager in Schlesien,* composed for the reopening of the Berlin Opernhaus after a destructive fire, and first heard there on December 7, 1844.[1] The opera was sung at the Comique one hundred times during its first year.

L'Étoile du nord was staged at Covent Garden, London, on July 19, 1855, in an Italian translation by S. Manfredo Maggioni. Sir Michael Costa conducted, and the cast included Angiolina Bosio (Catherine), Mlle Marai (Prescovia), Luigi Lablache (Gritzenko), Karl Formes (Peter), and Italo Gardoni (Danilowitz). The composer, attending

the performance, was so overcome with emotion generated by the applause that he forgot the speech in English which he had memorized, and stammered out: "Gentlemen, the heart is so full that the words are nowhere!" His opera reached nine performances that season. It was not heard at Covent Garden again until July 21, 1864, when Costa again conducted, and the cast included Marie Miolan-Carvalho, Jean-Baptiste Faure, and Emilio Naudin. When Adelina Patti first sang Catherine during the 1866 season, Faure was again the Peter and Naudin the Danilowitz; the Gritzenko was Giuseppe Ciampi. Patti held the role of Catherine through the season of 1882. Then, in 1883, Marcella Sembrich was heard at Covent Garden in the role, which she repeated during the 1884 season, after which *L'Étoile du nord* was heard no more there.

On April 1, 1855, New Orleans was the first city in the United States to hear *L'Étoile du nord,* in French. It reached New York, in Italian, on September 24, 1856, and in English on March 3, 1876. It has never been played at the Metropolitan.

73. Eugene Onegin
(Tchaikovsky)

Three acts; libretto, based on Pushkin's poem of the same name, by the composer and Constantine Shilovsky; Moscow, Little Theater of the Imperial College of Music, March 29, 1879.

Although *Eugene Onegin* became very successful in Russia, Tchiakovsky had to suffer some suspense: certain people could not bear to think of a libretto being made from Pushkin's masterpiece,

[1] Jenny Lind scored one of her first great successes in the name role of this opera when it was produced at the Theater an der Wien, Vienna, as *Vielka* on February 18, 1847. Although she never appeared in *L'Étoile du nord,* having retired from the operatic

stage five years before its *première,* she sang "Là, là, là, air chéri," the heroine's mimetic bout with two flutes in the Mad Scene, at concerts, thus helping to keep the revised opera alive.

and they "resented the appearance of the almost canonized figure of Tatiana upon the stage" (Rosa Newmarch, *The Russian Opera*). It had been given, outside Russia, only at Prague (1888) and Hamburg (January, 1892)[1] before reaching London, in English translation by H. Sutherland Edwards, at the Olympic Theatre on October 17, 1892. Fanny Moody (Tatiana), Eugène Oudin (Eugene Onegin), Iver McKay (Lensky), and Charles Manners (Gremin) were the principals. Covent Garden, despite Emmy Destinn, Mattia Battistini, and Ivan Altchevsky, did not like the opera in 1906, and it was laid aside after three performances. The Sadler's Wells revivals of 1934 and 1952 should be noted. Ljuba Welitch was a fine Tatiana at the Vienna revival in 1950.

Eugene Onegin, first given at the Metropolitan, New York, on March 24, 1920 (there had been a New York concert version as early as 1908), had Claudia Muzio (Tatiana), Giuseppe de Luca (Onegin), and Giovanni Martinelli (Lensky) to attract critics and public; the former liked the opera not at all, the latter only enough to keep it in the repertoire for seven performances spaced out through two seasons. Lucine Amara, George London, and Richard Tucker were the principals of a dull Metropolitan revival, in English, on October 28, 1957, when *Eugene Onegin* opened the season.

74. Euridice (Peri)

Prologue and six scenes; libretto by Ottavio Rinuccini; Florence, Pitti Palace, October 6, 1600.

With a dedication to Maria de' Medici, Rinuccini's libretto was published in the month of the opera's first pro-duction; the score was issued in 1601. The opera has had numerous modern revivals in Italy and Germany in the twentieth century, but the only known seventeenth-century performance outside Florence occurred at the Casa Marescotti, Bologna, on April 27, 1616. A notable modern production was that given in the Boboli Gardens, Florence (just behind the structure in which the original singing was given), on June 28 and 30, 1960. Bruno Rigacci conducted a reduced orchestra, to which had been added a group of eleven stage musicians (lute, viola da gamba, viola da braccio, basso de viola, flauto diritto, and spinet). The cast consisted of Giuliana Matteini (Prologue and Venus), Jolanda Meneiguzzer (Euridice), Marco Stecchi (Orpheus), Laura Londi (Nymph), and Paolo Washington (Pluto).

75. Euryanthe (Weber)

Three acts; libretto by Helmine von Chézy; Vienna, Kärntnertortheater, October 25, 1823.

Weber had bad luck with this, his only opera without spoken dialogue, from the start. Perhaps Henrietta Sontag, who created the name role, helped it to last for twenty performances that first season in Vienna, after which it was not heard there for many years. London did not like it in 1833, and not much better in 1882, though the Euryanthe was Rosa Sucher, with Eugen Gura as Lysiart. New York tried harder during two widely separated seasons. On December 23, 1887, Anton Seidl began his vain attempt to establish *Euryanthe* solidly at the Metropolitan. Under his baton, Lilli Lehmann (Euryanthe), Marianne Brandt (Eglantine), Max Alvary (Adolar), and Emil Fischer

---

[1] The first Hamburg performance (January 18, 1892) was conducted by Gustav Mahler, with the following leading singers: Kathi Bettaque (Tatiana), Kolun (Olga), Cron-berger (Lensky), Rudolf Eichhorn (Onegin), and Heinrich Wiegand (Gremin). Tchaikovsky, who was present, called the performance "positively superb."

(Lysiart) worked nobly; but after four performances the opera was dropped until Arturo Toscanini revived it on December 19, 1914, when Frieda Hempel (Euryanthe) and Johannes Sembach (Adolar) sang well beyond the abilities of their colleagues. There were five performances that season, and since then *Euryanthe* has not been heard at the Metropolitan. *Euryanthe* was presented in concert form at Carnegie Hall, however, on January 13, 1953, by The Little Orchestra Society, Thomas Scherman conducting. The cast consisted of Helen Laird (Euryanthe), Irene Jordan (Eglantine), David Garen (Adolar), Luis Pichardo (Lysiart), and Kenneth Smith (The King).

76. The Fair at Sorochintzy (Mussorgsky)

Three acts; libretto by the composer, after an episode in Nikolai Gogol's Evenings on a Farm near Dekanka; *left incomplete by the composer. Apart from a private concert version, its* première, *probably semipublic, seems to have been given at the Comedia Theater, St. Petersburg, on December 30, 1911; some of the numbers had been orchestrated by Anatol Liadov. The version orchestrated by Yuri Sergeyevich Sakhnovsky which was staged at the Free Theater, Moscow, on November 3, 1913, was a hopeless hybrid with added spoken dialogue. Alfred Loewenberg, in* Annals of Opera, *plumps for the César Cui version (Petrograd, Musical Drama Theater, October 26, 1917) as the true vehicle of the* première *(Cui at least was a survivor of the Five). Nikolai Tcherepnin, adding little of his own, tried out a fourth version, in French, at Monte Carlo on March 7, 1923; Vissarion Shebalin and Paul Lamm gave Leningrad their reading of Mussorgsky's ideas at the Little Opera Theater on December 21, 1941.*

When *The Fair at Sorochintzy* was given at the Metropolitan Opera House, New York, for the first time, at a matinee on November 29, 1930, public and critical response was on the chilly side. Tullio Serafin conducted. As the opera was sung in Italian, Ina Bourskaya's Russian accent did not help; Maria Müller, Ezio Pinza, and Frederick Jagel also sang leading roles. In the early 1940's, The New Opera Company offered *The Fair at Sorochinsk* (so spelled) at New York's Broadway Theatre as a companion to the Balanchine *Ballet Imperial*. Emil Cooper conducted his own new version, based on the Tcherepnin version, and the language purported to be English. Not only, as at the Metropolitan, was Mussorgsky's added interlude, *A Night on Bald Mountain,* played between the second and third acts, but also Conductor Cooper supplied music of his own composition "on themes of Mussorgsky" in all three acts. The cast included Marina Koshetz, Winifred Heidt, Michael Bartlett, Carlton Gauld, Donald Dame, Paul King, and Hugh Thompson; the leading dancers were William Dollar and Gisella Caccialanza.

First heard in London at the Fortune Theatre, in Russian, on February 17, 1934, *The Fair* reached Covent Garden on a double bill with *Pagliacci* on November 24, 1936. Albert Coates conducted (the London Symphony Orchestra was in the pit that season), and the cast included Elena Danieli (Parassia), Vera de Villiers (Khivria), Francis Russel (Gritzko), and Gerald Kassen. An English translation by Edward Agate was used.

77. The Fairy Queen (Purcell)

Prologue and five acts; libretto adapted (perhaps by Elkanah Settle) from Shakespeare's A Midsummer Night's Dream; *London, Dorset Gardens, April (?), 1692.*

Lost for more than two centuries, the score, partly in Purcell's autograph, was found in the Royal Academy of Music Library by John South Shedlock, who conducted a performance, in concert form, at St. George's Hall, London, on June 15, 1901. Not until February 10, 1920, when Cyril Bradley Rootham conducted it at Cambridge, was *The Fairy Queen* heard in a modern staging. In an arrangement by Constant Lambert, it was used to open the first (1946) season of opera at Covent Garden after World War II; Lambert conducted the first performance, on December 12; the cast included Audrey Bowman, Muriel Burnett, Constance Shacklock, Bruce Dargavel, Rhydderch Davies, Olive Dyer, Edgar Evans, David Franklin, Hubert Norville, Muriel Rae, and Dennis Stephenson. The producer was Malcolm Baker-Smith; the scenery and costumes were by Michael Ayrton.

78. Falstaff (Verdi)

Three acts: libretto by Arrigo Boito, after Shakespeare's The Merry Wives of Windsor *and* Henry IV; *Milan, Teatro alla Scala, February 9, 1893.*

The most renowned of the Falstaff operas [1] was sung for the first time at La Scala, Milan, on February 9, 1893, when Verdi was seventy-nine. At the composer's request, Edoardo Mascheroni conducted. The cast included Victor Maurel (Falstaff), Edoardo Garbin (Fenton), Antonio Pini-Corsi (Ford), Paroli (Cajus), Pelagalli-Rosetti (Bardolfo), Vittorio Arimondi (Pistola), E. Zilli (Alice Ford), Adelina Stehle (Nannetta), Fuerrini (Meg), and Pasqua-

Giacomelli (Dame Quickly). Among those in the brilliant audience were noted Teresina Stolz, Maria Waldmann, Princess Letizia Bonaparte, Giuseppe Giacosa, Giosuè Carducci, Giacomo Puccini, Pietro Mascagni—and, of course, Giuseppina Strepponi Verdi, who had created the role of Leonora in Verdi's first opera, *Oberto, conte di San Bonifacio,* more than fifty-three years before.

Falstaff quickly was staged throughout Italy; before 1893 was over, it had been heard also in Trieste, Vienna, Berlin, Buenos Aires, Rio de Janeiro, Stuttgart, Mexico City, and Prague. It reached Paris, at the Opéra-Comique, on April 18, 1894, in a French translation prepared by Boito and Paul Solanges; London on May 19, 1894, at Covent Garden; and New York on February 4, 1895, at the Metropolitan.

Luigi Mancinelli conducted the Covent Garden *première,* on May 19, 1894; the cast included Arturo Pessina (Falstaff), Umberto Beduschi (Fenton), Pini-Corsi (Ford), Zilli (Alice Ford), and Giulia Ravogli (Dame Quickly). The opera was played eight times that season. Maurel was heard in the title role during 1895, and Fernando de Lucia sang Fenton. After the four performances of that year, *Falstaff* was not heard at Covent Garden again until July 21, 1914, when Giorgio Polacco conducted and leading roles were sung by Antonio Scotti (Falstaff), Giuseppe Armanini (Fenton), Armand Crabbé (Ford), Claudia Muzio (Alice), Louise Kirkby-Lunn (Quickly), Alice Zeppilli (Nannetta), and Violet Hume (Meg). On June 29, 1926, *Falstaff* was revived again at Covent Garden; Mariano Stabile, considered by many the

---

[1] Other operas in which the character of Sir John Falstaff appears include Antonio Salieri's *Falstaff ossia Le Tre Burle,* 1799 (Beethoven composed a set of piano variations on the aria "La stessa, la stessissima" from this opera); Giovanni Pacini's *La Gioventù di Enrico V,* 1820; Michael William Balfe's *Falstaff,* 1838; Otto Nicolai's *Die lustigen Weiber von Windsor,* 1849; Ambroise Thomas's *Le Songe d'une nuit d'été,* 1850—in which Shakespeare himself and Queen Elizabeth also are characters; Adolphe Adam's *Falstaff,* 1856; Gustav Holst's *At the Boar's Head,* 1925; and Ralph Vaughan Williams' *Sir John in Love,* 1929.

greatest Falstaff after Maurel, had the title role, Charles Hackett was the Fenton—and otherwise the excellence of the ensemble was praised more than any of the individual singers. A second singing of *Falstaff* closed the season on July 2.

Stabile was again the Covent Garden Falstaff when Tullio Serafin conducted the opera during the 1931 season; Dino Borgioli was the Fenton, and Elvira Casazza and Ernesto Badini were praised for their interpretations, respectively of Dame Quickly and Ford. Less appreciated were three singings of *Falstaff* during the 1937 Coronation season, the first on May 31, with Beecham conducting,[2] Cesare Formichi a poor Falstaff, Maria Caniglia, Licia Albanese, Angelica Cravcenco, and Amalia Bertola excelling as, respectively, Alice, Nannetta, Quickly, and Meg.

When a company from La Scala, Milan, visited London in September, 1950, *Falstaff* was one of the three operas that it presented at Covent Garden. At the first performance, on September 19, Victor de Sabata and the La Scala Orchestra starred. Gino Bechi was not admired as Falstaff; others in the cast were Cesare Valletti (Fenton), Paolo Silveri (Ford),[3] Giuseppe Nessi (Bardolfo), Cesare Siepi (Pistola), Caniglia (Alice), Alda Noni (Nannetta), Anna Maria Canali (Meg), and Fedora Barbieri (Quickly). Since 1950, *Falstaff* has not been heard at Covent Garden, but has been staged at Glyndebourne and Sadler's Wells.

The first New York *Falstaff*, at the Metropolitan on February 4, 1895, was conducted by Mancinelli. Maurel had the title role; the others in the cast were Giuseppe Rusitano (Fenton), Giuseppe Campanari—who shared Maurel's triumph (Ford), Roberto Vanni (Cajus), Rinaldini (Bardolfo), Nicolini (Pistola), Emma Eames (Alice Ford), Zélie de Lussan (Nannetta), Jane de Vigne (Meg), and Sofia Scalchi (Quickly). Although the critics knew what they were hearing—H. E. Krehbiel called the music "a perfect sea of melodic champagne," W. J. Henderson called Maurel's fat knight "one of the great creations of the lyric stage"—the audiences apparently did not. Two repetitions that season and three the next preceded a banishment of thirteen years. Revival came under Toscanini during his first Metropolitan season, when, at a matinee on March 20, 1909, Scotti as Falstaff had around him Emmy Destinn (Alice Ford), Frances Alda (Nannetta), Maria Gay (Quickly), and Campanari (Ford). This time, five performances in two seasons sufficed. During the second season, on February 16, 1910, Louise Homer was heard as Dame Quickly, Edmond Clément as Fenton and Pini-Corsi, in the role he had created at La Scala in 1893, as Ford.

After the 1909–10 season, New York did not hear *Falstaff* until January 2, 1925,[4] when Lawrence Tibbett, as Ford, received a clamorous ovation that did much to win the opera the unprecedented total of six performances that season. Tibbett's associates on that night were Scotti (Falstaff), Beniamino Gigli (Fenton), Angelo Bada (Cajus), Giordano Paltrinieri (Bardolfo), Adamo Didur (Pistola), Lucrezia Bori (Alice Ford), Alda (Nannetta), Kathleen

---

[2] Of this performance, Ernest Newman wrote that "the statement current during the intervals that the orchestra and singers were never together may be dismissed as a calumnious exaggeration. I myself counted more than one occasion when they were." The trouble seems to have been inadequate rehearsals.

[3] Silveri was announced to sing this role at the second *Falstaff*, which concluded this eleven-day season on September 23. But he was also announced to sing at an Albert Hall concert that night. The Albert Hall management went to law to prevent Covent Garden and the La Scala troupe from advertising Silveri for the *Falstaff* performance, and it was sung instead by Tito Gobbi.

[4] Except for a single performance at the Lexington Theater in 1920 by the Chicago company, with Giacomo Rimini as Falstaff, Rosa Raïsa as Alice Ford, Désiré Defrere as Ford, and Tito Schipa as Fenton.

Howard (Meg), and Marion Telva (Quickly). After another ten performances during the 1925–26 and 1926–27 seasons, *Falstaff* was absent from the Metropolitan until, at a matinee on December 16, 1938, Tibbett was heard in the title role; Ettore Panizza was in the pit, and others in the cast were Charles Kullmann (Fenton), John Brownlee (Ford), Caniglia (Alice Ford), and Bruna Castagna (Quickly). Four performances sufficed.

In 1944, with Sir Thomas Beecham conducting, the Metropolitan erred by presenting *Falstaff* in English (largely, it was said, the conductor's English). Tibbett, in fading voice, was assisted in these rather pale proceedings by a variable cast including Eleanor Steber (Alice Ford), Frances Greer (Nannetta), and Margaret Harshaw (Quickly). At a matinee on March 11, 1944, Leonard Warren's admired Falstaff did what it was possible to do toward reviving an opera so poorly staged,[5] directed, and treated. Although Salvatore Baccaloni, much praised elsewhere for his Falstaff, was on the Metropolitan roster from 1947 on, he never sang the role there.[6] When Fritz Reiner conducted a superb *Falstaff* at the Metropolitan at a matinee on February 26, 1949, the language was again Italian and the Falstaff was Warren, who was given superior assistance by his colleagues: Giuseppe di Stefano (Fenton), Giuseppe Valdengo (Ford), Leslie Chabay (Cajus), Alessio de Paolis (Bardolfo), Lorenzo Alvary (Pistola), Regina Resnik (Alice Ford), Licia Albanese (Nannetta), Martha Lipton (Meg), and Cloe Elmo (Quickly). Although, as Olin Downes wrote, "The net result was a performance of 'Falstaff' that we have not seen equaled on

this side of the Atlantic," it was followed by only two repetitions that season—its fortieth and forty-first singings in the house—and *Falstaff* has not been heard since.

The 1956 Holland Festival presented an intensely admired *Falstaff* under the baton of Carlo Maria Giulini, with Fernando Corena excelling in the title role, Eugenia Ratti as Nannetta, and superior décor and direction by Franco Zeffirelli. Later that year, the Teatro San Carlo at Naples opened its season with a *Falstaff* conducted by Mario Rossi. Giuseppe Taddei had the title role, and his chief colleagues were Luigi Alva (Fenton), Clara Petrella (Alice Ford), Anna Moffo (Nannetta), Miriam Pirazzini (Meg), and Ebe Stignani (Quickly). On October 10, 1958, the Chicago Lyric Opera opened its season with Serafin conducting an insufficiently rehearsed *Falstaff* made notable by the superb knight of Gobbi, the excellence of Cornell MacNeil as Ford, Moffo's Nannetta, the Dame Quickly of Giulietta Simionato, and the beautifully sung (though poorly acted) Alice Ford of Renata Tebaldi. Perhaps unparalleled was the *Falstaff* that opened a season at the Teatro La Fenice, Venice, on January 14, 1959. Mariano Stabile, at the age of seventy (he had been singing in opera for about fifty years), not only produced the opera but also sang the title role. Richard Bonynge, in *Opera,* reported: "I had expected, naturally enough, a great performance by an ageing man with not too much voice left—I had not expected to hear, as I did, a wonderfully youthful sound, resonant and with the required staying-power for this mammoth part and a line to be

---

[5] In a typical half-measure of the period, the Metropolitan Opera Guild had contributed $5,000 for the restoration of Joseph Urban's sets, which had been in use since 1925.

[6] With William Steinberg conducting, Baccaloni sang the role of Falstaff so successfully with the San Francisco Opera Company on October 16, 1944, that four years later he was again starred in it when it was used

to open the 1948 San Francisco season (September 14). On the latter occasion, his principal companions were Regina Resnik (Mistress Ford), Hertha Glaz (Mistress Page), Ebe Stignani (Mistress Quickly), Licia Albanese (Nannetta), Robert Weede (Ford), and Max Lichtegg (Fenton). Steinberg again conducted.

envied and copied by most singers half his age." Overshadowed by Stabile's classic portrayal, but excellent in their roles, were the current Nannetta extraordinary, Anna Moffo, and Fedora Barbieri as Dame Quickly. When it is added that the Bardolfo was the veteran Giuseppe Nessi and that Serafin, as so often, conducted, it can be seen that all the victories in this opera of Verdi's old age do not go to the young.

79. La Fanciulla del West (Puccini)

Three acts; libretto by Guelfo Civinini and Carlo Zangarini, after David Belasco's play The Girl of the Golden West; *New York, Metropolitan Opera House, December 10, 1910.*

With Arturo Toscanini conducting, the three chief principals of the Metropolitan world *première* were Emmy Destinn (Minnie), Enrico Caruso (Dick Johnson), and Antonio Scotti (Jack Rance). (The Chicago *première*, two weeks after the New York world *première*, starred Carolina White, Amadeo Bassi, and Maurice Renaud.) Although the opera had been composed for the Metropolitan, New York did not particularly like it. After twenty-two performances distributed over four seasons, it was dropped until 1929, when it amassed twelve more performances in three seasons. In the 1929 revival (November 2), Maria Jeritza, Edward Johnson, and Lawrence Tibbett were starred. San Francisco tried vainly to revive American interest in *La Fanciulla del West* in 1943 and again in 1960.

On October 23, 1961, the Metropolitan Opera opened its season with *La Fanciulla del West,* using the Chicago production, which the magazine *Opera* had described well (December, 1956)

when it said that the sets were "of 1922 vintage" and looked their age.[1] Leontyne Price was an excelling, though badly costumed, Minnie under the surprisingly vivid conducting of Fausto Cleva. Her chief colleagues were Richard Tucker (Dick Johnson) and Anselmo Colzani (Jack Rance). During the first repeat performance, on October 31, Miss Price became so hoarse during the climactic game of poker in Act II that Dorothy Kirsten had to be summoned from her nearby hotel to replace her in Act III.

La Fanciulla del West reached the homeland of her composer and her operatic style on June 12, 1911, at the Teatro Costanzi, Rome. Before that, however, opera and composer both had stopped off in London, where the Covent Garden *première* of May 29, 1911, provided a great triumph for both, as well as for the singers (notably Destinn, Bassi, and Dinh Gilly), and for the public, which applauded until its hands were sore (perhaps not unmindful of the fact that Puccini had dedicated the opera to Queen Alexandra). Cleofonte Campanini conducted. Before London's interest flagged (eight performances in two seasons) and *La Fanciulla* disappeared from the Covent Garden repertoire, both Riccardo Martin and Giovanni Martinelli had been heard as Dick Johnson. The opera still is often sung in Italy.

80. Faust (Gounod)

Five acts; libretto by Jules Barbier and Michel Carré, after Part 1 of Goethe's Faust; *Paris, Théâtre-Lyrique, March 19, 1859.*

The cast assembled for the *première* was mediocre enough, excepting Marie Miolan-Carvalho (Marguerite), who, however, had not yet attracted much

---

[1] *La Fanciulla del West* had last been heard in Chicago in 1922 (with Rosa Raïsa as Minnie) when it was revived there on October 10, 1956, with Dimitri Mitropoulos conducting and a cast headed by Eleanor Steber—who rode a horse on stage in Act III (Minnie), Mario del Monaco (Dick Johnson), and Tito Gobbi (Jack Rance).

attention. Joseph Barbot, the Faust, was literally a pensioned teacher at the Conservatoire: he was very definitely chosen *faute de mieux*. The opera caught on slowly, and its greatest rash of popularity in Paris came not merely after its transference to the Opéra (with ballet music added) on March 3, 1869, but after its first five hundred performances. The second five hundred, from mid-November, 1887, through mid-December, 1894, was not again equaled: an average of roughly seventy performances a year. The first Opéra cast presented Christine Nilsson (Marguerite) and Jean-Baptiste Faure (Méphistophélès), but the other principals were indifferent.

Faust migrated to London in 1863, where it had two separate *premières* within three weeks. In the first, on June 11, Colonel Mapleson brought forward Therese Tietjens (Marguerite), Zelia Trebelli (Siebel), and Sir Charles Santley (Valentine) as the chief singing attractions. Luigi Arditi, the sprightly composer of "Il Bacio," conducted. On July 2, Gye's rival company produced *Faust* at Covent Garden, with Miolan-Carvalho in her old role, Enrico Tamberlik as Faust, and Faure as Méphistophélès. Arditi records, in *My Reminiscences,* that *Faust* "did not immediately force its way into the hearts of the people," and that for Mapleson, at least, twenty performances the first season resulted in a financial loss. On January 23, 1864, an English text by Henry Fothergill Chorley was first used, as was an interpolated song, "Avant de quitter ces lieux," which Gounod, who had been much impressed by Santley's pure intonation the previous year, had consented to write for the great baritone as a way of making the secondary role of Valentine more worthy of his talents.

As *Faust* began to settle into its place in English life, it became a favorite of Victoria herself. As late as 1900, when the Queen had but several more months of life, she wanted the De Reszkes to sing certain scenes from it at Windsor. Édouard, a famed Méphistophélès, could meet her command, but Jean could not, and in his place Albert Saléza, a fine French tenor, sang Faust. Klein, who was present, testifies that his ailing sovereign's "face lighted up and her lips parted with a transient smile of recognition whenever some well-known phrase occurred."

The first New York Marguerite (the first American, except for whoever sang the role, in German, in Philadelphia exactly one week before) had a realistic —that is to say, low—opinion of the role. "Stupidity is the real keynote of Marguerite's character," she wrote fifty years after that New York *première,* adding, "She was a well-brought-up but uneducated young person of an ignorant age and of a stupid class, and innocent to the verge of idiocy." Thus Clara Louise Kellogg, who, nevertheless, was much admired in the part, "dear Longfellow" (as she calls him), who was present at the Academy of Music on that November 25 in 1863, summoning lines from Dryden to describe the quality of her performance:

So pois'd, so gently she descends from high,
It seems a soft dimission from the sky.

By 1883, *Faust* had become so popular in the United States that it was chosen to open the first season of the Metropolitan Opera House, on October 22, 1883. Naturally, for this great occasion, an impressive cast was assembled by Manager Abbey. The Marguerite was Nilsson, no longer in her best voice, singing opposite Italo Campanini, one of the most satisfactory of Fausts. Others in the cast were Sofia Scalchi (Siebel), Giuseppe del Puente (Valentine), and, as Méphistophélès, Franco Novara (*né* Nash), a much valued bass during the early years of the Metropolitan. As all these artists had been heard in precisely the same roles at the Academy of Music, this was not an epochal performance, except as it initiated a better-equipped house. Patrons of the Academy were enjoying, the same evening, a performance of *La Sonnambula,* with Etelka Gerster as Amina; New Yorkers must have felt that there was to be healthy competition between the two houses. When fashion finally decreed the extinction of the Mapleson company, that sane hope was, for all practical purposes, thwarted until the challenge of Oscar Hammerstein.[1]

Faust became epidemic in New York with the arrival of the De Reszkes at the Metropolitan. Jean, with his chivalrous bearing and silvery voice, suffused the title role with unequaled romance. Édouard, whose interpretation of Méphistophélès impressed Bernard Shaw as a caricature, was nevertheless hardly less admired. In the season of 1896–97, they pulled the repetitions of *Faust* up to ten, provoking W. J. Henderson to dub the Metropolitan "Das Faustspielhaus." Édouard, who remained in the company two years after his brother's retirement, used Mephistopheles as his Metropolitan farewell role, on March 21, 1903, when the other principals were Lillian Nordica (Marguerite), Albert Alvarez (Faust), and Antonio Scotti (Valentine). Also, this was the afternoon performance on the last day of the Grau regime.[2] The *Faust* furore waned with the departure of the De Reszkes, though the opera was still important enough to be used to inaugurate, on November 14, 1908, at the Brooklyn Academy of Music, the Dippel and Gatti-Casazza joint management of the Metropolitan company, the cast being headed by Geraldine Farrar and Enrico Caruso, both of whom had made their world debuts in these roles, the former at Berlin (October 15, 1901), the latter at the Teatro Bellini, Naples (1894).

Among the most intelligent interpreters of Méphistophélès have been Pol Plançon, Feodor Chaliapin, and Clarence Whitehill, the last of whom, on April 19, 1920, sang in an admired all-American aggregation of principals, including Farrar (Marguerite), Mary Ellis (Siebel), Kathleen Howard (Marthe), Orville Harrold (Faust), and Thomas Chalmers (Valentine). Chaliapin, on November 30, 1923, returning to the role after sixteen years, caused some scandal among lovers of tradition by encoring his first-act aria. The Valentine of that performance was Lawrence Tibbett, in his first important role. Emma Calvé was an excellent Marguerite—it was the role in which she had made her debut, at the Théâtre de la Monnaie, Brussels, on September 29, 1882—but could not persuade New Yorkers to accept from her anything but her literally adored Carmen.

Although the lyric soprano, a species said to have been invented by Gounod, is far from extinct, it cannot now be said that every young soprano dreams of singing Marguerite, despite its great tradition from Adelina Patti, Nellie Melba, Emma Eames, Nordica, and Suzanne Adams to Victoria de los Angeles. Nor does every young tenor dream of singing Faust, with its equally great tradition from Jean de Reszke, Italo Campanini, Caruso, Lucien Muratore, Charles Dalmorès, and Fernand Ansseau to Jussi Björling and Giuseppe di Stefano. *Faust* has been out of the repertoire of Covent Garden for years, while at the Metropolitan it is a bad fourth after *Aïda, La Bohème,* and

---

[1] The Academy of Music lingered on, occasionally housing frail operatic ventures, then spoken drama, and, finally, motion pictures. In 1925, it was torn down, and the northeast corner of Fourteenth Street and Irving Place is now occupied by the tower of the Consolidated Edison Company of New York.

[2] Édouard actually appeared once more at the Metropolitan, again as Méphistophélès, when the fifth act of *Faust* was presented as part of a gala farewell for Grau. Emma Eames was the Marguerite, Alvarez again the Faust.

Carmen. Nobody is likely to equal in the near future the astonishing record of the great French bass Marcel Journet, who sang his one-thousandth Méphistophélès in *Faust* at San Francisco on September 23, 1926, thirty-three years after his operatic debut at Montpellier, France, in 1893.

The lore of *Faust* is naturally enormous. One of its adventures in the Soviet Union would have infuriated the clerical Gounod. Frederick H. Martens, in his *A Thousand and One Nights of Opera,* summarized the transformed libretto fitted to *Faust* by order of the Commissar of Public Art, when it was revived in Moscow in 1925:

Faust becomes "Harry," an American millionaire who, in his luxurious Berlin apartment, tells "Mr. Mephistopheles" life is vain unless he wins Margaret, a Hungarian moving picture actress, poor but pretty. Margaret, Siebel her lover, and Valentine, her brother, all communistically inclined, are tracked by the malefactor of great wealth to a Bavarian village (Act II) where, the girl's noble ideals succumbing to the lure of an enormous package of thousand-dollar bills laid temptingly on her window sill, she breaks out into a "Money Waltz" (Jewel Song) and allows Faust to lead her from the straight and narrow Marxian path while Mephistopheles, evil spirit of capitalism, laughs hideously. She is deserted by "Harry" (Act III) and condemned to death for the murder of her babe. When the millionaire, stung by remorse, comes to prison to rescue her, she kills him and is saved by the timely arrival of revolutionary troops. Gounod's music has been "pepped up" by the interpolation of jazz tunes (Acts II, III) to lend it "modern color."

81. La Favorite (Donizetti)

Four acts; libretto after François Baculard d'Arnaud's play Le Comte de Commingues, *by Alphonse Royer and Gustave Vaëz (pseudonym of Jean-Nicolas-Gustave van Nieuvenhuysen), reworked by Augustin-Eugène Scribe; Paris, Opéra, December 2, 1840.*

The third Donizetti opera produced in 1840 in Paris was conceived in three acts and entitled *L'Ange de Niside;* it was intended for performance at the Théâtre de la Renaissance, but was expanded to four acts and retitled *La Favorite* for staging instead at the Opéra, where, up until 1904, it had rung up more than 650 repetitions. During 1841, it was heard in Brussels, The Hague, Kassel, Frankfurt-am-Main, and Vienna, at the last-three-named cities in German. The first Italian-language performance occurred at Padua in 1842. It was sung at New Orleans in French on February 9, 1843; at Drury Lane, London, in English on October 18, 1843, and at New York in French on June 25, 1845. The variety of titles under which it was played in several languages is astonishing; some of its disguises were *Richard und Mathilde, Leonore, Leonora di Guzman, Riccardo e Matilda, Die Templer in Sidon.*

The Leonora di Guzman of the original Opéra cast had been the spectacular Rosine Stoltz. The success of *La Favorita* in London dated from May 23, 1848, when Giulia Grisi, though a soprano, sang Leonora, Mario was the Fernando, Ignazio Marini was the Baldassare, and Corradi-Seti was the Alfonso. Mario was still the Fernando elect sixteen years later when, in 1866, Pauline Lucca made her London debut as Leonora; the Alfonso was Jean-Baptiste Faure. During his last London season, Mario sang Fernando on April 29, 1871, opposite Sofia Scalchi as Leonora. In 1873, at Drury Lane, Therese Tietjens sang her first London Leonora; at the same theater, in 1874, the "Sgr. de Reschi" who sang Alfonso was the baritone who would later become the idolized tenor Jean de Reszke; as Giovanni de Reschi, he had made his operatic debut earlier that year at Venice in this role. In 1877, the Spanish tenor Julian Gayarré made his Covent Garden debut as Fernando on April 7. On the opening night of the 1887 season, he sang in a cast on May 24 which included Medea Mei as Leonora, Francesco D'Andrade as Alfonso, and Campello as Baldassare. Later in that season, the Fernando was Nicolai Figner, whom (as all collectors of old operatic recordings know) Medea

Mei married, becoming known as Medea Mei-Figner. And on May 13, 1896, at Covent Garden, the Leonora was Eugenia Mantelli.

Just as the early success of *La Favorite* in London had depended upon the husband-wife team of Mario and Giulia Grisi as Fernando and Leonora, so its fame in New York, at the Academy of Music, was a result of the popularity of the Maine contralto Annie Louise Cary in the title role.[1] The

---

[1] Something of the difficulty of producing opera is suggested by the following excerpt from *The Mapleson Memoirs*, referring to Colonel Mapleson's vicissitudes at the New York Academy of Music:

"Early in December I was within a very close shave of closing the theatre. The opera announced for the evening in question was *William Tell*. At about four o'clock, I received a doctor's certificate from Mdlle. Dotti, who performed the principal female character, notifying me that she had been attacked with diphtheria. I therefore had to set about to find a substitute, having decided to give the opera anyhow. Shortly after a notification came from Mierwinski, the tenor, who was also indisposed, though after a deal of trouble he promised to go on and do his best.

"I was, however, compelled to change the opera to *Lucia di Lammermoor*, as the lady who had undertaken to replace the prima donna in *William Tell* was in such a nervous state. There was no time for a rehearsal; I therefore decided to give *Lucia* instead. On the notice being sent to Mdlle. Laura Zagury, the soprano, she informed me that although *Lucia* was in the *répertoire* she furnished me on her engagement she had never sung that *rôle*. The opera therefore had to be changed to *Aïda*. Orders had just been given to the various departments as to the scenery, dresses, music, etc., when the news came that Mdlle. Rossini, whom I had counted upon for the principal part, was lying ill at her house on Fifth Avenue.

"I now changed the opera to *Rigoletto;* but Mdme. Zagury was not ready with the part of 'Gilda,' and absolutely refused to appear. *Les Huguenots* was next announced, it being now half-past five. Everything was set in motion for the production of that opera, when Mdme. Fursch-Madi declared her inability to assume the part of the heroine, as she had taken some medicine, believing that her services would not be required until the early part of the following week. Thereupon an attack was made on Mdme. Savio, who however, regretted that she was unable to

appear as 'Valentine.'

"Nothing was left but to try *La Favorita;* but Signor Ravelli, who had just finished a *Carmen* rehearsal, declared it would be utterly impossible for him to sing the *rôle* of 'Fernando.' Then Minnie Hauk was sought for; but she was saving herself for her appearance in Brooklyn on the morrow, and distinctly declined.

"I now took a decision either to perform *La Favorita*, or to close up, as it was already 6:30 P.M. I at length persuaded Signor Clodio, one of the tenors, to assume the part of 'Fernando.' But a new difficulty arose, as, being a very portly gentleman, there were no costumes in the house to fit him. The tailors were then set to work, who promised to have the dress ready in time. At this juncture word came from Mdme. Galassi, who was to have taken the part of 'Leonora,' that she was in bed suffering, and that it would be impossible for her to appear. I immediately went off to Mdme. Galassi myself. She assured me of her willingness to do her best; but she had two large boils under her right arm which caused her acute agony. At that moment she nearly swooned from the pain. To fetch Dr. Mott, our talented theatrical surgeon, was the work of a moment. We raised her up and the boils were lanced, which at once gave her relief, and I got her down to the theatre just at five minutes to eight. She had time to dress, as 'Leonora' does not appear until the second act. The performance went off successfully; I had got out of another serious difficulty after changing the opera seven times.

"In the midst of my trouble a deputation arrived from Kalakaua I, King of the Sandwich Islands, informing me that they were commanded by his Majesty the King of Hawaii to confer on Mdme. Patti the Royal Order of Kapirlani. They had the diploma and jewels with them, and they were accompanied by the King's Chamberlain. I had to entreat them to wait 'a moment' while I got through my troubles. That moment must have been nearly two hours."

Metropolitan failed to produce *La Favorite* or *La Favorita* during its first dozen years: the taste was beginning to run against anything but high sopranos as heroines, and Leonora is (despite Giulia Grisi) a mezzo or contralto role. But when Manager Grau finally did get around to presenting it, on November 29, 1895, with Enrico Bevignani as conductor, he provided the truly magnificent cast of Mantelli (Leonora), Mathilde Bauermeister (Inez), Giuseppe Cremonini (Fernando), Mario Ancona (Alfonso), Roberto Vanni (Gasparo), and Pol Plançon (Baldassare). Plançon retained his role in the revival of November 29, 1905, when Edyth Walker (Leonora), Enrico Caruso (Fernando), and Antonio Scotti (Alfonso) were his colleagues. Since the 1905–6 season, *La Favorita* has not been heard at the Metropolitan.

Beginning with a revival at La Scala, Milan, in 1934, Ebe Stignani became identified in Italy with the role of Leonora. She sang it there again in 1939, for example, in a cast that also included Giovanni Malipiero, Carlo Tagliabue, and Tancredi Pasero; at Rome in 1946 with Giacomo Lauri-Volpi and Gino Bechi; and once again at La Scala in 1949 with Gianni Poggi, Paolo Silveri, and Cesare Siepi. At Rome in 1951, however, again with Lauri-Volpi, the Leonora was Fedora Barbieri. And at the Roman Arena in Verona, on August 16, 1958, Giulietta Simionato sang Leonora, with Gianni Poggi (Fernando), Ettore Bastianini (Alfonso), and Ivo Vinco (Baldassare).

82. Fedora (Giordano)

Three acts; libretto by Arturo Colautti, after the play by Victorien Sardou; Milan, Teatro Lirico, November 17, 1898.

Gemma Bellincioni, Enrico Caruso, and Delfino Menotti participated in the world *première,* which was conducted by the composer. London heard *Fedora* precisely a month before New York: Covent Garden, November 5, 1906, with Rina Giachetti, Giovanni Zenatello, and Mario Sammarco. It was revived for Maria Jeritza in 1925, when Ulisse Lappas and Ernesto Badini were her partners. *Fedora* had much the same sort of history at the Metropolitan, where it was first performed on December 5, 1906. Lina Cavalieri, the Fedora, was so beautiful that both press and public somewhat neglected the fine work of Caruso and Antonio Scotti. It disappeared after two seasons, and was not revived until 1923, when Jeritza, Giovanni Martinelli, and Scotti gave it a new lease of life. It was last sung at the Metropolitan in 1925, but it is still very popular in Italy.

83. Fernand Cortez, ou La Conquête du Mexique (Spontini)

Three acts; libretto by Joseph-Alphonse Esménard and Victor-Joseph Étienne de Jouy; Paris, Opéra, November 28, 1809.

Fernand Cortez was performed at the Opéra almost 250 times by 1840, after mid-1817 in a revised version. Carl Maria von Weber used it for his debut as a conductor in Prague (September 9, 1813). It never reached London because Sir Henry Rowley Bishop's mediocre opera on the same subject thwarted a rival work. As early as January 6, 1888, the Metropolitan Opera House, New York, gave a most spectacular production of *Fernand Cortez*. This setting by an Italian of a French libretto about the Spanish conquest of Mexico was sung in an English-speaking country in German, by Germans, among them such stars as Emil Fischer, Albert Niemann, and the Teuton Adonis, Max Alvary. "The people employed in the representation," H. E. Krehbiel wrote, "rivaled in numbers those who constituted the veritable Cortez's army, while the horses came within three of the number that the Spaniards took into Mexico." These facts (if facts they were) would have delighted Spontini, who was a precursor of Rossini and Meyerbeer in vast spectacle operas.

84. Fidelio (Beethoven)

Three acts; libretto a German translation and semiadaptation, by Josef von Sonnleithner, of Jean-Nicolas Bouilly's Lénore, ou l'amour conjugal; *Vienna, Theater an der Wien, November 20, 1805; Originally a three-act opera,* Fidelio *was reduced to two acts (Theater an der Wien, March 29, 1806), the libretto being revised by Stephan von Breuning; after tampering further with the text in 1814, Georg Friedrich Treitschke and Beethoven left it in a somewhat amended two-act form (Kärntnertortheater, May 23, 1814).*

Beethoven conducted the *première* on November 20, 1805. The Leonore was a nineteen-year-old girl named Anna Milder; as Anna Milder-Hauptmann she was later to become an unrivaled interpreter of Gluck's monumental female roles (Haydn once said to her: "Dear child, you have a voice like a house"). The Florestan of that ill-starred first performance was one Demmer, an aging tenor of local eminence; the Pizarro was Friedrich Sebastian Mayer. Milder won a notable success in the part of Leonore at Berlin on October 14, 1815. Among the most renowned of Milder's successors have been Maria Malibran, Pauline Viardot-García, Therese Tietjens, Katharina Klafsky, Milka Ternina, Lilli Lehmann, Marianne Brandt, Margarete Matzenauer, Lotte Lehmann, Kirsten Flagstad, and Birgit Nilsson. But the most famous of all

Leonores was Wagner's tempestuous friend and onetime idol, Wilhelmine Schröder-Devrient, who made her debut in this role, at the Royal Opera House, Dresden, under Carl Maria von Weber's direction, on April 29, 1823 (Weber had conducted *Fidelio* at Prague as early as November 21, 1814). Henry Fothergill Chorley, dean of mid-nineteenth-century English music critics, wrote of Malibran and Schröder-Devrient as Leonore thus: "The Spaniard threw more horror into the scene in the vault than her predecessor; but the German is before me when, in the introduction to the Chorus of Prisoners, as they creep out of their cells, she questioned one ghastly face after another with the heart-piercing wistfulness of hope long deferred."

Beginning in 1814, *Fidelio* began to be produced throughout Europe. It was staged at the Théâtre-Italien, Paris, in German, on May 30, 1829. The first performance in London was at Her Majesty's Theatre, May 18, 1832, in German; Covent Garden first staged *Fidelio* shortly later, both Malibran and Schröder-Devrient being heard there. On July 1, 1835, for her farewell benefit, Malibran appeared in both *Fidelio* and *La Sonnambula.* Thereafter, Covent Garden was to hear *Fidelio* with most of the great international stars. On July 2, 1892, Gustav Mahler conducted *Fidelio* at Drury Lane Theatre, repeating the performance at Covent Garden on July 20; the cast included Katharina Klafsky (Leonore), Sophie Traubmann (Marzelline), Seidel (Florestan), Heinrich Fritz Lissman (Pizarro), Landau (Jaquino), and Heinrich Wiegand (Rocco). In more recent years, too, Covent Garden *Fidelios* often have found outstanding English singers in leading roles.

Fidelio reached New York, in English, on September 9, 1839, and in German on December 29, 1856. New York also had heard the opera in

Italian (March 10, 1882) when it was staged for the first time by the Metropolitan Opera on November 19, 1884, in German, with Leopold Damrosch conducting and Marianne Brandt making her New York debut; others in the cast were Auguste Kraus (Marzelline), Anton Schott (Florestan), Adolf Robinson (Pizarro), Josef Staudigl Jr. (Don Fernando), and Josef Miller (Rocco). Thereafter, *Fidelio* was in and out of the Metropolitan repertoire a dozen times.[1] It won its greatest popularity after Flagstad first sang Leonore there on March 7, 1936, with René Maison an appealing Florestan. *Fidelio* left the Metropolitan when Flagstad departed in 1941, not to be revived again until she returned. Bruno Walter conducted the performance of March 6, 1950, with Flagstad (Leonore), Nadine Conner (Marzelline), Günther Treptow (Florestan), Paul Schöffler (Pizarro), Jerome Hines (Don Fernando), and Dezso Ernster (Rocco). After five performances that season, *Fidelio* lapsed at the Metropolitan until January 28, 1960. Karl Böhm then conducted, and the cast included Aase Nordmo Loevberg (Leonore), Laurel Hurley (Marzelline), Jon Vickers (Florestan), Hermann Uhde (Pizarro), Cesare Siepi, singing his first role in German (Don Fernando), and Oskar Czerwenka (Rocco). Matters improved vastly on February 13, 1960, when at a matinee, Birgit Nilsson's Leonore was heard in New York for the first time. By the end of the 1959–60 season, *Fidelio* had been heard six times, sixty-nine times in Metropolitan history.

Jon Vickers was a tower of strength in the most recent Metropolitan performances. But what *Fidelio* requires

most certainly is an overpowering Leonore. Beethoven needed her so, and a *Fidelio* with a merely adequate heroine can prove both artistically and financially direful. These remarks do not apply to Vienna, Berlin, and other German-speaking cities, where *Fidelio* remains a popular opera under almost any circumstances.

85. La Fille du régiment (Donizetti)

Two acts; libretto by Jules-Henri Vernoy de Saint-Georges and Jean-François-Alfred Bayard; Paris, Opéra-Comique, February 11, 1840.

At the Salle des Nouveautés on February 11, 1840, the original cast of this, the first of Donizetti's French operas, was: Juliette Borghese (Marie), Mlle Boulanger (La Marquise), Mlle Blanchard (La Duchesse), M. Henry (Sulpice), Mécène Marié de l'Isle (Tonio), M. Ricquier (Hortensius), M. Léon (Un Notaire), and M. Palianti (Un Soldat). On January 12, 1841, the Comique presented its fiftieth performance of the opera, with the original cast. The one-thousandth Comique singing took place on January 2, 1908. It had been sung at the Comique 1,044 times up to 1950, 110 of them in this century, the last on December 6, 1914, when the Salle Favart was reopened to give its first wartime performance.

The first performance outside France appears to have been at Copenhagen, in Danish, on October 6, 1840. But the Italians heard what came to be known as *La Figlia del reggimento* at Milan, in Italian, later that same month (October 30). New Orleans was the first American city in which the opera was produced—in French, March 6, 1843. New York heard it, again in French, on July 19, 1843; in English on June 5, 1844; and in German on

---

[1] During a season of German opera at the Academy of Music conducted by Walter Damrosch, Katharina Klafsky made her New York debut as Leonore in *Fidelio* on the opening night, March 2, 1896.

May 15, 1855. An English version was presented in San Francisco in 1854. The opera reached London, Her Majesty's Theatre, in Italian, on May 27, 1847,[1] with Jenny Lind as Marie. Henriette Sontag was much admired in this role in London, and Adelina Patti sang it at Covent Garden in 1863. Désirée Artôt, to whom Tchaikovsky once proposed marriage, appeared at Covent Garden as Marie in 1864. The opera has not been sung at Covent Garden for almost a century.

La Fille du régiment entered the Metropolitan repertoire on January 6, 1902, on a double bill with *Cavalleria rusticana*. Philippe Flon conducted. The Marie was Marcella Sembrich, and others in the cast were Thomas Salignac (Sulpice) and Eugène Dufriche (Hortensius). Much the same cast was heard on March 20, 1903, when the other opera on the double bill was Dame Ethel Smyth's *Der Wald,* the only opera composed by a woman ever staged at the Metropolitan. During the brightest days of Oscar Hammerstein's Manhattan Opera House, *La Fille* was heard there (1909–10) with such a cast as Luisa Tetrazzini, John McCormack, Charles Gilibert, and Maria Duchène. During World War I, on December 17, 1917, *La Figlia del reggimento* naturally reappeared at the Metropolitan, in Italian. Gennaro Papi conducted, and the cast included Frieda Hempel (Marie), Antonio Scotti (Sulpice), and Vincenzo Reschiglian (Hortensius). One war later, on December 28, 1940, Papi again conducted, and this time the stars of the cast were, in her best role, Lily Pons (Marie), Salvatore Baccaloni (Sulpice), Raoul Jobin (Tonio), and Louis d'Angelo (Hortensius). *La Fille* opened the 1942–43 season on November 23, 1942, again with Pons. Since that season, it has not been heard at the Metropolitan.

At the Florence Maggio Musicale of 1933, *La Figlia* was brilliantly staged, with Giannina Arangi-Lombardi, Gianna Pederzini, Beniamino Gigli, and Tancredi Pasero; Gino Marinuzzi conducted. At a La Scala, Milan, revival in 1951, Franco Capuana conducted, and the cast included Caterina Mancini, Miriam Pirazzini, Mirto Picchi, and Nicola Rossi-Lemeni; this was the first La Scala performance of the opera since Toti dal Monte had sung the title role there in 1928. In 1959, the Teatro Massimo, Palermo, heard a fine revival in a production by Franco Zeffirelli. Tullio Serafin conducted, and the leading roles were sung by Eugenia Ratti (Maria), Fiorenza Cossotto (Marchesa), Luigi Alva (Tonio), and Renato Capecchi (Sulpizio).

86. The Flaming Angel (Prokofiev)

Five acts; libretto by Prokofiev, after Valery Bryusov's story; concert performance, Paris Radio, January 15, 1954.

The actual *première* of *The Flaming Angel* is in dispute. There seems to have been no complete performance before that given by the Paris Radio on January 15, 1954. A concert performance conducted by Charles Bruck was heard at the Théâtre des Champs-Élysées, Paris, on November 25, 1954. Fragments from the opera had been heard, also in Paris, at one of the Concerts Koussevitzky, as early as June 14, 1928, and it is possible that records of other performances may still be found to fill in the gap from 1928 to 1954. The stage *première* of *The Angel of Fire* (in Italian as *L'Angelo di fuoco*) seems to have been the production at the Teatro La Fenice, Venice,

---

[1] *Madelaine, or The Daughter of the Regiment,* Edward Fitzball's adaptation of the opera as a play with incidental music, had been heard at Drury Lane on November 30, 1843.

in September, 1955.[1] This was staged by Giorgio Strehler of Milan's Piccolo Teatro, with sets by Luciano Damiani and costumes by Ezio Frigerio. Nino Sanzogno conducted, and the cast was headed by Dorothy Dow (Renata), Rolando Panerai (Ronald), and Enrico Campi (Inquisitor). Much the same production was put on at La Scala, Milan, in January, 1957. Sanzogno again conducted. Christel Goltz was the Renata, Panerai the Ronald, and Gabriella Carturan the Mother Superior.

Italy continued to present *The Flaming Angel*. At the Spoleto Festival of Two Worlds, on June 26, 1959, it was given in a sadly truncated version[2] staged by Frank Corsaro, with sets by Paul Sylbert. Istvan Kertesz conducted, and the leading roles were sung by Leyla Gencer (Renata), Panerai (Ronald), Campi (Inquisitor), and Carturan (Mother Superior). Criticizing the production and performance mercilessly, Andrew Porter ended his report to *Opera* this way: "Perhaps no other work of its time save Strauss's *Frau ohne Schatten* has so much of a claim to be seen and heard."[3]

87. Der fliegende Holländer (Wagner)

Three acts; libretto by the composer, based in part on an episide in Heinrich Heine's Memoiren des Herrn von Schnabelewopski;[1] *Dresden, January 2, 1843.*

Among the principals at the world *première* were Wilhelmine Schröder-Devrient (Senta), Johann Michael Wächter (Vanderdecken), and Karl Risse (Daland). There were only four performances, but after the revival of 1865 Dresden became enamored of *Der fliegende Holländer,* the three-hundredth performance taking place on February 13, 1910. It was the first Wagner opera to reach England, where, at the Drury Lane Theatre, London, it was given in Italian on July 23, 1870, with Sir Charles Santley as the Dutchman and Ilma di Murska as Senta. Emma Albani as Senta and Victor Maurel as Vanderdecken headed the first Covent Garden cast (1877). In America, the *première,* also in Italian, occurred at the Philadelphia Academy of Music, on November 8, 1876, with Eugenia Pappenheim as Senta. The next year, on January 26, Clara Louise Kellogg, ill-supported by a cast of nonentities, presented it in English at the New York Academy of Music. George A. Conly, a former printer, sang the bass role of Daland, Senta's sea-captain father—Miss Kellogg records, apparently without seeing the sardonic humor of the fact, that Conly died by drowning. The *Holländer* was finally presented in the United States in German when the Metropoli-

---

[1] Reporting the occasion for *Opera News,* William Weaver wrote: "In the virtually unanimous opinion of both Italian and foreign critics, the opera was not only a major Prokofiev work but one of the great operas of our century, to be set beside *Wozzeck, Mathis der Maler* and *The Rake's Progress.*" To many it seemed curious that both the Prokofiev and the Stravinsky should have had their first stage performances at a Venetian theater that had first opened its doors in 1792.

[2] The programs carried the following insert: "The Direction of the Festival of Two Worlds informs the public that, for artistic reasons, it has thought it opportune to reduce to four the number of acts in the opera *The*

Angel of Fire, suppressing the two scenes of the fourth act." As the second scene of the suppressed act contains an inn scene in which Mephistopheles cuts up and eats a boy, many spectators felt the more cheated by this arbitrary act.

[3] In 1959 a remarkable recording of *L'Ange de feu* became available. Charles Bruck conducted the orchestra of the Paris Opéra, the chorus of Radiodiffusion-Télévision Française, and a cast including Jane Rhodes, Irma Kolassi, Xavier Depraz, and Jean Giraudeau.

---

[1] For further minutiae of digging among the sources, see the chapter on *Der fliegende Holländer* in Ernest Newman, *The Wagner Operas.*

tan undertook it on November 27, 1889, with Theodor Reichmann, the original Amfortas of the Bayreuth *Parsifal,* as Vanderdecken, Kalisch as Erik, Fischer as Daland, and Sophie Wiesner as Senta. On March 31, 1892, an Italian version brought forward Albani, making her last operatic appearance in the United States, Jean Lassalle singing Vanderdecken for the first time anywhere, and Édouard de Reszke. Milka Ternina or Johanna Gadski was the Senta of some later performances, while Ernestine Schumann-Heink sometimes sang the secondary role of Mary. After dropping the *Holländer* for twenty-three seasons, the Metropolitan revived it on November 1, 1930, with Friedrich Schorr a superb Vanderdecken and Maria Jeritza hopelessly miscast as Senta. Kirsten Flagstad (Senta), Kerstin Thorborg (Mary), Schorr (Vanderdecken), Emanuel List (Daland), and Charles Kullmann (Erik) were the principals of a notable Metropolitan revival in 1937, and this was brought almost to perfection when René Maison replaced Kullmann. Astrid Varnay was the Senta of the 1950 revival; Hans Hotter (Vanderdecken) drew from Olin Downes the remark that "his interpretation was greater than the music . . . Wagner could give him in this early romantic score"—which is not quite fair to, for instance, "Die Frist ist um." Beginning on January 13, 1960, *Der fliegende Holländer* chalked up eight performances at the Metropolitan during the second half of the 1959–60 season, thanks largely to the conducting of Thomas Schippers and to the impassioned teamwork of Leonie Rysanek (Senta) and George London (Vanderdecken), who had sung together in this opera at Bayreuth; they received excellent support from Giorgio Tozzi as Daland.

---

[1] Frederick Gye had wanted to stage *La Forza del destino* at Covent Garden in the 1860's, but had found exclusive rights in England in the hands of Colonel Mapleson.

88. La Forza del destino (Verdi)

Four acts; libretto by Francesco Maria Piave, after Don Álvaro o La Fuerza del sino, by Ángel Pérez de Saavedra, Duque de Rivas; St. Petersburg, November 10, 1862.

At the St. Petersburg *première,* the cast singing *La Forza del destino* included Barbot (Leonora), Constance-Betsy-Rosabella Nantier-Didiée (Preziosilla), Enrico Tamberlik (Alvaro), Francesco Graziani (Don Carlo), Angelini (Guardiano), Achille de Bassini (Melitone), and Bettini (Trabucco). As *Don Alvaro* it was heard at the Teatro Apollo, Rome, on February 7, 1863; two weeks later, also in Italian, it was sung in Madrid (February 21, 1863). This original version was heard in New York (February 24, 1865), in Vienna (May 2, 1865), in Buenos Aires (July 9, 1866), and at Her Majesty's Theatre, London, on June 22, 1867, this last with Luigi Arditi conducting a cast that included Therese Tietjens, Zelia Trebelli, Pietro Mongini, Sir Charles Santley, and Gassie.

Verdi was not happy with *La Forza del destino* and its destiny. In 1869, using the libretto as revised by Antonio Ghislanzoni, he somewhat abbreviated the opera, this revised version being sung for the first time at Milan on February 27, 1869. This version (as re-edited, shortened, mixed up, and generally tampered with) is what is now usually presented as *La Forza del destino.* It was heard at the Academy of Music, New York, in 1881, with a cast including Annie Louise Cary, Italo Campanini, Antonio Galassi, and Giuseppe del Puente. The Metropolitan Opera did not get around to staging the opera until 1918, Covent Garden until 1931.[1]

On November 15, 1918, four days after the *Samson et Dalila* that had marked both the Armistice ending

World War I and the opening of another Metropolitan season, Gennaro Papi conducted the first Metropolitan presentation of *La Forza del destino.* It was a historic occcasion, for it happened that that night Rosa Ponselle (called Poncelle on the program), an ambitious refugee from vaudeville (where she had made up the Ponzillo Sisters act with her sister Carmela), was making her operatic debut as Leonora opposite Caruso's Alvaro.[2] Oddly, in view of the future extraordinary popularity of the Red Seal record (Victor 89001) of Caruso and Antonio Scotti's dramatic singing of the third-act duet, "Solenne in quest'ora," not Scotti but Giuseppe de Luca was the Don Carlo. Others in that remarkable cast were Louis d'Angelo (Marchese di Calatrava), José Mardones (Guardiano), Thomas Chalmers (Melitone), Marie Mattfeld (Curra), Paolo Ananian (The Alcalde), and Vincenzo Reschiglian (The Surgeon). New York liked the opera, and before Caruso died, he had sung in it at the Metropolitan nineteen times. Ponselle sang the role of Leonora for the last time on January 22, 1932 (with Gladys Swarthout as Preziosilla, Giovanni Martinelli as Alvaro, and Mario Basiola as Carlo). After that season, except for three singings in the 1934–35 season with Elisabeth Rethberg as Leonora, *La Forza* lapsed at the Metropolitan for eight years.

When Bruno Walter conducted *La Forza del destino* (with the libretto as revised by Franz Werfel) at the Metropolitan on January 9, 1943, he was presiding over the birth of one of the New York operatic traditions of the next decade: Zinka Milanov as Leonora, often one of the most exquisitely sung (though never one

of the most dramatically convincing) of Leonoras. Others in the cast on that evening were Irra Petina (Preziosilla), Kurt Baum (Alvaro), Lawrence Tibbett (Carlo), Ezio Pinza (Guardiano), and Salvatore Baccaloni (Melitone). When *La Forza del destino* was given on November 10, 1952, to open the season, Milanov was still the Leonora, but Richard Tucker was the Alvaro, Leonard Warren the Carlo, and Cesare Siepi the Guardiano. In *The New York Times,* Olin Downes noted that the opera was performed in a mixture of the 1862 and 1869 versions.

After the 1957–58 season, *La Forza del destino* went unsung at the Metropolitan until February 1, 1960, when a changed cast showed Leonie Rysanek as Leonora, Mignon Dunn as Preziosilla, Tucker as Alvaro, Ettore Bastianini as Carlo, Siepi as Guardiano, and Fernando Corena as Melitone; Thomas Schippers conducted. For the evening of March 4, 1960, no unusual drama was promised beyond the fact that the Leonora would be Renata Tebaldi (her first appearance of the season) and that Warren would return to the role of Don Carlo. He was also announced to repeat the role on Saturday afternoon, March 12, a performance that would be broadcast. But on the evening of March 4 he had just completed the recitative beginning "Morir! . . . Tremenda cosa!" and the aria "Urna fatale," had acknowledged the audience's enthusiastic applause and begun the ensuing recitative, when he fell to the stage. Roald Reitan as the Surgeon entered to pronounce the phrase "Lieta novella, è salvo." Warren did not answer. Reitan rushed to his side, called out "Help!"—and Schippers ordered the curtain down. At about ten-thirty, after a long wait, Mr. Bing appeared before the curtain to say that Warren was dead. The rest of that performance was suspended. At the March 12 broadcast, the role of Carlo was sung by Mario Sereni.

[2] It was a night of debuts, for Alice Gentle, a Manhattan Opera House recruit, and the tenor Giordano Paltrinieri were also making their Metropolitan bows—in the roles, respectively, of Preziosilla and Trabuco.

After a one-season absence, *La Forza* returned to the Metropolitan on December 12, 1961, with George Schick conducting, Eileen Farrell as Leonora, Helen Vanni (Preziosilla), Tucker (Alvaro), Robert Merrill (Carlo), Jerome Hines (Guardiano), and Fernando Corena (Melitone) (ninety house performances by the end of the 1961–62 season).

The history of *La Forza del destino* at Covent Garden, London, has been shorter and less dramatic. It was first staged there on June 1, 1931, when Tullio Serafin conducted a cast that included Ponselle (Leonora), Gianna Pederzini (Preziosilla), Aureliano Pertile (Alvaro), Benvenuto Franci (Carlo), and Tancredi Pasero (Guardiano). After four performances that season, the opera was heard no more at Covent Garden.

Franci and Pasero also had taken part in the notable La Scala, Milan, performances of *La Forza* in 1928, when Toscanini had conducted, the Leonora had been Bianca Scacciati, the Alvaro, Francesco Merli. At Buenos Aires in 1933, Gino Marinuzzi had conducted a cast made notable by the Leonora of Claudia Muzio and the Alvaro of Beniamino Gigli. He conducted again—and the durable Pasero was still on hand—at La Scala in 1940 when Gigli repeated his Alvaro, the Leonora was Gina Cigna, and the Carlo was Armando Borgioli. The opera continues to be widely and frequently performed on the Continent.

89. Four Saints in Three Acts (Thomson)

Four acts; scenario (An Opera To Be Sung) *arranged by Maurice Grosser from a text by Gertrude Stein; Hartford, Connecticut, Avery Memorial Theater, February 7, 1934.*

The Hartford *première* was sponsored by the Society of Friends and Enemies of Modern Music. The singers, all of them Negroes, included, besides Edward Matthews as Saint Ignatius, Beatrice Robinson Wayne, Bruce Howard, Bertha Fitzhugh Baker, Altonell Hines, Embry Bonner, and Abner Dorsey. *Four Saints* was later given successfully at the Forty-fourth Street Theater, New York, and has been widely performed elsewhere. In 1952 it was sung by a Negro company, headed by Inez Matthews and Edward Matthews, at the Festival of Twentieth-century Art, Paris.

90. Fra Diavolo, ou L'Hôtellerie de Terracine (Auber)

Three acts; libretto by Augustin-Eugène Scribe; Paris, Opéra-Comique, January 28, 1830.

Among the principals at the world *première* were Jean-Baptiste Chollet (Fra Diavolo) and Marie Boulanger (Zerlina). By 1911 *Fra Diavolo* had been given over nine hundred times at the Opéra-Comique, and it is still given in France, Germany, and Italy.[1] It had an early popularity in both England and the United States. John Braham, the first tenor of the age, took over the name role at Covent Garden on November 3, 1831 (the London *première* had occurred on February 1, 1831). In these early days the Zerlina in London was preferably Elizabeth Rainforth or Mrs. Wood (Mary Ann Paton). Angiolina Bosio was a fine Zerlina of the fifties. Later Pauline Lucca showed herself supreme in the role. The final Covent Garden revival (1910) was undistinguished, as befitted an admittedly fading Victorian favorite. In New York, which first welcomed

---

[1] Alessandro Bonci and Tito Schipa distinguished themselves in the name role. Aureliano Pertile and Margherita Carosio headed the La Scala, Milan, production of 1924.

Fra Diavolo on October 17, 1831, the opera had a long career in four languages, in the following order: French, English, German, Italian. Edmond Clément (Fra Diavolo) and Bella Alten (Zerlina) headed the only cast at the Metropolitan; Jeanne Maubourg (Pamela) alone rose to distinction. The *première* was February 3, 1910; after two repeats the opera was dropped.

91. Francesca da Rimini (Zandonai)

Four acts; libretto by Tito Ricordi, after Gabriele D'Annunzio's play of the same name; Turin, Teatro Regio, February 19, 1914.

Louise Edvina (Francesca), Giovanni Martinelli (Paolo il Bello), and Francesco Cigada (Giovanni lo Sciancato) sang leading roles at the London (Covent Garden) *première* of *Francesca da Rimini*, on July 16, 1914. The opera was sung three times, but never was revived thereafter despite a generally favorable reception by press and public. When it was staged at La Scala, Milan, on February 22, 1916, the three leading roles were sung by Rosa Raïsa, Aureliano Pertile, and Giuseppe Danise. Martinelli was again the Paolo at the New York (Metropolitan Opera House) *première* on December 22, 1916, with Frances Alda and Pasquale Amato as his chief associates; Giorgio Polacco conducted. New York was slightly kinder than London: the Zandonai opera won nine performances in two successive seasons. In Chicago, meanwhile, the three principal characters had been portrayed by Raïsa, Giulio Crimi, and Giacomo Rimini. The opera still is frequently heard in Italy, where Gilda Dalla Rizza, Gina Cigna, and Maria Caniglia all have been well-known Francescas. A new production at La Scala, Milan, on May 21, 1959,

was conducted by Gianandrea Gavazzeni, and starred Magda Olivero, Mario del Monaco, and Gian Giacomo Guelfi.

92. Die Frau ohne Schatten (Strauss)

Three acts; libretto by Hugo von Hofmannsthal; Vienna, Opera, October 10, 1919.

Franz Schalk conducted the world *première* of *Die Frau ohne Schatten;* the cast included Karl Aagard-Oestvig (Kaiser), Maria Jeritza (Kaiserin), Lucie Weidt (Amme), Richard Mayr (Barak), and Lotte Lehmann (Sein Weib). Extravagantly admired by some German critics and audiences, it has not won continuing performance outside Germany and Austria. It was staged at Dresden twelve days after the Vienna *première*—and at Berlin on April 18, 1920, when the cast included Karin Branzell. It was sung at the Teatro La Fenice, Venice, on September 16, 1934, by the visiting Vienna Opera Company, and at Rome, at the Teatro Reale, on April 20, 1938, in an Italian translation by Rinaldo Küfferle. La Scala, Milan, mounted it on January 5, 1940, and it was heard at the Teatro Colón, Buenos Aires, in 1949, when Erich Kleiber conducted a cast including Hilde Konetzni, Elisabeth Höngen, and Ludwig Suthaus. Clemens Krauss conducted a Salzburg staging in 1932, with Lehmann, Viorica Ursuleac (Frau Krauss), Gertrud Rünger, Franz Völker, and Josef von Manowarda. A Munich staging in 1954 was conducted by Rudolf Kempe, and the cast included Marianne Schech, Leonie Rysanek, Lilian Benningsen, Hans Hopf, and Josef Metternich.

Die Frau ohne Schatten has not been staged at either the Metropolitan Opera House, New York, or Covent Garden, London. It had been given only in

German-speaking countries and in Italy when, on September 17, 1959, the San Francisco Opera Company presented it at the War Memorial Opera House. Leopold Ludwig conducted, and the cast included Sebastian Feiersinger (Kaiser), Edith Lang (Kaiserin), Irene Dalis (Amme), Mino Yahia (Barak), and Marianne Schech (Sein Weib). The roles of the Kaiserin, Barak, and Sein Weib had been intended for, respectively, Rysanek, Otto Edelmann, and Eleanor Steber, all of whom had had to withdraw because of illness. The production was regarded by many critics as the most important in the thirty-seven-year existence of the San Francisco company. When *Die Frau ohne Schatten* was heard in San Francisco again on September 20, 1960, Rysanek was the Kaiserin, Paul Schöffler the Barak, and Ticho Parly the Kaiser.

93. Der Freischütz (Weber)

Three acts; libretto by Friedrich Kind, after a story in Johann August Apel and Friedrich Laun's Gespensterbuch *(1811); Berlin, Schauspielhaus, June 18, 1821.*

Weber conducted the triumphant *première*. His Agathe was Karoline Seidler; she was supported by Eunicke (Ännchen), Stümer (Max), and Heinrich Blume (Caspar). *Der Freischütz* at once became a craze, and in Germany, at least, its powerful attractiveness has continued. In Berlin it is approaching its thousandth performance. At Vienna, on March 7, 1822, Wilhelmine Schröder-Devrient sang her first Agathe, with Weber conducting. The great John Braham, with a mediocre supporting cast, was the Max of the first London performance (1824). It was the second opera to be sung there in German. At least four, possibly five, versions communicated a *Freischütz* craze to Lon-don the same year; some of them used only parts of the opera. While Weber was there during his fatal last adventure, he rejoiced in Braham's Max, which had a fine vis-à-vis in Mary Ann Paton. After Schröder-Devrient's Agathe (1833), her successors were inevitably placed at a disadvantage, though it was allowed that Marie Stöckel-Heinefetter (1842) sang exquisitely. Frederick Gye's 1850 production had but one satisfactory singer-actor: Karl Formes (Caspar). When Therese Tietjens took over the role of Agathe in the late sixties, her best support came from Sir Charles Santley (Caspar). Emmy Fursch-Madi (1881) was a fine Agathe, but the opera was little heard in London after that. The splendid Agathe of Eva Turner made Sir Thomas Beecham's Covent Garden revival of 1935 a notable event. The 1954 revival, finally, brought Joan Sutherland to the role; Otakar Kraus (Caspar) proved himself a splendid singer-actor.

New York has heard *Der Freischütz* in four languages, in this order: English, French, German, Italian; the first performance took place on March 2, 1825, only four years after the world *première*. The Metropolitan first, on November 24, 1884, gave leading roles to Marie Schröder-Hanfstängl (Agathe), Auguste Kraus—later Seidl-Kraus (Ännchen), Anton Udvardy (Max), and Josef Kögel (Caspar). The superb Agathe of Johanna Gadski could not alone bring audiences to the 1910 revival, and Elisabeth Rethberg, with a perfect voice for the role, found herself in much the same position in 1924 (March 22), though she was finally provided with a reliable Max (April 7) in the person of George Meader. Michael Bohnen (Caspar) and Editha Fleischer (Ännchen) far outdistanced their colleagues in the final Metropolitan try of February 23, 1929. After two repetitions *Der Freischütz* left the Metropolitan; it has not been revived there since.

94. La Gazza ladra (Rossini)

Two acts; libretto by Giovanni Ghe-rardini, after the play La Pie voleuse, *by Jean-Marie-Théodore Baudouin d'Au-bigny and Louis-Charles Caigniez; Mi-lan, Teatro alla Scala, May 31, 1817.*

Stendhal called the first night of *La Gazza ladra* the most successful he had ever attended. Besides running up and down the length of the Italian peninsula very quickly, the opera was soon being played, in several languages, in Ger-many, Vienna, Budapest, Spain, Lisbon, Amsterdam, St. Petersburg, Paris and Lille, Dublin, Brussels, Cluj, Copen-hagen, Warsaw, Riga, Mexico City, Edinburgh, Buenos Aires, Santiago, Lima, Switzerland, Malta, Stockholm, and Constantinople. It held its place on Italian stages past the middle of the nineteenth century.

New York first heard *La Gazza ladra* in French, on August 28, 1830. On No-vember 18, 1833, the Italian Opera House, at Church and Leonard streets, New York, the first theater built there specifically for producing opera, opened with a performance of this opera. The theater was a joint project of Lorenzo da Ponte and the Chevalier Riva-Finoli. An English translation was sung in New York on January 14, 1839. It is to be noted that the first singing in America, in French, had taken place in Philadel-phia in October, 1827. The opera has never been staged at the Metropolitan in New York.

The first London presentation, in Ital-ian, was staged at the Haymarket Thea-tre on March 10, 1821. Covent Garden heard it on February 4, 1830, as *Ninetta,*

or The Maid of Palaiseau, the music adapted by Sir Henry Rowley Bishop, the English translation by Edward Fitz-ball. Pippo, the leading role, was sung at the 1821 *première* by Lucia Elizabeth Vestris,[1] at the 1830 English perform-ance by Mary Anne Paton. The role was later sung at Covent Garden by both Marietta Alboni and Adelina Patti. The widespread revival of interest in Rossini's operas since World War II strangely has produced few revivals of *La Gazza ladra,* which so shrewd a judge as Francis Toye has judged "one of the most likely, perhaps, to repay the trouble of resuscitation." It was sung in concert performance by what was then called the American Chamber Opera Society (the word Chamber later was dropped) at Town Hall, New York, on March 10, 1954. Arnold U. Gamson conducted, and the chief roles were sung by Jean Schneck (Pippo), Ruth Kobart (Lucia), Laurel Hurley (Ninetta), Lee Cass (Fabrizio Vingradito), Lawrence Avery (Isacco), Charles Anthony (Gi-anetto), and Salvatore Baccaloni (The Podestà).

95. Gianni Schicchi (Puccini)

One act; libretto by Giovacchino For-zano, who based his text on a hint from Dante (Commedia I, xxx, 32ff.); pro-duced as the third of the three one-act operas that together are called Il Trittico *(q.v., No. 235), New York, Metropoli-tan Opera House, December 14, 1918.*

Florence Easton (Lauretta), Giu-seppe de Luca (Gianni Schicchi), Giulio Crimi (Rinuccio), and Adamo Didur (Simone) participated in the world *pre-mière. Gianni Schicchi* at once showed

[1] Madame Vestris, as she was usually called, was a granddaughter of the renowned Italian engraver Francesco Bartolozzi. Her second husband was Charles James Mathews, with whom she managed Covent Garden from 1839 to 1842 and the Lyceum Theatre from

1847 to 1854. Her stage name derived from her having married, at the age of sixteen, the dancer Armand Vestris, grandson of the *dieu de la danse.* She was a fine contralto, especially fitted for comic roles.

a vitality of its own; its popularity is chiefly limited by the necessity of having a fine singing actor available for the role of Gianni. Edward Johnson, Nino Martini, and Giacomo Lauri-Volpi successively sang the role of Rinuccio. A truly superb performance, on January 6, 1944, presented Licia Albanese (Lauretta), Salvatore Baccaloni (Gianni), Martini (Rinuccio), and Virgilio Lazzari (Simone). In the late 1940's, Italo Tajo was a bad choice for Gianni, being as absurd a caricature as Lawrence Tibbett had been in his earlier try.

As the third opera in the Covent Garden, London, production of *Il Trittico* (June 18, 1920), *Gianni Schicchi* enlisted Gilda Dalla Rizza, Ernesto Badini, and Thomas Burke as the chief principals. Heddle Nash became a fine Rinuccio, but the history of *Gianni Schicchi* at Covent Garden must in the main be a tribute to Badini's Gianni Schicchi.

96. La Gioconda (Ponchielli)

Four acts; libretto by Arrigo Boito (under his pseudonym of Tobia Gorrio), after Victor Hugo's Angelo, tyran de Padoue; Milan, Teatro alla Scala, April 8, 1876.

Although the cast of the world *première* was not of the first brilliance, later performances of *La Gioconda* often attracted the best voices of the age. The New York constellations have been, on the whole, more glittering than the London ones. It was "the single unfamiliar work of the first Metropolitan season" (December 20, 1883); thus Irving Kolodin, who adds that at the Metropolitan it was "perpetually revived, but rarely vivified," the brutal truth. Christine Nilsson (Gioconda), Emmy Fursch-Madi (Laura), Sofia Scalchi (La Cieca), Roberto Stagno (Enzo Grimaldo), Giu-

seppe del Puente (Barnaba), and Franco Novara (Alvise Badoero) introduced the opera at the Metropolitan. After three performances it was dropped for twenty years. Then, on November 28, 1904, Lillian Nordica, Louise Homer, Edyth Walker, Enrico Caruso, Eugenio Giraldoni, and Pol Plançon constituted an unquestionably star cast, though Giraldoni, who had created the role of Scarpia at the world *première* of *Tosca,* disappointed. The opera was dropped for four years, after eight performances in two seasons. In 1909 it returned for six seasons (there had been a notable revival at Oscar Hammerstein's Manhattan Opera House, on November 4, 1907, with Nordica, Eleanora de Cisneros, Jeanne Gerville-Réache, Giovanni Zenatello, Mario Ancona, and Adamo Didur). The six seasons were informed by the fervor of Arturo Toscanini, whose weakness for agreeable, second-rate operas of his native Italy was joined to an understanding of other, more profound matters. At any rate, *La Gioconda* blossomed under his baton, besides which it opened the 1909–10 season, with Emmy Destinn, Homer, Anna Meitschik, Caruso, Pasquale Amato, and Andrés de Segurola. Later, Margarete Matzenauer was much admired as La Cieca, Margarete Ober equally admired as Laura. With Toscanini's departure, this popular opera also departed, and for a decade. In the revival of 1924, Florence Easton was the new Gioconda, Beniamino Gigli the new Enzo. The new run of *La Gioconda* was to be, and was to remain, unprecedented: eleven seasons, with very few unified productions. Rosa Ponselle's Gioconda and Gigli's Enzo were soon to become musts for the seasoned operagoer, with irritating false notes, quite literally, in the choice of and performances given by some of the other artists. Ezio Pinza became a notable Barnaba or Alvise, and Titta Ruffo an authoritative Barnaba. Gladys Swarthout inaugurated her

Metropolitan career as a very intelligent La Cieca (November 15, 1929). Three years later, Rose Bampton, then a fine contralto or, as W. J. Henderson described her, a "rich, powerful, sensitive mezzo-soprano," sang Laura at her Metropolitan debut. Bruna Castagna was a great Laura in the revival of December 30, 1939, Zinka Milanov (Gioconda) erratic but capable of splendor at times, and Giovanni Martinelli (Enzo) unassertive. Richard Tucker, previously a successful cantor, sang a superb Enzo at his Metropolitan debut (January 25, 1945), and made the role his own. Leonard Warren became the best recent Barnaba. The opera had had one hundred forty-five house performances by the end of the 1961–62 season.

At Covent Garden, London, La Gioconda has been in the repertoire rarely since its first performance there, on May 31, 1883, with a not uniformly brilliant cast headed by Marie Durand, with Francesco Marconi (Enzo), Antonio Cotogni (Barnaba), and Édouard de Reszke (Alvise). A 1907 revival assembled Emmy Destinn, Louise Kirkby-Lunn, Edna Thornton, Amadeo Bassi, Mario Sammarco, and Marcel Journet; later that season Félia Litvinne was heard as La Gioconda and Giuseppe de Luca replaced Sammarco. The last revival at Covent Garden was as long ago as 1929, with Ponselle as La Gioconda and Aureliano Pertile as Enzo.

It was as La Gioconda, at the Roman Arena, Verona, on August 3, 1947, that Maria Callas made the international[1] debut that launched her cometlike career; in the cast with her on that occasion was Richard Tucker, who was thus making his Italian debut. Another noted Gioconda of recent years, Eileen Farrell, was heard at the Metropolitan Opera in this role for the first time on February 25, 1961.

---

[1] She had previously sung opera only in Greece.

97. I Gioielli della Madonna (Wolf-Ferrari)

Three acts; libretto by Enrico Golisciani and Carlo Zangarini, but translated into German by Hans Liebstöckl (as Der Schmuck der Madonna) *for the* première; *Berlin, Kurfürsten-Oper, December 23, 1911.*

Chicago had the first American performance, the first in Italian anywhere, of Wolf-Ferrari's very successful attempt at *verismo* (little in it is Germanic); the date was January 16, 1912, and the chief singers were Carolina White, Amadeo Bassi, and Mario Sammarco. Less than two months later, on March 5, the same principals appeared in the opera at the Metropolitan Opera House, New York. The response was almost as coruscating as the music. One of the Chicago Opera Association's later casts included Rosa Raïsa and her husband, Giacomo Rimini. The Metropolitan revival of December 12, 1925, showed, somewhat surprisingly, that the critical press had largely changed its collective mind about the qualities of I Gioielli. Yet Maria Jeritza received twenty recalls, Giovanni Martinelli was scarcely less favored, and Giuseppe Danise was criticized only because he seemed rather old for the role of Rafaele the roué. Nevertheless, the work did not survive beyond the season of 1926–27. A Chicago revival in 1940 found, in Dusolina Giannini, a soprano who knew precisely how to sing Maliella's music.

The London story, though similar, profoundly differed because, at Covent Garden on May 30, 1912, Louise Edvina (who created more roles at Covent Garden than any singer after Adelina Patti), Martinelli, and Sammarco were adversely criticized—there seemed to be no doubt that Edvina, whose beauty of voice and perfection of technique were beyond cavil, was too refined for the role of Maliella the vixen. Carmen Melis was better in the role. When the opera was revived for Jeritza in 1926, she was supported by Francesco Merli and Giuseppe Noto. It was then dropped.

98. Giulio Cesare in Egitto (Handel)

Three acts; libretto by Niccolò Francesco Haym; London, Haymarket (King's) Theatre, February 20, 1724.

The cast of the first performance included Francesca Cuzzoni (Cleopatra), Margherita Durastanti (Sesto Pompeo), Anastasia Robinson (Cornelia), Senesino (Giulio Cesare), Signor Bigonsi (Noreno), Signor Lagarde (Curio), Gaëtan Berenstadt (Tolomeo), and Giuseppe Maria Boschi (Achillas). The performance was sung fourteen times up to April 11, and the opera was revived twice during Handel's lifetime. In Oskar Hagen's German revision it was heard at Göttingen on July 5, 1922, the fourth opera of the so-called "Handel Renaissance." In more recent years it has been widely revived in concert performances, most often in truncated "editions" omitting many numbers and even some of the characters. In July, 1952, the opera was revived at Pompeii, in the ruins of the Teatro Grande, in a nineteenth-century version; the cast included Renata Tebaldi, Cesare Siepi, Elena Nicolai, and Gino Sinimberghi. It was mounted at La Scala, Milan, in the 1956–57 season, again adapted and arranged; the cast included Virginia Zeani (Cleopatra), Giulietta Simionato (Cornelia), Nicola Rossi-Lemeni (Giulio Cesare), Mario Petri (Tolomeo), Antonio Cassinelli (Achillas), Franco Corelli (Sesto), and Ferruccio Mazzoli (Noreno). As part of the celebration of the two-thousandth anniversary of the foundation of Basel, Switzerland, the Stadt-theater there staged *Giulio Cesare* in August, 1957; Silvio Varviso conducted, and the cast, studded with guest stars, included Hilda Zadek (Cleopatra), Grace Hoffman (Cornelia), Ernst Hä-fliger (Sesto), Heinz Rehfuss (Giulio Cesare), and Derrik Olsen (Tolomeo). On November 18, 1958, the American Opera Society presented at Carnegie Hall, New York, a version of *Giulio Cesare* starring Maureen Forrester, Elisabeth Schwarzkopf (her New York operatic debut), Cesare Siepi, and the countertenor Russell Oberlin.

Giulio Cesare was one of the four Handel operas (the others being *Admeto, Poro,* and *Ariodante*) staged in 1959 at the Theater des Friedens, Halle, as part of the celebration by the composer's birthplace of the bicentenary of his death.

99. Die glückliche Hand (Schoenberg)

One act (four scenes); libretto by the composer; Vienna, Volksoper, October 14, 1924.

Schoenberg's *Drama mit Musik* was staged at the Vienna Volksoper little more than four months after the Prague *première* of *Erwartung*. The opera had been completed nearly eleven years earlier. This work, in which the composer intended that color dynamics should parallel musical dynamics—increasing orchestral volume being accompanied by a shift in colors from red to brown to green to dark blue to purple—was heard again at Breslau on March 24, 1928. In 1930, seeking a short work with which to precede the New York *première* of Stravinsky's *Le Sacre du printemps* in danced form, the League of Composers chose *Die glückliche Hand.* Both were staged by the League under Leopold Stokowski's conductorial hands at the Metropolitan Opera House on

April 22, 1930. The Schoenberg was played in a set designed by Robert Edmond Jones and was directed by Rouben Mamoulian. The chorus was in the pit with the orchestra, the Chimera was represented by a gigantic bat with outspread wings, and the mimed roles of the three people were done by Doris Humphrey, Charles Weidman, and Charles Howland. Shortly later (June 7, 1930), *Die glückliche Hand* was heard in Berlin. It was heard in England for the first time on December 11, 1957, when the BBC Third Programme broadcast a Viennese recording with Eberhard Wächter singing the role of The Man, with the Vienna Symphony Orchestra and members of the chorus of the Österreichischer Rundfunk under the baton of Michael Gielen.

100. Die Götterdämmerung (Wagner)

Three acts; libretto by the composer, being Part IV ("drittes Tag") of Der Ring des Nibelungen; Bayreuth, Festspielhaus, August 17, 1876, as part of the first Ring cycle. See also Der Ring des Nibelungen (No. 197).

With Hans Richter conducting, principals in the world *première* were Georg Unger (Siegfried), Eugen Gura (Gunther), Karl Hill (Alberich), Gustav Siehr (Hagen), Amalie Materna (Brünnhilde), and Mathilde Weckerlin (Gutrune). As in *Das Rheingold,* Lilli Lehmann sang the relatively unimportant role of Wellgunde. When the Metropolitan Opera, New York, first staged *Götterdämmerung* on January 25, 1888, with Anton Seidl conducting, the cast was: Albert Niemann (Siegfried), Adolf Robinson (Gunther), Emil Fischer (Hagen), Rudolph von Milde (Alberich), Lehmann (Brünnhilde), Auguste Seidl-Krauss—the conductor's wife (Gutrune), Sophie Traubmann (Woglinde), Marianne Brandt (Well-

gunde), and Louise Meisslinger (Flosshilde). The Norn and Waltraute scenes were omitted.

At the first London *Götterdämmerung,* on May 9, 1882, at Her Majesty's Theatre, Heinrich Vogl (Siegfried), Heinrich Wiegand (Gunther), and Therese Vogl (Brünnhilde) were among the principals. Gustav Mahler conducted the first Covent Garden production (July 13, 1892), featuring Katharina Klafsky (Brünnhilde), Kathi Bettaque (Gutrune), Ernestine Schumann-Heink (Waltraute), Max Alvary (Siegfried), Theodor Reichmann (Wotan), and Heinrich Wiegand (Hagen).

101. Goyescas (Granados)

One act (three scenes); libretto by Fernando Periquet y Zuaznabar; New York, Metropolitan Opera House, January 28, 1916.

The composer was present when, on January 28, 1916, the Metropolitan staged *Goyescas,* the first opera in Spanish ever to be sung there. Gaetano Bavagnoli conducted, and the cast consisted of: Anna Fitziu, making her Metropolitan debut (Rosario), Flora Perini (Pepa), Giovanni Martinelli (Fernando), Giuseppe de Luca (Paquiro), and Max Bloch (Public Singer). The work was performed five times and then dropped from the Metropolitan repertoire. It was heard at the Opéra, Paris, in French, on December 17, 1919; at La Scala, Milan, in Italian, on December 28, 1937; and has had occasional later performances in Spain and elsewhere.

102. Guillaume Tell (Rossini)

Four acts; libretto derived from Schiller's Wilhelm Tell by Victor-Joseph Étienne de Jouy and later worked on by Hippolyte-Louis-Florent Bis; Paris, Opéra, August 3, 1829. Three-act version first presented at the Opéra on June 1, 1831.

Rossini's last opera, heard fifty-six times in its first season, ran up one hundred performances at the Opéra in five years; on February 10, 1868, the year of his death, it was sung there for the five-hundredth time, and by 1912 the total had reached 868. It was sung in Italian for the first time in Paris, Théâtre-Italien, on December 26, 1836. During the nineteenth century, its popularity was truly world-wide (it was heard in such unlikely places as Soerabaja, Java, and Malta), and it was translated into numerous languages, appearing under an astonishing variety of titles, many of them designed to cover up its political implications.

The original cast of *Guillaume Tell* included Laure Cinti-Damoreau (Mathilde), Adolphe Nourrit (Arnold), Nicholas Levasseur (Walter), and Dabadie (Tell). On April 17, 1837, Gilbert-Louis Duprez made his triumphant debut at the Opéra as Arnold. In London, *Tell* was first heard at Drury Lane, in English, as *Hofer, or The Tell of the Tyrol,* the text being by James Robinson Planché, the librettist of Weber's *Oberon,* the music having been arranged by Sir Henry Rowley Bishop. London heard Bishop's arrangement, but with a new text by Alfred Bunn, at Drury Lane, on December 3, 1838. The Italian version finally reached London, Her Majesty's Theatre, on July 11, 1839. When a company from the Théâtre Royal, Brussels, visited Covent Garden in 1845, the French original (in cut form) was sung on June 13 to open the season. In 1848, the resident Covent Garden company presented *Tell* in Italian, with a cast including Jeanne Castellan (Mathilde), Gustave Roger (Arnold), and Antonio Tamburini (Tell). Becoming something of a fixture at Covent Garden, the opera was used to inaugurate the 1854 sea-

son, on April 1, when the role of Mathilde was sung by Mlle Marai, that of Arnold by Enrico Tamberlik, and Tell by Giorgio Ronconi. In later Covent Garden performances, Marie Miolan-Carvalho was heard as Mathilde, and both Jean-Baptiste Faure and Victor Maurel as Tell. The most recent London performance of the opera seems to have been that at the London Opera House in 1911.

Guillaume Tell was heard in New York, in English, on September 19, 1831, in French on June 16, 1845, in Italian on April 9, 1855, and in German on April 18, 1866. It was also heard in New Orleans, in French, on December 13, 1842. On November 28, 1884, during the Metropolitan's second (and first all-German) season, *Tell,* under the untiring baton of Leopold Damrosch, was sung by the following cast: Marie Schröder-Hanfstängl (Mathilde), Marianne Brandt (Hedwig), Anna Slach (Jemmy), Anton Udvardy (Arnold), Adolf Robinson (Tell), Josef Kögel (Walter Furst), Josef Miller (Melchthal), Ludwig Wolf (Leuthold), Emil Tiferro (Fisherman), Josef Staudigl Jr. (Gessler), and Otto Kemlitz (Rudolf). Ten years later, almost to a day (November 21, 1894), *Tell* was the occasion of a contretemps on the second night of a Metropolitan season. Libia Drog, a well-equipped young Italian soprano, substituting at the last moment for Lucille Hill, forgot the words of Mathilde's famous florid aria in Act II, "Selva opaca," better known by its opening words in French, "Sombre forêt." It took all the efforts of Francesco Tamagno (Arnold) and Mario Ancona (Tell) to save the evening. Yet Signorina Drog sang the name role of *Aïda* the very next night with perfect composure. On the night of her misfortune, the Jemmy had been Mathilde Bauermeister, the Walter Furst, Édouard de Reszke, and the Gessler, Pol Plançon.

On January 5, 1923, *Tell* was revived in Italian at the Metropolitan. Gennaro

Papi conducted,[1] and the cast included Rosa Ponselle (Mathilde), Giovanni Martinelli (Arnold), Giuseppe Danise (Tell), Adamo Didur (Gessler), Angelo Bada (Rudolf), José Mardones (Walter Furst), and Louis d'Angelo (Melchthal). In the next season, Elisabeth Rethberg also sang the role of Mathilde. In these two seasons, nine performances were given. The opera was revived again on March 21, 1931, when Tullio Serafin conducted and the cast included Editha Fleischer (Mathilde), Giacomo Lauri-Volpi (Arnold), Giuseppe Danise (Tell), Ezio Pinza (Walter Furst), and Pavel Ludikar (Gessler); at the only repetition that season, Léon Rothier assumed the role of Walter Furst. With the fourth singing of this revival (December 5, 1931), *Tell* disappeared from the Metropolitan repertoire.

Beginning with a revival at La Scala, Milan, in 1930, and at Rome the same year (with Giannina Arangi-Lombardi as Mathilde), *Tell* has continued to show new signs of life. The Paris Opéra restaged it in 1932, with a cast that included Eidé Noréna, Albert Huberty, and Marcel Journet. Robert Heger conducted a Berlin revival in 1934, the singers including Helge Roswaenge, Michael Bohnen, and Alexander Kipnis. It has been staged twice at the Florentine Maggio Musicale—in 1939, with Gino Marinuzzi conducting, and a cast including Gabriella Gatti, Todor Mazaroff, Alexander Sved, and Tancredi Pasero, and under Tullio Serafin in 1952, with Renata Tebaldi, Kurt Baum, and Nicola Rossi-Lemeni (who, though a bass, sang the role of Tell). *Tell* opened the season at the outdoor Terme di Caracalla, Rome, on June 27, 1957; Gabriele Santini conducted, and the cast was headed by Marcella Pobbe (Mathilde), Mario Filippeschi (Arnold), and Giuseppe Taddei (Tell). A scratch

group trying *Tell* at Drury Lane Theater, London, on February 28, 1958, skirted disaster when the Mathilde, Onelia Fineschi, met difficulties and had to skip "Sombre forêt." A concert performance of *Tell* at Philharmonic Hall, New York, was announced for March 18, 1963, by the Concert Opera Association, Thomas Scherman conducting, with the New York debuts of Gré Brouwenstijn and Rolf Björling.

103. Halka (Moniuszko)

Two acts (later four); libretto by Wlodzimierz Wolski, after a story by Kazimierz Wójcicki; first public performance at Vilna, February 16, 1854, in four acts (the original two-act version had been given by amateurs at the Sala Miller, Vilna, on December 20, 1847).

This is the most popular of Polish operas; it received its thousandth performance at Warsaw in 1935. It was given in New York, in Russian, in June 1903, and revived at Mecca Temple, New York, in Polish, on February 18, 1940. It has had frequent performances throughout Poland and the rest of Central Europe, as in foreign cities with large Polish populations. In August, 1912, it was sung at Cracow, Poland, in a translation into Esperanto by Antoni Grabowski. A rare American performance, in Polish, was staged at Milwaukee, Wisconsin, on May 13, 1923.

104. Hamlet (Thomas)

Five acts; libretto by Jules Barbier and Michel Carré, after Shakespeare; Paris, Opéra, March 9, 1868.

With Jean-Baptiste Faure as Hamlet, and Christine Nilsson—in 1868, as Ophélie, probably supreme among sopranos —*Hamlet* did brilliantly at first, but soon slowed down: in rather more than thirty years the Opéra showed it three hundred times—it was slow as compared with *Mignon*. Thomas had had the cour-

---

[1] Exercising the conductor's immemorial right to outguess the composer, Papi played the well-known Overture before Act II.

age to make his hero a baritone, and he needed a sequence of great baritones to keep Hamlet on the boards. Such, of course, was Faure. Great, too, were Jean Lassalle and Victor Maurel, who helped to make the opera familiar to audiences during the last three decades of the nineteenth century. Such baritones could make the interpolated Drinking Song convincing. So, too, could the great Italian baritone Titta Ruffo, who, making his New York debut on November 19, 1912, at the Metropolitan (with, however, the Philadelphia-Chicago Opera Company), broke a long-standing house rule by encoring this elegantly Parisian prayer to Bacchus. Obviously, Ophélie's florid Mad Scene wants a Sembrich or a Melba to make it anything more than a too, too difficult race to run.

Mounted at Covent Garden by the Gye-Mapleson coalition, *Hamlet* was first heard in London on June 19, 1869 (in Italian), with Nilsson (Ofelia), Clarice Sinico (Gertrude), and Sir Charles Santley (Amleto). Successive heroines were Ilma de Murska, Therese Tietjens, Emma Albani (who sang the role for several seasons), Nellie Melba, and Emma Calvé. Despite Clarence Whitehill's fine Hamlet of Beecham's 1910 season, the opera thereafter vanished from the Covent Garden repertoire. It had a similar fate in New York, which it first reached on March 22, 1872 (in Italian). That was the language of the Metropolitan *première* (during its first season), when Marcella Sembrich, Sofia Scalchi, and Giuseppe Kaschmann starred. Marie Van Zandt, Giulia Ravogli (Gertrude), Lassalle, and Édouard de Reszke made a strong cast in 1892. Melba, Calvé, and Clementine de Vere were the last interpreters of Ophélie. After 1896 *Hamlet* was not again heard at the Metropolitan. Nevertheless, it cannot be considered without vitality. The great baritone Mattia Battistini was playing the name role triumphantly long after *Hamlet* had ceased to find favor in the United States and England.

105. Hans Heiling (Marschner)

Three acts; libretto by Eduard Devrient; Berlin, Königliches Opernhaus, May 24, 1833.

One of the curiosities of operatic history is that this, one of the most significant works of pre-Wagnerian romanticism, has never been given in either the United States or England. Nevertheless, Marschner's earlier *Der Vampyr* (1828), translated into English by James Robinson Planché, had had a run of sixty performances at the Lyceum Theater, London, from August 25, 1829.

106. Hänsel und Gretel (Humperdinck)

Three acts; libretto by Adelheid Wette, the composer's sister, after a fairy tale by the brothers Grimm; Weimar, Hoftheater, December 23, 1893.

The opera immediately became epidemic throughout Germany, and in Berlin alone had been performed more than three hundred times by 1925. Translated into English by Constance Bache, it was given at Daly's Theatre, London, on December 26, 1894, with Marie Elba (Hänsel), Jeanne Drouste (Gretel), and Edith Miller (Witch). The first Covent Garden performances (1896) were also in English, with Elba, Jessie Huddleston, and Lilian Tree in the aforementioned roles, Luise Meisslinger (Mother), and David Bispham (Father). It was not given in German until 1901 (Covent Garden). Later Frieda Hempel was an admired Gretel, and in 1922 was so charming as Hänsel that the opera was given twelve times. In 1936 Maggie Teyte as Hänsel had, in Irene Eisinger, an admirable Gretel.

As a thrice-convinced Wagnerian, Anton Seidl was instrumental in bringing *Hänsel und Gretel* to New York by October 8, 1895, but only as far as Daly's, with a "poorish" cast. The Metropolitan first mounted it on November 25, 1905, with Lina Abarbanell, Bella Alten, Louise Homer, Marion Weed, and Otto Goritz as the principals; Alfred Hertz conducted. For a few seasons, beginning with Humperdinck's visit in 1910, the tenor Albert Reiss sang the Witch, but in 1916 Homer took over her old chore, with Raymonde Delaunois (Hänsel) and Mabel Garrison (Gretel). For the Christmas season of 1927, the Metropolitan had Joseph Urban redesign the stage sets for *Hänsel und Gretel;* the carefully picked cast was excellent: Editha Fleischer, Queena Mario, Dorothee Manski (debut; she remained a most popular Witch), Gustav Schützendorf, and Gertrude Wakefield. The same principals appeared on Christmas Day 1931, when this holiday staple was the first complete opera ever broadcast, by NBC, in the United States. (As early as January 6, 1923, *Hänsel und Gretel* had been the first opera ever broadcast in Europe: from Covent Garden, with Doris Lemon, Lillian Stanford, and Sydney Russell [Witch].) The switch to the English version on December 27, 1946, brought forward Risë Stevens, Nadine Conner, Thelma Votipka, John Brownlee, and Claramae Turner in leading roles. *Hänsel und Gretel* has not been heard at the Metropolitan since a matinee on December 28, 1947; on that occasion Max Rudolf conducted, the language was English, and the leading roles were sung by the singers who had been heard in them the preceding season.

107. Háry János (Kodály)

*Prologue, five parts, and an epilogue (sometimes reduced to three acts); libretto by Béla Paulini and Zsolt Har-*sányi, *after a poem by János Garay; Budapest, Royal Opera, October 16, 1926.*

Although the success of *Háry János* as a staged opera has been confined largely to Hungary, it has had a few performances elsewhere. For a staging at Cologne on September 26, 1931, its text was translated into German by Rudolf Stephan Hoffmann. Andreas Böhm and Ira Malaniuk had leading roles when *Háry János* was presented at Zurich in 1950. What appears to have been the first American production was seen at the Juilliard School of Music, New York, on March 18, 1960, in an English translation by David Shaber and Peggy Simon; Frederic Waldman conducted.

108. L'Heure espagnole (Ravel)

One act; libretto by Franc-Nohain (pseudonym of Maurice Legrand); Paris, Opéra-Comique, May 19, 1911.

François Ruhlmann conducted the world *première* of *L'Heure espagnole.* The cast was: Geneviève Vix (Concepcion), Delvoye (Don Inigo), Jean Périer (Ramiro), Coulomb (Gonzalve), and Cazeneuve (Torquemada). It was first heard at the Paris Opéra on December 5, 1921, when Philippe Gaubert conducted and the singers were Fany Heldy (Concepcion), Albert Huberty (Don Inigo), Robert Couzinou (Ramiro), Dubois (Gonzalve), and Henry Fabert (Torquemada). It returned to the Comique on November 7, 1945 (its tenth performance there), with Roger Desormière conducting this cast: Ellen Dosia (Concepcion), Louis Guenot (Don Inigo), José Beckmans (Ramiro), Louis Arnoult (Gonzalve), and Paul Payen (Torquemada). The fiftieth performance of *L'Heure espagnole* at the Comique occurred on March 1, 1950; André Cluytens was the conductor, and the cast was made up of Denise Duval (Concepcion), Charles Clavensy (Don Inigo), Jean Vieuille (Ramiro), Raymond Amade (Gonzalve), and Payen (Torquemada).

The first performance of *L'Heure espagnole* outside France was delayed by World War I until July 24, 1919, when the opera was staged at Covent Garden, London, where audiences responded to it enthusiastically enough to warrant four performances. Percy Pitt conducted; the cast was: Pauline Donalda (Concepcion), Édouard Cotreuil (Don Inigo), Alfred Maguenat (Ramiro), André Gilly (Gonzalve), and Octave Dua (Torquemada). When the opera was heard at Covent Garden again in the summer of 1924, Pierre Renaud was the conductor, Couzinou and Cotreuil were in their former roles, Edna di Lima was the Concepcion, and Edmond Warnery was Gonzalve. Pitt was again the conductor on June 23, 1926, when Fany Heldy sang Concepcion in a cast that also included Fabert, Maguenat, and Cotreuil. Since the two performances of that season, *L'Heure espagnole* has not been sung at Covent Garden.

The Chicago Opera Company staged *L'Heure espagnole* on January 5, 1920 (and this production was heard in New York on January 28), with Louis Hasselmans conducting and the roles sung by Yvonne Gall (Concepcion), Cotreuil (Don Inigo), Maguenat (Ramiro), Warnery (Gonzalve), and Désiré Defrère (Torquemada). The little opera reached the Metropolitan, on a double bill with Peter Cornelius's *Der Barbier von Bagdad,* at a matinee on November 7, 1925. Hasselmans again conducted, and the cast was: Lucrezia Bori (Concepcion), Adamo Didur (Don Inigo), Lawrence Tibbett (Ramiro), Ralph Errolle (Gonzalve), and Angelo Bada (Torquemada). The five performances of that season constitute the work's whole Metropolitan history. It has fared much better in European opera houses. At a semiamateur performance at the Juilliard School, New York, on March 9, 1936, the opera was sung in an English translation by Robert A. Simon.

L'Heure espagnole has been heard in Dutch translation (Rotterdam, 1923), German (Prague, 1924), Swedish (Stockholm, 1925), Hungarian (Budapest, 1928), Polish (Warsaw, 1928), English (Liverpool, 1928), Italian (La Scala, Milan, 1929, with Conchita Supervia as Concepcion and Salvatore Baccaloni as Don Inigo), Romanian (Bucharest, 1932), and Danish (Copenhagen, 1940). The San Francisco Opera Company staged it on October 23, 1945, when Gaetano Merola conducted this cast: Licia Albanese (Concepcion), John Garris (Gonzalve), Alessio de Paolis (Torquemada), Mack Harrell (Ramiro), and Baccaloni (Torquemada). At a revival at the Teatro San Carlo, Naples, in 1952, Cluytens conducted and the Concepcion was Marthe Luccioni.

109. Hin und zurück (Hindemith)

One act; libretto by Marcellus Schiffer; Baden-Baden, July 17, 1927.

Four short operas formed the bill of July 17, 1927, at the Baden-Baden Chamber Music Festival: Hindemith's *Hin und zurück,* a preliminary version of Kurt Weill's *Mahagonny,* Ernst Toch's *Die Prinzessin auf de Erbse,* and Darius Milhaud's *Die Entführung der Europa (L'Enlèvement d'Europe).* Hindemith called his hilarious opera a "film sketch" because it leads up to a climax and then runs backwards to the beginning like a film reversed. It was played at Basel on May 9, 1928, at Prague in December, 1929, at Zurich in 1930, and at Berlin on November 29, 1930. In a Hungarian translation by Markus László, it was staged in Budapest on January 13, 1929. Silent in Nazi-dominated areas during World War II, it has been restaged occasionally since then.

At a Berlin Festival in the fall of 1957, *Hin und zurück* was presented by the Studio der Städtischen Oper, with Hermann Scherchen conducting. This production was repeated in 1958 at Naples. And in July, 1958, the Opera da Camera di Buenos Aires presented the farce at Sadler's Wells, London, during a pair of double bills that included also Georg Philipp Telemann's *Pimpinone,* Cimarosa's *Il Maestro di capella,* and Haydn's *Il Filosofo di campagna.* At Los Angeles on June 6, 1958, City College presented a triple bill of Purcell's *Dido and Aeneas, Hin und zurück,* and Pergolesi's *La Serva padrona,* all in English. Mansouri directed, Leonard Stein conducted the augmented College orchestra, and the stylishly presented Hindemith got an uproarious reception from the audience.

110. Les Huguenots (Meyerbeer)

Five acts; libretto by Augustin-Eugène Scribe and Émile Deschamps; Paris, Opéra, February 29, 1836.

One of the most frequently performed of all operas during the first eighty years after its *première, Les Huguenots* began its career with a stellar cast: Cornélie Falcon (Valentine), Julie Dorus-Gras (Marguerite de Valois), Adolphe Nourrit (Raoul de Nangis), Nicholas Levasseur (Marcel). The opera reached its one-hundredth singing at the Opéra on July 22, 1839, its five-hundredth on

April 4, 1872, its one-thousandth on May 16, 1906. It left the Opéra repertoire after 1,080 performances, in 1914, but was revived there on January 13, 1930, and again on March 23, 1936, this last time with Germaine Hoerner (Valentine), Solange Delmas (Marguerite), Georges Thill (Raoul), Albert Huberty (Marcel), and André Pernet (St.-Bris).

When the first performance of *Les Huguenots* outside France was staged at Cologne on March 21, 1837, it was billed as *Margaretha von Navarra,* thus initiating a long career of aliases designed to disguise the nature of its religious subject; it was to be heard also as *Die Anglicaner und Puritaner, Die Gibellinen in Pisa, Die Welfen und die Gibellinen, I Guelfi e i Ghibellini, Renato di Croenwald,* and *Raoul und Valentine.* The opera had been staged widely on the Continent when it reached Covent Garden, London, in German, on June 20, 1842, with Marie Stöckl-Heinefetter as Valentine and the highly regarded Grete Lutzer as Marguerite. Queen Victoria made her first state visit to the Royal Italian Opera at Covent Garden on July 20, 1848, when *Gli Ugonotti* was sung there, in Italian, by a starry cast including Pauline Viardot-García (Valentine), Jeanne Castellan (Marguerite), Marietta Alboni—Meyerbeer having transposed the soprano role of the page for her contralto voice (Urbain), Mario (Raoul), Ignazio Marini (Marcello), Antonio Tamburini (St.-Bris), and Joseph-Dieudonné Tagliafico (De Nevers).[1] Tag-

[1] This production reached eight performances that season. Of the fifth (August 3), Harold Rosenthal wrote: "(it) was the occasion of Viardot's benefit; the soprano was informed during the morning that Mario was too ill to sing that evening, but that Grisi was only too willing to appear in *Norma* for her rival's benefit if that opera should be substituted. Viardot thanked Grisi for her courtesy and kindness and then asked whether the costumes and scenery were ready to play either opera. On being informed that this was the case, she told the management that Gustave Roger, the French tenor who

had been singing in other operas during the season, was still in London, and that she would ask him to play Raoul in place of the indisposed Mario. 'But,' she added, 'if he cannot do that, *Norma* can of course be given instead, but I will sing Norma.' Roger agreed to appear and sang Raoul in the original French, not having learned the rôle in Italian. Viardot, on her part, demanded a copy of the French words and, during the times when she was not on the stage, quickly memorized as much of the French text as she could, taking up the rôle in that language from about half-way through the opera. The liafico became the St.-Bris when, on May 24, 1849, Giulia Grisi sang Valentine, Dorus-Gras as Marguerite repeated the role she had created thirteen years earlier, and Jean-Étienne Massol was the De Nevers.

Grisi was again the Valentine when *Les Huguenots* opened the first Covent Garden season in the new (present) house, on May 15, 1858. Sir Michael Costa was the conductor; others in the cast included Constance-Betsy-Rosabella Nantier-Didiée as Urbain, Mario as Raoul, and Tagliafico back in the role of De Nevers. The season at Her Majesty's Theatre had also opened (April 13), with *Les Huguenots,* in the presence of Queen Victoria, and with Therese Tietjens making her London debut as Valentine. Mario (by then fifty-two years old) was still the Raoul when, on July 18, 1863, Pauline Lucca made her London debut at Covent Garden as Valentine; the Marcel on that occasion was Karl Formes. Christine Nilsson sang her first London Valentine at Drury Lane in 1874. Édouard de Reszke's first London St.-Bris (a baritone role that he later abandoned for the bass role of Marcel) was sung at Covent Garden on April 26, 1880, and on May 9, 1881, a soprano then billed as Emmy Fürsch-Madier (she became Fursch-Madi the next season) made her London debut as Valentine. During the year of Victoria's Jubilee, Drury Lane mustered this cast for a *Huguenots* on July 11, 1887: Lillian Nordica (Valentine), Marie Engle (Marguerite), Jean de Reszke (Raoul), Édouard de Reszke (St.-Bris), Victor Maurel (De Nevers), and "Signor Foli" (Allan James Foley) as Marcel.

On July 20, 1891, *Les Huguenots* reached two hundred performances at Covent Garden. Five years later, on July 24, 1896, the opera served as the farewell to London opera audiences, after twenty-four years of popularity, of Emma Albani (Valentine); the Marguerite was Nellie Melba. A cast surely equaling that of Drury Lane in 1887 was heard at Covent Garden in 1905 (June 3): Emmy Destinn (Valentine), Selma Kurz (Marguerite), Enrico Caruso (Raoul), Clarence Whitehill (St.-Bris), Antonio Scotti (De Nevers), and Marcel Journet (Marcel). During 1908, the fiftieth anniversary year of the existing Covent Garden house, a July 11 *Huguenots* presented Destinn, Luisa Tetrazzini (Marguerite), Giovanni Zenatello (Raoul), and Vanni Marcoux (Marcel). *Les Huguenots* was last heard at Covent Garden in 1927, nearly eighty-five years after its first performance there. George V and Queen Mary were in the house on May 30 when a very poor performance included Bianca Scacciati as Valentine, Anna Maria Guglielmetti as Marguerite, John O'Sullivan [2] as a struggling Raoul, Mariano Stabile as De Nevers, and Alexander Kipnis as Marcel. The King and Queen departed before the final curtain—after which loud boos were heard from the upper part of the theater.

The New York career of *Les Huguenots* began with a performance in the original French on August 11, 1845; [3] it was heard there in Italian on June 24, 1850, in German on April 23, 1866, and in English on December 6, 1869. But it was not until the Academy of Music casts of the seventies and eighties that New York savored the real quality

excitement engendered by these two artists in the great conspiracy scene produced an atmosphere in the house such as had not been experienced in any of the previous performances; not only were there encores, but solo calls for both soprano and tenor. It need hardly be added that Roger never again sang Raoul at Covent Garden—nor was Mario ever indisposed when *Les Huguenots*

was listed for performance!"

[2] The Irish tenor on whose career James Joyce wasted so much energy.

[3] It had been sung in French in New Orleans on April 29, 1839. Eighty years later, in December 1919, *Les Huguenots* was the last opera sung in the French Opera House before the fire that destroyed it. At that final performance, the Valentine was Eva Grippon.

of the opera. The first noteworthy one was assembled in 1872 by Carl Rosa; it included his wife, Euphrosyne Parepa-Rosa, Theodor Wachtel, and Sir Charles Santley. The next year came Christine Nilsson, Annie Louise Cary, Giuseppe del Puente, and Italo Campanini. The Metropolitan presented *Gli Ugonotti* during its first season,[4] on March 19, 1884; Nilsson was the Valentine, Marcella Sembrich the Marguerite, Sofia Scalchi the Urbain, and the four leading male roles were in the hands of Campanini (Raoul), Giuseppe Kaschmann (St.-Bris), Del Puente (De Nevers), and Giovanni Mirabella (Marcel).

Before leaving the Metropolitan repertoire during the 1914–15 season, *Les Huguenots* was to be sung in the house sixty-one times. When Emma Albani was indisposed on December 18, 1891, her replacement was Nordica (Valentine) making her Metropolitan debut in a cast that included both Jean and Édouard de Reszke. A cast on December 18, 1893, included Nordica (Valentine), Sigrid Arnoldson (Marguerite), Scalchi (Urbain), Jean de Reszke (Raoul), Jean Lassalle (St.-Bris), Mario Ancona (De Nevers), and Édouard de Reszke (Marcel). With the performance of December 26, 1894, Abbey and Grau began the experiment of raising the top price to $7.00 per seat for "seven-star casts" of *Les Huguenots;* that night the seven were Nordica, Melba, Scalchi, the De Reszkes, Maurel, and Pol Plançon. During succeeding seasons, Lilli Lehmann was at times the Valentine, Sembrich the Marguerite, Eugenia Mantelli or Louise Homer the Urbain, Lassalle the St.-Bris. By 1901, however, the "seven-star cast" was beginning to wear thin as an attraction. W. J. Henderson wrote in *The New York Times:* ". . . as for 'Les Huguenots,' what is there in our performances but the im-

posing line-up of celebrities before the curtain at the end of the garden scene?"

But *Les Huguenots* (still as *Gli Ugonotti,* of course) took on a new lease on life on February 3, 1905, when Caruso sang his first Raoul, his colleagues being Nordica (Valentine), Sembrich (Marguerite), Edyth Walker (Urbain), Journet (Marcel), Plançon (St.-Bris), and Antonio Scotti (De Nevers). How little respect was paid to the dramatic aspect of the opera may be judged by the fact that when Sembrich finished singing "O beau pays de la Touraine," the other singers on the stage joined the audience in applauding. Nearing the end of its Metropolitan career, *Gli Ugonotti,* on December 27, 1912, was the occasion of Frieda Hempel's Metropolitan debut (Marguerite); Giorgio Polacco conducted, and others in the cast were Destinn (Valentine), Bella Alten (Urbain), Caruso (Raoul), Léon Rothier (St.-Bris), Scotti (De Nevers), and Adamo Didur (Marcel). With its third performance during the 1914–15 season, *Gli Ugonotti* departed the Metropolitan on February 8, 1915, when the cast included Destinn, Hempel, Mabel Garrison (Urbain), Caruso, Rothier, Scotti, and Carl Braun (Marcel).

The "seven stars" of the revival at La Scala, Milan, on May 28, 1962, were Joan Sutherland, Giulietta Simionato, Fiorenza Cossotto, Franco Corelli, Wladimiro Ganzarolli, Nicolai Ghiaurov, and Giorgio Tozzi. This was, of course, *Gli Ugonotti.*

111. Idomeneo (Mozart)

Three acts; libretto by Giovanni Battista Varesco, after a libretto by Antoine Danchet; Munich, January 29, 1781.

Anton Raaff (Idomeneo), Vincenzo dal Prato (Idamante), Dorothea Wendling (Ilia), Elisabeth Wendling (Elec-

---

[4] During that same season, Adelina Patti sang Marguerite at the Academy of Music.

tra) and Domenico Panzacchi (Arbace) sang at the *première*. Except for a private performance at Prince Auersperg's, in Vienna in March, 1786, the opera was not otherwise given in Mozart's lifetime. It was eventually presented on many German stages throughout the nineteenth century. In 1931, its 150th anniversary, Richard Strauss put forth a somewhat controversial version, as did Ermanno Wolf-Ferrari. In Great Britain, *Idomeneo* was first heard at Glasgow in 1934. Richard Lewis, Léopold Simoneau, Sena Jurinac, and Birgit Nilsson were the principals in the first Glyndebourne performance in 1951. *Idomeneo* first reached the United States in 1947, when it was given in concert form at the Berkshire Festival. A notable concert presentation of the opera took place at Town Hall, New York, on April 24, 1951, when The Little Orchestra Society, with Thomas Scherman conducting, had a cast made up of Camilla Williams (Klia), Brenda Lewis (Idamante), Mariquita Moll (Electra), William Hess (Idomeneo), and Howard Fried (Arbace).

1926; the opera was also heard in New York, at the Juilliard School of Music, February 23, 1933. The first performance in England (in English) seems to have been that given at Oxford by the Opera Club, December 6, 1927. A notable revival was that in the Boboli Gardens, Florence, June 3, 1937, in a version prepared by Giacomo Benvenuti. Later that year (December 23), a version arranged by G. Francesco Malipiero (French text by Charles van den Borren) was staged at the Opéra-Comique, Paris; Gustave Cloëz conducted, and the cast included Renée Gilly (Poppée) and Georges Jouatte (Néron). In New York, the opera has been heard as presented in concert form by the American Opera Society (first performance, February 8, 1953); English translation by Chester Kallman; two-act version prepared by Arnold U. Gamson, who conducted; in a 1958 repetition, the cast included Leontyne Price (Poppea) and Robert Rounseville (Nero). A German version has been prepared by Ernst Křenek.

112. L'Incoronazione di Poppea (Monteverdi)

Prologue and three acts; libretto by Giovanni Francesco Busenello; Venice, Teatro Santi Giovanni e Paolo, late 1642.

This was one of the first—perhaps the first—operas heard at Naples, where it was sung in 1651. The first modern (concert) performance was heard in Paris, February 24, 1905, in a version prepared by Vincent d'Indy. D'Indy conducted the first modern stage presentation, in his own version, at the Théâtre des Arts, Paris, February 5, 1913; the cast included Claire Croiza (Poppée) and M.-A. Coulomb (Néron). The American *première* occurred at Northampton, Massachusetts, on April 27,

113. Intermezzo (Strauss)

Two acts; libretto by the composer; Dresden, November 4, 1924.

At the Dresden *première*, Fritz Busch conducted. Lotte Lehmann was the Christine, supported by Joseph Correck (Storch), Theo Strack, Hans Lange, Lisel von Schuch, and Ludwig Ermold. George Szell conducted a Berlin production on March 28, 1925, with Maria Hussa, Theodor Scheidl, Guszalewicz, and Leo Schützendorf. When Strauss conducted *Intermezzo* in Vienna on January 15, 1927, Lehmann again was the Christine. The opera was revived at the Munich Opera Festival of 1960, at the Cuvilliéstheater, with Joseph Keilberth conducting. The skat game that occurs at the climax of the plot was much admired; the cast included Hermann Prey (Storch—*i.e.*, Strauss himself), Hans Hermann Nissen (Justizrat), Max Pröbstl (Kammersänger), Hanny Steffek (Christine), Gertrud Freedman (Anna), Karl Schmitt-Walter (Notary), Ferry Gruber (Baron Lummer). The United States *première* was scheduled for Philharmonic Hall, New York, on February 11, 1963, by the Concert Opera Association, Thomas Scherman conducting an English version by Alice Hammerstein Mathias, with Phyllis Curtin, Richard Lewis, and Donald Bell.

114. Iphigénie en Aulide (Gluck)

Three acts; libretto by Marie-François-Louis Gand-Leblanc, Bailli du Rollet, based on the tragedy by Racine; Paris, Opéra, April 19, 1774.

The cast of the first performance included Sophie Arnould (Iphigénie), Mlle Duplant (Clytemnestre), Alice Berelli (Diane), Joseph Legros (Achille), M. Larrivée (Agamemnon), M. Gelin (Calchas), M. Durans (Patrocle), and M. Beauvallet (Arcas); Gaëtan-Apolline-Balthasar Vestris, then called *"le dieu de la danse,"* took part in the ballet. The Dauphine Marie Antoinette was in the royal loge. The death of Louis XV on May 10 stopped the opera's successful run after the fifth singing, but it was put on again on January 10, 1775, and ran up a tally of 428 performances at the Opéra by 1824. By 1800 it had also been heard at Lille and in Belgium, Germany, and Sweden, and it has since been performed widely throughout Europe. It reached the Opéra-Comique, Paris, on December 18, 1907, when François Ruhlmann conducted; the cast was headed by Lucienne Bréval, and the

première danseuse was Régina Badet.

Richard Wagner drastically revised the score in 1846, even adding a new character, Artemis;[1] his version was first heard, in German translation, at Dresden on February 24, 1847; it was revived at Zurich as late as October 17, 1936. After its 1847 *première*, however, its most famous production occurred at Vienna in 1904, when Gustav Mahler conducted and the cast included Marie Gutheil-Schoder, Anna von Mildenburg, Erik Schmedes, and Leopold Demuth. The opera's first staging in England occurred at Oxford on November 20, 1933, in an English version by the Reverend John Troutbeck. It was first given in the United States by the Philadelphia Orchestra Association, at Philadelphia, on February 22, 1935, in French; Alexander Smallens conducted, and the cast included Rosa Tentoni (Iphigénie), Cyrena Van Gordon (Clytemnestre), Joseph Bentonelli (Achille), and Georges Baklanoff (Agamemnon). As part of the Florence Maggio Musicale of 1950, *Iphigénie en Aulide* was staged in Italian, with leading roles assigned to Adrianna Guerrini, Elena Nicolai, Gino Penno, and Boris Christoff. Christoff was again the Agamemnon when La Scala, Milan, completed its 1959 spring season with a new production of *Ifigenia in Aulide.* Bernhard Conz conducted, and the cast was filled out by Giulietta Simionato (Iphigenia), Adriana Lazzarini (Clytemnestra), Pier Miranda Ferraro (Achilles), and Nicola Zaccaria (Calchas).

115. Iphigénie en Tauride (Gluck)

Four acts; libretto by Nicolas-François Guillard, after the tragedy by Euripides; Paris, Opéra, May 18, 1779.

In the original cast were Marie-Rosalie Levasseur (Iphigénie), Mlle Châteauvieux (Diane), M. Larrivée

---

[1] Wagner also supplied the familiar Overture with the ending (Gluck's original overture runs without full close into the opening scene) with which it is now always performed in concerts.

(Oreste), Joseph Legros (Pylade), and M. Moreau (Thoas). By 1829, the opera had been sung 408 times at the Opéra. By 1800 it had also been staged at Lille, as well as in Vienna (in German in 1781; in Lorenzo da Ponte's Italian translation on December 14, 1783), several German cities, Stockholm, Copenhagen, and London (in Da Ponte's Italian version, April 7, 1796). It has since been performed widely throughout Europe in many languages and editions. It reached the Opéra-Comique, Paris, on June 18, 1900, when Georges Marty conducted and the cast included Rose Caron (Iphigénie), Mlle Dhumont (Diane), Max Bouvet (Oreste), Léon Beyle (Pylade), Hector Dufranne (Thoas), and Gustave Huberdeau (Un Prêtre).

The first performance in America took place at the Metropolitan Opera House, New York, on November 25, 1916, in a German version arranged (and cut) by Richard Strauss and edited further by the conductor, Artur Bodanzky, who introduced ballet music from *Orfeo ed Euridice*. The cast included Melanie Kurt (Iphigénie), Marie Rappold (Diane), Hermann Weil (Oreste), Johannes Sembach (Pylade), and Carl Braun (Thoas); Rosina Galli danced. The first Italian staging seems to have been that at the Teatro Olimpico, Vicenza, on August 28, 1922; La Scala, Milan, put on a vivid production on March 11, 1937, when Victor de Sabata conducted and the cast included Maria Caniglia and Armando Borgioli. In June, 1957, La Scala remounted the opera, with a permanent set by Nicola Benois, Nino Sanzogno conducting, costumes of Gluck's period rather than Euripides', and a cast that included Maria Meneghini Callas (Iphigénie), Dino Dondi (Oreste), Francesco Albanese (Pylade), and Anselmo Colzani (Thoas).

Iphigénie en Tauride was first heard in New York in the original French in a concert performance at Town Hall on February 15, 1955, by the American Opera Society. Arnold U. Gamson conducted; the cast consisted of Lucine Amara (Iphigénie), Rosemary Carlos (Diane), Léopold Simoneau (Pylade), Chester Watson (Thoas), and Hugh Thompson (Oreste). When the Society repeated the Tauric *Iphigénie* at Carnegie Hall, New York, on January 9, 1962, the listless performance was galvanized into intermittent vividness by the stylish singing of Gabriel Bacquier, in his United States debut (Oreste); Edouard Van Remoortel was the inept conductor, and the cast also included Marilyn Horne (Iphigénie), Johanna Meier (Diane), Simoneau (Pylade), and Morley Meredith (Thoas).

Iphigénie en Tauride was also heard in the original French in a concert performance at Carnegie Hall, New York, on January 19, 1959; Thomas Scherman conducted, and the cast included Gloria Davy (Iphigénie), Margaret Kalil (Diane), Martial Singher (Oreste), Simoneau (Pylade), and Louis Quilico (Thoas). A notable performance of *Iphigénie en Tauride* was heard at Covent Garden, London, on September 14, 1961, when Georg Solti's conducting was greatly praised. The cast was headed by Rita Gorr (Iphigénie); with her were Robert Massard (Oreste), André Turp (Pylade), Louis Quilico (Thoas), and Margreta Elkins (Diane). The production, by Göran Gentele, failed to live up to the music, as did the sets by Carl Toms.

116. L'Italiana in Algeri (Rossini)

Two acts; libretto by Angelo Anelli, originally set by Luigi Mosca in a version presented at Milan, Teatro alla Scala, on August 16, 1808; Venice, Teatro San Benedetto, May 22, 1813.

The cast of the Venice *première* included Marietta Marcolini (Isabella),

Filippo Galli[1] (Mustafà), Serafino Gentili (Lindoro), and Paolo Rosich (Taddeo). This, Rossini's first comic success, was also heard at Rome in 1815 (as *Il Naufragio felice*) and on January 13, 1816 (as *Il Pampaluco*). It was widely performed throughout Italy during most of the nineteenth century. In the first three decades of its existence, it was also sung in nearly forty cities in some twenty-four countries in Europe, North and South America, and Africa—in a total of seven languages (to which Czech was to be added in 1933). It was the first Rossini opera heard in Germany (Munich, June 18, 1816) and in Paris (Théâtre-Italien, February 1, 1817, with Rosa Morandi and Manuel del Popolo Vicente García in the cast).

L'Italiana in Algeri, heard in Italian in New York on November 5, 1832, and in Philadelphia on February 4, 1833, did not reach the Metropolitan Opera House, New York, until December 5, 1919. On that occasion, Gennaro Papi conducted, and the cast consisted of Gabriella Besanzoni (Isabella), Marie Sundelius (Elvira), Kathleen Howard (Zulma), Charles Hackett (Lindoro), Millo Picco (Haly), Giuseppe de Luca (Taddeo), and Adamo Didur (Mustafà). Besanzoni was badly miscast, and the successes were largely reserved for De Luca and Didur. After four performances that season, the opera dropped from the Metropolitan repertoire.

The first performance in England appears to have occurred at the Haymarket Theatre, London, on January 26, 1819, with Teresa Belloc, Giuseppe Ambrogetti, and Manuel del Popolo Vicente García, in Italian. During the Covent Garden season of 1847, Marietta Alboni sang Isabella in a cast that also included Luigi Salvi (Lindoro) and Agos-

[1] Galli, previously a tenor, had made his debut as a bass in the *première* of Rossini's *L'Inganno felice* at Venice, Teatro San Moisè, on January 8, 1812. He went on to become an extravagantly admired *basso cantante*.

tino Rovere (Haly). A noted modern staging of the opera took place at Glyndebourne on June 11, 1957, when Vittorio Gui conducted and the cast included Oralia Domínguez (Isabella), Antonietta Pastori (Elvira), Josephine Veasey (Zulma), Juan Oncina (Lindoro), Thomas Hemsley (Haly), Marcello Cortis (Taddeo), and Paolo Montarsolo (Mustafà).

The restoration of *L'Italiana in Algeri* to a relatively secure position in the modern repertoire dates from November 26, 1925, when, at Turin, the small Teatro di Torino—a joint project of Vittorio Gui and Guido Gatti—opened with a performance of it conducted by Gui. The cast included Conchita Supervia (Isabella), Tedeschi (Lindoro), Vincenzo Bettoni (Mustafà), and Carlo Scattola (Taddeo). Supervia's Isabella was also heard at the Opéra-Comique, Paris, on October 18, 1933, with Tullio Serafin conducting; when she sang the role at Covent Garden on May 16, 1935, Nino Ederle was the Lindoro and the conductor was Vincenzo Bellezza. After Supervia's death in 1936, Isabella was often sung by Gianna Pederzini (Buenos Aires, Teatro Colón, 1938; Maggio Musicale, Florence, 1941; Rome, 1948). But when Gui conducted a revival at the Teatro La Fenice, Venice, in 1946, the Isabella was Suzanne Danco. Giulietta Simionato asserted her claim to the mantle of Supervia when La Scala, Milan, staged the opera in 1953; her colleagues included Mattiwilda Dobbs, Cesare Valletti, Sesto Bruscantini, and Mario Petri. She repeated her success in the role when *L'Italiana,* on November 22, 1957, became the first opera of the opening season of the Dallas (Texas) Civic Opera Company; Nicola Rescigno conducted, and among Simionato's colleagues were Nicola Monti, Giuseppe Taddei, Paolo Montarsolo, and Umberto Borghi. In the Dallas repetitions of 1958, however, the Isabella was Teresa Berganza.

117. Jenufa (Janáček)

Three acts; libretto by the composer, after a story by Gabriela Preissová; Brno, January 21, 1904, as Její Pastorkyňa (Her Foster Daughter); under the title Jenufa, the name of its heroine, it was first performed at the Czech Theater, Prague, on May 26, 1916, and under this title became well known.

The first of Janáček's operas to be staged, *Jenufa* was heard at Brno on January 21, 1904, with a cast headed by Marie Kabelacova, Leopolda Svobodova, Stanek-Doubrovsky, and Prochazka. Max Brod's translation into German—from which most later versions have flowed—was first heard at Vienna on February 16, 1918. The Metropolitan Opera, New York, staged this translated version on December 6, 1924. Artur Bodanzky conducted, and the large cast was headed by Maria Jeritza (Jenufa), Margarete Matzenauer (Sexton's Widow), Kathleen Howard (Grandmother Buryja), Martin Oehman (Laca Kliemen), Rudolf Laubenthal (Stewa Buryja), and Gustav Schützendorf (Mill Foreman). Five performances in one season sufficed. Ernest Newman, then guest critic of the *New York Evening Post*, wrote: "To [the] crude story, Janacek has written music that is obviously the work of a man who, however many works he may have to his credit, is only a cut above the amateur."

Eight performances of *Jenufa* during the Covent Garden 1956–57 season (its first in England) brought to the box office the lowest postwar receipts except those for *Elektra, The Midsummer Marriage,* and *Wozzeck,* a list that seems to suggest little fondness for twentieth-century opera on the part of London audiences. At the first *Jenufa* (December 10, 1956), Rafael Kubelik conducted, and the principal singers were Amy Shuard (Jenufa), Sylvia Fisher, John Lanigan, and Edgar Evans.

Jenufa, like several others of Janáček's operas, is much more popular on the Continent than in either England or the United States. Borrowing the 1956 Covent Garden production, the Chicago Lyric Opera presented *Jenufa* on November 2, 1959. Lovro von Matacic conducted, and the leading roles were taken by Gré Brouwenstijn (Jenufa), Fisher (Sexton's Widow), Richard Cassilly (Laca Klemen), and Robert Charlebois (Stewa).

118. La Jolie Fille de Perth (Bizet)

Four acts; libretto, after Sir Walter Scott's novel The Fair Maid of Perth, *by Jules-Henri Vernoy de Saint-Georges and Jules Adenis; Paris, Théâtre-Lyrique, December 26, 1867.*

Christine Nilsson had been engaged to create the role of Catherine, but broke her contract with the Lyrique in order to create instead that of Ophélie in Ambroise Thomas's *Hamlet* at the Opéra. The role of the Fair Maid was then given to Jane Devriès; M. Massy was Smith; Ralph was sung by M. Lutz. After its *première* and a run of eighteen performances, the opera was not heard in Paris again until it was staged at the Opéra-Comique on November 3, 1890. It was, however, staged at Brussels on April 14, 1868; Bizet attended, and called the performance monstrous. Other stagings occurred at Weimar on April 8, 1883, and at Vienna on May 5, 1883—both in German; at Parma on January 14, 1885, and at Barcelona in September of that year—both in Italian. It was staged in Russian at Kiev on January 2, 1887, and at both Manchester and London (Drury Lane Theatre) in English in 1917. Mina Curtiss reported that the Oxford University Opera Club revived it in 1955 (November 30) and that it was broadcast by the BBC in 1956. It has never been staged at the Metropolitan Opera, New York.

Two performances of *The Fair Maid of Perth* were sung at Covent Garden, London, the first on February 26, 1920, during a season under Sir Thomas Beecham's direction. The Catherine was Sylvia Nelis, and others in the cast were Walter Hyde, Webster Millar, and Foster Richardson; Beecham conducted the first performance, Eugene Goossens the second. Since 1920, *La Jolie Fille* has had astonishingly few performances anywhere.

119. Le Jongleur de Notre Dame (Massenet)

Three acts; libretto (miracle) *by Maurice Léna; Monte Carlo, February 18, 1902.*

Among the leads at the world *première* were Charles Maréchal and Maurice Renaud. Jean was originally a tenor role. Mary Garden took it over so authoritatively that for a time even wise operagoers forgot that she was an innovator. *Le Jongleur* was admirably produced at Covent Garden, London, on June 15, 1906, with Léon Laffitte and Charles Gilibert. It soon was dropped. New York heard the opera by way of Oscar Hammerstein's Manhattan Opera House on November 27, 1908, with Garden as Jean. The finest Chicago cast included Garden, Renaud, and Hector Dufranne.

120. La Juive (Halévy)

Five acts; libretto by Augustin-Eugène Scribe; Paris, Opéra, February 23, 1835.

The cast of the *première* of Halévy's most successful opera included Julie Dorus-Gras (Eudoxie), Cornélie Falcon (Rachel), Adolphe Nourrit (Eléa-

zar), and Nicholas Levasseur (Cardinal de Brogni). Among the tenors of the era, Gilbert-Louis Duprez was said to have been superb as Eléazar, Mario insufferable—possibly because the role gave him too little opportunity to show his good looks. The twenty-four-year-old Marie Bischoff—later a great Wagnerian contralto—made her operatic debut as Rachel at Graz in 1867, and did not change her name to Marianne Brandt for some time.

On April 10, 1835, Donizetti, returning to Naples from Paris—where he had supervised the staging of his *Marin Falliero* and had attended the *première* of *I Puritani* and either the *première* or a very early performance of *La Juive*—wrote as follows from Leghorn to his friend Innocenzo Giampieri: "I saw *La Juive* at the Grand Opéra . . . and I say that I saw it because as for popular music it has none. Illusion is carried to the extreme . . . You would swear that everything is real. Real silver and cardinals who are almost real. The king's armory real, the costumes of the armed men, doublets, lances, etc., real; and those which were false—the doublets of the extras —were copied from real ones and cost 1500 francs each. Too much truth . . . the final scene too horrible and the more horrible because of so much illusion. At Constance [the scene of the opera]! A Jewess, because of her relations with a Christian, is thrown with her father into a caldron of boiling oil. Before it comes to that, we go through a thousand surprises, but everything is rich and everything is magnificent—if one closes one eye."

La Juive reached 100 singings at the Opéra on June 3, 1840; 500 on May 26, 1886; 550 in 1893. It was revived in Paris at the Gaîté-Lyrique on November 21, 1903, and at the Opéra on April 3, 1933. During the year of its first performance it was also sung at Brussels and, in German, at Leipzig. Beginning in 1836, it spread throughout

Europe; it was sung at New Orleans on February 13, 1844. New York heard it before London—in the original French on July 16, 1845. (There were New York performances in Italian in 1860, in German in 1864, in Yiddish in 1921, and in Russian in 1922). When Leopold Damrosch conducted its first Metropolitan performance, on January 16, 1885, the cast included Amalia Materna (Princess Eudoxie), Marie Schröder-Hanfstängl (Rachel), Anton Udvardy (Eléazar), and Josef Kögel (Cardinal de Brogni); in Act III, Schröder-Hanfstängl interpolated an aria from *Robert le Diable*. A performance on December 7, 1887 (matinee), brought together this largely Wagnerian cast: Biro de Marion (Eudoxie), Lilli Lehmann (Rachel), Albert Niemann (Eléazar), and Emil Fischer (Cardinal de Brogni). The opera temporarily left the Metropolitan repertoire after the 1889–90 season.

On November 22, 1919, the Metropolitan revived *La Juive* in French, at a matinee conducted by Artur Bodanzky. Evelyn Scotney was the Princess, Rosa Ponselle the Rachel, Enrico Caruso the Eléazar, and Léon Rothier the Cardinal; also in the cast were Orville Harrold, Thomas Chalmers, Louis d'Angelo, Vincenzo Reschiglian, and Pompilio Malatesta. Caruso was singing his thirty-sixth, and last new, Metropolitan role; Harrold was making his Metropolitan debut. Of Caruso's performance, Irving Kolodin has written: "It was without doubt the most striking artistic triumph of his career. Some quality in the character had inflamed Caruso's imagination; and the impersonation he finally presented was the product of more care and study, especially dramatically, than any of the

thirty-five other roles he sang during his career in New York. It was particularly impressive as the accomplishment of a singer whose position in the esteem of the public was inviolate; and spoke more highly for his development as an artist than any verbal tribute could." A year later, on November 15, 1920, *La Juive,* with the same principals, opened the Metropolitan season; it was Caruso's seventeenth and last Metropolitan opening. On December 24, with Florence Easton replacing Ponselle, he sang *La Juive* once more, his 607th Metropolitan performance. He was a sick man, and this proved to be his farewell to the Metropolitan—and to opera. Eight months later, after apparent recovery, he died at his native Naples.[1]

When Halévy's opera was next heard at the Metropolitan, on December 12, 1924, Easton was again the Rachel, Giovanni Martinelli the Eléazar. At a performance on December 23, 1927, the Rachel was Tullio Serafin's wife, Elena Rakowska. On January 28, 1931, Elisabeth Rethberg sang Rachel. After that season, *La Juive* again left the Metropolitan, not to be heard again until January 11, 1936, when Ezio Pinza played the Cardinal, opposite Rethberg and Martinelli. At a performance nine days later, Marjorie Lawrence was heard as Rachel. With a repetition on January 31, the opera left the Metropolitan repertoire for a third—to date, the last—time, having been sung there nearly fifty times.

Although a spoken version of Scribe's drama, adapted by James Robinson Planché, and with incidental music by Thomas Simpson Cooke, had been given at Drury Lane on November 16, 1835, London did not hear Halévy's opera

---

[1] Comedy as well as tragedy is connected with the American history of *La Juive.* At a performance at the Auditorium, Chicago, in the early 1920's, Rosa Raïsa, until then a passionately doleful Rachel, was the blameless victim of a ludicrous anticlimax in the final scene. Thrown into what purported to be a huge caldron of boiling oil, she bounced practically back onto the stage. A too-coddling stage director had overcushioned her landing by flooring the caldron with some too-elastic material. Even those in the pit, who seldom have any fun, could see Raïsa's death gymnastics.

until July 29, 1846, again at Drury Lane, in French. When it was sung at Covent Garden in Italian on July 25, 1850, the cast included Pauline Viardot-García, Enrico Tamberlik, Karl Formes, and Entimio Polonini. Mario had been announced to sing the Eléazar, but, as Harold Rosenthal has written, ". . . the success of the première was threatened by Grisi's jealousy of Viardot. During the afternoon of the twenty-fifth a message came to the opera house that Mario was too ill to sing. Viardot, remembering the trick that had been played on her two years previously on the night of her benefit, was again ready with a suggestion. [Enrico] Maralti, who had sung Eleazar in Brussels, was available, and he could sing the role in the original French. This he did and his success was even greater than had been Roger's at the famous *Huguenots* performance in similar circumstances. In the second act the tenor raised the house to great enthusiasm and the audience insisted on an encore, much to the annoyance of Grisi who was sitting in full view of the audience in a private box. A regular subscriber was heard to remark as the curtain fell, 'He will never sing that part again.' He did not. Mario had sufficiently recovered to sing at the second performance . . ." *La Juive* was sung five times at Covent Garden that season, twice in 1852 (with Dejean Jullienne as Rachel), and once in 1893 (with a cast including Italia Vasquez, Sigrid Arnoldson, Ferruccio Giannini, and Pol Plançon), and then vanished from the repertoire.

On June 17, 1924, *La Juive* was sung in Jerusalem in a Hebrew translation by M. Freidmann. It does not seem to have been produced in a major opera house anywhere since it was heard in Paris in 1933, San Francisco in 1935 and 1936, and Brussels in 1938. In its first San Francisco Opera Company performance (November 18, 1935) it was conducted by Richard Lert. The cast included Elisabeth Rethberg (Rachel), Emily Hardy (Eudoxie), Giovanni Martinelli (Eléazar), Hans Clemens (Léopold), and Ezio Pinza (Cardinal).

121. Káta Kabanová (Janáček)

Three acts; libretto by Vincenc Červinka, after Alexander Ostrovsky's play Groza; *Brno, October 23, 1921.*

Franz Neumann conducted the first performance of *Katya Kabanova* (now commonly so written outside Czechoslovakia); the cast included Marie Vesela and Karel Zavrel. Staging in Prague followed on November 30, 1922, when Otakar Ostrčil conducted. The German translation, by Max Brod, was first heard at Cologne on November 9, 1922, when Otto Klemperer conducted and the title role was sung by Rose Pauly. The decision by the Sadler's Wells company to produce the opera in 1951 (April 10) had far-reaching effects. Amy Shuard, then a promising young British dramatic soprano, was vaulted to fame overnight, soon to become one of the regular star singers at Covent Garden. The other effect was the decision, because of the opera's success, to invite Rafael Kubelik to conduct the 1954 revival, which action in turn led to his becoming musical director of Covent Garden in 1955. *Katya Kabanova* has been performed frequently throughout Europe since World War II. It received its first complete performance in the United States [1] as part of the Empire State Music Festival, at Harriman State Park, New York, on August 2, 1960. Laszlo Halasz conducted; the partially comprehensible English translation was by Norman Tucker; the cast included Amy Shuard (Katya), Doris Doree (Marfa Kabanova), Giulio Gari (Tichon Kabanov), and Rudolf Petrak (Boris Grigoryevich).

---

[1] An earlier performance, at Karamu House, Cleveland, Ohio, by students, had had only piano accompaniment.

122. Khovanshchina
(Mussorgsky)

Five acts; libretto by the composer after sketches by Vladimir Vasilyevich Stassov, which were given continuity by the composer; St. Petersburg, Kononov's Hall, February 9 (O.S.), 1886,[1] having been completed and orchestrated by Rimsky-Korsakov.

Because *Khovanshchina* was not accepted for production by the imperial theaters until a quarter of a century after 1886, it had its official *première* at the Maryinsky Theater, St. Petersburg, on November 20 (N.S.), 1911, with Feodor Chaliapin in a leading role. Chaliapin also was heard in the Russian company that—under the aegis of Sir Thomas Beecham, but with Emil Cooper conducting—gave *Khovanshchina* at Drury Lane Theatre, London, on July 1, 1913. The opera did not reach the Metropolitan Opera, New York, until February 16, 1950, with Cooper conducting. The cast included Risë Stevens (Marfa), Polyna Stoska (Susanna), Charles Kullmann (Golitsin), Jerome Hines (Dossifé), and Lawrence Tibbett (Prince Ivan Khovansky). This elaborate production was the last new one of Edward Johnson's regime; it did not outlast its first season. It was, indeed, a singular performance, not least in that it omitted the most familiar excerpt from the score, the Act IV entr'acte.

123. The King's Henchman
(Taylor)

Three acts; libretto by Edna St. Vincent Millay; New York, Metropolitan Opera House, February 17, 1927.

Tullio Serafin conducted at the world *première,* and the enormous cast was headed by Florence Easton (Aelfrida), Merle Alcock (Ase), Edward Johnson (Aethelwold), and Lawrence Tibbett (Eadgar). Of the critical press, only Pitts Sanborn saw with the eye of posterity: "For the most part, *The King's Henchman* is based firmly upon Wagner." The work lasted through fourteen performances during three successive seasons, but apparently was not seen elsewhere.

124. Lady Macbeth of Mzensk
(Shostakovich)

Four acts; libretto by Shostakovich and Y. Preiss after the novel by Nikolai Leskov; Leningrad, January 22, 1934.

The title of Leskov's novel and Shostakovich's opera actually is *A Lady Macbeth of the Mzensk District,* but in the Soviet Union it was also referred to as *Katerina Ismailova,* its heroine's name. Two days after the Leningrad *première,* it was heard at Moscow. When it was repeated as part of the First Leningrad Theater Festival, on May 27, 1934, its fame was spread by foreign critics attending. It was heard outside Russia for the first time at Cleveland, Ohio, on January 31, 1935. Artur Rodzinski conducted an aggregation called The Art of Musical Russia and the Cleveland Symphony Orchestra. This performance was repeated by the same forces at the Metropolitan Opera House in New York on February 5, 1935. Despite snow and cold, a line of would-be standees was outside the Metropolitan long before performance time, and *The New York Times* noted that among those present

---

[1] Although Alfred Loewenberg calls this performance "a private one," Rimsky-Korsakov seems to belie this in his autobiography, *My Musical Life:* ". . . let me note a very fair first performance . . . by

amateur members of the dramatic Circle, under [E.] Goldstein's leadership. The opera took the fancy of the public and had three or four performances."

inside were Mr. and Mrs. John D. Rockefeller, Jr., Mrs. Vincent Astor, Mrs. Cornelius Vanderbilt, Arturo Toscanini, and Leopold Stokowski.

One month after a Moscow revival on December 26, 1935, *Pravda* thundered against *Lady Macbeth*, calling the opera deliberately antimelodic and subservient to Western modernism, thus effectively curtailing its previously successful career in Russia. So great was international interest in this first opera of a young man who had become famous far beyond his due that it was staged in Swedish at Stockholm (1935), Prague and Zurich in German (1936), Ljubljana in Slovenian (1936), Copenhagen in Danish (1936), Zagreb in Croatian (1937), and Bratislava in Slovakian (1938). London heard a concert performance of it on March 18, 1936, in an English translation by Michel D. Calvocoressi. The opera was received with scant admiration when it was staged at the Teatro La Fenice, Venice, in 1947, with Nino Sanzogno conducting and a cast that included Mercedes Fortunati, Antonio Cassinelli, and Giovanny Voyer.

Later performances of *Lady Macbeth of Mzensk* have been few. First the score and parts mysteriously "disappeared." Then, when the Deutsche Oper am Rhein, Düsseldorf, "rediscovered" them and produced the opera late in 1959, Shostakovich himself forbade further singings of it. The Düsseldorf production was directed by Bohumil Herlischka and designed by Teo Otto. Alberto Erede conducted, and the cast included Erika Wien (Katerina Ismailova), Rudolf Franci (Serge), and Randolph Symonette (Boris).

125. Lakmé (Delibes)

Three acts; libretto by Edmond Gondinet and Philippe Gille; Paris, Opéra-Comique, April 14, 1883.

Marie Van Zandt, the beautiful Brooklyn soprano for whom Delibes had composed the title role of *Lakmé*, and whom he himself coached, was the hapless Hindu maid of the world *première*. With many rival singers spitefully arrayed against her, she nevertheless secured a clear triumph for herself and immediate success for the opera. Van Zandt, whose Paris career was virtually ended by a never-proved accusation of having appeared drunk on the stage, was not, however, the first New York Lakmé. Pauline l'Allemand, a native of Syracuse, New York, headed the Academy of Music cast which, singing in English, introduced the opera to the United States on March 1, 1886. With her were William Candidus (Gerald), Jessie Bartlett Davis (Mallika), and other Americans of chiefly local eminence. Theodore Thomas conducted. *Lakmé* was not particularly liked, and efforts to restage it were attended by discouraging vicissitudes.

On April 2, 1890, Adelina Patti sang the role of Lakmé once at the Metropolitan, but not with the resident company. Van Zandt tried to endear it to New Yorkers in 1892, but without success, and after two attempts the Metropolitan dropped the item until 1907, when Marcella Sembrich carried it through three performances. Three years later, Oscar Hammerstein made a gallant effort to convince skeptics that *Lakmé* was indeed worth their time, and put the responsibility of proving it onto the shoulders of Luisa Tetrazzini and John McCormack. This also failed, as did Giulio Gatti-Casazza's effort in 1917, with María Barrientos and Giovanni Martinelli. Amelita Galli-Curci, who had won Chicago for *Lakmé*, was an interesting interim interpreter, but it was not until the advent of Lily Pons that Delibes's masterpiece was finally established in New York. She first sang it at the Metropolitan on February 19, 1932, in a performance notable for the advanced dishabille of the ballet. Pons did not elect to sing it after 1947; that year, after a single mediocre performance with Patrice Munsel, it vanished from the Metropolitan repertoire.

Van Zandt had introduced *Lakmé* to London on June 6, 1885. It had a curious career at Covent Garden, where Tetrazzini and McCormack introduced it on June 18, 1910. No one could profitably try to criticize their artistry, but the work itself far from enchanted the British audiences. Yet it was chosen to open the 1911 season—the coronation year of King George V and Queen Mary. After eight performances in these two seasons, the opera was dropped. *Lakmé* can be resuscitated only for a prima donna with a flawless coloratura voice, personal charm, and physical loveliness.

126. Die Liebe der Danae (Strauss)

Three acts; libretto by Joseph Gregor, after an idea by Hugo von Hofmannsthal; Salzburg, Festspielhaus, August 14, 1952.

Die Liebe der Danae was composed in 1938–40. It was to have been staged in 1944, and was in rehearsal when all German theaters were shuttered temporarily because of an attempt to assassinate Adolf Hitler. A dress rehearsal was held, however, with Clemens Krauss conducting (August 16, 1944), and with a cast including his wife, Viorica Ursuleac (Danae), Taubmann, and Hans Hotter. Because of this delay, the official *première* is always listed as that of the Salzburg Festival of 1952, again with Krauss conducting, but with Annelies Kupper in the title role, supported by Josef Gostic (Midas), Julius Patzak, and Alfred Poell. Berlin and Milan performances followed, but the opera has been heard relatively few times since 1952. It was introduced to England during a September, 1953, visit to Cov-

ent Garden by the Bayerische Staatsoper (first of four performances, September 16). Rudolf Kempe conducted (he was replaced at the repetitions by Kurt Eichorn); the singers included Kupper (Danae, a role sung at two of the performances by Leonie Rysanek), Käthe Nentwig, Gerda Sommerschuh, Elisabeth Lindermeier, Antonie Fahberg, Lillian Benningsen, Irmgard Barth, the American Howard Vandenburg (Midas), August Seider, and Ferdinand Frantz (Jupiter). The only London critic who strongly admired the opera was Ernest Newman.

127. A Life for the Tsar (Glinka)

Four acts and an epilogue; libretto by Baron Georgy Fedorovich Rosen; used for the opening of the rebuilt Bolshoi Theater, St. Petersburg, November 27 (O.S.), 1836.

Glinka had first called his opera *Ivan Susanin,* after the peasant who had saved the Tsar at the cost of his own life, but renamed it *A Life for the Tsar* upon dedicating it to Nicholas I. The Susanin of the world *première* was Ossip Afanasyevich Petrov (1807–78), the greatest Russian bass-baritone of the age. His wife, the almost equally famed contralto Ann Petrova-Vorobyeva, was the Vanya. The opera was immensely popular throughout Russia until the 1917 Revolution, until which time it was used to open every new season at St. Petersburg and Moscow. Again christened *Ivan Susanin,* it is by no means dead. Among the oddities of its career, *A Life for the Tsar* was the first opera ever sung in Lettish (Riga, 1886). Also, although it was not given in Paris until 1896, Berlioz had played an air from it in a concert there on March 16, 1845.

As *La Vita per lo czar,* it was sung at Covent Garden, London, on July 12, 1887, and repeated only once, despite a fine cast and a good press. The principals were Emma Albani (Antonida), Sofia Scalchi (Vanya), Julian Gayarré (Sobinjin), and Jules Devoyod (Susanin). Only parts of it were offered at the concert version by the Schola Cantorum, New York, on February 4, 1936.

128. Linda di Chamounix
(Donizetti)

Three acts; libretto by Gaetano Rossi; Vienna, Kärntnertortheater, May 19, 1842.

Linda di Chamounix was the first of two operas that Donizetti composed especially for Vienna (the other, *Maria di Rohan,* was presented at the Kärntnertortheater on June 5, 1843). After its Italian *première* at the Teatro Carignano, Turin, on August 24, 1842, it became exceedingly popular throughout Italy. It was sung at the Théâtre-Italien, Paris, on November 17, 1842, and at Her Majesty's Theatre, London, also in Italian, on June 1, 1843.

During Louis-Antoine Jullien's disastrous Drury Lane season in 1847, he staged *Linda.* The opera was first heard at Covent Garden on April 10, 1849, with Sir Michael Costa conducting, and a cast including Catherine Hayes (Linda), Mlle de Méric, the contralto daughter of Henriette-Clémentine Méric-Lalande (Pierotto), Luigi Salvi (Charles), Antonio Tamburini (Antonio), and Entimio Polonini (Prefect); both Hayes and Méric were making Covent Garden debuts. When *Linda* was heard again on June 6, 1865, Adelina Patti was the heroine, supported by Pasquale Brignoli (Charles) and Giorgio Ronconi (Antonio). Ilma di Murska was heard at Covent Garden as Linda on November 12, 1868, with Sofia Scalchi (Pierotto) and Sir Charles Santley (Antonio). On June 27, 1872, Emma Albani sang the title role, again with Scalchi, but with Ernest Nicolini as Charles: when Al-

bani repeated the role the next year on May 10, Victor Maurel was her Antonio. Patti took up the role at Covent Garden during the 1881 season, during which Édouard de Reszke sang the Prefect. The American soprano Ella Russell was heard as Linda on June 22, 1886. With a single repetition of her performance in 1887, *Linda di Chamounix* left Covent Garden. The last London performance to date seems to have occurred in 1888, when the cast included Emmy Fursch-Madi, Zelia Trebelli, and Vittorio Navarrini.

Linda was heard in New York, in Italian, at Palmo's Opera House on January 4, 1847, with Clothilda Barili as the heroine, and in English on August 4 of that year, when Mme Anna Bishop, the wife of Sir Henry Rowley Bishop, made her American debut as Linda. Numerous performances of the opera were heard in New York later in the century, often with Clara Louise Kellogg as Linda, but the Metropolitan was not stirred to mount it even when Amelita Galli-Curci, on February 4, 1920, sang "O luce di quest'anima" with tripping ease during a Chicago Opera Association visit to the Lexington Theater, New York. Finally, on March 1, 1934, *Linda* was heard at the Metropolitan[1] at a matinee, with Tullio Serafin conducting a cast that included Lily Pons (Linda), Gladys Swarthout (Pierotto), Richard Crooks (Charles), Giuseppe de Luca (Antonio), and Ezio Pinza (Prefect). With a total of seven performances in that season and the next, it vanished from the Metropolitan stage.

Toti dal Monte was heard as Linda at the Teatro San Carlo, Naples, in 1934, and again at a La Scala, Milan, revival on December 9, 1939, when Gino Marinuzzi conducted, the Pierotto was Cloe Elmo, Giovanni Malipiero was the Charles, Mario Basiola the An-

---

[1] It had been heard *in* the Metropolitan in 1890, when Patti had sung the title role there during a series of postseason performances.

tonio, and Tancredi Pasero the Prefect. Margherita Carosio was heard as Linda during the next decade. At Palermo in 1957, Rosanna Carteri sang this role, with Giuseppe Taddei as Antonio, with Serafin conducting. In 1958, the opera was heard at the Teatro San Carlo, Naples, under Franco Capuana's direction, with Antonietta Stella terribly miscast (as her recorded version cruelly proved) as Linda, Miriam Pirazzini (Pierotto), Doro Antonioli (Charles), Aldo Protti (Antonio), and Giuseppe Modesti (Prefect).

129. Lohengrin (Wagner)

Three acts; libretto by the composer; Weimar, August 28, 1850.

Liszt, who conducted the world *première* at Weimar, had not been able to secure first-class singers. Ernest Newman (*The Life of Richard Wagner*, II, p. 233) comments: "All in all, the presumption is that these first performances of *Lohengrin* were hardly on the level of those of a small English touring company to-day."

The English *première,* such as it was, took place at Covent Garden, on May 8, 1875, with Emma Albani as Elsa, supported—unreliably—by one of Patti's husbands, a French tenor who called himself Nicolini. Victor Maurel was the Telramund of a production marred by many un-Bayreuthian cuts. Several days later, Colonel Mapleson staged his version at Her Majesty's. Sir Michael Costa, whose wry sense of humor was provoked by a badly mismanaged swan, to which he referred as "dat goose," held his superior orchestra, cast, and chorus in a firm rein.[1] Christine Nilsson was perhaps not ponderably better than Albani, but Therese Tietjens, the Or-

[1] Nevertheless, Costa used a score and parts that Hans Richter, a few years later, found to contain over four hundred mistakes.

trud, was so far superior to her rival in the Covent Garden cast as to make comparisons irrelevant. Italo Campanini sang Lohengrin superbly, while Antonio Galassi "appeared," wrote Herman Klein, "to step naturally into the part of a Telramund only too ready to hearken to his wicked spouse." When London finally heard *Lohengrin* in German, Rosa Sucher, a future heroine of many Bayreuth festivals, quickly established herself as a thoroughly admirable Elsa, while Hermann Winkelmann, whose English debut was as the Knight of the Swan, was her peer.

As with *Tannhäuser,* America was ahead of England in getting *Lohengrin.* Four years before the London productions, on April 3, 1871, Adolf Neuendorff conducted the New York *première* at the Stadt Theater. Three years later, at the Academy of Music, an Italian version was given by the Strakosch company—in every way superior to the Stadt Theater attempt. With Nilsson and Campanini were associated Annie Louise Cary as Ortrud and Giuseppe del Puente as Telramund. Nilsson and Campanini again headed the cast when, as the seventh offering of its first season, the Metropolitan staged *Lohengrin* on November 7, 1883. The Ortrud of that occasion was the eminent French dramatic mezzo, Emmy Fursch-Madi, the Telramund the Italian baritone Giuseppe Kaschmann.

Almost at once, *Lohengrin* became, in New York, the favorite it has remained, but to all early Wagnerians the announcement that it was at last to be sung adequately in German came as a relief. On November 23, 1885, the occasion being Anton Seidl's debut as a conductor in the United States, *Lohengrin* was given as the opening opera of the season. Seidl's wife, Auguste Seidl-Kraus, was Elsa, while the Ortrud was Marianne Brandt, the Viennese contralto who introduced many late Wagnerian roles in America, and who was unquestionably among the first half-dozen of magnificently voiced, intelligent Wagnerian interpreters. Until Brandt left the company, Ortrud was as clearly her property as it became that of Ernestine Schumann-Heink, who, after using it as her American debut role, in Chicago, on November 7, 1898, likewise chose it for her first Metropolitan appearance, on the following January 9, when her associates were Jean de Reszke (Lohengrin), Lillian Nordica (Elsa), David Bispham (Telramund), and Édouard de Reszke (the King).

The De Reszkes sang Wagner in both German and Italian. *Lohengrin* had been their first Wagnerian opera, when, on June 22, 1888, at Covent Garden, Jean sang Lohengrin, and Édouard the King. It was in these roles that they made their American debuts, at the Chicago Auditorium, on November 9, 1891. Both of these performances were sung in Italian, as was that of December 5, 1894, when Jean headed a cast that included Nordica, Eugenia Mantelli (Ortrud), Mario Ancona (Telramund), and Pol Plançon (the King). On January 2, 1896, however, the brothers sang in the German version of *Lohengrin,* assisted by Nordica, Marie Brema, and Kaschmann. It was not unnatural, therefore, that Jean, who had made his New York debut as Lohengrin, chose that role for his farewell to the Metropolitan, on March 29, 1901, with Milka Ternina, Schumann-Heink, Bispham, and Édouard.

As *Lohengrin* had been presented at the Metropolitan 333 times through the 1961–62 season, it is impossible to mention even one-twentieth of the famous artists who have sung it there. In the Metropolitan's first *Lohengrin* of the 1961–62 season (its 328th singing in the house), three house debuts were made: those of Ingrid Bjoner (Elsa), Sandor Konya (Lohengrin), and Norman Mittelmann (Herald); Joseph Ro-senstock conducted, and the cast was filled out by Irene Dalis (Ortrud), Walter Cassel (Telramund), and Jerome Hines (King Henry).

After Albani finally gave up the role of Elsa, at Covent Garden, Nordica and Nellie Melba alternated in it for some years. An 1891 *Lohengrin* starred Emma Eames (Elsa) and Giulia Ravogli (Ortrud), with Victor Maurel and the De Reszkes. Ernest Van Dyck was occasionally heard as Lohengrin. Leo Slezak, making his Covent Garden debut on May 18, 1900, was a superb Lohengrin, finely supported by Ternina (Elsa) and Louise Homer (Ortrud), but the musical effects were somewhat lessened by the delirious joy of the audience, informed after the second act that Mafeking had been relieved. Emmy Destinn sang Elsa in 1904, Aïno Ackté in 1907, and Frieda Hempel later that year. After 1907 *Lohengrin* was not heard at Covent Garden until 1913. After the performance of May 23, 1913, with Clarence Whitehill outstanding as the King, German ceased to be used at Covent Garden for precisely a decade. The revival of 1925 was a triumph for Lotte Lehmann (Elsa), Maria Olczewska (Ortrud), Emil Schipper (Telramund), and Otto Helgers (Heinrich). Some of the casts that looked so well on paper did not live up to expectations: for instance, the Elsa of Tiana Lemnitz (1938) was thought to be a "trifle over-sophisticated"—a fairly damning judgment; but toward the end of that season Karin Branzell revealed herself as a thrilling Ortrud. *Lohengrin* thereafter left the Covent Garden repertoire until 1950. Among the recent Elsas have been Sylvia Fisher and Victoria de los Angeles.

Lohengrin performance data are almost endless, in part because it was the first Wagner opera given in many cities. It was the first opera sung in German in Australia (Melbourne, March 30, 1907).

130. I Lombardi alla Prima Crociata (Verdi)

Four acts; libretto by Temistocle Solera, after Tommaso Grossi's poem of the same name; Milan, Teatro alla Scala, February 11, 1843.

Erminia Frezzolini was the Giselda of the *première* of *I Lombardi* at La Scala. The opera was even more immediately successful than *Nabucco* had been the year before, though the critics were generally cool—as were Venetian audiences shortly later. It did not spread throughout Europe as widely as *Nabucco* had, nor has it kept the stage, even in Italy, to the same extent as *Nabucco*. It was sung in Italian at Her Majesty's Theatre, London, on May 12, 1846, and became the first Verdi opera to be sung in New York when it was staged at Palmo's Opera House there on March 3, 1847.

The history of *I Lombardi* in Paris is singular and complex. In a translation by Alphonse Royer and "Gustave Vaëz" (pseudonym of Jean-Nicolas-Gustave van Nieuvenhuysen), and with several additional numbers (a long ballet included) supplied by Verdi, it was produced at the Opéra on November 26, 1847, as *Jérusalem*. It was a success. And soon this version was being played outside Paris, not only in French, but also in Polish, German, Portuguese, Russian, Dutch—and Italian. For, retranslated by Calisto Bassi, *Gerusalemme* was produced at La Scala, Milan, on December 26, 1850; still in Italian, it even reached Paris, at the Théâtre-Italien, on January 10, 1863. The fortunes of *I Lombardi–Jérusalem* thus curiously paralleled those of Rossini's *Mosè-Moïse*.

I Lombardi in its original form was revived at the Teatro Regio, Turin, on December 16, 1926, and at La Scala, Milan, on December 7, 1931. The Welsh National Opera Company, which has turned its attention to several early Verdi operas, has performed *I Lombardi* in London and elsewhere in recent years.

131. Louise (Charpentier)

Four acts; libretto (roman musical) by the composer; Paris, Opéra-Comique, February 2, 1900.

Marthe Rioton was the Louise of the world *première*. *Louise*, which soon became a fixture at the Comique (one thousand performances by 1959), was rather slow (in view of the pervading excitement about the opera) in getting to New York: Oscar Hammerstein first staged it at the Manhattan Opera House on January 3, 1908, with Mary Garden, Clotilde Bressler-Gianoli, Charles Dalmorès, and Charles Gilibert. The work passed into the Metropolitan repertoire on January 15, 1921, when Geraldine Farrar, who had learned nothing from Garden's thoughtful interpretation, appeared as a too well-dressed working girl. Louise Bérat (Mother) and Clarence Whitehill (Father) were excellent, but Orville Harrold was a disappointing Julien. Oddly enough, the Metropolitan had to wait for Grace Moore's first Louise, on January 8, 1939, for the best interpretation of the role since Garden's, though it was utterly unlike Garden's. René Maison was an excellent Julien, and Ezio Pinza, as the Father, gave everything to the role except Gallicism. Dorothy Kirsten, a Moore protegée, was a superficial Louise, with a more than adequate Julien in Raoul Jobin.

Louise Edvina, too refined for a working girl,[1] but vocally impeccable, was the Louise of the Covent Garden *première* on June 18, 1909. Histrionically, she was at least conscientious, and thus the opera, with Bérat, Dalmorès, and Gilibert, was well received, and was

---

[1] She was, in private life, the Hon. Mrs. Cecil Edwardes.

heard every year until 1914. After World War I Fernand Ansseau sang Julien to Edvina's familiar Louise. Later revivals had small distinctions, and the casting was reckless.

132. The Love for Three Oranges (Prokofiev)

Prologue and four acts; libretto by Prokofiev after Carlo Gozzi's L'Amore delle tre melarancie; *Chicago, Auditorium, December 30, 1921.*

A French translation by Vera Janacopulos was used when Prokofiev conducted the world *première* of *The Love for Three Oranges*. On that occasion, the large cast included Nina Koshetz (Fata Morgana), Irene Pavloska, Philine Falco, Dusseau, José Mojica (The Prince), Octave Dua, Désiré Defrère, Édouard Cotreuil, and Hector Dufranne. This production was heard at the Manhattan Opera House, New York, on February 14, 1922. Performances followed at Cologne (1925) and Berlin (1926) in German; at both Leningrad (1926) and Moscow (1927) in Russian; and at Ljubljana (1927) in Slovenian. La Scala, Milan, staged the opera in 1947, when Angelo Questa conducted and the cast included Dora Gatta, Scipio Colombo, Raphael Arié, and Cristiano Dalamangas.

Neither Covent Garden, London, nor the Metropolitan Opera, New York, ever has staged a Prokofiev opera. On November 1, 1949, however, the New York City Opera Company presented *The Love for Three Oranges* at the City Center in an English translation by Victor Seroff staged by Vladimir Rosing in a production described as "devised by Theodore Komisarjevsky." The cast included Ellen Faull (Fata Morgana), Margery Mayer (Clarissa), Virginia Haskins (Ninetta), Rosalind Nadell (Smeraldine), Robert Rounseville (The Prince), Carlton Gauld (Leandro), John Tyers (Pantalone), and Lawrence Winters (Celio); Laszlo Halasz conducted. This production won a large public. In Europe in more recent years, the highly colorful productions sent out by both the Ljubljana Slovenian National Opera and the Belgrade National Opera have been greatly admired.

133. Lucia di Lammermoor (Donizetti)

Three acts; libretto by Salvatore Cammarano, after Sir Walter Scott's The Bride of Lammermoor; *Naples, Teatro San Carlo, September 26, 1835.*

Among the singers in the Naples *première* of *Lucia di Lammermoor* were Fanny Persiani (Lucia), Gilbert-Louis Duprez (Edgardo), Cosselli, and Porto. On the heels of the opera's tremendous, immediate popularity in Italy, foreign stagings proliferated. It was heard on April 13, 1837, in Vienna; on August 2, 1837, in Madrid; and on December 12, 1837, in Paris—all in Italian. The first translation appears to have been that staged in French at the Théâtre de la Renaissance, Paris, on August 6, 1839; the opera was soon heard in many other languages.

The first London *Lucia*, in Italian, was sung at Her Majesty's Theatre on April 5, 1838. A performance in English was heard at the Princess's Theatre on January 19, 1843—and Drury Lane presented the opera in French on July 16, 1845. During 1847, Fanny Persiani was heard at Covent Garden in the role she had created; her Edgardo was Luigi Salvi; in December of that same year John Sims Reeves, who had been singing the role of Edgardo successfully at La Scala, Milan, made his English stage debut in the role at Drury Lane [1] (he

---

[1] This was the strange season put on by the eccentric Louis-Antoine Jullien, with Berlioz as conductor, Sir Henry Rowley Bishop as "inspector-superintendent at rehearsals," and Frederic Gye as manager. The season was a financial fiasco.

was later heard in this role at Covent Garden). During 1849, Jenny Lind sang Lucia at Her Majesty's during her third, and final, London opera season. A decade later, the Lucia at Drury Lane was Therese Tietjens. During the 1861 Covent Garden season, Adelina Patti chose Lucia as her second role in that theater, playing opposite (May 25) Mario Tiberini (Edgardo), Francesco Graziani (Enrico), and Zelger (Raimondo). The next year, Patti, on June 7, had as her Edgardo the German Theodor Wachtel, who was described as "the most robust of all robust tenors."

During 1866, Ilma di Murska was singing Lucia at Her Majesty's (she would make her Covent Garden debut in this role on November 5, 1868), and at Covent Garden on May 29, the French tenor Ernest Nicolini made his London debut as Edgardo opposite Patti, whom he married twenty years later. On May 4, 1869, Christine Nilsson made her first Covent Garden appearance as Lucia. *Lucia* opened the Covent Garden season both in 1870 (March 29) and 1871 (March 28), both times with Mathilde Sessi as Lucia and Augusto Vianesi conducting. On April 9, 1872, Emma Albani sang Lucia at Covent Garden for the first time, with Emilio Naudin (Edgardo), Antonio Cotogni (Enrico), and Capponi (Raimondo). Eight years later (June 12, 1880), Lucia was the London debut role of Marcella Sembrich, at Covent Garden (it would also be her New York debut role three years later). The young American soprano Ella Russell was heard at Covent Garden as Lucia on June 1, 1886. And on May 24, 1888, Nellie Melba was heard in London for the first time (Covent Garden), as Lu-

cia opposite Luigi Ravelli (Edgardo), Cotogni (Enrico), and Vittorio Navarrini (Raimondo); Luigi Mancinelli conducted.[2]

During Enrico Caruso's first (1902) London season, he sang Edgardo at Covent Garden on June 4 (its two-hundredth singing in that theater), with Regina Pacini (Lucia), Antonio Scotti (Enrico), and Marcel Journet (Raimondo). When Caruso did not return in 1903, Edgardo was sung on June 5 by Alessandro Bonci; the Lucia was Erika Wedekind, the Enrico—making his London debut, which turned out to be his only London appearance—Titta Ruffo. Luisa Tetrazzini first essayed the role of Lucia in London at Covent Garden on November 15, 1907, when the Enrico was Giuseppe de Luca. Oscar Hammerstein included *Lucia* in the first (it proved also to be the last) season (1911–12) of his London Opera House. On June 15, 1925, Toti dal Monte made her London debut, at Covent Garden, as Lucia opposite Dino Borgioli (Edgardo), Ernesto Badini (Enrico), and Édouard Cotreuil (Raimondo); an announced repetition did not materialize, and *Lucia* was heard no more in London for thirty-two years.

On May 13, 1957, at the Stoll Theatre (since torn down), London, Vincenzo Bellezza conducted a *Lucia* in which the title role was sung by Virginia Zeani; Giacinto Prandelli was the Edgardo, Enzo Sordello the Enrico. London audiences appeared to like the unfamiliar opera. And on February 17, 1959, the Australian soprano Joan Sutherland won a genuine triumph in a Covent Garden revival produced by Franco Zeffirelli and conducted by Tullio Serafin. The other leading roles

---

[2] During the summer of 1889, Nasr-ed-Din, Shah of Persia, was visiting London. Covent Garden put on (July 2) in his honor what must have been an endless evening, made up of the Mad Scene from *Lucia*, with Melba; Act IV of *Faust,* with Emma Albani, Jean and Édouard de Reszke, Sofia Scalchi, and Jean Lassalle; Act IV of *Mefistofele,* with Margaret Macintyre, Sofia Scalchi, Antonio d'Andrade, and Édouard de Reszke; isolated numbers sung by Marie Roze, Ella Russell, and Lillian Nordica; and—as if that had not been enough—in addition to the national anthems of both England and Persia, the Overture to *Guillaume Tell* and the "Leonore" Overture No. 3.

were sung by Geraint Evans (Enrico), Kenneth Neate (Edgardo), Kenneth Macdonald (Arturo), and Michael Langdon (Raimondo); there was not an Italian in the cast. Sutherland's success was so notable that the BBC altered its announced schedule so as to broadcast a complete *Lucia*. At the Opéra, Paris, Sutherland was the triumphant Lucia of that house's 301st performance of the opera. Franco Zeffirelli's Palermo production was used; the principals sang Italian, the chorus French. Pierre Dervaux conducted, and Miss Sutherland's colleagues on the stage were Alain Vanzo (Enrico), Robert Massard (Edgardo), Guy Chauvet (Arturo), Raoul Gourgues (Normanno), and Elise Kahn (Alisa). It soon became clear that no European or American opera company could hold up its head among its colleagues until it had presented Sutherland as Lucia, which San Francisco, Dallas, Chicago, and New York (the Metropolitan) hastened to do in 1961–62.

New Orleans had been the first city in the United States to hear *Lucia* (in French), on December 28, 1841. It reached New York, in Italian, on September 15, 1843, and was heard there in an English translation by G. Bowes and Michael Rophino Lacy on November 17, 1845. Two days after the opening *Faust* of its first (1883–84) season, the Metropolitan presented *Lucia* (October 24), with Augusto Vianesi conducting, Marcella Sembrich making her New York debut (Lucia), and a supporting cast including Italo Campanini (Edgardo), Giuseppe Kaschmann (Enrico), and Achile Augier (Raimondo). In *The New York Times,* W. J. Henderson wrote: "No singer ever won the recognition of a New York audience more easily than Mme. Sembrich did," and in the *Tribune* H. E. Krehbiel said of her voice that it wakened "echoes of Mme. Patti's [3] organ, but has warmer life-blood in it." Through the 1961–62 season, *Lucia*

had been sung 209 times at the Metropolitan.

After the otherwise exclusively German-language 1888–89 season, a benefit performance of *Lucia* in Italian (the beneficiary was the Edgardo, Italo Campanini) had Clementine de Vere as Lucia, Giuseppe del Puente as Enrico. Patti, who had sung Lucia at the Metropolitan as a member of her own touring company, was with the resident company during the 1891–92 season, as a guest artist, and sang Lucia on April 6, 1892. Enrico Caruso, who on November 23, 1903, had sung the first of 607 performances at the Metropolitan, first sang Edgardo there, opposite Sembrich, on January 8, 1904, with the result, as Irving Kolodin wrote, that "Thanks to his superb singing of the tomb scene, Edgardo was now a character with an end as well as a beginning."

At Oscar Hammerstein's Manhattan Opera House, during its final season, the greatly admired Luisa Tetrazzini sang Lucia, to John McCormack's Edgardo, on November 15, 1909. During the preceding season the Metropolitan had tried to challenge Tetrazzini's preeminence in this role by assigning it to Ellen Beach Yaw (March 21, 1908), a vocal phenomenon who could sing the C above high C; according to Kolodin, "she went no higher than G (in alt) during '*Quando rapito*,' and was not asked back." Tetrazzini finally made her Metropolitan debut on December 27, 1911, in a *Lucia* in which the Sextet had to be repeated. The Edgardo was Florencio Constantino, Pasquale Amato was the Enrico, and Herbert Witherspoon sang Raimondo. Frieda Hempel sang Lucia at the Metropolitan on November 26, 1913, for the first time. The role was sung by Mabel Garrison on January 25, 1919,

---

[3] Patti, aged sixteen, had made her operatic debut as Lucia on November 24, 1859, at the Academy of Music; the Edgardo on that occasion was Pasquale Brignoli.

when Giovanni Martinelli was the Edgardo, Giuseppe de Luca the Enrico, and Léon Rothier the Raimondo. When Amelita Galli-Curci joined the Metropolitan company during the 1921–22 season, she sang Lucia on November 17, 1921; she had been heard in the role with the Chicago Opera Association for some time in both Chicago and New York.

The highly publicized Marion Talley sang Lucia at a matinee on February 22, 1926, during her first Metropolitan season; Giacomo Lauri-Volpi was the Edgardo, and other roles were sung by De Luca (Enrico) and José Mardones (Raimondo). And on January 3, 1931, Lily Pons made her Metropolitan debut in a *Lucia* conducted by Vincenzo Bellezza, with Beniamino Gigli as Edgardo, De Luca as Enrico, and Ezio Pinza as Raimondo. Pons was occasionally appearing to sing this same role at the Metropolitan more than a quarter of a century later. A Pons *Lucia* on December 9, 1940, had radio's Nino Martini as Edgardo, Francesco Valentino (real name Frank Valentine) in his Metropolitan debut as Enrico, and Norman Cordon as Raimondo. When the Metropolitan mounted a new production of *Lucia* on November 28, 1942, Jan Peerce sang his first Edgardo; Pons was, as usual, the Lucia. On December 13, 1944, however, the Lucia was Patrice Munsel, with Peerce (Edgardo), Leonard Warren (Enrico), and Nicola Moscona (Raimondo). Robert Merrill first sang the role of Enrico at the Metropolitan on January 10, 1946, with Pons, James Melton (Edgardo), and Virgilio Lazzari (Raimondo). On February 21, 1947, Ferruccio Tagliavini's first Metropolitan Edgardo, with Munsel as Lucia, was enlivened by the failure of Francesco Valentino to arrive (he had been delayed by a snowstorm) in time to sing Enrico in the first act. Hugh Thompson was rushed into the gap; Valentino arrived in time to carry on after the first intermission. At a matinee student performance on January 14, 1949, the Lucia was Carmen Gracia; Richard Tucker sang Edgardo, Valentino was the Enrico, and Jerome Hines sang Raimondo; the next evening Munsel had replaced Gracia, Melton was heard instead of Tucker, and Giuseppe Valdengo was the Enrico. Mario del Monaco was heard as Edgardo on January 3, 1952, with Pons, Renato Capecchi (Enrico), and Moscona (Raimondo). On February 4, 1952, Graciela Rivera was the Lucia to Peerce's Edgardo, a role in which Eugene Conley was also heard that season. In a January 13, 1954, singing, with Pons, the Edgardo was Peerce, the Enrico being sung by Ettore Bastianini. On February 8, 1954, Dolores Wilson was heard as Lucia. On January 3, 1956, a "Lily Pons Gala," celebrating her twenty-fifth anniversary at the Metropolitan, presented the diminutive soprano in Act II of *Rigoletto,* the Mad Scene from *Lucia* (with Moscona as Raimondo), and arias from four other operas. Roberta Peters was heard as Lucia on February 1, 1956, and Giuseppe Campora as Edgardo on March 16.

Maria Meneghini Callas was first heard at the Metropolitan as Lucia on December 3, 1956; Campora was the Edgardo, Sordello the Enrico, Moscona the Raimondo. A near-riot occurred in the Broadway lobby of the Metropolitan on the night of December 11, 1956, the cause being the announcement that a scheduled Callas *Lucia* would be a Dolores Wilson *Lucia* instead. The 1957–58 season of the Metropolitan closed with Lily Pons's only appearance of that season—as Lucy Ashton. The opera was dropped from the Metropolitan repertoire during the 1959–60 and 1960–61 seasons.

In 1960 and 1961 it began to seem that the role of Lucia might become the exclusive property of the phenomenally agile and accurate Australian soprano Joan Sutherland, whose impersonation of the unhappy Bride of Lammermoor first had been heard at Covent Garden, London, on February 17, 1959. She since has sung the role many times in many opera houses, including the Paris Opéra and La Scala, Milan. A Sutherland *Lucia* was announced to open the 1961 San Francisco Opera season on September 15, but the star fell ill, and the role was taken by Anna Moffo; San Francisco finally heard Sutherland in her most famous role on September 23, when Francesco Molinari-Pradelli conducted, Renato Cioni was the Edgardo, and the Enrico was Vladimir Ruzdak. She also sang in this opera at Dallas on November 16, 1961. And her Metropolitan Opera debut (a special Sunday-night benefit performance), again as Lucia, occurred on November 29, 1961, evoking prolonged roars of approval which she admitted to having found somewhat frightening. The young Swiss conductor Silvio Varviso also made his Metropolitan debut that evening; the cast was filled out by Thelma Votipka (Alisa), Richard Tucker (Edgardo), Charles Anthony (Arturo), Robert Nagy (Normanno), Lorenzo Testi (Enrico), and Nicola Moscona (Raimondo).

134. Lucrezia Borgia (Donizetti)

Prologue and two acts; libretto by Felice Romani, after Victor Hugo's Lucrèce Borgia; *Milan, Teatro alla Scala, December 26, 1833.*

The fourth new Donizetti opera to be staged during 1833,[1] *Lucrezia Borgia,* though successful with the public,

quickly ran into complex difficulties. In Italy, its subject matter was censorable, and it appeared disguised under such pseudonyms as *Eustorgia da Romano, Alfonso duca di Ferrara, Giovanni I di Napoli,* and *Elisa da Fosco.* After it was sung at the Théâtre-Italien, Paris, on October 27, 1840, Victor Hugo brought suit, claiming that his auctorial rights had been infringed. He won his case, and the opera became *La Rinnegata,* with scenes laid in Turkey. Still further to add to the historical confusion, it was sung in Lyon in French on March 6, 1843, as *Nizza de Grenade.*

The Lucrezia Borgia of the original Milan production was Henriette-Clémentine Méric-Lalande.[2] In 1843, Marietta Alboni made her debut at La Scala, Milan, in the travesty role of Maffio Orsini (who sings the well-known *Brindisi*); Alboni also sang this role in London, at Covent Garden, during 1847, her first season there. A favorite Lucrezia at the Haymarket for a short period was Sophie Cruvelli. At Covent Garden on June 2, 1855, *Lucrezia Borgia* was sung by a cast including Giulia Grisi (Lucrezia), Constance-Betsy-Rosabella Nantier-Didiée (Maffio Orsini), Mario (Gennaro), and Antonio Tamburini (Alfonso). Eleven years later, at the Haymarket, Grisi made the mistake (it was 1866, and she was fifty-five) of singing this role again; the evening was a fiasco. The most famous of Lucrezias was Therese Tietjens, who sang the role at Drury Lane in 1859, and then used it for her Covent Garden debut on October 24, 1868, the first night of the season. Luigi Arditi conducted, and the cast included two other Covent Garden debutantes—Zelia Trebelli (Maffio Orsini) and Pietro Mongini (Gennaro)—as well as Sir Charles Santley (Al-

---

[1] The other three were *Il Furioso nell'isola di San Domingo* (Rome, January 2), *Parisina* (Florence, March 17), and *Torquato Tasso* (Rome, September 9).

[2] Others in that first cast were Marietta Brambilla, Francesco Pedrazzi, Luciano Mariani, and Domenico Spiaggi.

fonso). On May 19, 1877, suffering from cancer, Tietjens made her final operatic appearance as Lucrezia Borgia at Her Majesty's Theatre. In severe pain, she fainted at the end of every act, and at the final curtain could not rise from the floor to acknowledge the applause. She died less than five months later. Italo Campanini's London debut was made in the role of Gennaro at Drury Lane early in 1872. *Lucrezia Borgia* opened the Covent Garden season on May 25, 1886. The Prince and Princess of Wales were present; Enrico Bevignani conducted, and the cast included Anna Cepada (Lucrezia), Julian Gayarré (Gennaro), and Francesco Pandolfini (Alfonso). The future Edward VII and Queen Alexandra were again present when this opera opened another season—Sir Augustus Harris' first as manager—at Covent Garden on May 14, 1888. On that occasion the Lucrezia was Emmy Fursch-Madi; Trebelli was the Maffio Orsini, Luigi Ravelli the Gennaro, and Vittorio Navarrini the much-applauded Alfonso.

Lucrezia Borgia was the last role sung by both Giulia Grisi and Henriette Sontag, the first sung by Marietta Piccolomini, a capable actress whose voice was better suited to lighter roles. During the middle years of the nineteenth century, the opera was sung constantly throughout Europe and America in many versions and in many languages. It was first heard in New York in Italian on November 25, 1844; in German on March 18, 1856; and in English on October 13, 1871. It has had only one performance at the Metropolitan—on December 5, 1904, when Arturo Vigna conducted, and the cast included Maria de Macchi (Lucrezia), Edyth Walker (Maffio Orsini), Enrico Caruso (Gennaro), and Antonio Scotti

(Alfonso). One of its most recent revivals occurred on April 24, 1933, at the first Maggio Musicale Fiorentino.

135. Luisa Miller (Verdi)

Three acts; libretto by Salvatore Cammarano, after Schiller's play Kabale und Liebe; *Naples, Teatro San Carlo, December 8, 1849.*

The original San Carlo cast of *Luisa Miller* included Gavazzaniga, Della Salandri, Settimio Malvezzi, Antonio Selva, and Achille de Bassini. The opera traveled slowly throughout Italy and the rest of Europe, reaching Paris on December 7, 1852, and Her Majesty's Theatre, London, on June 8, 1858, at the latter with Marietta Piccolomini (Luisa), Antonio Giuglini (Rodolfo), Signor Vialetti (Miller), and Giuseppe Beneventano (Conte Walter). When Covent Garden first staged *Luisa Miller,* under the baton of Enrico Bevignani, on June 27, 1874, the Luisa was Adelina Patti, and with her were her future husband, Ernest Nicolini (Rodolfo), Francesco Graziani (Miller), and Anacleto Bagaggiolo (Conte Walter). Nicolini garnered a huge burst of applause for his singing of the fine Act II aria "Quando le sere al placido." But after two performances that season, the opera disappeared from the Covent Garden repertoire. It was restaged, however, as the opening opera of the 1953–54 Sadler's Wells season in London.

Luisa Miller, first sung in New York at Castle Garden on July 20, 1854, reached the Metropolitan Opera on December 21, 1929.[1] Tullio Serafin was the conductor, and the cast included Rosa Ponselle (Luisa), Marion Telva (Federica), Giacomo Lauri-Volpi (Ro-

---

[1] At a performance at the Academy of Music, New York, on October 20, 1886, the Luisa was Giulia Valda, a Boston soprano whose real name was Julia Wheelock, and who had made her operatic debut at Pavia in Italy seven years earlier, as Leonora in *Il Trovatore.*

dolfo), Giuseppe de Luca (Miller), Tancredi Pasero (Conte Walter), and Pavel Ludikar (Wurm). In a repetition nine days later, Federica was sung by Gladys Swarthout. The opera rang up four performances that season and one the next, after which it left the Metropolitan.

136. Lulu (Berg)

Three acts (unfinished); libretto adapted by the composer from Frank Wedekind's Erdgeist and Die Büchse der Pandora; Zurich, Municipal Theater, June 2, 1937.

The world *première* of *Lulu,* in the unfinished form in which Berg left it at his death in 1935, was conducted at Zurich on June 2, 1937, by Robert Denzler. The cast included Nuri Hadzic (Lulu), Maria Bernhard (Gräfin Geschwitz), Feichtinger (Wardrobe Mistress and Gymnasiast), Aster Stig (Dr. Schön), Emmerich (Animal Tamer and Rodrig, An Athelete), Peter Baxeranos (Alwa), Paul Feher (Painter), and Honisch (Schigolch). The opera was staged at the Teatro La Fenice, Venice, in 1949; Nino Sanzogno conducted, and the cast included Lydia Styx, Heinz Rehfuss, Demetz, and Eugenia Zareska. At a notable Hamburg performance in 1957 (a production by Günther Rennert which has been seen also in Berlin and other cities), Leopold Ludwig conducted and some of the chief singers were Helga Pilarczyk (Lulu), Gisela Litz (Gräfin Geschwitz), Toni Blankenheim (Dr. Schön), and Kurt Rüsche (Alwa). On October 16 and 17, 1959, a remarkable tape recording of *Lulu* was made in Rome for broadcasting later on RAI. Bruno Maderna conducted, the orchestra was that of the Rome Radio, and leading roles were sung by Ilona Steingruber (Lulu), Eugenia Zareska (Gräfin Geschwitz), Heinz Rehfuss (Dr. Schön), Kurt Rüsche (Alwa), Ratko

Delorko (Painter), Scipio Colombo (Animal Tamer), James Loomis (Rodrig), and Dimitri Lopatto (Schigolch).

137. Die lustigen Weiber von Windsor (Nicolai)

Three acts; libretto by Salomon Hermann Mosenthal, after Shakespeare's The Merry Wives of Windsor; Berlin, Königliches Opernhaus, March 9, 1849.

Nicolai's best-known opera reached New York on May 3, 1864, having been heard in Philadelphia a year earlier, on March 16, 1863. Just as London in 1864 had squandered the gifts of Therese Tietjens and Sir Charles Santley on the music of Mistress Ford and Fenton respectively, so, at the Metropolitan *première,* on March 9, 1900, leading roles were given to such first-rate artists as Marcella Sembrich, Ernestine Schumann-Heink, and Antonio Pini-Corsi, though by this time *Die lustigen Weiber* had certainly entered the class of inexplicable productions. Finally, to quote Alfred Loewenberg: "Very popular on German stages, and successful also abroad; not even Verdi's *Falstaff* (1893) was able to displace it." Anyhow, it has vanished from the Metropolitan repertoire. It was very temporarily revived by the New York City Opera Company at the New York City Center on March 31, 1955, in English. Joseph Rosenstock conducted, and leading roles were taken by Phyllis Curtin (Mistress Ford), Edith Evans (Mistress Page), Peggy Bonini (Anne Page), William Wilderman (Falstaff), William Shriner (Ford), Leon Lishner (Page), and Jon Crain (Fenton).

138. Macbeth (Verdi)

Four acts; libretto by Verdi and Francesco Maria Piave with additional verse by Andrea Maffei, after Shakespeare's play; Florence, Teatro della

Pergola, March 14, 1847. Revised version, in French translation by Charles Nuitter (pseudonym of Charles-Louis-Étienne Truinet) and Beaumont (pseudonym of Alexandre Beaune); Paris, Théâtre-Italien, April 21, 1865.

Felice Varesi was the Macbeth, Marianna Barbieri-Nini the Lady Macbeth, of the Florence *première*. Although not truly successful at first, the opera soon spread throughout Italy, and then the rest of Europe—though, curiously, it was not to be heard in England until 1938. It was staged at Havana, in Italian, in 1849, and at Niblo's Garden, New York, on April 24, 1850. Pauline Viardot-García was the Lady Macbeth of a Dublin performance in Italian on March 30, 1859, with Luigi Arditi conducting. *Macbeth* had been sung also in Polish, German, Hungarian, and Swedish when it was first staged in Paris, in French, on April 21, 1865, at the Théâtre-Italien. For this version, Verdi added Lady Macbeth's aria "La luce langue" (Act II), the duet of Macbeth and Lady Macbeth at the end of Act III, the ballet music, and various small touches. It was sung at the Italien only fourteen times, and Verdi regarded the production as a failure. This version, translated back into Italian, however, was eventually to become the standard one.

The twentieth-century revival of interest in Verdi's *Macbeth* began in Germany, where a new German version had been prepared by Georg Göhler. First heard at Dresden on April 21, 1928, this *Macbeth* was also sung at Berlin on October 1, 1931, when Gertrud Bindernagel (and later Sigrid Onégin) was the Lady Macbeth, with Hans Reinmar (Macbeth) and Ivar Andrésen (Banquo). Göhler's version was also staged at Zurich, Vienna (with Rose Pauly as Lady Macbeth), and Prague. In 1932, *Macbeth* was revived at Rome with Bianca Scacciati (Lady Macbeth) and Benvenuto

Franci (Macbeth). La Scala, Milan, mounted the opera on December 26, 1938, under the baton of Gino Marinuzzi; the cast included Gina Cigna (Lady Macbeth), Alexander Sved (Macbeth), and Tancredi Pasero (Banquo). As part of the commemoration of the fiftieth anniversary of Verdi's death, in 1951 the Maggio Musicale, Florence, staged *Macbeth;* Vittorio Gui conducted, and the cast included Astrid Varnay (Lady Macbeth), Ivan Petroff (Macbeth), Italo Tajo (Banquo), and Gino Penno (Macduff). A notable revival occurred at La Scala, Milan, in 1952, when Victor de Sabata conducted, the Lady Macbeth was Maria Meneghini Callas, and the Macbeth was Enzo Mascherini.

England at last heard *Macbeth* when it was staged at Glyndebourne on May 21, 1938, in a production by Carl Ebert conducted by Fritz Busch. The Lady Macbeth was Vera Schwarz (succeeded in the 1939 repetitions by the spectacular Irish-Italian soprano from Tasmania, Margherita Grandi); others in the notable cast were Francesco Valentino (Macbeth), David Franklin (Banquo), and David Lloyd (Macduff). The opera was sung ten times in 1938, ten in 1939, nine at the Edinburgh Festival of 1947, and eight in 1952 (plus a special televised performance)—a total to date of thirty-eight performances by the Glyndebourne company. London heard *Macbeth* at last on March 31, 1960, when it became the eighth Verdi opera to be staged at Covent Garden after World War II. Francesco Molinari-Pradelli conducted; the scenery and costumes were by Georges Wakhévitch; the principal roles were sung by Tito Gobbi (Macbeth), Amy Shuard (Lady Macbeth), Joseph Rouleau (Banquo), and André Turp (Macduff).

The San Francisco Opera Company staged *Macbeth* on September 27, 1955, with Fausto Cleva conducting. Inge Borkh as Lady Macbeth and Robert Weede as Macbeth made the opera vibrate with life in the appropriately gloomy sets of Leo Kerz. The Banquo of Giorgio Tozzi also was much admired. When the opera returned to San Francisco in 1957 (October 11), Francesco Molinari-Pradelli conducted and the three leading roles were in the hands of Leonie Rysanek (Lady Macbeth), Giuseppe Taddei (Macbeth), and Lorenzo Alvary (Banquo).

The Metropolitan Opera, New York, projected a Carl Ebert production of *Macbeth*, with decor and costumes by Caspar Neher, as a starring vehicle for Maria Meneghini Callas for its 1958–59 season. When Callas was separated from the company after a much-publicized quarrel, the role was assigned to Leonie Rysanek. With her in the first Metropolitan singing, on February 5, 1959, were Leonard Warren (Macbeth), Jerome Hines (Banquo), and Carlo Bergonzi (Macduff). The first night was disturbed when, upon Rysanek's first appearing on the stage, someone in the upper reaches of the house shouted: "Viva Callas!" The opera had had sixteen house performances by the end of the 1961–62 season. A well-remembered, New York *Macbeth* had been that of the short-lived New Opera Company, during the 1941–42 season (repeated the following year), with Florence Kirk (Lady Macbeth) and Jess Walters (Macbeth).

During its 1957 autumn season, the New York City Opera Company staged *Macbeth* at the City Center. Irene Jordan, a mezzo-soprano turned soprano, was the Lady Macbeth; the Macbeth was William Chapman, the Banquo, Norman Treigle. Chapman was again the Macbeth when the opera was staged by Luchino Visconti and conducted by Thomas Schippers as a leading attraction of the 1958 Spoleto Festival of Two Worlds. Shakeh Vartenissian sang Lady Macbeth; Ferruccio Mazzoli and Ugo Trama alternated as Banquo, Angelo Rossi and Nicola Nicoloff as Macduff.

Shakespeare's *Macbeth* has supplied material for the texts of several operas besides Verdi's. Hippolyte Chélard's *Macbeth*, with a libretto by Claude-Joseph Rouget de Lisle, author-composer of "La Marseillaise," was produced at the Paris Opéra on June 29, 1827. A *Macbeth* by Wilhelm Taubert, with libretto by Friedrich Eggers, was staged at the Opernhaus, Berlin, on November 16, 1857. Frank Marshall supplied the peculiar libretto, with scenes laid in Norway, of *Biorn*, a Macbeth opera by Lauro Rossi, staged at the Queen's Theatre, Long Acre, London, on January 17, 1877. Ernest Bloch's *Macbeth*, its libretto by Edmond Fleg, was first heard at the Opéra-Comique, Paris, on November 30, 1910. Lawrance Arthur Collingwood composed, to his own libretto, a *Macbeth* that was staged at the Sadler's Wells Theatre, on April 12, 1934 (the year also of Dmitri Shostakovich's wholly non-Shakespearean *Lady Macbeth of Mzensk*).

139. Madama Butterfly (Puccini)

Two acts (later changed to three by the division of Act II into two parts); libretto by Giuseppe Giacosa and Luigi Illica, after David Belasco's dramatization of a story by John Luther Long; Milan, Teatro alla Scala, February 17, 1904.

The principals at the world *première* were Rosina Storchio (Butterfly), Giovanni Zenatello (Pinkerton), and Giuseppe de Luca (Sharpless). The opera was a fiasco, and Puccini drastically revised the score. The revised version, first given at the Teatro Grande, Brescia, on May 28, 1904, was a huge success; Salomea Krucenisca (often spelled Krusciniski) was the Butterfly, Storchio having departed for Buenos Aires, where she was to sing the first performance of *Madama Butterfly* outside Italy on July 2, 1904. The Covent Garden, London, *première* assembled one of the classic casts of operatic history: Emmy Destinn, Enrico Caruso, and Antonio Scotti. Destinn was a peerless Cio-Cio-San, and the verbal tradition is that none of her successors truly equaled her. At Covent Garden *Butterfly* was an immediate success of tremendous proportions; it was symptomatic that Queen Alexandra attended the first three performances. Rina Giachetti, Florence Easton (whose Pinkerton was her husband, Francis Maclennan), Maggie Teyte, Margaret Sheridan, Dusolina Giannini, Victoria de los Angeles, and Amy Shuard had much to bring to the role. After Caruso, Zenatello, Amadeo Bassi, Riccardo Martin, and Giovanni Martinelli were favored Pinkertons. The new production of January 17, 1950, brought forward Elisabeth Schwarzkopf (Cio-Cio-San), Monica Sinclair (Suzuki), Kenneth Neate (Pinkerton), and Tom Williams (Sharpless).

In the first New York performance, at the Metropolitan Opera House, on February 11, 1907, Geraldine Farrar, Caruso, and Scotti had the leads, with Louise Homer as a sympathetic Suzuki. Destinn was able to repeat her London triumph as Cio-Cio-San, though Farrar was heard in the role off and on until her retirement. During the war years Paul Althouse and Thomas Chalmers were reasonably effective as, respectively, Pinkerton and Sharpless, again with Farrar—the tendency at the time was all for Americans in leading roles. Farrar last played the role in 1922. Easton, a better singer, was one of her successors, Elisabeth Rethberg another. Cio-Cio-San was Licia Albanese's best role, but neither Charles Kullmann nor Richard Bonelli matched her art. Dorothy Kirsten was much liked in the role: she was a sort of latter-day Farrar. Victoria de los Angeles sang better but was less satisfactory as an actress, even with such effective support as Mario del Mon-

aco and Frank Guarrera. Misled by the apparently plausible idea that approximately realistic Japanese settings, costumes, and stage actions would mix well with the Italianate music of Puccini as married to the ideas of John Luther Long and David Belasco, the Metropolitan, on March 12, 1958, remounted *Madama Butterfly* in a staging by Yoshio Aoyama, with sets and costumes by Motohiro Nagasaka. The cast glittered much less than the décor, consisting as it did of Antonietta Stella, Margaret Roggero, Eugenio Fernandi, and Mario Zanasi in the principal roles; the secondary roles were generally in such more competent hands as those of Alessio de Paolis, George Cehanovsky, and Ezio Flagello. *Madama Butterfly* had been heard at the Metropolitan 293 times through the 1961–62 season, when its title role was sung by Leontyne Price. Jarmila Novotna, the aristocratic Czech soprano who was to grace the Metropolitan for some seventeen seasons, made her United States debut as Cio-Cio-San with the San Francisco Opera on October 18, 1939, under the baton of Gennaro Papi. In support of the debutante were heard Michael Bartlett (Pinkerton), Julius Huehn (Sharpless), and Hertha Glaz (Suzuki).

140. Les Mamelles de Tirésias (Poulenc)

Prologue and two acts; libretto, after Guillaume Apollinaire, by Claude Rostand; Paris, Opéra-Comique, June 10, 1947.

When Poulenc's uproarious *opérabouffe* was staged at the Paris Opéra-Comique on June 10, 1947, Albert Wolff conducted; the direction was by Max de Rieux and the costumes and sets had been designed by Romain Erté. Denise Duval, who since has become the Poulenc soprano extraordinary, created the role of Thérèse; with her were Irène Gromova (Une Dame élégante), Jane Atty (La Marchande de journaux), Yvonne Girard-Ducy (Une Grosse Dame), Paul Payen (Le Mari), Émile Rousseau (Le Gendarme), Robert Jeantet (Le Directeur), Alban Derroja (Lacouf), Marcel Enot (Presto), Jacques Hivert (Le Fils), Serge Rallier (Le Journaliste), and Gabriel Jullia (Un Monsieur barbu). By 1950, *Les Mamelles de Tirésias* had rung up twenty-seven singings at the Comique.

On February 26, 1957, *Les Mamelles de Tirésias* and Denise Duval both made their New York debuts in an American Opera Society concert performance at Town Hall, sharing a double bill with Manuel de Falla's *El Retablo de Maese Pedro*. Arnold U. Gamson conducted, and the cast also included Mignon Dunn, Martial Singher, Donald Gramm, Robert Goss. John Kuhn, Paul Franke, and Loren Driscoll. At the Jubilee Hall, Aldeburgh, England, *Les Mamelles* was sung in anonymous English translation as half of a double bill with Monteverdi's *Il Ballo delle ingrate* on June 16, 1958. The accompaniment was supplied by two pianos played by Benjamin Britten and Viola Tunnard. Charles Mackerras was the director, Osbert Lancaster the designer. The two leading roles were sung by Jennifer Vyvyan and Peter Pears.

141. Manon (Massenet)

Five acts; libretto by Henri Meilhac and Philippe Gille, after the novel by the Abbé Prévost; Paris, Opéra-Comique, January 19, 1884.

Marie Heilbronn was the Manon of the world *première;* Alessandro Talazac was the Chevalier des Grieux.

The New York Academy of Music, in its dying days, introduced *Manon* to America, in Italian, with Minnie Hauk

as Manon; also in the cast was Ferruccio Giannini, father of Dusolina Giannini. The date was December 23, 1885. Sybil Sanderson, who had made her debut in this role at The Hague in 1888, was chosen for the Metropolitan *première*, when, on January 16, 1895, New York first heard the French text. Sanderson's chief associates were Jean de Reszke (Des Grieux), Mario Ancona (Lescaut), and Pol Plançon (Comte des Grieux). Geraldine Farrar, most pathetic of Manons, first interpreted the role on February 3, 1909, opposite Enrico Caruso, whose Des Grieux, though untouchable vocally, did not come up dramatically to that of Edmond Clément, who used the role for his Metropolitan debut early the next season. Farrar alternated with Frances Alda, whose world debut, at the Comique in 1904, had been as Manon. After six years' absence, the opera was revived for Lucrezia Bori in 1929, and she rapidly became an intensely admired Manon. Later lovers at the Metropolitan were Jarmila Novotna, the Czech soprano, and Richard Crooks, who, in 1935, had made his Metropolitan debut in the same role. Bidu Sayão and Charles Kullmann succeeded them; praise was accorded to Sayão's "intimate, piteous" interpretation. Licia Albanese's assumption of the role put her opposite the "suave, well-turned" Chevalier des Grieux of Giuseppe di Stefano on March 29, 1948. Eleanor Steber and Victoria de los Angeles have since sung the name role, but *Manon* has not been heard at the Metropolitan since the 1954–55 season.

To England *Manon* never truly appealed, and indeed French opera has had difficulties both in England and the United States. After the days of Oscar Hammerstein and Mary Garden, Sir Thomas Beecham alone did anything for the French section of the operatic repertoire. *Manon* first reached London on May 7, 1885, with Marie Roze and Joseph Maas. Sanderson, Ernest Van Dyck, and Eugène Dufriche sang leading roles at the Covent Garden *première* of May 19, 1891. Mary Garden's Covent Garden debut, on July 3, 1901, displayed a great Manon, but the next year, supported by Albert Alvarez (or Thomas Salignac), Maurice Renaud, and Marcel Journet, she appeared to even greater advantage. Unfortunately for Covent Garden, she went on to greater triumphs in the United States, and did not return. Fernand Ansseau, first heard as Des Grieux at a revival of *Manon* on May 23, 1920, was greatly admired in the role; with him were Louise Edvina (Manon), Alfred Maguenat (Lescaut), and Gustave Huberdeau (Comte des Grieux). The great Belgian soprano Fany Heldy was heard as Manon at Covent Garden on June 21, 1926, with Ansseau, Maguenat, and Édouard Cotreuil (Comte des Grieux). After that season, Massenet's *Manon* went unsung at Covent Garden until January 30, 1947, when the American soprano Virginia McWatters, whose singing was criticized, at least communicated more impression of the heroine's being French than was achieved by Elisabeth Schwarzkopf when she was the Covent Garden Manon on May 18, 1950, with an otherwise British cast.

142. Manon Lescaut (Puccini)

Four acts: (anonymous) libretto by Marco Praga, Domenico Oliva, and Luigi Illica, after the novel by the Abbé Prévost; Turin, Teatro Regio, February 1, 1893.

The principals of the world *première* were Cesira Ferrani (Manon) and Giuseppe Cremonini (Des Grieux). When Arturo Toscanini conducted the opera at the Teatro dal Verme, Milan, in the fall of 1897, Ferrani was again the Manon; the rest of the cast was: Emilio d'Albore (Lescaut), Fiorello Giraud (Des Grieux), Vittorio Arimondi (Geronte de Ravoir), Eugenio Grossi (De-

mondo), Pietro Francalancia (L'Oste), and Aurelia Kitzu-Arimondi (Un Musico). The first English production (London, Covent Garden, May 14, 1894) had evoked these words from Bernard Shaw: "Puccini looks to me more like the heir of Verdi than any other of his rivals." Antonio Pini-Corsi, the Lescaut, was probably the best member of the poorish cast assembled for this event. Fortunately, when the opera was revived at Covent Garden ten years later, it had, in Rina Giachetti, a wonderful Manon, unhappily supported by Enrico Caruso, who had a bad cold; later, Giovanni Zenatello was her Des Grieux, Mario Sammarco her Lescaut. Lina Cavalieri, a beautiful woman and fine actress, was histrionically poignant as Manon, but London did not care overmuch for her voice, and only Antonio Scotti (Lescaut) gave her adequate support. Riccardo Martin, briefly a London favorite, sang an excellent Des Grieux, with Marie Kousnietzoff and Sammarco. Giovanni Martinelli was a very successful Des Grieux (1911). Later Covent Garden productions of *Manon Lescaut* were scarcely memorable, and it is among the bad jests of history that a revival for Mafalda Favero had to be canceled when that fine singer bowed out—she had thought that Massenet's *Manon* was the work in question.

Although *Manon Lescaut* had been heard in New York as early as May 27, 1898, it did not get to the Metropolitan Opera House until January 18, 1907, with Cavalieri, Caruso, and Scotti. At the Metropolitan it never has had more than a mild success. Yet it has twice opened a season: in 1912, with Lucrezia Bori, Caruso, and Scotti; in 1929, with Bori, Beniamino Gigli, and Giuseppe de Luca, on the evening of October 28. The next day witnessed the stock-market crash, and that evening the house was dark. Martinelli and Pasquale Amato were other Bori associates in *Manon Lescaut;* eventually, Frances Alda was heard as Manon. The new production accorded the opera in 1949 brought forward various casts: the Manons were Dorothy Kirsten, Licia Albanese, Stella Roman, and Eleanor Steber; Jussi Björling [1] and Richard Tucker were equally fine as Des Grieux.

143. Martha, oder Der Markt von Richmond (Flotow)

Four acts; libretto by W. Friedrich (pseudonym of Friedrich Wilhelm Riese), after the ballet-pantomime Lady Henriette, ou La Servante de Greenwich, scenario by Jules-Henri Vernoy de Saint-Georges, music by Flotow, Norbert Burgmüller, and Édouard-Marie-Ernest Deldevez; Vienna, Kärntnertortheater, November 25, 1847.

Leading roles at the *première* were sung by Anna Zerr (Lady Harriet), Anton Erl (Lionel), and Karl Formes (Plunkett). The opera's career has been more honorable than its music. It reached Drury Lane, London, on June 4, 1849, and New York, in English, on November 1, 1852, with Anna Bishop as Lady Harriet. Almost every famed coloratura of the second half of the nineteenth century sang the role of Harriet, while not a few eminent tenors were attracted by that of Lionel, particularly after the famous tenor ario, "M'appari," was interpolated (its source was Flotow's opera *L'Âme en peine*) at the production at the Théâtre-Lyrique, Paris, on December 16, 1865.

Marta—the Italian version—reached the Metropolitan during its first season, on March 14, 1884, with Marcella Sembrich (Harriet), Zelia Trebelli (Nancy), Roberto Stagno (Lionel), and Franco Novara (Plunkett). At the Metropolitan, *Martha* became a favorite in spurts, not a perennial, and the death of the bass, Armand Castelmary, during a performance of the Italian version on Feb-

ruary 10, 1897, was not calculated to increase the opera's popularity among either singers or audiences. Castelmary's death had been the final touch on a memorable hit of energetic stage business between him and Jean de Reszke, the Lionel of the evening; it was too much for his heart, and he collapsed, dying in Jean's arms while the unsuspecting audience applauded. The cluster of Metropolitan performances that occurred from 1906 to the season of 1907–8 depended upon the magnificent quartet of Sembrich (Harriet), Edyth Walker (Nancy), Enrico Caruso (Lionel), and Pol Plançon (Plunkett). With a revival on December 14, 1923, Frances Alda, Kathleen Howard, Beniamino Gigli, and Giuseppe de Luca established a record of six performances the first season. The cast assembled by the San Francisco Opera for a *Martha* on September 30, 1925, under the baton of Pietro Cimini, included: Elvira de Hidalgo (Lady Harriet), Tito Schipa (Lionel), Marcel Journet (Plunkett), and Vittorio Trevisan (Sir Tristan). When San Francisco heard the opera again on the opening night (September 21) of the 1926 season, the Lady Harriet was the American soprano Florence Macbeth. Still faithful to this fading opera, Director Merola himself conducted it at San Francisco on October 3, 1944, when the cast included Licia Albanese (Lady Harriet), Hertha Glaz (Nancy), Bruno Landi (Lionel), Lorenzo Alvary (Plunkett), Salvatore Baccaloni (Sir Tristan), and Charles Goodwin (Sheriff). The Flotow opera has not been heard in San Francisco since that season.

One of the Bing regime's open confessions of unsure judgment was the revival of *Martha* on January 26, 1961, in a poor English translation, limply conducted by Nino Verchi, and acted and sung without approach to the essential style (though often with vocal

---

[1] Björling had made his actual (unofficial) debut in the minor role of the Lamplighter in this opera at the Stockholm Opera on June 21, 1930.

sounds lovely in themselves) by a cast including Victoria de los Angeles (Harriet), Rosalind Elias (Nancy), Richard Tucker (Lionel), Giorgio Tozzi (Plunkett), and Lorenzo Alvary (Tristram). According to a listing in *Opera News* (January 28, 1961), the role of Queen was played by King. The general confusion of the performance was not reduced when, at a later singing, Tucker decided, unannounced, to sing "M'appari" in Italian.

Les Martyrs (Donizetti)

See *Poliuto* (No. 183).

144. I Masnadieri (Verdi)

Four acts; libretto by Andrea Maffei, after Schiller's play Die Räuber; *London, Her Majesty's Theatre, July 22, 1847.*

I Masnadieri was the only opera that Verdi composed especially for London, the only one of his operas in which Jenny Lind created a role. When it was first staged, under the managership of Benjamin Lumley, at Her Majesty's Theatre on July 22, 1847, the cast included Lind (Amalia), Italo Gardoni (Carlo), and Luigi Lablache (Massimiliano Moor). The glittering audience was headed by Queen Victoria, Prince Albert, the Prince of Wales, and the aged Duke of Wellington.

The opera was first heard in Italy at Rome, Teatro Apollo, on February 12, 1848, and was soon sung throughout the peninsula. It reached Rio de Janeiro and Havana in 1849, New York on June 2, 1860. It has been revived rarely in more recent decades.

145. Mathis der Maler (Hindemith)

Seven scenes; libretto by the composer; Zurich, Municipal Theater, May 28, 1938.

Robert Denzler conducted the *première* of *Mathis der Maler;* the principal singers were Judith Hellwig, Funk, Aster Stig, Peter Baxeranos, Fridolin Mosbacher, Honisch, Marko Rothmüller, and Emmerich. The Zurich troupe also presented the opera at Amsterdam on March 9, 1939. A concert version, in an English translation by D. Millar Craig, was given at Queen's Hall, London, on March 15, 1939. Clarence Raybould conducted, and the singers included Stiles-Allen, Noël Eadie, Dennis Noble, Fullard, Parry Jones, and Francis Russell. In 1946, *Mathis der Maler* no longer being *musica non grata* in post-Nazi Germany, the opera was staged at Stuttgart. Under the baton of Ferdinand Leitner, the chief roles were sung by Wissmann, Stoll, Czubok, Wolfgang Windgassen, and Von Rohr. The Stuttgart Opera, with Leitner conducting, presented *Mathis der Maler* at Rome in 1951. Several productions in Germany followed, a notable one occurring at Hamburg in 1952, when Leopold Ludwig was the conductor and the singers included Elfriede Wasserthal, Anneliese Rothenberger, Matthieu Ahlersmayer, Helmut Melchert, Theo Herrmann, and Bensing. In the Günther Rennert production, the Hamburg Opera presented the opera during the Edinburgh Festival of 1952.

At the redecorated Graz Opera in late 1956, *Mathis* was staged by André Diehl with costumes by Lotte Pieczka and sets by Heinz Ludwig. Gustav Cerny conducted and a cast including Gertrud Hopf (Ursula), Otto Wiener (Mathis), and Josef Janko (Schwalb) was completed by three young American singers —Eleanor Schneider (Regina), Robert L. Charlebois (Cardinal), and Daniel Ferro (Commander of the Guard). On December 26, 1957, the opera was given at La Scala, Milan, for the first time in a production by Adolf Rott with scenery and costumes by Robert Kautsky. Nino Sanzogno conducted, Rolando Panerai sang the title role, and others in the cast were Cesy Broggini, Aureliana Beltrami, Gabriella Carturan, Nicola Filacuridi, Francesco Albanese, Ferrando Ferrari, and Antonio Cassinelli. The Rott-Kautsky production was seen at the first Vienna performance of *Mathis* in 1958, when Karl Böhm conducted and the leading singers were Paul Schöffler (Mathis), Lisa della Casa (Ursula), Wilma Lipp (Regina), Karl Liebl (Cardinal), Edmund Hurshell, Laszlo Szemere, Oscar Czerwenka, Anton Dermota, Hans Braun, Karl Terkal, and Margarita Kenney.

At the Städtische Oper, Berlin, in 1959, *Mathis der Maler* had Dietrich Fischer-Dieskau in the title role. Wolf Völker was the producer, Richard Kraus the conductor, and Peter Roth-Ehrang the designer of the much-ridiculed costumes and scenery. The rest of the cast was Gladys Kuchta (Ursula), Pilar Lorengar (Regina), Helmut Melchert (Cardinal), Walter Geisler (Schwalb), Theo Altmeyer (Capito), and Peter Roth-Ehrang (Riedinger). *Mathis der Maler* never has been staged at either Covent Garden or the Metropolitan Opera.

atres" of Naples. By 1793 *Il Matrimonio segreto* had been heard throughout Italy. London heard it in 1794. The revival of June 17, 1849, at Her Majesty's, brought forward the great Fanny Persiani as Carolina, with Giulia Grisi (Elisetta), Elena Angri (Fidelma), Mario (Paolino), Antonio Tamburini (Geronimo), and Joseph Tagliafico (Count Robinson). An ideal cast of the period would certainly find Luigi Lablache as Count Robinson, most effective with Tamburini in the patter duet of Act II. New York first heard *Il Matrimonio segreto* in 1834. In an English version by Reginald Gatty, it was crudely done at the Metropolitan on February 25, 1937, with Muriel Dickson, Irra Petina, Natalie Bodanya, George Rasely, Louis d'Angelo, and Julius Huehn, and withdrawn after a single repetition. The work is still popular in Italy: for instance, it was chosen for the opening of La Piccola Scala,[1] Milan, in December, 1955. Nino Sanzogno conducted, and the principal singers were Graziella Sciutti, Giulietta Simionato, Eugenia Ratti, and Luigi Alva.

146. Il Matrimonio segreto (Cimarosa)

Two acts; libretto by Giovanni Bertati after The Clandestine Marriage *by George Colman the elder and David Garrick; Vienna, Burgtheater, February 7, 1792.*

One of the few *opere buffe* still in the repertoire, *Il Matrimonio segreto* was hurriedly composed for the Emperor Leopold II. The story goes, in one version, that Leopold missed the *première* and at the second performance demanded that the opera be encored in its entirety: "You have heard it twice," he told Cimarosa, "and I must have the same pleasure before I go to bed." Spike Hughes states (in *Great Opera Houses*) that Cimarosa "was welcomed home with fifty-seven consecutive performances . . . at one of the smaller the-

147. Mavra (Stravinsky)

One act; libretto by Boris Kochno, after Pushkin's The Little House at Kolomna; *Paris, Opéra, June 3, 1922.*

Before the official *première* of *Mavra* —on a double bill with that of Stravinsky's *Renard*—the little opera had been performed privately at the Hôtel Continental, Paris. The Opéra performance was by Diaghilev's company; Gregor Fitelberg conducted, and the scenery and costumes were by Leopold Survage. The role of Parasha was sung by the noted Russian soprano Oda Slobodskaya. *Mavra* was sung in German at Kiel on November 7, 1925; at Prague

---

[1] "The little 600-seat theatre . . . tucked away inside the Scala building like an infant kangaroo in its mother's pouch" (Spike Hughes, *Great Opera Houses*).

in Czech in 1927; at Leningrad in Russian in 1928—and had been broadcast in English translation in London (April 27, 1934) when it was first heard in America, at Philadelphia, on December 28, 1934. For this Academy of Music performance, in an English translation by E. Robert Burness, the role of Parasha was sung by another noted Russian soprano, Maria Kurenko.

Mavra has not become a repertoire opera, but is revived more than occasionally. At Town Hall, New York, on October 19, 1953, The Little Orchestra Society presented it in English translation. Thomas Scherman conducted, and the singers were Ann Ayars (Parasha), Sandra Warfield (Mother), Ruth Kobart (Neighbor), and John Druary (Hussar-"Mavra").

148. Médée (Cherubini)

Three acts; libretto by François-Benoît Hoffman; Paris, Théâtre Feydeau, March 13, 1797.

After the year of the *première, Médée* was not revived in Paris, but was not neglected on German stages (it was for a performance at Frankfurt-am-Main in 1855 that Franz Lachner substituted for the original spoken dialogue the recitatives now inevitably used). In 1851, Henry Fothergill Chorley wrote resignedly: "The transcendent *Medea* of Cherubini is inaccessible. There is a time for everything. A new Parthenon is almost as improbable to be built as a new Bamberg Cathedral." *Medea,* in Italian, was staged at Her Majesty's Theatre, London, on June 6, 1865. Cherubini's statements in regard to an earlier projected production were so lofty that his acerb temper and extremely high standards may have frightened off possible producers. Certainly this was the situation in Paris, where he reigned for many years, from his throne room at the Conservatoire de Musique, as dictator of French music.

Medea is a role that, for more than half a century, challenged the indomitable will of every possessor of a stentorian and untiring soprano voice. Julie Scio created the role, and is said to have injured her lungs fatally while singing it—her death, in turn, was attributed to the lung complaint. Other famous artists followed her, including Margarethe Schick, whom Mozart so admired, and who created the role in Berlin in 1800. Clara Stöckl-Heinefetter, one of six singing sisters (the others were Sabina, Mathinka, Eva, Nanette, and Fatima) essayed the part and had even worse luck than Scio: she died insane. Pauline Anna Milder-Hauptmann, for whom Beethoven had designed the part of Leonore, sang Medea in Vienna. The undisciplined Wilhelmine Schröder-Devrient tried it. Unfortunately, Giuditta Pasta wasted her Medean talents on a tame version of the story set by Simon Mayr, Donizetti's teacher, instead of trying Cherubini's "grand fiendish part." So there was none to touch Therese Tietjens when, on June 6, 1865, that favorite English household institution revived the role under Colonel Mapleson's regime at Drury Lane. Sir Charles Santley was the Creon, but the heroine dominated the performance: evidently her Medea was an unforgettable experience. Her last presentation of this *tour de force* occurred in 1870; although she continued to appear in opera almost up to the day of her death in 1877, she dropped this role, apparently because it was too exacting.

Médée followed a largely Central European career during the late nineteenth century, but was staged in Italy for the first time (La Scala, Milan, December 30, 1909) in a version edited by Carlo Zangarini and translated into Italian. The opera's more recent burst of life has depended largely upon two sopranos, Maria Meneghini Callas and Eileen Farrell. Callas' assumption of the role (in Italian) at the 1953 Florentine Maggio Musicale, and later that season at La Scala, Milan, produced one of the great operatic characterizations of this century. She later sang it (1955) in Dallas, Texas, at Covent Garden (1959), to an audience estimated at 17,000 people, at Epidauros, Greece (1961), and again at La Scala (December 11, 1961). The news from Florence and Milan led the American Opera Society to present *Medea,* again in Italian, in concert form at Town Hall, New York, on November 8, 1955, with Farrell in the title role. Not an actress of the Callas genius, Farrell displayed a dramatic soprano voice of enormous range and volume. She has repeated Medea for the American Opera Society with constant success; she was again the Medea when, on September 12, 1958, the San Francisco Opera Company opened its season with the first performance of the opera ever staged in the United States. With her that night under the baton of Jean Fournet were Sylvia Stahlman (Glauce), Claramae Turner (Neris), Richard Lewis (Jason), and Giuseppe Modesti (Creon). Despite the fact that both Callas and Farrell have been on the Metropolitan's roster of singers, no staged performance of *Medea* ever has been seen in New York.

149. The Medium (Menotti)

Two acts; libretto by the composer; New York, Brander Matthews Theater, Columbia University, May 8, 1946.

Evelyn Keller and Claramae Turner participated in the world *première.* Marie Powers later brought suspense and terror to her interpretation of the role of Madame Flora (the medium), in both New York and London; Leo Coleman became internationally familiar in the mute role of Toby. In many productions throughout Italy, Gianna Pederzini for some time all but made singing Madame Flora her career; she was often supported by Dora Gatta as Monica and Coleman as Toby. *The Medium* also has been heard across the United States and, as sharing a double bill with Menotti's *The Telephone,* went on a European tour under the auspices of the State Department in 1955.

150. Mefistofele (Boito)

Prologue, four acts, and epilogue; libretto by the composer; Milan, Teatro alla Scala, March 5, 1868.

The cast of the world *première* was not of the first quality. Erminia Borghi-Mamo, Italo Campanini, and Romano Nannetti were the principals of the Bologna *première* of the much-revised version, which met with immense success on October 4, 1875. Outside Italy, it was first produced at London, in Italian, at Her Majesty's, on July 6, 1880, with Christine Nilsson, Zelia Trebelli, Campanini, and Nannetti. The Covent Garden *première,* July 11, 1882, evoked one of Emma Albani's greatest achievements (Margherita and Elena), with Wladyslaw Mierzwinski (Faust) and Pierre Gailhard (Mefistofele). The revival of 1914, with Claudia Muzio, Rosa Raïsa, John McCormack, and Adamo Didur, was much praised, the youthful Muzio getting full measure. Feodor Chaliapin's Covent Garden debut took place on May 25, 1926, in the name role of *Mefistofele.*

The United States was the next country to hear *Mefistofele,* at Boston, on November 16, 1880, an English translation being used. Eight days later, on November 24, the language was Italian for the first New York hearing, at the Academy of Music, with Alwina Valleria, Annie Louise Cary, Campanini, and Franco Novara (*né* Nash). The opera was popular enough to be featured in the Metropolitan's first season, on December 5, 1883, with Christine Nilsson, Zelia Trebelli, Campanini, and Giovanni Mirabella. Thus far, in Metropolitan history, *Mefistofele* has been given forty-four times in eleven seasons—but has not been heard since January 16, 1926. Lilli Lehmann and Emma Calvé were notable Margheritas, Édouard de Reszke was a very remarkable Mefistofele, and quite as good was Pol Plançon in the revival of 1900. Chaliapin's Mefistofele was criticized for its overt realism when he used it for his Metropolitan debut on November 20, 1907 (the gleam of his naked, oiled torso was thought especially shocking). On that occasion, Geraldine Farrar was the Margherita, Marie Rappold the Elena, and Riccardo Martin—also making his Metropolitan debut—the Faust, in which role Beniamino Gigli also made his Metropolitan bow on November 26, 1920 (in a cast headed by Adamo Didur and including Frances Alda, Florence Easton, and Kathleen Howard).

Although New York has not heard Boito's impressive opera since 1926, other American cities have not been thus deprived. The San Francisco Opera Company, which had staged this opera during its first (1923) season,[1] returned to the charge on September 20, 1952, when Fausto Cleva conducted the following cast: Nicola Rossi-Lemeni (Mefistofele), Ferruccio Tagliavini (Faust), Bidu Sayão (Margherita), Jean Fenn (Elena), Virginio Assandri (Wagner), Thelma Votipka (Martha), Margaret Roggero (Pantalis), and Cesare Curzi (Nereo). This time the company gave three performances of *Mefistofele*, at the third of which (October 11, matinee), the Faust was Mario del Monaco. And in 1961 the Chicago Lyric Opera presented a *Mefistofele* conducted by

Antonino Votto, with a cast that included Ilva Ligabue, Christa Ludwig, Carlo Bergonzi, Gian Giacomo Guelfi, and Boris Christoff (three performances, the first on October 21). New Yorkers, then, may still hope that Boito's masterpiece has not been taken from them forever.

151. Die Meistersinger von Nürnberg (Wagner)

Three acts; libretto by the composer; Munich, June 21, 1868.

Hans von Bülow conducted the world *première*, with Franz Betz (Hans Sachs), Kaspar Bausewein (Pogner), Gustav Hölzel (Beckmesser), Franz Nachbaur (Walther von Stolzing), Karl Schlosser (David), Mathilde Mallinger (Eva), and Sophie Dietz (Magdalena). To quote Alfred Loewenberg's *Annals of Opera:* "Of all Wagner operas *Die Meistersinger* was the one which made its way most quietly and steadily, and without that note of sensation and hostility so characteristic of the earlier (and later) operas."

It was in German, on May 30, 1882, that *Die Meistersinger* was first given in London. That night, the Drury Laners heard Rosa Sucher as Eva, Hermann Winkelmann as Walther, and Eugen Gura, a famous *Ring* baritone at Bayreuth, in the leading role of Hans Sachs. Hans Richter conducted, and magnificently. Seven years later, to mark Jean de Reszke's growing interest in Wagnerian roles, Covent Garden staged an Italian version in which, according to Bernard Shaw, Jean's sing-

---

[1] Dishearteningly, the gross box-office receipts on that October 1, 1923 (according to Arthur J. Bloomfield's book *The San Francisco Opera 1923–1961*), were only $9,925, whereas a *Rigoletto* one week later grossed $16,822. Gaetano Merola had conducted, and the cast had been made up of Adamo Didur (Mefistofele), Beniamino Gigli (Faust), Bianca Saroya (Margherita and Elena), Giordano Paltrinieri (Wagner), and Doria Fernanda (Martha and Pantalis). Hoping to obviate further additional losses, the management replaced a scheduled second *Mefistofele* with a repeat of a Gigli-Saroya *Andrea Chénier*—in vain, for the take on that October 6 proved to be only $9,030.

ing was far better than his understanding of the part of Walther. The top honors of this performance of *I Maestri cantori* went to Jean Lassalle, the Sachs, and to Emma Albani, the Eva.

Meanwhile, three years earlier, on January 4, 1886, the ambitious Anton Seidl had trotted out an uneven cast for the Metropolitan *première* of the German version, which, because of its excessive length, was much cut—to this day a complete *Meistersinger* has never been heard at the Metropolitan. In the cast were Emil Fischer (Sachs), Auguste Seidl-Kraus (Eva), and Marianne Brandt (Magdalena), with most of the other roles taken by relatively second-flight artists. The work was repeated seven times that season. Given twenty-eight times in German in the course of six seasons, it was kept in the repertoire when the Italian regime took over in the fall of 1891. Then New York heard almost precisely the same stars who had sung *I Maestri cantori* at Covent Garden in 1889. On March 25, 1901, the De Reszkes having for some time increased their fame by singing Wagner in German, the Metropolitan presented their first German *Meistersinger,* with Jean a more understanding Walther, and Édouard a lusty Sachs; Johanna Gadski was the Eva, Ernestine Schumann-Heink the Magdalena, and David Bispham the Beckmesser. This performance occurred just four days before Jean's Metropolitan farewell. It is pleasant to record that Marcella Sembrich, an artist who did only what she could do perfectly, sang the role of Eva "with her customary finesse"—her only Wagnerian Metropolitan role, though she sang Elsa (*Lohengrin,* in Italian) elsewhere. Heinrich Knote made his debut as Walther in 1904, with Aïno Ackté (Eva), Anton Van Rooy (Sachs), and Otto Goritz (Beckmesser). In 1910 the alternating Evas were Johanna Gadski and Emmy Destinn, the Walther either Leo Slezak or Carl Jorn. A few years later Frieda Hempel sang a delightful Eva. On March 19, 1917, Clarence Whitehill, one of the greatest Wagnerian baritones, first sang, after careful preparation, the role of Hans Sachs. This was to become one of his most splendid achievements, and he was succeeded by Friedrich Schorr, almost as fine an artist. To Whitehill and to Schorr the Metropolitan productions of *Die Meistersinger* owed a basic vitality, even though a thoroughly satisfactory performance was a rarity; the coming of Greta Stückgold (Eva) and Richard Mayr (Pogner) helped. An Eva worthy of Schorr's Sachs was Lotte Lehmann (March 15, 1934). After Schorr's farewell, the Sachs of the forties and fifties were adequate rather than satisfying. Torsten Ralf (Walther) was agreeable but scarcely imaginative, and Eleanor Steber, a conscientious artist, could not point to her Eva without qualification. Set Svanholm (Walther) reached a higher level of distinction. Lisa della Casa and Lucine Amara were later Evas; Karl Dönch excelled as Beckmesser.

London productions of *Die Meistersinger* suffered from the troubles that beset the Metropolitan ones: with a cast so large, total perfection is all but impossible. That Édouard de Reszke was a glorious Hans Sachs no one can doubt, and he was well supported by his brother Jean (Walther), Emma Eames (Eva), Pol Plançon (Pogner), and David Bispham (Beckmesser) in an Italian version in 1896. Many of the Covent Garden casts in pre-World War I days were almost exact duplicates of Metropolitan ones, but Claire Dux, the delightful Eva of Beecham's 1913 and 1914 seasons, was never heard at the Metropolitan. With Lehmann alternating with Elisabeth Schumann as Eva, the 1925 *Meistersinger,* which also rejoiced in Mayr and Schorr, was a triumph. With Heddle Nash as David (1930), satisfaction was extended except that Bruno Walter whipped the orchestra up to a din. Tiana Lemnitz' Eva passed Ernest Newman's severe test (1936), and was generally much liked. Recent productions have been ragged, but there are good words to be said for the Sachs of James Pease and the Eva of Una Hale.

Die Meistersinger was chosen as the first opera to be presented at the new Leipzig Opera House in 1960, with Walter Ulbricht, Secretary of the Central Committee of the East German Communist Party, as guest of honor. The opera was given a "Socialist" interpretation, without pomp, with Hans Sachs, a man of the people, reconciled with Beckmesser at the close. Helmut Seydelmann conducted, and leading roles were sung by Ladislav Mraz (Hans Sachs) and Gustav Papp (Walther).

152. The Midsummer Marriage (Tippett)

Three acts; libretto by the composer; London, Covent Garden, January 27, 1955.

John Pritchard conducted the *première;* the principal roles were taken by Joan Sutherland (Jenifer), Adele Leigh (Bella), Monica Sinclair (A Voice), Oralia Domínguez (Sosostris), Richard Lewis (Mark), Otakar Kraus (King Fisher), and John Lanigan (Jack). The extremely ambiguous text was not helped by the poor English enunciation of Domínguez and Kraus. "The reception was mixed," Harold Rosenthal wrote (*Two Centuries of Opera at Covent Garden*). "The final ballet had been greeted by boos and cries of 'rubbish' from the gallery; and after the final curtain there was sporadic applause for about five minutes, mingled with some cries of dissension." The opera received five performances that season, none in the 1955–56 season, and two more in the season of 1956–57, with Jeanette Sinclair replacing Leigh.

153. A Midsummer Night's Dream (Britten)

Three acts; libretto by Peter Pears and the composer, after Shakespeare; Aldeburgh, England, Jubilee Hall, June 11, 1960.

At the *première* of Britten's ninth opera, leading roles were taken by Alfred Deller, a countertenor (Oberon), Jennifer Vyvyan (Titania), Marjorie Thomas (Hermia), April Cantelo (Helena), Johanna Peters (Hippolyta), Forbes Robinson (Theseus), George Maran (Lysander), Thomas Hemsley (Demetrius), Owen Brannigan (Bottom), Peter Pears (Flute), and Leonid Massine II (Puck). The opera was staged at Covent Garden on February 2, 1961, with Georg Solti conducting; changes in the cast from the Aldeburgh *première* included: Russell Oberlin (Oberon), Joan Carlyle (Titania), Irene Salemka (Helena), Margreta Elkins (Hippolyta), André Turp (Lysander), Louis Quilico (Demetrius), Geraint Evans (Bottom), John Lanigan (Flute), and Nicholas Chagrin (Puck). The opera also had been sung during the June–July, 1960, Holland Festival—one night in Amsterdam, the next in The Hague. The cast was substantially that to be heard later at Covent Garden, except that Alfred Deller retained his Aldeburgh role.

On February 21, 1961, opening a modern opera week of the Hamburg State Opera (which also afforded Stravinsky's *Oedipus Rex*, Honegger's *Antigone*, Liebermann's *School for Wives*, Berg's *Lulu* and *Wozzeck*, Henze's *Der Prinz von Homburg*, and Karl-Birger Blomdahl's "space-age opera," *Aniara*[1]), *A Midsummer Night's Dream*

[1] The world *première* of this opera, which takes place in a space ship that becomes lost for twenty years, finally becoming a flying coffin for its passengers, was given in Stockholm on May 31, 1959. The music is said to echo Bartók and Stravinsky. Margaret

received its first German performance. The countertenor role of Oberon was sung by a tenor, Alfred Stolze; Stina-Britta Melander was the Titania, and others in the cast included Heinz Hoppe (Lysander), Vladimir Ruzdak (Demetrius), Cvetka Ahlin (Hermia), and Helga Pilarczyk (Helena). Britten's opera also was staged in 1961 in a Walter Felsenstein production at the Komische Oper in East Berlin, in Vancouver, British Columbia, and by the San Francisco Opera Company.

154. Mignon (Thomas)

Three acts; libretto by Jules Barbier and Michel Carré, after Goethe's Wilhelm Meister; *Paris, Opéra-Comique, November 17, 1866.*

Marie-Célestine Galli-Marié, a mezzo-soprano, was the first Mignon, and did much to make the world *première* an unmistakable success; the Philine was Marie Cabel, a popular singer at the Comique and a protégée of Pauline Viardot-García. When it became obvious that *Mignon* was to become a staple, Thomas decided to make over the title role for Christine Nilsson, who first sang it in England and the United States. It was a wise move, for in her day the Swedish soprano was surpassed by none in the role and equaled only by the vivid Pauline Lucca. For the original London production, at Drury Lane, on July 5, 1870, Thomas not only composed a special number for Nilsson, but he also devised for Zelia Trebelli, the Frederick (*sic*), a charming gavotte based on the entr'acte between Acts I and II; Jean-Baptiste Faure was the Lothario. Maurice Strakosch staged *Mignon* at the New York

Academy of Music, on November 22, 1871. Victor Capoul, a glamorous-voiced tenor who had come up from the ranks of *opéra-bouffe,* was Nilsson's Wilhelm Meister, and this pair resumed their roles at the first Metropolitan *Mignon,* on October 31, 1883, when Alwina Valleria was Philine, Sofia Scalchi the Frederick, and Giuseppe del Puente the Lothario. The opera did not succeed, despite Capoul's convincing transports of love, and it had been given only eight times during the four scattered Metropolitan seasons when it was revived, on March 6, 1908, for Geraldine Farrar, supported by Bessie Abott, whose light voice showed to advantage in Philine's music, Alessandro Bonci (Wilhelm Meister), and Pol Plançon (Lothario). Even then New York heard *Mignon* coldly.

It was not until 1927 that *Mignon* established itself so solidly in New York that for a time a season without it became a rarity. On March 10 of that year, Lucrezia Bori was the Mignon, and a superb one, the usually maladroit Marion Talley the Philine (her best role); Beniamino Gigli sang Wilhelm Meister, Clarence Whitehill Lothario. Later, Lily Pons became a favorite Philine, and when Bori dropped from the company, Gladys Swarthout or Risë Stevens revived the mezzo version of the name role, the latter making her Metropolitan debut in it, on December 17, 1938, with Richard Crooks and Ezio Pinza. In the 1948–49 season Stevens (in the best cast) was assisted by Patrice Munsel, Giuseppe di Stefano, and Jerome Hines. Oddly enough, during a season when its popularity was by no means striking, *Mignon* was used for the first commercially sponsored Metropolitan broadcast, the sponsor being Lucky Strike, the singers Bori, Pons, Swarthout (on this occasion Frederick), and Tito Schipa, the date December 30, 1933. An interesting interim performance of *Mignon* occurred at the Park Theater in 1918, when the ex-Metro-

Hallin as the Blind Poetess (one of the eight thousand doomed passengers) was extravagantly praised for her singing of a wordless aria, a singular means of expression for a writer.

politan bass, William Wade Hinshaw, presented the fascinating English soprano Maggie Teyte in the name role.

Although absent from Covent Garden for forty years and from the Metropolitan for almost fifteen, *Mignon*, with about two thousand performances to date at the Comique, may well be revived any day, at least when the French repertoire can be re-examined by a friendly eye.

155. Mireille (Gounod)

Five acts, later in the year reduced to three; libretto by Michel Carré, after Mireïo, *a poem in Provençal by Frédéric Mistral; Paris, Théâtre-Lyrique, March 19, 1864.*

Marie Miolan-Carvalho, who had created the role of Marguerite in Gounod's *Faust*, was the Mireille of the world *première*. The three-act version, which allows a happy ending to an intrinsically tragic situation, was probably that in which Edmond Clément inaugurated, on November 29, 1889, his twenty-one-year reign as leading tenor of the Opéra-Comique, Paris. London heard the longer version first, at Her Majesty's, on July 5, 1864, with Therese Tietjens, Antonio Giuglini, and Sir Charles Santley in leading roles. Two acts of *Mireille* were produced in Philadelphia, in German, only eight months after its Paris *première*, and in the eighties the entire opera was heard, in English or Italian, in Chicago, Brooklyn, and New York. It did not secure a Metropolitan mounting until February 28, 1919, when Pierre Monteux conducted the French version in shortened form. The principals then were María Barrientos (Mireille), Charles Hackett (Vincent), Clarence Whitehill (Ourrias), and Léon Rothier (Ramon). Victor Maurel, who had settled in New York after his great career on the operatic stage, was a Provençal by birth and upbringing, as well as a former art student. He was therefore chosen to design the Metropolitan settings for Gounod and Carré's version of *Mireïo*, Frédéric Mistral's charming poem of Provençal life. After four performances, *Mireille* was dropped from the Metropolitan repertoire.

A remarkable production of *Mireille* was seen at Les Baux, in Provence, on July 24, 1954. The outdoor setting of the Val d'Enfer and its suggestive rocks was made to provide seats for more than six thousand spectators in the very setting of Mistral's poem. In a letter to his wife written on March 12, 1863, Gounod himself had said that it was "so fantastic in appearance that it would make a magnificent stage setting." Georges Wahkévitch provided the *mise en scène;* André Cluytens conducted, and the cast included Janette Vivalda (Mireille), Christiane Gayraud (Taven), Madeleine Ignal (Vincenette), Christiane Jacquin (Clémence), Nicolai Gedda (Vincent), Michel Dens (Ourrias), André Vessières (Ramon), Marcello Cortis (Ambroise), and Robert Tropin (The Ferryman). A few days after the first performance, the entire original cast recorded the opera at nearby Aix-en-Provence.

156. Mona (Parker)

Three acts; libretto by Brian Hooker; New York, Metropolitan Opera House, March 14, 1912.

Alfred Hertz conducted the *première* of this opera, with which Horatio Parker had won the $10,000 prize offered by the Metropolitan for the best opera in English by an American composer. The cast was: Louise Homer (Mona), Rita Fornia (Enya), Herbert Witherspoon (Arth), William Hinshaw (Gloom), Albert Reiss (Nial), Lambert Murphy (Caradoc), Putnam Griswold (Roman Governor), Riccardo Martin (Quintus, known as Gwynn), and Basil Ruysdael (Old Man). With its fourth performance that season (April 1, 1912), *Mona* vanished from the Metropolitan repertoire. It seems never to have been staged elsewhere. On February 22, 1961, however, the Orchestra of America, with Richard Korn conducting, included sections of it in an all-American concert at Carnegie Hall, New York. The Prelude, Sword Song, Love Duet, Entr'acte, and Finale were heard, with Arlene Saunders as Mona and Enrico di Giuseppe as Gwynn.

157. Mosè in Egitto (Rossini)

Three acts; libretto by Andrea Leone Tottola; Naples, Teatro San Carlo, March 5, 1818. The later French version, Moïse et Pharaon, ou le Passage de la Mer Rouge (*known in Italian as* Mosè Nuovo), *in four acts; libretto by Giuseppe Luigi Balochi and Victor-Joseph Étienne de Jouy; Paris, Opéra, March 26, 1827.*

Actually an oratorio to be staged (*azione tragico-sacra*), *Mosè in Egitto* was produced during Lent. The Anaïde of the Naples *première* was Rossini's mistress and future wife, Isabella Colbran. The opera, immediately successful in Italy, became even more popular after Rossini added to it, for a San Carlo singing on March 7, 1819, the prayer beginning "Dal tuo stellato soglio." During Rossini's lifetime, it was sung—in the original Italian version, in the French version, in translations of both, as staged and in concert form —in at least six languages in nearly thirty cities in some twenty-two countries. The Italian version of the French version was sung at Rome in concert form in 1827, and was staged in Perugia on February 4, 1829.

On February 22, 1833, at Covent Garden, London, was heard *The Israelites in Egypt, or The Passage of the Red Sea,* Michael Rophino Lacy's pas-

ticcio in English of music from Rossini's opera and Handel's *Israel in Egypt.*[1] The cast included Jane Shirreff, Miss Cawse, Joseph Wood, and Arthur Seguin.[2] The second version of the opera was sung at Covent Garden on April 20, 1850, as *Zora,* when the cast included Jeanne Castellan (Anaïde), Enrico Tamberlik (Amenophi), Zelger (Mosè), Antonio Tamburini (Merismane), and Mlle Vera (Sinaïde).

Paris, which had heard the Italian *Mosè* approvingly at the Théâtre-Italien on October 20, 1822, received even more warmly its own version, *Moïse et Pharaon,* when it was staged at the Opéra on March 26, 1827, with a cast including Laure Cinti-Damoreau, Adolphe Nourrit, and Nicholas Levasseur; by 1865, this version had been heard 187 times at the Opéra.

The original Italian version was sung in New York on March 2, 1835, the second version, in Italian translation, on May 7, 1860. Between them there was sandwiched in a performance in English of Lacy's *The Israelites in Egypt,* October 31, 1842 (also at Philadelphia, December 16, 1842). The work has never been staged at the Metropolitan in any version.

During the fall of 1957, RAI (Radio Italiana) broadcast a much-admired studio performance of the opera, the director being Tullio Serafin, the cast including Anita Cerquetti, Rosanna Carteri, Gianna Iaja, Giuseppe Taddei, and Nicola Rossi-Lemeni. And on December 2, 1958, at Carnegie Hall, New York, the American Opera Society presented a concert performance of *Mosè.* Arnold U. Gamson conducted, and principal roles were sung by Gloria Davy (Anaïde), Jennie Tourel (Sinaïde), Jon Crain (Amenophi), and—in

---

[1] London had heard an earlier bowdlerized version, as *Pietro l'Eremita,* in Italian, on April 23, 1822, at the Haymarket Theatre.

[2] Arthur Seguin and his wife Anne, with an operatic troupe of their own, went to the United States and Canada in 1838, touring extensively. He was elected a chief of an In-

his New York debut—Boris Christoff (Mosè).

158. Moses und Aron (Schoenberg)

Three acts (third act never composed); libretto by the composer; Zurich, June 6, 1957.

Why Schoenberg, who completed two of the proposed three acts of *Moses und Aron* in 1932, failed to compose the third act during the remaining nineteen years of his life (he took up work on it again only in the year of his death, 1951) is not clear. A concert performance of the two completed acts was broadcast from Hamburg on March 12, 1954, with Hermann Spitz conducting. The first staged performance[1] occurred at Zurich on June 6, 1957, produced by Karl Heinz Krahl, conducted by Hans Rosbaud, and with the title roles performed by Hans Herbert Fiedler (Moses) and Helmut Melchert (Aron). A peculiar performance of *Moses und Aron* was put on at the Berlin State Opera in 1959. Produced by Gustav Rudolf Sellner, with settings by Michel Raffaelli, and conducted by Hermann Scherchen, it was in part live, in part prerecorded. In the first scene, for example, Josef Greindl as Moses spoke his lines against a recording of the half-spoken, half-sung chorus; also, as a conclusion, this choral tape was repeated as a background for the spoken lines of the uncomposed third act. As at Zurich, the Aron was Helmut Melchert. A small but very raucous part of the Berlin audience demonstrated against the opera—Desmond Shawe-Taylor, reporting the event for *Opera*,

referred to the "disgusting behavior" of these people. The Berlin production, with Scherchen conducting and Greindl and Melchert as, respectively, Moses and Aron, was seen at La Scala, Milan, on June 19, 1961.

159. Nabucco [Nabucodonosor] (Verdi)

Four acts; libretto by Temistocle Solera; Milan, Teatro alla Scala, March 9, 1842.

The cast of the *première* of *Nabucodonosor* (soon to become known to all Italians as *Nabucco*) was: Giuseppina Strepponi, Verdi's future second wife (Abigaille), Giovannina Bellinzaghi (Fenena), Teresa Ruggeri (Anna), Giorgio Ronconi (Nabucodonosor), Corrado Miraglia (Ismaele), Prosper Derivis (Zaccaria), Gaetano Rossi (High Priest of Baal), and Napoleone Marconi (Abdallo). By December 4, 1842, it had been sung sixty-seven times at La Scala. On April 3, 1843, in Italian, it became the first Verdi opera to be staged in Vienna, and soon it was being sung throughout Europe. It reached Paris on October 16, 1845, in Italian; Her Majesty's Theatre, London, in Italian (billed as *Nino* and revamped to detour the English prejudice against Biblical subjects on the stage), on March 3, 1846; and Covent Garden (as *Anato*) on May 30, 1850.

Sophie Cruvelli had been the Abigaille of the London *première* at Her Majesty's, but the role was sung by Jeanne Castellan at Covent Garden. Others in the Covent Garden cast were Mlle Vera as Fenena, Enrico Tamberlik as Ismaele, Giorgio Ronconi

dian tribe. His sister Elizabeth married a Wallachian baron named Demetrius Parepa; their daughter Euphrosyne became a well-known soprano, who, having married Carl Rosa in 1867, became known as Euphrosyne Parepa-Rosa. From 1875 to the present there

has been a Carl Rosa Opera Company in England.

[1] A performance of *Moses und Aron* scheduled for the eleventh Sagra Musicale Umbra at Perugia on September 20, 1956, appears not to have taken place.

as Nabucco, and Joseph-Dieudonné Tagliafico as Zaccaria.[1] This proved to be the only performance of *Nabucco* ever heard at Covent Garden. The middle two acts were, however, played there on June 4, 1850, after a singing of Rossini's *Il Barbiere di Siviglia*. In more recent decades, England has heard *Nabucco* only as staged by smaller regional companies and semi-amateurs.

New York first heard *Nabucco*, in Italian, when it was sung at the Astor Place Opera House on April 4, 1848. Michele Rapetti was the conductor; the name role was sung by a man who himself sounds like an aria—Giuseppe Federico Del Bosco Beneventano. The cast was filled out by Teresa Truffi (Abigaille), Amalia Patti (Fenena), Mme Avogadro (Anna), Francesco Bailini (Ismaele), Settimo Rossi (Zaccaria), Lorenzo Biondi (High Priest), and Giuseppe Piamontesi (Abdallo). No other professional performances of *Nabucco* appear to have been heard in New York until the Metropolitan finally staged it on October 24, 1960, as the opening opera of its 1960–61 season. "Edited" into a three-act, seven-scene version, confusingly staged by Günther Rennert, curiously costumed by Teo Otto and Wolfgang Roth (the whole production breathed obviously German air), and somewhat raucously conducted by Thomas Schippers, it naturally failed to exercise all of its potential effectiveness. Leonie Rysanek, damagingly miscast in the vocally strenuous role of Abigaille, sang well the much simplified music handed her; the cast otherwise consisted of Rosalind Elias (Fenena), Carlotta Ordassy (Anna), Cornell MacNeil (Nabucco), Eugenio Fernandi (Ismaele), Cesare Siepi (Zaccaria), Bonaldo Giaiotti (debut, the High Priest), and Paul

Franke (Abdallo). In more than a century, New York has still not been given an opportunity to hear Verdi's first resounding success as he conceived it.

In Italy, however, *Nabucco* continues to hold the affection of impresarios and audiences. It was used to open the first Florentine Maggio Musicale, April 22, 1933, with a cast including Gina Cigna (Abigaille), Ebe Stignani (Fenena), Alessandro Dolci (Ismaele), Carlo Galeffi (Nabucco), and Tancredi Pasero (Zaccaria); the conductor was Vittorio Gui. The opera was heard at La Scala, Milan, on December 26 of that year with much the same cast (Giovanny Voyer replacing Dolci as Ismaele). *Nabucco* also reopened the rebuilt Scala after World War II, when Tullio Serafin conducted, and the cast included Maria Pedrini (Abigaille), Fedora Barbieri (Fenena), Mario Binci (Ismaele), Gino Bechi (Nabucco), and Siepi (Zaccaria). Gui again conducted when the opera was sung at Rome in 1951, with Maria Caniglia (Abigaille), Miriam Pirazzini (Fenena), Francesco Albanese (Ismaele), Bechi (Nabucco), and •Nicola Rossi-Lemeni (Zaccaria). It has been heard in the open air at the Terme di Caracalla in Rome, and was again staged at Florence during the 1959 Maggio Musicale, when the cast included Margherita Roberti (Abigaille), Gastone Limarilli (Ismaele), Ettore Bastianini (Nabucco), and Paolo Washington (Zaccaria).

160. Natoma (Herbert)

Three acts; libretto by Joseph Deighn Redding; Philadelphia, February 25, 1911.

On the night of its Philadelphia *première*, *Natoma* also was heard (though not seen) at Ladbroke Hall, London, the purpose of the performance being

---

[1] As given here, the names of the roles are not those of *Anato*, but of the original form of *Nabucco*. In *Anato*, for example, the role of Ismaele was called Dario.

the establishment of British copyright. Later it was staged in New York, Baltimore, Chicago, Los Angeles, and San Francisco, but it never won true popularity. During that section of the Metropolitan Opera's 1910–11 season which saw Cleofonte Campanini conducting there operas from the recently defunct Oscar Hammerstein company's repertoire, *Natoma* was heard at the Metropolitan on February 28, 1911, with the Philadelphia cast. Mary Garden did much for the name role, but John McCormack was hopelessly miscast as Lieutenant (naval) Paul Merrill.[1] When the opera was first staged at the Auditorium, Chicago, by the Chicago Grand Opera Company, on December 13, 1911, the cast was: Mary Garden (Natoma), Carolina White (Barbara), George Hamlin (Lieutenant Paul Merrill), Henri Scott (Don Francisco), Mario Sammarco (Juan Bautista Alvarado), Hector Dufranne (Father Peralta), Armand Crabbé (Pico), Constantin Nicolay (Kagama), Frank Preisch (José Castro), Rosina Galli—the future Signora Gatti-Casazza (Chiquita), Minnie Egener (A Voice), and Desiré Defrère (Sergeant); Cleofonte Campanini conducted.

161. Neues vom Tage (Hindemith)

Three parts; libretto by Marcellus Schiffer; Berlin, Kroll's Opera House, June 8, 1929.

Hindemith's *Gebrauchsoper* was produced at Kroll's Opera House, Berlin, on June 8, 1929. Its notorious scene

showing the heroine in a bathtub singing in a flood of cotton soapsuds was virulently attacked by Dr. Joseph Goebbels, Nazi Minister of Propaganda, on December 6, 1934, the sentence referring to it being as notable for musical inexactness as for its tone: "Opportunity creates not only thieves but also atonal musicians who in order to create a sensation will exhibit on the stage naked women in the bathtub in the most disgusting and obscene situations and will further befoul these scenes with the most atrocious dissonance of musical impotence." Hindemith's next true opera, *Mathis der Maler*, had its *première* in Switzerland. Having revised *Neues vom Tage*, Hindemith conducted the first performance of the revised version at Naples on April 7, 1954.

162. Norma (Bellini)

Two acts; libretto by Felice Romani, after Louis-Alexandre Soumet's tragedy Norma; *Milan, Teatro alla Scala, December 26, 1831.*

Bellini's second 1831 success (its *première* followed that of *La Sonnambula* by not quite ten months) eventually became the most popular of his works. Alfred Loewenberg's *Annals of Opera* lists, outside of Italy, performances in sixteen different languages, in some thirty-five different countries, up to the beginning of the twentieth century. *Norma* was the first Italian opera ever staged at Constantinople (November 18, 1841) and the first opera sung in Italian at Bucharest (September 15, 1843), where, five years

---

[1] In *Forty Years of Opera in Chicago*, Edward Moore wrote: "As a matter of fact 'Natoma' was older than the date of its first performance. Herbert had written it several years before at the invitation of Hammerstein, when that impresario still was a power in New York. He told me once that he had

had an entirely different cast in mind at the time of its composition, that if, for instance, he had known in advance that Miss Garden was to have had the leading part, he would have constructed her music in quite another manner."

earlier, a translation of its libretto, by Gheorghe Asachi, had become the first libretto ever printed in Romanian. When *Norma* first reached the United States, it was staged at two theaters on the same night (Philadelphia, January 11, 1841) in a translation by Joseph Reese Fry, brother of William Henry Fry, the American opera composer. Within twenty-five years of its Milan *première, Norma* had been heard in most Western metropolises, as well as in such outposts as Corfu, Algiers, Palma, Malta, Jassy, Guayaquil, Nizhni Novgorod, and Soerabaja.

Vienna was the first non-Italian city to hear *Norma* (in German translation by Joseph von Seyfried, May 11, 1833), but London heard it in Italian, at the Haymarket, six weeks later (June 20, 1833). At Drury Lane, on June 24, 1837, the opera was heard in the English version of James Robinson Planché. The cast of the Milan *première* had included Giuditta Pasta (Norma), Giulia Grisi (Adalgisa), Domenico Donzelli (Pollione), and Vincenzo Negrini (Oroveso), and at the 1833 Haymarket staging, Pasta and Donzelli sang their original roles, with Henriette-Clémentine Méric-Lalande as Adalgisa and Filippo Galli as Oroveso. Bellini, who was visiting London, was called to the stage with Pasta and Donzelli by the enthusiastic audience. Pasta sang the role of Norma only once at Covent Garden (July 12, 1833), with Mme Castelli (Adalgisa), Donzelli, and Galli; on that occasion the opera was billed as "compressed into one act."

An extraordinary event occurred at Covent Garden on November 2, 1841, when Adelaide Kemble, the daughter of Charles Kemble and sister of Fanny Kemble, making her operatic debut as Norma, created such a sensation that the performance had to be repeated forty-one times up to the Easter of 1842. Sir Julius Benedict conducted, at least on the first night (and substituted for Bellini's overture one by C. Raper "as performed at Her Majesty's Theatre"). In support of Kemble were Elizabeth Rainforth (Adalgisa), William Harrison (Pollione), and Adam Leffler (Oroveso). On December 23, 1842, as Norma, Adelaide Kemble, though not yet thirty years old, made her final operatic appearance. On April 11, 1850, the enduring London popularity of Enrico Tamberlik was initiated when he appeared at Covent Garden as Pollione, with Giulia Grisi now the Norma, Mlle Vera the Adalgisa, and Karl Formes the Oroveso (Tamberlik was still singing in London twenty-seven years later). On May 18, 1861, Grisi made one of her series of London "farewell appearances" (actually she sang in London again five years later) as Norma. On March 30, 1869, the first Covent Garden season under the joint managership of Frederick Gye and James Henry Mapleson opened with a *Norma* in which Therese Tietjens sang the title role, Clarice Sinico was the Adalgisa, Pietro Mongini the Pollione, and Allan James Foley—"Signor Foli"—the Oroveso. One of the last sopranos to sing Norma at Covent Garden before the opera lapsed there for more than half a century was "Maria Vilda," in reality the Marie Wilt who in 1878 was to be the Brünnhilde of the Leipzig *Ring* cycle conducted by Anton Seidl, the first cycle sung in Germany outside of Bayreuth.

New York first heard *Norma* in English—the Fry translation—on February 25, 1841; and in Italian on September 20, 1843. It really came into its own in New York, however, only on October 2, 1854, when it was staged at the Academy of Music as the inaugural opera of that successor to the Astor Place Opera House. Giulia Grisi was the Norma of that gala occasion, and as her Pollione she had her husband, Mario. The opera was introduced to the Metropolitan on February 27, 1890, in German, with Walter Damrosch conducting and the following cast: Lilli Lehmann (Norma), Betty Frank (Adalgisa), Louise Meisslinger (Clotilde), Paul Kalisch—Lehmann's husband (Pollione), Emil Fischer (Oroveso), and Albert Mittelhauser (Flavio). Lehmann made the statement that it was easier to sing all three Brünnhildes than one Norma. In Wagner, she explained, "You are so carried away by the dramatic emotion, the action, and the scene that you do not have to think how to sing the words. That comes of itself. But in Bellini you must always have a care for beauty of tone and correct emission."

After that single *Norma* in 1890 and two more performances, both with Lehmann, in the 1891–92 season, the opera was heard no more at the Metropolitan until a revival for Rosa Ponselle on November 16, 1927.[1] Tullio Serafin conducted, and in support of the great soprano were Marion Telva (Adalgisa), Minnie Egener (Clotilde), Giacomo Lauri-Volpi (Pollione), Ezio Pinza (Oroveso), and Giordano Paltrinieri (Flavio). Ponselle sang this taxing role at the Metropolitan nineteen times, the last on January 25, 1932; Frederick Jagel and Armand Tokatyan both replaced Lauri-Volpi several times; Léon Rothier sang the Oroveso on December 14, 1928, but beginning on January 31, 1930, the Oroveso was usually Tancredi Pasero; Philine Falco was heard as Clotilde on December 14, 1928, and Angelo Bada as Flavio at several performances. On December 26, 1931, one century to the day after the Milan *première* of *Norma,* Gladys Swarthout made a much-admired appearance as Adalgisa. After 1932, *Norma* was unheard at

the Metropolitan for five years.[2] Then, on February 20 (matinee), 1937, it reappeared under the baton of Ettore Panizza, with Gina Cigna (Norma), Bruna Castagna (Adalgisa), Thelma Votipka (Clotilde), Giovanni Martinelli (Pollione), Ezio Pinza (Oroveso), and Giordano Paltrinieri (Flavio). This revival chalked up five performances in two seasons. Another new Norma made her appearance on December 29, 1943: Zinka Milanov, who was supported by Castagna (Adalgisa), Votipka (Clotilde), Jagel (Pollione), Norman Cordon (Oroveso), and Alessio de Paolis (Flavio), with Cesare Sodero conducting. Milanov sang the role eight times in two seasons, during which—on December 15, 1944—Jennie Tourel made rather more than is usually made of the character of Adalgisa. In 1954, Milanov made four more appearances as Norma, though her never entirely dependable voice was beginning to vary alarmingly; at the first of these, on March 9, 1954, with Fausto Cleva conducting, the Adalgisa was Fedora Barbieri, Gino Penno was the stentorian Pollione, and Cesare Siepi the Oroveso.

Norma finally opened a Metropolitan season on October 29, 1956, when it provided Maria Meneghini Callas with her Metropolitan debut role. Fausto Cleva again conducted, and the Adalgisa and Pollione again were respectively Barbieri and Siepi; the Pollione was Mario del Monaco. With Callas' abrupt departure from the Metropolitan roster in 1958, *Norma* again left that house without promise of return. Callas' Norma had been heard first at La Scala, Milan, in 1952, under the baton of Franco Ghione, with Ebe Stignani (Adalgisa), Gino Penno (Pollione), and Nicola Rossi-

---

[1] *Norma* was, however, sung in New York. The Chicago Opera Association, during an extensive 1920 season at the Lexington Theater, presented it, with Gino Marinuzzi conducting, Rosa Raïsa as an excelling Norma, Myrna Sharlow as Adalgisa, Alessandro Dolci as Pollione, and Virgilio Lazzari as Oroveso.

[2] A revival of *Norma* announced for February 26, 1936, with Dusolina Giannini in the title role, did not materialize.

Lemeni (Oroveso). What happened when Callas sang the druid priestess in London (with Vittorio Gui conducting, Stignani as Adalgisa, Mirto Picchi as Pollione, and Giacomo Vaghi as Oroveso), at Covent Garden on November 8, 1952, was thus described by Harold Rosenthal: "The occasion was one to remember; the audience was both brilliant and enthusiastic, and the ovations that greeted the Greek-American prima donna were of the kind usually reserved for Margot Fonteyn on ballet evenings. Callas took more than a dozen curtain calls at the close of the performance, and began the controversy about her voice and art that still exists among critics, musicians, and opera-goers wherever, and whenever, she appears." [3]

A notable revival of *Norma* occurred in the Roman Arena at Verona during the summer of 1957, with Francesco Molinari-Pradelli conducting, and a cast headed by Anita Cerquetti (Norma), Giulietta Simionato (Adalgisa), Salvatore Puma (Pollione), and Giulio Neri (Oroveso). It was Cerquetti who took over the role of Norma (which she had been singing at the Teatro San Carlo, Naples) on the stormy opening night of the Rome Opera season of 1958, when Callas refused to return to the stage after the intermission between Act I and Act II. Cerquetti also sang this role at Philadelphia later that year. For opera's contribution to the two-thousandth anniversary of the founding of Lyon, *Norma* was produced in the Roman amphitheater at Fourvière; Bruno Bogo conducted, and the cast was headed by Mary Curtis-Verna (Norma), Simionato (Adalgisa), Del Monaco (Pollione), and Plinio Clabassi (Oroveso). And on August 24, 1960, an audience

of more than twelve thousand people heard Callas as Norma in the Greek amphitheater at Epidauros in Greece. The performance was conducted by the eighty-two-year-old Tullio Serafin; others in the cast included Kiki Morfoniou (Adalgisa), Mirto Picchi (Pollione), and Ferruccio Mazzoli (Oroveso). Especially admired was the way in which the director, Alexis Minotis, had used as advantages those physical aspects of the natural setting which had seemed likely to prove disadvantages. More than a century and a quarter after its first production, Bellini's *Norma* clearly remains very much alive.

163. Le Nozze di Figaro (Mozart)

Four acts; libretto by Lorenzo da Ponte after Beaumarchais's La Folle Journée, ou Le Mariage de Figaro; *Vienna, Burgtheater, May 1, 1786.*

The cast of the world *première* included Nancy (*i.e.*, Anna Selina) Storace (Countess Almaviva), Luisa Lanchi (Susanna), Signora Mandini (Cherubino), Dorotea Bussani (Marcellina), Nannina Gottlieb (Barbarina). Stefano Mandini (Count Almaviva), Francesco Benucci (Figaro), Michael Kelly (Basilio and Don Curzio),[1] and Francesco Bussani (Bartolo). Despite the tremendous ovation of the *première*, at which every number was encored, the Viennese shelved the opera until the brilliant revival of August 29, 1789, when Adriana Ferrarese del Bene appeared as Countess Almaviva and Caterina Cavalieri as Susanna; for each of these newcomers Mozart wrote a new aria. Meanwhile the music-lovers of Prague had taken *Le Nozze* to their hearts. There, after the Italian first, it was soon given in German (June, 1787). For the

---

[3] The Clotilde of this performance made a stir even in the presence of Callas and Stignani. She was the Australian soprano Joan Sutherland, who had made her Covent Garden debut eleven days before, as the First Lady in *Die Zauberflöte.*

[1] See his *Reminiscences* (written by Theodore Hook), Vol. I, pp. 258–62, for an account of the first performance.

first performance in Italy, at Monza (which of course was still Hapsburg territory) in the autumn of 1787, the third and fourth acts were wholly rewritten by Angelo Tarchi.

As *The Follies of a Day, Le Nozze* may have been (not certainly was) sung in New York as early as 1799. Its authenticated *première* in England, at the Haymarket, London, occurred on June 18, 1812, when Angelica Catalani, one of the first women ever to manage an opera house, sang the role of Susanna. This pushing beauty, quite without taste, but with a voice of incomparable beauty and a technique that effortlessly conquered difficulties, doubtless dominated this performance. The Countess Almaviva was Maria Dickons, whose earlier experiences as an admired Polly in *The Beggar's Opera* gave zest to her interpretation. Giuseppe Naldi was the Figaro. The Covent Garden revival was in English, with Mozart "improved" by Sir Henry Rowley Bishop. The Glyndebourne *première* in 1934 employed a brilliant cast headed by Aulikki Rautawaara, Audrey Mildmay, Luise Helletsgruber, Willi Domgraf-Fassbänder, and Roy Henderson. Among favored singers in various London revivals were: (Susanna) Mary Ann Paton, the contralto Lucia Elizabeth Vestris (for whom the role was transposed down), Maria Malibran, Jenny Lind, Giulia Grisi, Adelina Patti, Marcella Sembrich, Elisabeth Schumann, and Elisabeth Schwarzkopf; (the Countess) Henriette-Clémentine Méric-Lalande, Sophie Cruvelli (*née* Crüwell),[2] Fanny Persiani, Therese Tietjens, Eugenia Pappenheim, Emma Albani, Emma Eames, Lotte Lehmann, Lisa della Casa, and Una Hale; (Cherubino) Marietta Alboni, Pauline Lucca—here unsurpassed—Marie Van Zandt, Maggie Teyte, Hilde Gueden, Anna Pollak, and Sena Juri-

nac; (Figaro) Sir Charles Santley (the most admired of English Figaros), Jean-Baptiste Faure, Antonio Cotogni, Mario Ancona, Richard Mayr, Ernest Badini, and Geraint Evans; and (the Count) Antonio Tamburini, Victor Maurel, Édouard de Reszke, Francesco d'Andrade, John Brownlee, and Eberhard Wächter. In reading these lists, we can scarcely believe that a famous tenor had once refused the baritone role of Count Almaviva because he considered it beneath his dignity to sing in a comic opera: this had happened at the London *première*. Herman Klein, in *The Golden Age of Opera,* singled out for peculiar favor the May 1884, cast: Sembrich, Albani, Lucca, Cotogni, and Édouard de Reszke.

The first authenticated performance of *Le Nozze* in the United States took place at the Park Theater, New York, on May 10, 1824, an English version being used. When Joseph Wood and his better-known wife, Mary Ann Paton, gave the opera in Boston on April 8, 1835, Charlotte Cushman, later a famous tragedy queen, was the Countess —it was her operatic debut. Once more in its original Italian, *Le Nozze* entered the repertoire of the Academy of Music, New York, on November 23, 1858. On January 31, 1894, it was first heard at the Metropolitan Opera House, with Lillian Nordica, Eames, Sigrid Arnoldson, Ancona, and Édouard de Reszke as the leading artists. The following have been outstanding interpreters of *Le Nozze* at the Metropolitan: (Susanna) Sembrich, Frieda Hempel, Bidu Sayão, Nadine Conner, and Hilde Gueden; (the Countess) Johanna Gadski, Margarete Matzenauer, Eleanor Steber, Victoria de los Angeles, and Lisa della Casa; (Cherubino) Zélie de Lussan, Suzanne Adams, Fritzi Scheff, Geraldine Farrar, Jarmila Novotna, and Risë Stevens; (Figaro) Maurel, Giuseppe Campanari, Giuseppe de Luca. Ezio Pinza, Martial Singher, Italo Tajo, Cesare

---

[2] She had made her debut in Venice, in 1847, in this role.

Siepi, and Erich Kunz; and (the Count) Antonio Scotti, Adamo Didur, John Brownlee, and George London. For the revival of February 20, 1940, after twenty-one years, Sayão, Rethberg, Stevens, Pinza, and Brownlee were the principals.

On the second night (November 20) of the 1953–54 season, the Metropolitan *Figaro,* with Fritz Stiedry conducting, marked the New York operatic debuts of Lisa della Casa (Countess) and Irmgard Seefried (Susanna); others in the cast were Frank Guarrera (Count), Erich Kunz (Figaro), Mildred Miller (Cherubino), Herta Glaz (Marcellina), and Salvatore Baccaloni (Bartolo). During the 1959–60 season, the audiences at five performances of *Figaro* were polled as to the language they would prefer for future performances of the opera. The published figures of the vote were: Italian, 6,129; English, 2,952; and German, 22. On January 28, 1961, the Metropolitan broadcast its 124th *Figaro,* happily still sung in Italian.

Statistics published in the September, 1960, issue of the English magazine *Opera* showed that of the 565 operas by 280 composers played on German-speaking stages in Germany, Austria, and Switzerland during the 1958–59 season, *Le Nozze di Figaro*—with 452 performances in 28 theaters—led all the rest. Among composers, Mozart was second (1,699 performances in 111 theaters), being preceded by Verdi (2,267 in 170 theaters) and followed by Puccini (1,351 in 108), Lortzing (1,044 in 62), and Richard Strauss (509 in 74). The ten most-performed operas were: *Figaro, Der Wildschütz, Die Zauberflöte, La Bohème, La Traviata, Carmen, Un Ballo in maschera, Der Freischütz, Tosca,* and Lortzing's *Zaar und Zimmermann.* Of the forty-two operas that received more than one hundred performances each, only five were of the twentieth century: *Madama Butterfly,*

Turandot, Ariadne auf Naxos, Jenufa, and *Der Rosenkavalier;* nine were by Verdi (*La Traviata, Un Ballo in maschera, Rigoletto, Aïda, Il Trovatore, Otello, Nabucco, La Forza del destino,* and *Don Carlos*); and only two (and they the forty-first and forty-second— *Die Meistersinger* and *Lohengrin*) were by Wagner.

164. Oberon (Weber)

Three acts; libretto by James Robinson Planché, after William Sotheby's English translation of Christoph Martin Wieland's Oberon; London, Covent Garden, April 12, 1826.

Principals in the *première* were Mary Ann Paton (Rezia), Lucia Elizabeth Vestris (Fatima), John Braham (Huon), and James Bland (Oberon), with Weber conducting. After the 1826 season, *Oberon* was not revived at Covent Garden until 1870, when the powers of Therese Tietjens pulled it through three performances, her chief colleagues being Zelia Trebelli (Fatima), Sofia Scalchi (Puck), and Giuseppe Fancelli (Huon). Thus it was that in England *Oberon* scarcely outlived the furore attending the performances that the composer himself had conducted. Similarly, although it reached New York two years after its London *première,* it then disappeared from the American stage for ninety years. On December 28, 1918, when German operas still were banned because of the bitter feelings attendant on World War I, *Oberon,* by the quite obviously German Carl Maria von Weber, was put on at the Metropolitan because it had been written to an English text. Artur Bodanzky collected the acceptable cast of Rosa Ponselle (who was not quite ready for the exigencies of "Ocean, thou mighty monster"), Alice Gentle,

Marie Sundelius (who in the minor role of the Mermaid did quite the best singing of the group), Giovanni Martinelli (who made sad business of the English allotted to Huon), and Paul Althouse. Florence Easton, who replaced Ponselle once, took over Rezia's formidable music with great authority. *Oberon* lasted three seasons, and has not since been heard at the Metropolitan.

165. Oberto, conte di San Bonifacio (Verdi)

Two acts; libretto by Antonio Piazza, revised by Bartolommeo Merelli and Temistocle Solera; Milan, Teatro alla Scala, November 17, 1839.

Verdi's first opera, counted reasonably successful as the introduction of a twenty-six-year-old tyro, is notable for the fact that the soprano and contralto who played its two principal female roles were destined for future fame. The Leonora of that first cast was Giuseppina Strepponi, who twenty years later became Verdi's second wife; the Cuniza was a young English girl making her operatic debut—Mary Postans Shaw, who was to have a brilliant brief career at Covent Garden, and who had sung at the Gewandhaus, Leipzig, under Mendelssohn's direction. *Oberto* was staged at Turin in 1840, at Genoa in January, 1841, and at the Teatro San Carlo, Naples, in the spring of that same year. It was to be restaged at Milan on November 17, 1889, the fiftieth anniversary of its *première*, and at Busseto, Verdi's childhood home, on July 30, 1939, prematurely, to celebrate its centenary. Very few other productions have been noted. During the Italian celebrations of the fiftieth anniversary (1951) of Verdi's death, *Oberto* was revived at La Scala under the baton of Franco Capuana; the cast included Maria Caniglia, Ebe Stignani, and Gianni Poggi.

166. Orfeo [La Favola d'Orfeo] (Monteverdi)

Prologue and five acts; libretto by Alessandro Striggio; performed privately, Accademia degl' Invaghiti, Mantua, February, 1607; also at the court theater, Mantua, February 24, 1607.

The role of Orfeo was sung at the Mantuan *première* by Giovanni Gualberto. The first modern stage performance occurred at the Théâtre Réjane, Paris, May 2, 1911; a French version prepared by Vincent d'Indy was used. The earliest American (concert) performance, condensed and in English, took place during a Metropolitan Opera House (New York) Sunday night concert, April 14, 1912; Josef Pasternack conducted, and the cast included Hermann Weil (Orfeo), Rita Fornia (Euridice), Anna Case (Nymph), Herbert Witherspoon (Pluto), and Basil Ruysdael (Charon). The first American staging occurred at Northampton, Massachusetts, May 12, 1929; a version prepared by G. Francesco Malipiero was used; Werner Josten conducted; the Orfeo was Charles Kullmann. The first performance in England (the D'Indy version in concert form) took place in London, March 8, 1924; the first staging in England, in an English translation arranged by J. A. Westrup and W. H. Harris, occurred at Oxford, December 7, 1925. Notable among numerous recent revivals in Italy was that at the Florentine Maggio Musicale in 1949; the arrangement was by Vito Frazzi; Fedora Barbieri was the Orfeo. Other versions have been edited or prepared by Giacomo Benvenuti, Giacomo Orefice, Ottorino Respighi, Hans Erdmann-Guckel, Carl Orff, and Hans Ferdinand Redlich.

Orfeo was at last staged in New York on September 29, 1960. On that evening, sharing a double bill with the New York *première* (in English translation) of Luigi Dallapiccola's *Il Prigioniero,* it opened a season of the New

York City Opera at the City Center. Drastically shortened and revised by the conductor, Leopold Stokowski, the venerable opera made a considerable effect largely because of the excellent singing of Gérard Souzay in the title role.

167. Orfeo ed Euridice (Gluck)

Three acts; libretto by Raniero de' Calzabigi; Vienna, Burgtheater, October 5, 1762; the reworked French version, Orphée et Eurydice, *with text translated by Pierre-Louis Moline, was first sung at the Opéra, Paris, on August 2, 1774.*

In the original Vienna production, the role of Orfeo was sung by an alto *castrato,* Gaetano Guadagni. The first cast of the French version included Joseph Legros, a tenor (Orphée), Sophie Arnould (Eurydice), and Marie-Rosalie Levasseur (Cupidon). The Vienna production had not been a success (only seven performances up to July 24, 1763), but the Paris version had been given 297 times by July 28, 1848.

London heard an Italian version first (April 7, 1770), but the text had been edited by Giovanni Gualberto Bottarelli, and music had been added by Johann Christian Bach and Pietro Guglielmi; the original Italian score was sung in London on March 9, 1773. Alfred Loewenberg asserts that when the opera was first performed in London in English translation (Covent Garden, February 28, 1792), it contained additional music by Johann Christian Bach, Handel, William Reeve, Antonio Maria Gasparo Sacchini, and Charles Weichsel.

It is possible that the first performance in the United States took place at Charleston, South Carolina, on June 24, 1794, in French. But the first certain American singing occurred at the Winter Garden, New York, on May 25, 1863, in an English translation by Fanny Malone Raymond. The opera was also heard in English at the Academy of Music, New York, on January 8, 1886. Perhaps the most renowned revival of all was that first sung at the Théâtre-Lyrique, Paris, on November 18, 1859, for which Berlioz had crossed the Italian and French scores, but kept the French text; the Orphée was Pauline Viardot-García, who won a resounding personal triumph. Berlioz' version was heard at Covent Garden, London, June 27, 1860; Rosa Czillag was the Orpheus, Marie Miolan-Carvalho the Eurydice. Gluck's original French version finally reached Covent Garden on June 22, 1905, conducted by André Messager, and with Louise Kirkby-Lunn as Orphée, Jeanne Raunay as Eurydice; a few days later (July 3), the ailing Kirkby-Lunn was replaced by Jeanne Gerville-Réache, who was greatly praised.

Other notable Covent Garden performances of *Orfeo ed Euridice* occurred in 1890 when, beginning on November 6, Giulia Ravogli triumphantly assumed the role of Orfeo opposite her sister Sofia as Euridice; the six performances of the season were all completely sold out, and George Bernard Shaw wrote idolatrously of Giulia Ravogli's "perfectly original artistic impulse." On July 1, 1920, Sir Thomas Beecham conducted a revival of *Orphée et Eurydice* at Covent Garden, with Clara Butt, making her first official operatic appearance, as Orphée, and Miriam Licette as Eurydice. In 1947, at Glyndebourne, Kathleen Ferrier won one of her greatest successes as Orfeo, a success she repeated when the opera was sung at Town Hall, New York, on March 2, 1949, in concert form under the direction of Thomas Scherman; in New York the Euridice was Ann Ayars, the Amor "Louisa Kinlock"— the temporary stage name of Ethel

Barrymore Colt. Ferrier's final appearance was as Orfeo at Covent Garden on February 6, 1953.

The first Metropolitan staging of *Orfeo ed Euridice* was conducted by Augusto Vianesi, with Giulia Ravogli as Orfeo, Sofia Ravogli as Euridice, and Mathilde Bauermeister as Amor. The date was December 30, 1891, and the other half of the double bill was the first Metropolitan singing of *Cavalleria rusticana,* in which Giulia Ravogli was the Lola, Bauermeister the Mamma Lucia. New York did not share London's admiration for the Ravoglis in the Gluck opera, which seems to have been haphazardly staged: according to Irving Kolodin, "Odds and ends from *Merlin* [Goldmark] and *Asraël* [Franchetti] were utilized to dress the stage for *Orfeo.*"

On December 23, 1909, Arturo Toscanini conducted a still-remembered *Orfeo* at the Metropolitan,[1] with Louise Homer (Orfeo), Johanna Gadski (Euridice), Bella Alten (Amor), and Alma Gluck (Happy Shade). The stage designs were by Puvis de Chavannes. Later Metropolitan Orfeos under Toscanini's baton were Marie Delna (her American debut, January 29, 1910) and Margarete Matzenauer (December 25, 1911). After April 3, 1914, *Orfeo* left the Metropolitan repertoire for twenty-two years, being revived during the resident company's first spring season, on May 22, 1936, under the baton of Richard Hageman. The action was mimed in a ludicrous "experimental" manner by the American Ballet Ensemble; the singers—not much better—were relegated to the orchestra pit; for the record, the double cast (mime-singer) consisted of Lew Christensen–Anna Kaskas (Orfeo), Daphne Vane–Jeanne Pengelly (Euridice), and William Dollar–Max-

ine Stellman (Amor). On November 29, 1939, the Metropolitan partially redeemed itself by presenting, under Erich Leinsdorf's direction, the magnificently sung Orfeo of Kerstin Thorborg, who unfortunately was given wretched support by Irene Jessner (Euridice), Marita Farell (Amor), and Annamary Dickey (Happy Shade). Jarmila Novotna was the admired Euridice of some later Thorborg performances. The most recent Metropolitan incarnation of *Orfeo* was first heard on February 24, 1954, when Pierre Monteux conducted and the cast included Risë Stevens (Orfeo), Hilde Gueden (Euridice), Roberta Peters (Amor), and Laurel Hurley (Happy Shade); much attention was concentrated on the dancing of Alicia Markova in the Elysian Fields scene. Miss Stevens, possibly the handsomest Orfeo of all time, never was Thorborg's equal as a singer, and in later years her vocalization of this role notably failed to match her acting of it. On November 1, 1960, at Town Hall, New York, the American Opera Society presented *Orfeo ed Euridice* in a concert arrangement that appeared to be the French version translated back into Italian. Antonio de Almeida conducted, and the wholly dominant star of the performance was Giulietta Simionato, who again asserted her position as one of the foremost operatic personalities of her time.

At the 1951 Maggio Musicale Fiorentino, one of the operas was billed as Joseph Haydn's *Orfeo ed Euridice.* Actually, this was a cut version of the opera *L'Anima del filosofo,* with libretto by Carlo Francesco Badini, which Haydn composed for presentation in London in 1791, but which was not performed, having fallen innocent victim to the strained relations

---

[1] In view of Toscanini's reputation as a purist, it is worth noting that he was not satisfied with the Gevaert edition used, but interpolated into the performance "Divinités du Styx" from *Alceste,* a trio from *Paride ed Elena,* and a chorus from *Echo et Narcisse,* the last as a substitute for Gluck's own finale.

between George III and the Prince of Wales. This *Orfeo ed Euridice* had some partial concert performances in Leipzig and Königsberg early in the nineteenth century, but the Florence production appears to have been its first staging. Leading roles were sung by Maria Meneghini Callas and Boris Christoff; the conductor was Erich Kleiber.

168. Otello, ossia Il Moro di Venezia (Rossini)

Three acts; libretto by the Marchese Francesco Berio di Salsa, after Shakespeare's Othello; Naples, Teatro del Fondo, December 4, 1816.

This very successful opera was widely sung throughout Italy—and in a few decades had been heard in German, Hungarian, English, French, Spanish, Polish, and Russian. The original Desdemona was Isabella Colbran, later Rossini's wife; famed later performers of this role included Giuditta Pasta, Henriette Sontag, Maria Malibran, Pauline Viardot-García, and Christine Nilsson. Annoyed by what she took to be the pallidness of Desdemona's character, Pasta also attempted the part of Otello, securing for herself a *succès de scandale*. Most renowned of the Rossini Otellos was Enrico Tamberlik.

London first heard *Otello* at the Haymarket Theatre on May 16, 1822, in Italian. Its first production at Covent Garden occurred in 1850, when the cast included Tamberlik (Otello), Giulia Grisi (Desdemona), and Giorgio Ronconi (Iago); on August 7, 1855, the opera was repeated there with Tamberlik again in the title role, Viardot-García (Desdemona), and Francesco Graziani (Iago). On June 21, 1870, at the Drury Lane Theatre, Christine Nilsson was the Desdemona, with Pietro Mongini (Otello) and

Jean-Baptiste Faure (Iago). On May 12, 1871, at Covent Garden, Mongini repeated his Otello, with Graziani as Iago and Adelina Patti the Desdemona.

Otello reached New York, in Italian, on February 7, 1826, being presented by the visiting troupe headed by Manuel del Popolo Vicente García, which included his daughter, the future Maria Malibran. The opera has never been sung at New York's Metropolitan, and in the years following the great success of Verdi's *Otello* has been heard rarely. It was sung in concert performance by the American Opera Society at Town Hall, New York, on November 23, 1954. Arnold U. Gamson conducted, and leading roles were sung by Thomas Hayward (Otello), Jennie Tourel (Desdemona), Thomas Lo Monaco (Iago), Albert Da Costa (Rodrigo), and Carol Brice (Emilia). When the Society revived it at Town Hall on December 10, 1957, Gamson again conducted and Hayward was the Otello; the other chief roles had passed into the hands of Eileen Farrell (Desdemona), Hugh Thompson (Iago), Loren Driscoll (Rodrigo), and Martha Lipton (Emilia).

169. Otello (Verdi)

Four acts; libretto by Arrigo Boito, after Shakespeare's Othello; Milan, Teatro alla Scala, February 5, 1887.

Romilda Pantaleoni, the Desdemona of the La Scala *première* of *Otello*, was of local celebrity and largely so remained. But the Otello and Iago of that triumphant night— respectively Francesco Tamagno and Victor Maurel—were destined to become world-famous in the parts they created. Franco Faccio conducted. Before 1887 was over, *Otello* had been heard in five more Italian cities. During 1888, ten more of them were added. The first singing outside Italy must have been a strange performance. It took place in Mexico City on November 18, 1887. Paolo Valline had orchestrated the opera from a vocal score in order to avoid paying the composer and his publisher their just due. The opera was sung in a variety of translations in St. Petersburg, Budapest, Prague, Hamburg, Brünn, Amsterdam, and Vienna before it reached New York.

On April 16, 1888, at the Academy of Music, New York heard *Otello* in Italian, thus becoming the first non-Italian city to hear it as Boito had written it and Verdi composed it. As lessee of the Academy, Italo Campanini had his brother Cleofonte conduct and cast his sister-in-law, Eva Tetrazzini (sister of the more famous Luisa), as Desdemona; others in the cast were Francesco Marconi (Otello), Sofia Scalchi (Emilia), and Antonio Galassi (Iago). Marconi, primarily a lyric tenor, was terribly miscast as the dramatic Otello; after two performances, Italo Campanini sent him back to Europe and himself assumed the role. In vain, for after seven repetitions of *Otello,* the Academy had to close its doors temporarily.

Otello was not sung in New York again until March 24, 1890, when the management of Abbey and Grau presented it at the Metropolitan. (This was a postseason performance, and is not credited historically to the resident Metropolitan company. It was sung in Italian, whereas all of the preceding regular season's operas had been sung in German.) Tamagno was intensely admired in the title role, Giuseppe del Puente was the Iago, and Emma Albani—already well known in New York—made her Metropolitan Opera House debut as Desdemona. The resident company followed suit not quite two years later, when, on January 11, 1892, Louis Victor Saar conducted, Albani was the Desdemona, Scalchi

the Emilia, Eduardo Camera the Iago —and Jean de Reszke the Otello.

At various times, *Otello* has enlisted magnificent Metropolitan casts. One of the most remarkable was that of December 3, 1894, when, under the baton of Luigi Mancinelli, Emma Eames was the Desdemona, Eugenia Mantelli the Emilia, Tamagno the Otello, Maurel the Iago. As the opening opera of the 1902–3 season (November 24, 1902), *Otello* had this cast: Eames (Desdemona), Louise Homer (Emilia), Albert Alvarez (Otello), Antonio Scotti (Iago), Marcel Journet (Lodovico), and Eugène Dufriche (Montano). A tenor who rivaled Tamagno's Moor was Leo Slezak, who made his Metropolitan debut in the first Toscanini *Otello,* on November 17, 1909. Florence Wickham, the Emilia, also made her first Metropolitan bow that evening; others in the cast were Frances Alda (Desdemona), Scotti (Iago), Angelo Bada (Cassio), Herbert Witherspoon (Lodovico), and Vincenzo Reschiglian (Montano). Six performances were attained that season, equaling the number reached the season before at Hammerstein's Manhattan Opera House, where Nellie Melba, Giovanni Zenatello, and Mario Sammarco had made an unforgettable impression.

Otello remained in the Metropolitan repertoire until Slezak's departure— after his final *Otello,* on January 31, 1913, a performance during which Scotti, replacing the indisposed Pasquale Amato at short notice, had to sing the first-act Iago costumed as Barnaba in *La Gioconda,* his costumes being delayed en route from Boston. Thereafter, *Otello* was not heard at the Metropolitan until December 22, 1937, on which date Martinelli, vocally past his prime, had, as the Moor, perhaps the greatest musicodramatic triumph of his career, sharing the honors with Donald

Oenslager's new décors and such other singers as Elisabeth Rethberg (Desdemona), Thelma Votipka (Emilia), and Lawrence Tibbett (Iago). Eight singings that season indicated that the opera was solidly established with the New York public.

On November 21, 1938, the opera opened a Metropolitan season, again with Martinelli and Tibbett, but with Maria Caniglia as Desdemona. It opened another Metropolitan season, under Fritz Busch's baton, on November 29, 1948 (the first opening night to be televised), when Ramón Vinay was the Otello, Leonard Warren the Iago, Licia Albanese the Desdemona, and Martha Lipton the Emilia. At a Saturday matinee performance on November 15, 1958, a favorite latter-day trio of singers was heard in the three chief roles: Mario del Monaco, Warren, and Renata Tebaldi. At the end of that season, *Otello* had been given eighty-seven performances during regular Metropolitan seasons.

When *Otello* was first sung at the Paris Opéra (October 12, 1894), the French translation of the libretto was the work of Boito himself and Camille du Locle; the Otello was Albert Saléza. Five years earlier, the first London staging, in Italian, had been at the Lyceum Theatre; Franco Faccio had conducted the orchestra of La Scala, imported for the occasion, and the principal roles had been in the hands of Tamagno, Maurel, and Cattaneo. Covent Garden presented *Otello* in 1891, when Albani and Eames alternated as Desdemona, Maurel and Dufriche as Iago, the Emilia was Mme Passana, Jean de Reszke had the title role, and Mancinelli conducted. On November 19, 1892, Melba was the Desdemona, Olimpia Guercia the Emilia, Ferruccio Giannini the Otello, Dufriche the Iago, and Enrico Bevignani the conductor. Tamagno made his Covent Garden debut as

Otello in the opening-night performance of the 1895 spring-summer season, with Albani, Rosa Olitzka, and Arturo Pessina. He returned six years later to sing the role again (June 15, 1901), this time with Eames, Olitzka, and Scotti. Maurel, at the age of fifty-six—thirty-six years after his operatic debut—sang Iago at Covent Garden on November 24, 1904, the year of his retirement. His Desdemona was Rina Giachetti; the Otello was one "Signor Duc," from whom little was expected or received.

In a Covent Garden *Otello* of July 11, 1908, with Cleofonte Campanini conducting (and with Melba as Desdemona, Scotti as Iago), Zenatello began to encounter vocal troubles during Act II. In the succeeding intermission, the management asked the audience for its indulgence—and it has been said that Zenatello never again, at least in Covent Garden, sang Otello's opening "Esultate" in full voice. On June 2, 1909, Slezak, returning to Covent Garden after a nine-year absence, sang his first Otello there, triumphing despite the audience's affection for Zenatello in this part. Melba, by then fifty-four, was still the Desdemona of the first *Otello* of the 1914 spring-summer season (Covent Garden's last until 1919), but in the second she was replaced with a twenty-five-year-old Italian singer, Claudia Muzio; others in the cast were Ruby Heyl (Emilia), the much-admired Paul Franz (Otello), and Scotti (Iago).

After some postwar seasons in which *Otello* was occasionally heard at Covent Garden with casts of local singers, part of it was part of a memento to a great past when, on June 8, 1926, George V and Queen Mary were in the house to attend Melba's farewell. The sixty-five-year-old soprano sang the second act of Gounod's *Roméo et Juliette,* the third and fourth acts of *La Bohème,* and the opening section of the last act of *Otello* (with Jane Bourguignon as Emilia). It was announced during the 1927 season that the Irish tenor whom James Joyce labored to promote, John O'Sullivan (or Sullivan), would sing the role of Otello. But when a singing of *Les Huguenots* in which he was the Raoul proved to be a crushing fiasco—and not least because of him—these plans were canceled; he was not heard further at Covent Garden, and neither was *Les Huguenots*. *Otello* was postponed until 1928, when the title role was sung by the Chilean tenor Renato Zanelli, Slezak's true successor.

On June 2, 1933, Lauritz Melchior sang the role of Otello at Covent Garden—in German, much to the displeasure of parts of the audience, perhaps because his colleagues (Rosetta Pampanini as Desdemona, Constance Willis as Emilia, Giacomo Rimini as Iago) stuck to the original Italian. By the following season, however, Melchior was singing in something resembling Italian, this time in a cast in which only the Cassio and the Lodovico were Italians, the other principal roles being sung by Viorica Ursuleac (Desdemona), Jane Bourguignon (Emilia), and John Brownlee (Iago). Melchior never sang the Moor at the Metropolitan, but he did try the role with the San Francisco Opera on December 5, 1934, when the Desdemona was another non-Italian, Elisabeth Rethberg. On the opening night of the 1937 (Coronation) season, Martinelli, singing in London for the first time in eighteen years, was the Otello. Sir Thomas Beecham conducted, Fernanda Ciani was the Desdemona, Ebe Ticozzi the Emilia, and Cesare Formichi the Iago. Melchior returned during the 1939 season (the last until 1946 in the house), having Caniglia as his Desdemona; Mario Basiola was the Iago.

When a company from La Scala, Milan, played a ten-day season at Covent Garden in September, 1950, it opened on September 12 with an *Otello* that rubbed away much of the tarnish the opera had been acquiring. Victor de Sabata conducted, and the cast included Vinay (Otello), Tebaldi (Desdemona), Anna Maria Canali (Emilia), and Gino Bechi (Iago). And on October 17, 1955, Rafael Kubelik began his brief tenure as musical director of Covent Garden by presenting *Otello*. He himself conducted, and the stars of the cast were Gré Brouwenstijn (Desdemona), Vinay (Otello), and Otakar Kraus (Iago).[1]

Otello has been—and continues to be—performed frequently almost everywhere in the operatic world. Toscanini conducted an often-recalled performance of it at La Scala, Milan, in 1927, when Bianca Scacciati was the Desdemona—and Trantoul, the Otello, was outshone by the Iago, Mariano Stabile. The line of renowned Otellos, begun by Tamagno and continued by Zenatello, Slezak, Zanelli, Martinelli, Vinay, and Del Monaco, also included Aureliano Pertile.

170. Pagliacci (Leoncavallo)

Prologue and two acts; libretto by the composer; Milan, Teatro dal Verme, May 21, 1892.

The first cast of *Pagliacci* was notable chiefly for including both Victor Maurel and Mario Ancona. The opera's success was immediate, and its staying power has more than equaled that of *Cavalleria rusticana*. For instance, since its *première* at the Metropolitan Opera on December 11, 1893,

---

[1] Tito Gobbi had been engaged to sing Iago, but when he had not yet reached London at 5:30 P.M. on October 11, six days before the opening night, Kubelik decided to discipline him—and perhaps to save the performance—by substituting Kraus.

it has been out of that house's repertoire only twelve seasons—quite different from the situation at Covent Garden, where it has been rarely heard since 1928. The first Metropolitan cast follows: Nellie Melba (Nedda), Ancona (Tonio), Fernando de Lucia (Canio), Victor de Gromzeski (Silvio), and Pedro Guetary (Beppe). Oddly enough, Melba, in her first Metropolitan season, had not, despite critical acclaim, been winning the public. Her Nedda, however, was warmly received. Antonio Scotti soon made the role of Tonio his, and somewhat later Enrico Caruso began to evolve what doubtless became the most famous of Canios. Geraldine Farrar made Nedda a favorite role, so that a Farrar, Caruso, and Scotti performance, with whomever else, became somewhat of a fixture. Claudia Muzio and Florence Easton were successful Neddas. Unhappily, Caruso wrenched a muscle in his back during a performance of *Pagliacci* on December 8, 1911, and the results were so lamentable that he broke down during *L'Elisir d'amore* three days later. Giulio Crimi was to succeed him for a few years. Elisabeth Rethberg was a bit too Germanic for Nedda, though she sang the Ballatella exquisitely. Giovanni Martinelli had the ample voice needed for Canio. Eventually John Charles Thomas sang his sonorous Tonio, and Grace Moore was a popular Nedda. Leonard Warren's Tonio was one of the better interpretations of the *Pagliacci* performances during the fifties, and Mario del Monaco was a brilliant Canio. Lucine Amara's Nedda, though often heard, never achieved the dash and glitter needed for the role. As with *Cavalleria,* the Metropolitan management has ever been too willing to produce *Pagliacci* with a slapdash cast, relying on its perdurable popularity to bring in the audience. It was as Canio that, on January 17, 1960, the excellent Canadian tenor Jon

Vickers made his Metropolitan debut.

Melba, Ancona, and De Lucia were in the first Convent Garden cast (May 19, 1893), and achieved ovation after ovation. Yet, *Pagliacci,* again like *Cavalleria,* did not take London by a storm that lasted, as it has taken New York. Fritzi Scheff, who made her London debut on May 19, 1900, as Nedda, was thought delectable, and the entire performance was deemed the best heard there; Thomas Salignac and Scotti were the other stars. A bit later, Emmy Destinn, Caruso, and Scotti were a familiar, popular triangle. Amadeo Bassi was an interim Canio. Caruso's return to the role in 1913 brought forth a newspaper comment that "no singer of our time has ever made a more triumphant *rentrée* at the opera." Fernand Ansseau, bravely trying Canio, in an—at first— far from perfect Italian, became a popular Canio. An effective Canio in the thirties was Dennis Noble. One of the last notable performances (October 1, 1946) of *Pagliacci* at Covent Garden starred Margherita Carosio, Mario del Monaco, and Paolo Silveri, during a season of Italian opera by the visiting San Carlo, Naples, company.

Pagliacci was the first opera ever sung in Bulgarian (Sofia, May 5, 1909).

171. Palestrina (Pfitzner)

Three acts; libretto by the composer; Munich, June 12, 1917.

Bruno Walter conducted the world *première,* in which the role of Palestrina was sung by Karl Erb; others in the cast included Maria Ivogün (Ighino), Fritz Feinhals, Friedrich Brodersen, Paul Bender, and Gustav Schützendorf. In November of that year, the Munich troupe performed the opera in Basel, Bern, and Zurich. Bruno Kittel was the conductor when the opera was staged at Vienna on March 1, 1919, with Emil Schmedes as Palestrina, supported by Lotte Lehmann (Ighino), Feinhals, Hans Duhan, Richard Mayr, Viktor Madin, and Georg Maikl. Pfitzner conducted the Berlin *première*, on October 11, 1919. Other tenors who sang the title role in German and Viennese productions were Marcel Wittrisch, Julius Patzak, and Lorenz Fehenberger. The opera does not appear to have been staged outside German-speaking countries, except for a production at Antwerp in February, 1939, and that too was sung in German.

172. Le Pardon de Ploërmel [Dinorah] (Meyerbeer)

Three acts; libretto by Jules Barbier and Michel Carré; Paris, Opéra-Comique, April 4, 1859.

Napoleon III and the Empress Eugénie were in the house when Meyerbeer conducted the first performance of *Le Pardon de Ploërmel.* Leading roles were sung by Marie Cabel (Dinorah), Sainte-Foy (Corentin), and Jean-Baptiste Faure (Hoël). The opera was an immediate success. At its one-hundredth performance, on September 26, 1874, the roles of Hoël and Correntin were sung by Jacques-Joseph-André Bouhy and Paul Lhérie, respectively the Escamillo and the Don José of the following year's first performance of *Carmen.* The opera had been sung at the Comique 216 times through 1950.

Le Pardon de Ploërmel has almost always been known outside France by the name of its heroine, *Dinorah.* Meyerbeer himself arranged the Italian version of the opera (translation by Achille de Lauzières de Thémines) and supervised the rehearsals when

Dinorah was sung outside France for the first time, at Covent Garden, London, on July 26, 1859, less than four months after the Paris *première.* The Dinorah was Marie Miolan-Carvalho, the Corentino Italo Gardoni, the Hoël Francesco Graziani; Constance-Betsy-Rosabella Nantier-Didiée sang a minor role. When the "Royal English Opera" that had been organized by Louisa Pyne and William Harrison gave the second of its eight seasons at Covent Garden, it opened on October 3, 1859, with Henry Fothergill Chorley's English translation of *Dinorah.* Louisa Pyne sang the Dinorah, Harrison the Corentin, and Sir Charles Santley the Hoël; during the forty-six performances of that season, Euphrosyne Parepa also sang the title role.

Ilma di Murska was heard as Dinorah at Her Majesty's Theatre, London, in 1866. When she sang the role at Covent Garden on November 21, 1868, Luigi Arditi conducted, Signor Bettini was the Corentin, Santley the Hoël; a minor role was sung by Sofia Scalchi. Five years later, on May 19, 1873, Adelina Patti sang Dinorah to the Hoël of Victor Maurel, with Bettini and Scalchi. When Marcella Sembrich sang her first Covent Garden Dinorah on May 23, 1881, her Hoël was Jean Lassalle, with Ignazio Marini and Zelia Trebelli. Patti also sang in *Dinorah* that season. The Jubilee year, 1887, proved to be *Dinorah*'s last at Covent Garden. Ella Russell sang the title role, Francesco d'Andrade the Corentin; Enrico Bevignani conducted. Two performances that season, and *Dinorah* was heard at Covent Garden no more.

New Orleans was the first city in the United States to hear *Le Pardon de Ploërmel,* in French, on March 4, 1861. The first New York performance, in Italian, occurred on November 24, 1862. A single performance of the opera was sung at the Metropolitan during the 1891–92 season

(January 29, 1892); Marie Van Zandt was the Dinorah, Signor Gianini the Corentino, Lassalle the Hoël; Giulia Ravogli was one of the two Goatherds. During her first New York season, Luisa Tetrazzini sang Dinorah at the Manhattan Opera House (1907). When the Chicago Opera Association visited New York in 1918, Amelita Galli-Curci, on the night of January 28, 1918, created a true triumph for herself as Dinorah under the baton of Cleofonte Campanini; her colleagues were Gustave Huberdeau, Giacomo Rimini, and Octava Dua. The soprano took some twenty-four curtain calls after singing "Ombra leggiera" (the "Shadow Song"), and about sixty at the close of the opera. Nevertheless, when she sang in *Dinorah* as a member of the Metropolitan company on January 22, 1925, with Armand Tokatyan as Corentino and Giuseppe de Luca as Hoël, and repeated the performance eight days later, the Metropolitan was through with another Meyerbeer opera.

The first time that Galli-Curci had sung in *Dinorah* in Chicago had turned out to be a very peculiar occasion. Someone threw a stench bomb and all but caused a panic. Cleofonte Campanini, who was conducting, immediately switched from Meyerbeer to "The Star-Spangled Banner"; Galli-Curci, who did not know the words, vocalized the melody, a brave fireman carried the hissing bomb to the street, and the evening was saved. It is said that Galli-Curci became so attached to the role of Dinorah that she left the Chicago Opera Company because the management insisted that she sing it less often.

Recent revivals of *Dinorah* have been few in any language anywhere.

173. Paride ed Elena (Gluck)

*Five acts; libretto by Raniero de' Calzabigi; Vienna, Burgtheater, No-*vember 3 (*not 30, as often asserted*), *1770.*

In the original performance, the role of Paride was sung by Giuseppe Milico, that of Elena by Katharine Schindler, and that of Amor by Theresia Kurz; the dances were directed by Jean-Georges Noverre. It was a failure, and the only other eighteenth-century performance of it seems to have occurred at Naples in 1777. There have been several twentieth-century revivals, mostly in concert form, but *Paride ed Elena* survives chiefly because of Paride's famous aria with oboe obbligato, "O del mio dolce ardor bramato oggetto . . ."

The American Opera Society, which had presented the New York *première* of *Paride en Elena,* in concert form, at Town Hall, New York, on January 15, 1954 (with Paul Franke as Paride, Mariquita Moll as Elena, Laurel Hurley as Amor, and Maria Leona as Pallade Atena), repeated it, somewhat more sensationally, again at Town Hall, on November 5, 1957. On the latter occasion, David Poleri was the Paride, Miss Hurley and Miss Moll repeated their earlier performances— and the Pallade Atena, making a striking (some thought it almost a frightening) New York operatic debut was Anita Cerquetti. The sheer impact of size (of both physical presence and voice) as she stood before the audience holding a huge score in both hands made all that had gone before seem puny by comparison.

174. Parsifal (Wagner)

Three acts; libretto by the composer; Bayreuth, Festspielhaus, July 26, 1882.

The chief singers at the world *première* were Hermann Winkelmann (Parsifal), Emil Scaria (Gurnemanz),

Karl Hill (Klingsor), Theodor Reichmann (Amfortas), and Amalie Materna (Kundry). Hermann Levi was the conductor.

Because of its quasi-religious character, Wagner did not wish to have *Parsifal* performed outside Bayreuth: there the special facilities for its production had been brought into being under his own supervision, and there, too, a tradition of reverence had, from its first performance, clung to this last of the *Meister's* music dramas. Yet, there is evidence that, toward the end of 1882, he had so relaxed his point of view that he was willing to give Angelo Neumann a contract to take *Parsifal* on tour. He died, however, on February 13, 1883, without giving Neumann the precious document. Frau Cosima, *plus royaliste que le roi,* was fanatical in her efforts to restrict stage performances to Bayreuth. Oratorio versions and concert excerpts were another matter, and almost at once advantage was taken of this concession. During the Edmond C. Stanton regime at the Metropolitan occurred, on March 4, 1886, under Walter Damrosch, the first oratorio presentation of *Parsifal* in America, the principals, including Marianne Brandt and Emil Fischer, singing in German; the Oratorio Society chorus sang in English.

Late in 1886, Stanton played with the idea of giving *Parsifal* as an opera, but was dissuaded by, among others, Lilli Lehmann, who considered the scheme a sacrilege. It was shelved for fifteen years. Then Heinrich Conried, desiring something unusual for his first season at the Metropolitan, determined to brook all protest, and scheduled *Parsifal,* as a music drama, for Christmas Eve, 1903. It was a publicity move of genius: ministers thundered at him from their pulpits, Mayor Seth Low was asked to intervene, and the Wagner family, through its American representative,

brought suit against Conried. But he was unmoved, confident in his knowledge that Wagner's operas were not protected by copyright in the United States. He won the suit, and produced the opera in an atmosphere of excitement comparable to that attending the election of a president. Fannie Bloomfield Zeisler, the pianist, chartered a special "Parsifal" Limited from Chicago, and the *New York Evening Telegram* brought out a "Parsifal" extra. At the *première,* Alfred Hertz conducted, with Milka Ternina (Kundry) and Aloys Burgstaller (Parsifal) heading a fine cast, including Anton Van Rooy, Marcel Journet, Robert Blass, Otto Goritz, and Louise Homer. The performance went off magnificently, and ten repetitions were called for that season. Only the new Italian tenor, Enrico Caruso, measured up to the furore created by *Parsifal.* Since then, despite its great length and difficulties of staging, *Parsifal* has been out of the Metropolitan only those two years when German art was being excoriated along with the Kaiser and the seasons of 1950–51 (which was an experimental moment) 1959–60, and 1961–62. It has become a fixture of the Lenten season.[1] In later years, Lauritz Melchior was the Parsifal, Kirsten Flagstad the Kundry, and Friedrich Schorr the Amfortas. After Flagstad's departure, Kerstin Thorborg and Rose Bampton alternated as the Kundry; after Melchior's departure, Torsten Ralf succeeded to the role of Parsifal for several years, and after him Charles Kullman. Helen Traubel was a latecomer to the role of Kundry. After the respite of 1950–51 (no *Parsifal*), Set Svanholm was the Parsifal, Astrid Varnay the Kundry, and Hans Hotter the Amfortas, a role

[1] During Gatti-Casazza's first season at the Metropolitan, *Parsifal* was apparently an integral outgrowth of American history, for of the five performances during 1908–9, three took place on Thanksgiving, Lincoln's Birthday, and Washington's Birthday.

later taken by George London. Of the three Varnay played her role longest: she left the Metropolitan in 1956.

With a solemnity that must have been impressive at the time, but is a bit absurd in retrospect, Covent Garden first produced *Parsifal* on February 2, 1914. Eva von der Osten was the "truly remarkable Kundry," and Heinrich Hensel was the Parsifal. Other singers were Paul Bender (Amfortas), Paul Knüpfer (Gurnemanz), August Kiess (Klingsor), and Murray Davey (Titurel). The conductor was Artur Bodanzky, then director of the Mannheim Opera, and later for a number of years director of the German-opera division of the Metropolitan Opera House. *Parsifal* was sung no less than nineteen times at Covent Garden in 1914, and there were inevitable replacements in the cast, the most interesting being Margarete Matzenauer as Kundry and Karl Burrian as Parsifal. Covent Garden was shuttered during World War I (as it was through World War II), and the first postwar *Parsifal* was in English. Although some performers sang well, and moreover could be understood, the experiment, which was not unconnected with a possibly unconscious attempt to turn *Parsifal* into a cosy semioperatic English oratorio, was not altogether successful. Glady Ancrum (Kundry) and Norman Allin (Gurnemanz) were the stars of this occasion. It should be said at once, however, that after the stuffiness of the first years, the English managed to take their *Parsifal* or leave it, and it was almost as often out of the repertoire as in. It is worth noting the wonderful performances of Gertrud Rünger (Kundry), Friedrich Schorr (Amfortas), and Alexander Kipnis (Gurnemanz). The last season (1939) before World War II brought the best *Parsifal* in many a year, and even Ernest Newman was satisfied; he particularly praised Torsten Ralf (Parsifal), Her-

bert Janssen (Amfortas), and Ludwig Weber (Gurnemanz), but his chief salvo went to Kerstin Thorborg's Kundry: "I would rank her as the greatest Wagnerian actress of the present day." In 1951, just before Covent Garden dropped *Parsifal* for years, the sole great impersonation was Weber's Gurnemanz; Flagstad's Kundry was considered mediocre.

Somewhat surprisingly, *Parsifal* has invaded Italy successfully, having been heard there first on January 9, 1914, at La Scala, Milan, in an Italian translation by Giovanni Pozza. In more recent years, La Scala has taken to presenting German opera in German. In 1960, for example, a notable German-singing cast was heard in a performance there conducted by André Cluytens: Sandor Konya (Parsifal), Rita Gorr (Kundry), Gustav Neidlinger (Amfortas), Boris Christoff (Gurnemanz), Silvio Maionica (Titurel), and Georg Stern (Klingsor). What must have been an especially wearying performance of *Parsifal* was staged at Barcelona, in Angelo Zanardini's Italian translation, at the very first opportunity after the expiration of the copyright on December 31, 1913: it began at midnight, running into the white hours of the early morning of January 1, 1914, on which day performances also were heard in Berlin, Breslau, Bremen, Kiel, Prague (two performances, one in German and one in Czech), Budapest, Bologna, Rome, and Madrid.

175. Les Pêcheurs de perles (Bizet)

Three acts; libretto by "E. Cormon" (pseudonym of Pierre-Étienne Piestre) and Michel Carré; Paris, Théâtre-Lyrique, September 30, 1863.

When *Les Pêcheurs de perles* was sung at the Théâtre-Lyrique, Paris, on

September 30, 1863 (exactly five weeks before the first performance in the same theater of Berlioz' *Les Troyens à Carthage*), the cast included Léontine de Maësen (Leïla), M. Morini (Nadir), "Ismaël"—pseudonym of Jean-Vital-Ismaël Jammes (Zurga), and M. Guyot (Nourabad); Louis-Michel Deloffre conducted. Alternating with performances of *Le Nozze di Figaro,* the new opera ran up eighteen singings, the last on November 23, and then was not revived until Bizet had been dead eleven years. In 1886 it was heard in Italian at Milan and Lisbon, in French at Aix-les-Bains, and in German at Coburg. Under the baton of the noted Italian conductor Leopoldo Mugnone, *Les Pêcheurs* was revived in Italian at the Gaïté-Lyrique, Paris, on April 20, 1889, with Emma Calvé (Leïla), Alessandro Talazac (Nadir), Paul Lhérie—the original Don José in *Carmen* (Zurga), and M. Navarri (Nourabad). Calvé was again the Leïla when the opera was staged at the Opéra-Comique (Salle du Châtelet) for the first time on April 24, 1893; her colleagues were Jean-François Delmas (Nadir), Gabriel-Valentin Soulacroix (Zurga), and M. Challet (Nourabad). *Les Pêcheurs* reached fifty performances at the Comique on April 2, 1932, one hundred on May 21, 1936—and had been sung there 359 times by January 1, 1958.

In Italian and billed as *Leila,* the opera was first heard in London, at Covent Garden, on April 22, 1887. Lhérie repeated his greatly admired Zurga; other roles were taken by Anna Fohström (Leila), Alfonso Garulli (Nadir), and Miranda (Nourabad). Still in Italian, but now billed as *I Pescatori di perle,* Bizet's opera was sung at Covent Garden again on May 18, 1889, this time with Ella Russell (Leila), Talazac (Nadir), Francesco d'Andrade (Zurga), and Miranda (Nourabad). Covent Garden finally heard it with an all-star cast in June,

1908, when Cleofonte Campanini conducted and the singers were Luisa Tetrazzini (Leila), Alessandro Bonci (Nadir), Mario Sammarco (Zurga), and Vanni Marcoux (Nourabad). After three performances that season, it lapsed at Covent Garden until May 12, 1920, when Sir Thomas Beecham conducted a revival of it, again in Italian, with Graziella Pareto (Leila), Thomas Burke (Nadir), Ernesto Badini (Zurga), and Edmund Burke (Nourabad). Four performances— and the end of the opera's Covent Garden career, as that season was the end of the Beecham company. The Sadler's Wells Opera Company, however, revived Bizet's opera in 1956.

Philadelphia was the first city in the United States to hear *Les Pêcheurs* (in Italian, August 25, 1893). But New York was at last permitted to hear part of the opera when—on January 11, 1896, as a curtain raiser to Massenet's *La Navarraise* with Calvé as Anita—Acts I and II of the Bizet opera were presented at the Metropolitan, also with Calvé (Leila), with whom were Giuseppe Cremonini (Nadir), Mario Ancona (Zurga), and Vittorio Arimondi (Nourabad). Finally, on November 13, 1916, to open the season, the Metropolitan staged *Les Pêcheurs* complete. Giorgio Polacco conducted, and the admirable cast included Frieda Hempel (Leila), Enrico Caruso (Nadir), Giuseppe de Luca (Zurga), and Léon Rothier (Nourabad). Interestingly, a photograph of Caruso and De Luca in these same roles survives from a Genoa performance in 1899. After three performances in the 1916–17 season, *Les Pêcheurs* left the Metropolitan repertoire.

La Scala, Milan, has staged some notable revivals of *I Pescatori di perle* —on February 23, 1938, with Margherita Carosio as Leila; and in 1948 with Onelia Fineschi as Leila and Luigi Infantino as Nadir. Leo Blech conducted a highly praised staging in Berlin in 1934, starring Erna Berger (Leila), Marcel Wittrisch (Nadir), and Heinrich Schlusnus (Zurga). It has had occasional revivals elsewhere in recent years, but its hold on the repertoire seems tenuous. One of its few recent performances outside France occurred at Harriman State Park, New York, during an Empire State Music Festival, on July 12, 1961. Laszlo Halasz conducted; the production was by Hugh Thompson, who also sang the role of Zurga. Others in the stylistically uncertain cast were Lee Venora (Leila), Giuseppe Campora (Nadir), and Ara Berberian (Nourabad).

176. Pelléas et Mélisande (Debussy)

Five acts; libretto is Maurice Maeterlinck's play (1892) of the same name, very slightly altered; Paris, Opéra-Comique, April 30, 1902.

Mary Garden (Mélisande), Jeanne Gerville-Réache (Geneviève), Jean Périer (Pelléas), Hector Dufranne (Golaud), and Jean Vieuille (Arkel) participated in the world *première*. This cast was never bettered, but that assembled for the New York *première*, on February 19, 1908, at the Manhattan Opera House, had the same artists except Vieuille; Vittorio Arimondi sang Arkel. The Debussy work did not reach the Metropolitan until March 21, 1925, with Lucrezia Bori, Kathleen Howard, Edward Johnson, and Clarence Whitehill. Bori's Mé-

lisande and Johnson's Pelléas were eventually subtilized almost to perfection, and there is little doubt that Pelléas was Johnson's finest role—one that he never took for granted. Throughout the remaining years of Gatti-Casazza's regime—eleven more seasons—*Pelléas* remained in the Metropolitan repertoire. The revivals in the late thirties were unfortunate: Helen Jepson was certainly no authentic Mélisande.[1] The revival of January 26, 1944, was a return to better days, with Bidu Sayão, Margaret Harshaw, Martial Singher, Lawrence Tibbett, and Alexander Kipnis. But this was the last New York cast that seemed relevant to the opera: the New York City Center's 1948 production, with Maggie Teyte looking middle-aged, did no good for the cause of French opera, while the Metropolitan's revival in the winter of 1953 had only Pierre Monteux's conducting and Singher's Golaud (he had been graduated from the role of Pelléas) to recommend it. Neither Nadine Conner nor Victoria de los Angeles, the latter making ravishing sounds, came close to creating the character of Mélisande.

With the Mélisande and the Pelléas specially chosen for the Covent Garden *première*, things went well on May 21, 1909, with Rose Féart, Jane Bourgeois, Edmond Warnery, Jean Bourbon, and Vanni Marcoux. Louise Edvina, a new Mélisande in 1910, did wonders with the music, having studied the role with Debussy. A very fine cast, besides Edvina, included Jacqueline Royer, Alfred Maguenat, Édouard

---

[1] San Francisco heard a much more stylish *Pelléas et Mélisande* on October 19, 1938, when the Mélisande was Janine Micheau, later a reigning star of Parisian opera stages, and the Pelléas was the handsome Georges Cathelat, another Parisian, who also sang this role opposite Helen Jepson at the Metropolitan in New York in 1940. Erich Leinsdorf conducted the San Francisco performance, and the cast was filled out by Carlton Gauld (Golaud), Louis d'Angelo (Arkel), Doris Doe (Geneviève), and Anne Jamison (Yniold). Nine years later, San Francisco heard *Pelléas* again (October 10, 1947), this time with Wilfred Pelletier conducting and a cast headed by Bidu Sayão (Mélisande), Martial Singher (Pelléas), Lawrence Tibbett (Golaud), Lorenzo Alvary (Arkel), Margaret Harshaw (Geneviève), and Martina Zubiri (Yniold).

Cotreuil, and Gustave Huberdeau. Teyte's Mélisande was first heard at Covent Garden in 1930, with Roger Bourdin, John Brownlee, and Fernando Autori. The 1937 revival had Lisa Perli and André Gaudin as the lovers, Vanni Marcoux as Golaud.

177. Peter Grimes (Britten)

Prologue, three acts, and epilogue; libretto by Montagu Slater, after a story in George Crabbe's The Borough; London, Sadler's Wells Theatre, June 7, 1945.

Reginald Goodall conducted the world *première* of *Peter Grimes* at the Sadler's Wells Theatre, marking the company's return to its own auditorium. The cast included Joan Cross (Ellen), Edith Coates (Auntie), Iacopi, Blanche Turner, Bower, Peter Pears (Grimes), Roderick Jones, Edmund Donlevy, Owen Brannigan (Swallow), Morgan Jones, and Culbert. An immediate success, it was staged at Stockholm that same year with a cast headed by Sundström, Set Svanholm, and Sigurd Björling. Leonard Bernstein conducted the United States *première,* at the Berkshire Festival, Tanglewood, in 1946. A notable staging occurred at Zurich, also in 1946, when Robert Denzler conducted and the large cast included Joan Cross, Lisa della Casa, Pears, Heinz Rehfuss, Lubomir Vichegonov, and Libero de Luca. Performances followed in Basel, Hamburg, and Berlin.

The first Covent Garden staging of *Peter Grimes* was seen on November 7, 1947. Karl Rankl was the conductor, and Cross, Coates, Turner, Pears, and Brannigan repeated their Sadler's Wells roles; new to the cast were Tom Williams (Balstrode), Graham Clifford (Keene), Hubert Norville (Boles), and Constance Shacklock (Mrs. Sedley). The opera

was heard fourteen times that season, five times during 1948–49, and six times during 1949–50. It was revived on November 14, 1953, for seven more performances, with Goodall conducting; Joan Cross was heard at some of them, Sylvia Fisher at others. In another revival, first heard on January 29, 1958, Pears and Fisher sang the leading roles, supported by James Pease (Balstrode), Geraint Evans (Keene), Jean Watson (Auntie), Joan Carlyle and Iris Kells (Nieces), Brannigan (Swallow), John Lanigan (Rector), Raymond Nilsson (Boles), and Lauris Elms (Mrs. Sedley); Rafael Kubelik conducted.

Peter Grimes also had been heard in many other places, including Milan, when, on February 12, 1948, it reached the Metropolitan Opera, New York. Emil Cooper led rather heavy-handedly a performance that managed to seem Slavic, or at least Central European. Leading roles were sung by Frederick Jagel (Grimes), Regina Resnik (Ellen), John Brownlee (Balstrode), Claramae Turner (Auntie), Paula Lenchner and Maxine Stellman (Nieces), Thomas Hayward (Boles), Jerome Hines (Swallow), Martha Lipton (Mrs. Sedley), John Garris (Rector), and Hugh Thompson (Keene). Dramatically, at least, matters improved at a February 23 performance, when Brian Sullivan sang Peter Grimes, Polyna Stoska was the Ellen Orford, and Mack Harrell was the Balstrode. On January 21, 1949, designated to celebrate Lawrence Tibbett's twenty-fifth season with the Metropolitan, he assumed the role of Balstrode, with Stoska and Sullivan. Nonetheless, *Peter Grimes* disappeared from the Metropolitan repertoire after eight performances in two seasons, the last on February 26, 1949. In the opinion of many, it had been killed by totally inappropriate staging and unsympathetic conducting.

178. Peter Ibbetson (Taylor)

Three acts; libretto by the composer and Constance Collier, after the novel by George du Maurier; New York, Metropolitan Opera House, February 7, 1931.

Tullio Serafin conducted at the *première;* leading roles were taken by Lucrezia Bori (Mary), Edward Johnson (Peter), and Lawrence Tibbett (Colonel Ibbetson); others in the large cast were Marion Telva, Ina Bourskaya, Angelo Bada, Léon Rothier, and Louis d'Angelo. During the four seasons it remained in the repertoire, *Peter Ibbetson* ran up a total of sixteen performances, thus making Taylor the American composer heard most frequently at the Metropolitan. On December 26, 1933, too, it became the first American opera to open a Metropolitan season.[1] It has been heard rarely since then. On July 22, 1961, however, it was presented by the Empire State Music Festival at Harriman State Park, New York, with Wilfrid Pelletier conducting and a cast that included Licia Albanese, in her first English role (Mary), Charles K. L. Davis (Peter), and Peter van Ginkel (Colonel Ibbetson).

179. La Pietra del paragone (Rossini)

Two acts; libretto by Luigi Romanelli; Milan, Teatro alla Scala, September 26, 1812.

Rossini's first opera for La Scala was also heard during his lifetime in Munich, Berlin, Vienna, Graz, Lisbon, Oporto, Barcelona, Cagliari,

---

[1] In fact, a matinée performance of *Hänsel und Gretel* had begun the season the preceding day (Christmas), but December 26 was made the official opening by fiat.

Paris, and Mexico City. There were revivals in Warsaw in 1866 and at the Teatro Pagliano, Florence, on September 1, 1868, while he still lived.

The original cast at La Scala included Marietta Marcolini and Filippo Galli. When the Piccola Scala revived the opera on May 29, 1959, the conductor was Nino Sanzogno, the cast as follows: Eugenia Ratti (Donna Fulvia), Fiorenza Cossotto (La Marchesa Clarice), Silvana Zanolli (La Baronessa Aspasia), Alvinio Misciano (Il Cavalier Giocondo), Ivo Vinco (Il Conte Asdrubale), Giulio Fioravanti (Pacuvio), Renato Capecchi (Macrobio), and Franco Calabrese (Fabrizio); the producer was Eduardo de Filipo. It had also been staged as part of the 1952 Florence Maggio Musicale, when Tullio Serafin conducted and the cast included Giulietta Simionato, Rina Corsi, Mario Petri, and Melchiorre Luise.

180. The Pipe of Desire (Converse)

One act; libretto by George Edward Barton; Boston, January 31, 1906.

On March 18, 1910—more than four years after its Boston *première* —*The Pipe of Desire* became the first opera by an American composer to be presented by a Metropolitan Opera company; it shared a double bill with *Pagliacci.* The all-American cast consisted of Louise Homer (Naioia), Leonora Sparkes (First Sylph), Lillia Snelling (First Undine), Riccardo Martin (Iolan), Clarence Whitehill (Old One), Glenn Hall (First Salamander), and Herbert Witherspoon (First Gnome); Alfred Hertz conducted. Two performances sufficed, but Boston showed its defiance by reviving the opera almost a year later.

181. Pique Dame (Tchaikovsky)

Three acts; libretto by Modest Tchaikovsky, after Pushkin's long short story of the same name; St. Petersburg, Maryinsky Theater, December 19, 1890.

Pique Dame had won very considerable success throughout Russia, as well as in Central Europe, Milan (La Scala, January 18, 1906), and Stockholm, before it reached either the United States or England. Powerfully sponsored by Gustav Mahler, who conducted, it reached the Metropolitan Opera House at a matinee on March 5, 1910, in German. That first New York cast included Emmy Destinn (Lisa), Anna Meitschik (Countess), Alma Gluck (Chloë), Leo Slezak (Hermann), and Adamo Didur (Tomsky and Plutus). Despite critical acclaim, the opera was retired after four performances. Jennie Tourel sang an excellent Lisa in the New Opera Company's *Pique Dame* at the Forty-fourth Street Theatre, New York, in 1941.

Although *Pique Dame* was heard at the London Opera House, in Russian, on May 29, 1915, it was not staged at Covent Garden until December 21, 1950, and then in English, as *The Queen of Spades*. Erich Kleiber conducted, and the cast included Hilde Zadek (Lisa), Edith Coates (superb as the Countess), Edgar Evans (Hermann), Monica Sinclair (Pauline), Jess Walters —a baritone in a bass role (Yeletsky), and Marko Rothmüller (Tomsky). Six performances that season, three in 1951–52, three in 1952–53 (with Ljuba Welitch as Lisa), and seven in 1955–56 (with Amy Shuard as Lisa) "failed to attract the public" (Harold Rosenthal, *Two Centuries of Opera at Covent Garden*). *Pique Dame* continues, however, to exercise its sway over Central Europe, where it is performed frequently.

182. Il Pirata (Bellini)

Two acts; libretto by Felice Romani; Milan, Teatro alla Scala, October 27, 1827.

Bellini's first international success and third opera (the first two were *Adelson e Salvini*, 1825, and *Bianca e Gernando*, 1826), *Il Pirata* was soon heard, in Italian, in Vienna, Dresden, London (April 17, 1830), and Madrid. It reached Paris, at the Théâtre-Italien, on February 1, 1832, New York on December 5, 1832. It seems to have won special favor in Latin America, having been sung in Havana, Mexico City, Valparaiso, and Buenos Aires by 1850. German and French translations meanwhile had proliferated.

The original Milanese cast of *Il Pirata* had included Henriette-Clémentine Méric-Lalande (Imogene), Giovanni Battista Rubini (Gualtiero), and Antonio Tamburini (Ernesto). The Scala being closed in 1829, a season was given instead at the Canobbiana, where, from July 16 to August 28, the original cast sang twenty-four consecutive performances of *Il Pirata*. Méric-Lalande was again the Imogene when, on April 17, 1830, at Her Majesty's Theatre, *Il Pirata* became the first Bellini opera heard in London. It has never been sung at either Covent Garden or the Metropolitan Opera, New York.

After long neglect, *Il Pirata* was revived at Rome on January 1, 1935. On January 21, 1958, the opera opened the season at the Teatro Massimo, Palermo; Franco Capuana conducted, and the cast included Lucia (Lucy) Kelston, Mirto Picchi, Giuseppe Taddei, Enrico Campi, and Mariano Caruso. Later in 1958, the opera received a magnificent production at La Scala, Milan, providing Maria Meneghini Callas with one of her greatest triumphs. She was admirably supported by Franco Corelli as Gualtiero and Ettore Bastianini as Ernesto. On January 27, 1959, Callas sang the role of Imogene in a concert performance of *Il Pirata* at Carnegie Hall, New York, under the auspices of the American Opera Society; on that occasion, Piero Miranda Ferraro was the Gualtiero, Constantine Ego the Ernesto.

183. Poliuto [Les Martyrs] (Donizetti)

Three acts (four as Les Martyrs); *original Italian libretto, after Corneille's drama* Polyeucte, *by Salvatore Cammarano, French libretto by Augustin-Eugène Scribe; Paris, Opéra, April 10, 1840 (the first performance in Italy seems to have been in the original three-act version, at Naples, Teatro San Carlo, November 30, 1848).*

Designing the title role for the French tenor Adolphe Nourrit, Donizetti composed *Poliuto* in 1838. Its performance was prohibited by the Neapolitan censor. When, after the composer's death, it was at last staged at Naples in its original form, the cast included Eugenia Tadolini, Carlo Baucardé, Filippo Colini, Elisa Rossi, Marco Arati, and Domenico Ceci.

Recomposing *Poliuto* as a five-act opera to a libretto by Scribe, Donizetti saw it staged at the Paris Opéra as *Les Martyrs* on April 10, 1840, with a cast including Julie Dorus-Gras, Gilbert Duprez, Jean-Étienne Massol, Prosper Derivis, Pierre-François Wartel, and Serda. It achieved only twenty performances at the Opéra, but quickly spread, in French, German, and Italian, to many other European opera houses. As *I Martiri*—the French opera translated into Italian—it was sung at Lisbon on February 15, 1843. When it was staged at Rome on December 26, 1849, it was called *Paolina e Severo;* in Vienna on March 10, 1853, it was called *Paolina e Poliuto.*

As *I Martiri, Poliuto* reached Covent Garden, London, on April 20, 1852, when leading roles were sung by Dejean Jullienne (Paolina), Enrico Tamberlik (Poliuto), and Giorgio Ronconi (Severo); this was the first of the only nine performances of the opera ever sung in London. New York finally heard the opera, in Italian, on May 25, 1859 (it had been sung in concert form in Boston on December 16, 1849). In more recent times, *Poliuto* was staged as the inaugural opera at the Teatro Rubini, Bergamo, on November 16, 1907, and in Malta in 1926. In 1960, La Scala, Milan, announced that its winter season would open with a revival of *Poliuto* to signalize the return to that house of Maria Callas. This performance took place on December 7, 1960, with Callas (Paolina), Franco Corelli (Poliuto), and Ettore Bastianini (Severo). A capacity audience of 3,800 (including 600 standees) had purchased tickets at face values up to $60 each; the black market price for a single seat was reported by the Associated Press to have mounted to $800.

184. Porgy and Bess (Gershwin)

Three acts; libretto by DuBose Heyward and Ira Gershwin, after a play by DuBose and Dorothy Heyward based on DuBose Heyward's novel Porgy; *Boston, Colonial Theatre, September 30, 1935.*

Todd Duncan and Anne Brown were respectively the Porgy and the Bess of the world *première,* their chief associates being Abbie Mitchell, Warren Coleman, and Edward Matthews. *Porgy* has been the most widely performed of American operas, having been revived frequently in the United States and played all over America and Europe, including (1955–56) the Soviet Union. A pirated "blackface" production of it was produced in a small basement theater in Moscow in 1961 by Boris Alexandrovich Pokrovsky of the Bolshoi Theater. Reporting on this production to *The New York Times,* Osgood Caruthers wrote: "He has created a passable copy of the original. However, he has deleted some of what he called 'more exotic and erotic passages.' The deletions were made in accordance with the strict Soviet moral standards. . . . With a few minor errors, such as having Crown guzzle vodka and Jake quaff a bottle of Georgian wine with his breakfast, scenery, properties and costumes are well done." While this Sovietized *Porgy and Bess* was running in Moscow, a revival—in the "operatic" as contrasted with the "musical comedy" interpretation—was running at the New York City Center, with William Warfield as Porgy.

185. Le Postillon de Longjumeau (Adam)

Three acts; libretto by Léon-Lévy Brunswick and Adolph de Leuven; Paris, Opéra-Comique, October 13, 1836.

Jean-Baptiste Chollet, as Chappelou the postillion, headed the first cast. In London, which *Le Postillon* reached on March 13, 1837, its adventures had, it seems, more to do with operetta than opera. It was never heard at Covent Garden, nor did the Metropolitan mount it in New York, where it was first produced on March 30, 1840. Although it had reached five hundred performances at the Opéra-Comique, Paris, by October 24, 1873, its popularity could not compete with that of *Le Chalet* (1834)—Adam's first great hit—which achieved its fourteen-hundredth performance at the Opéra-Comique on July 8, 1899. The role of Chappelou became inextricably associated with the name of Theodor Wachtel, a leather-lunged German tenor, of whom

The Times (London) wrote in 1862: "He sings vigorously but does not sing well." For such a voice Adam designed Chappelou's famous air near the beginning of the first act. Wachtel is said to have sung the role more than a thousand times.

186. Prince Igor (Borodin)

Prologue and four acts; libretto by the composer, after a scenario by Vladimir Vassilyevich Stassov; St. Petersburg, Maryinsky Theater, November 4, 1890, with additions by Rimsky-Korsakov and Alexander Konstantinovich Glazunov.

Prince Igor was not notably successful at the *première,* and the Maryinsky Theater management eventually made some sad cuts in this opera, which is still known chiefly because of the Polovtsian Dances. Outside Russia, Feodor Chaliapin's unforgettable Prince Galitzky became known in Paris as early as 1909 (in a Diaghilev production), and in London, at Drury Lane, on June 8, 1914, with Marie Kousnietsoff as Jaroslavna. Chaliapin, with Sinaide Lissitchkina as Jaroslavna, took *Prince Igor* to London again in 1931, this time at the Lyceum. Meanwhile, Covent Garden had heard the opera, in English, in 1919. The Covent Garden revival of 1935 was sung in German by a "nearly all-German cast," including Elisabeth Rethberg, Karin Branzell, Charles Kullmann, Herbert Janssen, Alexander Kipnis, and Paul Schöffler. But the dancing of the De Basil troupe, starring Tamara Toumanova, and the playing of Sir Thomas Beecham's orchestra captured the audience. Beecham's 1937 effort brought forward a French-singing constellation of poorish singers as well as a magnificent diatribe from Ernest Newman.[1]

Prince Igor, in Italian, arrived in

---

[1] He wrote that the work had been "disarranged" for Covent Garden.

New York on December 30, 1915, at the Metropolitan Opera House. The chief singers were Adamo Didur (doubling Prince Galitzky and Kontchak), Pasquale Amato (Igor), and Frances Alda (Jaroslavna). It lasted for eight performances scattered through three seasons.

187. Der Prinz von Homburg (Henze)

Three acts; libretto by Ingeborg Bachmann, after Heinrich von Kleist's play of the same name; Hamburg, Staatsoper, 1960.

Leopold Ludwig conducted the world *première* of Hans Werner Henze's opera, one of the most successful of recently composed large-scale works. The cast was headed by Liselotte Fölser (Natalia), Mimi Aarden (The Electress), Vladimir Ruzdak (The Prince), Helmut Melchert (The Elector), Toni Blankenheim (Kottwitz), Heinz Hoppe (Hohenzollern), and Herbert Fliether (The Field Marshal).

188. Le Prophète (Meyerbeer)

Five acts; libretto by Augustin-Eugène Scribe; Paris, Opéra, April 16, 1849.

At the Paris *première,* the role of Fidès was created by Pauline Viardot-García, that of John of Leyden by Gustave Roger. The opera was heard at the Opéra one hundred times up to July 14, 1851, five hundred times up to November 26, 1898—and was last heard there in a revival first sung on February 26, 1912.

London was the first foreign city to hear *Le Prophète*—in an Italian trans-

lation by S. Manfredo Maggioni, at Covent Garden on July 24, 1849. Viardot-García was the Fidès (a role on which she held a substantial London monopoly for the next six years), Catherine Hayes the Bertha, and Mario the John; the cast was filled out by Ignazio Marini, Entimio Polonini, Joseph-Dieudonné Tagliafico, and Luigi Mei. Seven performances were heard that season. When, in 1852, Giulia Grisi tried the role of Fidès during Viardot-García's absence, she was judged a total failure. The original French text was used at Covent Garden in 1890, when Hélène Richard was the Fidès, Nuovina the Berthe, Jean de Reszke the Jean, and Édouard de Reszke the Zacharie. *Le Prophète* was last heard at Covent Garden in 1895, when Giulia Ravogli was the Fidès, Gabrielle Lejeune the Berthe, Francesco Tamagno the Jean, and Armand Castelmary the Zacharie. During the 1860's at Covent Garden, both Rosa Czillag and Therese Tietjens had been admired as Fidès, Enrico Tamberlik as John of Leyden.

Le Prophète was first heard in the United States at New Orleans, in French, on April 2, 1850. When it reached Niblo's Gardens, New York, in Italian, on November 25, 1853, Luigi Salvi was the John, and others in the cast were Steffanoni and Mme Maretzek. The opera's Metropolitan *première* occurred during the house's opening season, on March 21, 1884. Augusto Vianesi conducted, and the Italian-singing cast included Sofia Scalchi as Fidès, Alwina Valleria as Bertha, Roberto Stagno as John, and Giovanni Mirabella as Zacharias. After that single performance, the opera was heard again during the all-German Damrosch 1884–85 season, on December 17, 1884, with Marie Schröder-Hanfstängl as Bertha, Marianne Brandt as Fidès, Anton Schott as John, and Josef Kögel as Zacharias. During this and the four succeeding German seasons, *Le Prophète* was heard twenty-two times. On December 9, 1885, Lilli Lehmann was the Bertha.

On March 8, 1899, Jean de Reszke was the Metropolitan John, with Marie Bréma (Fidès), Lilli Lehmann (Bertha), Édouard de Reszke (Zacharias), Pol Plançon (Oberthal), and Herman Devries—later well known in Chicago as a music critic (Mathisen). On January 10, 1900, Ernestine Schumann-Heink was the intensely admired Fidès, with Suzanne Adams (Bertha), Albert Alvarez (John), Édouard de Reszke (Zacharias), and Plançon (Oberthal). Enrico Caruso first sang his highly praised John of Leyden at the Metropolitan on February 7, 1918, with Artur Bodanzky conducting; Claudia Muzio was the Bertha, Margarete Matzenauer the Fidès, José Mardones the Zacharias, and Adamo Didur the Oberthal. The last revival of *Le Prophète* at the Metropolitan began its career on December 31, 1927 (matinee). Again Bodanzky conducted; Leonora Corona was the Bertha, and others in the cast included Matzenauer (Fidès), Giovanni Martinelli (John), Ezio Pinza (Zacharias), Léon Rothier (Oberthal), and Gustav Schützendorf (Mathisen). In the third performance (January 28, 1928), Karin Branzell was the Fidès—as she was in the fourth (February 29, 1928), with which the opera left the Metropolitan repertoire.

Alfred Loewenberg reported that journals of the period had stated that *Le Prophète* was sung at Brisbane, Australia, on July 1, 1889, in Volapük, an artificial "universal" language invented about ten years earlier. A revival in French at Brussels on August 1, 1926, and one in Russian at Leningrad in 1934 have had few echoes in more recent decades.

189. Pskovityanka (Rimsky-Korsakov)

Four acts; libretto by the composer, after a play by Lev Alexandrovich

Mey; *St. Petersburg, Maryinsky Theater, January 1 (O.S.), 1873.*

Pskovityanka was revived in St. Petersburg on April 18, 1895, in a revised version that included a new prologue. Its first performance outside Russia was given, in the original language, at the Théâtre du Châtelet, Paris, on May 26, 1909, by the Diaghilev company, having been rechristened *Ivan the Terrible*. That aggregation took it to London, under the aegis of Sir Thomas Beecham, presenting it at Drury Lane Theatre on July 8, 1913. Feodor Chaliapin was the fervently admired Ivan the Terrible. In 1917 (September 22), Drury Lane heard the opera again, this time in Rosa Newmarch's English translation. *Pskovityanka* subsequently has won few performances anywhere outside Russia.

190. I Puritani di Scozia (Bellini)

Three parts; libretto by Count Carlo Pepoli, after the play Têtes rondes et cavaliers, *by François Ancelot and Xavier-Boniface Saintine; Paris, Théâtre-Italien, January 24 (not 25, as stated by Alfred Loewenberg), 1835.*

Bellini's final opera had a truly remarkable cast at its *première:* Giulia Grisi (Elvira), Giovanni Battista Rubini (Arturo), Antonio Tamburini (Riccardo), and Luigi Lablache (Giorgio). The opera was an instant success. It reached Italy, at La Scala, Milan, and Palermo, both on December 26, 1835, and was sung in Rome as *Elvira Walton* on February 6, 1836; it was repeated in Palermo in 1840 as *Elvira ed Arturo.* The first performance outside Paris, however, had taken place at the Haymarket, London, on May 21, 1835, in Italian. Berlin heard the opera in German on February 10, 1836; Vienna, at the Kärntnertortheater, on May 16, 1836, in Italian. It reached New York, also in Italian, on February 3, 1844, the opera that opened Palmo's Opera House, on Broadway above Duane Street. It was sung at the Academy of Music, New York, in 1883 by a cast headed by Etelka Gerster.[1] Angiolina Bosio was a renowned Elvira. When, at Athens, on June 7, 1877, Marcella Sembrich made her first appearance on an operatic stage,[2] she chose Elvira as her debut role.

Sembrich was the first Elvira at the Metropolitan Opera House when, on October 29, 1883 (one week after the inaugural *Faust*), *I Puritani* was conducted by Augusto Vianesi and the rest of the cast consisted of Ida Corani (Enrichetta), Roberto Stagno (Arturo), Giuseppe Kaschmann (Riccardo), Giovanni Mirabella (Giorgio), Achile Augier (Gualtieri), and Amadeo Grazzi (Benno). That single performance remained the only one in Metropolitan history until February 18, 1918. In the interim, however, Oscar Hammerstein staged *I Puritani* as the first offering at his Manhattan Opera House, December 3, 1906, when Cleofonte Campanini conducted and the cast included Regina Pinkert (Elvira), Alessandro Bonci (Arturo), and Mario Ancona (Riccardo). Luisa Tetrazzini and the Spanish tenor Florencio Constantino also sang in *I Puritani* under the Hammerstein aegis. At the Metropolitan revival of February 18, 1918, María Barrientos was the Elvira, Hipólito Lázaro the Arturo, and José Mardones the Giorgio—a heavily Spanish contingent with which Giuseppe de Luca sang the Riccardo. With four singings during that season, *I Puritani* disappeared from the Metropolitan stage.

A revival of *I Puritani* was a feature of the first Maggio Musicale Fiorentino, being sung on May 25, 1933, by a cast including Mercedes Capsir, Giacomo Lauri-Volpi, Mario Basiola, and Ezio Pinza; Tullio Serafin conducted. Margherita Carosio was the Elvira of a La Scala, Milan, staging in 1942 and again in 1949. The opera was staged at the Rome Opera in 1948, with a cast including Lina Pagliughi, Mario Filippeschi, Carlo Tagliabue, and Luciano Neroni. Maria Meneghini Callas was first heard as Elvira at the Teatro La Fenice, Venice, in 1949, with Serafin conducting and a supporting cast that included Ugo Savarese and Boris Christoff. Callas sang Elvira in the Chicago Lyric Opera's *Puritani* on October 31, 1955, with the excellent supporting cast of Giuseppe di Stefano, Ettore Bastianini, and Nicola Rossi-Lemeni.

On May 24, 1960, the Glyndebourne Festival Opera opened its season with a revival of *I Puritani*. Vittorio Gui conducted, and the cast was: Joan Sutherland (Elvira), Monica Sinclair (Enrichetta), Nicola Filacuridi (Arturo), Ernest Blanc (Riccardo), Giuseppe Modesti (Giorgio), David Ward (Lord Walton), and John Kentish (Bruno Robertson).

Some words should be said about the opera's complete title, *I Puritani di Scozia,* puzzling because Count Pepoli had specified the locale as "near Plymouth." The explanation is simple: Pepoli cavalierly had located Plymouth in Scotland.

191. The Rake's Progress (Stravinsky)

Three acts and an epilogue; libretto by Wystan Hugh Auden and Chester Kallman; Venice, Teatro La Fenice, September 11, 1951.

---

[1] Of a Gerster revival, Gustav Kobbé wrote: "It was in the duet at the end of Act II . . . that I heard break and go to pieces the voice of Antonio Galassi, the great baritone of the heyday of Italian opera at the Academy of Music. '*Suoni la tromba!*'—he could sound it no more. The career of a great artist was at an end."

[2] The daughter of a famous violinist, Praxede Marcelline Kochanska (as she was called in her preoperatic days) studied violin and piano until she was eighteen. Liszt granted her an audience, at which she performed as violinist, pianist, and vocalist. The Abbé advised her to sing.

Stravinsky conducted the world *première* of *The Rake's Progress*. The cast was as follows: Elisabeth Schwarzkopf (Anne Trulove), Jennie Tourel (Baba the Turk), Nell Tangeman (Mother Goose), Robert Rounseville (Tom Rakewell), Otakar Kraus (Nick Shadow), Hugues Cuénod (Sellem), and Raphael Arié (Trulove). The opera was also sung at Zurich, Stuttgart, and La Scala, Milan, in 1951. At Milan, Schwarzkopf, Kraus, and Cuénod repeated their Venice roles, but others in the cast included Cloe Elmo and Mirto Picchi; Ferdinand Leitner conducted. It was staged in Vienna in 1952 under Franz Hollreiser's baton, with a cast headed by Erna Berger, Elisabeth Höngen, Rudolf Schock, and Alfred Jerger. And it was broadcast in England by the BBC in 1953 with Paul Sacher conducting a cast that included Gwen Catley, Anna Pollak, Alexander Young, and Otakar Kraus.

The Metropolitan Opera, New York, presented *The Rake's Progress* at a matinee on February 14, 1953, as staged by George Balanchine and conducted by Fritz Reiner, with this cast: Hilde Gueden (Anne), Blanche Thebom (Baba), Martha Lipton (Mother Goose), Eugene Conley (Tom), Mack Harrell (Nick), Paul Franke (Sellem), Norman Scott (Trulove), and Lawrence Davidson (Keeper of the Madhouse). Heard five times that season and two the next, *The Rake's Progress* was then dropped from the Metropolitan repertoire.

Alfred Wallenstein conducted when *The Rake's Progress* began its much more successful career in Great Britain in 1953. The Glyndebourne company staged the work at the Edinburgh Festival in a production by Carl Ebert. Leading roles were sung by Elsie Morison (Anne), Nan Merriman (Baba), Richard Lewis (Tom), and Jerome Hines (Nick). The opera has been heard since at Glyndebourne and in London. At the end of the 1958 season, the Glyndebourne production had been heard twenty-three times, including five singings at Edinburgh and one special television performance.

192. The Rape of Lucretia (Britten)

Two acts; libretto by Ronald Duncan, after André Obey's play, Le Viol de Lucrèce; Glyndebourne, England, July 12, 1946.

The Glyndebourne world *première* of *The Rape of Lucretia* had the following cast: Joan Cross (Female Chorus), Kathleen Ferrier (Lucretia), Margaret Ritchie (Lucia), Anna Pollak (Bianca), Peter Pears (Male Chorus), Otakar Kraus (Tarquinius), Edmund Donlevy (Junius), and Owen Brannigan (Collatinus); the composer conducted. A total of eighty-two performances was run up by the Glyndebourne company (including six on tour, a special broadcast, and six at the Holland Festival); Flora Nielsen sometimes was the Female Chorus, Frank Rogier the Tarquinius, and Aksel Schiøtz the Male Chorus. In 1947, the opera was staged at Basel and Chicago, at the latter being conducted by Paul Breisach, with a cast that included Regina Resnik. Breisach also conducted the first New York performance, in 1949. *The Rape of Lucretia* was staged at Mulhouse, Paris, and Rome. At Salzburg, during the 1950 Festival, Josef Krips conducted it; the singers included Annelies Kupper, Elisabeth Höngen, Hilde Gueden, Julius Patzak, Hermann Uhde, and Alfred Poell. On October 23, 1958, the New York City Opera Company staged this opera for the first time (though its first United States performance had occurred eleven years before). At the New York City Center, the cast included David Lloyd, Brenda Lewis, Joshua Hecht, Emile Renan, William Chapman, Frances

Bible, and Ruth Kobart. *The Rape of Lucretia* has won very numerous other performances.

193. Das Rheingold (Wagner)

One act (four scenes); libretto by the composer, being the Vorabend *of* Der Ring des Nibelungen; *Munich, September 22, 1869. See also* Der Ring des Nibelungen (*No. 197*).

With Franz Wüllner conducting, the world *première* of *Das Rheingold* had the following cast: August Kindermann (Wotan), Franz Nachbaur (Froh), Heinrich Vogl (Loge), Toni Petzer (Fasolt), Kaspar Bausewein (Fafner), Karl Fischer (Alberich), Karl Schlosser (Mime), Sophie Stehle (Fricka) and Seehofer (Erda). At the first *Rheingold* in London, at Her Majesty's Theatre on May 5, 1882, among the principals were Emil Scaria (Wotan), Heinrich Vogl (Loge), Otto Schelper (Alberich), Karl Schlosser (Mime), and Hedwig Reicher-Kindermann (Fricka). It had its first American production at the Metropolitan, New York, on January 4, 1889, with Emil Fischer (Wotan), Max Alvary (Loge), Albert Mittelhauser (Froh), Joseph Beck (Alberich), Wilhelm Sedlmayer (Mime), and Fanny Moran-Olden (Fricka); Anton Seidl conducted. The first Covent Garden production, on June 22, 1892, starred Karl Grengg (Wotan), Alvary (Loge), and Kathi Bettaque (Freia— her debut role there); Gustav Mahler conducted.

194. Richard Coeur-de-lion (Grétry)

Three acts; libretto by Jean-Michel Sedaine; Paris, Comédie-Italienne, October 21, 1784.

Although but mildly successful at first, *Richard* gradually gathered partisans. Its fame soon crossed the Channel: in 1786 Covent Garden (October 16) and Drury Lane (October 24) had rival productions. The first used an English translation by Leonard Mac-Nally, with the music adapted by William Shield; the second version of the text was made by "Gentleman John" Burgoyne, the absent-minded blunderer of Saratoga, with the music adapted by Thomas Linley. The latter version was used in Dublin later that year, and also at Edinburgh in 1792. In the United States, Boston was the first to hear *Richard* (January 23, 1797); Philadelphia was next (March 23, 1798), and New York last (May 21, 1800). The opera was rather extensively revived during the fifties and sixties of the last century, and is still occasionally heard on French stages.

195. Rienzi (Wagner)

Five acts; libretto by the composer, after Bulwer-Lytton's novel Rienzi, or The Last of the Tribunes (*the formal title of the opera is* Cola Rienzi, der Letzte der Tribunen); *Dresden, October 20, 1842.*

Among the principals at the world *première* were Joseph Aloys Tichatschek (Rienzi), Wilhelmine Schröder-Devrient (Adriano),[1] Henriette Wüst (Irene), Wilhelm Dettmer (Colonna), and Johann Michael Wächter (Orsini). For many years *Rienzi* was a mild fixture in Dresden and by the end of August, 1908, it had been given there two hundred times.

---

[1] The great soprano, who was inclined to sulk at having to impersonate a male, unnerved Wagner, who had an uncanny prescience about the importance of this fine singing actress. Ernest Newman, citing Ferdinand Heine, relates that she was "the last to master her part, and then, at the performance, had astonished and transported everyone with the sheer genius of her impersonation."

Rienzi has always, except for its initial spurt, been the least popular of Wagner's major operas. In the United States, it was preceded by *Tannhäuser, Lohengrin,* and *Der fliegende Holländer.* Max Maretzek conducted its first American performance, at the New York Academy of Music, on March 4, 1878, with Charles R. Adams, a Boston tenor who was one of the first American singers to win laurels in Europe, as Rienzi, and Eugenia Pappenheim as Adriano. *Rienzi* reached the Metropolitan in its third season, on February 3, 1886, when Anton Seidl conducted a distinguished cast, including Marianne Brandt, Lilli Lehmann, and Emil Fischer. The last of the total of thirteen performances given at the Metropolitan occurred on February 26, 1890, when the singers, except for Sophie Traubman, the Irene, were second-raters. The German Opera Company, on December 26, 1923, revived *Rienzi* at the Manhattan Opera House, with Heinrich Knote as the Roman tribune. At that performance, Editha Fleischer, later one of the most serviceable all-round sopranos of the Metropolitan, appeared in a minor role. Since then, *Rienzi* has not been heard in New York. The London history of *Rienzi* has been negligible. First produced in London at Her Majesty's Theatre (in English), on January 27, 1879, it has yet to have a Covent Garden performance.

196. Rigoletto (Verdi)

Three acts; libretto by Francesco Maria Piave, after Victor Hugo's play Le Roi s'amuse; Venice, Teatro La Fenice, March 11, 1851.

Because of censorship trouble, the opera was billed at its *première* as *La Maledizione,* and at some later Italian performances as *Viscardello, Clara di Pert,* and *Lionello.* The original cast at the Fenice included Teresa Brambilla (Gilda), Annetta Casaloni (Maddalena), Raffaele Mirate (Duca di Mantova), Felice Varesi [1] (Rigoletto), Feliciano Pons, and Paolo Damini—the roles of the two last singers being impossible to determine. From that performance *Rigoletto* quickly became a hit. After running like wildfire the entire length of the Italian peninsula, it was heard within four years in Austria, Hungary, Germany, Bohemia, Russia, England, Poland, Spain, Greece, Portugal, Turkey, the United States, Argentina, and Cuba.

Rigoletto was first heard at Covent Garden, London, on May 14, 1853. Sir Michael Costa conducted, and the cast included Angiolina Bosio (Gilda), Constance-Betsy-Rosabella Nantier-Didiée (Maddalena), Mario (Duca di Mantova), Giorgio Ronconi (Rigoletto), and Joseph-Dieudonné Tagliafico (Sparafucile). By June 3, 1911, the opera had been sung at Covent Garden two hundred times. Lists of some of the singers who have portrayed the principal roles in *Rigoletto* at Covent Garden in something over one century tell much, not only of the opera's continuing popularity, but also of the quality of singers with which London operagoers often have been blessed. Thus, the Gildas have included Marie Miolan-Carvalho, Adelina Patti, Emma Albani, Marcella Sembrich, Lillian Nordica, Nellie Melba, Suzanne Adams, Selma Kurz, Luisa Tetrazzini, Elvira de Hidalgo, Maria Ivogün, Edith Mason, Lina Pagliughi, Erna Berger, Elisabeth Schwarzkopf, Wilma Lipp, Mattiwilda Dobbs, Hilde Gueden, and Joan Sutherland; the Duke of Mantua has been sung by, among many others, Enrico Tamberlik, Julian Gayarré, Fernando de Lucia, Alessandro Bonci, Florencio Constantino, Enrico Caruso, John McCormack, Alfred Piccaver, Dino Borgioli, Giacomo Lauri-Volpi, and Beni-

---

[1] This notable baritone had created the role of Macbeth in 1847, and would be the first Germont *père* in *La Traviata* in 1853.

amino Gigli; the Rigolettos have included Sir Charles Santley, Victor Maurel, Jean Lassalle, Mario Ancona, Antonio Scotti, Maurice Renaud, Mario Sammarco, Pasquale Amato, Riccardo Stracciari, Mattia Battistini, Georges Baklanoff, Giuseppe de Luca, Dinh Gilly, Mariano Stabile, John Brownlee, Carlo Tabliabue, Tito Gobbi, and Otakar Kraus; notable Maddalenas have included Sofia Scalchi, Zelia Trebelli, and Louise Homer; and Sparafucile has been sung by Marcel Journet, Vanni Marcoux, Adamo Didur, Gustave Huberdeau, Alexander Kipnis, and Ezio Pinza.

In Paris, at the Théâtre-Italien, on January 19, 1857, *Rigoletto* had a cast including Erminia Frezzolini—whom Verdi had tried vainly to secure for the Venice *première*—as Gilda, Mario as the Duke, and Marietta Alboni as Maddalena. Brussels and Marseille were both to hear the opera in French before the translated version was sung at the Théâtre-Lyrique, Paris, on December 24, 1863.

Frezzolini was also the Gilda of the first New York performance, at the Academy of Music, then under lease to the violinist Ole Bull, on February 19, 1855, after which the opera was rarely out of the Academy's repertoire, Ronconi being a greatly admired Rigoletto of this period. On February 27, 1861, Clara Louise Kellogg made her operatic debut at the Academy as Gilda, Adelaide Phillipps being the Maddalena. At the Teatro La Fenice, Venice, on January 8, 1876, Etelka Gerster, a future Academy of Music idol, made her operatic entry as Gilda.

The Metropolitan Opera, New York, staged *Rigoletto* as the ninth opera of its inaugural season, on November 16, 1883. The cast included Sembrich (Gilda), Scalchi (Maddalena), Roberto Stagno (Duca di Mantova),

Luigi Guadagnini (Rigoletto), and Franco Novara (Sparafucile). For the two repetitions of that season, the Rigoletto was Giuseppe del Puente. Twenty years later, on November 23, 1903, when the Metropolitan used *Rigoletto* to open its season, Sembrich was still the Gilda; with her were Scotti (Rigoletto), Homer (Maddalena), and—making his New York debut—Caruso, as the Duke. Thus astutely did Heinrich Conried inaugurate his regime and start Caruso on his unparalleled series of 607 Metropolitan appearances in leading roles. Caruso had captured London as signally the preceding year, when he had used the same role for his first appearance there, playing opposite Melba (Gilda) and Renaud, one of the greatest impersonators of the hunchback jester; the date was May 14, 1902, the locale Covent Garden. Renaud, in turn, used Rigoletto as his New York debut role, at the Manhattan Opera House, on December 5, 1906, with Regina Pinkert as Gilda and Bonci as the Duke. Frances Alda made her Metropolitan bow as Gilda, on December 7, 1908, and on November 4, 1912, Titta Ruffo, as Rigoletto, made his American debut at Philadelphia.

Since 1915, *Rigoletto* has been a staple of the Metropolitan repertoire, which has included it in most seasons, total singings having reached 288 by the end of the 1961–62 season. To name those who have interpreted its principal parts would be to call the roll of most of the foremost Italian-singing stars, but Amelita Galli-Curci must be specially mentioned: it was as Gilda that she made her operatic debut at Trani, Italy, in 1907, and as Gilda, too, that she provoked riotous demonstrations at her North American debut, at the Auditorium, Chicago, on November 18, 1916.[2] After joining

---

[2] In 1914, the Auditorium had been the scene of a quite different demonstration as the crisis of a quarrel between Cleofonte Campanini, generalissimo of the Chicago Opera Company, and his sister-in-law, Luisa Tetrazzini. Edward Moore, in his *Forty Years*

the Metropolitan, Galli-Curci finally sang Gilda there on November 26, 1921 (matinee), opposite Telva (Maddalena), Mario Chamlee (Duca di Mantova), and Giuseppe de Luca (Rigoletto). Mention must also be made of Lily Pons, who first sang Gilda at the Metropolitan on January 7, 1931 at a matinee; on that occasion, Ina Bourskaya was the Maddalena, Armand Tokatyan the Duke, Giuseppe Danise the Rigoletto, and Pinza the Sparafucile. When, on January 3, 1956, a Lily Pons Gala marked the twenty-fifth anniversary of her Metropolitan debut as Lucia di Lammermoor (January 3, 1931), the program included Act II of *Rigoletto*, with Jan Peerce as the Duke, Robert Merrill as Rigoletto, and Nicola Moscona as Sparafucile.

Some notable recent interpreters of the leading *Rigoletto* roles at the Metropolitan have been: Gilda—Mattiwilda Dobbs, Hilde Gueden, Pons, Roberta Peters, Genevieve Warner, Patrice Munsel, and Erna Berger; the Duke—Jan Peerce, Richard Tucker, Giuseppe di Stefano, Gianni Poggi, Eugene Conley, Jussi Björling, and Ferruccio Tagliavini; Rigoletto—Tito Gobbi, Merrill, Leonard Warren, Ettore Bastianini, Frank Guarrera, and Paolo Silveri; Sparafucile—Giorgio Tozzi, Nicola Moscona, and Jerome Hines.

197. Der Ring des Nibelungen (Wagner)

Stage-festival play for three days and a prelude (more properly, fore-evening): Ein Bühnenfestspiel für drei Tage und einen Vorabend; *poems by the composer; first cyclic performance, Bayreuth, Festspielhaus, August 13, 14, 16, 17, 1876. See also separate performance data on* Das Rheingold (*No. 193*), Die Walküre (*No. 248*), Siegfried (*No. 218*), Die Götterdämmerung (*No. 100*). *For further data on the first* Ring *cycle at Bayreuth, see Chapter XIV, pp. 240–3.*

The first cyclic performance of *Der Ring des Nibelungen* outside Bayreuth occurred, both in England and in the United States, after separate performances of some of its component parts had been given. Angelo Neumann, in 1882, convinced the reluctant *Meister* of the practicability of touring Europe with a *Ring* stock company. Wagner, though shocked by the sacrilege, succumbed to the dazzle of possible profit. It was the Neumann troupe that carried the cycle to Austria, Italy, Paris, and London, where, on May 5, 6, 8, 9, 1882, the English first heard the *Ring* entire. Except for Hedwig Reicher-Kindermann, who had sung only a minor part at the 1876 Bayreuth performances, and was now promoted to be the Brünnhilde, most of the leading artists from that epochal world

of Opera in Chicago, thus recounts the incident that followed close on Tetrazzini's having indiscreetly referred to Director Campanini as "merely a conductor": "She was singing Gilda in *Rigoletto* and he was conducting. She had reached '*Caro nome*,' and had skyrocketed into the cadenza with which she ended the aria when somehow or other she lost her place and her pitch, ending on a note which was high enough but many degrees away from the true one. Campanini's quick ear caught the mistake. Now a kind-hearted conductor, even Campanini, if he had not had the previous row in his mind, would have allowed her note to die away, and while applause was raging, brought the orchestra in gently and softly, and probably no one

in the audience would have detected the mistake. Instead, he sensed a devastating revenge. He took a firm grip of the baton, signaled the orchestra, and produced a crashing chord that jarred the roof and showed every one in the opera house the discordant spine-chilling distance that she had removed herself from the correct pitch. This is what 'merely a conductor' can do when unamiable. The two never appeared in the same performance again, never spoke again, in fact Mme. Tetrazzini never sang in Chicago again until after Campanini's death. And when she came to get out her autobiography, she made no mention of ever having sung in Chicago, and of Campanini only the fact that he had married her sister."

première—Albert Niemann, Georg Unger, Heinrich Vogl, and Lilli Lehmann—sustained their original roles.

Die Walküre was the first section of the *Ring* to reach America. In that sadly truncated, badly given performance at the New York Academy of Music, on April 2, 1877, Eugenia Pappenheim was the Brünnhilde. Bad as it was, it was doubly historic, being the first time any part of the *Ring* was given outside Munich and Vienna. The real American "first" took place at the Metropolitan on January 30, 1885, under Leopold Damrosch, with the Bayreuth Brünnhilde in the person of Amalie Materna, whose principal colleagues were Auguste Seidl-Kraus, Marianne Brandt, Anton Schott, and Josef Staudigl Jr. Two years later, on November 9, 1887, *Siegfried* had its Metropolitan *première*. Anton Seidl conducted, the chief roles being taken by Lilli Lehmann (Brünnhilde), Seidl-Kraus (the Forest Bird), Brandt (Erda), Max Alvary (Siegfried), and Emil Fischer (Wotan). Ten weeks later, on January 25, *Die Götterdämmerung*, also under Seidl's baton, followed, with Lehmann again as Brünnhilde, Seidl-Kraus (Gutrune), Brandt, Sophie Traubmann, and Louise Meisslinger (Rhinemaidens), Niemann (Siegfried), Adolf Robinson (Gunther), and Fischer (Hagen). Then, on January 30, 1888, the Metropolitan did an extraordinary thing: it began a cyclic production of the *Ring* without *Das Rheingold*, which had to wait until January 4, 1889, for its *première*, with Alvary and Fischer, respectively Loge and Wotan, heading the cast. Finally, on the following March 4, began the first complete cyclic performance of the *Ring* in America,

with Seidl on the podium, and Lehmann, Alvary, and Fischer taking the leading roles.[1]

At the Metropolitan, as at Covent Garden, the greatest—and sometimes the worst—artists of the German wing have competed for the honor of appearing in the *Ring*. To list them all would be an endless task. Some outside it, like the De Reszkes, whose early successes were made in Italian and French opera, lived to become applauded in Wagnerian roles: for example, Jean for years was the favorite Siegfried, Édouard the favorite Wotan or Hagen.

Their debuts in *Siegfried*, on December 30, 1896, brought laurels to the De Reszkes, but disgrace to their Brünnhilde, and serious trouble to the Grau management. Lillian Nordica, a magnificent Brünnhilde, who had once cowed the formidable Cosima Wagner into letting her future husband, an indifferent Hungarian tenor named Zoltán Doeme, sing Parsifal at Bayreuth, had failed to convince Grau that he should not give Melba exclusive rights for a whole year to the role of Brünnhilde, and angrily left the company for two years. She had her revenge. Melba sang Brünnhilde, and very badly, so hurting her voice in the attempt that she had to retire from the stage for a long rest. The final irony of the situation lies in the story that her singing Brünnhilde at all came about through a misconception of Jean de Reszke's recommendation that she sing in *Siegfried*: it seems that he had intended to advise her selection as the Voice of the Forest Bird—a warbling part that would have suited her admirably—and not as Wotan's lusty-throated

---

[1] Seidl felt that an uncut *Ring* was properly a Bayreuth task. After he left, Franz Schalk, a Viennese conductor, in the season of 1898–99, initiated the pious but ill-advised course of giving the *Ring* in its pristine entirety. The Schalk idea was revived on February 21, 1930, by Artur Bodanzky, who held the first-day audience in its seats for two hours and a half without an intermission. As *Das Rheingold* is the shortest of the *Ring* dramas, what followed tried the patience even more. Yet, such has been the popularity of Wagner in New York that this exhausting custom has been adhered to ever since.

daughter. Melba's teacher, the great Marchesi, had warned her against attempting Brünnhilde, but she had persisted. About the resulting disaster, she wrote candidly in her memoirs: "The music was too much for me. I felt as though I were struggling with something beyond my strength. I had a sensation almost of suffocation, of battling with some immense monster. . . ."[2]

Those who have heard the *Ring* year after year for a quarter of a century or more (or at least those sections which were available—*Die Walküre* could have been heard at the Metropolitan for thirty seasons, 1921–51) agree that they do not remember a perfect *Ring*. Yet, although Franz Schalk's uncut *Ring* brought new terrors to being a Wagnerian (W. J. Henderson: "I am first, last, and all the time in favor of the customary cuts"), it could boast of performances never to be bettered in Ernest Van Dyck's Loge and Ernestine Schumann-Heink's Waltraute (Henderson: "No greater piece of declamation has ever been heard on the stage here"). A few seasons later the same critic called Van Dyck's Loge "a finer creation than Edwin Booth's Iago."

Excitement could scarcely be lacking with a Fremstad or even a Gadski as the Brünnhilde, but some of this might be canceled out if the cycle alternated conductors for different parts: Gustav Mahler and Alfred Hertz.

Clarence Whitehill began his twenty-year career as a leading Wagnerian singer at the Metropolitan with three *Ring* interpretations: Wotan, The Wanderer, and Gunther. In 1912 Margarete Matzenauer rose to such distinction among the Wagnerian singers that Irving Kolodin's summation cannot be bettered: "In all, Matzenauer came to recognition as a paragon of the Schumann-Heink order, and more versatile." While the truncated three-part *Ring* had become more or less routine, in 1916 the whole cycle was heard, with a fine *Rheingold,* absent from the Metropolitan repertoire for a quarter of a century, starring Johannes Sembach as Loge, Matzenauer as Fricka, and Margarete Ober as Erda. In 1924 came the first postwar *Ring* cycle; the sequence was not to be interrupted until 1946. Unhappily, neither Siegfried nor Brünnhilde lived up to such confreres as Michael Bohnen, Friedrich Schorr, Karin Branzell, and Maria Müller. The *Ring* section recruited Lauritz Melchior in 1926 and Kirsten Flagstad (Metropolitan debut, as Sieglinde in *Die Walküre,* February 2, 1935). Thenceforward, until Flagstad's return to Norway in 1941, she and Melchior were almost inevitably paired as Sieglinde and Siegmund, Brünnhilde[3] and Siegfried. For almost a decade thereafter Melchior's Wagnerian partner was usually Helen Traubel: they left the Metropolitan after the 1949–50 season, but for quite different reasons. The name of Marjo-

---

[2] *Siegfried* was the setting of another Metropolitan casualty of a quite different nature. On March 19, 1925, Curt Taucher, singing the name role, stepped into an open trapdoor, and disappeared from view. He fell twenty feet, and was so bruised that, though he finished his performance, he sang little during the rest of the season.

[3] Flagstad had sung the *Siegfried* Brünnhilde for the first time at San Francisco (November 6, 1935) during a cyclic presentation of the *Ring* under the baton of Artur Bodanzky. With her that night were Melchior (Siegfried), Friedrich Schorr

(Wotan), Chase Baromeo (Fafner), Gustav Schützendorf (Alberich), Marek Windheim (Mime), Kathryn Meisle (Erda), and Emily Hardy (Forest Bird). This was the third night of a *Ring* cycle that must be almost or entirely unique in American operatic history: it opened the season. Perhaps out of deference to the first-nighters, accustomed to something more ceremonial, the management had flown in the face of Wagnerian tradition by authorizing an intermission after the second scene of *Das Rheingold* (November 1, 1935).

rie Lawrence, whose debut as Brünnhilde in *Die Walküre* was promising,
might have figured prominently in this
sketch if she had not been stricken by
polio. The 1960's may well be notable
to Wagnerians for the dominance of
Birgit Nilsson in the heroic soprano
roles; it was as the *Götterdämmerung*
Brünnhilde that, for example, she
made her Covent Garden debut in
1957. Reviving the *Ring* with Nilsson
in the 1961–62 season, the Metropolitan
had to add a third cycle to the two
originally announced; one cycle was
broadcast.

198. Rita ou Le Mari Battu (Donizetti)

*One act; libretto by Gustave Vaëz
(pseudonym of Jean-Nicolas-Gustave
van Nieuvenhuysen); Paris, Opéra-
Comique, May 7, 1860.*

Composed in 1840, but not produced during Donizetti's lifetime, *Rita*
was first sung in Paris twelve years
after his death. Although the French
version was also staged at Brussels on
December 27, 1860, and was revived
in Paris at the Opéra-Populaire on
November 22, 1879, and an Italian
translation was sung at Naples on
May 18, 1876, a Hungarian version
at Budapest in 1879, *Rita* began to
be widely staged only in the twentieth
century. There was a revival at Verona
on March 21, 1924. The Piccola Scala,
Milan, presented the work in 1957 (on
a double bill with *Il Campanello di
notte*); Nino Sanzogno conducted, and
the three singing characters were handled by Eugenia Ratti, Luigi Alva, and
Renato Capecchi; the Milan audience
was pleased to hear Giuseppe Nessi, a
long-time favorite, in the speaking role
of the elderly gardener. Performances
of *Rita* were also given in 1957 in
Berlin and Buenos Aires by visiting

Italian groups. In 1958, it was heard
at the Teatro Carignano, Turin (with
Dora Gatta, Carlo Franzini, and
Capecchi). Semiprofessional performances have become widespread, including several in English in the
United States.

199. Il Ritorno d'Ulisse in patria (Monteverdi)

*Prologue and five acts; libretto by
Giacomo Badoaro; Venice, Teatro San
Cassiano, February, 1641.*

Fragments were performed in a
French version prepared by Charles
van den Borren, Brussels, January 9,
1925. The first modern staging seems
to have been that at the Petite Scène,
Paris, May 16, 1925, of a French
three-act version prepared by Vincent
d'Indy. At the Florentine Maggio
Musicale of 1942, in an edition prepared by Luigi Dallapiccola, the opera was conducted by Mario Rossi;
the cast included Jolanda Magnoni,
Cloe Elmo, Fedora Barbieri, and Tancredi Pasero. For musicological reasons, doubts have often been cast on
the authenticity of the score. The most
recent scholars, including the scrupulous Leo Schrade, in his *Monteverdi:
Creator of Modern Music*, nonetheless
continue to assign the music to Monteverdi, as does Luigi Dallapiccola, who
studied the matter thoroughly while
working on his edition of the opera.

200. Robert le Diable (Meyerbeer)

*Five acts; libretto by Augustin-Eu-
gène Scribe and Germain Delavigne;
Paris, Opéra, November 21, 1831.*

Described succinctly by Alfred Loewenberg as "Meyerbeer's first French

opera; one of the greatest operatic successes of all time," *Robert le Diable* ran up a tally of 100 singings at the Opéra by April 20, 1834, 500 by March 1, 1867, 758 by August 9, 1893. London first heard approximations of the opera, in two varying adaptations in English, on two successive days: at Drury Lane, the music adapted by Sir Henry Rowley Bishop, as *The Daemon, or The Mystic Branch,* on February 20, 1832;[1] at Covent Garden, adapted by Michael Rophino Lacy, as *The Fiend-Father, or Robert of Normandy,* on February 21, 1832. The unadapted opera was sung, in French, at the Haymarket on June 11, 1832. It was last revived at Covent Garden in 1890, in Italian, the one-hundredth Covent Garden performance occurring on October 25, 1890.

Performances in many languages, in an astonishing variety of places, including Bucharest, Calcutta, Odessa, Batavia, Constantinople, Zagreb, and Corfu, followed in the twenty-five years after the Paris *première. Robert le Diable* was heard in New York for the first time on April 7, 1834, in English—but it was also sung there in Italian (December 17, 1841), French (July 2, 1845), and German (September 16, 1856). New Orleans had heard the original French version earlier (November, 1840), and the success of the opera coursed through Latin America, beginning with a staging at Valparaiso in January, 1847.

At the Paris *première,* the cast included: Julie Dorus-Gras (Alice), Laure Cinti-Damoreau (Isabelle), Adolphe Nourrit (Robert), Nicholas Levasseur (Bertram), and, in the mimed role of the Abbess, the great dancer Maria Taglioni. The elaborate scenery was the work of P.-L.-C.

---

[1] With a cast including Elizabeth Inverarity (Alice), Jane Shirreff (Isabel), John Braham (Robert), and Reynoldson (Bertram).

Cicéri. The popularity of the opera in Paris was not at first repeated in London—the wretched "adaptations" heard there suffice to explain why. But then Jenny Lind made her London debut as Alice on May 4, 1847, at Her Majesty's Theatre—after which *Robert* became so popular as a vehicle for her that the score was cut to reduce the role of the rival soprano, the Isabelle. Alice was one of the four roles that Lind repeated during her final London season in opera (1849). On May 12, 1849, Dorus-Gras was heard at Covent Garden in the role she had created more than seventeen years earlier—but this time with so weak a supporting cast that only one performance was called for. Things looked up for *Robert* at Covent Garden when, on May 23, 1850, it was heard with Giulia Grisi (Alice), Jeanne Castellan (Isabelle), Enrico Tamberlik (Robert), Mario (Raimbaut), and Karl Formes (Bertram). During the early 1860's, Marie Miolan-Carvalho sang the role of Isabelle at Covent Garden. Then, on May 14, 1870, Christine Nilsson was heard as Alice, Ilma di Murska as Isabelle, the stentorian Pietro Mongini as Robert, Italo Gardoni as Raimbaut, and Allan Foley of Tipperary ("Signor Foli") as Bertram. At the last Covent Garden performance to date (October 25, 1890), Fanny Moody was the Alice, under Luigi Arditi's baton, with her husband, Charles Manners, as Bertram, Stromfield as Robert, and Pedro Guetary as Raimbaut.

On November 9, 1879, at Madrid, a performance of *Robert le Diable* presented a popular baritone by the name of Jean de Reszke as Robert. Having raised his voice to sing this tenor role, he never sang low again. At this historic event, his sister Josephine sang the role of Alice.

When *Robert le Diable* reached New York, the Park Theater, on

April 7, 1834, Mary Anne Paton ("Mrs. Wood") was the Isabelle, or, rather, Isobel—for the performance was in English. When the opera was heard at the Astor Place Opera House in 1851, the cast included Steffanoni (Alice), Angiolina Bosio (Isabelle), Bettini (Robert), and Ignazio Marini (Bertram). Formes was heard as Bertram at the Academy of Music in 1857. The Metropolitan, during its first season, on November 19, 1883, presented *Robert* under Augusto Vianesi's direction, with this cast: Emmy Fursch-Madi (Alice), Alwina Valleria (Isabelle), Roberto Stagno (Robert), Victor Capoul (Raimbaut), Giovanni Mirabella (Bertram), Vincenzo Fornaris (a Herald), and the dancer Malvina Cavallazi as the Abbess. After two repetitions, the last on March 28, 1884, *Robert le Diable* disappeared from the Metropolitan repertoire—a surprising fact in view of the enormous success of other Meyerbeer operas in the house later on.

Robert le Diable seems not to have been staged at a major opera house during the twentieth century.

201. Rodelinda (Handel)

Three acts; libretto arranged by Niccolò Francesco Haym from a text by Antonio Salvi first set by Jacopo Antonio Perti in 1710; London, Haymarket Theatre, February 13, 1725 (not February 24, as stated by Alfred Loewenberg).

At the *première*, the cast included Francesca Cuzzoni (Rodelinda), Anna Dotti (Eduige), Senesino (Bertarido), Francesco Borosini (Grimoaldo), Andrea Pacini (Unulfo), and Giuseppe Maria Boschi (Garibaldo); it was played fourteen times up to April 6. It was one of the earliest operas in

which an important role (Grimoaldo) was assigned to a tenor.

Rodelinda was the first opera of the so-called "Handel Renaissance" in Germany, where it was performed at Göttingen on June 26, 1930, in a German version by Oskar Hagen. It was revived at Smith College, Northampton, Massachusetts, in English, on May 9, 1931, and was also heard in English at the Old Vic, London, on June 5, 1939. The Handel Opera Society staged *Rodelinda* at Sadler's Wells on June 24, 1959. Charles Farncombe prepared and conducted it, and the cast included Joan Sutherland in the title role, Janet Baker (Eduige), Margreta Elkins (Bertarido), Raimund Herincx (Garibaldo), Alfred Hallet (Grimoaldo), and Patricia Kern (Unulfo).

202. Le Roi d'Ys (Lalo)

Three acts; libretto by Édouard Blau; Paris, Opéra-Comique, May 7, 1888.

Marie-Blanche Deschamps-Jehin was the Rozenn of the world *première*. *Le Roi d'Ys* had, and still has, a substantial career in France, but it has not gone well elsewhere. It was slow in getting to London and New York, though it had a New Orleans hearing as early as January 23, 1890. Covent Garden presented it twice in 1901 (the first time on July 17), and then dropped it; Suzanne Adams, Pol Plançon, and Marcel Journet knew what they were about, but the rest of the cast was colorless. The Metropolitan first produced *Le Roi d'Ys* on January 27, 1922, and retired it after four more performances that season. Neither public nor critics took to it, despite the fine cast—Rosa Ponselle, Frances Alda, Beniamino Gigli, Giuseppe Danise, and Léon Rothier had leading roles—and the frequently beautiful music.

203. Roméo et Juliette (Gounod)

Five acts; libretto by Jules Barbier and Michel Carré, after Shakespeare; Paris, Théâtre-Lyrique, April 27, 1867.

Marie Miolan-Carvalho was in every sense the heroine of the world *première*. When the Opéra welcomed *Roméo et Juliette* on November 28, 1888, Adelina Patti, Jean and Édouard de Reske, and Jean-François Delmas had leading roles. After Paris, *Roméo* first reached London (Covent Garden) on July 11, 1867, in Italian, with Patti, Mario, Antonio Cotogni, and Joseph Tagliafico. Then for some years Londoners had their choice of Nellie Melba or Emma Eames, with the De Reszkes and Pol Plançon. Eventually, Juliette so became a Melba property that Covent Garden used it as a closing-night fixture for no less than five consecutive seasons. With obstinacy undiminished, Melba sang it when Covent Garden reopened after World War I: 1919 was her last season there. *Roméo* has rarely been heard at Covent Garden since.

With its New York history dating back to November 15, 1867, when Minnie Hauk sang Giulietta in Italian at the Academy of Music, *Roméo* was chosen to open the Metropolitan season of 1891–92. This was in some respects a more significant performance than the *Faust* of 1883, for whereas in the earlier performance familiar artists had merely moved uptown, this first Metropolitan *Roméo*, on December 14, 1891, introduced three artists who were to become mainstays of many succeeding seasons—Eames and Jean and Édouard de Reszke in the respective roles of Ju-

liette, Roméo, and Frère Laurent. As the De Reszkes had created these roles at the Opéra *première* of *Roméo,* and as Eames had made her world debut as Juliette at the same institution on March 13, 1889, replacing Patti, they had a thorough understanding of their roles, besides a sense of teamwork that had come from singing them often together. This performance was also the beginning of an—at that time —bold experiment of turning away from giving little but German opera, and most of that little in German. *Roméo* was excellently enough produced to make the Metropolitan patrons breathe more easily. The same trio sang *Roméo* for the opening of the 1894–95 season, and would have done so for that of 1899–1900 but for the absence of Jean: in his place was Albert Alvarez, who had made his world debut at the Opéra as Roméo, and on this occasion made his Metropolitan debut.

On November 26, 1906, Geraldine Farrar made her Metropolitan debut as Juliette, opening that season. But she was not happy in the part, and during the reign of this gifted lyric soprano *Roméo et Juliette* was all but allowed to lapse. On November 25, 1922, with new settings designed by Josef Urban, it was revived for Lucrezia Bori, supported by Beniamino Gigli (Roméo), Giuseppe de Luca (Mercutio), and Léon Rothier (Frère Laurent). Thereafter it was heard at least once a year until the season of 1935–36, with Grace Moore or Eidé Noréna (*née* Kaja Hansen Eidé), the Norwegian soprano, as Juliette. More recently, the role has been sung by the Brazilian Bidu Sayão, the Flemish Vina Bovy, and the Americans Helen Jepson, Dorothy Kirsten, and Patrice Munsel.[1]

---

[1] *Roméo et Juliette,* having opened six Metropolitan seasons, thus has outdistanced all other operas except *Aïda,* which has opened eight.

In Chicago, too, *Roméo* has had an exciting history. Not only did it open the Auditorium, on December 10, 1899, with Patti, but it was also the last opera to be given there—January 26, 1929—before the resident company moved to the luxurious Insull-sponsored skyscraper on the Chicago River. There it was that, with Roméo's sword, Jean de Reszke held at bay a lunatic who had leaped upon the stage, pinning him to a wall until members of the behind-the-scenes crew could some to his assistance, thus permitting the opera to continue. On January 26, 1918, at the Lexington Theater, the Chicago Opera Association gave New Yorkers an excellent *Roméo* with singers almost unknown to the Atlantic seaboard. Lucien Muratore, a second Jean de Reszke in the elegant suavity of his acting and in his glamorous stage presence, sang Roméo. His Juliette was not his songstress wife, the widely advertised "most beautiful woman in the world," the Roman Lina Cavalieri, but the lovely Breton soprano, Geneviève Vix. Others in that interesting cast were Hector Dufranne, Gustave Huberdeau, and Alfred Maguenat.

204. La Rondine (Puccini)

Two acts; libretto by Alfred Maria Willner and Heinrich Reichert, adapted and translated into Italian by Giuseppe Adami; Monte Carlo, March 27, 1917.

The principals of the world *première* were Gilda Dalla Rizza (Magda), Ines Ferraris (Lisette), and Tito Schipa (Ruggero). *La Rondine* reached Vienna (but not the Carl-Theater, for which it had been intended) on October 9, 1920, in a translation back into German by Rudolf Stephan Hoffmann and with changes in the score by Puccini, who later made a third version, again in Italian, which largely returned to the first. The Metropolitan Opera, New York, staged *La Rondine* on March 10, 1928. Vincenzo Bellezza conducted, and the cast included Lucrezia Bori (Magda), Editha Fleischer (Lisette), Beniamino Gigli (Ruggero), and Armand Tokatyan (Prunier). It survived through ten performances in three successive seasons. A revival for Bori, with Ettore Panizza conducting (January 17, 1936), substituted Nino Martini for Gigli, Marek Windheim for Tokatyan. This added three more performances only to the opera's Metropolitan history. *La Rondine* has not been heard in England except for what Mosco Carner called "a potted version in English" broadcast by the BBC in 1938.

205. Der Rosenkavalier (Strauss)

Three acts; libretto by Hugo von Hofmannsthal; Dresden, Königliches Opernhaus, January 26, 1911.

Ernst von Schuch, Strauss conductor extraordinary, was at the conductorial helm when, on January 26, 1911, *Der Rosenkavalier* began its highly successful career. This was the cast: Margarethe Siems (Die Feldmarschallin), Karl Perron (Ochs von Lerchenau), Eva von der Osten (Octavian), Karl Scheidemantel (Faninal), Minnie Nast (Sophie), Riza Eibenschütz (Marianne Leitmetzerin), Hans Rüdiger (Valzacchi), Erna Freund (Annina), Anton Erl (Der Haushofmeister bei der Marschallin), Fritz Soot (Der Haushofmeister bei Faninal), Ludwig Ermold (Ein Notar), Josef Pauli (Ein Wirt), and Fritz Soot (Ein Sänger). The opera was heard at Nuremberg the very next night, at Munich on February 1, Bremen on February 28, Frankfurt on March 1, and Berlin on April

4.[1] In the Berlin cast were Frieda Hempel (Marschallin), Claire Dux (Sophie), Lola Artôt de Padilla, the daughter of Tchaikovsky's friend Desirée Artôt (Octavian), and Paul Knüpfer (Ochs).

The first *Rosenkavalier* outside Germany was staged at Basel, Switzerland, on February 15, 1911. Two weeks later (March 1), it was sung in Italian at La Scala, Milan, in a translation by Ottone Schanzer. Under the direction of Tullio Serafin, the Milan cast included Adelina Agostinelli (Marschallin), Ines Ferraris (Sophie), Lucrezia Bori (Octavian), and Pavel Ludikar (Ochs). For the third of three Beecham Opera Seasons at Covent Garden, London, Sir Thomas (who had given London *Elektra* in 1910, *Salome* in 1911), chose *Der Rosenkavalier* as the opening opera, January 29, 1913. He conducted, and his cast included Siems (Marschallin) and Von der Osten (Octavian) of the original Dresden cast, Dux (Sophie), Knüpfer (Ochs), Friedrich Brodersen (Faninal), Hans Bechstein (Valzacchi), and Anna Gura-Hummel (Annina). When the Lord Chamberlain told Sir Thomas that he must remove either the bed in Act I or Baron Ochs' references to it in Act III, Beecham chose to do without the bed. The opera was sung eight times that season, which it closed on March 8.[2] George V, Queen Mary, and the Queen Mother Alexandra attended the February 8 performance. Dux sang the Sophie throughout the season, but many other changes in cast occurred, one of them presenting Marie Gutheil-Schoder as Octavian in the single Covent Garden performance of her life.

Prague had heard *Der Rosenkavalier* in Czech, Budapest in Hungarian, and Birmingham, England, in English be-

fore it reached New York, in German. The Metropolitan staged it on December 9, 1913, with Alfred Hertz conducting, and this cast: Hempel (Marschallin), Otto Goritz (Ochs), Margarete Ober (Octavian), Hermann Weil (Faninal), Anna Case (Sophie), Rita Fornia (Marianne), Albert Reiss (Valzacchi), Marie Mattfeld (Annina), Pietro Audisio (Marschallin's Majordomo), Lambert Murphy (Faninal's Majordomo), Basil Ruysdael (Notary), and Carl Jörn (Italian Singer).[3] Hertz later bade farewell (April 24, 1915) to the Metropolitan with the same opera and almost the same cast, the substitutions being Elisabeth Schumann as Sophie (she had made her Metropolitan debut in this role on November 20, 1914), Vera Curtis as Marianne, Max Bloch as Faninal's Majordomo, and Paul Althouse as the Italian Singer. On November 20, 1915, at a matinee, Edith Mason made her Metropolitan bow in the first Bodanzky *Rosenkavalier*.

When the United States entered World War I, almost the entire German repertoire was dropped by the Metropolitan. *Der Rosenkavalier,* last heard there on January 8, 1917, vanished until November 17, 1922, when Bodanzky again conducted, and the principal singers were Florence Easton (Marschallin), Paul Bender, making his Metropolitan debut (Ochs), Maria Jeritza (Octavian), Gustav Schützendorf, making his Metropolitan debut (Faninal), and Marie Sundelius (Sophie); the Italian Singer was Orville Harrold. At a December 23 matinee, Elisabeth Rethberg was heard as Sophie.

The flamboyant Ochs of Michael Bohnen was on view at the Metropolitan in a performance on March 16, 1927, as were the Marschallin of Easton, the Octavian of Maria Müller, the Faninal of Schützendorf, and the

---

[1] The three-hundredth Berlin performance occurred on June 28, 1933.

[2] The programs of three of these performances listed the composer as Richard Wagner, though *Der Rosenkavalier* is one of the least Wagnerian of the operas of Richard II.

[3] Minor roles were taken by Sophie Braslau, Jeanne Maubourg, and Ludwig Burgstaller.

Sophie of Editha Fleischer. The most renowned of Ochses, Richard Mayr, sang the role at the Metropolitan on November 17, 1927, when Grete Stückgold was the Octavian. Stückgold had been graduated, not happily, to the Marschallin's role when *Der Rosenkavalier*—with the coldly greeted Joseph Rosenstock replacing Bodanzky—was sung at the Metropolitan on November 4, 1927. Lotte Lehmann, most admired of Marschallins after Hempel, appeared in this role at the Metropolitan for the first time at a matinee on January 4, 1935, when Bodanzky was back in the pit, and other leading singers were Emanuel List (Ochs), Maria Olszewska (Octavian), Schützendorf (Faninal), and Fleischer (Sophie).

Risë Stevens, whose exceedingly handsome Octavian was to become an enduring Metropolitan fixture, sang the role for the first time there on December 19, 1938, with Lehmann (Marschallin), List (Ochs), Friedrich Schorr (Faninal), and Marita Farell (Sophie). Bodanzky, who conducted that night, led two more *Rosenkavalier*s that season, his last at the Metropolitan. Erich Leinsdorf had replaced Bodanzky when, on December 7, 1940, Eleanor Steber as Sophie sang her first Metropolitan role; on that occasion, Maria Hussa replaced the indisposed Lehmann and Walter Olitzki was the Faninal. Minor roles provided Metropolitan debuts for singers of some lasting prominence in a Lehmann-List-Stevens-Olitzki-Steber *Rosenkavalier* on November 27, 1941: the Notary was Gerhard Pechner, the Italian Singer Kurt Baum. On January 15, 1944, another conductor—George Szell—had before him on the stage Irene Jessner (Marschallin), List (Ochs), Jarmila Novotna (Octavian), Olitzki (Faninal), and Nadine Conner (Sophie).

Max Rudolf made his Metropolitan bow as a conductor with a *Rosenkavalier* on March 2, 1946. But when this highly popular opera opened the Metropolitan's 1949–50 season, the last under Edward Johnson's management, on November 21, 1949, Fritz Reiner was the conductor. Steber, just short of ten years after her debut as Sophie, was now the Marschallin; List and Stevens were in their accustomed roles; Erna Berger was making her Metropolitan debut (Sophie), and Hugh Thompson was the Faninal. The Italian Singer was a genuine Italian this time: Giuseppe di Stefano. Another Metropolitan Marschallin, Helen Traubel, sang under Reiner's direction on January 5, 1951, with Fritz Krenn (Ochs), Stevens (Octavian), John Brownlee (Faninal), and Berger (Sophie). Astrid Varnay sang the Marschallin in a Saturday afternoon broadcast on February 28, 1953, with Reiner conducting, Stevens (Octavian), Endré Koreh (Ochs), Brownlee (Faninal), and Conner (Sophie). Except for Stevens' enduring Octavian, all the roles had changed hands when the Metropolitan again broadcast *Rosenkavalier* on February 18, 1956: Rudolf Kempe conducted, the Marschallin was Lisa della Casa, and the others were Otto Edelmann (Ochs), Ralph Herbert (Faninal), and Hilde Gueden (Sophie). And in the Metropolitan's most recent *Rosenkavalier* broadcast to date, even the Octavian had changed: on December 26, 1959, Christa Ludwig was the Octavian to the Marschallin of Lisa della Casa, the Ochs of Oscar Czerwenka (who was making his Metropolitan debut), the Faninal of Ralph Herbert, and the Sophie of Elisabeth Soederstroem. When the 1959–60 season ended, *Der Rosenkavalier* had been sung at the Metropolitan 134 times in forty-six years.

In view of Lotte Lehmann's future greatness as the Marschallin, it is fascinating to note that she made her London debut at Drury Lane Theater in 1914, during a Beecham season there, as Sophie in *Der Rosenkavalier*

—and that the Marschallin on that occasion was Frieda Hempel, by general consent Lehmann's foremost predecessor in that role. Lehmann made her Covent Garden debut on May 21, 1924, as the Marschallin (in the ten-year interval she had sung Octavian, too!), with Delia Reinhardt (Octavian), Richard Mayr (Ochs), Elisabeth Schumann (Sophie)—and Bruno Walter conducting. (Later in that season, Frida Leider also was heard as the Marschallin.) The same conductor and leading singers were on hand to open the season on May 2, 1927. The "classic cast" was weakened when *Der Rosenkavalier* opened another season on April 22, 1929, and Gita Alpar had replaced Schumann as Sophie. In addition to Lehmann, both Leider and Elisabeth Ohms were heard as the Marschallin—and Schumann returned to sing the final Sophie. Walter conducted the opera in London for the last time when it opened yet another season on April 27, 1931, with Lehmann, Schumann, and Mayr, but with Margit Angerer as Octavian. At other performances during that season, Leider was heard as the Marschallin, Olszewska as Octavian.

Sir Thomas Beecham conducted his first London *Rosenkavalier* in nineteen years to open a Covent Garden season on May 1, 1933. Lehmann was the ever-reigning Marschallin, Eva Hadrabova the Octavian, Adele Kern the Sophie, Alexander Kipnis the Ochs, and Eduard Habich the Faninal. On June 1, 1936, a Lehmann-less *Rosenkavalier* was heard at Covent Garden under Fritz Reiner's direction; Rethberg was the tepidly admired Marschallin, and others in the cast were Tiana Lemnitz—who was ardently admired (Octavian), Stella Andreva (Sophie), List (Ochs), and August Neumann (Faninal). A historic Covent Garden performance of the opera occurred on the opening night (November 2) of the 1936 season by the visiting Dresden State Opera Company. The sets of the 1911 Dresden world *première* were used. Karl Böhm conducted, and the chief roles were sung by Marta Fuchs (Marschallin), Marta Rohs (Octavian), Maria Cebotari (Sophie), Ludwig Ermold (Ochs), and Arno Schellenberg (Faninal). Strauss, then seventy-two, sat in a box with the German ambassador to London, Joachim von Ribbentrop, and was on stage to accept applause after both the second and the final acts.

Lotte Lehmann was the Marschallin of a *Rosenkavalier* at Covent Garden under Erich Kleiber's baton on May 4, 1938 (with Lemnitz, Berger, Krenn, and Habich). At the end of the levée in Act I, left by herself on stage, she should have pronounced the line "Als musst's so ein." Instead, she said— the words were heard by the audience in the house and the one listening by radio—"I can't go on . . . finish." The curtain was rung down, and shortly Walter Legge, the assistant director of Covent Garden, announced that because she was ill, Hilde Konetzni, who had been in the audience, would take over her role for the rest of the performance (Konetzni was to have made her London debut as Chrysothemis in *Elektra* the next night). Six days later, however, Lehmann sang the Marschallin when *Der Rosenkavalier* had to be substituted at the final hour for *Die Entführung aus dem Serail,* made impossible by the illness of Richard Tauber. This, too, was a heart-in-the-mouth performance: it had to be delayed from seven forty-five until eight-thirty to allow for the arrival by plane from Berlin of Lemnitz and Marie Louise Schilp, the Annina, who had been enlisted by telephone. After that evening, Lehmann never again sang in opera in London, though she remained a member of the Metropolitan Opera in New York through the 1945–46 season.

A notable *Rosenkavalier* was heard

in San Francisco on September 20, 1955. Erich Leinsdorf conducted, and the cast included Elisabeth Schwarzkopf, making her American operatic debut (Marschallin), Dorothy Warenskjold (Sophie), Frances Bible (Octavian), and Otto Edelmann (Ochs). In a repetition during the company's twenty-fifth anniversary season in the War Memorial Opera House (October 1, 1957), Schwarzkopf, Bible, and Edelmann were again heard, but the Sophie was Rita Streich, making her American operatic debut. What many critics have called the finest impersonation of the Marschallin since Lotte Lehmann's great days, that of Régine Crespin, was heard at Glyndebourne in 1959 and 1960, and at Covent Garden on October 24 of the latter year, with Edward Downes conducting, Michael Langdon as Baron Ochs, Hertha Töpper as Octavian, and Joan Carlyle as Sophie.

206. Le Rossignol (Stravinsky)

Three acts; libretto by Stravinsky and Stepan Nikolayevich Mitusov after the story by Hans Christian Andersen; Paris, Opéra, May 26, 1914.

The first performance of *Le Rossignol* was given by Diaghilev's company at the Paris Opéra with Pierre Monteux conducting. The elaborate décors of Alexandre Benois were transported to London, where, on June 18, 1914, Sir Thomas Beecham sponsored the Diaghilev production of the opera at Drury Lane Theatre, with Emil Cooper conducting and with a case including Dobrolovska, Petrenko, Andreef, and Warfolomeiev.[1] When Covent Garden mounted *The Nightingale* (so billed) on November 12, 1919, it was heard in an English translation by Edward Agate. Eugene Goossens, Sr., conducted, and the cast included Sylvia Nelis, Edith Clegg, Maurice d'Oisly, and Frederick Austin. It was sung four times.

There seems to have been a performance of *Le Rossignol* in Leningrad in the autumn of 1920; it was also sung in German at Mannheim on May 5, 1923. But when it reached the Metropolitan Opera, New York, at a matinee on March 6, 1926, it was heard in a French translation by the noted Greco-French musicologist, Michel D. Calvocoressi, and shared a double bill with the American *première* of Manuel de Falla's *La Vida Breve*. Tullio Serafin conducted; leading roles were sung by Marion Talley (The Nightingale), Ina Bourskaya (The Cook), Ralph Errolle (The Fisherman), Adamo Didur (Emperor of China), Gustav Schützendorf (Chamberlain), and James Wolfe (Priest). The gorgeous settings by Serge Soudeikine were admired more than the singing of Talley, who was only eighteen, and who had made her Metropolitan debut, as Gilda in *Rigoletto*, exactly seventeen days earlier. In part because of the incredible flood of publicity surrounding Talley, *Le Rossignol* won four performances that season and three the next, since when it has not been heard at the Metropolitan.

The operatic version of *Le Rossignol*[2] was staged at La Scala, Milan, in an Italian translation by Rinaldo Küfferle, on May 14, 1926. Küfferle's translation was also used when the opera was put on at the Teatro Colón, Buenos Aires, on June 28, 1927. Stravinsky conducted at Milan; at Buenos Aires, under the baton of Ferruccio Calusio, the Nightingale was sung by Toti dal Monte. Others who have sung

---

[1] The two performances in Paris and four in London completed the career of the elaborate stage investiture, which was destroyed in the Drury Lane Theatre's cellar storehouse during World War I.

[2] There are, additionally, a ballet version and a symphonic poem (*Le Chant du rossignol*), both based on the opera score.

the title role in the relatively few performances in later years have been Lina Pagliughi (Genoa, 1937) and Mattiwilda Dobbs (Holland Festival, 1952). Stravinsky conducted a performance of *Le Rossignol* at Lisner Auditorium, Washington, D. C., under the auspices of the Opera Society of Washington, on December 28, 1960. Reri Grist was the highly praised Nightingale; other roles were sung by Marina Picassi (The Cook), Loren Driscoll (The Fisherman), Donald Gramm (The Emperor of China), Kenneth Smith (The Chamberlain), and Herbert Beattie (The Priest); the opera was sung in the original Russian.

207. Ruslan and Lyudmila (Glinka)

Five acts; libretto by V. F. Shirkov and others, after Pushkin;[1] *St. Petersburg, November 27 (O.S.), 1842.*

Presented exactly six years after the world *première* of *A Life for the Tsar, Ruslan and Lyudmila,* the first opera to be based on a Pushkin text, a far more original and interesting work than its predecessor, never attained, even in Russia, the celebrity of Glinka's first opera. Hissing disrupted the *première,* but A. M. Gedeonov, the director of the imperial theaters, held firm; at the third performance, Ann Petrova-Vorobyeva, the famous contralto, assumed the important role of Ratmir, and the tide turned.

Ruslan and Lyudmila had its English *première* at the Lyceum Theatre, London, on June 4, 1931, with Sinaide Lissitchkina, Rebane, Pozemkovsky, and Kaidanov in leading roles. Apparently it has not been heard in the United States.

---

[1] The idea was suggested to Glinka by Prince A. A. Shakhovskoy, the librettist of Catterino Cavos' *Ivan Susanin,* the precursor of Glinka's *A Life for the Tsar,* for performance data of which see No. 127.

208. Russalka (Dargomizhsky)

Four acts; libretto by the composer, after Pushkin; St. Petersburg, Cirque Theater, May 16, 1856.

Ossip Afanasyevich Petrov, Bulakhova, and Daria Leonova gave superb performances at the *première,* but could not push the opera beyond a short run. Within a decade it had established itself, for the sole argument against a quicker success was the management's lack of confidence. Outside Russia, where it finally became very popular and still is revived, *Russalka* is rarely played. In the United States, it was first heard at San Francisco, in Russian, on October 1, 1922, and in New York on May 8, 1922. Feodor Chaliapin, with his Russian company, headed the cast that first took *Russalka* to London (Lyceum Theatre, May 18, 1931).

209. Sadko (Rimsky-Korsakov)

Seven scenes (divided into three or five acts); libretto by the composer and Vladimir I. Byelsky; Moscow, Solodovnikov's Theater, December 26 (O.S.), 1897.

Sadko became very popular in Russia, but except for a fragmentary production in Paris by Diaghilev in 1911, it was not heard elsewhere for many years. Eventually piling up sixteen performances in three successive seasons, it was first given at the Metropolitan, New York, on January 25, 1930. It was sung in French, with Edward Johnson (Sadko), Ina Bourskaya (Lioubova), and Editha Fleischer (Volkhova). London first heard *Sadko* at the Lyceum Theatre, in Russian, on June 9, 1931, with Sinaide Lissitchkina as Volkhova. Margherita Carosio and Erna Berger have both sung Volkhova.

210. Salome (Strauss)

One act; libretto a translation into German, by Hedwig Lachmann, of Oscar Wilde's poetic play; Dresden, Königliches Opernhaus, December 9, 1905.

Ernst von Schuch conducted the Dresden world *première* of *Salome*. Marie Wittich, the Salome, allowed a ballerina to perform the Dance of the Seven Veils—though at a later singing she distressed the composer by doing it herself. Others in the original cast were Irene von Chavanne (Herodias), Karl Burian (Herod), and Karl Perron (Jokanaan). Without moral scruple the audience accepted the opera enthusiastically. Soon, despite the temporary ban laid upon it in Berlin by Wilhelm II, patron of Leoncavallo, it was produced in many German cities; Strauss himself conducted it at Graz on May 16, 1906. It was a shocking show, but those who flocked to hear and see it left their hypocrisy at home. Its first staging outside Germany occurred in Italian, at Turin, on December 22, 1906.

Salome had breached the defenses of Berlin (December 5, 1906) when its encounters with Anglo-Saxon morality began in New York, at the Metropolitan, on January 22, 1907.[1] Heinrich Conried staged this first performance of a Strauss opera in America as his own annual benefit, at doubled prices. After a concert in which songs and operatic excerpts were sung by sixteen Metropolitan singers, among them Celestina Boninsegna, Enrico Caruso, Lina Cavalieri, Geraldine Farrar, Editha Fleischer, Otto Goritz, Louise Homer, Marcel Journet, Antonio Scotti, Marcella Sembrich, and Riccardo Stracciari, Alfred Hertz conducted *Salome*. Olive Fremstad had the title role; the Herodias was Marion Weed; Burrian (one *r* in Europe, two in New York) repeated the role he had created in Dresden; Anton Van Rooy was Jokanaan, and Andreas Dippel was the Narraboth. Mme Fremstad permitted Bianca Froelich of the ballet to perform the by then notorious dance.

A journalistic tempest broke over the heads of Conried and his associates the next morning. The newspapers' morals had been outraged; they demanded that *Salome* be suppressed. The management could have weathered that (perhaps profited by it), but when the directors of the Metropolitan Opera and Real Estate Company threatened to cancel Conried's lease, he withdrew the opera.[2] Seven years were to pass before a Strauss opera would be heard at the Metropolitan again, twenty-seven before *Salome* would be restaged there. Meanwhile, Oscar Hammerstein had taken up arms against the freedom to stifle novelty in America. On January 28, 1909, he produced *Salome* in French at the Manhattan Opera House, with Mary Garden rivaling Fremstad's realistic portrayal of the bad little girl, yet failing to get Hammerstein into trouble. Cleofonte Campanini conducted, and others in Hammerstein's cast were Augusta Doria (Herodias), Charles Dalmorès (Herod), and Hector Dufranne (Jokanaan). The notoriety surrounding the opera itself and Garden's magnificently conceived Salome filled the Manhattan ten times that season.[3] It was also sung in Philadelphia.

---

[1] A Tuesday, this performance followed a semipublic dress rehearsal on the preceding Sunday morning, when a thousand guests had been allowed a first clandestine glance. Although a Sabbath, that day had produced no outbreaks.

[2] The influence of J. P. Morgan was said at the time to have been decisive in forcing Conried's decision.

[3] In 1910, when Garden sang the role in Chicago for the first time—with Eleanora de Cisneros (Herodias), Dalmorès (Herod), and Dufranne (Jokanaan)—the most flattering vituperation came her way, and the opera was shelved temporarily after a single performance.

Maria Jeritza's Salome never was seen (or heard) in New York, but was on display in both San Francisco and Chicago. In a long-discussed San Francisco performance on September 12, 1930, her Herod was Sydney Rayner; John Charles Thomas was the Jokanaan, Dorothee Manski the Herodias, and Gaetano Merola the conductor. Arthur J. Bloomfield reported that the head of Jokanaan on the salver was covered with an opaque veil as "a concession to certain pressures."

Salome returned to the Metropolitan on January 13, 1934, when Göta Ljungberg was totally inadequate in the title role. Artur Bodanzky's conducting was praised, as were the Jokanaan of Friedrich Schorr and the Herod of Max Lorenz; Dorothee Manski as Herodias was forgiven much because she was substituting for an indisposed Karin Branzell, who later brought great distinction to the role. *Salome* was heard seven times that season without incident. When it was sung again four seasons later (February 4, 1938), Ettore Panizza was in the pit. Marjorie Lawrence was an uninflamed Salome, quite outshone by the neurotic Herod of René Maison, the Herodias of Branzell, and the Jokanaan of Julius Huehn. The problem of where to find a Salome had not been solved on December 9, 1942, when George Szell made his Metropolitan conducting debut with *Salome:* Lily Djanel in the title role was not the answer, and again was outshone by Branzell as Herodias— as, on this occasion, were Frederick Jagel as Herod and Herbert Janssen as Jokanaan. Nothing about Ella Flesch's Metropolitan debut as Salome on January 6, 1944, suggested that she was the answer either.

On February 4, 1949, however, New York heard a Salome to be compared with Fremstad and Garden. Fritz Reiner conducted magnificently a cast headed by Ljuba Welitsch (later Welitch), who at once became, as Irving Kolodin wrote, "a new figure of legend." Other singers in a cast remarkable for its ensemble were Kerstin Thorborg (Herodias), Max Lorenz (Herod), and Joel Berglund (Jokanaan). When Astrid Varnay sang Salome at the Metropolitan on January 26, 1950, it was her misfortune to be in the shadow of Welitch, as well as in that of Paul Schöffler, making an impressive Metropolitan debut as Jokanaan. Reiner and Thorborg continued their admired contributions to the totality of the opera; Set Svanholm was a serviceable Herod. When Welitch returned to her greatest role in the 1949–50 season, it was evident that her voice was in the decline that was to lead in a few years to its almost total eclipse. She still held the role when, on January 19, 1952, *Gianni Schicchi* and *Salome* were performed at a Saturday matinee performance that was broadcast.[4] Elisabeth Höngen was the Herodias, Svanholm the Herod, and Hans Hotter the Jokanaan.

When Christel Goltz made her Metropolitan debut on December 15, 1954, as Salome, her performance was astonishing in ways that seemed to make reasonable the gossip that she had originally been a circus contortionist. Her incessant movement was, however, combined with a clear, powerful voice equipped to be heard above Strauss's orchestra in full cry. Her comparatively static companions on the stage were Blanche Thebom (Herodias), Ramón Vinay (Herod), and

---

[4] Unbelievably, in view of British attitudes toward *Salome*, the opera was telecast complete by the BBC on September 26, 1958. The London Symphony Orchestra was conducted by Walter Goehr, and the chief roles were sung and acted by Helga Pilarczyk as Salome, Hasso Eschert (replacing an indisposed Jon Vickers) as Herod, Monica Sinclair as Herodias, and Norman Foster as Jokanaan. The performance was in English, or partly so: Eschert, having had insufficient time to master the English text, was reported to have sung such lines as *"Was ist's, das du einer* silver charger *haben möchtest?"*

Schöffler (Jokanaan). All were heard, under Dimitri Mitropoulos' baton, when *Salome* again was broadcast on January 8, 1955. Perhaps *Salome* broadcasts have become a Metropolitan tradition, for on February 8, 1958, a different Metropolitan Salome—Inge Borkh, who first sang the role there on January 24, 1958—was heard during a Saturday matinee broadcast, with Thebom and Vinay in their former roles, Mack Harrell as Jokanaan. Mitropoulos again conducted; Borkh was both less mobile than Goltz and less demonic than Welitch. The suggestion was that another interregnum between veritable Salomes had set in.[5]

Salome's difficulties in England were of a different nature. The censors having been placated by extraordinary changes in the text, Sir Thomas Beecham was permitted to let the music say what it would when London first exposed to *Salome*, at Covent Garden, on December 8, 1910. The Salome was the Finnish soprano Aïno Ackté, the Herodias was Ottilie Metzger, and other leading roles were sung by Ernst Kraus (Herod) and Clarence Whitehill (Jokanaan). Actually, Jokanaan was called Mattaniah the Prophet. The scenes were laid, with supreme inappropriateness, in Greece, where the Jews and Nazarenes had been metamorphosed into, respectively, Learned Men and Cappadocians.

According to Harold Rosenthal: "No biblical phrase was allowed to remain, and the prophecies of 'The Prophet' were concerned with social and political affairs. Salome's sensual utterances were toned down, and her desire to kiss the Prophet was turned into an appeal to let her follow him or a resolution to be with him until death. No head of the dead prophet was allowed for the final scene, only a dish of blood—which all agreed looked like pink blancmange. The sale of an English translation of this new version was prohibited by the executors of Wilde; but this did not matter, for as Beecham recalls, the performers got so carried away during the performance, that one by one they lapsed into the original unbowdlerized German text. The Lord Chamberlain's representatives were not one bit the wiser, and even congratulated Beecham at the end of the performance for having acceded to their wishes with so little fuss!" The season ended twenty-three days later, by which time London had heard this compromise *Salome* ten times without noticeably becoming more wicked.

On May 10, 1924, a Covent Garden *Salome* had Ljungberg as the title character, Maria Olczewska (so spelled at Covent Garden) as Herodias, Walter Kirchoff as Herod, and Emil Schipper as The Prophet-Jokanaan. For January 11, 1937, the Covent Garden management promised a double bill of *Salome* and *Elektra*, but when a cast for the latter could not be rallied, took pity on the audience's constitutions and put *Gianni Schicchi* in its place. The Salome of the occasion was

---

[5] After Jane Rhodes' single appearance in New York as Carmen (Metropolitan, November 7, 1960), it was rumored that she might return during the 1961–62 season to sing Salome. But when she first sang this part at the Paris Opéra in 1958, Elliott Stein reported in *Opera:* "Her voice is not mature enough [she was then twenty-seven, but Strauss had asked for "a sixteen-year-old princess with an Isolde voice"] for the exacting role, and she is a clumsy actress, suggesting a petulant *midinette* rather than a monstrous princess." Her companions in the performance he described had been Rita Gorr,

a tremendously effective Herodias; Ramón Vinay, ill and singing Herod in French for the first time; René Bianco as Jokanaan; and —in the pit—André Cluytens. Mlle Rhodes finally repeated her very French Salome (even her German was French) at the Metropolitan on February 3, 1962, to vituperation from the leading critics, though in her conception of the role, and certainly in appearance, she was much closer to the character conceived by Wilde and Strauss than even the greatest of her more ample and more powerful predecessors at the Metropolitan.

Hildegarde Ranczak and the Jokanaan Paul Schöffler; Hans Knappertsbusch conducted. The greatest of recent Salomes was heard at Covent Garden during a visit of the Vienna State Opera, on September 22, 1947, when Welitsch gave the role the demonic quality inherent in text and music. Others in that well-remembered cast were Höngen (Herodias), Julius Patzak (Herod), Marko Rothmüller (Jokanaan), and Anton Dermota (Narraboth). At a performance on September 30 the less psychotic Salome of Maria Cebotari won admirers. At all these performances, Clemens Krauss, who had become a sort of court conductor to Strauss, displayed his mastery.

Salome blew up another London storm when it was staged in settings by Salvador Dali on November 11, 1949, at Covent Garden. Karl Rankl, the musical director, disapproved of this production; as conductor, he refused to appear on the stage at the end of the performance. The musical press leaped to the fray—and soon Peter Brook, who had produced the opera, resigned. The cast, overwhelmed by Dali's macabre sets, included Welitsch (Salome), Constance Shacklock (Herodias), Franz Lechleitner (Herod), and Kenneth Schon (Jokanaan). Lechleitner had considerable difficulty singing his lines in the English translation used, and when Goltz appeared to sing the title role on January 25, 1950, this difficulty became almost total unintelligibility.

Salome blew up still another storm —stylistic this time—when, on June 30, 1961, it was presented at the Festival of Two Worlds at Spoleto, Italy, in a production by Luchino Visconti. The young American Negro soprano Margaret Tynes was praised more for her physical charm and sinuous movements than for her understanding or projection of the title role. Others in the cast were Lili Chookasian (Her-

odias), George Shirley (Herod), Robert Anderson (Jokanaan), and Paul Arnold (Narraboth). The orchestra was the Trieste Philharmonic; Thomas Schippers conducted.

211. Samson et Dalila (Saint-Saëns)

Three acts; libretto by Ferdinand Lemaire; Weimar (in German), December 2, 1877.

Samson et Dalila has had a curious history. When Saint-Saëns had completed it, no French theater would stage it, despite the fact that its composer was already very distinguished. Its alleged seriousness and gloom were held against it. Fragments were publicly performed, and Pauline Viardot-García gave the second act at her summer place, herself singing Delilah. Liszt, from whom Saint-Saëns had already borrowed copiously in forging his instrumental style, now came forward with his usual generosity and offered to stage the opera at Weimar. There, accordingly, a German version was brought out on December 2, 1877. The next year, Brussels heard *Samson*, and Hamburg followed in 1882, with the composer conducting, and Rosa Sucher as the heroine. (Sucher was a dramatic soprano, but the role is most often sung by mezzos or contraltos.) In 1890, *Samson et Dalila* finally arrived in France, though not in Paris, when it was performed at Rouen. Seven months later, on October 31, it reached the capital, but still not the Opéra, which did not capitulate until November 23, 1892, when the cast included Jean Lassalle as the High Priest. Since then, in France, *Samson* has joined the company of such overplayed favorites as *Faust, Mignon, Carmen,* and *Manon.*

The Anglo-Saxon prejudice against

representing Biblical characters on the stage led to oratorio performances of *Samson and Delilah,* in English, in both England and the United States. In the former country, it was not heard as an opera until 1909. New Orleans, then a predominantly Catholic city of liberal cosmopolitan cast, heard the first American *Samson* at the French Opera House (January 4, 1893). Little more than two years later, on February 8, 1895, the Metropolitan gathered a magnificent cast for a polyglot *première.* Francesco Tamagno was the Samson, Eugenia Mantelli the Delilah, Giuseppe Campanari the High Priest, and Pol Plançon both Abimelech and an Old Hebrew. Possibly the confusion of tongues was too much for the staid patrons of Grau, and the opera was immediately retired.

Oscar Hammerstein is credited by Pitts Sanborn with having established *Samson* in New York by his superb revival of November 13, 1908, when Jeanne Gerville-Réache sang Delilah to Charles Dalmorès' Samson, Hector Dufranne's High Priest, and Félix Vieuille's Old Hebrew. Cleofonte Campanini conducted, and in the bacchanale Odette Valéry, later a music-hall queen, writhed voluptuously with a pet snake. *Samson et Dalila* did not crop up again at the Metropolitan until it was used to open the season of 1915–16. On that November 15, Giorgio Polacco conducted, Enrico Caruso and Margarete Matzenauer were the lovers, and other principals were Pasquale Amato and Léon Rothier. For eleven seasons, *Samson* remained

in the Metropolitan repertoire, and was used, moreover, to open another season—that of 1918–19, when Caruso and Louise Homer were supported by the High Priest of Robert Couzinou.[1] After Caruso's death, Giovanni Martinelli succeeded, and admirably, to the role of Samson, playing opposite a series of Dalilas, including Matzenauer and Karin Branzell. After ten years' inexplicable absence, *Samson* again returned to the Metropolitan on December 26, 1936, with a new hero and heroine—the Belgian René Maison and the Swedish Gertrud Wettergren. Later performances continued Maison's excellent Samson, and both Bruna Castagna and Risë Stevens were heard as Dalila. The latter singer went on through the season of 1955–56, after which the opera was dropped, doubtless only temporarily.

The Americans seem to care more for *Samson et Dalila* than do the British. When it was first given in London as a real opera, it was chosen to open the Covent Garden season of 1909 on April 26. Louise Kirkby-Lunn was in every way impressive, but her Samson was feeble even before his hair was clipped. At the fifth performance, Charles Affre, a tenor from the Paris Opéra, came to her rescue. For the last three performances he was replaced by Dalmorès. Kirkby-Lunn's fine interpretation was heard last on the eve of World War I, and postwar casts were not inspired. *Samson et Dalila* has not been heard at Covent Garden since 1928.[2]

---

[1] The date—November 11, 1918—was epochal. To meet the emotions of a resplendent first-night audience throbbing with the excitement of the signing of the Armistice, the management staged a tableau that was more effective than artistic. After Act I of *Samson,* the curtains parted to reveal the Allied flags held aloft by singers of more or less appropriate nationalities. Homer, Caruso, and Rothier accounted for three of the chief victors. As there was no English singer in the cast, the British flag was carried by Paolo Ananian.

[2] One of the most dramatic, almost terrifying incidents in the voluminous *Samson* lore occurred at the Chicago Auditorium during a performance starring the ample Marguerite d'Alvarez, Lucien Muratore, and Dufranne. Edward Moore tells the story in his *Forty Years of Opera in Chicago:* "Mme. D'Alvarez on her first entrance, standing at the top of the steps of the temple, slipped and fell all

212. Schwanda the Bagpiper (Weinberger)

Two acts; libretto by Miloš Kareš; Prague, Czech Theater, April 27, 1927.

The complaint about the casting of the New York *première* at the Metropolitan, on November 7, 1931, was that what would have done well for Wagner was not for Weinberger, whose chief desideratum was resilience. Anyhow, Friedrich Schorr was excellent in the name role, and Maria Müller, Karin Branzell, Rudolf Laubenthal, and Ivar Andrésen were satisfactory. Five performances in one season sufficed. *Schwanda* also had five performances at Covent Garden, London, in two successive seasons. The *première* was May 11, 1934. The stars were unquestionably Paul Schöffler (Schwanda), Charles Kullmann (Babinsky), and Alexander Kipnis (Magician); Viorica Ursuleac (Dorota) and Gertrud Rünger (Ice Queen) "were quite equal to the little they had to sing." Elisabeth Rethberg was the Dorota in 1935.

213. Die schweigsame Frau (Strauss)

Three acts; libretto by Stefan Zweig, after Ben Jonson's Epicœne *or The Silent Woman; Dresden, June 24, 1935.*

Karl Böhm conducted the world *première* of *Die schweigsame Frau,* which was produced by Josef Gielen and designed by Adolf Mahnke. The cast included Maria Cebotari (Aminta), Erna Sack (Isotta), Helene Jung, Friedrich Plaschke (Morosus), Matthieu Ahlersmeyer (Barber), Martin Kremer (Henry), Kurt Böhme, and Ludwig Ermold. The Nazis were in power in Germany, which explained why the name of Stefan Zweig, a Jew, which appeared on the first programs, quickly was dropped. The political venom of the critics was so lethal that *Die schweigsame Frau* was removed very quickly from the Dresden repertoire; a few months later, Strauss resigned his position as chief of the *Reichsmusikkammer.* It was revived in non-Nazi Switzerland, at Zurich, on May 16, 1936, and in Prague on June 3, 1937. Meanwhile La Scala, Milan, had staged it (March 11, 1936) in an Italian translation by Ottone Schanzer.

Sir Thomas Beecham wanted to stage *Die schweigsame Frau* at Covent Garden, London, in 1938, but was balked by casting difficulties growing out of political differences among singers aware that the opera was in severe Nazi disfavor. The opera never has been sung at the Metropolitan Opera in New York, and has had comparatively few performances anywhere. But the New York City Opera Company staged it at the City Center on October 7, 1958, when Peter Herman Adler conducted and the cast included Ruth Kobart, Jacquelynne Moody, Regina Sarfaty, Joan Carroll, Paul Ukena, Herbert Beattie, John Alexander, Arnold Voketaitis, Arthur Newman, and Joshua Hecht. The opera was sung in an English translation (mostly incomprehensible) by Herbert Bedford, and was presented in a cripplingly "adapted" version.

Another attempt, somewhat more successful, to bring life to *Die schweigsame Frau* was made during

---

the way to the bottom. In fact she slid into the middle of the stage. It was one of the most striking instances of the self-discipline of artists on record, for while the audience gasped, thinking she might have cracked her spine, she, with practically a continuation of the same motion, rolled to her feet and came up with the note between her teeth and on pitch. She finished the opera with no delay and no complaint, though she was rather lame the next day. But the next time she took the precaution to apply rosin to her sandals until you could have heard their squeak to the back of the house."

the 1959 Salzburg Festival. The production, by Günther Rennert, was much admired, as were the performances of Hilde Gueden in the vocally trying role of Aminta and of Hans Hotter as Sir Morosus Blunt. It still seems possible, though not likely, that *Die schweigsame Frau* may one day be heard with enough frequency to become a repertoire opera rather than an occasional novelty. In an English translation by Arthur Jacobs, it was presented at Covent Garden, London, on November 20, 1961, as produced by Franz Josef Wild, designed by Martin Battersby, and conducted by Rudolf Kempe. The cast included Barbara Holt (Aminta), Monica Sinclair (Theodosia Featherbed), Elizabeth Vaughan (Isotta), Noreen Berry (Carlotta), David Ward (Sir John Morosus), Kenneth Macdonald (Henry Morosus), Joseph Ward (Tobias Razorblade), David Kelly (Vanuzzi), Ronald Lewis (Morbio), and Michael Langdon (Farfallo). This was *The Silent Woman*'s first hearing in England.

214. Il Segreto di Susanna (Wolf-Ferrari)

One act; libretto by Enrico Golisciani, but translated from Italian into German (as Susannens Geheimnis) *by Max Kalbeck for the* première; *Munich, December 4, 1909.*

Felix Mottl conducted the world première. Thereafter the little *intermezzo* was heard in German at Strasbourg, Prague, and Vienna, and in Swedish at Stockholm. The New York première, by the visiting Chicago company, at the Metropolitan Opera House on March 14, 1911, used the original Italian text for the first time anywhere; Carolina White was the Susanna, Mario Sammarco the Count. The Metropolitan company staged *Il Segreto di Susanna* for the first time

on December 13, 1912 (on a double bill with *Pagliacci*). Giorgio Polacco conducted, and the two singing roles (Sante, the servant, is a mute) were played by Geraldine Farrar and Antonio Scotti. A revival for Lucrezia Bori and Scotti on March 9, 1921 (double bill with the American *première* of Karel Weiss's *Der polnische Jude*), ran the Metropolitan total of performances up to eleven in four seasons before *Il Segreto* vanished from that opera house.

The first *Segreto* at Covent Garden, London, on July 11, 1911, presented Lydia Lipkowska and Sammarco; Cleofonte Campanini conducted. After Sammarco's farewell (August 1, 1919) to Covent Garden, where he had been much valued for fifteen years, there was less reason to preserve the little Wolf-Ferrari opera that had been so closely associated with his adroit performance of Count Gil. After three performances in the 1919–20 Beecham season, with Albert Coates and Aylmer Buesst conducting, and with Jeanne Brola (Countess) and Frederick Ranalow (Count), the opera had only one more performance before disappearing from Covent Garden.

215. Semiramide (Rossini)

Two acts; libretto by Gaetano Rossi, after Voltaire's tragedy Sémirame; *Venice, Teatro La Fenice, February 3, 1823.*

Immensely successful, *Semiramide* proved to be the last of the nearly thirty operas composed by Rossini in Italy. It reached London, the Haymarket Theatre, on July 15, 1824, and Paris, the Théâtre-Italien, on December 8, 1825. On February 20, 1832, it was first heard in America, at Mexico City. The earliest performance in the United States occurred at New Orleans on May 1, 1837. Sections of the opera had been heard in New York on April 29, 1835, but the complete work was not sung there until January 3, 1845.

At the London *première* of *Semiramide* (July 15, 1824), the Semiramide was Giuditta Pasta, the Arsace Lucia Elizabeth Vestris. Nearly five years later, the first complete Rossini opera (if such it could be called) to be heard at Covent Garden was *The Maid of Judah,* an English adaptation of *Semiramide* made by the busy Michael Rophino Lacy, who had twisted Rossini's music to fit a libretto based on Scott's *Ivanhoe.*[1] On October 1, 1842, *Semiramide* was conducted by Julius Benedict, the cast including Adelaide Kemble (Semiramide), Mrs. Alfred Shaw (Arsace), Signor Giubilei (Assur), and Adam Leffler (Oroe). It opened the Covent Garden season in 1851, with Giulia Grisi in the title role, Elena Angri (Arsace), Signor Salvatore (Assur), and Luigi Mei (Idreno). In 1860, at Her Majesty's Theatre, Therese Tietjens created a sensation as Semiramide. She sang it at the new Covent Garden on November 15, 1870, with Zelia Trebelli (Arsace), "Signor Foli," whose real name was Allan James Foley (Assur), and Signor Bettini (Idreno). In a revival in 1875, the Semiramide, Maria Vilda (Marie Wilt), was outshone by both the Arsace (Sofia Scalchi) and the Assur (Jean-Baptiste Faure). But probably the most sensational Covent Garden performances of *Semiramide* began on June 23, 1885, when the title role was sung by Adelina Patti,

the Arsace was again Scalchi, and the role of Assur was handled by Giuseppe del Puente.

Patti also sang the role of Semiramide at New York's Academy of Music in 1883; she sang it at the Metropolitan in the spring of 1887 when a touring company followed the regular German season there, and was still repeating that performance there on March 27, 1890. The opera entered the repertoire of a resident Metropolitan company only in the 1893–94 season: it was first heard on January 12, 1894, with Luigi Mancinelli conducting and a cast made up of Nellie Melba (Semiramide), Sofia Scalchi (Arsace), Édouard de Reszke (Assur), Pedro Guetary (Idreno), Armand Castelmary (Oroe), and Antonio de Vaschetti (Ghost of Nino), and was repeated with the identical cast three times that season. With a fifth performance, on January 25, 1894, the opera disappeared from the Metropolitan roster. It is still very occasionally revived in Europe. On April 28, 1940, *Semiramide* opened the sixth Florentine Maggio Musicale; Tullio Serafin conducted, and the cast included Gabriella Gatti, Ebe Stignani, Ferruccio Tagliavini, Tancredi Pasero, and Alfredo Colella.

216. Serse (Handel)

Three acts; libretto an adaptation of Niccolò Minato's Xerse, *first set in 1654 by Francesco Cavalli*[1]; *London,*

---

[1] Lacy no doubt had taken the idea from *Ivanhoé;* this pastiche of music from Rossini's *Semiramide, Mosè, Tancredi,* and *La Gazza ladra,* fitted to a libretto by Émile Deschamps and Gabriel-Gustave de Wailly based on Scott's novel, was first sung at the Odéon, Paris, on September 15, 1826. The adapting had been done by Antonio Pacini—a fact, as Alfred Loewenberg pointed out, which has led to much confusion in reference works, the more renowned Italian composer Giovanni Pacini having himself

also composed an *Ivanhoe* (Venice, March 19, 1832), in Italian.

[1] Cavalli's *Xerse,* first produced at the Teatro Santi Giovanni e Paolo, Venice, on January 12 (?), 1654, is said to have been the first opera ever sung (1658) at Palermo. It was also produced in the Grande Galerie du Louvre, Paris, on November 22, 1660, with ballet music supplied by Lully, as part of the festivities surrounding the wedding of Louis XIV and Maria Theresa of Austria.

Haymarket Theatre, April 15, 1738 (not April 26, as stated by Alfred Loewenberg).

The original cast included La Lucchesina (Arsamene), Antonia Margherita Merighi (Amastre), Signora Francesina (Romilda), Margherita Chimenti, known as La Droghierina (Atalanta), Caffarelli (Serse), Antonio Lottini (Elviro), and Antonio Montagnana (Ariodate). This, Handel's only opera with a comic libretto, achieved only five performances in its first season (up to May 2); it remains familiar chiefly because it contains the ever-popular "Largo," to text lines beginning "Ombra mai fu."

Serse was revived in German translation by Oskar Hagen, as part of the so-called "Handel Renaissance," at Göttingen on July 5, 1924. It was also sung, in an English translation by Thornton Wilder, at Smith College, Northampton, Massachusetts, on May 12, 1928, the version being repeated later at the Juilliard School of Music in New York (December 15, 1932) and at the University of Chicago (February 16, 1935). Geoffrey Thomas Dunn's English translation has been heard in England (Loughton, Essex, June 15, 1935; Duke's Theatre, London, November 28, 1935, produced by the Royal Academy of Music). As part of the world-wide celebration of the Handel Bicentenary in 1959, the Württemberg State Opera, Stuttgart, staged *Serse* in a production by Caspar Neher; the cast included Friederike Sailer (Romilda), Franziska Wachmann (Atalanta), and Joseph Traxel (Serse).

217. La Serva padrona (Pergolesi)

Two parts; libretto by Gennaro Antonio Federico; Naples, Teatro San Bartolommeo, August 28, 1733.

Until the relatively recent operatic persistence of Monteverdi and Purcell, *La Serva padrona* was the oldest fixture in the standard repertoire. The two parts (*intermezzi*) were first given between the acts of Pergolesi's *Il Prigionier superbo*, an *opera seria* (librettist unknown). It reached Paris in 1746; a revival there, at the Opéra, on August 1, 1752, was historic: from it grew the notorious *querelle des bouffons*. Its adventures in London after its *première* at the Haymarket, April 7, 1750, included that sure gauge of popularity: not merely translation into English (1758), but also its acceptance, in that language, as an almost native product. However, the French versions had the wider range, and it was in French that the opera first came to the United States: Baltimore and New York, both in 1790. *La Serva padrona* did not reach the Metropolitan Opera House until February 23, 1935, the last novelty mounted during the regime of Giulio Gatti-Casazza. Editha Fleischer was the Serpina, Louis d'Angelo the Uberto, in this stylish production. Bidu Sayão and Salvatore Baccaloni were true *buffa* characters in the revival of December 9, 1942, when the opera was a curtain raiser for Strauss's *Salome*. Meanwhile, *La Serva padrona* runs around the world, in a variety of languages. Despite several new versions in English, it has not yet reached Covent Garden.

218. Siegfried (Wagner)

Prologue and three acts; libretto by the composer, being Part III ("zweites Tag") of Der Ring des Nibelungen; Bayreuth, Festspielhaus, August 16, 1876, as part of the first Ring cycle. See also Der Ring des Nibelungen (No. 197).

With Hans Richter conducting, principals at the world *première* were Franz Betz (Wanderer), Georg Unger (Siegfried), Karl Hill (Alberich), Karl Schlosser (Mime), Amalie Materna (Brünnhilde), Jaïde (Erda) and Marie Haupt (Forest Bird). The stars of the first New York performance, at the Metropolitan Opera House on November 9, 1887, were Emil Fischer (Wanderer), Max Alvary (Siegfried), Lilli Lehmann (Brünnhilde), and Marianne Brandt (Erda). At the first London performance, at Her Majesty's Theatre on May 8, 1882, Emil Scaria was the Wanderer, Heinrich Vogl the Siegfried, and Therese Vogl the Brünnhilde. A fine cast was assembled for the first Covent Garden performance, on June 8, 1892, with Gustav Mahler conducting: Karl Grengg (Wanderer), Alvary (Siegfried), Rosa Sucher (Brünnhilde), Sophie Traubmann (Forest Bird), Ernestine Schumann-Heink (Erda), Julius Lieban (Mime), Lorent (Alberich), and Heinrich Wiegand (Fafner). Later that season, Katharina Klafsky was heard as Brünnhilde.

219. Il Signor Bruschino, ossia Il Figlio per azzardo (Rossini)

One act; libretto by Giuseppe Maria Foppa, after a comedy by André-René-Polydore Alisan de Chazet and E.-T.-Maurice Ourry; Venice, Teatro San Moisè, late January, 1813.

Although not a real success, the opera was heard in Milan, at the Teatro della Canobbiana, in 1844; in a French version prepared by Philippe-Auguste-Alfred Pittaud de Forges and Jacques Offenbach, at the Bouffes-Parisiens, Paris, on December 28, 1857; at Brussels; and at Berlin in both French and German—all during Rossini's lifetime.

Il Signor Bruschino was first heard in New York, at the Metropolitan Opera, on December 8, 1932, when it served as a curtain raiser for Strauss's *Elektra*. Irving Kolodin noted that many of the vocal lines had been transposed. Tullio Serafin conducted, and the cast included Editha Fleischer (Sofia), Giuseppe de Luca (Bruschino), and Ezio Pinza (Gaudenzio). Its four performances during the 1932–33 season ended its Metropolitan career, as well as that of the prolific designer of scenery, Joseph Urban, whose final illness had prevented him from completing the *Bruschino* designs (they were actually completed by Joseph Novak).

In 1957, the Piccola Scala, Milan, revived *Il Signor Bruschino* as part of a double bill with Riccardo Malipiero's *La Donna è mobile*. Gianandrea Gavazzeni conducted, and the cast included Mariella Adani, Luis Mandelli, Paolo Montarsolo, Paolo Pedani, Franco Ricciardi, Mario Spina, Michele Cazzato, and Franco Iglesias. Many of the same singers appeared in the opera when the Teatro da Camera of Milan performed it at the Teatro Colón, Buenos Aires, that same year.

220. Simon Boccanegra (Verdi)

Prologue and three acts; text by Francesco Maria Piave, after the play of the same name by Antonio García Gutiérrez; Venice, Teatro La Fenice, March 12, 1857; revised version, with libretto altered by Arrigo Boito, Milan, Teatro alla Scala, March 24, 1881.

The cast of the Venice *première* included Luigia Bendazzi (Amelia), Carlo Negrini (Gabriele Adorno), Leone Giraldoni (Simon Boccanegra), and Giuseppe Echeverria (Jacopo Fiesco). It was not a success, and only the fact that for the revised version of 1881 La Scala billed three of the greatest singers then alive—Victor Maurel (Simon Boccanegra), Francesco Tamagno (Gabriele Adorno), and Édouard de Reszke (Jacopo Fiesco)—the conductor was Franco Faccio and Anna d'Angeri was the Amelia—sufficed to make *Simon Boccanegra* more than a temporary *succès d'estime*. For real success, the opera had to wait until 1930, when Franz Werfel's German translation was used for a mounting at Vienna on January 12. This version soon was heard in Berlin, Prague, and Basel—and made the rounds of German-language opera houses.

Simon Boccanegra was staged for the first time in the United States at the Metropolitan Opera, New York, on January 28, 1932. Tullio Serafin conducted, and the cast included Maria Müller (Maria—that is, Amelia—Boccanegra), Giovanni Martinelli (Gabriele), Lawrence Tibbett (Simon Boccanegra), and Ezio Pinza (Fiesco). Pinza gave a magnificent account of the best-known excerpt from the opera, the dramatic apostrophe, "Il lacerato spirito," and Tibbett was altogether admirable as Boccanegra. The production achieved probably its best performance on February 24, 1932, when Elisabeth Rethberg was the Amelia. On the following November 21, the twenty-fifth opening night at the Metropolitan under the managership of Giulio Gatti-Casazza, Arturo Toscanini was in the audience as the manager's guest[1] when *Simon Boccanegra* inaugurated the 1932–33 season, with the cast of the first Metropolitan singing. During the 1938–39 season, the role of Amelia was sung by Maria Caniglia (January 13, 1939). After a lapse of eleven seasons, the opera was revived at the Metropolitan on No-

vember 28, 1949. Fritz Stiedry conducted, and the cast included Astrid Varnay (Amelia), Richard Tucker (Adorno), Leonard Warren (Boccanegra), Mihaly Szekely (Fiesco), and Giuseppe Valdengo (Paolo Albiani). Warren became much admired in the title role. After his dramatic death, it was assumed (April 7, 1960) by Anselmo Colzani, making his Metropolitan debut. In the final *Boccanegra* of the 1959–60 season (its twenty-ninth performance in the house), Colzani was supported by Zinka Milanov (Amelia), Carlo Bergonzi (Adorno), Giorgio Tozzi (Fiesco), and Enzo Flagello (Paolo Albiani).

Simon Boccanegra reached London in 1948, when it was staged by the Sadler's Wells group, with Joyce Gartside (Amelia), James Johnston (Adorno), Arnold Matters (Boccanegra), and Howell Glynne (Fiesco). It was revived at Rome in 1949 with a cast including Onelia Fineschi, Mirto Picchi, Tito Gobbi, and Cesare Siepi, under Tullo Serafin's baton; at Venice in 1950 with Caterina Mancini, Gino Penno, Carlo Tagliabue, Boris Christoff, and Rolando Panerai. It is still frequently revived throughout Europe.

221. Snegurochka (Rimsky-Korsakov)

Prologue and four acts; libretto by the composer, after a play by Alexander Ostrovsky; St. Petersburg, Maryinsky Theater, January 29 (O.S.), 1882.

New York's *Snegurochka*, first heard at the Metropolitan Opera on January 23, 1922, starred Lucrezia Bori

---

[1] As the culmination of a disagreement with Gatti-Casazza, the details of which remain unclear, Toscanini had left the Metropolitan after conducting Mascagni's *Iris* there on April 14, 1915. He never conducted opera for the Metropolitan again, but his willingness to be seen there with Gatti more than seventeen years later was taken to indicate some degree of personal reconciliation between the two men.

(Snegurochka) and Orville Harrold (Tsar Berendey). It was sung in French, and lasted out nine performances in two seasons. The Chicago production, also in French, starred Edith Mason in the name role; Georges Baklanoff was an excellent Misgir. London first heard the opera, in English (translation by Edward Agate), at Sadler's Wells, on April 12, 1933; Olive Dyer had the name role.

222. Socrate (Satie)

Three parts; libretto from Victor Cousin's French translation of Plato's Dialogues; Paris, Société Nationale de Musique, February 14, 1920.

Satie's *drame symphonique avec voix* was first heard, in concert form, as presented in Paris by the Société Nationale de Musique on February 14, 1920. It seems to have been staged before 1925 in the private theater of the Princesse Edmond de Polignac in Paris. Its first public staged performance occurred at Prague in May 1925, during a festival of the International Society for Contemporary Music; it was sung in a Czech translation. At Naples in 1959, the third part of *Socrate, La Mort de Socrate*, was staged by the visiting Berlin Städtische Opers Opernstudio at the Teatro San Carlo as one-fourth of a quadruple bill that also included Boris Blacher's *Abstract Opera No. 1*, Hindemith's *Hin und zurück*, and *Il Cuore*, this last being Anton von Webern's Cantata No. 2 with added text by Hildegard Jone. The productions were by Wolf Völker, a founder of the Opernstudio, and Hermann Scherchen conducted. Satie also composed a *comédie-lyrique* to his own libretto entitled *Le Piège de Méduse*.

223. La Sonnambula (Bellini)

Two acts; libretto by Felice Romani; Milan, Teatro Carcano, March 6, 1831.

The cast of the Milan *première* of *La Sonnambula* included Giuditta Pasta (Amina), Giovanni Battista Rubini (Elvino), and Luciano Mariani (Rodolfo). An immediate success, the opera was sung in some forty-five cities in twelve different countries by 1850— in addition to numerous performances in Italy itself. On July 29, 1850, it became the first opera heard in Chicago; Eliza Brienti was the Amina, and after Act I on the second night, the Chicago Theater took fire and burned to the ground.

London heard it in Italian at the Haymarket on July 28, 1831; in the English of Samuel Beazley, edited by Sir Henry Bishop, it was sung at Drury Lane on May 1, 1833, with Maria Malibran making her English stage debut as Amina; this production was transferred bodily to Covent Garden on June 14, 1833. Supporting Mme Malibran were John Templeton (Elvino) and Arthur Seguin (Rodolfo); the opera was sung twenty-four times that season. The opening opera of the 1843 summer season was *Sonnambula* again (April 24), this time with Malibran's sister-in-law, Eugenia García (Amina), William Harrison (Elvino), and Adam Leffler (Rodolfo). Malibran's sister, Pauline Viardot-García, made her Covent Garden debut as Amina on May 9, 1848. And in the autumn of that year the great English tenor John Sims Reeves made his first Covent Garden appearance as Elvino (October 18). During the 1849 season, on May 22, Fanny Persiani sang Amina with Sims Reeves and Antonio Tamburini (Rodolfo).

During 1849, too, Jenny Lind was singing her hysterically admired Amina at Her Majesty's Theatre during the last of her three seasons on the London operatic stage. Of Lind's singing of the aria "Ah! non credea," Queen Victoria rhapsodized in her diary: "It was all *piano* and clear and sweet, and like the sighing of a zephyr; yet all heard. Who could describe those long notes, drawn out until they quite melt away; that shake which becomes softer and softer; those very piano- and flute-like notes, and those round, fresh tones that are so youthful?"

Adelina Patti made both her Paris and her London debut as Amina, the latter at Covent Garden on May 14, 1861. Sir Michael Costa conducted, and others in the cast were Mario Tiberini (Elvino) and Joseph-Dieu-donné Tagliafico (Rodolfo); thus began for England what is justly called "Patti's reign." On October 26, 1868, the sixteen-year-old American soprano Minnie Hauk made her Covent Garden debut as Amina.[1] On November 23, 1869, the Amina was Ilma di Murska. The Canadian soprano Emma Albani—who had made her world debut at Messina in 1870, and would make her New York debut at the Academy of Music on October 21, 1874, as Amina—first appeared at Covent Garden in a *Sonnambula* in which the Elvino was Julian Gayarré, the Rodolfo Édouard de Reszke. The twenty-six-year-old bass was encored for his masterly singing of "Vi rav-viso." He was still singing Rodolfo when Marie Van Zandt made her Covent Garden debut as Amina on June 3, 1889. After 1890, *La Sonnambula* was not heard at Covent Garden until May 29, 1909, when it was put on as a starring vehicle for Luisa Tetrazzini, supported by John McCormack (Elvino) and Scandiani (Rodolfo). With a 1910 repetition in which Edmund

---

[1] Hauk had been only fourteen when she had made her first operatic appearance, as Amina, at the old Brooklyn Academy of Music on October 13, 1866.

Burke replaced Scandiani, *Sonnambula* passed from the stage of Covent Garden.

New York heard *La Sonnambula* first in English, on November 13, 1835; in Italian on May 13, 1844; and in German on January 4, 1871. Etelka Gerster made her New York debut as Amina at the Academy of Music on November 18, 1878. The opera was sung at the Metropolitan during that house's first season: the cast on November 14, 1883, was: Marcella Sembrich (Amina), Emily Lablache (Teresa), Ida Corani (Lisa), Italo Campanini (Elvino), Franco Novara—whose real name was Frank Nash (Rodolfo), Baldassare Corsini (Alessio), and Amadeo Grazzi (the Notary). Cleofonte Campanini, Italo's younger brother, conducted. After the two performances of that first season, *Sonnambula* lapsed at the Metropolitan until December 21, 1891, when Marie Van Zandt was the Amina; again two performances sufficed. Then, on December 15, 1905, Sembrich returned to the title role in a cast that included Enrico Caruso (Elvino) and Pol Plançon (Rodolfo). After one repetition that season, there was a gap until a single matinee performance late in the 1909–10 season (April 2, 1910) brought forth Elvira de Hidalgo as Amina, Alessandro Bonci as Elvino, and Andrés de Segu-rola as Rodolfo; the double bill was filled out with *Hungary,* a ballet to music by Alexander Glazunov in which Anna Pavlova and Mikhail Mordkin danced. Malibran and Lind no doubt had considered themselves realists in the role of Amina, but Hidalgo outdistanced all comers by playing the sleepwalker barefooted.

On March 3, 1915, the Metropolitan again tackled *La Sonnambula,* this time with Giorgio Polacco conducting a cast that included María Barrientos (Amina), Giacomo Damacco (Elvino), and Adamo Didur (Rodolfo);

this time, too, the opera ran up three performances in a single season. Although Amelita Galli-Curci, who had sung Amina with the Chicago company, was at the Metropolitan from November 14, 1921, to January, 1930, she never sang the role at the Metropolitan. On March 16, 1931—during a season in which Rosa Ponselle also appeared in *Norma*—Tullio Serafin conducted a *Sonnambula* with Lily Pons as Amina, Beniamino Gigli as Elvino, and Ezio Pinza as Rodolfo; again, three performances in a season. During the 1932–33 season there were three more performances, the first, a matinee on February 11, 1933, with Giacomo Lauri-Volpi replacing Gigli. After two performances in 1935, the second, on March 11, with Pons supported by Tito Schipa as Elvino and Virgilio Lazzari as Rodolfo, and with Ettore Panizza conducting, *La Sonnambula* left the Metropolitan repertoire for more than a quarter-century, having been sung there eighteen times.

At La Scala, Milan, in 1935, Toti dal Monte was the Amina, Tito Schipa the Elvino, and Tancredi Pasero the Rodolfo. At a Florentine production in 1942, the Amina was Margherita Carosio, who was supported by Ferruccio Tagliavini and Pasero. At Rome in 1951, Carosio repeated her excellent Amina under Gianandrea Gavazzeni's direction, with Cesare Valletti as Elvino and Boris Christoff as Rodolfo. Perhaps the outstanding *Sonnambula* of recent years was produced for La Scala in 1957 by Luchino Visconti, with Maria Meneghini Callas (Amina), Nicola Monti (Elvino), Nicola Zaccaria (Rodolfo), and Eugenia Ratti (Lisa); Antonino Votto conducted. This production was also heard, during 1957, at the Edinburgh Festival and at Cologne during the festivities marking the opening of the new opera house there. The opera was heard at the Teatro Massimo in Catania, Bellini's birthplace, in April 1958, with Gianna d'Angelo (Amina), Luigi Pontiggia (Elvino), and Plinio Clabassi (Rodolfo); Franco Capuana conducted. At Trieste's Teatro Giuseppe Verdi in 1958, under Oliviero de Fabritiis' baton, the Amina was Renata Scotto, supported by Alvinio Misciano (Elvino) and Clabassi (Rodolfo).

On February 12, 1851, *La Sonnambula* became the first opera performed in San Francisco. More than a century later (October 1, 1960), it was heard there when a San Francisco Opera Company performance was conducted by Francesco Molinari-Pradelli; the Amina was Anna Moffo, who was supported by Sylvia Stahlman (Lisa), Nicola Monti (Elvino), and Giorgio Tozzi (Rodolfo). On December 5, 1961, the American Opera Society presented Joan Sutherland in a concert performance of *La Sonnambula* at Carnegie Hall, New York. Nicola Rescigno conducted, and others in the cast were Betty Allen, Eileen di Tullio, Renato Cioni, Armand McLane, and Ezio Flagello. The Metropolitan Opera announced that it would revive *La Sonnambula* for Sutherland during the 1962–63 season.

224. Stiffelio [Aroldo] (Verdi)

Three acts; libretto by Francesco Maria Piave, after a play by Émile Souvestre and Eugène Bourgeois; Trieste, November 16, 1850. Revised, in four acts, as Aroldo; Rimini, Teatro Nuovo, August 16, 1857.

Stiffelio in its original form was a failure, and it was with extreme misgivings that Verdi recast it in four acts to an almost entirely new libretto, transferring the action from early nineteenth-century Germany to medieval Scotland and England. The revised version, *Aroldo*, was used to inaugurate the Teatro Nuovo at Rimini on August 16, 1857. *Aroldo* was somewhat more successful than *Stiffelio*, being staged in several other Italian cities, elsewhere in Europe, in South America, and—on May 4, 1863 —in New York.

As part of the 1951 commemoration of the fiftieth anniversary of Verdi's death, *Aroldo* was given over the Italian radio; Arturo Basile conducted, and the cast included Maria Vitali (Mina), Vasco Campagnano (Aroldo), and Rolando Panerai (Egberto). In 1953 *Aroldo* was staged during the Florentine Maggio Musicale. Tullio Serafin conducted, and the leading singers were Antonietta Stella (Mina), Gino Penno (Aroldo), and Aldo Protti (Egberto). In 1955—105 years after the original *Stiffelio*'s *première* at Trieste—*Aroldo* was restaged at that city's Teatro Giuseppe Verdi. Franco Capuana conducted, and the three principal protagonists were Anna Maria Rovere (Mina), Roberto Turrini (Aroldo), and Ugo Savarese (Egberto).

A notable revival of *Aroldo* occurred early in 1957 at the newly opened opera house of Wuppertal, Germany. This centenary production of the revised opera had a cast including Margrit Wieden (Mina), Georg Paskuda (Aroldo), and Ronald Jackson (Egberto). Dissenting from the generally adverse pronouncements of many past and present critics, Ralf Steyer wrote in *Opera:* "There is a certain Baroque size about the work and the line-drawing is apt to recall Handel. The music follows the tradition of Donizetti and Bellini without giving so much scope for coloratura. Verdi's genius is everywhere in evidence, his melodic opulence, his dramatic verve; and as the libretto is also very effective it is difficult to see why the piece is not given more often."

On March 7, 1961, at Town Hall, New York, the Amato Opera Theatre presented a semistaged concert version of *Aroldo* which underlined Mr. Steyer's opinion. Anthony Amato conducted, and the leading roles were sung by Anne Ottaviano (Mina) and—impressively—as Aroldo, George Shirley.

225. The Stone Guest (Dargomizhsky)

Three acts; libretto uses Pushkin's short play, The Stone Guest *(1830), without changes; St. Petersburg, Maryinsky Theater, February 16 (O.S.), 1872, orchestrated by Rimsky-Korsakov; César Cui furnished the overture.*

Eduard Napravnik, the Czech conductor and composer, conducted the *première,* with the best singers of the age in principal roles: F. P. Komissarjevsky, Ossip Afanasyevich Petrov, Melnikov, Y. F. Platonova, and Ilissa. Rimsky-Korsakov wrote somewhat ambiguously in *My Musical Life:* "The audiences were perplexed, but the opera had success nevertheless." There have been occasional revivals in Russia, but few performances are noted elsewhere.

226. Suor Angelica (Puccini)

One act; libretto by Giovacchino Forzano; produced as the second of the three one-act operas called Il Trittico *(q.v., No. 235), New York, Metropolitan Opera House, December 14, 1918.*

Geraldine Farrar (Suor Angelica), Flora Perini (Princess), and Marie Sundelius (Alms Collector) were the principals at the world *première.* There were ten performances in two successive seasons, and the opera was not revived. At the Covent Garden, London, *première,* it also was given as the second of the three parts of *Il Trittico.* Gilda Dalla Rizza was Suor

Angelica, Jacqueline Royer the Princess. The opera was not revived at Covent Garden, and indeed it has been given rarely anywhere. It was as Suor Angelica, at San Francisco on December 2, 1935, that Helen Gahagan, later well known in both the legitimate theater and politics, made her American debut in opera.

227. Il Tabarro (Puccini)

One act; libretto by Giuseppe Adami, after Didier Gold's play La Houppelande; *produced as the first of the three one-act operas called* Il Trittico (q.v., *No. 235*), *New York, Metropolitan Opera House, December 14, 1918.*

The principals of the world *première* were Claudia Muzio (Giorgetta), Luigi Montesanto (Michele), Giulio Crimi (Luigi), and Adamo Didur (Talpa). Edward Johnson sang Luigi the next season. When the opera was revived in 1946, Licia Albanese was Giorgetta and Lawrence Tibbett was Michele, "hard put to produce the vocal power the role required" (Irving Kolodin); Frederick Jagel was the Luigi.

At Covent Garden, London, where *Il Tabarro* was first given on June 18, 1920 (as part of *Il Trittico*), the principals were Ida Quaiatti, Dinh Gilly, and Thomas Burke. In 1935 it was heard at Sadler's Wells, in English, with Winifred Kennard, Arnold Matters, and Henry Wendon.

228. Tancredi (Rossini)

Two acts; libretto by Gaetano Rossi, derived from Voltaire's tragedy Tancrède *and Tasso's* Gerusalemme liberata; *Venice, Teatro La Fenice, February 6, 1813.*

This second of Rossini's three 1813 operas established his fame, becoming a truly world-wide favorite in a few years. In its first twenty-two years of existence, in fact, it was heard in some thirty-six cities in twenty-five countries, including Russia, Mexico, the United States, Brazil, Argentina, Chile, Peru, Romania, and Finland—in twelve different languages. It remained a fixture of the repertoire in Europe until the 1860's.

A notable performance of *Tancredi* opened a Covent Garden, London, season on March 9, 1848, when the cast included Marietta Alboni (Tancredi), Fanny Persiani (Amenaide), Entimio Polonini (Orbazzano), and Luigi Mei (Argirio). The opera was never staged at the Metropolitan in New York. It was revived at the Florence Maggio Musicale in 1952 under the baton of Tullio Serafin, with the American soprano Teresa Stich-Randall, Giulietta Simionato, Francesco Albanese, and Mario Petri.

229. Tannhäuser (Wagner)

Three acts; libretto by the composer (*his ultimate title was* Tannhäuser und der Sängerkrieg auf Wartburg);[1] *Dresden, October 19, 1845.*

At the world *première* Johanna Wagner was the Elisabeth, Wilhelmine Schröder-Devrient the Venus, Joseph Aloys Tichatschek the Tannhäuser, and Anton Mitterwurzer the Wolfram. The opera soon achieved popularity: five-hundredth performance in Dresden on November 16, 1913; five-hundredth performance in Berlin on August 26, 1907. *Tannhäuser* had traveled far (to New York, among other places) before the notorious night at the Paris Opéra

[1] Wagner had planned to call the opera *Der Venusberg*, but his publisher feared that the title might cause "ribald comment"— bad enough that some of the action be located on the Mountain of Venus. . . . (See the chapter on *Tannhäuser* in Ernest Newman, *The Wagner Operas*.)

(March 13, 1861), with Marie Saxe (Elisabeth), Fortunata Tedesco (Venus), and Albert Niemann (Tannhäuser—the first Wagnerian role of one of the greatest of Wagnerian tenors). Wagner insisted upon withdrawing the opera after the third performance (see p. 230), and *Tannhäuser* was not thereafter heard in Paris for over a quarter of a century, until Charles Lamoureux's courageous production of *Lohengrin*, in 1887, opened the French market to a Wagnerian invasion. A famous revival of *Tannhäuser* occurred at the Opéra on May 13, 1895, when Ernest Van Dyck, a Belgian tenor who had actually been greeted with plaudits when he essayed the role of Parsifal at Bayreuth, took the lead, his Elisabeth being Rose Caron, and his Venus the powerful Swiss dramatic soprano, Lucienne Bréval; Maurice Renaud was the Wolfram, Jean-François Delmas the Landgrave.

London heard its first *Tannhäuser*, in Italian, at Covent Garden, with Emma Albani (Elisabeth), Anna d'Angeri (Venus), Fernando Carpi (Tannhäuser), and Victor Maurel (Wolfram), on May 6, 1876. This was seventeen years later than the American *première*, which, moreover, was in the language in which the opera was written. In fact, that performance at the Stadt Theater, New York, on April 4, 1859, was the first opera by Wagner ever to be given in the Americas. "Some objections," wrote Henry Lahee, "were made . . . to the thoroughly German atmosphere pervading the whole affair. Boys went through the aisles with beer in stone mugs for the thirsty, and huge chunks of *Schweizerkäs* for the hungry." That, of course, was the Dresden version, which was also used when to *Tannhäuser* fell the honor of opening the second Metropolitan season, on November 17, 1884. It marked, also, the beginning of a heavy wave of operatic Teutonism, when, in addition to naturally German operas, French and Ital-

ian works were given in German. Leopold Damrosch conducted a performance that might not be considered notable today, but was then a revelation because of the *chef d'orchestre*'s fine command of his ensemble. Auguste Seidl-Kraus, Anton Seidl's wife, was Elisabeth; Anton Schott was an explosive Tannhäuser (H. E. Krehbiel called his singing "monstrous"); and Anna Slach was Venus.

Tannhäuser was in the repertoire of the Metropolitan almost uninterruptedly until 1949. Oddly enough, it had been given over thirty times before the much more attractive and spectacular Paris version was first used there, on January 30, 1889, with Lilli Lehmann as Venus and Paul Kalisch as Tannhäuser. In the late nineties, Emma Eames was a favorite Elisabeth, though some of the performances in which she sang were a little less than artistic, with French and Italian mingled indiscriminately. After the World War I interim of eight seasons, *Tannhäuser* was revived on February 1, 1923, for Maria Jeritza, with Margarete Matzenauer as the ample but golden-voiced Venus; Curt Taucher was the Tannhäuser, Clarence Whitehill the Wolfram. It was as Wolfram that, on February 14, 1924, Friedrich Schorr, the Hungarian baritone, began a distinguished Metropolitan career. A list of the Metropolitan Tannhäusers, Elisabeths, Venuses, and Wolframs would include most of its greatest non-Italian alumni. Florence Easton, a superb Elisabeth, had made her world debut as Newcastle-on-Tyne, in 1903, in the minor role of the Shepherd. Oscar Hammerstein, during the brilliant seasons when his Manhattan Opera House rivaled the Metropolitan, brought forward some notable casts, one of them presenting Mariette Mazarin, a fine singing actress, as Elisabeth, with Maurice Renaud as Wolfram, and Giovanni Zenatello an unfortunate choice as Tannhäuser. Later Elisabeths at the Metropolitan included Elisabeth Rethberg, Lotte Lehmann, Kirsten Flagstad, and Helen Traubel. Kerstin Thorborg was an altogether memorable Venus, and Lauritz Melchior was, at least in his prime, a fine Tannhäuser. But the Metropolitan performances of *Tannhäuser* seemed to suggest that the opera was losing its hold on both sides of the footlights, and the revival on December 17, 1960, after a six-season lapse, told the sad story that *Tannhäuser* was no longer an old-time favorite.

The English data are not quite so copious, for *Tannhäuser* was not, for so long a time as at the Metropolitan, an apparently perdurable staple in London. A fine Drury Lane production in 1882 brought forward the peerless Rosa Sucher (Elisabeth), supported by Hermann Winkelmann (Tannhäuser) and Eugen Gura (Wolfram). On July 16, 1892, Covent Garden audiences were delighted by Katharina Klafsky (Elisabeth) and Max Alvary (Tannhäuser); Gustav Mahler conducted. In 1897 Emma Eames, Van Dyck, Renaud, and Pol Plançon were memorable. Two years later Johanna Gadski made an impressive Covent Garden debut as Elisabeth, and in 1903 Olive Fremstad provided a Venus resplendent to the eye as well as to the ear. Milka Ternina and Karl Burrian produced a great impression. The last pre-World War I productions in 1913 starred Louise Petzl-Perard and Gertrud Kappel (who alternated as Elisabeth and Venus—a somewhat shattering experience for those who had rigorous ideas about *amor sacro e profano*), Heinrich Hensel (Tannhäuser), and Rudolf Hofbauer (Wolfram). A 1928 revival starred Göta Ljungberg, Frida Leider, Melchior, Herbert Janssen, and Ivar Andrésen (Landgraf).

Post-Hitler Bayreuth has had two productions of *Tannhäuser,* both by Wieland Wagner, one in 1954, one to open the 1961 Festival on July 23. The latter, which aroused prolonged arguments, was conducted by Wolfgang Sawallisch, with the chief attention focused on the "Black Venus," the American Negro Grace Bumbry. Others in the cast were Victoria de los Angeles (Elisabeth), Wolfgang Windgassen (Tannhäuser), Dietrich Fischer-Dieskau (Wolfram), and Josef Greindl (Landgraf).

230. Thaïs (Massenet)

Three acts; libretto by Louis Gallet; Paris, Opéra, March 16, 1894.

Sybil Sanderson, Solange Delmas, and Albert Alvarez participated in the world *première. Thaïs* was first heard in New York on November 25, 1907, but the Metropolitan did not stage it until February 16, 1917, with Geraldine Farrar, Luca Botta, and Pasquale Amato. Unhappily for Farrar, Mary Garden's incursions into New York reminded her that she could not compete in *Thaïs,* in the name role of which Garden never was surpassed. Maria Jeritza, Orville Harrold, and Clarence Whitehill showed more authority (first performance, December 14, 1922), and Jeritza was so much favored that the opera was chosen to open the 1923–24 season, on November 5, 1923, with Armand Tokatyan replacing Harrold. In the 1939 revival both Helen Jepson and Marjorie Lawrence attempted the role, with varying success, with Tokatyan and John Charles Thomas, and later John Brownlee. *Thaïs* has not been heard at the Metropolitan since March 6, 1939, when Jepson was the Thaïs, Armand Tokatyan the Nicias, and John Brownlee the Athanael. But on November 8, 1961, the Dallas Civic Opera presented a Franco Zeffirelli production of the opera as a starring vehicle for Denise Duval in her American stage debut. The Nicias was Luigi Alva, the Athanael Aurelio Oppicelli.

The first Covent Garden *Thaïs* failed chiefly because the leading roles, which went to Louise Edvina, François Darmel, and Dinh Gilly, were unconvincingly projected. Edvina was better in the first postwar London revival. *Thaïs* was last revived at Covent Garden in 1926, for Jeritza.

231. Tiefland (D'Albert)

Prologue and three acts; libretto by Rudolf Lothar (pseudonym of Rudolf Spitzer), after Angel Guimerà's Catalan play, Terra Baixa; *Prague, Neues Deutsches Theater, November 15, 1903.*

No doubt Emmy Destinn had sung Marta elsewhere before singing it at the New York *première* of *Tiefland*, on November 23, 1908, at the Metropolitan. She was showered with praise, and fine things were also said about Erik Schmedes (Pedro) and Fritz Feinhals (Sebastiano). The opera did not get beyond four performances in one season. Covent Garden treated it somewhat better: five performances in one season. Muriel Terry (Marta) and John Coates (Pedro) had the leading roles on October 5, 1910, with Maggie Teyte in the relatively small role of Nuri. *Tiefland,* as the principal musical text of German verism, is still heard throughout Germany. When Kirsten Flagstad became for a time director of the Norwegian National Opera at Oslo, she opened her first season with *Tiefland* (Folketeatret, February 16, 1959), the opera in which she herself had made her operatic debut forty-six years before. King Olav V and Princess Astrid attended, but the theater was not full, and the production was widely regarded as a disaster.

232. Tosca (Puccini)

Three acts; libretto by Giuseppe Giacosa and Luigi Illica, after the play La Tosca *by Victorien Sardou; Rome, Teatro Costanzi, January 14, 1900.*

Leopoldo Mugnone conducted at the world *première*, the three chief roles being assigned to Hariclea Darclée (Tosca), Emilio de Marchi (Cavaradossi), and Eugenio Giraldoni (Scarpia). When Covent Garden first produced the opera, on July 12, 1900, Milka Ternina, the Tosca, exhausted the superlatives of the critics, just as Antonio Scotti at once established himself as a peerless Scarpia—indeed, if Scotti was available, it was pointless to try another Scarpia; Fernando de Lucia was the Cavaradossi. The casting of *Tosca* is thus relatively simple, and its history is that at least two of the trio usually are superb; oddly, the third often is weak. At Covent Garden, the fine combination of Lina Cavalieri and Scotti was all but destroyed by Edoardo Garbin. One thinks of Emmy Destinn, Giovanni Zenatello, and Scotti, of Claudia Muzio, Enrico Caruso, and Scotti. Later, a great cast included Gina Cigna, Giovanni Martinelli, and Lawrence Tibbett; another, Cigna, Beniamino Gigli, and Mario Basiola. Unhappily, Maria Jeritza was ill supported in her famous characterization. Recent Covent Garden casts have included Renata Tebaldi, Ferruccio Tagliavini, and Tito Gobbi, and Zinka Milanov, Franco Corelli, and Gian Giacomo Guelfi.

At the New York *première*, at the Metropolitan, on February 4, 1901, Ternina and Scotti repeated their London triumphs; Giuseppe Cremonini was a weak Cavaradossi. Irving Kolodin is authority for the statement that "Scotti sang every performance of Scarpia in *Tosca* until 1910, when [Pasquale] Amato had a chance, and most of those until his retirement in 1932." As Amato was also a fine artist, this simplifies one-third of the Metropolitan history of *Tosca* up to the year 1932. Also, Caruso was a perennial Cavaradossi whenever available, though Martinelli later invaded his territory. Gigli began to make his powerful bid in 1920. Tibbett succeeded Scotti, and John Charles Thomas occasionally alternated with Tibbett. Emma Eames, a great artist, was doubtless somewhat remote for Tosca, and Olive Fremstad, though courageous, was not right. Geraldine Farrar, Destinn, Muzio, Jeritza: each of these made Tosca her proper role. Maria Caniglia did not quite fit the part. It was, no matter what qualifications were made, Grace Moore's best role: Floria Tosca was theatrical, and so was Grace Moore. Ljuba Welitch's Tosca was merely idiosyncratic. In recent years Tebaldi and Richard Tucker have made *Tosca* certainly theirs, with the Scarpia ranging from a Cesare Siepi to a George London. Maria Meneghini Callas' far more impassioned and convincing impersonation of Tosca was heard at the Metropolitan for the first time on November 15, 1956, with Dimitri Mitropoulos matching her fire.

Tosca opened the War Memorial Opera House, San Francisco, on October 15, 1932, with Gaetano Merola conducting. Claudia Muzio was the Tosca, Dino Borgioli the Cavaradossi, Alfredo Gandolfi the Scarpia. Act I was heard throughout the United States over the Red Network of NBC. Two years later (November 16, 1934), with the same conductor, Cavaradossi, and Scarpia, the Tosca, highly lauded by the local critics, was Lotte Lehmann.

233. La Traviata (Verdi)

Three acts; libretto by Francesco Maria Piave, after the play La Dame

aux camélias,[1] *by Alexandre Dumas* fils; *Venice, Teatro La Fenice, March 6, 1853.*

The Violetta of the first, unsuccessful, Venice performance of *La Traviata* was Fanny Salvini-Donatelli, wife of the famous actor Tommaso Salvini; with her were Lodovico Graziani (Alfredo) and Felice Varesi (Giorgio Germont). At the second, successful, Venice production—the Teatro San Benedetto, May 6, 1854—the Violetta was Maria Spezia, the Alfredo a tenor named Landi, and the Giorgio Germont a baritone named Filippo Coletti. On December 30, 1854, at the Teatro Apollo, Rome heard the opera as *Violetta*. From that time forward, the popularity of *La Traviata* grew world-wide.

La Traviata was heard in London for the first time, at Her Majesty's Theatre, in Italian, on May 24, 1856; the Violetta was the aristocratic and beautiful Marietta Piccolomini, and with her were Calzolari (Alfredo) and Beneventano (Giorgio Germont). During that year, also, Angiolina Bosio was heard as Violetta at the Lyceum Theatre. Adelina Patti first sang Violetta at Covent Garden on July 4, 1861, and was praised more for her acting than for her singing; with her were Mario Tiberini (Alfredo) and Francesco Graziani (Giorgio Germont); Sir Michael Costa conducted.

Violetta soon became, in both Europe and America, a favorite debut role. Christine Nilsson began her operatic career with it, at the Théâtre-Lyrique, Paris, on October 27, 1864,[2] and also used it for her first appearance in London. Lilli Lehmann, who sang everything from the First Boy in *Die Zau-*

---

[1] The incorrect spelling is Dumas's own. When he was reminded that the correct form was *caméllias*, he replied that George Sand had written the word with one *l*, and that he would rather be wrong with her than right with others.

[2] The first Paris singing of *La Traviata* had occurred, in Italian, at the Théâtre-Italien, on December 6, 1856, with Piccolomini (Violetta), Mario (Alfredo), and

Graziani (Giorgio Germont). The opera entered the repertoire of the Opéra-Comique on June 12, 1866, and by 1950 had been sung there 430 times, the Violettas having included Mary Garden and Fany Heldy. In Édouard Duprez's French translation, Flora has become Clara, Alfredo is known as Rodolphe, and his father is called D'Orbel. *La Traviata* has also been sung at the Opéra.

berflöte to Brünnhilde, and who is erroneously limited, in popular memory, to Wagnerian roles, burst on London as Violetta at Her Majesty's Theatre on June 3, 1880.

Rio de Janeiro, Buenos Aires, and Mexico City all had heard *La Traviata* before it was sung in New York for the first time, on December 3, 1856, at the Academy of Music, where Anna Caroline de La Grange was Violetta, Pasquale Brignoli the Alfredo, and Amodio the Germont *père*. Marcella Sembrich was the first Metropolitan Violetta, when the opera was staged as the sixth offering of the house's first season, on November 5, 1883; her Alfredo was Victor Capoul, and Giorgio Germont was sung by Giuseppe del Puente. Sembrich chose this role, too, for her Metropolitan farewell more than twenty-five years later, when, on January 23, 1909, the Alfredo was Enrico Caruso, the Giorgio Germont, Pasquale Amato. Among the three excerpts selected for her official farewell on February 6, 1909, was Act I of *La Traviata,* with the remarkable supporting cast of Geraldine Farrar (Flora), Caruso (Alfredo), Antonio Scotti (Douphol), Adamo Didur (Doctor Grenvil), Amato (Marquis D'Obigny), and Angelo Bada (Gastone).

Luisa Tetrazzini made her London debut as Violetta at Covent Garden on November 2, 1907, with Fernando Carpi (Alfredo) and Mario Sammarco (Giorgio Germont), her New York debut at the Manhattan Opera House in the same role on January 15, 1908, with Amadeo Bassi as Alfredo and Mario Ancona as Giorgio Germont. It was at the Manhattan Opera House, too —on November 10, 1909—that John McCormack made his New York debut as Alfredo. And it was as Violetta that, on November 14, 1921, the opening night of the Metropolitan's 1921–22 season, Amelita Galli-Curci (already a great star in Chicago, and familiar to New Yorkers through appearances with the Chicago company), making her Metropolitan debut, brought to their feet thousands of cheering opera-lovers.

The Covent Garden career of *La Traviata* has been strewn with glamorous names. On May 9, 1882, the cast included Emma Albani, and five years later, Colonel Mapleson opened the season on March 12, 1887, with Lillian Nordica (Violetta), one Signor Ria (Alfredo), and Del Puente (Giorgio Germont); at a repetition on April 4, Del Puente was replaced by Paul Lhérie, who had been the original Don José in *Carmen* in 1875, but had meanwhile become a baritone. Nearly thirty-four years after her first Covent Garden Violetta, Patti returned to the role there on June 11, 1895, when she was supported by Fernando de Lucia (Alfredo) and Ancona (Giorgio Germont). Nellie Melba sang Violetta during the 1898 season. Selma Kurz, who had made her Covent Garden debut in 1905, sang Violetta there during the 1924 season, as did Eidé Noréna; in both cases, the elder Germont was Dinh Gilly. Rosa Ponselle sang Violetta for the first time anywhere at Covent Garden on June 13, 1930, with Vincenzo Bellezza conducting, Beniamino Gigli as Alfredo, and Giovanni Inghilleri as Germont *père*. Gigli was still the Alfredo of the last prewar (1939) season, when the Violetta was Maria Caniglia, Mario Basiola was the elder Germont, and Vittorio Gui conducted. After the six silent seasons during the war, *La Traviata* was again heard at Covent Garden on September 5, 1946, as the opening performance of a guest season by the San Carlo company from Naples; Franco Capuana conducted, and the cast included Margherita Carosio (Violetta), Gustavo Gallo (Alfredo), and Carlo Tagliabue (Giorgio Germont). Elisabeth Schwarzkopf's Violetta, heard at Covent Garden on April 6, 1948, aroused controversy; the performance was in English, and the names of the characters were those of the original

Dumas play. Maria Meneghini Callas' greatly admired Violetta was heard at Covent Garden on June 20, 1958, when she was supported by Cesare Valletti (Alfredo) and Mario Zanasi (Giorgio Germont).

The Metropolitan Opera chronicles of *La Traviata* are no less starred with great names and colorful occasions. Melba was heard as Violetta on December 21, 1896, when her Alfredo was Giuseppe Cremonini, and Ancona sang the elder Germont. On November 29, 1902, Antonio Scotti sang the elder Germont for the first time, in a cast that also boasted Sembrich (Violetta), Emilio de Marchi (Alfredo), Eugène Dufriche (D'Obigny), and Charles Gilibert (Doctor Grenvil). On February 28, 1908, Farrar was the Violetta, supported by Caruso (Alfredo) and Riccardo Stracciari (Giorgio Germont). On the fourth night (November 20) of the 1908–9 season, Amato made his debut as the elder Germont opposite Sembrich and Caruso. McCormack made his Metropolitan debut on November 29, 1910, as Alfredo, which had also been his New York debut role, at the Manhattan Opera House, on November 10, 1909; with him at the Metropolitan were Melba (Violetta) and Carlo Galeffi (Giorgio Germont). On November 30, 1922, Lucrezia Bori sang a Metropolitan Violetta for the first time, with her being Gigli (Alfredo) and Giuseppe Danise (Giorgio Germont); thirteen years later, on December 16, 1935, the Metropolitan would open with a Bori *Traviata,* when Richard Crooks would be the Alfredo and Lawrence Tibbett would sing the elder Germont.

Ponselle's always controversial Violetta was heard at the Metropolitan for the first time on January 16, 1931, and was used to open the following season (November 2, 1931). On both occasions she was supported by Giacomo Lauri-Volpi (Alfredo) and Giuseppe de Luca (Giorgio Germont). On January 1, 1934, Claudia Muzio, who had not been heard at the Metropolitan since the 1921–22 season, returned to sing Violetta opposite Tito Schipa (Alfredo) and Richard Bonelli (Giorgio Germont). Bidu Sayão sang her much-admired Violetta for the first time at a matinee on March 6, 1937, opposite Charles Kullmann as Alfredo and John Brownlee as Germont *père*. On February 7, 1940, the Violetta was Jarmila Novotna, with Kullmann as Alfredo— and the sixty-four-year-old De Luca (who had been singing in opera since 1897) as an excellent elder Germont.

Jan Peerce made his Metropolitan debut, as Alfredo, in a Saturday broadcast matinee on November 29, 1941— a performance conducted by Ettore Panizza because Gennaro Papi, who was scheduled to conduct it, had died that morning; Novotna was the Violetta, Tibbett the Germont *père*. It was at another matinee, December 5, 1942, that Licia Albanese, destined to become a sort of standard Violetta at the Metropolitan, first sang the role; on February 17, 1959, she sang it at a performance commemorating her twentieth season with the Metropolitan. During 1945, both Eleanor Steber and Dorothy Kirsten were heard as Violetta. Robert Merrill made his Metropolitan debut, as the elder Germont, in a *Traviata* on December 15, 1945, opposite Albanese (Violetta) and Richard Tucker (Alfredo). Ferruccio Tagliavini was heard as Alfredo during the 1946–47 season, Giuseppe di Stefano during that of 1948–49. Renata Tebaldi was heard as Violetta on February 21, 1957, opposite Giuseppe Campora (Alfredo) and Leonard Warren (Giorgio Germont). Callas, who had sung Violetta at La Scala, Milan, in 1955 opposite Di Stefano and Ettore Bastianini (Giorgio Germont), was heard in the role at the Metropolitan during the 1957–58 season. The final *Traviata* of the 1959–60 season (its 304th performance in the house), April 1, 1960, had Anna Moffo as Violetta, Peerce as Alfredo, and Robert Merrill as the elder Germont. By the end of the 1961–62 season, *Traviata* had been sung 321 times at the Metropolitan.

234. Tristan und Isolde (Wagner)

Three acts; libretto by the composer; Munich, June 10, 1865.

The Tristan and Isolde of the world *première* were husband and wife: Ludwig Schnorr von Carolsfeld and Malwine Schnorr von Carolsfeld; other leading roles went to Anne Deinet (Brangäne), Zottmayer (King Mark), Anton Mitterwurzer (Kurwenal), and Heinrich (Melot); Hans von Bülow conducted. In view of the opera's subsequent stupendous popularity, which began to build up during the eighties and nineties, the coolness of early audiences may seem like restraint carried to intemperate ends. Outside of nine performances in Munich, up to October, 1872, *Tristan* was not asked for. It reached Weimar in 1874, Berlin in 1876, Könisberg in 1881, and Leipzig in 1882. The leap to London later that year was important in the spreading of the Wagnerian gospel.

Announcement of the first London performance of *Tristan und Isolde* for June 20, 1882, raised high expectations among critics, musicians, and operagoers. Hans Richter, who had been associated personally with Wagner, and who had taken upon himself the heavy burden of converting a skeptical England to the *Meister*'s gospel, conducted. Rosa Sucher was the Isolde, Hermann Winkelmann the Tristan, while Marianne Brandt, whom Wagner had pronounced ideal in the role, sang Brangäne. Sucher and Winkelmann were singing the lovers for the first time. The event produced a great, if mixed, impression. Herman Klein, then music critic of *The Sunday Times,* later wrote of his reactions: "My first action on re-

gaining my mental equilibrium was to solemnly vow that I would never write another word in disparagement of Richard Wagner or his music so long as I lived." The performance left London an armed camp of critics spitting at each other, but nevertheless *Tristan,* rather than the previously produced *Meistersinger,* established the later Wagner as a staple of the English stage.

The American *première* of *Tristan* at the Metropolitan on December 1, 1886, was, if anything, more of a sensation. Another Wagnerian apostle, Anton Seidl, conducted. Albert Niemann and Lilli Lehmann were the guilty pair; Brandt was the Brangäne, Emil Fischer the King Mark, and Adolf Robinson the Kurwenal. The relatively unimportant role of a sailor was assigned to Max Alvary. The opera was in every way a huge success: it was repeated seven times that season and was used to open the following one. H. E. Krehbiel led the chorus of excited Wagnerians who acted as if a new dispensation had arrived. Yet, exciting as these first performances were, *Tristan und Isolde* attained its greatest vogue in 1895, when Lillian Nordica and the De Reszkes, a trio as famous as the "Puritani" Quartet, began to sing in it. To their Isolde, Tristan, and King Mark, on November 27 of that year, Marie Brema was the Brangäne, Giuseppe Kaschmann the Kurwenal. The honor of being the greatest of Tristans lies between Niemann and Jean de Reszke. On January 1, 1908, Olive Fremstad first sang Isolde at Gustav Mahler's debut as a Metropolitan conductor, and went on to become one of the most admired interpreters of the role. (This versatile Swedish woman also tried singing Brangäne, a role usually left to such deeper voices as those of Margarete Matzenauer, Sigrid Onégin, and Kerstin Thorborg, but she never repeated the attempt.) What many who were present always have remembered as perhaps the most thrilling performance of *Tristan* was that of January 16, 1933, which marked the Metropolitan debuts of both Frida Leider (Isolde) and Maria Olszewska (Brangäne); Lauritz Melchior was the excelling Tristan. In the remembering eyes and ears of many hardened Wagnerians, Leider never has been surpassed as Isolde.

For a number of years (from February 6, 1935, until April 12, 1941) *Tristan* became such a favorite of New York audiences that it often was the most frequently performed opera of a Metropolitan season. On the latter date, Kirsten Flagstad felt that she must go back to Norway, and when she returned to New York during the 1950–51 season, Melchior had left the Metropolitan—for some seasons his voice had been frayed, but his immense popularity might have made his Tristan the oldest on record if he had not maneuvered himself into an untenable position *vis-à-vis* the management. In the interval, Flagstad's role had fallen first to Helen Traubel and then to Astrid Varnay. On December 18, 1959, Birgit Nilsson made her sensational Metropolitan debut as Isolde, signaling the real possibility of a Wagner renaissance, particularly as Jon Vickers was also on the roster. Unhappily, Vickers has not sung Tristan at the Metropolitan, where recent Isoldes have had no efficient partner, Ramón Vinay having become more and more weak-voiced with the years. On December 28, 1959, a Metropolitan audience was subjected to three Tristans in a single performance: Vinay in Act I, Karl Liebl in Act II, and Albert Da Costa in Act III. A patron who had missed the announcements of these cast changes was said to have remarked wonderingly that Tristan seemed to be getting younger as the evening progressed. The San Francisco Opera Company gave its first *Tristan* on September 16, 1927, when Alfred Hertz conducted, the Isolde was Elsa Alsen, the Tristan Rudolf Laubenthal, and others in the cast were Kathryn Meisle (Brangäne), Fred

Patton (König Mark), and—strangely —Pasquale Amato (Kurwenal). On October 2, 1953, during the tenth season in which *Tristan* had been heard in San Francisco, Georg Solti conducted it; Gertrud Grob-Prandl was the Isolde, Ludwig Suthaus the Tristan, and the cast included Margarete Klose (Brangäne), Dezso Ernster (König Mark), and Paul Schöffler (Kurwenal).

235. Il Trittico (Puccini)

Three one-act operas: Il Tabarro, *libretto by Giuseppe Adami, after Didier Gold's play* La Houppelande; Suor Angelica, *libretto by Giovacchino Forzano;* Gianni Schicchi, *libretto by Forzano, who based his text on a hint from Dante* (Commedia 1, xxx, 32ff.); *première of the triptych, New York, Metropolitan Opera House, December 14, 1918. See also under performance data for the separate parts of* Il Trittico, *Nos. 95, 226, and 227.*

Because *Il Trittico* need not be presented in its entirety, cyclic performances after the world *première* have been few if compared with those of, notably, *Gianni Schicchi.* Exactly four weeks after the New York first night, the *Trittico* was heard at the Teatro Costanzi, Rome. Gino Marinuzzi (not Arturo Toscanini, as stated in many books) conducted, and the leading singers were: in *Il Tabarro*, Maria Labia (Giorgetta), Eduardo di Giovanni—the temporary pseudonym of Edward Johnson (Luigi), and Carlo Galeffi (Michele); in *Suor Angelica*, Gilda Dalla Rizza (Angelica); in *Gianni Schicchi*, Galeffi (Gianni Schicchi), Dalla Rizza (Lauretta), and Johnson (Rinuccio).

Il Trittico was staged by the San Francisco Opera during its first season, on September 29, 1923 (matinee). Gaetano Merola conducted; the casts included: in *Il Tabarro*—Bianca Saroya (Giorgetta), Armand Tokatyan (Luigi),

Alfredo Gandolfi (Michele), Giordano Paltrinieri (Tinca), and Adamo Didur (Talpa); in *Suor Angelica*—Saroya (Suor Angelica), Doria Fernanda (Princess), and Lela Johnstone (Abbess); in *Gianni Schicchi*—Giuseppe de Luca (Gianni), Tokatyan (Rinuccio), Merle Epton (Lauretta), Didur (Simone), Paolo Ananian (Betto), Paltrinieri (Gherardo), and Louis d'Angelo (Marco). When *Il Trittico* returned to San Francisco on September 26, 1952, it had three conductors: Glauco Curiel (*Il Tabarro*), Kurt Herbert Adler, who became the company's artistic director the next year (*Suor Angelica*), and Karl Kritz (*Gianni Schicchi*). Leading parts were sung by: in *Il Tabarro*—Brenda Lewis (Giorgetta), Mario del Monaco (Luigi), Robert Weede (Michele), Virginio Assandri (Tinca), and Nicola Moscona (Talpa); in *Suor Angelica*—Mary Curtis (later Curtis-Verna, Suor Angelica), Claramae Turner (Princess), and Dorothy Throndson (Abbess); in *Gianni Schicchi*—Italo Tajo (Gianni), Eugene Conley (Rinuccio), Dorothy Warenskjold (Lauretta), and Lorenzo Alvary (Simone).

London first heard *Il Trittico* at Covent Garden on June 18, 1920, when Gaetano Bavagnoli conducted. The chief roles in the three operas were sung by: *Il Tabarro*, Ida Quaiatti (Giorgetta), Thomas Burke (Luigi), and Dinh Gilly (Michele); in *Suor Angelica*, Dalla Rizza (Angelica) and Jacqueline Royer (Princess); in *Gianni Schicchi*, Dalla Rizza (Lauretta), Burke (Rinuccio), and Ernesto Badini (Gianni Schicchi). King George V and Queen Mary attended the second performance, but were spared (perhaps intentionally) the rigors of *Il Tabarro* by late arrival at the opera house. Thereafter, *Suor Angelica* was dropped, the other two operas being played either as an entire performance or as companion pieces with ballet.

On October 5, 1961, the New York City Opera opened a season at the New York City Center with a performance of the *Trittico*. *Suor Angelica* came off best among the three stylistically vague investitures; *Il Tabarro* lacked the flaming passion without which it loses all significance; and not even the wit and vividness of the score could save *Gianni Schicchi* from a wholly inept production that tried to turn it into *commedia dell'arte*.

236. Troilus and Cressida (Walton)

Three acts; libretto by Christopher Hassall, after the poem by Chaucer; London, Covent Garden, December 3, 1954.

Sir Malcolm Sargent conducted the world *première;* the chief roles were sung by Magda Laszlò (Cressida, a role for which Walton vainly had tried to obtain several other sopranos, including Elisabeth Schwarzkopf and Maria Meneghini Callas), Monica Sinclair (Voice of the Oracle), Richard Lewis (Troilus), Frederick Dalberg (Calkas), Geraint Evans (Antenor), Peter Pears (Pandarus), Forbes Robinson (Horaste), and Otakar Kraus (Diomede). Writing in *Opera,* Paul Müller stated accurately: "Walton's opera is a significant addition to the repertory, but the musical theatre of the twentieth century has gained no fresh impetus from it." It was sung twelve times that season, five times more in that of 1955–56. The New York *première* of *Troilus and Cressida* was given at the New York City Center, by the New York City Opera Company, on October 21, 1955. Joseph Rosenstock conducted; leading parts were sung by Phyllis Curtin (Cressida), Gloria Lane (Evadne), Jon Crain (Troilus), Yi-Kwei-Sze, in his debut (Calkas), Richard Torigi (Antenor), Norman Kelley (Pandarus), John Reardon (Horaste), and Lawrence Winters (Diomede). Performances also were staged by La Scala, Milan, and by the San Francisco Opera Company. Erich Leinsdorf conducted in San Francisco (October 7, 1955), where leading roles were sung by Dorothy Kirsten (Cressida), Richard Lewis (Troilus), Robert Weede (Diomede), Giorgio Tozzi (Calkas), and Ernest McChesney (Pandarus).

237. Il Trovatore (Verdi)

Four acts; libretto by Salvatore Cammarano, completed by Leone Emanuele Bardare, after Antonio García Gutiérrez's play El Trovador; *Rome, Teatro Apollo, January 19, 1853.*

The Leonora of the Rome *première* of *Il Trovatore* was Rosina Penco; others in that cast were the aging Emilia Goggi (Azucena), Carlo Baucardé (Manrico), Giovanni Guicciardi (Di Luna), and Balderi. An immediate and enduring success, the opera was soon sung throughout Italy, and within five years of its first performance had been staged in many other European countries, South America, Egypt, and North America. The first performances outside Italy appear to have been given at Corfu, Malta, and Trieste, all in 1853. Rio de Janeiro heard it on September 7, 1854; Paris—in Italian at the Théâtre-Italien—on December 23, 1854; New York—in Italian at the Academy of Music—on May 2, 1855; and London—in Italian at Covent Garden—on May 10, 1855. It has since been sung in many languages in almost every center of civilized life, performances being recorded even in Croatian, Slovenian, Lettish, Bulgarian, Serbian, Hebrew, Estonian, and Lithuanian.

The singers at the original Rome *Il Trovatore* had been, except for Penco, of only local importance, but the Leonora and Manrico of the Paris, London, and St. Petersburg (December, 1855) *premières* were respectively Erminia Frezzolini and Mario, Pauline Viardot-García and Enrico Tamberlik, and Angiolina Bosio and Tamberlik, proving that the opera was taken up quickly by stars of international reputation. When, little more than two years after its Roman birth, *Il Trovatore* was staged by Max Maretzek at the New York Academy of Music, the Manrico was Pasquale Brignoli, a luscious Italian tenor who was for many years a favorite on Fourteenth Street; others in that cast were Steffanoni (Leonora), Vestvali, and Amodio. Annie Louise Cary, whose rich, pure contralto Anton Rubinstein called the most beautiful in the world, made her operatic debut at Copenhagen in 1867 as Azucena, which became a popular fixture of her repertoire. In the heyday of the Academy of Music, she often sang it in a galaxy that included Christine Nilsson (Leonora), Italo Campanini (Manrico), and Giuseppe del Puente (Di Luna).

The Metropolitan Opera, New York, staged *Il Trovatore* as the third opera of its first season, on October 26, 1883; that first cast included Alwina Valleria (Leonora), Zelia Trebelli (Azucena), Roberto Stagno (Manrico), and Giuseppe Kaschmann (Di Luna). Later that season, Leonora was sung by Emmy Fursch-Madi, Azucena by Emily Lablache. Through the 1960–61 season, the Metropolitan had given 222 performances of *Il Trovatore,* which often has been allowed to degenerate into a mere routine penny-catcher. Lilli Lehmann sang a role (Leonora) in Italian for the first time when, on December 16, 1891, the second night of the season, *Il Trovatore* was produced; the cast also included Giulia Ravogli (Azucena), Paul Kalisch (Manrico), and Eduardo Camera (Di Luna). On January 5, 1901, the Metropolitan cast of the opera included Lillian Nordica (Leonora), Rosa Olitzka (Azucena), Andreas Dippel (Manrico), and Giuseppe Campanari (Di Luna).[1]

[1] Verdi's death, on January 27, 1901, was signalized at the Metropolitan by that house's first performance of the "Manzoni"

Enrico Caruso sang Manrico for the first time on February 26, 1908, when Emma Eames was the Leonora and other roles were taken by Louise Homer (Azucena) and Riccardo Stracciari (Di Luna). On December 1, 1909, the troubadour was Leo Slezak; his colleagues were Johanna Gadski (Leonora), Anna Meitschik (Azucena), and Dinh Gilly (Di Luna). On February 20, 1915, *Il Trovatore* was completely restaged at the Metropolitan under Arturo Toscanini's baton, at a matinee. The cast was headed by Emmy Destinn (Leonora), Margarete Ober (Azucena), Giovanni Martinelli (Manrico), and Pasquale Amato (Di Luna). When Claudia Muzio sang her first Leonora at the Metropolitan on December 18, 1916, Homer was the Azucena, while Martinelli and Amato were held over from the Toscanini cast. Martinelli was still the Manrico on April 19, 1924, when Karin Branzell sang her first Metropolitan Azucena; Rosa Ponselle was Leonora, and Count di Luna was sung by Giuseppe Danise. By November 11, 1929, when Elisabeth Rethberg was the Leonora, the cast was entirely new: Julia Claussen (Azucena), Giacomo Lauri-Volpi (Manrico), and Mario Basiola (Di Luna). Gina Cigna was heard as Leonora at the Metropolitan for the first time on February 11, 1937, with Martinelli again the Manrico, Bruna Castagna as Azucena, and Carlo Morelli (Renato Zanelli's brother) as Di Luna.

Zinka Milanov made her Metropolitan debut, as Leonora, on December 17, 1937, with Castagna (Azucena), Frederick Jagel (Manrico), and Carlo Tagliabue (Di Luna). By the season of 1940–41, *Il Trovatore* had slipped so far into routine that—at Toscanini's suggestion, it was rumored—it was again restudied, and once more with impressive results. The chief roles on December 12, 1940, were taken by Norina Greco (Leonora), Castagna (Azucena), Jussi Björling (Manrico), and the Bronx-born Francesco Valentino (Di Luna). When Milanov was indisposed for an *Il Trovatore* on December 6, 1944, the young Regina Resnik, then a soprano, sang Leonora without a full rehearsal; with her were Margaret Harshaw, then a contralto (Azucena), Kurt Baum (Manrico), and Leonard Warren (Di Luna). On November 19, 1947, Cloe Elmo made her Metropolitan debut, as Azucena; the Leonora was Stella Roman, and others in the cast were Baum (Manrico) and Warren (Di Luna). On October 26, 1959, still another newly staged *Il Trovatore* opened the Metropolitan season and provided Giulietta Simionato, as Azucena, with the occasion of her Metropolitan debut; with her were Antonietta Stella (Leonora), Carlo Bergonzi (Manrico), and Warren (Di Luna). *Il Trovatore* at the Metropolitan took back a fiery verisimilitude that it long had lacked on January 27, 1961, when both Leontyne Price (Leonora) and Franco Corelli (Manrico) made their Metropolitan debuts; the Di Luna of Robert Merrill, the Azucena of Irene Dalis, and the conducting of Fausto Cleva contributed less to the excitement of the occasion.

The first London singing of *Il Trovatore* occurred at Covent Garden on May 10, 1855. Jenny Ney, a German soprano, was the Leonora, and with her were Pauline Viardot-García (Azucena), Enrico Tamberlik (Manrico), Francesco Graziani (Di Luna), and Joseph-Dieudonné Tagliafico (Ferrando). During the season, Leonora was also sung by Angiolina Bosio, Azucena by Constance-Betsy-Rosabella Nantier-Didiée, and during the following season, Giulia Grisi was heard as Leonora, Mario as Manrico. Penco, the Leonora of the Rome *première,* sang the role at Covent Garden in 1861, Adelina Patti (whose interpretation of the role Verdi admired) in 1863. On October 27, 1868,

Requiem, February 17, 1901, with Luigi Mancinelli conducting; the soloists were Nordica, Ernestine Schumann-Heink, Thomas Salignac, and Pol Plançon.

Therese Tietjens was the Leonora, Zelia Trebelli the Azucena, Pietro Mongini the Manrico, and Sir Charles Santley the Di Luna. At Drury Lane Theatre, where *Il Trovatore* had been sung in English in 1856, Christine Nilsson sang Leonora in 1874.

In May 15, 1883, Pauline Lucca sang Leonora in London for the first time, at Covent Garden, part of a cast that also included Mattia Battistini as Di Luna. When Eva Tetrazzini, sister of the more famous Luisa, sang Leonora at Covent Garden on May 24, 1890, Sofia Scalchi was the Azucena, Francesco d'Andrade the Di Luna. A greatly admired cast (October 23, 1890) included Sofia Ravogli (Leonora), Giulia Ravogli (Azucena), Ferruccio Giannini (Manrico), and Antonio Galassi (Di Luna).

In 1905, *Il Trovatore* was heard at Covent Garden with Celestina Boninsegna as Leonora, Eleanora de Cisneros as Azucena, Julian Biel as Manrico, and Riccardo Stracciari as Di Luna. After a Carl Rosa season in the autumn of 1909, *Il Trovatore* lapsed at Covent Garden until 1920, and another Carl Rosa season—which presented the much-admired English soprano Eva Turner as Leonora. A striking international cast took up the opera on June 14, 1927: Vincenzo Bellezza conducted, and the principal roles were sung by Frida Leider (Leonora), Maria Olczewska (Azucena), Aureliano Pertile (Manrico), and Armando Borgioli (Di Luna). The opera then lapsed again for a dozen years. On May 12, 1939, the Covent Garden cast, conducted by Vittorio Gui, included Gina Cigna (Leonora), Gertrud Wettergren (Azucena), Jussi Björling (Manrico), and Mario Basiola (Di Luna); during the season, Ebe Stignani also sang Azucena, Arthur Carron was heard as Manrico, and Armando Borgioli appeared as Di Luna. During the late 1940's, Joan Hammond, Doris Doree, and Margherita Grandi were heard as Leonora, Edith Coates and Constance Shacklock as Azucena, Libero de Luca and Carron as Manrico, Paolo Silveri and Jess Walters as Di Luna. On June 26, 1952, Maria Meneghini Callas was the Leonora, Giulietta Simionato the Azucena, James Johnston the Manrico, and Walters the Di Luna. Gré Brouwenstijn was heard as Leonora in 1953–54, with Nell Rankin and Coates alternating as Azucena, Johnston as Manrico, and Walters and Marko Rothmüller alternating as Di Luna. And during the 1956–57 season, the Covent Garden *Trovatore* casts included Zinka Milanov and Victoria Elliott as Leonora, Fedora Barbieri as Azucena, Johnston and Kurt Baum as Manrico, and Walters as the continuing Di Luna.

Il Trovatore continues to be staged all over the world. A very intensely applauded performance, for example, took place at the Palacio de Bellas Artes, Mexico City, in October, 1957: Anita Cerquetti was the Leonora, Jean Madeira the Azucena, Carlo Bergonzi the Manrico, and Gian Giacomo Guelfi the Di Luna. At the Roman Amphitheater in Cagliari, Sardinia, in the summer of 1958, this cast was heard: Elisabetta Barbato (Leonora), Miriam Pirazzini (Azucena), Mario Filippeschi (Manrico), and Aldo Protti (Di Luna). And at San Francisco on September 16, 1956 (matinee), Eileen Farrell was the Leonora, Oralia Domínguez the Azucena, Jussi Björling the Manrico, and Anselmo Colzani the Di Luna of a *Trovatore* conducted by Oliviero de Fabritiis. Björling was again the Manrico when San Francisco heard the opera on September 26, 1958, with George Sebastian conducting; his colleagues on that night included Leontyne Price (Leonora), Claramae Turner (Azucena), and Louis Quilico (Di Luna). These are but a scattering of samples.

238. Les Troyens (Berlioz)

Five acts; libretto by the composer, after Vergil; Karlsruhe, December 6 and

*7, 1890. The vicissitudes of this operatic epic, because of which it had to be divided into two parts—*La Prise de Troie *and* Les Troyens à Carthage*—are discussed on pages 205–6.*

Les Troyens à Carthage, Part II of the whole, was first given (as *Les Troyens*) at the Théâtre-Lyrique, Paris, on November 4, 1863, with Anne Arsène Charton-Demeur as Dido and Monjauze as Aeneas; Berlioz conducted. By December 20, *Les Troyens* had been sung at the Lyrique twenty-one times. Part I (for its world *première*) and Part II were given, respectively on December 6 and 7, 1890, at Karlsruhe in their entirety, but in a German translation by Otto Neitzel; Felix Mottl conducted. *La Prise de Troie* was first performed in French at Nice in February, 1891; when it reached the Opéra, Paris, on November 15, 1899, Marie Delna was the Cassandra, with Lucas and Maurice Renaud; this was, however, a "reduced" version of the whole. Dr. Erik Chisholm staged *Les Troyens* intact at Glasgow, Scotland, in 1935.

Les Troyens received a modern performance worthy of it in all respects but one (it was sung in Edward J. Dent's English translation) when Covent Garden presented it, with only twenty minutes of cuts in the four-hour score, on June 6, 1957. Produced by Sir John Gielgud, conducted by Rafael Kubelik, it ran from six o'clock until eleven, with three brief intermissions. The generally excellent cast was headed by Amy Shuard (Cassandra), Blanche Thebom (Dido), Jess Walters (Choroebus), and John Vickers (Aeneas); Dermot Troy made a notable impression in the brief role of Hylas. In relative terms, *Les Troyens* became a smash hit of the London opera world. For a revival on April 29, 1960, Kerstin Meyer was the Dido.

On December 29, 1959, and January 12, 1960, at Carnegie Hall, New York, the American Opera Society, with Robert Lawrence as a late-hour replacement for Sir Thomas Beecham, presented *Les Troyens* in a concert performance in French. The cast included Eleanor Steber (Cassandra), Regina Resnik (Dido), Martial Singher (Choroebus), and Richard Cassilly (Aeneas). The performances were generally considered unsatisfactory, as perhaps even a finer concert performance would be.

Early in the summer of 1960, La Scala, Milan, staged the first complete Italian *I Troiani*; Rafael Kubelik conducted. The much-admired staging and choreography were by Margherita Wallman. Leading roles were sung by Nell Rankin (Cassandra), Giulietta Simionato (Dido), and Mario del Monaco (Aeneas). On November 17, 1961, after postponements caused by a chorus strike, the Paris Opéra presented *Les Troyens*. Margherita Wallmann repeated her Scala production, using the Piero Zuffi scenery and costumes made for it. *La Prise de Troie* was given without intermission; only about a half hour was cut from the entire work. Régine Crespin won unstinted critical praise as Dido. The Cassandra was Geneviève Serres, the Aeneas Guy Chauvet. The conducting of Pierre Dervaux and the singing of the chorus were praised, and only the flimsy, unconvincing Wooden Horse was criticized adversely. Few of the world's major opera houses—most noticeably those in Berlin, New York, and Vienna —now have failed to present Berlioz' towering masterpiece.

239. Turandot (Puccini)

Three acts; libretto by Giuseppe Adami and Renato Simoni, after a fiaba *(fable) by Carlo Gozzi; Milan, Teatro alla Scala, April 25, 1926, Franco Alfano having arranged the last duet and final scene.*

Arturo Toscanini conducted at the world *première;* leading roles were sung by Rosa Raïsa (Turandot), Maria Zamboni (Liù), Miguel Fleta (Calaf),[1] Giacomo Rimini (Ping), and Giuseppe Nessi (Pong). The opera was sung at Rome four days later, and then traveled throughout Italy. Its first foreign performances were staged at Buenos Aires, Rio de Janeiro, and Dresden (in German) in June and July, 1926, and on October 14 and November 6 of that year it was heard, still in German, at Vienna and Berlin respectively.

The first performance in the United States, at the Metropolitan Opera House, New York, on November 16, 1926, was conducted by Tullio Serafin. Unwise casting—or casting that looked well enough on paper—dogged it from the start, and as a result it was not widely considered, as it now is, one of Puccini's masterpieces. The New York critics took that first cast apart one by one: Maria Jeritza (Turandot), Martha Attwood (Liù), Giacomo Lauri-Volpi (Calaf), and Giuseppe de Luca (Ping). Jeritza and Lauri-Volpi were particularly attacked. Things improved when Nanette Guilford took over the role of Liù on the opening night—October 31 —of the 1927–28 season, but when Florence Easton replaced Jeritza on March 16, 1929, she could do no better than her predecessor with the Princess Turandot. Anne Roselle, a Hungarian soprano, was the intensely admired Turandot of a San Francisco Opera Company performance on September 19, 1927. Gaetano Merola conducted, and the cast also included Myrtle Donnelly as Liù, Armand Tokatyan as Calaf, Ezio Pinza as Timur, Angelo Bada as Pang, and Lodovico Oliviero as Pong. *Turandot* opened a San Francisco season on September 17, 1957, when Francesco Molinari-Pradelli conducted a cast including Leonie Rysanek

(Turandot), Licia Albanese (Liù), Eugene Tobin (Calaf), Nicola Moscona (Timur), and Heinz Blankenburg (Ping). On September 16, 1961, San Francisco heard one of its native daughters, Lucille Udovick, as the icy princess (a role she had sung very successfully in Europe); with her, under Francesco Molinari-Pradelli's baton, were Leontyne Price as Liù and Sandor Konya as Calaf.

On April 26, 1950, honoring the twenty-fifth anniversary of Puccini's death, the New York City Opera Company performed the feat, almost incredible in view of its straitly limited financial and mechanical resources, of staging *Turandot*, which had last been heard in New York more than twenty years earlier (January 8, 1930). However happy enthusiasts of *Turandot* may have been with this brave, partly successful attempt, another eleven years had to pass before New York would see and hear a *Turandot* almost entirely worthy of the score. On February 24, 1961, the Metropolitan performed the opera for the first time in more than thirty-one years. Leopold Stokowski, making his Metropolitan debut on crutches, conducted; Yoshio Aoyama had originated the fantastic China of this opera with more success than he had achieved with a pseudorealistic Japan for *Madama Butterfly;* and Cecil Beaton's costumes and scenery were vigorously colorful. The generally excellent cast was headed by Birgit Nilsson (Turandot), Anna Moffo (Liù), and Franco Corelli (Calaf). The opera immediately became a major box-office attraction: eight sold-out houses by the end of the season.[2] No reason for its leaving the repertoire again, except the possible absence of Nilsson and Corelli or their peers, was easy to foresee.

---

[1] Puccini had had Beniamino Gigli in mind for the role of Calaf.

[2] When *Turandot* was heard at the Metropolitan on November 4, 1961, with Nilsson (Turandot), Lucine Amara (Liù), Richard

Tucker (Calaf), and Ezio Flagello (Timur), it was noted that the audience included Rosa Raïsa, who had created the title role more than thirty-five years before.

Covent Garden had troubles like the Metropolitan's when it first produced *Turandot* on June 7, 1927; the first cast was thought scarcely more than competent. Bianca Scacciati was the Turandot, Aroldo Lindi the Calaf; only the Liù, Lotte Schöne, won much praise. Things improved greatly after the debutante Eva Turner assumed the role of Turandot, with Rosetta Pampanini as an intelligent Liù and, on at least one occasion, Salvatore Baccaloni as Timur. Soon there was Ina Souez, an even finer Liù. Later, Eidé Noréna was another expressive Liù. The constellation of Turner, Mafalda Favero, and Giovanni Martinelli proved altogether satisfactory, and in the eyes and ears of many, Turner never has been surpassed as the icy princess. Gertrud Grob-Prandl, Adele Leigh, and James Johnston were a fine combination during the 1951–52 season, whereas in that of 1956–57, the all-British trio of Johnston, Sylvia Fisher, and Amy Shuard was much praised. Other recent Turandots of international renown have been Inge Borkh (who sang the role at San Francisco in 1953) and Maria Meneghini Callas.

240. Il Turco in Italia (Rossini)

Two acts; libretto by Felice Romani; Milan, Teatro alla Scala, August 14, 1814.

Not so successful as *L'Italiana in Algeri*, this opera nonetheless reached performance at Vicenza (as *Il Tutore deluso*) in 1816, Rome (as *La Capricciosa corretta*) in 1819. In a little more than thirty years, it was heard in some eighteen European cities and New York in a total of six different languages.

London first welcomed *Il Turco*, in Italian, at the Haymarket Theatre, on May 19, 1821; it was repeated at the Drury Lane Theatre on May 1, 1827, in an English adaptation, called *The Turkish Lovers,* by the Irish musician Michael Rophino Lacy. It was heard in New York for the first time on March 14, 1826, in Italian, as presented by a troupe headed by Manuel del Popolo Vicente García. New York heard it again on December 18, 1840, but it never has been sung at the Metropolitan.

A notably successful revival of *Il Turco in Italia* was staged at Rome in 1950 by Amfiparnasso; Fernando Previtali conducted, and the cast was headed by Maria Meneghini Callas (Fiorilla), Cesare Valletti (Narciso), Sesto Bruscantini (Selim), and Mariano Stabile (Prodoscino). In the spring of 1957, the opera was revived under Vittorio Gui's direction at Genoa's Teatro Carlo Felice; the cast included Graziella Sciutti, Fernanda Cadoni, Nicola Monti, Bruscantini, Melchiorre Luise, and Renato Capecchi. When a company from La Scala, Milan, sang *Il Turco* at the Edinburgh Festival on August 30, 1957, Gianandrea Gavazzeni conducted; the cast included Eugenia Ratti (Fiorilla), Bruscantini (Selim), Franco Calabrese (Geronio), Fiorenza Cossotto (Zaïda), Luigi Alva (Narciso), and Fernando Corena (Prodoscino).

241. Vanessa (Barber)

Four acts; libretto by Gian-Carlo Menotti; New York, Metropolitan Opera, January 15, 1958; revised version, with libretto translated into Italian by Fidele d'Amico: three acts; Spoleto, Teatro Nuovo, June 15, 1961.

As the first opera by an American composer to reach the Metropolitan Opera, New York, in eleven years (Bernard Rogers's *The Warrior* had received the second of its two Metropolitan singings on January 31, 1947), *Vanessa* was mounted with sumptuous costumes and scenery by Cecil Beaton, staged by Menotti, and conducted by Dimitri Mitropoulos. The cast, of widely varying aptness, was: Eleanor Steber[1] (Vanessa), Rosalind Elias (Erika), Regina Resnik (The Old Baroness), Nicolai Gedda (Anatol), Giorgio Tozzi (The Old Doctor), George Cehanovsky (The Majordomo), and Robert Nagy (A Footman). *Vanessa* was sung six times that season, four the next—and was heard in New York last on February 23, 1959. Translated into Italian, contracted to three acts (the original Act I and Act II having become two scenes of Act I), it was produced as the opening attraction of the 1961 Festival of Two Worlds at Spoleto, Italy (June 15). The scene had been transferred from "a Northern Country about the year 1905" to upper New York State in the eighteenth century. Sets and costumes were by Beni Montresor, Werner Torkanowsky conducted, and the chief members of the cast were Ivana Tosini (Vanessa), Mietta Sighele (Erika), Giovanna Fioroni (The Grandmother—no longer a Baroness), Alvinio Misciano (Anatol), Giulio Bardi (The Old Doctor), and Harold Lara (The Majordomo). Operagoers who heard both versions unanimously preferred the tightened-up Spoleto incarnation to the diffuse Metropolitan original.

242. Les Vêpres siciliennes (Verdi)

Five acts; libretto by Augustin-Eugène Scribe and Charles Duveyrier (written originally for Donizetti as Le Duc d'Albe*); Paris, Opéra, June 13, 1855.*

---

[1] Louis Sherry's Metropolitan Opera Restaurant that evening of the *première* served a dinner that included "Vanilla Ice Cream with Strawberries Eleanor" and "Breast of Pheasant, Vanessa, with Wild Rice."

Ill luck dogged the fortunes of this first of Verdi's two French operas. Johanne-Sophie-Charlotte Cruvelli (real name Sophie Crüwell), the diva chosen to create the role of Helène, disappeared before the *première,* giving rise to a scandal that the Parisian newspapers delightedly played up under such captions as "Where is Cruvelli?" She turned up in time to fulfill her obligations in a composed manner. ("She seems," Francis Toye wrote, "to have gone on a kind of anticipatory honeymoon with one Baron Vigier, whom she married shortly afterwards.") *Les Vêpres siciliennes* failed, on June 13, 1855, to please its first-night audience. Poor Verdi was in a dilemma with the libretto, which pleased neither the Italians, whom it represents as murderous desperadoes, nor the French, whom—greater insult—it shows as the Italians' stupid victims. In ten years, the opera reached sixty-two performances in Paris.

Les Vêpres siciliennes was staged at Brussels on November 18, 1856, and was soon sung in Italian, under a variety of names, both in Italy and elsewhere, finally settling down as *I Vespri siciliani.* It had been heard in Spain, Portugal, Russia, and Chile when it was staged in London, Drury Lane Theatre, for the first time on July 27, 1859, with Therese Tietjens as Elena. New York heard it that same year, on November 7. Since then, though never becoming a genuinely popular opera, it has been revived with some frequency.

On June 5, 1932, in a German version revised by Julius Kapp, *I Vespri* was sung in Berlin by a cast including Anny Konetzni (Elena), Helge Roswaenge (Arrigo), Heinrich Schlusnus (Guido di Monforte), and Emanuel List (Giovanni da Procida); Erich Kleiber conducted. At the Teatro Massimo, Palermo, in 1937, Franco Capuana conducted a performance in which the cast was headed by Giannina Arangi-Lombardi (Elena), Franco lo Giudice (Arrigo), Guicciardi (Guido), and Giacomo Vaghi (Giovanni). At Genoa two years later (1939), Vittorio Gui was the conductor, and the cast included Bianca Scacciati (Elena), Olivato (Arrigo), Armando Borgioli (Guido), and Tancredi Pasero (Giovanni). A spectacular revival occurred at the Florentine Maggio Musicale of 1951, when Kleiber conducted, Maria Meneghini Callas was the Elena, and the supporting cast showed Mafalda Masini (Ninetta), Giorgio Kokolios (Arrigo), Enzo Mascherini (Guido), and Boris Christoff (Giovanni). Victor de Sabata conducted a restaging at La Scala, Milan, later that year with much the same cast. On January 18, 1957, the Teatro Massimo at Palermo opened its season with *I Vespri siciliani;* Antonietta Stella was the Elena, Tullio Serafin conducted, and the supporting cast included Mario Filippeschi (Arrigo), Giuseppe Taddei (Guido), and Bernard Ladysz (Giovanni).

son, Giuseppe de Luca, José Mardones, and Paolo Ananian. The Vestal's role showed, as Irving Kolodin has said, the "real range of Ponselle's gifts," and the opera was chosen to open the 1925–26 season, with Giacomo Lauri-Volpi substituting for Johnson, and Ezio Pinza (beginning his Metropolitan career) substituting for Mardones as the Pontifex Maximus. Altogether, it was magnificent—and it was dropped after eight performances spaced out in two seasons. In 1933, *La Vestale* had a handsome production at Florence: the Vestal, with her selfless devotion to the will of the State, was approved subject matter in Fascist Italy.

In German *La Vestale* long remained verdant. Wagner staged it at Dresden in 1844, with Wilhelmine Schröder-Devrient as the Vestal. Eventually Sophie Cruvelli and Jenny Lind annexed the Vestal as their own: Henry Fothergill Chorley preferred Lind vocally, but admitted that she was a bit prissy.

243. La Vestale (Spontini)

Three acts; libretto by Victor-Joseph Étienne de Jouy; Paris, Opéra, December 16, 1807.

At first *La Vestale* was reasonably popular at the Opéra: two-hundredth performance on January 4, 1830. London first heard it in Italian at the Haymarket Theatre on December 2, 1826, and in German at Covent Garden on June 9, 1842. It reached New Orleans and Philadelphia (October 30, 1828) just over twenty years after its world *première,* but almost a whole century passed before New York heard it at the Metropolitan Opera on November 13, 1925. Giulio Gatti-Casazza's production seemed, in its magnificence, to expiate this neglect. Joseph Urban designed the sets, Tullio Serafin conducted, and Rosa Ponselle headed a superb cast, including Margarete Matzenauer, Edward John-

244. La Vida Breve (Falla)

Two acts; libretto by Carlos Fernández Shaw, but translated from Spanish into French by Paul Milliet for the première; Nice, Casino Municipal, April 1, 1913.

Lillian Grenville (Salud), David Devriès (Paco), and Édouard Cotreuil (Uncle Salvador) participated in the world *première.* The opera was staged at the Opéra-Comique, Paris, on December 13, 1914, with Fritz Ruhlmann conducting; the cast included Marguerite Carré (Salud), Suzanne Brohly (The Grandmother), Fernand Francell (Paco), Félix Vieuille (Uncle Salvador), and Daniel Vigneau (The Singer). In a 1928 performance at the Comique, Ninon Vallin was the Salud, Gaston Micheletti the Paco; Albert Wolff conducted. *La Vida Breve* was heard in Spanish for the first time when it was staged at the

Teatro de la Zarzuela, Madrid, on November 14, 1914. It has been heard since in many parts of Europe in many languages. The Metropolitan Opera, New York, staged it in Spanish at a matinee on March 6, 1926 (on a double bill with Stravinsky's *Le Rossignol*). Tullio Serafin conducted; the leading roles were sung by Lucrezia Bori (Salud), Kathleen Howard (The Grandmother), Armand Tokatyan (Paco), and Louis d'Angelo (Uncle Salvador). The opera vanished from the Metropolitan repertoire after four performances that season.

245. Le Villi (Puccini)

One act; libretto by Ferdinando Fontana; Milan, Teatro dal Verme, May 31, 1884.

The conductor of the world *première* of Puccini's first opera was not (as is stated in many books) Ettore Panizza—who was only eight years old at the time—but an already elderly man named Achille Panizza. The cast was headed by Caporetti (Anna) and Antonio d'Andrade, a brother of Francesco d'Andrade (Roberto). The orchestra included a double-bass player who was soon to become world-famous, Pietro Mascagni. The little one-acter, which shared a triple bill with Filippo Marchetti's opera *Ruy Blas* and a ballet entitled *La Contessa d'Egmont*, was an immediate success. Puccini revised it as a two-act opera, in which version it was first heard at the Teatro Regio, Turin, on December 26, 1884, again winning success. It was much less well liked at La Scala, Milan (January 24, 1885), and was a thunderous failure at the Teatro San Carlo, Naples, four months later.

Le Villi was staged at Buenos Aires on June 10, 1886, and at Hamburg, in a German translation by Ludwig Hartmann, on November 29, 1892; Gustav Mahler conducted. On September 24, 1897, the Carl Rosa Opera Company, at Manchester, presented *Le Villi* as *The Witch-Dancers* (English translation by Percy E. Pinkerton). It was heard in Italian at the Metropolitan Opera, New York, on December 17, 1908. Arturo Toscanini conducted (he had conducted this opera earlier, at Brescia), and the cast consisted of Frances Alda (Anna), Alessandro Bonci (Roberto), and Pasquale Amato (Guglielmo Wolf). Its partner on this Toscanini double bill was a *Cavalleria rusticana* with Emmy Destinn and Enrico Caruso. *Le Villi* endured for five performances that season, since when it has not been heard in New York. It never has been staged at Covent Garden, London, but occasionally it wins revivals at Continental opera houses.

246. La Voix humaine (Poulenc)

One act; the libretto is Jean Cocteau's play of the same name; Paris, Opéra-Comique, February 6, 1959.

Except for a few lines excised, the libretto of *La Voix humaine* is the intact text of Jean Cocteau's 1930 monodrama. Georges Prêtre conducted at the *première;* the opera's only role, Elle, was sung and acted spectacularly by Denise Duval, for whom it was written. The date was February 6, 1959, and the opera shared a double bill with André Messager's *Isoline;* at some later performances the other opera was Puccini's *La Bohème*. When Duval repeated her Paris success at the Piccola Scala, Milan, shortly after the Paris *première,* the Poulenc was part of a triple bill shared with Goffredo Petrassi's *Il Cordovano* and Falla's *El Retablo de Maese Pedro*. Later in the year, Duval also sang Elle at a performance of *La Voix humaine* at Charleroi, Belgium. She sang it, too, in its United States *première,* in a concert performance in New York by the

American Opera Society, on February 23, 1960, when it shared a double bill with another Poulenc opera, *Les Mamelles de Tirésias,* both conducted by Prêtre. The composer was present.

247. Von Heute auf Morgen (Schoenberg)

One act; libretto by Max Blonda (pseudonym); Frankfurt-am-Main, February 1, 1930.

Schoenberg's only comic opera has had very few performances since its *première.* In 1958, however, the Holland Festival gave it on a double bill with Schoenberg's *Erwartung.* Hans Rosbaud conducted, and the cast consisted of Erika Schmidt (The Wife), Derrik Olsen (The Husband), Herbert Schachtschneider (The Singer), and Magda Laszlò (The Friend). A taping of this performance later (September 21, 1958) was broadcast in England by the BBC. The opera was also staged at Naples in 1953, when Hermann Scherchen conducted.

248. Die Walküre (Wagner)

Three acts; libretto by the composer, being Part II ("erster Tag") of Der Ring des Nibelungen; Munich, June 26, 1870. See also Der Ring des Nibelungen (No. 197).

The principals of the world *première* were August Kindermann (Wotan), Heinrich Vogl (Siegmund), Karl Bausewein (Hunding), Sophie Stehle (Brünnhilde), Therese Vogl (Sieglinde), and Anna Kaufmann (Fricka); Franz Wüllner conducted. The first American production, rough and truncated, took place at the Academy of Music, New York, on April 2, 1877, under the direction of Adolf Neuendorf, with Eugenia Pappenheim as Brünnhilde. The London first, at Her Majesty's Theatre, on May 6, 1882, was conducted by Anton Seidl, with such well-trained voices as those of Emil Scaria, Albert Niemann, Therese Vogl, and Hedwig Reicher-Kindermann at his command. The first Metropolitan performance, Leopold Damrosch conducting, took place on January 30, 1885, with Josef Staudigl Jr. (Wotan), Anton Schott (Siegmund), Amalie Materna (Brünnhilde), Auguste Seidl-Kraus (Sieglinde), and Marianne Brandt (Fricka). The Covent Garden *première,* on June 29, 1892, under Gustav Mahler, gave important roles to Theodor Reichmann, Max Alvary, Pelagie Ende-Andriessen, Kathi Bettaque, and Ernestine Schumann-Heink.

249. War and Peace (Prokofiev)

Thirty scenes (eleven in revised version); libretto by Prokofiev and Mira Mendelson after Tolstoy's novel; first version—Leningrad, June 12, 1946; revised version—Leningrad, April 1, 1955.

Although the official *première* of the original version of Prokofiev's *War and Peace* took place in Leningrad on June 12, 1946, some preliminary performances in concert form had taken place earlier—one of them at the Bolshoi Theater in Moscow on June 7, 1945, with Samuel A. Samosud conducting the State Symphony Orchestra. The first performance outside Russia was staged at the Florentine Maggio Musicale in 1953, when Artur Rodzinski conducted his own shortened version of the opera and the cast included Rosanna Carteri, Fedora Barbieri, Franco Corelli, and Italo Tajo. On January 13, 1957, the NBC-TV Opera Company broadcast what was described as the first performance outside Russia of *War and Peace* as Prokofiev had revised it just before his death in 1953. The eleven scenes, lasting two hours and a half, were sung in an English translation by Joseph Machlis. Peter Herman Adler conducted, and the cast included Helena Scott (Natasha), Gloria Lane (Helene), Davis Cunningham (Anatol), Leon Lishner (Napoleon), Kenneth Smith (Kutuzov), Morley Meredith (Andrey), and David Lloyd (Pierre). During the season of 1957–58, *War and Peace* was staged at the Stanislavsky Theater, Moscow; the thirty scenes which, in one version, Prokofiev had wanted performed during two evenings were condensed into one evening. The performance of Alexander Pirogov as Kutuzov was lauded by Moscow critics. When the opera appeared in a recorded version conducted by Werner Janssen, it was noted that the soloists of the Belgrade National Opera, with the Vienna Chamber Chorus and Vienna State Opera Orchestra, performed only 3,178 of the 6,938 measures of music in the score (Moscow, 1958) used.

250. Werther (Massenet)

Four acts; libretto by Édouard Blau, Paul Milliet, and Georges Hartmann, after Goethe's novel Die Leiden des jungen Werthers (1774), *but translated from French into German by Max Kalbeck for the* première; *Vienna, Opernhaus, February 16, 1892.*

Marie Renard (Charlotte), Forster (Sophie), Ernest Van Dyck (Werther), and Neidl (Albert) participated in the world *première*. The opera was first heard in French at Geneva, Switzerland, on December 27, 1892. It moved to the Opéra-Comique, Paris, on January 16, 1893, and there it has been played about thirteen hundred times; Marie Delna sang the role of Charlotte at the Paris *première*. At the one-thousandth performance (October 10, 1928), Roger Desormière conducted, and the cast was headed by Ninon Vallin (Charlotte), Giuseppe Lugo (Werther), and Roger Bourdin (Albert).

Chicago was the first American city to hear *Werther* (March 29, 1894); on April 19 of that year, the Metropolitan produced it in New York, with Emma Eames (Charlotte), Sigrid Arnoldson (Sophie), Jean de Reszke (Werther), and Henri Albers (Albert). The 1909 revival presented Geraldine Farrar, Alma Gluck, Edmond Clément, and Dinh Gilly. In Chicago, Mary Garden made Charlotte one of her great interpretations. In the autumn of 1947, the New York City Opera Company revived *Werther* at the New York City Center; Jean Morel conducted, and the cast was headed by Winifred Heidt, Virginia Haskins, Eugene Conley, and Norman Young. The San Francisco Opera Company staged *Werther* for the first time on November 22, 1935, when Coe Glade was the Charlotte, Anna Young the Sophie, Tito Schipa the Werther, and Alfredo Gandolfi the Albert; Gaetano Merola conducted. Eighteen years later, Tullio Serafin was the conductor when San Francisco heard the opera again, this time with Giulietta Simionato as Charlotte, Dorothy Warenskjold as Sophie, Cesare Valletti as Werther, and John Lombardi as Albert (September 19, 1953).

A notable performance of *Werther* occurred in St. Petersburg on January 16, 1902: the name role, originally composed for tenor, had been recast for this occasion so that Mattia Battistini, a baritone, could sing it. The first Covent Garden performance introduced the opera to England on June 11, 1894; Luigi Mancinelli conducted; the cast, as at the Metropolitan two months before, was headed by Eames, Arnoldson, Jean de Reszke, and Albers. The Sadler's Wells company, in January, 1952, gave London its first opportunity since 1910 to hear *Werther*.

251. Wozzeck (Berg)

Three acts (fifteen scenes); libretto a reduction by the composer of Georg

Büchner's drama Woyzeck; *Berlin, Staatsoper, December 14, 1925.*

Wozzeck was conducted by Erich Kleiber at its world *première.* Leading members of that cast were Sigrid Johannsen (Marie), Ida von Scheele-Müller (Margret), Leo Schützendorf (Wozzeck), Waldemar Henke (Captain), Martin Abendroth (Doctor), and Fritz Soot (Drum Major). By 1933, when—the Nazis having achieved power—further performances of *Wozzeck* in Germany became impossible, it had been sung twenty-one times in Berlin and uncounted times in sixteen other German cities, beginning with Oldenburg on March 5, 1929. It was staged at the National Theater, Prague, in Czech on November 11, 1926, arousing such demonstrations of protest that eighteen days later the city authorities forbade further performances of it there. It was also staged, in Russian, at Leningrad on June 13, 1927.

Clemens Krauss conducted the Vienna *première* of *Wozzeck* on March 30, 1930; Rose Pauly was Marie and the Wozzeck was Josef von Manowarda. A company from Aachen presented the opera in German at Amsterdam and Rotterdam in October, 1930. Its first performance in America occurred at Philadelphia, the Metropolitan Opera House, on March 19, 1931, when Leopold Stokowski conducted. Leading members of that cast were Anne Roselle (Marie), Edwina Eustis (Margret), Ivan Ivantzoff (Wozzeck), Bruno Korell (Captain), Ivan Steschenko (Doctor), and Gabriel Leonoff (Drum Major). The Philadelphia performance was repeated in New York on November 24, 1931, when the Drum Major was sung by Nelson Eddy.

At Brussels on February 29, 1932, *Wozzeck* was sung in a French translation by Paul Spaak. The opera was heard in England for the first time in concert form, at Queen's Hall, London, with Sir Adrian Boult conducting, on March 14, 1934. Tullio Serafin conducted the Italian *première*, in Italian, at Rome in 1942; Gabriella Gatti was Marie, Tito Gobbi was Wozzeck. Other Italian performances occurred at Naples in 1949, again with Gobbi, but with Suzanne Danco as Marie and Karl Böhm conducting, and at La Scala, Milan, in 1952, when Dimitri Mitropoulos conducted, Gobbi was Wozzeck, and Dorothy Dow sang Marie. The first London stage performance of *Wozzeck* was at Covent Garden on January 22, 1952, with Kleiber conducting. Marko Rothmüller (Wozzeck), Christel Goltz (Marie), Monica Sinclair (Margret), Frederick Dalberg (Doctor), Parry Jones (Captain), and Thorsteinn Hennesson (Drum Major) headed the cast. Goltz sang Marie in all six performances heard that season, but some other replacements were heard: Jess Walters (Wozzeck), Otakar Kraus (Doctor), Max Worthley (Captain), Frank Sale (Drum Major), and Edith Coates (Margret). When *Wozzeck* was repeated three times during the 1954–55 season, Reginald Goodall conducted and the Marie was Elfriede Wasserthal.

On April 12, 1951, *Wozzeck* was given in concert form at Carnegie Hall, New York, by the New York Philharmonic-Symphony Orchestra, with Mitropoulos conducting. The chief singers were Eileen Farrell (Marie), Edwina Eustis (Margret), Mack Harrell (Wozzeck), Joseph Mordino (Captain, Soldier, Idiot), Ralph Herbert (Doctor), and Frederick Jagel (Drum Major). This performance was in German, but when the New York City Opera Company staged the work at the New York City Center in 1952, it introduced the Eric Blackall–Vida Harford English translation that had been used at Covent Garden and would be used at the Metropolitan. The City Center production by Komisarjevsky and the settings by Mstislav Dobujinsky were much more Russian than German; Joseph Rosenstock's conducting was not destructive. As at Covent Garden, Marko Rothmüller was the Wozzeck; Patricia Neway (later Brenda Lewis) was the Marie; others in the cast were Howard Vandenburg (Drum Major), Ralph Herbert (Doctor), and Luigi Vellucci (Captain).

Wozzeck was presented by the Metropolitan Opera Company for the first time on March 5, 1959. Böhm conducted; the opera was staged by Herbert Graf with sets and costumes by Caspar Neher. The leading roles were sung by Hermann Uhde (Wozzeck), Eleanor Steber (Marie), Margaret Roggero (Margret), Paul Franke (Captain), Karl Dönch (Doctor), and Kurt Baum (Drum Major). This production, which was broadcast on March 14, 1959, was heard five times that season, dropped for the 1959–60 season, and restored to the repertoire on March 10, 1961, for five more performances. During its remarkable 1960 season (which also included *Die Frau ohne Schatten, La Fanciulla del West,* and *La Sonnambula,* the San Francisco Opera Company presented *Wozzeck* for the first time (October 4). Leopold Ludwig conducted, and the cast included Geraint Evans (Wozzeck), Marilyn Horne (Marie), Richard Lewis (Captain), Lorenzo Alvary (Doctor), Ticho Parly (Drum Major), and Raymond Manton (Andres).

Berg's *Wozzeck* is not the only operatic setting of Büchner's play. Manfred Gurlitt, a prolific German conductor-composer born in 1890, composed a *Wozzeck* almost simultaneously with Berg. His opera, which inevitably suffered by the comparison, followed Berg's by a little more than four months, having its *première* at Bremen on April 22, 1926. It is set in eighteen scenes and an epilogue.

252. Die Zauberflöte (Mozart)

Two acts; libretto by Emmanuel Schikaneder, probably helped by Karl Ludwig Giesecke (born Johann Georg Metzler); Vienna, Theater auf der Wieden, September 30, 1791.

Among the principals at the *première* were Nannina Gottlieb (Pamina), Josefa Hofer—Mozart's wife's sister (Queen of the Night), Benedict Schack (Tamino), Thaddäus Gerl (Sarastro), and Schikaneder (Papageno). By the end of the eighteenth century *Die Zauberflöte* had received over two hundred performances at the Theater auf der Wieden, and it has been solidly successful in Vienna ever since. Some of *Die Zauberflöte*'s early history outside Vienna was most curious. In 1801, Paris heard a pastiche called *Les Mystères d'Isis,* which consisted largely of sections of *Die Zauberflöte,* plus bits of *Don Giovanni, Le Nozze di Figaro, La Clemenza di Tito,* and Haydn symphonies. This potpourri, not unusual for the period, was enthusiastically received. The untainted version of *Die Zauberflöte* did not reach Paris for many years. Meanwhile, it was faring better in London, being introduced at the Haymarket Theatre by Giuseppe Naldi, who, impressed by the welcome accorded to *Così fan tutte* at its first London performance (May 9, 1811), chose *Die Zauberflöte*—as *Il Flauto magico*—for his closing-night benefit that same season (June 6, 1811). And, although Victoria's subjects showed only a mild interest in the opera, it was heard in London from time to time, often with the greatest vocal galaxies. In 1833, Wilhelmine Schröder-Devrient sang Pamina at Covent Garden (it had been her world debut role in Vienna in 1821). In 1851 the constellation of Giulia Grisi (Pamina), Mario (Tamino), Giorgio Ronconi (Papageno), Karl Formes (Sarastro), and Pauline Viardot-García (Papagena) was dimmed by the meager gifts of Anna Zerr (Queen of the Night); "in her bravuras," Henry Fothergill Chorley wrote, she "reminded the listener of a pea-hen masquerading as a lark."

Fräulein Zerr was replaced by the youthful Louisa Fanny Pyne, better in both cantabile and bravura. Ilma di Murska was, according to Herman Klein, the most nearly perfect Queen of the Night ever heard in London. And it was in London that Christine Nilsson, singing the first aria of the Queen of the Night, took the last two notes in *chest tones*. (The italics are borrowed from Clara Louise Kellogg, who tells the tragic story in her *Memoirs of an American Prima Donna*, adding, "Her beautiful high tones were gone forever.") Sir Thomas Beecham revived *Die Zauberflöte* in 1914, at Drury Lane, with Claire Dux, Margarete Siems, Walter Kirchoff, Paul Knüpfer, and Hans Bechstein in leading roles. Sir Thomas' revival of 1938, at Covent Garden, was notable for the resurgence of Richard Tauber, a great Mozart singer in the twenties, who had declined into operetta roles. His Tamino was matched by the Pamina—Tiana Lemnitz, the equal of Claire Dux; both Erna Berger (Queen of the Night) and Gerhard Hüsch sang to perfection. *Die Zauberflöte,* under Fritz Busch, entered the Glyndebourne repertoire in 1935, with Aulikki Rautawaara, Ivan Andrésen, and Willi Domgraf-Fassbänder in leading roles.

On April 17, 1833, New York heard an English version at the Park Theater, the original text and uncut score having to wait for a hearing there until November 10, 1862, when it was sung at the German Opera House. The first Metropolitan production was heard in Italian, on March 30, 1900, with Marcella Sembrich, Emma Eames, Zélie de Lussan, Andreas Dippel, Giuseppe Campanari, and Pol Plançon; in minor roles were such celebrated artists as Milka Ternina, Eugenia Mantelli, Suzanne Adams, Rosa Olitzka, and Antonio Pini-Corsi. For the Metropolitan revival of November 6, 1926, in the original German, the principals were Marion Talley, Elisabeth Rethberg, Louise Homer, Rudolf Laubenthal,

Gustav Schützendorf, Paul Bender, and George Meader. Rethberg, Meader, and Editha Fleischer (First Lady), the last making her Metropolitan debut, alone understood the subtleties of Mozartian style. It was no wonder that Giulio Gatti-Casazza retired the opera after four performances. Unhappily, the later adventures of *The Magic Flute* (for in 1941 it was revived to the English text of Ruth and Thomas P. Martin) may be described as hectically experimental. The first try, on December 11, 1946, gave leading roles to several singers whose English ranged from nonexistent to awkward: Jarmila Novotna (Pamina), Rosa Bok (Queen of the Night), Alexander Kipnis (Sarastro), Friedrich Schorr (High Priest), and Karl Laufkötter (Monostatos). Charles Kullmann (Tamino) and John Brownlee (Papageno) were models of diction and style, but could not rescue a babel so carelessly assembled. Before Ezio Pinza left the Metropolitan for Rodgers and Hammerstein he added another unforgettable role to his Mozart gallery: that of Sarastro (November 27, 1942), "performing with implacable dignity and nobility of style" (Irving Kolodin). At that stage of the Johnson regime nothing seemed planned, except, perhaps, the stubborn whimsicality that characterized casting around for an unsuitable Queen of the Night. Under the Bing regime, imagination arrived triumphantly at a cast that by and large should have had no difficulties with the English language. With Jerome Hines and George London as Sarastro and the High Priest respectively, the omens sounded right; a born Papageno (Theodor Uppman) could not have been bettered. But Brian Sullivan had little understanding of how to sing or how to act Tamino, while the Pamina (Lucine Amara), despite her lovely voice and undoubted conscientiousness, simply failed to qualify. Roberta Peters was an altogether ineffective Queen of the Night. It may be said without exaggeration that this sad state of affairs can be traced back to the idea that the most important thing about *Die Zauberflöte* is to know what the characters are saying and singing. Thus the integrated English-speaking and English-singing cast (not necessarily enlisting the most capable artists)—and the inevitable decline of the music itself. This is possibly one of the most notorious cases of imbalance that the Metropolitan Opera has achieved.[1]

253. Zazà (Leoncavallo)

Four acts; libretto by the composer, after a play by Charles Simon and Pierre Berton; *Milan, Teatro Lirico, November 10, 1900.*

A fine cast was assembled for the world *première* of *Zazà;* Rosina Storchio had the name role. Although given in London as early as April 30, 1909, at the Coronet Theatre, it has never reached Covent Garden. At the Metropolitan Opera House, New York, *Zazà* had its *première* on January 16, 1920. Given twenty performances in three seasons, and then dropped, it was chosen to display the charms, vocal and otherwise, of Geraldine Farrar. Her principal confreres were Giulio Crimi and Pasquale Amato.

---

[1] One of the ironies of the situation is that *The Magic Flute* does not communicate so well as does *Die Zauberflöte*, even to those whose German does not go beyond the recognition of an occasional cognate. Can anyone who listens to the opera as a totality, to Mozart's German *Singspiel*, miss its range of expressiveness, from the most poignant to the most farcical, or miss, finally, its explicit jokes, which the opera-in-translation people seem to regard with humorless piety?

INDEX

Names beginning with the particule de (and such related forms as da, dal, del, delle, dello, des, di, du, la, le, les, lo, van, and von) have been alphabetized under the part of the name following (*e. g.,* Camille du Locle under Locle, Camille du) except where common usage dictates otherwise (*e. g.,* D'Avenant, Sir William). Umlauts have been treated as implying a following e (*e. g.,* Büchner is alphabetized as though spelled Buechner). Names beginning with Mc follow those beginning with Ma. All theaters and opera houses appear under their official names, largely as Teatro, Theater, and Théâtre, but where confusion is possible, cross references have been supplied.

Index

For Index to Annals of Performance see page 679

Index to Annals of Performance

Names beginning with the particle de (and such related forms as da, dal, del, delle, dello, des, di, la, le, les, lo, van, and von) have been alphabetized under the part of the name following (e. g., Zélie de Lussan under Lussan, Zélie de) except where common usages dictates otherwise (e. g., D'Annunzio, Gabriele). Umlauts have been treated as implying a following e (e. g., Hüsch is alphabetized as though spelled Huesch). Names beginning with Mc follow those beginning with Ma. All theaters and opera houses appear under their official names, largely as Teatro, Theater, and Théâtre, but where confusion is possible, cross references have been supplied.